{ Word • Nerd }

Barbara Ann Kipfer, PhD

SOURCEBOOKS, INC.
NAPERVILLE, ILLINOIS

Published by Sourcebooks, Inc.
P.O. Box 4410, Naperville, Illinois 60567-4410
(630) 961-3900
Fax: (630) 961-2168
www.sourcebooks.com

Library of Congress Cataloging-in-Publication Data

Kipfer, Barbara Ann.
  Word nerd : more than 18,000 fascinating facts about words / Barbara
Ann Kipfer.
     p. cm.
  ISBN 978-1-4022-0851-5 (trade pbk.)
  1. English language–Etymology. 2. Vocabulary. I. Title.

PE1574.K47 2007
422–dc22

                              2007016208

          Printed and bound in the United States of America.
          DR 10 9 8 7 6 5 4 3 2

To Paul, my Sherpa

Thank You

At the Thanksgiving feast about three years ago, I explained some of the words pertaining to the holiday. Everybody had so much fun and so many new questions and tidbits came up. My husband, Paul Magoulas, reminded me of the word notes I had made over the years as a lexicographer, and encouraged me to compile them to share with others. Thank you to Paul, who endured my endless dictionary reading (and talking about words) for three years while I went over my notes to ensure I found the most interesting tidbit about every word on my list. Thank you, also, to my boys Kyle and Keir, who were the unwitting recipients of much word knowledge during this time!

 Introduction

This book is a collection of a-really-interesting-thing-you-probably-do-not-know about thousands and thousands of words. It is the result of a hobby of gathering observations about words, something that has just come naturally during my twenty-seven years as a professional lexicographer. It is a delightful hobby, writing down what I find to be truly interesting definitions, fascinating origins or histories, details of usage, surprising trivia, useful synonyms, or unexpected connections between words. In *Word Nerd*, I have "caught" the interesting details about thousands of words and now present them to the wide world of word-lovers.

I have read dictionaries, etymology books, tomes on usage and grammar, books of unusual or old words, word trivia, and vocabulary books—for fun! The entries offer information that would otherwise be elusive to readers who do not have access to numerous books about language and words. The book is intended for reader exploration and then as the stimulus for readers to dig up interesting information on their own.

I have never met a person who is not interested in language. Mostly, people are curious about etymologies, unusual words, definitions, and points about usage and grammar. But there are no browsable books with a combination of these types of information about words. I know, because I have been a lexicographer for twenty-seven years and it is my business to be aware of all the books written about language. I have been writing down cool stuff about words for many years. Up to now, you could not find a book that contained word origins and changes of meaning and cool-but-rarely-used words in concise, easy-to-grasp snippets. You could only find books focused on and extensively explaining a specific language topic or dictionaries with a myriad of facts, but which few people decide to tackle cover-to-cover.

So, here comes *Word Nerd*. You see, I *do* read dictionaries from A-to-Z. *Word Nerd* contains my notes from books about word history and etymology, unusual or lost or uncommon words, grammar instruction and usage, word trivia, differences between confusable words, how words are formed—from all the general and specialized dictionaries and language books that I have read. In *Word Nerd*, I have distilled many, many bookshelves' worth of books in each of these areas and now they are presented together for others to enjoy.

Readers will be inspired by *Word Nerd* to explore further. They will find that any trip through *Word Nerd* is a really cool way to learn things about words, things that may be useful or things that they can then turn around and describe to their friends and families. In opening to any page, readers can have experiences like, "wow, I had forgotten that," or "that is certainly something I did not know," or "aha! that is what that means!" or "oh, that is where that came from!"

Word-of-the-day services and calendars flourish, online dictionary sites prosper, and print dictionaries and word books continue to sell very well—all due to our unending curiosity about the English language. People are infinitely curious about where a word came from (etymology/word history), words that elude them (tip-of-the-tongue syndrome), new words, unusual or old words that could be revived, and correct usage and grammar. There is something for every sort of word lover in this book. Dip into *Word Nerd* at any point and discover fresh, entertaining insights into the world of words. I present a fantastic trip through English vocabulary. The focus is on single words, not phrases, in this book.

The fun and fascinating tidbits about our language and culture found in *Word Nerd* will provide endless hours of pleasurable browsing. This is a connoisseur's collection of information about words. More importantly, it fuels the reader's desire to learn even more. *Word Nerd* is a mix of all types of information about a huge range of vocabulary. It is great for learning something in a snap, for an "aha! I didn't know that!" moment, for chatting with and quizzing friends and family. *Word Nerd* is a book to share. And before you know it, there may be scores of people reading dictionaries for fun!

A Note on Sources

I am deeply indebted to Oxford University Press and all of its wonderful lexicographic resources. I wish I could have read the whole *Oxford English Dictionary*, but I settled for the *Shorter Oxford English Dictionary*—three times! Most of the word origin information that I gathered was from Oxford sources and they are the ones to turn to as you, the reader, do your own investigations and word trivia collecting. I read many other books on etymology and I found lots of good information, but one must always go back to Oxford as the "authority."

I encourage all word nerds to dive into books on word history and etymology, books about unusual or uncommon words, grammar and usage instruction, books on word differences, and Latin and Greek roots. There are so many great word books out there; I read literally hundreds when compiling this, and there is not room to list them all—but I am deeply indebted to all the lexicographers and linguists who wrote them.

A Note on Errors

In the 17,000 notes on words' origins, meanings, and other details in this work, it is not unlikely that an error has crept into the copy along the way. So if you find one, please feel free to write to me at barbara@word-nerd.com so I can research it and correct it in subsequent editions.

{ The letter **A** evolved from the Hebrew and Phoenician character *aleph*, 'ox' }

use "**a hold**" or "**hold**," not "ahold"

use "**a lot**," not "**alot**"

awhile means "for a time" and **a while** means "a period of time"

a is the determiner to use for consonant sounds; **an** is for vowel sounds

the lightest weight of sandpaper is **A** and the heaviest is **E**

A ranks third in frequency for printed English behind **E** and **T**

A-1 was orginally an abbreviation in the Register of Shipping for Lloyds of London—used to describe ships in first-class condition

everyone knows that the **aa** of crossword puzzles is rough lava of Hawaii

aardvark is from Afrikaners who called the beast an "earth pig"; a synonym is antbear

the **aardwolf** is also known as the maned jackal

aargh is a lengthening of "ah" to represent a prolonged cry

the term **aback** originated in sailing—as a ship was taken **aback** when a strong gust of wind suddenly blew the sails back against the mast, causing the ship to stop momentarily

abacus comes from Greek *abax*, "drawing board"; abacuses or abaci are plurals of **abacus**

abaft has the element *baft*, which is an archaic word meaning "in the rear"

an **abalone** is also called an earshell or sea ear or ormer

a pickpocket specializing in bandannas or handkerchiefs is an **abandannad**

abandon (from French) originally meant "bring under control"; **abandon** suggests that the thing or person left may be helpless without protection

abase first meant "to lower physically" or "bring or cast down"

abash and **abeyance** share a common ancestry, going back to a Latin verb *batare*, "yawn, gape"; **abash** originally meant "stand amazed" as well as "embarrass"

abate stresses the idea of progressive diminishing

an **abatis** or abattis is a defense made of felled trees with the boughs pointed outward

an **abattoir** is a slaughterhouse for cattle

a lazy monk is also called an **abbey-lubber**

abbot comes from Greek *abbas*, "father"

a preliminary or rough sketch is an **abbozzo**

abbreviating words was widely condemned until the late eighteenth century; an element of **abbreviate** is Latin *brevis*, "short"

abbreviate and **abridge** come from Latin *brevis*, "short," with **abridge** taking a trip through Old French

an **ABC** was formerly a child's reading primer

abc, **alphabet**, and **abecedarian** are the only words in English based on the sequence of letters in the **alphabet**

abdabs or **habdabs** is a state of extreme nervousness or the jitters

abdicate implies a giving up of sovereign power or the evasion of responsibility (as a parent)

an **abditory** is a hidden or secret place and **abditive** means "hidden, hiding"

abdomen is straight from Latin and originally denoted the fat deposited around the belly

anyone with an overly large abdomen is **abdominous** and can be called a gorbelly, gundygut, greedigut, swillbelly, porksnell, pangut, or tenterbelly

{ to **abduct** is to move a limb or body part away from the body }

one's **abearance** is his/her behavior

an **abecedary** or **abecedarian** is a person just learning the alphabet

in biology, the discovery of an **aberrant** (i.e., different from normal or natural) variety of a species can be exciting

the long tool for pruning tree branches is an **aberuncator**; to **aberuncate** is to pull up by the roots or extirpate

abet also means "assist or support in achievement of a purpose," from French meaning "to bait" or "encourage a hound to bite"

abeyance literally means "hold your mouth open," from French *bayer*, "to gape"; it originated as a legal term meaning "state of expectation"

abhor is from Latin meaning "shrink back in terror"

abide has the past participle abode, but also abidden

to **abilitate** is to enable

applied to a person, **ability** and **capacity** mean about the same thing but are grammatically different: an **ability** to do something, a **capacity** for doing something; **ability** is qualitative while **capacity** is quantitative

abiology is the study of inanimate things

abjection (casting down, rejection) refers more to the act; **abjectness** refers to the condition or state of mind (depression, humiliation) created

abjunct means disconnected or severed as does **abjunctive**

abjure is "swear off" or "swear away" and **adjure** is "command earnestly"; **abjure** implies a firm and final rejecting or abandoning often made under oath

to **ablaqueate** is to expose the roots of a tree by loosening or removing soil

ablation is the evaporation or melting of part of the outer surface of a spacecraft, through heating by friction with the atmosphere

ablatitious means "diminishing, lessening"

a vowel change in related words—e.g., sing, sang, sung,—is called an **ablaut** (from German *ab*, "off," and *Laut*, "sound") or **gradation**

only a human is "**able**" to do anything (not an animal or thing)

as a general rule, words of English or French origin take-**able** (portable, washable) while words of Latin origin take-**ible** (audible)

ablegate means to send away or abroad

abominate's root sense is "to turn away from a thing of ill omen"

aborigines is from Latin "ancestors" and was spelled with a capital A as the name of the primeval Romans; the first people called aborigines were the original inhabitants of Italy and Greece and **aborigine** was specifically applied to the inhabitants of a country *ab origine*, "from the beginning"

an attempt, effort, mission, or proposal that is unsuccessful can be described as **abortive**

{ an **abortorium** is a hospital or place that specializes in performing abortions (*ab-*, "from" and *oriri*, "come into being") }

when you squander your money on treats and comfort foods, you are engaging in **abligurition** (excessive spending on food and drink)

to **ablocate** means to rent or rent out

ablude is to differ from or not be in keeping with

ablution is the act of washing something clean, especially as a religious rite

abnegate means renounce or reject something desired or valuable

abnormal means "not normal, different from normal" while **subnormal** means "below normal"

abnormous is a blend of abnormal and enormous

aboard is "on base" in baseball

abode originally meant "delay" or "stay"

abolish can only describe customs, institutions, and practices

the **abomasum** is the fourth stomach of a ruminant, which receives food from the omasum and passes it to the small intestine

some say **abominable** comes from *ab hominus*, "away from man"

the roots of **abound** are *ab-*, "from," and *undare*, from *unda*, "wave"

say "**about**" not "at about"

the word **above** traces back to an Old English word first meaning "north" and later taking the meaning of "overhead"

aboveboard is a term based on the trickery of card sharps and magicians with their hands under the board or table

abracadabra derives from the Gnostic term *Abraxus*, Greek for "almighty God," which the Gnostics used to call up power; the supreme deity of the Assyrians was called with this term as a charm against ague and flux; the word **abracadabra** was arranged in an inverted pyramid amulet with one less letter on each line and as the letters disappeared so also (supposedly) did disease or trouble

abracadabrant means "marvelous or stunning"

to **abraid** is to awake, arouse, or startle

abrasions, contusions, and lacerations are more commonly called scrapes, bruises, and cuts/tears, respectively an **abrazo** is a greeting of a bear hug and a back pat

the release of repressed emotions or ideas during psychoanalysis is known as **abreaction**

in regard to ships, **abreast** can mean equally distant and parallel

an **abreuvoir** is a space between bricks or masonry

abridge can mean "deprive a person of"

abroad first meant "widely" and "at large"

abrupt comes from Latin elements *ab-*, "away, from" and *rumpere*, "break"

an **abruption** is an interruption or sudden break

to **abscede** is to move away or go elsewhere, losing contact

an **abscess** is, technically, a localized glob of pus within the body

the **abscissa** (horizontal or x-axis) in mathematics is from a Latin phrase meaning "cutoff (line)," and it denotes the part of a line between a point on it and the points of intersection with an **ordinate** (vertical or y-axis)

abscond's original meaning was "to hide away, to conceal"

absent as a verb means "keep away" or "stay away"

Absolut is short for **Absolut** Rent Brannvin, Swedish for "Absolute Pure Vodka"

absolute is from a Latin wordmeaning "freed" or "completed"; in philosophy,

absolute means "existing without relation to other things" or "able to be thought of without relation to other things"

absolution can mean the general forgiveness of offenses

one is **absolved** of blame or responsibility but is **acquit**ted of a charge, usually a crime

absorb is based on Latin *sorbere*, "suck in"

absquatulate is a blend of abscond, squattle ("depart"), and perambulate

abstain, from Latin *abs-*, "from" and *tenere*, "hold," means basically "keep or withhold from oneself"

abstract can be used euphemistically to mean "steal something"

something that is **abstruse** is concealed, hidden, or secret

absumption is what happens in a compost pile (the process of being consumed or wasted away)

to **abseil** is to descend a steep rock face by using a doubled rope coiled around one's body and fixed to a higher point

absinthe is an aromatic herb of temperate Eurasia and North Africa having a bitter taste used in making a liqueur; the synonym is wormwood

an **absit** is a student's brief leave of absence

absurd is from Latin *ab-*, "completely," and *surdus*, "deaf," hence it implies deaf to the truth or deaf to reason; **absurd** can mean "musically inharmonious, insufferable to the ear"

inability to make decisions is **abulia** or **aboulia**

if one is all **abubble**, he/she is full of excitement and enthusiasm

someone who is **abulic** is unusually ambivalent about acting on or making decisions

abundant is related to abound

an **abundary** is an abundant source

a snow-and-wind storm in Alaska is an **aburga**

abuse usually implies the anger of the speaker and stresses the harshness of the language (from Latin, literally "wrongly use")

abuse carries with it some sense of harm; **misuse** refers to an incorrect use that may not lead to harm

to **abut** means to be next to or have a common boundary with; an **abutter** is the owner of an adjoining property

bridge **abutments** support the lateral pressure of an arch or span

to **abvolate** is to fly away

abysmal can mean "very bad" or "very deep"

abyss is from Greek *abussos*, "bottomless"— first used in the Bible, Genesis 1:2 and Revelation 9:1

acacia is from a Greek word for the shittah tree, from which the Ark of the Covenant was made

academic can mean "having no practical applications, merely theoretical"

academy came from Akademos, the man or demigod for whom Plato's garden, where he taught, was named

Acadia is the former name of Nova Scotia

acalculia is the inability to perform simple arithmetic

the **acanthus** is the leaf often used to decorate the capitals of Corinthian and Composite columns in architecture

a nonsmoker can also be called an **acapnotic**

an **acaricide** is a substance poisonous to ticks

acatalepsy in Greek is "not thoroughly seizing" or "incomprehensibility"

things purchased can be called **acate**(s) and the purchaser an **acatour**; **acates** or **acatery** are things bought or a storeroom for provisions, respectively

acatharsia or **acatharsy** are fancy words for "filth"

you can **accede** (join) a group

the Latin base of **accelerate** is *celer*, "swift"

accent comes from Latin *acentum*, "song added to speech," from *ad cantum*, "to singing"; the original meaning of **accent** is "singing speech"

when an inanimate object "**accepts**," it physically receives or absorbs something

accept is "take or agree to" and **except** means "exclude, leave out"

acceptation means "the particular sense or the generally accepted meaning of a word or phrase"

in general senses, use **accepter** to mean someone or something which accepts— but in legal and scientific contexts, use **acceptor**

to **accerse** is to summon

access can mean "an attack or outburst of an emotion"

accession can be the "onset of illness or a powerful feeling"

an **accession** is a new item added to an existing collection of books, paintings, artifacts, etc.

an **accessory** is a person who helps in an act, such as a crime

accidence is the part of grammar that deals with the variable forms of words, like inflections; a grammar book or the fundamentals of a subject is an **accidence**

until the nineteenth century, an **accident** was anything that happened, good or bad

an **accidental** color is a property depending on the relations of light to the eye, by which individual and specific differences in the hues and tints of objects are apprehended in vision—as, happy colors; sad colors, etc.

accidental stresses chance; **fortuitous** so strongly suggests chance that it often connotes absence of cause

accidie is another word for apathy, laziness, or sloth

to **accinge** is to apply oneself to a task

the adjective form of falcon is **accipitrine**

{ **accismus** is the pretended refusal of something that is actually coveted }

an **acclivity** is an upward slope

acclumsid is "numb, paralyzed; clumsy"

accolade is French for "around the neck" (from Latin *ad*, "to" and *collum*, "neck") as it was originally an embrace of the neck by which knighthood was bestowed

if you are neighboring or living nearby, you are **accolent**

accommodate's adjectival forms are accommodable, accommodating, accommodative, and accommodatory

accommodate and **accommodation** have two cs and two ms

someone who accompanies in music is an **accompanier** or **accompanyist**

accomplice was borrowed into English from French as *complice* and originally meant "an associate" with no negative sense

to **accomplish** can mean "to equip completely"

accord can mean a harmony of colors or agreement in pitch or tone

something (a quality) is in **accord** with something else; something acts in **accordance** with something else (an activity)

accordion derives from Italian *accordare*, "to tune" and both it and the **concertina** operate on the same basic principle—but the **accordion** has a pianolike keyboard and is rectangular and bulky while the **concertina** has buttons in headboards and is hexagonal and more portable

accost comes from Latin *costa*, "rib, side" and literally means "at the side"—if you **accost** someone, it can mean that the two of you are standing rib to rib

account can mean "a performance (of a piece of music, etc.)"

accountant originally was an adjective meaning "liable to give an account"

accouter is related to both the words "couture" and "sew"

accouterments describes equipment or trappings

to **accoy** is to quiet or soothe

to **accrete** is to grow by accumulation

accrue can mean "gather up, collect"

if you are living together in the same bed but not having sex, that is **accubitus**

to adjust to a new environment is to **acculturate** or **assimilate**

one of the Latin elements of **accumulate** is *cumulus*, "a heap"

accumulative is a synonym for **cumulative**

a calculator's register for counting and accumulating data is the **accumulator**

accurate can describe a thing or person as being correct or exact as the result of care

accuse is based on Latin *causa*, "cause," in the sense of "legal action"

ace is traced to ancient Rome's *as*, a unit of weight which meant "one" or "unit"

acedia is spiritual sluggishness, indifference, or apathy

acedolagnia is complete indifference to sex

an **acephalist** is someone who does not acknowledge a superior

a manuscript lacking a beginning could be called **acephalous**

acerbic often describes sharp or biting mood, temper, tone, or wit; **acerbity** is normally a bit less sharp than sarcasm

acerbity first referred to the taste of unripe fruit

acervation is an accumulation or heating up

you might throw out food that is **acescent** (turning sour)

the **acetabulum** is the socket of the hip bone, into which the head of the femur fits

acetarious pertains to plants used in salads

acetous means "producing or resembling vinegar"

ache comes from Old English and originally rhymed with "batch"—but changed spelling and pronunciation when lexicographer Samuel Johnson mistakenly said it was derived from Greek *akhos*, "pain"

a **pain** is something that hurts; an **ache** is a prolonged dull **pain**

an **achene** is a one-seeded fruit that does not open to release the seed—examples are the many achenes on a strawberry or sunflower

Acheron is another name for infernal regions or a river in Hell

achieve means "to bring to a successful conclusion" (literally French "to bring to a head") and **accomplish** means "to perform fully"; the completion of achievement is more comprehensive

color blindness is **achromatopsia**

{ the original notion contained in the word **acid** is "pointedness" }

acid/acidic is the opposite of basic

the sections of a raspberry are **acini** and the stem is the **cane**

a bunch of grapes is an **acinus**

acknowledge implies the disclosing of something that has been or might be concealed

aclinal is another word for horizontal

acme is from Greek *akme*, "highest point"; the word **acne** came erroneously from Greek *aknus*, a misreading of another word *akmas*, plural of *akme*, "facial eruption"

acokoinonia is sex without passion or desire

acolastic means "incorrigible"

acolyte comes from Greek *akolcuthos*, "follower"

acomous is a cute word for "bald"

coffee is usually **acopic**, "relieving tiredness"

acorn is from German *aecern*, "fruit of the unenclosed land," possibly from an Indo-European root meaning "berry, fruit"

an **acouasm** is an imagined ringing in the head

acoustic is from Greek *akouein*, "hear"

acoustics is a singular noun when referring to the science of sound but is a plural noun when used to mean the sound properties of a building

acquaint is from a French word, from a Latin root *cognoscere*, "know"

acquiesce's original and literal sense was "to remain quiet; stay at rest"

{ a radar **"acquires"** when it begins receiving signals }

a person or thing is the subject of (**acquire**) the acquiring process; a person or thing is the object or goal of (**accrue**) the accruing process

acquisition is a material possession while an **acquirement** is a personal skill or knowledge that one gains

acquisitive means "very interested in acquiring money or material things"

acquit originally meant "pay a debt" or "discharge a duty"

acquitment is the series of moves that a magician makes to convince the audience that his/her hands are empty

acrasia is acting against your better judgment or a lack of self-control

Old English *aecer*, now **acre**, was originally the amount of land a yoke of oxen could plow in a day; the Old English word came from Latin *ager*, "fertile field" and became **acre**, which first meant any field

acrid is a blend of acrimonious and acid to mean "bitter and fiery"

acridulous means tart or acid; **assiduous** means diligent

acrimony comes from Latin acrimonia, meaning sharpness and pungency of

flavor, a quality prized by the Romans, who were very fond of mustard and red pepper

sex without orgasm is **acrition**

an **acroama** is a dramatic recitation during a meal

acrobat derived from Greek *akrobatos*, "walking on tiptoe," from Greek *akron*, "summit," and *baino*, "walk"

acrohypothermy is cold feet

an **acrolect** is the most prestigious dialect or variety of a particular language

acronical means happening at sunset or twilight

the term **acronym** was formed from the combining forms *acro-*, "tip, end," and *-onym*, "name," on the analogy of words like synonym, homonym, etc.; the test of a true **acronym** is often assumed to be that it should be pronounceable as a word within the normal word patterns of English

an abbreviation pronounced as a word is an **acronym**; one pronounced letter by letter is an **initialism**

an ingrown nail is an **acronyx**

acropolis is Greek for "peak of the city"

the first leaf that sprouts from a germinating seed is the **acrospire**

in Middle English, **across** was an adverb meaning "in the form of a cross"

acrostic is from Greek *akron*, "end," and *stikhos*, "row, line of verse"

acrylic comes from Latin *acer/acri*, "pungent," and *ol(eum)*, "oil"

act usually means something brought about at a stroke—or something of short duration; an **act** is a fact or reality as opposed to intention or possibility

an **act** is the main dramatic unit and a **scene** is a division within an **act**

act-drop is a curtain let down between theater acts

when light causes a chemical change, as in photography, it is called **actinism**

action items are things to do or discuss, **thoughtware** are things we know about, and **bandwidth** is basically "time" or the "inability to think about or do multiple things at once"

an **action** applies in particular to the doing of something, whereas an act refers to the thing done; an **action** is punctual, an **activity** is durative—and an **action** takes place, an **activity** takes time

an **actioner** is an exciting action-and-adventure film

with mechanical action—while **activate** is used mainly in scientific expressions

acturience is the desire for or impulse to act

acuate is "sharp-pointed"

acuity pertains principally to hearing, vision, understanding, and wit

acumen suggests that keenness relates to a person's mind, whereas **acuity** suggests that it relates to a person's performance; **acumen** is something that a person has, whereas **acuity** is something that a person displays

an **aculeate** is any stinging insect of a group including bees, wasps, and ants

{ when something is **activated**, it is made active; when something is **actuated**, it is moved to take action (or produce a consequence) }

active is literally "preferring action to con-templation"

active knowledge is the knowledge of a language which a user actively employs in speech or writing, as opposed to **pas-sive** knowledge, which is what a person understands in what he/she hears or reads

the word "**actor**" is preferred now for both men and women; **actor** was originally an agent or administrator and in Latin it meant "doer"

actual first meant, literally, "relating to acts, active"

actuals are actual qualities

actuary originally denoted a clerk or regis-trar of a court

to **actuate** is a general word meaning "to set working" and has more to do

acumen, the ability to make good judg-ments and quick decisions, is Latin, literally "sharpness, point"

acupoints are the energy points where needles are inserted for acupuncture or where pressure is applied for acupressure

acupressure is a blend of "acupuncture" and "pressure"

to **acupunctuate** is to prick or poke with a pin or needle

acupuncture derives from Latin *acu*, "with a needle," and *pungere*, "to prick, pierce," and was developed around 2500 BC to address imbalances in a person's yin and yang and unblock the obstruction of ch'i (life force) which flows through the body's twelve meridians

acutance is the sharpness of a photographic or printed image

something is **acutangular** if it has acute angles

adder (the snake) was first "a nadder," which was misanalyzed to "an **adder**"

adderbolt is an old name for the dragonfly, i.e., "arrow of a crossbow"

 acute is used for a sudden onset and short duration; **chronic** is for conditions that are slow to develop and of long duration

acute comes from the Latin word for "needle"

acute is an angle of less than 90 degrees; **obtuse** is one of more than 90 degrees

AD should be placed before numerals, **AD** 700 (except when the date is spelled out; it is normal to write the seventh century **AD**)—and be in small caps when printed, but **BC** should come after the year

adage, from a Latin word meaning "saying" is from the earlier *aio*, "I say"

adagio is music played "at ease"

adamant has no corresponding noun form

adamant was the word for a legendary rock or mineral once associated with diamond or lodestone and meant "untamable, invincible" in Latin; **adamantine** means "unbreakable" and is pronounced ad-uh-MAN-tin

adapter is now more usual for a person, **adaptor** for a device

add is from Latin *addere*, from *ad-*, "toward," and *dare*, "give, put"

addenda is occasionally singular when it means "a list of additional items"

an **addition** is something that, when added, serves simply to augment or extend that to which it has been added, leaving the character of the original unchanged; an **addendum** forms a separate distinguishable portion of the whole and it first meant "a thing to be added"

to **addict** originally meant "to award as a slave"; an **addict** now is a slave to his/her habit and comes from Latin *addictus*, which in Roman law meant "a debtor awarded as a slave to his creditor"

addiction is mainly physical while **dependency** is mostly psychological

the classes of **additives** are preservatives, antioxidants, emulsifiers, coloring matter, sweeteners, and flavoring agents/enhancers

if you are **addled**, you are mixed up; if a egg is **addled**, it is rotten

addled refers to mental confusion; **muddled** is anything confused or in a mess

both eggs and brains are capable of **addling**

to **address** something can mean "to make straight or right" or "erect, raise, set up"

addubitation is the suggestion of a doubt

to **adduce** is to cite as an instance or as proof or evidence

-ade is a suffix meaning "produced from," as in lemonade

the **adenoids** are technically the pharyngeal tonsils

adeps is another word for "animal fat"

adeptship is the state or condition of being thoroughly proficient

adequate comes from Latin *adaequatus*, "made equal to"

adequate tends toward the qualitative and **sufficient** toward the quantitative, so **adequate** is "suitable to something" and **sufficient** is "enough for something"

there is an opposite of dharma (eternal law of the cosmos)—**adharma**, which means unrighteousness

to **adhere** first meant "to be a follower" and is based on Latin *haerere*, "to stick"

only things of a different nature can **adhere**; **cohere** is for things of the same kind that stick together and form a whole

adherence is mostly used in figurative senses while **adhesion** is literal and implies physical contact between surfaces and has a technical sense in medicine

> the frictional grip of a wheel on a rail or road surface is called **adhesion**

adhesive is a substance for sticking one thing to another; **cohesive** refers to particles of the same substance sticking together

to grant admittance is to **adhibit**

an **adiaphoron** is a matter of ethical indifference

Adidas is a blend of the first syllables of Adolf (Adi) Dassler, inventor of these athletic shoes

adieu and **adios** are both, literally "to God" (Dieu, Dios); **adieu** is an elliptical form for "I commend you to God"

instead of saying "fat" or "fatty," say **adipose** or **pinguid**

adit "approach or entrance" is the opposite of **exit**

adjacent means next to but not necessarily connected with, while **adjoining** means next to and connected—**adjacent** rooms are separated by a wall, **adjoining** are

connected by a common door; things are **adjacent** when they are side by side, they are **adjoining** when they share a common boundary, and **adjacent** may or may not imply contact but always implies absence of anything of the same kind in between

an **adjectament** is an addition

adjective is from Latin *adject-*, "added," and was first part of the phrase "noun **adjective**"—a translation of Latin *nomen adjectivum* and Greek *onoma epitheton*, "attributive name"

adjoining implies meeting and touching at some point or line

adjourn is from French *à jorn nommè*, "to an appointed day" and originally meant "to summon someone to appear on a particular day"

in grammar, an **adjunct** is a word or words modifying or amplifying a word(s) in a sentence

adjust is based on Latin *ad-* and *juxta*, "close to"

adjutant is from Latin meaning "being of service to"; an **adjutator** is a helper or assistant

to **admarginate** is to note in the margin

an **adminicle** is something that helps and **adminicular** means "corroborative"

administer first meant "to be a servant to"

admiral was first used in English to mean "an emir or prince under the Sultan" coming from Arabic *amir al*, "commander of"; **admiral** was originally a sea lord due to the office of *amir-al-bahr* or *amir-al-ma* (Arabic) "ameer/emir of the sea"

admire can mean "to wonder at, to be slightly surprised"

admission implies a physical entrance, whereas **admittance** implies some sort of procedural or merely formal entry; **admission** correlates with permission to move into a room or building but **admittance** correlates with acceptance into a group or organization

admission falls short of an acknowledgment of all elements of a crime—which would be a **confession**

with **admit**, the acknowledgment of something being true applies to one's own sphere of conduct, whereas with **concede** the acknowledgment applies to another's; **admit** implies reluctance to disclose, grant, or **concede** and refers usually to facts rather than their implications

admixture is the process of mingling one substance with another

admonish can mean "warn or caution against danger or error" or "warn or criticize mildly"

adnexa are the parts adjoining a human organ

an adjective used as a noun is an **adnoun**

ado literally means "to do"

adobe is from Arabic meaning "the bricks"

adolescence is the period of transition from childhood to adulthood; **puberty** is the time of sexual development

the elements of **adolescent** are *ad-*, "in the direction of," and *alescere*, "grow up" (from *alere*, "nourish")

to **adonize** is to dress up or beautify

adopt implies accepting something created by another or foreign to one's nature

adoptive is the active form, applied to the parents, and **adopted** is the passive form for the children

in Roman times, **adore** meant "to pray to a god"

adorn implies an enhancing by something beautiful in itself

adoxography is good writing on a trivial subject

adrenaline is sometimes called epinephrine

adret is a mountain slope which faces the sun; the opposite is **ubac**

adroit comes from French *a*, "with," and *droit*, "straight, correct" meaning nimble in body or mind

adscititious means "additional, supplemental"

{ **adsorbent** is the surface and **adsorbate** is the material adsorbed }

adulation derives from *adulari*, which meant "to fawn over someone like a dog wagging its tail"

adult comes from Latin *adultus*, the past participle of *adolescere*, "to grow to maturity"

an **adulterine** is a child born of an adultress

neither **adultery** nor **adulterate** have any connection with adult; they come from Latin *adulterare*, "corrupt, debauch"

an **adultescent** is a middle-aged person who wants to be associated with youth culture and whose choices in clothing, activities, etc. reflect this

adumbrate means "to give a sketchy outline or disclose only in part; hint" and its root is Latin *umbra*, "shadow"

adunation is the union or combination into one

advance is steady progress and stresses effective assisting in hastening a process or bringing about a desired end, while **advancement** suggests progression that is bigger, more, or beyond normal

to **advantage** is to further the progress of something

advectitious is a synonym for imported

advent, from Latin *adventus*, "arrival," is the four weeks before Christmas

when someone sneaks in the parking spot you have targeted, that is **adventitious**, "accidentally intruding from an unexpected place"

adventure comes from a Latin word meaning "about to happen" and first meant "chance" or "fortune"

adventurous may be predicated of both a person and an undertaking and implies a willingness to accept risks but not necessarily imprudence; **adventuresome** is predicated only of a person

an **adverb** can modify an adjective, **adverb**, or verb

adversaria are miscellaneous remarks and observations—as in a commonplace book

adverse refers to reluctance or unwillingness and it is more often a thing than a person that is **adverse**—like **adverse** circumstances

aversion is something that originates from within, whereas adversity is something that originates from without; **adverse** is usually applied to situations while **averse** is used to describe a person's attitude

advertent means "giving attention; heedful" (opposite of inadvertent)

an **advertique** is an antique advertisement, a piece of early advertising material

the Latin word that begat **advertise** meant "to turn toward"

advertisement is from *advertir*, Old French for "to notice" and ultimately from Latin *advertere*, "to turn toward"

advice first meant "way of looking at something" or "judgment"

to **advigilate** is to watch diligently

the original senses of **advise** included "look at" and "consider"—hence, "consider jointly, consult with others"

adviser might be more informal than **advisor**; **advisory** is the adjectival form

any lawyer can be called an **advocate**; **advocate** comes from Latin *advocare*, "call (to one's aid), summon"

adytum, the inner sanctum of a temple, comes from Greek *adytos*, "impenetrable"

an **adz/adze** is an ancient woodcutting tool similar to an ax with the blade set at right angles to the handle and curving in toward it

aeaeae is "magic"—and is derived from *aealae artes*, "magic arts"

an **aedicule** is a small room or structure used as a shrine—or a niche for a statue

aegis comes directly from Latin, which in turn comes from Greek *aigis*, "goatskin," from which Athena's protective shield was made; **aegis** originally meant shield

aeolian describes a sighing or moaning sound similar to wind

aeolistic is long-winded

aeon is pronounced E-un or E-ahn

aequor is the sea or a similar flat surface and aequorial is marine or oceanic

{ the filter piece on your faucet spout is the **aerator** }

aerial first meant "thin as air" or "imaginary"

an **aerie** (or **eyrie**, **eyry**) is the nest of any bird of prey

sewage treatment plants rely on **aerobic** (oxygen-loving) bacteria to do the work; septic tanks use **anaerobic** (oxygen-hating or that which is killed by oxygen) bacteria

the study of meteors is **aerolithology**

aerometry is the measurement of airflow through the nose and mouth during speech

aerose means brassy or coppery

Aesop, of Greek fables, is pronounced E-sup

aesthesics is a synonym for pronunciation

the perception of the external world by the senses is **aesthesis**

an **aesthete** is someone who claims to be sensitive to and appreciate beauty and thereby feels superior to others

aesthetic is from Greek *aistheta/aisthesis,* "things perceptible by the senses"

affinal means "related by marriage"; an **affine** is an in-law or any relative via marriage

aesthetics first denoted the study of sense-experience generally and then emerged as a subfield of philosophy in the nineteenth century

the root sense of **affable** is "easy to talk to" from Latin *fari,* "to talk"—related to *fable,* "a spoken tale"

affair is derived from French *faire,* "to do"

as a noun, **affect** means "a feeling or emotion," whereas **effect** means "the result or consequence of some action or process"; as a verb, to **affect** means "to exert an influence upon," and implies the action of a stimulus that can produce a response or reaction, whereas to **effect** means "to bring about as a result"

affection can be used as a verb to mean "like, love"

the original meaning of **affectionate** was "affected," especially unduly so

affective meaning is the emotional meaning of an utterance

the **affenpinscher,** German for "monkey terrier," is a dog resembling the griffon

afferent describes nerve fibers that carry messages to the brain

an **affiant** is a person who swears to an affidavit

affiche is a synonym for poster or placard

affidation is a vow to be faithful

an **affidavit** (literally "he has stated on oath") is taken by a judge, while the **deponent** swears, makes, or takes an **affidavit**

affiliate is from Latin meaning "adopted as a son"

affined means closely related or connected

affinity really means a feeling of kinship or an emotional bond and the prepositions that follow it are between, to, or with—not "for"; **affinity** is mutual: except in chemistry, you cannot have an **affinity** in one direction; and it can also mean "a family resemblance," as between cats and lions

an **affinity** is a relationship by marriage and **consanguinity** is a blood relationship

affirm first meant "make firm or strengthen" **afflated** means "inspired," as a poet would be

having an **afflatus** is a sudden rush of divine or poetic inspiration, a creative impulse, from Latin *afflare,* "to breathe or blow on," referring to the breath of gods or muses

the first meaning of **afflict** was close to the Latin original *affligere,* "to throw down"

afflict is generally used with living beings; **inflict** is generally used with inanimate objects

affluence's first meaning was "a plentiful flow"

affluent first meant "flowing freely or in great quantity"; **affluent** should be pronounced AF-loo-uhnt

affluential is a blend of affluent and influential

the original sense of **afford** was "accomplish, perform, promote"—then, "be in a position to do" or "manage"

the underlying meaning of **affray** is "take away someone's peace" an **affront** is a deliberate insult while **effrontery** is insolence

affrontee is an insulted person; **affrontive** is insulting

an **afghan** is a knitted quilt, first made on the Indian continent

aficionado means "amateur" in Spanish, coming from Latin *aficion*, "become fond of" and it first referred to a devotee of bullfighting—but now an ardent follower of any activity

if you are all **aflunters**, you are in a state of disorder

aforcing is the term for stretching the amount of a dish to accommodate more people

afraid was originally a form of the word affray, "to disturb, brawl"

Afrikaans is the principal language of South Africa

the **aft** is the stern or tail of a boat or other vessel, from Dutch *achter*, "after"

after was first the comparative form of aft

an instance of being blindsided is **afterclap**

{ **aftercare is childcare from after school till the end of the parental workday** }

aftermath was originally spelled "aftermowth"—which is a second or later mowing, the crop of grass that grows after the first mowing of early summer

afterward once had the nautical meaning "towards the stern"

wisdom or cleverness that comes too late is **after-wit**, also called **staircase wit**

again is sometimes spelled agen or agin when it is used jocularly or by certain dialects

an **agape** is a love feast

the medium in a petri dish is **agar**

agate, a form of quartz, got its name from the River Achates in Sicily, near which it is found in abundance; it usually contains variegated colors in bands

if you accompany someone partway home, you have gone **a-gatewards** with them

agathism is the belief that things tend to work out for the better

agathokakological means "made of good and evil"

age is a word used in mythology, geology, archaeology, history, etc. to denote a period of time marked by particular characteristics; a space of one hundred years can be called an **age**

an **agelast** is a person who never laughs

agenda is based on a Latin element meaning "do" and was originally the plural of **agendum** (a thing to be done); now it is singular, with agendas being the plural

agennesis is another word for impotence"

in grammar, the entity performing the action of the verb is the **agent**, which is the opposite of the patient or instrument (thing used in or for performing an action)

agerasia is looking young for your age or not appearing to age

an **aggie** is any person attending an agricultural school or is applied to the school itself

an **aggie** is a playing marble that resembles agate; an **immie** is imitation agate

aggiornamento is the process of making the life, doctrine, and worship of the Roman Catholic Church effective in the modern world

agglomerate is an adjective meaning "gathered into a ball or cluster" in geology, an **agglomerate** is a mass consisting of volcanic or eruptive fragments which have united under the action of heat - as opposed to a **conglomerate**, composed of waterworn fragments united by some substance in aqueous solution

agglutination is the formation of new words by combining other words or word elements

people can never be aggravated, only circumstances or situations (but people can be annoyed); **aggravate**'s historical meaning is "to make heavier; to pile on," "increase the gravity of," or "make more burdensome"

agile means having quick motion and being nimble (from Latin *agere*, "to do")

to **aginate** is to sell small things

agiotage, speculation in the stock market, was borrowed from French *agioter*, "speculate"

agitate (from Latin *agere*, "drive") first meant "drive away"

agitprop, political propaganda or cultural works which have adopted an ideological stance, is a blend of agitation and propaganda

the wavy lines drawn in comic strips to represent movement are **agitrons**

{ to **aggravate** is to make something worse, while to **exacerbate** is to increase something's bitterness or harshness }

aggravate means "to add to" an already troublesome or vexing matter or condition while **irritate** means "to vex, annoy, or chafe"

an **aggregate** is fragments or particles loosely grouped or held together

aggression developed from the milder action of "approaching" somebody—from *ad-*, "towards," and *gradi*, "walk"

if something is physically injured or one's rights are injured, one is **aggrieved**

aggro is deliberate troublemaking (an abbreviation of aggravation or aggression)

aggry is a kind of variegated glass bead from West Africa—and joins angry and hungry in answering the Riddle about three English words ending in -gry

aghast was from a verb *agastea*, "frighten," based on an Old English word meaning "torment"

an **aglet** is the plastic or metal covering on the end of a shoelace (formerly called point) that makes it easier to thread through the eyelet holes

the speech sound represented by "ng" in "thing" is an **agma**

agminate means "grouped together in a cluster"

agnail is actually the torn skin around a fingernail (from Old High German ungnagel)

agnoiology is the branch of philosophy studying human ignorance

small ravioli are called **agnolotti**

if you have a nickname, it is an **agnomen**

agnostic was coined by T.H. Huxley, based on gnostic (an early Christian sect claiming mystic knowledge) and adding a- "without" (such knowledge); Huxley got tired of being called an atheist, so he coined **"agnostic"** to indicate that he had no evidence of God's existence one way or the other

agnosy is another word for ignorance and **agnoiology** is the study of human ignorance

when **ago** is followed by a clause, the clause normally starts with "that" (rather than "since"): "it was ten years **ago** that I left that company"; in fact, there is no need to use "ago" and "since" together—one or the other is fine

agog comes from Old French *en gogues*, "in a merry mood"

agomphosis/agomphiasis is looseness of teeth

agon was Greek for competitive event and *agonia* was the struggle to win ("contest") as well as the accompanying pain of the struggle, hence **agony** and the extended meaning of "mental anguish"

agoraphobia is based on Greek *agora*, "open space"—but it was not the first phobia described, which was actually hydrophobia in the mid-sixteenth century

{ an **agraffe** is a hook-and-loop arrangement used for a clasp on clothing }

agree is based on Latin *ad-*, "to," and *gratus*, "pleasing," and we **agree** to a plan or idea or **agree** with a person

agrestal is "living or growing in the wild"

agriculture is based on the Latin root *ager*, "field"

agroforestry is the cultivation and alternation of tree or bush crops with annual food crops

agronomy is the management and husbandry of land

agrostology is the study of grasses

agrypnia is a synonym for insomnia

a fit of shivering is **ague**

ahi is yellowfish tuna

ahimsa is the spiritual doctrine of not harming any living thing (nonviolence)

animals are **ahistoric** or **ahistorical**: having no concern or awareness of the history of their kind

ahoy was once a Viking battle cry and is from "ah" and *hoy*, "look!"

aid is assistance or a source of assistance; **aide** is an assistant

aidance is another word for aid

aide is an abbreviation of aide-de-camp, for which the plural is aides-de-camp

the **aigrette** is the feathery top of a dandelion

a steep, pointed mountain is an **aiguille**

aikido comes from Japanese *ai*, "together, unify," *ki*, "spirit," and *do*, "way," meaning "the way of unifying the spirit" or "way of harmony"

ail comes from Old English meaning "troublesome"

aileron is literally "little or small wing"

when you **aim** a weapon, you are estimating the path of the missile to the target (from Latin *aestimare*, "to estimate")

aioli is French for *ai*, "garlic" and *oli*, "oil"—mayonnaise seasoned with garlic

an **air** is an expressive succession of musical sounds—a melody or tune

an **airbrush** is a device for spraying color over a surface by means of compressed air; when used in photography, its purpose is to retouch or obliterate parts of an image

airglow is the light of the night sky (excluding starlight and moonlight), that lends itself to spectroscopic examination and has been found to contain light emissions characteristic of nitrogen, oxygen, and sodium

airish is a synonym for "drafty"

to go directly by the shortest route can be described as "taking the **air-line**" (also bee-line)

airplane is based on Greek *planos*, meaning "wandering"

airstream is the source of energy for speech sound production

an **airt** is a quarter of a compass

aisle first meant "wing of a church" and the word is based on Latin *ala*, "wing"

ait (a favorite crossword puzzle word) is a small island in a river or lake; synonyms for this are **eyot** and **holm**

the **aitchbone** is the rump bone in cattle or a cut of beef from it or including it

a narrative devised to explain the origin of a religious observance is an **aition**

ajar is from a phrase meaning "on turn" as a door or window that was in the act of turning is neither completely shut or open

AK-47 means Automat Kalashnikov, the latter the name of its designer

if you are restless and cannot sit, you suffer from **akathisia**

akimbo is derived from Old Norse *kengboggin*, "bent bows" or "bent in a curve," and describes one's position of hands on the hips and elbows pointed outward

akrasia is weakness of will (Greek *a-*, "without," and *kratos*, "power") when someone acts against their better judgment through weakness of will

Alabama's name comes from Choctaw *alba ayamule*, "I open the thicket (to obtain food)"

alabaster is a light-colored gypsum that was used for cat coffins in ancient Egypt; hence a-la-Baste, Baste being the cat-headed goddess

alack comes from alackaday and **alas** comes from French *ah las*, "oh weary (me)"

alacrity comes from Latin words meaning "briskness, liveliness"

Alamo is a Spanish term for the cottonwood and other poplar trees

alamodality is fashionableness

alamode is a type of thin glossy black silk

alarm comes from Italian *all'arme*, "to arms!," the call to equip oneself with weapons in preparation for battle

alas comes from a combination of the interjection "ah" and Latin *lasse/lassus*, "weary," and usually expresses unhappiness, grief, or concern

Alaska's name comes from Inuit *alakshak* or *Ayayeks*, "great land, mainland," and we use the Russian version of the name

albacore comes via Portuguese from Arabic *al-bakurah*, "the tuna"

{ **albatross** is a double eagle, three under par on a single golf hole }

golf words having to do with birds are **albatross** (three strokes under, also called double **eagle**), **eagle** (two strokes under), **birdie** (one stroke under), and **buzzard** (two strokes over)

albedo is the ratio of the radiation reflected by a surface to the total incoming solar radiation, hence in extended use, applied to the proportion of light reflected from various surfaces

the white pithy inner peel of citrus fruit is the **albedo**

albeit is a shortened version of "all be it (that)"

the plural of **albino** is albinos

the white of the eye is the **albuginea**

{ **album** means "white," which comes from the tablets on which Roman edicts were written; **album** should be pronounced AL-buhm }

albumen is the white of an egg, from Latin *albus*, "white"; **albumin** is a protein within the **albumen**

albus "white" is the base of the word albino

alcatraz is another name for a pelican

alchemy is from Arabic *al-kimya*, "the transmutation"; the first reference to **alchemy** is by a Chinese Taoist in 140 BC

the process that distinguished **alchemy** from **chemistry** was similar to that which later distinguished **astrology** and **astronomy**

the adjective form for **auk** is **alcidine**

alcohol is from Arabic *al-kohl*, a substance obtained by distillation, and came to be used of any distillate; its first meaning was finely ground powder, kohl—c 1000 AD, Arabian alchemists invented the distillation of **alcohol** by a similar process to that used to make the cosmetic kohl, so they borrowed the name of the process "alkohl"

alcopop is a ready-mixed carbonated drink containing alcohol

alcove derives from Arabic *al-gobbah*, "the dome vault"

alder is an ancient tree name

alderman preserves the notion that those who are old (elders) are automatically in charge (based on *eald*, "old")

an **ale** is a social gathering at which much **ale** is drunk

aleatory derives from the Latin word for the game of dice *alea jacta est*, "the die is cast"; **aleatory** means "depending on the throw of a die" (Latin *alea*, "a die")—

"random by chance" or "depending on certain contingencies"

aleatory refers to the present or future while fortuitous is more about past events

an **alector** is a person who is unable to sleep (from Homer's *Odyssey*)

malt vinegar can also be called **alegar**

fear of chickens is **alektorophobia**

an **alembic** is a device or method that tests, transforms, or purifies

alembicated is a word for "overly subtle or refined in thought or expression"

alert is from Italian *all'erta*, "on the watch; on the lookout" or "to the watch-tower"

aletude is another word for obesity

alewife is the landlady of an alehouse, and the fish got its name from resembling such a person's plump appearance

an antidote can also be called an **alexipharmic** (from Greek *alexein*, "ward off" and *pharmakon*, "poison")

Charles Darwin was the first writer to use the word **alfalfa** in English (from Arabic *al-fasfasah*)

Alfredo sauce is named for Alfredo di Lelio, the Italian chef who invented it

alfresco means "in the cool"

alga is the Latin word for "seaweed"; **algae** is the plural

algebra comes from Arab words meaning "reunion of broken parts" (from *jabara*, "set broken bones")—and became popular when a mathematician published the book

"The science of restoring what is missing and equating like with like"—but the word's first meaning was "the surgical treatment of fractures"

if something is **algedonic**, it is characterized by pleasure and pain, reward and punishment (from Greek *algos*, "pain," and *hedone*, "pleasure")

algefacient or **algific** means "cooling"

algesia is sensitiveness to pain

algid means "cold, chilly" from Latin *algere*, "be cold"

aliment can be used figuratively to mean "mental sustenance or support"; **alimentary** means "providing nourishment"

alimentotherapy is the assignment of dietary therapy to treat a disease

alimonious means "nourishing"

alimony is from Latin *alimonia*, "nourishment" or "eating money," from *alere*, "to nourish," and *mony*, "result, resulting condition," and first meant "nourishment, support"

aliquant means "contained in a larger quantity or number but not an exact number of times"—as four is an **aliquant** part of fifteen

an **algorithm** is a calculating procedure using a series of steps; an example of an **algorithm** is the set of rules for doing simple multiplication, which are precise and can be applied without judgment, part of the definition of "**algorithm**"

alias is Latin for "at another time; otherwise"

in Latin, **alibi** was an adverb that meant "elsewhere" or "at another place" and when it first came into English it was limited to adverbial use; an **alibi** is in one sense an excuse, but a specific one

an **alien** is a word from one language that is used but not naturalized in another

alieniloquy is a word for rambling or evasive talk

aliety is the state of being different and **aliud** is something else or another thing

align is from French *a ligne*, "into line"

alike is an ancient word whose ultimate Germanic source (*galikam*) meant something like "associated form"

the **A-line**, a dress or skirt shaped like an A, was created by Christian Dior

aliquot means "contained in a larger whole an exact number of times"—like four is an **aliquot** part of sixteen

if your legs are across each other or two legs lie crossing each other, they are **aliry**

aliunde means "from another person or place; from elsewhere"

alive comes from the Old English phrase "on life"; **alive** is a derivative of "life," not of the verb "live"

alkali is from Arabic *al-galiy*, "the ashes," in reference to the plant saltwort (Salsola kali) which was burnt to get its alkaline ashes

all together means "collectively," "in one place," "all at once"; **altogether** means "in sum, entirely"

all-American is the noun form; **all-America** is the adjective

allay is from Old English "lay down or aside"

allege first meant "to declare under oath before a tribunal" (Latin *ex-* and *lis/lit,* "lawsuit")

allegiance first meant the duty of a liegeman to his liege lord or a subject to his monarch or government

allegory is another word for "emblem" or "a picture in which the meaning is symbolically represented"—from Greek *allegoria,* "speaking otherwise,"—and indicates another level of meaning concealed within a story of some kind

allemang means "mixed together" as when two flocks of sheep are accidentally driven together

allergens themselves are not harmful, but when combined with certain antibodies a reaction liberates substances that damage body cells and tissues (i.e. the allergy)

allergy is derived from Greek *allos,* "other, different," and *energie,* "energy," as it is the altered reactivity of the body towards an antigen

alleviate can mean "diminish the weight of"; to **alleviate** is not to cure but rather to lighten, lessen, or relieve to some degree

originally an **alley** was a passageway in or into a house

alley-oop may come from French *alles!* "go on!" and the French pronunciation of "up"

if you just ate Italian food, your breath is probably **alliaceous,** "smelling or tasting of garlic or onion"

allicient is "attractive" and **alliciency** is "attractiveness"

alligator is Spanish *el lagarto,* "the lizard," which may have come from Latin *lacerta;* the **alligator** has a shorter, blunter snout than a crocodile

an **alligator pear** is another name for **avocado**

the striking of a stationary ship by one that is moving or the ramming of one object by another is **allision**

alliteration is based on Latin *ad-,* "to," and *litera,* "letter," from the notion of an accumulation of words beginning with the same letter (and **alliterate** is a back-formation of this)

alliteration is the repetition of a consonantal sound(s) while **assonance** is the repetition of a vowel sound

a person who hates garlic is an **alliumphobe**

to **allocate** something is to set it aside for a specific purpose; to **allot** something is to give it with an implied restriction and an understanding of sharing

allodoxaphobia is a fear of others' opinions

geological material that has been transported and then accumulates elsewhere is **allochthonous** and sediment carried by a river is **allogenic**

{ an **allograph** is a signature or writing done for another person }

the grooming of one cat by another is **allogrooming**

if your feet are growing faster than your body as a whole, they are **allometric**

an **allonym** is a pen name that is borrowed, not made-up like a **pseudonym**

another word for conventional medical treatment is **allopathy** and an **allopath** or **allopathist** is a physician

allopathy is treatment to suppress the symptoms of illness using the principle of opposites while **homeopathy** encourages rather than suppresses the body's reaction to an illness

an **allotrope** is an element in different molecular forms like O_2 and O_3 or two crystal variations—like diamond and graphite are variations of carbon

an **allottery** is an allotted share

feeling slightly indisposed? say you are feeling "**all-overish**"

allow first meant "praise, commend"

alloy was the comparative purity of gold or silver and originally a mixture of a precious metal with a baser one; now it is any mixture of something which diminishes the character or value

allspice is also **pimento**, which should not be confused with the pimiento, a pepper

allude can mean "to play on words" and **allusion** was once a "play on words, pun"

allude is "mention indirectly, hint at" and **refer** is "mention directly"

allure first meant "to attract or tempt; entice"

allusion is an "indirect mention," **illusion** is "false impression," and **delusion** is "deception" which is much stronger than **illusion**

alluvial, "washed down and deposited by running water," is from Latin *lavare*, "wash"

alluvium is a deposit of earth, sand, and other transported matter left by water flowing over land, but it can also mean the overflow or flood itself

in Chaucer's day, **ally** meant "relative, kinsman"

almanac is from Arabic *al-manakh*, "the calendar"

a compiler of almanacs is an **almanagist**

almond should be pronounced AH-muhnd and is mentioned seventy-three times in the Old Testament

almost first meant "mostly all"

alms goes back to Greek *eleemosune*, "compassion, pity," and *eleos*, "mercy"

alogy is unreasonableness or absurdity

aloha is Hawaiian for both hello and goodbye and also means "love"

alone first meant "the all is one"

along once meant "at a distance"

alongside should never be followed by "of"

a potato or potato dish in Indian cooking is an **aloo**

aloof comes from sailing, to keep clear of coastal rocks by holding the vessel "luff" meaning "to the windward"—so, to hold "a-luff" means to "keep clear"

alopecia (hair loss, baldness) comes from Greek *alopekia*, "fox mange" or "baldness in man"

aloud first meant "in a loud voice"

an **alpaca** resembles a **llama** but has long fine woolly hair and usually brown-and-white coloring

alpenglow is the rosy lighting of the setting or rising sun as seen on high mountains

one of **alphabet**'s original meanings was "knowledge acquired from written works"

alphabetology or **alphabetics** is the science or study of alphabets

some passwords have to be **alphameric** or **alphanumeric**, made up of letters and numbers

alpine, fast downhill skiing, originated in the Alps

a synonym for German shepherd is **Alsatian**

also was an Old English compound formed from *all*, "exactly, *even*," and *swa*, "so"—meaning "in just this way; thus"

also-ran came from the heading used in daily published racing results for horses that finished out of the money ("also ran but did not win money")

altar comes from Latin *altus*, meaning "high," as this is usually a raised structure

an individual's conception of another person is called **alter**

an **altercation** is a heated exchange of words, not a fight

the state of being different is **alterity**

altern, "every other," is the base of alternate

alternate means "one after the other" or "each succeeding the other in turn, especially continuously," and **alternative** means "one instead of the other" or "allowing or necessitating a choice between two or more things"

an **alternator** produces alternating current while a **generator** (or dynamo) produces direct current

although and **though** are interchangeable as conjunctions, but to start a clause, use "**although**"

altitude figuratively means "lofty feeling or attitude" as well as "eminence"

altivolent means "flying high," as an eagle

alto, which means "high," was formerly the highest male voice (now countertenor) but is now the lowest female voice

altocumulus undulatus are the clouds in a herringbone sky (there are other forms of **altocumulus**: castellanus, duplicatus, floccus, lacunaris, lenticularis, opacus, perlucidus, radiatus, stratiformis, and translucidus)

Altoids (the breath mint) is from Latin *altus*, "highest, best," and *-oid*, an older pharmaceutical suffix

the word for the condition of being born blind and helpless, like chicks, is **altricial**

altrigenderism is the stage at which one develops interest in the opposite sex

etymologically as well as semantically, **altruism** contains the notion of "other people" (from Italian *altrui*, "that which belongs to other people") and it is contrasted with egoism

English chemist Sir Humphry Davy coined the term **aluminum** in 1812

alumnus and **alumna** stem from Latin *alere*, "to nourish or be nourished," now by a university; originally **alumnus** was a pupil and now it is a male graduate; **alumni** refers to either sex

prunes are **alviducous**, "purgative"

Alzheimer's is named for neurologist/psychiatrist Alois Alzheimer (1864-1915) who identified the dementia

an **amalgam** is what follows upon an **amalgamation**; **amalgamation** is a process in which things are combined and an **amalgam** is the result or consequence—of that process—so **amalgam** means "combination," while **amalgamation** means "the act of combining or uniting; consolidation"

{ **amalgamate** seems to go back to Greek malagma "softening" }

amandine means "served or cooked with almonds"

amanuensis is literally "slave at hand"— for a literary assistant, especially one who takes dictation or copies manuscripts

one meaning of **amaranth** is a "flower that never fades"

amaretto takes its name from Italian *amaro*, "bitter," for the bitter almonds which flavor it; the plural of **amaretto** is amaretti

the **amaryllis** gets its name from Linnaeus, who adopted it from a Greek personal name of a country girl used in the writings of Theocritus, Ovid, and Virgil

someone amasses something; things do not simply "**amass**"; an **amass** (noun) is an accumulation

amateur is based on the Latin word for "love," as an **amateur** engages in a pursuit for the love of it, not for pay; its original meaning was "person who is fond of or has a taste for something"

amation is the activity of love

amative means "inclined to be loving"

amaze once meant "alarm, terrify" but now means "astonish"; **surprise** means "meet with suddenly or without warning"

amazon is probably a Greek form of the Iranian *ha-mazan,* "fighting together"

Amazon.com was so named because its founder wanted the store's inventory to be as deep and wide as the Amazon River

encompassing" or "existing or present on all sides"

an old name for a banquet offering a medley of dishes is **ambigu**

lexical **ambiguity** is seen in a word like chip, which can be related to a computer or a potato

ambiguous is vague by accident or intent; **equivocal** is vague by intent

ambilingualism is the ability to speak two languages with equal facility

if you are awkward with your hands, that is being **ambisinister**

an **ambit** is a boundary, circuit, or circumference—or a limit, range, or scope of something

{ **ambages** is Latin for "drive both ways" and means "roundabout path or speech"; **ambagious** is "not straightforward; roundabout" }

ambassador is based on Latin *ambactus,* "servant"

amber is easily electrified by rubbing and is the name of the color for the caution road traffic signal

ambergris was originally amber but was distinguished as *ambre gris* (French for "gray amber" as it is waxy matter from the stomach of the sperm whale)

ambidextrous means literally "right-handed on both sides" from *ambi-,* "both," and *dexter,* "right-handed"

ambience describes the accessory and surrounding elements of a painting

ambient means "pertaining to the immediate surroundings" (as in **ambient** temperature); the stem of **ambient** is Latin *ambire,* "go round," and it means "surrounding,

ambition is from Latin *ambitio,* "running around," for what Roman politicians did to get votes—and because this was motivated by a desire for honor or power, **ambition** came to denote this desire itself

the exterior edge of an object, such as a leaf, is the **ambitus**

ambivalent is patterned on the word equivalent; an **ambivalent** person is someone who has strong feelings on more than one side of a question or issue

a person balanced between extrovert and introvert characteristics is an **ambivert**

amble originally referred to a horse's gait

an **ambodexter** is an unethical lawyer or bribed juror

ambrosia comes from the Greek elements *am-*, "not," and *-brosos*, "mortal," meaning it is a substance for immortals, literally "elixir of life"

another word for a treasury, storehouse, place to keep things, is an **ambry**

ambsace means both "bad luck, worthlessness," and a "pair of aces on dice"

an **ambulance** once brought the hospital to the patient—and it kept the name when it reversed the process and started bringing the patients to the hospital; its original meaning was "mobile hospital following an army"

an **ambulatory** is a place for walking

ambush is based on a Latin word meaning "to place in a wood"

ameba/amoeba comes from a Greek word meaning "alternation, change"

to **ameed** is to reward

ameliorate, an alteration of meliorate, is based on Latin *melior*, "better"

amen is from Hebrew meaning "truth, certainty" and it is generally accepted as meaning "so be it"

amenable first meant "liable to answer (to a law or tribunal)" and now means "open to suggestion or advice"

to **amenage** something is to domesticate or tame it

amend first meant "to reform or convert" a person

when you **amend** a text, you change it—usually for the better—and when you **emend** a text, you simply correct the mistakes; whereas one can **amend** various aspects of conduct or behavior, **emend** is used if the issue at hand is that of a manuscript, speech, or literary product

amenity is the pleasantness of a place or person

amentia is being out of one's mind with joy, in a rapturous daze

America is believed to derive from the Latin form, Americus, of the name of Amerigo Vespucci, who followed after Columbus and extended his discoveries, sailing along the west coast of South America in 1501

the earliest **Americanisms** were probably words borrowed from Native American languages indicating natural objects that had no counterparts in England

the **amethyst** was believed by the Greeks to protect against the effects of overdrinking and Greek *amethystos* means literally "not inducing drunkenness" (from *methy*, "wine"); the literal translation of **amethyst** is "not to be drunk"

amicable implies being well disposed; **amiable** is acting well disposed and **amiable** is commonly applied only to people—though sometimes it is used for occasions, while **amicable** is not applied to people at all but to human interactions and their outcomes; **amiable** first meant "kind" or "lovely, lovable" and **amicable** first applied to things and meant "pleasant, benign"

when **amicable** describes personal relations, it tends to indicate a rather formal friendliness

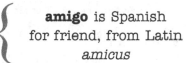
{ **amigo** is Spanish for friend, from Latin *amicus* }

the **Amish** people got the name from Jacob Amen or Amman or Ammon, a Swiss Mennonite preacher active at the end of the seventeenth century

amiture is another word for friendship

amity pertains specifically to friendly relations between public individuals or governments

ammonia gets it name from Ammon, the oracle of Jupiter, from sal ammoniac "salt of Ammon," and **ammonia** was first made from the dung of camels in Ammon, Egypt the fossil **ammonite** got its name from Latin *cornu Ammonis*, "horn of Ammon," from its resemblance to Ammon, the oracle of Jupiter's ram's horn

ammunition originally applied to all military supplies generally

amnesia and **amnesty** are based on Greek **amnesia** "forgetfulness" (from *a-*, "not," + *mnasthai*, "to remember"); **amnesty** is another word for forgetfulness

amniocentesis is *amnion* (the innermost membrane enclosing a fetus), and Greek *kentesis*, "pricking"; the **amnion** is the innermost membrane that encloses the embryo of a mammal, bird, or reptile

amok is from a Malay *amuk*, "fighting furiously" or "rushing in a frenzy"

among applies to things that can be separated and counted; **amid** to things that cannot

for physical presence, **amongst** is used; if no physical presence is indicated, then **among** is used

the sherry called **amontillado** was first made in Montilla, Spain

a person who is **amoral** does not understand the difference between right and wrong, so it means that one is neither moral nor **immoral**, while a person who is **immoral** understands the difference but does wrong anyway; **amoral** means "not concerned with morality" while **immoral** means "not conforming to moral standards" or "evil"

pudding; an **amorphous** solid lacks the perfect ordered structure of crystals—and other examples are glass, polymers, and rubber

to **amortize** is to pay a mortgage in installments

amount is based on Latin *ad montem*, "uphill"

use **amount** with things that cannot be counted but **number** with things that can be counted

one's **amour-propre** is one's awareness of what is right and proper for oneself

the **ampere** unit of electrical current was named for Andre-Marle **Ampere**, the French physicist

the **ampersand** is a stylized *et*, Latin for "and," and the name is a combination of "and, per se, and"

amphibian from Greek *amphibios* (*amphi*, "both," and *bios*, "life") means "living a double life, having two modes of life" (aquatic and terrestrial); **amphibian** as an adjective can mean "of doubtful nature"

if there is ambiguous wording or equivocation, there is **amphibology**

an **amphigory** is a nonsensical piece of writing, often in verse and usually a parody

amphitheater is from Greek elements meaning "on both sides of the theater" and can refer to a level piece of ground surrounded by naturally rising slopes or sides

 amphoric or **amphorous** is hollow-sounding, "like the sound made by blowing across the top of an open bottle"

an **amorist** is a person who is in love

something **amorphous** has no real shape or is irregularly shaped—like

writing or speech that treats a subject in full can be called **ample**

amplexation is embracing

amplexus is the mating position of frogs and toads, literally "an embrace" in Latin—an embrace during which the eggs are fertilized externally

ampliative means "adding to what is already known"

amplify is from a Latin word meaning "enlarge"

amplivagant or **amplivagous** means "wide in scope; extensive"

amputate comes from Latin *ambi*, "around," and *putare*, "to prune, trim"

sediment in olive oil is **amurca**

the first meaning of **amuse** was "to divert the attention of in order to mislead," "delude, deceive," and now means "entertain, make smile or laugh"; **bemuse** means "confuse, bewilder, puzzle"

an **amuse-bouche** is a small complimentary appetizer offered at some restaurants

another word for appetizer is **amuse-guele**

a word for almond-shaped is **amygdaline** or **amygdaloid**

if you are weak or lacking muscle, you are **amyous**

ana originally was a collection of the wit and wisdom of a particular person and can describe any collection of unusual bits of information on a particular subject of interest

an **anabasis** is a military expedition and **catabasis** is the retreat of an army

an **anachronism** is something which is more appropriate to another period of time (Greek *ana-*, "backward," and *khronos*, "time")

anaclitic is "characterized by a strong emotional dependence on another" or "overly dependent"

anaconda comes from a Sinhalese term for "whip snake"

a head wreath is an **anadem**

in the summer you may have **anadipsia**, great or excessive thirst

a fish that migrates upriver to spawn is **anadromous**; downriver to spawn at sea is **catadromous** and **diadromous** refers to fish that migrate between fresh and salt water

lack of interest in former loved ones is **anagapesis**

when a hair is growing, it is in the **anagen** stage of its life cycle

anagram's elements mean "anew, back" and "letter" as this is a word or phrase rearranged to form another

analects first meant "crumbs, gleanings," from Greek *analekta*, "things gathered up"; **analects** are randomly picked written passages

{ **analgesia** is Greek, literally "painlessness" }

an **analog** is a person or thing seen as comparable to another

analog is a traditional watch face and **digital** is the time shown in figures

homologus features are those that were originally the same in evolutionary development but have adapted differently (arms of humans, forelegs of cats, etc.); **analogous** features are those that resemble one another in function but are traceable back to completely different origins

an **analogue** is a synthetic food product resembling a natural food in taste and texture

analogy comes from Greek *analogia*, a proportion like $2/10 = 10/X$, a way of calculating unknown quantities

analogy is when two different things share characteristics that lead to a comparison between them; an **analogue** is one of the things compared

an **analysand** is a person undergoing psychoanalysis

analysis is from Greek elements meaning "loosen up"

analysis is breaking down or taking apart; **synthesis** is bringing together

the original sense of **analyze** was "dissect"

when you tell your medical history to a doctor, that is your **anamnesis**

ananas is a pineapple plant

in some Eastern religions, **ananda** means "bliss, extreme happiness"

an **ananym** is a pseudonym, arrived at by spelling the author's name backwards— e.g., REFPIK for KIPFER

an **anapest** is a metrical foot made up of two short syllables preceding one long syllable

{ **anaphora** is the central prayer sequence of the Eucharist }

if one is **anaphroditous**, one lacks sexual desire

anarchy is from Greek *anarkhos*, "without a chief"

an **anastigmat** is a lens that corrects astigmatism

word-order inversion is termed **anastrophe** or hyperbaton

anathema originally meant "something dedicated to God" which could be either a revered object or an object representing destruction brought about in the name of God (and is pronounced uh-NATH-uh-muh)

the adjective form for duck is **anatine**

another word for dissect or cut up an animal or human is **anatomize**

anatomy is from Greek *ana*, "up," and *temnien*, "to cut"

anaudia is loss of voice

ancestor is from Latin *ante*, "before," and *cedere*, "go"

ancestry can also be used in reference to animals or other organisms

an appliance mooring a balloon (etc.) to the ground is the **anchor**

anchorage is an area off the coast that is suitable for ships to anchor

anchorite (hermit) is derived from Greek *ana-*, "back," and *chorein*, "to withdraw"

the **anchorperson** is the one at the back of a tug-of-war team or the last runner in a relay race

anchovy comes from Spanish and Portuguese, but the word is of unknown origin

ancient is from Latin *ante*, "before," and *anus*, "of or belonging to"

your **ancon** is your elbow and the bend of the elbow is the **bought**

and is as ancient as the English language itself, and it has persisted virtually unchanged since at least 700 AD

and/or means "either both or only one" and indicates that the idea expressed is both distributive and inclusive

andiron is from Old French *andier* and has nothing to do with iron

andragogy are the methods or techniques used to teach adults

androgens are male sex hormones like testosterone; **estrogens** are female sex hormones

androgenous pertains to making male offspring; **androgynous** means having male and female characteristics

an **android** is an automation of human form

an **androsphinx** is a sphinx with the head of a man

anecdotage is an advanced age when it is accompanied by a tendency to reminisce

the adjectival forms of anecdote are **anecdotal**, **anecdotical**, anecdotic (from Greek *anekdotos*, "not made public")

anecdote comes from the title of a sixth century AD book by the historian Procopius, *Anecdota* (*Unpublished Tidbits*); the first meaning of **anecdote** was "secret history"

anemia is from Greek *an*, "without," and *haima*, "blood," as it is a deficiency of red blood cells

if something is **anemic**, it is "spiritless, weak"

anemone, or the windflower, comes from Greek words for "wind" and "habitation"

an **anesthetic** induces insensibility and an **analgesic** makes you feel no pain, while an **anodyne** removes your cares

a dill seed is an **anet**

an **aneurysm** is an excessive enlargement of an artery

anfractuosity means circuitousness or intricacy and **anfracture** is a mazelike winding

in aviation, an **angel** is one thousand feet of altitude

the word **angel** was one of the earliest Germanic adoptions from Latin, which came from Greek *aggelos*, "messenger," and it originally meant "hireling" or "messenger"

angelology is the hierarchy of angels

anger comes from an Old Norse word meaning "grief"

angina "severe pain," is from Latin *angere*, "to choke, strangle"

if a dish is done **anglaise**, it is boiled and served without sauce

the fishing term **angle** dates back to Old English meaning "fish-hook"

angler probably derives from the ancient tribe of fishermen in England, the Angles (which became Angli and then English)

angora as in cat, goat, and rabbit, comes from the Turkish capital **Angora** (till 1930), now Ankara

a wound or sore is **angry** if it is red and inflamed

angst is a German word (pronounced AHNGST) that originally meant constriction; anxiety that is strong but unspecific is **angst**

the **angstrom** took the name of Anders Angstrom (1814-1874), a pioneer in (light) spectrum analysis

anguish, **anxious**, and **anxiety** come from Latin *angere*, "to choke, squeeze, strangle"

anguria is a gourd or watermelon

> { if one is **anhelous**, one is short of breath or panting }

anhidrotic is another word for antiperspirant

anile is the female equivalent of senile (the male)

anima is the source of the female part of personality and **animus** is the source of the male part

anima is Carl Jung's term for the inner part of the personality or character, as opposed to the **persona** or outer part

to **animadvert** can mean "to turn the mind or attention to, pay attention to (something)" or "to comment critically (on)"

the Latin noun **animal**, derived from *animalis*, "having breath, living," designates those living beings that breathe perceptibly

animism is the belief that inanimate things have a spirit and an awareness

animosity first meant "boldness, high spirits," so courage or spirit can also be called **animosity**

animus was Carl Jung's term for the masculine part of the female personality (compared to anima, the feminine component of the male personality)

the **ankh** is also called the ansate cross

to **ankle** is slang for "to walk"

ankylosis is stiffness or immobility in a joint

one's **anlage** is an inherited disposition to certain traits or a particular character development; **atavism** is the reappearance of characteristics after skipping one or more generations

the first, medial/internal, and final sounds in a word are **anlaut**, **inlaut**, and **auslaut**, respectively

annealing is the heat treatment of metals to allow for molecular and crystalline rearrangement before cooling—to improve or restore a metal's properties

annex can apply to something that is joined—without subordination—or appended as an accessory (with the idea of subordination)

annihilate once meant "made null and void" as an adjective, now it means "reduced to nothing"

Latin *anniversarius*, "returning yearly," (*annus*, "year," and *versus*, "turning") is the base of **anniversary**

annotate first meant "make a mark on"

announce can mean "make known to the senses," not involving words

annoy derives from Latin *in odio*, from *mihi in odio est*, "it is hateful to me," and first meant "injury" or "molestation"; **annoy** implies a persistent petty unpleasantness that wears on someone's nerves

annuated is slightly aged

annular is another word for ring-shaped and an **annulus** is a ring

your **annulary** is your ring finger

anode is from Greek *anodus*, "way up"; it is the positive electrode or terminal

anomaly comes from Greek roots meaning "uneven"

anomy or **anomie** is lawlessness or an absence of social standards or values

an **anonym** is a concept or idea that has no word to express or describe it (which some may call "Sniglets")

in its earliest uses, **anonymous** meant "unacknowledged, illegitimate"

anophelosis is a morbid state due to extreme frustration

anopisthographic (or -ical) means something has writing on only one side (usually paper)

anorak was borrowed from Inuit *annoraaq*; another meaning is "a socially inept or studious person"—the type who might wear an unfashionable **anorak**

anorchous means "lacking testicles"

anorectic means "suffering from a loss of appetite"

anorexia is from Greek *an-*, "without," and *orexis*, "appetite"

anosmia is the loss of the sense of smell

anotherguess is an adjective for "of another type or sort"

ansal means "two-edged, cutting both ways"

if something has a handle, it is **ansate**

annual can mean lasting for one year or recurring once every year; an **annual** plant lasts for one year/season only

the adjective form of goose is **anserine**

Anglo-Saxon *andswerian*, the forebear of **answer**, meant "to swear in opposition to"; **answer** once meant "to swear a solemn oath in reply to a charge or *accusation*"—*an*, "against," and *swer*, "to swear against"

an **answer** is something said, written, or done in return; a **reply** is an **answer** that satisfies a detail in a question

an **answer-jobber** is one who makes a living of writing answers

ant comes from Old English *aemete*, "cut off"

antagonize first meant "struggle against"

antapology is the reply to an apology like "That's all right"

ante is an advance payment

anteambulate means "to walk in front of or before"

antebellum means "existing before a war," especially the American Civil War

the noun to which a pronoun refers is the **antecedent**

an **antechamber** is any room leading to a more important one and suggests a room somewhat more formal than an anteroom

antecubital is pertaining to the inner surface of the forearm and **antebrachial** is pertaining to the forearm

an **antedating** is an example or instance of (a sense of) a word, phrase, etc., at a date earlier than previously known or recorded or a citation of this

an **antefact** is a previous or earlier act

many people need an **ante-jentacular** (pre-breakfast) coffee

antelope was originally the name of a fierce mythological creature said to live on the banks of the Euphrates

antelucan is "happening before dawn" (*as luc* is "light")

antenna has an odd etymology, being the alteration of Latin *antenna*, "sailyard," a translation of Aristotle's *keratoi*, "horns" of insects

antennae is the preferred plural for living organisms (insects) and **antennas** is the plural for manmade objects (cell phones)

the hanging cloth on the front of an altar is the **antependium**

the third from last syllable is the **antepenultimate**

anterior/ventral means "front, situated at the front" and **posterior/dorsal** means "rear, situated at the rear"

anthem is ultimately an alteration of antiphon "scriptural verse said or sung as a response—and they started out as compositions from the Book of Psalms, then evolved to national (patriotic) anthems

the **anther**, the pollen-bearing part of a flower's stamen, originally meant "part of a plant which grows above ground"

the process or period of blooming in plants or the full bloom of a flower is called **anthesis**

anthology is from Greek *anthos*, "flower," so it is a "bouquet" of literary pieces

anthrax is from Greek, literally "coal," and Louis Pasteur used it for the animal disease that causes large ulcers on the body

the parrot is an **anthropoglot**, an animal with a tongue like that of a human

anthropomorphism is the ascription of a human attribute or personality to anything impersonal or irrational

anthurium's etymology is Greek for "flower tail" as it has a long appendage drooping from a brilliant, heart-shaped leaf

antibiotic is from *anti-*, "against, not," and *biotikos*, "fit for life"

antic originally meant "grotesque posture" or "absurd action"

anticipate is etymologically "takes before"

antidote comes from Greek *anti-*, "against," and *didonai*, "to give"

antigens (*-gen*, "beget") stimulate production of antibodies (proteins of the body)

Antigua is pronounced an-TEE-guh or an-TEE-gwuh

an **antimacassar** is a cloth put on the back of a chair to protect it from hair oil (macassar)

antimony is a poisonous metal and **antinomy** is contradiction between two authorities

antipastic means pertaining to appetizers or hors d'oeuvres (or the eating of them)

the pasto in **antipasto** is not related to pasta—pasto derives from Latin *pastus*, meaning "food" (and *anti*, "go before," was changed from *ante*)

antipasto and **hors d'oeuvre** are different terms—first Italian, second French—for the same thing, appetizers or starters

antipathy is a natural tendency toward contrariness or incompatibility

antipelargy is the reciprocal love of children for their parents

a collection of antiphons (chants for a psalm) is an **antiphoner**

{ a word used in a sense opposite of the usual is an **antiphrasis** }

antipodes are two points on the surface of the earth that are diametrically opposite each other or people who live on the other side of the earth from you; the literal meaning of **antipodes** is "with feet opposite"

antique comes from Latin *antiquus*, "in front, existing earlier"; in legal terms, an **antique** is defined as being more than one hundred years old

people who live in the same longitude but on opposite sides of the equator are **antiscians**

antiseptic literally means "preventing sepsis" by chemically destroying bacteria

if something is **antithetical**, it is characterized by direct opposition

antitwilight is the sky's pink or purple glow after sunset

antler first only denoted the lowest forward-directed branch of the **antler**; when antlers are growing, they are covered in soft skin called **velvet** and the spikes on an **antler** are called tines

using a title instead of a name (e.g., "the Boss" or "Prince") is **antonomasia**

antonym, the term, made its debut in C.J. Smith's *Synonyms and Antonyms* (1870) and was coined in the 1860s from the combining forms ant(i)- "opposed to" and -onym, on the model of the classically derived synonym

antonymous is **antonymous** to synonymous

fear of remaining single is **anuptaphobia**

anus is Latin for "ring"

an **anvil** is the horizontally extended top of a cumulonimbus cloud

anxiolytic means serving to reduce anxiety and phrontifugic is helping one escape one's thoughts or cares

anxious implies being worried or fearful

any is descended from a Proto-Germanic compound, literally meaning "one-y"

use **any more** if you mean "any additional," but **anymore** if you mean "nowadays" or "any longer"

anyone is correct if you can substitute **anybody** (in the sense of "any person") for it

anyway is correct if you mean "in any case"; otherwise, use **any way**

anywhen means "at any time"

astronauts on the Mercury Project in 1961 popularized **A-OK**, meaning "excellent, perfect," and it was coined by blending the adjective "A," as in A-one or A1, meaning "first-class" with "OK"

aorta/aortae was used by Hippocrates to describe the branches of the windpipe—then Aristotle used it to describe the "great artery"

aosmic is another word for odorless

the Zuni named the **Apache** apachu, "the enemy"

apanthropy is a dislike of being with people and a love of solitude

apart's first meaning was "at the side, to one side"

apartheid is from Dutch apart, "separate," and -heid, "-hood," and it is pronounced uh-PAHR-tayt or uh-PAHR-tight

apartment can refer to a single room in a house

apathy is from Greek a-, "without," and pathos, "suffering"

an animal of the monkey tribe was called by the generic name of "**ape**" before being called "monkey"

a perceptive comment is an **apercu**

an **aperient** is a laxative drink

aperitif comes from Latin aperire, "to open," the idea being that the drink opens the stomach and stimulates the appetite (**aperitif** is literally "opening the apetite up"); this alcoholic drink can also be called a preprandial libation

aperitif is a drink to stimulate the appetite and **appetizer** is food that does this before a meal

apert means "bold" and **malapert** means "inappropriately bold"

aperture is based on Latin aperire, "to open," and it first meant "the process of opening"

apex's plural is apices in math and science, but otherwise it is apexes

the tip of the tongue is the **apex**

aphesis is the language process by which the initial part of a word is dropped, as possum from opossum

aphetic means "life-giving"—but it has a second meaning: "pertaining to the loss of a short unaccented vowel at the beginning of a word" (see asparagus)

to **aphetize** a word is to shorten it by removing an initial, usually unstressed vowel

aphorism comes from the title of a fifth century BC book by Greek physician Hippocrates, and his title meant "terse sentences"

aphrodisiac is derived from the name of the Greek goddess of love, Aphrodite

{ an unpronounced letter or letter combination is an **aphthong** }

aviary is a building for the birds; **apiary** for the bees

a blanket used under a saddle is an **apishamore**

aplomb comes from French meaning "according to the plumb bob" (perfectly balanced, straight up and down) and it originally meant "perpendicularity" or "steadiness"

apocalypse comes from Greek meaning "uncover" as it was the supposed revelation or uncovering of the future made to St. John

dunkin 'instead of dunking and thinkin' instead of thinking are examples of an **apocope** the word **apocrypha** was first used in reference to scriptural writings that were "hidden" from the general public and it was once used adjectivally to mean "of unknown authorship"

apocryphal is a 'second-generation' adjective—after apocrypha, which was the first adjective, from Greek *apokruptein*, "hideaway"

if something is **apodictic**, it is established on incontrovertible evidence

another way to say conclusion is **apodosis**

apogee is the point where an orbiting body is at its farthest from the Earth (from Greek meaning "far from the Earth" (*apo-*, "away," and *ge*, "earth")); **perigee** is the point where the orbiting body is closest to Earth

if something is intended for enjoyment, it is **apolaustic**

Apollonian means "rational, well-ordered; harmonious"

apology once meant the act of defending against an accusation, from Greek *apologia*, "a speech in defense"

apophasis is mentioning a subject by saying one is not going to mention it

the curve where a column merges to its base or capital is the **apophyge**

apoplexy is another word for stroke

aporetic means "doubting, skeptical"

an **aporia** is an espression of doubt, but can also describe a contradiction or paradox over conflicting propositions

aposematic coloring or markings on an animal serve to warn or repel

aposiopesis is stopping in the middle of a statement upon realizing that someone's feelings are hurt or about to be hurt; when a sentence trails off or falls silent, that is an **aposiopesis**

an aversion to food is **apositia**

apositic is "taking away the appetite"

apostasy is abandonment or renunciation of one's religion or morals

aprioristic is based on reasoning rather than experience; **aposterioristic** is based on knowledge from experience

an **apostil** is a marginal note

apostle comes from Greek *apostolos*, "messenger"

apostrophe originally referred to an omission of one or more letters (Greek *apostrophus*, "accent of elision"); **apostrophe** in Greek meant "turned away"—and in punctuation means something is omitted

the **apostrophe** no longer has to appear in the plurals of abbreviations (MPs) or plural dates (1980s)

an **apothecary** sold general merchandise until the seventeenth century as well as prepared and sold drugs

an **apothegm** (pronounced AP-uh-them) is a terse, pointed saying or pithy maxim; it may also be spelled apophthegm

apotheosis, the highest point in the development of something or a perfect example, is from Greek *apotheoun*, "make a god of"

appal (once spelled appale) first meant "grow or make pale; fade"

Appalachian is from Choctaw *appalachee*, "people on the other side"

appall literally meant, "to make pale"

{ a natural or necessary accompaniment can be called an **appanage** }

an **apparat** is the structure or mechanism of an organization, especially a political one

an **apparatus** is an organization within a political party

apparel once meant "embellishment, ornament"

the furniture of a ship is its **apparel**, including the sails, rigging, and anchor; to **apparel**, in early use, meant "make ready or fit"

apparel highlights the sense of clothes as material; **attire**, the sense of clothes as dress

apparent and **appear** come from the same Latin stem, *apparere*, "to come into sight," "show, become visible"

early on, **applicable** meant "pliable, well-disposed"; **applicable** should be pronounced AP-li-kuh-buhl

an **applicant** is one who applies him/herself closely to his/her studies

appliqué is any work applied to or laid on another material

{ **apparition** first meant the action of appearing or becoming visible, the supernatural appearance of invisible beings }

in astronomy, an **apparition** is the appearance of a comet or other body after a period of invisibility

appeal has a nautical background of "direct a ship towards a particular landing"

appease first meant "bring to peace"

append originally meant "hang on" or "attach as a pendant"

appendix is Latin, literally meant "part that hangs"—which makes sense for the leftover organ in the digestive tract that hangs at the end of the large intestine, and supplementary material that is "hung" at the end of a book

appetence is desire or longing

appetible is a synonym for desirable

appetite comes from Latin *appetitus*, "desire for"

applaud, plaudit, and **explode** are based on Latin *plaudere*, "clap"

applause once meant "an object of approval"

apple is one of the oldest English words and first referred to fruit in general

applesquire is an obsolete term for a pimp

appliance first was the use or application of a technique, putting a technique into practice

apply, from a Latin base meaning "to fold," first meant "put close or in contact with"

appoint, from French *à point*, "to a point," first meant "come or bring matters to a point"

apposite means apt or appropriate

appraise is "evaluate, size up" and **apprise** is "inform"

an **appraisee** is one whose work performance has been reviewed

an **apprecation** is a devout wish

the use of "**appreciate**" should involve valuing something or understanding it sympathetically, and when there is no value or sympathy, use "**recognize**" or "**understand**"; **appreciate** first meant "set at a price; appraised"

apprehend once meant "learn"

apprentice comes from French *apprendre*, "learn"

apprise means to inform; **appraise** means to assess or evaluate

approach comes from Latin elements *ad-*, "to" and *propius*, "near"

approbation indicates both formal recognition of an accomplishment and happy acceptance of it

appropinquity means "nearness"

an **appropriament** is an individual characteristic

appropriate derives from Latin *propius*, "own, proper"

the original sense of **approve** was "prove, demonstrate"

there is no need to use **approximate** or **approximately** when about or almost or nearly will do

to **apricate** is to bask in the sun, to sunbathe

apricot is from Arabic *al-barquq*, and the Latin *praecoquum*, "early-ripening peach," and *praecoquere*, "to cook or ripen before," due to the **apricot**'s tendency to ripen early

April is from Latin *aperire*, "to open," (*aperia*, "open") as it is when trees unfold and the earth opens with new life

apron is from Old French *naperon*, a diminutive of *nape/nappe*, "tablecloth, napkin" and the initial n was lost by corruption of Old English *a napron* to "an **apron**"

{
the **apron** is the part of the stage in front of the curtain
}

the **apron** is the large concrete area at an airport for refueling and parking; the **tarmac** is the material used to create aprons

aprosexia is the inability to concentrate

apse, from Greek meaning "fastening together," is based on the notion that a vaulted space seems to be the joining together of arcs to form a circle

apsis is the extreme point of an orbit

apt can mean "ready to learn"

apt is for general probabilities, **likely** is for specific probabilities; **liable** and **prone** indicate a probability arising as a regrettable consequence

the **apterium** is the part of a bird's body that has no feathers

aptitude and **attitude** derive from Latin *aptitudo*, "fitness," the first through French, the second through a French borrowing of Italian *attitudine*

an **aptronym** is a name that fits a person's nature or occupation, like Jane House for a real estate agent

aqua, the color, is an abbreviation of aquamarine, from Latin, literally "sea water"

an **aquabib** is a water drinker

an **aquabob** is a cute name for an icicle

aquaculture is the cultivation of marine life

aquamarine is literally "sea water" in Latin

in wet weather, a vehicle can **aquaplane**—plane here meaning "lose adhesion"

in classical Latin, **aquarium** meant "watering place for cattle"

aquatic can mean "watery" or "rainy"

aquiline (from Latin *aquila*, "eagle") means of or belonging to an eagle; it also means having a curved or hooked beak like an eagle's

aquose is a synonym for watery

aquosity is a fancy word for moisture

Arab (pronounced AHR-ub) describes people; **Arabian** is the historical term, "belonging to Arabia"

arabesque literally means "in the Arabic style"

arable as in farming means that it involves regular plowing, aerating of the soil, and planting of regular crops

arachnid (arthropods including spiders, mites, ticks) comes from Arachne, a Greek girl in myth who challenged Athena to a weaving contest

arain is another word for spider

arbiter is Latin for "judge, supreme ruler"

arbitrament is free will or free choice

arbitrariness describes the absence of physical correspondence between a word and the entity to which it refers, e.g., the word table does not physically resemble the thing table

arbitrary can mean despotic or tyrranical

arbitrate can mean "give an authoritative decision" (from Latin arbiter "judge")

an **arbitrator** is appointed; an **arbiter** has no such authority, but his/her opinion is valued

an existence ideally rural is **arcadian**

arcane "hidden, secret; mysterious, abstruse" is from Latin arcere, "shut up," from arca, "chest"

carefully hidden knowledge is **arcanum**

arch can describe any part of a curve

archaeology originally meant "ancient history" or "antiquities" and only in the nineteenth century did the modern scientific sense develop; in American English, **archaeology** is the preferred spelling

{ **architrave** is the collective term for the various parts (lintel, jambs, and their moldings) that surround a doorway or window }

arbitrators make a decision/judgment but mediators do not

arbor originally referred to a garden lawn or green as well as an herb or flower garden

an **arborescence** is a treelike growth or formation

an **arboretum** is a botanical garden devoted to trees

arborization is the production of a tree-like structure

an **arbovirus** (arthropod-borne) is transmitted mainly by mosquitos and ticks

a dwarf tree is also called an **arbuscle**

an **arc** started out as a term for the path of the Sun or other celestial object from horizon to horizon

arcade was first a passage arched over, an arched opening

Arcadia is an "ideal region of rural contentment," from Greek Arkadia, a district in the Peloponnese

archaic is from a Greek word meaning "beginning"

archer and **archery** are based on Latin arcus, "bow"

archetype comes from Greek arkhetupos, literally "first-molded" or "original pattern"

an **archimage** is a great magician (from Greek archi-, "chief, principal," and Latin magus, "magician")

archipelago originally meant Aegean Sea—which has a number of islands, so the word came to mean that; **archipelago** translates to "chief sea"—now meaning a large group of islands or a sea containing such a group

architect is from Greek askhi-, "chief," and tekton, "builder"

architectural is the literal form and **architectonic** is the figurative term

archive is based on Greek arkhe, "government," and it evolved to mean "public office or records"

another way of saying multicolored is **arci-pluvian** (literally, like a rainbow)

arctic comes from the ancient Greeks' word for north, *arktikos*, literally "of the bear"; **arctic** should be pronounced AHRK-tik

the suffix **-ard** generally is pejorative (bastard, coward, dastard, drunkard)

{ **ardent** means "burning, fiery" or "glowing like fire" }

ardor can mean "fierce or burning heat"

arduous, from Latin *arduus*, "difficult, steep," can be used to mean "energetic" when referring to a person making an exertion

are is one hundred square meters

area originally meant space allocated for a specific purpose

arena comes from the Latin word *(h)arena* "sand, sand-strewn place" which was what it was originally; **arena** is specifically the field as distinct from the area and seating around it

areology is the study of Mars—from Greek Ares, the counterpart of Roman war god Mars

an **arête** is a sharp mountain ridge with steep sides, usually separating valleys, and it is derived from Latin *arista*, "fish bone or spine, ear of corn"

argent is a poetic word for "silver"

if someone is **argh**, they are timid and cowardly

argil is a clay especially used in pottery

other words for "argue about" are **argle**, **argle-bargle**, **argy-bargy**

argosy's present-day spelling evolves from Italian *ragusea*, literally "vessel from Ragusa" (city on the Dalmatian coast)

argot is the jargon or slang of a class of people, such as thieves

argue comes from the Indo-European base *arg-*, "be or make clear"

you can describe a shrill sound as being **argute**

argyle is based on the tartan of the Argyll branch of the Campbell clan

rare four-letter, three-syllable words are **aria** and **Oreo**

arid figuratively means "dull, uninteresting"

arise is from Latin *a-*, "away, out," and probably *tivus*, "stream" (which rises)

arisings are materials forming waste or secondary products of a process

aristocracy comes from Greek *aristos*, "best," and originally meant government of a state by its best citizens

aristology is the art or science of dining (Greek *ariston*, "breakfast, lunch") or luncheon talk

arithmetic is from Greek *arithmetike*, "(art) of counting" (from *arithmos*, "number")

Arizona is from Pagago Arizonac, "small spring place"

an **ark** was originally a large chest or cupboard in farmhouses for keeping meal or flour, which is what arkwrights make

Arkansas, formerly Arkansaw, is from Sioux for "south wind people/place"

arm as a limb and weapon go back to Indo-European *ar-*, "fit, join"

armada, a fleet of warships, traces back from Spanish to Latin *armata*, "army"

armadillo is from Spanish, the diminutive of *armad*, "armed man"

a naval force equipped for war is an **armament**

the equipment of a medical institution or physician is the **armamentarium**

armipotence is strength in battle

armistice comes from Latin (*armistitium*) *arma*, "arms," and *-stitium*, "stoppage," and means a temporary cessation from fighting or the use of arms, or a short truce

an **armoire** was originally a place for storing arms

a synonym for fighting or warfare is **armor**, and a diver's suit can be called **armor**

armory and **heraldry** each originally meant "arms, military equipment, and their employment"

{ **arms** can describe defensive or offensive parts of animals or plants }

armsaye or **armscye** (or **armseye** or **scye**) is the armhole in clothing, the hole in a shirt, sweater, jumper etc. through which you put your hand and arm

if something is at **armshot**, it is at arm's length

the literary use of the word **army** is "any armed expedition by land or sea"

aroma is Greek for "spice" and originally meant "a fragrant plant, spice"; **aroma** started out as a plural denoting fragrant plants or spices—and it can only be applied to pleasant smells

aromatherapy is first attested in 1949

around probably comes from French *a la reond*, "in the round"

arouse, first used by Shakespeare, is a combination of a- (intensive) and rouse, which first meant, in falconry, "plump up the feathers"

arpeggio is the playing of notes of a chord in usually rapid ascending or descending succession—and it is from Italian *arpeggiare*, "play on the harp"

arrack is an Asian alcoholic drink distilled from rice or molasses

to **arraign** can mean "find fault with" or "call into question"

arrange first meant "draw up in ranks or in lines for battle"

arrant means "complete, utter" as in **arrant** knave "an extremely untrustworthy individual"

an **arras** is a tapestry hanging, formerly hung to cover or hide an alcove

array is a state of preparedness, as for war or festivities

to stand still or stop in one's course is to **arrest**

arrehenotokous is "giving birth to only boys"

arrhythmic refers to lacking rhythm or regularity of rhythm; **eurhythmic** refers to the art of graceful and harmonious movement

to **arride** is "to please, gratify, delight"

arrière-pensée is French for "backward thought" and we use it to mean "mental reservation" or "concealed motive"

arrive comes from Latin *ar-*, "to," and *ripa*, "shore, bank"; **arrive** first meant "come or bring to shore"

arrogant comes from Latin *arrogare*, meaning "claim for oneself"

to **arrogate** first meant "to adopt" and now means "to lay claim to something to which one is not entitled"

arrow was the original meaning of bolt

arrowroot is so called because the tubers can be used to absorb poison from arrow wounds; it is an alteration of Arawak *aru-aru*, "meal of meals"

an **arroyo** is a brook or stream, also a gulley

arsenal is from Arabic *dar al sindah*, meaning "workshop for art, manufacture" and was originally used in English to mean "naval dock" or workshops for making ships and arms

arsenic, a yellow compound, takes its name from Persian *zar*, "gold"; **arsenicated** or **arseniuretted** means "combined with **arsenic**"

to **arsle** is to move backward or retreat

arson is based on Latin *adere*, "to burn"

art comes from a base word meaning "put together" and the original general meaning of **art** referred to any kind of skill

arteriosclerosis is brought about by a thickening or calcification of the arterial walls and consequent loss of elasticity; **atherosclerosis** is caused by deposits of plaques of cholesterol and cellular debris—with both resulting in decrease in blood supply to parts fed by the arteries involved

arteries carry clean oxygenated blood from the heart, **veins** return impure blood back to the heart, and **capillaries** connect the ends of arteries to the beginnings of veins

arthralgia is pain in a joint, from Greek *arthron*, "joint," which also gives us the word **arthritis**

arthropod is Greek for "jointed feet" of crustaceans, insects, and spiders

the **artichoke** is also the globe **artichoke**, and it was originally Arabic *al-karsufa*

article comes from Latin *articulus*, "small connecting part," and originated in English in the sense "clause of the Apostles Creed"; it can also mean "a portion of time" or "a critical point or moment"

{ **articulate** first meant "formulate in articles" }

on a windshield wiper blade, the point where it pivots a bit is the **articulation**

artifact is from Latin elements *arte*, "by or using art," and *factum*, "something made" ("art that is made"), and it is literally "something made with skill"

artificial comes from Latin *artificium*, "handicraft"

an **artigrapher** is a grammarian

artillery is a poetic term for thunder and lightning

artisan is based on Latin *artire*, "instruct in the arts," and artisans collectively are **artisanate**; **artisan** cheese, bread, etc. is handmade or created with non-mechanized methods or techniques

artist first referred to a master of the liberal arts or scholars of grammar, logic, rhetoric, arithmetic, geometry, music, or astronomy

English poet Robert Browning coined the word **artistry** (1873)

arugula is an Italian dialect word from Latin *eruca*, "colewort," a Mediterranean salad green; **arugula** is also known as the rocket plant

an **arval** is a supper served after a funeral

asana, meaning "posture, yoga posture" is from Sanskrit "manner of sitting" from *aste*, "to sit"

asbestos is from Greek words meaning "unquenchable"

a planet **ascends** when it moves toward the zenith or comes above the horizon

in typography, **ascenders** are the parts of characters that extend above x-height (b, d, f, h, k, l, t), while **descenders** are the parts of characters that extend below the base line (g, j, p, q, y); x-height refers to the vertical depth of the characters (a, c, e, l, m, n, o, r, s, u, v, w, x, z—sometimes called "x-high")

ascension is "rising"; **accension** is "kindling" or "being kindled"

ascension or **ascent** also mean "a going back in genealogical succession; reversion to an ancestor"

ascesis is the practice of self-discipline

ascetic (pronounced uh-SET-ik) is derived from Greek *asketes*, "monk, hermit" an **ascian** is one who has no shadow

ascriptitious means "added to a list"

aseptic means "keep from germs or disease"

the Runic letter Æ {runash} is called the **ash** and it corresponds to Œ in Old English

ashamed is an Old English compound ultimately from *scamu*, "shame"

an **ashram** is a place of religious retreat, sanctuary, or hermitage in India, etc., from Sanskrit *asrama*, "hermitage"

ashtanga yoga is Sanskrit for "having eight parts"—referring to the eight limbs or sutras of yoga; it is also known as power yoga

an **aside** is words spoken in an undertone

an **ask** is a request or question

askance first meant "obliquely, sideways"

asked should be pronounced ASKT

a sail that is **asleep** is filled with just enough wind to prevent flapping

asparagus was first called sperage in English in sixteenth and early seventeenth centuries and also sperach or sparage. About 1600, the influence of herbalists and horticultural writers made **asparagus** familiar, in the aphetic form "sparagus," which by folk etymology was corrupted before 1650 to sparagrass or sparrowgrass, which remained the name during the eighteenth century. Botanists still wrote **asparagus** and then during the nineteenth century, **asparagus** returned into literary and polite use. There is a slight possibility the word comes from Greek *ana*, "up," and *spargan*, "to swell" also.

symbols used to denote the positions of planets are called **aspects**

if something is visible, it is **aspectable**

do you know someone who is **aspectabund** (has an expressive face)?

the **aspen** is a species of poplar

to **asperge** is to sprinkle

asperity can refer to the roughness, ruggedness, or unevenness of a surface

baptism by sprinkling is **aspersion**, by dipping is **immersion**, by pouring water is **affusion**

asphalt's synonyms are mineral pitch, Jews' pitch, and slime

a synonym for communism is **aspheterism**

stoppage of the pulse was the original meaning of **asphyxia**

aspic was borrowed from French where it meant "snake"—possibly because the colors and patterns of **aspic** molds resembled a snake's coloration

{ an **aspirant** is one who is seeking a higher position or some distinction }

aspirate means "to articulate to produce an audible puff of breath" as with the first t of total

aspire (from Latin *spirare*, "breathe") first meant "breathe into" or "rise, rise up"

aspirin comes from German *acetylierte Spirsaure* (acetylated salicylic acid)

ass comes ultimately from Latin *asinus*, "donkey"

ass, as in buttocks or rear end, is a euphemistic spelling derived from arse

to **assail** a task is to approach it with the intent of mastering it, from Latin *salire*, "to leap"; **assault** is also based on this word, and **assail** and **assault** can be synonyms

assassin derives from an Arabian word, literally "a hashish-eater, one addicted to hashish," applied in Arabic to the sectarians who used to intoxicate themselves with hashish or hemp when preparing to murder a king or other public person

assation is another term for roasting or baking

assault is an attempt or threat to do physical harm while **battery** is unjustified application of force; **assault** and **battery** is carrying out of threatened physical harm or violence

assemble has the Latin base of *simul*, "together"

assent is based on Latin *sentire*, "feel, think"

assert comes from Latin *asserere*, "join oneself to something"

assertory is a synonym for assertive the literal meaning of Latin *assidere*, the source of **assess**, was "sit beside someone"— which evolved to "sit next to a judge and assist in deliberations"; **assize** also comes from this source and came to mean, generally, "act of sitting" or "seat"

asset comes from French *asez/asetz*, "enough," from Latin *ad-*, "to," and *satis*, "enough"—for "enough to settle claims against an estate"

to **asseverate** is to affirm solemnly or declare positively

assiduous is another word for persistent

a prepared dish of food can be called an **assiette** (French for "plate, course of a meal")

assimilation is the name of the process where iced cream and iced tea change to ice cream and ice tea (the dropping of the -ed); it is also the tendency of a sound to become more like a neighboring sound, as in congratulate

assist can mean "be present" as a spectator or participant

an **assize** is a court session (from Latin *assidere*, "to sit")

associate, from Latin *socius*, "companion"— was first an adjective, then a verb, then a noun

to **assoil** is to pardon or atone for a sin

{ **assonance** is where the words of a phrase or verse have the same sound or termination and yet do not rhyme }

to **assort** can mean "fall into a class with" and **assorted** may mean "matched to" or "suited to one another"

to **assot** is to make an ass of oneself or someone else

assuage (pronounced uh-SWAYJ) has the Latin base *suavis*, "sweet"

something that is calming is **assuasive**

assume can mean "receive up into heaven"

assume means "suppose to be the case, without proof; take for granted"; **presume** means "suppose that something is the case on the basis of probability; take for granted that something exists or is the case"

the word **assumption** was first used with reference to the reception of the Virgin Mary into Heaven

an ingenious polite insult or mockery is an **asteism**

aster is from Greek for "star" (which also gives us asterisk)

asterisk comes from the Greek word *aster*, "star," and it can be used to describe a little star or something starlike; **asterisk** should be pronounced AS-tuh-risk

an **asterism** is a triangular cluster of (three) asterisks

the Big Dipper is both an **asterism** (group of stars) and **constellation**, a prominent formation of seven stars in the **constellation** Ursa Major

asteroid is from Greek *asteroeides*, "starlike"

Greek *azein*, "breathe hard," evolved into the word **asthma**

astound, **astonish**, and **stun** all ultimately come from an obsolete verb astony, "**stun**," based on Latin *extonare*, "leave someone thunderstruck" (from *tonare*, "thunder")

astrakhan is the skin of stillborn or very young lambs from **Astrakhan**, Russia—the curly wool of which resembles fur

someone energetically struggling can be described as **astrive**

a crater caused by a meteor is an **astrobleme**

an **astrologamage** is a wise person or wizard who predicts events based on celestial influences

originally, **astrology** was referred to as natural **astrology** and denoted practical uses of astronomy, including the measurement of time and the prediction of natural phenomena; the two words and studies parted company in the seventeenth century

{ **astrometry** is the precise measurement of celestial objects }

astronaut is literally "star sailor" (Greek *astron nautes*); originally at NASA it denoted a pilot and now it is used for scientists and payload specialists, too

it is only recently that **astronomy** and **astrology** have been distinguished—and they were formerly known as judicial astrology (astrology in the modern sense) and natural astrology (modern astronomy); astronomy is from Greek *astronomos*, "star-arranging"

astrut is openly showing pleasure about an accomplishment

the Latin *astus*, "crafty, cunning" gave us **astute**

asylum comes from Greek *asulon*, "refuge," from *asulos*, "inviolable"

words can have more than one prefix (**asymmetry**) or suffix (**tyrannical**)

asymptotically means getting closer but never quite meeting

the preposition **at** was originally found throughout Germanic languages

ataraxy or **ataraxia** is imperturbability or stoical indifference, a state of serene calmness or tranquility

an **atavism** is a reversion or throwback to an earlier style or form, such as resembling one's grandparents instead of one's parents

an **atelier** is an artist's workshop or studio, an abbreviation of French *atelier libre*, "free studio"

athambia is another word for imperturbability

atheism is Greek *a-*, "without" and *theos*, "god"

athenaeum can describe "an association of persons interested in scientific and literary pursuits, meeting for the purpose of mutual improvement" or refers to a reading room or library

atherosclerosis (or **atheroma**) is a form of arteriosclerosis with fatty degeneration of blood-vessel walls

athlon in Greek is "prize" or "contest"—which gives us **athlete** as well as biathlon (etc.); **athlete** should be pronounced ATH-leet—with two syllables, not three

a collection of maps is called an **atlas** because the cartographer Mercator put the image of the Greek god Atlas on his map collection—and this was copied by other cartographers and the collection name changed to "atlas"

the first vertebra of the neck is called the **atlas**—because it holds up your head

a seal's breathing hole in the ice is an **atluk**

ATM machine is actually redundant, as the M stands for "machine"

atmosphere derives from Greek *atmos*, "vapor," and *sphaira*, "globe," and is literally "ball of vapor"

atoll was borrowed from Malayalam *atolu,* "reef"

atom comes from Greek *atomos,* "uncut, indivisible,"—based on *a-,* "not," and *temneir,* "to cut," and it is the smallest unit of matter that retains the characteristics of an element; a **molecule** is the smallest unit of matter that retains the characteristics of a compound

an **atomy** is a skeleton or emaciated body

atone comes from the phrase "at one" meaning "united, in harmony"

atonement is the condition of being AT ONE with others, from the earlier word onement and the phrase "to be atone" or "at onement"

atrament is a synonym for ink

atrocious literally meant something like "having a black eye" (*ater,* "black," and *oclox,* "looking, appearing")

atrophy is from Greek *atrophos,* "unfed, not nourished"

attaboy may come from "That's the boy!"

attach first had the legal sense of "to place or take under the control of a court or authority"

to begin a music piece decisively or confidently is to **attack**

attain first meant "bring to justice"

the **attar** is a flower's essence used for perfume

attelets are the small thin top-ornamented skewers used decoratively for serving sandwiches and hors d'oeuvres

the base of **attempt** is Latin *temptare,* "tempt"

attend, as in "apply one's mind or energies to" is from Latin *ad-,* "to," and *tendere,* "stretch"

the military command "**attention**" is sometimes pronounced ten-HUT

attenuate can apply to actual thinning by means of some mechanical process or can refer to the loss (or thinning out) of whatever gives a thing its strength or vitality

attenuation is the reduction in magnitude of some quantity, caused by either absorption or distance from the source

 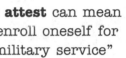

to **attest** can mean "enroll oneself for military service"

attic is short for **attic** storey, the top story of a classical building using **Attic** design; the **Attic** order originally consisted of a small order placed above another at a much greater height, hence, **attic** for top story of a building or home, and the earliest use of the word **attic** was as an architectural term for a small column and entablature above a taller one

to **attinge** is to touch or come into contact with; **attingent** is touching or being in contact

attire originally meant a headdress, from French *a tour de tete;* **attire**'s earliest meaning as a verb was "put in order" or "equip"

attitude is the orientation of an aircraft relative to its direction of travel

some say **attorney** comes from a French word for turn and was first applied to someone to whom people turned for help, others say it is from a French word meaning "one appointed or constituted"

a euphemistic use of **attract** is "pilfer" or "come by dishonestly"

attrahent means attracting or magnetic

attribute can mean "assign or give as a right"

an **attributive** (that expresses an attribute) adjective is usually directly in front of the noun, e.g. lonely planet, red sky most adjectives can be used both **attributively** (black cat) and **predicatively** (the cat is black)

attrition is wearing away by friction or abrasion

a love song sung at dawn is an **aubade**, the opposite of **serenade**

etymologically, **aubergine** is "fruit of the eggplant" (French), ultimately from Spanish *alberchigo*, "apricot"

auburn was originally a brownish-white color, coming from Latin *albus*, "white," and later associated with brown by false etymology

the original meaning of **auction** was "increase"

auctorial means "of or pertaining to an author"

aucupate "lie in wait for, gain by craft" is from Latin, literally "go bird catching"

audaculous means slightly bold

an **audible** is a play called at the line of scrimmage in football, changing what was called in the huddle

audient is "listening or paying attention"; it is also a noun for a listener

audile is another word for auditory, pertaining to the sense of hearing

an **audit**, from Latin *audire*, "hear," was originally listened to as an oral presentation, and **audition** first meant "the faculty of hearing"; **audition**, **audio**, and **audience** come from the same root as **audit**

when you attend an academic course without credit, you are **auditing**

an **auditor**, based on a root meaning "hearing," does have to listen to people's explanations and is "one who examines accounts," though an earlier meaning was "hearer"

auditorium first meant "a place for hearing"

augean means "abominably filthy"—based on the nasty stables of Augeus in Greek myth

auger (like adder and apron) was the victim of wrong division of the word; it was originally nauger

an **auger** is a tool and to **augur** is to foretell or betoken

{ **aught** is another word for "nothing, zero" }

augment comes from Latin *augere*, "to increase"

augment means to add more of the same thing; **supplement** means to add something, usually to make up for a deficiency

a word or word element indicating largeness or intensity is an **augmentative**, the opposite of diminutive

augur comes from a Latin word meaning diviner, for a person responsible for interpreting signs and omens for guiding decisions

omen has a negative connotation, a connotation absent from the word **augury**; generally, **augury** bodes well for the future, an **omen** bodes ill

August is so-called for Augustus Caesar, the first Roman emperor

an **aumbry** or **ambry** is a place for keeping things

an **aunt** can be a woman one turns to for help, an unrelated older woman friend; **aunt** was formerly applied to any old woman

aura (with plurals auras or aurae), originally denoted a gentle breeze, now is more used to describe the energy field that radiates from all living organisms

orange peel can be called **aurantii-cortex**

an **aureole** is the radiant circle of light or halo around a head

doctors look inside your ears with an **auriscope**

 the plural of **aurochs**, an extinct species of wild ox, is aurochsen

aurora means "dawn, early morning"—and it is a diffuse, colored light in the upper atmosphere over polar regions

aurum is the Latin name for gold, from which its chemical symbol Au is derived

when a doctor listens with a stethoscopre, that is **auscultation**

auspice originally denoted the observation of bird flight as a form of divination

auspicious implies success in the future while **propitious** means favorable conditions are present; **auspicious** means promising or of good omen—not just special or memorable

austere can mean "grave, serious; sober" and **austerulous** means "somewhat harsh"

another way to say southern is **austral** or **austrine**

austral means "southern" while **boreal** means "northern" (as does **septentrional**)

Australia means "southern land"

autarchy means "absolute power" while **autarky** means "self-sufficiency," especially national economic self-sufficiency or isolationism

an **auteur** is a film director whose influence qualifies him or her as its author

authentic comes from Latin *authenticus*, "asserted by authority, verifiable"

author and **authority** are based on Latin *auctor*, "originator, promoter"; the early general sense of **author** was "a person who

invents or causes something" and **authority** is basically the right to issue commands without that right being questioned

authoritarian is tyrannical while **authoritative** commands respect

autochthon is from the Greek word for indigenous and is used for someone or something who is an original inhabitant or living in their place of origin

an **autoclave** is a pressure cooker, from Latin *autom* and *clavis* ("key") because it is self-fastening

autocracy is a synonym for autonomy

an **autodidact** is a self-taught person

autograph comes from Greek words meaning "self" and "written"; **autograph** originally meant "author's own manuscript"

automation, from Greek meaning "acting of itself" came first before automate and automatic

automaton (pronounced aw-TAH-muh-tahn) is from Greek *automatos*, "acting of itself"

to **automobile** is to drive or travel in a motor vehicle

autonomy is from Greek *autos*, "self," and *nomos*, "law," i.e. a person or unit that makes its own laws

an early sense of **autopsy** was "personal observation"; **autoptic** means "based on personal observation"

autotelic means "having or being an end or purpose in itself"

the shedding of a part by a living being, such as a crab or salamander or lizard, is called **autotomy**

to **autumn** is "to ripen, bring or come to maturity"

Autumn or **Fall** is regarded as the third season of the year, from the descending or autumnal equinox to the winter solstice, approximately September 21 to December 21. Chaucer first used the word **autumn** c 1374, which is derived from Latin autumnus/auctumnus. The use of **fall** to mean **autumn** in North American English comes from the phrase **fall** of the leaf, and it came into use by 1545 for this time of year when the leaves **fall** from the trees. The term **autumn** is still preferred in British English.

auturgy is any independent activity

in botany, **auxesis** is when the size of individual cells increase and **merisis** is when the number of cells increase

auxiliary (pronounced awg-ZIL-yuh-ree) is from a Latin word meaning "help"

avail comes from the obsolete vail, "be of use or value"—apparently on the pattern of pairs like amount/mount

aval means "grandparental"

avalanche means literally "a gulp, something swallowed" from French avaler, "to swallow," and Italian lava, "torrent," and refers to snow, rocks, or other debris coming down a mountainside—whereas a **landslide** is an entire mountainside coming down

avant-garde is from French and first meant vanguard; it should be hyphenated

avarice is greed or eager desire for something

avast is a command meaning "Halt!"

avatar can mean "manifestation" or "incarnation"

the early meaning of **avenue** (from French avenir) was "way of approaching a problem" and as a street it originally meant an access road by which to "come toward" something

aver first meant "confirm or declare to be true" (from Latin verus, "true")

average was first a maritime term for shipping damages and the monetary responsibility for these damages was distributed among all parties involved in the venture

to **averruncate** is to avert or ward off

averse can mean turned away or in the reverse direction

averse means reluctant or disinclined; **adverse** means hostile and antagonistic

etymologically, **avert** means "to turn away": blows can be averted, but not pain, a snub can be averted, but not a humiliation, and violence can be averted, but not damage

avert means "prevent, turn away" and **avoid** means "stay clear of, shun"

aviary and **aviation** are based on Latin avis, "bird"

avifauna is the bird life of a particular area

> { **avigation** is a synonym for aerial navigation }

avinosis is another word for airsickness

avionics is a blend of aviation and electronics

avocado comes from the Aztec word ahucatl, "testicle," and **guacamole** comes from ahuacatl-molli, "**avocado** sauce"; the plural of **avocado** is avocados

avoid's original meaning was "empty; make void"

avoirdupois (pronounced ah-vur-duh-POIZ) is French for "to have goods," and is an Anglo-American system of weights based on an ounce equalling sixteen drams

avow implies boldly declaring, often in the face of hostility, what one might be expected to be silent about

to **avulse** is to tear or pull away or pluck off

avuncular means "behaving like or acting as an uncle"

the adjective **awake** was first a variant form of the past participle of the verb

award was first a judicial decision

away was formed in Old English by conflating the phrase *on weg*, "on one's way, departing"

awe first meant terror or dread

aweigh, when an anchor is no longer hooked to the bottom, is based on the word weighed, "taken up like a weight"

awful literally and originally meant "full of awe"

awhile is an adverb and so must occur as a modifier to a verb; the form **while** is a noun meaning "period of time"

awk means "in the wrong direction"

awkward comes from Old Norse *awk*, "perverse," and *weard*, "in the direction of," i.e., "turned back upon itself" or "turned backward"

an **awl** is a small tool with a point used for poking or piercing holes, as by shoemakers

wheat's whiskers are the **awk**

though **AWOL** stands for "absent without leave," no one is certain what the "o" stands for—possibly the complete phrase was "absent without official leave"

axes is the plural of both **axis** and **ax**

in archaeology, an **axe** (sometimes ax) is a double-edged or wedge-shaped stone tool

{ **axel** is the figure-skating jump; **axle** is the pin or rod between two wheels }

axiom comes from Greek *axioma*, "what is thought fitting" or "a self-evident principle"

the quality that makes something believable is **axiopisty**

axle was originally **axle**-tree, the "tree" being the beam of wood carrying the opposite wheels of a carriage

ayatollah is Persian for "sign of God"

Ayurveda is Sanskrit for "life science"

azalea is from Greek *azaleo*, "dry," because it flourishes in dry soil

Aztec is from Nahuatl Aztecatl, "person from Aztlan," their legendary place of origin

azuki is from Chinese *xiao dou*, "small bean"—so you should not say **azuki** bean or that is redundant

azure is from Persian, from lazhuward, the source of lazuli in lapis lazuli

unleavened breads—like Jewish matzoh or Christian wafers at Eucharist—are called **azyme** or **azym**

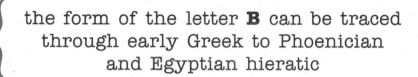

{ the form of the letter **B** can be traced through early Greek to Phoenician and Egyptian hieratic }

babble is based on the repeated ba-ba-ba made by a **baby** or young child; **babe** and **baby** are also probably imitative of an infant's speech

according to the Bible, the tower of **Babel** was built to reach Heaven, but God punished the presumptuous builders by making them unable to understand each other by creating the various languages of the world—hence, the metaphorical "confused medley of sounds" is **babble**

babies-in-the-eyes is the phenomenon of seeing yourself in another person's pupils

a **bablatrice** or **chaterestre** is a female babbler

baboons—which have large muzzles—have a name derived from Old French *baboue*, "muzzle"

a woman's scarf folded into a triangle and used as a head covering with the ends tied under the chin is a **babushka**

the word **baby** is probably imitative of an infant's first attempts at speech

baccalaureate, from word play on *bacca lauri*, "laurel berry" originally referred to the laurels awarded to congratulate Greek

scholars—however, the current use of **baccalaureate** as a farewell speech to a graduating class dates only to 1970

baccate and **bacciferous** mean "bearing berries, berrylike"

bacchanalian and **bacchanal** "given to drunken revelry" are named for Bakkhos (Roman Bacchus), the Greek god of wine

bachelor came from Old French *bacheler*, "a young man hoping to become a knight"; originally a **bachelor** was a young poor soldier and then a person of inferior rank and now can mean a male bird or mammal without a mate

bachelor first meant a junior member or apprentice, hence **bachelor's** degree—for one who has passed the lowest level of training but is not yet a master

a **back** is a tub or vat for brewing, dyeing, or pickling

backdate or **predate** is writing a date on something that is earlier than the actual date; **postdate** is to write a date on something that is later than the actual date

a **backfriend** is a secret enemy, a pretended or false friend

backgammon appears to mean literally "back game" and it was first called tables; gammon is the ancestor of game

older books kept in print by a publisher are the **backlist**

to **background** is to surreptitiously perform a task in the **background** while one's attention is supposed to be on another task

backlog was originally the big log put in the back of a log fire that will usually go on smoldering for days

backslang is reversing the pronunciation of words like "look" to "cool" and "dog" to "god" and "ynnep" to "penny"

a **backsplash** is a vertical surface (as of tiles) designed to protect the wall behind a stove or countertop

backwater is water fed by the backflow of a stream or river

bacon is derived from German *bach*, "back," since it is cut from the back of the pig (as well as the sides)—though at first the word referred to any part of a pig; **flitch** (the old word for **bacon**) designates a whole chunk of **bacon** before it is cut into slices

the Greek word *bakterion*, "rod, stick," is the source of **bacteria/bacterium**; the first **bacteria** discovered were rod-shaped

bacutum is the official name for the penis bone

the comparative and superlative of **bad** used to be worse and worst, now it is badder and baddest

the **badger**, the burrowing member of the weasel family, was probably named for the white "badge" on its forehead (from badgeard) though the animal was originally called a brawson, brock, or gray; the word **badger** as a verb comes from

badger- baiting, a pastime where badgers were drawn from their holes (sets) by dogs and killed for sport

badinage is humorous banter

badland is desert with eroded ridges and peaks

badling was an effeminate or worthless man and a **badling** is a small group of ducks

badly is an adverb to describe an activity; **bad** is an adjective to describe a condition or state

badminton was named for the country house in England where the game was first played in the mid nineteenth century and also used to be called poona; the word **badminton** also referred to a summer drink of claret, sugar, and soda water

a **baffle** is a device to restrain the flow or spread of something

to **baffound** is to baffle and confound, stun and perplex

the bulging part of a sail is the **bag**

to **bag** can mean "to cut wheat with a reaping hook"

bagatelle is from French or Italian for "trick" or "trifle"

bagels take their name from the Austrian-German word for stirrup—beugel or bugel

baggage was originally portable equipment for an army

bagnio has several meanings, but the first was bathhouse, especially a sauna or or Turkish bath

baguette means "little rod" and is derived from Latin *baculum*, "staff, stick"

bail once meant "a water carrier" or "a person charged with the weight of a responsibility" (from French *baillier*, "to carry, to take charge"); to **bail** can mean "abandon a commitment"

the handle of a bucket or kettle is the **bail**

the outer wall of a castle is the **bailey** (from French *baile*, "enclosure, palisade")

the base of **bailiff** was Latin *bajulus*, "carrier," which became "administrator"

bailiwick comes from *bailie*, "custody," and *-wick*, "function of an official" or "place of jurisdiction"

bain-marie was originally alchemical equipment named for Mary/Miriam, the sister of Moses, literally "the bath of Mary"; now it is a vessel of water in which saucepans, etc. are placed to warm food—or the bottom part of a double boiler

bait seems to trace back to Old Norse *beit*, "food, pasture," or *beita*, "to chase or hunt"

baize is the green material that covers a billiards table

baklava (from Turkish) is a rich sweet pastry; **balaclava** is a tight-fitting wool head-covering

baksheesh is a small sum of money given as a tip or as alms

the root of **balance** is Latin *bi*, "two," and *lanx*, "large plate" or "scale pan," i.e., "two large plates" or "two scale pans"

a **balatron** is a contemptible buffoon and **balatronic** means "buffoonish"

balcony came from Italian *balcone* "**balcony**, full-length window" or "scaffold"

bald in **bald** eagle means "white," not "hairless"; eagle comes from the Latin word *aquila*, "black eagle," from *aquilus*, "dark-colored," which it is until it gets the white head plumage as an adult

balderdash first denoted a frothy liquid, later an unappetizing mixture of drinks

a **bale** is a package of merchandise

whalebone is actually made of **baleen**—and it is not actually bone but an elastic horny substance

something is **baleful** that intends or portends harm or injury; something is **baneful** that produces harm or injury—thus, a glance may be **baleful**, an herb or poison **baneful**

balk was first spelled balc, from an Old Norse word for "partition" and its first meaning was "land left unplowed" or "unplowed ridge," and then it became an obstacle or to avoid an obstacle

{ **Balkan** is derived from a Turkish word signifying "mountain" }

at early dances, sometimes a **ball** was thrown; the name was retained even though people stopped throwing a **ball** at these events

the word **ball** has the Indo-European root for "swelling/swollen" and "rounded," whence "balls" for "testicles"

on a clothing snap, there is a **ball** and a **socket**

ballad traces to Provençal *balada*, "song to dance to"

a **ballade** is a verse or poem made up of three stanzas of equal length with a recurrent line or refrain at the end of each of the stanzas

if you are maintaining a course toward an ultimate target, you are **balladromic**

ballast was first a heavy substance put in the bilge of a ship to ensure its stability, then the same used in a balloon or airship

ballerina is the feminine of Italian *ballerino*, "dancing master"

ballet is borrowed from French "little dance," the diminutive of *bal*, "dance"

the phrase go **ballistic** probably refers to a **ballistic** missile which is guided during the propulsion phase but then goes into freefall

ballistics is the study of what takes place when a projectile is fired from a firearm

a **balloon** was originally a game played with a large inflated leather ball—and derives from French *ballon* or Italian *ballone*, "large ball"

ballot is Italian for small ball or pebble, as its citizens once voted by casting the same into one of several boxes

the special decorative boxes for chocolates are called **ballotins**

ballyhoo was originally a showman's touting speech

Greek *balsamon* is the source of both **balm** and **balsam** and it was an oily resin of various trees and shrubs

something **balneal** relates to bathing, especially in medicinal waters or hot springs"

nonsense is **baloney**; sausage is **bologna**

balsa is Spanish for raft and it was the name given to a tropical American tree which has strong, light wood that is used for rafts

balsam first referred to an aromatic resinous substance with healing or soothing properties

balsamic vinegar is a dark, sweet Italian vinegar from the Modena region, matured in wooden casks

to **balter** is to tangle the hair

a **balthazar** is a huge wine container holding the amount of sixteen bottles

baluster is so named as it resembles the curved calyx tube of a flower—from *balaustra*, "wild pomegranate flower" (banister is an alteration of **baluster**)

{ a **balustrade** of a stairway is the banister plus all the balusters that hold it up }

bamboo is ultimately derived from Malay *mamby*

bamboozle may have been a cant term of Scottish origin, from the verb *bombaze*, "perplex"

to **ban** can mean "to curse" or "to speak angrily to, chide"

ban is typically consequent upon a formal proclamation, law, or edict, whereas that effected by **bar** is usually the result of a physical barrier

banal is pronounced BAY-nuhl and it means "common, commonplace; trite"

banana comes from Arabic *banayna*, meaning "fingers, toes," and bananas were once called Indian figs; the **banana** "tree" is really a giant herb with a rhizome instead of roots and its "trunk" is made of leaves, not wood

originally **banana** was restricted to the fruit and **banano** was used to signify the tree

banausic can mean uncultivated or suitable only for artisans, two quite opposite meanings

band, mainly used in musical contexts, started out as a military usage

bandanna comes from Hindi *badhnu*, "tie-dyeing, cloth so dyed"; **bandanna** is the proper spelling, though bandana is acceptable

a **bandbox** first carried clergymen's clerical collars

a **bandeau** is a narrow band for holding the hair—or a strapless bra

a **banderole** (or banderol) is a long narrow flag, like a streamer on a knight's lance

bandicoot is from the Teluga word *pandikokku*, "pig rat"

bandit is derived from Italian *bandito*, literally "banned person"; **bandit**'s plural is bandits or banditti

bandwagon was first used for bands and then adopted for election campaigns, which were "hopped upon" by supporters of the candidate

to **bandy** words with someone may go back to "banding together to oppose others"

the original sense of **bane** was "murderer"

baneful has the meaning of poisonous or toxic while **baleful** implies the quality of evil

bang is printer's slang for an exclamation point

a **banger** is an enthusiastic kiss

the source of **bangle** is Hindi *bangri*, "glass bracelet"

a **banns** is a proclamation of intended marriage

banquet is literally "little bench" in French and at first it meant light snack or single course and it has evolved from a snack taken from a small side table to an elaborate ceremonial feast; what we now call dessert was once called a **banquet**

an upholstered bench against a wall is a **banquette**; in the U.S. south, **banquette** is a synonym for sidewalk

banshee is from Irish words *bean sidhe*, "women of the fairy world"

bantam comes from the name of a district in Java

to **banter** can mean "to make fun of (a person) in a good-humored way"

> cutting horses' tails the same length was called "banging off," which led to **bangs** as a women's hairstyle

banish first meant "proclaim a person to be an outlaw"

banjo is a black American alteration of bandore, probably based on Greek *pandoura*, "three-stringed lute"

a **banjulele** is a cross between a banjo and ukelele

the financial **bank** was originally a money dealer's table (from French *banque* or Italian *banca*)

bankbook and **passbook** are synonyms

a money lender in medieval Italy worked from a *banca* (bench) until there was a shortage of funds—then, the bench was broken up and he was referred to as *bancarotta*, "bench broken"—which is where we get **bankrupt**

a **banner** headline is a conspicuous headline

banting is a former method for dieting by avoiding fat, starch, and sugar

bantling "young child" may come from German *Bankling*, "bastard"

banyan originally meant "Hindu trader" and when European traders visited Bandar Abbas on the Persian Gulf, there was a pagoda in the shade of a large Indian fig tree—which is why they called it a **banyan** tree

banzai literally means "May you live 10,000 years!" and **kamikaze** means "wind of God"

bap is a small soft roll of bread

baptism can be the naming of church bells or naming of ships

baptize is from Greek *baptein*, "dip"

the legal use of **bar** was from its use as a partition in a court between the lecturers and the rest of the hall

barathrum is a bottomless pit or hell

barb, as any type of spike or projection, is based on Latin *barba*, "beard"; a **barb** is also a piece of vertically pleated linen worn over or under the chin, as by nuns

barbarian is based on Greek *barbaros*, "stranger" or "enemy"

barbaric pertains to crudeness and uncivility (based on Greek *barbaros*, "foreign"); **barbarous** pertains to cruelty, harshness, and immorality

barbate means "bearded" and **barbatulous** is "having a small beard"

barbecue was originally a word for a wooden framework for sleeping or for drying or storing meat or fish and the word derives from Arawak or Haitian or Taina *barbacoa* and became Spanish *barbacoa*, "wooden frame on posts" or "framework for meat over fire." Barbeque is the variant spelling. In English, the word's first meanings were the framework and the animal roasted on it; the usage of "social entertainment" is not recorded until 1733.

barber comes from Latin *barba*, "beard," because a **barber**'s work consisted of trimming beards—and originally they also performed surgery and dentistry!

barbet was the name for a poodle until the early nineteenth century

barbican first described an outer fortification or defense for a city or castle

Barbie's original name was Barbara, after the inventor's daughter

barbiturate is named for a person, Barbara, who helped Johann Bayer, the discoverer of the narcotic drug

the **barcarolle** is the type of song performed by Venetian gondoliers

bard was originally used for poets who composed and recited epic or heroic tales of chiefs and warriors

to cover meat (like meatloaf) with strips of bacon is to **bard**

bardo is the intermediate space between death and rebirth

bardolatry is excessive admiration for Shakespeare

to unsheath a weapon is to **bare** it

barefoot has the synonyms **discalced** or **discalceate**

bargain traces back to a German word meaning "borrow"

barge may come from Greek *baris*, "Egyptian boat"

a **bargee** is a person who works on a barge

{ **bariatrics** is the branch of medicine dealing with obesity }

bariolage is a synonym for medley

a **barista** is a person who serves coffee in a coffeehouse

baritone derives from Greek words *barus*, "heavy," and *tonon*, "tone, tension"

dogs, foxes, and seals **bark**

barker is another term for baseball coach

if a person wants a breather or timeout during play or wrestling, he/she should call out **barlafumble**—a call for a truce

barley was originally an adjective meaning "flour" and it was not until the twelfth century that it came to be used as a noun

barleyhood or **barlihood** is a bad temper induced by drinking

the yeast formed during fermentation of alcoholic beverages like beer is called **barm**; beer foam is also called **barm**

barmy can mean "foamy, frothy"

Old English *bere*, "barley," and *ern*, "house," combined to give us **barn**, literally barley house

a **barnacle** is a tenacious person or thing

barnacle first referred to a species of waterfowl; for the longest time, no one saw these geese breeding, so there was a myth that the geese spontaneously generated from wood rotting in the ocean (the dots on rotting wood later taking the name **barnacle**)

barnstorm was originally a theatrical term, describing itinerant stock companies that occasionally performed in barns; the word storming meant "moving impetuously" (around the country)

{ a **baron** of beef is a double sirloin joined at the backbone }

baron, first meaning "tenant under the feudal system who got his land and title directly from the king" probably comes from Latin *baro*, "man" or "vassal"

baroque is from Portuguese *baroco*, "rough or imperfectly shaped pearl" or "rocky mountainous country," and is used to describe a florid style of art, architecture, and music—though at first it denoted an irregularly shaped pearl

the music genres originating in the **Baroque** period include the opera, oratorio, cantata, sonata, and concerto

ear pain due to change of pressure during air travel is **barotitis**

to **barrack** is to shout or interrupt with rude comments

barracking, "loud vocal criticism," is not from the military barracks but may derive from an Irish word meaning "boast"

barracks, as in military, probably derives from Spanish *barraca*, "soldier's tent"

a movable dam wall across a waterway is a **barrage**

barrage comes from French *tirde barrage*, "curtain of fire," from World War I

a dancer's practice handrail is the **barre**

barrel comes from medieval Latin *barriclus*, "small cask"; **barrel** is also the belly and loins of a four-legged animal such as a horse or cow

barricade comes from a French word *barrique*, meaning "barrel, hoghead," as the first street barricades in Paris were casks filled with earth and stones

barrister (a lawyer) may have been patterned on the word minister

barrow, the burial mound, is related to German *berg*, "hill, mountain"

barter probably comes from the French word *barater*, "deceive"

barton is a word for a farmyard, specifically a barley farm, or for the lands or farm of a lord of a manor or grange

basalt goes back to Greek *basanites lithos*, "touchstone"

a **base** is part of an English word derived from a word (maybe Greek or Latin) that has a constant meaning and form—also a word to which derivational or inflectional morphemes are added

The word **baseball** is formed from base + ball, so called from the four bases that are the boundaries of the infield and the circuit run by a player after hitting the ball. It is first attested in writing by Jane Austen in *Northanger Abbey* (1815), when she wrote about New England colonists playing a version of rounders in the 1700s, but the game as we know it was not really played until the 1820s.

basement first meant "toilet"

the oldest formation of rocks underlying a particular area is the **basement**

bash may be a blend of bang and smash or dash

a **basho** is a sumo wrestling tournament

basil, from Greek *basilikos*, "little *king*," or *basilikon*, "royal," is so named for its being used in royal potions, medicines, and perfumes

a prisoner's ankle-iron is a **basil** or **basilisk**

basilica is literally "royal palace" in Latin (from Greek *basileus*, "king")

basilisk is a person who casts a malicious look

basin dates back to Latin *bachinus*, "eating bowl"

the small depression at the bottom of a fruit like an apple is the **basin**

the medieval metal helmet with visor was a **basinet**

the earliest literal sense of **bask** was "bathe" or "wallow in"

figuratively, a **basket** means a group or category

basketball got its name from the half-bushel peach baskets used as goals by its creator, James Naismith

basmati (the rice) is from the Hindu word meaning "fragrant" as this rice has a delicate fragrance

bas-relief is pronounced baa-rih-LEEF or BAA-rih-leef, and the term refers to sculpture or carved work in which the figures project less than one half of their true proportions from the surface on which they are carved

a **bass** is really the common perch

bass is an obsolete word for kiss

bassinet is a diminutive of French *bassin*, "basin," and means child's cradle

bassoon is from Italian *bassone*, "deep," with the augmentative (big) ending -*one* (as in *minestrone*, "big serving of soup")

bast is a word for an asylum, refuge, or sanctuary

basta in Italian means "Enough!" or "No matter!"

bastard may come from *bastum*, "packsaddle," and is literally "packsaddle son"—the offspring of an amorous itinerant mule driver

in printing, a type font combining elements of two others is called a **bastard**

figuratively, **baste** means "thrash, beat soundly"

bastinado is punishment by beating the soles of the feet with a stick

a **bastion** can be a person, a fortified structure, or a natural rock formation

bat, the animal, is an alteration of Middle English *bakke*, which was from Scandinavian

batch is based on a word related to bake and first meant "process of baking" before "quantity produced at one baking"

{ **bated** breath is based on the idea that the breath is abated or stopped }

the origins of **bath** indicate a first sense of "heat" rather than "washing"—as preserved in steam **bath** and Turkish **bath**

a **Bathazar** is a very large wine bottle holding the quantity of sixteen regular bottles

bathos (from Greek for "depth") is a descent from exalted to trite or sublime to ridiculous

batik is Javanese, literally "painted"

a long loaf or stick of bread can be called a **baton**

when a clock has bars in place of numbers on its dial, they are called **batons**

a battle between frogs and mice is **batrachomyomachy**

a **batsman** is the signaler on an airfield or aircraft carrier who uses a pair of light-weight bats to guide the pilot of an aircraft when taking off or landing

another sense of **batten** (on) is "to thrive or prosper at the expense of someone"

{ **batter** is based on a French word *bateure*, "action of beating" }

batter is a thin mixture of flour and liquid (usually pourable) while **dough** is a thick mixture of flour, liquid, and other things

the original sense of **battery** was "metal articles wrought by hammering"; a synonym for **battery** is accumulator

battle is based on Latin *battuere*, "to beat"

battledore can describe various tools, such as the paddle of a canoe or a utensil for inserting loaves into an oven or wares into a kiln

a **battlement** is an indented parapet at the top of a wall, first used only in fortified buildings for defense, but later becoming an architectural decoration; the raised parts are called cops or merlons, the indentations embrasures or crenelles

battleship is actually a shortening of line-of-battle ship, originally the largest type of wooden warship

you know at least one person who engages in **battology** (tiresome repetition and idle talk); a **battologist** is one who needlessly repeats the same thing

bauble is from Old French *baubel*, "play-thing"

the unit **baud** got its name from the French engineer J.M.E. Baudot (1845–1903)

a balustrade is a railing held up by balusters and a **banister** is a handrail held up by balusters; the post at the top or bottom is the **newel** or **newel** post

bavardage is idle talk or chitchat

bavin is a bundle of light wood or brush used for kindling

a **bawd** is a woman in charge of a brothel; **bawd** and **bawdy** either come from French *baude*, "shameless," or from Welsh *bawaidd*, "dirty, vile," from *baw*, "dirt, mud"

bawl is a word imitative of the sound

a **bay** is an indentation in a range of hills

bay is the position or action of a cornered animal when it turns and defends itself

bayonet is probably a diminutive form of *bayon*, "shaft of a crossbow"

Creole **bayou** meant "river forming part of a delta" but others say **bayou** is from Choctaw *bayuk*, "creek"

bazaar is from a Persian word meaning "market"

bazillion is a large exaggerated number

BC means Before Christ, the years before the modern era of history, but now many use **BCE**, meaning Before Common Era; **AD** is Latin for anno Domini, "in the year of our Lord" to denote time after the birth of Christ, but many now use **CE** for Common Era

be has several distinct components derived from three different Indo-European bases

beach can mean "cause someone to suffer a loss"

a **beachcomber** is a long wave rolling in from the sea

the first achievement toward success is called the **beachhead** or **bridgehead** or **foothold** or **salient**

beacon first meant "sign, portent"; **beacon** and **beckon** are related (Old English béacn, "sign")

the small timed-release balls in capsules are called **beadlets**

{ **bead** comes from an Old English word meaning prayer and it derives from the use of a rosary, each **bead** representing a prayer }

beagle comes from French words meaning "open-wide throat"

some insects, like weevils, have a **beak**, which is the proboscis or sucker mouth and head

the **beak/bill/nib** of a bird are used synonymously for the horny jaws usually projecting to a point

beaker comes from Greek *bikos*, "drinking bowl"

the **beakhead** is the ornamented projection on the prow of an ancient warship

in Old English **beam** had a basic sense "tree"

beano is an old British word for a festive entertainment frequently ending in rowdy behavior, a party with plentiful food and drink—but it is also the name of the game of bingo played with beans as markers

a **bear** is a stock speculator who anticipates lower market prices or a fall in the market

bear and **beaver** are etymologically "brown animal"

the hairlike feathers on a turkey's head is its **beard**

a **bearing** is so named because it is a part of a machine that bears friction

Béarnaise sauce is from Béarn, a region of Southwest France

beast can only refer to quadruped mammals—not birds, reptiles, fish, or insects

the **beat** is the tract of land covered by a hunter searching for game or the waters fished by a fisherman

beatific means "giving a blessing" or "imparting much happiness"; **beatitude** is supreme blessedness or happiness

the **Beatles**' name was imitative of Buddy Holly's band the Crickets and the spelling is a reference to "beat" music

beatnik was coined by a newspaper columnist in 1958—an allusion to deadbeat

beau has plurals beaus or beaux

beauism is excessive attention to dress and etiquette

beaujolais wine is named for its region of origin in France

beautiful traces back to Latin *bellus*, "fine, beautiful"

beauty is based on Latin *bellus*, "beautiful, fine"

beaux-arts, pronounced bo-ZAR, is French for "fine arts"

beaver goes back to an Indo-European base meaning "brown"

the lower face-guard of a helmet is the **beaver**

to **beaze** is to dry in the sun

beblubbered is another word for "swollen"

because is from the earlier "by cause," in turn based on French *par cause de*, "by reason of," and it originally meant "arrive, come"

Bechamel sauce is named after Marquis de **Bechamel**, a French financier and steward of Louis XIV

beck, as in **beck** and call, means "summoning gesture"

a **becket** is any simple device for holding something in place

beckon implies a movement of the head, hand, or finger

bed is related to Latin *fodere*, "to *dig*," and Greek *bothros*, "pit"—probably the connection is a place dug out of the earth as a place for an animal or person to lie in

bedfellow implies great intimacy

the **bedhead** is the upper end of a bed

the word **bedlam** is a contraction of Bethlehem, a hospital in London which became a lunatic asylum

the **bedrail** connects a bed's **headboard** to the **footboard**; the whole framework on which the springs and mattress are placed is the **bedstead**

a **bedswerver** is an adulteress

bee alludes to "busy workers" on a project; the first use was for corn-husking, then other social activities

beech traces back to Greek *phagos*, "edible oak"; **beech** and **book** derive from the same root as **beech** strips were written on by Germanic peoples

beef (from Latin *bos*, "ox") as meat is beefs in plural; in reference to cattle, it is beeves

cattle driven for a long way begin to bellow because of their suffering—giving us the slang "to **beef**" (complain)

to **beek** is to bask in the sun or before a fire

a **bee-master** is one who tends to bee hives

beer's etymology is uncertain but it came to us through West Germanic, perhaps from Latin *biber*, "drink," from *bibere*, "to drink"; **beer** originally distinguished a drink flavored with hops from (unhopped) ale—and now it is mainly a more general term that encompasses ale, lager, and stout

beestings (or beastings or biestings) is the first milk of a cow, especially after giving birth

to **beet** is to repair or mend—or to make good

beetle as an insect is from Old English *bitela*, meaning "biter" or "biting"

the Volkswagen **Beetle** was originally called the KdF Wagen

to **beetle** is to make one's way hurriedly with short quick steps

beezer is slang for a person's nose

before is from a Germanic compound of *bi-*, "by," and *forana*, "from the front"

{ a warning shock for
an earthquake is a
before-shock }

beg comes from French *begard*, "a begging monk"

begin comes from a prehistoric West Germanic compound verb *biginnan*

to be **begrumpled** is to be displeased

begrutten is having a face swollen from weeping

beguile includes the obsolete *guile*, "to deceive"

behalf is a mixture of the earlier phrases "on his halve" and "bihalve him," both meaning "on his side"

behave comes from Middle English meaning "have or bear (oneself) in a particular way"

beheadment is the removal of an initial letter of a word to form a new word (blather became lather)

behemoth is from Hebrew *behemot*, the plural of *behema*, "big beast"

behest is a stronger term than **request**

behind is from Old English *bi-*, "by," and *hindan*, "from **behind**"

behold first meant "hold, retain"

beige was originally a type of undyed, unbleached fabric

a square doughnut is a **beignet**

the unit **bel** (of which **decibel** is one/tenth) was named for Alexander Graham Bell (1847–1922)

belch was originally a perfectly inoffensive word, until the seventeenth century

beleaguer is from Dutch *belegeren*, "camp around," from *be-*, "(all) around" and *leger*, "camp"

belfry originally was a siege tower, from Middle English *berfrey* (the initial part meaning "protecting, defending" and the latter meaning "shelter")

a **belgard** is a longing, loving look (from Italian *bel guardo*)

to **belie** can mean to tell lies about, to deceive by lying

believe first meant "hold dear, love"

Belize was formerly British Honduras

the flared open end of a wind instrument is the **bell**

bellboy first referred to a ship's boy who rang a bell

bellhop derived from a clerk ringing a bell on the counter and the worker "hopping" to see what was wanted

a **bellibone** is a woman who is beautiful and good

bellicose orients "prone to fighting" toward an individual while **belligerent** refers to an organized body, a national or political entity— a person is **bellicose**, a nation is **belligerent**

belligerent is from Latin *belliger*, "waging war"; a synonym is belligerous

the beauty of a person is his/her **bellitude**

bellman is the historical term for a town crier

the side of a paper bag is the **bellows**

wether is an Old English word for castrated sheep and a **bellwether** is a sheep with a bell by which it leads the flock

belly has its origin in *belig*, "skin bag," which was used to carry beans and peas

in the violin family, the **belly** is the top surface of an instrument, across which the strings are placed

{ **bellygod** is another word for glutton or epicure }

to be **belly-pinched** is to be starved and hungry

bellysinkers, **doorknobs**, and **burl cakes** are nicknames for doughnuts

bellytimber is hearty, nourishing food

belong is from an Old English verb *langian*, "pertain to"

below is a lexicalization of the phrase by low, replacing on low, the opposite of on high

in boxing, the "**belt**" is the imaginary line between the navel and top of the hips

beluga comes from a Russian word meaning "white"—and it is also called the white whale

to **belute** is to cover or spatter with dirt or mud

bemoan is motivated when pity or grief is over an event that is joined to a consequence, whereas **lament** is motivated when the grief is over the event itself

to **bench** is to exhibit a dog at a show

bend is the name of a number of nautical knots, based on the word "band"

beneath is partially based on Old English *nithan/neothan*, "below"

kindliness in speech is **benedicence**

a long-time bachelor who is newly married is a **benedick** or **benedict**

a **benefactor** is someone who provides a gift; a **beneficiary** is someone who receives benefits or favors

benzene started as benzine, then benzol, and then its final form in the 1870s

etymologically, what you **bequeath** is what you "say" you will leave someone in your will—but the original sense "say, utter" died out, leaving the legal sense

{ **bender**, "drinking spree," comes from the drinker bending his/her elbow every time he/she picks up a glass to take a drink }

benefit originally denoted a kind deed or something well done (from Latin *benefactum*, "good deed")

beneplacit is "a good pleasure" or a gift

Latin *bene volent*, "well wishing," gave us **benevolent**

benign probably comes from Latin *bene*, "well," and *genus*, "born," and first meant "of kindly disposition; gentle"; a **benign** climate or environment is mild and favorable

benign refers to a trait or characteristic; **benignant** to a tendency or disposition

benignity is kindness or tolerance toward others

Benin was formerly Dahomey

a **benison** is a blessing or benediction, the saying of grace

the stiff flowering stalk of a grass is the **bent**

benthos is the flora and fauna at the bottom of a sea or lake

bento/obento is a complete Japanese meal served in a lacquered box or lunchbox divided into sections

bentwood is wood that is artificially shaped for use in making furniture

bereave first meant "deprive of a possession"

bereft means dispossessed of something, not just lacking it

beret is based on Latin *birrus*, "hooded cape"

a deep glacial fissure is a **bergschrund** or **crevasse**

beriberi is a Sinhalese reduplication of *beri*, "weakness"

for a fort, the **berm** is the space between a ditch and the base of the parapet

Bermuda is named for sea captain Juan de Bermudez, who first sited the islands c. 1503

berried describes crustaceans or fish that are bearing eggs

a **berry** is any fruit enclosed in a fleshy pulp—like a banana or tomato

Berserk was a fearless hero of an old Viking tale and the name means "bear shirt," which is all that crazy **Berserk** wore into battle—and it is said he fought in an erratic frenzied way

berth first meant "adequate sea room"

beryl once meant "perfect clarity"—but that has been replaced by the word "crystal"

beseech first meant "search for, try to obtain"

beside is a preposition meaning "next to, alongside, by the side of"; **besides** is a conjunction or adverb meaning "in addition, moreover, at the same time" or "also" but it does not mean "alternatively"

besiege was first assiege

a **besom** is a fireplace broom and **besom-clean** is "as clean as a broom can make a floor"

the curling broom is the **besom** and the stone is the **clint**

to **besot** is to cause to dote on or be infatuated with, e.g., "I am besotted with words."

bespoke means "tailor-made" or "custom-made"

best and **better** go back to a base meaning "advantage, improvement"

bestiality is pronounced bess-chee-AH-luh-tee

a **bestiarian** advocates kindness to animals

besuited means "wearing a suit"

the past tense and past participle of **bet** can be **bet** or betted

the star **Betelgeuse** started out as Arabic *yad al-jawza*, but changed quite a bit in translations into Greek, Latin, and French

Bethlehem is Hebrew for "house of bread"

betray is based on Latin *tradere*, "hand over"

betroth is from the elements "be" and "truth," as in "be true to (somebody)"

a **betty** is a baked pudding made of layers of sugared and spiced fruit and buttered bread crumbs

a husband who does a lot of housework is a **betty**, **cotquean**, or **henhussy**

between is from Old Saxon *tweho* and Old High German *zweho*, "difference"

use **between** when referring to two, use **among** for three or more entities, and use **amid** for a quantity that is not made up of separate items; **between** applies to reciprocal arrangements and **among** to collective arrangements

betweenity is another word for indecision

a sloping edge is a **bevel**

to cut the edges or corners is to **bevel** or **chamfer**

a chisel's slanted surface is the **bevel** and the handle is the **helve**

beverage, from French *be(u)vrage* (*breuvage*), goes back to Latin *bibere*, "to drink"

figuratively, **beverage** can mean "suffering" or "a bitter experience"

bevue is an inadvertent error

bevy can describe a throng of girls, women, roebucks, quails, or larks

beyond is a lexicalization of Old English *be geondan*, "from the farther side"

bi- means two and **semi-** means half

bialy, a roll topped with chopped onions, originated in Bialystok, Poland

bias originated in bowling as a weight that was once placed within the ball to make it deviate from a straight line

a person's **bias** is based on facts, but **prejudice** occurs without a person knowing or examining the facts

a **biathlon** consists of cross-country skiing and rifle shooting

bib means to drink alcohol (Latin *ibibere*)

a faucet with a bent-down nozzle is a **bibcock**, **bibb**, or **bib** the muscle that draws the eye down towards the cup when one drinks is the **bibitory**

bible is derived from *biblios*, the name for the papyrus produced in Byblos'

bibliobibuli are people who read too much

bibliography first meant "the writing of books"

a **biblioklept** is a book thief

bibliomania is a "concern with reading or buying books"

a **bibliophage** is a devourer of books

a **bibliopole** is a dealer in books, especially rare ones

a **bibliothecary** is the keeper of a library

bibulous first meant "absorbent, like a sponge" and later figuratively meant "addicted to alcohol"

biceps is Latin for "two-headed" because the muscle has two points of attachment; the plural is **biceps** or bicepses

bicker as a noun first meant "skirmish"

to **bicker** is to quarrel and to **dicker** is to haggle or bargain

a **bicuspid** is a tooth with two cusps, from Latin *cuspis*, "sharp point"

bicycle's base is Greek *kuklos*, "circle, wheel"

referring to the position one must assume to use a **bidet**

biduous means lasting two days

plants taking two growing seasons to complete the life cycle (usually including flowering) are **biennials**

etymologically, a **bier** is "something used for carrying"

a **biff** is a sharp blow with the fist

big first meant "powerful, strong"

bigamy breaks down to *bi-*, "twice" and *gamos*, "married"

an uprising of women is a **biggening**

the perforated basket holding the grounds in a coffeepot is the **biggin** or **filter**

a **bight** is a curve or recess in a coastline or a loop or slack of a rope—from Old English *byht*, "bend or angle"

bigot was originally a derogatory name applied by the French to the Normans

bigwig is so named from the large wigs formerly worn by distinguished men

bijou means small and elegant when describing a business or residence

bijouterie is a term for jewelry or trinkets

bilberries—also called whortleberries, blaeberries, or whinberries—are the same genus as the blueberry

{ **bikini** was named for the atoll in the Pacific where an atom bomb was exploded—alluding to the explosive effect of the garment }

bid derives from Old English *beodan*, "to offer or command"

biddy was originally a term for an old chicken

bidet (a low bathing vessel for the genitals) originally meant "pony"—

a **bilbo** is a very flexible sword or a type of ankle shackle for prisoners

bildungsroman, from German *bildung*, "education," and *roman*, "novel," refers to a novel with the main theme being the formative years or spiritual education of one person

bile figuratively means "anger" or "peevishness"

a **bilf** or **bulf** is something large and clumsy

bilge can mean "nonsense, rubbish"

> { **bilk** is a term originally used in cribbage meaning "spoil one's opponent's score" }

bill's original sense was simply "written document"—either a general one or a legal statement to the master of a ship by the consul of the port from which he comes—certifying that when the ship sailed there were no infectious diseases onboard

a **billabong** is the branch of a river in Australia that runs to a dead end and forms a backwater or stagnant pool, *billa*, "river," and *bong*, "dead," in Australian Wiradhuri

a **billet** is a civilian house where soldiers are lodged temporarily; a **billet** is also a thick piece of wood, from Latin *billa*, *billus*, "branch, trunk"

billet-doux, a love letter, is French for "sweet note"

billiards is from French *billard*, "cue," or "bent stick" or "stick to push balls"; **billiards** is the general name though Americans mainly play **pool** or **pocket billiards**—with **eight ball** and **snooker** being forms of **pool**

Billingsgate was a wall built around the city of London, by which a fish market was soon established—the fishmongers' loud and vulgar language giving the word a new meaning; **billingsgate** implies practiced fluency and a variety of profane or obscene abuse

a British **billion** is an American **trillion** and an American **billion** is a **milliard** in England

a **billow** is the swell on the ocean produced by the wind, or on a river or estuary by the tide or wind

biloquism is the ability to speak in two distinct voices

bimanous is two-handed and **bicrural** is two-footed

bimbo comes from Italian "little child"; **bimbo** once meant "tough guy" or "one of the boys"

a partitioned stand for storing wine bottles is a **bin**; **binned** is the term for bottles stored in tiers

binary derives from Latin *bini*, "two together"

binate means "composed of two equal parts."

a **bind** is a curved line above or below notes of the same pitch to show that they are to be joined in a continuous sound

the Old English ancestor of **bind** meant "strong" and the past participle once was bounden

a long flexible stem of a climbing plant is a **bine**

to **binge** can also mean "to liven up"

to **binger** is to prevent an activity by saying no to it

bingo is a play in Scrabble using all seven of a player's letters

bingo was first called beano because players put beans on corresponding squares on their cards; the word **bingo** probably imitates the ping of a bell formerly rung to announce a win

the compass stand on a ship is the **binnacle**

binocular is Latin *bini-*, "two together," and *oculus*, "eye," and it means "having two eyes" (adjective); a synonym is field glasses

decomposing naturally or by bacteria is being **biodegradable**

biography can mean "the life course of a human being"

examples of **biological** rhythms in humans are breathing, sleep, and waking; for plants, photosynthesis and the daily opening and closing of flowers

biology came to us via Greek *bios*, "life," and *logia*, "discourse, study," having been coined in German by naturalist Gottfried Reinhold in 1802

bionic means "having artificial body parts, especially electromechanical (from bio- "human" and patterned on "electronic")

there are three types of **biorhythm** cycle: the physical cycle (twenty-three days), the emotional cycle (twenty-eight days), and the intellectual cycle (thirty-three days)

the **biota** is the animal and plant life of a particular region, habitat, or geological period

biotic means "of or relating to life" (opposite of antibiotic)

birch may be related to bright with reference to the tree's light-colored bark

birchen means "made of birch" or "pertaining to birch"

bird was *brid* in Old English

the golf term **birdie** is a diminutive of bird "first-rate thing" as it is one stroke under par for a hole

to revolve a log in the water while standing on it is **birling**

the **birn** is the socket in a clarinet or other woodwind into which the mouthpiece fits

birse is a synonym for bristle

birth is from Old Norse *byro* and shares its base with bear

biscotti is from Latin *bis coctus*, "twice cooked," and zwieback is German for "twice baked"; **biscotti** is actually plural— one is a biscotto

biscuit is Latin for *biscotum panem*, "twice-cooked bread"

Greek *episkopos*, "overseer," became **bishop** in English

the European **bison** is also called the **wisent**, the North American **bison** is also called the **buffalo**, and the Indian **bison** is the **gaur**

bisque is a French word meaning "crayfish soup," but now it describes rich shellfish soup, especially from a lobster

bisque is an extra turn, point, or stroke allowed to a weaker player in croquet, court tennis, or golf

 bisque or biscuit can describe fired unglazed pottery

bissextus is another term for February 29 and that day is **intercalary**, i.e., inserted into the calendar, in leap years

bistro may come from French *bistrouille*, a drink of coffee and brandy

the **bit** is the part of a key that turns the lock

a **bit** is a single unit of computer information and a **byte** is eight

the word **bitch** has meant female dog since before the tenth century, but in the fifteenth century began to be used for an immoral or despicable woman

bite's semantic root is "cleave, split" as in splitting with the teeth

a scissor's **bite** is the distance it cuts in a single stroke

bittern (a bird) evolved from *bitoure*, perhaps on the analogy of heron

bivouac first referred to an army remaining on alert during the night

bizarre once meant "warlike, menacing"

the term to describe variegated garden flowers such as carnations and tulips is **bizarre**

the pupil of the eye was once called the **black**

black comes from a root word meaning "burnt" and **white** from one meaning "shining brightness"

blackball derives from the practice of registering a nay vote by placing a black ball in a ballot box

blackberry is the same as black currant or bilberry

blackguard, pronounced BLAH-gurd, is a hoodlum or scoundrel

blackhead and **comedo** are synonyms

blackjack and **twenty-one** are synonyms

the "mail" in **blackmail** is Scottish for "tax, tribute," referring to the tribute demanded by rebel chiefs in return for their protection

blackout was originally a theatrical term for the extinguishing of all lights on the stage when scenery was shifted

blacktop refers to a material, usually asphalt, that is used to pave roads or cover roofs

the shape containing the words coming from the mouths of cartoon characters is a **bladder**

scalding almonds to remove their skin is **blanching**

bland derives from Latin *blandus*, "soft, smooth"

to **blandish** is to flatter by kind words or affectionate actions

blank was first a small French coin; as an adjective it originally meant "white, colorless, pale" (from Old Norse *blakkr*, "pale (horse)")

a layer of blubber in a whale is a **blanket**

Blarney, Ireland, was the site of a castle where its owner in 1602 talked the British out of taking it over, hence **blarney**

blasé is a French word meaning "worn out" and means bored with the simple things that others still find delightful

the origin of **blasphemy** and **blaspheme** is Greek *blasphemos*, "evil-speaking" (*blapsis* and *pheme*)

the suffix **-blast** is used to form nouns denoting embryonic cells

blatant first meant "clamorous, offensive to the ear"

 a **blazer** was originally a brightly colored ("blazing") jacket used in boating, cricket, and other sports

a **bladderskate** is an indistinct or indiscreet talker

a broad flat bone is a **blade**, as in the shoulder of man

a **blag** is a violent robbery

blame actually derives from Greek *blasphemein*, "reviling, blasphemous"

blamestorming is an intense discussion for the purposes of placing blame or assigning responsibility for a misdeed or failure

blanch and **blank** come from Old French *blanc* "white"

a **blatteroon** is a person who will not shut up

a **blaze** is a white mark made on a tree by chipping off a piece of bark (and a white spot or strip on the face of an animal), hence, to **blaze** a trail by marking trees in this way to mark a route when exploring or pioneering

the **blea** is the wood of a tree beneath the bark

bleach is from a Germanic base meaning "white, colorless, pale" or "shining"

bleak first meant "shining, white" and shares its base with bleach

a **bleat** is a feebly expressed complaint

a **bleb** is an air bubble—like a bubble trapped in glass—and a **spiracle** is an air hole

someone's complexion or color can be called his/her **blee**

a plant emitting sap is **bleeding**

bleezed refers to the state of one on whom intoxicating liquor begins to operate

a **blench** is a trick or strategem

a **blend** is a combination of different types or grades of fabric, spirits, tea, tobacco, etc.

blends are also called **blend** words, amalgams, fusions, hybrids, telescoped words, and, notably, portmanteau words

blepharon means "having huge eyebrows"

bless originally meant "to redden with blood" as in sacrifice—hence, God **bless** you literally means "God bathe you in blood"

a group of unicorns is a **blessing**

bletting is the spotted appearance of a ripe fruit, like on a banana, and these are also called sugar spots; a **blet** is a form of near-decay seen on overripe pears and other fruit

blighty are wounds that secure a soldier his/her return home

a **blik** is a personal slant on something or one's conviction, especially religious

World War II's two types of dirigibles were A-rigid and B-limp—hence, **blimp**

blin (as in blini and blintze) is Russian for "pancake"

a stake put up in poker by a player before seeing his/her cards is a **blind**

blindfold was originally *blindfelle*, meaning "strike someone blind," and was perverted to the notion of folding something around the eyes

to **blink** can mean "to turn sour"

a **blinkard** is a person who lacks intellectual perception

a horse's eye screen is a **blinker** or **blinkers**

blintz(e) is from Russian *blinets*, "little pancake"

a **blipvert** is a TV advertisement of a few seconds' length

an outburst of tears is a **blirt**; a **blirt** is also a squall, a gust of wind and rain

bliss originally meant kindness of manner

a swelling filled with air or water, as on a painted surface, is a **blister**

blithe first meant "being kind, gentle, clement"

{ **blitz** is an abbreviation of *blitzkrieg* (German "lightning war") }

blive means "before long, soon"

a **blivit** is something pointless, useless, or impossible—or a gadget

blizz, a violent rainstorm, is not related to the word blizzard

blizzard was originally a sharp blow or knock

bloat first meant "flabby, soft" before "puffed up"

block derives from Middle Dutch *blok*, "tree trunk"

blockbuster was originally a bomb that could blow up a city block

blockhead relates to the head-shaped blocks of wood used for the design and fitting of hats; blockheads purportedly having no more brains than the hatmakers' blocks of wood

blocking is the physical arrangement of actors on a stage or film set

to flow with a gurgling sound out of a narrow opening is to **blodder**

blog, formed by contraction of Web log (or

weblog), is essentially an online personal diary or journal available to the public on a website

blond/blonde derive from Latin *blondus*, "yellow"

bloom comes from Old Norse *blom*, "flower, blossom"

the waxy coating on some fruits like plums is called **bloom**

blue chips used in gambling games usually have a high value, thereby the adjective **blue-chip**

the blueness of **bluegrass** only becomes visible when the grass is allowed to go to seed, the seed covering having a distinctly blue cast

a **bluenose** is a person from Nova Scotia or a puritanical person

{ **bloomers** were named, tongue-in-cheek, for Amelia Jenks Bloomer, an early feminist—and were also known as "rational dress" }

the Indo-European root *blo* eventually yielded both "**blossom**" (the old word for **flower**) and "**flower**"

a **blot** in backgammon is an exposed piece liable to be taken

blister and botch blended to make **blotch**

bloten means "fond," as children are of their care-givers

blouse was first a garment, usually belted at the waist, worn by peasants or workmen

to **bloviate** is to talk at length

a brilliant display, as of blossoms, can be called a **blow**

a sea rock opening through which water intermittently spouts is a **blowhole** or **gloup**

the annoying cards in magazines are called **blow-ins** and **bound-ins**

a **blowtop** is someone who gets mad easily or quickly

to **blub** is to complain

the original notion underlying **blubber** is "bubbling, foaming" particularly in reference to the sea—and it lies behind the verbal sense of "cry copiously"

blueprint originated from the (original) process in which prints were composed of white lines on a blue ground or blue lines on a white ground

the adjective **blue-rinse** means "pertaining to elderly women"

the **blues** is a shortened form of "blue devils," a type of music that first expressed depression, despair, or hopelessness of African-Americans

bluestocking refers to a female intellectual

bluff as in cliff comes from a nautical word meaning "broad" as in a ship's bow

the early meanings of **bluff** were "to blindfold" and "to hoodwink" from Dutch words meaning "brag" or "bragging"

blunder comes from Old Norse for "to shut the eyes"

blunderbuss was derived from Dutch *donderbus*, "thunder gun, thunder tube"

a **blunger** is a machine to mix clay (etc.) with water

blunt orginally meant "dull, obtuse, foolish"

American humorist Gelett Burgess coined **blurb**—and he made a comic book with a character named Miss Blinda Blurb

blush may have derived from Old English *blysa*, "firebrand, torch"

to blurt out is to **blutter**

blutterbunged is another word for "confounded, overcome by surprise"

skin that peels off after a sunburn is called **blype**

BMX stands for Bicycle Moto Cross (X)

a full-grown male badger, guinea pig, or hedgehog is a **boar**

a table set for a meal was once called a "**board**"

the name Border signified a feudal tenant and this may have become **boarder** (one who pays for food and lodging)

boardsailing is another word for **windsurfing**

boast first meant "threaten" or "threat"

a **boat** is a vessel that can be hauled aboard a **ship**, according to the Navy, with a **ship** being somewhat larger

the **boater** or **boater** straw is so called because the hat was first worn when boating

a **boatswain** (pronounced BO-suhn) is a ship's officer in charge of the deck crew

a **bob** in Middle English denoted a bunch or cluster; a suckling calf is also called a **bob**

to **bob** is to ride on a bobsled—which gets its name "bob" from being a short sled

a **bobber** is a person who rides a bobsled or bobsleigh (meaning "short sled")

a **bobbit** is an old word for "hopeless little bit of something that must be found"

a **bobble** is a small ball of wool (etc.) as a decoration on a hat or other knitted clothing

bobbies are named for Sir Robert (Bobby) Peel, the Prime Minister who established the Metropolitan Police in London

a **bobolink** was originally Bob o' Lincoln or Bob Lincoln, which is imitative of its call—also is true for the **bobwhite**

a **bobweight** is a counterweight to a moving part in a machine

bocce is Italian for "bowls"

small balls of mozzarella cheese are **bocconcini**

bock is an abbreviation of German *Eimbockbier*, beer from Einbeck (in Hanover)

bodacious is a blend of bold and audacious

boda is messenger in Germanic, hence **bode**; at first, a **bode** was a command—then an omen or premonition

bodega first meant "wine shop" and now is used for "grocery store" or a combined wine shop and grocery store, especially an Hispanic one; it derives from Spanish for "storehouse"

a **bodhisattva** has attained the enlightenment of a Buddha but has chosen not to pass into Nirvana so that he or she can stay and help lesser beings attain enlightenment

originally, **bodice** was identical to bodies, that is, the plural of body

a **bodkin** was originally a small dagger (kin is a diminutive suffix)

{ the consecrated bread (or crackers) in the Eucharist is the "**body**" }

a **bodyscape** is a map of the body

boffo was originally "a hearty belly laugh"—a comedian's big reward, which later changed into meaning "a great success"

a joke that gets a hearty laugh is a **boffola**

a **bog** (from Irish or Scottish Gaelic **bog**, "soft") is wetland covered with mats of moss and decaying vegetation—with or without shrubs and evergreens

to **bogart** is to hog or take more than one's fair share—or in some way act like a bully

bogey, originally a proper noun applied to the Devil, is probably related to **bogle**, "goblin, phantom"

to **boggle** means "to start with fright," like a horse

bogglish means "uncertain, doubtful" or "skittish"

the wheel inside the tread of a tractor or tank is the **bogie** or **bogy**

bogus originally denoted a machine for making counterfeit money

Bohemian is from French *bohemien*, "gypsy"

a **bohunk** is a lout—but first was a derogatory term for a Hungarian or person of east-central Europe, based on Bohemian Hungarian

the sudden rise of a fish at a fly is a **boil**

text that is recyclable is called "**boilerplate**"

Boise is from French and means "wooded"

boite, literally French for "box," is a small restaurant or nightclub

to **bold** a fire is to kindle glowing coals

bole is another name for the trunk of a tree

a **bollard** is the fat post to which a boat is tied or a fixed post used to prevent traffic access, as well as the name for an inverted rubber traffic cone

Bologna, Italy, was once known for its sausage of dubious quality

bolshevik comes from *bol' shoy*, "big," and originally applied to supporters of extreme socialism

bolster, originally a long thick pillow, comes from a Germanic base meaning "swell"

bolt originally referred to a short thick arrow with a blunt head, fired from a crossbow

bolus is chewed food ready for swallowing and **chyme** is swallowed, partially digested food

bomb derives from Latin *bombus*, from Greek *bombos*, "booming, humming"

bombardier first denoted a soldier in charge of a bombard, an early form of cannon

bombast is literally the produce of the bombyx or silkworm (Greek *bombux*) and the soft down of the cotton plant is the **bombast**, which was used for padding clothing; hence, **bombast** describing "padding" in speeches

{ to **bombinate** or **bombilate** is to buzz or hum }

bombshell was first literal for an artillery shell and later figurative for anything or anyone with a shattering effect

bombus is a buzzing in the ears, stomach, etc.

a **bonamano** is a tip or gratuity

bonanza is a Spanish word meaning "fair weather, prosperity" (from Latin *bonus*, "good" and *malacia*, "dead calm"); one of the meanings of **bonanza** is "a very rich vein or pocket of ore"

bonbon is a French word for sweet

the pattern in which a wall is laid is its **bond**

bonds are securities but differ from shares of **stock** in that **stock** is an ownership interest (termed "equity"), but bonds are "debt"; therefore a shareholder is an owner, but a bond-holder is a creditor

bone is slang for a dollar

boned means either "with the bones in" or "deboned, boneless"

bonfire comes from the words bone and fire, referring to an open-air burning of bones or funeral pyre

when a cyclist or runner **bonks** they have reached the point of exhaustion and cannot go further

a **bonne-bouche** is a tasty morsel kept for last—to leave a last good taste in the mouth

a cap on a fire hydrant is called a **bonnet**

bonsai comes from Japanese words meaning "tray planting"; **bonsai** involves growing and pruning so that all parts of the plant—flowers, leaves, and stems—are in proportion

to **boodle** is to practice bribery; a **boodler** is one who practices boodling

boodles is a great quantity, especially of money

before the invention of paper, the thin inner bark of certain trees was used for writing— **book** is of Germanic origin and is related to beech, on which runes were carved; the Latin word for this was *liber*, which later also came to mean "**book**"

bookkeeper is the only English word with three consecutive repeated letters (not including its other forms) in which omission of the **medial hyphen** is a practical option, which it is not in, for example, hoof-footed or sweet-toothed

Boolean as in algebra, logic, and search, is named for mathematician George Boole (1815–1864)

{ **boom** was originally a long beam or pole and came from Dutch }

Australian aborigines coined the word **boomerang** as possibly "weapon that flies through the air and returns to part the throwers hair"

boon once meant "request for a favor"

boondocks is from Tagalog *bunok*, meaning "mountain"—a word misheard during World War II in the Philippines and now used to mean "backwoods, remote rural area"

a **boondoggle** is a task of little practical value; to **boondoggle** is to do useless or futile work

the leather knot under a Boy Scout's hat is a **boondoggle**

a **boonfellow** is a warm companion

boor is derived from Dutch *boer*, "peasant, farmer"

boom and hoist combined to make **boost**

a navy or marine recruit is a **boot**

a **booth** was first a temporary dwelling made of branches, material, etc.

illicit merchandise was carried in the legs of high boots in the nineteenth century— hence, **bootlegger**

bootless means "useless, fruitless; to no avail"

booty has no connection with boots, but is from a German base meaning "exchange"

Middle Dutch *busen* or *buizen*, "to drink to excess; tipple," brought us **booze**

borasca or **borasco** is a thunderstorm or squall

stomach rumbling can be called **borborygmus** or **gurgulation** or **borborygm**

bordelaise is the feminine form of Bordeaux and it is a red wine sauce

border shares a background with board as in "side of a ship"

bore connoting "tiresomeness" became a buzzword in the 1760s

bore "tidal wave" is from Old Norse *bara*, "billow"

boreal winds are northern

a **boreen** is a narrow country road

around 1600, **born** was established for obstetrics and **borne** became the past participle of **bear**

borough was originally a fortress or castle or manor house

when putting in golf, to **borrow** means to allow for sideways motion due to slope or wind

in Russian, **borscht** means "cow parsnip"; **borscht** first referred to turnip or parsnip, not beet, soup

a **borstal** is a correction or detention center for young offenders

a **boscage** is a mass of growing trees or shrubs—or a depiction of a wooded landscape

{ **bosh,** "nonsense, foolish talk," is from Turkish *bos,* "empty, worthless" }

the surface of the sea, river, or ground can be called the **bosom**

boss derives from the Dutch word *baas*, "master"

a **bosset** is a small protuberance or knob

bos, Greek or Latin for cow, evolved into **Bossy**, a traditional name for a milk cow

Greek *botane*, "plant" gives us **botany**

both is from an Indo-European base meaning "each of two"

bother first meant "noise, chatter"

Botswana was formerly Bechuanaland

bottega is another word for workshop or studio; the plural is bottegas or botteghe

a **bottle** of wine is a **bottle** full of wine and a wine **bottle** is an empty **bottle** used to hold wine

bottle now means glass but originally denoted a vessel of any material, especially leather

bottom is related to the word foundation through their shared Indo-European base

botulism is from a German word translated to "sausage poisoning" (from Latin *botulus*, "sausage")

boudoir is from *bouder*, "to pout or sulk," and originally meant a room where one went when feeling depressed or unsociable (literally French "sulking place")

a **bouffage** is a satisfying meal or meat eaten greedily

bouffant is French, literally "swelling"

the greatest circumference of a cask is the **bouge** or **bilge**

bouillabaisse is French for "to boil and settle or lower," which is how it is cooked

bouillon is literally French "liquid in which something has boiled"

boulder is shortened from the earlier *boulderstone* of Scandinavian origin

a rounded loaf of bread, as sourdough is sometimes, is a **boule**

boulevard is from French, literally "rampart" or a "promenade on the site of a rampart"

bounce may come from Dutch *bons*, "a thump"

bouncing in bouncing baby means "vigorous"

in grammar, an element that is **bound** occurs only in combination with another form

bounty's origin is Latin *bonus*, "good"

bouquet comes from French *bosquet*, originally meaning "a little forest" or "clump of trees"

bourbon (named for **Bourbon** County, Kentucky) is an American **whiskey** made from at least 51 percent corn, plus other grains (all bourbons are **whiskey**, but not all whiskeys are **bourbon**); **whiskey** is an alcoholic liquor distilled from grain, such as corn, rye, or barley, and containing approximately 40 to 50 percent ethyl alcohol by volume—and the varieties include **bourbon whiskey**, corn **whiskey**, and rye **whiskey**

a bagpipe's bass drone is a **bourdon**

bourgeois came from French from Latin *burgus*, "castle"

bourgeoisie is the middle class, while the **proletariat** is a lower working class

a **bourn** or **bourne** can be a small stream or brook—or a boundary between fields, or the limit or terminus of a course, journey, or race

a curve in the side of a guitar, violin, or other musical instrument is a **bout**

boutique first meant a small shop of any kind (literally French for this); now it is a small fashionable retail store

boutonniere is French for "buttonhole" as that is where these flowers are usually worn

bovarism is the condition of having a magnified opinion of one's own abilities

linguistically related **bovine** words include boustrophedon, beef, bulimia, butter, and bugle

the looped end of a key is the **bow**

bowdlerize is censoring or sanitizing written material in the style of physician and editor, Dr Thomas Bowdler (1754–1825)

{ **bowel** derives from Latin *botellus*, diminutive of *botulus*, "sausage" }

bower was once a lady's private room or bedroom

Bowl as in Super Bowl derives from the eating vessel bowl. Its first sports meaning was "football stadium," though such a stadium is no longer necessarily bowl-shaped. The Yale Bowl is an example of a football stadium so named. As a sporting event, it first referred to the Rose Bowl (1923) and, later, the Super Bowl.

the **bowl** you eat cereal from takes its name from the same source as "ball, balloon" and "ballot"—Latin *bulla*, "bubble"

bowl and **bowling** have roots in words meaning "globular vessel" or "swell, swelling" or "round pod"

the **bowshot** is the distance to which a bow can send an arrow

box descends from Latin *pyxis*, "boxwood **box**"

to **box** is to recite the compass points in correct order

the inside pocket on a coat or jacket is a **boxter**

in Greek and Roman times, a **boy** was one who wore shackles and was a slave

boycott was named for a person who was excluded from the Irish Land League after charging his tenants unreasonable rents

a **boycott** is an organized popular protest, while an **embargo** is usually imposed by a government

bozos originally were rather naive or inexperienced youngsters, the Spanish word it comes from meaning the peach fuzz of a near-man

bra is an abbreviation of brassiere

to **brabble** is to quarrel over nothing

brace is from Old French meaning "two arms," the distance between the fingertips with the arms extended, from Latin *bracchium*, "arm"

bracelet comes from Old French *bras*, "arm" from the Latin base *bracchium*

when apes swing from branch to branch by the arms, they are **brachiating**

bracken is a a warm orangey-brown, based on the fern of the same name

square **brackets** were formerly called crotchets, round brackets are commonly designated parentheses, curly brackets are called braces; the punctuation called brackets derives from the bookshelf type, implying that in writing these marks "lift up" a section of a sentence

to break bread is to **brackle**

brad—a small or thin wire nail—is from Old Norse broddr "spike"

the bray of a trumpet can be called the **brag**

bragging is more obnoxious than **boasting** and is always exaggerated and crude

the handle of a pump is the **brake**

bramble comes from Germanic meaning "thorny bush"

brambles refer specifically to blackberry bushes; **briers** normally means the thorny branches of the rose

branch is derived from Latin *branca*, "paw"

brand originally meant "burning" or "to mark by burning"

originally, a **brand** was a flame or fire; when a product was **brand-new**, it was fresh out of the **brand** (as horseshoes) and was only used in reference to metal "fresh from the fire"—as a newly forged sword

brandish can also describe scattering rays of light

a **brandreth** is a tripod or trivet—or a wooden framework to hold a cask

brandy is made from grapes and other fruits and is short for brandywine, from Dutch *brandewijn*, "burnt (distilled) wine," which was untrue, though it was distilled over a hot fire

the poet **Braggadochio** in Edmund Spenser's "The Faerie Queene" is the source of braggadocio, "cowardly boaster"

the ultimate source of **braid** meant "make sudden jerky movements from side to side"

braille was devised by Louis **Braille** (1809–1852)

brainstorm was a medical term for "mental explosion" by the 1890s

the Chinese combination of *hsi*, "brain," and *nao*, "wash," gave us **brainwash**

the origin of **braise** is a French word meaning "live coals"—in which the container was formerly placed

to **brangle** is to squabble or brawl

a **brannigan** is a spree or binge

branular means pertaining to or affecting the brain

a euphemism for vomit is **brash**

brash is "loose broken rock or ice; rubble"

brass is from German *bras*, "metal," and originally was an alloy of copper with tin, zinc, or another metal—now copper and zinc

a band worn around the arm is a **brassard**

brasserie comes from French, literally "brewery"

names for a **brat**: awp, azzard, birsie, cade, gobbin, carker, rantipole, bratchet, smatchet

bratwurst is German *Brat*, "meat without waste," and *Wurst*, "sausage"

brave once meant "showy, gaudy"

bravo is directed to a male performer and **brava** to a female

the meat of a boar is called **brawn**

to **bray** is to crush something with a mortar and pestle

to **braze** is to unite pieces of metal using a **solder** containing brass or another high melting-point material; **weld** is to unite pieces of metal by fusing them at a high temperature—usually with a flame or acetylene torch; **solder** is to unite pieces of metal by bonding them using another metal (called the **solder**) that has a melting point lower than either metal to be joined— usually done with electric heat

brazen means belonging to or made of brass

breach is the leap of a whale out of the water or the breaking of waves over a vessel or onto a coast; **breach** is also the act of breaking

breach is an infraction, gap, or break; **breech** is the rear or lower portion of things

in Old English the word **bread** meant "piece, morsel" while actual **bread** was known as "loaf"

breadfruit, which grows on South Pacific islands, was so named because the soft white pulp resembles fresh baked bread

breadth is *brede*, "broaden, extend," and -th, patterned after length

the first appearance of light or the onset of something is the **break**

breakfast literally means "breaking the fast"—of the night, as it is the first meal after sleeping

a **breakfront** is a piece of furniture having the line of its front broken by a curve or angle

in the Congreve poem, it is "music has charms to soothe a savage **breast**, to soften rocks, or bend a knotted oak" (not beast)

breath is from an Old English word meaning "scent, smell"

when you use the word **breathe** in reference to the skin or to wine, it means how it is affected by contact with air

breccia is another word for gravel or pieces of angular rock fragments (often in a matrix)—the opposite of conglomerate

a baby delivered feet- or bottom-first is **breech**

a **breech-cloth** or **Indian waist-band** was once called a **gee-string**

{ **breeches** and **britches** are synonymous and both are pronounced BRICH-iz }

when kids start to get teeth, this can be called **breed**, "to exhibit naturally"

a **breedbate** likes to start arguments

breeks is another word for britches/ breeches

the original sense of **breeze** was "northeastern wind," from Old Spanish/Portuguese *briza*

a **breezeway** is a roofed passage, usually open at the sides, connecting two buildings or parts of a house

brephic means pertaining to an early stage of growth

a **brevet** is an official or authoritative message in writing

a **breviary** or **breviate** is a brief statement or summary the ancestral meaning of **brew** has to do with "heat"

brewis is bread soaked in broth—or a broth thickened with bread

a **brew-up** is a pause for the making of tea

briar is wild heather

bribe, from Old French, was originally a piece of bread given to beggars; the original sense of **bribe** is "extort, rob"

bric-a-brac comes from French *à brie et à brac*, "at random"

calling a person a **brick** is a compliment

bricolage is the creation of an artwork or literary work from a diverse range of available things

bridal comes from Old English "bride's ale"

a **bride** is a link or thread in a network of lace that connects the patterns

bridegroom comes from Old English *brydguma*, "bride's man"

the **bridge** of the nose is the upper bony part and the **bridge** of eyeglasses is the central/middle part that lies on the nose

the verb **bridle** is a metaphor from a horse being pulled up suddenly and sharply

brief derives from Latin *brevis*, "short"

brier is the wild rose or any prickly bush like the bramble

brig is an abbreviation of brigantine

brigade, **brigand**, and **brigantine** go back to Italian *briga*, "strife"

brightwork is the chrome or other polished metal on a vehicle or appliance

a perfect **brilliant** diamond has fifty-eight facets

brilliant can be traced to Italian *brillare*, "shine, shining"

brim first denoted the edge of the sea or other body of water

{ when your glass or cup is filled to the brim, you have a **brimmer** }

brimstone is an old word for the element sulfur

the juice in a pickle jar is the **brine**

the brim of a hat is the **brink**

brio is from Italian, literally "fire, mettle, vivacity"

brioche in French is literally "split up into small pieces"

a small brick or block of ice cream is a **briquette**

brisket seems to be from Old Norse *brjosk*, "cartilage, gristle"

brit are tiny sea creatures that are dinner for a whale

British was first *Bruttische* or *Bryttische* in Middle English, from Latin *Britto*, the name used by the Roman invaders for the Briton tribe

brittle probably comes from the Germanic stem *brut*, "break"

to burn slightly or singe is to **brizzle**

broach comes from Latin *brocchus*, *broccus*, "projecting"

broach is what a fish or sea mammal does when it rises through the water and breaks the surface

the word **broad** meaning "woman" or "prostitute" may come from the slang use "playing card" but the reason is obscure; the term may be suggestive of **broad** hips, but it also may trace to American English abroadwife, for a woman away from her husband, often a slave

in athletics, the track and field **broad jump** was changed to the **long jump** c. 1967 because of the negative association with "broad" for a low-class woman

broadcast was first a farming method of sowing small seed with a broad casting motion of the arm

broadcloth started out as fine, plain-woven, double-width black cloth used chiefly for men's garments

in naval language, the whole side of a ship is called this—so firing all the guns on one side simultaneously is to fire a **broadside**; later this meant a verbal onslaught and then was a synonym for a **broadsheet** (large piece of paper with printing on one side)

when something is described as **broad-spectrum**, it is effective against a wide variety of organisms, e.g., antibiotics and pesticides

broasting is a combination of cooking by broiling and roasting

brobdingnagian, "enormous, huge," is from the race of giants in Jonathan Swift's "Gulliver's Travels"

> **brocade** comes from the Italian *broccato*, from *brocco*, "twisted thread"

broccoli comes from Latin *bracchium*, "strong arm or branch" in reference to its shape; **broccoli** is the Italian plural of *broccolo*, "cabbage sprout, head," and is literally "little shoots"

brochure is from a French word meaning "a stitched work"

brockie is a cow with a black-and-white face or any person with a dirty face

a **brogue** was originally a rudimentary sort of shoe worn in Celtic areas of the British Isles, from Old Norse *brok*, "leg covering"

broil comes from Old French *bruler*, "to burn"

in football, **broken-field** describes an area where the defenders are relatively scattered

originally a **broker** or brokour bought wine cheaply in quantity and sold it at a profit; **broker** came to mean any retailer who did this or a middleman/agent

an essay, discourse, or study of food is a **bromatology**

a **bromide** is a commonplace saying, trite remark, or conventionalism meant to soothe

bad body odor is **bromidrosis** or **kakidrosis** or **osmidrosis**

bronco is Spanish for "rough, rude"

brontide is a low, rumbling sound like thunder or an earthquake

bronze is probably derived from Persian *birinj*, "brass"

bronze is copper and tin, **brass** is copper and zinc, and **pewter** is lead and tin

brooch first meant "skewer"

to sit on eggs is to **brood**

a hen sitting on eggs is a **broody**

a **brook** is a small stream

brooms were first called besoms but evolved because many were made of twigs from the wild **broom** shrub

broth etymologically means "that which has been brewed"

a **brothel** at first was a person, not a place: "scoundrel, low life, worthless person" and eventually "harlot, prostitute"

brethren is a plural of **brother**

a **half-brother** can also be called a **brother-in-law**

brou ha ha! was an exclamation used by characters playing the devil in sixteenth century French dramas—coming from the Hebrew *barukh habba* (*beshem adhonai*), "blessed is he who comes (in the name of the Lord)"

{ the **brougham** was a four-wheeled one-horse carriage, named for Henry Peter **Brougham** (1778–1868), who designed it in 1838 }

a **brow** is a gangway from ship to shore

brown first meant "dark, dusky"

brown is a former name for a penny or any copper coin

brownette is a person who has light brown hair

the first meaning of **brownie** was a benevolent spirit or goblin, of shaggy appearance, supposed to haunt old houses, especially farmhouses, in Scotland, and sometimes performing useful household tasks while the family was asleep

a **brownout** is a period of low voltage when lights are apt to dim

browse comes from French *broust*, the young shoots, leaves, etc. that animals feed on

bruin comes from the Dutch word for "brown"

bruise is a blend of Old English *brysan*, "crush to pieces," and Old French *bruisier*, "break"

a sound heard through a stethoscope is a **bruit**

brumal means wintry, belonging to winter—from Latin *brumalis*, from *bruma*, "winter," which is a contraction of *brevima*, "shortest (day), winter"

brume is a poetic term meaning "mist, fog, or vapor" and **brumous** means "foggy"

brummagem means "cheap, gaudy"

a **brunch** is the perfect name for a meal between breakfast and lunch

brunet(te) is seldom applied to males; **brunette** is a diminutive of French *brun*, "brown"

bruschetta should be pronounced BROO-sketuh; it is derived from Italian *bruscare*, "to toast"

a bushy dog tail is a **brush** and a smooth dog tail is a **stern**

brusque comes ultimately from the name of an unpleasant spiky shrub, the butcher's broom, which instead of normal branches and leaves has flattened twigs with stiff spines at the ends; this came to be used as an adjective meaning "sharp, tart" and then "fierce"

brut is unsweetened champagne

brute comes from Latin *brutus*, "dull, stupid"

habitual grinding of the teeth is **bruxism**

to **bruzzle** is to make a stir or to-do

bubba is a term of address meaning "brother"

bubble is partly imitative and partly an alteration of burble

bubbler is the metal part of a drinking fountain out of which the water comes

bubkes (absolutely nothing) is Yiddish, from Russian for "beans," and is also written bupkis, bupkes, bupkus

those who cured their meat on barbecues were first called **buccaneers** and both derived from Tupi *boucan*

if you have a double chin, you can call it a **buccula**

buck is the male of several animal species: antelope, deer, goat, rabbit, sheep

buck, as a dollar, comes from buckskin, an early unit of exchange

it may be that **buck** naked came from the color of buckskin or as an alteration of the word "butt"

buckaroo, a working cowboy, is a corruption of the Spanish word *vaquero*, "cowboy"

bucket is *buc*, "container; heavy thing," and -*et*, a diminutive suffix

a **buckeye** is a backwoodsman

buckle is a streusel-topped fruit coffee cake

Latin bucca meant "cheek" and a warrior's helmet had a strap across the cheek, a *buccala*, "cheek strap of a helmet" (the diminutive of *bucca*)—and this became the word "**buckle**"

buckwheat comes from Middle Dutch meaning "beech wheat" as its grains are shaped like beech mast, the nuts of the beech tree

bucolic means "pertaining to country life; rural, rustic"

buculets are the little bumpers on the underside of a toilet seat

the wad of cotton on a Q-tip is the **bud**

broccoli is a **flower cluster**, the Brussels sprout is a **bud**

buddha is Sanskrit, literally "enlightened"

budge is derived from French *bouger*, "to stir," from Latin *bullire*, "to boil"

the small parrot, the **budgerigar**, translates to *budgeri*, "good," and *gar*, "cockatoo" (Australian)

budget is derived from Old French *bougette*, "leather bag," and in English originally meant a pouch or wallet—and later its contents—and also has an archaic meaning "a quantity of material, especially written or printed"; formerly, the **budget** was literally a sack full of money, with sums appropriated to specific purposes being sorted into little bags

Budweiser is named for the Czech town of Ceske Budejovice, known in Germany as "Budweis"

the word **buff** "someone interested in and knowledgeable about a subject" was originally used for fire-watchers because of the buff-colored uniforms worn by New York firefighters; **buff** the color came from the whitish-yellow skin of buffalo

buffalo probably came from Portuguese *bufalo*, from Greek *boubalos*, "antelope, wild ox"; strictly speaking, neither **buffalo** nor antelope live in North America and the American **bison** is what we call a **buffalo**

buffer is based on the word buff, which is imitative of the sound of a blow to a soft body

buffet was first the sideboard or cupboard, then the food served on it

buffoon comes from Latin *buffo*, "clown"

bug is a slang synonym for lobster

bug is the transparent network logo that appears in the lower corner of a TV screen

the first use of **bug** as a defect or glitch in a machine seems to be around 1889 in reference to Thomas Edison's phonograph when he used the expression, implying that some imaginary insect has secreted itself inside and was causing trouble

bugs suck and **beetles** chew

a **bug** is a particular kind of **insect**, specifically belonging to the order Hemiptera (tough leathery forewings attached to the body—like ladybugs, beetles) while insects generally belong to the class Insecta, which have bodies in three segments, usually two pairs or wings and three pairs of legs (like bees, mosquitoes); spiders are not technically insects because they have four pairs of legs

{ a **bugaboo** is something which one finds terrifying }

early references to **bugbear** suggest it was a "frightening creature" conjured up to frighten naughty children

the Bulgarians, belonging to the Eastern Orthodox Church, were regarded by Western Europeans as heretics in the early Christian era; the Latin *Bulgarus* came to be applied to any heretic and passed into English as **bugger**, now generally a term of abuse

bugle was originally the word for ox, whose horn was used to give signals—and it came to mean such a musical instrument

build comes from the Germanic base *bu-*, "dwell"; Old English *bold*, "house," formed *byldan*, "construct a house," before it became **build**

bulb descends from Greek *bolbos*, "onion, bulbous root," and first meant "onion," then evolved to mean the underground spheroid part of the onion, lily, or similar plants

if it is **buldering**, it is hot and muggy

bulgar or **bulgur** is Turkish for "bruised grain"

the original meaning of **bulge** was "wallet or bag" and later "a ship's bilge"—with other senses derived by association with the shape of a full bag

bulimia comes from Greek words meaning ox (*bous*) and hunger (*limos*), "the hunger of an ox"

bulk probably comes from Old Norse *bulki*, "cargo"

a section divider in an aircraft is a **bulkhead**

bull, as in exaggeration or lying, is based on French *boule*, "deceit, fraud"

to plunge into a situation without preparation is to **bull**

bulldog is the first newspaper edition of the day, usually available the night before

the sport of setting dogs upon a bull in an arena started by the twelfth century and special dogs—**bulldogs**—were bred for the event

bulldoze was originally bulldose, a "dose" being a whipping sufficient for a bull—later used for the idea of pushing others or things around

a **bulldozer** was originally a person, especially one who intimidated others by violence

a dot setting off an item on a list is a **bullet**; **bullet** is from a French word meaning "small ball," from Latin *bulla*, "bubble"

bulletin is from French *bulle* (from Latin *bulla*), "papal edict," and the earliest bulletins were from the pope

bullion came from Anglo-Norman *bullion*, "mint; place where coins are made," and has the underlying connotation of melting or boiling

bullition is the act or state of boiling

baseball's **bullpen** may have come from a game of this name in which opponents lined up in a rectangle and threw balls at each other or it may come from a newspaper reporter comparing pitchers with bulls and the game with a bullfight

bullshit started as army slang for excessive spit and polish and the unnecessary cleaning of equipment

bully first meant lover or sweetheart, then fine fellow, then blusterer, then "person who harms or threatens weaker people"

bulwark comes from German *bole*, "plank," and *werc*, "work," and originally meant "rampart made out of planks or tree trunks"

bum as in vagrant comes from German *bumm-ler*, "loafer," and *bummelem*, "waste time"

to **bumbaste** is to spank

a **bumbershoot** is an umbrella

the **bumblebee** is of the genus Bombus, from which it gets its name (it also was called a humblebee, from its loud humming sound)

bumbledom is the world of incompetent people or self-importance while in a minor office

bumf or **bumph** is a great British term for "useless or tedious printed information"

the primary meaning of **bump** seems to be "knock" and this led to "swelling" as the result of being hit

bumpkin is derived from Dutch *boomkin*, "little stunted tree"

bumwhush is a state of annihilation or ruin or obscurity

bun is derived from French *bugne*, "bump or swelling on the head"

Bunbury is the name of an imaginary person used as a fictitious excuse for visiting a place or avoiding obligations (from "The Importance of Being Earnest")

bunion is probably a modification of the East Anglian *bunny*, "lump, swelling," borrowed from Old French *bugne*, "bump on the head"

bunk as in bed is probably short for bunker, which was "box, chest" in Scottish English

a prattling congressman from Buncombe County, North Carolina around 1820, was the origin of **bunk** and **bunkum** (first spelled buncombe), "nonsense"

a **bunkie** is a person who shares a bunk with another

bunny is a lengthening of *bun*, a Scottish Gaelic term for "the tail of a rabbit"

the cloth from which flags are made and the material decorating a stage or platform is **bunting**

buoy (pronounced BOO-ee) may come from Old French *boie*, "chain"; **buoyant** comes from Spanish *boyar*, "float," from French *boie*, "chain"

burble, a blend of burst and bubble, means "to talk quickly and incoherently"

the **burden** is the main theme or gist of a speech, book, or argument—or the **refrain** or **chorus** of a song

{ **bumper**, originally meaning "full glass or cup" was extended to anything large or abundant, as in **bumper** crop }

to **bunch** is to present a person with a **bunch** of flowers

to **bundle** (in, off, out) is to pack for a journey

bungalow, from Hindi *bangla*, "of Bengal, belonging to Bengal," was originally the house of a European in India—usually one story with a veranda all the way around

bungersome is awkward or clumsy

the French word **bureau** (before it meant desk) was a kind of woolen cloth used to cover desks (from Latin *burra*, "woolly cloth")

bureaucracy is literally "rule by writing desk"—i.e., professional paper shuffling

a network of fine lines or dots, as on a postage stamp, is called burelè or **burelage**

burgeon means to bud or sprout; it does not mean expand or thrive

burglar is literally "town thief," ultimately from Latin *borgus/burgus*, "(walled) city," then Anglo-Latin *burgulator/burglator*, and related to Old French *burgier*, "pillage"

burglary first meant breaking into a house by night with the intent to commit a felony

burglary can take place when the victim is not there and is the theft of property without the owner being aware of the crime; in **robbery**, the victim is present and is confronted

burgoo is a nautical slang term for porridge

burial originally meant a burying place and later came to denote the act

a knot in cloth is a **burl**, a knot in wool is a **nep**, a knot in wood is a **knar** or **nar**

burlesque is from French, which got it from Italian *burlesco*, a derivative of *burla*, "joke, fun"—which may have come from Latin *burra*, "trifle"

burly originally meant "excellent, noble, stately" and it gradually came to mean "stout, sturdy, heavily built"

burn is a conflation of two Old English verbs, *birnan* and *boernan*, and is ultimately from the Germanic base *bren-/bran-*

a **burr** is a rough edge of something, such as metal, after it has been cut

the **burrito** was so named "little donkey" for its curved shape when filled, like a donkey's back

the donkey as a pack animal is the **burro**

the underlying meaning of the base of **bury** was "protection, shelter" and in the case of **bury** this meant "covering a dead body with earth"

bus is a shortened form of Latin *omnibus*, "for all"

busboy is a person who clears the dirty dishes from diners' tables, so called from his "bus" or trolley

{ **bush**, as in the Australian wild, is from Dutch *bosch*, "wood" }

bush and **shrub** are used interchangeably for relatively low woody perennials with many stems and branches that grow from a complex close to the ground; a **tree** is a woody perennial, usually taller, with branches starting higher up

bushed in Canadian use means mentally disturbed from living in isolation, especially in the north

business originally meant "anxiety, uneasiness," as it was simply a derivative formed from busy by adding the suffix -ness

a **busker** is an itinerant entertainer or musician

a bad hand at cards can be called a **bust**

bustard came from two French terms which came from Latin *avis tarda*, literally "slow bird"

a **bustle** is a stuffed pad or cushion worn under the skirt of a woman's dress and it had a synonym of "dress-improver"

busy goes back to Old English *bisig*, "occupied"

but originally meant "outside," formed in prehistoric West Germanic

butcher comes via Anglo-Norman from Old French *bouchier*, a derivative of *boc*, "male goat" and the original sense was "dealer in goat's flesh"

the adjective form for buzzard is **buteonine**

butler comes from French *boutellier*, "bottle or cup bearer" as originally it was an officer of high rank in charge of wine for the royal table (also Old French *bouteillier*, "a man who puts wine into bottles")

butment is another word for **abutment**

a **butt** is a cask or barrel for ale or wine

a **butte** (from French) is an isolated hill or peak rising abruptly, especially in the American West

butter derives from Greek *bouturon*, "cow," and *turos*, "cheese"

the **buttercup** was so named because cows that ate it produced rich yellow butter (through their milk)

Old English folklore said butterflies sucked milk and just-churned butter, but they actually suck flower nectar; the word **butterfly** may refer to the yellow color of certain species

both the **butterfly** and **moth** belong to the order Lepidoptera (Greek "scale-winged") but butterflies have clubbed antenna and moths do not, butterflies fly during the day while moths are out at night

butterine is a substance prepared from animal fat with some other ingredients inter-mixed, as an imitation of butter

there is no butter in **buttermilk**, egg in **eggplant**, worms or wood in **worm-wood**, pine or apple in **pineapple**, or ham in **hamburger**

the **butternut** is also called a white walnut

butterscotch has no liquor in it; the original meaning of scotch is "to score, cut, or mark" and **butterscotch** may be so-named as the toffee may perhaps have been first made by the Scotch or the root may be "cut butter squares"

a **buttery** was first a place where liquor was kept and supplied, especially at a college or other establishment; **buttery** can mean "pantry"—possibly from having been a storage place for butter

to **buttle** is to serve drink or do a butler's work

yes, there is such a thing as **buttock**, singular

the last line of a commercial is called the **button**

buttonhole was once buttonhold, sweet-heart was originally sweetard, penthouse was pentice, shamefaced was originally shamefast, and chaise lounge was chaise longue

a **butty** is a slice of bread and butter

butyric means pertaining to butter

a **buvette** is another name for tavern or refreshment bar

the original meaning of **buxom** was "compliant, meek; obedient, humble" and "physically pliable, flexible"

BVD (lightweight boxer shorts) is an acronum for the proprietary name of Bradley, Voorhees & Day

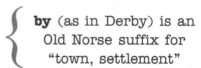

{ **by** (as in Derby) is an Old Norse suffix for "town, settlement" }

the -**by** ending in place names comes from the Scandinavian word for "farm" or "town"

by- as a prefix usually means "subordinate, secondary"

another word for an illegitimate person is a **by-child**

a **by-corner** is an out-of-the-way corner or nook

bye first meant "secondary object or undertaking; a side issue"—before it took on sporting senses

a subordinate goal is the **by-end**

bylaw comes from *byr law*, "law or custom of a town" (*byr* = town) in Old Norse

nicknames were once **bynames**

a **byre** is a barn or shed for cows

byte is a word formed arbitrarily from bit and bite

a **byword** is a prime example

Byzantium became Constantinople and then Istanbul

C is the only major scale played solely on the white keys on a piano

cab is a shortening of cabriolet, which took its name from French *cabriole*, "goat's leap"—from the motion of the carriage

cabal (pronounced kuh-BAL) is a plot woven with intrigues by a small group of people

cabana is pronounced kuh-BAHN-yuh, from Spanish for "hut, cabin"

a **cabaret** in early use described a French inn, and is derived from *camberet*, "little room"

ask for a head of **cabbage** and you are repeating yourself because **cabbage** means "head" (from Latin *caput*, "head")—and it is probably the most ancient of vegetables

the enclosed compartment of a crane, the driver's cab, can be called the **cabin**

a **cabinet** is a milkshake in Boston, possibly named after the square wooden **cabinet** in which the mixer was encased

cabinet is from Old French, which translates to "little gambling house," which was

what it first was; the word **cabinet** is a diminutive of the word cabin and meant "small repository"

the word **cabinet** originally meant a small room, and it came to apply to the group of politicians who met in the room

the ultimate source of **cable** is Latin *capulum*, "lasso"

cablese is an extremely brief or shorthand style of writing, as in a telegram

to **cabobble** is to mystify, puzzle, or confuse

caboose originally signified the kitchen on merchant ships or fishing boats, having come from Dutch *kabuis*, "ship's gallery"

the right of a country to regulate its air traffic is **cabotage**; this word can also mean "coastal trade"

a **cabriole** leg on furniture is one that resembles the front leg of a leaping animal

cacciatore means "hunter" in Italian and possibly alludes to the ingredients a hunter might have had handy—tomatoes, mushrooms, herbs

cache first meant "a hiding place"

cachet is French literally meaning "something compressed to a small size" and also "a seal, a stamp of individuality"

cachexia is a chronically bad outlook or way of thinking

a **cacchinnator** is a very loud laugher

a **cachou** is a breath-freshening mint or pastille

cachpule is the ancestral name for tennis or a tennis court

cacoepy is a word for incorrect pronunciation

cacoethes from Greek *kakos*, "bad" and *ethos*, "habit" is just that, or an insatiable or uncontrollable urge, desire, or itch, especially to do something harmful; **cacoethes loquendi** is an insatiable urge to talk, **cacoethes carpendi** is a compulsion to criticize, and **cacoethes scribendi** is a habitual urge to write

cadaver comes from Latin *cadere*, "to fall"

a **caddie** is a person who runs errands or delivers messages, and **caddie** in golf is a form of the word cadet; a **caddy** is a container, as for tea

a **cadence** is a harmonious combination of colors

the first use of **cadet** meant "younger son or daughter" and its notion of "little or inferior head" gave way to "trainee"

to **cadge** is to beg or mooch off of someone

the serpent-entwined staff representing the medical profession is called a **caduceus**

caducity means "senility," "frailty," or "transitory nature"

a **caesura** in prose is a pause or breathing place around the middle of a metrical line— and the word generally describes a break, interruption, or interval (Latin "cutting, metrical pause")

{ the name **Caesar,** that of a number of Roman emperors, eventually gave rise to the German title *kaiser* and Russian *czar/tsar* }

a **cacogen** is a hostile, unfriendly, or antisocial person

cacography is bad handwriting or poor spelling

cacology is a bad choice of words (or poor pronunciation)

a **caconym** is a "bad name" or "bad terminology"

cacophemism is the opposite of **euphemism**

an imaginary place where things are worse than real life is **cacotopia** or **dystopia**

cactus was first another name for the cardoon plant

cafè is French for both coffee and coffeehouse

cafeteria is literally Latin American Spanish for "coffee shop, coffeehouse"

caffeine literally means "something found in coffee"

caffeism is a very serious condition arising from the prolonged or excessive use of beverages containing caffeine

to **caffle** is to argue or prevaricate

a **caftan** is a wide-sleeved, loose-fitting shirt or dress

cagamosis is marital unhappiness

cage came to English from Latin *cavea*, "enclosure for animals; coop, hive, or stall" or "dungeon"

cagg is a solemn vow not to drink for a certain period of time

a **cahier** is an exercise book or notebook

a **cairn** is a pyramid of stones made as a memorial or mark of some kind, as over the grave of some person of distinction

 a **caisson** is a chest holding ammunition or explosives

a **caitiff** person is base, mean, vile

Cajun, a French-speaking culture of Louisiana, is an alteration of Acadian, as Acadia was the name of a French colony in Canada whose inhabitants were driven out by the British and who migrated to the southern states of the U.S.

cake is a Viking contribution, from Old Norse *kaka*—and is related to "cook"; **cake** first meant small, flat bread roll baked on both sides by being turned—as in pancake, potato **cake**

cakewalk started out as a competitive dance and the winner of the **cakewalk** got a cake as a prize

squirrel fur is called **calaber**

another name for a prison or lock-up is **calaboose**

calamari (deep-fried squid) comes from Latin meaning "pen case"—because of its long tapering shell and its ink; it is also spelled *calamary*

to **calamistrate** is to curl the hair

the comblike structure on the fourth pair of legs of certain spiders, which "cards" the silk as it is secreted, is the **calamistrum** (Latin "curling iron")

a folding hood on a baby carriage is the **calash** or **calèche**

tartar, also known as **calculus**, is hardened **plaque**; when the bacteria interact with saliva and food particles (sugars, starches especially) **tartar** forms at the gum line through a process called **calcification**

calcium was coined by the English chemist Sir Humphry Davy in 1808 on the basis of Latin *calx*, "limestone"—probably from the earlier Greek *khalix*, "pebble" or "limestone"

a person who draws with crayons is a **calcographer**

calculate comes from *calculus*, "a pebble used for counting and calculating"

calculus meant "a pebble"—used when ancient Romans calculated, as on an abacus

a bandage or substance applied to produce warmth is **calefacient**

Latin *kalendae* referred to the time when accounts were due, usually the first day of the month, which gave us **calendar**

a **calender** is a pair of rollers for pressing paper or cloth

calenture is burning passion or zeal

a dictionary, especially a polyglot (written in several languages) dictionary, can also be called a **calepin**

a **calf**, an iceberg detached from a glacier, is a transferred use of something born from something larger

caliber's first sense was "social standing or importance," coming from a Greek term for shoemaker's last, of which "weight" is a feature

calico was originally Calicut-cloth, as it was the main export of Calicut, India in the sixteenth-seventeenth centuries

calid is another way of saying "warm, tepid"

California used to be Alta **California** (upper) and Baja **California** (lower)—both from Spanish

calipash is the fatty, dull greenish substance of the upper turtle shell and **calipee** is the light yellow fatty substance of the lower turtle shell

calisthenics comes from Greek *cali-*, "beauty, especially elegant" and *sthenos* "strong"

the projections at the ends of horseshoes are the **calks**

calligraphy is from Greek meaning "beautiful writing"

calliope comes from Greek *Kalliope* ("beautiful-voiced"), the muse of epic poetry

callipygian means "having beautiful buttocks" while **steatopygia** is the condition of "having excess fat on the buttocks" (pygian is from Greek *puge*, "buttocks")

callisteia is another word for beauty prizes

callithumpian means "pertaining to a band of discordant instruments"

in its earliest sense, **callow** meant "bald"

callus is a hard patch of skin; **callous** is an adjective meaning "indifferent to suffering" or "hardened"

calm came via one of the Romance languages and first meant "heat of the day"

calorie is from Latin *color*, "heat"

a **calque** is a loan translation from another language, like English "superman" derived from German *Ubermensch*

calumet, a peace pipe, is from Latin *calamellus*, "little reed," referring to the pipe's reed stem

calumny is a false charge or imputation intended to damage another's reputation

Latin *calvaria* meant literally "skull" (from *calva* "scalp") and this led to the word **calvary**

calvity is another word for baldness

when a shirt's tails are tied in a knot at the waist, the style is called **calypso**

from Italian for "pant leg" comes **calzone**—ultimately from Latin *calceus*, "shoe" which evolved to *calza*, "sock" before **calzone**

cam, a projection on a rotating part in machinery, is from a Dutch word *kam*, "comb" as in *kamrad*, "cogwheel"

Cambodia was formerly the Khmer Republic

cambric tea (origin is Cambria, Wales) is a beverage for children containing hot water, milk, and sugar and a small amount of tea

camcorder is a blend of video camera and video recorder

camel is of Semitic origin (Hebrew *gamal*, Arabic *jamal*), from Greek *kamelos*; **camel** replaced Old English *olfend* for "the animal," a word based on the misconception that the **camel** was a type of elephant

the **camellia** was named by Linnaeus after Joseph Kamel, a Moravian botanist

camelopard is an old-fashioned word for giraffe

cameo is from Italian **cameo**/cammeo and may ultimately have an Oriental source such as Arabic *qamaa'il*, "flower buds"

camera first meant "vault, chamber"

camerate is "divided into chambers"

{ **camisated** is wearing a shirt on the outside over other clothing }

camisole derives from a diminutive of Latin *camisia*, "shirt or nightgown"

camouflage derives from French *camouflet*, "a puff of smoke"

camp comes from Latin *campus* "level field" or "place for games," and **camp** first meant "battle" or "combat, war" (in *Beowulf*)

campaign first meant open tract of land, from Latin *campus*, "level ground," and the change to a military meaning came from troops "taking the field" (moving from fortress or town to open country), from which the political sense evolved, referring to the organized efforts of office-seekers to sway public opinion or influence their vote at an upcoming election

a **campanile** (from Italian *campana*, "bell") is a bell tower

campestral means "relating to open country, uncultivated fields"

a **campion** is one who fights on behalf of another or on behalf of any cause

another name for quarrel or dispute is **cample**

campus is "field" in Latin

a **can** (*canne* in Old English) was originally a container of any material, shape, or size for holding liquids; "**can**" is purportedly an abbreviation of "canister"

can applies to what is possible and **may** to what is permissible; **can** means "able to," **may** means "permitted to"

Canada, the world's second largest country, comes from Huron-Iroquoian *kanata*, "village, settlement"

a **canaille** is "the rabble, the populace," from Italian *canaglia*, "pack of dogs"

canal is a refashioning of channel and first was used generally for a pipe or tube conveying liquid

the holes in a sponge are called **canals**

canapé is French for "couch, mosquito-netted sofa" or "covering" and is bread upon which other items sit on for their being served before dinner

canard, the French word for duck, gave rise to **cancan** because of the dance's resemblance to the wiggling bottoms of ducks

canary as in "jail bird" comes from the yellow suits of English convicts sent to jail in Australia

the **Canary Islands** were named for the large wild dogs (Latin *canes*) encountered there by the Romans; the birds got their name from the islands

cancel comes from a Latin word for "crossbars" as it originally meant "to delete or obliterate writing by drawing or stamping lines across it"

cancellate means "marked with crossing lines"

cancer is a Latin word for "crab" or "creeping ulcer," a translation of Greek *karkinos*—which was applied to tumors because the swollen veins around them resembled crab legs. **Canker** meant the same and was used until the seventeenth century, then replaced by "**cancer**."

a **candelabrum** is one large branched candleholder; **candelabra** is the plural

candent means "glowing with heat, glowing white"

candid comes from Latin *candidus*, "white" and first meant "pure, innocent"; **candidate** is based on the same Latin word, and became Latin *candidatus*, "white-robed" as the traditional attire of a **candidate** for office was a white toga because it symbolized honesty

candle is from Latin *candere*, "to be white or glisten, to shine"

{ to **candle** is to hold an egg to the light as a check of freshness }

the **candle-end** is the stub of a candle

candy comes into English from Arabic *qandi*, "sugar," which may be related to Sanskrit *khandakah*, "sugar in crystalline pieces" or *khanda*, "broken piece" applied to sugar pieces broken off a large block of crystallized sugar

the stem of the raspberry is called **cane**

canel or **canella** are old words for cinnamon

canister comes from a word related to cane and originally was a basket for bread, fruit, or flowers

canities is the medical term for the graying or whitening of hair

the bevel on the edge of a chisel is the **cannel**

cannellini is literally "small tubes" and **cannelloni** is "large tubes" in Italian—and the word "cannon" is derived from Italian *cannone*, "large tube"

when Columbus was trying to find the Spice Islands, he was told of a tribe of man-eating natives in Cuba and Haiti called Caribs (from which we get Caribbean) or Caniba (Columbus' rendition of the name); the word *canib* meaning "brave and fierce" became **cannibal**, "anthropophagite"

to dismantle a machine to get parts for another is to **cannibalize**

a small can is a **cannikin**; a small pan is a **pannikin**

> **cannoli**'s origin is Italian *canna*, "reed"

cannon comes from Italian for "large tube"

canny is "free from weird qualities or unnatural powers" (opposite of uncanny)

canoe is purported to be the first word from Native American languages to pass into European usage

canola comes from a variety of Canadian oilseed rape, so its name is Canada + *-ola* (Latin "oil")

canon comes from Greek *kanon*, meaning "rule, law, decree"

canopy comes from a Greek word *konopelon*, "couch with mosquito curtains," and from Greek *konops*, "mosquito, gnat"

the **canopy** is the spread cloth of a parachute in descent

something that is pleasant-sounding, melodious, and resonant is **canorous**

the early meaning of **cant** was "musical sound, singing"

cantaloupe was first cultivated outside Rome at a villa called Cantalupo, hence the name; the "cantaloupes" you buy in stores are actually muskmelons—why grocers (etc.) prefer to call them by the wrong name is unclear as real cantaloupes are rarely grown or sold in the United States

cantankerous may be from Middle English *contak/conteke*, "contention, quarreling" (from an earlier Scandinavian word) and modeled on and rancorous

cantata in Italian means "sung air"

a **canteen** is a set of cooking, eating, or drinking utensils

canter is short for Canterbury pace or gallop, the supposed easy pace of medieval pilgrims to Canterbury

the angle formed where the upper and lower eyelids come together is the **canthus**

a little song or hymn is a **canticle**

cantilever (pronounced KAN-tuh-lee-vur) can be, in bridge building, a projecting support or arm of great length, two of which, stretching out from adjacent piers, are used to support a girder which unites them and completes the span

the raised curved part at the back of a horse's saddle is the **cantle**

canton (small division of a country) is literally French for "corner" a **cantonment** is temporary living quarters built for housing military troops

basically, **cantor** means "singer"

a witch's trick or mischievous device is a **cantrip**

Canuck is used in Canada for Canadians of French descent

canvas, literally "cloth made of hemp," is based on Latin *cannabis* and Greek *kannabis*, "hemp"

canvas is the noun (fabric, etc.) and **canvass** is generally a verb (to solicit, question)—though a **canvass** can be an examination of pros and cons

canyon gets its name from Spanish *cañón* "tube"

cap probably comes from Latin *capo*, "head"

capable first meant "having sufficient room or capacity"

capable, **capacity**, **captive**, and **capture** are based on Latin *capere*, "hold or take"

capacious means "roomy, spacious, wide"

capacity refers to a general ability to comprehend an issue or perform a task; **capability** implies a reference to one of a set of such abilities

cap-a-pie means "from head to foot"

the **caparison** is a cloth or covering spread over the saddle or harness of a horse, often ornamented; this word can also mean "housings, trappings"

caper, the edible bud, came from Greek *kapparis*

being slightly intoxicated is **capernoited**

capital, from Latin *caput*, "head," is the head of a pillar or column

capitalism is a nineteenth century term drawing on earlier references to capital as financial ownership of, or investment in, economic enterprises—denoting a distinctive form of private property

a **capitalist** is a person who uses capital "goods, money" to increase production and make more goods and money

the word **capitol** is from the Roman Capitoline Hill and the similarity between **capitol** and **capital** is purely coincidental; **capitol** applies to the building and **capital** to the seat of a government

a **capitonym** is when the meaning of a word changes according to whether it starts with a capital letter, e.g. earth/Earth, herb/Herb

a **capitulant** is a person who surrenders

capitulate once meant "negotiate"—now it means "surrender, acquiesce"

a daisy's dense disk cluster is the **capitulum**;

the movable bar on a guitar fingerboard is a **capo**

you can call a dull-witted person a **capon**

caponata is a Sicilian dish similar to ratatouille

> **cape** is a headland or promontory and derives from Latin *caput*, "head" (**capital** and **captain** come from the same Latin root)

capeesh is a slang term from Italian *capisce*, a form of *capire*, "understand"

caper "jump about" is a shortening of *capriole*, "leap," from Latin **caper** "goat"

cappelletti pasta is literally "little hats"

cappuccino commemorates the dull gray-brown clothing of the (Italian) Capuchin monks and its "formula" is one-third espresso, one-third steamed milk, and one-third foamed/frothed milk

caprice comes from an Italian word *capriccio*, literally "head with the hair standing on end"—hence, "horror" or "sudden start"—from earlier Latin *capo*, "head" and *riccio*, "hedgehog"

a **capsa** is a cylindrical box for holding upright rolls of documents

capsize may be based on Spanish *capuzar*, "sink a ship by the head"

capstan (revolving cylinder) was borrowed from Old Provençal *cabestan*, from Latin *capistrum*, "fasten, bind fast, halter"

the foil/metal or plastic that covers the top of a wine bottle and must be removed before the cork is called the **capsule**

captain is ultimately derived from Latin *caput*, "head"

caption's early senses of "arrest; warrant for arrest" gave rise to "a statement of where, when, and by whose authority a warrant was issued" which was added to a legal document

captious means "disposed to find fault, cavil, or raise objections"

captivate originally meant "to make prisoner"

to **capture** data is to cause it to be stored in a computer

the hood of a cloak may also be called a **capuche/capouch**

capybara, the South American mammal, is Tupi for "grass eater"

car comes from Latin *carrus*, "two-wheeled wagon"

carabiner is shortened German *Karabinerhaken*, "spring hook"

carafe comes from Arabic *gharafa*, "to draw or lift water"

caramel comes from Spanish *caramelo* and is literally "honey cane," possibly from Latin *cannamella*, "sugar cane plant"; **caramel** should be pronounced KAR-uh-muhl or KAR-uh-mel or KAHR-muhl (in that order)

caramelized means cooked over moderate heat until the natural sugars break down and leave a sweet flavor

carat comes from Greek *keration*, "fruit of the karob/carob," whose seed was once used as a unit of weight and is still the unit of weight for pearls and some other gemstones; **karat** is the Canadian spelling for **carat**

caravan is from Persian *karwan*, "company of travelers"

a **caravanserai** is a type of inn in Eastern countries where caravans are put up

the ultimate source of **caraway** is probably Greek *karon* "cumin" as **caraway** and cumin seeds are very similar

carbon's root is Latin meaning "coal"

carbonara, though literally "in a charcoal kiln," is a dish of pasta with bacon or ham, egg, and cream; spaghetti alla **carbonara** used to be spaghetti sauce with meat grilled over charcoal

etymologically, a **carbuncle** is a "small piece of coal," ultimately from Latin *carbunculus*, diminutive of carbo "coal" and the metaphorical meanings are based on the idea of a glowing coal

carburetor comes from words meaning "charged with carbon or hydrocarbons"

the bones of a cooked bird are the **carcass**

carceral is an adjective meaning "imprisoning"

carcinology is the branch of zoology that studies crustaceans

{ **card** goes back to Greek *khartes/chartes* "papyrus leaf" }

cardamom can also be spelled cardamum and cardamon—from Greek *kardamomon*, "peppergrass" and "a variety of Indian spice"

a fancy name for heartburn is **cardialgia**

the **cardigan** was named for James Thomas Brudenell, the seventh Earl of **Cardigan**, who popularized the clothing item

the bird **cardinal** got its name from the red-robed official of the Roman Catholic Church—which, in turn, got its name from *cardo*, "hinge, pivot" or "hinge that upon which things turn"

cardinal as an adjective means "on which something hinges; crucial, fundamental"—from Latin **cardo**/cardin "hinge" and the hinge of a bivalve is a **cardo**

a **cardoon** is a thistlelike southern European plant—and it was first likened to the American **cactus**, which takes its name from Greek *kaktos*, "**cardoon**"

care first had the meaning of "grief, sorrow; mental suffering" or "poverty"

careen has a nautical origin and is a side-to-side trajectory while **career** is a headlong high-speed trajectory

career first referred to a race course, then a course or road in general

careful first meant "full of anxiety"

caress is from Latin *carus*, "dear"

caret (^), the proofreader's mark indicating that material is to be inserted, comes from Latin *carere*, "be without, lack"

a cut or notch in timber is a **carf** or **kerf**— and is used to describe the width of such a cut

a **carfax** or **carrefour** is a place where (usually four) roads or streets meet (from French *carrefurcs*, from Latin *quadrifurcus*, "four forks")

cargo is based on Latin *carrus*, "wagon"

Caribbean is pronounced kair-uh-BEE-un since it was first the land of the Caribs or Caribals

caribou is from Micmac *yalipu/yalipi* "shovel snow" (or *maccaribpoo* "he who paws the ground") from its habit of scraping snow with its hoofs when looking for food

caricature is from Italian *caricare*, "exaggerate, load"

carillon, a set of bells in a tower, is from French *quarregnon*, "peal of four bells"

something **cariogenic** promotes or causes tooth decay

caritas is another word for charity

cark (noun) is solicitude or sympathetic feeling; to **cark** is to fret anxiously or to cause distress or worry

something that is **carminative** relieves flatulence

carmine is the red color of the cochineal (insect), from Spanish *carmesì*, "crimson"

carnage goes back to Latin *carnaticum*, "flesh"

carnal means literally "of the flesh," from Latin *caro*, "flesh, meat"

the **carnation**'s name means "fleshlike" possibly because its pink color reminded people of flesh though the name may derive from coronation, as the flower's dented leaves somewhat resemble a crown; **carnation** is the general name for the cultivated variety of the clove-pink

a **carnet** is a book of postage stamps or tickets or a permit allowing use of a campsite

---

literally, **carnival** means "flesh, farewell!" as Lent meant giving up food such as meat, so the big meal before Lent was a farewell to meat

the people Christopher Columbus met in Cuba called themselves Canibales—and they were known to eat human flesh—which gave us **carnivore**

Christmas **carol** is a term which originally referred to a non-religious ring dance accompanied by singing. Eventually it came to mean a merry song with a tune that could be danced to. The Italian friars who lived with St. Francis of Assisi were the first to compose these songs, c. 1410.

carousal is a drunken spree; **carousel** is a merry-go-round or baggage machine at an airport

carouse comes from a German expression "time to leave the bar" or "last drink before closing" and the original meaning of **carouse** was "(drink) to the bottom of the glass"

carp's root sense was "to crow and croak" (like a raven or stork)

a dish called **carpaccio** was named for artist Vittore **Carpaccio**, whose art was bright red, which inspired the name for thinly sliced raw meat

carpenter comes from Latin *carpentarius* (artifex) "carriage (-maker)" (*carpentum* is "wagon"), and it first meant carriage or wagon maker

a **carpet** originally denoted a thick fabric that covered a table or bed; a **rug** is generally smaller than a **carpet**

carpology is the study of fruits and seeds

Frank Lloyd Wright invented the word **carport**

the human **carpus** is the eight bones that form the wrist and part of the hand

a reader's cubicle in a library is a **carrel**

the cost of conveying goods is **carriage**

carriage trade referred to the upper class who arrived as clients via private carriage

ultimately, **carrion** is a derivative of Latin *caro*, "flesh" and at first it meant "dead

body" before becoming "flesh unfit for human consumption"

the distance traversed by a golf ball or its trajectory is called the **carry**

cart may be a diminutive of car and is related to Dutch *krat*, "hind part of a **cart**"

cartel comes from Italian *cartello*, which meant "written challenge to a duel" and acquired the meaning of a cooperating group that seeks power or the promotion of a cause

cartography is based on French carte "map"

the disk within the bull's-eye of a target is the **carton**

carton and **cartoon** come from Italian *cartone*, "card or pasteboard"

a **cartoon** first described a full-size drawing of a design for a painting or other work of art

cartouche is the name given to the oval or oblong figures in Egyptian hieroglyphics, enclosing names or titles

the head that holds the needle for a record player is the **cartridge**

the supermarket shopping cart was first called a "**cartwheel**"

very heavy sleep is **carus**

carve first meant cut (in general)

a column in the shape of a female is a **caryatid**; the same for a man is a **telamon**

Casanova was the name of an Italian writer (1725–1798) known for his amorous adventures

a **cascade** is a waterfall that falls in stages

{ **case** as an adjective can refer to the last one of anything }

case "container" is based on Latin *capsa* and *capere*, "to hold"

to **case** also means "to skin an animal"

casein is the main protein in milk and cheese

if something is **caseous**, it is cheeselike

cash as a verb first meant "to disband or dismiss troops"

> **cash** first meant "money box," and came from Latin *capsa*, "box"

cashier is from French *casse*, "money chest"

cashiered means "dismissed in disgrace"

cashmere is an early spelling of Kashmir, the goat from which it was originally made

casino is Italian for "small house" and first meant a summer house in Italy or a club house for music and dancing

casita is from Spanish and it is the diminutive of *casa*, "house"

originally a **casket** was a container for jewels, letters, cremated ashes, or other things of value

to **cass** is to make void or annul; **cassation** is annulment or cancellation

a prepared form of **cassava** flour is tapioca

casserole came from *casse*, "pan" or "ladle," which probably comes from Greek *kuathos*, "serving cup"; **casserole** is a diminutive of *casse*, "spoonlike container" (cassette is also a diminutive of *casse*)

a frame for an X-ray plate or film is a **cassette**

etymologically, a **cassock** is probably a cloak worn by a Cossack and first meant "cloak, long coat"

cast is from a hunting term meaning (of a hound) "go in all directions looking for game or for a lost scent"

castanet comes from Latin *castanea*, "chestnut" because of its resemblance in shape

castaway was first an adjective meaning "rejected"

something that is **castellated** is shaped like a castle or built like a castle, with battlements and turrets

a **caster** is a container with holes in the top for sprinkling something like sugar or pepper

castigate has a meaning close to chasten except that the punishment inflicted is often verbal and the aim is to correct

the rook is also the **castle** in chess

castle and **chateau** derive from Latin *castellum*, a diminutive form of castrum "fort"; **chateau** is the modern French version that has been borrowed into English "as is"

castor as in the oil, originally meant "beaver" and **castor** oil was the reddish-brown unctuous substance, having a strong smell and nauseous bitter taste, obtained from two sacs in the inguinal region of the beaver

castorial means pertaining to a hat

a synonym for expurgate, as a text, is **castrate**

castrensian is "pertaining to a camp"

casual stresses lack of real or apparent premeditation or intent

casualty simply meant "a chance occurrence" when it entered English in the 1400s

casuistry is a quibbling or evasive way of dealing with difficult cases of duty—as well as the use of clever but false reasoning, especially in relation to moral issues

a draw in tick-tack-toe is a **cat**

the word **cat** is from Latin *catta/cattus* and it appeared around 1000 AD

catabolism is the metabolic process in which energy is liberated for use

catachresis, the incorrect use of a word or phrase, comes from Greek *katakhresthai*, "to misuse"

a **cataclasm**, literally "washing down, deluge" from Greek *kataklusmos*, is a disruption of the normal order of things

the first **catacomb** (Latin *catacumbas*) was the subterranean cemetery of St. Sebastian on the Appian Way near Rome

catacosmesis is an ordering of words in descending order of importance, such as "Give me peace, prosperity, and a coffee."

cataglottal is pertaining to passionate kissing with tongues

a **catalog** can be a series of bad or unfortunate things

of the two forms, **catalog** and **catalogue**, many U.S. dictionaries show that their preference of use is in that order

catalogue comes from a Greek word *katalegein*, "pick out, enroll,"—formed on *cata-* and *legein*, "choose"

a **catalupe** is a waterfall

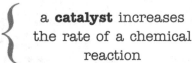

{ a **catalyst** increases the rate of a chemical reaction }

catamaran can mean "a quarrelsome woman"; the word comes from Tamil *katta-maram* "tied wood or tree"

a **catamite** is a boy kept for homosexual purposes

the word **catamount**, "pard, panther," is reduced from cat-o-mountain

catapult is from two Greek words meaning "hurl" (*pallein*) "down" (*kata-*); castastrophe

comes from *kata-* "down" and *strophe* "turning"

cataract comes from a Latin word that meant "floodgate, waterfall" (giving us a word for large waterfall) but also Latin *portcullis*, which led to the medical sense involving opacity in eyesight

letting off steam by cursing is **catarolysis**

etymologically, **catarrh** is "something that flows down," from Greek *katarrhein* (*kata*, "down" and *rhein*, "flow"), and **catarrh** is excessive mucus in the nose or throat

catastrophe comes from Greek *katastrophe*, "overturning, sudden turn" and it originally meant the final resolution of a novel or play, an "overturning" of the beginning of the plot

catawba grapes and wine are named for a river in the Carolinas

a snatch of a song is a **catch**

catch-22 is from the title of Joseph Heller's 1961 novel; the "catch" is that a bomber pilot is insane if he flies combat missions without asking to be relieved from duty, and is thus eligible to be relieved from duty—but if he asks to be relieved from duty, that means he's sane and has to keep flying

catchword, **guideword**, or **running head** are the word(s) at top of reference book pages

cate is a dainty or choice food

catechism comes from Greek meaning "instruction by word of mouth" and is literally a series of questions and answers; a **catechumen** is a young Christian preparing for confirmation

categoric and **categorical** are from Greek meaning "affirmative," and they mean "unconditional, absolute, explicit"

the word **category** was first used in philosophy and meant "statement, accusation," from Greek *kategoria*; the first categories were the ten postulated by Aristotle as the set among which all things might be distributed

catenary is the name of the curve formed when two ends of a flexible object are hung at equal heights

at first, **cater** was a noun, from French *acatour* meaning "a buyer of provisions" and when a verb **cater** was needed, the noun was changed to caterer

the "cater" in **catercorner** means "diagonally"; cater-cornered is also cater-corner or catty-cornered or kitty-corner

a female caterer is a **cateress**

caterpillar is from Old French *chatepelose*, "hairy cat"

the first part of **caterwaul** is presumed to be cat while the second is onomatopoeic, imitating the sound of a cat wailing or yowling—possibly from German *katerwaulen*, (kater "tom cat")

catgut, which is not from cats, may be a shortening of "cattlegut"

catharsis can describe purging of the bowels

cathedral derives from Latin meaning "seat" as it was first a church containing the bishop's throne

catheter (a tube inserted for withdrawing bodily fluids) comes from Greek *kathienai*, "send or let down"

cathexis is the concentration of emotional energy on one person or thing (activity, idea, object); **countercathexis** is an attempt to block from one's consciousness anyone or anything that is objectionable; (and then there is **hypercathexis**, desire amounting to mania for an object)

etymologically, the **Catholic** Church is the "universal" church, comprising all Christians for **catholic** comes ultimately from Greek *katholikos*, "relating to all, general" (from *kata*, "relating to" and *holos*, "whole"); its

original meaning is preserved in such contexts as **catholic** tastes, "wide-ranging tastes"

the flower of the willow tree is the **catkin**

catlap is a weak drink, fit only for cats to lap

catnap came from "a cat's nap"

catnip is also called catmint

catoptric is "pertaining to a mirror, reflection, or reflector"

{ a reflecting road marker is often referred to as a **catseye** }

indentations on a hillside are called **catsteps** or **terracettes**

the word **catsup** was dropped by Del Monte in 1988 as they followed Heinz and Hunt's by using **ketchup** instead; this word is apparently originally from the Amoy dialect of Chinese *koe-chiap*, *ke-tsiap* "brine of pickled fish or shellfish," borrowed into Malay as *kechap*, taken by the Dutch as *ketjap*, then to English

cattle is derived from Anglo-Norman *catel*, "movable property" and first meant "personal property"; a rancher driving **cattle** would call them chattels or capital

caucus may come from Algonquian *cau'-cau-as'u*, "adviser"

having a tail is **caudate**; having no tail is **anurous**

etymologically, **cauldrons** are for heating not food but people, from Latin *calidarium*, "hot bath"

cauliflower, **collard greens**, **kale**, and **kohlrabi** are all derived from Latin *caulis*, "cabbage" and **cauliflower** is, literally, "flowering cabbage"; the original English form of **cauliflower** was "colieflorie" or "cale-flory"

causatum is that which is caused, a result or effect

cause derives from Latin *causa*, "reason"

causerie is a light conversation

a **causeway** is a raised path, road, or way across a wet place or stretch of water—based on "causey," "a mound, embankment, or dam to retain water"

a **caution** is an amusing or surprising person or thing; **caution** first meant guarantee or security given (from Latin *cavere*, "take heed")

originally, a **cavalcade** was simply a ride on horseback, often for the purpose of attack (from Latin *caballus*, "horse") and later meant the more general "procession"; "-cade" has come into being a suffix in its own right, meaning "procession, show"

cavalier as a noun is a horseman or cavalryman, and cavalry comes from Italian *cavallo*, "horse" and Latin *caballus*, "horse"

cave is from Latin *cava/cavus* "hollow"

cavern is more vague and rhetorical than **cave**; a **cavern** is a large **cave**

cease and **cede** come from Latin *cedere*, "go away, withdraw"

cecity is blindness of the eye or mind

three English words end in **"ceed"**—succeed, proceed, exceed

at first, **ceiling** was the "lining of the interior of a room with plaster or paneling"

ceiling can describe the inside planking of a ship's bottom and sides

in meteorology, the **ceiling** is the highest level from which the Earth's surface can be seen, effectively—the cloud base

a **ceilometer** means the height of clouds

celebrants take part in religious ceremonies; **celebrators** or revelers gather for purposes of revelry

celebrate comes from Latin meaning "to fill often or numerous times"—alluding to the drinking involved in festivities

 caviar (or *caviare*) started out as a four-syllable word, following the Italian borrowing; the modern pronunciation was influenced by French

to **cavil** is to raise frivolous objections, find fault unfairly

caving means staying inside one's home as much as possible

cay and **key** mean a small, low islet or abovewater coral reef or sandbar

cayenne comes from Tupi *quiynha/kyinha*, "capsicum" or "pepper"—but by folk etymology came to be named after the French Guiana town of **Cayenne**, where it was mistakenly thought to originate

CE or Common Era (or Christian Era) means the same thing as A.D., the time period beginning with Christ's birth

celebrity was, at first, another word for celebration and "due observance of rites and ceremonies"

the ultimate source of **celery** is Greek *selinon*, "parsley"

celestial comes from Latin *caelum*, "heaven"

traditionally, **celibacy** is the state of being unmarried

celibataire is another word for bachelor

celibate does not mean abstaining from sexual relations (that is chaste) but rather means unmarried, especially due to religious vows

cell is from Latin *cella*, "storeroom, chamber"

the origin of **cellar** is Latin *cellarium*, "set of cells, storehouse for food"

a **cellar** is a storage place, usually underground, for foodstuffs, etc; **basement** is the lowest story of a building, part or wholly below ground level

cello is a shortening of violoncello

cellophane was originally a trademark

a **cellular** phone system is divided into sections or "cells"—circular areas of a number-of-miles radius—each having its own short-range transmitter/receiver linked to a switching center which relays waves from **cell** to **cell**

a **cellule** is a small compartment or pigeonhole, and is the root of **cellulose**

Anders **Celsius** (1701–1744) devised the scale to standardize thermometers

cement comes from Latin *caementum*, "chips of stone"; **cement** is an ingredient of **concrete**, but is not a synonym and **cement** should be pronounced suh-MENT

cemetery comes from Greek *koimeterion*, "dormitory" or "sleeping place," from *koiman*, "put to sleep"

a **cenacle** is a discussion group or literary clique—also, a small dining room where a literary or philosophic group eats and talks (from Latin cena "dinner"), such as the room in which the Last Supper was held

cenal is "pertaining to the midday meal"

{ **cenatory** is pertaining to dinner and **jentacular** is pertaining to breakfast }

a **cenotaph** is a monument to a person(s) buried elsewhere

to **cense** is to burn incense

a **censer** or **thurible** is a vessel in which incense is burnt

censor comes from Latin *censere*, "pronounce as an opinion" or "assess"

to **censor** is to disallow portions or the entireties of books, plays, etc., on the grounds that they transgress propriety, "to scrutinize, revise, or cut," expurgate or suppress; to **censure** is to criticize vehemently or harshly, or condemn

a **census** was originally a tax or tribute paid

cent, a 100th of a dollar, is from Latin *centum*, "hundred," and is also used in this sense in percent/per **cent**

a **centaur** is body of a horse with the head and upper torso of a man

the word **center** came originally from the spike or stationary point of a pair of compasses which is stuck into a surface while the other arm describes a circle around it; Greek *kentron* meant "sharp point" and was applied to a compass spike and this spread metaphorically to "mid-point of a circle"

a **centiday** is a period of 14 minutes 24 seconds, or a hundredth of a day, used especially in the study of plant growth

centipedes (Latin "hundred feet") generally have more body segments than the **millipede** (Latin "thousand feet"), the former only has one pair of feet on each segment, while the latter has two pairs; centipedes have fifteen–170 segments and millipedes from twenty–sixty thereabouts

centrifugal force pulls away or pushes outward; **centripetal** draws toward or pulls inward

centuries are hyphenated as adjectives: twelfth-**century** artifacts

century first described a hundred-man, ancient Roman army

cephalgia is a medical term for a headache

pottery made from clay is called **ceramic** or **earthenware** the ancient Roman goddess of agriculture was Ceres, giving us the word **cereal**

cerebrum is Latin for "brain" and it is the main part of the brain, divided into left and right hemispheres by the central groove (sulcus); the **cerebellum** is a smaller part in the rear below the **cerebrum** and it is involved in voluntary muscular activity and balance

ceremonial is more often applied to things (clothing, etc.) and **ceremonious** is used for persons and things (occasion, venue)

ceremonially relates to the performance of a procedure; **ceremoniously** relates to the performer of the procedure

ceremony started out in the religious sense and then for solemn ritual observances

cerise is French for "cherry"

if a plant is drooping, it is **cernuous**

certain comes ultimately from Latin *certus*, "fixed, sure," from the verb *cernere*, "decide"

the words **certainer** and **certainest** were common until the mid-18th century, but are now rare

certitude is a measure of a person's positive feeling about something; **certainty** is a measure of the degree to which a process or development may be realized

cerulean is the color of the cloudless sky, pure deep blue, azure

cervisial means "pertaining to beer" as it is from Latin *cervisia*, "beer"

cesspit was coined on analogy with cesspool, though there is not a word "cess" meaning "sewage"

cesspool has no direct etymological connection with pool; it comes from Old French *suspirail*, "ventilator, breathing hole" from *souspirer*, "breathe" (from Latin *suspirare*) which came into English as "suspiral" or

"cesperalle," "drainpipe"—and the change to **cesspool** was a "reinterpretation" of the word's final element through the process of folk etymology

a diesel fuel rating is the **cetane** number; regular fuel ratings are **octane** numbers

chads are the holes poked out of cards or paper

{ if someone is in need of a shave, they are **chaetophorous** }

to **chafe** means to rub until sore or worn; to **chaff** means to tease good-naturedly

to **chaffer** is to bargain over price, to haggle

chagrin literally means "tough skin" (French)

chai is tea boiled with milk, sugar, cardamom, and other spices; **chai** is pronounced CHIE (**chai** and tea are really the same word, borrowed from two different Chinese dialects)

in chemistry, a **chain** is a number of similar atoms, usually carbon, joined in a series

chair comes from Greek kathedra "seat"

to be **chairborne** is to be assigned to a desk job rather than field or combat duty, as in the military

chakra, one of the Indian centers of spiritual power in the body, is Sanskrit for "circle or wheel"

the membranous strands which join the yolk to the ends of an egg are the **chalazae** (from Greek *khalaza*, "small knot")

chalet is a diminutive of French chasel "farmstead" (from Latin *casa*, "cottage, hut")

Latin *calix*, "cup" and Greek *kalux*, "pod" brought us **chalice**

Latin *calx*, "lime, limestone" applied to soft white limestone became the English word **chalk**

the original notion of **challenge** was "accusation" or "charge" as it comes from Latin *calumnia*, "false charge, deception"

chalupa is from Spanish "boat, sloop," from French *chaloupe*—as it is the shape of a boat

chamber derives from Greek *kamara*, "object with an arched cover"

chamberlain was first a servant in a bedchamber

chambray is a type of gingham and its name is from Cambray (Cambrai), France, where it was originally made

wine at room temperature is **chambré**

chameleon is Greek *khamaileon*, "lion on the ground"

chamois (soft pliant leather) is pronounced SHAM-ee

champion is based on Latin *campus*, "field" and literally means "one who has the field when the fighting is over"; **champion** first meant "fighting man," from Latin *campio(n-)*, "fighter"

chance originally meant "that which befalls (by accident)" and ultimately comes from Latin *cadere*, "fall"

the **chancel** is the area around the altar of a church for the clergy and choir, often separated by a railing

a **chancellor** originally was a court official stationed at the grating separating the public from the judges

chandeliers are "candlesticks" in French

a **chandler** is a candle and oil dealer

change is the different permutations in which bells may be rung

a **changeling** is an elf child

chankings is food that you spit out—bones, pits, seeds, stems, etc.

{ **chaparral** is derived via Spanish *chaparro*, "evergreen oak" from Basque *tshapar* and *ñal*, a collective suffix for "grove of trees" }

chamomile is from Greek *khamaimelon*, "apple on the ground" and is pronounced KAM-uh-meel

horses **champ** at the bit, though **chomp** is also ok to use

Champagne is the name of a province in eastern France and the varieties of still or sparkling wine made from the grapes there. As defined by French law, only sparkling wine from **Champagne** can be called "**champagne**."

there are eight sizes of **Champagne** container, from a bottle to the Nebuchadnezzar

channel and **canal** are ultimately the same word as their common ancestor was Latin *canalis*, "**channel**, groove," a derivative of *canna*, "pipe"

the Latin verb for "sing" was *canere* and then *cantare*, "keep on singing" which eventually gave us **chant**

to **chantepleure** is to sing and weep at the same time

a violin string is a **chanterelle**

chantry first meant singing or chanting

chaogenous means "born into or among chaos"

chaos originally meant "vast chasm, gaping void" as did the Greek word *khaos*, from which it came

either of the jaws of an animal or either half of the bill of a bird is the **chap**

chaparajos is the full form of chaps

a buckle's metal prong is the **chape**

chapel originally referred to the sanctuary in which the cloak of St. Martin was kept, then denoted a chest of relics or the shrine of such relics

chaperone comes from French "hood" from Middle French "cowl, head covering" which was worn from the 16th century by ladies who served as guides and guardians; **chaperon** is the standard spelling and **chaperone** is a variant only caused because of pronunciation

a **chaplain** conducts services in a chapel

a string of 55 prayer beads is a **chaplet**

a **chapman**, "merchant dealer, peddler," comes from Old English *ceapman*, "trade man"

chapter is based on Latin caput "head"

char as a verb is a back-formation of charcoal

char is a name for an odd job of domestic work or a piece of business

character comes from Greek *kharassein*, "engrave" as it first meant a distinctive mark impressed or engraved; **character** also has a sense of " branding-iron"

character is what one is; **reputation** is what one is thought to be by others

charactery is another word for writing

charade comes from Provençal *charrado*, "conversation"

charcoal may come from Old French *charbon*, "**charcoal**" or from the Old English *chare* or *cerran*, "turn" which would make the etymological meaning of the word "turning

into **charcoal**" for in Old English coal meant "**charcoal**" as well as "coal"

 chard (the potherb) is from a Latin word meaning "thistle"

the notion underlying the word **charge** is of a "burden" or "load"; it ultimately comes from Latin *carrus*, "two-wheeled wagon"

the large plate sometimes placed under a dinner plate (or for carrying meat) is the **charger**

a **charientism** is an elegantly veiled insult

chariot is from Old French, literally "large car"

charisma first meant "the god-given power to perform miracles" (from Greek *kharis*, "God-given grace; favor"); a variant form of the word is **charism**

charity was first Christian love, between man and God and between men and their neighbors (then also called benevolence)

to **chark** is to burn wood into charcoal

charlatan comes from Italian *ciarlatano* from the verb *cialare*, "to chatter"—as charlatans need the gift of gab

charm and **charming** originally were only related to magic

an intensive, eleventh-hour effort to accomplish or finish something before a deadline is **charrette**

card and **chart** are related, both coming from Latin *charta*, "paper" or "leaf of the papyrus plant" from the earlier Greek *khartes*

a **charter** confers powers and rights from the state or an organization to people, local chapters, or corporations

it should be **chartered** plane, not charter plane

chartreuse, the color, got its name from the color of a French liqueur which gots its name from the place in France where it was first made

charwoman comes from *cierran*, "to turn" (to do a turn of work) and is related to chore

something **chary** can be "causing sorrow" or "feeling, showing sorrow"

chase, as in pursue, traces back to Latin *captare*, "try to seize" from *capere*, "take"

a **chasmophile** is a lover and seeker of nooks and crannies

a **chasmophyte** is a plant that grows in the crevices of rock

chassis (pronounced SHA-see, not CHAS-ee) was originally a window frame or sash, coming from Latin *capsa*, "case"

chaste comes via Old French from Latin *castus*, "pure"

chastise is a variant of **chasten** with the basic meaning "inflict corporal punishment"

the **chaston** or **collet** is the part of a jewelry ring that holds a stone

to call a swine is to **chat**

the dish **Chateaubriand** was named after French diplomat and writer Vicomte François René de **Chateaubriand** (1768–1848)

a **chatelaine** is the lady or mistress of a household

chatoyancy is the condition of changing color or luster depending on the angle of light, as with a gemstone

chatoyant derives from French, literally "to shimmer like cats' eyes"

a **chauffeur** originally stoked stoves and when steam cars were invented it was a **chauffeur**'s job to heat the engine

a **chauffeuse** is a female hired to drive— also, a low seat near a hearth

Nicolas Chauvin, a French veteran known for extreme patriotism, was the origin for the word **chauvinism**

chav is a British derogatory term for a person or group of people described as lower class, often wearing fake designer clothes

chavish is the sound of many birds chirping or singing at once

cheap as an adjective is quite recent but its ultimate source goes back to the Latin noun *caupo*, "tradesman" and evolved into the Old English noun *ceap*, "trade"; the original sense of "trade" is preserved in the personal name Chapman

cheat is a shortened form of *escheat*, "reversion of property to the state," which was the original sense

{ **check** goes back to French *èschec*, "play chess; put in **check**" }

checkers used to be called "chess for ladies"

if you **checkle**, you laugh heartily

a **checkmark** was originally an X, then later a V with an elongated right arm

the word **checkmate** comes from Persian *shahmat*, "the king is dead"

a **cheek** can be a side piece of something, like the side post of a door

to be **cheeping-merry** is to be half-drunk

cheer's original sense was "face," hence, "mood, expression"

cheerlead is a verb, and cheerled is the past tense

cheese derives from Latin *caseus*, "to ferment or become sour" (which became *queso* in Spanish)

the **cheese** was once used to mean "first-rate," i.e., the thing; **cheese** as an "important person" is from Persian *ciz*, "thing"

cheeseburgers appeared around 1939, as did the plain term **burger**

cheesecake (slang) comes from photos of women's legs by newspaper photographers and the comments that the photos were "better than **cheesecake**"

cheesehead is a nickname for a resident of Wisconsin or the Netherlands

cheetah was taken from Sanskrit *citraka*, "leopard" related to *citra*, "spotted, speckled, variegated"

chef is short for the French **chef** de cuisine "head of the kitchen"

the large claw of a crab or lobster is the **chela**; two pincers are **chelae**

chemical, chemistry, and **chemist** come from alchemy with the "al-" dropped, which was part of the Arabic ancestor and meant "the"

chemise is a word for a loose covering for a book

in the U.S., one says **druggist**, but **chemist** in the UK; **pharmacist** is a formal term in both countries and **apothecary** is the old-fashioned term

chenille is French for "hairy caterpillar"— now applied to fabrics whose pile protrudes like the hairs of a caterpillar

the Chinese/Asian silk dress with a high neck, short sleeves, and a slit skirt is a **cheongsam**—pronounced chiongSAM

an old word for "keep warm" is **cherish**

cherish comes from French *cher*, "dear"

Cherokee is the Creek word for "people of different speech"

a **cheroot** is a cigar with both ends cut off, from Tamil *curuttu*, "curl, roll"

a **cherophobe** is afraid of having fun

cherry comes ultimately from Greek *kerasos*, "**cherry** tree"

cherte is tenderness or affection

cherub is from an Akkadian word meaning "to pray" or "to bless"; the plural of

cherub is cherubim for angels, but cherubs in all other circumstances

chess, from French *esches*, "game of the two kings," is ultimately from Sanskrit *chaturanga*, "four members of an army"

chessman was first *chessemeyne*, "chess company"

chest ultimately comes from Greek *kiste*, "box, basket" which became *cista* in Latin; **chest** as in thorax is a metaphor based on the ribs enclosing the heart and lungs like a box

the town endings -**chester** and -**caster** mean "military camp"

a **chesterfield**, an over-stuffed couch or sofa with a back and two ends, was named for the Earl of **Chesterfield** (nineteenth century)

chestnut comes from a Greek word meaning nut of Castanaea (Pontus) or Castana (Thessaly)

the word **chestnut**, for stale joke, comes from an 1816 play "The Broken Sword" by William Dimond

{ **chevelure** is the trail of a comet or a fancy word for a head of hair }

chèvre is French for goat's milk cheese

the first meaning of **chevron** was a beam or rafter (especially in plural) as the rafters or couples of the roof, which meet at an angle at the ridge

the definition of **chew** involves the molar teeth

chez as a preposition means "at the home of"

chianti is named for the **Chianti** mountains in Tuscany

the **chiaroscuro** light-and-shadow painting technique is from Italian *chiaro*, "bright" and *oscuro*, "dark"

chic comes from German *shick*, "deftness, skill" and *schicken*, "appearance"

the suffix **-chic** denotes a fashion or style

Chicago is Algonquian for "place of the wild onion"

a **chicane** is an artificial narrowing or turn on a road or course

chicanery comes from Persian meaning "crooked mallet"—which equates to cheating

a **chickadee**'s name is imitative of its call

chicken à la king was said to be named after E. Clark King, proprietor of a hotel in New York

chicken is a Germanic word whose ancestor has been reconstructed as *kiuki-nam*; **chick** is a fourteenth-century abbreviation

chicken-pecked means under the rule of a child

chickenpox is not connected to chickens but was far less dangerous than smallpox, so there may be an implication of its being "chickenfeed" compared to smallpox—or it may refer to the marks resembling chickpeas

the **chickpea** is not related to chicks but is from Latin *cicer*, the Roman name for the plant—which became *ciche pease* until the eighteenth century; it is synonymous with **garbanzo**

what the British call **endive**, Americans call **chicory** and vice versa; Americans say **chicory** is synonymous with **radic-chio** and **endive** is synonymous with **escarole**

chide first meant quarrel or contend loudly

{ **chief** ultimately comes from Latin caput, "head" }

chiffon was first a fabric, then a type of pie

a bureau of drawers with a mirror is a **chiffonier** and **chiffonier**'s root sense is rag chest (-ier is a suffix of function and French *chiffe* was "old rag")

chignon was originally French for "nape of the neck"

chilblain is a compound formed from "chill" and *blain*, "blister"

child is from a Gothic word meaning "fruit of the womb"; the Anglo-Saxon word for **child** is *cild* and some did not pronounce the "l"—giving us kid as a synonym for **child**

childlike refers to a person's temperament, whereas **childish** refers to a person's behavior

for the name of the fiery vegetable, the U.S. spelling is **chili** (plural chilis) while the British spelling is **chilli** (plural chillies); guesses at the etymology of **chili/chilli** include that it comes from a Nahuatl word meaning "sharp, pointed"

a figure of one thousand equal sides is a **chiliahedron**

Old English had a noun *cele/ciele*, "cold" which developed into *chile*, "cold, frost" and probably, eventually, **chill**

to crumble into very small fragments or gnaw is to **chimble**

chime was first a cymbal or something for striking a set of bells, then came to mean a set of bells

figuratively, **chime** can mean a system by which all the parts work in harmony

a **chimera** (pronounced kuh-MIR-uh) is the head of a lion, body of a goat, and tail of a serpent

chimerical means "fantastically conceived, imaginary, fanciful"

chimichanga (deep-fried burrito with a spicy meat filling) means "trinket" in Mexican Spanish a **chiminea/chimenea** is an earthenware outdoor fireplace shaped like a lightbulb, with the bulbous end housing the fire and typically supported by a wrought-iron stand

chimney, via Latin *caminus*, "fireplace, oven" from Greek *kaminos*, "heating chamber, furnace," first meant the hearth or fireplace itself and the opening for the smoke

a **chimp** is a grown-out shoot of a stored potato

a talk or conversation can be called a **chin**

china comes from Persian *chini* for the delicate and valuable ware first made in **China**; the word describes pieces made from certain kinds of clay that have been glazed, usually decorated, and fired in a kiln at high temperatures

China has one main written language and about 35 spoken languages

chino is American Spanish, literally "toasted"—referring to its typical color

chintz comes from the plural of Hindu *chint*, a printed Indian calico, from earlier Sanskrit *chitra*, "variegated"

the original meaning of **chip** as a verb was to remove the crust of bread

to **chipe** is to cheep and whine, to speak in a high-pitched voice in a persistent, complaining manner

Chipmunk (also chipmuck) is an American English word, first written "chitmunk," that was borrowed from Algonquian *atchitamon*, meaning "one who descends trees headlong." It is a species of ground squirrel and has the synonyms chipping squirrel, hackee, and striped squirrel. The first record of the word in writing is around 1841, though chitmunk was written about in 1832.

a shop that sells fish and chips can be called a **chippy**

to be **chirk** is to be lively and in good spirits

chirm is the blended singing of many birds, the sound of a swarm of insects, or the noise of many children

{ **chiropractic** breaks down to mean "with the hands" and "practicing" }

to **chirotonize** is to elect by voting or to vote

grasshoppers **chirr**—make a sound by rubbing rough surfaces together (their legs)

to **chirrup** is to say or make high-pitched sounds

chisel's Latin root is *caedere*, "to cut"

chit derives from Hindu *citthi*, "a short note"

chitlins or **chitterlings** (the small intestines of pigs, etc., cooked as food) is probably a diminutive of Old English *cieter*, "intestines"

to **chitter** is to "shiver with cold"

a potato sprouting or germinating is **chitting**

etymologically, **chivalry** is the practice of riding horses and comes from Latin *caballarius*, "horseman," from Latin *caballus*, "horse"

chive is derived from Latin *cepa*, "onion"—and the plant resembles an onion

chivvy means "tell someone to do something repeatedly"

to **chizz** someone is to cheat or swindle them

chlorine, a yellowish-green chemical element, is from Greek *khloros*, "green" (the combining form chloro- also means green) a **choana** is a funnel-shaped opening, like either of those connecting the nasal cavities to the pharynx (the plural is **choanae**)

choate means "finished, complete" or "well-established, completely formed" and is a back-formation of inchoate

a wedge to keep a vehicle from rolling or sliding when parked is a **chock**; **chock** seems to come from a French word meaning "block, log"

chock-full has one meaning of "full to suffocation" as the meaning of chock in this instance is "choke"

chocolate is from Mexican/Nahuatl *chocolatl*, "food made of cacao seeds and pochotl seeds"; in English it was originally a drink, then a paste, then a confection

choice and **choose** derive from the Germanic base *kaus-* or *keus-*

the point on a knife where the cutting edge ends and it adjoins the tang is the **choil**

choir was once spelled *quere/quer* in English (from French) but changed because of its Latin root *chorus*

to stop the vibration of a cymbal is to **choke** it

an artichoke center is the **choke** or **heart**

choler is another word for anger or bad temper

cholesterol comes from Greek words meaning "bile, gall" and "stiff, solid" plus the ending "-ol"

{ a **choller** is a double chin or the hanging lip of a hound }

choosehow means "under any circumstances" as in "He will have to do it **choosehow**."

a snap with the jaws or mouth is a **chop**

chop as in "cut" is from chap, as in "cracked skin"

chop-chop for "quick, quickly" is pidgin English based on Chinese dialect *kuai-kuai*

chopper comes from the chop-chop noises made by helicopter rotors

chops is a slang term for extreme proficiency

in Chinese, **chopsticks** originally meant "quick sticks" or "nimble ones"

a **chord** is three or more notes sounded together; the original sense of **chord** was "agreement, reconciliation"

chord and **cord** may derive from Greek *chorde*, "length of catgut"—which was first used for stringed instruments and which resembles string

to **chore** is to do household or routine tasks; chores, from the beginning, implied light tasks as opposed to real work

choreography is based on Greek *khoreia*, "dancing in unison," from *khoros*, "chorus"

a **chorine** is a chorus girl

chorometry or **embadometry** is the science of land surveying; **geomatics** is the mathematics of the earth

the study of place names and geographical phenomena is **choronymy**

a **choropleth** map is a map in which areas are shaded or patterned in proportion to the measurement of the statistical variable being displayed on the map, such as population density or per-capita income

chortle is probably a blend of chuckle and snort and was coined by Lewis Carroll

chorus originally meant a character speaking the prologue or epilogue in a play

chou or **choux** is a pastry, at first a round cream-filled pastry cake, from French *choul*

choux "cabbage(s), rosette(s)," from Latin *coulis*, "cabbage"

choucroute is a synonym for sauerkraut

chow is an abbreviation of Pidgin English **chow-chow**

chow mein is an alteration of Chinese *ch'ao mein*, "fried flour"

chowder derives from French chaudière, "pot" and was originally a hodge-podge prepared in the fishing villages of Brittany, who probably carried the custom to Newfoundland, from which it spread to Nova Scotia, New Brunswick, and New England

if something is undertaken to make money, it is **chrematistic** or **quaestuary**

chreotechnics describes "useful arts" such as agriculture, commerce, and manufacturing

chrism, oil and balm mixed for religious anointments, is from Greek *khrisma*, "anointing" or "unction"

Christ is from Greek *Kristos*, "anointed one"; **Christ** was not Jesus's last name, just his title

christen comes from an Old English word meaning "make Christian"

Christian is derived from the name of Christ, but it is a surprisingly recent word, introduced in the sixteenth century

Christmas is from the Old English words *Cristes moesse*, "the mass or festival of Christ"; the abbreviation **Xmas**, thought as sacrilegious by some, is entirely appropriate as the letter X (chi) is the first letter in the Greek word for Christ

chrome gets its name from the brilliant colors of its compounds

chromosome originates from Greek words meaning "color" and "body" because the surface of **chromosome** is easily stained by basic dyes

chronic is contrasted with **acute** as **chronic** pain persists over a longer period of time than **acute** pain and is resistant to most medical treatments

chronicle comes from Greek *khronika*, "annals"

to **chronologize** is to establish the order in time of (documents, events)

{ **chronology** means literally "the study of time" }

one's **chronotype** is the factor that determines if one is an early bird or an owl

etymologically, a **chrysalis** is a "gold-colored" pupa, from Greek *khrusos*, "gold," and many butterflies do have pupae that have a metallic sheen at some point

chrysanthemum is Greek *chrys-*, "gold" *anthemon*, "flower," which they mostly were in ancient times

chthonic "inhabiting or pertaining to the underworld," is from Greek *khthon*, "earth"

chubby is derived from chub, a thick-bodied European river fish

chuckle in its original sense was almost the opposite of what it is today, as it meant "laugh vehemently"

chug and huff makes **chuff**

the periods of a polo game are called chukkas; **chukka** boots were ankle-high boots first worn by polo players

chum was short for chamber-fellow and first meant someone who shared an apartment with another, probably originating at Oxford University

refuse from fish is called **chum**

the sharing of a room by two or more people who are initially strangers (as at college) is called **chummage**

a log of wood for burning is a **chump**; **chump** is probably a blend of chunk and lump to **chunk** is to group together words so they can be stored or processed as single concepts

to **chunter** is to murmur, mutter, grumble, complain

church is derived from Greek *kyriakon doma*, "the Lord's house"

churchianity is excessive devotion to a particular church

a **churchkey** is a bottle opener at one end and a can-opener punch on the other end

churl is a term of contempt for a low-bred or rude person

churn may be based on the granular appearance that cream takes on when it is stirred or agitated

chute is from French, meaning "fall of water"

chutney is from Hindi *chatni*, a strong hot relish or condiment of ripe fruits and sour herbs, flavored with chilies, spices, etc.

chutzpah is Yiddish and is pronounced HUTZ-puh

ciabatta is Italian for "slipper" from the shape of the bread

ciao (or *ciau*), from Italian, is an alteration of *schiavo*, "(I am your) slave"

cibation is feeding or taking food

the scar of a healed wound or burn—or a scar on tree bark—is a **cicatrice** or **cicatrix**

a **cicerone** is a person who acts as a guide, especially to historical and antiquities sites; the word is from Latin *Cicero*, alluding to his eloquence

to **cicurate** is to tame or domesticate, render mild or harmless

cider comes from Greek *sikera* and Hebrew *shekar*, "strong drink" and at first denoted an intoxicating beverage

apple juice if unfermented is **cider** or **sweet cider**; if fermented, it is **hard cider** (apple **cider** is redundant)

cigar comes from Spanish *cigarro*, from the Mayan verb *sik'ar*, "to smoke" or "smoking"

cigarettes have a name of French origin, as a diminutive of *cigare*, thus "little cigars"

cilantro is the leaves of coriander

the **cilia** are the eyelashes or eyelids (especially the outer edges of the eyelids); the singular is **cilium**

cinch is from Spanish *cincha*, "girth" and it means something securing a saddle, pack, or article of clothing; **cinch** "certainty" is from the Mexican saddle girth—which was strong, tight, and safe

cincinate means curled in ringlets and **cingular** means ring-shaped

the molding around a column is the **cincture**

cinder comes from Latin *cinis*, "ashes"

a **cineaste** is a person with a deep interest in movies and moviemaking

cinema comes from Greek *kinema*, "motion"

a small movie theater specializing in art or classic films is a **cinematheque**

cinemese is language typical of the cinema or film criticism

cingular means "encircling, girdling, surrounding" (from Latin *cingulum*, "girdle," *cingere*, "to gird")

the source of the word **cinnamon** is Semitic or Hebrew *qinnamon* and was borrowed into Greek as *kunnamon*—and it is the inner bark of an East Indian tree

the five on dice is called **cinque**

cipher comes from Arabic *sifr*, "nought, zero," which is from Sanskrit *sunya*, "empty"

cipherdom is the state of being a nobody, a nonentity

circle is a diminutive of *circus*, "ring"

a series of exercises is a **circuit**

to **circumambulate** is to beat around the bush or to approach something indirectly

circumcize is from Latin meaning "cut around"

circumference means literally "carrying around"—that is, around the boundary of a circle or other geometric figure

> **circumflex** (accent mark as ê) is, literally, "bending around"

anything that wanders from house to house is **circumforaneous**

circumspect as a noun is a state of watchfulness, from Latin *circumspectus*, "a looking round"

circumstance is, literally, "that which stands around (something)"

circumvallation is a rampart or entrenchment constructed around a place for defense

the first use of **circus** (Latin "ring") was for the arena of Roman antiquity, an oval or circular area enclosed by tiers of seats and usually covered by a tent

a bowl-like mountain basin with steep walls is a **cirque**, **cum**, **corrie**, or **corry**

cirrus, a wispy cloud, means "tuft of hair" in Latin

a **cistern** is an artificial reservoir for the storage of water or a large vessel for water or liquor

citadel's etymology is "little city," i.e. the smaller or inner fortified city, usually on a higher ground, around which the larger city of later times gradually formed itself

Latin *citare*, "cause to move" or "call, summon" came into English as **cite**, "summon

officially," and then was used metaphorically to mean "calling forth" of a quotation

citizen is based on *civitas*, "city" and, from the thirteenth century, a **citizen** was simply a member or denizen of a city or borough

citriculture is the cultivation of citrus fruits and **pomiculture** is the cultivation of fruit trees

citronella is a fragrant Asian grass whose oils are used in anti-insect candles

Latin **citrus** signified the **citron**, an Asian tree with lemonlike fruit; **citron** is a French derivative of **citrus**, coined on the model of French *limon*, "lemon"

the Latin word for **city** was *urbs*, but a citizen was *civis*—from which came *civitas*, "citizenship" and, eventually, **city**, which is a town incorporated by charter

city first was used for any settlement regardless of size; the modern distinction between **town** and **city** developed during the fourteenth century

the original use of **civic** was **civic** garland, something given to a Roman person who saved a fellow citizen's life

civil as in **civil** engineer means "not military or naval"—as **civil** engineers were distinguished from those who designed military works; **civil** derives from Latin *civis*, "citizen," which passed into English via *civilis*, "of or pertaining to citizens"

civilian was first a student or practitioner of civil law

civilization (like culture) referred originally to a process—to bring within a form of social organization, civilizing or being civilized

the etymological notion behind **claim** is "calling out," from Latin *clamare*, "cry out, shout"

clairvoyance is a form of ESP, **precognition** is seeing into the future, and **telepathy** is mind training and thought transference

clairvoyant is literally (French) "clear seeing"

clam comes from Old English *clamm*, "fetter, constriction" and, hence, "clamp"

clamant, from Latin "crying out," means "forcing itself gently upon the attention"

another word for the common people or a mob is **clamjamfrie**

to be **clammed** is to be damp and cold

etymologically, **clammy** means "sticky as if smeared with clay" and comes from the now-obsolete verb *clam*, "smear, stick" and back further to Germanic *klaimaz*, "clay"

a **clamp** is a pile or stack of something—garden matter, peat, turf

clan is ultimately from Latin *planta*, "plant, sprout"

clancular means secret or underhanded

clapboard (pronounced KLA-burd) comes from German that translates into "to crack" and "wood"

to **clapperclaw** is to scold

claptrap first meant a trick or device to catch applause or an expression designed to get applause

a **claque** is a group of people hired to applaud an act or performer

claret first pertained to light-red wine, now red wine in general or the English name for the red wines of Bordeaux

to purify butter by melting is to **clarify**, to make clear by removing impurities or solid matter, as by heating gently

clarinet is borrowed from French *clarinette*, "little clear-sounding instrument, little bell" (a diminutive of *clarine*, a type of bell)

the colors of cigars are: green (**clarissimo**) to blonde (**claro claro**) to cafè au lait (**claro**) to light-brown (**colorado claro**) to reddish-brown

(**maduro colorado**) to dark brown (**maduro**) to black (**oscuro**)

clash is the sound of heavy rainfall

> **class**, from Latin *classis*, first referred to a division of the Roman people

for **classic**, assume the meaning "of the highest class" and "typical, excellent as an example; timeless," and for **classical**, "pertaining to or characteristic of Greek or Roman antiquity or civilization"

clastic is having separable pieces, being able to be taken apart; **clastic** in geology refers to rocks made of broken pieces of older rocks

a **clatterfart** or **clatterfeit** is a babbler

clause first referred to the close of a rhetorical period, then came to mean "a section of the law"; a **clause** is a type of grammatical construction intermediate between a sentence and a phrase

claustrophobia is from Latin *claustrum*, "lock, bolt" and *phobia*, "fear"

clavate is having one thickened end

a **claviature** is a musical keyboard, as a piano

clavichord comes from Latin *clavis*, "key" and *chorda*, "string"

the **clavicle** or **collarbone** gets its name from its key (Latin *clavis*) shape

clay had an early meaning "material of the human body"

clean traces to Germanic *klainoz*, "clear, pure"

clear comes via Old French from Latin *clarum*, "bright, **clear**, plain"

cleave means chop apart or rend, but also the opposite, adhere or stick together

clef comes from Middle French meaning "key"

cleg is a synonym for **horsefly**

clematis (an ornamental plant) comes from Greek *klematis* from *klema*, "wine branch"

clement basically means "gentle, mild, placid" (opposite of inclement)

the **clementine**, a type of tangerine, was named for the French priest who first cultivated it, Pere Clement

to **clepe** is to call or name; its past forms are cleped/clept or ycleped/yclept

an hourglass with sand that measures time other than an hour is a **clepsammia**

late-night refrigerator raiding is called **cleptobiosis**

clerestory's etymology is *clere*, "clear" and *story*, "floor, stage" of a building and it generally describes an upper story of a church or other building containing windows that admit light to the center of the building

the cords of a hammock are the **clews**

a **cliché** is a frying noise

cliché (from French) was first a metal stereotype, then was used figuratively

click comes from French *clique*, "tick of a clock" and Dutch *flik*, "tick"

in ancient Rome, **clients** were often poets and philosophers who lived under the patronage of a patrician

cliff comes from Proto-Germanic *kliban*

cliffhanger comes from serial movies of the 1930s where, at the end of each episode, some person was left in a perilous situation such as hanging off the edge of a cliff

in medical terms, **climacteric** is the period of life when fertility and sexual activity are in decline; otherwise, a **climacteric** is a supposed critical period in life, especially occurring every seven years (i.e., the "seven-year itch")

 clergy first meant "learning, scholarship" and **clerk** had the original meaning "man ordained to the Christian ministry"

satirical verses of two rhyming couplets of uneven length—like the old Burma Shave slogans—are called **clerihews**, for writer Edmund **Clerihew** Bentley (1875–1956)

the **clerisy** is the collective group of educated people, intellectuals, literati, or scholars

clerk (and cleric, clergy) owe their existence to a Biblical reference to the Levites, members of an Israelite tribe whose men were assistants to the Temple priests, which mentions "inheritance," and Greek for that is *kleros* and that begat the adjective *klerikos*, which eventually became English **clerk**

clever can mean "manually dexterous," and in the case of a horse means it is a good-natured one

climactic means appearing at a climax; **climatic** relates to weather and climate; one can speak of poor **climatic** conditions or of a certain **climactic** development

climate originally denoted a zone of the earth between two lines of latitude, then any region known for an atmospheric condition

climax first described propositions in rhetoric, one rising above the other in effectiveness and it comes from Greek *klimax*, "ladder"

the original notion in **climb** was "holding on"; the original past tense of **climb** was *clamb*

to leave fingerprint smudges on a clean surface like windows is to **climp**

clinamen is an inclination or bias

boxers in a **clinch** are too close for a full-arm punch, often holding after an exchange of punches (**clinch** is a variant of clench)

in biology, a **cline** is a graded series of changes in size or function exhibited by related organisms in response to changes in the environment

cling can mean "shrink" or "cause shrinking" of an animal or vegetable body

in **clingstone** peaches, the flesh adheres to the stone; in **freestone** peaches, it is the opposite

clinic first meant "teaching of medicine at the bedside"

a well-known jail was once located on **Clink** Street in London, which is why jails are sometimes called **clinks**

clink (as in the sound and a crack in metal) comes from a Dutch term for a kind of brick that was made by firing clay until it was extremely hard—and the word comes from the sound of these bricks hitting each other

clinker is a stonelike furnace or coal residue

clinker-built means made with overlapping planks; **carvel-built** is made with planks laid flush

clinomania is an excessive desire to stay in bed

clinquant means glittering, as tinsel or spangles

Clipping or shortening is the creation of short variants of complex words. In some, the initial or first part of the longer word is used: ad from advertisement, chimp from chimpanzee, deli from delicatessen, lab from laboratory. In others, the beginning of the word is dropped: burger for hamburger, phone from telephone. Occasionally, the middle part is dropped to create an "elliptical word," such as flu from influenza.

clips are sheers for wool

clique is actually pronounced KLEEK

a **clitic** is the 'm in I'm—an unstressed word that only occurs in combination with another word

to **clitter** is to make a thin vibrating or rattling sound

clivose means hilly or steep

{ **clo** is the unit of measurement for the thermal insulation value of clothing }

a **cloacal** is a waste pipe that carries away sewage or surface water

cloak and **clock** both originate in Medieval Latin *clocca*, "bell," by way of Old French *cloque*; a **cloak** was so called from its shape resembling that of a bell and **clock** meant originally a timepiece in which each hour was marked by the sound of a bell

a bell-shaped cover for plants is a **cloche**

a woman's close-fitting, bell-shaped hat is a **cloche**

clod first meant the same as clot

a dog that is **cloddy** is thickset and close to the ground

clodpate is a combo of a clod and a blockhead

to **cloffin** is to sit idly by a fire

clog, from Middle English, originally meant "block of wood to impede an animal's movement"

to **clointer** is to make a noise with the feet, like treading heavily in shoes

cloissoné is from a French word meaning "to partition or divide" as the art is enamel in which colors of a pattern are kept apart with thin metal strips (etc.)

cloister, the part of the abbey restricted to members, comes from Latin *claustrum/clostrum* "monastic cell," "enclosed place," or "lock," from Latin *claudere*, "to close"

close, from Latin *clausum*, "closed place," first meant "enclosure"

closet first denoted a private or small room

in theater, **cloth** can mean a large piece of painted scenery

to **clothe** a ship is to rig it

cloture is the closing of a debate by calling for an immediate vote

the **clou** is the main attraction of an event or the center of attention

cloud from Old English *clud* meant "hill" or "rock" at first; the name of a **cloud** describes both its appearance and its height above the ground

cloudberry derives from the obsolete sense of *cloud*, "hill" (and berry)

> a **cloudburst** is a torrential local downpour of rain of short duration

clout once meant "heavy blow"

a **clove** is 8-10 pounds of cheese

clove comes from Old French *clou de girofle*, "nail of gillyflower (**clove** tree)," from its shape, and gillyflower originally being the name of the spice

cloven can mean "divided by two"

the **clover** takes its name from the suit of clubs in cards (which was *claver* in Old English), not the other way around

clown may derive from Northern Frisian meaning "clumsy fellow" or "clod" and it first referred to an unrefined person

cloy originally meant "fasten with a nail," reduced from the obsolete *acloy*, based on Latin *clavus*, "nail"

cloying means "overly sweet"—from the verb *cloy*, "to overload, to surfeit with food" or "to gratify beyond desire"

club implies that the stick gets thicker on one end

club soda (also sometimes called **soda water**) is a flavorless soft drink that also gets its effervescence from an infusion of carbon dioxide; the distinction between **seltzer** and **club soda** is that **club soda** also contains a bit of sodium bicarbonate

clubs in cards comes from Spanish *basto* or Italian *bastone*, "**clubs**, cudgels"

a **clue** is literally "a ball of thread or twine" (which is why one unravels clues)—and in the old Cretan Minotaur fable, the only way Theseus could get out of the labyrinth was by unrolling a ball of thread as he went in

chunk and lump = **clump**

hands stiff with cold are said to be **clumpst**

if you are **clumse**, you are stiff from the cold

clumsy may come from Swedish *klumsi*, "benumbed with cold" (the original sense of the word) or *clumse* (plus -y), "drowsy"

a **clutch** is a group of eggs laid in a single session

clutch is a variant of the obsolete *clitch*, "close the hand"

clutter is a variant of *clotter*, "to clot"

clyssus means quintessence

coach first referred to a cart or carriage and came to mean "a private tutor" in British universities around 1848; the sense of "an athletic trainer" (especially for a boat race) was first recorded in 1885 and is a figurative use of the vehicle **coach**, from the concept "move forward or along"

coal originally meant "a glowing piece of wood or a cinder"

coalesce, "cause to grow together," is from Latin *co-* and *alere*, "nourish"

coalition comes from Latin *coalescere*, "grow together"

the **coaming** is the raised borders about the edge of the hatches and scuttles of a ship which prevent water on deck from getting below

the original meaning of **coarse** was "common, ordinary"

cobble as in cobblestone comes from *cob*, "rounded lump" with the diminutive suffix -le

a **cobbler** is fruit topped with tender biscuits and the dessert may have gotten its name from its top crust's resemblance to cobblestones

the last sheep to be sheared is the **cobbler**

cobra is from Portuguese **cobra** *de capello*, "snake with hood"—based on Latin *colubra*, "snake"

{ the difference between a **coast** and the **shore** is the **coast** is the seaward limit of the land and the **shore** is the landward limit of the sea }

coast first meant "side of the body" (from Latin *costa*, "flank, rib, side")

to cycle without pedalling is to **coast** or **freewheel**

coaster (a mat for a bottle, glass, or cup) comes from the idea of making the circuit of the table after dinner

coat seems originally to have signified a sort of short, close-fitting cloth tunic with sleeves for men; originally, as a woman's garment, a **coat** was a skirt, a sense preserved in petticoat

the original senses of **coax** were "fondle, pet" or "make a simpleton of"

a **cob** is a male swan

cob meaning "spider" survives only in the word cobweb (from Old English, literally "poison head or cup"); **cob** was first spelled *cop(pe)web* as *coppe* meant "spider"

German *kobold* means "goblin" and in early times it was believed that impurities in silver ore made the miners sick and those impurities were put there by goblins; the silver-white metallic element that was the impurity was named kobalt/**cobalt**

a **cobweb** is a single thread spun by a spider

Coca-Cola is from *Quecha kuku*, "coca leaves, coca bush," borrowed via Spanish coca + cola from languages of West Africa *kola*, "cola nut"

the **coccyx**, the bone at the bottom of the spinal column, is so named as it is shaped like the bill of a *kokkux*, "cuckoo"

cochineal, "red dye," comes from Spanish *cochinilla*, a term for the dye and insect from whose dried body it is made

your ear's inner spiral, the **cochlea**, is from Greek *kochlos*, "snail with a spiral shell"; **cochlea** can be used to denote spiral objects like the Archimedean screw or a spiral staircase

cochleare is a spoon or spoonful of a medical prescription

a cone-shaped tied bundle of straw or hay is a **cock**

the male crab or lobster is a **cock**; the female, a **hen** a **cockade** is a rosette or knot of ribbon worn on a hat

cockamamie, "nonsensical, ridiculous," may be a corruption of *decalcomania*

cockapoo is a hybrid of cocker spaniel and poodle

cockatoo was originally a Malay word *kakatua*, and **cockatiel** is also from that root

cockatrice, a mythical serpent, started as Latin *calcatrix*, "hunter, tracker" from Greek *ikhneumon*, "track," a name given to a mysterious creature said to prey on crocodiles

cockcrow is a literary word for "dawn"

to **cockerate** is to brag

a candy heart with a message is called a **cockle**

a **cockle** is a bulge, pucker, or wrinkle in paper, glass, etc.

cockle, as in shell, is from Greek *konkhulion*, "little mussel"

some words that only exist as part of an idiom are: **cockles**, **fritz**, **lam**, **QT**, **zoot**

cockney (a dialect) started as a word for a misshapen hen's egg, "cock's egg," and also meant "spoiled child"

in its earliest sense, **cockpit** literally referred to cockfighting pits

in **cocksure**, cock is an euphemism for "God"

a cock-tailed horse was one with a docked tail, usually non-thoroughbreds which raced, and this led to the sense of "lack of purity; adulteration" which probably led to the **cocktail** as drink sense for an "adulterated" spirit

{ if your Adam's apple is larger than normal, you are **cock-throppled** }

cocoa is an alteration of Spanish *cacao*

coconut is the nut or seed of the coco-palm, from Portuguese *côco*, literally, "bogeyman," from the resemblance of a **coconut** to a grotesque head

cocoon is a diminutive of *coque*, "shell"

a **cocotte** is a a high-sided cooking pot (casserole) with a lid or a small ramekin dish for baking and serving eggs and other preparations

coctile means "made by baking or exposure to heat"

the origin of many fish names are obscure—as **cod**, which may come from Old English meaning "bag, pouch"

to **cod** is to tease or deceive

a **coda** is a concluding event, passage, or section (Latin *cauda*, "tail")

an egg cooked in water just below boiling is **coddled**

code, from Latin **codex**, "block of wood split into tablets, document written on wood tablets," was first a set of laws

a **codger** is a mildly eccentric person

codicil is a diminutive of *codex*, a "small part of a legal document," usually used to add to or change something about a larger piece of writing

an unripe apple is a **codling**

young cod are **codling** or **sprag** or **scrod**

a **codpiece**, earlier codde-piece, is a piece of fabric used to mimic the male genitalia; cod was once a common name for a bag and, by extension, the scrotum

codswallop means "nonsense, drivel"

coelacanth, the "living fossil" of the lungfish, is pronounced SEE-luh-kanth

in order to answer "How are you?," you need **coenesthesia** or **cenesthesia**—the totality of impressions you get from organic sensations forming the basis of your awareness of your bodily state

coerce derives from Latin *arcere*, "restrain"

coeval usually describes things that existed together for a very long time or that originated at the same time in the distant past—and is also used as a noun, usually referring to a person

the word **coffee** derives from Arabic *qahwah*, a word originally used for wine or a drink made by infusion; when **coffee** first arrived in Europe, it was known as "Arabian wine"

a **coffered** ceiling is one with ornamental sunken panels in a box-like structure

coffin is French for "little basket"—from Greek *kophinos*, "basket," and first generally meant "box, case, casket, chest"

a **coffle** is a line of animals or slaves fastened or driven along together

cogitabund is being deep in thought

cognac is named for a town in western France

a blood relative is a **cognate**

words in different languages coming from the same root are **cognates**

cognitive skills and knowledge involve the ability to acquire factual information, often the kind of knowledge that can be easily tested—so **cognition** is different from creative, emotional, and social development and ability

Latin *gnoscene*, "know" begat *cognoscere*, "get to know; recognize" and it moved through French *connoissance* to English to become **cognizance**

cognomen is literally "name by which one is known"

if you are making an inquiry, you can say you **cognosce**

a **cognoscente** is a connoisseur

coherent first meant "logically related"

silver salmon is the same as **coho**

cohonestation is honoring another with one's company

cohort first referred to an ancient Roman military unit (one/tenth of legion); **cohort** is an accomplice or conspirator, not a colleague, counterpart, or friend

cohort and **court** derive from Latin *cohortem* (later, *cortem*) "**court**, enclosure," with **cohort** entering French first (*cohorte*)

coif, **coiffure**, and **coiffeur** (hairdo, hairstyle) derive from Latin *cofia*, "helmet"

coign is a position of advantage or a favorable viewpoint

a **coil** once was a noisy disturbance or confused noise

coin comes from the wedge-shaped tool or die (Latin *cuneus*, "wedge") that was used to hammer or stamp pieces of money

coincide can mean "occupy the same portion of space"

{ a word inventor is a **coiner** or **neologist** }

coir is the fiber from the outer husk of a coconut

a **coistril** is a horse groomer

a **col** is an area of low pressure between two high-pressure systems

a saddle between two mountain peaks is a **col**, from Latin *collum*, "neck"

cola is from Temne *k'ola*, "**cola** nut"; **cola** seeds are used to make Coca-**Cola** and Pepsi-**Cola**

a drainer for washed foods is a **colander** and the word may come from Latin *colare*, "strain"; **colation** is the action of straining something and **colature** is the product of straining the word **cold** is related to Latin *gelu*, "frost"

{ when the moon is far to the north it is popularly called a **cold** moon }

cold-blooded (*poikilothermic, poikilothermal*) is used for creatures whose blood takes on the temperature of their environment; **warm-blooded** (*homoiothermic, homeothermal*) is having a fairly steady body temperature governed by the thermotaxic nerve mechanism

cold-fire is fuel laid for a fire, but unlit

beetle specialists are **coleopterists**

Dutch *koolsla*, "cabbage salad" gave us **coleslaw**

colic is, literally, "pertaining to the colon"

collaborate is a combination of *col-* and *labor* and *-ate*

collage, meaning "a pasting" (French *colle*, "paste, glue"), is bits pasted together; **decoupage**, "to cut out," is designs cut out and mounted, then varnished or lacquered; and **montage** is a composition of complete or partial photographs or prints—superimposed to make a blended whole

collagen, the fibrous protein of connective tissue, comes from Greek *kolla*, "glue"

collapse is a back-formation of collapsed

collar descends from Latin *collum*, "neck"

collards take their name from Anglo-Saxon *coleworts*, "cabbage plants"

collate first meant "to bring together for comparison; compare copies carefully" before it meant "put together sheets to make two or more copies of a document"

a **collation** is a light meal at an unusual time—a bringing together of elements required for a meal—and the verb can mean "have lunch with"

a **colleague** is literally "one chosen or delegated to be or work with another" and comes via French from Latin *collega* (*com-* "with" and *leg-* "choose")

collectibles are items collected by people because they like them or regard them as representative mementos of a time past; **memorabilia** is another word to describe the latter

The word **college** comes from Latin *collegium*, "association, partnership," from *collega*, "partner in office." The word **university** is from Latin *universitas*, "the whole," from *universus*, "combined into one." The difference between a **college** and a **university** is that a **college** offers degrees in one or a few specific areas, while a **university** is a collection of colleges.

collegial is the adjective for colleague

a **collegienne** is a girl attending college

colletic means adhesive or adhesive substance

collibration is comparison

the Latin base of **collide** is *laedere*, "hurt by striking"

collies get their name from their original color, which was like coal or black and white, from *col*, "live ember, charred coal"

to talk secretly is to **collifobble**

a **colligation** is the connection of a number of isolated facts by a general notion or hypothesis

collision involves two or more moving objects, not a moving object and something stationary

if two things are found in or belong to the same place, they are **collocal**

collocate is "to place side by side"

a typical arrangement or combination of words is a **collocation**, such as "red apple," "nice day"

to **collogue** is to influence by flattery and also to talk confidentially or conspiratorially

a fold of flesh is called a **collop**

collop is fried bacon or a slice of meat fried or grilled, from Scandinavian *kolhuppadher*, "roasted on coals"

colloquial is Latin *col-* and *loqui*, "speak" and it describes a term used in ordinary or informal conversation

a **colloquium** was first a conversation or dialogue, which gives us **colloquial**, "conversational"

colloquy is a conversation (from Latin *colloquium*)

if you are wrestling or struggling with another that is **colluctation**

a **collocutor** is a participant in a conversation or dialogue; one's **collocutor** is the person with whom one is talking

collusion and **collude** contain the Latin prefix *col-*, "with" and *ludere*, "play," so they mean "play along with"

a **collup** is a small piece or slice

collutory or **collutorium** is mouthwash

collected garbage is **colluvies**

collyrium is another word for eyewash

collywobbles is a humorous term for stomach pain, queasiness, intense anxiety, or nervousness (from colic + wobble)

cologne was created in **Cologne**, Germany and first called Eau-de-**Cologne** or **Cologne** water

a **colon** (from Greek meaning "limb, member or clause of sentence") introduces a part of a sentence that exemplifies, elaborates, balances, or undermines the preceding part

colon, the greater portion of the large intestine, comes from Greek *kolon*, "food, meat"

colonel comes from the Italian *colonna*, "column," from the arrangement of troops who were led by the head officer of a regiment; in Spanish it was *coronel* and it was so spelled in English at first and pronounced KORR-o-nel

a **colonnade** is a series of columns placed at regular intervals, or a similar row of trees or other objects

{ a **colony** was first a farm or rural settlement }

a **colophon** is a crowning or finishing touch, from Greek *kolophon*, "summit" or "finishing stroke"

color refers to the wavelength composition of light; **shade** is a gradation of **color** referring to its degree of darkness; **tint** is a gradation referring to its degree of lightness; and **hue** indicates a modification of a basic **color**

Colorado means "red earth" in Spanish

colossal comes from Greek *kolossos*, the name given by Herodotus to the larger-than-life-size statues in Egyptian temples

a peddler of religious literature is a **colporteur**

a **colt** is a rope with a knotted end

baby seahorses are called **colts**

columbine means "dove's plant" as the inverted flower has some resemblance to five pigeons clustered together

the adjective form for dove is **columbine**

the notion underlying **column** is of "height, command, extremity" and it comes from Latin *columna*, "pillar" which probably came from *columen/culmen*, "top, summit"

coma derives from Greek words translating to "lying down in bed"

comb comes from *gombhos* (pre-Teutonic) for teeth, as the first combs were dried backbones or jawbones of fish

combat started out meaning just a fight between two persons

a long curving wave is a **comber**, a wave that curls over and dissolves into foam is a **breaker**, and a long wave moving steadily shorewards is a **roller**

the notion underlying **combine** is simply "two together," from Latin *combinare* (*com-*, "together" and *bini*, "two at a time")

come is a basic word of English and it has Indo-European roots in the base *gwem-* which also produced Greek *bainein*, "go, walk" and Latin *venire*, "**come**"

a **comediographer** is a writer of comedies

if something is tending to produce or aggravate acne, it is **comedogenic**

comedy comes from Greek *komos*, literally meaning "village bard" or "village merrymaker"

comely is from a Dutch word *komlick*, "fitting"

{ **come-on** was first a slang term for a con man or swindler }

comestion is a fancy word for eating

comets, which have tails, get their name from Greek *kometes*, "long-haired star"

comfit, "sugar-coated sweet," is from Latin *confectum*, the same root as for confectionery (literally something "put together")

comfort is from Latin *con-*, an intensifier, and *fortis*, "strong"

comic means "intended to be funny" while **comical** is "funny unintentionally"

comity is courtesy and considerate behavior toward others

comma (from Greek "a piece cut off") first meant a short clause or phrase within a sentence—and then came to be the name for the punctuation mark

ultimately, **command** and **commend** are the same word—from Latin *com-* and *mandare*, "entrust, commit to someone's charge"

commando is from Afrikaans *kommando*, "raid, raiding party"

commence is based on Latin *com-* (for emphasis) and *initiare*, "begin"

commensal means "eating at the same table"

the **comment** is the part of a sentence offering new information

commerce is another word for conversation

the fully critical word **commercialism** indicates a system which puts financial profit before any other consideration

a cafeteria in the entertainment business is often called the **commissary**

a **commisure** is a juncture or seam—also a joint between two bones or the line where the lips or eyelids meet

etymologically, **commit** simply means "put together"—from Latin *committere* (*com-*, "together" and *mittere*, "put, send"); **commit** originally meant "connect, join"

committee's original meaning was "an individual to whom some charge, function, or trust is committed"

commode is another word for toilet

Latin **commodus** meant "convenient" and it was a compound formed from *com-*, "with" and *modus*, "measure," literally "conforming with due measure" and originally the English form commodious meant "advantageous, useful, convenient" until the 16th century when it developed the meaning "affording a conveniently large amount of space"

commodity first meant "convenience, suitability" and then "a person's benefit, convenience, interest" and its Latin root meant "due measure, fitness, convenience, complaisance"

a yacht club chairman is the **commodore**

common can be compared either with commoner/commonest or more **common**/most **common**

a **commonplace** book is a personal journal in which quotable passages, literary excerpts, and comments are written

commonplace was originally written as two words, from Greek *koinos topos* "general theme"

a resident can be called a **commorant**

a **commoratory** is a place to live

a **commorient** is a person killed in a disaster that claimed other lives

a **communard** is a member of a commune

{ **commune** first referred to a French (etc.) territorial division }

one who partakes of or receives the Holy Communion is a **communicant**

the base meaning of **communication** is "to make common to many" and its oldest sense in English is perhaps "the action of imparting things material"

communion is sharing or having in common, "fellowship"

communism's name is based on its definition as "working for the common benefit by the community"

a group of animals or plants living together can be called a **community**; **community** was first used to refer to a "body of commons" or a social or political entity

when regular travelers on nineteenth-century railroads could first buy a ticket for a month at a time at a reduced rate, that was **commuting**, "exchanging" many tickets for one; and also **commuting**, "making less severe" the price paid; and **commuter** came to mean any regular traveler to work

compact (adjective) can mean "made up or composed of"

a **compact** is a formal agreement on rights and conduct, a **treaty** is a **compact** between nations, and a **contract** is a **compact** between two business entities

compadre in Spanish means "godfather"

food eaten with bread is **companage**

companion is from French *compagnon*, "one who eats bread with another" from Latin *com*, "with" and *panis*, "bread"; **companion** was once used with contempt and implied an attendant or person of inferior social position

a **companionway** is a stairway or ladder from a deck to the cabin below

company once meant "sexual intercourse"

a group of actors is a **company**; a group of critics is a **shrivel**

comparable should be pronounced COM-puh-ruh-buhl

positive is the ordinary form of a word, with **comparative** conveying the sense of greater intensity of the adjective and **superlative** reflecting the greatest intensity of the adjective

a **compare** is an equal or a rival

compare emphasizes the similarities between or among things, though not losing sight of the differences; **contrast** emphasizes the differences

compartition is the distribution of the parts of a plan

a **compartment** describes a watertight division of a ship

compass (noun) first meant "cunning, cleverness, ingenuity"

anything patched together is a **compatchment**

compathy is shared feeling

the base of **compatible** is Latin *compati*, "suffer with"

one's addressed name is a **compellative** or **compellation**

to **compendiate** is to sum up concisely

compendious means "abridged, succinct" not "voluminous"

compendium (Latin "that which is weighed together") is a complete summary or abridgment or a concise collection of materials—not an all-encompassing or comprehensive work (plural is **compendiums** or **compendia**)

to **comperendinate** is to defer or delay, put off from day to day

compete comes from Latin *competere*, "come together," but in later Latin it developed the sense "strive together," which was the basis for the English term

competence is a measure of the ability to perform a task; **efficiency** is a measure of the success achieved in the performance of a task

competent once meant "appropriate, suitable"

competition refers to an abstract quality, whereas **competitiveness** implies a practical activity whose manifestation can be observed

dictionaries are described as "**compiled**" rather than "written"

compital means "pertaining to a crossroads"

complacent means "pleased or satisfied with how things are, with how they affect one's self," "self-satisfied, snug"; **complaisant** means "attempting or eager to please or satisfy," "obliging, affable"—**complacent** thus refers to a state of mind and **complaisant** to a disposition to behave or conduct oneself in a way that pleases or satisfies others

complain is from Latin meaning "to beat the breast" or "to lament"

complaisance is the action or habit of making oneself agreeable or deferential

complanate means "even horizontally"

complement is "to complete, round out" and **compliment** is "to praise or admire" and as a noun it is an expression of praise or admiration

complement means an addition will serve to complete something or form with it to make a whole while a **supplement** is an addition to something already regarded as complete or whole; **complement** can also mean "the full quantity, number, or amount"

complete used to be spelled compleat and is based on Latin *complere*, "to fill up, finish"; **comply** also comes from this Latin base

 a **completist** is an obsessive and often indiscriminate collector

a **complex** is a combination of memories, ideas, and wishes that exercise an influence on the personality

something **complex** may be well-organized, logically constructed as well as subtle and intricate, while a thing that is **complicated** will have something irregular, perverse, asymmetrical in addition to fundamental intricacy; **complex** is more formal and technical (a problem in mathematics is **complex**) while something like personal life can be **complicated**

complexion first meant a person's physical nature and because that was thought to be revealed by the color and texture of the skin, it came to mean the appearance of (facial) skin; **complexion** also originally meant "combination" or "combining," especially related to the four body humors

complicate, from Latin *plicare*, "fold," first meant "fold together, entangle, intertwine"

compliment and complement—which are often confused—are actually doublets, coming from the same ultimate source, Latin *complementum*, from *complere* "fill up, finish"

something is **complimentary** when it has the property embodied in such an expression; **complementary** describes an addition that produces completeness or perfection in something

component specifically implies that it is part of a machine or vehicle

deportment adds the sense of action or activity to a mode of conduct or behavior; **comportment** ("behavior or bearing") does not have this

compose is preferred when the parts of the whole being assembled are regarded as nonconcrete and more general; when the parts are concrete and specific, then **constitute** is more appropriate; and then there is **comprise**, which can mean "comprehending or encompassing certain parts"

when type is set, as for a book or newspaper, it is "**composed**"

a daisy, dandelion, or other plant with a compound flower head is a **composite**

a word that is **compositional** is one whose semantic interpretation is predictable

from the meaning of its parts, like prearranged or farmer, and these are not given entries in print dictionaries

compossible is "compatible or possible in conjunction with another thing"

compost is partly decomposed organic material put on soil to fertilize it and replenish its humus (organic component of soil that supplies nutrients to plants)

compost was first, generally, a composition or compound—then a compote, or mixture of fruit

{ **compotation** is another word for drinking session or drinking together }

a **compotator** is a drinking companion

a **compote** is a bowl-shaped dessert dish with a stem

compound meaning "combine" comes from Latin *componere*, "put together"; **compound** the enclosure is from Malay *kampong* "group of buildings; village" and came through Portuguese or Dutch

comprehend literally means "seize with the senses"

comprise means literally "embrace": a zoo comprises mammals, reptiles, and birds (because it "embraces" or includes them), but animals do not **comprise** ("embrace") a zoo, they **constitute** a zoo

compromise started literally as a "joint promise"

compt is an old word for "having the hair dressed" or otherwise being "elegant; polished"

comptroller is an erroneous spelling of controller; **comptroller** should be pronounced kuhn-TROH-luhr

a **compulsive** eater is compelled by an exterior force to eat and eats constantly;

an **impulsive** eater is impelled (has an impulse) to eat, occurring sporadically, and eats only from time to time

etymologically, to do something "without **compunction**" means literally to do it without one's conscience pricking, from Latin *compungere*, "prick hard"; a **compunction** is either anxiety caused by guilt or a slight misgiving or scruple

a **compurgator** is a sworn witness to the innocence or good character of a person

compursion is wrinkling one's face

compute and **computer**'s base is Latin *com-*, "together" and *putare*, "reckon, settle (an account)"

computeracy is a blend of computer literacy

computerate is another word for computer-literate

originally, **comrades** (from Spanish *camarada*, "roommate") were "chamber mates," men who shared sleeping quarters

to **con** a ship is to steer it; to **con** is also "to learn by heart or study attentively"

conation is the conscious desire or will to perform an action, the mental processes or behaviors that lead toward some action or change

> { **conatus** is the vital force in plants or animals that is similar to human effort }

a **concatenation** is literally a "chain" of events or occurrences, from Latin *concatenare*, "chain together, link"

a group of interrelated causes that works together is made up of **concauses**

conceal is based on Latin *con-* and *celare*, "hide"

conceit first meant "a conception, idea" as the word came from conceive, patterned on deceit

conceive is literally "take on" (as a pregnancy) or means "take in" (as mentally)

if you celebrate together, you **concelebrate**

concent is a harmony of sounds or a harmonious combination of voices

concentrate literally means "bring toward or to a center"

concentric means "sharing the same center"

a **concept** is a more definite, more unitary, more complete type of notion than is a **conception**, which is more of an ideational structure with a potential for realization (rather like a schema)

conceptacle is a word for any vessel or cavity of the body

the **conceptus** is the technical name for the embryo during the early stages of pregnancy

a **concern** is a complicated or cumbersome contrivance

concert first meant a harmony of sounds, voices, or instruments, and it can also be used as a synonym for choir or set of musicians

concertina (accordion-like instrument) means "opening or closing in multiple folds"

conch comes from Greek *koghke*, "mussel; shell-like cavity," Latin *concha*, "shell" or "shellfish" and is either conchs or conches in plural; **conchology** is the study of shells and shellfish

the ear's large shell-like hollow is the **concha**

conchiglie is another word for conch shells

concierge should be pronounced kon-see-AIRZH

to **concinnate** is "to put or arrange neatly; fit together skillfully"

concinnity is elegance in artistic or literary style or skillful blending and harmony, as a harmonious arrangement of parts (Latin *concinnus*, "skillfully put together")

a person who conceives something is **concipient**

concise comes from Latin *concisus*, "brief" or "divided"

conclave is based on *con-* and *clavis*, "key," as it was first an inner chamber or private room to which one would have needed a key, literally a "place that can be locked up" or a room or set of rooms that can be opened with only one key

conclude's elements are *con-* and Latin *claudere*, "close, shut"

if something is **conclusible**, it is able to be concluded

the original meaning of **concoct** was "digest food," though it comes from Latin *concoquere*, "cook together"

concoction derives from Latin *concoctio*, "digestion"—of which there were three types: digestion of the stomach and intestines, the chyme-changing process, and secretion

a **concomitant** is an accompanying thing

concord is literally "of one mind" in Latin

a **concordance** is an index of all the words in a text, lined up by the keywords

an open space for people to move about in an airport terminal (or a set of gates) or other transport station is a **concourse**

concrete comes from a Latin word that means "grow together" and **concrete**'s original sense was "composite"

concur tends to suggest cooperative thinking or acting toward an end but sometimes implies no more than approval; in its original literal sense, **concur** meant "collide, converge," reflecting its Latin source meaning "run together"

the etymological notion underlying **concussion** is of "violent shaking," from Latin *concutere*, "shake violently"

condemn is based on Latin *damnare*, the root of "damn"

the white cloud left by a jet is the **condensation trail** or **contrail**

condense has both adjective forms— condensable and condensible

a group of actors is a **condescension**

condign etymologically signifies "fully deserved," from Latin *condignus* (*com-* an intensive and *dignus*, "worthy")

condiment is from Latin *condimentum* from *condire*, "to pickle, preserve"; condiments are food substances used to heighten the natural flavor of foods, to stimulate the appetite, to aid digestion, or to preserve certain foods

a **condisciple** is a fellow student

Latin *condicere* originally meant "talk together" and it became *conditio*, "agreement," giving us **condition** in English

condole means to grieve over or grieve with

{ **condolence** and **sympathy** are parallel formations going back to Latin *condolere* and Greek *sumpatheia*, meaning "together-suffering" }

concubinage is a word for cohabitation of the unmarried

concubine's roots are *con-*, "with" and *cubare*, "to lie"

concupiscence is another word for "lust"

condom may have been named for the doctor who invented it, but the search for that person and the etymology has been fruitless

condominium once meant "joint rule or sovereignty"

condone (from Latin *condonare*, "refrain from punishing") does not mean "approve of, endorse"; it means "let something pass without interference even though you probably disapprove" or "pardon, forgive, overlook"

conduce means "to help bring about"

conduct first meant provision for a safe passage, such as an escort or pass, and the original form of the word was conduit

conductor was a term initially for a military leader

a **condyle** is a rounded bulge on bones that occur in pairs, as those in a knuckle

a **cone** in early use referred to an apex or vertex

a synonym for conversation is **confariation**

to **confect** is to put together from various ingredients

confection had the early general sense "something made by mixing," coming from Latin *conficere*, "put together"; a fashionable article of women's dress is a **confection**

confectionery is sweets and chocolates collectively; **confectionary** is a place where you buy confections

confederacy comes from Latin *confoederare*, "join together in league" based on *foedus* "league, treaty"

{ a **conferee** is a recipient of an honor or a participant in a conference }

conference first meant "conversation, talk"

confess may apply to an admission of a weakness, failure, omission, or guilt

confetti is the plural of Italian *confetto*, "small sweet" as this was originally real or imitation bon-bons thrown during carnival or after a wedding

a person entrusted with private information is a **confidante** (feminine) or **confidant** (masculine)

in **confide** and **confident**, part of the word is from Latin *fidere*, "trust"

configure first meant "fashion according to a model"

confine's earliest meaning was "have a common boundary with; border on"

confirm first meant "make firm or firmer"

a **confirmand** is someone about to undergo a religious confirmation rite

corroborate is used in a narrower context, usually by way of providing support for testimony in a legal proceeding; **confirm** is to lend support to a much wider array of things

confiscate is from Latin *con*, "together" and *fiscus*, "chest, treasury," which made Latin *confiscare*, "store in a chest or treasury"

confit is duck or other meat cooked slowly in its own fat

one who confesses is a **confitent**

conflagration is etymologically "completely blazing"

if something is **conflate**, it is blown together or brought together from various sources

Latin *fligere*, "strike," is the base of **conflict**

confound's base is Latin *confundere*, "mix up," and it first meant "to defeat, overthrow, ruin"

a **confrere** is a fellow member of a fraternity or college, or a colleague at the office

to **confront** can mean to bring things face to face or side by side for comparison

confuse originally meant "rout" or "bring to ruin"

to **confute** is to overwhelm by argument

if you perform the **conga**, the verb forms are congas, congaing, congaed

conge is a formal permission for departure or a curt dismissal

congeal (become semi-solid, especially upon cooling) is from Latin *con*, "together" and *gelare*, "freeze"

congee is water in which rice has been boiled

a **congener** is a person or thing of the same class or kind as another; **congeneric** means "of the same genus or kind"

congenial first meant "kindred" or "sharing the same disposition"

congenital means "existing from birth" while hereditary is "transmitted from one generation to another"

the **conger** eel's name is from Latin **conger** and Greek *gongros*, "sea eel"

congeries is a Latin word meaning "heap or pile of disparate items" or "disorderly collection"

congestion in the body is an accumulation of fluid

congle is Chinese porridge made from rice

conglomerate's root meaning is "gathered together in a rounded mass"

congratulate's etymology is *con-* and Latin *gratulari*, "manifest one's joy" and first meant "to celebrate with some act"

congregate derives from *congregare* (Latin), "collect into a flock"

etymologically, a church's **congregation** is comparable to a pastor's flock, coming from Latin *congregare*, "flock together"

congress comes from Latin elements meaning "walk together"

congruent means "agreeing or corresponding with" in a strict, technical sense while **congruous** indicates that the correspondence is looser, more general

conifer literally is Latin meaning "cone-bearing"

conite is a very poisonous plant is also known as **wolfsbane** (poisonous to wolves) and **monkshood** (since it resembles a monk's hood)

conjecture first meant "the interpretation of omens or signs" or "divination" and it means literally "to throw together," that is, to produce a theory by putting together a number of facts

to **conjobble** is to arrange matters or discuss

the underlying notion of **conjugal** is "joining together" from Latin *conjugare*, "join together (in marriage)" (from *com-*, "together" and *jugare*, "yoke")

the grammatical connotations of **conjugate** arise from the notion of a "connected" set of verb forms, from Latin *conjugare* "join together"—for to **conjugate** a verb is to inflect it in its various forms of mood, number, person, tense, and voice

in the jargon of grammar, the forms of nouns, pronouns, and adjectives can be arrayed in **declensions** or **inflections**; the forms of verbs are said to be arrayed in **conjugations**

a **conjunction** is a word that connects: a **coordinating conjunction** connects similar elements (you and I), while a **correlative conjunction** has related parts (either/or)

a word connecting elements with meaning in sentence is a **conjunctive**; a word connecting words, phrases, clauses, sentences is a **conjunction**

another name for pink eye is **conjunctivitis**

conjure comes from Latin words meaning "band together by an oath; conspire"; it can also mean to beg or implore

conky is anybody with a big nose

{ **connatural** means "innate; belonging inherently or naturally to" }

connect's Latin base is *nectere*, "bind, fasten"

Connecticut is Mohican *quinnitukqut*, "at the long tidal river" and is called the Nutmeg state because its inhabitants reputedly passed off pieces of wood as the spice nutmeg; a native or inhabitant of **Connecticut** can be called a **Connecticutter**

connivance first meant winking and **connive** meant "to shut one's eyes (to something), pretend ignorance"—both descending from Latin *con-* and *nictare*, "to wink"

one **connives** at something but **conspires** with somebody

connoisseur in French meant "knower, judge" and it indicates an expert in a particular area whose recognized knowledge and good taste have established his/her reputation

adjective meaning "aware of something, being awake"

another word for conscious is **conscient**

conscionable "having a conscience" is the opposite of unconscionable

conscious first meant "having guilty knowledge of"

consecrate's root is Latin *sacer*, "sacred"

consectaneous or **consectary** means following as a consequence; the noun **consectary** means "consequence," also "a deduction or conclusion"

consecutive derives from Latin *consecut-*, "follow closely"

consenescence is a word to describe "growing old together"

consent first meant "feel the same; agree"

consensus came into English in a physiological sense—"a set of organs" or the "involuntary or reflex actions of the nervous system"

connotation is from Latin *connotare*, "mark in addition"

connubial is a synonym for "married, wedded"

to **conquassate** is to shake violently

conquer comes from Latin elements *con-* and *quaerere*, "seek," meaning "seek to attain, acquire"

conquistador is pronounced kahn-KWIS-tuh-door

consanguineous means "related by blood"

in early use, **conscience** meant "inner thoughts or knowledge" (from Latin *conscire*, "to know")

conscience is the noun meaning "a sense of right and wrong" while **conscious** is the

a synonym for unanimous is **consentient**

a **consequent** is a thing that follows something else in time or order, or following as a direct result

conservation is the creation of the environment in which a work of art is properly preserved

conservatism's earliest meaning spoke more generally about a state of affairs remaining intact or unchanged

the term musical **conservatory** comes from an Italian word for a hospital for foundlings, to whom music was taught

conserve once meant "observe a custom or rite"

conserves are jams thick with citrus fruit and nuts, possibly coconut or raisins

consider's root is from Latin literally "to study with the influence of the stars; to cast a horoscope"

consign first meant "mark with the sign of the cross," coming from Latin *consignare*, "mark with a seal"—and now means to "put into a person's custody"

a **consilience** is a chance happening or coincidence

consist once meant "stand or remain firm"

consolate means "consoled, comforted"—the opposite of disconsolate

the Latin elements of **consolation** are *con*-"with" and *solari*, "soothe"

a **console** is a cabinet for controls and switches, as for an organ—or it is a cabinet for audio/visual equipment

consolidate is from Latin *con*, "together" and *solidare*, "make firm," from *solidus* "solid"

consommé (meat stock soup) is so called from its being the last goodness of the meat consumed or used up in the making of the soup

consonance first meant "correspondence of sounds in words or syllables"

consonant comes from Latin *consonans*, "sounding along with"; a **consonant** cannot be pronounced except in connection with a vowel

{ a **consort** is a husband or wife of a monarch }

the early sense of **consortium** was "partnership"

conspectable means obvious

a **conspectus** is a comprehensive mental survey

conspire first meant "combine in action or aim," from Latin literally "breathe together"

constable derives from Latin *comes stabuli* "count or officer of the stable"

a certainty or verification is a **constatation**; to **constate** is "to establish; ascertain"

constellation was first an astrological term, referring to the influence of planets and stars on events and personality

a paralyzing fear is **consternation**, from Latin that meant "lay prostrate; terrify"

Latin *stipare*, "cram, press," is the base of the word **constipate**

constipation is based on Latin elements meaning "press or cram together"

constitute can mean "make laws" and a **constitution** is a "how-to" document for a government or organization

constrain can mean "compel to do," "bring about by compulsion"

construct was generalized from "piling up together" as in stones to make a house, to meanings like "piling up words to make a sentence" or "a group of words forming a phrase"

construe first meant "to analyze the construction of a sentence" and "to explain the arrangement and meaning of words in a sentence"

consubstantial means "regarded as the same in substance or essence"—as of the three persons of the Trinity (Father, Son, Holy Ghost)

a **consuetude** is a social custom or convention

the first **consuls** were magistrates in either the Roman Republic or Roman Empire

a **consulate** is essentially a junior embassy

in **consult**, the -sult element is from Indo-European *sal-* or Sanskrit *sar-*, "go," becoming Latin *consulere*, "**consult**, discuss"

consume's original meaning was "destroy by fire or disease"

early uses of **consumer** had the general sense of destruction or waste

consumption, from the Latin root *consumere*, designated not only the use of things but also any type of removal and various forms of disposal

the disease one may read about in older literature called **consumption** is what we now call pulmonary phthisis

the underlying notion of **contact** is "touching," from Latin *tangere*, "touch"

diseases spread by contact are **contagious** and those spread by air or water are **infectious**

contain comes from Latin *tenere*, "hold" and then *continere*, "hold together, enclose"

contaminate seems to come from the base *tag-*, "touch," which became Latin *contagmen*, "contact," and then Latin *contamen*

conte is another word for adventure story

the base of **contemplate** and comtemplation is Latin *templum*, "open space for observation"

contemporary can be predicated of persons, conditions, or events; **contemporaneous** is predicable only of occurrences or events

contempt is a more engaged, more involved feeling of disapproval than **disdain**

contemptible means deserving contempt, while **contemptuous** means bestowing contempt; the first sense of **contemptuous** was "despising law and order"

{ **content** comes from the Latin plural *contenta*, "things contained" }

contentation is a contented condition

contentment first referred to payment of a claim which "satisfied" the obligation

conterminous is "sharing a common boundary"

contes are short tales of derring-do or adventure

the base of **contest** is "bearing witness," from Latin *contestari* (*com-*, "together" and *testari*, "bear witness") meaning "calling witnesses together" from both sides

contexture is the putting together of words or sentences in a connected whole or text

if something is hushed or quiet, it is **conticent**

contiguous implies having contact on all or most of one side

all the **continent** names begin and end with the same letter (if you count America as one **continent**); **continent** derives from Latin *terra continuens*, "continuous land"

continent is "able to control the bowels and bladder" or "exercising self-restraint"

contingent suggests the possibility of happening but stresses uncertainty and dependence on other future events for existence or occurrence

continually means "repeatedly, with breaks in between" and **continuously** means "without interruption, in an unbroken stream"; **continual** typically refers to time while **continuous** can refer to space as well as time

Latin *continere*, "hang together," begat *continuus*, "uninterrupted," then *continuare*, "make or be continuous" and eventually the English word **continue**

a **contour** line on a map passes through points of equal elevation or depth

contraband literally means "proclamation against," from Italian *contrabbando* (*contra*, "against" and *bando*, "proclamation")

contraception is from Latin *contra*, "against" and *conceptio*, "conception"; **contraceptive** is, literally, "against conception"

the words **contraconscientious** or **contraconscient** indicate something that is "against (one's) conscience"

the ultimate source of **contract** was Latin *contractus* (*com-*, "together" and *trahere*, "draw, pull")

a word shortened by omitting letters is a **contraction** ("won't" from "will not")

contradict is from Latin *contra dicere*, "speak against"

the cloud behind jets, **contrail**, is a word combining condensation and trail

contralto is the voice intermediate between soprano and tenor

a **contranym** (or contronym) is a word that can mean the opposite of itself; examples are aloha, bimonthly, bolt, bound, buckle, cheerio, cleave, commencement, dust, fast, give out, handicap, hold up, impregnable, left, overlook, put out, ravel, root, scan, screen, seed, shank, temper, trim, vital, weather, wind up

for a photo or portrait, when the chest and shoulders face one direction and the hips and legs go in another, that is **contrapposto**

contrivance and trap and invention combined to make the word **contraption**

a **contrary** is an adversary

contrary describes something that contradicts a proposition; **converse** is used when the elements of a proposition are reversed; **opposite** pertains to that which is diametrically opposed to a proposition; and **reverse** can mean each of those

if something is unusual for the time of year, it is **contra-seasonal**

contrast was first used as a term in fine art; on a TV or computer monitor, it is a control that increases or decreases the difference between the dark and light areas of the screen

contrectation is handling, fingering, or touching something

contretemps is from French meaning "against the time" or "out of time," indicating a misstep in a dance or a mistake is one's social rhythm

a **contribution** used to refer specifically to a tax or levy

to **contrist** means to sadden

contrite is "bruised, crushed" or "worn or broken by rubbing"

contrive was once controve, from Latin *contropare*, "represent metaphorically"

control first meant "to check or verify accounts" and referred to a duplicate or keeping a copy; a **control** is the standard comparison in a statistical analysis or scientific experiment

a **control character** is typed by depressing a key and the **control key** at the same time; the **control key** is the key on a computer keyboard that is used (in combination with some other key) to type control characters

{ to push, thrust, or crowd together is to **contrude** }

contubernal is a tentmate or a person you live with, as an intimate companion

the idea underlying **contumely** "insolence" is "swelling up," from Latin *contumelia* (*com-* and *tumere*, "swell")

contusion comes from Latin *com-* (intensive) and *tundere*, "beat, hit"

conundrum first meant "whim" and then "pun" and then its current sense of "puzzling problem"; the plural is **conundra**

a **conurbation** is a large urban area created by several contiguous areas that keep expanding (*con-* "together," *urb-* "city") the base of **convalesce** is Latin *valere*, "be strong, well"

convenience originally meant "suitability" or "commodiousness"

convenient comes from Latin *convenire*, "come together" or "be suitable, agree"

convent originally applied to a body of monks, friars, or nuns that lived together

a **convention** in card games is a pre-arranged method of play

conventional usually expresses the unfavorable senses of "artificial" or "formal" or "old-fashioned"

converge means "to approach as if to meet or join" but does not mean things have joined

conversant means "having familiarity through study or experience"

conversation once had meanings "intimacy, familiarity" and "living" or "way of life" as it came from Latin *conversari*, "keep company (with)"

> **converse** is a noun meaning "social communication"

convert into means to change from one thing to another; **convert to** means to switch allegiance, loyalty, or obligation

if terms are interchangeable or synonymous, they are **convertible**

a **convertite** is a reformed prostitute

convex (from Latin *convexus*, "arched, vaulted") refers to a surface that curves outward, **concave** (from Latin *concavus*, "hollow") to a surface that curves inward

to **convey** can mean "to steal"

convince started out meaning "overcome, conquer"

you **convince** someone to believe—but **persuade** someone to act

convolution originally meant a complex winding pattern such as those on the brain

great putdown names for stupid people are: **coof**, **dizzard**, **gomeril**, **gump**, **lobcock**, **loord**, and **mome**

cook came from popular Latin *cocus* from Latin *coquus*; to **cook** can mean "to falsify; concoct, make up"

cookie comes from Dutch *koekje*, a diminutive of *koek* "cake"

jazz music that is **cool** is "relaxed"

coolant, based on cool, was formed on the pattern of lubricant

coolth is a state of pleasantly low temperature

coomb can describe a deep hollow or valley

coop is based on Latin *cupa*, "barrel" and originally referred to a basket placed over fowl when sitting or being fattened (as in hen **coop**), hence the occupation of a cooper

a **coop** is a cage or enclosure; a **co-op** is a cooperative organization

a **co-op/cooperative** is a multiunit building that a corporation owns and leases units to its owners; a **condo/condominium** is a multiunit building with units owned by individuals

cooperation is always positive; **collaboration** is positive except in wartime (working with the enemy); and **collusion** is always negative (working together in secret for a dishonest purpose)

coordinate first meant "of the same rank" or "place in the same rank"

coot is a word for a silly person or simpleton

cootie may come from Malayan-Polynesian *kutu*, "louse, parasitic biting insect"

a cone-shaped roll of yarn or thread is a **cop**

the verb **cop**, "catch," may be from the obsolete **cap**, "arrest" from Latin *capere*, "seize"

to **cope** was "to come to blows" as it came from French *colper*, "to strike" your **copemate** is your partner, lover, or spouse

the top of a brick or stone wall is the **coping**

copious comes from Latin *copia*, "plenty" (as in cornucopia)

a sherry glass is called a **copita**

if you collect key rings, you are a **copoclephilist**

copper in ancient times was mainly found in Cyprus and gets its name (Latin *copreum* or *cypriumaes* "Cyprus metal") from the island's Cyprium/Cuprium; the Latin name for **copper** is *cuprum*, from which its chemical symbol Cu is derived

used and distributed on the condition that anything derived is bound by the same condition

copyright is, literally, "the right to reproduce" one's own work or authorize others to do so; **copyright** protects original artistic, literary, dramatic, musical, and intellectual work in a tangible medium

coquette first meant a strutting male fop, but it underwent a sex-change operation

coquina is a clam used for broth or chowder; its also the name broken shells used in road-making

the impregnated roe of lobster, which turns red when boiled, is called **coral**

{ a **corbel** is a projection of stone, brick, timber, iron, etc., jutting out from the face of a wall to support something }

---

a red nose from drunkenness is a **coppernose**

the notion behind **coppice** (dense growth of bushes) is of "cutting" and it comes from Greek *kolaphos*, "blow," which became Latin *colpare*, "cut"

copra is the dried meat of the coconut

coprolite, fossilized feces, is Greek, literally "dung" (*kopros*) "stone" (*lithos*)

a thicket of small trees is called a **copse**, **coppice**, or **arbustum**

a **copula** is a connecting word, especially forms of "be" linking a subject and complement

copulate first meant "join or link together"

copy is based on Latin *copia*, "abundance, plenty"

copyleft is an arrangement for artistic works or software in which they may be

a **cord** of wood should have 128 cubic feet of wood (4x4x8 feet) and the name comes from the old practice of measuring a stack of firewood with a **cord** of a certain length; to **cord** is to stack or put up wood in cords

cord comes from Greek *khorde*, "gut, string of a musical instrument" and **chord** is a refashioning of **cord**

cordate means heart-shaped

if a muscle is **corded**, it is tensed and standing out

cordial (literally "from the heart") translates (Latin *cordialis* from *cor(d-)*, "heart") to drinks that are "comforting" or "invigorating the heart"; a synonym of **cordial** is liqueur

cordovan used to be goatskin and now is horsehide—and it is named for Cordoba, Spain

a **corduroy** road is formed by tree trunks sawn lengthwise and laid transversely, creating a ribbed effect like **corduroy** fabric

corduroy, the fabric, may come from French *corde du roi* "the king's cord"

a **cordwainer** is an old term for shoemaker

the central strand of a rope is the **core**

a **corespondent** is a person charged with adultery

corgi is literally dwarf dog

coriaceous describes something leatherlike or leathery

coriander is the same as **cilantro**

cork, generally made from oak, derives from Latin *quercus*, "oak" or "**cork**-oak"

corked, said of wine, means tainted through reacting with the tannin in the cork of the bottle

if you are fretfully anxious, you are **corked**

the word **corker** is based on the idea of something so good that it settles a dispute so one can "put a cork in it"

corn derives from Old Teutonic *kurnom*, which is akin to Latin *granum*, "grain"; to American colonists, "**corn**" meant any common grain

a **cornel** is a corner or angle of a house

the underlying idea of **corner** is of a "projecting part" or "point," coming from Latin *cornu*, "point"

to **corner**, "buy up a stock," is from the idea that goods are piled and hidden in a **corner** out of sight

cornice is another word for picture molding and can also mean a decorative framework to conceal curtain fixtures at the top of a window casing

a **corniche** is a road that winds along a cliff or steep slope

cornucopia is a Latin form evolved from two words *cornu copiae*, "horn of plenty," and it was fabled to be the horn of the goat nymph Amalthaea, whose milk was fed to the baby Zeus in Greek mythology

corny derives from comedians playing to unsophisticated, "corn-fed" audiences in the Midwest

corolla is the most conspicuous part of a flower, the whorl of leaves or petals forming the inner envelope of the flower

in Latin, *corolla* was "little crown or garland," a diminutive form of *corona*, "crown" and Latin *corollarium* was "money paid for a little garland" and by extention, "gratuity," which became the word **corollary**

{ a **corona** can be a small circle of light around the sun or moon }

coronary comes from Latin *corona*, "garland, crown" and it was applied to anatomical structures like arteries that encircle others like a crown—with the main example being the heart with its encircling blood vessels

a **coroner** was once an official responsible for safeguarding the private property of the Crown (literally "guardian of the pleas of the Crown")

a **coronet** is a small crown and a **tiara** is a jeweled **coronet**

the **corporal** in the military came from "the head of a body of troops" (Latin *caporal*)

corporation derives from Latin *corporare*, "combine in one body," or *corporatus*, "formed into a body"; one's **corporation** is one's entire body of work

in legal use, **corporeal** describes physical property such as houses and cars

corpse originally meant a body or person, not one that was dead

to **corrade** is to gather together from various sources

corral is from Latin *currale*, "enclosure for carts"

correct comes from Latin *corrigere*, "make straight; amend"

correctitude is correctness of behavior with adherence to rules of etiquette

a **corrida** is a bullfight

corridor comes from an Italian word meaning "running place" as it runs from one place to another

a substance added to a medicine to counteract undesirable side effects is a **corrigent**

corrigible is "capable of being corrected or reformed"—the opposite of incorrigible

corroborate was first recorded in the sense "make physically stronger"

a **corroboree** is a large, noisy gathering

corrode comes from Latin *rodere*, "gnaw," and **corrosion** from *corrodere*, "gnaw through"

the muscles that contract the eyebrows when frowning are the **corrugators**

corrupt comes from Latin *corrumpere*, "destroy completely" and first meant "to destroy or spoil the flesh, fruit, or organic matter by dissolution or decomposition"

corsage first meant the bodice of a woman's dress and also can mean the body as distinct from the limbs

a **corsair** is a pirate or privateer operating in the Mediterranean

etymologically, a **corsair** is someone who goes on a "course," from Latin *currere*, "run" and it moved from meaning "expedition" to a "hostile expedition" to the plunder gotten from this

originally **corset** in Old French meant "little body" and was a close-fitting garment worn on the outside of other clothes in the Middle Ages

cortex is a Latin word meaning "bark"

to **coruscate** is to give forth intermittent or vibratory flashes of light, to shine with a quivering light—as light does between the trees as one drives along a road

a **corvée** is an unpleasant or unavoidable task or job

corvine means like a raven or crow, especially in color

{ a cluster of ivy berries or grapes is a **corymb** }

a **coryphaeus** is a leader of a party, sect, school of thought, etc. (from a Greek word meaning "chief")

coryza is a head cold

to make oneself cosy is to **cose**

a **cosh** is a small cottage or hut

co-sleeping is when parents allow a child to sleep in their bed

if something is merely decorative, it is **cosmetic**

cosmetics comes from Greek *kosmetikos*, "skilled in decorating" from *kosmein*, "arrange, adorn"

cosmolatry or **physitism** is the worship of nature

cosmology is the study of the world as a totality of all phenomena in space and time

a plant or animal found all over the world is **cosmopolitan**; for people, it literally means "citizen of the world"

a **cosmorama** is a display of scenes from different parts of the world

cosmos is from Greek *kosmos*, "order of world" and is often used to suggest an orderly or harmonious universe

cosset first pertained to a lamb brought up by hand, a pet lamb

cossis is a synonym for algebraic and is literally "unknown quantity in an equation"

a **costa** is a rib or riblike structure

cost-benefit refers to assessing the benefits of an undertaking in relation to its cost

cost-effective is anything effective and productive in relation to its cost

costermonger is, literally, apple dealer

a kinder word for constipation or causing constipation is **costive**

costume and **custom** were actually two forms of the same Latin root *consuetudinem*, "habit, **custom**," with **costume** first meaning "manners and customs belonging to a particular time and place"

when a cat sits with its body resting on the legs and its head raised, that is **couchant**

the same feline is called a **cougar**, **puma**, **mountain lion**, **panther**, **painter**, **catamount**, and **American lion**

cough is of onomatopoeic origin

could started as *cuthe* in Old English and by the sixteenth century the spelling had evolved and taked on an "l" to bring it in line with "would" and "should"

coulis is a thick fruit or vegetable purée (from French *couler*, "to flow")

 something that **costs** a particular amount literally "stands at or with" that price (Latin *constare*, "to be settled or fixed, stand at a price, **cost**")

cot is ultimately derived from Sanskrit *khatva*, "bedstead, couch, hammock," then Hindi *khat*, and was first a small cottage or humble dwelling

a **cote** is a shelter for birds or mammals

a **coterie**, from French, is literally "tenants holding land together" and now a circle of persons who associate with one another, as distinguished from "outsiders"; a **coterie** is also a group of prairie dogs occupying a communal burrow

cotillion is borrowed from French, meaning "petticoat," an object of apparel worn to such a formal ball

the Old English words for a small house or hut were *cot* and *cote* and they are probably the base of **cottage**

cotton is actually from Arabic *qutun*

cotyledon, the embryonic leaf of seed-bearing plants, is from Greek *kotuledon*, "cup-shaped cavity"

to **couch** can mean "to include in a list"

coulrophobia is the fear of clowns

council comes from Latin words meaning "summon" and "together"

counsel is "advice, guidance" and a **counsel** is a lawyer; a **council** is a deliberative body of people assembled for some purpose and members are councillors (especially in Britain)

count comes from Latin *computare*, "calculate"; the noble title of **count** comes from Old French *conte* from Latin *comes*, "attendant, companion" and when it came into English it was used to translate "earl," and countess was used for the wife of an earl

countenance is the face together with its expression—and the mood or character which is revealed; to **countenance** is to sanction or support

the **counter** on a shoe is the stiff piece of leather backing the heel

counterfeit once meant a legitimate copy

counterpane is a coverlet for a bed, such as a quilt or bedspread

when two people or things occupy comparable positions, they should be called **counterparts**

etymologically, the meaning of **country** is "surroundings" and it originated in Latin *contratus*, "lying on the opposite side" and *terra contrata* was "land opposite or before one, spread out around one"

country really refers to geographical characteristics while **nation** refers to political and social characteristics; **country** comes from Latin *contrata* (*terra*), "the landscape in front of one, the landscape lying opposite to the view" and **nation** is from Latin *nation/natio* "race, class of person"

county, acquired via Anglo-Norman *counte* from French *conté* "land belonging to a count," first meant a meeting held periodically to transact the business of a shire

coup was first a blow or stroke, from Greek *kolaphos*, "blow with the fist"

a **coupe** is defined as a closed, two-door, two-seat motor car and is short for French *carosse* **coupe** "shortened coach"

coupe is a shallow dish or glass with a stem, for serving champagne or dessert

the notion underlying **couple** is of "joining," coming from Latin *copula*, "connection, tie"

a **coupling** is a connection (like a clamp or vise) between two things so they move together

coupon is French for "piece cut off" and originally denoted a detachable portion of a bond to be given in return for payment of interest; **coupon** should be pronounced KOO-pon

courage comes from Latin *cor*, "heart" and denotes this as the seat of feelings

courbette is when a trained horse rears up and jumps forward on the hind legs

without the forelegs touching the ground (also called **curvet**)

courier is based on Latin *currere*, "to run"

etymologically, **course** denotes "running," from Latin *currere*, "run," and its earliest meaning was "onward movement in a particular direction"

court comes from Latin *cohors*, "enclosed yard" (the yard was the central point of a farm and its buildings, hence for other buildings, a town, etc.), which was extended to being a crowd assembled in such a yard and then "area enclosed by walls or buildings"

{ **courteous** first meant "having manners fit for a royal court" }

courtesan is another word for prostitute

couscous comes from an Arabic *kaskasa*, "to pound, grind small" as it is made from crushed durum wheat

cousin comes from Latin *consobrinus*, "mother's sister's child"

couth is a back-formation of uncouth

couther is to comfort with refreshment, remedies, and/or warmth

couturier literally in French is "one who sews" and couturière is "seamstress"

cove comes from Old English *cofa*, "small room" from a Germanic root *kubon* and came to mean "small hollow place in coastal rocks" and then "small bay"

a **coven** is a gathering of witches, especially thirteen of them

covenant's literal meaning is "coming together" from Latin *convenire*

coventry is a state of ostracism or exclusion from the society of one's fellows

cover utlimately comes from Latin *cooperire*, com- "completely" and *operire* "**cover**"

the **coverlet** is the uppermost covering of a bed—a bedspread or quilt

covert (concealed, covered, hidden) is the opposite of **overt** (apparent, open to view, plain, public)

covetousness and **cupidity** are etymologically and semantically related, coming from Latin *cupere*, "desire"

covey comes from French for the act of sitting on eggs to hatch them ("covering" them)

cowabunga may have been derived from an interjection used on the Howdy Doody Show for surprise and anger (kawaboŋga)

coward is literally French *cove*, "tail" (from Latin *cauda*, "tail") + *-ard*, "tail person," because a frightened animal "turns tail" or has its tail between its legs

cowl is the section of a car that holds the windshield and dashboard

the **cowlick** is presumably so-named because the hair looks as though it has been licked askew by a cow

cowslip, from Old English *cuslyppe*, literally was "cow dung" and came to be applied to the plant because it grew in cow pastures

the **coxcomb** is the cap worn by a professional fool

a **coxswain** was originally a servant (swain) whose job it was to steer a boat (cock or cockboat)

coy and **quiet** derive from Latin *quietus*, "at rest, in repose," with **coy** coming from the Old French form *coi* (earlier *quei*), and **quiet** coming straight from Latin; the original sense of **coy** was "**quiet**, still"

the **coyote** is also called a prairie wolf and **coyote** word is Spanish, from Nahuatl *koyotl*, "**coyote**" (actually pronounced KI-oat)

to **cozen** is to cheat, dupe, beguile, defraud

besides a tea **cozy**, there are egg **cozies**

crab comes from Old English *crabba* and Old Norse *krabbi*, "to scratch and claw"

crabby and **crabbed** derive from a crab's sideways movement and habit of snapping (thought to suggest a perverse or irritable nature)

{ **crack**, the drug, got its name because it crackles when you smoke it }

the "**crack**" of a whip is a miniature sonic boom as the tip breaks the sound barrier

crackerjack is from crack, "excellent" and jack, "man"

crackpot was originally "cracked pot"

a rest or support for a telephone receiver not in use is a **cradle**

craft started out meaning art or skill, ingenuity

cram comes from a Germanic base *kram-/krem-* which denoted "compression" or "bending" which begat Old English *crammian*, "press something into something else; stuff"

a **cramp** is a clamp with a movable part that can be tightened as a screw

cranberry was first crane berry, named this because the plant grows on a stalk that looks like a crane's neck

when you **crane** your neck, you are imitating the bird

crank was first a weaver's tool and it is related to *crincan*, "to bend"

cranky literally means "having a crooked temper"

cranny seems to come from Latin *crena*, "notched"

crap comes from Latin *crappa*, "chaff; residue"

if something, like a door, swings on top and bottom pivots, it is **crapaudine** the dice game **craps** was first called hazard and crab—or two aces—was the lowest throw at hazard, which may be how the game came to be renamed

crapula is a synonym for hangover and **crapulent** or **crapulous** mean "drunk"; words for feeling ill from overeating or drinking are **crapulent, crapulous, cropsick**

crapulence is the intestinal and cranial distress arising from intemperance and debauchery

the web of hairlike cracks in older oil paintings is **craquelure**

crash may have been created as an imitation of the sound of noisy breaking or may be a blend of craze and dash

crass means stupid and grossly ignorant, not just coarse or tasteless

crastin is the morrow or the day after

{ to **crastine** is to put off from day to day }

a fodder rack or trough is a **cratch, crib,** or **manger**

crate seems to have come from Latin *cratis*, "hurdle," but no explanation has related that meaning to "large case or box"

crater comes from Greek *krater*, "mixing bowl"

a **craton** is a large stable block of the earth's crust, forming the center of a continent

the **Croats** were called **Cravates** by the French and their neckerchiefs came to be known as **cravates** and then **cravats**

crave first meant "demand as a legal right"

craven originally meant simply "defeated" and gradually took on the pejorative sense of "cowardly," coming from Latin *crepare*, "creak, rattle"

to **crawfish** is to retreat from a position taken up, to "back out"

the data along the bottom of a television news station is **crawl**—which is also the term for the rolling credits after a television show or film

crayfish/crawfish is adapted from Old French *crevice*, "edible crustacean"; **crawfish**, like **crawdad**, is a corruption of **crayfish**

Crayola comes from French *craie*, "chalk" and *olea*, "oleaginous, oily" (as it is a wax crayon)

crayon derives from French *craie*, and earlier Latin *creta*, "chalk, clay"; in art, a **crayon** is any drawing material in stick form

craze was first a crack or flaw; to **craze** is to produce minute cracks on the surface of pottery

the cracks that form in the glaze of a piece of pottery are called **crazing**

crazy goes back to a Scandinavian word *krasa*, "broken"

many slang words for **crazy** end in -tty such as batty, dotty, nutty, potty, etc.

cream may come from Latin *cranum*, "**cream**" and *chrisma*, "ointment," which were probably blended to make Old French *cresme/craime*, which preceded English **cream**

creance is the mental action or condition of believing or faith

crease can mean to crumple, but it can also mean the opposite, to press—as with an iron

creative was coined in association with art, not with the divine

something's **crebity** is its frequency

crebrous means frequent

something is credible to the extent that it is worthy of belief, so that **credibility** is worthiness of belief; **credence** is an acknowledgment of such worthiness

credenda are the constituent elements of what forms your belief about something—or things to be believed

credenza, a buffet or sideboard, originally meant "belief or confidence" because a nobleman's meal was first placed on a sideboard or buffet and tasted by a servant. If the servant did not die, the food was believed to be safe.

credible means "believable" and **credulous** means "gullible"

creosote comes from Greek meaning "preserver of flesh"

crêpe derives from French and, earlier, Latin meaning "curled" or "frizzed, frizzled," i.e., **crêpe** paper

a **creperie** is a restaurant specializing in crepes

crepitation is the sounds of Rice Krispies cereal (snap, crackle, pop); **crepitate** or **crepitant** is "making a crackling sound"

 **creature** and **creator** predate the verb create, coming from Latin *creatus*, "produce"; **creature** is literally "that which is created"

creed comes from Latin *credo*, "I believe"

creek has the root sense "crooked waterway" (from Old Norse *kriki*, "crook, twist")

a fisherman's basket is a **creel**

creep has been traced to Indo-European *greub-*, and it was a common Teutonic strong verb

the board on wheels used for working under cars is a **creeper** or **cradle**

crema is the frothy topping on a dessert or an espresso coffee

cremains are the ashes of a cremated body

the **cremaster** is the muscle of the spermatic cord by which the testicle can be partially raised

a scum gathering on the top of a liquid is the **cremor**

the crease in the buttocks is the **crena**

a **crenelation** (from Latin *crena*, "notch") is a series of indentations or loopholes around the top of a castle, battlement, or wall—with each indentation being a **crenelle** (or crenel)

to **creolize** is to relax in an elegant fashion in a warm climate

crepitus is the breaking of wind

crepuscular is "of or like twilight"

crepusculum is the period of half-dark at the beginning or end of the day

crescendo is often mistakenly used to mean "reaching a pinnacle" when, in fact, it should be used only to describe a gradual increase in intensity or volume

crescent comes to English from Latin *crescere*, "grow"

crescive means "growing"

a **crest** (from Latin *crista*, "plume, tuft") was first erect feathers of a plume on a helmet or headdress

a wave's foamy top is its **crest**; spray blown up from wave tops is **spindrift**

crestfallen is an allusion to fighting cocks, whose crests fall in defeat and rise in victory

if someone is **cresty**, they are afflicted with hemorrhoids

cretaceous means "chalking," and the **Cretaceous** Period (about

146 to 65 million years ago) was when many chalk deposits were formed and flowering plants first appeared

cretin comes from the Swiss-French *creitin/crestin*, their version of Christian, and it was applied to mentally and physically handicapped people, to emphasize that despite their abnormalities, they were human beings like any other Christian

crevasse is a deep crack or opening, especially in a glacier or ice field; **crevice** is a narrow opening or fissure in a rock, wall, or floor

crew was originally the reinforcement or increase in a military force

the **crewcut** was first adopted by boat crews at Harvard and Yale universities

a cattle stall is a **crib**

cribration is sifting

the adjective form of hamster is **cricetine**

cricket, the insect, is from French *criquet* from *criquer*, "crackle" and is of imitative origin for its sound

cricket's (the game) name is derived from French *criquet*, "goal post, wicket"

crime is from Latin *crimen*, "judgment, accusation, offense" and a **crime** is an act in violation of a law; a **misdemeanor** is a less serious **crime** while a **felony** is a major **crime**

criminy is a mild old-fashioned euphemism for Christ

crimson comes from a Sanskrit word which had to do with the red color of an insect; **crimson** is a deep red, while **scarlet** is a bright red

cringe seems to come from the Germanic base *krank* with the original meaning of "bend" or "curl up," which produced Old English *crincan*, "yield" or "cause to curl up"

cringle-crangle is similar to zigzag

crinicultural means "of or pertaining to the growth or culture of hair"

crinite is another word for "hairy"; **crinosity** is hairiness, the state of being hairy

crinkum-crankum is an intricate or convoluted thing; an elaborate device

crinoline gets its name from a stiff fabric woven from horsehair and linen, from Latin *crinus*, "hair" and lino "flax"

{ a vehicle or ship unfit for service is a **cripple** }

crisic means pertaining to a crisis

crisis, from Greek *krisis*, "decision; turning point," in English first meant "the turning point of a disease" or "a vitally important or decisive stage or point"

a **crisp** is fruit sprinkled with streusel

crisp describes closely curled or frizzy hair

a slight contraction of a muscle—like the skin in goose-flesh—is **crispation**

crispature is a crisp or curled condition

the **crisper** is the part of the refrigerator for fruits and vegetables— a humidity compartment that allows more or less cold air in through small vents located by the slide control

the sign of the cross, sometimes marked as an X, was called the Christcross, which became slurred over time into "**crisscross**"

criterion comes from Greek *kriterion*, "means of judging"

critic and crisis both ultimately come from Greek *kritos*, "judge, discern" and then *kritikos*, "able to make judgments" and "one who makes judgments," which passed into Latin *criticus* and then to English **critic**

a **criticism** is an evaluation or judgment of something, while **critique** is a somewhat elevated term for the same thing; **review** is used as a synonym for these but may also imply a more comprehensive study

when water begins to freeze, it becomes rough on the surface, which is to **crizzle**

a crow **croaks** (so does a frog)

to **croak**, meaning "to die," is probably from the hoarse death rattle or **croak** of the expiring breath

a person who talks dismally or pessimistically is a **croaker**

crochet is from French "little hook" (diminutive of *croc*, "hook") which is what is used for such needlework

a **crock** was first an old ewe or old horse

crockery gets its name from the obsolete *crocker*, "potter"

a long line of children walking together is a **crocodile**

crocodile is based on Greek *krokodilos*, "worm of the stones"

a person who makes a hypocritical or malicious show of sorrow is a **crocodile** (as the **crocodile** was said to do in fable) and **crocodilian** is "treacherous; that feigns sorrow"

cromlech is Welsh for "arched stone" and means any "megalithic chamber tomb"

cromulent means "acceptable" or "legitimate"

a **crone** is a very old woman

crony was originally university slang, from Greek *khronios*, "long-lasting" and means "contemporary"

the low music of birds is **croodle**

to **croodle** is to cling to or nestle together, crouch down or snuggle, especially for warmth

a **crook**, "criminal," is literally a "bent" person, and first meant "crooked deed, piece of trickery," from Old Norse *krokr*, "hook, corner"

to **croosle** is to make a low, whimpering noise

a **crop** was originally the top or head of a plant—and these were gathered during the harvest and came to be the general name for what was collected

 a **cropper** is a severe misfortune or personal failure, and "come a **cropper**" means to suffer sudden misfortune or to fall heavily

crocodility is false reasoning

crocus takes its name from the Greek word for saffron as it has been used to make saffron since prehistoric times

a Viennese baker created croissants by copying the shape of the crescent Islamic symbol on the Turkish flag in 1683; the proper pronunciation of **croissant** is krwah-SSAHN and it can also be called a crescent

Cro-Magnon was the name of a hill in France with the cave in which the first skeletons of this type were found

croque-monsieur, literally French "sir muncher" or "bite man," is a grilled or toasted ham and cheese sandwich

Old Norse *krokr*, "hook," was borrowed into Old French as *croc* and formed the basis of the diminutive crochet "little hook" and **croquet**, a variant of French crochet, possibly for its mallets shaped like hockey sticks

croquette is a small cake of minced food usually coated in bread crumbs and deep-fried

to whine along with another person is to **crose**

the curled tip of a young fern is the **crosier**

the early use of **cross** was for a monument in that form and the adjective meant "transverse, lying across"—then "adverse," which led to "angry"

the X-shaped warning sign for a railroad is a **crossbuck**

the stick used in lacrosse is the **crosse**

the opposite of **cross-eyed** is **wall-eyed**

to **cross-index** is to index (a particular item) under more than one heading or to furnish (an index in a book, for example) with cross-references; to **cross-reference** is to place a reference from one part of a book, index, catalog, or file into another part containing related information

a **crosspatch** is constitutionally ill-natured and disagreeable

a drawing of a slice of something is a **cross-section**; a drawing with the casing removed is a **cutaway**; and a drawing with the parts separated out is an **exploded view**

to **cross-train** is to learn another skill, especially one related to one's current job

crostini, pieces of toasted or fried bread, is the Italian plural of crostino, "little crust"

crotch was first a fork or forked tool and came to mean a forked road, tree, or body area

a **crotchet** is a perverse belief or preference, usually about a trivial matter—or a quirk or eccentricity

a **croup** is an animal's rump, so a croupier is a person who stands behind or assists (riding on the **croup**)

crouton is from French croute, "crust or hunk"

the raven, rook, and jackdaw are all really crows—**crow** being the term for any bird in the genus Corvus, family Corvidae

crowbar gets its name from the two-pronged end that resembles the foot of a crow

the notion behind **crowd** is of "pushing, pressing," from Old English crudan, "press"

crowd-surfing is when someone is passed in a prone position over the heads of an audience, as at a rock concert

to **crowl** is to rumble or make sounds in the stomach

crown derives from Latin corona, "wreath"

a **crozier/crosier**, a bishop's crook, is from Old French crosse, "hooked stick"

crucial originally meant "cross-shaped"

the words **crucial**, **essential**, and **vital** cannot be qualified (cannot be more or less...)

 cruciation is another word for torment or torture

in Christian processions, the cross-bearer is the **crucifer**, the censer-bearer is the **thurifer**

cruciform is "shaped like a cross"

crucify comes from Latin cruci figere "fix to a cross" and **crucifix** comes from Latin crucifixus, "fixed to a cross"

crosswords are the most popular hobby on earth and a crossword maniac is a **cruciverbalist**

crude is from Latin crudus, "raw, rough"

crudites, mixed raw vegetables used as an hors d'oeuvres, is literally "rawness" from Latin crudus, "raw, unprocessed"

cruel and **crude** are linked etymologically by Latin crudus, "**cruel**," "raw, bloody"

a **cruellie** is a cruel joke or remark

cruet comes from Old French crue, "pot," borrowed from Old Saxon kruka—and it is a diminutive form and is related to crock

cruise probably comes from Dutch kruisen, "to cross"

cruller is from Danish *krulle-koken*, "rolled-up cake" (from *krul*, "curly")

the soft inner part of a bread roll, slice, or loaf is called the **crumb**

crumbs! is an expression of astonishment or dismay

crummy was first used to describe something desirable, or it meant "plump, well developed"

to **crump** is to eat with a muffled crunch or walk over snow-covered ground making a crunching noise

crompid cake may be the ancestor of **crumpet**, literally "curled-up cake"

the harsh cry of a bird is a **crunk**

to **crunkle** is to crinkle, rumple, or wrinkle

crural refers to the area between the knee and ankle

crusade was originally spelled croisade, from French literally meaning "state of being marked by the cross"

crust is from French *crouste* from Latin *crusta*, "rind, shell; incrustation"

crustaceans have a hard integument and Latin *crusta* means "rind, shell; crust"

crux originated as a reference to a real cross and its association with torment and trouble

cry comes via Old French *crier* from Latin *quiritare*, "call for the help of the Quirites" (those who held the rank of Roman citizen)

crypt is from Greek *kryptos*, "concealed"

cryptic comes from Greek *kryptikos*, "hidden"

cryptic coloration helps conceal an animal; phaneric coloration makes an animal stand out

the **cryptoclimate** is the climate within a small enclosed structure

cryptodynamic means "pertaining to or having hidden power"

a **cryptonym** is a code name or secret name

crystal from Greek *krustallos*, originally meant "ice" and it is, properly, **rock crystal**—describing ornamental pieces or items of crystallized quartz; fine **glass**, when cut or etched, is called **crystal**—but often there is no crystallized quartz but rather lead and it is properly called **lead crystal**

if you have an urge to look in the windows of the homes you pass, that's **crytoscopophilia**

C-SPAN stands for Cable Satellite Public Affairs Network

ctenoid means "resembling a thin-toothed comb"—as the scales of some fish

an extremely conservative person can be called a **cube**

cubical originally meant "bedroom" and **cubicular** means "pertaining ot the bedroom"

a **cubicle** was originally a small room for sleeping (Latin *cumb*, "lie down") that was separated from a larger room

cubit comes from Latin *cubitum*, "forearm" and it is a unit of length approximately equal to a forearm's length; **cubital** means "as long as the forearm"

cuckold is a derivative of cuckoo, the cuckoo's invasion of other birds' nests perhaps being viewed as analogous to the stealing of a wife's affections by another man

cuckoo has similar names in a variety of languages, possibly because they are all based on its call

 the **cuckquean** is the female counterpart of the cuckold

the adjective form for cuckoo is **cuculine**

Latin *cucumis*, "**cucumber**" is **cucumber**'s base

the etymological base of **cud** appears to be "glutinous substance"; **quid** "piece of tobacco for chewing" is a variant of **cud**

the word **cue** as in the billiards stick is related to **cue**/queue for long braid or pigtail

cuff first meant "glove or mitten"

the inflatable bag that is put around the arm when blood pressure is measured is the **cuff**

a **cuirass**, "breastplate" is literally and originally a piece of body armor made of leather, from Latin *coriaceus*, "made of leather," from *corium*, "leather"

cuisine is French for "kitchen" and first meant that or "a culinary establishment"

culch is rubbish or refuse (also meat scraps) and **quisquilian** means "consisting of trash or rubbish"

cul-de-sac is French, literally, "bottom of a sack," and it also means "situation from which there is no escape"; the plural of **cul-de-sac** is cul-de-sacs or culs-de-sac

a **culet** is a small face that forms the bottom of the facet of a gemstone

the **culex** is the common mosquito

culinary should be pronounced KYOO-luh-ner-ee, but many say KULL-uh-ner-ee (from Latin *culinarius*, "kitchen")

cull means "obtain from a variety of sources or an assortment" and "select either the best or worst in a batch of something"

cullet is recycled broken or waste glass that is used in glassmaking

if you are **culling** things, you are selecting inferior or surplus items

a **cullion** is a rude, mean-spirited person

a **cully** is a person who is easily duped, a simpleton

an individual cane or shoot of bamboo is a **culm**

culminate is to mark a high point, not just any result or outcome; **culminate**'s meaning

of "reach the top of a hill" was generalized to "reach a decisive point after struggling"

culottes is a divided skirt (French "knee breeches")

the legal term culpable prit. ("ready") was abbreviated to cul. prit. and then became **culprit**—a term of address to an accused person

cult comes from Latin *cultus*, "worship," from *colere*, "to cultivate" and was originally homage paid to a divine being

a **sect** is a rule defined by some doctrinal difference, a **cult** by allegiance to an idea or commanding personality

a **cultivar**, cultivated variety, is an organism resulting from cultivation

culturati are well-educated people who appreciate the arts

bacteria grown for experimentation is a **culture**

culture is acquired by study and application; **cultivation** is developed by training and exposure

cultured refers to people and pearls; **cultivated** refers to mind, tastes, speech, or behavior

a **culvert** is a drain or waterway under a road or embankment

to **cumber** is to overwhelm or rout or harass/trouble

cumbered is "benumbed; stiffened with cold"

cumber-ground is a person who needlessly takes up space, especially someone useless at their job

the Greek name for **cumin** became the English name for **caraway**

the wide waist sash worn with formalwear (tuxedo) is a **cummerbund**

cumshaw is another word for gift or tip (from Chinese, literally "grateful thanks")

cumulus means "cloud"; the plural is **cumuli** and the adjective is **cumulous**

cunctation is the habit or practice of delay or tardiness, also a synonym for procrastination

another word for procrastinator is **cunctator**

cunning is from Old Norse *kunnandi*, "knowledge, accomplishments"; like artful and crafty, **cunning** was originally a favorable word

{ if you tend to be tardy or are prone to delay, you are **cuntatious** }

the Age of Exploration brought hot drinks to the world, which created a need for bowl-shaped vessels called **cups**, from Sanskrit *kupa*, meaning "water well," and Latin *cupa* meaning "cask" or "tub"

cupboard was originally a "board" or table to place cups and other vessels (etc.) on or a piece of furniture for the display of plates, like a sideboard or buffet, then "a set of vessels for the table"; **cupboard** also can mean "clothes closet" or "wardrobe"

in Latin, the name of **cupid** was Cupidines, a personification of cupido, "desire, love" (from *cupere*, "to desire or long for") and **Cupid** was the Roman god of love; **cupidity** is inordinate desire or covetousness

cupola generally refers to a small domed structure

the cuplike base of an acorn is the **cupule**

curator comes from Latin *curare*, "care for"

the chain or strap under the lower jaw of a horse and attached to the bit is the **curb**

the edible head of broccoli or cauliflower is the **curd**

curdle was once cruddle

curds are the coagulated semisolid residue of milk and **whey** is the thin watery remains of cheese-making

cure first meant "anxiety, concern" or "care, heed"

curfew comes from French *coeverfu/cuevre-fu* "cover the fire" from the medieval regulation of the time by which fires had to be extinguished in the evening, which was indicated by the ringing of a bell

the shock felt when one first plunges into cold water is **curglaff**

strange subject matter is **curiosa**

curious has the obsolete meanings of "careful, studious; attentive" and "carefully made; excellent" (from Latin *curiosus*, "careful" from *cura*, "care")

curl is a disease of plants in which the leaves or shoots are curled up and not developed perfectly

curmudgeon is probably related to *cur*, "to growl"

curple is a synonym for buttocks

currant developed from Middle English *raison of Corauntz* "a raisin of Corinth" from where the fruit came

currency is so called because it is money flowing as a medium of exchange (from Latin *currere*, "to run")

a **current** event is one flowing or passing during the present period of time (from Latin *currere*, "to run")

curricle, from Latin *curriculum*, is the running or course of one continuous thing or several consecutive things

curriculum is a complete course of study offered by a school; **syllabus** is the outline of a single course

curry can mean "to brush a horse" or "to dress (tanned) leather"

curriculum, from Latin *currer* "to run" evolved into "to run a course" and then to the full slate of courses offered for study

curry is from Tamil *kari*, "sauce"—as it first meant spicy sauce for wheat cakes or rice

curse first was an utterance of God or other deity

to **cursitate** is to flit, run here and there

cursive comes from Latin *currere*, "to run" and it means running hand, writing in which the pen is not raised after each character

cursor first meant "runner" or "running messenger" and now it is the moving/movable indicator on a computer screen

cursory means "superficial"; **cursorial** is "pertaining or adapted to running"

curt is from Latin *curtus*, "abridged, cut short"

curtail meant "horse with a docked tail" and comes from Latin *curtus*, "cut off, shortened"

curtailment is the removal of the last letter of a word to leave another word (goon becoming goo)

a **curtain-lecture** is a scolding given by a wife to her husband in bed

curtate means "shortened, reduced" or "comparatively short in time"

a widower's use of his deceased wife's property when they have had children is known as **curtesy**

curve is from Latin *curvus*, "curved" and Greek *kurtos*, "curved"

curvulate means "slightly curved"

a **curwhibble** is another word for thingamajig

cushion is ultimately from Latin *coxa*, "hip, thigh"

cushy comes from Urdu *kushi*, "pleasure" (from Persian *kus*)

the transitional period from one zodiac sign to the next is the **cusp**

cuspidor is Portuguese for "spitter"

cuss is a variant of curse and it first referred to a detestable or obstinate person

custard was first an open pie (French *crouste*, "crust") with meat or fruit in thickened sweetened milk or broth—now it is thickened sweetened sauce; early spellings were crustarde and custarde

custom comes ultimately from Latin *consuescere*, *com-* and *suescere*, "become accustomed"

early on, **customer** was the word for a customary tenant or a collector of customs

cute is actually a shortened form of "acute" meaning "keenly perceptive, shrewd"

the waxy layer covering a leaf is the **cuticle**

dead skin at the base of a nail is the **cuticle** (diminutive of Latin *cutis*, "skin"); a piece of torn skin beside a nail is a **hangnail** or agnail

cutlery includes knives but there is no association with "cut," rather being from Old French *coutelier*, "cutler's art" from *coutel*, "knife"

cutlet is not based on "cut" but rather on Latin *costa*, "rib" which later became French *cùtelette*, "little rib piece"

the caption beneath or beside a newspaper photograph is the **cutline**

the **cutwater** is the most forward part of a ship

cutlass has no etymological connection with cut but rather comes from Latin *cultellus*, a diminutive of culter "knife"

a fair-haired, brown-eyed individual is a **cyanope** and a fair-haired blue-eyed person is a **glaucope**

cybernetics was coined in French as *cybernetique* in the 1830s but meant "art of governing" and in English it came to mean "theory of control and communication processes"—something founded in the late 1940s by mathematician Norbert Wiener

a **cyborg** is a human who has received mechanical implants that he/she controls with his/her brain; the term stands for cybernetic organism

cycle is from Greek *kuklos*, "wheel"

a single to-and-fro movement of an air particle is called a **cycle** and the number of cycles that occur in a second is known as the **frequency** of a sound

cyclical is pronounced SY-kli-kuhl

cyclone probably comes from Greek words meaning "circle eye"; it is the general term for a storm that can be called, depending on features and where it occurs, a hurricane, typhoon, or tornado

not quite a manic-depressive but with tendencies in that direction is a **cyclothyme**

cygnet is literally a "small swan" from Latin *cygnus*, "swan"

the adjective form of swan is **cygnine**

cylinder derives from Greek *kulindein*, "to roll"

the notion underlying **cymbal** is of "hollow vessel" from Greek *kumbe*, "bowl, cup" through Latin *cymbalum* to French *cimbal*, "metal plate struck to make noise"

cyme is the unopened head of a plant

cynics doubt because they question motives (**Cynic** was first a school of philosophy expressing contempt for wealth and pleasure; the word **cynic** comes from Greek *cyniko*, "doglike"); skeptics doubt reports of what they hear or read

a **cynologist** is a dog trainer

cynophobia is the morbid fear of dogs

a **cynosure** is an admired person or thing, the focus of attention; the base of **cynosure** is "dog's tail"—referring to the star called Polaris (North Star), a reference point for mariners

cypress foliage is a symbol of mourning

cyst derives from Greek *kustis*, "bladder"

czar, which came through Polish, Russian, Old Slavic, Gothic, and Greek—goes back to Latin, *Caesar*

{ the letter **D** is from the shape of a doorway or archway }

dachshund in German means "badger hound" from its original breeding purpose to pursue a badger (etc.) that has taken refuge in a burrow

dacity is a word to describe ability, activity, capacity, or energy

your **dactyls** are your toes

display the **dactylion** is the same as giving someone the finger

counting on your fingers is **dactylonomy** and a **dactylogram** is a fingerprint

to **dad** is to beat one thing against another

a **dado** is a section of a pedestal between the top and the base—or it is the lower part of the wall of a room

any intricate, cunningly formed object can be called **daedal**

The early Spring flower, **daffodil**, is a variant of affodill, borrowed from Latin *affodillus* and *asphodelus*, from Greek *asphodelos*. The initial added "d" has not been explained, but could be related to the d' or *de*, "the" in French. This flower is also playfully called the daffadilly. Though the **daffodil** was originally the asphodel, there was some controversy among

botanists and the affodil was designated as part of the Asphodel species and the **daffodil** as part of the Narcissus but, later, affodil was changed to asfodyl/asphodel to finalize the distinction. What we now call the **daffodil** is the Yellow Narcissus.

daft first meant "mild and meek" before it meant "crazy and silly"

a **dag** is a portion of a serrated edge

dag, a pointed implement, was probably the root of the word **dagger**

a **dagwood** is an enormous multilayered sandwich—after **Dagwood** Bumstead, a character who made such sandwiches in the comic strip Blondie by M.B. "Chic" Young(1901–1973)

the **dahlia** was named for Swedish botanist Andreas Dahl (1751–1789)

a **daibutsu** is a giant Buddha in Japan

the original sense of **dainty** was "substantial and able," a reversal of the current sense

daiquiri comes from **Daiquiri**, Cuba

dairy, first spelled deierie, came from *deie*, "dairymaid" which was *daege*, "female servant" in Old English; originally, **dairy** was applied to a female breadmaker

dais and **disc** come from Latin *discus*, "quoit" or "table"

daisy—from "day's eye" or "eye of the day" is so named because it closes its ray in the evening to conceal its yellow disk and opens again in the morning

Dakota is a Native American name for the Sioux meaning "allies, friends"

a **dale** is a broad valley

danger's origin goes back to Latin *domnus, dominus*, "lord, master" and it first meant "power of a lord or master" and "power to harm or injure"

dangle would be considered an imitative word

dangwallet means "abundantly, excessively, plentifully"

what we call **Danish** is called Vienna bread in Denmark

dank may come from Swedish **dank** "mushy spot" or Icelandic *dokk/danku* "pit, pool"

the bounce of a ball or the skip of a stone on water is a **dap**; a **dap** is also a bait made to bob lightly on water's surface

a **dam** is a rubber sheet used to keepsaliva from the teeth during a dental operation

a horse's mother is a **dam**; the father is a **sire**

damage comes from Latin *damnum*, "**damage**, loss"

Latin *domina* came through Old French to give us **dame** and it is also the source of **damsel**

damn is from Latin *damnum*, "loss,injury," *damnare*, "to inflict damage or loss upon"

damp (the noun) first meant "vapor, steam" or "smoke"—especially that was harmful or noxious

the **damper** is the movable plate adjusting airflow in a fireplace or furnace or stove flue

dandelion means "tooth of the lion" from French, because of the leaves' jagged edges

to bounce a baby on one's knee is to **dandle**

it is said that **dang**, a euphemism for damn, is a blend of damn and hang

dapper experienced an ironical change of meaning from "heavy" to "neat and lively"

dapple is any roundish spots or small blotches of coloring on a surface, as a horse

dare goes back to Greek *tharsein*, "be bold"

daredevil is a contraction of "someone ready to dare the devil"

a day's work is a **darg** and dirty work is **glorg**

daring implies fearlessness in courting danger

the application of **dark** to colors did not occur till the Sixteenth century; before that it denoted the absence of light

darling derives from "dear"

darn ("to mend") comes from Dutch *dernen*, "stop holes (in a dike)"

dart is from French/Frankish for "lance, spear"

dash is probably of Scandinavian origin, in imitation of rapid violent movement

the stick used in a churn is the **dash** or **dasher**

dashboard dates to horse-and-buggy days when a board was installed on the front of the carriage to deflect mud of dashing horses

dasypodid is pertaining to armadillos

dasypygal means "having hairy buttocks"

strictly speaking, **data** is the plural of **datum** and should be used with a plural verb, but in American English it is now acceptable as an uncountable noun followed by a singular verb; **data** started out meaning "things given or granted"

date (the fruit) takes its name from Latin *dactylus*, "finger" as people believed this fruit resembled the human finger

dation is the act of giving something, like a dose of medicine

daub comes from Latin *dealbare* meaning "whiten, whitewash plaster"

Daughter is a very old English word, first recorded c 1000 as *dohtor*. It descends from Old English and is related to words in many other Indo-European languages, such as Greek *thugater*. The modern spelling **daughter** was first used in a sixteenth-century Bible and was popularized by Shakespeare. The word "son" is quite a bit older, found in Beowulf in 645. It also descends from Old English and is related to words in many other Indo-European languages, such as Greek *huios*.

daunt comes from a Latin word meaning "to tame"

davenport was first a small writing desk, probably named for the manufacturer

davering is riding or walking in a dazed condition

a **davit** is the shipboard crane used for raising and lowering lifeboats or the anchor

to **daw** is to awaken and to be dawed is to be fully awakened from a deep sleep

daw, meaning "to **dawn**," was the base of **dawning**—and **dawn** is a back-formation of **dawning**

any of the perpendicular divisions or "lights" of a mullioned window are the **days**

{ **daylight** is the light seen between the wine and the rim of a wineglass }

a person's **daylights** are their vital organs, though originally the term referred to the eyes

an anxiety attack during the day is a **daymare**

dayspring is an early stage of any promising development or the first appearance of light in the morning

daze is from Old Norse and first meant "exhausted from cold or exertion"

dazzle first had to do with the result of gazing at too bright a light

D-Day actually means "day day"—as redundancy was common in military correspondence referring to a top-secret time

the prefix **de-** can mean 1) down, down from, down to; aside, away, off; completely, thoroughly; to exhaustion, 2) over again, repeatedly; formed from; or 3) denoting removal or reversal

to remove an item from a museum collection is to **deaccession** it

deacon comes from Greek *diakonos*, "servant"

to **deacon** is to arrange or pack fruit so that the best specimens are on top

dead cat bounce is a slang term for an apparent recovery from a major decline in stock prices resulting from speculators rebuying stock that they previously sold rather than from a genuine upturn in the market—an allusion to free-fall descent and then a brief rally—if you threw a dead cat off a 50-story building, it might bounce when it hit the sidewalk, but you would not confuse that bounce with renewed life; it is still a dead cat

in the U.S. Civil War, a beat was a soldier who shirked duty and a **deadbeat** was one who shirked duty by faking illness or injury

a **deadfall** is a type of trap in which a large weight falls and kills or disables the prey

to **deadhead** is to complete a trip in an empty truck (or other commercial vehicle); a pilot traveling as a passenger or in the cockpit to an airport for an assignment is **deadheading**, and an empty aircraft or truck is a **deadhead**

a **deadlight** is a skylight that cannot be opened

deadline is a Civil War term for a line that marked the distance a prisoner could go before being shot on sight

a **deadlock** was first a lock with no spring catch

in **deadpan**, pan means "face"

deadstock is agricultural machinery, as opposed to livestock

deal first meant a part, portion, or division of a whole

dean comes from Latin decanum," chief of a group of ten," and Greek dekanos, "a monk or dignitary in charge of ten others"

dear is one of the English language's more semantically stable words

dearth means "scarcity," not complete lack

to **deasil** is to travel in the direction of the sun

deasil means clockwise (toward the right) and **widdershins** means counterclockwise

death means "act or process of dying"— much the same as birth and strength were formed

debacle comes from French debacler, "to unbar, free" with the root sense being "to shatter with one's rod"; its original meaning was "a breaking-up of ice in a river" or a "sudden flood or rush of water carrying debris"

debar means to bar from a place or prevent from exercising a right; **disbar** means to expel from the bar or legal profession

to **debark** a dog is to deprive it of its ability to bark

to **debarrass** is to disembarrass or disencumber from anything that embarrasses

{ **debate** is from Latin de-, "down, completely" and battere, "to fight, beat" }

debauch first meant "to turn or lead away, entice, seduce, from one's master or spouse"

debellation is the process of conquering or defeating

debenture is from Latin debentur, "there are due"

debility comes from Latin debilis, "weak," and has no connection with the word ability

debitage in archaeology is the waste material from stone tool-making and is literally in French, "cutting of stone"

debonair comes from Old French "de bonne aire" meaning "of good disposition"

to **debord** is said of a body of water that overflows or goes beyond its margins

to **debouch** is "to issue or emerge from a narrower into a wider place or space"

debris comes from French de- and briser, "break"

debt is based on Latin debere, "owe"

billiards gave us the word **debut**, derived from French débuter "to make the first stroke in billiards, to lead off the game"

a **debut** is a first public appearance; a **premiere** is a first performance, showing, or broadcast

decade first meant "each of ten books or parts of a single literary work"

decadence is from Latin *decadentia*, "a falling away" (from *decadere*, "to fall away")

decadescent is beginning or tending to decay

decal is an abbreviation of decalcomania, the process of transferring pictures from special paper onto glass or ceramic surfaces" (from French décalquer "transfer a tracing")

decant means to pour wine, taking pains not to disturb any sediment at the bottom; **decant** comes from Latin *de-* + *canthus*, "angular lip of a jug"

the underlying notion of **decay** and **decadence** is of "falling off" from a condition of health—both going back to Latin decidere

decease actually means "departure from life," from Latin *decessus*, "departure"

etymologically, to **deceive** someone is to "catch, ensnare" them (from Latin *decipere*, "ensnare, take in")

December was originally so named because it was the tenth month in the Roman calendar, derived from Latin *decem*, "ten"

decent ultimately comes from Latin *decere*, "be fitting, suitable"

deceptious means "tending to deceive"

decibel is literally one-tenth of a bel, a unit of sound intensity

the base of **decide** is Latin *decidere*, "cut off, determine"

{ **deciduous** derives from Latin *deciduus*, "falling down" }

decimal is from Latin *decimus*, "tenth" from *decem*, "ten"

decimate means "to destroy in part," not entirely; the literal and original sense of **decimate** was "put to death one person in ten"

decipher can also be spelled decypher and it first meant "discover, find out"; a synonym is **decrypt**

to **deck** implies adding something that contributes to gaiety, showiness, or splendor

to **declaim** is "to speak aloud in an impassioned oratorical manner"

to **declare** in horse racing is to withdraw from a race

the sinking of the sun toward its setting is the **decline**

one **declines** (or accepts) something that is offered; one **refuses** (or agrees) to accept something offered

declivity is a fancy name for a downward slope

decoction is the process of boiling a substance in water to extract its essence or boiling a substance down or away

décolletage is from French *decolleter*, "expose the neck"

deconstruct was coined in 1973 to describe analyzing and interpreting a text as proposed by French philosopher Jacques Derrida

decorate suggests relieving plainness or monotony by adding beauty through color or design

the word **decoration** comes from Latin *decorationem*, from *decorare*, "to adorn or beautify"

decorticate means "to remove the bark, husk, or other outer layer"

decoy, derived from a Dutch word for "cage" was originally a place, a netted area of a lake into which game birds were lured for capture

decrease literally means "ungrow" (Latin *decrescere*)

the base of **decrepit** is Latin *crepare*, "creak, rattle"

decry is literally to "cry down," i.e. "denounce, condemn"

decubation means lying down

decubitus and **decumbent** mean "reclining, lying down"; your position in bed is your **decubitus**

decumbiture is the act of going to bed when sick

to be **decussate** is to have an X shape or to have leaves arranged oppositely in pairs

dedans are the spectators at a tennis match

deduce first meant "to lead" (from Latin *ducere*, "to lead")

etymologically, a **deed** is "that which is done"

the only word in English that consists of two letters used three times is **deeded**

deely-bobber was originally a U.S. proprietary name for a construction toy with interlocking parts

deep/depth is the same pattern as **long/length**

deep and **dip** come from the Germanic base d(e)up- "**deep**, hollow"

deep-dish can mean "extreme" or "thoroughgoing"—as in "she's a **deep-dish** Jets fan"

deep-fry means to fry food in an amount of fat or oil sufficient to cover it completely (-deep)

deepies is another name for 3-D movies

the adjective **deepmusing** means "contemplative, lost in thought"

to be **deep-read** means to be "skilled from extensive reading; erudite"

originally, the general word for animal was "**deer**"—which was displaced by "beast" in the thirteenth century, and later by "animal" in the fourteenth century

a Sherlock Holmes hat is a **deerstalker** and his coat with detachable cape is an **Inverness**

defalcation is the misappropriation of funds by someone entrusted with them

defatigable is "apt to or capable of being wearied"

default first had to do with lack or deficiency—then failure

etymologically, to **defeat** someone is to "undo" them, from Latin *disfacere*

something's **defeature** is its undoing or ruin

defecate first meant "purify, clear from impurities or dregs"

the fend in **defend**, from Latin *defendre*, "ward off," survives only in compound forms like offend

defenestration is the act of throwing someone out the window (French *fenestra*, "window")

defer is from Latin *differre*, "to carry apart, delay"

defervescence is a cooling down

deficient comes from Latin *deficere*, "fail, be lacking"

defile is an alteration of defoul, "to trample down, to tread on"

define comes from *de-* "completely, thoroughly" and *finire*, "finish," and first meant "bring to an end, settle"—hence, **definite**

a dictionary definition or statement of meaning is the **definiens** and the **definiendum** is the headword or the word or phrase to be defined

definite means "precise and unmistakable," "clear, sharply delineated"; **definitive** means "final and conclusive," "complete, final, ultimate"—so a **definitive** example is a perfect example

a fancy word for "runny nose" is **defluxion**

in **defray**, *de-* means "reverse" and *frai* is French for "cost, expenses"

deft originally meant "gentle, meek"

a synonym for dead person is a **defunct** and **defunction** is death

defuse means to remove a fuse, usually from an explosive

defy first meant "renounce faith" and it comes from Latin *dis-*, and *fidus*, "faithful"

dégagé means "casual or easygoing"

to **degenerate** means "to decline in value, move lower on a scale" but to **deteriorate** means "to worsen, to become lowered, or be reduced in value"; **degenerate** pertains more to character and virtue while **deteriorate** is more about loss of strength or vitality

deglutition is the act of swallowing

degree comes from Latin *de-* and *gradus*, "step"; a rung of a ladder or a step on a flight of steps is a **degree**

degressive means "reducing by gradual amounts"

dégringolade is a rapid descent or deterioration from bad to worse; as a verb, it means "to fall and disintegrate"

to **degust** is to taste carefully or appreciate fully

dehisce is to burst or gape open

the antonym of exhort is **dehort**—to discourage someone from a course or purpose

a **deictic** word like "yesterday" or "here" can be determined only by considering its context of use; a **nondeictic** word like horse has a meaning which it has regardless of the context

the base of **deign** is Latin *dignus*, "worthy"

if you are skilled at table talk, you are a **deipnosophist**

learned conversation conducted while dining is **deisidaimonia**

deity comes from Latin *deus*, "god"

to take an oath is to **dejerate**

a late breakfast can be called a **dejeuner**

deke is a shortened form of decoy

to **delaminate** is to separate into layers

delassation is fatigue or tiredness

to accuse or inform on someone concerning an offense is to **delate**

an accuser and informer is a **delator**

Delaware was named for colonial governor Lord de la Warr

various things may cause a **delay**, but a **postponement** will result from the action of a person

the simplification of an organization's hierarchy is **delayering**

the proof correction mark for deletion is a **deleatur**

delectation is another word for pleasure or enjoyment

delegate is based on Latin *legare*, "send on a commission"

a **delegation** differs from a **legation** in that the members of a **delegation** are usually not charged with a specific mission but merely with the overall task of representing the interests of a body of people, often at a conference during an assembly's regular session; a **legate** usually acts alone while a **delegate** acts as part of a group

deleterious is based on a Greek word for "noxious"

deletitious means pertaining to erasing

delibation is a taste or sip

deliberate comes from Latin *deliberare*, "consider carefully" from *de*, "down" and *librare*, "weigh" (*libra*, "scales")

delicate's first senses were "delightful," "elegant," or "nice"

delicatessen is literally "delicate eating, good things to eat" in German, from French *delicat*, "delicacy"

to **deliciate** is to make yourself happy or to indulge

delicious has the underlying meaning of "tempting, luring from the straight and narrow," from Latin *delicia*, "delight"

delight is from French *delitier* from Latin *delectare*, "to charm" and the change in spelling to "gh" was patterned on words like "light"

delightful is more general than **delectable** which describes a sensual experience

deligible means "worthy to be chosen"

delinquent is, literally, "completely having left" one's duty or obligation

delirious, from Latin *de-* "out of, away from" and *lira*, "a furrow, track," first meant "away from the furrow" and was applied to farm animals that would not obey commands to plow; **delirium** is "out of the furrow," referring to a reeling plow

{ **deliver** comes from Latin *de-* "away" and *liberare*, "liberate, set free" }

a **dell** is a small, secluded valley

delphic means "ambiguous, confusing; obscure in meaning"

the adjective form for dolphin is **delphine**

delphinium is Greek (*delfinium*) for "little dolphin" because the nectary/spur is shaped like the marine mammal

delta, as in river-mouth island, is named for its resemblance to the Greek letter

deltiology is collecting or studying postcards

the root of **delude** is Latin *ludere*, "play" and it first meant "play with under the pretense of seriousness"

deluged is best pronounced DELL-youjd

delushious is something that is delicious and luscious

deluxe, once two words, is French for "of luxury"

originally, **demagogue** was a popular leader, not a derogatory term

demagoguery or **demagogy** are the practices or rhetoric of a demagogue

the Latin base of **demand** is *mandare*, "to commission or order"

demean first meant "drive on (animals) with threats"

demeanor comes from the obsolete verb demean, "behave"

demerara is a kind of brown crystallized sugar named after a river in Guyana

demerlayk is a word for the practice of magic and occult arts or the practice of juggling

a fish that is **demersal** lives close to the floor of the sea or a lake

demesne, **domain**, and **dominion** come from Latin *dominicus*, "of a lord"

hemi-, "half," comes from Greek, **semi-**, "half," comes from Latin, and **demi-**, "half," also comes from Latin; they all appear together in hemidemisemiquaver "sixty-fourth note"

demi-island or **demi-isle** are synonyms for **peninsula**

a narrow-necked bottle with wicker basket woven around it is a **demijohn**

demise means death, not decline

to **demit** is to relinquish an office or function

demitoilet means semiformal dress

demiurge is the creator of a world, real or imaginary

a woman who behaves licentiously while remaining a virgin is a **demi-vierge** ("half virgin")

demo- in demography, democracy, etc., is "people"

democracy is derived from Greek for "power or rule by the people" and **democrat** first indicated an opponent of the aristocrats of the French Revolution of 1790 and the word is patterned on aristocrat

a **democracy** is confined to a small spot while a **republic** is extended over a large region

demurral is the act of taking exception

den's origin are words that mean "low ground" or "threshing floor," and **den** first meant the lair or habitat of an animal

the reading of tree rings for dating purposes is **dendrochronology**

to **denegate** is to deny or refuse

denigrate (from Latin *de-* + *nigare*, "blacken") first meant + "make black or dark in color" and came to mean "blacken the reputation of"

denim was first a type of serge (fabric) produced in Nimes, France—serge de Nimes—the last two words coming together to form the English word

denizen originates from Latin *de intus*, "from within" and *ñein* (assimilated to citizen); a foreign word which has become naturalized is a **denizen**

{ the **denominator** in a fraction is the part below the horizontal line (called the **separatrix**) and the **numerator** is above the line }

a **Democrat** is a member of the political party; a **democrat** is one who supports democracy

a **Democrat** was once a **Republican**—as the party was first the Democratic-**Republican** Party before "**Republican**" was dropped in 1828

demolish comes from Latin *de-* and *moliri*, "construct"

demon comes from Greek *daimon*, "divine power, fate"

a medicine that is **demulcent** relieves inflammation or irritation

demur is the verb "to object or voice opposition" while **demure** is the adjective meaning "modest, shy"

a word's **denotation** is its reference to the things it designates, its direct, explicit meaning; a word's **connotation** is things or attributes that the word brings to mind, any idea or notion suggested or associated with the word

denouement is French literally "untying" and it is the unraveling of the complications of a plot, the final part of a story, play, or movie when things are explained and resolved; also, **denouement** is the climax of any chain of events

denounce (from Latin *denuntiare*) first meant "give official information" and "declare, proclaim"

dent as in "notch" comes from the French word for tooth; **dent**'s original meaning was "blow, stroke" in general

dens/dentem, "tooth" in Latin give us **dental**, dentist, etc.

the **dentary** is the bone of the lower jaw that bears the teeth

dentifrice, another word for "toothpaste," is from Latin *dent-*, "tooth" and *fricare*, "to rub"

dentiscalp is a fancy word for toothpick

dentist was borrowed from French *dentiste* and was first considered a highfalutin' term

deny comes from Latin *de-*, "completely" and *negare*, "say no, refuse"

a **deodorant** neutralizes or masks body odors; an **antiperspirant** includes cosmetic chemical(s) to inhibit perspiration

to **deosculate** is to kiss affectionately

The etymology of **depart** starts with its initial use being restricted to wedding ceremonies to mean "separate" in the expression, "till death us **depart**." So, at first, **depart** meant "separate into two or more parts" or "part thoroughly." Later, the verb became obsolete and was analyzed as do and part, hence the changed expression "till death do us part."

department has an obsolete sense of "departure"

if something is **depascent**, it is consuming

{ **depend** first meant "hang down, be suspended from," as an icicle }

depend is invoked when the expectation is that the person will provide something that need not involve physical activity, whereas **rely** is used when the person is needed to physically do something

dependent's meaning of "hanging from something" was generalized to "supported financially by someone else"

depict first meant "represent in colors"

to **depilate** is to remove the hair from; if something is **depilatory**, it removes hair

you may **deplore** a thing but not a person

deploy, based on Latin *plicare*, "fold," first meant "display, unfold"

to **depone** is to swear under oath or testify

the earliest sense of **deport** was "bear with; refrain"

depository and **repository** are basically synonymous, but there are special senses like a bank's (night) **depository** and a sepulchre as a **repository**

depot can mean "act of depositing"

depraved means "morally bad or corrupt"

to **deprecate** can mean to pray for deliverance from evil, to make prayer or supplication to—but it can also mean "to express disapproval of, to disparage"

the base of **depreciate** is Latin *pretium*, "price"

depredation is robbery, pillaging, plundering

deprehension is "catching in the act" or detection

something that depresses is a **depriment**

depth from deep is the same pattern as length from long

deputy is from Latin *deputare*, "assign, allot"

to **deracinate** is "to pluck or tear up by the roots" (Latin *racine*, "root")

range in **derange** is from French *rang*, meaning "rank"—which gives the meaning "disturb the arrangement or order"

Derby, a city and county in England, gave its name to cheese and porcelain; the race and hat were named for the Twelfth Earl of **Derby** who founded an annual race at Epsom, England

derelict comes from Latin *de-*, "completely" and *relinquere*, "leave, forsake"

deride is from Latin *de-*, "completely" and *ridere*, "laugh at"

derivation is the process through which new words are formed by adding a prefix, suffix, or other word element to an existing word, or by which complex words are formed from less complex ones

a **derivative**, word formed from another such as electricity from electric, may also be called paronyms and conjugates if the root is shared (like beautiful and beauteous, foul and filth)

derive first meant "conduct (water or another fluid) from a source; channel; drain" and comes from Latin *de-*, and *rivus*, "brook, stream"

dermagraphism and **passion purpura** are the giving of love bites or hickeys

the patterns on the palms of your hands and soles of your feet are **dermatoglyphics**

the **dermis** is also called the true skin and it forms the bulk of the thickness of the skin

derogate means "to destroy or impair the authority of" and "to detract from; dispar-age," hence **derogatory**

derrick first denoted a hangman and the gallows itself—and is derived from the last name of a London hangman

derring-do is from Middle English *dorry-ing do*, "daring to do"

{ **dervish** comes from Persian *darvesh*, "religious mendicant" }

descant is an additional melody sung above the principal melody (from *des-*, "two; apart" + *cant*, literally "second song")

descend's base meaning is "climb down," from Latin *scandere*, "climb"; it should be pronounced di-SENT

to **describe** something is to literally "write it down"

descript means "described; inscribed"—the opposite of **nondescript**

to **descry** is to cry out, announce, proclaim

desert is from Latin *desertum*, "something left to waste" and implies that the object left may be weakened but not destroyed by one's absence

that impoverished stretch of sand called a **desert** can only afford one "S"; that rich gooey extra thing at the end of the meal called a **dessert** indulges in two of them

deserve is from Latin *deservire*, "serve well or enthusiastically"

desiccate has the Latin base *siccare*, "make dry"

do you **desiderate**?—feel that something is missing, regret the absence of something, or feel a keen wish to have something?

desiderium is a feeling of deep yearning or loss

design was first a plan or scheme

a **desinence** is an ending, or inflection, of a word

desipience is another word for silliness

a fancy way to say "silly, trifling, foolish" is **desipient**

desire literally began as "to examine the stars carefully"—based on Roman beliefs in astrology

desition is "ending" or "termination of being"

desk may be based on Provençal *desc(a)*, "basket" or Italian *desco*, "butcher's block" or "table"

despair is literally "lack of hope"

the act of despising is **despisal**

to be **despiteous** is to be full of contempt or ill will

to **despoil** is to strip of possessions through violence

despond is from Latin *despondere*, "lose heart"

the ultimate source of **despot** is Greek *despotes*, "lord"

dessert comes from a French word that means "clear the table" as it is the course served at the end of a meal

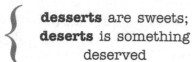

{ **desserts** are sweets; **deserts** is something deserved }

etymologically, one's **destiny** is that which has been firmly established or determined for one, as if by fate

destroy is literally "to unbuild"

depriving of sugar is **desucration**

desuetude is a state of disuse

desultory ("flitting, wavering") is from the days of the Roman circus, from *desultor*, "a circus horse-leaper"

detail comes from French *de-*, "removal" and *tailler*, "cut in pieces," and means "to relate or describe minutely"

to **detail** a car is to touch it up and polish it to conceal flaws

detain first meant "be ill or infirm"

detect originally meant "uncover" and "expose"

the root sense of **detective** is "one who strips (others) bare"

détente is an "easing of tensions" and **entente** means "understanding"

deter is from *de-* and *terrere*, "frighten" and it means to restrain or discourage by use of fear, doubt, etc.

detergent, **detergency**, and **deterge** come from Latin *de-* and *tergere*, "wipe"

deteriorate's meaning lies in the first syllable *de-* "down," that became *deter-*, "bad," then *deterior*, "worse"

determine is based on Latin *de-*, "completely" and *terminare*, "set bounds to"

a **determiner** is a word that limits or indicates the scope of a noun

detest originally meant "to bear witness against"

one would tend to **detest** someone for behavior, **despise** someone for character

detonate is from Latin *detonare*, "thunder down, cause to explode"

detract derives from Latin *trahere*, "draw"

detriment denotes damage caused by "wearing away"

detritus originally meant "wearing away by rubbing"—the action, not the product; now **detritus** is rubble or debris and **detrition** is erosion by friction

Detroit should be pronounced di-TROYT

detumescence is the subsiding of swelling

deuce in tennis comes from French *à deux*, "at two," which signifies that a player must score two successive points to win a game

deuterogamy is one's second marriage

devastate is Latin *de-* "completely" and *vastare*, "lay waste"

to **develop** is to bring a piece in chess into position for effective use

develop is from *dis-* and *voloper*, "envelop" and first meant "unfold, unfurl, unroll" or "uncover"; **development** was based on the root sense of unfolding, unrolling

device first meant "desire, intent" or "inclination, will"

devil is from Greek *diabolos*, "accuser, slanderer"

to **devil** means to cook with peppery hot condiments—and deviled eggs are sprinkled with paprika

the literal meaning of **devious** is "out of the way," from Latin *de via*—applied to a place that was remote because it was off the main road

devise first meant "distribute, divide"

devolution is a passing down from stage to stage or the passing of property, rights, or authority from one person to another—and implies moving backward

the literal sense of **devolve** is "to roll down"

{ **devout** and **devote** come from Latin *de-* and *vovere*, "promise" }

dew can be traced back to the Indo-European base *dheu-*

dewfall is the time of evening when dew begins to form

the **dewlap** is the loose fold of skin below the throat in cattle, dogs, etc.

though **dexterous** (skillful with the hands) is preferably spelled with two e's, **ambidextrous** has only one

dextrous/dexterous is from Latin *dexter*, "on the right side," "skillful," and originally meant right-handed

dharma means "something established; decree, custom" from Sanskskrit

dhyana is meditation upon a single object

diabetes in Greek is literally "siphon," from *diabaino*, "go through" or "passing through"—and it is marked by excessive production of urine

diabolic is based on Latin *diabolus*, "devil"

diachronic, "through time" in Greek, is that which is concerned with historical development, especially of a language

diacritic, from Greek *diakrinein*, "distinguish from" denotes marks or signs that distinguish different values or sounds (pronunciation) of a letter

a **diadem** (jeweled headdress) was originally something bound around someone's head (Greek *dia-*, "across" and *dein*, "bind")

diadromous fishes migrate between fresh and salt waters

diagnose developed from diagnostic, from Greek meaning "the art of distinguishing diseases" (*diagignoskein*, "to distinguish, to discern"); the disease is diagnosed, not the patient

a **diagnosis** is the process of identifying or determining the nature of a diseased condition or the conclusion reached; a **prognosis** is a prediction of the probable course of a disease or likely outcome of a problem

diagonal comes from Greek *diagonios*, "from angle to angle"

the first meanings of **dial** were as a mariner's or miner's compass—and then as a timepiece or part of a timepiece

a **dialect** is geographical or social variety of speech, whereas **dialectic** is a form of reasoning or argumentation that focuses on resolving contradictions

dialect is formed from Greek *dia-* and *legein*, "speak" (which meant "discourse" or "conversation") and **dialogue** is from *dialogos*, "conversation, discourse"

the underlying meaning of **dialysis** (separation of particles in a liquid to purify it) is "undoing" or "loosening"

diameter is from Greek meaning "measure through" (a circle or sphere, etc.)

diamond is from Latin *adamans*, from Greek *adamas*, "invincible," and adamant was the name of the hardest stone or mineral of the time—and the word **diamond** developed from that word (*a-*, "not" and *daman*, "to tame")

diapason, "a grand swelling harmony," is literally "through all (notes)"

diaper is from the Greek word *diaspros*, "pure white"; **diaper** was originally a textile with a pattern of small diamonds

the process of imitating stained glass by means of transparent colored paper is **diaphanie**

diaphanous can mean transparent or translucent; light mist is **diaphanous** since things may be seen at least faintly through it

a low-pitched, grunting fog signal is a **diaphone**

the flexible corridor between railroad passenger cars is the **diaphragm**

diaresis (two dots over a letter) is used to show that a vowel is sounded separately and **diaresis** is based on a Greek word for "separation"

diarrhea is made of Greek elements *dia*, "through" and *rhein*, "to flow"

diary can mean "lasting for one day" or "ephemeral"

diary and **journal**, which are synonyms, also come from the same Latin word *dies*, "day"

a **diaskeuast** is an editor or reviser of works

diaspora (pronounced die-AS-puh-ruh) literally means "the scattering of seeds" and is derived from Greek *dia*, "over" and *speiro*, "to sow" and its most well-known use describes Jews living outside of Palestine

{ a **diastema** is a gap between a person's two upper front teeth }

damning with faint praise is **diasyrm**

diatribe originally meant "learned discourse or disquisition" from Greek **diatribe** "that which passes the time" or "study"

a **dibble** is a pointed gardening tool for making holes in the ground for planting bulbs

to **dibble** means "to drink like a duck," lifting up the head after each sip

dibs may come from the old game dibstones in which **Dibs**! was yelled, meaning "I claim"

historically, **dice** is the plural of die—but in modern English, **dice** is the singular and plural; **dice** are often called **bones** because in play they are rattled together and sound like castanets—and castanets were once made of **bones**

dickens as an interjectional expression signifying astonishment, impatience, or irritation is not related to the surname of Charles **Dickens**, the novelist; it is probably a euphemism for deuce or devil; what the **dickens** was first in Shakespeare's "The Merry Wives of Windsor"

dicker can be a noun for articles exchanged in barter or any deal made

dickey was originally a detachable shirt-front worn by men (Dick) only

dict, now **dictum**, meant "maxim, saying"; to dict is to put into words

a female dictator is a **dictatress**

diction first meant simply "word" or "phrase"

dictionary is based on Latin *dictio(n-)*, "mode of expression" or "word," then di*ctionarius*, "a repertory of words or phrases"

the word **dictionary** was first recorded in 1526; though there were some 642 books known as dictionaries in print before 1746, the standard was, at best, questionable

didactics is the art or science of teaching

one who disappears and then pops up again is a **didapper**

to **didder** or **dither** is to tremble or shake

diddledees are fallen pine needles

diddler—a cheat or swindler—probably came from Jeremy Diddles, a character in the farce "Raising the Wind," who constantly borrowed small sums of money

diddly-squat was originally doodly-squat

a **dido** is a prank or antic; to **dido** is to play pranks

didy is how you spell the slang word for diaper

die, "stop living," probably came from Old Norse *deyja*, "**die**"

the **diegesis** is the narrative or plot

diesel gets its name from Rudolph **Diesel** (1858–1913), a German engineer

diet comes from Greek *diaita*, "a way of life, mode of living"

{ **different** is from Latin *differre*, "carry apart, separate" }

different is from Latin *differre*, "carry apart, separate"

difficult is a back-formation from difficulty—from Latin *dis-*, "reversal" and *facultas*, "ability, opportunity"

diffident comes from the older verb *diffide*, "lack confidence (in)"

diffract comes from Latin meaning "break in pieces"

diffuse is based on Latin *diffundere*, "pour out" (*fundere*, "pour") and means "to spread out"

dig was first a tool for digging

digamy is a second marriage, **trigamy** a third, and **quadrigamy**, a fourth

Latin *digesta*, "matters methodically arranged" (from *di-* and *gerere*, "bear, carry") gave us **digest**, with the root sense of the verb being "separate into basic elements"

a **digestif** is an alcoholic drink taken to aid digestion

the extent of the occultation of a partial eclipse is measured in digits—a **digit** is half the apparent diameter of the Sun or Moon

to **digitate** is to speak with the fingers

digitigrade is tiptoeing or on tiptoes

a silent machine for piano practicing is a **digitorium**

the first nine numerals are called **digits** from the habit of counting them on the fingers (Latin *digitus*, "finger")

digladiation is verbal wrangling

dignity can be a synonym for **dignitary**

a distinguishing mark or sign can be called a **dignotion**

digress is *di-* "away from" and *gradus*, "step"

digs, as in lodging, is a colloquial term—possibly related to the gold rush diggings

an arbitrary command is called a **diktat** or **ukase**

to tear or rip something or someone to shreds is to **dilacerate** or **dilaniate**

dilapidate, adopted from Latin *dilapidare*, literally meant "to scatter, as throwing stones," as *lapidem* meant "stone"

dilapidated literally means "to have stones missing from"

to **dilate** is to write or speak about at great length

dilatory means "slow to act" or "delaying, causing delay"

a **dilemma** (from Greek meaning *di-*, "twice" and *lemma*, "premise") is a specific type of problem, one that presents a person with two equally balanced courses of action, either one usually entailing unwanted consequences

a **dilettante** (plural dilettanti or dilettantes) is a person who cultivates an area of interest—but without commitment or knowledge (from Italian, literally "person loving the arts") and first meant "devoted amateur" or "one with love of a subject"

the underlying meaning of **diligent** is "loving" from Latin *diligere*, "love, esteem highly"

an old name for **dill**, the herb, was **anet**

dilly, meaning an excellent example of something, is an alteration of delightful or delicious

{ a **dimble** or **dingle** is a deep and shady dell or hollow }

dime meant "one tenth" until it became the name of a coin

dimension derives from Latin *di-* and *metiri*, "measure"

a **dimication** is a contest or fight

dimidiate means to divide into half (or something divided in half)

dimidiation is the process of dividing in half

diminish is a blend of *diminue*, "speak disparagingly" and *minish*, "reduce in amount, degree, influence, power"

A **diminutive** is a word denoting something small or endearing of its kind. There are many words denoting a smaller or affectionate version of an original (e.g. auntie, sonny, starlet). Diminutiveness is sometimes contained in etymologies and is not evident to those using the words (e.g. catkin, originally "little cat"). Examples of diminutives are cigarette from cigar, rivulet from river, and princeling from prince. Diminutives are also formed by the addition of a combining forms like mini-.

Diminutive words can be literal or metaphorical, are often terms of endearment or affection, familiarity or intimacy, but sometimes also suggest condescension or dismissal. The contrasting word form is "**augmentative**," whose general meaning is "large," often implying awkwardness or ugliness. An example is "up" in eat up, hurry up. Augmentatives are common in Latinate languages. In English, **augmentative** words are generally formed by the addition of **augmentative** affixes.

dimissory means giving permission to go

dimple first meant "hollow in the ground" before "hollow in the cheek"

dimpse is the dimming of daylight

din is ancient and traceable to Indo-European *dhun-*, "loud noise"

dine and **dinner** come from French *désner*, from *desjeuner*, "to break a fast"; in Middle English **dinner** meant "breakfast" or "first big meal of the day"

dinful means "noisy"

a **dinge** is a depression in the surface of something, caused by a blow; to **dinge** is to make such an impression

dinghy comes from Hindi *dingi*, the diminutive form of *dinga*, "boat, sloop"

to **dingle** is to ring

another word for whoozit or whatsisname is **dinglefuzzie**

a **dingo** is a wild Australian dog

a **dingus**, "doodad," gets it name from Dutch *ding*, "thing" and a **dinglet** is a "small thing"; a **dingus** is something one cannot or does not wish to specifically name

dingy derived from Old English *dynge*, "dung, manured land"

dinner is the main meal of the day, and **supper** is the last meal of the day and lighter than **dinner**

dinosaur, Greek *deinos*, + *sauros*, means "terrible lizard"

dinosaurs named for head features include: corythosaurus (helmet), dilophosaurus (two-ridged), ornatotholus (ornate), pachyrhinosaurus (thick-nosed), pentaceratops (five-horned), saurolophus (crested), triceratops (three-horned)

diocese is based on Greek words meaning "administer, keep house" (*oikos*, "house")

the act of putting straight or in order is **diorthosis**

in **diphtheria**, a false membrane forms and obstructs breathing; the term was based on Greek *diphthera*, "piece of leather"

diphthong (pronounced DIF-thawng) is from Greek *di-*, "twice" and *phthongus*, "sound, voice"; there is actually a **monophthong** and a **triphthong** also

diploma is Latin/Greek for "folded paper" and originally meant an official state document

diplomacy is from diplomatic and diplomat is a back-formation of diplomatic—all patterned on aristocrat, aristocratic

dirt comes from Old Norse *drit* and first meant "excrement, feces"

the prefix **dis-** from disrespect actually became a word itself, **dis**, "to show disrespect toward"

some of the earliest uses of **disability** (sixteenth–seventeenth centuries) are related to law and contract rather than to physical impairment

disappoint originally meant "remove from a post or office"

disarray can mean "to undress"

disastrous is literally "ill-starred" (*dis-*, "bad" and *astrum*, "star")

> **disaster** is from Italian *disastro*, literally "ill-starred event" and was first "the influence of an unlucky planet or evil star"

diplomat is Greek for "folded twice," as a person dealing in secret matters needed to take this precaution with documents

diplopia is another word for "double vision"

dipsomania is an insatiable desire for alcoholic beverages

a **dipstick** is a graduated rod dipped into a container to indicate the fluid level, as for the oil in an automobile

direct is based on Latin *regere*, "put straight" or "rule"

dirge (song for the dead) is an anglicization of Latin *dirigere*, "direct, guide"

a double six-sided pyramid whose faces are identical isosceles triangles is a **dirhombohedron**

dirigent means "guiding, directive"

dirigible was originally an adjective meaning "capable of being directed; steerable"

dirndl is short for German **dirndl** *kleid*, "young woman's dress" or "peasant dress"

to **disbosom** is to reveal or confess

to **disburse** means to pay out or expend; to **disperse** is to scatter something

the **disc** is the central part of the flower of a daisy or other composite plant

some make a distinction between **disks**—magnetic media like floppy disks and hard disks—and **discs**, optical media like CD-ROMs and DVDs

discard first meant "throw out or reject a card from a hand"

discern was once spelled *decern*

discerp is to shred or tear something apart

discharge is the process of removing the color from a fabric

disciple comes from a Latin word meaning "learner," and **discipline** from one meaning "instruction, knowledge"

disclose once meant "to open, to hatch"

disco in Latin means "I learn"

a **discography** is a list of musical recordings by a person or group

discoid pertains to something flat and circular

discolored can mean "colorless"

discomfit is from Latin *discomficere*, "destroy, undo"

discord is literally "severance of hearts," from Latin *discordia* (cord "heart")

{ **discotheque** is French originally meaning "record library" }

discount is from Latin *dis-* and *computare*, "count, compute"

discourage literally means "deprive of courage"

discourse derives from Latin *discursus*, "running to and fro" and its meanings move from "thought" to speech in its various forms and thence to a sustained conversation or text, sometimes with a didactic orientation; the corresponding adjective is **discursive** and means "rambling, digressive" or "proceedings by reasoning or argument"

The word **discover** goes back to Latin *dis-* and *cooperire*, meaning "to remove the covering; completely uncover." By 1553, it was used to mean "seeing or gaining knowledge of something previously unknown" and "finding out; bringing to light." You **discover** ("uncover") something that is already there, something that has existed but is generally unknown—but you **invent** something that has never existed before.

discreet means "judicious, prudent, showing discernment," while **discrete** means "detached, separate" and "individually distinct"

discrepant is from *dis-* and *crepare* (Latin), "to creak, be discordant"

discrepate means "differ from" or "distinguish between"

discretionary income or excess income is what is left over after bills for home, food, clothes, etc.—that with which one has the freedom to decide how to spend

discriminal pertains to the line on the palm between the hand and the arm

a person confined to bed is **discumbent**

one meaning of **discursion** is "the action of running or moving to and fro"

discuss comes from Latin *discutere* first meaning "dash to pieces," then "investigate"

disdain is based on *de-* and *dignare*, "deign," literally "deign (unworthy)"

disease originally meant "uneasiness; annoyance"

disedifying speech or action is that which shocks or disturbs (morally or religiously)

to **disembogue** is to discharge or pour out, as from a river

in **disgruntled**, *dis-* means "twice" and *gruntle* is "grunt (complain) repeatedly"—hence, "double gruntled"

the earliest meaning of **disguise** (from Old French *desguisier*) was "change one's usual style of dress"

disgust is, literally, "have no taste for," "have strong distaste for"

dish is a more general term and **plate** is more specialized

dishabille and **discinct** mean "loosely dressed or partly undressed"

to **disheir** is to deprive of an heir, to stop a lineage

dishevelled is based on *dis-*, "not" and Old French *cheval*, "hair," and the first meaning was "wearing nothing on the head"

disinflation means the rate of inflation is going down and prices are rising but at a slower pace; **deflation** means that prices are going down—which is negative inflation

disinformation is that which is deliberately misleading

if you are **disinterested**, you have no stake in the outcome of an event and you are impartial—but if you are **uninterested**, you simply don't care; **disinterested** is "impartial, neutral," and **uninterested** is "bored, lacking interest"

a word contrasting elements or giving a choice between possibilities in a sentence is a **disjunctive**

disks are the layers of cartilage and pulp between vertebrae

in the military sense, **dislodge** means "leave a place of encampment"

dismal comes from French *dies mali*, "evil days" and first meant the 24 evil or unlucky days of the medieval calendar (two per month)

dismantle is Latin *dis-* and *manteler*, "fortify"

dismay is from Latin *dismagare*, "deprive of power"

dismiss has the Latin base *mittere*, "send"

disorganized means "not properly planned and controlled; (of a person) unable to plan one's activities efficiently"; **unorganized** means "not organized"

disparage as a noun can mean "inequality of rank in marriage"

disparity means "a great difference"

dispatch is from an Italian or Spanish word meaning "expedite"

dispel, "to drive away," is based on Latin *dis-* and *pellere*, "to drive"

dispense is ultimately from Latin *dispendere*, "weigh out"

if something is **displaced**, it has been shifted from its customary place; if something is **misplaced**, it has been lost or taken or has wandered off

displacement or **ellipsis** is when one word absorbs part or all of the meaning of

another word with which it is linked in a phrase—usually adjective-noun—for example contact(s) from contact lens(es)

display first meant "to unfold," coming from Latin *dis-* and *plicare*, "fold"

displode means "burst with a noise"

disport is any diversion from serious duties

a discussion may be called **disputatious**, and so may a subject about which people disagree, but normally we use the word to describe individuals

dispute first meant "logical argument"

a **disquisition** is a diligent or systematic search, a thorough investigation or research

disrupt first meant "break apart, separate forcibly"

only a person can be **dissatisfied** while an abstract thing can be **unsatisfied** (hunger)

the opposite of save is **dissave**; **dissaving** is spending more than one has earned

{ to **dissect** language is to parse it—as analyzing the structure of a sentence }

dissemble means to conceal, to give a false appearance; **disassemble** means to take apart

dissensus is widespread dissent

dissent is, literally, "feel or think differently" and **dissident** means "sit apart, disagree"

dissertation is from Latin literally "continue to discuss"; to **dissert** is to discuss or examine

to **dissimulate** is to pretend not to see

the figurative meaning of **dissipate** is to dispel care, fear, doubt, or anything compared to clouds or darkness

if something is **dissolute**, it is completely relaxed to the point of being feeble or weak

distaff is based on *dis*, "bunch of flax" and it first was a staff on which wool or flax was wound for spinning

the counter to the female "**distaff-side**" is the male "**spear-side**"; in medieval times, the distaff was a rod used to hold wool during weaving—and it became a symbol of the values of a woman's work

distant and **distance** have the Latin base *stare*, "stand" and *dis-*, "apart"

distemper is from *dis-*, "reversal" and *temperare*, "mingle in proper proportion"

distill first meant to trickle down or fall in minute drops, from Latin *de-* and *stilla*, "a drop"

distinct means something stands out—while **distinctive** implies that an attribute or quality make something recognizable or distinguishable

distort first meant "twist to one side"

distract derives from Latin *trahere*, "drag, draw" and *dis-*, "away"

a **distracter** or **distractor** is one of the incorrect answers presented as a choice in a multiple-choice test

distrait means "absent-minded as a result of apprehension, worry, etc." while **distraught** means "agitated" and "bewildered, distracted"

material that is aged artificially is **distressed**

district originally meant "compelled, seized," from Latin *districtus*

to **distrust** is to suspect someone is dishonest; to **mistrust** is to merely lack confidence in someone

to **dither** is to be indecisive

a poem, song, or speech delivered in an impassioned manner is a **dithyramb**

ditionary means "under rule or dominion; subject," and the noun means "subject; one who is under rule"

ditransitive means that a verb can take an indirect object as well as a direct object

to **dittify** is to turn into a ditty

ditto is from Italian *detto*, "said, aforesaid, spoken," and is abbreviated do, or expressed by two dots or commas or a dash

a **dittology** is a double reading or interpretation

diuturnal means lasting

diva is Italian, literally "goddess"

divan comes from Persian *diwan* meaning "anthology, register" and "court, bench" and as furniture it was originally a low bench or raised section of floor against a wall

dive originally was any establishment one would reach by descending into a building's depths

something that is **divellent** causes things to separate or come apart

divergent means steadily moving farther apart

divers has the meaning "several, many, various," while **diverse** has the meaning "different, unlike, variegated"; **diverse** derived from **divers** and was influenced by adverse and perverse

if someone is looking for trouble or an argument, they are **diversivolent**

a **diversory** is a place of shelter along the way, a temporary lodging place

divert is literally "to turn aside" from a course or direction

disturb is based on Latin *turba*, "tumult," and **disturb** applies better to physical agitation and **perturb** to mental agitation

divertissement is a diversion or entertainment as well as a short ballet—from French for "ballet interlude"

the base of **divide** is Latin *videre*, "separate" and *dis-*, "apart"

a **dividend** can be a portion or share of anything divided

divine is from an Indo-European root *deiwos* that probably meant "shining"

divining is any of a number of methods to discover, explain, or interpret what is hidden, obscure, or unintelligible

the **division** symbol ÷ is called an **obelus**

if something is **divulgate**, it is published

divulge is from Latin *dis-*, "widely" and *vulgare*, "make common"

divvy first meant "extremely pleasant" and can be a synonym for divine or heavenly

Dixie may be a corruption of dix/dixes, the name of a banknote issued by Citizen's Bank of Louisiana in the 1830s—and the famous song actually first said, "I wish I was in the land of the dixes"

a **dixit** is an utterance

dizzy first meant "foolish, stupid"

Djibouti was formerly Afars and Issas

DNA is the prime constituent of chromosomes and it controls the hereditary characteristics and synthesis of proteins within the cells of virtually all living beings; **RNA** is a complex nucleic acid in cells that is involved in the synthesis of protein

do is ancient and goes back to Indo-European *dhe-*, "place, put"

to **doattee** is to nod the head when sleep comes on while one is sitting

the float of a fishing line is the **dobber**—which is also the name of a large marble

dobbin is a general or familiar name for any horse, a diminutive of the proper name Dob, which is a variation of Robin and Robert

Dobermanns are named for German dog breeder Ludwig **Dobermann**; **pinscher** means "terrier" in German

docent comes from Latin *docere*, "to teach"; **docible** is "capable of learning" and **docile** first meant "teachable," and **doctor** in Latin means "teacher"

docity is the ability to learn quickly

dock as "deduct" originates from the cutting short of an animals tail, which was later generalized

a **dock** is the water next to a **wharf** or **pier** and it is not a solid thing, a **wharf** is built along and parallel to the shore, while a **pier** runs out and away from or at a right angle to the shore; **dock** was first a "natural hollow or creek where a ship could stay at low water"

the word **doctor** is derived from Latin *doctus*, "having been taught; learned" (from *docere*, "to teach"); **physician** comes from Latin *physica*, "natural science; physics"

a **doctress** or **doctrix** is a female doctor

doctrinaire describes a person or an attitude based on a particular set of ideas that are absurd or undesirable

another name for a textbook is **doctrinal**

doctrine, **novice**, **office** changed from a religious context to more general, secular meanings

{ **document** first meant "instruction" or "evidence," whether written or not }

an easy task is a **doddle**

a lot of people refer to **dodgeball** when they really mean **bombardment**—two teams squaring off from opposite sides of the gym and unable to cross the center line; **dodgeball** is a game with a circle of attackers and the victims in the middle

dodo comes from Portuguese *doudo*, "fool, simpleton" from the bird's awkward appearance

doff, "remove," is a contraction of "do off," and **don** is a contraction of "do on"

dog first appeared with the more specific meaning of "a powerful breed of **dog**," and **dog** did not replace the word hound until the sixteenth century

dogfall is a draw or tie

dogged originally meant "malicious, spiteful"—anything that had the bad qualities of a dog

doggerel is loosely styled verse with an irregular rhythm, usually intended to be comical

doggone is not derived from dog but is a euphemism for "God damn" with a reversal of "God"

an orphaned calf is a **dogie**

dogma is Greek for "opinion"—but now it means principle(s) laid down as incontrovertible

dogwood is so named because the wood was formerly used to make skewers called "dogs"

dohada (from Sanskrit) is the word for the unusual appetites and cravings of pregnant women

doily is probably from Doiley or Doyley, the name of a seventeenth-century London draper

a very small amount of money is **doit**

dojo is the room or hall in which judo or other martial arts are practiced (from Japanese *do*, "way, pursuit" and *jo*, "a place")

a **doke** is a hollow, dent, or dimple

dol is a unit for measuring pain intensity (from Latin *dolor*, "pain")

dolatry is excessive admiration

engineer Ray **Dolby** (1933–) devised the noise reduction technology named for him

doldrum may have come from the adjective "dull" and may be modeled on tantrum

dole can mean "state of being divided"

doless can mean lacking in energy or lacking in ambition

doll evolved first as a pet name for Dorothy, first meaning "mistress"

dollar ultimately derives from German *Taler*, short for *Joachimstaler*, a silver coin of the 16th century; the Spanish *dolar*, a coin also known as piece of eight or peso, derived from that and influenced Thomas Jefferson's choice of name for our monetary unit

a **dollop** first denoted a clump of grass or weeds in a field, perhaps from Scandinavian *dolp*, "lump"; now **dollop** refers to a shapeless mass or lump, especially of soft food

dollum is to spoil something through too much handling

dolly, a nickname for Dorothy, was then shortened to doll

dolmen, a prehistoric megalith typically having two upright stones and a capstone, is a Celtic word

dolomite, a type of limestone, was named for its identifier, Deodat de Dolomieu

dolor is mental pain or suffering, but it first meant physical pain

{ something that relieves or drives away sadness is **dolorifuge** }

Greek *delphis* is the source of **dolphin**

a **dolphinarium** is an aquarium in which dolphins are kept and trained for public entertainment

a **dolphinet** is a female dolphin

domain is associated with Latin *dominus*, "lord" and first meant "heritable or landed property"

another word for vineyard is **domaine**, literally "estate" in French

domal means of or pertaining to a house or houses

dome first meant a stately building, coming from Latin *domus*, "house" (hence, domestic)

a **domestic** animal is a pet; a **domesticated** animal is a formerly wild animal bred for human use

domicile and **domestic** derive from Latin *domus*, "house"

only a person can be **domineering**

dominical means "pertaining to Sunday"

domino was a French word for a hood worn by priests in winter and then at masquerades to conceal a person's identity—probably ultimately from Latin *dominus*, "lord, master"

domino was once slang for the teeth and also for the keys of a piano

to **dompt** is "to tame or subdue; daunt"

donate is a back-formation of donation

the **donjon** is the great tower of a castle

donkey may come from Old English *dun*, "grayish brown" and *ky*, "small"; **donkey** was originally pronounced to rhyme with monkey

a **donkey** is a domesticated ass and so is a **burro**, but it is used as pack animal

a **donnée** is literally French for "a given," a basic fact or assumption

Donnybrook is a suburb of Dublin, Ireland, once famous for its annual fair and now used to describe a scene of uproar or disorder

dontopedalogy is a propensity for putting one's foot in one's mouth, a tendency to say something inappropriate or indiscreet

donut is the U.S. spelling of doughnut

doodle was originally a noun meaning "fool, simpleton" from German *dudeltopf*, and came to mean absent-minded scribbling

one meaning of **doodle**, "to play the bagpipe," comes from German *dudeln*, from *dudelsack*, "bagpipe"

doolally is a shortening of the slang term **doolally** tap "characterized by an unbalanced state of mind"

originally, **doom** was a statute, law, judgment, or decree and because **doom** came to mean judgment or sentence; **doomsday** is a judgment day

the bottom timber of a door frame is the **doorsill** or the **groundsill/groundsel**

the rubber-tipped projection attached to the wall behind an opening door is a **doorstop**

> **doozie** is derived from Duesenberg (originally Duesie), the car

a **dop** is a quick bob or curtsy

dope comes from Dutch *doop*, "sauce or liquid," from the viscous goo created by heating opium—but the word originally denoted a thick lubricating liquid or gravy

doppelganger is borrowed from a German word meaning "double-goer"

Doppler radar is named for Austrian physicist and mathematician Christian Johann **Doppler**, who articulated the **Doppler** effect

a whale's penis is called a **dork**

dormant comes from the Latin word *dormire*, "to sleep," and its original meaning was sleeping, literally or figuratively; **dormant** and **dormancy** later were used to describe plants and seeds as well as animals, especially during the winter season

dormer first meant dormitory or bedroom windows from Latin *dormire*, "to sleep"

dormition is a peaceful and painless death, also the act of sleeping or falling asleep

dormitory comes from Latin *dormitorium*, "sleeping place"

the **dormouse**, which is a rodent but not a mouse, may be corrupted form of French *dormeus*, "sleepy"

dorsa or **dorsum** is the back of any bodily structure, like the back of a hand

the back part of the tongue is the **dorsum**; the thin muscle under the tongue is the **frenulum**

a **dose** is a quantity taken at one time; a **dosage** is any amount prescribed for a given period of time

do-si-do is an alteration of French *dos-a-dos*, "back-to-back"

a **doss** is a place for sleeping; to **doss** is "to butt, gore, or toss (a person) with horns" or "to sleep, bed down"

dossier comes from French denoting a bundle of papers in a wrapper with a label on the back (from *dos*, "back" based on Latin *dorsum*)

dot first meant the "head of a boil" or "small lump or **dot**"

dotage is another word for senility, also called **second childhood**

a **dotard** is a tree that has lost its branches through age or decay

dottle is any tobacco left in a pipe after smoking

double is from *duo*, "two" and the Indo-European element *pl-*, "folding"

double-cross was originally the cheating of two parties who tried to win a game after promising to lose it

double-quick or **double time** is the quickest step next to a run

A **doublet** is one of two or more words derived ultimately from a single source: abbreviate/abridge, fragile/frail, guardian/warden. The doublets may or may not show much resemblance and they also vary in closeness of meaning. Somewhere along their line of development they diverge and go off in different paths. The term **cognate** is usually reserved for two or more words in different languages that share a common ancestor as English father, Latin Pater, Greek pater, Spanish and Italian padre, French pere, and German Vater.

doublethink is acceptance or promotion of conflicting ideas

a **double-wide** is two connected mobile homes

doublure is the lining of the covers of a book as with marble papers and gold tooling at the edges

doubt is from Latin *dubitare*, "to go two ways at once" or "to move from one side to the other"

a person is capable of **doubting**, whereas a thing is **dubitable**; dubious, unlike **doubtful**, carries the connotation of suspicion

dote comes from a Dutch word meaning "to be silly"

silly persons can be called: gilly-zaupus, gaupus, chrisom, **dotterel**

douche comes from Italian *doccia* for "conduit pipe" and also means a shower of water

dough, as in money, almost certainly came from bread (another slang term for it) because bread is the staff of life

the words **dough**, **figure**, **lady**, and **paradise** all come in part from the Indo-European root *dheigh-*, "to knead"

the small round doughnuts served to sailors in the nineteenth century were called **doughboys**—and they resembled the round buttons on the sailors' uniforms—so the sailors came to be known as this

doughnuts were first called *oly-cooks* (from Dutch "oilcake") and can also be called dunkers or sinkers

{ to be **doughty** is to be capable, fearless, valiant, and worthy }

afternoon drinking is called **doundrins**

douse first meant "knock, punch, strike" and now means "to extinguish or wet thoroughly"; **dowse** means to look for water or minerals with a divining rod

a **doust** is a firm blow or punch

the word **dove** derives from Dutch *duyve*, "diver"

doves and **pigeons** are in the same family; the smaller species are doves and the larger are called pigeons

a **dowager** is a wealthy widow

down is the soft fluffy plumage beneath the feathers and on the breasts of many birds

down was the Old English word for "hill" and hill was originally a general word for any height, including a mountain; **downs** is an open expanse of high ground with few trees

the allusion behind **down-and-out** is to boxing

an emphasized beat is the **downbeat** and unemphasized beat is **upbeat**

to **down-lie** is to lie down or go to bed

downsteepy is steeply descending or precipitous

downwind means the wind is at your back; **upwind** is when the wind is against your face

doxastic means "pertaining to an individual's beliefs"

a **doxology** is a short utterance of praise to God, such as the "Gloria Patri"

doxy can mean "mistress, sweetheart"

doyen is the female counterpart to dean

a **doyer** or **doyenne** is a senior member of a group or profession

dozen derives from Latin *duodecim*

to **dozzle** is to make stupid or to stupefy

DPT stands for diphtheria, pertussis (whooping cough), and tetanus

drab first referred to undyed cloth of dull neutral color

to **drabble** is to become or make dirty and wet

around 600 BCE, a stateman named Draco drew up a codified, systematic set of laws that were unusually harsh—giving us the word **draconian**

draconic can mean "pertaining to a dragon"

a **draegerman** is a crew member trained for underground rescue work—and is named for the German inventor of a type of breathing apparatus

draft is the phonetic spelling of draught

the tiny silver candy balls for decorating cakes and cookies are **dragées**

drag and straggle makes **draggle**, "to make dirty or wet"

dragon is from a Greek word meaning "serpent"

a **dragonfly** can also be called darner, sewing-needle, devil's darning needle, snake doctor, and horse stinger

the underlying meaning of **drain** seems to be "making dry"

dram "small drink" is related to *drachm*, the measure

drama is literally "that which is done," from Greek **drama** "deed, action"

Drambuie, a type of liqueur, is from Gaelic meaning "satisfying drink"

to coat food with flour before cooking is to **dredge** it

dree is suffering or grief

to **dreep** is to fall in drops or drip

dreg (singular) is a small remnant or a small quantity

dreidel (four-sided Jewish toy) comes from the German word *drehen* meaning "to turn"

the way a garment or fabric hangs is its **drape**

originally **draper** was a dealer in cloth only, derived from French *drap*, "cloth"

drapetomania is an intense desire to run away from home

drastic first referred to medicine as acting strongly or violently

drat is a shortening of 'od rat, which was a euphemism for God rot

the billiard ball's recoil after impact is the **draw**

the movable part of a drawbridge is the **draw**

drawers, based on drawer, "something pulled or drawn out," literally are "garments pulled on"

dreadnought was any of a class of British battleships, named after a particular battleship

dream is from the Old English word *dream* meaning "noise, music" or "joy, mirth"

dreamt is the only English word that ends in "mt"

dreary first meant "dripping with blood; gory"

dreck, derived from Yiddish *drek*, "filth, dregs, dung," is probably connected with Greek *skatos* and/or Latin *stercus* "excrement"

a **drench** is a dose of medicine given to an animal

the earliest noun sense of **dress** meant "speech, talk"

to apply a bandage is to **dress**

dressage, the art of riding and training horses is from French *dresser*, "to train"

to **dretch** is to torment

dretched is "troubled in sleep"

a **drew** is a drop or very small amount of liquid

a **drey** is a squirrel's nest of twigs in a tree

dribble first meant "to shoot an arrow short or wide of its target"

a **driblet** is a small drop of liquid or an insignificant amount or part of something

drier is the adjective; **dryer** is the appliance

drift originally referred to snow

drill can mean "to flow in a small stream"

someone who likes to waste time is a **dringle**; to **dringle** is to waste time

a large body of water can be called the **drink**

drinkdom is the power of alcoholic beverages or the alcoholic beverage industry

drintling refers to turkeys' clucking noises

drips are each of a series of steps on a gently sloping roof

dripple means to trickle or to drip with moisture

a molding over a door or window that deflects rain is a **dripstone**—and anything formed in a cave by dripping water is **dripstone**

drisk is a drizzly mist

drive, as in car, came from the earlier notion of driving a horse, ox, etc. by pushing or forcing

driven snow is that formed into drifts by the wind

driveway first meant a passageway by which grain, hay, etc. could be taken to a barn

drix is the rotten or decayed part of timber or wood

drizzle is defined as 14 drops per square foot per second; light rain is 26 drops per square foot per second

a **droid**, shortening of android, is a robot in science fiction

droit is a right or legal claim, a due; **droitural** means relating to a right to property

droll means "unintentionally funny"

a one-hump camel is **Dromedary** (Latin meaning "swift camel" from Greek *dromas*, "runner") and a two-hump is **Bactrian** (from Bactria in Asia)

dromomania is a mania for roaming or running (from Latin *dromas*, "runner")

drone derives from an Old English word for "male bee," from a Germanic verb meaning "resound; boom"

a **drool** is a slow or slothful person; a **drumble** is an inert or sluggish person

drop, **droop**, and **drip** go back to Indo-European *dhreub*-

drop-ship refers to goods sent from a manufacturer directly to a customer

drop-stitch is a pattern in knitted garments made by dropping a made stitch at intervals

dropsy is a synonym for **edema**

a **drosometer** is an instrument for measuring the amount of dew on a surface

to **drowse** is to be half asleep or to doze

the etymological notion of **drowsy** seems to be heaviness

drub originally referred to punishment by bastinado

the body of a banjo is the **drum**; the cylindrical rotating part of a clothes dryer is a **drum**

{ to **drumble** is to move in a slow, sluggish way }

a small chicken wing that resembles a drumstick is a **drumette**

as an adjective, **drunken** can only precede the noun, while **drunk** follows a verb

drupe, a fleshy fruit with thin skin and a central stone (e.g. almond, cherry, plum, olive) comes from Latin *drupa*, "overripe olive" and from Greek *druppa*, "olive"

a **drupel** or **drupelet** is one of the individual drupes (balls) on an aggregate fruit such as a raspberry or blackberry

druther is a changed pronunciation of "would rather"

when timber has decayed spots hidden by healthy wood, it is **druxy**

if bread or toast is served without butter or another spread, it is "**dry**"

dryad, a tree nymph, derives from Greek *dryas*, "tree"

dry-roasted means roasted without fat or oil

drywall is a building material made of a sheet of plaster covered with heavy paper on both sides and it is also called **plasterboard**

DSL stands for digital subscriber line

dual's original sense was "two people or things"

dub as in "to provide a film with a soundtrack" is an abbreviation of "double"

duberous is a synonym for dubious and doubtful; to **dubitate** is to doubt or waver

ducat is another name for admission ticket

a **duchesse** is a chaise lounge consisting of two facing armchairs connected by a detachable footstool

duck comes from Old English *duke*, "diver"

duct first meant the action of leading or "guidance" as it derives from Latin *ducere*, "to lead"

the original meaning of **dud** was "an article of clothing," then "things" in general, then "rags," and eventually, a "counterfeit or useless thing"

dudgeon is sullen or angry disposition

a female dude is actually a **dudine**

unpopped popcorn kernels are called **duds**

duel comes from Latin *duellum*, an archaic form of *bellum*, "war," used to describe a single fight to settle a matter

a **duettino** is a short duet

a **duettist** is a person who takes part in a duet

duff is the decaying leaves of a forest floor

duffel as in "bag," was at first a thick woolen cloth, got its name from **Duffel**, Belgium, where it was originally made; **duffel** is a variant spelling of duffle and vice versa

dugong is the whalelike creature supposed to be the origin of the mermaid (from Malay *duyong*, "sea cow")

duh is first recorded in a 1943 Merrie Melodies cartoon as an expression of confusion and inarticulacy

duke comes from Latin *ducere*, "lead"

duke of York was rhyming slang for "forks," meaning "fingers, fists, hands"—which later became **dukes**

a dilemma is a **dulcarnon**

dulciloquent means "speaking sweetly"

{ the **dulcimer** gets its name from Latin *dulce melos*, "sweet song" }

dull originally meant "slow-witted"

dumb as in "stupid" comes from German *dum* (as in *dumkopf*, "stupid head")

dumbbell was something used to ring a church bell, but alone this apparatus was "dumb" or "noiseless"; it was a bar with two rounded masses on the ends

dumbfound is dumb and confound

a **dumble** is another name for a bumblebee; **dumbledore** is the name of two different insects, including the bumblebee

"dumb" in **dumbwaiter** means "lacking some property normally belonging to things of the name"

dumducketty means "of a dull, drab color"

a **dumdum** bullet is named for a town and arsenal near Calcutta, India, where the bullets were first produced

mockups of newspaper or magazine pages before they are produced are called **dummies**

dumosity is dense bushy growth, like a mass of bushes or brambles

dump once meant reverie or "absence of mind"; **dumps** is probably a figurative use of middle Dutch *domp*, "haze, mist"

dumpster, a very large trash container, was originally Dempster **Dumpster**, a proprietary name of the U.S. manufacturer Dempster Brothers of Tennessee

a **dumpy** level in surveying gets its name for being a short telescope with a large aperture

dun (a debt collector) may be from Dunkirk "privateer" (hinting piratical demands) or from the name Joe **Dun**, a well-known bailiff

dunce was originally an epithet for John Duns Scotus, a scholastic theologian who was ridiculed for making what seemed to be useless distinctions; the obstinance of Scotus and his followers led to the idea of a person unable to learn—hence, **dunce**

if bread is **dunch**, it is doughy and heavy

dungaree is from Hindu *dungri*, **denim** is from "de Nimes," the town in France, and **jeans** came from a cloth called jean, once made in Genoa, Italy

dungeon first meant "castle, fortress," "keep of a castle," or "prison cell under the keep of a castle"

the word **dunk** came from Pennsylvania/German *dunke*, "dip" from German *tunken*, "dip or plunge"

packing material like bubble wrap can collectively be called **dunnage**

to **dunt** is to bump into or hit heavily

the body's **duodenum** (pronounced doo-uh-DEE-numb) was so named because its length is approximately the breadth of twelve fingers (Latin *duodeni*, "in twelves")

a **duologue** is a lengthy conversation between two people

dupe comes from a French word for a hoopoe, a bird with a supposedly stupid appearance

a **duplet** is a set of two things

duplication may be regarded as an activity because one duplicates (makes again) something, but **replication** is a process in which something is replicated (copied)

duplicity implies double-dealing while **chicanery** suggests trickery and wiliness

to **dure** is to last, hold out, continue in existence—hence, **durable** and **duration**

a **durance** is a long confinement

durative or **continuative** in grammar means "denoting continuing action"—as in "She is going"

duress comes from Latin *durus*, "hard"

during is an extension of meaning from Latin *durare*, "harden"

dusk is the darker stage of twilight

dusky can figuratively mean "gloomy, melancholy"

the material of the human frame is figuratively called **dust**

{ **duty** is, literally, "that which is due," "one's due" }

the stuffing **duxelles**, made from mushrooms, onions, shallots, and parsley—is named after the Marquis d'Uxelles, a 17th century French nobleman

DVD stands for digital versatile disk

a **dwarf** is smaller and not proportioned like an average person; a **midget** is smaller but is proportioned like an average full-grown person; a **pygmy** is perfectly proportioned but smaller than a **midget**

dweeb is a blend of dwarf and feeb, "a feeble-minded person"

a **dwell** is a slight regular pause in the motion of a machine or part of a machine, usually so another part can operate

to **dwizzen** is to shrink and dry up or look parched

dybbuk is a dead person's wandering soul that comes to inhabit the body of a living person

dye's original meaning was simply "color"

dynamic is the opposite force of static

Alfred Nobel, who invented **dynamite**, also coined its name

dynasty is from Greek *dunasteia*, "domination, power"

dysania is the state of having a hard time waking up and getting out of bed in the morning

dysentry derives from Greek *dus*, "bad" and *entera*, "bowels"

not healing quickly means you are **dysepulotic**

dysgeusia is a metallic taste in one's mouth

dyslogistic is expressing disapproval

if you give someone a **dyslogy**, you make a speech with a number of uncomplimentary remarks about them (the opposite of **eulogy**)

dyspathy is antipathy—either dislike or disagreement in feeling

dysphemism is the substitution of a disagreeable word or phrase for a neutral or positive one (also a word or phrase so substituted); it is the opposite of **euphemism**

you ate a carton of ice cream? you probably feel **dysphoria** (an unwell feeling, generally unwholesome state; also, chronic discontent)

some people have **dyspnea** (labored breathing) at night

jet lag is **dysrhythmia**

{ **dystocia** is slow or difficult labor or childbirth }

dystopia is a failed **utopia**; **utopia**, literally Greek *ou*, "no" and *topos*, "place"—"no place" conveys an expectation of failure

a **dzo** is a hybrid of a cow and a yak

{ Easily the most-often-used letter in English-language print, **E** outdistances runners-up T, A, and I by a wide margin. One reason is the many shades (about 15) of vowel sounds E can represent }

e.g. (*exempli gratia*) means "for example" while i.e. (*id est*) means "that is," explaining a subject further

eadness is happiness derived from luxury and wealth

early on, **eager** meant "sharp, biting" (as in air) and "pungent, sour"

eagle at first referred to the black **eagle** from Latin *aquilus*, "dark-colored"

an abrupt tide rise is an **eagre**

a mug's handle is the **ear**

a small box of information at the top of a newspaper's front page is an **ear**

the word **earl** originally denoted a man of noble rank, as opposed to a **churl** "peasant" or ordinary freeman; **earl** is below duke and marquis, above viscount and baron

early is based on *ere*, "before"

earmark was first a mark on the ear of sheep or other animals to indicate ownership or identity

earnest was first a noun meaning "seriousness of feeling"

earshell is a common alternative name for the **abalone**

Earth the planet is capitalized, while **earth** the ground is not

earthenware is low-fired clay, **porcelain** is high-fired, **stoneware** is about halfway between **earthenware** and **porcelain** in quality and durability, and the term **china** can be applied to any **porcelain**, **earthenware**, or ceramic ware dishes or crockery

the opposite of moonlight on the Earth is **earthshine** or **earthlight** on the Moon; **earthshine** is the glow caused by sunlight reflected by the Earth, especially on the darker part of a crescent moon

earthy is "similar to earth; hearty" or "coarse, vulgar" while **earthly** is "pertaining to human existence on earth"; **earthen** means "made of earth or clay"

an Old English word for insect was *wicga*, part of the eventual **earwig**

ease first meant "opportunity, ability, or 'means to do something'"

ease is the extra fabric in a piece of clothing that allows the wearer to move more easily

the Dutch word for donkey, "*ezel*," gave us **easel** because of the analogy that a donkey carried equipment and an **easel** carried the artist's canvas during the painting

the root of **east** is Latin *aurora*, meaning "dawn" and **west** came from a root meaning "sunset or evening"

easy first meant "nearby," then "handy, convenient" and eventually "comfortable"

easy-peel is a grocer's term for small citrus fruit like the tangerine

eat is a very ancient basic verb, going back to Indo-European *ed-*, "eat" and first referred to solid food and to fluid (like soup) for which a spoon is used

eatage is grass available for grazing

eatertainment is dining combined with entertainment

eau is the French word for "water" as in **eau** de cologne and **eau** de toilette

the etymological meaning of **eaves** is "going over the edge, projecting"

ebullition is a sudden outburst of emotion or violence

ecceity is "the quality of being present"

eccentric first meant "not concentric" as it referred to an orbit in which the Earth was not precisely in the center or straying from a circular path; the area where two circles overlap is the **eccentric**

ecclesiastic is from Greek *ekklesia*, "assembly, church"

ecdysiast is a stripteaser, a word coined by the writer and social critic H. L. Mencken (1880–1956) from *ecdysis*, a technical term for the shedding of the outer skin by a reptile or insect, plus the ending *ñast*

an animal or plant's adjustment to a new environment is **ecesis**

echelon comes from French *echelle*, "ladder" (from Latin *scala*) and first meant a formation of troops

echinate means covered with rigid bristles, prickles, or spines

eavesdrop was originally the dripping of water from the eaves of a house and the verb is a back-formation from the noun eavesdropper

eBay was chosen by its founder for his own Echo Bay Technology Group, but since the domain name echobay.com was taken, he settled for **ebay**.com

ebb suggests the receding of something (tides) that commonly comes and goes

to **eblandish** is to get something by coaxing or flattery

Ebonics is another word for Black English

ebony is ultimately of Semitic origin

ebriety is another word for drunkenness

ebullient is literally "boiling" from Latin *ebullire*; **ebullient** should be pronounced i-BUUL-yuhnt

echo is from Greek *ekho*, from *ekhe* "sound"

éclair is French for lightning bolt—perhaps for the speed with which one is eaten

to **eclaircise** means "to make clear, elucidate"

eclectic first entered English as a philosophical term, from Greek *eklektikos*, "selecting"; it now means "drawn from many sources"

eclipse comes from Greek *ekleipein* (*ek*, "out" and *leipein*, "to leave") meaning "fail to appear, forsake its customary place"

ecmnesia is the loss of memory of events of a particular period (as opposed to **amnesia**, for all of one's past)

ecology comes from Greek *okologie*, from *oikos*, "home, habitat" and -ology

economic means "pertaining to the production and use of income" and **economical** is "avoiding waste, being careful of resources"

economics first meant "treatise on household management" and is derived from the title by Aristotle "*ta oikonomika*"; **home economics** could be redundant except that the word **economics** has had its meaning extended

economy comes from Greek *oikos*, "home, habitat" and *nomos*, "manager" and meant "household management, steward of an estate"—home being the place where we originate most expenditures

écorché is an anatomical model of part or all of the human body with the skin removed to allow study of the muscle structure

{ **ecphrasis** is a lucid, self-contained explanation or description }

ecru is French for "unbleached"

ecstasy, which first meant "bewilderment; insanity" comes from Greek *ekstasis*, "standing outside oneself" or "displacement, being out of one's condition or place"

ecstatic should be pronounced ek-STA-dik

ectal means exterior or outside

ectomorphic is having a thin body build, **endomorphic** is short and broad, and **mesomorphic** is being big-boned and muscular

the abnormal positioning of a body part is **ectopia**

an **ectotherm** is an animal whose body temperature varies with the temperature of its surroundings—which is any animal except birds and mammals (also known as **cold-blooded**!)

a two-handled soup bowl is an **ecuelle**

ecumenical first meant "belonging to the universal church"—from Greek *oikoumenikos/oikoumene*, "the inhabited earth"

eczema is from Greek *ekzema*, "eruption"

edacious means pertaining to eating; **edacity** is a voracious appetite

the ultimate source of **eddy** (miniature whirlpool) seems to be a Proto-Germanic particle meaning "back, again"

edelweiss, the alpine plant, translates to "noble" and "pure, white"

edema is a synonym for **dropsy**

edentate means "without teeth"

edge's meaning of "border, boundary" dates from the late fourteenth century

an **edict** is literally that which is "spoken out" or "proclaimed"

an **edifice** is a large, stately building

edify originally meant "construct a building," now can mean "to instruct and improve spiritually and morally; enlighten"

edit first meant "give it out, put out, publish"; **edit** as in "prepare for publication" is a back-formation from editor

editor is a Latin word meaning literally "producer (of games), publisher" from *edere*, "to put out, produce"

an **editrix** is a female editor

a student is an **educand**

to **educate** people is literally "to lead them out" (Latin *ex-*, "out" and *ducere*, "lead")

the etymology of **education** leads back to two separate but not dissimilar Latin roots: *educare* with connotations of "drawing out" or "bringing up" and *educere* with connotations of "leading forth" to **educe** is to draw out, elicit, or evoke—or to infer from a set of data, as a principle

{ **eerie** probably comes from Old English earg "cowardly" }

Eeyore's name (in Winnie the Pooh) is a phonetic representation of the donkey's bray (onomatopoeia)

efface means "to cause an emotion or memory to completely disappear"

effect is from *ef-* and *facere*, "do, make," which became *efficere*, "accomplish"

effect is a noun referring to a thing, but if you mean an action, that is **affect**; if you want the verb meaning "achieve, bring about," that is **effect**

effective means "having a (desired) result or effect," **effectual** is "succeeding in producing a desired result or effect," and **efficacious** means the same as **effectual** as well as "serving as an **effective** solution or remedy"

effects as personal belongings arose from an obsolete sense of the word meaning "something acquired on completion of an action"

effete comes from Latin *effetus* meaning "worn out by bearing young"; in English it means "barren, used up, worn out," not weak

if something is **efficacious**, it is able to produce the desired result; **efficacy** means the power to produce effects

to **effigiate** is "to make a picture or sculpture of, present a likeness of, portray"

effigy had the early senses of "portrait" and "image"

to **efflagitate** is to desire or demand eagerly

effluent is Latin *ex-*, "out" and *fluere*, "flow" the smell of decaying matter is **effluvium**

effort first meant power and it comes from Latin *ef-* and *fortis*, "strong"

effossion is the act of digging up from the ground

another word for breaking and entering is **effraction**

effrontery is from Latin *effroms*, "barefaced, shameless"

effulgent means "shining brilliantly"

an **eft** is a small lizard or lizard-like animal, like a newt

egads originated in a military acronym for Ground Automatic Destruct System

an **egeria** is a female advisor

egest means to excrete waste matter, especially of a cell

egg was borrowed from Old Norse **egg** and is akin to Old English *[œ]g*, **egg**, Old High German *ei*, Crimean Gothic *ada*, Latin *ovum*, Welsh *wy*, Greek *omacrion*, and Old Persian *xamacrya*

an **egger** is a collector of birds' eggs

an **egghead** was originally a bald person—being an analogy of a bald head with age and wisdom

an **eggler** is an egg dealer

eggnog is also called egg-flip, from egg + nog, "a strong ale," and the drink was originally made with either hot beer, cider, wine, or spirits

eggplant was so named because the delicate white varieties resemble eggs

to **eggtaggle** is to waste time in the company of people who misbehave

ego means "I" in Latin

an **egoist** thinks the world revolves around him, an **egotist** is someone who cannot stop talking about himself

egoity is the essence of personal identity

egregious first meant "remarkably good" and "standing out or apart from the flock or herd; eminent"; its later derogatory sense (conspicuously and outrageously bad) is probably an ironical use

egression is the action of going out or leaving a place

teenagers are **egressors**—people who go out all the time

egritude or **aegritude** are words that mean "sickness"

the base of **eight** was Greek *okto* or Sanskrit *asht·u*

{ **eighty-six**—"reject, discard"—may be rhyming slang for "nix" }

eisegesis is the interpretation of a word or passage by reading into it one's own ideas

either is the descendant of an ancient Germanic phrase meaning "always each of two"

either and **neither** are correctly pronounced two ways—i as in like or ee as in queen, though the latter is more frequent

ejaculate and **eject** come from Latin *jacere*, "to throw"; **ejaculate** used to be a synonym for exclaim

ejecta is material forced or thrown out—especially in an eruption, explosion, or impact—as from vomit or a volcano

ejulate is to wail or lament

eke was a noun meaning "addition, extension, increase"

ekistics is a science dealing with human settlements and draws on the research of professionals in archaeology, architecture, city planning, engineering, and sociology

elaborate first meant "produced by effort of labor" and as a verb it meant "to produce a substance from elements or simple constituents"

élan is impetuousness or vivacity

elanguescence is the process of gradually fading away into non-existence

to **elaqueate** is to free from a noose or other entanglement

elastic originally described a gas that expanded to fill the available space, from Greek *elastikos*, "propulsive"

a generic name for a Band-Aid is **elastoplast**

elate derives from a Latin verb meaning "raise" and now means "to raise the spirits"

elbow literally means "arm-bend" from Proto-Germanic *alino*, "forearm" and *bugon*, "bend, bow" (Old English *elboga*) is related to Dutch *elleboog*—and ell is a former measure equivalent to six handbreadths

elbow-lifting is an euphemism for a fondness for drinking

elder is used when precedence with respect to birth order is the point; **older** is used when the point is seniority with respect to age

to **elder** is to become older or start to show signs of age

the card player who is dealt to first is the **elder, elder** hand, or **forehand**

eldorado means "the gilded one"

God can "**elect**" a person for salvation

election came via French from Latin *electionem* from the earlier *eligere*, "to choose, pick out"

electric means "relating, pertaining, derived from, or producing electricity" and **electrical** means "involving or concerned with electricity"

electric and **electricity** are from Latin *electrum* and Greek *elektron*, "amber" as this phenomenon (electrostatic) was first noted when amber was rubbed

electrocute is a blend of electric and execute

electron is actually a combination of electric and -on

electronica is a collective term for electronic devices and technology

an **electuary** is a medicine mixed with honey or syrup

elegant comes from Latin *eligere*, "select"

elegiac can mean "melancholy, mournful"

elegy is from Greek *elegos*, "mournful poem"

to be unhappily alone is to be **elenge**

an alpine forest's stunted trees are **elfinwood** or **krummholz**

elicit comes from a Latin stem meaning "draw forth by magic or trickery"

elicit, **extract**, and **extort** are synonymous in general, meaning "to draw or coax out"—but the degree goes from mild to medium to strong

element comes from Latin *elementum*, "letter of the alphabet" or "principle, rudiment"—a translation of Greek *stoikheion*, "component, part, step"

elephant is made up of Greek *ele*, "arch" and the Latin *phant*, "huge"—a reference to its arched back

a refrigerator raid is an act of **eleptobiosis**

a fancy name for a deliverer is **eleutherian**

elevate, from Latin *elevare*, "to raise," is based on *levis*, "light"

an **elevation** is a two-dimensional scale drawing of something as if one were viewing it from one side; a **section** is a two-dimensional scale drawing of one part or detail of an object or structure; and a **plan** is a two-dimensional scale drawing showing the view of an object or structure as if one were looking down on it from above

an **élève** is a French term we use for a pupil or scholar

eleven comes from "leave one"—you count ten fingers and that leaves one (literally "one over"); **twelve** is "twa" or "two left" ("two over") and **thirteen** is "three plus ten" ("three over")

midmorning tea or coffee with a snack is **elevenses**

elf comes from a German word meaning nightmare as originally these supernatural beings were thought to cause them

to **elide** is to omit a vowel or syllable in pronunciation

eligible means "fit or entitled to be chosen" and comes from Latin *eligere*, "choose"

eliminate derives from Latin *eliminare*, "turn out of doors" (*limen*, "threshold")

elint is another way of saying electronic intelligence, which is usually covert

to **eliquate** is to melt or liquefy

elite comes from Latin *elire*, "to elect, pick out"

elixir derives from Arabic *al-'iksir*, "the powder for drying wounds"

elk is the largest living deer

ellipse is from Greek meaning "defect, failure"

ellipsis is the old name for a dash as used in writing to indicate the omission of letters in a word

elliptic corresponds to the ellipse while **elliptical** corresponds to the ellipsis

elocution is related to eloquent (from Latin *eloqui*, "speak out")

to **eloin** or **eloign** is to remove oneself to or set something at a distance

elongate first meant "to remove" or "to move away"

at first, **elope** meant a wife running away from her husband in the company of a lover

when one composes by working at night, one **elucubrates**; **elucubration** is another word for studying or composing at night

{ **elude** comes from *e-*, "out, away from" and *ludere*, "to play" }

elusion is the action of deluding someone—or an escape or evasion

elusive is used when what is being avoided is physical capture or apprehension, whereas **evasive** is used when what is being avoided is direct or relevant response to a verbal challenge

baby eels are **elver**

the **em** (long dash) in printing is a measure based on a capital M, measuring 12 points or 4.5 mm; an **en** is half an **em**

emaciate is based on Latin *macies*, "leanness"

emacity is an urge to buy

emanate first referred to courses of action, ideas, and principles originating from a person or other source

emancipate derives from Latin *e-*, "out" and *mancipare*, "deliver as property; transfer, sell"

emargination is a word for notching on a book, as a reference book with thumb indexing

the base of **emasculate** is Latin *emasculare*, "castrate"

to **embale** is to wrap up in packages; **emballage** is wrappings or packaging

enbalm is literally "putting on balm"

embargo comes from the word *embargar* meaning "to arrest or impede" and was originally an order prohibiting foreign ships to enter or leave a harbor in wartime

embark is from French *embarquer*, *em-*, "in" and *barque*, "ship"

embarrass first meant "hamper, impede, obstruct"

embassy originally had the spelling variant ambassy and is based on Latin *ambactus*, "servant"; an **embassy** is the one entity maintained by a foreign country by each nation, whereas a **consulate** may be situated in a number of cities of a foreign country

embellish had the early sense of "make beautiful," from Latin *bellus* and the word suggests adding something, often stressing a superfluous or adventitious ornament

originally, **embezzle** simply meant "steal"

emblem, from Latin *emblema* and Greek *emballein*, "throw in," first was an ornament of inlaid work and an **emblem** is usually inserted or cast into something

emblements is the growing of crops and the profits reaped

embolalia are useless or hesitation words or utterances in speech like oh, uh, you know, I mean

embonpoint means plumpness, though in French *en bon point* means "in good shape"

embrace's source is Latin *in-* and *bracchium*, "arm" and the word implies a ready or happy acceptance

to **embrangle** or **imbrangle** is to confuse, entangle, or perplex

have you been flossing your **embrasures** (the spaces between your teeth)?

to **embrocate** is to bathe a painful part of the body, but it can also mean "to apply lotion"

the shape of the mouth when blowing on a musical instrument's mouthpiece is **embrochure**

broid means "interweave, plait" and *broider* means "**embroider**"—and **embroider** was formed from broid

embryo comes from *em-*, "into" and *bruein*, "swell, grow"

a human **embryo** is the earliest stage of development while a **fetus** is from the eighth week of development to birth

emend originally meant "free a person from faults"

emerald traces its history to an ancient Semitic verb *baraq*, "shine" and it went into Greek as *maragdos*, "green gem"

{ **emerge** is a combination of *e-*, "from" and Latin *mergere*, "to dip, plunge" }

emergency comes from Latin *emergere* (*e-*, "from" and *mergere*, "to dip, plunge") and first meant "unforeseen occurrence"

emerited is "retired from active service"

originally **emeritus** meant "a veteran"

emery (as in board) comes from French *esmeri* and Italian *smeriglio*, based on Greek *smuris/smiris*, "polishing powder"

emesis is a kinder word for vomiting and an **emetic** is a substance causing vomiting

emiction is the passing of urine

an **emigrant** is a person who leaves their country to settle in another

to **emigrate** or **immigrate** is to enter a new country to take up residency; the only real difference between these words is you **emigrate** from your country to another country and you **immigrate** into (or to) another country

eminence can describe height, altitude, or degree of elevation

eminent can mean "projecting, protruding" and it is based on *eminere*, "project"

if you mean "famous" or "superior," you want **eminent**; if you mean "impending, about to happen" that is **imminent**; and if you mean "present, inherent," your word is **immanent**

an **emissary** is more likely to be representing governments, political leaders, or institutions other than churches (for which there are missionaries)

emit, **emission**, and **emissary** come from Latin *emittere*, "send out" and **emit** once meant "publish a book or notice"

ants used to be called **emmets**

emmetropia is the condition of perfect vision in which light rays from distant objects, which are approximately parallel, are focused on the retina without accommodation or distortion, as compared to hyperopia (far-sightedness) and myopia (near-sightedness)

the **Emmy** Award is an alteration of Immy, nickname for image orthicon, a camera tube used in television production

emollient is from Latin *emolliere*, "to soften"; to **emolliate** is to soften or make effeminate

emolument's original meaning was "fee paid to a miller for grinding grain"

emote is derived (a back-formation) from emotion

an **emoticon** is a texting symbol made from standard characters; the word is a blend of emotion and icon

emotion first described a commotion or public disturbance (from Latin *movere*, "move")

emotional means "affected by an emotion" while **emotive** means "drawing out or evoking emotion"

an **empanada** is a turnover with a filling of meat, cheese, or vegetables (Spanish, from *empanar*, "roll in pastry")

empathy denotes a deep emotional understanding of another's feelings or problems, while **sympathy** is more general and can apply to small annoyances or setbacks

emperor derives from Latin *imperator*, "military commander"

the dominion of an emperor is his **empery**

from Greek, **emphasis** originally meant "appearance"

empire comes from Latin *imperium*, related to *imperator*, "military commander, emperor"

empirical describes results determined by experiment and observed behavior or facts; **theoretical** describes results that are based on guesswork or hypothesis—and **pragmatic** is contrasted with **theoretical** on the grounds that the former proceeds from what is demonstrably practical, the latter from conjecture

Employ comes from a French word employer, which first meant "to apply or make something for a specific purpose." The French word traces back to Latin *implicare*, "to involve or engage." By the late 16th century, the sense of "to use the services of a person in a business or professional capacity" was recorded. The word employer was coined by Shakespeare (c 1599) and he also used **employ** and **employment**. **Employee** was first recorded in 1850 according to the "Oxford English Dictionary," though previously it was spelled **employé** and was used by 1834 for "one who is employed."

emporeutic is pertaining to merchandise or to trade

emporium is from a Greek word for "merchant"

empressement is a show of affection

{ to **empt** can mean "to be at leisure" or "to drain, pour, or clear out" }

emption is the act of purchasing, **emptional** means "buyable," and **emptor** is another word for "buyer"

empty first meant "at leisure, unoccupied" and it could also mean "unmarried"

empyrean refers to the highest heaven

empyreuma is the burnt smell of an organic substance, like toast; **nidor** is the burnt smell of an animal substance, like bacon

emulate means "try to equal or surpass, especially by copying"

emulous is "closely resembling, imitative of," "wanting to imitate," or "motivated by rivalry"

an **emulsifier** is an additive that binds water and fat in foods

an **emulsion** is slowly mixing two liquids that don't easily combine and the word is based on *emulgere*, "drain out, milk out"

emunction is nose wiping and **emunctory** is pertaining to nose-blowing

to **emunge** is to wipe or clean out

the **en** is the short dash, a longer one is the **em**, and the longest is a **z-em** (two-**em**) dash

in **enallage**, one part of speech is used for another, like a noun or adjective for a verb, as in "You want peace? I'll peace you."

the underlying meaning element in **enamel** is "melting"

enantiodromia is the adoption of a set of beliefs which are opposite to those previously held

enascent means "just coming into being"

enatation is escape by swimming

a fancy name for headache is **encephalalgia**

exhaustion due to emotional stress rather than overwork or lack of sleep is called **encephalesthenia**

to **enchafe** is to "make hot," "excite; anger"

enchilada comes from American Spanish meaning "season with chili"

an **enchiridion** is a book containing essential information on a subject

enchorial is used in or belonging to a particular country

an **enclave** is a group or area different from the surroundings, a secured area within another secured area (Latin *clavis*, "key"); an **exclave** is the same thing, but usually describes a portion of a country which is separated from the main part and surrounded by politically alien territory

else that is "native to a particular region," as a panda is in central China and eastern Tibet

the **endgame** in chess is the final stage of the game when there are only a few pieces left

endocrine glands (like pituitary, throid) are ductless and secrete hormones directly into the bloodstream, serving to control the functions of various organs; **exocrine** glands (like sweat, salivary) have ducts and secrete directly to the surface of an organ or tissue

an example of an **enclitic** is "n't" in can't—a word pronounced with very little emphasis and simply part of the preceding word

encomium means "high praise"

encore is French for "again" or "still"

encounter is formed from Latin *in-*, "in" and *contra*, "against"

encratic means self-controlled or abstinent and **encraty** is mastery over the senses or abstinence from pleasures of sense

something that **encroaches** on something else literally seizes it with its hooks (en- and croc, "hook")

encyclopedia comes from Greek *enkuklios*, "all-around, general" and *paideia*, "education"

end is an ancient word traced back to Indo-European *antjo*

endeavor is literally "put oneself in *devoir* (duty, service; effort)"

endeictic means "serving to show or demonstrate"

an **endemic** is a disease that is constantly present in a community or region—like diarrhea; it can also refer to something

endoderm (or entoderm) is the innermost cell layer, **mesoderm** is the enclosing layer, and **ectoderm** is the outmost layer of a human body's skin

endogenous is originating within and **exogenous** is originating externally

endolated is "spun in a large ridged drum to break up insect eggs to prevent them from hatching (in flour)"

the early sense of **endorse** was "write on the back of"

an **endoskeleton** is contained entirely within the body of an animal (like the mammal), while an **exoskeleton** is entirely outside the animal (e.g. mollusks, snails, tortoises)

endow first meant "provide a dower or dowry"

the **endpin** (or tail-spike) is the adjustable thin leg at the bottom of a cello or double bass that the instrument rests on while being played

to **endue** is to put on an item of clothing

endure first meant "harden, strengthen" and its Latin roots are *en-* and *durus*, "hard"

{ **endysis** is the growth of new hair, plumage, scales, etc. }

enecate is a synonym for "kill, destroy"

enema comes from Greek *emienai*, "send or put in"

enemy comes from Latin *inimicus*, *in-*, "not" and *amicus*, "friend"

energy is from Greek *energeia*, from *en-*, "within" and *ergon*, "work"

enervate means "drain energy or vigor from" (from Latin *enervare*, "weaken by extraction of the sinews") and **innervate** means "supply with energy" (Latin *in-*, "in" and *nervus*, "strength, vigor, energy")

an **enfilade** is a suite of rooms with doorways in line with each other—or a vista between rows of trees

enfleurage is the extraction of perfumes from flowers by means of oils and fats

the origin of **enforce** is Latin *in-*, "in" and *fortis*, "strong"

enfranchise literally means "make free" from *in-* (expressing a change of state) and *franc*/*franche* "free"

engage originally meant "to pawn or pledge something" and later it meant "pledge oneself to do something," which led to "enter into a contract"

engender first meant beget or conceive offspring

engine derives from Latin *ingenium*, "device" or "talent" and its original meaning was "cunning, ingenuity" and then a "product of ingenuity" and later "tool," "weapon," "machine"

engine is the more general term; **motor** is a special kind of **engine**

engineers first designed and constructed military works or were builders of engines of war (large offensive weapons)

technically, **England** is not a country and neither are **Scotland** or **Wales**; **England** and **Scotland** are kingdoms and **Wales** is a principality. All occupy **Great Britain**, the largest island of Europe. Add **Northern Ireland** and you've got the **United Kingdom**, which is a country.

English is a member of the western branch of the Germanic family of languages, which is, in turn, a branch of the Indo-European language family

the billiards player's "body **english**" results in putting "**english**" on the ball

the name **English** is older than the name **England**; the spelling **England** no longer represents the pronunciation of the word (Ingland)

engorge comes from French *en-*, "into" and *gorge*, "throat"

engrave can mean "portray or represent by sculpture"

engross originally meant "use large handwriting, write out in large clear handwriting" and then "enter in a formal document, make a written record of"; another early meaning was "buy wholesale"

when a river **engulfs**, it is discharging itself into the sea or disappearing underground

enhance originally meant "elevate," both literally and figuratively

an **enigma** was originally a riddle, usually involving metaphor, from Greek *ainigma*, "riddle" from *ainos*, "fable"

enjoy probably comes from Old French *enjoir*, "in rejoice"

enlighten can mean "make luminous"

enmity is "hatred, ill will," the feelings of an enemy

an **enneagon** is a nine-sided figure

ennui (pronounced ahn-WEE) means "boredom" and comes from Latin *inodiare*, "make odious"; synonyms are **accidie** or **acedia**

ennuyant is "giving rise to ennui," or is a synonym for "boring"

an **enophile** or **oenophile** is a connoisseur or lover of wines

enormity is not about size alone, it refers to something monstrous or outrageous; **enormity** first meant "a crime"

{ **enormous** is literally *e-*, "deprived of" and *norma*, "pattern" (and -ous) }

enough is from an Indo-European root meaning "attain, reach"

the base of **enquire** and **inquire** is Latin *quaerere*, "ask, seek"

ens (plural entia) is "an abstract being, an **entity**" and it is the stem of **entity**; **entity** can also mean "all that exists"

to **ensanguine** is to stain with blood

ensconce comes from the archaic noun sconce meaning "small fort"

the lumbar incurvation of a woman is the **ensellure**

ensemble means "at the same time, together" and is from *in-*, and Latin *simul*, "at the same time"

to store something for the winter is to **ensile** it

to **ensorcell** is to bewitch, fascinate

enstasy means "to stand inside the self"; **ecstasy** means "to stand outside the ordinary self"

ensue is from Latin *insequi*, literally "follow in (the steps of someone)"

ensure is an alteration of French *asseurer*, "assure"

ensynopticity refers to the ability to take a general or overall view

on a column, the **entablature** is the top part containing the architrave (also called epistyle), the frieze, and the cornice

entail first meant "carve, cut" from Latin *in-*, and *taleare*, "to cut"

ental means inner or inside

the state of actuality is **entelechy**, as opposed to **potentiality**

enter's Latin base is *intra*, "within"

to **entermete** is to meddle or concern oneself with another's business

the underlying meaning of **enterprise** is "taking something in or between one's hands"

entertain, first meaning "keep up, maintain" is from Latin *inter*, "among" and *tenere*, "to hold"

enthasy is a soft, quiet death

enthrall once had the sense "enslave"

enthuse is a back-formation from enthusiasm

enthusiasm, from Greek *enthous*, first meant "possessed or inspired by a god"

entice probably derives from Proto-Romance "set on fire" from the Latin root *titio*, "firebrand"

to **entify** is to make into an entity

entire also used to be spelled intire, based on Latin *integer*, "untouched, whole"

entomologists study insects; **etymologists** study word histories

entomology—the science of bugs/insects—is based on Greek *entomos*, "insect"

entopic means occurring in the usual place

entortillation is the action of entwining or twisting

entourage comes from French *entourer*, "to surround, to hedge"

entrails comes from Latin *intralia*, an alteration of *interanea*, "internal things"

entreat first meant "treat in a specified way"

entrechat, the ballet move, is from Italian *capriola intrecciata*, "complicated caper"

{ a light dish served between two courses of a formal meal or dishes served in addition to the main course of a meal is **entremets** }

entrepreneur was once a job title for the director of a musical institution, from French *entreprendre*, "undertake"

entropy is the theory that the amount of disorder in the universe is bound to increase

a person gathering census data is an **enumerator**

enunciate derives from Latin *nuntius*, "messenger"

to **enurn** is to put in an urn
envelop is the verb; **envelope** is the noun

the basic part of a balloon is the **envelope**

environment emerged linked with nature, implying "natural" (not human, not cultural) surroundings; **ecology** emerged as a scientific effort to connect organisms (such as the human) to their environments

envisage originally meant "look straight at; face"

envisage refers to an image that is delineated, whereas **envision** can refer to an appearance that is indefinite or immaterial; **envisage** is "contemplate or view in a certain way," and **envision** means "picture to oneself; visualize"

envoi is the final communication or send-off

envoy (pronounced EN-voy) is literally "sent on one's way"

envy comes from Latin *invidere*, "grudge, look maliciously upon"

eoan is pertaining to dawn or to the east

an **epact** is the difference in time between the solar year (365 days) and the lunar year

(354)—from the last new moon of the old year to the first of the following January

epalperbrate means "without eyebrows"

épater is from French, literally "to flabbergast"

a fencing sword with a bowl-shaped guard and flexible blade is an **épée**; the one with a circular guard is a **foil**

epeiric means "connected with the ocean but situated on a continent or continental shelf"

epenthesis is the development of an unetymological sound or letter in a word, such as "b" in thimble

epeolatry is the worship of words

epergne is the centerpiece of a table, especially a large one with many compartments for sauces and condiments

epexegesis is the addition of a word(s) to convey meaning more clearly

ephebiatrics is the branch of medicine dealing with adolescents (patterned on pediatrics, geriatrics)

a freckle can also be called an **ephelis**

ephemera is the plural of **ephemeron** "an item of short-term interest or use," from Greek for "lasting only a day"

ephemeral originally meant specifically "lasting only one day" (Greek *epi-*, "on" + *hemera*, "day") and it literally refers to something that is "over" in a day

an **ephialtes** is an evil spirit thought to cause nightmares and it is a synonym for nightmare

Greek *epos*, "song, word" is the base of **epic**

epics are long poems about legendary heroes; **sagas** are prose epics about famous men and women especially of medieval times

epicene means "having an ambiguous sexual identity"

the meaning of *epi-*, in **epicenter** is "over, upon" so the **epicenter** of an earthquake lies over the center or "focus" of the earthquake; **epicenter** is never the center of a thing, but what is above the center

Epicurus, a Greek philosopher (341–270 BC) gives us **epicurean** or **epicure** "person devoted to enjoyment of the best things in life"

epidemic comes from Greek *epidemios*, *epi-*, "upon" and *demos*, "the people"

epidural means "administered in the spinal canal just outside the dura mater"

epifauna is underwater animal life

a follower of an important person, like an artist or writer, is an **epigone**

epigoni are close followers who imitate a star

an **epigram** is a short statement that makes an interesting, frequently profound, observation about life or the world; an **epigraph** is a statement culled from the writings or sayings of someone else and used as the heading

etymologically, **epilepsy** is the Greek equivalent of "attack, seizure" from Greek *epilambanein* "seize upon"

epilogue is taken from Greek *epilogos* from *epi*, "in additon" and *logos*, "speech"

the **epimyth** is the moral of a story

epincian means "celebrating victory"

epiphany was originally the appearance or manifestation of a divinity

an **epiphenomenon** is something that appears in addition, a secondary symptom

an exclamatory sentence or reflection summing up a discourse is an **epiphonema**

epiphytic plants are sometimes called "air plants" because they seemingly survive on thin air; tropical epiphytes include orchids, ferns, and members of the pineapple family

an argument that begins by insulting, bullying, or shaming someone is an **epiplexis**

epipterous describes seeds that have wings

an **epirot** is a person who lives inland or on the mainland away from the coast

episode, first a Greek dialogue between two songs, is from *eis*, "into" and *hodos*, "way"

epistaxis is a word for nosebleed

epistemology is the theory or science of the methods or grounds of knowledge

epistle is from Greek *epistole*, "something sent to someone"

epistolary means "of the nature of letters, contained in letters"

epitaph is from Greek *epi*, "upon, over" and *taphos*, "tomb" or "funeral"

epitaxis is a fancy word for nosebleed

a poem written to celebrate a wedding is an **epithalamium**

{ literally, an **epithet** is a word "put on" or "added" to another }

epoch (pronounced EH-puhk) is from Greek *epokhe*, "fixed point in time, stoppage" and it first was the initial point in a chronology from which succeeding years were numbered

epoch applies to the beginning of a new **period** marked by radical changes and new developments—while **era** applies to the entire **period**; **age** denotes a **period** identified with some dominant personality or characteristic and **period** pertains to any portion of time

a word derived from a person's name is an **eponym**; **eponymous** is pronounced uh-PON-uh-mus and **eponym** is EPP-uh-nim

{ an **epopt** is an overseer, watcher, or beholder }

ept means adroit or competent

an **epulation** is a feast

equable means steady or unvarying and far from extremes; **equitable** means fair and impartial

equaeval means "belonging to the same period"—as pieces of furniture might

Latin *aequus*, "even, level" gives us **equal**

the earliest uses of **equality** are in relation to physical quantity

equanimity comes from Latin words meaning "even mind"

equator comes from Latin *aequator*, "in full", *circulus aequator diei et noctis*, "circle equalizing day and night"

equerry, a person in charge of stables, is derived from Latin *scuria*, "stable" and erroneously evolved due to a connection with Latin *equus*, "horse"

equestrian comes from Latin *eques*, "horseman" from *equus*, "horse"

an **equilibrist** is one who performs feats requiring an unusual sense of balance, like a tightrope walker

equilibrium derives from *aequi-*, "equal" and *libra*, "balance"

equinecessary means "needful to the same degree"

equinoctial is that pertaining to a state of equal day and night (as in equinox)

the word **equinox** means "equal night"

equip literally means "fit out or provide crew for a ship"

equipage can be used for articles of personal adornment or use

to **equiparate** is to regard as equivalent

equirotal means having back and front wheels of equal diameter or size

equitant means "overlapping or straddling"

equivalent derives from *aequi-*, "equal" and *valere*, "worth"; two things are **equivalent** when one can be substituted for another

equivocate, from the root *equi*, "equal," suggests that whatever is said has two equally possible meanings

an **equivoque** or **equivoke** is an ambiguous expression or term

an **era** (pronounced EER-uh) is a system of numbering years from an important event

eradicate is from Latin *e-*, "out" and *radix*, "root," "to pull up by the roots"

erase is from Latin *e-*, "out" and *radere*, "scrape"

erect is derived from Latin *erigere*, "raise up, set up"

eremitic is the adjective belonging to a hermit or recluse

eremology is a science concerned with the desert and its phenomena

erenow means "before this time"

to **erept** is to snatch or take away

the day before a Jewish holiday is the **erev**

an **ergophile** is a person who loves to work

a two-year-old canary is an **eriff**

eristic means "enjoying argument for its own sake" or "of or pertaining to controversy"

an **erlang** is an international unit of measurement for telephone use, equal to one caller using the telephone for one hour

ermine came to English from Old French as a name for the stoat or fur of the stoat

erode comes from *rodere*, "gnaw" as **erosion** occurs gradually

the question mark can also be called an **eroteme**

erotic comes from Eros, the winged god of love

erotology is the "science of love"

err first meant "roam, wander, go astray" and it is the basis of **error**, which can mean "action of wandering" or a "winding course"

errand first meant "message"

errant was first used to mean "traveling in search of adventure" as in knight **errant**

erratic comes from Latin *errare*, "to stray, err"

erroneous seems to be used most often with words that suggest mental activity, i.e. assumptions, ideas

an **errorist** is one who errs or who propagates error

ersatz comes from German *ersetzen*, "to replace, compensate" and now means "artificial, synthetic"

erstwhile, quondam, sometime, and **whilom** all mean "onetime, former, at a former time"

to **ert** is to incite, urge on, encourage

an **eructation** is a belch

erudite ("having or showing knowledge") traces to Latin *eruditus/erudire* "bring out of an untrained state" with the base being *rudis* "untrained; rude"

erumpent means "bursting open or apart"

erupt is literally "break out"

eruption is breaking out; **irruption** is breaking in

to **escalade** is to climb or get over by means of ladders

escalate is a back-formation from escalator—a verb back-formed from a trademark

most people used the term movable stairway before **escalator** caught on

escapade is from Spanish *escapar*, "to escape"

escape comes from Latin *ex-*, "out" and *cappa*, "cloak" as one who flees usually wriggles out of a garment and runs; **escape** should be pronounced es-KAYP

escarole (a type of endive) is literally "something edible"

a cliff formation or line of cliffs can be called **escarpment**, **scarp** (from Italian *scarpa*, "slope"), or palisade(s)

eschaton is the end of the world or the end of time

an **escort** was originally a body of armed men accompanying travelers

{ an **escritoire** is a writing desk with a top section for holding books }

esculent means "fit to be eaten"

a decorative plate around a keyhole, lock, doorknob, or drawer handle is an **escutcheon** (from Latin *scutum*, "shield")

the root sense of **esoteric** is "for the initiates of a religious mystery" and it means "confined to or understood by just a few people"

espadrille, the shoe, is from a Provençal word *esparto* for the kind of rush used to make the cordage bottoms of the shoes

an **espalier** is a stake(s) or lattice for training fruit trees or ornamental shrubs

especially means "particularly" or "exceptionally" while **specially** means "for a specific purpose"; **especially** comes from Latin meaning "belonging to a particular species," it now is restricted to mean "important"

esperance is another word for expectation or hope

espial is the act of spying or keeping watch

espionage is based on French *espion*, "spy"

esplanade originally was a "large level area"

espouse implies close attachment to a cause and a sharing of its fortunes

espresso (pronounced es-PRES-oh) is strong black coffee; **cappuccino** is **espresso** to which foamy steamed milk has been added

esquire at root means "shield bearer (in service to a knight)" from Latin *scutarius*

the early sense of **essay** was "test the quality of"

estrange is based on Latin *extraneus*, "not belonging to the family"

estrus is a glow of passion

an **estuary** is a tidal opening or inlet or the tidal mouth of a large river

if you are **esurient**, you are hungry

etape is a place where troops pitch their tents after a day's march and also refers to the length of a day's march

etch comes from a base meaning "cause to eat"

a thing or substance that etches is an **etchant**

eternal's ultimate base is Latin *aevum*, "age"

{ **ether** was once considered to be the fine air above the earth that also constituted the material of the soul—the finest, most perfect matter }

the **esse** is something's essential nature or essence (Latin "to be")

essence is from Latin *esse*, "be"

essorant means soaring in spirit

the base of **establish** is Latin *stabilis*, "stable"

state or condition" was the early meaning of **estate**, as in "holy **estate** of matrimony"

esteem and **estimate** are from Latin *aestimare*, "assess, **estimate**"

estimable means "worthy of esteem or regard" and "of considerable importance"

estimate implies a calculation has been performed and it is on that basis that a judgment or valuation is being made, while **estimation** implies that an on-the-spot evaluation is being performed and that it is an opinion based on that evaluation; an **estimate** conveys a more reasoned or impersonal judgment than an **estimation**

estival (or **aestival**) describes things relating to summer

ethereal first meant "resembling the ether or lightest and most subtle of elements" and now means that something is impalpable or unearthly

ethic(s) is based on Greek *ethos*, "nature, disposition"

Ethiopia was formerly Abyssinia

ethnic, like gentile, was first used for a person not belonging to the Christian or Jewish faith and it now pertains to race, not foreignness (from Greek *ethnikos*, "heathen" and *ethnos*, "nation, people")

ethnicity can be defined as a quasi-primordial collective sense of shared descent and distinct cultural traditions

ethnocentric is based on Greek *ethnos*, "nation, people" and an **ethnocentric** person feels that his or her own nation or group is the cultural center of the world

to **etiolate** is to become whiter or lighter, especially by not getting enough light

etiology is the study of causes, origins, or reasons

etiquette is almost literally "just the ticket"

ettle means "to intend, plan, prepare, attempt"

an **etymologicon** is a book of etymologies

the underlying meaning of **etymology** is "finding the underlying or true meaning of words" (from Greek *etumos*, "real, true" and *elumon*, "true thing")

the earliest known form of a root word is an **etymon**, the original or primary meaning of a word

eucalyptus was coined on the fact that its flower buds have a characteristic conical cover (Greek *eu-*, "well" and *kaluptos*, "covered")

Eucharist is an ancient name for the Lord's Supper, Holy Communion, or Mass; **Eucharist** is from *eu*, "well" and *kharizesthai* (Greek), "offer graciously"

eudemonics or **eudemonism** is the art or a means of acquiring happiness—or a theory of happiness

eugeria is a normal and happy old age

an individual cane or shoot of bamboo is a **eulm**

since the prefix *eu-* means "well or good," a **eulogy** speaks well of a person or thing

eunuch is from Greek *eunoukhos*, literally "bedroom guard" (*eune*, "bed" and *ekhein*, "keep")

an appropriate, apt, or fitting name for a person, place, or thing is a **euonym**

good digestion is **eupepsia** and poor digestion is **dyspepsia**

the opposite of **euphemism** is **dysphemism** (an unpleasant word for something normally pleasant or neutral); **euphemism** comes from Greek *eu*, "well" and *pheme*, "speaking"

eupnea is normal breathing

eureka derives from Greek *heureca*, "I have found (it)!"

Europe is Semitic for "land of the setting sun"

the **Eustachian** tube of the ear was named for Italian anatomist Bartolommeo Eustachio

eustress is good stress, like that from a promotion

the adjective form for alligator is **eusuchian**

eutaxy is an established order or arrangement

euthanasia is from Greek *eu*, "well" and thanatos "death"

eutocia is normal or easy childbirth and dystocia is difficult or abnormal childbirth

eutrapely means pleasantness in conversation and being easy to talk to

eutrophic means "promoting good nutrition; nutritional" and **eutrophy** is "good nutrition"

evade is Latin *e-* and *vadere*, "go"

evagation means mental wandering or digression, also a digression in speech or writing

something that is **evanescent** is at the point of vanishing or becoming imperceptible

> **evangelism** is from Greek *euangelion*, "gospel" or "good news"

evangel was an angel that brought good news—hence, **evangelist**

the salt left after evaporation is **evaporite**

if something is **evasible**, it is able to be evaded

even can be traced back to Proto-Germanic *ebnaz*

even-aged describes a woodland with trees of approximately the same age

the Old English base of **evening** meant "grow towards night" as **evening** extends from sunset to dark

event is from Latin *e-*, "out of" and *venire*, "come"

eventual first meant "pertaining to events"

eventually means "finally, at a future point in time"; **ultimately** means "last, final, or furthest in some projected scheme or time frame"

every is literally a compound word meaning "ever each"

everyday is an adjective and it means "casual" or "informal" with an implied contrast to formality, as well as the meaning of "familiar, ordinary" in contrast with "strange, unusual"; the time expression is written separately—**every day**

little-used adjectives include **everydeal** (in every part), **everyhow** (in every way), **everylike** (always in a similar fashion), and **everywhither** (in every direction)

everyone is correct if you can substitute the word everybody—as it is a noun that means "every person"; **every one** is a pronoun meaning "each one"

evict first meant "conquer, overcome"

evidence (from Latin *e-*, "out" + *videre*, "to see") is information that helps form a conclusion; **proof** is factual information that verifies a conclusion

evil originally signified nothing more sinister than "uppity"

{ to **evince** is to indicate, to reveal the presence of a quality or feeling }

if something is **evitable**, it is avoidable

evoke is from Latin *e-*, "out of, from" and *vocare*, "to call"

evolution comes from Latin (*evolvere*, "roll out") meaning the "unrolling and reading of a papyrus roll"

an **evolvant** is an evolved or deliberately modified form of an organism, especially a bacteria or enzyme, while an **evolvent** is something that gives rise to or evolves something else

an **ewer** was a wide-mouthed water jug formerly used in bedrooms

exact was first a verb, from Latin *ex-*, "thoroughly" and *agere*, "perform"

exaggerate once meant "accumulate, pile up"

exalt means to elevate, praise, or raise a person or thing; **exult** means to rejoice greatly

an **exaltation** is a group of larks in flight

an **examen** is a critical study

examine comes from Latin meaning "weigh accurately"

example is based on Latin *eximere*, "take out"—as it is a typical instance singled out

exempt is from Latin roots *ex-*, "out" and *emere*, "take"

exasperate, based on Latin *exasperare*, "irritate to anger" is based on *asper*, "rough"

excandescence is the state of being glowing hot, anger or passion

excavate is from Latin *excavare*, "hollow out" from *ex-*, "out" and *cavare*, "make or become hollow" (from *cavus* "hollow")

the early sense of **exceed** was "go over a boundary or specific point"

excel comes from *ex-*, "out" and *celsus*, "lofty" (Latin)

the underlying notion of **excellent** is of physically "rising above" others

excelsior is an interjection meaning "go higher!"

the curled shavings of soft wood used for packing and stuffing are **excelsior**

except is from Latin *ex-*, "out of" and *capere*, "take"

excubation is the act of watching all night

to **exculpate** is "to free from accusation or blame" while **exonerate** is literally "to free from a burden"

excursion's first sense was "act of running out, escape"

exceptional means "exceeding the ordinary or expected"; **exceptionable** refers to something "liable to objection or rejection"

a person who expresses many objections is **exceptious**

excerpt derives from Latin *ex-*, "out of" and *carpere*, "to pluck"

exchange comes from Latin *cambire*, "barter"

the original sense of **exchequer** was "chessboard" and it comes from medieval Latin *scarcarium*, "chessboard"

an inactive substance that serves as the vehicle or medium for a drug is the **excipient**; excepient is also the material or surface that receives the pigments in painting

excise as in "remove by cutting" is from Latin *excidere*, "cut out"

excise as in tax is from Middle Dutch *excijs*, from Latin *accensum*, "to tax"

to pluck, bow, or strike a guitar, violin, etc. is to **excite**

exclaustration is being expelled from or leaving a religious retreat and it is also the return to secular life by someone who has been released from their religious vows

Latin *claudere*, "to shut" combines with *ex-*, "out" to give us **exclude**, **exclusion**, and **exclusive**

to **excoriate** something is to pull the skin or hide off it (from Latin *corium*, "hide")

excrement comes from Latin *ex-*, "out" and *cernere*, "to sift"

excruciating's root sense is "to crucify"

excuse is from Latin *ex-*, "out" and *causa*, "cause, blame, accusation"

an **exeat** is a leave of absence

to be **execrable** is to be horrifying

to **execrate** is pronounce a curse upon

execute derives from Latin *exsequi*, "carry out, follow up; punish"

executive first meant "pertaining to execution; putting something into effect"

exegematic is a synonym for explanatory

an **exegesis** is an analysis of a word

an **exegete** is a person who explains or interprets difficult literary passages

exemplar or **exemplary** is an ideal or typical example

exemplify can mean "make an official copy of a document"

an **exemplum** is an illustrative story

exercise comes from the Latin word *exercere*, "keep busy, practice, keep at work" and the notion underlying **exercise** is of "removal of restraint" (from *ex-*, and *arcere*, "restrain")

a person engaged in spiritual exercises is an **exercitant**

the place on a coin for the date, engraver's initials, etc., is the **exergue**

exert can refer to a seed's pushing out or up

to **exflunct** is to overcome or beat thoroughly—or to use up completely

exfodiate means to dig out

exgorgitation is matter vomited

haurire, "drain, draw" is the Latin base of **exhaust**

to cut off someone's inheritance is to **exheridate**

exhibit derives from Latin *ex-*, "out" and *habere*, "hold"

exhilarate comes from Latin *ex*, "out of" and *hilarare*, "to cheer" and originally meant "bringing out happiness"

exhort implies praise and recommendation

exhume is from Latin *ex-*, "out of" and *humus*, "ground"

exigency is anything needed, demanded, or required

a good word to write on letters or packages is **EXIGENT**, since everyone else writes "urgent" or "rush"

exile as an adjective can mean "slender or thin; diminutive"

eximious means "choice, excellent, select" or "distinguished"

exist is probably a back-formation from existence

{ **existential** started out as expressing and predicating actuality }

Latin **exit** meant "he or she goes out," from *ex-*, "out" and *ire*, "go"; **exit** was originally a direction for an actor to leave the stage

a point of exit or departure is the **exition**

an **exlex**, from Latin *ex*, "out" and *lex*, "law," is a synonym for outlaw

on a grape or apple, the skin is called the **exocarp** and the inside is the **mesocarp**; the stem of either is the **pedicel**

mass **exodus** is a redundancy

a fancy word for faintness or lightheadedness is **exolution**

exonerate comes from Latin *ex-*, "from" and *onus*, "a burden"

exonumia are objects that resemble, but cannot be used as, money—such as coupons or tokens

an **exonym** is a name that foreigners use for a place, like Florence for Firenze, or for a people or social group—a name which that group does not use for itself

exorbitant was originally a legal term for a case outside of the scope of a law and since it implies going "out of orbit," also first meant "deviating from the true path"

exorcise derives from Latin *ex-*, "out" and *horkos*, "oath" and first meant to "conjure up or command an evil spirit"

exoteric means readily understandable (also suitable) to most people

exotic once meant "belonging to another country"; **exotic** plants are introduced from abroad—the opposite of endemic and indigenous

expand comes from Latin *ex-*, "out" and *pandere*, "to spread"

expatiate first meant "roam freely" or "move beyond one's usual bounds" and now can mean "wander" or "talking about a subject at length"

part of **expatriate**'s history is Latin *patria*, "fatherland" and *ex-*, "out of, away from"

someone who **expects** something literally "looks out" for it

expectorant and **expectorate** are partly based on *pectus/pector*, "breast" as this action involves expelling from the chest or lungs

expedient means "convenient in the circumstances" and suggests unfairness or dishonesty

expedite comes from a Latin word (literally "free the feet") meaning "put in order by freeing from difficulties"

expeditious means "quick and efficient" and only applies to actions and procedures; **expedition** retains the notions of speed and purpose

expend comes from *ex-*, "out" and *pendere*, "weigh; pay" and, originally, **expend** referred to spending money with the root sense being "to weigh out money"

expenditure refers to an actual outlay of money or goods, whereas **expense** has a more general sense, a charge or cost of goods or property; we have expenses, but we make expenditures

a synonym for awakening is **expergefacient**; **expergefaction** is waking up and an alarm clock is an **expergefactor**

experience and **experiment** and **expert** derive from Latin *experiri*, "try"

{ **experimental** first meant "having personal experience" }

experrection is waking up or awakening

to **expiate** is to make amends or reparation for

expire is, literally, "breathe out (the soul)" and first meant "to die"

to **expiscate** is to fish out, to find out by scrutiny

explaterate is to run off at the mouth or have verbal diarrhea

expletive's first meaning was "a word or phrase serving to fill out a line" and another meaning was "a person or thing which serves merely to fill up space"; now we use it to mean a vulgar or obscene word or expression

the thing to be explained is the **explicandum** and the explanation is the **explicans**

explicate also contains the implication that the something of which an account is being given is more complicated or detailed—so

while one may **explain** why a child is crying, one would **explicate** the meaning of a poem or implications of a legal document; early senses of **explain** were "smooth out" and "spread flat"

explicate comes from Latin *ex-*, "out" and *plicare*, "to fold," as does **explicit**, literally "unfolded" or "unwrapped"

explode, from Latin *explodere*, originally meant "to drive out by clapping, to hiss off the stage"

explode is to blow up from a confined area outwards; **implode** means blow inwards, as a lightbulb does when it burns out

exploit originally meant "progress, success" and "speed"

explore comes from Latin meaning "search out" from ex- "out" and plorare "utter a cry"

exponent as an adjective means "expounding, interpreting"

to reason earnestly is to **expostulate**

something that is **expressed** is literally "pressed out"

expressionism is a style of painting, drama, music, etc. that expresses the inner experience of the artist rather than impressions of the physical world

expropriate is from *ex-*, "out, from" and *proprium*, "property"

expunge is *ex-*, "out" and *pungere*, "to prick" and literally means "to mark for deletion with dots"

expurgate originally meant "purge of excrement"

etymologically, **exquisite** means "sought out"

exsuccous means devoid of all juices or sap

extant comes from Latin *ex-*, "out" and *stare*, "to stand" and it means "currently or actually in existence"

extemporaneous means "prepared in advance and carried out with few or no notes" while **impromptu** means "totally unprepared, performed on the spur of the moment"—but this distinction has been all but lost

extempore was literally "out of the time" in Latin

to **extemporize** can mean "do something in a makeshift manner"

extend and **extent** are based on Latin tendere "stretch"

extenuate comes from the Latin verb extenuare, "make thin or lean" and it originally meant "to treat as of small importance, make light of"

to **exter** is to dig out of the earth, the opposite of **inter**

exterior was first a Latin word, the comparative form of exter, "outer"

extimate is an adjective meaning "the most distant; outermost"—as a planet

extinct is, literally, "with the light put out" from Latin ex-, and stinguere, "quench" (and extinguish has the same base)

extol is from ex-, "out, upward" and tollere, "to raise"

{ a synonym for astonishing is **extonious** }

extort and extortion are from Latin ex-, "out" and torquere, "to twist"

extra is probably a shortening of extraordinary

extradite is a back-formation from extradition

the upper or outer curve of an arch is the **extrados**

a fancy word for outdoor is **extraforaneous**

the **extramundane** is the infinite empty space supposed to be extended from the bounds of the universe

extramural is from Latin extra muros, "outside the walls"

an **extranean** is an outsider or stranger, a person not belonging to a household

extraordinary should be pronounced ek-STROR-di-nair-ee

to **extrapolate** is to deduce from information known

extrapunitive means "blaming other people or events unreasonably; reacting aggressively to frustration"

extravagant was first used to mean "wandering, roaming," from Latin extra-, "outside" and vagari, "wander"

extreme and **extremity** are from Latin exter, "outer"

Latin ex-, "out" and tricae, "perplexities" are the origins of **extricate**

extrovert derived from extro-, and vertere, "to turn"

trudere, "thrust" is the Latin base of **extrude**

to **extund** is to produce with effort

the base of **exuberant** is Latin uber, "fertile" and the word can mean "big-breasted"

exude comes from Latin sudare, "to sweat"

exulant means "living in exile"

exult is from Latin ex-, "out, upward" and salire, "to leap"

trimming your nails is to **exungulate**

Exxon is the only word in English with a double x

the holes in Swiss cheese are technically called **eyes**

eyeblack is the stuff that athletes put under their eyes to deflect the glare of light

an **eyelet** is a small hole for a lace, rope, or ring—it is actually a diminutive form of the word "eye"

you can call the burners on a stove the "**eyes**"

an **eye-servant** or **eye-waiter** is a domestic or other employee who only performs duties when within eyeshot of his or her master, this insincerity known as **eye-service**

eyeshot (and sight-shot) is "glance, sight, or view" as in "She was out of **eyeshot**."

the **eyetooth** is so called because the nerves of the upper teeth pass close to the eyes

{ a small island in a river or lake is an **eyot** or **ait** }

an **eyrie** is the nest of a bird of prey

an **e-zine** is a magazine published only in electronic form

{ Forever saddled with an obscenity, the letter **F** can seem vulgar or comical by itself. F's crude sound attracted comment even before English was born. Cicero called it the "unsweetest" sound in Latin. }

fable goes back to a Latin word *fari*, "to speak"

a **fable** is a short instructional tale, while a **fairytale** (or fairy tale) is told as amusement

fabric was originally a building, then later a machine or appliance

fabrile means "pertaining to a skilled artisan or mechanic"

a collective term for the tools used by a craftperson is **fabrilia**

to **fabulate** is to tell invented stories

a **fabulist** is a great euphemism for liar

fabulosity is the quality of being fabulous

façade, a front—especially a false one—is pronounced fuh-SAHD

face is a colloquial term for makeup; the word **face** is from Latin *facies*, "form, aspect"

facepainting is another term for the art of drawing portraits

facet is a diminutive of face, literally "little or small face"

facetious originally meant "having polished or urbane manners" and along with sequoia, uses all five vowels

the nameplate over a shop front with the occupier's name and trade is the **facia**

facial started out as a religious term meaning "face to face; open"

facile can mean "affable, relaxed"—a **facile** writer seems to write too quickly and easily, a **facile** suggestion does not deal with the issue in any depth, and a **facile** solution may be only temporarily effective

facile, **facility**, **fact**, **faction**, and **factor** are all based on Latin *facere*, "do, make"

facility once meant "gentleness, lightness"

facinorous means extremely wicked

facsimile is from Latin *fac simile*, "do the same" (from *facere*, "do, make" and *similis*, "like, similar")

fact originally meant a brave or noble action, a feat

a **faction** can be a way of acting or behaving

Faction and **fashion** come from Latin faction-, *factio*, "a doing or making" (from facere "to do, make"). French **faction** was a learned borrowing from Latin before coming into English with the meaning "a class or party of people," while **fashion** took the longer route through Old French *façon* in the sense of form, shape, appearance, **fashion**.

factitious refers to "made up, contrived" as opposed to what is genuine while **fictitious** is "made up, contrived" as opposed to what is real; a **factitious** story might be designed to serve a purpose, but a **fictitious** story is intended to deceive

a verb that expresses something is being made, e.g. to paint, is a **factitive**

a **factlet** is a piece of trivia

factoid is an unsubstantiated statement, account, or report published as if it were factual, coined by the novelist Norman Mailer from fact + -oid (as in android, humanoid), in reference to his fictionalized biography of Marilyn Monroe

faerie is the land of the fairies

another word for dregs/sediment is **faex**

to **faff** is said of wind, meaning "to blow in puffs"—but it can also mean "to bustle about ineffectually; fuss"

faffle describes work which occupies a lot of time but does not produce commensurate results

the **fag-end** was originally the last part of a piece of cloth and then became the last part or tail end of other things; **fag** as in cigarette is an abbreviation of **fag-end**, which originally meant generally "extreme end"

Gabriel **Fahrenheit** (1686–1736) devised the temperature scale named for him

faience gets its name from Faenza, Italy

fail (and fallacy, fallible, false, fault) comes from Latin *fallere*, "deceive someone" or "disappoint someone"

{ **factory** was originally a place where traders did their business in another country, based on Latin *factorium*, "an oil press" (for olive oil) }

factotum is from Latin, literally, "do the whole thing"

facture is something made or constructed

if someone or something is full of facts, they are **facty**

facultative means occurring in response to circumstances rather than by nature

faculty first meant an ability or aptitude and is based on Latin facilis "easily done"

facund means eloquent

fad is a shortening of fiddle-faddle "trifling talk or action"

fade may come from a Proto-Romance blending of Latin *fatuus*, "fatuous" and *vapidus*, "vapid"

fadoodle is a good synonym for nonsense

fain as an adverb means "rather" or "gladly, unwillingly"

a **faineant** is a person who does nothing, an idler

faint in "faint of heart" means "lacking in courage"

fair comes from Latin *ferial*, "holy days," times when this type of event was held

fairway is a way that is "fair," i.e. "obstacle-free"

fairy comes from fay "**fairy**" which came through French from Latin *fata*, "the Fates" and the word first referred to the mythical land of the fays

faith's root is Latin fides from *fidere*, "trust"

faitour is a cheat or imposter

fajita is Spanish for "little strip or belt" and the dish uses small strips of meat; it is pronounced fuh-HEE-tuh

a **fake** is a work of art that is deliberately made or altered to appear better, older, or other than what is is; a **forgery** is a fraudulent imitation of another thing that already exists

falafel comes from an Arabic word for pepper and falafels are deep-fried balls of ground chickpea, small peppers, and pickled cucumbers, served hot in pita bread

falbala is the trimming or flounce on a woman's petticoat

falcate means "curved like a sickle; hooked"

falcon probably comes ultimately from Germanic *falkon*; a **falcon**'s wings are longer and more pointed than **hawk** wings and they are fast, frenzied fliers as opposed to hawks which have a flap-soar pattern of flying

fall as a season is from the 16th century phrase "**fall** of the leaf"

fall as in landfall and nightfall is "a first occurrence" in the sighting of land or the coming of night

fallacy was first "fallace" and both derived from fallere "deceive"—as is **false**

the **fallboard** is the hinged protective covering that protects the keyboard of a piano when it is not being played

fallow "uncultivated" originally meant "plowed land"

false came from Latin *falsus*, from *fallere* "deceive"

a statement which is self-evidently false is a **falsism**

another name for a hand is a **famble**; to **famble** means "to stammer, stutter"

fame also meant "reputation" in early contexts

to **famigerate** is to divulge

familiar comes from Latin *familiaris*, from *familia*, "household servants; household, family"

The word **family** first referred to the servants of a household and then to both the servants and the descendants of a common ancestor. It comes from Latin *familia*, "household; household servants," which came from another Latin term *famulus*, "servant." It was not until 1667 that the term was used specifically for the group of persons consisting of parents and their children.

famine and **famish** come from Latin *fames*, "hunger"

an assistant to a scholar is a **famulus**

a **fan** was originally a device for winnowing grain, from Latin *vannus*, "winnowing **fan**" (winnowing is separating the grain from chaff by tossing it in the air)

fan, as in enthusiast, is an abbreviation of fanatic, from Greek *phanatikos*, "person from the temple"—a god-intoxicated person

a **fanal** is a lighthouse or beacon

fanatic comes from a Latin word for "pertaining to a temple" or "inspired by or frenzied by a god"

fanboy is a term for a passionate enthusiast of a geek culture item, such as a game or comic, without question and also pushing the enthusiasm on acquaintances

the root of the word **fancy** is "the ability to project mental images"

fane is an old word for temple or shrine

fanfaronade is a euphonious word for "bluster" or "ostentation"

> **fang** originally meant "something caught or taken; booty, spoils"

a **fanlight** is a semicircular or rectangular window over a door or other window

fantastic, from Greek *phantos*, "visible," was spelled phantastic from the 16th–19th centuries (same with phantasy)

fantasy can be used as a verb to mean "imagine" or "fantasize"

{ **fantigue** is a state of excitement, anxiety, or tension }

another name for the fidgets or the willies is **fantods**

far has the comparative forms farther and further, superlative forms farthest and furthest

farce first meant forcemeat stuffing and came to be used metaphorically when a humorous play was "stuffed" in between two more serious acts of the main theatrical presentation—or for interludes of impromptu buffoonery in a dramatic presentation

a **farctated** diner is one who cannot eat another bite; if you are **farctate**, you are stuffed to the gills or bloated from eating a large meal

to put on makeup is to **fard** and makeup can also be called **fard**; **farded** means covered with makeup, as a clown might be

fare first meant "traveling, journey, expedition" for which a sum was paid and then became "amount paid for a journey"

farewell is literally, "go well"

farfalle, pasta shaped like bowties or butterflies, is the Italian plural for "butterfly"

far-fetched originally meant "brought from far"

farina comes from far, the Latin word for spelt (a type of wheat)

farinaceous means "containing or made of starch"

a **farl** is a chunk of bread

the word **farm** comes from medieval Latin *firma*, "fixed annual payment or rent"

farmer in late Middle English was a tax collector; its modern use stems from the word's use for a tenant who tended the land on behalf of an owner

farouche means "sullen or shy in company"

farrago, from Latin, originally meant "a mash for feeding cattle"; later, figuratively, a medley or hodgepodge

a blacksmith who only shoes horses is a **farrier**

farrow (litter of pigs) originally meant "young pig," from Indo-European *porkos*

a **farshtinker** is a selfish or insecure person

fart is an ancient word in the Indo-European languages, with the root of *perd-*, perhaps an imitation of the sound

farther is generally preferred over **further** when the context is distance in space or time; use **farther** when talking about physical distance and use **further** when talking about abstract ideas or extent/degree

farthing literally means "quarter" and was first used to translate Latin *quadrans*, "quarter of a denarius"

the hoops of a hoop skirt is the **farthingale**—and the word is a corruption of Spanish verdugado "**farthingale**," from verdugo "rod, stick"—so called because a **farthingale** is distended by cane hoops or rods inserted underneath

excrement clinging to hairs of a backside can be called **fartleberries** or **dilberries**

fartlek, a method of fast and slow training for running, is from Swedish *fart*, "speed" and *lek*, "play"

a cover (especially detachable) for the front part of a cell phone is a **fascia**; **fascia** is pronounced FASH-ee-uh or FASH-uh

fasciation is bandaging or becoming bound or bandaged

fascinate is derived from Latin fascinare "to bewitch or enchant" and a **fascinator** was a magician

the **Fascist** party's name, literally "bundle, group" was based on the fasces which was the party's symbol and the word **Fascism** was formed on analogy with Communism

fashion (noun) first meant "make" or "shape, style" as the word is based on Latin facere, "do, make"

{ a **fashionista** is an avid follower of fashion or a haute couture designer }

if something is troublesome, it is **fashious**

fast as in "quick" and **fast** "abstain from food" come from the same ultimate source, Germanic fastuz, "firm" and the application to "eating no food" comes from "holding **fast** to a particular observance"

fasten etymologically means "make fast," coming from Germanic fastuz, and **fasten** was first used to mean "establish, settle"

fastidious is from a root meaning "squeamish, easily moved to disgust" and it first meant "disdainful"

to **fastigate** is to make pointed

fastigiate means "sloping up to a point"

fastuous means haughty, pretentious

a **"fat"** acting part is one that allows the person to be impressive

fatal first meant "decreed by fate"

use **fatal** for something which has caused someone's death; use **lethal** for something which is capable of killing someone

etymologically, **fate** is "that which is spoken"—by the gods—going back to Indo-European bha-, "speak"

The word **father** first appeared in Old English spelled as fæder (c 825), having derived from assumed Germanic fadar. It has cognates (relatives) in many other languages: Dutch vader and German Vater, as well as forms in Old Norse, Swedish, Danish, Gothic, etc., Latin and Greek pater, Old Irish athir, and Sanskrit pitar; all of these words share an Indo-European root. The use of the word **father** as a verb did not occur until 1483. Common synonyms for **father** are dad and daddy (c 1500), papa (c 1681), pa (c 1811), pop (c 1838), poppa (c 1897), and pops (c 1928).

father and **mother** should be capitalized in direct address or in reference to one's own parents

fathom is Germanic in origin, meaning "six feet" (tracing back to Old Norse "embrace, bosom") and the original sense was "something which embraces"—giving rise to the unit of measurement based on arm span, generally around six feet; the sense of "understand" for **fathom** is from the notion "embrace"

other words for prophetic are **fatidic** or **fatiloquent**

fatigue first meant "a task or duty causing weariness"—and it also refers to the weakening of metal

fatiscent means having chinks or clefts

fatstock is livestock fattened for slaughter

fatuous is derived from Latin fatuus, "foolish"

the passage between the mouth and the pharynx is the **fauces**

faucet probably comes from French meaning "bore, tap"

fault, from Latin fallere, "be wanting, be defective," is related to the word failure

a **faun** is upper body of a man with the ears, horns, tail, legs of a goat

Fauna, an Italian rural goddess, and her brother Faunus, an Italian rural god, were worshipped by shepherds and farmers—and brought us the word **fauna** for animal life

the plural of **fauna** is faunae or faunas and for **flora** it is floras or florae

a **faunule** is the fauna of a small habitat, especially fossils from a small area

faust is an adjective meaning happy

favaginous is "like a honeycomb"

when you **favor** a body part, as a limb, you deal with it gently and avoid putting strain on it

fawn, from Latin *feto*, first meant "young of an animal" before it became specialized to "a young deer"

an informal plural of fact is **fax**

fax is an obsolete word for the hair of the head

fax, as the machine, is from Latin *fac simile*, "make alike"

The word **feast** comes from the Latin *festa* (plural of *festum*), "festive ceremonies" and was originally a religious celebration commemorating a person, like the Bible's Passover. There are movable feasts like Easter, whose date changes each year, and immovable feasts, like Christmas and saints' days. The word **feast** came into English in the 13th century.

feat can be described as the art or knack of doing something and it once meant "fact" (as it is from Latin *factum*, "fact")

feather is a word for the rising of cream on the surface of a cup of coffee

featous means well-proportioned or handsome

feature comes from Latin *facere*, "do, make" and then *factura*, "making, formation"

featurely means "having strongly marked features"

to **faze** is to "disconcert, embarrass"; **phase** as a verb is used with "in" or "out" to mean appear and disappear by stages

faze, to disconcert or perturb, is a variant of feeze, "drive off or away; frighten"

feag comes from German *feige*, "cowardly" and first meant "fated to die; at the point of death"

slovenly, slobby people are **feague** or **shabbaroon** (male) and **callet**, **dratchell**, or **slattern** (female)

a **feak** is a dangling curl of hair

fear first meant "sudden calamity" or "danger"

someone may be **fearful**; someone or something may be **fearsome**

feasible means capable of being done (not probable or plausible)

to **feaze** is to fray or unravel at the end; feazings are the frayed or unraveled ends of something

febricula is a slight fever

febrile is a synonym for feverish

February was the month of the festival of purification for the ancient Romans "februa," from Latin *februum*, "purgation"

februation is religious purification or exorcism

feckful means "efficient, vigorous" or "powerful"

literally, **feckless** is another way of saying ineffective, from feck "effect"

fecund is another word for "fertile, fruitful, productive" and is pronounced FEH-kund; **fecundation** is another word for "fertilization, impregnation"

federal first referred to a covenant or treaty and the word is derived from Latin *foedus*, "covenant"

fedity means foulness, turpitude, or vileness

the hat "**fedora**" is named for an 1882 play "Fédora" which featured Sarah Bernhardt in a large soft felt hat with an upturned brim

fee first referred to movable property or tenure in an estate or land and evolved to its monetary senses

feeble is from Latin *flebilis*, "that is to be wept over," from *flere*, "weep"

a **feed** or **feeder** in theater is someone who provides lines to react to, like a comedian's straight man

the shortest English word that contains A,B,C,D,E,F is **feedback**

to **feek** is to wander aimlessly

feel's ultimate ancestor is Indo-European *pol-/pal-*

the obnoxious sounds made by a computer, especially to denote user error, are called **feeps**

to **feer** is to mark off land for plowing

feesks are tufts of unruly hair

to **feeze** is to brighten and to be in a **feeze** is to be in a state of alarm or perturbation; **feezy** is "worried, mildly confused or alarmed"

a **feff** or **natkin** is a disagreeable smell

feign is based on Latin *fingere*, "conceive, contrive"

feint paper is paper printed with faint lines as a handwriting guide

feisty comes from fist "a small dog" which came from fisting cur, a derogatory term for a lapdog; fist or **feist** was the name of a small mongrel or terrier, hence "**feisty**"— which is also a word for a farting dog

feldspar comes from German words meaning "field" feld and "spar" spath (crystalline minerals)

{ **felicity** comes from Latin *felix* and originally meant "fruitful" }

fell as in "cut down" originated as a causative version of fall "cause to fall"

in "one **fell** swoop" the word **fell** means "fierce, lethal"

a **fellow** is a person who shares with another in anything, literally "one who lays down money in a joint enterprise," and it originally was a man or a woman

fellowfeel is to share the feelings of others, sympathize with

the **felly** or **felloe** is the exterior rim on a wheel or the section of rim supported by a spoke

Latin *fello* meant "evil-doer" and eventually gave us **felon**

etymologically, **felt** is a fabric that is formed by beating as it is made from compressed fibers, from Indo-European root *peldos*

felth is the power of feeling in the fingers

the word **female** is unrelated to the word **male** except to be influenced by its spelling; it is a diminutive of *femina*, "woman" and **male** comes from Latin *masculus*

the **femur** is the third segment of an insect's leg

fen is low land covered with water or a marsh

fenberry is a synonym for cranberry

fence as in stolen goods is a shortening of defence (defense, defend)

fender is a shortened form of "defender"—originally the name given to iron cable hung on the sides of sailing vessels to minimize damage in case of collision, so called because it "defends" the vehicle

a **fenestra** is a small mark or scar left by the separation of a plant seed from the ovary (from Latin for "window")

a **fenestral** is a window with panes of paper or cloth instead of glass

fenestrated means "having windows"

the pattern or scheme of a building's windows is its **fenestration**; **interfenestral** means between windows

the refuse of whale blubber when melted is **fenks**

fennel means "little hay" and this spice is mainly used in sauces

a short slit or opening in a robe, especially by the throat, is a **fent**

fenugreek literally means "Greek hay" as the Romans used this dried plant for fodder

feracious means "fruitful, prolific"

feral pertains to domestic cats that once lived under human control but have returned to live and breed in the wild; **feral** cats are often found on islands where they were left by sailors, but where there are now few humans

feriation is the celebration of a holiday by not working—or simply going on vacation

something wonderful or strange, a marvel or curiosity, can be called a **ferly**

ferment is based on a Latin word meaning "boil"—and a figurative meaning is "to excite or become excited or agitated"

if something is **fermentescible**, it is capable of causing or undergoing fermentation

fern traces back to the Indo-European root porno-

extremely freckled is **fernticled**; a fernticle is a freckle

etymologically, **ferocious** means "wild-eyed," from Latin *ferus*, "fierce, wild" and *oc/ox*, "appearing, looking"

the **ferret**'s name comes from Latin *furritus*, "little thief"—alluding to ferrets" stealing of hens" eggs

ferriage is the fare paid for the use of a ferry and a **ferrier** is a person who operates a ferry

a **ferrule** is a ring or cap that strenthens the end of a handle, stick, or tube; a **ferule** is a flat ruler, rod, or cane used for punishment

ferrum, the Latin name for iron, is the origin of its symbol Fe

ferry originally was a place where people could cross water by boat, not the boat itself, and the word is based on an Old Teutonic word for "fare"

{ **fertile** and **fertilizer** have the Latin base *ferre*, "to bear" }

the intensity of heat or feeling can be described as **fervency** (from Latin *fervere*, "boil"); an instance of this heat or feeling is **fervor**

something that is **fervent** or **fervid** is "burning, glowing, hot"

a synonym for obscene is **Fescennine**

a **fescue** is a pointer, such as that used by a teacher, having originally meant "a straw or twig"

if food **festers**, it becomes rotten

if something is hasty or hurried, it is **festinate** and to **festinate** is to walk fast, make haste; **festination** is "haste, speed"

festival was for some time an adjective referring to a feast day of the church

festive, when said of a person, can mean "fond of feasting"

a decorative chain is a **festoon**

a **Festschrift** is a collection of writings forming a volume presented to a scholar at a certain age or at the high point in his/her career

feta (cheese) translates to "slice"—one of the stages in its making

fetch has some nautical uses, including "get into the wake of a boat" or "get into the course of the wind"

fetid is a synonym for stinking

fetish goes back to a Latin *facticius* meaning "made by art"—and the word probably pertained to charms and talismans worshipped or thought superstitious by the inhabitants of the Guinea coast of Africa in the 1600s

to **fetishize** is to overvalue

a **fetlock** is a tuft of hair on a horse's leg

fetters are shackles for the feet, from the Germanic root *fetero*, which came from the Indo-European base *ped-*

a **fettle** is a bandage or strap, especially on a pannier (basket); to **fettle** is to get oneself ready or prepare

Fewer means a smaller number of individual things and **less** means a small quantity of something. A traditional rule of English usage holds that **less** should be used only of uncountable things, that is, things that can be measured but not counted as discrete units. Thus "**less** electricity," "**less** than a quart," "**less** doubt." **Fewer**, on the other hand, should be used only of things that can be counted: "**fewer** people," "**fewer** cars." In actual usage, **fewer** almost always adheres to the traditional rule; the "problem" is that **less** is often used with countable things.

a **fewterer** or **feuterer** is someone who keeps a dog, especially a greyhound

fey means "fated to die"

the **fez** is named after **Fez** (Fes), Morocco, once its chief place of manufacture

the s-shaped opening in a violin is the **f-hole**

fiancé is French for "a promise"

fiasco is a bulbous long-necked bottle for wine encased in raffia or straw—originally "flask, bottle"

a lobe of the liver was once called a **fiber**

{ a **fiat** (pronounced FEE-ut) is a command by which something is brought into being (Latin for "let it be done" or "let there be made") }

to trim or clean the edges of pottery before firing is to **fettle**

fettuccine is the Italian plural and diminutive of *fetta*, "slice, ribbon"

a human embryo starts to be called a **fetus** at three months

feud is from the Germanic base of *foe*

few goes back to Indo-European *pau-*, denoting smallness of quantity or number

the **fibula** is the outer of the two bones between the knee and ankle; the **tibia** is the one in front (shinbone)

fico is another way of saying "giving the finger"

fictile is an adjective meaning "pertaining to pottery" or "suitable for making pottery"

the early sense of **fiction** was "invented statement"—which is also the earliest sense of **figment**

fictional is pertaining to or found in fiction; **fictitious** is "false, fraudulent" or "non-existent"

Fictionary or **Balderdash** are games for a group using a dictionary, with one person finding a really odd word and everyone trying to come up with a dictionary definition of it

fiddle may derive from Latin *vitulari*, "celebrate a festival"—as Vitula was the goddess of victory and jubilation

fidelity (pronounced fuh-DEL-uh-tee) comes from fides, the Latin word for "faith"

to **fidget** is also to figgle, fissle, jiffle, nestle, sessle, tiddle, or trifle

fidicinal means "pertaining to stringed instruments" or a person who plays one

fidimplicitary is "fully trusting someone"

fiduciary can mean "held in trust for another" or "having to do with a confidence or trust"

a **fief** is a person's sphere of operation or control

field originally meant "area of flat, open land" and comes from the Indo-European root *plth-*

fiend first described an enemy or foe

fierce is from Latin *ferus*, "untamed"

{ **fifth-generation** means "using artificial intelligence" }

a small valueless thing may be called a **fig**

fig or **full fig** is the complete set of clothes for an occasion

fighting seems to have had its etymological origins in the petty act of pulling someone's hair

figment comes from Latin *figmentum*, "something created or invented"

if something is **figulate**, it is made of clay

a **figurant** is an actor appearing only in crowd scenes

figure comes via Old French from Latin *figura*, "**figure**, form, shape"

figurehead literally is a bust or full-length figure carved into the cutwater of a ship

a **fike** is an itch or anything causing one to fidget

filberts were named for Frankish Saint Philibert, whose feast day falls in the height of nut-harvesting season

filch comes from the jargon of thieves for a rod with a hook on the end of it, used for stealing

file for smoothing comes from Germanic *fikhala*, back to Indo-European *pik-/peik-* denoting "cut"

file for storing something is from Latin *filum*, "thread," applied to the string or wire suspended and first used for hanging documents and records

a boned piece of meat is a **filet** (preferred in U.S.) or **fillet**, a thin slice of meat is an **escalope**, and a thick slice is a **steak**; a **fillet/filet** is a narrow band (from Latin *filum*, "thread")—as in a band of nerve or muscle fiber

a **filial** (noun) is an offshoot

filibuster is from Dutch *vrijbuiter*, "freebooter"—its original meaning

the formative elements of **filigree** are Latin *filum*, "thread" and *granum*, "grain"

filipendulous is another word for "hanging by a thread"

fill is from Germanic as a derivative of *fullaz*, "full"

another name for a headband is **fillet**

any short, sharp blow is a **fillip**—like snapping your fingers or a flick of a finger

filly is from Old Norse *fylja*, of Germanic origin and related to foal

the notion underlying **film** is of a thin "skin," from German *fellam*, and Latin *pellis*, "skin"

filo or **phyllo** comes from a Greek word for "leaf"

filter first meant "felt" and came from Latin *filtrum* and Germanic *filtiz*

{ to **fimble** is to move the fingers lightly and frequently over something }

a lying answer or phony excuse is **fimblefamble**

fimbriate means "fringed"

fimbulwinter is the winter of winters

fin, as in fish, is actually etymologically related to Latin *pinna*, "feather, wing"

fin, slang for $5, is a clipping of *finif*, a borrowing from Yiddish for "five"

final is from Latin *finis*, "end"

finally is used when the item being introduced figures as part of a process or development; **lastly** should be used when the item introduced counts as part of a list

finance comes from Old French finer "make an end; settle a debt" and Old French fin "payment, end" (from Latin *finis*, "end")

fine (monetary penalty) first meant "end"—from Latin *finis*, "end; a sum to be paid on concluding a lawsuit"

finesse is the clarity or purity of metals

we actually have eight **fingers**, unless you count the thumbs

a **fingerfull** is a pinch or small quantity

each of the fingers of a glove is a **fingerling**

a **fingerpost** is a sign at a road junction with attached signs pointing in the directions of places indicated

a decorative knob on the top of a lamp, holding the shade on, is a **finial**

a **finific** is a limiting quality

finifugal means shunning the end of something

the final taste from a sip or drink of wine is its **finish**

the horizon is the **finitor**

finny is another way of saying "teeming with fish"

the **fipple** is the mouthpiece of a flute, recorder, or whistle

your lower lip is your **fipple**

the Douglas **fir**, the Chinese **fir**, and the big cone **spruce** are not true firs or spruces

Fire is often associated with winter, for its great contribution to keeping us warm. The English word has many cognates (words related by descent from the same ancestral language) in the Germanic languages and corresponds to Greek, Umbrian, Armenian, and Sanskrit terms. Originally, the word described emotion and passion; by 1300, it described one of the four "elements" (with earth, wind, water). The spelling **fire** was first recorded around 1200, but it did not become fully established until the early 1600s.

the back wall of a fireplace is the **fire-back** or **reredos**

a piece of burning wood is a **firebrand**

firebug is fire plus bug meaning "maniac"

firedog is one of the two metal supports for burning logs in a grate—and we also know these as andirons

fireflies are not flies, they are beetles

fire-iron pertains to any implement for tending to a domestic fire, usually tongs, poker, and shovel

the instrument for stirring up a fire is the **fire-pike**

The term for a combustible or explosive or pyrotechnic ("pertaining to fire art") projectile was "**rocket**" until **fireworks** was used in 1777 to describe these in connection with the first Fourth of July celebration. "Rockets" are still the most popular form of firework. Rockets are lifted by recoil from the jet of fire created by the burning ingredients—and they are designed for maximum combustion and maximum thrust.

Fireworks originated in ancient China. The word **firecracker** refers to those that make loud sounds and sparklers are those that send off a shower of sparks.

to **firk** is to urge oneself forward or press on

firkin comes from a Dutch word for fourth and originally was a cask containing a quarter of a barrel (for liquids, fish, butter, etc.)

firm as in "business, company" comes from Latin *firmare*, "fix, settle; confirm by signature"—as in the name by which a company's business was transacted

the "vault of the sky" as a fixed structure is the basis for the word "**firmament**"

first was originally a superlative form "most in front" as it comes from Indo-European *pro-*, "in front, before"

first-foot means "to be the first person to cross someone's threshold in the New Year"

the term **first-rate** originally indicated the highest of the "rates" by which vessels of war were distinguished according to size and equipment

a **firth** is a narrow inlet from the sea

the Latin base of **fiscal** (fiscus) meant "purse, treasury"

fish in Old English first meant any animal living exclusively in water; **fish** is the plural when referring to **fish** in general or a quantity of **fish** of the same kind and **fishes** is the plural to refer to a quantity with variety

a **fishplate** is a type of metal plate used to strengthen a joint (from fish meaning "mend")

sea urchins' reproduction by splitting in two is called **fissiparity**

fissiparous (from Latin *fissus*, "split") is patterned on viviparous

fist literally refers to the number of fingers on the hand

fisticuffs is from fisty "related to fist fighting" and cuff "strike with the open hand"

a whale's spout is the **fistula** and that was the name of an ancient Roman flutelike reed instrument

fit can mean "section of a poem"

fitful "irregular" is from fit meaning "sudden attack"

a **fitten** is a lie or invention

five is one of a general Indo-European family of words (*pengke*) meaning "**five**"

fix comes ultimately from Latin *figere*, "fasten"

{ preservative applied to a drawing to prevent smudging is a **fixative** }

fixings are foods that are usually served with a main dish

fixture, which started as fixure, got its t when it was patterned after mixture

a piece of furniture that cannot be moved is a **fixture**; a piece of furniture that can be moved is a **fitment**

a firework that hisses is a **fizgig**

a **fizgig** is a frivolous woman

if food **fizzes**, it makes a sizzling noise when frying

fizzle derives from *fisten*, "to fart" and **fizzle**'s original definition is "the action of breaking wind, noiseless fart"

flab is a back-formation of flabby

for **flabbergast**, flabber is probably from flap and the second element is aghast

flabby was once used to mean "damp, clammy"

flabellation is the use of a fan to cool something

flaccid should be pronounced FLAK-sid

to **flack** is a synonym for to flap or flutter

to **flacket** is to rustle like a taffeta dress

flag is a "flat stone slab," so flagstone is somewhat redundant

strawberry plants **flagellate**—send out long threadlike runners

flagitious is "criminally wicked"

an early sense of **flagrant** was "blazing, resplendent"

flagrant implies shocking and reprehensible, while **blatant** is obvious, contrived, and usually obnoxious; **flagrant** is a stronger term than **blatant**

flagstone (properly just "flag") is not based on flag "banner" but is derived from Old Norse *flaga*, "slab" and its original meaning was "turf" or "piece cut out of grass"

flail is based on Latin *flagellum*, "whip"

flair comes from Latin *fragrare*, "smell sweet" and was first the ability to detect the "essence" or "scent" of something and know how to act accordingly

{ **flak** is short for German *fliegerabwehrkanone*, "pilot defense gun" }

an ignited fragment thrown off by a fire is a **flake**

flambé is literally "singed," as food that is **flambéd** is passed through a flame

a **flambeau** is a flaming torch

the base of the word **flamboyant** is French flambé "a flame" and it originally was an architectural term "having waving curves that resemble flames" and now can mean "flaming, blazing" or "having a wavy form, like a flame"

flamdoodle is exaggerated, boastful speech or pretentious nonsense

flame traces back to Indo-European *bhleg-/phleg-*

the **flamingo** is named for the people of Flanders, the Flemings who often were gypsys, and **flamenco** was once a disparaging term for them

if you are **flammulated**, you are ruddy or reddish

flan comes from Latin meaning "flat cake" and was first flawn

to **flanch** is to spread out or slope outwards towards the top

to **flane** is to laze or saunter

a **flaneur** is an idler or loafer

the double-pointed pick can also be called a **flang**

a thing can only have two **flanks** and they fall on either side of a body or entity—nowhere else

flannel is evasive or flattering talk

flannel, the fabric, probably comes from Welsh *gwlanen*, "woollen article"

any vain, ostentatious person is a **flapadosha**

a powder compact is sometimes known as a **flapjack**

a **flappet** is a little flap

flare is a blend of flame and glare

the **flarepath** is an area illuminated to enable an aircraft to land or take off

flarting is another word for mocking or jeering

flapdragon is an old game in which players grab raisins out of burning brandy and swallow them immediately

flash was first a verb for the swift turbulent splashing movement of water (as in "**flash flood**")

the **flashlight** was first called an electric hand torch

flaskisable means changeable

a **flat** is a a shallow box in which seedlings are started or refers to a tray full of plants, fruit, or vegetables

an exhausted battery is "**flat**"

flat as an apartment (a British usage) comes from an obsolete word *flet*, "floor dwelling" of Germanic origin

flathers is a synonym for rubbish or dirt

etymologically, **flatter** means "smooth down or caress with the flat of the hand"; **flattery** and **flatter** are ultimately from the Germanic base of flat "pat, smooth, caress"

flatulent comes from Latin *flatus*, "blowing, blast"

another term for windiness is **flatuosity**

flatware is knives, forks, and/or spoons not made of silver

a **flaughen** is a flake of flame or snow

to be **flaughtbred** is to be "with arms spread like a bird, thus eager and ecstatic"

one **flaunts** (makes much of) something of one's own (wealth, good looks, education) while one **flouts** (disregards or violates) something outside oneself (convention, law, regulation); to **flaunt** is to show off and to **flout** is to treat with contempt or disregard with smugness

flautist, one who plays the flute, is formed from *flauto*, the Latin word for flute

flavor first meant fragrance or smell and may be a blend of Latin *flatus*, "blowing, breath" and *foetor*, "stench"

the original sense of **flaw** was "flake of snow" and then "fragment or splinter"

to **flax** someone is to beat them, with the allusion to the beating of **flax** (the plant)

flaxseed is crushed to obtain **linseed oil**

a synonym for tearful is **flebile**

fleck, of Scandinavian origin, came from the adjective flecked "spotted"

to cover with feathers is to **fledge**

fledge was first an adjective meaning "ready to fly" and fledging, a newly feathered bird, is based on the pattern of nestling

fleece comes from a West Germanic base but is probably ultimately related to the base of Latin *pluma*, "feather"

fleechment is flattery or cajoling

to **fleer** is to laugh in a disrespectful or jeering way

fleet can mean "float," "rest on the surface of the water" and **fleeting** can mean "floating, swimming"

fleeted pertains to something felicitous or piquant

the underlip is the **flepper**

flerd means deceit or fraud

flerking is jerking or twitching

flesh may trace back to Old Norse *flesk*, "bacon, pork"

fleshment is excitement from a first success

flet is the floor or ground beneath one's feet

an arrow-maker is a **fletcher**

to **fletcherize** is to chew each bite of food at least 30 times (from nutritionist Horace Fletcher)

the feathers on an arrow is **fletching**

the fleshy flaps on the sides of a dog's mouth are **flews**

flexanimous means "mentally flexible" or "having the power to move, affect, or change others' minds"

a **flexitarian** is one who eats vegetarian at home but who will eat meat or fish in a restaurant or as a guest

a step in a straight stairway is a **flier** and a step in a winding stairway is a **winder**

a dusting of snow is a **flight**

{ one meaning of **flight** is "state of agitation or trembling" }

three wines served together in a tasting menu is a **flight**

flinch used to mean "slink, sneak off"

a moth or butterfly can also be called a **flinder**

flinders is fragments, pieces, or splinters

to **flink** is to behave in a cowardly manner

twelve or more cows is a **flink**

a **flip** is a drink of spirits or wine beaten with egg or sugar

flippant once meant "flexible, nimble, pliant"

a limb adapted for swimming is a **flipper**—like that of a penguin, seal, or turtle

flirt is either imitative of flick or spurt or both words

a side of bacon is a **flitch**, which is also the name for an outside slice of tree trunk or a strengthening plate added to a beam, joist, or other woodwork

flite is an archaic verb meaning "to quarrel"

flivver originally meant anything that was a failure or flop

the fur of an animal is its **flix**

to **flizzen** is to laugh with the whole face

a mass of weeds on the surface of water is a **float**

a root beer **float** is so-named for the ice cream floating in it

the boards and paddle of a waterwheel or paddlewheel are the **floats**

to **flob** is to move clumsily or aimlessly

flobbage is an old word for phlegm

to **floccify** is to value little or consider worthless

floccinaucinihilipilification is estimating or categorizing something as worthless and **floccipend** means "regard as insignificant" (from Latin *flocci pendere* "hold at little value")

to **flodder** is to disfigure the face from crying

floe (sheet of ice) comes from Old Norse *fló*, "layer, stratum"

a floating sheet of ice is a **floe** or pack ice, a large floating block of ice is an **iceberg**, and a small **iceberg** is a **growler**

flonker is anything very large or outrageous

the word **flood** was first *flod* in English and meant "a river or stream"

floor goes back to Proto-Germanic floruz "flat surface"

flora, plants and flowers as a group, is named after the Roman goddess of plant life and fertility

the earliest sense of **floozy** (late 19c-early 20c) is "a girl or young woman" and evolved quickly to one of questionable character

Florentine means "containing spinach" in cooking

florescent refers to a time of blossoming or flowering

a **floretum** is a garden specifically for the scientific study of flowers

floriated means "decorated with flowers" while **florid** is "blooming with flowers"

floribunda is a plant, like the rose, with dense clusters of flowers

Ponce de Leon discovered **Florida** (Spanish "flowery") during flowering season—hence, its name

a **florilegium** is a gathering of poems

floruit is a period during which something or someone thrived

floss is a word for untwisted filaments of silk used in making embroidery or satin

flotsam are goods floating on the sea (French floter) and **jetsam** are things thrown into the sea (short for jettison, from French jeter)

flounce can mean a sudden fling or jerk of the body or a limb

to **flounder** is to "stumble awkwardly" or "thrash about" while founder is to "get stuck, fail, or sink"; **flounder** may be a blend of founder and blunder

etymologically, **flour** is the same word as flower and it originally meant "flower" and became the differentiated sense of "finest or best part of the meal" of wheat or another grain

to **flourish** is etymologically to "flower" and it first meant "bloom, come into flower"

flout means "to treat or behave with disdain," "express contempt for" and is possibly derived from Dutch *fluiten*, "whistle; play the flute"; a **flout** is an insult

flout means "defy, ignore" and **flaunt** means "show off"

flowage is an overflowing onto adjacent land

The word **flower** (first flur or flour) came from Latin *florem*, and the spelling changed to **flower** around the mid-14th century; however, it was also spelled flour, which caused some confusion with the milled grain. Flour is taken from the French *fleur de farine*, literally "the **flower**, or finest, of the meal (of grain)."

flu is an abbreviation of influenza

if something has the sound of rolling waves, it is **fluctisonant** or **fluctisonous**

fluctuate, **fluent**, and **fluid** are all based on Latin *fluere*, "flow"

flue can mean "a loose, fluffy mass, as of lint"

to put the **fluence** on is to use one's mysterious, magical, or hypnotic power

fluff may come from the Dutch *fluweel*, "velvet"

fluids include liquids and gases; a **liquid** is a **fluid** with a fixed volume and a **gas** is a **fluid** that can expand indefinitely

the two lobes of a whale's tail are the **flukes**

two words meaning "pertaining to rivers" are **fluminous** and **potamic**

a **flummery** is an empty compliment

a **flump** is a heavy sound of something moving, falling, or dropping heavily

flunky is from Scottish where it meant "footman, liveried manservant," "one who attends another at the flank"

{ a **flurch** is a multitude or great many things (not persons) }

to **flurn** is to show contempt by looks

flurry may be a blend of flutter and hurry

flush may be a blend of flash and gush

if something is aligned with a margin, it is **flush**

fluster first meant "make slightly drunk"

fluster and frustrate makes **flustrate**

a tall slender glass for sparkling wine is a **flute**

a synonym for diarrhea is **flux**

a tent's flap is the **fly**

fly was once used generally for any winged insect

to **flychter** is to run with outstretched arms

a blank page at the beginning or end of a book is a **flyleaf**

a migratory route is called a **flyway**

an elephant or camel soon after birth is a **foal**; **foal** goes back to a prehistoric source meaning "offspring, young"

a **fob** is a small pocket close to the waistband of trousers

focus in ancient times meant "fireplace, hearth" which was the center of family activity; the plural of **focus** is focuses or foci

fodder is a name for food in general

fodient means "pertaining to digging"; a **fodient** animal is burrowing or digging

foe originally meant adversary in a feud

fog is a back-formation from foggy; **foggage** is a synonym for **fog**

fogdom is a region where nothing is clear, the state of fog

foggy first meant "covered with a grass; mossy; boggy" as **fog** first meant "coarse grass" and evolved to mean "thick, murky" in relation to atmosphere

a **fogram** is an old-fashioned person

fogy (person who is behind the times) is the preferred spelling over **fogey**

a **foible** is a minor eccentricity—or a fencing blade from the middle to the point

foil as in aluminum (etc.) comes from the original meaning of "leaf of a plant" and then anything flat and thin, then a substance like metal hammered or rolled into a thin sheet (i.e. gold **foil**, silver **foil**, tin **foil**)

foil, as a person or thing that sets off another to advantage, is an allusion to metallic leaf used by jewelers to set off stones

the track or scent of a hunted animal is the **foil**

to **foin** is to make a thrust or lunge with a pointed weapon

a **foison** is a plentiful supply or an abundance

foist is a wooden cask for wine—or a fusty smell

a pen for sheep is a **fold**

folderol is trivial or nonsensical fuss, nonsense, or a useless trifle

foliage was first spelled foilage, and meant "a design resembling leaves" though quite quickly it took on the collective meaning of "leaves of a plant or tree"; it is from Latin folium, "leaf," which influenced the later spelling change

folio originally designated the largest size of book

a **folivore** is an animal that feeds mainly on leaves

follicle, a saclike structure, is from Latin folliculus "little bag"

folly comes from French fol "foolish, mad"

to **foment** is to instigate or stir up

a **fomentation** is a hot moist medicinal application

fond first meant "foolish, silly"

fondle is a back-formation from fondling

fondling can refer to a much-loved person

fondue comes from French fondre, "to melt"

font originally referred to the action or process of casting or founding in printing and comes from French fondre, "to melt"; in the days of hot type, a **font** was one set of a typeface in a single size and style

fontanelle, the gap or soft spot on a baby's skull, is from the French word for "little fountain"; **fontanelle** formerly also referred to a hollow of the skin between muscles

food is derived from Middle English fode, from Old English fomacrda and is related to Latin panis, "bread" and pascere, "to feed"

a **food processor** is an electric kitchen tool that is used to chop, grate, mince, slice, puree, and blend food ingredients while a **blender** is an electric kitchen appliance that consists of a tall container with a removable lid and motor driven blades at the bottom that blend, chop, mix, or liquefy foods depending on the speed setting selected; in general, blenders are better suited to working with liquids (they are also called liquidizers or liquefiers), and food processors work wonders with more solid foods and of the two, the **food processor** is the more versatile

when a dog **foofs**, it howls or whines in a melancholic manner

fool comes from Latin follis, "inflated ball" and later, figuratively, "windbag" empty-headed person"

foolhardy suggests recklessness involving lack of common sense

foolscap is a large size of paper, approximately 13.5 inches by 17 inches, mostly used for writing and printing in the UK

foot traces back to Indo-European pod-/ped-

lower hills beneath mountains are **foothills**

to **footle** is to talk or act foolishly, from the old verb **footle** "bungle"; **footle** or **footling** as an adjective refers to something trifling or silly

{ **footloose** may have a nautical origin in "being unshackled" }

footmanship is the art of running

other terms for a mugger are: **footpad**, **ladrone**, or **lowpad**

the surface area taken up by a machine, building, etc. is its **footprint**

fop describes a foolish person or a person who pays too much attention to how they look

for first meant "before"

forage comes from the Germanic base of fodder

foray is a back-formation from forayer "raider"

forbear (verb) means "to cease or refrain from," "control oneself, abstain"; **forebear** (noun) means ancestor, literally "a person existing before"

forbysen is an "example or parable"; **bysen** is a "shocking thing"

force is derived from Latin fortis, "strong"

{ **forcible** indicates the use of brute force, **forced** means done involuntarily, and **forceful** suggests a potential for force }

forcibly connotes physical force, whereas the force suggested by **forcefully** need not be physical and can be of any nature aimed at producing a desired effect

forcemeat is a highly seasoned mixture containing chopped meat and it is an alteration of *farcemeat*, "stuffing"—and has a synonym, **farce**

forceps originally denoted smith's tongs

to **fordo** is "to do away with," "to destroy, ruin"

in golf, the warning call is **fore**! (from before "in front of") and in archery, it is **fast**!

early meanings of **foreclose** were "bar from escaping," "shut out," and "bar from doing something"

forego means to go before or precede (as in fore) and to do without is to **forgo**

forehead once had the meaning of "a feeling easily expressed by the face"—as innocence

foreign comes from Latin foris meaning "door" or "outside" and its early meanings were "out of doors," "outside one's home"

foremost, which looks like a combination of fore and most, actually comes from Old English fyrmest, meaning "earliest, first," and the superlative of forma, related to fruma "beginning"

your first name is also your **forename**, **given name**, or **Christian name**

forensic means "pertaining to courts of law," "pertaining to evidence for a court of law"

the part of a sleeve nearest the hand is the **foresleeve**

forest is from Latin *forestis* (*silva*), "outside wood," referring to a **forest** reserved for royals to hunt

forestial is "of or pertaining to a forest"

the **foreword** is written by someone other than the author; the **preface** is written by the author or editor

the counterpart of backyard is **foreyard**

forfeit comes from a French word meaning "minor crime, misdeed" and that was its original meaning—then becoming something or some right lost due to one's committing a crime

to **forfend** is to protect by precautionary measures

a **forfex** is a pair of scissors and **forficate** is "shaped or working like a pair of scissors"

nail scissors can be called **forficula**

forge comes from Latin *fabrica*, "trade, workshop" or "fabric" and it first meant "smithy" or "manufacture"

forget is literally "not get" as this "for" is a prefix of negation or exclusion

forgetive is a synonym for creative and inventive

forget-me-nots may have gotten their name from the last words of a knight who drowned while trying to pick these flowers by a riverside

forgive is a calque or loan translation, from Latin *perdonare*, "**forgive**," then German *fergeban*, before English

forgiveness is the only verb with a -ness form

a **fork** was first a pronged agricultural implement

forlorn originally meant "morally lost or ruined"

a long backless bench is a **form**

formal was first a philosophical term to say that something was "pertaining to the form or essence of something; essential"

formalism first was used as if equivalent to ideas of "art for art's sake"

format originally pertained to the physical characteristics of a book or other object—especially the shape or size

a **former** is a person or tool or machine that forms things

Formica got its name from being created as a substitute "for mica," a mineral

a **formicary** is an anthill; to **formicate** is to swarm like ants

{ **formication** is a sensation of ants creeping over one's skin }

the adjective form for ant is **formicine**

formidable comes from Latin *formidere*, "fear"

in math, the plural of **formula** is formulae; otherwise the plural is formulas

a collection or book of formulas is a **formulary**

formulate can mean "reduce to a formula"

formulistic means "fond of formulas"

fornicate or **fornicated** in architecture means "arched, vaulted" (Latin *fornix* which meant "brothel" as well as "arch, vault") and the root sense is "built like an arched brick oven" (Italian *forno* is "oven")

vaulted underground dwellings of Rome were used by tramps, criminals, and prostitutes—giving us Latin *fornicari*,

"have illicit intercourse" and then **fornication** in English

the upper shell of an oyster is the **fornix**

to **forold** is to "wear out with age" or "grow old"

forsake suggests an action likely to bring bereavement or impoverishment to that which is forsaken; **forsake** comes from for- and Old English *sacan*, "quarrel, accuse"

to **forslack** is to hinder or delay by laziness

forswear contains an implication of perjury or betrayal

to be **forswunk** is to be utterly worn out by hard labor (which is **swink**)

forsythia is named for English botanist William Forsyth (1737–1804)

forte is the strongest section of a sword blade and **foible** is the weakest

forte as in "personal strength, strong point" is from Latin *fortem*, "powerful, strong"; **fort**, **fortify**, and **fortress** also come from Latin *fortem*, "strong"

forthward became forward

fortnight is a shortening of "fourteen nights" (from Old English *feowertiene niht*) and there was a term **sennight** for "seven nights"

fortuitous means accidental or by chance, not necessarily fortunate or lucky

fortunate means good fortune, while **fortuitous** means merely happening by chance or accident

Latin *fors*, "chance" formed *fortuna*, "that which fate brings along," hence **fortune** "luck" or "good luck"

forum in Latin means an enclosure surrounding a house and was first a term for a public place or marketplace of a Roman city

a **fosse** is a canal, ditch, or trench and a **fossette** is a small hollow or depression (as in bone or shell) to undermine some else's digging is to **fossick**

a **fossil** is any word preserved only in isolated regions or in set phrases or forms; tell once meant "to count," and it is preserved in the expression "bank teller"—and other examples of fossils are short shrift, hem and haw, rank and file, out of kilter

fossil comes from Latin fossilis "dug up" and a **fossil** originally was any rock or mineral dug out of the earth

foster comes from the Germanic base for "food" and it originally meant "food, nourishment"

foudroyant means "dazzling, flashing, stunning"

the **fouette** is a spectacular pirouette in which the ballerina whips her raised leg around in an eggbeater motion while spinning on the other leg

foul came from Germanic words meaning "rotten, stinking" or "lazy"

found is from Latin fundus, "bottom, foundation"; **founder** is also from this and means "knock or fall to the ground"

founder means to sink, while **flounder** means to flail helplessly

fount is a poetic word meaning "fountain, spring, source"

a **fountain** originally was a natural spring (Latin font)

Greek tessares and Latin quattuor are the bases for "**four**"

fourchettes are the slender pieces of material that form the sides of the fingers of gloves; quirks are diamond-shaped pieces inserted at the bottom between the fingers of gloves

a **four-flusher** is a bluffer, braggart, or cheat—originating in poker, the pretending of having a full flush when one actually has a four flush (four cards of one suit)

the small depression in the yellow spot on the retina is the **foveola**

a **fowl** at first was any kind of bird

chickens, ducks, geese, pheasants, and turkey are **fowl** in the wild and poultry if domesticated

foxfire is the phosphorescent light emitted by decaying timber

foxtrot the dance comes from **foxtrot**, a horse's gait when it is slowing down from trotting to walking

foyer comes from Latin focus, "hearth" and originally was a room to which theater audiences went to warm themselves between acts of a play

to **frab** is to harass or worry

if something is **fracid**, it is rotten from overripeness

a **fractal** is a curve or surface of which any small part of it enlarged has the same statistical character as the whole

fraction is from Latin fractio, "breaking" (as of bread) from frangere, "break" (fragile and fragment also come from this base)

a **fractious** person is one whose self-control is easily broken

{ the way in which a rock or mineral breaks when struck is a **fracture** }

the initial sense of **fragile** was "morally weak," from Latin frangere, "to break"

fragor is a loud harsh noise—like a crash

fragrant and **fragrance** stem from Latin fragrare, "smell sweet"

a **frail** is 50 pounds of raisins

frail first meant "morally weak; unable to resist temptation"

fraise is white brandy distilled from strawberries; **framboise** is that distilled from raspberries (Latin *fraga ambrosia* "ambrosian strawberry") but **framboise** also means "raspberry"

frame's original meaning was "benefit, profit"

to **franch** is to eat greedily

franchise originally meant "freedom; exemption from servitude" and comes from Old French *franche*, "free"

frangibility is the condition of being very easily broken (Latin *frangere*, "break"); **friability** is the condition of being easily crumbled or pulverized

a **frank** was once a signature on a letter which entitled it to be sent free-of-charge (franking), especially by a member of Parliament; the idea of politcal freedom originally conveyed by "**frank**" was later extended to include freedom of expression

genetically modified food is called **Frankenfood**

frankfurter is short for **Frankfurter** wurst, literally, Frankfurt sausage

German cities, Frankfurt and Hamburg, gave us the perennial favorites, **frankfurter** and **hamburger**; "of Vienna" is the meaning of wiener

a **frankfurter** is a smoked sausage, **hot dog** describes a **frankfurter** served in a bun or roll, and **wiener** is actually "wienerwurst" or Vienna sausage and later became a synonym for **frankfurter**

frankincense is literally frank "high-quality" and incense

frankly first meant "freely; without restriction or restraint"

frantic (from Latin phrenecticus "**frenetic**") pertains to a mental state or condition, to a frame of mind, whereas that of **frenetic** pertains rather to a type of behavior or conduct

a **frap** is a noise made by knocking

something striking or impressive is **frappant**

frappé (from French *frapper*, "to ice") means "iced, cooled" (of a drink)

insect excrement or the refuse of boring insects is called **frass**

to be **fratchy** is to be quarrelsome

fraternal is "brotherly" from Latin **frater** "brother"; a **frater** is a brother

a dining hall in a monastery is a **fratery**

fraught means "laden with freight"

fray (from affray) was first an assault or attack and then became a quarrel or fight

frazil is an accumulation of ice crystals in water that is too turbulent to freeze solid

frazzle may be a blend of fray and *fazle/fasel*, "ravel"

freak first meant a caprice or whim

freck can mean "keen for mischief, ready for trouble"

freckle is an alteration of frecken and comes from Old Norse and is of Scandinavian origin

free goes way back to a base meaning "to love"

you get something **free**, not "for free"—because it's an adverb, not a noun

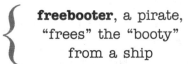

{ **freebooter**, a pirate, "frees" the "booty" from a ship }

the elements of **freedom** are free and doom, but when the word came into English, this combination meant "condition of being judged to be free" and doom then meant "deem"

freeganism is obtaining as much of one's food as possible from free sources

a **freeloader** "frees" a "load" from the person he/she is sponging off of

freemasons historically were masons who were "free"—not bound by guilds

free-range is a nonstandardized and misleading term regarding the way poultry is raised: **free-range** is defined as a system in which chickens have access to the outdoors—but often **free-range** chickens are mostly coop dwellers that do not get any living greens in their diet

freeze goes back to an Indo-European base of Latin *pruina*, "hoarfrost" and Sanskrit *prusva*, "frozen drop"

freeze-drying is preserving by rapidly freezing something and then subjecting it to a high vacuum to remove the ice

a **freeze-up** is a period of extreme cold

freight first meant "hiring of a craft for transporting goods"

freit is anything to which superstition attaches

the murmuring of a dissatisfied crowd is **fremescence**

if something is becoming noisy, it is **fremescent**

fremitus is a dull roar or other continuous noise

French-cut underpants are cut high on the sides to reveal the upper thigh

French-cut vegetables are sliced obliquely

frendent is an adjective for "pertaining to gnashing one's teeth"

the tendon holding your tongue to the bottom of your mouth is the **frenum**

the base of the word **frenzy** is a Greek word meaning "delirium"

frequent is from Latin *frequens*, "crowded" or "regularly repeated"

a **frequentative** is a verb expressing a repeated action, like dabble or curdle or dazzle

a **frescade** is a cool shady alley or walkway (fresco is Italian for "cool, fresh")

fresh "making presumptuous sexual advances" is from German *frech*, "cheeky"

a synonym for freshman is **fresher**

a **freshet** is a small stream of fresh water

freshman's origin is somewhat obvious, from fresh "inexperienced, new"

freshwater can be used as an adjective meaning "raw, unskilled, inexperienced"

Fresno is Spanish for "ash tree"

to **fress** is to eat a lot and often

fret is ultimately from Latin *fricare*, "rub"—as is friction

friable is "able to be crumbled, crushed into dust" while **fryable** is "able to be fried"

friand is an adjective meaning "delicious to the palate" or "fond of delicate food"

a foolish person can be called a **fribbler** or **twiddlepoop**; a **fribbler** is also a man who is infatuated with a woman but is unwilling to commit to her

fricassee (also fricassée) is (meat) cooked in a white sauce

a **fricative** is the sound produced by air flowing through a constriction in the oral cavity, such as for F and S

on a pierced earring, the part you put onto the post from the back is called the **friction nut**

Friday is named for Frigg, the ancient Germanic goddess of love

> **fridge** is short for the Fridgidare refrigerator; **frig** is a mild curse word

in Old English, **friend** meant "lover"

to **frieze** means "to embroider with gold," to cover with silver," or "to decorate by painting"

fright experienced the "vowel plus r" reversal (metathesis) from the Germanic *furkhtaz*

a **fritlag** is a worthless man

frigolabile means easily affected by cold

frijoles is the Spanish plural of *frijol*, "bean"

frim means "vigorous, flourishing"

Latin **fimbria** "fiber, thread" experienced metathesis (transposition of sounds or syllables within a word or words) and became frimbia before **fringe**

the early meaning of **frippery** was "secondhand clothes"—but now it means finery

a frivolous woman can be called a **frippet** or **fizgig**

Frisbees were modeled on pie tins from Mrs. Frisbie's Pies, made by the Frisbie Bakery of Bridgeport, CT, which students began tossing around in the 1920s

the thrill of excitement is **frisson**

a delay or respite can be called a **frist**

fritiniency is another word for twittering, like the various sounds of insects

{ **Frito** means "fried" in Spanish }

a **frittata** (from *fritta*, "fried") is an Italian omelet containing vegetables, cheese, or meat

fritter is from French *friture*, "to fry"

a **frixory** is a frying pan

if food **frizzles**, it burns or dries up during frying, toasting, or grilling

frock first meant "long cloak or tunic"

the triangular part of the underside of a horse's hoof is called a **frog**

frogs usually have smooth skin and **toads** have warty skin

frogging is catching or fishing for frogs

frogmarch is walking with your armed pinned behind you

frolic is derived from Dutch *vrolijk*, "joyful"

from goes back to Indo-European *pr* which also produced first, for, fore, before—and first denoted forward movement or advancement

fromology is a knowledge of cheeses or the collecting of cheese labels

a **frond** is a leaf (from Latin) of a fern and a **pinna** is a leaflet—and a **pinnule** is a leaflet of a **pinna**

frondescence is the period when leaves unfold, but also means foliage

frons is the middle of the face of an insect, between the eyes

the original meaning of **front** was "forehead"

frontier can mean "the front side, forepart"

the final syllable of **frontispiece** has no etymological connection with piece, as it comes from *spic-*, "see" (as in conspicuous)—and it first meant "judgment of character through interpretation of facial features"

the "forehead" of an animal or bird is the **frontlet**

the development of a weather front is **frontogenesis**

to **froonce** is to go about in an active, bustling manner

to **frot** is to rub or polish

to **frounce** is to wrinkle or fold

frown is from French *froigne*, "surly look"—ultimately of Celtic origin

frowst is extra time in bed in the morning—or in an armchair and as a verb can mean "to stay in a stuffy warm atmosphere"

fructification is the process of bearing fruit (Latin *fructus*, "fruit")

fructose (fruit sugar) is in green plants, fruits, and honey; **glucose** (also **dextrose**) is a simple sugar in grapes, corn, etc., **galactose** is another simple sugar—while **sucrose** (ordinary table sugar) is a disaccharide or double sugar as is **lactose** (milk sugar) and **maltose** (in beer)

fructuous means producing a great deal of fruit

frugal refers more directly to practicing economy in the course of shopping for goods or services, whereas **thrifty** applies more to the preservation of funds

a **frugivore** is an animal that feeds on fruit

fruit comes from Latin *frui*, "to enjoy" which became French *frut*, "means of enjoyment"; **fruit**, a true scientific term, describes a very specific part of a plant—edible or not

the following are botanically "**fruits**" though we normally think of them as "vegetables': buckwheat, acorn, almond, corn, cucumber, coconut, chestnut, okra, rice, sugar pea, eggplant, tomato, string bean, pumpkin, and olive

fruit is the name given to those plants which have an ovary used for food; **vegetable** is the name given to a large category of herbaceous plants with parts used for food

fruitage is the collective term for fruit

frump also means a snort or a sneer or jeer

frustrate as an adjective means "invalid, null" or "pointless"

a **frustrum** is a part or fragment

to **fruzz** is to rub the hair the wrong way

fry as in cook is from Latin *frigere*, "roasting and frying"

fry as in young of animals is from French *frier/froyer*, "to spawn"

a small chubby person is a **fub** and **fubsy** means fat and squat

fubbery is another word for cheating or deception

fucate means artificially colored

fuchsia was named for German botanist Leonhard Fuchs (16th c)

to **fuddle** is to tipple or confuse with drink

a piece of late news inserted in a newspaper is called **fudge**

fudge was first an interjection meaning "stuff and nonsense!"

fuel traces back to Latin *focalis*, "hearth"

an engine without carburetors or internal combustion is a **fuel-injection** engine

fug is a thick stuffy atmosphere

nouns ending in -**ful** regularly form their plurals by adding -s at the end, not internally, e.g. cupfuls, mouthfuls

fulcrum originally meant "bed post," coming from Latin *fulcire*, "to support or prop up"

fulfill originally meant "fill full, fill up"

fulgent means "dazzlingly bright"

dazzling brightness is **fulgor**

full is from Indo-European *ple-*, "full"

etymologically, **fulminate** means "strike with lighting"

{ **fulsome** means offensively insincere or overdone/excessive }

fulvous means "dull brownish yellow"

fumarole is from Latin *fumariolum*, "vent" and it is what you call a volcanic vapor hole

fume comes from Old French *fum*, from Latin *fumus*, "smoke, steam"

fumet is deer poop

if something is **fumose**, it gives off fumes or smoke

fun was first a cheat, hoax, or trick

before the sixteenth century, animal functions were those of the brain and nervous system, vital functions were the heart, lungs, and other essential organs, while natural functions involved assimilation and nutrition; the source of **function** is Latin *fungi/fungor*, "discharge, perform"

fund's original and literal meaning is "bottom" (Latin *fundus*) but changed to "basic supply, as of money"

the basis of **fundamental** is "found"

fur comes from a Germanic word meaning "sheath"

furbish first meant "remove the rust from"

furciferous means rascal-like

a **furcula** is a forked bone, an example being the wishbone

dandruff is also known by a cuter name, **furfur**

another word for furious or raging is **furibund**

furiosity is another word for fury or rage

to **furl** something is to roll up and bind, draw in and secure

fundamentalism is now employed to refer to any person or group that is characterized as unbending, rigorous, intolerant, and militant

a **funeral** once was a torchlight procession from Latin funis "torch"—because funerals of the Romans took place at night by torchlight

funge is another word for fungus and **fungology** is the science of **fungi** (which is pronounced FUN-ji)

if something is **fungible**, it is interchangeable, returnable, or easily replaced

fungo (probably from Scottish *fung*, "to pitch, toss, fling") is a baseball drill in which a batter tosses a ball in the air and hits it as it descends

fungus probably derived from Greek *sphoggos*, "sponge"

funicular is literally "running on a rope"

to run away in fright is to **funkify**

French *funkier*, "to smoke" gave us the slang word **funky** for "smelly" (etc.)

funnel is from Latin *fundere*, "pour"

furlong, 1/8 of a mile or 201 meters, dates from the days when a race was a furrow long, the length of a plowed field

furlough comes from Dutch *verlof*, modeled on German *Verlaub*, "for leave"

Latin formus "heat" and *fornus/fornax*, "oven, kiln" are the sources of **furnace**

furnish derives from Old French *furniss-*, from *furnier*, "accommodate, promote"

furniture once signified any kind of movable property

further suggests a removing of obstacles in the way of a desired advance

someone who is **furtive** literally "carries things away like a thief"

furze is another word for a beard or a bushy growth of hair

a charcoal drawing or a charcoal drawing stick is a **fusain** (French for charcoal)

fuse comes from Italian *fuso*, "spindle" (from Latin *fusus*, "spindle") as it originally referred to the casing or tube filled with combustible matter

fuselage, the part of an airplane in which the passengers or cargo are stowed, is pronounced FYOO-suh-lawzh

fusillade, a rapid and continuous discharge, is pronounced FYOO-suh-lade

fusilli (short spiral pasta) means "little spindles"

fusk or **fusc** means dark brown or dusky

to **fustle** is to exhibit a state of restless activity or agitation

fusty means stale smelling

futile is based on Latin *futilis*, "that easily pours out" or "leaky"—which intimates the meaning "useless" or "lacking in purpose"

a Japanese mattress that acts as a bed or couch is a **futon**, from Chinese *putvan*, "rush-mat seat"

future comes from Latin *futurus*, "going to be, about to be"

futures are stocks (and goods) bought and sold for future delivery

futurology is the art or practice of forecasting trends or developments

> **futz** may be an alteration of Yiddish *arumfartzen*, "fart about"

fuzz and fuzzy come from German *fussig*, "spongy"

the slang term **fuzz** comes from London police once wearing fuzzy helmets

to **fuzzle** is to intoxicate or confuse

a **fuzzword** (fuzzy + buzzword) is a deliberately confusing or imprecise term

a flick with the finger and thumb is a **fyerk**

a person with no curiosity is a **fysigunkus**

{ the **G** in G-string probably stands for "groin" }

in mechanics, a hook or a notch in a rod or lever which then engages with a pin or, needle is called a **gab**

gabardine is from German *walle vant*, "pilgrimage" (then French *gauvardine*) because it first was a garment worn by Jews, almsmen, and beggars

gable seems to have a Germanic origin meaning "fork" as it is a triangular piece or structure

an iron **crowbar** is a **gablock**; a **crowbar** is so-called for its curved beaklike end

gaccade is pressure on violin strings that makes two or more sound at once

to **gad** is to wander about from place to place—or go astray in thought

another way of saying a plant is straggling is **gadding**

a **gadfly** is an annoying person or persistent irritation

gadget may come from French *g,chette*, which is or has been applied to various pieces of mechanism or from Gaget, the person who created the first so-called gadgets—miniature Statues of Liberty sold in Paris, or from a Navy term for a tool or mechanical device for which one could not recall the name

the inverted fluting on silverware is **gadroons**—which are described as a series of convex curves or arcs joined to form a decorative edge

gadzooks is an abridgment of God's hooks, "nails of the cross"

Gaelic means Irish or Scottish; **Gallic** means French

gaffe is actually French for "blunder"

in television and film, a **gaffer** is the senior electrician

gag was originally an ad-lib joke thrown in by an actor to throw another actor off his lines

gaga is French and originally meant "senile person"

gage in "engage" means "pledge, promise"

a group of geese is a **gaggle**, but only when they are on the ground; in the air, the group is a **skein**

comedians are **gagsters**

Gaia (Greek for "the earth") is the planet regarded as a self-regulating system of living matter

to **gainsay** is to contradict or deny (gain "against" + say)

> { **gait** can refer to the manner of forward movement of a vehicle }

gaiters are waterproof fabric coverings that go from the instep to either the ankle or the knee

the original meaning of **gala** was "fine or showy dress" before it meant "a festive occasion"; it is pronounced GAY-luh, though optionally GAH-luh and GAL-uh

know a big milk drinker? call him/her a **galactophagist**; babies are **galactophagous** (milk-drinking)

the **Galapagos** Islands take their name from Spanish galapago "tortoise"

galaxy is from Greek gala, galaktos "milk"—as in Milky Way—and **galaxy** actually means "circle of milk"

the general contour of a rounded object is its **galbe**

gale, a very strong wind, is probably related to Old Norse *galinn*, "frantic, mad"

galeated is "shaped like a helmet" or "wearing a helmet"

Galileo is properly pronounced gah-luh-LEE-oh

gall as in gallbladder refers to a secretion of the liver or to bile

gallant language is ornate

gallant with the first syllable stressed means "brave, honorable"; with the second syllable stressed it means "chivalrous, attentive to women"

a mall or court covered by skylights is a **galleria**

the spectators at a golf match are the **gallery**

a **gallet** is a rounded beach pebble, a chip or splinter of stone

galley is a term used for a first set of proofs for a printing project—getting its name from the original long metal tray for holding type for a hand-operated press

the kitchen of a boat, aircraft, or camper is the **galley**

a man of courage and spirit can be called a **galliard**

a **gallicism** is a French phrase or idiom appearing in another language

gallimaufry is a medley or confused jumble, especially a dish made of leftovers, from French **gallimaufry** "ragout, hash"

gallinippers are large mosquitoes

gallivant may come from French gallant "ladies' man" (from *galer*, "to revel") and *avant*, "forward"

a **gallon** in the U.S. measures liquid while in Britain it is used for dry capacity; these two are different, not equivalent

gallon in ten-**gallon** hat is from Spanish galon "ribbon"—and the larger the hat, the more galones (ribbons) it could have around it

gallop is the fastest pace of a horse or quadruped

on a carousel, the horses that don't move are **gallopers** and the ones that move up and down are **jumpers**

the plurality of **gallows** probably comes from its two upright poles as opposed to a gibbet with a single upright

galluses is another name for suspenders for trousers

galoot first had a nautical use "an inexperienced marine"

galore comes from Irish Gaelic *go leor*, "enough or plenty; to sufficiency"

galosh originally applied to a wooden shoe or clog attached to the foot with a leather thong

another word for yawn or gape is **galp**

anatony professor Luigi Galvani (1737–1798) gave his name to **galvanize**, which is a process he figured out by experimenting with frogs and first meant "to stimulate by means of a galvanic (chemically induced electrical) current"

a **gambit** is an early sacrifice designed to gain a later advantage, an opening move that involves some strategic sacrifice or concession

the Middle English form of game, *gamen*, became **gamble**

a **gambrel** roof is a curved or hipped roof, so called from its resemblance to the shape of a horse's hind leg

gambrinous means "being full of beer"

game as a pastime/sport goes back to Germanic meaning "people together, participating"

to **gamel** is to "play games," "frolic"

a **gamin** is a neglected boy or waif; a **gamine** is the girl counterpart

gangplank and **gangway** preserve an old meaning of gang "action of walking" or "a manner of going" or "alley"

a child just beginning to walk is a **gangrel**

the figurative sense of **gangrene** is "moral corruption"

fish scales that are smooth and shiny are **ganoid**

to **gant** is to "yawn or gape"

gantlet refers to a section of railroad track at which two parallel pairs of tracks converge for a space into a single track and then diverge again

the supportive structure for a rocket to be launched is a **gantry**

the **Gap** (store) is named for "generation **gap**"

to **gape** can mean "to open the mouth wide to bite or swallow something"

a **gapesnest** is a wonderment or strange site and is also called a **gazingstock**

gaposis is a gap or series of gaps between buttoned buttons or closed snaps on a garment

gaptoothed is having teeth set wide apart

garage is a direct borrowing from French "place where one docks"

garb first meant "grace, elegance"

gamut comes from "gamma" being the last note on Guido d'Arezzo's musical scale and "ut" the first note in his singing scale

a **gammerstang** is a tall awkward person

gammon is another word for bacon

ganache is an icing made from chocolate and heavy cream

gander can mean "wander aimlessly" or "ramble" in speaking

garbage may come from Italian *garbuglio*, "mess" and a special meaning is "the fruit or vegetable garnishesof a cocktail"; the first use of the word **garbage** was for the offal (entrails, internal organs) of an animal used as food

garbanzo is chickpea in Spanish

garble originally meant "to sort out" or "to select in a biased way" and was applied to the selection and sorting out of individual passages from a person's writings or any separation of the good from the bad, of a selection of the worst and setting aside the better; it evolved to mean "to jumble, scramble"

{
garble is extraneous matter, especially the refuse of spices
}

garbology is the anthropological study of a society or culture by examining or analyzing its refuse

garden may come from Latin *hortus gardinus*, "cultivated plot guarded by a wall" but it is likely to be of Germanic origin and related to "yard"

the **gardenia** was named for amateur botanist, Alexander Garden, a Scottish-American physician (1730–1791)

botanists have had flowers named for them, including Alexander Garden (**gardenia**), Pierre Magnol (**magnolia**), Johann Zinn (**zinnia**)

gardyloo is a warning cry derived from French *gare l'eau*, "beware of the water"—the water and slops which were once thrown by servants from higher stories of a building onto the street

gargalesthesia is the feeling caused by tickling

in Celtic myth, Gargantua was a giant with a large appetite, giving us the word **gargantuan**

gargoyle is an old French word literally meaning "throat" and is literally "thing that spews from its gorge"—as these architectural devices were originally used as projections from gutters to carry rainwater clear of the walls

garland can figuratively mean "the thing most prized"

garlic comes from Old English *gar*, "spear" and *leac*, "leek"

garner was originally a storehouse or granary

garnet is from Middle Dutch garnate from Old French grenat "dark red"

garnish was first a set of vessels for use at a table, then became "trimming, embellishment"; **garnish** suggests decorating with a small final touch, especially referring to food

garniture is a cooking term for the trimming or garnish on a prepared dish

garret is the same as an attic; **garret** first meant "high watch post, watchtower, turret"

at first, **garrison** meant "store, treasure"

garrote is from Spanish **garrote** "cudgel" and is pronounced guh-RAHT

garrulity is talkativeness

the ultimate source of **garter** was a Gaulish word meaning "leg"

a small enclosed area or ground beside a house is a **garth**; a **garth** is also a wooden hoop on a barrel

Dutch chemist JB van Helmont (1577–1644) invented the word **gas** from Greek chaos "atmosphere" (ch in Greek is g in Dutch)

for the verb **gas**, the forms are gassed, gasses, gassing; for the noun **gas**, the plural is gases

gasconade is extravagant boasting, based on Gascon, natives of a former province of France—who were notorious for bragging

gaseity is the state of being a gas

gash is slang for something extra

gashful or **gashly** means "ghastly"

gash-gabbit means having a protruding chin

gasket was first a cord or rope for securing sails, then a strip of material on postons or joints

gasoline was originally a petroleum distillate for use in heating or lighting

Greek *gaster*, "stomach" gave us **gastric**

a **gat** is a hole in the ground

the earliest sense of **gate** was "opening in a fence"

the flight of a bird, especially a hawk, is the **gate**

gâteau is French for "cake"—especially a light sponge cake with rich icing or filling

in glass-blowing, you start with a "**gather**" or gob of molten glass

each of the front teeth of a horse is called a **gatherer**

the football team of the University of Florida, the Gators, were the guinea pigs for the development of the drink **Gatorade**

gauche is French meaning "left, left-handed" and has come to mean "awkward, crude, tactless"; **gaucherie** is more correct than **gaucheness**

gaud is a deceitful trick

one of the large ornamental beads in a rosary is a **gaud** (Latin *quinque gaudia*, "five joyful mysteries" of a rosary)

the distance between train track rails is the **gauge**

gauntlet comes from Old French *gantelet*, a diminutive of *gant*, "glove"

to **gaure** is to stare in astonishment

gauze may get its name from Gaza in Palestine

a **gavel** was originally a stonemason's mallet

French gai became associated with effeminate roles in French burlesque played by men, and the use gave us **gay**, "homosexual"

gaydom is the world of homosexuals

gazebo comes from the Victorian expression "gaze about," for a shelter from where you can see your whole garden; originally, a **gazebo** was a windowed turret in the roof of a house for gazing out over the landscape

a *gazzetta*, a Venetian coin of little value, gave rise to the phrase *gazzetta de la novita*, "halfpennyworth of news" and this eventually gave us **gazette**

the etymological meaning of **gear** is "that which puts one in a state of readiness"

geason is an adjective meaning "rare, uncommon; extraordinary"

in the early 1900s, carnival performers who swallowed swords or fire were called **geeks**

---

a **geek** is any smart person with an obsessive interest, a **nerd** is the same but also lacks social grace, and a **dweeb** is a mega-nerd

---

a luxurious feast or day of plenty is a **gaudy**
gaudy did not have a disparaging sense at first, but meant "fine, showy"

gee-up is an interjection to get a horse to move faster

geezer first meant "someone who goes around in disguise"

gegenschein is a faint reflection of the sun seen at night

geisha in Japanese means "arts person" as in "woman trained as singer, dancer, and companion"

the dimples that appear when you smile are **gelasins**

if something is laughable, it is **gelastic**— and funny is **gelogenic**

gelati is the plural of **gelato** (from Italian *gelare*, "to freeze")

gelatin is from Italian *gelata*, "jelly"

gem comes from Italian *gamba*, "leg"

gemelli, pasta pieces made of two strands of pasta twisted together, is literally "twins" in Italian

things associated in pairs are **gemels**

long consonants are called **geminates**

a **gemma** is a leaf bud, as distinct from a flower bud (plural is gemmae); a small **gemma** is a **gemmule**

gender first meant "kind, sort; class, genus"

gene is from German Gen, short for pangene, coined by Danis scientist W. L. Johannsen (1857–1927), from Greek *genea*, "generation, race"

{ **genealogy**'s root is Greek *genea*, "race, generation" and once had the meaning "offspring, progeny" }

generable means "able to or capable of generating or being generated"

general is based on Latin *genus*, "class, kind, race"

a **generality** is an indefinite, nonspecific statement or observation, one that describes a condition, situation, or set of facts in general; a **generalization** is a statement or conclusion inferred from a set of descriptions, experiments, or observations

there are early uses of **generation** for reckoning historical time at the rate of 30 years (which referred to the interval of time between the birth of parents and that of their children) or three to a century (grandparents, parents, children)

generic is "characteristic of or belonging to a genus or class"

an early sense of **generous** was "highly, nobly born" from Latin generosus

the word **genesis** was first the name of the Old Testament book and genetic(s) derive from this word on the pattern of antithetic/antithesis

another name for astrologer or one who casts horoscopes is **genethliac** and as an adjective this means "pertaining to birthdays"

genetic first came into English as a reference to origins (then formation and development)

a mom can be called a **genetrix**

genial derived from Latin *genialis*, "nuptial" and it first pertained to marriage and reproduction

a **genicon** is a sexual partner imagined by one who is dissatisfied with his/her actual partner

geniculate is "bent at a sharp angle," like the knee

genie is from Arabic meaning "demon"

genital derives from Latin *gignere*, "beget"

a **genitory** is a testicle

genius is Latin for "attendant spirit," coming from Greek for "to be born, to come into being" and is related to genie and jinn, other spirits; the plural of **genius** is genii or geniuses

genocide was coined in 1945 as a combination of Greek *genos*, "race" and Latin *caedere*, "to kill"

to **gentle** is "to ease, soften, soothe," especially in taming horses

gentleman originally meant "a man of gentle (noble) birth" and came from French *gentilz hom*

genu is Latin for knee, so if you are **genuant**, you are kneeling

genuflect's Latin base is *genu*, "knee" and *flectere*, "to bend"

genuine originally meant "placed on the knees" as in ancient Rome a father legally claimed his newborn by doing this before the family; *genero*, Latin for "give birth to" is the root of **genuine**

genus is straight from Latin and means "birth," "family," or "nation"

a rock lined with crystals is a **geode**

if something is growing on or in the ground, it is **geogenous**

geology actually has a synonym: **geognosy**

the science or theories about the formation of the earth is **geogony**

geography is literally "written description of the earth"

until 1755, **geology** was a general term for a science dealing with the earth and encompassed geography, hydrography, phytography, and zoography

a feng shui practitioner is a **geomancer**

an expert in geometry is a **geometer**

geometry originally was the measurement (*metrein*) of the earth (*ge*)

geoponic means "relating to agriculture" (from Greek *geoponos*, "farmer") or as a noun refers to a book about agriculture or a writer on agricultural topics

the name **George** is derived from Greek *georgos*, "farmer," which comes from *geo*, "earth" and *ergein*, "to work"

geraniums resemble a crane's bill, which is the origin—Greek *geranion*, "crane"

the **gerbil** is a rodent native to deserts in Africa and Asia and they have long tufted tails; the **hamster** is a rodent native to Europe and Asia and its tail is stubby and bare

something to be done is a **gerendum**

the word **geriatric** is patterned after pediatric

germ is from Latin *germen*, "seed, sprout"

german, as in cousins **german**, meant "approaching a sibling in proximity"—thus, the children of brothers and sisters are called cousins **german**

germane and **relevant** indicate pertinence to a matter, but may not be essential; **material** means pertinent and necessary

germinate comes from Latin *germen*, "sprout"

Geronimo, a Native American chief (1829–1909) was the inspiration for the interjection, first used in World War II by U.S. participants

gerrymander is from the name Elbridge Gerry, U.S. governor, and salamander, from the supposed resemblance of the shape of the Massachusetts electoral district formed by Gerry in 1812 for political purposes

{ a **gerund** is a verb with an -ing ending and which functions as a noun }

gesso is a type of plaster sometimes used as a surface or ground for painting—and it is pronounced JESS-oh

gestalt is from German meaning "form, shape" and in psychology means "an integrated structure perceived as functionally more than a sum of its parts"

gestapo was an acronym for Geheime Staats Polizei, Hitler's secret police

gestation is literally the period during which unborn young are "carried" inside the womb—from Latin *gerere*, "carry" or "conduct"

to welcome as a guest is to **gesten**

gestic means "pertaining to body movement or dancing" (from Latin *gerere*, "to bear, deport (oneself)"); **gestion** is "performance," "conduct," or "management"

gesticulate and **gesture** are based on Latin *gerere*, "bear, carry, perform" and **gesticulation** is more exaggerated than a **gesture**, often involving flailing; originally, a person's **gesture** was their "bearing" or the way they "carried" themselves

gesundheit is "health" in German

get has only been in English for 800 years, borrowed from Old Norse *geta*, and Indo-European *ghed-*, "seize"

a **geta** (plural is getas) is the thick Japanese wooden shoe with a thong to pass between the first (big) toe and the second toe and two crosswise wooden pieces underneath

get-go is a nominalization of the verb phrase to get going "to begin"

Gewurztramier (wine) is from German *Gewurz*, "spice" and *Traminer*, a grape variety of Tramin

geyser is from Icelandic Geysir "hot spring" from *geysa*, "pour or rush forth" (Old Norse)

ghastly is not related to ghost but is from Middle English *gasten*, "terrify"

gherkin is from Dutch *gurkkijn*, a diminutive of *gurk*, "cucumber" and it is an immature or small cucumber

ghetto was first a site of an old foundry in Venice, Italy, to which Jews were restricted in 1516 (from Venetian *getto*, "foundry") and then any crowded section of a city in which people were forced to live

ghost first meant "the soul or spirit as the source of life" and once meant "breath" or "wind blast"

a martial arts outfit is called a **gi**, with loose-fitting pants and a jacket that is closed with a cloth belt

GI is an abbreviation for Government Issue

{ to **gibber** is to speak rapidly and inarticulately }

gibberish may come from the earlier word *gibber*, "speak rapidly and unintelligibly," with the added -ish as in other language names (English, Spanish)

to **gibbet** is to hold up to public contempt

gibbous means "curved around farther than a semicircle" and it is used to describe a moon or planet that was between half and full as well as something that is convex or protuberant

gibe (sometimes spelled **jibe**) means "taunt, jeer mock" and is semantically related to **jive** "tease, bluff"; another meaning of **jibe** is "agree, be in harmony with"

giblets is an adaption of French gibelet "game stew" as those parts of a bird usually went into such a stew; odds and ends can also be called **giblets**

giddy is literally "possessed by a god"

giffgaff is mutual accommodation

gift first meant "bride price" and was borrowed from Old Norse

gig first meant "a light two-wheeled carriage pulled by one horse" and then was applied to other objects that whirled

Samuel Johnson defined such words as **giglet** (a wanton), **fopdoodle** (a fool), **dandiprat** (an urchin), and **jobbenowl** (a blockhead)

gignate means to originate or produce

gill can mean "a deep rocky cleft or ravine, usually forming the course of a stream"

a **gimlet** is a boring tool with a metal screw tip and a crosspiece handle for one-handed turning (from Germanic "auger")

a **gimmal** is two or more interlocked rings or connecting parts in machinery for transmitting motion, as in a clock

gimmick originally meant "dishonest contrivance" or "device for making a game crooked"

gin is a spirit distilled from grain and once flavored with the juice of juniper berries and was first made in Holland and formerly called Hollands Geneva

gin, as a machine, started out with the meaning "skill, ingenuity"

ginger, the spice, gives us the figurative use of "mettle" or "spirit"

gingerbread is any elaborate or excessive ornamentation on a house

in origin, **gingerbread** (the cake) has nothing to do with "bread" but derives from gingebras "ginger paste" and **gingerbread** first meant "preserved ginger"; the association with "bread" led to the cake itself

gingerly has nothing to do with ginger—but may have arisen from French gent "well-born" or "dainty"

gingham is from Malay ginggang, "striped"

a **gink** is a person of no consequence

a **ginnel** is a long narrow passage between houses

Mandarin Chinese jen shen, "man root, man herb" describes **ginseng**'s forked root that looks like legs

to **gip** is to cut and clean fish

the **giraffe** was originally called a amelopard

a branched candleholder is a **girandole**

a **gird** is a hoop for a barrel

girdle is from Proto-Germanic denoting "surrounding"

from the thirteenth century, a **girl** first meant any young person—male or female—with a female was known as a "gay **girl**" and a male as a "knave **girl**"

to **girn** is to bare the teeth in anger

girouettism is changing one's opinion or position to match popular trends

gist is a broadening of a legal term meaning "the ground of a legal action"

gizzard is based on Latin gigeria, "cooked entrails of fowl" and it is the strong muscular second stomach of birds in which food is finely ground

the flat area of the forehead is the **glabella**

to be free from hair or down (as skin, a leaf) is to be **glabrous**

a fancy name for an ice skating rink is a **glaciarium**

glacier comes from Latin glacies, "ice"; a **glacialist** studies ice and its impact on geology

a gentle slope is a **glacis**; a percipitous slope is a **steep**

the original meaning of **glad** was "bright, shining"

glade originally referred to a part of water not frozen over, but surrounded by ice (analogy to **glade**, an opening in the woods)

the main Latin word for sword was gladius from which came **gladiator**; **gladiate** is an adjective meaning sword-shaped

gladius was a Roman sword, which gives us **gladiolus** "little sword," which has swordlike leaves; corn lily is an old name for the flower

glaikery is foolish conduct or giddiness

glair is another name for egg white

glam is a word for the loud noise of talking or merrymaking

glamour first meant "magic, enchantment" or "art of contriving magic spells"

a **glance** captures more than a **glimpse**; the verb **glance** takes no object while **glimpse** does

gland first meant acorn (or a similar nut) and it derives from Latin *glans*, "acorn"

glandiferous is "bearing acorns" or similar fruit

glasnost is Russian for "speaking aloud" and means "freedom of expression" or "the fact of being public" in politics

glass traces back to Old Teutonic *gla-/glae-*, a variant of *glô*, "to shine"

glaucoma comes from a Greek word meaning "bluish green or gray" from a type of color haze affecting the eyes; the word was formerly used to denote cataracts

the spidery **glia** of the brain is Greek for "glue"

a **gliff** is a brief look or passing glance

to **glimmer** is to look with half-closed eyes

glimpse originally meant "shine faintly"

a **glint** is a steep cliff of almost horizontal strata produced by erosion

to peep or take a glance is to **glint**

a **glisk** is a slight touch of pleasure that penetrates and quickly passes away

glitch is probably from Yiddish *glitsh*, "lapse, slip"

glitz is a back-formation from glitzy

gloaming is twilight

to **gloat** once had the meaning "to gaze, stare" or "to glow" (Danish gloe)

glob may be a blend of blob and gob

globe, from Latin globus, is related to gleba "lump of earth" and etymologically was "something rolled up into a ball"

the protective razor-sharp hairlike bristles on cacti are **glochidia**

glaucous means "of a dull bluish green or gray" or "covered with a powdery bloom" as of grapes, plums, etc.

to **glaze** means "to fill or fit a window with glass"

a person who cuts and fits glass is a **glazier**

gleam, of Germanic origin, first meant "brilliant light"

the literal sense of **glean** is "gather ears of corn left by the reapers"

gleet is sticky, slimy, or greasy filth

a **glen** is a mountain valley, usually forming the course of a stream

glockenspiel is literally "bell play" in German

a bright place in the sky or a clearing/open area is a **glode**

glom is a variant of glaum "snatch at"

glome is a name for a skein or ball of yarn or thread

to **gloom** is to look sullen or displeased, appear dejected or depressed

to be **gloppened** is to be surprised

a **glory** is a circle of light around the head of a saint or Jesus

gloss and **glossary** are based on Greek *glossa*, "word needing explanation" or "language"

glossal means "of or pertaining to the tongue"

glossolalia is the practice of speaking in foreign languages

glossology is the writing of glossaries

a **glout** is a frown or sullen look

glove is from Germanic *galofo* with *lofo*, "hand" as the main part

glow literally means "be heated to incandescence"

glox is the sound of liquids when shaken in a barrel

a marginal note or a comment is a **gloze**

gluck or **glug** is the light repetitive gurgling sound of liquid being poured from a bottle

Greek *glukus*, "sweet" is the ancestor of **glucose**; the variant glukeros was used by a chemist to coin **glycerin/glycerine** for "syrupy liquid"

the base of the word **glue** is Latin *gluten*; in its unaltered form, **glue** is brownish

gluhwein is literally mulled wine

to **glump** is to be sullen or glum; to **glunch** is to look sour or glum, to frown

someone who eats while gulping or making unpleasant noises is **glunshing**, **gruzzling**, or **yaffling**

a **glut** is the amount of liquid swallowed in a gulp

glutton comes from Latin *glutire*, "to swallow"

a **glyph** was first a carved ornamental groove or channel, then was used for characters and symbols

to **gnap** means to criticize

gnarled is a variant of knarled from *knur*, "knot in wood"

a knot in wood can also be called a **gnarr**

the tip of the chin is the **gnathion**

gnathonic means "sycophantic, parasitic"

if you are **gnatling**, you are busy doing nothing or engrossed with trifles

gnocchi (pronounced NYAWK-ee) is potato-stuffed pasta, getting its name from Italian *nocchio*, "knot in wood"

gnome (the creature) may derive from Greek *genomus*, "earth dweller" as they were thought to provide intelligence about the secret treasures of the earth

gnomic means "consisting of gnomes" and gnomes in this case are proverbs, aphorisms, or maxims

a **gnomology** is a collection of maxims, sayings, or precepts

a **gnomon** is the pillar or rod that casts a shadow on a sundial; **gnomonics** is the art or science of dialing or of constructing dials to show the hour of the day by the shadow of a **gnomon**

gnostic means "relating to knowledge" or "clever, knowing"

gnurr is the substance that collects over time in the bottoms of pockets or cuffs of trousers

go's original past tense was eode, then yode, then went

the shortest sentence in English is **Go!**

goal at first was a physical limit or boundary—and then came to be used figuratively

goat may etymologically be "animal that jumps about"

a piece, lump, or extract of something can be called a **gobbet**

gobbledygook was coined by Texas lawyer Maury Maverick, a descendant of Samuel Maverick; an alternative term for **gobbledygook** is **bafflegab**

goblet, from French, is a diminutive of *gobel*, "cup"

goblin may come from the name of an evil spirit that haunted Evreux, France, in the twelfth century

goblocks are large mouthfuls

gob originally meant "mouth" so **gobsmack** "astound" refers to the action of clapping a hand to one's mouth in astonishment; **gobsmacked** means "flabbergasted, speechless"

go-cart first meant "baby walker" as go has an obsolete sense "walk"

a wreck of a ship cast up on the shore is termed a **godsend**

another word for witchcraft or magic using evil spirits is **goety** (from Greek *goeteia*, "witchcraft")

another word for waffle is **gofer** (from French *gaufre*, "honeycomb")

you can also call a stupid person a **goff**

the verb for crimping or waving your hair with a heated iron is to **goffer**

gold comes from an Indo-European root shared by "yellow"

goldbrick comes from a con in which a gold-polished item is passed off as solid gold

{ for a female, the **gonads** are the ovaries; for a male, the testis }

gondola literally means "to roll or rock"

the word **gong** comes from Malay and is imitative in origin

a person who stares for prolonged periods at something unusual is a **gongoozler**, like a rubbernecker; this is also a term for an idler

either end of the lower jaw, the part just under each ear, is the **gonion** (from Greek *gonia*, "angle")

the word **gonzo** either comes from Italian meaning "foolish" or Spanish meaning "fool" or "goose"; in regard to journalism, it was first used by Bill Cardoso, editor, for Hunter S. Thompson's style of writing which was characterized by distortion of the facts and exaggerated rhetorical style

goo may be an abbreviation of burgoo

goober is probably related to Kimbundu/Angolese *nguba*, "peanut"

using **good** as an adverb in place of **well** ("she dances real **good**," "he did **good**") is nonstandard usage—so, it would be best to say "she dances very **well**," "he did **well**"

the Middle Ages" phrase "God be with ye" became **goodbye**

the action of improving land by adding manure is called **gooding**

goodish means "moderately good"

gooey has an adverb form: gooeyly

goof may have come from the earlier *goff*, an obsolete word meaning "stupid person"

Google is a variation of googol, as the company's mission is to organize the infinite amount of information on the Web

mathematician Edward Kasner asked his nephew to coin a word for the number 1 followed by a hundred zeros—and his nephew came up with **googol**

goon may be a blend of gorilla and baboon

Popeye popularized the words **goon** and **jeep**

goop may be a blend of goo and drip

a **goose** has a shorter neck than that of a swan and a shorter, more pointed bill than that of a duck

gooseflesh is so called because the skin resembles that of a plucked goose

to **gooze** or **gaum** is to stare aimlessly

gopher is from Canadian French *gaufre*, "honeycomb" as this is what it does to the ground with its burrows; the **gopher** is variously called pocket **gopher** or ground squirrel in different areas

the heel of a sock is called the **gore**

the original meaning of **gore** was "dung, feces" or "slime" before it meant "bloodshed"

the groove of a pulley is the **gorge**

the original sense of **gorge** was "throat," from Latin *gurga*

gorgeous is from French *gorgias*, "elegant, fashionable"

to stare at with a petrifying look is to **gorgonize**

Gorgonzola is a village near Milan, Italy, where the blue cheese was first made

the word **gorilla** (large ape) comes from the discovery by Greeks of a hairy tribe of West African island women called Gorillai

someone who is **gormless** is dull or stupid

gorp is another name for trail mix and it may stand for "good old raisins (and) peanuts"

gorse is "prickly bush" if explained by etymology

the exclamation **gosh** is a euphemism for God, as is **golly**

gospel is literally "good news"

gossamer comes from "goose summer," the feast day when geese are eaten; at

that time, tiny spiders spin filmy webs over long distances and the spiders are wafted along like geese on the breeze

the original name for table tennis was **Gossima**, then **ping pong**

an early verb sense of **gossip** was "make oneself at home" and "act familiar to another"

god and sibb "a relative" gave us godfather and godmother, a person with which one would talk a lot—giving us the later "**gossip**"

goulash is from Hungarian *gulyashus* "hordsman's meat"

the **gourmand** rates quantity higher than quality and the **gourmet** adopts the opposite approach; a **gourmand** is one whose chief pleasure is eating and a **gourmet** is a connoisseur of food and wines

groumet, a servant who tasted wine for his wealthy employers, became English **gourmet**, which originally meant "wine taster" or "wine merchant's assistant"

gout is from Latin *gutta*, "drop"—as the disease was believed to be caused by the dropping of diseased matter from the blood into the joints

govern is from Greek *kubernan*, "to steer"

gown is from Latin *gunna*, "fur garment"

two hands held together to form a bowl is a **gowpen**

to **grabble** is "to feel one's way" or "to feel or search with the hands; grope around," especially on the floor

grace is from *gratia*, "pleasure, thanks"

gracile, meaning handsomely thin or willowy, is pronounced GRASS'l

graciosity is a synonym for graciousness

gradatim means step-by-step or gradually

a **gradation** is a series made up of successive stages or a step in an ordered scale

a **gradatory** is a flight of steps

the word **grade** comes from Latin *gradus*, "step"

Latin gradus "step" gave us **gradual**

a **graduand** is a person about to receive a degree

graduate and **graduation** are based on Latin gradus "degree, step"; to **graduate** from a school means to obtain a new degree (degree originally meant "step") and pass on to a new stage

graffiti in Italian is literally "scratches" (*graffito*, "scratch, scribble")

a **graft** is one thing attached to another by insertion or implantation so it becomes part of it; a **splice** is the joining of two things end-to-end to make a new whole

in the mid-nineteenth century, vegetarianism was named **Grahamism** for Dr. Sylvester Graham, its biggest proponent—after whom crackers, crust, etc. are also named

gram comes from Latin *gramma*, "a small weight"

gramercy (from *grand merci*) is a way of saying thank you

a symbol used to indicate a word (@, $) is a **grammalogue**

in its earliest use, "**grammar**" meant "Latin," or "the study of Latin"—and it derives from Greek *grammatike tekhne*, "art of letters" (because Latin was the only language taught grammatically)

grammar consists of a description of all the elements in a language; **syntax** focuses on the relationships between words that **graft** is the amount of earth that can be dug out in one shoveling of a spade—from Old Norse *groftr*, "action of digging" determine their order in sentences—**grammar** is the entire study and **syntax** is one part only

a student of grammar is a **grammatist**

gramophone was coined by Emil Berliner by reversing the elements of phonogram

grampus is a person who breathes heavily and noisily

Latin grandis, "big, fully grown" is the base of the word **grand**

a great name for old age is **grandevity**

graham flour, bread, and crackers are named after Sylvester **Graham**, a U.S. dietary reformer

grail is a cup or chalice but it hardly ever appears without holy, so there is really only one **grail**, the Holy **Grail**

grain first referred to a single seed of a plant or the pip or stone of a fruit

the ring of grooves around the edge of a coin is the **graining**

a **grandgousier** will eat anything and everything, especially to excess

originally, a **grange** was "somewhere for storing grain" or a "barn"

a **granita** is a frozen liquid and sugar that is stirred frequently during freezing so it has a granular consistency

granite is from Italian *granito*, "grained, grainy"

W.K. Kellog invented **granola**—based it on the word granulated for the ingredients' texture

{ **grant** came through French from Latin *credere*, "believe, trust" }

the **grape** is named for the hook that the French used to harvest them (**grape**, grapple)

a botanist said that the citrus paradisi tasted like grapes, earning it the name **grapefruit** (it does not grow in grapelike clusters, an erroneous etymology); synonyms are **pomelo** and **shaddock**

grapevine is a shortening of **grapevine** telegraph, a sarcastic term comparing the twisted stems of the **grapevine** and the straight lines of the early electric telegraph

graph is short for graphic formula, a term used in chemistry for a diagram representing in lines the relationship between elements and also in mathematics

graphic is from Greek *graphein*, "write" or "scratch"

the ability to understand maps, graphs, and diagrams or to present information by this means is **graphicacy**

graphology is the writing system of a language and **phonology** is the pronunciation system

if you have writer's cramp, you have **graphospasm**

grass is ultimately from the Germanic base of green and grow

grassant means "lurking with evil intent"

a **grasshopper** was first called a grasshop

the **grate** is the thing upon which the logs are placed in a fireplace

the grate of **grateful** is an obsolete adjective meaning "pleasing, thankful" (from Latin *gratus*)

dividing something into squares is **graticulation**

gratuitous means "unearned" or "unwarranted"

to **gratulate** is to welcome or greet joyfully

gravalax or **gravlax** is Swedish for "trench salmon" as it was originally marinated and fermented in a hole in the ground

the word **grave** as a place of burial dates to c 1000, though the verb form (now obsolete) meaning "to dig," may have come first and is of Germanic origin, coming into Old English as *groef*, "pit, trench"

grave "heavy, important" from Latin gravis, gives us the word **gravity** and also **grieve**

feeling drowsy? you are **gravedinous**

instead of saying you have a cold, say you have **gravedo**

the earliest meaning of **gravel** was "sand" and **gravel** now often contains coarse sand

to **gravel** is "to bring to a standstill" or "confuse, perplex"

a strong offensive smell is **graveolence**

gravid means quite pregnant, quite far along in a pregnancy

to **gravitate** implies a natural, perhaps irresistible, response to a force that works like gravity, drawing things steadily to it as if by their own weight

gravitation is the mutual force by which all bodies attract one another and a function of the masses of the bodies, the distance between them, and the gravitational constant; **gravity** is the force of **gravitation** on the earth or other celestial object (and also called acceleration or free fall)

gravity comes from Latin *gravitas* from *gravis*, "heavy, important"—and it can apply to situations and problems as well as to people

gravy initially described a spicy **sauce**; **gravy** now is a souplike addition to meats, **sauce** is for meat and pastas, etc., and **dressing** is reserved for salads (and also means "stuffing" in the U.S.) while **au jus** is "with natural juices"

graze is literally "feed on grass"

grazing is eating a number of small meals throughout the day

grease originally referred to the fat of an animal or the fat part of the body of an animal

the use of **great** as an adverb (e.g. doing **great**) only dates back to the 1940s

greave is armor for below the knee

Greece was formerly Hellas

greed is a back-formation from greedy

to tease or tantalize with no intention of giving is to **greg**

gregarious was once used to describe species or classes of animals living in flocks or communities (from Latin *greg/grex*, "flock, herd")

grege or **greige** is a color between beige and gray

gremial is an adjective meaning "of or pertaining to the bosom or lap"

grenade comes from French *pomegrenade*, "pomegranate" because the first grenades were shaped like the fruit

a pomegranate's sweet syrup is **grenadine**

able to walk is **gressible**

gressorial means "adapted for walking and **cursorial** means "adapted for running"

 the distinction in spelling between British **grey** and American **gray** is recent, popping up in Samuel Johnson's dictionary

green is from the same Germanic base gro- as grow

green onions are also called bunching onions and **scallions** were originally specific green bunching onions from Ascalon in Palestine; **shallots** resemble these but have grayish bulbs

greenhorn was first applied to an ox with "green" or young horns

Eric the Red named **Greenland** to induce colonists from Iceland to settle in the new country

unfired pottery is called **greenware**

early meanings of **greet** were "to assail, attack"

greyhound is derived from Old Norse *grey*, "dog"—so it is etymologically a tautology (redundancy)

grid is a back-formation from gridiron

the crossword diagram itself is the **grid**

to **gride** is to scratch, scrape, or cut with a grating sound

gridiron was an alteration (influenced by iron) of the earlier spelling gridire "griddle," which was a variant of gridil, a variant of Old French *greil*, *gril*, "grill"; the name of the cooking device lent itself to the term for a football field which resembles it

gridlock is grid and deadlock combined

Latin *gravis*, "heavy, weighty" gave us **grief**

the **griffin** (or gryphon) is the creature with the head and wings of an eagle and the body of a lion

griffonage is sloppy or illegible handwriting

grill was originally a gridiron, an instrument of torture, then a cooker; technically, a **grill** emits heat downward

grille "grating" is from the diminutive of a Latin word meaning "hurdle"

Spanish *grima*, "fright" may have become English **grimace**

a **grimalkin** is an old female cat

a **grimoire** is a magician's manual

grin first meant "to scowl, to show the teeth as a sign of anger"

a **grinagog** is a person who grins for no reason or is perpetually smiling

gringo is an alteration of Mexican Spanish *griego* meaning "Greek," "strange," or "stranger"

grinning originally denoted either pain or anger and dogs and wolves were said to "grin" to show their ferocity

grip is another name for a piece of hand luggage

gripe first meant "the action of gripping"

grisly (from Germanic *gri-*, "fear, terror") is "gruesome" while **grizzly** means "streaked with gray"

grissini are long thin sticks of crisply baked bread (breadsticks)

grist first meant "gnashing of the teeth" or other grinding, but also "anger"

gristle is cartilage or cartilaginous material

grit(s) is any coarsely ground grain, especially when made into a porridge

grizzle can mean "complain, whine"

to **groak** is to watch people eating food in hopes that they will offer you some

a **grocer** (literally, "dealer in gross") was originally a wholesaler and the food in retail amounts was called a "spicer"—so a wholesale dealer in these goods was called a "spicer en gross" or "grosser" (from French *gros*, "great, large")

{ **grocery** should be pronounced GROHS-[uh]-ree or GROW-sur-ee }

a **grocery store** is smaller; a **supermarket** is big

a sloppy fellow is a **grod**; a girl, a **groddess**

grog was part of a nickname of a Royal Navy admiral who ordered rum rations watered down to curb drunkenness; the nickname came from his coat's material grogram (from French *gros grain*)

groggy, from grog "spirits mixed with water," first meant "intoxicated"

groin seems to be related to ground, as Old English *grynde*, "depression in the ground" corresponded to the Middle English *grynde*, "**groin**"

grok means "to understand intuitively or by empathy"

a **grommet** is a metal, plastic, or rubber eyelet fitted to a hole to protect cable, rope, or other material strung through it—and first had a nautical meaning "a circle of rope used as a fastening"

between your toes: **gronk**, **cheese**, or **toe-jam**

groom was first simply a word for "boy"

groove comes from a Dutch word meaning "ditch, furrow" and first referred to a mine shaft or pit

gropple means "to grope" or "to come to grips with"

gross is borrowed from Old French gros and Latin grossus "coarse, thick" and came to mean "unrefined" and later "disgusting"

grotesque, first a style of decorative painting, derives from Italian *pittura grotesca*, "cave painting"—which is related to the word **grotto**, an interweaving of animal and human forms with flowers and leaves

{ **grotesque** is, literally, grottolike; **grotty** is a slang derivative }

grotto comes via Latin *crupta*, "subterranean passage or chamber" from Greek *krypte*, "hidden place"

to **grouk** is to become gradually enlivened after waking

the third prong of a three-prong plug is called the **ground**

Dutch settlers called any animal that lived in the ground and looked pig-like, aardvark or "earth pig"; when this was done in America, it was re-translated to **groundhog**

a **groundhog** and **woodchuck** are the same and are also known as a **whistle pig**; the **woodchuck** has nothing to do with wood or chuck, but comes from Cree *otchock*

groundsel may etymologically mean "ground-swallower"

group was first a term in art criticism for the disposition of a set of figures or objects in a painting, drawing, etc.

grouse, the bird, comes from Latin *grus*, "crane"

when a pig turns up the ground with its snout, that is called **grouting** or **rooting**

grove is from Germanic meaning "brushwood, thicket"

grovel is a back-formation from **groveling**—which first meant "face downward in a prone or prostrate position"

grow originally referred chiefly to plants

an early meaning of **grub** as a noun was "short person"

grub first referred to root vegetables which had to be grubbed (dug) out of the ground

a **grubbery** is a room for hard work or study—or a place where one eats

a form of obsession in which even the simplest facts are compulsively questioned is known as **Grübelsucht**

grubstake is U.S. mining slang for "the provisions (grub) furnished to a prospector on condition of the profits (stake) on any finds he makes"

grudge once meant "open utterance of discontent or displeasure with another" and "discontent, complaint" in general

grudgement is "envy or resentment"

grue means a horrifying effect or quality

gruel is etymologically something that is "finely ground"—a "fine flour or meal"

gruelling comes from the verb *gruel*, "to exhaust, punish"

gruesome is from an earlier verb *grue*, "be terrified"

if someone is **gruffing**, they are grunting or snoring

grim and glum combine to make **grum** "gloomy, morose, surly"

thunder can be said to **grumble**

a **grume** is a clot, usually of blood

another word for coffee grounds or dregs is **grummel**

blood can be **grumous** "clotted, viscid," roots can be **grumous** (knotty), and rocks can be **grumous** (formed of aggregated grains)

grump is imitative of inarticulate sounds expressing displeasure

grunch is a crunching and grinding noise

a **grundy** or **Mrs. Grundy** is a person who is prudish and the picture of propriety

grunge is a back-formation from grungy

a **gruntle** is the snout of a pig

gruntle can be used for swine, meaning "to make a little grunt"

gruntle is an old word meaning "complain," **disgruntle** is *di-*, "double" and **gruntle**, so it is double-**gruntle**—or complain repeatedly

gubernatorial and **governor** trace back to Latin *gubernare*, "to govern"—but **governor** took a detour through French (*governeor*)

guck is a combination of goo and muck

a **gudgeon** is a pivot or spindle on which a bell or other object swings or rotates

guerrilla is from a Spanish diminutive of guerra "war" and refers to a soldier of an independent armed resistance force; **gorilla** is the ape

{ **g-string** was first spelled gee-string and is of Native American origin though not much else is certain about it }

guacamole is from Nahuatl *ahuacamolli*, "avocado sauce or stew"

guarantee is from Old French *garant*, "a warrant," while **warranty** is from Old North French *warantie*, derived from *warant*, "a warrant." Both *garant* and *warant* came from Frankish (the West Germanic language spoken in the 400s and 500s in the region of ancient Gaul that became France), represented by Old High German *weren*, "to confirm, warrant." **Guarantee** is a general term for a representation regarding a good's quality and performance—and **warranty** is the legal term for the document; the person to whom it is issued is the warrantee with the issuer being the warrantor.

guard first meant "care, keeping"

guardian is from Old French gardein "protector, custodian," while **warden** is from Old North French *wardein*, "**guardian**, custodian"; both words came from Frankish, reprsented by Old High German *warten*, "to watch, guard"

gubbins means "miscellaneous items" or "gadget"

gubernation is the act of controlling or governing

at first, to **guess** was to take aim at something, such as a target, with a weapon

guest and **host** came from the same Indo-European base and Latin *hosti-potis*, "**host, guest**"

the small window through which tickets are sold is the **guichet**

the ancestor of **guide** was Germanic *wit*, "know" (source of wise, wit, witness)

guidon, a military pennant, is pronounced GUY-d'n

guilds probably got their name from subscriptions paid by their members originating from Germanic *gelth-*, "pay"

the **guillotine** (pronounced GIL-uh-teen) was named for Dr. Joseph Guillotin (1738–1814) who proposed the method of decapitation

originally "**guilt**" was the offense or crime itself

a **guimpe** (or **guimp**) is a high-necked shirt or undergarment worn showing beneath a low-necked shirt or dress

guinea (money) got its name from its connection with the **Guinea** Coast and because it was made from gold obtained there

gulag, a type of labor camp and prison of Russia/Soviet Union, is an acronym from *Glavnoe upravlenie ispravitel'no-trudovkh lagere*

Greek *kithara* evolved into **guitar**

gulf comes from Greek *kolphos*, "bosom"

gullet is from Latin *gula*, "throat"

the hollows in front of each tooth of a saw (on alternate sides) are the **gullets**

gullible is a derivative of archaic gull "dupe" or "simpleton"

a **gullion** is a mean, worthless wretch

the ultimate source of **gum** is Egyptian *kemai*, "tree sap"

gumbo, a stew made with okra, is related to Umbundu *ochinggombo* and Luba *chinggombo*, "okra"; it was first a colloquial name for the okra plant or pods

a **gump** is a large umbrella

the word **gun** originally referred to cannons and other instruments of war

gung-ho comes from Chinese *kung go*, "work together"

gunk (probably gunge and junk combined) came from a proprietary name of a detergent

gunny, the material used for sacks, is made from jute or sunn-hemp (from Sanskrit *goni*, "sack")

the **gunwale** is the upper side of a ship from the quarterdeck to the forecastle and is supportive of the guns; it is pronounced GUH-n'l

guop means to throb

a clergyman of Trinidad name RJL **Guppy**, who studied fish, lent his name to Gemidinus **guppy** (now renamed), known commonly as **guppy**

a rumbling in the bowels is **gurgulation**

to **gurk** is to belch

a **gurney** is a stretcher with wheels

guru is from a Sanskrit word meaning "dignified, grave, weighty"; hence, "venerable, elder, or "teacher"

gust, from Latin *gustus*, "taste" can mean "sense of taste" or "flavor (of food)"—but also "inclination, liking" and the old sense of "the sense of or an act of tasting" gives us **gustatory**

gusted meant "having a particular taste" and was used with "well" and "sweetly"

gusto, from Italian, is from Latin *gustus*, "taste"; the plural is gustoes

gut first meant the contents of the abdominal cavity

a candle burning low or almost out is a **gutter**

in a book, the inner margins by the fold is the **gutter**

guttersnipe is literally "child brought up in the gutters" and also pertained to "a gatherer of refuse from street gutters"

to **guttle** is to eat gluttonously, voraciously

guttural is from Latin *guttur*, "throat"

guy comes from **Guy** Fawkes, leader of the 1605 Gunpowder Plot, and first meant "person of odd appearance"

the sound of squeaky shoes is **gweek-gwak**

gwenders is a disagreeable tingling from the cold

gwicking is making a loud swallowing sound with your throat

gymnasium was a school where Greek youths were given athletic training while naked (*gymnos*)

gymnastic describes a letter in a manuscript decorated with human figures performing athletic exercises

gynecology is from the Greek word for woman, *gune*

{ **gyp** comes from Greek and literally means "vulture" }

the words spelled with the most number of descenders are **gyp** and **gyppy**

gypsum is from Semitic, a relative or ancestor of Arabic *jibs* and Hebrew *gephes*, "plaster"

gypsy is short for Egyptian as gypsies were believed to have come from Egypt

wanderers in Britain in the sixteenth century were thought to come from Egypt and were called Egipcyans, which was later shortened to Gipcyan and then became **gypsy**

a **gyre** is a circular movement or revolution; to **gyre** is to cause to spin around or whirl

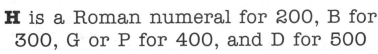
H is a Roman numeral for 200, B for 300, G or P for 400, and D for 500

Häagen-Dazs is made up; it does not mean anything in any known language

a **habanero** is a very hot roundish chili pepper (Capsicum chinense) that is usually orange when mature

the origin of **haberdasher** may be Anglo-Norman *hapertas*, "piece of cloth" or "small goods"

if someone is **habile**, they are able or skillful

habiliment can refer to one's attire but also to apparatus, fittings, gear, rigging—and to munitions and the apparatus of war

habit derives from the Latin stem *habere*, "have, hold"; we all know that a **habit**, good or bad, has a hold on you

habitacle is another word for dwelling-place

habitat, from Latin, is literally "it inhabits"

habitué (pronounced huh-BITCH-oo-way) is a resident of or frequent visitor to a particular place

hachure is a type of shading consisting of multiple crossing lines, especially to shade a map with hachures to represent the elevations

hacienda is a Spanish word taken from Latin *facienda*, "things to be done"

hack, as in a writer with marginal talent who works like a horse, is from hackney "a horse for hire"

to **hack** is to ride on a horse for pleasure—from whence we get **hacking jacket**

the top of a haystack is the **hackle**

hackles are the erectile hairs along an animal's back, like a dog

hackneyed "commonplace, used too often" is from Hackney, a town near London that was famous for its horses used for ordinary riding or driving

haecceity is the quality of a thing that makes it unique or describable as "this (one)"

hag first meant "witch"

originally, **haggard** was specific to falconry, referring to an adult hawk captured for training—which meant it was wild and often had ragged feathers

the probable source of **haggis** (a Scottish dish consisting of seasoned sheep's or calf's offal mixed with suet and oatmeal, boiled in a bag traditionally made from the animal's stomach) is Old French *agace*, "magpie" or from earlier *hag*, "hack, hew," from Old Norse

haggle first meant "hack, mangle; mutilate by cutting"

a **hagiography** is an overly praiseful biography

a **ha-ha** is a sunken trench or ditch not visible until one steps in it

haiku is an abbreviation of Japanese *haikai no ku*, "unserious or comic verse"

hail (ice pellets) traces to Greek *kakhlex*, "pebble"

hail is an exclamation of welcome like Latin *salve* (from Old Norse *heill*, "hale" or "whole")

hair can be traced back to Germanic *khaeran*, from Proto-Indo-European *ker(s)-*, "to bristle"

a **hairbreadth** is 1/48 of an inch

hair-trigger's underlying meaning is something may be triggered with the pressure of something as slight as a hair

hairy can mean "impressive"

a **halberd** is a combined spear and battle-ax (from German meaning "handle hatchet")

the **hale** is a handle of a plow or wheel-barrow

half, from Gothic *halba*, first meant "side"

half-cocked comes from hunting; a gun at half cock is in the safety position—so it came to mean "incompletely prepared"

half-light is dimness, such as at dusk

when one is **halflings**, one is between childhood and adulthood

a broad step or small landing between two half flights in a staircase is the **half-pace**

half-seas-over is halfway through a journey or course; figuratively, halfway through a matter

in Middle English, any flatfish was called a butte and fish was eaten on holy days, so *butte* was combined with *haly*, "holy" to form halybutte—now **halibut**

halidom is the condition or state of being holy or sacred or a sanctuary or sacred object

{ **halieutics** is the art or practice of fishing, from Greek *halieuein*, "to fish" }

hall was originally a roofed location in the center of a community for the communal use of a tribal chief and his people

hallelujah literally means "Praise (ye) the Lord" (Hebrew *hallelu-yah*, "praise Jehovah"); **alleluia** is also from this

if something is pertaining to hallelujahs, it is **hallelujatic**

the word **hallmark** (once hall-mark) comes from Goldsmiths' Hall in London, where precious metal articles were tested and stamped with a mark

hallow is essentially the same word as holy, from Old English *halig* and Germanic *khailag-*

November 1 became All Saints' Day (All Hallows' Day in England), by proclamation of Pope Boniface IV in the 7th century, a celebration of all the Christian saints. The evening before All Saints' Day, October 31, became a holy, or hallowed, eve and thus All Hallow Even or All Hallows' Eve (later Hallow-e'en, Hallowe'en, **Halloween**), considered "old-year's night." Despite the name change, this holiday's association with the supernatural persisted.

Latin *alucinari*, "wander in thought or speech," from Greek *alussein*, "be distraught or uneasy"—gave us **hallucinate**

hallucination is from disturbed sensory perceptions; **delusion** is from disturbed thinking

the **hallux** is a human big toe but also the name of the toe on a bird that is directed backwards

halo is from Greek *halos*, "disk of the moon or sun"; a synonym for **halo** is **nimbus**

sea flora and fauna collectively is **halobios**

hanaper "plate basket" or "repository for treasure"

at one time, second-rate actors who could not afford cold cream had to use ham fat—hence, "hamfatters," which became "**hams**"

the **hamster**'s name is from Old Slavic *chomestoru*, which came into German as *humustro*, then **hamster**; in the eighteenth century, the animal was also called the German rat

{ **halt** (noun) was first used in the military sense of "temporary stop in a march" and as a verb was "limp, walk lamely" }

halter as a woman's top came into English around 1935; it developed from the sense of **halter** for horses or cattle

originally the part of the leg behind the knee was called the **ham** and then the tendon near the **ham** was the **hamstring**; by extension, the **ham** became the thigh and buttock together

hamartia is a classic tragic or fatal flaw (from Greek *hamartanein*, "to miss the mark, err")

hamburger comes from the name of the German town, though it is disputed whether the **hamburger** steak (the earliest term (1889), which was a kind of sausage) originated there; it means "steak in Hamburg style" and it has spurred new forms such as cheeseburger, chiliburger, fishburger, veggieburger, burger, etc.

hamlet is a diminutive of a French word meaning "little village" (from Latin *hameletum*)

hammer goes back to Old Norse hamarr "back of an ax, crag"

hammocks were first made from the fibers of the hamack tree

hamous meaning "having hooks"

a food basket for a picnic is a **hamper**, which is a phonetic reduction of the word

hamstrung first referred to an animal crippled by the cutting of its hamstrings

a bunch of bananas is a **hand**

handbook first referred to a medieval ecclesiatical manual

to **handfast** is to cohabit for a trial period before marriage

hand-hot is a word to describe water that is hot but not too hot to put one's hands into

handicap comes from the drawing of lots out of a cap or hat by putting one's hand i(n the) cap; **handicap** can mean either disadvantage or advantage

handiwork comes from Old English *handgeweorc, hand + geweorc* "work"; the word was reformulated by folk etymology on the basis of handy + work

handcoverchief, showing that originally the cloth was a kerchief or cloth covering for the head that was carried in the hand, became **handkerchief**

etymologically, a **handle** is "something to be held in the hand"

an animal trainer is a **handler**

a gift made as a good-luck token, such as the first receipts of a new store, is a

handsel; it first meant "one's luck or fortune" or "an indication, omen, or token of luck" and it is the word for a gift given at the beginning of a new year

handsome (first hand-some) originally meant "easy to handle," then "handy, convenient" before its current meanings

hangar simple meant "shed" for carriages when it came into English

you put a plane in a **hangar**, but an item of clothing on a **hanger**

a **hangbird** is one which builds a hanging nest, such as the oriole

hangdog comes from the practice of convicting and executing dogs by hanging for crimes committed against humans

hangnail originally was angnail—meaning "anguish" caused by this condition

hangout originally meant a place of business—from the signs "hung out" by artisans, professionals, and tradespeople

a **hank** is a flexible loop of material or a skein or coil of rope, thread, or yarn

hanker is from Flemish *hankeren*, related to "hang" and first meant "to hang about, loiter" before it meant "to have a longing or craving"

hanky-panky may be an alteration of hokey-pokey

Hanukkah (also spelled Hanukka, Chanukah, Chanukkah) is from Hebrew and means "consecration, dedication"

a person who lives in Hawaii but is not a native is a **haole**

haphazard is redundant, with both components meaning "chance"

hapless means one is lacking hap "good fortune, luck"; the words happy and **happiness** also have the root "hap"

happen is fairly new to English, from hap "chance, luck" which was borrowed from Old Norse *happ*

happy comes from hap, an old word for "chance, luck, destiny" and the early sense of **happy** was "lucky"—but the modern meaning of "cheerful and contented" came much later

haptic means pertaining to the sense of touch

a synonym for cruel or violent is **harageous**

hara-kiri (suicide by disembowelment) is actually an impolite way of saying the Japanese word *seppuku*, "belly-splitting," literally "belly-cutting"

the original notion of **harangue** may have been of a large group of people crowded around, fom Latin *harenga*, "assembly"

harass comes from the French word harer "to incite dogs," "to set a dog after"; **harass** originally meant "trouble by repeated attacks" and should be pronounced HAIR-us, though her-ASS is acceptable

an **harbergery** is an inn or place of entertainment

originally, a **harbinger** was one who provided lodging or acted as a host

harbor first meant "shelter" and "lodging" and that is how the word first entered English place-names, as a "place of shelter; refuge" for a crowd of people; a **port** is a haven for vessels and it is equipped for loading and unloading ships, while a **harbor** is a haven for vessels but does not necessarily have onshore facilities

{ **hard** ultimately comes from Indo-European *kratus*, "power, strength" }

hardiment is a word for boldness, courage, or daring

hardy once meant "bold"—to describe an assertion or a person

hardy means "strong, durable, capable"—while **hearty** means "strong" in a more active way as in **hearty** appetite, applause, meal

foolish daring or willful recklessness is **hardydardy**

the **hare** was originally named for its color, possibly related to Old English *hasu*, "gray" and Latin *cascus*, "old"

hares live in the open and bear young that have fur at birth while **rabbits** live in burrows and bear young that are naked at birth; **jackrabbits** are **hares**, not **rabbits**

harem comes from Arabian *harim*, "sacred, forbidden place" (where Moslem women live)

Harlequin was a brightly dressed character in the Italian commedia dell'arte and before that was a mythical figure; other meanings of **harlequin** include any black-and-white dog or a variety of opal with a mosaic-like color pattern

harlot first meant "rascal, low fellow" or "vagabond, beggar" (Latin *harlotus*, "vagabond")

harm's original meanings were "grief" before "physical damage"

a **harmonica** is also called a mouth harp or mouth organ; Benjamin Franklin created the **harmonica**, but he called it an "armonica"

nest "provisions") or "armor," as in the phrase "to die in **harness**" (to die with one's armor on)

the pair of curved vertical metal supports for a lampshade is the **harp** (from its resemblance to the instrument)

harpsichord is literally "harp-string"

a **harridan** is an ill-tempered, scolding woman

a dog that is used to chase hares is a **harrier** and the first cross-country runs were made in the game Hare and Hound; hence, **harrier** is a name for a cross-country runner

to **harrow** is to wound the feelings or cause to suffer—which gives us **harrowing**

etymologically, to **harry** is to "go on a raid as an army does"

the word "**harsh**" used to be written "harsk" and is from German, literally "hairy"

harum-scarum is a reduplication based on hare and scare

harvest, literally "autumn," is Germanic in origin and that was the original meaning, later coming to reaping and gathering grain and other grown products during that season

a daddy longlegs is a **harvestman**, a name given to certain insects which abound in the fields in harvest-time

hashish is from Arabic meaning "dry herb" or "intoxicant made from dry herb or hemp leaves"

{ a **hasp** is a piece of hardware used to lock a door or gate; it fits over a staple or loop and a padlock through that secures the door or gate }

harmony comes from a Greek word *harmozein*, "fit together"

harness originally meant portable "military equipment" (Old Norse *herr*, "army"

hassle may be a blend of haggle and tussle

the root sense of **hassock** is "clump of matted vegetation"

haste comes from Germanic meaning "fury, violence"

an early-ripening fruit or vegetable is a **hasting** and such a food that ripens early is termed "**hasty**"

hat can be used to mean "a person's official capacity or status"

the **hatch** is the lower half of a divided door

shading done with parallel lines is **hatching** (or hachure); shading done with lines going two directions is **cross-hatching**—and artists use these techniques, varying the length, angle, closeness and other qualities of the lines

hate means to "dislike intensely, loathe" and **despise** means "look down on contemptuously"

a **hatful** is a considerable amount or number

hatter was a verb meaning "to entangle," "to wear out, weary"

haughty derives from obsolete haught, which came from Latin *altus*, "high"

haul originally had the nautical meaning of "to trim the sails to sail closer to the wind"

haulm is a collective term for the stalks or stems of beans, peas, or potatoes

the **haunch** is the buttock and thigh together

haunt first meant "to practice or use habitually or frequently"

hautain is "proud, arrogant" or describes a raised or loud voice

{ **hauteur** (from French *haut*, "high") means loftiness of manner or bearing }

have, coming through Proto-Germanic *khaben*, was from Indo-European *kap-* meaning "possession"

the cloth piece hanging down from the back of a (soldier's) hat as sun protection is the

havelock; it was named after English general Sir Henry **Havelock** (1795–1857)

the literal meaning of **haven** in English is "harbor"

haversack is from German Haber "oats" and Sack "bag, sack"

we are aware of the term "wreak **havoc**" and **havoc** was once part of a command for invaders to begin looting, plundering, pillaging, and killing (from French *havot*, "pillage"), but by the 1800s the term was being used for somewhat less aggressive activities

the third eyelid of dogs or cats is the **haw**

Hawaii was once called the Sandwich Islands and its native name Hawaiki or Owyekee means "homeland"

hawk "peddle" is a back-formation of hawker, from German *hoken*, "peddle"

if an animal **haws**, it turns or moves to the left

the hole in a ship's bow for an anchor is a **hawse** or **hawsehold**; the anchor rope or cable is the **hawser**

hawthorn appears to be etymologically the "hedgethorn"

etymologically, **hay** is "that which is cut down"

farmers used to tie hay bales with wire, but that wire would often get tangled in the machinery or when left exposed could hurt people or animals; so **haywire** came to mean malfunction

hazard started as the name of a game of dice but later extended to all kinds of risks and comes from Arabic *az-zahr*, "gaming die"

haze is probably a back-formation from hazy

hazel is a very ancient tree name, tracing back to Indo-European *kosolos* or *koselos*

HAZMAT stands for Hazardous Material

he ultimately comes from Indo-European ki-/ko- "this, here"—as opposed to "that, there"

a ship's bathroom is the **head**

on a celery bunch, the end where the branches come together is the **head**

a **header** is a piece of text in the top margin of a page and a **footer** is such in the bottom margin

a **headline** in palmistry refers to a fold in the palm of the hand that tells of abilities

wind blowing from in front is a **headwind** and blowing from behind is a **tailwind**

heal and **health** share a Germanic base meaning "whole"; etymologically, **health** is the "state of being whole"

healing is a process in which an organism's health is restored; **curing** is a method that promotes **healing**

healthcare as one word is preferred over two; as an adjective, **health-care** is usually hyphenated

healthy is a positive descriptive of a person's (or personified thing's) physical state; **healthful** of something that favorably affects or promotes that state

heap implies a roughly conical form

to **hearken** is to pay attention or listen and it can also mean "to return to a previous topic"

hearse was once the decorative bier, frame, or stand on which a corpse was laid, or a framework to carry candles over a coffin

a cabbage's tight head is the **heart**

Heart can be traced back from Old English (c 725) and the spelling was *herte* until about 1500 when it was spelled **heart** by analogy of pronunciation with heat, stream, etc. The Indo-European root

is shared with Latin *cor, cord-* and Greek *ker, kardia*. As the seat of feeling and intellect, **heart** has been used since around 825.

heartburn has an old meaning of "jealousy" or "hatred"

{ the **hearth** is the floor of a fireplace and the area in front of a fireplace }

the dent at the end of your sternum is the **heart-spoon**

a **heat** as a preliminary race for a sporting contest is so called because of its intensity

heath derives from Germanic for "untilled land, open country" and originally the word "**heath**" was used to denote any of the small northern and western European plants that grew on moorland, open woodland, or poor soil; a **heath** has sandy soil and a **moor** has peaty soil—but both are relatively barren tracts covered with shrubs

heathen literally meant "dweller on the heath"—a person living in a remote area that early Christianity had not yet reached

heather is also called **ling** or **broom**

the inflections of **heave** are heaved or hove, heaved, and hove or hoven

heave/heft is analogous to cleave/cleft, weave/weft

heaven's earliest meaning in English is "sky, firmament"—a overarching vault of sky

from the Proto-Germanic verb *khabjan*, "lift" came the noun *khabiz*, "weight" which begat the Dutch hevig and then English **heavy**

hebephrenic describes the condition of adolescent silliness

hebetate means "to make dull"

(mentally), something that makes you dull or stupid is **hebetating**, and **hebetude** is the state of being dull or lethargic

heckle was first a "flax comb" for splitting and straightening the fibers for spinning and its metaphorical sense developed from heckling being "to mangle by cutting, to cut roughly"

hectic was originally a medical term for a type of fever

hecto- (from Greek) means multiplied by 100 and **centi-** (from Latin) means divided by 100

a **hector** was first a valiant warrior

other names for a **hedgehog** are: ilspile, furze-pig, herisson, hurcheon, irspile, irchon, and tiggy

someone who is **hedgehoggy** has a defensive appearance or manner, like a hedgehog rolled into a ball with its prickly spines exposed

a baby hedgehog is a **hoglet** or **hedgehoglet**

hedonism comes from Greek *hedone,* "pleasure"

heebie-jeebies is a term that originated in the comic strip Barney Google

the crusty ends of a loaf of bread are its **heels**

heeltap is a small amount of liquid remaining in a glass after drinking

a **heffalump** is a child's word for elephant, popularized in Winnie the Pooh stories

hegemon is a Greek word for "leader"

hegemony (dominance, especially by one state or social group over others) is pronounced hi-JEM-uh-nee

{ **hegira** is a journey undertaken to escape a troublesome situation }

etymologically and semantically, **height** is the "condition of being high"; in Middle English this word rhymed with "hate"

heinous is from a French word haineus from an earlier form meaning "to hate"; **heinous** should be pronounced HAY-nuhs

heirloom is a combination of heir and loom "tool, utensil" and it describes any personal property that has been in a family for several generations

heist is a dialectal form of hoist, which has taken on life as a separate word

helical is a synonym for screw-shaped and spiral

a ramp that curves and goes up is a **helicline**

helicopter comes from Greek *heliko,* "screw" and *pteron,* "wing"; the word **helicopter** is first recorded in 1872, but the first **helicopter** flight took place only in 1907

using a mirror to send a signal is **heliography**

a **heliolater** is a sun worshiper

heliotherapy is the use of sun baths as treatment

the **heliotrope** got its name because its flowers always turn to face the sun, from Greek *heliotropion,* "sun-turning"; when plants bend toward the sun, that is **heliotropism**

heliport is a blend of helicopter and airport

helium gets its name from Greek *helios* for "sun" as the element was observed in the solar spectrum during the eclipse of August 18, 1868

helix has the plurals helixes and helices

Helladic pertains to the Bronze Age cultures of Greece, c 2900–1100 BC

Hellenistic denotes the culture and time from the death of Alexander the Great to the defeat of Antony and Cleopatra, roughly the 4th to the 1st century BC

helliborne means "carried by helicopter"

Thomas Edison popularized the greeting of "**hello**," which was an exclamation of surprise dating back to the Middle Ages, from French *hallow*, "to pursue by shouting," first becoming "hallo" in English

to **helm** is a nautical term "to steer"

a **helmet** is literally "a little protective hat," from a diminutive form of French *helme* "**helmet**" and an Indo-European base meaning "cover, hide"; a **helm** was originally armor for the head or a **helmet**

help seems to be a Germanic word from a Proto-Indo-European base *kelb-/kelp-*, "to **help**"

a female lobster or other crustacean is known as a **hen** or a **chicken**

hence means "from here, from now, thus," **thence** means "from that time" or "from that place," and **whence** means "from what place, source, or cause"

the base of **henchman** is an Old English word meaning gelding or stallion (+ man)

to **hend** is to seize or take; **hent** is the act of seizing

using two modifiers connected by "and" instead of just two words is called **hendiadys**

a stone that is suspended or overhangs is a **henge**

{ the Indo-European root of **hell** meant "covered or concealed" as **hell** is supposedly hidden in the dark regions near the earth's center }

---

helpmeet is another word for **helpmate**, especially a wife

the handle of a hammer, ax, etc. is a **helve**

a **hemera** is the period of geological time in which any particular species had its "day" or was most abundant

hemorrhoid (pronounced HEM-royd, HEM-uh-royd) is also called **piles** and is from Greek *haimorrhoides* (*phlebes*), "bleeding (veins)"

the **hemidemisemiquaver** is a 64th note; a 32nd note is a **demisemiquaver** and a 16th note is a **semiquaver**

hemorrhage is literally "bursting forth of blood," from Greek words *haima*, "blood" and *rhegnunai*, "break, burst"

hemp (Old Teutonic) is ultimately the same as *cannabis* (from Latin), probably sharing the Germanic ancestor and borrowed from the same Scythian word that became Greek *kannabis*

henpeck is a back-formation of **henpecked**; **henpecked** alludes to the plucking of a domestic fowl by his hens

the word **hep** comes from the Army, where it was a shortened step, so one who learned to "keep in step" was "**hep**"

hep, the slang and jazz term, evolved into **hip**

hepatic (pertaining to or affecting the liver) is from Greek *hepatikos*, "of the liver," and **hepatitis** is *hepatos*, "liver" and *-itis*, "inflammation"

herb (pronounced URB) comes from Latin *herba*, "grass" or "green crops"

her is the modern English descendant of Old English *hire*, a derivative of Germanic *khi-*, which also produced he etymologically, a **herald** is a "leader of an army," from Germanic *kharjaz*, "army"

herbs are, technically, plants with aerial

parts used for **seasoning** foods and a **spice** (also called **seasoning**) is any substance used for **seasoning** foods; many herbs are used as spices, but not all

grassy vegetation is **herbage**

herd as a verb first meant "keep safe, shelter"

here can be traced back to Indo-European *ki-/ko-* which denoted "thisness" or "hereness" as opposed to "thatness" or "thereness"

Latin *heres*, "**heir**" gives us **hereditary**, **heir**, **heritage**, and more

heresy, **heretic**, and **heretical** are based on Greek *haeresis*, "choosing, able to choose"—as a **heretic** literally chooses his/her own creed

in its earliest usages, **heritage** carried both spiritual and profane meanings, signifying a "people chosen by God as his peculiar possession" or as "inheritance" or "heirloom" for property passed through the generations

hermaphrodite is etymologically a blend of the names of Hermes, the messenger of the Greek gods, and Aphrodite, the Greek goddess of love; Hermaphroditos, son of Hermes and Aphrodite, had two bodies fused into one with dual sexual characteristics

hermeneutic is an adjective meaning "concerned with interpretation," especially of scripture

hermetic is related to Hermes and means impervious to outside influences; something that is firmly sealed and airtight is **hermetic**

hermit is from Greek *eremites*, "solitary"; a **hermitage** (pronounced HUR-muh-tij) is a place where a **hermit** or monks live

hernia is actually a Latin word with plurals hernias or herniae

hero is a Greek word (heros) applied to men of superhuman ability or courage

heroin (the drug) is based on Latin/Greek *heros*, "hero" because of its effects on the user's self-esteem; **heroine** is a courageous principal female character (the counterpart of hero)

heron may have originated in imitation of the bird's cry

herpes is Latin for "shingles," from Greek literally "creeping" (*herpein*, "creep")

herpetology, the branch of zoology dealing with amphibians and reptiles, is based on Greek *herpeton*, "creeping thing"

herptile is another word for reptile or amphibian

herring is etymologically "gray fish"

the bones of a herring are in a zigzag pattern, hence, **herringbone**

hesitancy is a quality or state, while **hesitation** is an act

hesitate is from the stem *haerere*, "hold fast, stick," "be undecided"

hesperian is western, **ortive** is eastern, **boreal** is northern, and **austral** is southern—of or relating to the time or act of rising in these directions

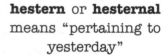

{ **hestern** or **hesternal** means "pertaining to yesterday" }

if you are keeping quiet, you are **hesychastic**

hetero-, from Greek, means "the other of two"

heterodox is from Greek words meaning "different, other" (*hetero-*) and "opinion" (*doxa*)

incorrect or poor spelling is **heterography** or **inorthography**

another name for hairball is **heterolith**

heuristic (enabling someone to learn something on their own) is from Greek *heuriskein,* "to find"

hex comes from German *hexen,* "to practice sorcery"

the six days of the Creation can be called the **hexameron**

hexanol is the chemical that gives freshly mowed grass its smell

heyday originally was an exclamation expressing excitement, happiness, surprise, or exuberance—and is from Saxon *heh-doeg,* "high day"

if something is **hiant**, it's gaping

hiatus is Latin, literally "gaping" or "gap"

hibachi is from Japanese meaning "fire bowl or pot"

hibernacle is a winter retreat or the winter home of a hibernating animal

the word **hibernate** derives from the Latin terms *hibernare,* "to winter," from *hiberna,* "winter quarters" and *hibernus,* "wintry"; Erasmus Darwin, grandfather of Charles Darwin, first used the word in 1802, according to Noah Webster

hibernation is a winter state of torpor and **estivation**/aestivation is the summer version

hiccup was originally called a **yex**

the word **hick** is actually a by-form (a secondary form of a word) of the name Richard

hickory (the tree) is actually an abbreviation of pohickory, from Algonquian *pawcohiccora,* "a milky drink made of these nuts"

hide "conceal" has no living relatives among the Germanic languages, but goes back to Indo-European *keudh-,* "cover, hide"

hide "skin" is from Indo-European *keut-,* which also produced Latin *cutis,* "skin"

hidebound first meant "having the skin stretched over bones, as in malnutrition"

hideous comes from a French base *hi(s)de,* "fear"

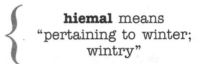

{ **hiemal** means "pertaining to winter; wintry" }

hierarchy is from Greek *hierarkhes,* "sacred ruler, holy ruler" and was first used for the three divisions of angels

hieratic means "pertaining to priests," but we know this word more in relation to the simplified cursive style of Egyptian hieroglyphics used in sacred and secular writings

etymologically, **hieroglyphic** means "of sacred carving" from Greek *hierogluphikos*

to **higgle** is to haggle or dispute the terms of a deal

high is ancient and goes back to Indo-European *koukos,* "rounded protuberance"; the notion of "tallness" is a secondary development from being "heaped up" or "arched up"

to **highball** is to signal a train to proceed

highbrow is a back-formation from highbrowed "having a high forehead"—which figuratively implied superior intelligence (etc.)

highfalutin actually has no apostrophe; its variant is highfaluting and its origin is unknown

highjack is said to derive from the gunman's command to the victim, "stick "em up high, Jack"

high-muck-a-muck is from Chinook *hayo makamak*, "plenty to eat" and evolved to mean "pompous important person"

hightail's derivation alludes to the erect tails of animals running away or in flight

a **highway** is a main road; an **expressway** is a multilane **highway**—and **freeway**, **parkway**, **turnpike** are types of expressways

vehicles and airplanes are **hijacked**, not people

hike as a walk evolved from its original meaning of "to jerk or pull" (oneself along)

hilarious comes from Greek *hilaros*, "cheerful"

hilarity was at first less boisterous, meaning "cheerfulness" or "calm joy"

hill shares the Indo-European base of Latin *collis* and Greek *kolomos/kolome*, "**hill**"

the outdoor equivalent of cabin fever is **hill-nutty**

a **hillock** is a little hill

the **hilum** is the scar on a seed marking the point where it is attached to its seed vessel

him was originally the dative case (indicating an indirect object or recipient) of the pronoun "he"

Himalaya is Sanskrit *hima*, "snow" and *alaya*, "abode"; **Himalayas** is pronounced hih-muh-LAY-uhs, also hih-MAHL-yuhz

in ancient Greece the outer garment worn over the left shoulder and under the right was called the **himation**

a **himbo** is an attractive but unintelligent man

hind once meant "female deer," "household servant," or "rustic"

> **Hind** is the Urdu word for "India"—giving us **Hindi** and **Hindu**

hinder first meant "do harm to or injure"

the **hinge** is another word for the earth's axis

the part of a hot dog roll that remains attached after the roll is sliced is the **hinge**

hinky means "dishonest" or "suspect"

a female donkey (jenny) and male horse (stallion) can make a **hinny**

hint first meant "an occasion or opportunity"

hinterland, remote parts or back country, comes from the original meaning of "area behind the coastal region" (from German *hinter*, "behind")

the fruit of the rose, especially wild, is the **hip**

hip dates back to 1904 while **groovy** predates the 1960s by some 30 years

hip-hop is a culture and **rap** is a style of music that is one of the components of **hip-hop**; **hip-hop** music is not the same as **rap**—it is a fusion of rapping and deejaying

hippie simply derives from hip/hep

the **hippocampus** (sea horse) derives from *hippos*, "horse" and *kampos*, "sea monster"

hippodrome "race track" is from Greek *hippo*, "horse" and *dromos*, "running"

hippomobile was once a word for a horse-drawn carriage

the plural of **hippopotamus** is hippopotamuses

hirable is the correct spelling (hireable is wrong)

armpit hair can be referred to as **hirci**

hire, as a noun, originally meant the payment for the use of something

hireling implies that the person is motivated by reward or payment

Hiroshima should be pronounced hi-roh-SHEE-muh

a cat's purr is **hirrient** (trilling)

a **hirsel** is a flock of sheep under a shepherd's charge

a man in need of a shave is **hirsute**

a **hithe** or **hythe** is a landing-place along a river

hitty-missy is another way of saying "at random" or "hit or miss"

hive comes from Indo-European *keup-*, "bowl, round container"

hiving is making one's home the focus of one's life, including work, while still connecting with the outside community (the opposite of **cocooning**)

> **hobble** is of Germanic origin, having to do with rocking from side to side; the noun can mean "an awkward situation"

his was originally the genitive form (indicating possession or close association) of the pronoun "he"

if you need to shave, you are **hispid** (bristly)

historic means "noteworthy, highly significant," whereas **historical** means "pertaining to history, relevant to the passage of time"; if something has a place in history, it is **historic**, and if something has to do with the subject of history, it is **historical**

historiography is the written history of something or the writing of history

history comes from Greek *histor*, "learned, wise man" but its first meaning in English was that of a "story"

histrionic is based on Latin histrio(n-) "actor"

hit is a relative latecomer to English, appearing at the end of Old English, borrowed from Old Norse *hitta*

hitch comes from a Scottish word meaning "motion by jerks" for a horse that is lame

hitchhike is literally hiking by "hitching" oneself to a vehicle; the word may only go back to World War I

hoar, now part of **hoary** and hoarfrost, is literally "white frost"; **hoary** is gray or white (or grayish white) with age (based on Germanic her "old")

hoard can describe an amassed (stock) of facts

a **hoard** is a collection or the action that creates one; a **horde** is a crowd, sometimes unfriendly

hoarfrost is the grayish-white frost on trees

hoax is probably a contraction of hocus

a male ferret is a **hob**

hobbit is a word invented by JRR Tolkein meaning "hole dweller"

a **hobbledehoy** is a gawky teenager

the diminutive **hobby** first meant "small horse or pony" and then a child's toy horse—a toy horse being for amusement and therefore it cannot be "worked"—so, we get **hobby** as "something for amusement which is not work"

in **hobgoblin**, hob means **hobgoblin**, sprite, elf—so the word is somewhat redundant a **hobnail**, a nail with a massive head, is based on the word hob "peg or pin used as a mark or target in games"

hobnob was once spelled habnab and its meaning was "have and not have" and it became "hob and nob" a synonym for "give and take"—as in an intimate conversation, and also hob or nob, "to drink to one another in turns" or "drink to each other"

a **hobo** is a migratory worker who likes to travel, a **tramp** travels without working, and a **bum** does not travel or work

hock as in "pawn, pledge" is from Dutch slang meaning "credit, debt"; "in **hock**" first meant "in prison"

hockey, first called hawkey, was first described in 1838 and the origin of the word is unknown but may be related to "hook"—as the sticks are hooked

the underside of the thigh is the **hockshin** or **gambrel**

hocus-pocus is a corruption of the sacred phrase hoc est corpus meum, "this is my body," used in the Eucharist

hodgepodge was originally spelled hotchpotch and meant "a type of stew"

hodiern or **hodiernal** is "pertaining to the present day"

a scarecrow can be called a **hodmandod**

hoe, the tool, is related to hew (verb) and a **hoeful** is as much as can be lifted on a **hoe**

hofles means "excessive, unreasonable"

a pig over 120 pounds is a **hog**

hogan is from Navajo hooghan, "home, home place" and is a dwelling made of logs or earth and covered with mud or sod

a **hogback** is sharply crested ridge, steep on each side and sloping gradually at each end

a **hogenhine** is a member of one's family

hogwash, from earlier hoggy swasch, is pig slops, swill of a kitchen or brewery given to hogs

flags grouped to make a signal is a **hoist**

hoity-toity is a reduplicative phrase based on obsolete hoit "to romp"

hokey-pokey was an early form of cheap ice cream, the name derived from hocus-pocus

{ **hokum** may be a combination of hocus-pocus and bunkum }

hold goes back to a Proto-Germanic source that meant "guard, watch," preserved in behold

seaweed attaches itself to the ocean floor by means of a **holdfast**

etymologically, a **hole** is a "hollow" place, from Old English hol, "hollow"

holiday, from holy day, first meant that

if something is "**holl**," it is "hollow, empty" or "deeply excavated"

holler is from French hola, "ho there!"

the strip of thick paper glued to the boards and back of a book in order to strengthen its spine is the **hollow**

hollyhock originally referred to the marsh mallow and it was from Middle English holy and the obsolete hock, "mallow"

holocaust, from Greek, literally means "burnt whole, slaughtered by fire" and was originally used of a burnt offering as a religious sacrifice; when in the 1940s, rumors of the mass murder of Jews leaked—the act had no precedent and thus no established vocabulary name, so the biblical term **holocaust** was recalled and redeployed

holster was probably borrowed from Dutch

a **holt** is an animal's lair, especially an otter's

holy started as a derivative of the adjective that produced "whole," so its etymological meaning is probably "inviolate, unimpaired"

homage (pronounced AH-mij) is worshipful reverence or veneration

the adjective form of lobster is **homarine**

Old English ham meant "place where one lives, house; village" and the last of these survives in place-names like Birmingham; the meaning "house, abode" evolved into the current use of **home**

home first meant "a collection of dwellings," "a town or village" and **homely** meant "of or belonging to a **home** or household"—as well as "friendly, intimate"

a **homeboy**, **homegirl**, **homie**, or **homey** is someone who likes to stay home or a friend from your neighborhood or a fellow member of a gang

homeopathy is a method in which a patient is given minute amounts of drugs that would produce symptoms in a healthy person similar to those of the disease being treated

a **homeotherm** is an animal maintaining a steady body temperature

the killing of one human being by another is a **homicide**—but it is not necessarily a crime in itself; **murder** and manslaughter are crimes, though

the general term for the killing of a person by another is **homicide**; **murder** is either the intentional killing or malicious killing of another while **manslaughter** is the unintentional, accidental killing of another through carelessness

a **homily** is a discourse offered to a crowd, as it derives from Greek homilos, "crowd" and Latin homilia, "discourse, sermon"

homing as in **homing** pigeon means "that goes home"

hominy is the inner part of corn that has been soaked to remove the hull, from Algonquian uskatahomen

if people have the same opinion, they are **homodox** or **homodoxian**

homogeneous means "of the same kind or nature, of a uniform structure"; **homogenized** refers to the fact that elements of a substance or population have been blended or processed into a uniform consistency

homogenous can refer to genetically related tissue or organs

homographs are spelled alike, have different meanings, sometimes have different pronunciations (lead); **homophones** are pronounced alike but have different spellings and meanings (rite, right, write), and **homonyms** are spelled and pronounced alike but have different meanings (bowl)

when several adjacent words have the same ending (like -ly), that's called **homoioteleuton**

a **homonym** is one of two or more words spelled and pronounced alike but different in meaning, i.e. the same name for different things, from homo-, "same" and onuma, "name"

homoousian means "consubstantial with others," as Jesus the Son of God is consubstantial (regarded as the same in substance or essence) with God the Father

{ **homosexual** contains Greek homos, "same" (not Latin homo, "human being") }

honcho is a direct borrowing of Japanese han, "squad" and cho, "leader"

the **honda** is the eye at the end of a lasso or lariat through which the rope passes to form a loop

hone was first a whetstone for sharpening tools, then became the action of sharpening

hone means to sharpen while **home** (in) means to seek out a target; you can **hone** a skill but you **home** in on something

honest comes from Latin *honor/honos*, "honor"

honey seems to come from Proto-Germanic *khunagom* or *khunanggom*, which may originally have described the color of **honey** (from Greek *knekos*, "pale yellow")

honeyflow is the period of secretion of honey or nectar by flowers

to **honeyfugle** or **honeyfuggle** is to dupe, deceive, or swindle

a **hoodoo** is an oddly or fantastically shaped rock column

a person who practices voodoo is a **hoodoo**, and the word also describes a person or thing whose presence is supposed to bring bad luck

hoodwinked's first sense was literally "blindfolded"

hoof has the plurals hoofs and hooves

hook goes back to Proto-Indo-European *keg-/keng*, "bent object"

etymologically, **hooker** may simply be "one who hooks" as such a person snares clients—but there are other stories, like **hooker** comes from an area of New York called "the Hook" where these ladies could be found

honky-tonk may come from a New England dialect word honk "to idle about" and is a rhyming duplication

honeymoon implied that everything was sweet after the wedding but, like a full moon, wanes with time; it later came to mean the first month after the wedding

honeysuckle was named erroneously in ancient times when people thought that bees extracted honey from the plant

Honolulu is "sheltered bay" in Hawaiian

the **honor** at a golf tee is the player who tees off first

the fee paid for a service done out of kindness is an **honorarium**

hooch comes from the Hoochinoo Indians, who made really strong liquor

ultimately, **hood** and hat are the same word, both meaning "head-covering" etymologically

hoodlum started as the name of a gang leader, Muldoon, and a reporter reversed it to Noodlum—but the typesetter could not read the reporter's handwriting and put it in the paper as "**Hoodlum**"

hookum-snivey is a deceit or fakery

hooligan probably comes from the Irish criminal Patrick **Hooligan** (Houlihan) of the 1890s

a circular wooden frame in which a cheese is molded is a **hoop**

hopefully is really supposed to be used for "in a hopeful manner"

Hopi is from *hopituh*, "peaceful ones"

a **hopper** is a funnel-shaped container in which the contents pass by via gravity into a receptacle below

in **hopscotch**, one must "hop" over the lines scratched in the ground—scotch meaning "scratched" or "to score"; it was once called hop-score

something that happens hourly is **horal**

horbgorbling is puttering around aimlessly

horde comes from Turkish *ordu*, "(royal) camp"

a **hordeolum** or **sty** is an inflamed and swollen sebaceous gland on the edge of the eyelid

horehound candy is made from the juice of the herb **horehound** (Marrubium vulgare), a juice also used as a cough remedy

in Greek, **horizon** meant "limiting circle"

in soil layers, the A **horizon** is characterized by weathering the the greatest proportion of organic matter, the middle layer or B **horizon** is not exposed to weathering but consists of humus and other organic materials leached into it through the A **horizon** by water, and the bottom layer or C **horizon** is partially decomposed rock and some elements leached through from the B **horizon**; below all three is bedrock

hormone comes from Greek *hormon*, "set in motion"—from *horme*, "impulse, onset"

horn comes from a very large Indo-European word family that has made a huge number of contributions to English, from Indo-European *ker-*, "animal's **horn**," "top," and "head"

a **hornbook** was a leaf of paper containing the alphabet (often with the addition of the ten digits, some elements of spelling, and the Lord's Prayer) protected by a thin plate of translucent horn, and mounted on a tablet of wood with a projecting piece for a handle

horoscope comes from Greek *hora*, "hour, time" and *skopos*, "observer"

evolving at the standard rate is **horotelic**, faster is **tachytelic**, and slower than standard is **bradytelic**

horrent hair is standing on end

horrible, **horror**, and **horrid** are from Latin horrere "stand on end" (hair) or "tremble, shudder" and the original sense of **horrid** was "bristly, shaggy, rough"

in decreasing degree of horror: **horrific**, **horrendous**, **horrible**, **horrid**

horripilating is getting goosebumps from the cold

if a tide or current **horses**, it carries or sweeps along

the Indo-European term for **horse** was *ekwos*, which produced Latin *equus* and Greek *hippos*—but our word "**horse**" descended from Proto-Germanic *khorsam/khorsaz*

horseplay originally was a play in which a horse was used or took part—or theatrical horsemanship

horsepower is so called from the supposed rate of work generated by a horse

horse in **horseradish** is an adjective meaning "pertaining to a large, strong, or coarse kind" of radish

a block of the Earth's crust that rises between two faults is a **horst**

{ **horticulture** comes from the Latin word *hortus* meaning "garden" }

hosanna is from Hebrew *hōšī'ā-nnā*, "save us we pray" ('save, we pray')

old plurals of **hose** were hosen and hoses

the **hosel** or **hose** is the socket of a golf club head into which the shaft is fitted

in the Middle Ages, **hospices** run by monks and nuns gave shelter and food to travelers and the poor (from Latin *hospitium*, "hospitality")

hospital first was a house for the reception and entertainment of travelers or pilgrims—based on Latin *hospitalis* (**hostel** is also from this)

hospitaler is a synonym for **hosteler**, the person in a hospice or hostel whose job is to receive and tend to visitors, pilgrims, and strangers to **hospitize** is to extend hospitality to

host, one who entertains guests, is from Latin hospes "a guest"

one early sense of **host** was "army"

hostage first referred to the state of someone handed over as a pledge or security (for the fulfillment of an undertaking)

hostel was the old word for hotel

hotbed originally was a bed of earth heated by fermenting manure and used for growing plants

hotchpotch / hodgepodge is an alteration of the earlier hotchpot, borrowed from Old French *hocher*, "shake" and *pot*, "pot" ("shake the pot")

hotdesking is the practice of allocating or using desks or workstations on an ad-hoc basis rather than assigning them permanently to particular individuals

hotel and **hospital** both go back to Latin hospitale "place where guests are received" or "**hospice**" but which developed into two different words in Old French

a **hotshot** was originally a reckless shooter of a firearm

a glass container, with black ridged neck and top, for keeping one cup of coffee hot is a **hottle**

the space behind the knee is the **hough**

before the word dog entered English, sometime before 1050, this animal was generally called *hund*, which became **hound**

Greek *hora* was vague, meaning "period of time, season" but came to be applied more specifically to **hour** "one twelfth of a day (from sunrise to sunset"; not until the Middle Ages did the term become fixed to a period of 60 minutes, or an **hour**

each square of a chessboard is a **house**

the audience at a theatre is called the **house**

{ to **hove** is to take shelter and a **hovel** is a sheltering place }

a **house** is the building or structure in which one lives; **home** is the place one lives with the pleasant connotations or family ties included

a sector on an astrological chart is a **house** or **sign**

a **housepainter** can be called a protective coating engineer

HOV stands for high-occupancy vehicle

a conical building enclosing a kiln is a **hovel**

the bump on the top of a whale's head is the **hovel**

hover comes from hove "raise, lift, rise" or "linger, wait"

how belongs to the large family of question-words which in Indo-European began with *qw-*

howdy is a shortened form of "How do you do?"

howitzer traces to the earlier howitz, to Czech *houfrice*, "catapult"

howl may derive from the word "owl"

hoyden can be applied to rude, ignorant people

huarache, a leather thong sandal, is a Mexican Spanish word

hub first meant "a shelf at the side of a fireplace used for heating pans"

hubbub may come from Irish or Gaelic battle cries *ub! ub! ubub!*—expressions of aversion or contempt

if a road is **hubby**, it is full of bumps

hubris is Greek, literally "insolence"

huckleberry is a synonym for blueberry

huckster is related to hawker "peddler" and probably borrowed from Middle Dutch *hokester*, "tradesman"

huddle originally meant "hide" or "hush up"

hue first meant "appearance, aspect," "form, shape"

hue and **cry** is somewhat redundant as **hue** means "shout, make an outcry"; **hue** and **cry** was a medieval law requiring that all citizens within earshot give chase to a fleeing criminal

hue is the quality of a color that makes it possible to call it bluish green, etc. (the color of a color), **shade** is a color variation having to do with the value of a **hue** (lightness or darkness), and **tint** is a pale variation of a color

PT Barnum popularized the word **humbug**

humbug and **hornswoggle** originally both meant "cheat, trick" (as verbs)

humdudgeon is imaginary pain or illness

to **humect** is to moisten or make wet and it comes from Latin *humere*, "be moist," as does **humid** and **humidity**

humectant means "retaining or preserving moisture"

to lie prone or prostrate is to **humicubate**

a **humidor** (from "humid") keeps cigars and tobacco moist and the word is patterned after *cuspidor* (spittoon)

---

hundredweight originally meant a weight of one hundred pounds, or C in Roman numerals, so the abbreviation is **cwt**.

---

hug is probably of Scandinavian origin—tracing to words meaning "comfort, console" and "affection"

hugger-mugger is concealment and secrecy or a person who keeps things secret or hidden

hulk comes from a Greek word meaning "ship that is towed"; **hulk** first designated a fast ship, then a cargo ship

an abandoned ship is a **hull**

human, from Latin *humanus*, is probably related to *homo*, "man," and was first just an adjective

humane was an earlier form of the word human

humanity's initial sense was much closer to the specialized "humane" than to the general "human"

humble derives from Latin *humus*, "earth, ground" and when used to describe a plant it means low-growing or low-lying

humiliate is from Latin *humilis*, "humble"

hummacky means "having an uneven surface"

Hummers were High-Mobility Multipurpose Wheeled Vehicles, called Hummvees, then Hummers

a **hummock** is a conical or dome-shaped protuberance of earth or rock, a low hillock or knoll

hummus (thick spread of mashed chickpeas, etc.) is from Arabic "chickpea"

humongous only dates back to around 1970 and started as college slang, probably a combination of huge and monstrous or stupendous or tremendous

humor first referred to the body fluid of an animal or plant

hump first appeared in English at the end of the seventeenth century in the compound **hump**-backed and was used on its own by the eighteenth century

humus (vegetable mold or decayed organic matter) is Latin for "ground, soil"

hunch once meant a lump or large slice

the main Old English word for **"hundred"** was hund; **hundred** should be pronounced HUHN-druhd

hunker can mean squat or crouch down low, or bend the top of one's body forward

hunkerousness is opposition to progress

if you have a short neck, you are **hunksit**

the **hunt** is the first or treble bell in a set of bells

hurdle refers to a difficulty or obstacle; **hurtle** means to move with great speed or violence

to **hurkle** or **hurple** is to draw one's limbs in and scrunch up the shoulders in reaction to the cold or in a storm

hurly-burly is turmoil or an uproar

hurrah, **hurray**, and **hooray** are alterations of huzza, a sailors" cheer

hurricane is from Carib huracan/furacan, "big wind," but it also may be from Taino hurakan, "god of the storm"

a **hurricane** is a severe tropical storm that starts east of the International Date Line (Atlantic Ocean, Caribbean Sea, Gulf of Mexico) anda **typhoon** is a severe tropical storm that starts west of this line (Pacific Ocean, China Sea)

hurry was first a commotion or disturbance

a **hurrygraph** is a hastily written letter

English borrowed **hurt** from Old French hurter "knock" and then came the metaphorical "harm, wound"

husband comes from the German words hus and bunda, meaning "house owner" and originally had nothing to do with marital status; in Old English, **husband** was literally "housebound"—bound to the house and family

husk is a shortening of Dutch huisken, "little house"

pea pods and nutshells are technically **husks**

husky, the dog, is a variation of the word hoskey, "Eskimo"

husky "hoarse" is from the obsolete verb husk "have a dry cough"; **husky** "big and burly" is from husk, the dry outer covering of a seed

the word **hussy** is just a corruption of "housewife" and originally had no unkind implications and for many years was not applied to a married woman

hustings' early meaning of "platform" led to its sense "any place from which campaign speeches are made" and "political campaigning"

hustle, from Dutch husselen, originally meant "to push or knock a person about roughly"

etymologically, **hut** is probably a "covering structure"

hyacinth is related to the Greek myth of Hyacinthus, a handsome youth loved by Apollo but accidentally killed by him—from whose blood Apollo caused a flower to grow

hybrids are words composed of morphemes from different languages—Greek tele- and Latin phone, Latin bi- and Greek cycle

{ **Hyde** is the bad side to a person's character or the unsuspected, hidden evil side }

hydrangea's seed capsule looks like a water cup so it was named from Greek hydr-,"water" and angos, "seed; capsule"

hydraulic comes from Greek hydor, "water" and aulos, "pipe"

Greek hydro, "water" contributed **hydrogen**, literally "generating water" coined in the late 1780s for **hydrogen's** property of forming water when oxidized

hydroponics comes from combining *hydro-* with *ponos*, "labor" and is patterned on geoponics; **hydroponics** is also known as aquaculture or tank farming

a **hydropot** is a water drinker and a **galactophagist** is a milk drinker

fanaticism about health is **hygeiolatry**

Hygeia, the goddess of health, gives us the word **hygiene**

hygienic is often misspelled hygenic

hygroscopic means the ability or tendency of a material to take up moisture readily

hymeneal means "of or relating to marriage"

hymn is from Greek *hymnos*, "song in praise of a god or hero"

hype had an early meaning of "cheating, deception, swindle"

hype is a slang abbreviation of hypodermic—implying the effect of injecting a drug

hyper- means "over" or "more"; **hypo-** means "under" or "less"

hyperbole (extravagant exaggeration) is Greek for "overcasting"

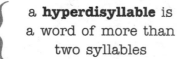

{ a **hyperdisyllable** is a word of more than two syllables }

high blood sugar is **hyperglycemia** and low blood sugar is **hypoglycemia**

gesturing or waving the hands a lot while talking is **hypermimia**

hypernym, a word that is more generic than a given word, is literally "the word above" and **hyponym** is literally "the word below," a word that is more specific than a given word

if you have a keen sense of smell, you are **hyperosmic**

hypertension is high blood pressure

hyphen is from Greek *hyph'hen*, "together"

teaching during sleep is **hypnopedia**

if you are in the fuzzy state between sleep and wakefulness, you are **hypnopompic**—while half-asleep is **semisomnous**; **hypnopompic** also means "causing to wake up"

hypnosis is based on a Greek word for sleep

hypnotism was originally called **neuro-hypnotism**

hypnotize should be pronounced HIP-nuh-tize

difficulty in making decisions is **hypobulia**

hypochondria first referred to the upper abdomen and the organs under the ribs (liver, gall bladder, spleen)—thought to be the source of melancholy

hypocorism is the creation or use of pet names, like Bob for Robert

Hypokrites was an ancient Greek actor who pretended to be another person, giving up **hypocrite**

hypogenous is "growing on the underside of something"—such as under a diner table

the **hypolimnion** is the lower layer of water in a lake that is stagnant and remains a constant temperature

hypomnematic is "having the form of memoranda or notes"

hyponoia is hidden meaning or significance

a vague feeling of sadness, seemingly without cause is **hypophrenia** and a vague feeling of mental discomfort is **malnoia**

hyposomnia is another way of saying lack of sleep

the **hypotenuse** is etymologically a line that is "stretched under" the right angle of a triangle (Greek *hypo-*, "under" and *teinein*, "stretch")

hypothesis is from Greek *hypo-*, "under" and *thesis*, "placing, proposition" which became **hypothesis** "foundation" as it is a basis for argument or reasoning

profound melancholy can be called **hypothimia**

hypotyposis is vivid description of a scene, event, or situation, bringing it, as it were, before the eyes of the hearer or reader

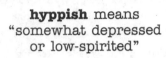

{ **hyppish** means "somewhat depressed or low-spirited" }

hysteria and hysteric(s) come from Greek hystera "womb/uterus" as the affliction was thought to be specific to women and originating in that area

the adjective form of porcupine is **hystricine**

{ I is from an Indo-European root shared by Latin and Greek "ego" }

an **iamb** or **iambus** is a metrical foot consisting of a short syllable followed by a long one, like "away" or "deduced"

iatrapistia is a lack of faith in doctors or medicine and **iatromisia** is a dislike of doctors

a word to describe making anything worse in an effort to make it better is **iatrogenic**, such as a disease caused by doctors or by a prescribed treatment

ibid is a contraction of the Latin adverb *ibidem* and literally means "in the same place," used to avoid repeating a reference in a piece of writing

the suffix **-ic** forms adjectives from other parts of speech while **-ical** forms adjectives from nouns and originally provided synonyms for adjectives ending in **-ic**

to **icchen** is to move or stir

to the Inuit, there are over 100 words for **ice**

Ice has cognates in Germanic languages and is ultimately from Proto-Germanic. Beowulf used an Old English form of it around 723. **Freeze** has a similar background and its sense of "chill" or "be chilled" was first used in a phrase meaning, "It is so cold that water turns to **ice**."

iceberg is from Dutch ijsberg "ice" and "hill"; an **iceberg** (figuratively) is something of which the greater part is unkown or unrecognized

ichabod is an exclamation of lament for the good old days

ichneumon (parasitic wasp or a mongoose) comes from a Greek word which meant literally "tracker," a derivative of *ikhnos*, "footstep, track"

an **ichnite** is a fossil footprint

ichnography is a floor plan for a building

the **ichthus** is the fish image used as a Christian symbol

the fish world is **ichthyarchy**

icicle goes back to Old English, when it was *gicel* and meant "a point of ice"

iconoclast is literally "image breaker"

an **icon** was originally a "simile" in rhetoric and the etymological idea of **icon** is of "similarity," from Greek *eikon*, "likeness, similarity"

iconodule is a worshipper of images (the opposite of iconoclast)

some words for yellowish are **icterical**, **luteolous**, **flavescate**

the beat of the pulse is called **ictus** (Latin "stroke")

ID is preferred over I.D. as the abbreviation for identification

id, from Freudian theory, simply means "it" in Latin

Idaho is Shoshone for "light on mountains"

idea was, at first, a term in philosophy adopted from Platonic thought—"an eternally existing pattern from which individual things derive their existence but are only imperfect copies"

idealism is contrasted with materialism

to **ideate** is to invent through thinking

idem is the Latin word for ditto

identity's root is Latin idem, "same"; the OED shows the first uses of the concept of **identity** with respect to the individual to occur only in the seventeenth century

when a word or phrase is depicted with a picture/figure or character without expressing the name of it, that is an **ideograph** (like the pictures in a book depicting words!)

the modern meaning of **ideology** was popularized by Napoleon Bonaparte after having been invented by a group of French philosophers in the *late eighteenth-early nineteenth* centuries

ides (literally, middle day of a Roman month) refers to the 15th day of March, May, July, or October as well as the 13th day of the other months in the ancient Roman calendar

{ another name for a trademark is an **idiograph** }

an **idiolect** is the combination of linguistic quirks and conventions that distinguish one group of language users from another; also, an individual's distinctive speech habits make up their **idiolect**

an artist's personal style is their **idiom** (from Greek idioma, "peculiar" from idiousthai, "makes one's own" and idios, "own, private")

an **idiopathy** is a disease of unknown origin or one having no apparent cause

a person who puts ideas into practice is an **idiopraxist**

idiosyncrasy comes from a Greek word that, when broken down, means idios, "own," sun, "with," krasis, "mixture"

an **idiot** once meant a layman as contrasted with a clergyman, and since few people outside the church were educated, it came to mean an uneducated or ignorant person

an **idioticon** is a dictionary of words for one region—a dialect dictionary

idle first meant "empty, vacant, void"

Greek eidos meant "form, shape" and from it was derived eidolon, "appearance" and "phantom," which developed into "image," then became Latin idolum, "image of a false god" before eventually becoming English **idol**

an **idolum** is a mental image

idyll comes from Greek eidullion, "little picture" and evolved to "small descriptive poem"; **idyll** is pronounced EYE-duhl (like idle)

idyllic (pronounced eye-DIL-ik) means "full of pastoral or rustic charm"

the Old English version of **if** was gif; the word is connected with German iba, "condition" and Old Norse **if**, "doubt"

use **if** or **whether** for a **whether**-or-not choice and it sounds fine to drop the "or not"

igloo is from Inuit/Inupiaq iglu, "house" and can also be spelled iglu

idleness or sloth can be described as **ignavia** or **ignavy**

ignition first denoted the heating of a substance to the point of chemical change or combustion (from Latin *ignire*, "set on fire," *ignis*, "fire")

if something is **ignominious**, it is shameful, disgraceful, discreditable (from ignominy "deep personal humiliation"—from *ig-*, "ignorant" and *nomen*, "name, repute")

ignoramus (Latin) is literally "we do not know" or "we take no notice"—and is pronounced ig-nuh-RAY-mus

ignore is properly used of things that are present in our surroundings; but for things like rules, conventions, stipulations, contracts, the right word is **disregard**

ignore and **ignorant** are from Latin *i-*, "not" and *gno-*, "know"

an **ignotism** is a mistake due to ignorance

ile meant island in the Middle Ages—then the "s" was added

historically, **ilk** means "same, identical"

ill's original meaning is not "sick" but "bad," borrowed from Old Norse *illr*; the sense of "sick" arrives in the fifteenth century

illapse is a gradual advance

illaqueable is "capable of being snared"

illation is the act of inferring—a deduction or conclusion

a word or phrase introducing or stating an influence—so, therefore—is called an **illative**

illatration is barking at someone or something

illecebrous is "attractive, alluring"

illegible refers to bad handwriting, while **unreadable** refers to poor writing

literally, **illegitimate** is "not lawful" and **illicit** is "not allowed"

illeism is the practice of referring to oneself in the third person

a form of conduct will be **illicit** and a type of practice will be **illegal**

Illinois is Algonquian *illiniwek* meaning "men, warriors" and should be pronounced il-uh-NOY

illth is the opposite of wealth

illude means "to trick or delude" or "ridicule or mock"

etymologically, **illuminate** is a parallel construction to enlighten, from Latin *in-* and *lumen*, "light"

illusion is based on a Latin word meaning "jest, mock, play"

an **illusion** is an image or conception of something actual or real that presents itself to the mind in an abnormal or distorted manner; a **delusion** is a false belief about oneself or other people that persists despite its being at variance with the facts

illustrate's meaning of "to light up, clear up" was generalized to "make clear by pictures, examples, etc., demonstrate visually or by reasoning"

IM (instant-messaging) as a verb has the inflections **IM**'s, **IM**'d, **IM**'ing

to **image** can mean "to describe graphically or vividly"; the original sense of the noun in the OED is "imitation in solid form, as a statue or effigy"

imagine comes from Latin *imaginare*, "form an image of; represent" and *imaginari*, "picture to oneself"

{ an **imaginator** originates, devises, and expresses something }

an **imagineer** is a person who devises a highly imaginative concept or technology

imago is the final, fully developed adult insect stage

imbecile, from Latin *imbecillus*, "without stick, staff" was someone without a crutch to lean on, and first meant "physically weak"

imberb and **imberbic** mean "beardless"

imbibe once had the meaning "to admit into the mind"; the corresponding noun for **imbibe** is **imbibition**

imbirferous means "raining, bringing rain"; **impluvious** is "wet with rain"

imbosk means to hide or conceal

the foam in "foaming at the mouth" is **imbost**; as a verb, it means to drive someone to madness

the overlapping of roof shingles or fish scales is **imbrication**

{ **imbroglio** originally meant "a confused heap" }

a person is imbued with values—values cannot be imbued onto someone; "saturate" was the early sense of **imbue**

imitate (and **image**) are based on Latin *imago*

immaculate comes from Latin words meaning "not stained"

immature comes from Latin words meaning "not ripe"

immediate is from Latin meaning "not intervening" and the first sense was "nearest in space or order"

immense comes from Latin meaning "not measurable"

in astronomy, **immersed** is a synonym for eclipsed

immersion comes from Latin words meaning "dip into"

immigrate means come to settle in a different country as a permanent resident

imminent is "about to happen" and **immanent** is "inherent" or "pervading the material world"

to **immit** is to "insert" or "introduce"

immolate means "to sacrifice to the gods" (not "to burn")

someone who is unyielding or inflexible is **immorigerous**

immote is a great word meaning "unmoved"

immune is from Latin *immunis*, "not ready for service" and first meant "free from a liability" or "exempt from public service"

to **immure** is to surround with or enclose within walls, confine or seclude

in Old English *impa* was a young shoot or sapling—from a Greek word meaning "to make grow; engraft"—and this eventually became **imp** "mischievous child"

impair is from Latin (*pejor*) meaning "make worse"

impale first meant "enclose with pales or stakes; surround with a palisade"

impanate means "contained or embodied in bread"

to **impark** is to enclose animals in a park

when one partner is more interested in sex than the other, their relationship is **imparlibidinous**

impart first meant "give a share of"

impartable means capable of being made known; **impartible** means indivisible

impasse is from French, originally "a road or way open only at one end"

impassible is incapable of feeling or suffering; **impassable** is not capable of being passed

impatient is from Latin (*pati*, "to suffer") meaning "not able to bear or suffer"

hinder or prevent was an early sense of **impeach**

the mere bringing of charges against a public official for crimes committed in office is **impeachment**—so **impeachment** does not imply definite conviction or removal from office

{ **impeccable** comes from Latin elements meaning "not liable to sin" }

impede is from Latin *impedire*, "shackle the feet of"

if someone gets in your way, they are **impeditive** (causing obstruction)

the base of **impel** is Latin *pellere*, "drive"

impel means to urge or encourage while **compel** means to take action as a result of pressure or coercion; **impel** is very similar in meaning to **compel** but suggests even more strongly an inner drive to do something and often a greater urgency in the desire to act

the literal sense of **impend** is "to hang towards or upon"

if one is **impenitible**, they are incapable of repentance or remorse

imperative in grammar expresses a command

imperial pertains to the qualities of power and royalty; **imperious** implies that someone is overbearing or domineering

imperium is supreme authority

impertinent first meant "not belonging (to); unrelated, unconnected" and eventually it came to mean "behaving without proper respect; presumptuous, intrusive"

etymologically, **impetuous** means "having impetus," from Latin *impetere*, "attack"—ultimately, "rushing towards something with great violence or aggression"

impetus meant "assault, force" in Latin and it can be something positive and pleasant or negative and unpleasant, but in either case it stimulates action

to **impignorate** or **pignorate** means to put up as security or to pawn

to **impinge** is to come into contact or encroach or have an impact; to **infringe** is to encroach on a right or privilege or to violate

to **impinguate** is to fatten

implacable means "irreconcilable" and "unable to be appeased"

the Latin base of **implement**, implere, means "fill, fulfill"

impletion is "filling up, making full" or the condition of being filled

implicate first meant "entangle, intertwine" and is based on Latin *plicare*, "to fold" and a person implicated for a crime is "wrapped up" in it somehow; **implication** is the noun corresponding to both **implicate** and imply

implicit has a root meaning of "wrapped up in" or "contained in"

implode, to collapse violently inward, is patterned on explode

implore comes from Latin *implorare*, "invoke with tears"

a speaker or writer implies, a hearer or reader infers, and implications are incorporated in statements while inferences are deduced from statements; **imply** means "suggest indirectly that something is true" while **infer** means "conclude or deduce something is true" and, further, to **imply** is to suggest or throw out a suggestion while to **infer** is to include or take in a suggestion

imponderabilia are matters or things beyond comprehension

import first meant "carry, cause, convey"

a product from abroad is an **import**; the process is **importation**

important and **import** come from Latin *importare* (in- and *portare*, "carry"); **important**'s original literal sense was "bring in"

the root of **importunate** is Latin *importunus*, "unfit, unsuitable," from Portunus, the protecting god of harbors

to **importune** is to trouble others with constant demands, to beg or beseech

an **impostor** is etymologically someone who "imposes" on others, from Latin *imponere*, "put on" or "inflict"—and note that it has two o's

impotence is the male's inability to copulate or get an erection; **sterility** is the inability of either a male or female to procreate

impractical means "not advisable to put into practice" while **impracticable** means "not capable of being put into practice"; **impractical** or **unpractical** is something that can be done but isn't worth doing while **impracticable** means it can't be done at all

impromptu conveys unrehearsed remarks or performance with an element of surprise, while **extempore** only suggests that this is done without notes or props

improve first meant "to make a profit for oneself" or "to employ to advantage; to make profitable use of"

the early spelling of **improvement** was emprowement, meaning "profit, profitable use or management"

etymologically, if you **improvise** something, it is because it has not been "provided" for in advance, from Latin *improvisus*, "unforeseen"

impuberty is the state of not yet having reached puberty

impudent is based on Latin *im-*, "not" and *pudere*, "feel ashamed"

impudicity is shamelessness or lack of modesty

to **imprecate** first meant "to pray for" (Latin *precari*, "to pray") but now means to wish harm upon or invoke evil upon

impregnable means "incapable of being taken by force" (from French *prendre*, "seize")

to saturate wood with preservative is to **impregnate** it

impresario comes from the Italian word *impresa*, "undertaking"

impress stresses the depth and persistence of the effect

an **imprest** is a monetary advance, from the obsolete verb **imprest** "to lend"

to **imprint** is to cause a young animal to accept its parent as the proper object of affection; the learning process of young animals is called **imprinting**

impromptu is based on Latin *in promptu*, "in readiness" from *promptus*, "prepared, ready"

to **impugn** is to dispute the truth, validity, or honesty of; to **oppugn** is to dispute the truth or validity of, to strive against

impunitive means "resigned to frustration"

impunity is protection from punishment, just as **immunity** is protection from disease

to **impute** means "to ascribe, to regard as resulting from"; to **impute** something to someone or something usually means observing something invisible in that person or thing

in is a widespread preposition (**in** various spellings) among Indo-European languages; however, the adverb **in** is a conflation of Old English inn and inne

an archaeological artifact found **in situ** is found "in place"—in its normal or natural or original position or place

in the pink comes from the English foxhunting tradition; people who foxhunt often wear scarlet jackets and are called pinks—so if you are **in the pink** you would be about to set off to gallop your horse across country

in the wings and **wing it** are expressions from the theatre

inalienable and **unalienable** are interchangeable for "unable to be taken away from or given away by the possessor"

{ **inamorata** comes from Italian *innamorare*, "to inflame with love" }

inane, from Latin *inanis*, first meant "empty"

words meaning "babbling, full of idle talk" include **inaniloquent** and **inaniloquous**

inanity is intellectual or spiritual emptiness; **inanition** is the lack of nourishment

inapposite means "out of place" or "not to the point"

inapt is "not suitable or appropriate" while **unapt** is "not likely or inclined"

inartistic refers to people who lack artistic taste or appreciation; **unartistic** refers to things as not relating or conforming to art

inaugurate is from Latin *inauguruat*, "interpreted as omens (from the flight of birds)"—from *augurare* "to auger"

the presidential induction ceremony is the **inauguration**; the speech made is the **inaugural** address or **inaugural**

Inca is a Quechua word meaning "king, lord, ruler"

incalescent means "growing warm"

incandescent means having a filament which glows white-hot when heated by a current passed through it; **fluorescent** means based on fluorescence from a substance illuminated by ultraviolet light

incapable is synonymous with unable

incapacitation is the action of making incapable; **incapacity** is a lack of ability or qualification

carcer is "prison" in Latin—giving us **incarcerate**

incarnadine can mean "flesh-colored or pink" but also "crimson, blood-red"

incarnate means "embodied in flesh; in human form"

incense once meant to kindle any passion, good or bad

to **incent** is a back-formation from incentive, appearing around 1977

incentive is from Latin *incentivum*, "something that incites or sets the tone" from incantare "to chant or charm"

the temporal orientation of **incentive** is toward the future; that of **inducement** is toward the past

incest is based on *castus*, "chaste" (and *in-*, "not")

inch, the unit of length, was adopted in Old English (ynce) from Latin *uncia*, "twelfth part (of a foot, pound, etc.)," while **ounce** came into Middle English through Old French from the same Latin *uncia*, meaning, in Troy weight, a twelfth of a pound (though inn avoirdupois or ordinary measure, it is a sixteenth of a pound)

inch-meal means gradually or by inches or small degrees

inchoate (imperfectly formed or developed) is pronounced in-KOH-it

an **incident** is technically an accessory or subordinate event the primary meaning of **incident** is that of occurrence or event; the primary meaning of **incidence** is that of the rate or number of times at which something occurs

incidently (not incidentally) means "be incident or resultant from"

the base of **incinerate** is Latin *ciner-*, "ashes"

an **incipient** is a beginner

{ to **incise** is to cut into and an **incisive** mark "cuts into" the matter at hand }

the base of **incite** is Latin *citare*, "rouse, set into motion quickly"; **inciteful** means "tending to **incite**"

the base of **incline** is Latin *clinare*, "to bend"

the Latin words leading to **include** meant "into" (*in-*) and "to shut" (*claudere*)

incognito is Italian "unknown, disguised," from Latin *incognitus*, "unknown"

income originally meant "arrival, entrance"; a place of entrance can be called an **incoming**

incompetence is unacceptable levels of performance; **incompetency** is insanity or inability to stand trial or testify

an **inconnu** is a stranger

inconsequentia are trifling facts or trivia

incontinent (not having control over bodily functions) is partly based on Latin *continent*—"holding together"

incorporate can mean "provide with a body" or "blend or combine into something already existing to form one whole"

incrassate means "to thicken in consistency"

the Latin base of **increase** and **increment** is *crescere*, "grow"

incredible means "unbelievable" and **incredulous** means "unbelieving"

we can say that a virus has been **incriminated** as the cause of a type of cancer, and that television has been **incriminated** in the decline of study skills among young people

incrispated means "stiffly curled"

Latin *incubare*, the source of **incubate**, meant literally "lie down on"; **incubation** once had the sense of sleeping in a sacred place or temple for oracular purposes

incubus can mean "a feeling of oppression during sleep, as feeling a weight on the chest and stomach"

one **inculcates** an idea or habit into people by persistent instruction; one **indoctrinates** people with certain values or beliefs through repeated instruction

to **inculpate** is to accuse or incriminate, show evidence of someone's involvement in a crime—the opposite of exculpate

if something is **incumbent** upon us, then it is a burden that has been laid on us and cannot be ignored

incunabula from Latin *in-* and *cunabula*, "cradle" or "printing press," refers to the first stages of anything, especially books printed before 1500

incur and **incursion** are from Latin *in-* and *currere*, "run," with the root meaning "run into, come upon" or "run towards"; **incurrence** is the noun corresponding to the verb **incur**

the anvil of the ear can also be called the **incus**

an impression stamped on a coin is the **incuse** and the ridges on the coin's edge are **milling**

indagatrix is a female searcher or investigator

indecision describes a general state or condition, one that can characterize a body or group, whereas **indecisiveness** describes an individual character trait

if someone is **indecorous**, they are acting in bad taste or behaving badly

indefatigable means "incapable of being wearied"

if something cannot be erased, it is **indelible**; the opposite is **delible**

the base of **indemnity** and **indemnify** is Latin *damnum*, "damage, loss"

indent first meant "to give a zigzag outline to" based on Latin *dens/dent*, "tooth"

servants were termed **indentured** because their contract was indented or folded and torn in two, with the master and servant each keeping half

indeterminable means impossible to decide, fix, or measure while **indeterminate** means unclear or vague

index (from Latin) first meant "forefinger," "sign, pointer," or "informer"; the plural of **index** in the back of a book is **indexes** but for all other uses, especially math, the plural is **indices**

index-learning is superficial knowledge, such as that may be gained from the cursory perusal of a book or study of its index

indicate has its origins in Latin *dik-*, "point out" and *dicare*, "show, make known"

indices should be pronounced IN-duh-seez

the formative elements of **indignation**, **indignant**, and **indignity** are *in-*, "not" and *dignus*, "worthy"

indigo is from Greek *indikos*, "Indian (dye)"

indiscreet means not showing prudent or good judgment; **indiscrete** means not divided or divisible into separate parts

indite means "to write, compose"

individual comes from a Latin word *individuum* meaning "not divisible" and in early English usage, it implied the inseparability of bonded elements

indivisibility has only one vowel and it occurs six times

indocible means unteachable as a pupil

Indo-European is a term invented in 1814 by Egyptologist Thomas Young to describe the racial and linguistic origins of the main Indian and European peoples

indolent means "habitually lazy"

one's natural or innate character or disposition is **indoles**

indomitable first meant "unable to be tamed"—and the opposite is **domitable**

indoors was initially "within-doors"

{ **induce** can mean "derive by reasoning from facts"; the base of **induce** and **induction** is Latin *ducere*, "to lead" }

---

an **indicium** is an indication, sign, or token—specifically, the stamp on mail indicating paid postage

indict (to accuse or formally charge) was first spelled endite or indite

you can be **indifferent** to, not **indifferent** as to

indigenous is based on Latin *indigena*, "native"

indulge came from Latin *indulgere*, "allow long enough for"

an **indult** is a special privilege or license

something that is hardened can be called **indurate**; someone morally hardened or rendered callous is also **indurate**

industry comes from Latin *industria*, "quality of being hard-working; diligent"

"the **industry**" is the movie **business** and "the **business**" is the television **industry**

the base of **inebriate** is Latin *ebrius*, "drunk"

ineffable literally means "that cannot be spoken" (opposite is **effable**)

ineffectual refers to a general or habitual lack of success in the carrying out of one's projects; **ineffective** refers to a specific or definite failure to perform a task or accomplish a purpose

ineluctable means "inescapable; that cannot be struggled out of"

inequity is "injustice, unfairness"; **iniquity** refers to "immorality, sin, wickedness"

inermous means "without thorns or prickles"

inert is literally, "having no art or skill"

inevitable comes from Latin *e-*, "out" and *vitare*, "shun" which became *evitabilis*, "avoidable" and then *inevitabilis*

etymologically, **inexorable** means "that cannot be removed by praying"—from Latin *orare* "pray" with *ex-*, "out" to make *exorare* and then further prefixation and suffixation to get Latin *inexorabilis*

infamous means "of ill fame or repute"—but being **infamous** is not necessarily being well-known as it can mean "deserving of infamy" something too horrible to mention is **infandous**

in Latin, **infant** means "unable to speak"; when first used in English, **infant** could apply to a child of any age

infantry was originally applied to soldiers who were too young to serve in the cavalry

infatuate is based on Latin elements meaning "make foolish"

infaust is "unlucky" and **infausting** is "making unlucky"

Latin *inficere*, "put in" or "dip in" came to mean "stain, taint, spoil" and became English **infect**

an **infectant** is an agent of infection (opposite is disinfectant)

infelicific means "making unhappy"

the Latin elements of **infer** are *in-*, "into" and *ferre*, "bring"

infer means "to deduce, reason" and **imply** means "to hint at, suggest"

{ an inhabitant of the underworld can be called an **infernal** }

one draws, not makes, **inferences**

inferior is a use of the Latin comparative of *inferus* "low"

infidel originally referred to a person of a religion other than one's own (Latin *in-*, "not" and *fidelis*, "faithful")

infill is material used to fill a space or hole—but also the development of vacant areas between existing buildings, especially as part of a planned growth or urban renewal program

the "to" form of a verb, e.g. "to read," is the **infinitive**

infinity comes from a Latin word meaning literally "not finished"

remember **inflammable** has *in-* which means "into," meaning it will burst into flame, but *non-* in **nonflammable** means "not," meaning will not burst into flame

inflate comes from Latin *inflatus*, a form of *inflare* "blow into"

inflict takes "on," **afflict** takes "with"

influence implies a force that brings about a change and one of the first meanings was astrological—the supposed flowing or streaming from the stars or heavens of an etherial fluid acting upon the character and destiny of men and affecting things generally; it should be pronounced IN-floo-uhnts

influenza is Italian for "**influence**" because the disease was thought to be influenced by the stars (see **influence**)

variants of the classic **infomercial** are **documercial** and **storymercial**

inform was first spelled enforme and informe

the primary definition of **information** is traceable to the fifteenth century, a record or communication of an event, fact, or subject; **information** is characteristically positioned on an ascending scale, above data, but below knowledge and wisdom

infra dig (or **infradig**) is short for Latin *infra dignitatem*, "beneath one's dignity"

infrared refers to electromagnetic radiation beyond the red end of the visible spectrum

to **infrendiate** is to gnash the teeth

infriction is the action of rubbing in, as a lotion

infringe first meant "break down, destroy"

infundibuliform is a complicated way of saying "funnel-shaped"

to **infuse** is to steep in a liquid to extract the soluble ingredients

the **-ing** ending in modern place names means "the people of"; **-ton** means "enclosure" or "village"; **-ham** means "farm"

ingenious is "clever, brilliant"; **ingenuous** is "frank, candid" or "naïve"

ingenuous means "naïve, easily deceived, unsuspecting; foolish"—and **disingenuous** means "calculating, deceptive"

ingle is an old name for a fire or fireplace; the **inglenook** is the nook or corner beside the **ingle**—the chimney-corner

ingot was first the mold in which metal was cast

ingrain literally means "work into the grain" (originally, of fabric) and **ingrained** is metaphorical "deep-seated"

the base of **ingredient** is Latin *ingredi*, "enter, go in"—as it is something which "goes into" a mixture

the Latin base of **inherent** means "stick to"

Latin *heres/hered-em* "heir" brings us **inherit** and **inheritance**

inheritance is a process by which characteristics of word parts are transferred to a new whole, as the Mc (pertaining to "mass-produced" or "cookie-cutter") in McDonald's is used to form McNuggets, McJob, McMansion, McWord

inhuman means "lacking human qualities such as kindness" while **inhumane** means "being cruel or insensitive to others"

inimical rarely describes a person but is generally used to describe forces, concepts, or situations—for example, high inflation may be called **inimical** to economic growth

inimitable means "unique; incapable of being imitated"

the bulge at the rear of the human skull is the **inion** (from Greek meaning "nape of the neck")

iniquity (absence of moral or spiritual values; an unjust act) is a combination of in- "not" and aequus "equal, just" from Latin

{ Latin *inire*, "go in(to)" is the base of **initial**, **initiate**, **initiation** }

initialisms (sometimes called **alphabetisms**) are formed from the initial letters of a string of words and are pronounced as a sequence of letters, e.g. BYOB, CIA, DVD

injure and **injury** come from Latin in- "against" and *jus/jur*, "right," i.e., wrongful action or treatment; **injure** is a back-formation from **injury**

ink was first spelled inke and enke—from Greek *enkauston*, the purple **ink** used by Roman emperors

an **inkhornism** is a literary composition that is overworked and unnecessarily intellectual

to **inkle** is to communicate in an undertone or whisper, to give a hint of something, which gives us **inkling**

inmate was initially a person who shared a house or a lodger/tenant in someone's house

an **inn** is etymologically a place "in" which people live or stay, from Proto-Germanic *innam*

innards is a dialect pronunciation of inwards

{ the base *nasci*, "be born" is the base of **innate** }

the word **innate** means "inborn" and should apply to living things; **inherent** is "essential, intrinsic" and applies best to nonliving things like ideas

innervate means "to stimulate or give nervous energy," the opposite of **enervate**

inning comes from an Old English word (*innung*), meaning "a putting or getting in"

innocent is *in-*, "free from" and *nocere*, "hurt, injure" (Latin)

innocuous is "harmless, not hurtful," from Latin *in-*, "not" and *nocere*, "to hurt"

innominate is a synonym for anonymous

innuendo is Latin for "by nodding at, pointing to" or "intimating" from *in-*, "toward" and *nuere*, "nod"

inoculate derives from Latin *inoculare*, "to graft by budding" or "into the bud or eye; implant" and first meant "graft a bud or shoot into a plant of a different type"

an early meaning of **inordinate** was "not ordered, intemperate"

inquilines are animals that move into the dwelling (nest or hole) of or made by a creature of a different species

to **inquinate** is to corrupt

inquire, first spelled enquere, is from Latin *quaerere*, "to seek"

an **inquirendo** is an investigation or inquiry

inquisitorial is being offensively or impertinently inquiring

inquorate pertains to a meeting attended by fewer people than needed for a quorum

an **inro** is a nest of boxes

inroad first meant "hostile incursion into a country"

sanus "healthy" is part of **insane** and **insanity**

to dedicate or sign a book is to **inscribe** it

insect (from Latin *animal insectum*) literally meant "divided animal" or "cut up or into" from the segments of its body (head, thorax, abdomen)—the common word being "**bug**"; **insect** is any of an extremely large group of small invertebrate animals—and most undergo metamorphosis while **bug** denotes a special group of insects with beaklike sucking mouth parts and partly membranous forewings

one major difference between **insect**, **spider**, and **crustacean** is the antennae; one pair on most insects, none on spiders, and two pairs for crustaceans

inscrutable first meant "that cannot be found" and then took the meaning of "unfathomable, impenetrable" and "entirely mysterious"

inseminate is derived from Latin *seminare*, "to sow, to plant"

insensate means without sensitivity or humane feeling; **insentient** means incapable of either

the Latin elements *in-*, and *serere*, "to join, plant" are part of **insert** and **insertion**

an **insessor** is one who sits in or on/upon something

insidiate means either "to lie in wait" or "to ambush"

insidious (Latin *insidere*, "to lie in wait for," from *sedere*, "sit") describes stealthy, treacherous behavior; **invidious** behavior arouses ill will, animosity, or hostility

insight is literally, internal sight or mental vision

insignia is singular and **insigniae** is its plural

only a human being can **insinuate** anything

insipid means tasteless or having only a slight taste

insist "to dwell at length (on or in)" is from Latin *sistere* "stand"

to **insolate** is to put something in the sunlight; **insolation** is exposure to the sun's rays

the base of **insolent** is Latin *in-*, "not" and *solere*, "to be accustomed" and means "contemptuous of the feelings and rights of others"

insoluble can be applied to problems that cannot be solved as well as substances that will not dissolve in liquids

synonyms for **insomnia** include agrypnia, ahypnia, anypnia, cacosomnia, insomnolence, pernoctation, and zoara

inspire comes from Latin meaning "breathe or blow into," its literal original sense

install's earliest sense was "place in office by seating in a stall or official seat" (from Old French *estaler*, "to place," from *estal*, "place")

an artifact or artwork displayed at an exhibition or gallery is an **installation**

instancy means "urgency, pressing nature"

instant is from Latin *instans*, "present moment of time"

instauration is the action of restoring or repairing; restoration, renovation, renewal

instead is the lexicalized form of "in the stead of" ("in place of")

to **instigate** is to incite someone else to start something

the etymological idea of **instinct** is of "goading onwards with a pointed stick," from Latin *instinguere*, "urge onward, incite"

an **institute** is etymologically something "established" or "set up," from Latin *instituere*, "establish"

institution was first a noun of action or process which became a general and abstract noun describing something objective and systematic

instruct is formed with Latin *in-*, and *struere*, "build, pile up"—and **instrument** also came from this base

if something is in a state of disuse, that is **insuetude**

insular was first a noun meaning "an islander"

{ **insulate,** from Latin *insula*, first meant "turn into an island" }

insulin gets its name from the body part called islets of Langerhans, from which the hormone involved is produced

insulse means "tasteless, flat," from Latin *insulsus*, literally "unsalted"

insult first meant "to leap on the prostrate body of a foe" or "attack or attacking," especially a surprise military assault, and the word comes from the Latin base of *saltus*, "leap"

insult, in medicine and science, can mean "trauma, something that disturbs normal functions"

insuperable means impossible to overcome; **insupportable** means impossible to tolerate

insurance should be pronounced in-SHUUR-uhnts

insure and **ensure** mean "to make certain" but only **insure** can mean "indemnify against loss"

if the sea is **insurgent**, it is a rushing in or surging up; **insurrect** and **insurrection** come from this same base (Latin *insurgere*, "to rise up")

insusurration is whispering in the ear

the pronunciation of **intaglio** is in-TAL-yo

integer is literally "intact" in Latin, as it describes a whole number; as an adjective, it means "entire, lacking no part" (and **integral** and **integrate** are formed from this also, from *in-*, "not" and *tangere*, "touch")

data's consistency and freedom from corruption is its **integrity**

intellect and **intelligent** come from Latin intelligere "perceive" or "understand"

intellection is the exercise of the intellect or a specific act of the intellect

intelligent is from Latin *inter-*, and *legere*, "gather, pick up, read"

people are **intelligent**; statements are **intelligible**

intelligentsia is from Latin *intelligentia*, "perceptiveness, discernment" and is used for people who regard themselves as the intellectual elite

intelligible means "understandable through the intellect"

intemperance first meant severity or inclemency in the weather or climate

intend had an early meaning "to stretch out, extend, intensify"

emotions are **intense** while sustained application or attention is **intensive**; **intense** arises from within and **intensive** comes from outside (it is imposed or assumed)

intent implies a sustained unbroken commitment or purpose, while **intention** would imply an intermittent resolution or an initial aim or plan

inter comes from Latin *interrare*, "to put into the ground" (*in-*, "into" and *terra*, "earth")

when you have an expression which can be either a question or an exclamation, you could use an exclamation point and a question mark together, which is an **interabang**

quilting? no! **interbastation**

intercede is from Latin words *inter-*, "between" and *cedere*, "go"

intercept first meant "contain between limits" or "include between two points or lines"

an **interchange** station is a place where passengers can change from one transportation line to another

the clear space between two columns is **intercolumniation**

intercom is an abbreviation of intercommunication

{ **intercourse** first had to do with commerce and exchange }

intercrural means "between the legs"

the Latin verb *interesse*, "be between" was used metaphorically for "be of concern, be important, matter" and was borrowed into Anglo-Norman, becoming **interest**

interesting should be pronounced IN-truh-sting

interim is from a Latin word meaning "meanwhile"

interior is Latin, literally "inner"

interjacent means "in between" (not "next to")

there are eight classes of **interjections**: exclamatory and emotive responses, expletives and their euphemisms, volitive and imperative, utilitarian, commentarial, greetings and farewells, affirmations and negations, and connecting **interjections**

to **interlard** is to mix irrelevant matter with the solid part of a discourse

a person taking part in a conversation or discussion is an **interlocutor** or **collocutor**

interloper is based on Latin elements *inter-*, "among, between" and Dutch *loopen*, "run, leap"

interlucent means "shining between"

interment is burial; **internment** is detention

intermit means stop or suspend in time

internecine first meant "fought to the death" (from Latin *necare*, "kill"); a mistake by Samuel Johnson led to the change in meaning "relating to internal struggle" and "endeavoring mutual destruction"

Internet should be capitalized, but **intranet** should be lowercase; **Internet** was coined from inter(national) + (Arpa)net and first popped up in 1974 as a descendant of Arpanet, a U.S. government information network (the Advanced Research Projects Agency network) that was created in 1968 to keep up with Soviet advances in aerospace and nuclear science

interplanetary refers to the space within the solar system that lies outside the atmospheres of the planets or their moons; **interstellar** refers to the space between the stars and galaxies

the Latin ancestor of **interpolate**, *interpolare*, meant literally "polish up" and this progressed to "refurbish" and "alter appearance" to "falsify by inserting new material"

interpret once meant "translate"

an **interpreter** converts speech to another language and a **translator** converts writing to another language

etymologically, **interrupt** means "break between," from Latin *interrumpere*, "break in"

if something is suddenly emerging in the midst of something, it is **intersilient**

an **interstate** is a highway that is part of the federal network of major roads but, despite the name, some interstates do not cross state lines

intertrigo is inflammation caused by the rubbing of one area of skin on another

to **interturb** is to disturb by interruption; an **interturber** is a person who does this

interval is from Latin *intervalla*, "between walls or palisades"

an **interval** is a gap in time or space, whereas an **interlude** (literally "between games") generally functions to fill such a gap, thus occupy an **interval**

{ **intervital** describes being between two lives or stages of existence }

intestate is from Latin *in-*, "not" and *testatus*, "testified" and the word refers to having made no legally valid will before death

intestine as an adjective can mean "domestic, taking place within a nation"

into is for entering something, for changing the form of something, or for making contact; otherwise use "**in to**" (if you can drop the "in" without losing the meaning, you want "**in to**")

if you twist or curl something around a fixed point, you **intort** it; **intorted** means "bent abruptly"

Latin *intoxicare* meant "to poison" as Greek soldiers dipped their arrows in *toxicum*, "poison"—later giving us **intoxicate**

intractable means stubborn or obstinate; **intransigent** is this, but implies being more intense and refusing to compromise or change

intramural literally is "inside the walls"

a Spanish political party of the eighteenth century was known as los intransigentes, from transigir "compromise" (from Latin *transigere*, "drive through") and this came through French to become English **intransigent** "uncompromising"

intravenous should be pronounced in-truh-VEE-nuhs

intrepid is based on Latin *trepidus*, "alarmed"

intricate is from Latin *in-*, "into" and *tricae*, "tricks, perplexities"

an **intrigant** is a person who plots something illicit or harmful

intrigue is from Latin *intricare*, "to entangle, entrap"

Latin *intrinsecus*, "on the inside" came to be the English **intrinsic** "inner, internal" and "inherent"

introduce means literally "lead inside" from Latin *introducere*, "lead in"

inveigh originally meant "carry in, introduce," from Latin *vehere*, "carry"

French *aveugler* "blind" may have come from Latin *ab oculus*, "without eyes," which passed into Anglo-Norman and then became English **inveigle**, "deceive, blind one's judgment"

invent first meant "discover, find out"

invest originally meant "to clothe or envelop in a garment" (*in-* + *vestire*, "to clothe"), which got the figurative meaning "to endow with certain qualities"; **investment** once meant "putting clothes or vestments on"

to **investigate** is literally to "look for vestiges or traces," from Latin *vestigare*, "track, trace," from *vestigium*, "footprint"

{ in its original meaning, **investiture** referred to clothing a new officeholder, such as a monarch, in the garments that symbolized power }

intropunitive means "blaming oneself rather than others or external events"

intuition is from Latin elements *in-*, "upon" and *tueri*, "to look"; **intuit** is a back-formation from **intuition**

Inuit is the plural of inuk "person"

inunction is the rubbing of oil or lotion into the skin

unda in Latin is "wave"—part of the word **inundate**

to accustom to hardship is to **inure**

the early sense of **invade** was "attack or assault someone"

invalescence is strength or health

Latin *validus* "strong" is part of **invalid** and **invalidate**

invective implies a comparable vehemence but suggests greater verbal and rhetorical skill and may apply to a public denunciation

invidious means "offensive, repulsive"

inviolable first meant "to be kept sacred and free from assault, desecration, infraction"

invious describes something that is pathless or without roads

invite comes from Latin *invitare*, from an Indo-European root meaning "to go after something, pursue with vigor, desire"

invoice is from *invoyes*, "message" (from *envoi*) from the phrase *lettre d'envoi*, "letter of consignment, **invoice**'"

invoke is to call upon or appeal to something or someone for help or inspiration while **evoke** is to bring or call something to the conscious mind; **evoke** is from Latin *evocare*, "to call out" while **invoke** is from *invocare*, "to call on"

involve first meant "enfold, surround, wrap"

inwit usually means "an inner sense of right or wrong" but its more general meaning is "reason, intellect, understanding, or wisdom"

inwit is the conscience or wisdom and **outwit** is acquired knowledge or information

iodine derives from the Greek word *iodes*, "like a violet," from Greek *ion*, "violet" (**iodine**, when heated, turns violet-colored)

ion (any individual atom, molecule, or group having a net electric charge) is a form of a Greek word for "go"

iota comes from its being the smallest letter of the Greek alphabet

Iowa is Dakota *ayuba*, "sleepy one"

someone who is easily angered is **iracundulous** or **iracund**

an **irade** is a decree

Iraq is pronounced ih-RAHK

irate means "angry" while **irascible** means "disposed toward or easily provoked to anger" (both are from Latin *ira*, "anger")

ire suggests greater intensity than anger, **rage** suggests loss of self-control, and **fury** is destructive **rage** verging on madness

two words that mean "promoting peace" are **irenic** and **henotic**

iridescent is from Latin *iris/irid*, "rainbow"

iris gets its name from **Iris**, the Greek goddess of the rainbow

irk originally meant "grow tired" and a possible source is Old Norse *yrkja*, "work"

ferrum is the Latin name for **iron**, from which its chemical symbol Fe is derived; **iron** exists in various states of impurity and it is processed to produce cast **iron**, wrought **iron**, etc. and **steel** (**steel** is **iron** to which carbon and other things have been added)

the golf clubs called **irons** and **woods** are named for the materials the heads were traditionally made of

irony is from Greek *eironeia*, "simulated ignorance" and **irony** is a device which may be employed in satire to say something couched in language that denotes quite the opposite of what is intended

if a statement or argument is **irrefragable** it is unanswerable

regardless is already a negative "without regard to; despite"—and **irregardless** is a redundant negative

people not answering your e-mails? that's **irrespondence**! (failure to reply)

irrevocable should be pronounced i-REV-uh-kuh-buhl

rigare, "moisten, wet" is the Latin base of **irrigate**

irritate means "inflame" (originally "excite, rouse"); **aggravate** means "worsen"

an **isagoge** is an introduction to a field of study

irruent means "rushing in" or "running rapidly"

to **irrupt** is to enter violently

ISBN stands for International Standard Book Number and each book has a unique one

island comes from Old Norse *ieg/ig/ey*, "water, sea" plus "land"

islomania is a passion for islands

an **isobar** is a line on a weather map connecting points having the same atmospheric pressure (from Greek *isobaros*, "of equal weight")

isochrous means "of the same color throughout"

words that don't repeat any letters are known as **isograms**

isolate comes from Italian *isolato*, "island"; **isolated** is literally "made an island"

an **isolato** (from Italian) is a person who feels fundamentally estranged from the time period or society he or she is stuck in

an **isomer** is each of two or more compounds with the same formula but a different arrangement of atoms and different properties or each of two or more atomic nuclei with the same atomic number and mass number but different energy states (from Greek *isomeres*, "sharing equally")

isometric is from Latin *isus*, "equal" and *metria*, "measuring"

the term **isotope** was coined in 1913 by British chemist Frederick Soddy and it means literally "equal place" formed from Greek *iso-*, "equal" and *topos*, "place"; although isotopes of the same element have different atomic weights, they occupy the same place in the periodic table

issue and exit are closely related, going back to Latin *exire* "go out," which became Old French *eissue* and later **issue**, and Latin *exitus* and then exit

Isuzu means "50 bells" in Japanese

the pronoun "**it**" has four uses: referring, anticipatory, cleft, and prop/empty; prop or empty **it** is used to fill the place of a function—such as the subject—but has little or no meaning and **it** is often used to refer to weather and time as in "**It**'s really hot in here." An example of anticipatory is "**It** is easy to play tennis," for referring **it**, "Isn't **it**

rather nice?," and cleft **it**, "**It** was John who broke the window."

item was a Latin word first used in English as an adverb meaning "also, in like manner"

iterate means "do or say something again" and **reiterate** is the result of the erroneous addition of a redundant prefix; **iterate** is used more for repeated actions like mathematical functions and **reiterate** tends to be used for things one says

itinerant is based on Latin *itinerare*, "to travel"

its is a possessive pronoun (as in "**its** purpose"); **it's** is the contracted or shortened for of "it is" (as in "**it's** definitely much faster")

{ **ivories** are teeth, dice, piano keys, billiard balls, and dominoes }

ivory comes from elephant, hippopotamus, mammoth, narwhal, or walrus

ivy was first grown on buildings to show that wine was sold inside

the suffix **-ize** (-ise in British English) is from the Greek infinitive verb ending *-dzein*

the sparks and embers rising from a fire are **izles**

the name of the letter Z is **izzard**

personal dignity or honor is **izzat**

{ **J** was formerly interchangeable with I and up to a point the two were not separated in English dictionaries, alphabetical lists, etcetera }

J was the last letter to be included in our alphabet; only in the mid-nineteenth century, under the influence of new dictionaries by Noah Webster and others, did the letters **J** and **V** gain full acceptance

jabble is turbulence on the surface of water; to **jabble** is "to splash or splatter"

the word **jabot** is French for "bird's crop or gullet"—which the frill on a shirt resembles

jacent means "lying, recumbent"—so **adjacent** means "lying next to"

jackal comes from Turkish *chacal*, from Persian *shaghal*, "wild animal related to the dog"

jackanapes originally referred to a tame ape or monkey

a jockey's colorful top is called a **jacket**

a **jackleg** is a reckless driver

A **jack-o'-lantern** (also jack-a-lantern) is a hollowed-out pumpkin, originally a turnip, carved into a demonic face and lit with a candle inside. The custom originated in the British Isles and the original meaning of the word **jack-o'-lantern** was "night watchman" or "man with a lantern," but it took on the Halloween sense by 1837, first in Nathaniel Hawthorne's *Twice-Told Tales*.

jackpot comes from draw-poker in which a pot/pool has to accumulate until one of the players can open the betting with a pair of jacks or better; several hands usually have to be dealt before this happens, adding to the ante

jacquard as in intricate fabric and weaving is named for Joseph Marie **Jacquard** of France who in the early nineteenth century invented an apparatus to facilitate the weaving of figured fabrics on a loom

a **jacquerie** is a communal uprising or revolt

if you toss and turn at night, you are **jactitating**; **jactitation** or **jactation** is restless tossing or twitching

to **jaculate** is to "dart" or "hurl"

the **jacuzzi** (a trademark) was created by U.S. engineer Candido **Jacuzzi** (1903–1986) who devised it for his son, who had rheumatoid arthritis

the term **jade** comes from Latin and was originally a description of the stone's medical applications to curing pain in the renal (ilia) area

jaded originally referred to a "worn-out" horse

jaguar came to us through Portuguese from Tupi-Guarani *yuguara*, "carnivorous animal"

jail is a diminutive of Latin *cavea*, "cage"

a **jail** is a short-term detention facility for those awaiting trial or convicted of minor offenses; a **prison** or **penitentiary** is a long-term detention facility for those convicted of major offenses

the word **jailbird** was coined with allusion to a caged bird

who had two faces—one looking forward to the future and one looking backward at the past

the hard lacquer varnish called **japan** got its name from **Japan**; the name **Japan** comes from Chinese *jih pun*, "sunrise" as it was thought of as the "land of the rising sun"

a **jape** is something designed to arouse amusement

japlish is a blend of Japanese and English spoken by Japanese people

jar comes from Arabic *jarrah*, "earthen water vessel" as it was originally a large earthenware vessel for holding water, oil, wine, etc.

jalapeño gets its name from Jalapa, Mexico

jam, the conserve, may get its name from the fact that its ingredients are crushed or squeezed (jammed)

jam is a thick mixture made from fruit pulp and sugar, **jelly** is made from fruit juice boiled with sugar, **preserves** are fruit preserved whole or in large pieces and cooked with sugar, and **marmalade** is boiled fruit pulp, rinds, and sugar

jamb, as in door, comes from French *jambe*, meaning "vertical support" or "leg"

jammy can mean "excellent" or "very lucky"

jamocha is a blend of java and mocha

jangle first meant "talk excessively or noisily"

janitor is based on Latin *janua*, "door" and first meant "doorkeeper; caretaker"

jannock means "fair, genuine"

a synonym for door is **janua**

January is named for Janus, the Roman god of gates and doors and beginnings,

jardiniere—a garnish of mixed vegetables—is French, literally "female gardener"

jargogle means "to confuse, to mix up"

the original sense of **jargon** was "chattering, twittering," and then "gibberish"—coming from French *jargoun*, "warbling of birds"

jarns, **nittles**, **grawlix**, and **quimp** are various squiggles used to denote cursing in comic strips and books

jasmine is the name of a pale yellow color

the **Jataka** are any of the stories of the past lives/incarnations of the Buddha

a **jaunce** is a long, tiring journey, which is what **jaunt** originally meant

jaundice is based on French *jaune*, "yellow"

a **jaup** or **jawp** is the splash of liquid against a surface or the sound made by liquid sloshing around in a container

Java was once the world's main producer of coffee beans, so coffee acquired the name of **java**

both pliers and wrenches have **jaws**

the **jawbone**, the **mandible**, takes its name from Latin *mandere*, "chew"

jaw-jaw is lengthy or pointless talk

{ like the robin, the **jay** may have been christened with a human name }

the blue **jay** inspired the name of **jay** for "country folk" and later the word "**jay-walk**"; the term **jaywalker** "one who crosses the road illegally" was based on an American use of **jay** for a "fool, simpleton"

jazz can mean "energy, excitement"

a **jazzbo** is a jazz musician

jealousy and **zeal** are etymologically related, coming from Greek *zelos*, "jealousy; fervor, enthusiasm"; **jealous** once meant "devoted, eager"

jealousy is reflective of a person's feelings or attitudes toward another person, whereas **envy** expresses a person's feelings or attitudes toward another person's advantages or accomplishments; **jealousy** pertains to emotional rivalry while **envy** is resentment of a more fortunate person

jeans are made of cloth that was originally called Gene fustian or Geane, the name for Genoa, Italy, in Middle English; **jeannette** is any fabric resembling jean

jeep is probably GP "general purpose," influenced by Eugene the **Jeep**, a powerful and resourceful character in the Popeye comic (1936)

a **jeeves** is a valet or personal attendant

jejune in English first referred to land as being barren or "without food"

between **Jekyll** and **Hyde**, the former is good and the latter is evil

nervous pudding is a term for **Jell-O**; **Jell-O** is named for jelly crystals in the invented gelatin dessert

jelly is based on words meaning "freeze, frost" presumably because of its firm shape

pertaining to breakfast is **jentacular** and another word for breakfast is **jentation**

jeopardy comes from French *ieu parti*, "(evenly) divided game" (from Latin *jocus partitus*, meant "divided game"), referring originally to chess where the chances of winning and losing are balanced

a **jeremiad**, a lamentation, is named for the "Lamentations of Jeremiah" in the Old Testament

jerk as in jerked meat (e.g. beef jerky) is from American Spanish and Quechua *charqui*, "dried flesh"

jerkwater refers to the days when railway engines needed water and, in remote areas, water had to be fetched or jerked out of a stream with a roped bucket (jerking out water)

jeroboam, a large wine bottle (four/fifths of a gallon), was named for a king of Israel

to **jerry-build** is to build unsubstantially and with poor materials; the origin of the term, attested to 1869, is unknown

jersey was originally a knitted fabric made in **Jersey** of the Channel Islands

the etymology of **Jerusalem** is "town of peace," a name that belies its turbulent history

something that is **jessant** is "shooting upward" or "springing up" (said of a plant or animal)

jest first meant "exploit, heroic deed" and then "a story of heroic deeds"—from Latin *gesta*, "exploits, actions"

Jesus means "anointed one" and **Buddha** means "the Enlightened"

jet was first a verb meaning "jut out," from French *jeter*, "to throw," based on Latin *jactare*

goods discarded from a ship and washed ashore are **jetsam**, a contraction of jettison

jettison comes from Latin *jacere*, "throw" and **jetty** from French *jeter*, "throw"

a counter or token used as a gambling chip or to operate slot machines is a **jetton**

a bridge or staircase used for aircraft passengers to get on or off a plane is a **jetty**, air bridge, or **jetway**

jewel may be from French *jeu*, "play," and some say from Latin *jocus*, "jest"

when a horse stops and refuses to move on, that is **jibbing**

jibe "be compatible, consistent" may come from the earlier **jibe** "to shift a sail from side to side while sailing in the wind"

jiffy is an actual unit of time—.01 seconds

jiggy originally meant "crazy" or "energetic" and now can be applied to anything one finds "cool" or "enjoyable" or "uninhibited"

{ **jihad** can refer to any campaign for an idea or belief }

the female ferret is called a **jill**

a **jilt** is a woman accomplice to a thief

the gold circles on a tambourine's edge are the **jingles**

jingo was originally a conjuror's word

to **jink** is to change direction suddenly and nimbly; a **jink** is a sudden quick change of direction

an extinct bird called the jynx supposedly had the ability to predict the future—but often the jynx's favorable predictions did not come true, but unfavorable ones did—and this seems to be the source of **jinx**

to **jirble** is to spill liquid by unsteady movement of the container

jitterbug was first a person who drank regularly and so had the jitters every morning

jizz describes the characteristic impression (color, size, shape, movement) of a particular animal or plant—especially to a birdwatcher or naturalist

to **job** is to peck at or suddenly stab

a long tedious scolding is a **jobation**

jobbie is a word used to describe an object or product of a certain kind, e.g., electronic **jobbie**

jockey first referred to a horse dealer or horse rider before it had the racing sense

jocose means "full of jokes" (from Latin *jocus*, "joke, jest")

jocund means "feeling pleasure at some particular event or circumstance" (Latin *jucundus*, "agreeable, delightful")

jodhpurs are named for Jodhpur, India

jog appears to be onomatopoeic in origin

johnnycake is an Americanism of uncertain origin; in the South, they are often made of cornmeal and it is generally believed that **johnnycake** is a corruption of journeycake—suggesting that it was adapted to being carried in a saddlebag during the pioneer days

join goes back ultimately to Indo-European *jug-*, which became Latin *jungere*, "**join**"

a woodworker making stairs, doors, etc. is a **joiner**

joinhand is an old name for cursive writing

a **joist** is a parallel timber to which floor boards or ceiling laths are fastened

Latin *jocus*, "jest, **joke**" gave us **joke**

jolly comes from Old French *jolif*, "merry, festive, pleasant"

a **jones** is an addiction or craving

a rope suspension bridge is a **joola**

josh "to joke, tease" may come from **Josh** "a country bumpkin"

the original sense of **jostle** was "have sexual intercourse with"

jot came via Latin from Greek *iota*, the smallest letter of the Greek alphabet

jouisance (or jouissance) is another word for "enjoyment" or "possession or use of something"

to **jounce** is to move roughly or violently up and down, as when one is riding a horse

originally, a **journal** was a book listing the times of daily prayer (from Latin *diurnalis*, "belonging to a day")

{ **journey**'s first sense was a day's (*jour*) travel }

journeyman preserves an older sense of journey "day" or "day's work"

the underlying meaning of **joust** is "an encounter" from Latin *juxtare*, "come together"; **jostle** is a derivative of **joust**

Jove is the poetic equivalent of Jupiter, the highest deity of the ancient Romans; from this we get **jovial**

jovial refers to a mood or disposition, **jocular** to a conduct or manner

the head and shoulders of certain fishes—salmon and sturgeon—are called the **jowl**

joy traces back to Latin *gaudere*, "rejoice"

if you have long hair, you are **jubate**

jubilate is from a Latin word meaning "shout for joy"

jubilee comes from Hebrew *yobhel*, "ram's horn," which was used as a trumpet to proclaim the **jubilee**, a year of emancipation and restoration (every fifty years)

when a partridge makes its noise, it is called **jucking**

a voice oscillating between greater and lesser intensity is **juddering**

judge is from Latin *jus*, "*law*," and *dicere*, "to say"

judicial means "pertaining to judges or the courts" and **judicious** means "prudent, carefully considered"; **judicial** refers to judgment as it is exercised by the court, **judicious** to judgment as exercised by an individual

judo is Japanese for "gentle way" and **jujitsu** is "gentle technique"

a **judoka** is a person who practices judo

juggernaut is derived from Sanskrit for "lord of the world," a title of Krishna, worshipped at an annual festival by the dragging of his image through the streets in a heavy chariot

juggle is from Latin *joculus*, a diminutive of *jocus*, "jest," and a **juggler** was originally a jester

juglandaceous is pertaining to walnuts

juice is from Latin *jus*, "broth"

a **juju** is a charm or fetish, or the power attributed to one

jujube is from Latin, originally a datelike fruit, then soft candy with date-like flavor, first recorded in 1835

juke was slang for "to have sex" and **jukeboxes** were originally in houses of prostitution

julep comes from Persian *gulab*, "rose-water"

julienne means cut into very thin strips

July and **August** were originally named, respectively, Quintilis (fifth) and Sextilis (sixth) month; **September** is *septem*, "seven," and **November** *novem*, "nine," and **December** *decem*, "ten"; both **July** and **August** are named for Roman Empire leaders: Julius Caesar and Augustus Caesar

jumble is a blend of jump and tumble

jumbo originally denoted a large and clumsy person and the word may come from Swahili *jambe*, "chief"

junket started off meaning a basket and there is an old-fashioned dessert (like sweetened cottage cheese) called **junket**

the art of taking photographs of people jumping, in order to capture their essence and also for scientific study, is **jumpology**

another word for twin or paired is **jumelle**

the continuation of a newspaper or magazine story on a later page is a **jump**

until early modern English, the words for "**jump**" were leap and spring

jumper was first a loose jacket worn by sailors, from jump "a short coat"

juncate is an old word for cheesecake

June is either named for Juno, the queen of the Roman gods and the goddess of marriage—or named for Junius, a prominent ancient Roman family

jungle derives from Sanskrit *jangala*, "rough and arid terrain" or "dry, waterless desert" which is quite opposite of its current meaning

junior is a Latin comparative form of juvenis "young"

junk was originally old or discarded rope, a nautical term

junta (pronounced HOON-tuh) is from Italian *giunta*, "meeting"

the **junters** is a state of sulking

jurisprudence literally means skill or proficiency in legal matters

juror and **jury** derive from Latin *jurare*, "to swear"

Latin *jus*, "right" or "sacred formula" came to be English **just**

early senses of **justify** were "administer justice to" and "inflict a judicial penalty on"

jute comes from Sanskrit *juta*, "braid of hair"

juvenilia are the writings of one's earlier years

juventude is another word for "youth"

juxtaposed means placed side by side especially so as to permit comparison and contrast

{ **K** for strike-out in baseball comes from the last letter of "struck" }

kabuki is Japanese and translates to *ka*, "song," *bu*, "dance," and *ki*, "skill"

in Native American Pueblo mythology, **kachina** is spirit of the invisible life forces, one of the deified ancestral spirits

the stump of a tree or a broken tooth is a **kag**

kahuna is Hawaiian for "witch doctor, medicine man, wise man"

kairos is a time when conditions are right for the accomplishment of a crucial action—the opportune and decisive moment

the **kaiser** ("emperor" in German) roll got its name from its resemblance to a monarch's crown

Japanese borrowings include **kaizen** "work philosophy," **karoshi** "death by job-related exhaustion," and **zaitech** "financial engineering"

kaleidoscope was coined using Greek *kalos*, "beautiful," *eidos*, "form," and *-scope* (skopein "look at") by the inventor of the instrument

kalon is the kind of beauty that is more than skin deep

when bees leave the hive, that is **kaming**

The explanation for the word **kangaroo** is that the Aborigines (in Guugu Yimidhirr) used the word *ganjurru*, which meant "large black **kangaroo**." The other more fanciful story is that when asked what the animal was by Captain Cook, the Australian Aborigines replied that large hopping animals were "**kangaroo**," but he did not know that the word meant "I don't know."

Kansas is Sioux for "south wind people/place"

kaolin clay is named for a mountain in China where the clay is found

kapok is a firm, fibrous, cotton-like substance found surrounding the seeds of a certain tropical tree (from Malay kapoq) and is used for stuffing things, like meditation cushions

kaput was originally a card game term for "being without tricks" in the game piquet

karabiner comes from a German phrase meaning "spring hook"

karakul is a breed of sheep with coarse wiry fur

karaoke means "empty orchestra" in Japanese

karate is literally "the way of the empty hand"

a **karateka** is a practitioner of karate

karma is from Sanskrit meaning "effect" or "fate"

karmadharaya is "a compound word in which the first part of the word describes the second part," like blackbird, gentleman

keep first appears in texts around 1000 AD, but its earlier history is unknown

the loop on a belt where the extra belt part is secured is the **keeper**

a guinea fowl chick is a **keet**

kef or **kif** is the tranquil or peaceful state of one who has smoked hallucinogenic or narcotic drugs

the squatting Cossack dance is the **kazachoc** (kazachok) or **kazatsky** (kazatske) and the characteristic kicking step is the **prisiadka**

karoshi is death caused by overwork

kata is a system of individual training exercises in karate and other martial arts

skiing is a **katabatic** sport (moving down a slope or valley)

a severe hangover can be called a **katzenjammer** (German for "cats wailing")

kayak was first called kaiak, or "man's boat," to distinguish it from umiak, the "woman's boat"

Dutch *bazu*, "trumpet" gives us the words **kazoo** and **bazooka**, the latter originally being a form of **kazoo** that was a long sounding-horn

keak is to cackle, laugh at

kebab, from Turkish *kebap*, "roast meat," can be spelled kabob, kabab, kebob, or cabob; *shish* is Turkish for "skewer"

kedogenous is "brought about by worry or anxiety"

Keds was first supposed to be called Peds (Latin *ped*, "foot") but it was already trademarked

a **keek** is a Peeping Tom or an industrial spy

the early meaning of **keen** was "brave"

kegler, a bowler, is from German *Kegel*, "skittle"

keister first meant "suitcase" or "satchel"

to **kelk** is to groan or belch

the first Baron **Kelvin** of Largs (1824–1907) invented the thermodynamic scale that bears his name

kempt means "combed" or "neatly kept"

ken first meant "make known," from Old Norse *kenna*, "know"

kenlore is the theory of knowledge

kennel is traceable back to Latin *canis*, "dog"

kennel once meant the hole of a fox; to **unkennel** is to drive from the hole

kenspeckle means "conspicuous, easily recognizable"

Kentucky is from Iroquois *kentake* meaning "meadow"

kerchief, from French *covrir*, "cover," and *chief*, "head," originally meant "head covering," and **handkerchief** was one of these carried in the hand

a **kerf** is a slit or notch made by a saw or other cutting instrument

the cut end of a felled or pruned tree is the **kerf**

a **kerfuffle** is a disorderly outburst or turmoil

kernel is a diminutive of corn "grain, seed"

kerosene is based on Greek *keros*, "wax"

to **kest** is to cast aside or throw away

ketchup comes from Malay *kechap*, "fish sauce" which may come from Chinese *ketsiap*, "brine of pickled fish"; there are other spellings like catsup and catchup

a pothole can also be called a **kettle**

kew-kaw is another way of saying upside-down

the dry winged fruit of an ash, elm, or sycamore is a **key**

KGB stands for Komitet gosudarstvennoi bezopasnosti (Committee of State Security)

khaki comes from Persian *khak*, "dust, earth"

dead leaves (etc.) swept up in gardens and yards are **kibble**

kibbutz is from a Hebrew word meaning "gathering"

kibe is a crack in one's skin due to the cold

kibitz (pronounced KIH-buts) derives from German *Kiebitz*, "interfering onlooker" or "lapwing," then *kiebitzen*, "to look on while others are playing cards, especially in an annoying way"

kibosh may be from the Gaelic phrase *cie bais* meaning "cap of death"

kick appears toward the end of the fourteenth century, but no one knows where it came from

the dent in the bottom of a wine or champagne bottle is the **kick** or **punt**

kickshaw, from French *quelque chose*, "something," first meant a fancy cooked dish, usually French

the **kickstand** is the metal piece that holds a bicycle upright when not being ridden

kid originally denoted a young goat

a **kiddleywink** (or kiddlywink, kiddliwink) is a beer shop or lowly public house

kidnap's second element is slang for "nab, seize"

the word **kidney** can mean "a kind or class of person"

kidology is the art or practice of kidding or teasing people

kielbasa is Polish for "sausage"

kill is not an old word (fourteenth century), and its first meaning was "strike" or "beat"

killarney is a moderate yellowish-green

{ **kiln** comes from Latin *culina*, "kitchen" or "cooking stove" }

khilioi was Greek for "thousand" and came through French to be English **kilo**

kilometer should be pronounced KILL-uh-me-tur (not kih-LAH-muh-tur)

kilt is of Scandinavian origin, first meaning "tuck up skirts around the body"

kilter can describe a poker hand consisting entirely of cards of low value

kilter or kelter is "good condition or order" or "good health or spirits"

a diamond-bearing rock is a **kimberlite**

kimono is from Japanese *ki*, "wearing," and *mono*, "thing"

kin and **kind** share an Indo-European base with Latin *genus* and Greek *genos*

your family or relatives are **kin**; your friends, neighbors, and acquaintances are **kith**

kindergarten is German for "children's garden"—a term for a school in which children's aptitude for learning is cultivated

kindle (verb) is related to Old Norse *kyndill*, "candle, torch"

the young of any animal can be called the **kindle**

a **kine** is an isolated body movement or gesture

kinemics is the study of gestures as units of expression

when you watch video of a car and the wheels appear to be going backward though they are going forward, the phenomenon is **kinephantom**

kinesics and **pasimology** are other terms for body language

kinetic is from Greek *kinein*, "to move"

king first appeared in Old English as the name of chiefs of Anglo or Saxon kins "clans or tribes" who invaded Britain, or the names of British chiefs who fought them

a **kingdom** is one of the five broad divisions of living things: Animalia, Plantae, Fungi, Protista, and Monera

kingbolt, the main or large bolt in a mechanical device or structure, became **kingpin**; the **kingpin** was first a vertical bolt used as a pivot or a main bolt in a central position

in chess, **kingside** is the side of the board on which the king is positioned at the start of the game

king-size is the preferred term and king-sized is a variant (this goes for other similar constructions)

kink is originally a nautical term for a twist in a rope

a **kinkle** is a slight kink or twist

kiosk first meant "pavilion" (from Turkish and Persian)

commotion or confusion can be called **kippage**

kirigami is the Japanese art involving cutting and folding paper into objects or designs, from *kiri*, "to cut," and *kami*, "paper"

a **kirkbuzzer** is someone who robs churches

Turkish *qismat*, "portion, lot" gave us **kismet** "fate"

when a ball lightly touches another in billiards, it **kisses** it

a message delivered with a kiss is a **kissogram**

a **kit** is a full set of drums used by a drummer in a group, especially jazz, pop, or rock

in colonial America, the **kitchen** was variously called the fire room, the hall, and the keeping room; **kitchen** is based on Latin *coquere*, "to cook"

kite (the hawk, then the toy that hovers like a bird) derives from an Old English name for a bird of prey, *cyta*

kitsch is borrowed from German *kitschen*, "to throw together a work of art"

baby beavers are called **kittens**

kitten is a variant of Old French *chitoun*, a diminutive of *chat*, "cat"

kittle means "difficult to deal with"

{ **kitty** (now pool of money) may be from the slang meaning of "jail" }

in Native American Pueblo practices, a **kiva** was an underground chamber used by the males for religious rites

klatsch is from a German word meaning "gossip"

the **Kleenex** was first used to remove cold cream—hence, Kleen (clean) and ex (out, away)

klutz comes from German *klotz*, "block of wood"

knabble means to bite or nibble

knackatory is a place to buy knickknacks

a **knag** is a peg for hanging things

knap is the crest or summit of a hill

knapsack is from German *knapper*, "to bite (food)," and *zak*, "sack"

a knot or protuberance in wood is called a **knar** or a **knag** or **knur**

knave is an example of degeneration where it once meant "child, youth" and now means "rogue, disreputable person"

the lowest court card of each suit, the jack, is also called the **knave**

knee traces back to an Indo-European root meaning "bend"

the **kneecap** has many names: knop, rotula, rowel, shive, whirl-bone, pattle-bone

knickerbockers (**knickers** for short) were short, baggy breeches gathered at the knee—named after Diedrich Knickerbocker, pretended author of Washington Irving's "History of New York" (1809)

knickknack has two k's in the middle

knickknack is an antiphonic (responsive in sound) reduplication of knack which first meant "stratagem, trick"; **kickshaw** and **gewgaw** are synonyms, also meaning "curious or pleasing trifle or ornament"

{ **knickknackatory** are small trivia items }

knife came from Old Norse *knifr*, from Germanic *knibaz*

knight first meant, simply, "boy, servant," or "youth"

knit literally first meant "tie with or in a knot"

a **knob** of butter is a lump

knock is a classic onomatopoeic word

knockwurst or **knackwurst** is from German *knack*, "to make a sudden cracking sound," and *wurst*, "sausage"—literally meaning "sausage that makes a crackling noise"

a **knoll**, the summit or rounded top of a mountain or hill, seems to derive from Old Teutonic meaning "ball, clod, knot"

a **knop** is a small rounded protuberance, especially ornamental

a **knot** is defined as a "nautical mile per hour"—so you write thirty knots (not thirty knots per hour)—since a **knot** is a measure of speed, not distance, it is redundant if you add "per hour"

knot as a unit of speed originated when a ship's speed was measured with a log line—a twine or rope marked at intervals with colored knots and attached to a log weighted with lead

know is from an Indo-European root shared by Latin (*g*)*noscere* and Greek *gignoskein*

knowledge is the information held on a computer system; the word was originally a verb meaning "acknowledge, recognize"

a **knuckle** is the end of a bone of any joint—knee, elbow, vertebral joints—as well as the fingers; **knuckle** first denoted the shape of an elbow or knee when bent

koala in Aboriginal language means "no drink" as it gets its liquid from eucalyptus leaves; technically, koalas are marsupials, not bears

a **koan** is a paradoxical statement used as a meditative technique in Zen Buddhism (from Japanese *ko*, "public" *an*, "matter" or "matter for thought")

koh-i-noor ("mountain of light") is used figuratively to mean something that is the most precious or superb of its kind

kohl, a powder used to darken the eyes, is from ancient Arabic and Egyptian times

kohlrabi is German, from Italian *cavolo rapa*, "cabbage turnip"

a **konimeter** measures impurities in the air

Kool-Aid was first called Kool-Ade, modeled on lemonade, and the final name choice gave the idea of "aiding" drinkers in remaining cool

kosher is Hebrew for "fit, proper"

kowtow comes from Chinese *kou tou*, "knock one's head" which would occur during prostration out of respect, worship, etc.

a **kraal** is an enclosure for animals or a native village community

the dormant area of land lying next to one that is prone to earthquakes is **kratogen**

krill comes from Norwegian meaning "very small fry of fish"; **krill** was originally (in Norwegian) any kind of buglike creature

{ applause measurement is done on a **krotoscope** }

kudos is best pronounced KYOO-dahs or KYOO-dohs and derives from Greek *kydos*, "glory, praise, renown"; in Greek, it means a single bit of praise or prestige, but the word looks like an English plural and is therefore treated as one

kumbaya (also spelled kumbayah) from the camp song is Creole for "come by here"

kumquat, from Cantones *kum kwat*, is from Mandarin Chinese *jin ju*, "golden orange"

kundalini yoga is a practice to uncoil "the coiled serpent" said to sleep at the base of the spine (Sanskrit *kundalin*, "coiled" from *kundala*, "ring")

kvetch—to complain chronically or habitually—is from Yiddish *kvetshn*, "pinch, squeeze; complain"

the name of **Kwanzaa** comes from Swahili *matunda ya* **kwanzaa**, "first fruits," as it was an African harvest celebration

a **kyle** is a narrow sea channel between two islands (from Scottish)

kyriolexy is the use of literal expressions

{ **L**, V, X, and D as Roman numerals are not abbreviations for Latin words but rather may commemorate primitive Roman symbols }

labefaction is a deterioration or downfall

label, originally meaning "narrow band or strip," comes from a French word meaning "ribbon"

an emotionally unstable, temperamental person can be described as **labile**; **labile** also can be used in reference to blood pressure that fluctuates (meaning "liable to change")

lability is the susceptibility to error or lapse, part of being human

the word for "the ability to read lips" is **labiomancy**

the word **labor** comes from Latin *laborem*, "distress, toil trouble; drudgery, **labor**," and first referred to work that was compulsory or painful; the meaning changed with the advent of the Industrial Revolution

laboratory is from Latin *labor*, "toil, work" and is, literally, "a place of labor"

the ear has a **labyrinth** and an inflammation of that area is **labyrinthitis**

lace, which first meant "noose," is from Latin *laqueus*, "noose"

laced can mean "diversified with streaks of color" from the earlier meaning of "ornamented or trimmed with lace"

the adjective form for lizard is **lacertine**

laches is carelessness or negligence

a **lachryma** is a tear; **lachrymose** is tearful

lack first meant "moral failing, crime, offense"

lackadaisical comes from an old term *lackaday*, which means "Shame on you, day!" as if it were a person

lackey is of Arabic origin, borrowed into English from French *laquais*, "footman" or "foot soldier"

laclabphily is said to be the collecting of cheese labels

laconic means sparing in speech and emotion and it comes from Laconia, a Spartan territory, as the Spartans were known for their brusque speech

lacquer comes from earlier *lac*, a secretion of certain homopteran insects parasitic on Asian trees, which was used to make dye and shellac

lacrosse is from French meaning "(the game of) the hooked stick"

lacto-ovo-vegetarians eat dairy products and eggs besides vegetables

a gap or a missing portion—as in the Nixon Watergate tapes—is a **lacuna**; **lacuna** also means "the hole in someone's learning"

> { **lad** meant "servant" before it acquired a more general sense of "youth" }

etymologically, a **ladder** is something that is "leaned up against a wall"

a vertical strip of unraveled fabric in knitted garments (as in nylons) is a **ladder** or **run**

to **lade** means "load cargo" or "work a soup ladle"

ladle comes from *lade*, "load" or "draw water"

lady is from Old English *hlaf*, "loaf" and a Germanic base meaning "knead" and first literally meant "one who kneads bread"

laetificant is an adjective meaning "cheering, antidepressant"

lag first meant the last person in a race or competition

to be flask-shaped is **lageniform**

lager, aged beer, comes from German *lagerbier*, "storehouse beer" from the beer's aging in a storehouse

a **lagniappe** is a gift given with a purchase, like a Christmas snow dome with the buying of a Christmas present

lagoon is derived from Latin *lacuna*, "pool, lake" or "hole, gap"

a **lagoon** is a shallow pond near a body of water; a long **lagoon** near the sea is a **haff**

laic is the adjective to describe the laity (lay people) and all things secular

lair first meant "grave, tomb" or "place where one sleeps"

lake first meant pool or pond

lama, from Tibetan *bla-ma*, means "superior one"

a **lama** is a Buddhist monk; a **llama** is a South American cud-chewing animal

in Gothic times, **lamb** was used for "adult sheep" as well as "baby sheep"

lambaste is a duplication for emphasis, with both parts meaning "to beat"

a medicine that is taken by licking is a **lambative** or a **lohock**

lambent can mean dealing gently but brilliantly with a subject

Lambrusco is Italian, literally "grape of the wild one"

lame came from Germanic *lamon*, "weak-limbed"

lamé is a material consisting of silk or other yarns interwoven with metallic threads

lamp is from Greek lampas "torch"

black pigment applied under an athlete's eyes is **lampblack**

lampoon probably comes from a French drinking song where *lampone/lampons* meant "let us drink or guzzle"

lamprey and **limpet** come from Latin *lampetra*, "stone-licker" as both cling to rocks

a private terrace or balcony on a hotel room is a **lanai**

lanate, from Latin *lana*, "wool," means "having a woolly surface"

lance may come from Latin *lancea*, or possibly a Spanish/Iberian source

lanceolate means "resembling a spearhead"

land goes back to Proto-Germanic *landam*, "particular (enclosed) area" the space between the grooves of a record are the **lands**

landlubber does not means "land lover" but comes from Danish *lobbes*, "clown" as one who is inexperienced or awkward aboard a ship

landscape comes from Dutch *landschap*, "region, tract of land"

the **landside** is the side or sections of an airport to which the public has admittance, contrasted with **airside**

a **lane** is a narrow, often bucolic, path that lacks a shoulder or median; **lane** can also be a division of a larger road

cross-country running or skiing can also be called **langlauf**

a **langoustine** is the Norway lobster

language is from Latin *lingua*

don't use "**language**" when you mean "**writing system**"—Chinese is a spoken **language** with no characters; the Chinese **writing system** uses thousands of characters

if someone is **languaged** or **well-languaged**, they are skilled in a language(s)

if you are becoming tired, you are **languescent**

languid is limp or listless; **limpid** means clear or calm

{ **languor** is any distressed condition, such as illness, sorrow, fatigue, etc. }

lank means "shrunken, spare" and "tall and thin"

lanolin comes from Latin *lana*, "wool" as it is the fatty matter which permeates sheep's wool

lantern traces back to Greek *lucerna*, "lamp"

the cord holding a whistle is a **lanyard**

any part of a garment that hangs down in front and can be folded over or up (to hold something) is a **lap**; hence, **lapel**

lapidary first meant "pertaining to stones"

to **lapidate** is to pelt someone with stones

the amount that layers overlap is **lappage**

lappet is a fold or hanging piece of flesh in some animals

lapwing has no etymological connection to lap or wing; its Old English form was *hleapwince* from leap and a base meaning "move from side to side" or "wink"

larceny comes from *larcin*, the French word for mercenary soldier—as they were expected to indulge in petty theft

lard was French for bacon, related to Greek *larinos*, "fat"

a **larder** was first a place for keeping bacon, from Old French *lardier* and Latin *laridum*, "bacon fat"

large once meant "generous, giving"

largesse (or **largess**) is pronounced lahr-ZHES and means "generosity"

larging is wasteful spending of money

largo is music played "broad, large" or grandly

a cattle herder's rope with a noose on one end is a **lariat** or a **riata**; **lariat** comes from Spanish *la reata*, "the rope, lasso"

the rings on a saddle through which the straps pass are **larigos**

the adjective form for gull is **larine**

lark "play about" is from Old English *lacan*, "to play"

the secretion from eucalyptus is **larp**

larva, from Latin, literally means "mask" (as well as "evil spirit") as this stage of an insect's life is hidden or masked

larynx is pronounced LAIR-inks

lasagna goes back to Latin *lasanum*, "cooking pot" and Greek *lasana*, "trivet" which became vulgar Latin *lasania*, "cooking pot"

lascivious means "inclined to lust"

laser is an acronym for Light Amplification by Stimulated Emission of Radiation

lash is the flexible part of a whip

a **lasque** is a flat piece of diamond

lassate means tired or weary

lassitude is mental weariness

lasso is from Spanish *lazo*, "knot, bow;" **lasso** from Latin *laqueus*, "noose, bond"

last once had the meaning "utmost, highest, greatest"

latch once was a loop or noose; a **latch** of links was a string of sausages

the leather strap on a shoe or sandal that fastens is a **latchet**

it is only correct to use the term "the **late**" for someone who has died within the past twenty years—and its use began with medieval rulers to distinguish living rulers from dead ones of the same name

late comes from Indo-European *lad-*, "slow, weary" which begat Latin *lassus*, "tired" before English **late** "slow"

some animals are **latebricole**, living in holes

{ **latent** means "hidden, concealed" and its opposite is **patent** }

latescent means "becoming obscure or hidden away"

latex is Latin for "fluid, liquid"

a **lath** (plural laths) is a narrow thin strip of wood or metal nailed into rows to be a backing for plaster, shingles, slates, or tiles

lathe may come from Danish for "saw bench"

lather first meant "washing soda"

you can call a hiding place a **latibule**

latitude comes from Latin *latus*, "broad"

latitudes are also called **parallels**; **longitudes** are also called **meridians**

latke is Yiddish, from Russian *latka*, "pastry," and it first appeared in English in 1927

if a dog is **latrant**, it is barking or snarling; to **latrate** is to bark like a dog

a **latrine** is a toilet for many at a camp

latter first meant "slower"

lattice is literally "a structure made of laths"

a **laud** is a hymn of praise

laud is the first of the daytime canonical hours

laudable means deserving praise; **laudatory** means expressing praise

laugh is ultimately onomatopoeic

launch first meant "to pierce, slit"

a **laund** is an open space in the woods, like a glade or pasture

launder was first used as a noun for a "person who washes linen," and is a contraction of lavender, based on Latin *lavare*, "to wash"

laundry comes from Latin *lavare*, "wash"—as does **lavatory**, which first meant "place or vessel for washing"

laureate can mean "crowned with laurel"

the miragelike shimmering above a paved road under hot sun is a **laurence**

lava is an Italian word first used to describe the matter coming from Mount Vesuvius but before that described a stream created by a sudden rain

lava is the molten rock from a volcano; it is called **magma** before it comes out

a mistress of Louis XIV, the Duchess de La Vallière popularized necklaces with a pendant ornament, spelled **lavaliere**, lavalier, or lavalliere

lavender got its name from the custom of adding it to the laundry and baths (Latin *lavare*, "to wash"); **lavender** once meant "laundress"

lavish traces back to French *lavache*, "deluge of rain"

law comes from an Old Norse word meaning "something laid down or fixed"

lawn comes from *laund*, "a glade or pasture"

lax (the noun) is a descriptive word for "diarrhea"

laxative can mean "having the power of relaxing" (from Latin *laxare*, "loosen")

lay as in layperson derives from Greek *laikos*, "of the people"—as opposed to clerics

to **lay** is to place something; to **lie** is to recline

a **layette** is a set of clothing, accessories, and equipment for a new baby

a cattle brand letter tipped on its side was called **lazy** and a line under a letter was a **bar**; a curved letter was called **running**—these became part of the names of ranches

lb originates with the Latin phrase *libra pondo*, "a unit of measurement by weight"—which was shortened to *pondo* and later changed to pound, but the abbreviation **lb** stuck

to **leach** is to drain through something

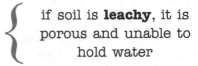
if soil is **leachy**, it is porous and unable to hold water

the first sentence or paragraph of an article (in a periodical) is the **lead**

the lines of dots in a table of contents or index (**leading**) between words and a page number or other information are called **leaders**

a **leaf**, in the description of wine, is a season or a year

a **leaf** is the term for a piece of paper with two sides; a **page** is one side of a piece of paper

other words for foliage are **leafage** and **leafery**

a **leak** was first a hole or a crack in a ship through which something either entered or escaped

Germanic *khlaupan* is the source of **leap**

the root sense of **learn** is "to track down"—from the Indo-European root *leis*, "trail, spoor, track down"

the etymology behind **lease** is "letting go," from Latin *laxus*, "loose"

in origin, **least** is the superlative form of less

the Indo-European ancestor of **leather** was *letrom*

one meaning of **leave** is "approval, pleasure"

leaven comes from Latin *levamen*, "means of raising" as **leaven**/leavening is an agent producing fermentation, like yeast which makes dough rise

etymologically, a **lecher** is a "licker"

a **lect** is a regional or social variety within a language, a form of speech defined by a homogenous set of rules

lectern comes from Latin *legere*, "to read" as it is a stand which holds a book or notes

a **lectern** is the stand on which the speaker's notes are placed, the **podium** is the platform on which the speaker and **lectern** stand, a platform for several people is a **dais**, and a **rostrum** is a platform for one or more

lecture first meant "the act of reading"

lederhosen, German for "leather pants," is pronounced LAY-dur-hose-un

a **ledger** originally was a large bible

a label or memo slip projecting from a book's pages is called a **ledgit**

lee also means "protection" or "shelter"

leech used to mean "cure, heal" as a verb and "healer, physician" as a noun

the edge of a sail is the **leech**

{ the finger next to the little finger is the **leech-finger** }

leek is from German and forms the second syllable of garlic

leer as an adjective means "empty" or "without a burden or load"

leeway started out as the lateral drift of a ship to leeward of the desired course

left originally meant "weak" and the **left** side of the body was regarded as the weaker side

left-handed had a meaning of "unlucky" or "unseasonable"

before **leftovers** were called **leftovers**, they were called relics and, before that, **relief**

streaks in a wine glass after swirling are called **legs**

legacy originally meant "the office, function, or commission of a legate" (an official representative)

legal, **legislate**, and **legitimate** come from Latin *leg/lex*, "law"; a **legist** is a person knowledgeable of the law

legend comes from Latin *legenda*, from *legere*, "to read"; the original legenda contained miraculous stories about the lives of saints

legerdemain is "slight of hand, conjuring tricks" from French, literally "light of hand"

legislator is from Latin *legis lator*, literally "the proposer of a law"

if someone is too drunk to stand, you can call them "**legless**"

Lego is from Danish "leg godt" meaning "play well," from *lege*, "to play"

leg-of-mutton sleeves means that they resemble a leg of mutton, very full and loose on the arm but close-fitting at the wrist

legume comes from Latin *legere*, "gather"— so called because the fruit may be gathered by hand

a **Lehrjahre** is a year of apprenticeship or learning

leisure is based on Latin *licere*, "be allowed"

a **leitmotif** (also leitmotiv) is a melodic phrase that accompanies the reappearance of a person or situation (from German, literally, "leading motive")

lekvar is prune jam

leman is an old word for "sweetheart, lover"

the form of a word or phrase chosen to represent all inflectional and spelling variants in a dictionary entry is the **lemma**; **lemma** has plurals lemmas and lemmata

an unthinking person can be called a **lemming**—with the literal meaning, the rodent, being the model due to its periodic mass migrations

the sign for infinity is called a **lemniscate**

lemon and **lime** likely get their names from the same source, Arabic *limah/laimun*, "citrus fruit" (or Persian *limun*)—with **lemon** reaching English via French "limon" and **lime** coming through Spanish, Provençal, and then French "**lime**"

lemur originally meant "ghost, the spirits of the dead"

lend (a verb) and **loan** (a noun or verb) come from the same source in Old English, *loenan*

length developed from Germanic *langitho*, from *langgaz* and the suffix *-itho*

to **lenify** is to alleviate or soothe an emotion or suffering (from Latin *lenire*, "soften"); **lenity** means kindness or gentleness

to be **lennow** is to be flabby

{ **lens** is from Latin for "lentil" because of the similarity in shape }

a slow fever or fire can be described as "**lent**"

The season of **Lent** was fixed at 40 days during the ninth century (with Sundays omitted). **Lent** comes from an Anglo-Saxon word meaning "spring" or "lengthening days." It is a period of preparation for Easter and a time to strengthen one's faith through repentance and prayer.

lenten-faced is an adjective for a dejected, emaciated, or mournful-looking person who has recently undergone the trials of fasting

lenticular, literally "shaped like a lentil," means something is double convex in shape

lentitude is slowness or lethargy

leopard got its name mistakenly as it was once believed to be a cross between a (Greek) *leon*, "lion" and *pardos*, "pard, white panther"

leopards are in Africa and Asia; jaguars are in Central and South America

Jules **Leotard** (1842-1870), the first flying trapeze artist, designed the body stocking that bears his name

the adjective form for rabbit is **leporine**

In Irish folklore, a **leprechaun** was a tiny sprite or fairy who carried a purse containing a shilling. The word is derived from Old Irish *luchorp·n*, "wee ones," from *lu*, "small" and *corp*, "body." Over the years, the word *luchorp·n* was confused with an Irish word meaning "one shoemaker" so the **leprechaun** started being depicted as a solitary creature working on a single shoe instead of a pair.

etymologically, a person suffering from **leprosy** has "scaly" skin (Greek *lepos/lepis*, "scale")

lesbian is based on the alleged homosexuality of Sappho, poetess of Lesbos, an island in the northern Aegean Sea; Aldous Huxley first used **lesbian** as a noun (1925)

Lesotho was formerly Basutoland

in origin, **less** is a comparative form, going back to Indo-European *loiso-*, "small"

generally, **less** applies to quantity while **fewer** applies to number; the traditional rule says that you should use **fewer** for things that can be counted (**fewer** than four players) but **less** with mass terms for things of measurable extent (**less** paper, **less** than a gallon of paint)

lesson, etymologically, is "something read," from Latin *lectio*, "reading" from *legere*, "read"—so **lesson** is literally the action of reading to oneself

stealing cookies from the cookie jar is the classic act of **lestobiosis** (pilfering food)

the underlying etymological meaning of **let** is "**let** go of something because one is too tired to hold on to it"

the early meaning of **lethal** was "causing spiritual death" and it was influenced by Greek *lethe*, "forgetfulness"—which is related to **lethargy** (Greek *lethargos*, "forgetful")

if someone or something is **lethe**, they are flexible and supple

if you cannot recall the precise word for something, you have a case of **letholog-ica** which may lead you to an obsession with trying to recall it—**loganamnosis**

lethonomia is the inability to recall the right name

letter is from Latin *littera*, "alphabetic symbol" or, in the plural, "document"

a **letteret** is a little or short letter

lettuce comes from Latin *lactuca*, "milk" because of the white liquid that oozes from broken stalks

leukemia is from Greek *leukos*, "white" and *emia* (from *haima*) "blood"

levant is French for "point where the sun rises"

as opposed to clergy—so it also came to mean "base, coarse, vulgar"

the headwords in a dictionary are all lexemes as a **lexeme** is a unit of lexical meaning which exists regardless of any inflectional endings it may have

lexicalization is the treatment of a formerly freely composed, grammatically regular, and semantically transparent phrase or inflected form as a formally or semantically idiomatic expression; to **lexicalize** is to form a single word from existing words in order to express something previously conveyed by several words or a phrase, for example front-runner was lexicalized from "runner at the front of the race"

leviathan is Hebrew for a sea monster which can only be subdued by God, so it came to mean a very large or powerful thing

levee is the action of rising from one's bed

levee, an embankment to prevent the overflow of a river, is from French *lever*, "to raise"

level is based on Latin *libella*, diminutive of *libra*, "balance; scales"

lever is literally "raise" in French

an archaic word for a flash of lightning or any bright light or flash is **levin**

levitate is patterned on gravitate

levity originally was thought to be a physical force exactly like gravity but pulling in the opposite direction

levy can mean "set up a fence" or "erect a house"

lewd comes from Anglo-Saxon *loewede*, "unlearned" and originally meant laypeople

a **lexicographer** is a writer or compiler of dictionaries; Samuel Johnson's famous definition was "a writer of dictionaries; a harmless drudge, that busies himself in tracing the original, and detailing the signification of words"

lexicography is the art of defining words or compiling lexicons

lexicology, the study of the structure of the vocabulary, was coined in 1828 by Noah Webster

a **lexicomane** is a dictionary lover

a dictionary and wordbook collector is a **lexiconophilist**

lexigraphy is a system of writing in which each character represents a word

if you like to use pretentious terms, you are **lexiphanic**; showing off your knowledge of words is **lexiphanicism** the **lexis** or **lexicon** is the total word-stock of a language

English has new verbs, like to **liaise** and to **diagnose**, based on nouns, like liaison and diagnosis; this is called back-formation

liaison first arose in English as a culinary term for a type of thickening or binding agent for sauces; **liaison** should be pronounced LEE-uh-zahn or LEE-ay-zahn

libation, any alcoholic beverage, comes from Liber, Roman god of fertility, who was worshipped by people spilling wine on the ground of his temple

libberwort is food or drink that makes one idle and stupid, food of no nutritional value, i.e., junk food

libel (from Latin libellus "little book") must be published, while spoken defamatory remarks are **slander**; **libel** first meant "document, written statement"

the early uses of **liberation** were administrative and legal, as in the discharge of a debt or exemption from military service

libertine first meant freedman or son of a freedman

a **libidinist** is one who is given to lewdness

Sigmund Freud defined **libido** as the psychic or instinctual energy associated with sexual drive

Library comes from Latin *libraria*, "bookshop," and *librarius*, "relating to books," from *liber*, "book." Chaucer was the first recorded user of the word **library** in English (c 1374) as a place set aside to hold books for reading, reference, and study. A Latinized Greek word, bibliotheca, is the origin of the word for **library** in German, Russian, and the Romance languages. Archaeologists have found a temple in the Babylonian town of Nippur, dating from the first half of the third millennium BC, in which a number of rooms were filled with clay tablets, suggesting a well-stocked

archive or **library**. **Library** should be pronounced LIE-brair-ee.

a person who reads in bed is a **librocubicularist**

licentious first meant "disregarding commonly accepted rules and correctness, especially in grammar or literary style"

lich is an old word for a living body or the torso

lichen, composed of a fungus and an alga in symbiotic association, is pronounced LIY-kun

{ **licit** means "not forbidden by law; allowable"—the opposite of illicit }

lickerish means "fond of delicious food" or "eager to eat" as well as "pleasant to the palate"

licorice comes from Greek words meaning "sweet root"

the top crust of a pie is the **lid**

Liebfraumilch or "milk of Our Lady" is a grape/wine that originated in the vineyards of a church by the name Our Lady

a **lief** is a beloved person or sweetheart

a **lienee** is an encumbered debtor

lieu "instead" is from Middle English via French from Latin *locus*, "place"

lieutenant comes from French *lieu*, "place," and *tenant*, "holding"—a commissioned officer who represents a higher official

the action of cutting a pack of cards used to be called the **lift**

ligaments hold bones together while **tendons** attach muscles to bones

two letters joined together like *ae* is a **ligature**; printed separately it is called a **digraph**

a **liger** is the offspring of a male lion and female tiger a **light** is a pane of glass forming the roof or side of a greenhouse or the top of a cold frame

in a crossword puzzle, a blank space to be filled in with a letter is a **light**

lighted and **lit** are equally correct as both past tense and past participial forms, though **lighted** is more usual and preferred as an adjective

lightening is a drop in the level of the womb during the last weeks of pregnancy as the head of the fetus engages in the pelvis

etymologically, **lightning** is simply something that illuminates or "lightens" the sky, a contraction of the earlier "lightening"

lightsome can mean "not weighed down by cares"

light-time is the time required for light to travel from a distant object to Earth

Jonathan Swift's *Gulliver's Travels* gave us the tiny people of Lilliput and, thereby, the word **lilliputian**

lilt comes from a word meaning "pipe" and the noun originally meant "song, tune"

lily probably originated in a pre-Indo-European language of the Mediterranean seaboard and it came to Latin as lilium

limaceous means sluglike or pertaining to slugs

either half of an archery bow is the "**limb**"

limbate means "having a border"—especially of a different color

to **limbeck** is to wear yourself out in an effort to come up with a new idea

limbo is from the Latin word *limbus*, "the edge"

the West Indian dance called the **limbo** is based on the adjective "limber"

limah, "citrus fruit" in Arabic gives us **lime**

 a spotlight was first created using a stream of oxygen and one of hydrogen burned on a ball of lime; hence, **limelight**

like comes from Germanic *likam*, "appearance, body, form"; the verb came from *likojam* which, as **like**, originally meant "please"

use "**like**" when no verb follows; use "**as**" when a clause follows (which has a subject and a verb)

when used as an adverb, **likely** needs a helping word: very, quite, most, or more

use **likely** if you mean "probable, expected"; use **liable** if you mean "bound by law or obligation"

the **lilac** shrub, cultivated for its fragrant blossoms, came into English in 1625, borrowed from French but traced back to Persian *nilak* and *nil*, "blue, indigo"; **lilac** also describes a pale pinkish-purple color

the **limerick** is named for a town in Ireland

sailors ate citrus fruits for their vitamin C to avoid scurvy, including limes, so they came to be called **limeys**

Latin *limes* originally denoted a "path between fields" but came to mean any "boundary" and it became **limit** in English

limit marks an end to something; **limitation** is the extent of one's capacity or a constraint that stops something

limited is now a stylish name for a fast train but it was first applied to railway trains that consisted of a **limited** number of cars and had **limited** seating

to **limn** is to capture through an artistic medium, either in drawing or in words

limoncello is an Italian lemon liqueur

limous means "muddy, slimy"

limousine is based on a French word for a caped cloak worn in the former French province of Limousin—and the early version of this car had a protective roof over the driver's seat

limp originally meant "fall short of" and then came to be applied to walking with an impairment

a style of writing, painting, architecture, or music is **limpid** if it is simple and clear

linage (pronounced LYE-nij) refers to the number of lines of printed material, as in a newspaper; **lineage** (pronounced LIN-ee-ij) refers to ancestry, derivation, or line of descent

linden is another name for a lime tree

line is the fiber of a flax plant

linen was originally an adjective meaning "made of flax" and **line** as in "cover the inside of something" is from the obsolete **line** meaning "flax"

a ferret on a leash (especially for rabbiting) is a **liner**

ling is an old word meaning "delay, lengthen, prolong"—and it is the base of **linger**

lingerie entered English meaning "linen articles collectively" (from French *linge*, "linen")

lingible is "meant to be licked"—as a lollipop

lingo traces back to Latin *lingua*, "tongue"

if someone is **linguacious**, they are talkative

linguini means "little tongues"; pastas named for everyday things is an Italian tradition—**spaghetti** is "strings," **farfale** is "butterfly," and **vermicelli** is "little worms"

a **linguipotence** is a mastery of languages

linguished means "skilled in languages"

linguister is a synonym for **linguist**

link goes back to Germanic *khlangkjaz*, "bending"

links became the name for a golf course because many Scottish golf courses were originally built along the seashore on *hlincs*, "slopes or ridges of land, gently undulating ground"

linoleum is actually canvas backing thickly coated with linseed (flax) oil (oleum) and powdered cork

lint derives from an Old French word for flax and first meant "flax prepared for spinning"

lintel (horizontal support across the top of a door or window) is a blend of two Latin words—*limes*, "boundary" and *limen*, "threshold"

liny is "marked with lines" and it has the comparative and superlative forms linier and liniest

the source of **lion** is Greek leon

lionize first meant "to visit the **lions** (things of note, celebrity, or curiosity, sights worth seeing) of a place"

each of the edges of a wound is a **lip**

lip comes from Latin *labrum*, "lip"

lip-clap is kissing

lipper is a rippling of the sea

after New Year's Eve, you may have **lippitude**, a soreness or bleariness of the eyes

liquefy is often misspelled (liquify)

liqueur is essentially the same word as **liquor** (from Latin), though the words have different meanings—**liqueur** is a strong highly flavored, often sweetened, alcoholic drink while **liquor** is an alcoholic beverage made by distillation rather than fermentation (which would be beer, wine)

liquid is a substance that flows and takes on the form of its container; a **fluid**—substance with no fixed shape and yields easily to external pressure—can be a **liquid** but it can also be a gas

an oyster's natural juices are referred to as its "**liquor**"

liquor comes from Latin *liquere*, "to be fluid" and it first meant any liquid or fluid and has an additional meaning as the broth derived by cooking meats or vegetables for a long time

a **liripipe** is something to be learned and acted or spoken

snapping the fingers is a **lirp** or **thrip**

liss is "abatement, remission" or "tranquility"

a stripe of color is a **list**

list as in "catalog" comes from French *liste*, "band, border" or "strip of paper, catalog," from Proto-Germanic *liston*; the sense of "enumeration" is from strips of paper used as a sort of catalog

{ **listen** is from the Indo-European base *klu-*, "hearing" }

to **listen** is to try to **hear**; to **hear** is simply to perceive with the ear

listless is based on the obsolete sense of list "appetite, desire, craving" and literally means "without desire"

a **litany** is a series of prayers; a **liturgy** is the canon of a religious service

a **litch** is a mass of tangled, matted hair

liter goes back to Greek *litra*, a Sicilian monetary unit

literally means "actually" or "to the letter"

a painting or sculpture that depicts a story can be described as "**literary**"

literature first meant "acquaintance with books" or "literary culture"; **literature** should be pronounced LIT-uhr-uh-chuur

lithification is the process of compaction of sediment into stone

lithography is etymologically "stone writing," from the fact that the original printing surfaces in this process were made of stone, but the word's first meanings were "a description of rocks or stones" and "the art of engraving on precious stones"

the **lithosphere** is the rigid outer portion of the earth, including the crust and the outermost mantle; the other two zones are the hydrosphere and atmosphere

litmus is probably so called for *lit*, "to color, dye" and *mosi*, "moss, lichen"—as this pigment is obtained from lichens

litotes is from Greek *litos*, "simple, single" and refers to an ironical understatement (e.g. no small amount) or two negatives used to make a positive (e.g. it was not unsuccessful); it is pronounced lie-TOH-teez, LEYED-uh-teez, LID-uh-teez, or leye-TOHD-eez

litter for animals started out as "material used as bedding" for them, evolving into "material used to absorb the urine and feces" of animals

littlemeal means little by little

littoral is "pertaining to the shore," from Latin *litus/littus*, "shore"

liturgy comes from Greek words *leitos*, "public" and *ergos*, "working" and it first meant "public service" or "service of the gods, public worship"

live (adjective) is a shortening of alive

livelihood is made up of Old English *lif*, "life" and *lad*, "course"

livelong "whole, entire" is etymologically "as long as you want it to be"

figuratively, the **liver** has been called the "seat of love" or other passionate emotions such as anger; **liver** is from Old English *lifer*, from Proto-Germanic *librn*, "fatten up" if someone is **liverish**, they are bad-tempered or peevish

a company's distinctive color scheme or emblem on vehicles is called the **livery**; **livery** first referred to the dispensing of clothes, food, or provisions to servants

liveware is working personnel, as opposed to abstract or inanimate things they work with

livid literally means "bluish, black-and-blue, ashen" and its figurative meaning of "furiously angry" is based on the liver's being considered the seat of passionate emotions

the base meaning of the word **lizard** is "muscle"

lizards are reptiles; **salamanders** are amphibians

the **llama** is a smaller humpless member of the camel family and the **alpaca** is a domesticated **llama** with long silky wool; there is also the **guanaco**, a wild **llama** with reddish-brown wool and the small **vicuna**, with soft shaggy wool

{ **load** originally meant "course, way" and "carriage, conveyance" }

a head on a cabbage is called **loaf**

loafer (the shoe) was once a trademarked term

the word **loam** descends from Latin *limus*, "mud"

a first use of **loan** was "a gift from a superior"

a **loanshift** is a change or extension of the meaning of a word through the influence of a foreign word, as in the application in English of the meaning "profession" to the word calling through the influence of Latin *vocatio*

loanwords and borrowings are words assimilated from one language into another, such as chic and restaurant, borrowed from French

loath is an adjective meaning "unwilling, reluctant, disinclined"; whereas **loathe** is a verb meaning "to dislike intensely, to feel revulsion toward, to despise"

lob comes from an old noun meaning "lout" or "pendulous object"

an early meaning of **lobby** was "monastic cloister" (from Latin *lobia*, "covered way") before it came to mean the passage or waiting area between rooms in a building

lobbying comes from the fact that those with special interests at legislative chambers were often asked to stay in the lobby

lobe (as in ear) is from Greek *lobos*, "something round"

lobster comes from Old English *loppestre*, "spider" because there is some resemblance

local and **locate** come from Latin *localis*, and *locus*, "place"

a **location** is a place, a **locality** is an area within a place, and a **locale** is a place regarded as an environment

when sleep overpowers you completely, it **locks** you up

lockage is the amount of rise and fall effected by canal locks—also, the construction or use of locks

locket comes from French *loquet*, "latch"

lockjaw was originally "locked jaw"

the **lockset** is the entire set of hardware involved in shutting or locking a door

to **loco** someone is to make them crazy

locomotive comes from Latin *in loco moveri*, "to move by change of position in space"

locution is speech as the expression of thought; to say, "an economy of truth," is an artful **locution**

lode originally was a course or way, specifically ditch that guided or led water into a river or sewer

loden first described a thick woolen cloth, then a dark green color

a **lodge** first was a temporary dwelling, as a hut or tent

loess, loam which is composed of matter transported by wind, is from German *losz*, "loosen"

loft comes from Old Norse *lopt*, "sky, upper room" and first meant "attic" or "air, sky"

log, as in "record," has a nautical origin from the apparatus used to determine the rate of a ship's motion, a piece of wood that floated upright in the water and fastened to a line wound on a reel—which became **log**-book, the journal into which the contents of the **log**-board or **log**-slate were daily transcribed

the **loganberry** is named for a U.S. horticulturist (J.H. Logan, 1841–1928)

logarithm is from Greek *logos*, "reckoning, ratio" and *arithmos*, "number"

a **loge** is a booth or stall, also a box in a theatre

loggerhead, first meaning "a stupid, thick-headed person" is based on logger being a word invented as expressing by its sound the notion of something heavy and clumsy; to be **at loggerheads** means "to be contending about differences of opinion"

logic comes from Greek *logos*, "discourse" or "reasoning"; **logistic** means "pertaining to reasoning" or "logical"

a **logion** is a traditional saying or proverb of a sage

you can call an expert accountant a **"logist"**

logo is an abbreviation or logogram or logotype

logodaedaly is the ingenious or cunning use of words (-*daedaly* referring to Daedalus, the designer of the Labyrinth for the Minotaur of Crete) and a **logodaedalist** is a person skilled in the use of words

logofascinated means "fascinated by words"

a word expert is a **logogogue**

a **logogram** or **logograph** is the same as a **grammalogue** (a word represented by a single sign), like $

logolatry is excessive admiration for words

{ **logology** is the pursuit of word puzzles; also the science of words }

logomachy is a dispute over or about words

a **logophile** is a lover of words

the **loins** (from Latin *lumbus*, "loin") are the parts of a human being or quadruped situated on both sides of the vertebral column between the false ribs and the hip bone

loiter may come from Middle Dutch *loteren*, "wag about"

a child that cries or screams all the time is a **lolaby**

to **loll** your tongue is to stick it out in a pendulous manner

a **lollapalooza** (also lallapaloosa) is something outstandingly good of its kind

lollipop is made up of lolly "tongue" and "pop" for popping it in and out of your mouth

to **lollop** is "to lounge or sprawl," but also "to bob up and down"

the tongue is also called the **lolly**

lollygag once meant "to kiss or to spoon"

loma is a hill with a broad top

a **loneling** is a single child, as opposed to a twin

lonely adds to solitary a suggestion of longing for companionship, while **lonesome** heightens the suggestion of sadness; **forlorn** and **desolate** are even more isolated and sad

the ability to suffer patiently or silently over a period of time is **longanimity** (endurance in the face of hardship; tolerance of mental or physical pain), but it usually implies that this is done while considering revenge

the long rein used to lead or guide a horse is a **longe** or **lunge**

longevity is from Latin *longus*, "long," and *aevum*, "age," literally "long life"

longinquity is long distance or remoteness

long-standing has a hyphen; **longtime** does not

boring periods of time or parts of a book, play, music, or movie are **longueurs**

when the sea has waves that are short and lumpy, this state is called "**lop**" (hence, "loppy" when it is choppy and lumpy)

loquacious, from Latin *loqu-*, "to speak," means talkative, chattering

lorate means shaped like a strap

lord and **lady** descend from Old English— from *hlafweard*, "bread-keeper" or "guardian of the bread or loaf," and *hlaefdige*, "loaf-kneader" or "bread-maker"

lore is a word for the space between a bird's eye and its bill

lore originally meant "the act of teaching" or a "piece of instruction, lesson"

when sailors passed goods from the ships to men along the shore—those men came to be called **longshoremen**

loo is probably a fanciful form of French *l'eau*, "the water"

the inside of a cat's paw or the palm of a hand is a **loof**

a **loofah** is not a sponge but a dried tropical fruit used as a sponge

lookism is prejudice or discrimination based on the grounds of appearance

loon's Old Norse root meant "creature (bird) that cries out"

loophole was first found in architecture as narrow vertical openings or windows in castles and fortresses— from Dutch *lupen*, "to lie in wait; peer"

the **loose** is a noun meaning "the close or conclusion of a matter"

loot comes from Hindu *lut*, from Sanskrit *loptra*, "booty, spoils"

the smaller branches and twigs of a tree is the **lop**

a **lorgnette**, an opera-glass or magnifier/glasses on a handle, is from the French word *lorgner*, "to squint"

loricate refers to being covered with scales, bony plates, or armor

a **lorimer** is a saddle-maker

lorn means "lost, perished" or "abandoned, desolate"

a **losel** is a worthless person

lotion is from Latin *lotion-em*, "washing"

if someone is **louche**, they are of questionable character (from French *louche*, "cross-eyed")

the underlying meaning of **loud** is "audible, heard"

a leisurely walk or stroll is a **lounge**

a half-mask, like Zorro's and Batman's, is a **loup**

a jeweler's magnifier is a **loupe**

lour (or **lower**) is a word for gloominess of the sky or weather—and also for a frown or scowl

to **lout** is to treat with contempt

louvre comes from French *lovier*, "skylight" and was first a domed turret-like part of a roof for smoke to leave or light to come in

love in tennis comes from *l'oeuf*, "egg" as a zero looks like an egg; we sometimes call zero a "goose egg"

love is from Old English *lufu*, connected with Sanskrit *lubh*, "to desire" and Latin *lubere*, "to please"

lowlights are dark streaks put into lighter hair—the opposite of **highlights**

lox, smoked salmon, comes from Yiddish *laks*, "salmon"

loyal comes from Latin *legalis*, "legal" (from *leg-*, *lex*, "law"), by way of Old French *loial*, *leial*, meaning "faithful, **loyal**"; the meaning "faithful" referred originally to allegiance to a country's law

the base of **lozenge** is a word that means "slab"

the amino acid **L-tryptophan** found on turkey skin is a natural sedative, which some blame for sleepiness after eating turkey

luau means "party, feast" in Hawaiian

lubber first referred to a clumsy, stupid fellow or a lout—before it took on a nautical meaning

{ **lubberwort** is food of little or no nutritional value, i.e., junk food }

lubricious means slippery (literally or figuratively)

lubricity is lewdness or wantonness

lucid, referring to temporary sanity or calm, comes from Latin *lucere*, "be evident" or

"shine," as does **lucent**, which can mean "luminous, shining" or "clear, transparent"

fireflie's light is from **luciferin**

a synonym for nocturnal (shunning the light) is **lucifugous**

luck was probably first a gambling term

lucre is from Latin *lucrum*, "monetary gain"

lucubration is working at night, especially by lamplight; a **lucubrator** is someone who studies at night

early senses of **ludicrous**, from the adjective *ludic*, were "sportive" and "intended as jest" and "spontaneously playful"

lugubrious means "mournful, sorrowful"

payment of ransom is **luition**

luke means "mild, warm"—an old word for **lukewarm** (making **lukewarm** somewhat redundant)

lull first referred to a soothing drink

lullaby derives from "lull" and "bye-bye" and is related to hushaby and rock-a-bye

lumbar comes from Latin *lumbus*, "loin"—the region which includes the small of the back

superfluous fat in horses is called **lumber**

what Americans call **lumber**, Britons call **timber**; **timbre** refers to the quality of sound

a well-lit room is **luminous**

to **lump** is to look sulky or disagreeable

lumpen means "ignorantly contented"

lumpens pertains to an amorphous group of dispossessed and uprooted people

luna is the personification of the moon

lunacy is insanity, once believed to be brought on by changes in the moon

lunar can be a synonym for menstrual

lunatic can mean "influenced by the moon"

lunch comes from Scottish *lonch*, a "hunk of meat" and it first meant "hunk, thick piece," a large piece of anything, especially edible like bread or cheese

luncheon is an extension of the word lunch, based on *nuncheon*, "a drink taken at noon"

lung goes back to an Indo-European root for "light," because of the lightness of these organs

lunge is from French *allonger*, "to lengthen"

{ a tall, lazy man who is slow about everything is a **lungis** }

a puff of smoke from a pipe (i.e., without flame) is a **lunt**

the **lupine** flower comes from Latin *lupus*, "wolf" and it is so named because of the way it thrives in poor soil

lurch comes from the game of cribbage—a term for winning a double game; hence, the opponent is so far behind that he/she has been left in the **lurch**

lurdane means dull and lazy

lure is from Germanic, probably *Luder*, "bait"

lurid originally meant "wan or yellow color"

something said by rote or a set speech is a **lurry**

luscious may be an alteration of obsolete *licious*, a shortened form of delicious

luscition means poor eyesight

to **lush** is to ply with or drink alcohol

you can use the slang term **lushington** for a drunkard

lusk means lazy or sluggish

lusory is "used as a pastime" or "playful"

lust first meant "delight" or "pleasure"

a glass pendant on a chandelier is called a **luster**

a **lustrum** is a period of five years

an airtight rubber seal for a jar is a **lute**

a **luthern** is a dormer window

lutose means "covered with mud"

the adjective form for otter is **lutrine**

luxuriant indicates profusion while **luxurious** means sumptuous and expensive

luxury was once a word for "lechery, lasciviousness"

lycanthropy is a type of insanity in which the patient imagines himself a beast

a **lychnobite** is someone who works at night

lymph, from Latin *limpa* or *lumpa*, first meant "water"

lynch is from Captain William **Lynch** (1742–1820), head of a self-determined tribunal in Virginia (1780)

lynx probably gets its name from its keen sight (from roots meaning "bright" and "to see")

lyric first meant "of or pertaining to a lyre"; a **lyrist** plays the lyre

antibodies destroying bacteria is the process of **lysis**

Lysol's name is a combination of its main ingredients, lye and cresol

{ Like B and P, **M** is in the category of consonants called labials, from Latin for "lip." Labials are formed with no need of teeth or tricky tongue movement. }

in Irish and Scottish names, **Mac** or **Mc** actually mean "son," so McDonald is "son of Donald"

the source of **macabre** may be the Maccabees, followers of a Jewish revolt leader, who themselves were slaughtered

macadam, the road material, was named for Scottish surveyor J.C. McAdam (1756–1836)

the **macadamia** nut was named for Scottish-Australian chemist John Macadam (1827–1865)

macaque is based on Bantu *kaku*, "monkey," and *ma* (denoting a plural, translating to "some monkeys")

macarism is pleasure in another's happiness

macaroni as in "Yankee Doodle" was referring to the demeanor or appearance of a dandy or fop

macaroni, the pasta, came through Italian from Greek *makaria*, "food made from barley"

macaronic describes a jumble or medley

macchiato is Italian for "stained or marked (coffee)" because of its frothy steamed milk

mace is the red fleshy outer covering of the nutmeg, dried and used as a spice and its name is from Latin *macir*, "red spicy bark from India"

a **macedoine** is a dish of mixed fruit or vegetables in small pieces—or any medley—based on Macedonia, an empire with great diversity of people

macerate (to soften) comes from Greek *massein*, "knead"

philosopher/physicist Ernst **Mach** (1838–1916) researched thermodynamics and his name is used for the scale measuring the speed of an object or fluid relative to the speed of sound; **Mach** is the ratio of the speed of something to the speed of sound in the surrounding medium

a **macher** is a person who gets things done

a **machete** was a small four-string guitar of Portugal and Madeira that was the forerunner of the ukelele, probably introduced to Hawaii by Portuguese sailors

machinate derives from Latin meaning "to contrive," from Latin *machina*, "device"

a **machine** was originally a structure of any kind or the "fabric" of a thing, from Latin *machina*, and Greek *makhana*, "device" and *mekhos*, "contrivance"

machine was first applied to a political organization by Aaron Burr

machinofacture is the making of items by machine

macho is from Mexican Spanish (from Latin *masculus*, "male") "male animal or plant" or "masculine, vigorous"; **machismo** (pronounced mah-CHEEZ-mo) is based on **macho**

macilent means "lean, thin" or "shriveled," i.e., lacking in substance

Charles **Macintosh** (Scottish inventor, 1766–1843) discovered how to waterproof fabric with rubber and his name is used for such a raincoat

a **macronutrient** is one required in relatively large amounts by organisms—like carbohydrates, fats, and proteins

macrophobia is a fear of long waits

the adjective form for kangaroo is **macropodine**

macroscopic describes anything large enough to be seen with the naked eye

macrosmatic is "having a highly developed sense of smell" or a supersensitive nose

maculate is "marked with spots; besmirched"—the opposite of **immaculate**

a leopard's spot is a **maculation**

macushla or **acushla** is an affectionate form of address (Irish)

mad's first sense was "insane" before it came to mean "angry"

madam is French, literally, "my lady"

mack first appeared with the meaning "a pimp" or "to pimp"—from French *maquereau*; **mack** now has the sense of "flirtatious talk"

a blurred impression in printing is a **mackle**

macramé comes from Arabic *miqramah*, "embroidered coverlet, bedspread"

macrobiotic is a diet of organic whole foods, based on Buddhist principles of balance

macrocosm combines *macro*, "large, long" with Greek *kosmos*, "world," and means "a complex structure or whole; great world"; **microcosm** is a "small world"

a **macrograph** is a life-size drawing or representation

macrology is long and tiresome talk

the long mark over a vowel (–) is a **macron**; the short mark (˘) over a vowel is the **breve**

to **madefy** is to dampen, wet, or moisten

the cake called a **madeleine** is associated with the nineteenth-century French pastry chef **Madeleine** Paulmier

madrigal comes from a Latin phrase meaning "simple song," so it also is the name of a short lyrical love poem that can be set to music

maelstrom comes from Dutch *malen/maalen*, "whirl around, grind," and *stroom*, "stream," and was first a proper name for a mythical whirlpool thought to exist in the Arctic Ocean west of Norway

maestro (Italian "master") has the plurals maestri and maestros

to **maffle** is to stammer or stutter or mumble

mafia in Sicilian means "boldness, bluster, swagger" or "beauty, excellence, bravery"; **mafia** is the organization and **mafioso** is an individual member

a **magazine** is considered a "storehouse" for articles—and it comes from Arabic *makhzan*, "storehouse"; it was first used in book titles presenting a "store" of information about specific topics

mage and **magian** are two other ways to say magician

magenta is named for a town in Italy that was the site of a battle shortly before the dye was discovered

magic is named for the magi who were regarded as magicians

magirics or **magirology** (from Greek) is the art and science of cooking; a **magirist** or **magirologist** is an expert cook

magirocophobia is intense fear of having to cook

magistrate and **magisterial** come from Latin *magister*, "master"—and **magistral** means "a problem or point of instruction," especially handed down from the masters of a branch of knowledge

magnanimous is from Latin words meaning "great" (*magnus*) "soul" (*animus*) and it means generous and equanimous, the opposite of petty

magnate is from Latin *magnas*, "great man"

{ **magnet** was originally a name for lodestone (*magnes lithos*, Greek) }

magnific is the old word for "glorious, renowned"—now **magnificent**; **magnify** first meant "praise highly" or "glorify"

magnificence was first a term in ethics, meaning "liberality of expenditure combined with good taste"

magniloquence refers to a language that is lofty and extravagant, whereas **grandiloquence** refers to a language that is pompous or bombastic

in astronomy, stars are classed by **magnitude**, a measure of their brilliancy

magnitude first meant "greatness of character"

the **magnolia** was named for French botanist Pierre Magnol (1638–1715)

magnolious means "magnificent, large"

a **magnum** is a bottle that is twice the standard size *(2/5 gallon, 1.5 liters)*—and it is derived from Latin *magnus*, "large"

a person regarded as having great wisdom or powers likened to those of a magician is a **magus**

mahal, as in Taj **Mahal**, is Arabic for "abode" or "stopping place"

maharajah is from a Sanskrit word meaning "great king"

mahatma is Sanskrit *maha*, "great," and *atman*, "soul"

mahimahi and **dorado** are synonyms for a Hawaiian food fish

some say that Confucius, who was said to be fond of birds, developed **mah-jong**, Chinese for "sparrows" or "hemp bird"; **mah-jong** is now thought to be the model for the rummy family of card games

mahogany was once a word for dining table

maid is a twelfth-century abbreviation of maiden

a feathery fern is the **maidenhair**

maieutic is pertaining to coaxing someone's latent ideas to the forefront of the consciousness

a lobster shell is called the **mail**

mail, as in armor, was originally any of the metal rings composing this type of armor

mail, as in postal, is of Germanic origin from a word meaning "bag, satchel"—as part of the early phrase **mail** of letters "a parcel or package of dispatches"; **mail** bag is etymologically redundant

{ **maillot** first referred to tights, then to a one-piece swimsuit }

maim figuratively means "render powerless"; **mayhem** is a variant of **maim**

an archery contest is a **main**

main comes from a Germanic base meaning "have power"

Maine is named for a province of France

a **mainpast** is a person's household or a household servant

maintain first meant "practice habitually" or "observe a custom" and it comes from Latin *manus*, "hand," and *tenere*, "to hold" ('hold with the hand" or "holds one's own"); **maintenance** first referred to a means of support or sustenance

the British call our corn "**maize**" and it derived from Caribbean Indian *mahiz*, "giver of life"

majesty first referred to the "greatness of God"

major is from Latin **major**, "larger," the comparative form of *magnus*, "large"

major-domo derives from Latin for "highest official or elder of the household" or "mayor of the palace"

majority's first sense was "state of being superior"

a **majority** is more than half the votes while a **plurality** is simply getting more votes than the other person(s)

a **majuscule** is a capital letter; a **minuscule** is a lowercase one

make goes back to an Indo-European root meaning "kneading"

makeup as a cosmetic was first used in the sense of the action or process of making up with cosmetics for a performance

maki is sushi and raw vegetables wrapped in a seaweed square

malacology is the study of mollusks

malady comes from Latin *male*, "ill," and *habitus*, "having (a condition)"

malaise comes from French words translating to "bad, ill" and "ease"

malaprop and **malapropism** come from a character, Mrs. **Malaprop**, in a 1775 play "The Rivals"—who uses language inappropriately; the word **malapropos** is from French *mal à propos*, "ill to the purpose; inappropriate"

malaria is from Italian *mala aria*, "bad air," as it was once thought to be contracted from the "bad air" given off in marshy places

Malawi was formerly Nyasaland

malaxate means "knead to softness" or "make soft by mixing"

the words **male** and **female** are not linked etymologically though **female**'s ending was changed due to association with **male**

maledicent means addicted to abusive speech

malefactor is the opposite of benefactor

something that is **malefic** is productive of disaster or evil

malevolent means "desirous of evil to others," and is based on Latin *male*, "badly, ill," and *volent*, "will, wish"

while **malevolent** suggests deep and lasting dislike, **malicious** usually means petty and spiteful

malic means "having to do with apples"

malign is from Latin *malignus*, "wicked," and is related to words like defame, slander, and libel—implying that the person or group being maligned is the victim of false or misleading statements; something that is frequently criticized is said to be "much maligned" which suggests that the criticism is not entirely fair or deserved

the origin of **malinger** is French *malingre*, "sickly (person)"

a **malist** believes that the whole world is bad or evil

mall first meant a mallet used in a game, the game itself, and also the alley in which the game was played—giving rise to its meaning as a sheltered area

{ etymologically, **mallard** seems to mean "male bird" }

malleable is based on mall as in mallet (for hammering metal); **malleated** describes "having a hammered appearance"

the bony bump on either side of the ankle is the **malleolus**

the light padded hammer for playing the xylophone is a **mallet**

the middle ear has three tiny bones: the **malleus** (hammer), **incus** (anvil), and **stapes** (stirrup) pronounced STAY-peez

malmy pertains to weather that is warm and sticky

malnoia is a vague feeling of mental discomfort

malt is a grain that has been steeped, germinated, and dried

a beverage that is **malted** is made from grain softened in water and allowed to germinate

malversation is corruption or misconduct in public office or plain old bad behavior

mammal comes from Latin *mamma*, "breast," as these animals make milk for their young; **mammalogy** is the study of mammals

a **mammock** is a scrap, shred, or piece that is torn or broken off

mammoth is a Russian contribution to English—from *mammot*, "earth," because the animal was discovered in the frozen soil of Siberia

a **mammothrept** is a spoiled or overindulged child

any of the pieces in chess or backgammon can be called a "**man**"

man originally referred to adult human beings of both sexes

a **manacle** (handcuff shackle) comes from Latin *manus*, "hand"; the ankle counterpart is **fetter**

manage first meant "to handle or train a horse" and it is based on Latin *manus*, "hand"

manage was once a noun meaning "age at which one becomes a man"

mañana is Spanish for "early tomorrow" but in English we use it to mean "tomorrow"

the game **mancala** is from Arabic meaning "remove, take away"

mancipation is enslavement; **emancipation** is freedom from slavery (Latin *manus*, "hand," *capere*, "take")

the circular Buddhist or Hindu sand design is a **mandala**, Sanskrit for "circle"

mandarin is from Sanskrit *mantrin*, "counselor"

a **mandatary** is a person to whom a **mandate** (Latin *mandatum*, "something commanded") is given; a **mandator** gives the **mandate**

mandible is derived from Latin *mandere*, "to chew"

manducate means "to chew or eat"

maneuver, based on Latin *manus*, "hand," was originally work using the hands

manga ('aimless or involuntary picture') are Japanese comics with vibrant characters with oversized eyes, spiked hair, nubs for noses, and exaggerated expressions; **anime** ('animation") refers to TV or film animation in the **manga** style

mange is a figurative word for "restless desire"

manger is literally a "feeding place" —from French **manger,** "food"

hot gases around a flame is the **mangle**

mango has plurals mangoes and mangos

the root sense of **mangy** is "chewed up"

manhandle can mean "handle or wield a tool"

mania is based on a Greek word meaning "madness," ultimately from an Indo-European root for "mind"

manicotti is "little muffs" or "little sleeves" in Italian

manicure is from Latin *manus*, "hand," and *cura*, "care"

a list of aircraft passengers is the **manifest**

manifesto is from Latin *manifestus*, "evident, palpable, disclosed"

Latin *manus*, "hand" is the base of **manipulate**, **manner**, and **manual**

{ a **manitou** is a supernatural force that pervades the world }

manky means "bad, inferior, or worthless"

a **manling** is a little man or dwarf

manna is "something beneficial provided unexpectedly"

mannequin and manikin come from Dutch *mannekijn*, "little man"

etymologically, a **manner** is a method of "handling" something

manor is from Latin *muneir*, "dwell"

manqué means "falling short of expectations; frustrated"

manscape is a sea of faces

manse is a synonym for mansion, the principal house of an estate

mansion first meant the action of living or remaining in a place (French *manere*, "remain," Latin *mansio*, "staying"); **mansionary** is an adjective meaning "resident"

mansuetude is tameness or sweetness of temper

mantel is what is above a fireplace and **mantle** is a cloak (Latin *mantellum*, "cloak")—though **mantel** is a variant of **mantle**

mantelpiece is the shelf over a fireplace, also called manteltree or mantelshelf

mantic is a synonym for prophetic

a **manticore** has body of lion, head of man, tail of dragon or scorpion

a small cape or mantle is a **mantilla** (from Spanish)

a repeated word or phrase or sound in meditation is a **mantra**, and it is literally Sanskrit for "thought, instrument of thought"

manual labor can also be called **manuary**

leading someone by the hand is **manuduction**

manufacture first meant "made by hand" (Latin *manu factum*)—but once mechanization was introduced, it came to mean "machine-made"

manumit means "set free," Latin literally "send out from one's hand"

manurage is the cultivation or occupation of land

manure was originally a verb meaning "to hold or manage land or property; administer"

manuscript was originally an adjective meaning "written by hand"; **manuscript** can refer to a handwritten piece of music

manutention is detaining or restraining with one's hands

many used to have comparative manier and superlative maniest; now it is more and **most**

map comes from Latin *mappa mundi*, "sheet of the world" from *mappa*, "napkin, tablecloth"

a room in miniature or other small-scale model is a **maquette**

maquillage is French, literally "makeup"

the word **mar** traces back to Gothic *marzjan*, "cause to stumble"

marabou is made of African stork down and the word comes from Arabic meaning "holy man"—as the stork was regarded as holy

the marasca (from Italian *amaro*, "bitter") cherry is the base for **maraschino** liqueur and **maraschino** (pronounced mair-uh-SKEE-no) cherry; **amaretto** is a diminutive of this same word and literally means "little bitter"

marathon, from the town in Greece, gets its meaning from the distance a messenger ran, carrying news of a victory over the Persians in 499 BC

marble derives from Greek *marmaros*, "shining stone"

{ the game of **marbles** originally used balls made of marble }

marcel hair waves are named for a French hairdresser, **Marcel** Grateau (1852–1936)

if leaves wither but remain attached to the stem, they are **marcescent**

marcescible is tending or likely to wither or fade

one of the early meanings of **march** as a noun was "the footprints or tracks of an animal"

a **marchioness** (MAR-shuh-nus) is the wife of a **marquis** (MAR-kwus)

mardy means sulky and moody

a **mare** is any large flat area on the moon which may once have been a sea(s) (**mare** being Latin for "sea")

mare first meant "horse," then just "female horse"

margarine comes from Greek *margaron*, "pearl" because the chemist who identified the fatty acid noted its pearly appearance; **margarine** is short for oleomargarine and is made of margaric acid

Margarita, now a tequila cocktail, was first the name of a Spanish wine

margaritiferous means "producing or wearing pearls" and **margaritaceous** is "pearly"

to **marge** is to border, edge, be adjacent to

marginal came into use in the late sixteenth century and originally referred to anything "written or printed in the margin of a page, rather than indented" and then was extended to the fields of botany, zoology, and psychology to refer to anything relating to "a border, boundary, edge, or limit"

mariachi is Mexican Spanish for "street singer"

mariculture is the cultivation of fish or other marine life for food

marigenous means produced in or by the sea

the **marigold** is named for the Virgin Mary and for its distinctive color

marijuana is a blend of Maria Juana, which really is Mary Jane in Spanish—but this may be a folk etymology

a **marimba** is a deep-toned xylophone

a dock for small boats is a **marina**

marinade comes from Spanish *marinar*, "to pickle in brine"

marinara's origin is *marinus*, "marine" (Italian *alla* **marinara** "sailor-fashion") and refers to its being a sailor-style sauce—containing ingredients that would not spoil at sea and could be prepared with minimal use of fire

marine traces to Latin *mare*, "sea"

marital comes from Latin *maritalis*, "conjugal, nuptial," from *maritus*, "husband"

maritime is from Latin *mare*, "sea" and *timus*, "near, neighboring"

ruthless domination by a husband is- **maritodespotism**

sweet **marjoram** is an herb for cooking; wild **marjoram** is another term for oregano

a **mark** was originally a boundary, frontier, or limit

market is from Old Provençal *mercari*, "buy," and the word originally denoted a place where people met to trade goods (from Latin *mercatus*); **mart** is a variant

marm is a respelling of ma'am

marmalade comes from Portuguese *marmelada*, "quince jam," from Latin *melomeli*, "honey flavored with quinces," and *melimela*, "sweet apple"

marmoreal is "resembling marble" (cold, smooth, etc.)

French *marron*, "chestnut," came into English to denote this, but gradually came to be its color, a deep brownish-red—spelled **maroon**

maroon "lost in the wilds" is either based on the name of a people in Suriname and the West Indies who live in forests and mountains or comes from the Spanish word cimarrón, meaning "wild" or "untamed"

a **marplot** is a person who spoils a plot or who ruins the success of an undertaking or process

the canopy over an entrance to a building (apartment, club, theater) is a **marquee**

marquetry (French *marqueter*, "variegate") is decoration using wood inlays of different colors; **parquetry** is a form of **marquetry** which is mosaic work in wood

a **marquis** is literally a lord of the marchers or frontier territory

marquisette is mosquito netting fabric

a **marriage** can be either valid or void (in legal terms)

marrow can mean one of a pair or a facsimile

marry traces back to Latin *maritus*, "husband"

Mars was the Roman god of war—hence, **martial** and **martian**

a **marsh** is wetland where woody plants (trees, shrubs) do not grow but herbaceous vegetation thrives

marshal is from German words meaning "horse" and "servant" and the word's first sense was "a person who tends horses"

marsh mallow plants have a jellylike gum in their roots and it was used as an ingredient in medicines and candy; today **marshmallows** contain no marsh mallow

the **marsupial** (Greek *marsipos*, "purse, pouch") is so called because of its **marsupium**, an external abdominal pouch for its newborn

martian can mean of or pertaining to the month of March

the **martin**, a small bird, is named after St. **Martin**, saint of publicans and reformed alcoholics; the **marten** is a fur-bearing weasel-like animal

the word **martinet** is from seventeenth century French colonel Jean Marquis de **Martinet**, who was a stickler for strictness and discipline

martini was first a **Martini** and Rossi vermouth, then a name for the cocktail using the vermouth; there are three types of **martini**: dry, medium, and sweet

a **martyr** (Greek "witness") originally was a person voluntarily undergoing the death penalty for refusing to renounce Christianity

marvel traces to Latin *mirabilia*, from *mirari*, "wonder at"

Maryland, originally Marieland, is named for Henrietta Maria (1609–69), queen of Charles I of England

marzipan and **marchpane** are synonyms for a sweet paste used in confectionery

mascara comes from an Italian word for "mask"

mascot is from Provençal *masco*, "sorcerer, witch"—a person or thing that is supposed to bring good luck

masculine first referred to grammar, designating the gender to which the majority of words denoting male people and animals belong

{ **mash** was originally malt mixed with hot water, to make wort }

mash comes from a German word for crushed grapes and a **masher** was a person who does this to create wine

mask came through French (*masque*) from Italian *maschera/mascara*, perhaps from Latin *masca*, "evil spirit, witch"

to **masker** is to bewilder

maslin is rye mixed with wheat or other mixed grains (from Latin *miscere*, "mix")

masochism is named for Austrian novelist Leopold von Sacher-Masoch (1836–1895), whose works described the disorder

to **mason** is to build from or strengthen with stone; structures built of stone or brick are called **masonry**

masonic means "utterly confidential," a tribute to the rigor with which a **masonic** oath is taken

mass (of a substance), tracing back to Greek for barley cake, was first a body of plastic material, like clay or dough—and in physics it is an agglomeration of matter

mass (the original sense of the word) in religion, from Latin *mittere*, "dismiss" may get its name from the last words of the service (*Ite, missa est*)

Massachusetts's name is Algonquian for "at the big hill"

massacre comes from Latin *mazacrium/masacrium*, "slaughter"

massage probably comes from Arabic *massa*, "to feel, handle, palpate"

the chewing muscle is the **masseter**

a **massif** is a compact group of mountains or mountain range section; it first meant "building block" and the word massive is derived from that

acorns as pig food are **mast**

master is from Latin *magister*, "chief"

masterate is the status of a person holding a master's degree

masterful can mean dominating, domineering, imperious, and imposing; **masterly** can describe having the skills of a master and means adoit and expert

masterpiece originally was used in a technical or academic sense to apply to a work that was presented to a medieval guild for qualification as a "master"

masticate is from Greek *mastikhan*, "gnash or grind the teeth"

mastiff's original meaning may be "tamed dog" or "dog accustomed to the hand"

the **mastodon**, "nipple-like teeth," got its name from the nipple-shaped (*mastos*, "breast") tubercles that were in pairs on the crowns of its molar teeth

mastodonic means unusually or surrealistically large

matador comes from Spanish *matar*, "to kill" and literally means "killer"

match first meant "wick of a candle or lamp," "spout of a lamp," before it was the item used to light candles and lamps

matchbox can mean "very small" as in **matchbox** apartment or **matchbox** car

a **matchmaker** is one who makes matches for burning

mate is from German *mat(e)*, "comrade," from a Germanic root with the underlying concept of "eating together"

one of a pair is a "**mate**" or "**fellow**"—as in gloves

material is based on Latin *materialis*, "formed of matter"; **materiel** means "personnel" or "military arms or equipment"

materialism is most often understood as a belief that the immediate physical world is the most important one that exists and a **materialist** is one who forswears any belief in a spiritual or otherworldly existence

maternal is from Latin *mater*

a **math** is "a crop of grass," "a mowing" and also "the amount of crop mowed"— and so an **aftermath** started out as a second crop of grass mowed in the same season

matins is a morning church service or the first mass of the day

matriculation is formal admission to a college or university and is based on Latin *matricula*, "register, catalog"

matrimony is from Latin *matrimonium*, "state of being married," from *mater*, "mother," and *monium*, "-mony" (state, condition)

a mold for casting is a **matrix**

matrix is from Latin meaning "breeding female" and it originally was used for the uterus or womb, then for a supporting or enclosing structure

looking more like mom is **matroclinous**; more like dad is **patroclinous**

matryoshka (Russian "little matron") are the nesting dolls shaped like skittles

matt/mat "dull, not glossy" traces back to Arabic meaning "dead"

matter is from Latin *materia*, "timber" or "stuff of which something is made" or "subject of discourse"

to **mattify** is to reduce the shine of the complexion

a **mattock** is a tool similar to a pick but with a point or chisel edge at one end of the head and an adzlike blade at the other

 mathematical is based on Greek *mathema*, "science," from *manthanein*, "learn"; **mathematic(s)** first referred to "something learned"

mental discipline is **mathesis**

matinee, literally French for morning, is so called because these performances once took place in the morning

mattoid means semi-nuts or behaving erratically

mattress comes from Arabic *al-matrah*, "bed, carpet, cushion, seat"

maturation is the formation of pus;

maturative is "causing the formation of pus"

the meaning of **maturation** is directed more at the process of development; in that of **maturity**, it is directed more at the attained state

earliness is the notion underlying the word **mature** (Latin *maturus*, "timely, early" as well as "ripe, fully developed")

{ breakfast is a **matutinal** meal (happening in the morning) }

matutolagnia is an urge to have sex in the morning

feeling like you got up on the wrong side of the bed? that is **matutolypea**

maudlin is a corruption of Magdalene, the woman who weeped at the feet of Jesus as he was crucified

maul was first a wooden club or massive hammer

a **maulifuff** is a woman without energy or one who makes a fuss but does little or nothing

to **maunder** is to grumble, moan, or mutter

maundy descends from a Latin word meaning commandment, so **Maundy** Thursday refers to the mandate given by Jesus at the Last Supper

mausoleum takes its name from the Greek governor Mausolus (d 353/352 BC) who had a magnificent tomb built at Halicarnassus (one of the Seven Wonders of the World) by his widow, Artemisia

mauve is more properly pronounced MOAV, like stove

maven is from a Hebrew word meaning "understanding" and it means "a connoisseur" or "an expert"

Texas cattleman Sam **Maverick** (1800s) did not brand his cattle, which gave birth to the word **maverick**

a **maw** is the stomach of an animal or person and can figuratively mean "appetite; inclination"

the loincloth of a sumo wrestler is a **mawashi**

the root sense of **mawkish** is "infected, maggoty" and now it means "nauseating, insipid"

maxim is from Latin phrase *propositio maxima*, "most important or largest proposition"

maximum is from Latin *maximus*, "largest," the superlative of *magnus*, "large"

may is more optimistic than **might**; **may** carries the idea of permission while **might** suggests likelihood

maybe is a shortening of the phrase "it may be that"

mayday the distress call is from French *venez m'aider*, "come help me!"

mayhem, from French *mahaing*, "maim," first meant "malicious injury or maiming" and then took on its figurative use

mayonnaise may mean "native to Mahon"—Port Mahon, France, and was first written Mahonnaise; the shortened mayo showed up in 1930

mayor's ancestor is Latin *maior*, "person in authority," from *maior*, "greater"

maze started as a verb (from amaze) meaning "daze, stupefy"

Mc or **Mac** as a prefix denoting inferiority owes its origin to the methods of mass production of McDonald's meals

a **McGuffin** is an object or device in a book, play, or film that is simply a trigger for the plot—from English film director Alfred Hitchcock for a humorous story involving such a pivotal factor

McJob is a low-paying job with few prospects

a **McMansion** is a large opulent house that does not fit in with the surrounding houses

a **McWar** is a military conflict that is fast and cheap

M.D. comes from Latin *medicinae*, doctor

a **meadow** originally was a piece of land permanently covered with grass to be mowed for hay

meager first meant "thin"

meal comes from an ancient word for "measure" that developed into Old English *mael*, "appointed eating time"

the quantity of milk given by a cow at one milking is a "**meal**"

mealy-mouthed is just a mispronunciation of the Greek *melimuthos*—*meli*, "honey," and *muthos*, "speech"

meander comes from the great winding Greek river Menderes (Maeander)

measles comes from Germanic *masel*, "pustule" or "spot" or early Dutch *masel*, "blister, pustle, spot"

measly can mean "of or pertaining to measles"

measure first meant "moderation"

meat first meant "food, nourishment"— especially solid food as opposed to drink

a **meatus** is a channel or passage

{ to be in the **mebby-scales** is to waver between two opinions }

mechanic first meant "pertaining to manual labor or skill," but this is now rare or obsolete

mechanical was earlier in English than machine and has long had certain separate senses, such as "an art, trade, or occupation: concerned with manual work" and "practical as opposed to theoretical"

a **mechanolater** is one who overestimates the importance of machines

medal comes from a Latin word meaning "small coin"

small round cuts of meat are **médallions**, **noisettes**, or **tournedos**

meddle first meant "mingle, mix"

magnetic disks for storing computer files are collectively called **media** or **mediums**

the **median** is the halfway point, dividing a series of numbers in half—while a **mean** is the average of the sum of the series

mediation is from three different senses of Latin *mediare*: to divide in half, to occupy a middle position, to act as an intermediary

Medicare and **Medicaid** are blends, respectively, of Medic(al) + care, and Medica(l) + aid

medieval comes from Latin *medium aevum*, "middle age"

mediocre is from Latin *mediocris*, "of middle height or degree"—from Latin *medius*, "mid," and *ocris*, "rugged mountain"

a **mediocrist** is one of mediocre ability or skill

mediocrity has an old meaning of "moderation in living"

meditation is based on Latin *meditari*, "contemplate"

Mediterranean is from Latin *mediterraneus*, "inland," from *medius*, "mid," and *terra*, "earth, land"

medium comes from Latin for "center; intermediary" and it moved from a broad sense of "the middle" to a narrower sense of "any intervening substance through which a force acts on objects at a distance or through which impressions are conveyed to the senses"

medley is a variant of French *melee* and it first meant "combat, conflict" before "-combination, mixture"

medicine's Indo-European root is "measure," and, literally means "the science of taking appropriate measures concerning one's health"

the **medulla**'s etymology is Latin "marrow, pith" as it first meant the inner substance of the brain and spinal cord as well as the soft internal tissue of a plant

meed is recompense or a reward

meek is from Old Norse *mjukr*, "gentle, pliant, soft" (**meeken** is to make **meek**); **meek** used to mean "courteous" or "indulgent"

meemie originally meant a state of drunkenness—and, later, hysterics

the word **meet** can be used to mean "appropriate, fitting, suitable"

megapixel is one million pixels, a measure of resolution in digital cameras

if you are **megapod**, it is a nice way of saying you have large feet

megrim is another word for a headache, especially a migraine

melancholy comes from Greek *melan-*, "black," and *cholos*, "bile"—as black bile caused a sorrowful feeling

mélange is a word for coffee served with whipped cream or hot milk

to **meld** is to declare a combination of cards in certain card games such as canasta, pinochle, rummy, etc.

the adjective form for turkey is **meleagrine**

mêlée can have the circumflex and acute accent—but in English these are generally dropped

meliorate is another term for ameliorate and is from a Latin base meaning "improve" and "better"

melliferous means "producing honey" (*mel/mell* meaning "honey" in Latin)

mellifluous, "pleasingly smooth and musical to hear," is based on Latin words meaning "to flow like honey"

Winnie the Pooh is **mellisugent** (honey-sucking) and **mellivorous** (feeding naturally on honey)

mellow fruit is soft, sweet, and juicy when ripe

melodrama's origin is Greek (*melos*, "music, song") meaning "song play" and it started out as a sensational play interspersed with songs

melody is from Greek *melos*, "song" and an early sense was "sweet music"

melon comes from Greek melopepon, from **melon** "apple" + pepon "an edible gourd"

{ **melt** goes all the way back to Sanskrit *mrdu*, "soft" }

member first meant "limb" (from Latin *membrum*, "limb, part of the body, constituent part") and **membrane** is from this same root

memorable and **memory** come from Latin *memor*, "mindful"

memorandum was originally an adjective meaning "to be remembered"

if someone is **memorious**, they have a good memory; a **memorist** is a person who memorizes things

to **memorize** can mean "to perpetuate the memory of in writing"

Latin *minax*, "threatening" begat *minacia*, "threatening things," and this eventually became **menace** a **ménage** was first a household or the members of a household

menalty is another word for the middle class

mend is a shortening of amend

a **mendacious** person is lying or untruthful

a **menhir**, a tall upright monumental stone of prehistoric times, gets its name from Breton meaning "stone" and "long"

menial first meant "pertaining to a household" or "domestic"

the curved surface of a liquid is the **meniscus**

a calendar of saints" days is a **menology**

menopause breaks down into roots meaning "month" and "cessation"

menorah is Hebrew for "candlestick, candelabrum," or "lamp stand"

the plurals of **mensch** (a decent upright honorable person) are menshen or mensches

a **menseful** person is one who is "considerate, neat, and clean," i.e., a great roommate

etymologically, **menstrual** means "monthly," coming from Latin mensis, "month"

menticulture means "cultivation of the mind"

mentimutation is a change of mind or the act of changing one's mind

the etymological notion of **mention** is "reminding," from Latin mentio, "remembrance"

mentor is the name of a character in Homer's "Odyssey" who was an advisor to Telemachus, son of Odysseus

the Latin base of **menu** is minutus, "very small" which led to French meaning "detailed list"

the fast-food restaurant lineup in the drive-through is the **menuboard**

meow is a variant of miaow

the adjective form of skunk is **mephitine**

something that is **meracious** is unadulterated and full-strength, pure or unmixed

{ **mercation** is the action or an act of purchasing something }

mercenary is from Latin mercenarius, "hireling," from merced/merces, "reward"

merchant and **merchandise** come from Latin mercari, "to trade"

the Roman god **Mercury** got his name from his original role as patron of trade and tradesmen, from Latin merx, "goods for sale"; the use of the term for the fluid metal comes from the planet name

Latin merces, "payment, reward" became metaphorical to "compassion given freely" and became English **mercy**

the early senses of **mere** were "pure" and "downright, sheer" from Latin merus, "undiluted"

a **merenda** is a light meal

meretricious "deceptively attractive" or "whore-like" is from Latin mereri, "to serve for hire" and **meretrix** "prostitute"; a **meretrician** or **meretrix** is a prostitute

merganser, a diving duck, is a combination of Latin anser, "goose," and mergere, "to plunge"

merge, from Latin mergere, "dip, plunge," first meant "immerse (oneself)"

meridian's root is Latin meridianum, "midday"

a **meridiation** is a midday nap or siesta

meringue may be related to Latin meringa or merenda, "afternoon meal"

merino wool is from a sheep first shorn in Spain but originating with a Berber people, the Banu Marin, in the former dynasty of Morocco

a whole expressed by contrasting words is a **merism** (e.g. young and old, head to foot)

merit originally meant "deserved reward or punishment" (from Latin *meritum*, "due reward")

merle is the bluish-gray color of a blue-heeler or Australian cattle dog/dingo

merlot is from French *merle*, "young blackbird" for the dark color of the grapes

mermaid is from *mere*, "sea" and maid

mero- is a prefix (from Greek *meros*) meaning "part"—so a **meronym** is a word denoting something which forms part of another object (pocket of jacket, handle of cup, etc.)

merry first meant "peaceful" or "pleasant" and that is what it first meant in "**Merry** Christmas"

merry-go-sorry is experiencing happiness and sadness simultaneously, laughing and crying at the same time

mesa is Spanish, literally "table"—and is similar to but larger than a butte

mesclun is French for "mixture" and pertains to a salad made from a number of different lettuces

to engage a gear is to **mesh**

a **meshuga** or **meshuggener** is a mad, crazy, or stupid person; **meshugas** is Yiddish for nonsense, foolishness or a foolish idea

if **mesic** is used to describe a habitat, it means "containing a moderate amount of moisture"

mesmeric is a synonym for hypnotic; **mesmerism** and **mesmerize** are named for physician F.A. Mesmer (1734–1815), who popularized this hypnotic activity

meso- is a prefix meaning "middle, intermediate" (Greek *mesos*) and from this we get words like **mesomorph**, a body build that is compact, muscular, and powerful

mesonoxian means "of or related to midnight"

Mesopotamia translates to "area or country between two rivers" (Tigris and Euphrates)

mesquite, the wood or charcoal to impart a hot smoky flavor, is from Nahuatl *mizquitl*

a group of army officers is a **mess**

mess originally meant "a serving of food" or "course of a meal" (from French *mes*) and also each of the groups, usually of four people, into which the guests of a banquet were commonly divided, so **mess** had an early meaning "party of four" and **mess**-making was the "act or practice of eating together"; to **mess** meant "to serve up food in portions"

message comes from Latin *mittere*, "send"; **messagerie** is the delivery or transport of goods, messages, or people and **messagery** is the occupation or function of a messenger

{ **messuage** is a house, its outbuildings, and the adjacent land }

meta- is a prefix meaning "after" or "with" or "across" and it can indicate a change of position or condition (**metamorphosis**), being in a position after or beyond (metatarsus), or being of a higher or second-order kind (**metalanguage**)

meta and **mete**, as nouns, both first meant "boundary" or "goal"

metabolism means specifically the chemical changes inside cells relating to the breaking down of food molecules to release energy—and the building up of new material

metacarpal bones are the hand bones that come right after the carpus "wrist bones" (meta meaning "after, behind")

the ability of some animals to change color is **metachrosis**

metadata is data that provides information about other data

metage is the official measurement of an object's contents or weight

metagnostic is "beyond human understanding"

molten glass before it is blown or cast is referred to as **metal**

metalanguage is language used to talk about language, such as dictionary definitions describing vocabulary

metaphysics is the branch of philosophy dealing with the first principles or nature of things—such as the concepts of being, cause, essence, identity, space, substance, time—describing what is "beyond" physics

a **metaplasm** is a change in a word through the addition, subtraction, or transposition of letters, sounds, or syllables—examples being the mispronunciations of library, nuclear, and sherbet

when a disease shifts to a different part of the body, that is **metastasis**

metathesis is the switching of the order of two sounds, as in third from *thridda* and the modern spelling of bird, a transposition of letters of Old English *brid*, "chick, fledgling"

metaxy is the recollection of a previous existence

 **mete**, the verb, first meant "measure the dimensions or quantity"—and **meter** was first "person who measures" (from Greek *metron*)

metallege is transposing two letters in a word to create another word (changing nuclear to unclear)

a **metalexicographer** is a person who conceives of or theorizes about dictionaries

advertising's subliminal message is the **metamessage**

metamorphosis comes from "Metamorphoses," a poem by Ovid about gods changing into objects, animals, or plants

metaphor is from Greek *metapherein*, "to transfer" as it is a word or phrase transferred from one context (meaning) to another

metaphrase is word-by-word translation, as opposed to paraphrase

when something is abstract and excessively complex, it is **metaphysical**

metempsychosis is the passage of the soul from one body to another, the soul beginning a new cycle of existence in another human body

a **meteor** is commonly called a "shooting star," a large bright **meteor** is a **fireball** and one of these that explodes is a **bolide**, and a **meteor** that reaches the planet is a **meteorite**

meteor (Greek "raised up, lofty") was first applied to any atmospheric phenomenon, e.g., watery (aqueous) meteors were precipitation such as rain, snow, hail, etc.—which is where meterorology gets its name

a meteor that survives and makes it to a planet is a **meteorite**; types of meteorites include siderites/irons, aerolites/stones, siderolites (iron/stone)

meteoroids are small pieces of galactic debris in space; **meteors** (shooting stars) enter the Earth's atmosphere, then become known as **meteorites** when they fall to earth

a **meteroid** is a rocky or metallic fragment floating through space, often a piece broken off from asteroids, comets, or other cosmic bodies

methinks preserves the Middle English phrase "me thinketh" and it means "it seems to me"

method comes from Greek *methodos*, "pursuit of knowledge, mode of investigation" from *meta*, which expresses development, and *hodos*, "way"; originally, **method** referred to a "prescribed medical treatment for a disease"

a **method** is a way of doing things; a **methodology** is a set or system of methods

meticulous first meant "fearful" or "timid" and now means "exact, finicky, or precise"; **scrupulous** means "conscientious or principled"

métier is something you are good at

a **metonym** is a substitute for something with which it is closely associated, like "Washington" for U.S. government or "crown" for the king or queen

metopic means "pertaining to the forehead"

while scientists' measurements are usually **metric**, the poets" are usually **metrical**

to **metricate** is to change to or adopt the metric system

metrology is the science of measurement

a young grandmother is a **metrona**

the musical tempo-keeping device is a **metronome**

metrophobia is a fear of poetry

metropolis first meant "capital city of a country" (Latin "mother city" of a colony)

mettle was first a variant spelling of metal, then took on figurative senses

irksome chores that must be done are **metutials**

a **meuse** is a gap in a fence or hedge through which rabbits or hares escape— and figuratively means "a way out of a difficulty"

a **mew** was first a place where trained falcons were kept and it means "molting place," coming from Old French *muer*, "molt"

the object attached to the doorway of Jewish houses and containing Pentateuchal texts is the **mezuzah**

a **mezzaluna** is a kitchen tool with a semicircular (half-moon) blade and a handle on each end—used for chopping food; a synonym is **hachoir**

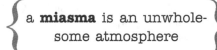

{ a **miasma** is an unwhole-some atmosphere }

mic and **mike** are shortened forms of microphone

mica is any of a group of minerals which occur in small glittering plates or scales in other rocks

Michigan is Chippewa *mica gama*, "big water"—referring to Lake **Michigan**; a **Michigander** is a native or inhabitant of **Michigan**

the prefix **micro-** comes from Greek *mikros*, "small" (a variant of *smikros*)

microbiology specializes in microbes (Greek "small life"), microorganisms commonly called germs

fiche in **microfiche** is French for index card, slip of paper

someone who gets all worked up about trivial things is a **microlipet**

micrology is the investigation and classification of trivial matters

micronutrients are vitamins and minerals

Microsoft is an abbreviation of microcomputer software

mid-air is between the sky/clouds and the ground, or a point or region in the air not immediately adjacent to the ground

midden traces back to Scandinavian forms *mog*, "muck," and *dynge*, "heap," and it first meant "dunghill" before it denoted a prehistoric or historic refuse heap

middle traces back to Indo-European *medhjo-*, which also produced Latin *medius*, "**middle**," and Greek *mesos*, "**middle**"

a middle-aged person can be described as **middlescent**, "exhibiting behavior or having interests more like an adolescent, especially in choice of activities and fashion"

midriff is based on the Old English *hrif*, "belly," and one's **midriff** is the front of the body between the chest and the waist

the term **midshipmen** originated in the British Navy centuries ago, from the fact that young men who were going through a course of training to become officers were assigned quarters amidships on the lower deck

the middle finger is also called the **midst** and **medicus**

the "wife" in **midwife** is based on an archaic sense "woman"—and thus means "woman who is with (the mother)"

mien is from Chinese for "wheat flour" and these are wheat flour noodles used in dishes like lo mein, chow mein (note change of spelling!)

{ if someone is in a **miff**, they are in a fit of pique or a huff }

might goes back to Indo-European *mag-*, "be able, have power," the same base that produced the word "may"

mignon as in filet **mignon** means "small or delicate"

migraine is literally a "half head" ache and in Latin it was *hemicrania*, "half skull"—but when it came through French, the first and last sounds were dropped and it became **migraine**

a wanderer can be called a **migrateur**

mild originally meant "gracious, merciful"

in Old English, **mildew** actually meant honeydew (*meli*, "honey") and was a sweet sticky substance deposited on plants by an insect; now it is described as a class of mold that grows on materials and a powdery mold that grows on plants

mile, from Latin *mil(l)e*, "thousand" originally was a Roman unit of distance of one thousand paces; in ancient Rome, milestones were placed along highways every thousand paces and outward, starting at the Forum

mileway is a word for "twenty minutes"—for the length of time it would take to travel a mile on foot

milieu is from Latin *medius*, "mid," and *lieu*, "place"

military is based on Latin *miles*, "soldier"

militia was first a system of military discipline

milk is intimately connected to the action of milking a cow or similar animal, coming from Proto-Indo-European *melg-*, "to stroke"

a **mill** is one-thousandth of a dollar

millenary refers to a thousand; **millinery** refers to women's hats

a **milliad** is a thousand years

Milaner, first someone from Milan or selling stylish goods there, became the word **milliner**—a designer or seller of women's hats

mille "thousand" in Italian is the base of the word **million**

in **millipede**, *milli-* simply means "many"

milquetoast comes from a comic strip character created in 1924 who was shy, timid, and unassertive

Milwaukee is Algonquian for "good land"

mimesis is the imitation of another person's words, mannerisms, actions, etc.

Greek *mimos*, "imitator" or "actor" became Latin *mimus*, and gave us English **mimic**

a cocktail consisting of champagne and orange juice is a **mimosa**—so called for its yellow color resembling the flowers of the **Mimosa** shrub

to purse one's lips is to **mimp**; **mimp** also means "to make believe" and "to sham"

minaret derives from Turkish *minare*, "lighthouse, tall tower"

mince can mean "lessen or diminish (something)" or "minimize"

mind comes from a large family of words that go back to the Indo-European base *men-*, "think"

mindshare is the consumer awareness of a brand or product

mineral is etymologically "something obtained by mining," from Latin *minera*, "ore"

in Italy, there are three versions of vegetable soup, minestrina (light and thin), **minestrone** ("big soup" in Italian, heavy and thick), and minestra (middle consistency)—from *minestrare*, "to serve or dish up"

to **ming** is to remind a person (and is followed by—of, on, that, to do)

the combining form **mini-** can indicate small, short, or minor: (small) minicalculator, minicomputer, minfestival, mininuke, minipark, minitank; (short) minicourse, minilecture, minidress, miniseries, miniskirt, miniwear; (minor) miniboom, minibudgdet, miniplanet, minirevolution, ministate

Smallness is a secondary semantic development for **miniature**; it comes from Latin *minium*, "red lead" which was used in ancient and medieval times for making red ink for illuminated manuscripts. This was taken into Italian as *miniare* and then *miniatura*, "painting, illustrating" and this particularly referred to small paintings in manuscripts. So when it was borrowed into English, **miniature** was broadened to mean "small image."

{ **minikin** refers to a petite or dainty person }

having almost no faith is **minimifidian**

minimize means to reduce to an absolute minimum—not to play down or soften

your little finger or toe is the **minimus**

minion is based on French *mignon*, "delicately small person" and evolved to mean servile attendant

minister was originally a person acting under the authority or as an agent of another

minister meant, etymologically, a small man, as opposed to **magister**, a big man

a **minister** is commonly a person who leads the congregation of a Protestant church; **pastor** is another word for **priest** or **minister** and **reverend** is a generic prefix for a Christian leader

Minnesota is Dakota Sioux for "sky-tinted water"

a **minnow** is someone or something considered insignificant

minonette was the original name of the game of volleyball

the word **minor** originally referred to a Franciscan friar

not being of legal age is **minority** or **nonage** or **underage**

originally, **minstrel**, like its relative "minister," meant "servant," going back to Latin *ministerialis*, "official"

mint as in money comes from Latin *moneta*, "**mint**, money" and it denoted "coin" until the fifteenth century when it became "place where money is made"

mint as in plant originated in Greek *minthe*, then Latin *mentha*

the number from which another number (subtrahend) is taken away in subtraction is the **minuend**

minuet comes from a French word meaning "delicate, fine"

in Renaissance mathematics, **minus** was written min (with a line over it), the overlining indicating that the form was an abbreviation; the "min" was later deleted and the overline became a dash, first used in print in 1489

minuscule comes from medieval manuscript writing, literally *minuscula littera*, "somewhat smaller letter"

Latin *minutus*, "small" came from *minuere*, "lessen," and the term *pars minuta prima*, "first small part" was applied to a sixtieth of a whole—a **minute**, originally of a circle and later of an hour; likewise, a **second** was originally a *secunda minuta*, a sixtieth of a sixtieth

minutes of a meeting may derive from Latin *minutus*, so called because the notes are about small details—or may derive from *minuta scriptura*, which denoted writing of a draft in "small" writing

minutiose or **minutious** means "dealing with minutiae or minor details"

minutissimic means "extremely minute or tiny"

to **minx** is to behave with bold flirtatiousness

miracle is from Latin *miraculum*, "object of wonder"; the ultimate root of **miracle** meant "to smile upon"

mirage is from French *se mirer*, "be reflected" from Latin *mirare*, "look at" (as is mirror)

a **miranym** is a word between two opposites: concave/flat/convex, hot/lukewarm/cold

to **mirate** is to express admiration or wonder—a back-formation of **miration** "a display of admiration, wonder"

deep mud is **mire**

mirific means "wonderful, causing wonder"

if you have dizziness, you have **mirligoes**

mireor is an old French word for "look at"; hence, **mirror**, which should be pronounced MIR-uhr

misacceptation is the taking of a word in the wrong sense or verbal misinterpretation

a **misandrist** hates persons of the male sex, a **misogynist** hates persons of the female sex, and a **misanthrope** is a hater of mankind

{ **miscellaneous** once described a person as "having various qualities" }

mischief once meant "distress" or "-misfortune," from a French word meaning "come to an unfortunate end"

mischievous should be pronounced MIS-chuh-vuhs

to **miscomfrumple** is to crease or rumple something

miscreant first meant "unbelieving; pagan, heretic"

miser and **misery** come from Latin, literally "wretched"

to **misgive** is to make or be apprehensive

misinformation is information that is false; **disinformation** is information that is more misleading or deceptive

if it is raining in minute drops, it is **misly** or **mizzly**

a **misnancy** is an effeminate character

a **misocapnist** dislikes tobacco smoke

a **misologist** is one who is averse to conflict, but a **misologist** may also be one who does not want to discuss something but prefers to plunge ahead

a person who cannot stand learning is a **misomusist**

people with a hatred of change or new things experience **misoneism**

a **misprision** is a failure to appreciate the value of something

miss as a verb comes from Proto-Germanic *missjan*, from the base *missa-*, "amiss, wrongly"

miss is a shortened form of mistress

missile was first an adjective meaning "suitable for throwing"

a **missile** is a whole vehicle ready for launching; a **rocket** is a type of engine that powers a **missile**

missiology is the study of methods, purpose, etc. of missions

mission first denoted sending the Holy Spirit into the world, from Latin *mittere* "send"

Mississippi is Chippewa *mici sibi*, "big river"

Missouri comes from Algonquian for "canoe"

dimness of vision is called **mist**; **mist** can also be "a state of obscurity or uncertainty," "an atmosphere of doubt"

mistake is a combo of mis- and take

mister is a weakened form of the word "master"

a **mistigris** is a joker that can be played as any card

mistletoe is literally "dung twig" and is based on German *mix*, "bird excrement," from the fact that the plant is propagated in it (though there is also a theory that the term derived from another German word (*mash*)

which refers to the stickiness of the berries) and Old English *tan/toe*, meaning "twig"

mistress first meant "a woman who rules or has control" or a "woman who employs others, as servants"

mistrust involves a withholding of confidence, whereas **distrust** involves a projection of lack of confidence or suspicion

to **misuse** is to use something wrongly, to **abuse** is to **misuse** something so badly that you damage it

the original meaning of **mite** "small thing" was "small coin" and came from Middle Dutch, going back to Germanic

the tall pointy hat and the staff of a bishop or abbot is the **miter/mitre** (Greek *mitra*, "headdress") or **crosier**

mitigating is lessening or moderating; **extenuating** is stretching out, thinning, making less dense or compact

} **Mitsubishi** is Japanese for "three diamonds" }

mitt is an abbreviation of mitten; **mittens** were first made of fur and the word may have come from a pet name for cats

a **mittimus** is an official order sending someone to prison

mix is a back-formation from mixed

mixology is skill in the mixing of cocktails

in a **mixture**, the combined elements lose their individual identities and are fused, blended, or compounded in the result; in a **mix**, the elements, though combined, retain their individual identities

mizle means "to lead astray, to deceive"

mizmaze is confusion or bewilderment

fine or light rain or drizzle can be called **mizzle**

mnemonic is from Mnemosyne, Greek goddess of memory and the mother of the nine Muses (Greek *mnemon*, "mindful"), and it is pronounced ni-MONN-ik

mnemotechnics is another name for memory techniques

mnestic or **mnesic** means pertaining to memory

moat is from a French word meaning "mound"

mob is from Latin *mobile vulgus*, which meant "the masses" or "disorderly crowd"

mobility first appeared in the sixteenth century to describe gatherings of people appraised as dangerous

mocassin is probably from Algonquian *mockasin*, but is also found in other Native American languages

mocha, originally a bitter coffee and now a coffee-and-chocolate flavoring, is named for **Mocha**, a seaport on the Red Sea in Yemen

mochaccino is cappuccino containing chocolate

mocteroof is an old term for dressing up damaged fruits and vegetables

mode was originally a tune or air—later, a scheme of sounds

model first meant "a set of plans for a building"

Latin *moderari* or *moderare* meant "control, reduce" and from this came **moderate**, etymologically "keep within due measure"

modern comes from Latin *modo*, "just now" and *-ernus* (after *hodiernus*) "of today"

modest comes from Latin *modestus*, "keeping due measure"

modicity is moderateness in price

modicum is Latin, literally "a short measure of quantity or time"

a word or phrase that limits or qualifies the sense of another is a **modifier** or **qualifier**

to adjust the tone is to **modulate**

module originally was "one's power or capabilities"

a **mogul** is a small mound of snow on a ski course, from Old Norse *mugl*, "little heap"

Mohave or **Mojave** is from Yuma Indian *hamok*, "three," and *avi*, "mountain"

moiety is one of two equal portions (half)

to **moil** is to work hard

wallowing in the mud is also called **moiling**

moiré is having a variegated or clouded appearance, like that of watered silk

moist has derivatives such as moistful, moistify, moistish, moistless

a **mojo** is a charmed object

a napkin tucked in a collar to protect clothes is a **mokador** or **bib**

molar comes from Latin *molaris*, meaning "of a mill" or "grindstone," from *mola*, "mill, millstone"

molasses derives from Latin *mel*, "honey"

mold was first a "matrix" in Old English—earth or soil

mole started out meaning a discolored spot on cloth or linen

molecule is Latin *moles*, "mass," and *-cule*, "small"

{ **molest** first meant "cause trouble to" or "annoy, vex" }

molimen is an old term for strenuous effort or labor

moliminous means "momentous, of great bulk or importance," the adjective form of molimen

moll as in gangster's **moll** is a pet form of Mary (also found in mollycoddle)

mollify first meant "make soft or supple"

mollusk comes from Latin *mollis*, "soft" as these animals have soft bodies and (usually) hard shells

the **molly** fish was named in honor of French statesman Comte Nicolas-Francois Mollien (1758–1850)

a **moloch** is any merciless all-devouring force

molt is based on Latin *mutare*, "to change"; to cast off dead skin is to **molt** or **slough**

capitalize **Mom** and **Dad** when you are talking about specific people, i.e., substituting these for their actual names

a **mome** is a stupid person or fool

a **moment** is when you suddenly forget where you are and what's going on, variously called a **blonde**, a **bristlecone**, **senior moment**, or **CRAFT** (can't remember a thing)

monastery is based on Greek words meaning "live alone"

Monday is "day of the Moon," a translation of *lunas dies* (Latin)

mondial means "involving the whole world; worldwide"

mondo "very remarkable" is from the title of a 1961 Italian movie, which was about bizarre behavior

monestrous describes an animal with only one estrus (period of heat) per breeding season

monetary means "pertaining or relating to money or currency" and **fiscal** means "pertaining or relating to finance and financial matters, especially of government and taxes"

> **money** comes from *moneta*, a Latin word that was an epithet of the goddess Juno, in whose temple a mint was housed

Latin **momentum**, from *movere*, "move," and -*mentum*, is the source of **moment**, which first meant "moving power" and is obviously the source of **momentum**

momentarily means "in a moment"; **presently** means "soon" or "shortly"

momentary means fleeting, brief; **momentous** means significant and having great consequence

momism is the practice of carping or fault-finding; a **momus** is a carping critic or faultfinder

another word for teeth is **mompyns**

momurdotes is a case of the sulks

monarch is based on Greek words meaning "rule alone"

to **mong** is to cause a thing to change

monger descends from Latin *mango*, "dealer, trader"

mongoose is of Indian origin and has no relation to the English goose; the plural is mongooses

mongrel's base meaning is "mix"

moniker originally meant a mark left by a tramp on a building or fence to indicate he/she had been there; therefore, a tramp's **moniker** identified him/her like a signature

monitor is from a Latin word meaning "advise, warn" and its first meaning was "an official letter conveying an admonition"

monitory is "giving a friendly warning or reminder"

monk traces all the way back to Greek *monos*, "alone"

the difference between a **monk** and a **friar** is that friars get out and do not stay in monasteries

monkey has a questionable origin, possibly from Arabic *maimun*, "**monkey**"

a **monkey** is a primate and not a type of **ape**, an **ape** is a primate and not a type of **monkey**, and a **chimpanzee** is a type of **ape** (so it's a primate but not a **monkey**)

monkeyshines is a combination of monkey and shines "capers, tricks"

monochrome's original meaning is "different shades of one color"

monocle, a one-lens eyeglass, once meant "one-eyed"

monogamy is from Greek meaning "marrying only once"

a **monoglot** speaks only one language

a **monograph** is a detailed written study of a single specialized topic

a colossal single rock or rock formation is a **monolith**

monologue comes from Greek and **soliloquy** from Latin, but both mean "speaking alone"

a **mononym** is a name or term that is only one word—like Madonna, Prince, Pele

monopoly is made up of *mono*- plus Greek *polein*, "sell"

a **monopolylogue** is an entertainment in which a single performer plays multiple characters

> **monops** means "having one eye"

monopsony is a situation in which there is one or a predominant consumer for a product

monosyllabic and **disyllabic** adjectives normally form their comparative and

superlative forms by adding -er and -est; **polysyllabic** with more and most

the word **monosyllable** has five syllables

monotremes get their name from the design of their urinogenital systems (*mono*, "one" *treme*, "aperture")

mawsim "season" in Arabic gives us **monsoon**

the ancient Romans believed the birth of a deformed animal was an omen of bad things to come, so the word **monster** comes from *monstrum*, Latin for "a divine portent or warning," ultimately from *monere*, "warn"

Montana is Spanish for "mountainous"

monte in cards is Spanish for "mountain," i.e., the pile of cards left after dealing

Montezuma II (1466–1520) was the Aztec emperor imprisoned by the Spanish conquistadors and then killed by his own subjects

in ancient times, time was recorded by noting the revolutions of the **moon**—so Indo-European had me(n)ses, "**moon; month**" and this was retained and passed on to English in words like **month** and **moon**

Monticello is properly pronounced mahn-tuh-SELL-oh

monture is either a mounting or the manner in which something is mounted

monument first meant "burial place, selpulchre"

in Old English, **mood** meant "mind" itself; early senses of **mood** and **moody** had to do with courage and bravery

the reflection of moonlight on water is **moonglade**

the half-moon of a fingernail is the **moonlet**

to **moonlight** means "to have a second job," originally secretly and done at night

moonshine was once called "jitter sauce" and Cab Calloway incorporated that into the coinage "**jitterbug**" for the intoxicated dance

moonwalk was coined in 1969, the year of the first moon landing

moor "tie up a boat" was probably borrowed from German or Dutch

moose is derived from Narragansett/ Passamaquoddy *moosu*, "he trims or cuts bark smooth"; a **moose** is actually an **elk** and the North American **moose** and the Eurasian **elk** are the same animal

etymologically, a **moot** point is one talked about at a "meeting" and it describes a point for discussion in a **moot**, or assembly, of law students

mop started as a sailor's term for a brush used for caulking a ship's seams with tar, possibly from Latin *mappula*, "cloth, towel"

moped comes from Swedish *mo-*, "motor," and *ped*, "pedal, cycle," as it is a motorized pedal cycle

moppet is from the obsolete *moppe*, "baby or rag doll"

a **moraine** is a mound, ridge, or other feature consisting of debris that has been carried and deposited by a glacier or ice sheet

Latin *mor/mos*, "custom" is the starting point of **moral**, **morality**, and other related words

morale was borrowed from French, where it is the feminine form of moral

morality is beliefs regarding appropriate behavior, while **ethics** is the formal study of **morality**

morass first meant "wet swampy tract" and then took the figurative meaning of "complicated or confused situation which it is difficult to escape from or make progress through"

morate means "well-mannered, moral, respectable"

moration, from the same root as moratorium, means "delay" or "tarrying"

morbid first meant "indicative of disease"

mordacious is "biting or inclined to bite"

{ to be **mordant** is to show a critical quality in one's remarks }

the Indo-European root for "**more**" was *meis*

more than refers to countable items (there are **more than** fifty pies); **over** refers to general or unspecified amounts (**over** half the church is full)

morel, as in mushroom, is from German *Morchel*, "fungus"

mores is the Latin plural of *mor/mos* and means "acquired customs and manners"; social and moral conventions are **mores** and lack of these is **anomie**

morganatic is a survival of an ancient Germanic marriage custom, a gift on the morning after the wedding from husband to wife called *morgangeba*, "morning" and "give"; now it describes a marriage between people of different social status, especially a man of superior rank and woman of inferior rank

morgue is from French and was originally the name of a Paris building where dead bodies were kept until identified

moribund means "in terminal decline; at the point of death"

morigerate means "compliant, obedient"

mornay is a cheese-flavored cream sauce

morning was created on the pattern of "evening"

a fool who speaks nonsense is a **morologist**

in medical terms, a **moron** is an adult with a mental age of 8–12

The parts that make up words are called by linguists "**morphemes**" and they are the smallest units of meaning in a language. **Morphemes** include things like prefixes (un- as in unbelievable) and suffixes (-able as in believable). A word in English may be simple, composed of one **morpheme** only, like bat or hammer, or it may be complex, containing more than one **morpheme**, as in blackboard (black + board), knowledgeable (knowledge + -able), and disestablishmentarianism, a word meaning opposition to established order, made up of six morphemes: dis-, establish, -ment, -ary, -an, and -ism.

morphine gets its name from the Greek god of dreams, Morpheus

morphology is the study of the form of words in a language, including change, formation, and inflection; the word **morphology** contains the root log-, "study," and it first referred to the study of biological forms

etymologically, the **morris** dance is a "Moorish dance," as it was probably borrowed from Flemish *mooriske dans*

morsel is a diminutive of French *mors*, "a bite"

a **mortar** was first the vessel (**mortar** and pestle—pronounced MORE-tur and PEH-sul) and then the meaning transferred to the mixture of lime or cement and sand and water made in the vessel

the graduation hat is a **mortarboard**, from its resemblance to a square board with a handle used for holding and carrying masonry mortar

mortgage, literally "dead pledge" was either constituting if it was not paid back, the property or pledge was forfeited (dead)—and if paid back, the pledge was void (dead)

the householder with a mortgage is a **mortgagor** and the bank or lender is the **mortgagee**

mortify (from Latin meaning "kill or subdue the flesh") originally meant "to kill," then "to destroy the vitality or vigor of" before it took on its present meaning

mortise may come from an Arabic word meaning "place of locking"

mortuary was originally a gift claimed by a parish priest from a dead person's estate

mosaic is etymologically "of the muses," coming from Greek *mouseion*, "place of the muses"

{ **mosey** derives from the Spanish term *vamose*, "let's go" }

mosque literally, from Arabic *masjid*, is a place where one "bows down" in prayer

mosquito is a Spanish diminutive of *mosca*, "fly"; the plural of **mosquito** is mosquitoes

moss originally meant "bog, swamp"

mossback was first a large old fish

most does not mean "nearly" and should not be substituted for "almost"

something that is **motatorious** is in constant motion

to eat in secret is to **motch** or **smouster**

motel is motor and hotel blended

originally, **moth** just referred to the larva of a clothes **moth**

Mother is one of the surviving words from Anglo-Saxon (starting as *modor*), which are among the most fundamental words in English. **Mother** has many cognates in other languages, including Old High German *muoter*, Dutch *moeder*, Old Norse *mothir*, Latin *mater*, Greek *meter*, and Sanskrit *mat*. These words share an Indo-European root. **Mother** is one of the Anglo-Saxon nouns that has an Anglo-Saxon adjective as well as a Latinate adjective—motherly and maternal—and motherly also came from Old English (*modorlic*). Mom, a shortened form of momma, was recorded in 1894; momma was first used in 1884. Both are chiefly North American uses. Mamma and mama, created by children reduplicating an instinctive sound, are much earlier terms showing up in the 1500s. In between came mommy (also North American in usage) in 1848, which was a variant of mammy (also 1500s).

a **motto** is a short phrase that usually expresses a moral aim or purpose; a **slogan** is a catch phrase used by a political party or other organization in advertising or promotion

moue is a pouting face

moulder/molder "to crumble" is based on mold "crumbling soft surface soil"

> when a tire mark or footprint or tooth print is used to make an impression for use as evidence in a criminal investigation, that is a **moulage**

freckles were once called **moth-patches**

in biology, if something is capable of moving, it is **motile**

motitation is a quivering movement

a **motive** is a reason for doing something or acting in a certain way; a **motivation** is the result of having been supplied with a **motive** and is thus a drive, stimulus, or impulsion for doing something

the multicolored costume of a fool or jester is a **motley**

an early use of **motor** was to describe a person who imparted motion and comes from Latin meaning "mover"

a **motor** is a small **engine** or a similar device powered by electricity; an **engine** is a machine that converts potential energy into kinetic energy to provide motive force in order to do work

a **motte** is a large artificial earthen mound with a flattened top, often with a castle or fort on it

mottle is likely a back-formation from motley

motto comes from Latin *muttum*, "sound, utterance," and is an adoption of Italian **motto** "word"

an early use of **mound** was "enclose with a fence or hedge" and "boundary fence or hedge"

a **mount** is a conical hill of moderate height

Latin *mons*, "**mountain**" is the source of **mount** and then **mountain**

mountebank is from Italian *montimbanco*, "one who climbs on a bench"

mourn's etymology goes back to Gothic *maurnan*, "be anxious"

mournival means group or set of four

mouse is another name for a black eye

mouses is correct when referring to timid people or the computer device; **mice** is the plural for the rodent

mousse (French "froth") is a word for the aggregation of tiny bubbles in sparkling wine, champagne, etc.

a **mousse** is a light aerated dish made of ingredients beaten with whipped cream, gelatine, or egg whites; a soufflé is not made with cream or gelatine but with beaten egg white, and a **pudding** is made from milk, eggs, and other ingredients and flavorings

moustache comes via French from Italian *mostaccio*, which goes back to Greek *mustax*, "upper lip, **moustache**"

mouth is traced back to Germanic *munthaz*

mouthfeel is physical sensation in the mouth produced by food or drink

{ **move** is from Latin *movere*, "move" }

movie is an abbreviation of moving picture

a **mow** is a stack of beans, corn, hay, or peas

Moxie was once a soft drink that made medical claims of providing nerve food; it came to mean figuratively that one was full of false nerve

mozzarella is the Italian diminutive of *mozza*, a kind of cheese—from *mozzare*, "cut off"—so called because the cheese was shaped into a bundle and then chopped

originally, **Mrs.** was a shortened version of mistress, a word that used to mean "wife"; **Mrs.** cannot be written out

mubblefubbles is depression for no reason

much goes back to the same Indo-European base that produced Latin *magis*, "more," and Greek *megas*, "large," starting as Old English *mycel*, then *muchel* in Middle English

mucid is a word to describe something that is moldy and musty

instead of saying you use glue or paste, call it **mucilage**

muck is probably of Scandinavian origin and first referred to dung or mud

muck-a-muck was first Chinook for food, then Chinook jargon for a person of great importance, from high **muck-a-muck** (a variant and derivative is mucketymuck)

a **muckender** is a handkerchief, a table napkin, or a bib

to **mucker** is to hoard money or goods

a **muckrake** is a rake for collecting or sifting through muck; the verb is mainly used in a figurative way

mucophagy is snot eating

mucous is the adjective from Latin meaning "slimy" and **mucus** is the noun from Latin but cognate with Greek *mussesthai*, "blow the nose"

muculency is an old word for snottiness

Greek *mukter*, "nose, nostril" is cognate with **mucus**

the Old English word for "**mud**" was **fen**, which now survives in the sense of "swamp"; **mud** is probably a borrowing from German *mudde*

muddle first meant "bathe or wallow in mud or muddy water"

to **muddle** a lemon is to lightly mash slices to release the essential oils

the technical name for a swizzle stick is **muddler** or **mosser**

mudras are codified hand signals, from Sanskrit *mudr*, "seal, mystery," from Iranian *mudr*, perhaps from Akkadian *musar°*, *muar°*, "object bearing a royal inscription," from Sumerian *mu-sar*, "name to write"

muesli (from German *Mus*, "stew, stewed fruit") is a German diminutive form of *mus*, "pulpy food; puree"

muff, when said of glass, means "frosted"

muffin comes from German *muffe*, "cake"

the **muffle** is a ruminant's upper lip and nose

to **muffle** the eyes is to cover them to prevent seeing something

mufti are civilian clothes worn by a person who usually wears a uniform

mug probably comes from Swedish *mugg*, "pitcher with a handle"; small jugs used for drinking in eighteenth century England were called "mugs" and were made to look like human faces—hence, **mug** being slang for "face"

mug, the verb, first meant "to strike in the face" or "strangle"; a **muggee** is a victim of a mugging

a **muggle** is a non-wizard

muggy descends from Old Norse *mugga*, "drizzle"

mugwump comes from an Algonquin word meaning "great chief"

mukluk is derived from Yupik *maklak*, "bearded seal" or "sealskin"—as the boots are made of this

mulch, often but not always organic, is a cover for soil for various reasons

a male donkey (jackass) and female horse (mare) can create a **mule**

the state of being a woman is **muliebrity**

to spice and heat wine is to **mull** it; **mulled** means "heated and spiced" in **mulled** cider

{ a **mullet** is a hairstyle that is short in front and on the sides, long in back }

a **mulligan** is an illegal golf practice where a mis-hit ball is respotted and reshot

mulligatawny is from Tamil *milagu-tannir*, "pepper water," which partially describes the highly seasoned soup

mulligrubs is a pretended or fake sullenness or displeasure in order to get something desired

the separators between panes of glass in windows can be called: **mullions, muntins, muttins, mutts**; the horizontal separators are **transoms**

mullock is worthless information

organic aquarium sediment in the bottom is **mulm**

multicolored is having all colors of the rainbow; **varicolored** and **particolored** is having a variety of colors

multiculturalism first came into wide circulation in the 1970s in Canada and Australia as the key plank of government policy to assist in the management of ethnic pluralism within the national polity

the **multiplier** in mathematics (in 8 x 20, the **multiplier** is 8) is also called the **facient**; a **facient** is a doer or agent

multiply comes from Latin *multus*, "much"

an orchestra is **multisonous**—having many sounds

multitask was first used in 1986

having many paths or roads is **multivious**

mum in medieval times meant hush! or shhh!

mumble can mean "to chew or bite softly" and is a frequentative based on mum "hush"

the children's game **mumbletypeg** was first mumble-the-peg, descriptive of one of the penalties imposed on the loser

to be **mumchance** is to be dumbstruck and silent

mummer first described a person who muttered or murmured

mummy comes from Arabic *mumiya*, "embalmed body," which may come from Persian *mumiya*, "pitch, ashphalt" from mum "wax"—an ingredient in embalming

mumper is one who sponges off others

mumps is the plural of mump, meaning "grimace," which is how people look who get the disease

munch is imitative of crunch and scrunch

mundane first meant "of this earthly world" (from Latin *mundus*, "world")

mundivagant means "wandering around the world"

mung is a crowd of people

mungency is nose noise

municipal's history includes Latin *municeps*, "citizen with privileges," from *munia*, "civic offices"

munificent means "characterized by abundance"

a **muniment** is an archived record

munition first meant a "granted privilege or right"

munitions include ammunition and weapons

munity is a granted right or privilege

A.H. **Munsell** was a U.S. painter (1858–1918) who developed a color classification system for chroma, hue, and value (brightness)

Muppet is a blend of marionette and puppet

mural is based on Latin *murus*, "wall"

a group of ravens or crows is called a "**murder**"—probably because they attack and kill in groups

murine means "pertaining to mice or rodents"

murmur comes from Latin meaning "rustling" and can mean "complain, grumble about"

murphy is slang for potato

murrey is another way of saying "mulberry-colored" (reddish purple)

muscle comes from Latin *musculus*, "little mouse" as the ancient Romans thought their muscles wriggled like mice

Muscovy duck's name is an alteration of "musk duck"

a **muselet** is the wire that holds a champagne cork in place

museum is Latin for "library, study" from Greek *mouseion*, "seat of the Muses" or "shrine to the Greek muses"

marchons or *marchez*—French for "let's go" or "move faster"—became "**mush** on" and then "**mush**"

mush and **moosh** (nouns) are variations on mash

a few words that originated in Alaska are **mush**, **no-see-um**, and **mukluk**

before it was a **mushroom**, it was called either toadstool or funge (from Latin *fungus*); small mushrooms are called "buttons," medium-sized are "cups," and the largest are "flat" or "open" mushrooms

{ **mushroom** and **mush** are slang for "umbrella" }

neither **mushroom** (possibly from "moss") nor **toadstool** (a fanciful name) is a scientific designation

music is from Greek meaning "of a **Muse** or the Muses"—especially a **muse** inspiring song; **muse** can mean "song" or "poem"

a **musicale** is a private music concert for social entertainment

musk may come from Sanskrit *muska*, "scrotum, testicle"—which alludes to the shape of the **musk** deer's muskbags

musket is from an Italian word meaning "bolt from a crossbow"

muslin is named after a place in Iraq (Mosul) where it used to be made

mussel gets its name from Latin *musculus*, "little mouse"

the sounds of a crabby teenager are **mussitation**

must is a variety of cider apple

mustache is a variant spelling of moustache

mustang comes from Spanish words meaning "wild or masterless cattle" (*mestenco*, "lacking an owner" or *mostrenco*, "a strayer")

mustard got its name from being made originally with grape must (juice)

mustard is slang for the velocity of a baseball

muster originally meant "to display, exhibit, or show"

musty may be an alteration of moisty

mutable means "liable to change or alteration" (from Latin *mutare*, "change")

semantically, **mutate** is probably a descendant of Indo-European *moi-/mei-* "change, exchange" then Latin *mutare* "change"

mute is the act of defecating by a bird

my is a reduced form of **mine** and in early Middle English both were used as first-person singular possessive adjectives meaning "of or belonging to me"—and early on the distinction was only that **mine** was used before a vowel sound while **my** was used before consonants

myriad originally meant a "unit of ten thousand"

the adjective form for anteater is **myrmecophagine**

a **myrmidon** follows orders without question

{ **mutual** applies to reciprocal relationships between two or more things; if something is held in **common**, use "**common**" instead }

mutuatitial means "borrowed" or "something borrowed"

mutine "popular disturbance or revolt" gave way to **mutiny**, both derived from French *muete*, "violent uprising"

mutt (as in dog) is an abbreviation of muttonhead

mutuatitial means "something borrowed"

in Hawaii, **muumuu** has four syllables

a mix of many things going through one's head is **mux**

Muzak is named for "music" and patterned on the brand name Kodak

to **muzz** is "to study intently"

the nose and chin are the **muzzle** of a human

if someone is feeling **muzzy**, they are spiritless, dull or dazed and confused

my bad is said to have originated in pick-up basketball

mystery traces back to Greek *mustikos*, "secret," and *musterion*, "secret rites"; the lesser-known meaning of **mystery** as "handicraft; art" is part of the phrase "**mystery** play"

mystic comes from Greek *mystikos*, "initiated person"—from *myein*, "dose (the eyes, lips)" or "initiate"

mystify is derived from mystery or mystic

myth is from Greek *mythos*, "a fable, story, or tale"

a **mytheme** is an element of a myth, as a relationship between a character, an event, and a theme

mythopoeic means "creating or giving rise to a myth or myths"

You need your nose to pronounce **N**. **N** and **M** are the only nasal sounds in English. **N** is basically three-quarters of an **M**'s shape.

nab the rust means "be angry or sulky"

nabe in U.S. slang means "local cinema" (from neighborhood)

the **nacelle**—the bulge of an aircraft's wing that encloses the engine—was originally the name for the cockpit (from Latin "ship")

naches is a sense of pleasure and pride in the achievements of one's children (Hebrew *nakat*, "contentment")

nachlass is the unpublished material left by an author after his/her death

nacho may derive from a nickname for Ignacio, purportedly the name of the chef that created it—or it may come from a Spanish word for "flat-nosed"

a tennis ballboy is also called a **nacket**

nadir (pronounced NAY-dur) is the point directly under your feet

naff is slang meaning "unfashionable, unstylish" or "worthless"

nag comes from German *nagen*, "to gnaw"

to **naggle** is "to nag or quarrel" or "gnaw, bite"

a **naiad** is a freshwater mussel or shell, as opposed to a marine one

a **naïf** is a **naïve** person (**naïve** is the adjective)

the Indo-European ancestor of **nail** was *nogh-/onogh-*

naissance is the birth or origin of a concept, idea, or movement

naïve can mean "not having been the subject of a particular experiment"

naivete is pronounced nah-eev-TAY

a **naked** sword is unsheathed

naked goes back to Indo-European *nogw-*, "unclothed," which also produced Latin *nudus*, the source of nude

namby-pamby was the nickname of English poet Ambrose Philips (1675–1749)

name is ancient and goes back to Indo-European *nomen*, then Latin *nomen*, and Greek *onoma*

to **name-check** is to mention or acknowledge by name

a person who lives on Nantucket is a **Nantucketer**

the inner sanctuary of a temple is the **naos**

a pretend hit or strike in a theatrical performance is a **nap**

nap, short sleep, comes from Old English *hnappian*, "to sleep lightly"

napalm is the compound naphthemic palmitate

{ the nasty-smelling mothball substance is **naphthalene** }

Latin *mappa*, "cloth" came through Old French and its m became n, produced nappa, then English **napkin** with the diminutive suffix -kin

napoo! means "done for, finished"

beer that has a head and is foaming is **nappy** and a person who is **nappy** is slightly intoxicated

the **narcissus** plant was so named because of its narcotic effects (Greek *narkissos*)

if you tend to fall asleep every time you are in a relaxing situation, you may have **narcolepsy**

narcotic is from Greek *narkoun*, "make numb"

nares is another word for nostrils

narial means "pertaining to the nose"

a **nark** is an annoying or unpleasant person, thing, or situation—also a bad mood

you can describe something as **narky** if it is annoying and irritating or irritable and bad-tempered

narp is a slang word for shirt

narratage is the technique of having one character in the role of storyteller, the insertion of bits of explanation or narrative

narrate is a back-formation from narration

narrative was first an adjective meaning "telling the facts of a story" (from Latin *narrare*, which is also the base of narrate)

to **narrowcast** is to transmit it to a small audience

the **narthex** is a vestibule or antechamber stretching across the western end of some churches, separated from the nave

nash-gab is an impertinent, gossiping person

you do not want hairs in the **nasion** (space between the eyebrows)

nasturtium in Latin means "nose-twitching" (*nasus*, "nose" and *torquere*, "to twist") because of its pungency

nasty started out meaning "disgusting, filthy, stinking" and this then extended from the physical to the moral

nasute means having an acute sense of smell

natalitial is "of or relating to a person's birth or birthday" and natalitials is a "birthday celebration"

a **natatorium** is a swimming pool

nates is a synonym for buttocks (and natal cleft is the crack in the buttocks)

nation was once an adjective meaning "very, exceedingly, extreme," derived from Latin *nasci*, "to be born," through *nationem*, "a breed or stock"

a **nation** is made up of states—and a **country** is a **nation** defined geographically

a person born under a specific horoscope sign is a **native**

a **natkin** is a disagreeable taste or smell

natter is imitative of fast chatter

somebody who is **natty** is tidy, neat, and smartly dressed

the **natural** keys on a keyboard instrument, as a piano, are those colored white which produce notes in the **natural** scale (not flat or sharp)

nature traces back to Latin *natura*, "birth; quality, **nature**" and *nasci*, "be born"

naturopathy is any course of treatment for disease by herbs, special diet, massage, acupuncture, and other methods not involving surgery or artificial drugs

naufrage is an old word for shipwreck or ruin

Naugahyde was first made in Naugatuck, Connecticut and the word combines *Nauga* and *hyde*, "hide, animal skin"

naught and **nought** both come from Old English *nawiht/nowiht*, "nothing"

{ **naughty** derived from naught and first meant "having nothing; needy" }

naupathia is seasickness

Nauru was formerly Pleasant Island

nauscopy is the ability to sight land or ships at a distance

nausea is Latin, literally, "seasickness"

nauseous ("sickening") is an adjective describing something that causes nausea; the adjective for the feeling ("made sick") is **nauseated**

nautical goes back to Greek *naus*, "ship"

Navajo comes from *Tewa navahu*, "fields adjoining arroyo"

the bride actually walks up the **nave** (from Latin *navis*, "ship") of a church, not one of the **aisles** (one of the two parts parallel to the **nave**)

the **navel** is also the **umbilicus, belly button**, or **omphalodium**; **navel** and **umbilicus** share the same Indo-European root

navel-gazing is absorption in oneself or a single issue

navigation first described the action of traveling on water and is traceable to Latin *navigare*, "to sail"; **navigate** originally

meant "to go from one place to another in a ship," from *navis*, "ship," and *igare/agere*, "drive, lead"

navigator once described someone who excavated or constructed a canal or other earthwork

navy blue refers to the traditional color of the naval uniform

navy comes from Latin *navis*, "ship"

Nazi is the shortened form of Nationalsozialist "National Socialist"

a **nazzard** is a lowly or weak person

a child who is guilty of deceptive practices is a **nazzle**

Neanderthal is pronounced ne-AH-dur-tawl

another word for childlike is **neanic**

neanimorphic means "looking younger than one's years"

if you are feeling hung out to dry, then you can say you feel **neaped**

just use "**near**," not "**near** to"—where "to" does not work

nearside is pertaining to the left side of an animal, but for a vehicle, it is the side nearest the curb

neat as in "clean, clear" comes from Latin *nidus*, "shining, clean"; **neat** first meant "free from impurities"

a drink without ice or anything added is "**neat**" or "**straight**"

nebbish is another word for a nobody, a nonentity

Nebraska is from Omaha *ni-bthaska*, "river in the flatness"—for the Platte River

a **nebula** is a dust cloud in outer space

to convert liquid to spray in an atomizer is to **nebulize**

hazy and confused? It could be said you are **nebulochaotic**.

a lavatory was once called a **necessary**

neck originally was just the back portion of the body connecting the head and shoulders

necklace once meant lace or ribbon for the neck—or a necktie

Greek *nekros*, "corpse" gives us **necrophilia**, **necropolis**, and **necromancy**

nectar is from Greek *nekros*, "dead," and Sanskrit *taras*, "victorious"—describing a victory over death

nectarine comes from an adjective of the same spelling meaning "sweet as nectar"

need originally meant "violence, force" or "compulsion"

needle has the same Indo-European base as Latin *nere*, "to spin," and Greek *nema*, "thread"

needment is a thing needed

a taboo subject could be called **nefandous**—"unmentionable, not to be spoken of"

Latin *nefas*, "sin" denoted something contrary to divine law and it gives us the word **nefarious**

negligée once meant "careless, incomplete attire" (from Latin *neglegere*, "to neglect"—as in housework)

the root sense of **negotiate** is "to be busy" or "to be ill at ease"—from Latin *otium*, "idleness, leisure" plus a negative prefix to make *negotiare*, "to carry on business"

neidfyre is the Old English word for a fire generated by the intense friction between two pieces of wood

{ **neighbor** is Germanic *nigh/neah*, "near," and *gebur*, "dweller" }

neither is an adjective, adverb, conjunction, determiner, and pronoun—formed from Old English *na* and whether

a **nemesis** is "an agent of vengeance and retribution," not a "persistent opponent" (from Greek **Nemesis**, goddess of divine punishment which begat *nemein*, "give what is due")

neomenia is the time of the new moon, the beginning of the lunar month

neon is from Greek *neos*, "new"—hence, the new (element) as named in 1898

neophyte goes back to Greek *neophutos*, "newly planted"

neoteny is the prolongation of the period of immaturity

when a person, especially an author, is described as **neoteric**, it means they belong to modern/recent times—but it might also refer to a person having a modern outlook or new ideas; of things, **neoteric** indicates that they are modern, new, or recent

nephalism is total abstinence from alcohol

nephew and **niece** both first meant "grandchild"—and at one time, **nephew** was the illegitimate son of a priest and **niece** was a priest's illegitimate daughter

a total abstainer from alcohol can be called a **nephralist**

nepimnemic means "pertaining to a childhood memory retained in the subconscious"

Dr. Seuss invented the word **nerd** (1950) but Dr. Seuss never defined the words he made up

nerve comes from Latin *nevus*, "sinew, bowstring"

a vein in an insect's wing or the principal vein of a leaf is a **nervure**

nescience and **inscience** both mean "ignorance"

nescient can mean "ignorant" or "agnostic" coming from Latin *ne*, "not," and *scire*, "know"

nesh means "soft in texture or consistency," or "lacking in energy; slack, negligent"

nesia as in the islands Micronesia and Polynesia is from Greek *nesos*, "island"

nesiote means "living on an island"

nest is from Indo-European *nizdos*, literally "(place where the bird) sits down"

an overindulged or spoiled child (or one who has never left home) is a **nest-cock**

nestle first meant "to build a nest"

nestorian means wise and aged and a **nestor** is a senior figure or leader in one's field

the **Netherlands** is a country and **Holland** comprises two of its twelve provinces

a nerve cell is called a **neuron** (or neurone) and it is made up of the **axon** which conducts electrical impulses away from the **neuron**, and dendrites, the branchlike processes that conduct impulses to the **neuron**—the synapses being the areas across which these electrical signals travel

neurosis is a disorder of the central nervous system and it has come to be used as a shortened form of psychoneurosis, a mildly disturbing emotional or physical condition brought on by a mental state, while **psychosis** is a severe emotional disturbance

neurotic is based on Greek *neuron*, "nerve" and first was a drug affecting the nervous system or meant "acting on the nerves"

neuter is from Latin *ne*, "not," and *uter*, "either of two"

Nevada is Spanish for "snowy, snowed upon"

{ **net** as in "without deductions" came from French **net** as "neat" and then evolved to **net** "free from any (further) deduction" }

---

netop is a synonym for friend

nettles got their name because people used to weave them into nets

network is traceable to the early sixteenth century and indicates a web of connectins which link objects, institutions, and/or people

neural comes from Greek *neuron*, "nerve"; **neural** network can now refer to computer architecture in which processors are connected in a manner suggestive of connections between neurons

we all have times when we feel we have **neurasthenia**: a disorder characterized by loss of energy, lack of motivation, and feelings of inadequacy, along with vague physical symptoms such as headache or muscle pain

never is formed from Old English *ne* and *ever*

new goes back to Indo-European *newos*, which produced Greek *neos*, and Latin *novus*

newbie perhaps came from "new boy"

the main post at the bottom of a banister or stairway is a **newel**

newelty is another word for novelty

news first meant "new things, novelties"

newt, a type of eft, comes from a misdivision of "an ewt"

etymologically, **next** means "nearest," from Proto-Germanic *nekh-*, "near" a **nexus** is a connected group or series

a **nib** is a cleaned cocoa bean for the process of chocolate-making

a half a (computer) byte, four bits, is a **nibble** or **nybble**

nice first meant "foolish, ignorant," derived from Latin *nescius*, "ignorant"; **nicety** first meant "stupidity"

niche is from Old French *nichier*, "make a nest"

a gap in a range of hills is a **nick**

Nickel was a mischievous demon or dwarf and the metal was so called because it yielded no copper (abbreviation of kupfernickel)

a **nicknackitorian** (or knickknackatorian) is a dealer in curiosities

nickname is from a misdivision of "an eke-name" (eke meaning "addition") into "neke-name"

nicotia is a poetic term for tobacco and **nicotian** is a tobacco-smoker

nicotine comes from the Latin name of the tobacco plant, named for Jean Nicot, French ambassador to Portugal, who brought it to France c1560

to **nictitate** is to blink or wink

niddering means "cowardly" or "wretched"

niddle-noddle and **nid-nod** mean "having a nodding head"; to **nidnod** is to allow the head to drop repeatedly from drowsiness

to **nidge** is to shake the head

nidicolous describes young birds that stay in the nest for some time

nidification is "nest-building," coming from Latin **nidus**, "nest," which is also used to mean a source or origin, a place where a quality or principle is fostered

the smell of burnt or cooked animal substances, especially fatty, is **nidor**

nidus is a word for a breeding place for bacteria or a place where the eggs of insects or spiders are deposited

niff is a smell, especially an unpleasant one

nifty is a name for a joke or witty remark

Nigeria is named for the river Niger, from *gher n'gherea*, "river among rivers"

niggardly (grudging, stingy) derives from Old Norse *hnoggr* (covetous), and is not racial in nature

minute or meticulous handwriting is **niggle**

night comes from a large Indo-European family *nokt-*

nightfoundered means distressed at night while finding one's way in the dark

nightingale literally means "night-singer" as gale was "to sing"

in eighth century England, people thought a female monster (mare) would sit upon a sleeper's chest, causing a feeling of suffocation—hence, a **nightmare**

ancient Germanic peoples recorded time in **nights** rather than **days**

night-shine is a term for faint light perceptible at night

nihilarian is a great word to describe "a person who deals with things of no importance"

Nike is named for the winged Greek goddess of victory

{ **nikhedonia** is the pleasure derived from anticipating success }

nil is a contraction of Latin *nihil*, "nothing"

nimbose means "cloudy" or "stormy"

a **nimbus** is a cloud of fine particles or other matter surrounding a person or thing

nimiety is "excess" or "too much"

nimrod first meant "skillful hunter"

nine traces back to Indo-European *newn/enewn* with the descendants Greek *ennea* and Latin *novem*

ninjas are experts in ninjutsu, a Japanese technique of espionage that has been used in the training of samurai; **ninja** is a combination of two Japanese words meaning "endurance" and "person"

ninny is actually a dialectic variant of "innocent"

ninny-broth was another name for coffee

a **nip** is one fourth of a bottle or a half-pint (of ale, especially), a **baby** is one eighth of a bottle of wine

nirvana comes from Sanskrit meaning "be extinguished, be blown out"—and it now means the experience when greed, hatred, and delusion are extinguished and enlightenment gained

nisus is a word for "effort, endeavor"

a **nitch** is a slight notch, break, or incision

nitchevo in Russian means "Never mind!"

an impulse or tendency can also be called a **nitency**

a **nitery** is another name for a nightclub

nithe is envy or hatred

a **nithing** is a contemptible or despicable person

nitid is a word for "bright, shining, polished, glossy"

a **nitpicker** was originally one who picked the eggs or young of lice or other parasites out of the hair; **nitpick** is a back-formation from **nitpicker**

nittiness is being filled with small air bubbles

nitwit comes from Dutch *niet wit*, "I don't know"

if an area is marked by perpetual snow, it is **nival**

niveous is "snowy, resembling snow"

nix comes from German *nichts*, "nothing"

any piece of mail that is unable to be forwarded because it is illegibly or incorrectly addressed is a **nixie**

no is a reduced form of the adjective none

{ a **nob** is a person of elegance and high social standing }

a **nobbler** is a small drink of spirits, wine, or beer

a winner of a Nobel Prize is a **Nobelist**

a **noble** metal is one resisting corrosion

etymologically, to be **noble** is simply to be "well known," coming from Latin *nobilis*, and the root *gno-*, "know"

noble comes from Latin meaning "to know," then **prince** "leader," **duke** "leader," **count** "companion," **viscount** "in place of a companion"

nocent and **nocuous** mean harmful (and are the basis for **innocent** and **innocuous**)

a **noceur** is a person who stays up late at night

noctidial means "lasting for or comprising a night and a day"

a **noctivagant** is a night wanderer

noctuary is the opposite of **diary**—a journal of the night's events

nocturia is the excessive need to urinate at night

a **nocturnal** is a person out at night

nocturne in music is a night piece and in painting is a night scene

nocuous "harmful, noxious" is based on Latin *nocere*, "to hurt"

a **noddary** is a foolish act

the **noddle** is the seat of the mind or thought

node is from Latin *nodus*, "knot"

the place where two lines cross is the **node** or **knot**

nodose or **nodous** is "knotty, knotted, knobbed" from Latin *nodus*, "knot"

noegenesis is the generating or obtaining of new knowledge from experience through observation and the inferring of relations

Noel, once a word shouted or sung to commemorate the birth of Jesus, comes from French *nouel*/**noel**, "Christmas season," from Latin *natalis*, "annual festival of the church"

a **noema** (Greek) is an object of perception or thought and **noesis** is the process or aspect of perceiving or thinking

{ **nog** was originally a term for a type of strong beer }

a **noggin** is another name for mug or cup

to **noggle** is to walk awkwardly

noise first meant quarreling and comes from Latin *nausea*, "feeling of disgust"

noisome means "evil-smelling, offensive" and it comes from "noy," a shortened form of annoy

nolition or **nolleity** is a state of unwillingness

nomad comes from the base of Greek *nemein*, "to pasture"

a **nomenclator** is a book containing collections or lists of names or words—or the person who makes the collection

nomenclature is from Latin elements meaning "name" and "calling, summoning"

a musical note giving its name to a scale is a **nominal**

nominal is "of or pertaining to a noun or nouns" and to **nominalize** is "to convert

into a noun"; nominalization describes the process of changing verbs into nouns

nominate means "call the name of" (Latin *nomen*), while **denominate** means "to give a name to"

nonage is being legally underage for something

nonce is from a phrase *then anes*, "the one (purpose)" which was altered by misdivision and became **nonce**; it means "occurring, used, or made only once or for a special occasion"

nonchalant comes from French *nonchaloir*, "not heated," ultimately from Latin *noncalere*, "not warm or aroused"

nondescript first meant "not previously described or identified"

none is from Old English *ne*, "not," and *an*, "one"

a **nonesuch** is a person or thing without equal

an anticlimactic outcome is a **non-event**

nonpareil "peerless, unrivaled" is pronounced nahn-puh-RELL

nonplus comes from Latin meaning "not more, no further" and etymologically it means "put in a position where no more can be done"

noodle comes from German, but is of uncertain origin

a silly act or idea is a **noodleism**

the difference between a **nook** and a **cranny** is that the **nook** is a corner and a **cranny** is a crack

noology is the science of intuition and reason as phenomena of the mind

noon is derived from the Latin word for "ninth" as it originally meant the ninth hour after sunrise, about 3 PM

neither **noon** nor **midnight** is 12 AM or 12 PM because neither comes before or after the moment the sun is on the meridian

the sharp point of the elbow is the **noop** and the funny "bone" is the **olecranon**

the underlying notion of **noose** is "knot," coming from Latin *nodus*, "knot"

nor is a contraction of Old English *nother*, "neither"

Nordic skiing is a ski competition featuring ski jumping and cross-country racing

normal first meant "right-angled" and comes from Latin *norma*, "carpenter's square" or "rule, pattern"

the word **normative** "serving as a norm or standard" is based on Latin *norma*, "square used by carpenters, masons, etc., for obtaining right angles"

the southern boundary of the U.S. **North** is Maryland, the Ohio River, and Missouri

the underlying meaning of **north** is "to the left as one faces the rising sun"

the odor or perfume of wine or tea is the **nose**; the taste is the **mouth**

nosegay, a bouquet, is from nose and gay "ornament"

the **nosing** is that part of a stair step that projects over the riser

the **nose-piece** is the part of eyeglasses that rest on the nose

a **nosh** (from Yiddish) was first a restaurant or snack bar, but it comes from German *naschen*, "to eat surreptitiously"

no-siree and **yes-indeedy** come from Irish

nosocomial is "pertaining to a hospital" or "originating in a hospital"

a **nosology** is a classification or list of diseases

nostalgia comes from Greek *nostos*, "homeward journey, return home" and *algos*, "pain"—the word *nostos* originally

referring to the journey of Odysseus and the heroes from Troy

nostril comes from Old English words meaning "nose hole"

a **nostrum** is a pet scheme or favorite remedy

not is a contraction of the adverb "nought" (a variant spelling of naught "no thing")

notabilia are things worthy of note

notable means "worthy of notice" and **noticeable** means "readily observed"

notaphily is collecting paper money and **numismatics** is collecting coins

 notary is from Latin *notarius*, "shorthand writer or clerk"

notation is the old term for the explanation of a word on the basis of its etymology

note is the milk given by a cow or the period of its giving milk

a **notelet** is a short note or notecard

a **nothingarian** is someone with no religious belief or political creed

notice once meant "knowledge"

notify first meant "take note of, notice, observe"

notionate means "headstrong, obstinate"

notorious first meant "generally known" (from Latin *notus*, "known")

nougat derives from Latin *nux*, "nut"

noun comes from Latin *nomen*, "name"

a **nouricery** is a place where growing things are loved and tended

nourish first meant "bring up, or rear (a child or animal)"

wine or spirits given medicinally can be called **nourishment**

nous is intuitive intelligence and common sense

nova was originally a new star or nebula

Italian *novella storia,* "new story" begat "**novel**"

> { **novelist** can be used to describe an inventor }

the ancient Roman calendar started with March, so the ninth month was novembris or **november** *mensis from novem,* "nine," giving us **November**

Novemberish or **Novembery** pertains to the allusion of cold, damp, or foggy days characteristic of the month in the northern hemisphere

novenary means "based on or relating to the number nine"

novercal is characteristic of a stepmother

now is part of a large Indo-European family *nu-* meaning "present time"

the **nowl** is the head of an animal (but not man)

noxa is a thing harmful to the body—from Latin "hurt, damage"

noxious comes from Latin *noxius,* "harmful"

Noxzema is so named for "knocks eczema"

to **noy** is to harass, trouble, or vex

a **nozzle** is that part of a candlestick or sconce in which the candle is set; **nozzle** is based on nose and at first was a slang term for it

nu is an interjection expressing impatient inquiry, surprise, emphasis, etc.

nuance comes from Latin *nubes,* "cloud," and then French *nuer,* "show cloudlike variations in color"

nubilation is the formation and arrangement of clouds; **nubilous** means "cloudy, foggy" or figuratively "obscure"

nubile etymologically means "suitable for marriage," from Latin *nubere,* "take a husband"

nucal means pertaining to nuts

nucha is the nape of the neck, from Arabic *nuka,* "spinal marrow"

nuclear should be pronounced NOO-klee-uhr

nucleus (Latin "kernel, inner part") in ancient Roman times meant "small nut"

the most prominent syllable or syllables in a word are the **nucleus**; the main word in a derivative is also called the **nucleus**

to push or butt something with the head is **nud**; to push something with the nose is to **nuddle**

nude first meant "explicit, plain"

pertaining to the day before yesterday is **nudiustertian**

nudnik is Yiddish, from Russian *nudnyi,* "boring, tedious"

nugacious and **nugatory** are synonyms for trivial

nugae are trifles or trivia

the base of **nuisance** is Latin *nocere,* "to harm"

null comes from Latin *ne,* "not," and *ullus,* "any"

sometimes you feel you are in a state of being nowhere—which is **nullibiety**

a **nullifidian** is someone having no faith or religion; a disbeliever

an obsolete verb *niman,* "to take" did leave us the adjective **numb** "taken, seized"

number is regularly used with count nouns, while **amount** is mainly used with mass nouns: **number** of mistakes, **amount** of money

numbles is a word meaning "animal intestines and internal organs" a **numen** is a resident spirit or power

numeracy is having arithmetic skills (like literacy for reading)

numerals are symbols; **numbers** are the things that **numerals** symbolize

numinous means "divine, spiritual; awe-inspiring"

nummary is an adjective for "pertaining to coins or money"

numptious is "cuddly and delightful"

a **numquid** is an inquisitive person

nun is derived from Latin *nonna*, the feminine of *nonnus*, "monk," originally a title given to an elderly person

nuncheon was the first name for lunch, from *noon schenche* (drink)—a drink taken at noon

nuncupative "declared orally," a legal term, is pronounced NUNG-kyoo-pay-tiv

and Old French. As a noun, **nurture** first referred (c 1330) to a person's training or breeding. The word can be traced back to Latin *nutritus*, meaning "to nourish."

nut comes from an Indo-European root meaning "lump"

the transitional paragraph where the lead passes into the body of the story is the **nut**

the **nuthatch** cracks or hacks nuts to eat and hatch is related to English hatchet and French *hache*, "ax"

etymologically, **nutmeg** means "nut that smells of musk," probably from Latin *nux muscata/muga*, "musky or musk-scented nut"

a **nutraceutical** is food that is thought to provide health benefits

nutrice is a synonym for "nurse"

nutriment is another word for food

nutrition can mean the adding of oil to an ointment or unguent

nuzzle once meant "grovel"—and it is a frequentative of "nose"

nuppence is British slang for "no money"

nuptial is from Latin *nuptiae*, "wedding," from *nubere*, "to marry"

a **nurgling** is a person with a catlike disposition

nurse goes back to Latin *nutricia*, "wet nurse," and *nutrire*, "to suckle"

nursery can be a pond in which fry are reared

To **nurture** means "to feed or nourish a child" and also "to raise and support to maturity." The verb was formed after the noun, which came into English via Anglo-Norman

to **nyaffle** is to eat in a hasty, gluttonous manner

nychthemeron is a 24-hour period

nyctalopia is poor vision in low light

nylon is an invented word patterned on "cotton" and "rayon"

nymph traces back to Greek meaning "bride" and Latin meaning "be married to (a man)"

nymphomania, excessive sexual desire in a female, has a male counterpart— **satyriasis**

{ **O** is the oldest letter of our alphabet }

in phrases using **o'**, the meaning is "of"

an **oaf** was originally the child of an elf or goblin

an **oafo** is a hooligan or a lout

oak flavor of wines comes from **oak** cases and is similar to coconut or vanilla

oakum is loose fibers from rope and it comes from an Old English word that literally meant "off-combings"

the origin of **oasis** is likely North African/Egyptian for "dwelling place," but the etymology is not formulated beyond Greek **oasis**

an **oast** is a kiln used to dry hops or malt or tobacco

unlike the names of other cereals (barley, wheat), **oat** is not a mass noun and its first meaning may have been that of an individual grain

to **obacerate** is to contradict

obdormition is numbness caused by pressure on a nerve, as when a limb is "asleep"

one who is **obdurate** is stubbornly impenitent

obelisk (pronounced AH-buh-lisk) is from a Greek diminutive of *obelos*, "pointed pillar"

the dagger mark used in dictionaries and other documents is an **obelus**

obese is from Latin *obesus*, literally "having eaten oneself fat"

an **obex** is any device that can hold a door shut (bolt, crossbar, latch, lock); it also means impediment or obstacle

obey comes from Latin *ob-*, "towards," and *audire*, "hear"

to **obganiate** is to irritate with reiteration

obi, a kimono sash, is Japanese for "belt"

the **Obie** award is named for the initials for "off Broadway"—as it is an award presented annually by a professional organization for notable achievement in plays performed off-Broadway

Latin *mortem obire*, "meet death," eventually gave us **obit**, which originally meant "departure from life" and then "a ceremony performed at the burial of a dead person" and the word "**obit**" actually came before the word "obituary" and is not an abbreviation of it

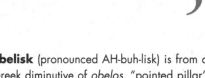

obituary goes back to a Latin euphemism for "die," *obire* meaning literally "go to meet"

object, the noun, comes from Latin *objectum*, meaning "thing presented to the mind"

object, the verb, comes from Latin *ob-* and *jacere*, "to throw," and first meant "put in the way" and "place to interrupt or hinder"

objective can describe something that exists as an object of consciousness as opposed to having a real existence

oblate means "flattened at the poles," and the opposite is **prolate**; the earth is an **oblate** spheroid

something offered to God or a god, like a sacrifice or donation, can be called an **oblation**

obligate first meant "attach, bind, connect, fasten"

to **oblige** someone is etymologically "bind them to" something with a promise, with the word coming from Latin *obligare*, "to tie, bind"

oblique can mean "indirect," as in a course or expression

a meaning of **obliterate** is to cancel a postage stamp

oblivescence is forgetfulness

to **obliviate** is to forget; an **oblivial** is anything that causes forgetfulness

oblivious can be followed by of or to

oblong comes from Latin meaning "somewhat long or elliptical"; **oblongitude** is the state of being **oblong**

obloquy suggests defamation and consequent shame and disgrace

obmutescence is the act of becoming mute or silent—usually a stubborn, willful act; if you are inclined to silence, you are **obmutescent**

obnounce is to report an unfavorable omen

obnoxious first meant "subject or liable to harm or injury" (Latin *ob-*, "toward," and *noxa*, "harm, injury")

to cover with clouds or fog is to **obnubilate**; a state of being cloudy or vague is **obnubilation**

the **oboe**, a woodwind instrument, gets its name from its high pitch, its ancestor being French *hautbois*, "high wood"

obreption is an attempt to obtain something by deceit or a false statement (and the actual obtaining by doing this)

obscene comes from Latin *obscenus*, "ill-omened" or "indecent"

obsequies comes from Latin meaning "funeral rites" and **obsequious** means "compliant to the will or wishes of another" but once meant "of or pertaining to funerals, mourning"

observance refers to the following of a custom, duty, or law; **observation** refers to the act of noticing or recording

an **observandum** is a thing to be observed or noted

observe comes from Latin *observare*, "watch, pay attention to" and "comply with"

the early sense of **obsess** was "to besiege, beset, harass" and **obsession** was the unexpected siege of a castle—and then the words took on the figurative sense

obsidian was erroneously formed from Greek *opsianos lithos*, "a black stone"—named after its supposed discoverer, Obsius

obsolagnium is waning sexual desire due to age

obsolescent is "passing out of use; becoming obsolete"

things that are no longer used or needed are **obsolete**; things that are becoming **obsolete** are **obsolescent**

obstacle, something that stands in the way, is from Latin *ob-*, "against," and *stare*, "stand,"

obstetrics is derived from Latin obstetrix "woman who is present, midwife," from earlier words meaning "to stand in the way," i.e., waiting for the baby to be delivered

severe constipation is **obstipation**

obstreperous "clamorous, noisy" and "argumentative" is from Latin ob-, "against," and strepere, "to make a noise"

an **obstriction** is an obligation

obtain can mean "prevail, succeed, win"

to **obtenebrate** is to cast a shadow over

to **obtrude** is to press, impose, or force on or upon (someone), to intrude

obvolution is a fold, turn, or twist of something coiled—like a bandage wrapped around a limb

the **ocarina**, a primitive musical instrument, is named for its resemblance to a goose, from Italian **ocarina**, "little goose"

occamy was an alloy imitating silver, the counterpart to **alchemy**, alloy imitating gold

occasion once had the specific sense of "an opportunity for finding fault or giving offense"

the **Occident** is the region of the sky where the sun sets—the west (the opposite of **Orient**, the east)

{ the **occiput** is the back of the head (Latin ob-, and caput, "head") }

obtruncate means "cut off the head or top of"

to **obturate** is to close up an opening, stopping a flow, and also has a meaning in dentistry—to fill a root canal

in botany and zoology, **obtuse** means "blunt, not pointed or sharp"

obumbrate means to darken, overshadow, or make difficult to see or understand

obvelation is the opposite of **revelation**—"the action of concealing something"

an occasional gift or treat is an **obvention**

the first meaning of **obverse** was "turned towards or facing the observer"

the side of a coin or medal with the main design is the **obverse** (head) and the other is the **reverse** (tail)

obviate literally means "meet in the way and prevent," from Latin obvium, "in the way"

the root sense of **obvious** is "like a thing met on one's way" (ob-, "in, toward," viam, "way")

occlude comes from Latin ob-, and claudere, "to close"; an **occlusion** occurs when something has been closed up or blocked off—as the teeth of the lower jaw with the teeth of the upper jaw

a stopper can be called an **occlusor**

occult first meant "hidden from sight; concealed" (Latin ob-, and celare, "conceal")

a meaning of **occultation** is "the disappearance from view of a star or planet in the sun's rays after sunset or before sunrise, when the star or planet is above the horizon"

occupy's Latin root is ob-, "over," and capere, "seize, take"

occur comes from Latin occurrere, "run to meet"

Ocean comes from Greek okeanos potamos, "the great river that encompasses the earth" (as it was believed to be a river that encircled the earth) and its former synonyms were "**ocean** sea" and "**ocean** stream." In early times, when only the one great mass of land, the Eastern hemisphere, with its islands, was known, the **ocean** was the "Great Outer Sea" and Greek cosmologists portrayed the world as a circular disk surrounded by a mighty stream named Okeanos, akin to Sanskrit *asayanas*, "the encompassing"—and Okeanos was the great primeval water, hence **ocean**.

ocelot comes from Nahuatl for "field tiger"

an **ocellus** is one of the eyelike spots on the tail of a peacock or on a butterfly's wing; the plural is **ocelli**

the line behind which the dart players must stand is the **oche** or **hockey**

ochre (or **ocher**) is any of various natural earthy materials or clays which are rich in iron oxides and vary in color from light yellow to deep orange-red or brown

ocivity is laziness

o'clock is an abbreviation for "of the clock"

the original meaning of **octave** was "eight-day festival"

octave is the distance covered by any eight notes of a **scale**; a **scale** is a series of eight notes played in alphabetical order

an **octavo** is a size of page traditionally produced by folding a standard printing sheet three times to form a section of eight leaves—making each 5 x 8"up to 6 x 9.5"

the Roman year originally began in March—so **October** (Latin *octo*, "eight") was the eighth month

an **octopus** means "eight-footed" so it is misnamed because it actually has eight arms; the plural is **octopuses** or **octopodes**

the pound key on a keyboard or keypad is technically an **octothorpe**

oculus is a term for the compound eye of an insect, an eyelike opening, or a circular window (as in a church or opening of a dome)

odd is from Old Norse *odda-maor*, "third or **odd** man who casts the deciding vote"

an **odditorium** is a shop for oddities or oddments (broken parts or parts of once-complete sets)

ode was first a poem that was to be sung

odium is another word for hatred

odobenid means "pertaining to a walrus"

to be in good or bad **odor** is to be in or out of favor

{ something's **odor** is its **reputation** or **estimation** }

odorant is an odorous substance, the opposite of **deodorant**

an **odoriferen** is a smell-producing or -bearing thing

odoriferous means "having an odor or fragrance" while **odorous** refers to something smelly

odyssey, not a common noun until the late nineteenth century, first meant "wayward travel"

another word for architectural is **oecodomic** or **oecodomical**

an **oenologist** is a "student of wine"

of is the only commonly used English word in which an "f" is pronounced like a "v"

there is no need to say "**off** of," just say **off**; the same with "outside"

off the wall alludes to squash or handball when a shot comes **off the wall** at an unexpected or erratic angle

offal first meant "refuse from a process"

off-capped means "having taken off one's cap or hat"

offend first meant "strike with the feet against something"

offer originally was "to present or sacrifice something to a religious entity"

office is actually a combination of Latin opus "work" and facere "do"—and the word first referred to a duty, service, or task attached to a person's employment

officious means "overeager to offer unwanted advice or help" and can also mean "unofficial"

offing is the distant sea visible from the shore

an **off-islander** is someone who is a visitor or temporary resident of an island

off-message means "departing from an expected or regular theme or issue"

to ski **off-piste** is to ski away from prepared ski runs

the **offscape** is a distant view or prospect; the background

offscourings is another word for riff-raff or rubbish/refuse

offset can mean "set at an angle" or "place off-center"

offshore denotes a wind blowing away from the land

often is an extended form of oft; **often** should be pronounced OF-en

an **ogee** in architecture is a molding consisting of two members, the one concave, the other convex, like an S

ogle "to cast amorous glances" comes from Dutch oog "eye"

an **ogre** is a man-eating monster; an **ogress** is a female **ogre**

ogygian means "incomparably ancient"

Ohio is Iroquois oheo "beautiful" referring to the **Ohio** River

an **ohrwurm** or **earworm** is a popular tune you "catch" like an infection

oikology is housekeeping

oil is from Latin oleum and that is from Greek elaion, "olive **oil**; other oily substance"

ok was first an abbreviation for Old Kinderhook, President Martin van Buren's birthplace, and it became a rallying cry for him during his reelection campaign

Oklahoma is Choctaw for "red people"

the Indian term for **okra** is bhindi

etymologically, **old** means "grown-up"

the bony tip of an elbow is the **olecranon**

the cultivation of vegetables is **olericulture**

to **olfact** is to detect the odor or scent of something

olfactory comes from Latin olere, "to smell," and facere, "make"

if something is **olid**, it has a strong and unpleasant smell

oligoria is a disinterest in former friends or hobbies

{ **olitory** means pertaining to or grown in a kitchen garden }

olive comes from Latin oliva, "oil"

an **olivet** is an olive garden or grove

ollapod is a mixture of language (from Spanish olla podrida); an **ollapodism** is a sentence made up of various languages

ollendorffian is an adjective describing the phenomenon of "representing or using stilted language of a kind characteristic of that found in some foreign-language phrasebooks"

Olmec literally means "inhabitant of the rubber country"

om is a Sanskrit sacred syllable or invocation traditionally uttered at the beginning and end of prayer and meditation; according to later classical Hindu thought, **om** is composed of three sounds, a, u, and m, interpreted as representing the three most important gods, Vishnu, Shiva, and Brahma, and a fourth element, which is silence

ombrology is the study of rain

ombud in **ombudsman** is from umbodh "commission, charge, administration"

omega is literally Greek for "Great O"

omelet has also been written **omelette**, amulet, and aumelet; **omelet**'s root sense is "thin layer" or "crepe" and it was first described in English as a "pancake of eggs"

omen is from classical Latin **omen**, "something that foreshadows an event"

the code of silence in the Mafia is the **omertà** ("humility")

if something is **omissible**, it is able to be omitted

a part of an invertebrate, like a tentacle, which has an eye is an **ommatophore**

omneity is the condition of being all; the prefix omni- means "all, in every way, of everything"

omniana is the word for "bits and pieces about almost anything"

an **omnibus** is a waiter's assistant who clears tables (etc.), i.e., a busboy

omnifarious means "dealing with all kinds of things" or "of all kinds or forms"

omnilegent is "reading or having read everything; characterized by encyclopedic reading"

omnistrain is the stress of trying to cope with everything at once, i.e., the stresses of everyday life

an **omnium** is the sum total of one's desires or values

an **omophore** is a giant who carries the earth on his shoulders

omphalophobia is a fear of belly buttons

omphalos describes the center, heart, or hub of a place, organization, or sphere of activity (from Greek meaning "navel"—for the round stone in the temple of Apollo at Delphi supposed to mark the center of the earth)

omphaloskepsis is contemplation of one's navel as an aid to meditation

on is an ancient Germanic preposition

before paved roads, horse-drawn water wagons sprayed the streets to settle the dust and anyone who had sworn abstinence from alcohol was said to have "climbed aboard the water wagon," later shortened to "**on the wagon**"

once originated as the genitive form of one; the genitive case was widely used in Old and Middle English for making adverbs out of nouns, as in always, towards

after **once**, **twice**, **thrice**—that's it, no comparable words for four, five, etc.

a **oncer** does something once and then never again

oncology (study and treatment of tumors) is based on Greek onco-, "mass"

> **ondinnonk** (from Iroquoian) describes the soul's innermost desires

one goes back to Latin *unus* and Indo-European *oinos*, "**one**, unique," a large ancient family of words

oneiric means "pertaining to dreams"

oneiromancy is dream interpretation

onerous "burdensome, oppressive" is from Latin *onus*, "burden, load"

one-time means "one time"; **onetime** means "former"

onewhere means "in one place only"

buying as a means of mental relaxation is **oniochalasia**

oniomania or **emacity** is an uncontrollable desire to buy things

onion comes from the Latin word *unio*, "oneness" (*unus* "one") as it consists of a single bulb

on-line should generally be hyphenated as an adjective or adverb

only is "one" suffixed with -ly

onomatomania is a fear of a particular word

words based on the imitation of natural sounds are called **onomatopoeias** (Greek *onoma*, "name," and *poi*, "maker") or **echoic words**

onset is the movement of the speech organs just before the articulation of a speech sound

onto is used where two elements function as a compound preposition and "**on to**" is used when on is an adverb; **onto** is when you mean "on top of, aware of"—otherwise, use "**on to**"

ontogenesis is the origin and development of an individual

ontology is the branch of metaphysics concerned with the nature or essence of being or existence, the opposite of **phenomenology** (the science of phenomena)

onychocryptosis or **onyxis** is an "ingrown toenail" (Latin *onycho-*, "nail")

onychophagia or **onychophagy** is the practice of biting one's nails

a scientific or technical name is an **onym**

onymous means "bearing the name of the author" (with the opposite being **anonymous**) or "having a name"

onyx comes from Greek *onux*, "claw, fingernail," and types of **onyx** are pink with white streaks, resembling fingernails, which is why it is so named

oof and **ooftish** are slang for cash or money and **oofy** means "rich"

an **oojah** or **ooja-ka-piv** or **oojiboo** is "a thing whose name one forgets, does not know, or prefers not to mention"

oolong, as in tea, is from Chinese *wulong*, "black dragon"

oose is the furry stuff that gathers under beds—also called **dust bunnies**, **trilbies**, or **kittens**

ooze, as in mud or slime, traces back to Old Norse "puddle, stagnant pool" and originally meant juice or sap from a plant or fruit

opal comes from Sanskrit *upala*, "precious stone"

opalescence is the condition of having various colors or milky iridescence like an opal

etymologically, **open** means "turned up" or "put up" from Germanic *upanaz*, denoting the raising of a lid or cover

the **opener** comes first in a three-comic show, followed by the **feature**, followed by the **headliner**

opera is actually the Latin plural of *opus*, "labor, work"

operate traces back to Latin *opus*, "work," and **operation** is from Latin *operari*, "expend labor on"

if one is diligently busy, one is **operose**; **operosity** is the quality or state of being busy or industrious

the ability to please generally is **ophelimity**

ophryon is the point between the eyes

a tough spelling is **ophthalmologist**, which starts with ophth- (pronounced "off" or ahf-thuhl-MAH-luh-jist); **ophthalmology** is based on Greek *ophthalmos*, "eye"

ophyron is the space between your eyebrows

{ **opinion** comes via Old French from Latin *opinari*, "think" }

opinional is "based on opinion"

the back of the human hand is the **opisthenar**

opium is from Greek *opion*, "poppy juice"

opossum is from Algonquian *op*, "white," and *assom*, "dog, doglike animal"

opponent was first a person who maintained a contrary argument in a dispute

opportune comes from Latin *ob-*, "in the direction of," and *portus*, "harbor" (opportunus) and **opportunity** first described wind driving towards a harbor, favorable winds

oppose is from Latin *ob-*, "against," and *ponere*, "to place," and first meant "to confront someone with hard questions"

opprobrium first meant "shameful or disgraceful conduct" and now means a bad reputation or disgrace based on such

to be **oppugnant** is to be antagonistic or opposing

opsigamy is marriage late in life

an **opsimath** is a person who begins to learn or study late in life

optimum has to do with harmony and the reconciliation of conflicting considerations and does not really mean greatest, fastest, or biggest; **optimism** is based on the word **optimum**

an **opulent** plant has a lot of color, fragrance, or blossom

an **opuscule** is a minor or small work, literary or musical (diminutive of opus)

the Old English word for "**or**" was *oththe*, and this changed in Middle English to "other" and other was soon contracted to "**or**"

an **ora** is a border or an edge

oracle and **orator** come from Latin *orare*, "to speak or pray"

oral comes from Latin *or/os*, "mouth"

orange comes from the Sanskrit word *naranga*, and the name of the fruit **orange** came first, then the color by association

oratorios are so named for the congregation of the Oratorians founded by St. Philip Neri in the sixteenth century—scenes from scripture set to music

opsony is anything eaten along with bread

opsophagy is the eating of delicacies

optable once meant "desirable"

optation is the action of wishing; a wish or desire

Greek *optos*, "visible," gives us **optical** and **optic**

opticians provide eyeglasses and contact lenses after an **optometrist** examines your eyes, after which you can see an **ophthalmologist** if you need treatment for diseases or disorders—though ophthalmologists also do regular exams

optimific means "producing the maximum good consequences"

orangutan is from Malay *orang*, "man," and *(h)utan*, "forest" (man of the forest)

an **orarian** is a dweller by the seashore, especially the coastal areas of Alaska

oration was originally a prayer to God and a private prayer chapel is an **oratory**

orb once denoted a circle

orbit first meant "eye socket"; the eye is located in the eye socket or **orbit**

orc can describe any large ferocious sea creature, like a killer whale

orchard (first spelled hortyard) originally meant "garden yard"

the earliest senses of **orchestra** were as "the semicircular area for the chorus to dance in an ancient Greek theatre" and the art of dancing itself (Greek *orkheisthai*, "to dance")

orchids got their name from Greek *orkhis*, "testicles," which is what their root system (tubers) looks like; orchids were once called ballock stones, sweet cods, fox stones, goatstones, dogstones

ordain first meant "to put in order; arrange; prepare"

ordeal is from Old English *ordel*, "judgment," figuratively, an experience testing endurance, patience, courage, etc.—also a test of guilt or innocence which was one of severe pain or torture

an **order** is being told to do something with no specific guidelines, a **command** is being told to do something in a specific way, and a **directive** is being told to do something and getting this information through channels

ordinance first meant arrangement in ranks or rows

an **ordinary** is a public house or restaurant offering regular meals at a fixed price

the **ordinate** or Y axis is vertical; the **abscissa** or X axis is horizontal

orecchiette pasta translates to "little ears"

oregano comes from Greek *origanon*, from *oros*, "mountain," and *ganos*, "joy"

Oregon is Algonquian *Waregan*, "beautiful water" for the Colorado River

{ **Ore-Ida** (food brand) is a combo of Oregon and Idaho }

organ comes from Latin *organum*, from Greek *oganon*, "implement, instrument, tool"; it was first a very general term but then was used for "wind instrument" and "functional part of the body"

if a compound contains carbon, it is **organic**; no carbon indicates **inorganic**

organize first meant "give organic structure to"—implying the interdependence of parts; also, it meant "form into a living being"

to **organize** can mean "covert into fibrous tissue during healing"

orgasm descends from Greek *orgasmos* (from organ), "swell with moisture" or "be excited" and the word first meant "excitement in a bodily organ or part, accompanied by turgescence"

orgy is from Greek and Latin *orgia*, the secret nocturnal revels or festivals in honor of Bacchus

an **oriel** is a large upper-story bay window, usually supported by brackets or on corbels

Orient was first defined as "that region of the heavens in which the sun and other heavenly bodies rise, or the corresponding region of the world, or quarter of the compass"

the special luster of a pearl of the best quality is called its **orient**

to **orient** was originally to make something face east (to the **Orient**), especially a church; use "**orient**," not "**orientate**"

the cross-country sport of map and compass reading is **orienteering**

an **orifice** is a small opening or aperture (from Latin for mouth)

origami is Japanese for "fold paper"

origin is from Latin *oriri*, "to rise"

originary is an adjective meaning "causing existence; productive" or "primitive; primary; original"

an **orihon** is a book or manuscript folded like an accordion (from Japanese *ori*, "fold," and *hon*, "book")

orismology is an explanation of technical terms or the science of defining technical terms

orison, a prayer, is from Latin *oratio*, "speech, oration"

orlings are the teeth of a comb

the lowest deck on a ship is the **orlop**

ornament implies adding something, stressing the heightening of the original

ornery is a dialectal corruption/variant of the word ordinary

orogenesis is the formation of mountains (Greek oros) and **orogeny** is the process by which mountains are formed

orotund (from Latin for "with round mouth") is a manner of speaking in clear, resonant tones—suited for public recitation

orphan is from Greek *orphanos*, "bereaved," and it originally meant a person who has lost one or both parents

an **orrery** is a mechanical model of the solar system and how the planets move around the Sun

an **ort** is a morsel or remaining scrap; **orts** is another name for leftovers

{ a cross between an orange and a tangerine is an **ortanique** }

ortho- and **orth-** come from Greek for "straight" or "right, true"

orthodontics, based on Greek *orthos*, "straight," is the branch of dentistry that aims to straighten crooked teeth

Greek *orthos*, "correct, straight" combined with *doxa*, "opinion" to make **orthodox** "having the right opinion"; **orthodoxy** is Greek for "right opinion"

orthoepy is the study of correct pronunciation and the relationship between pronunciation and spelling

orthograde animals walk with their bodies in a straight or vertical position

orthography is correct or proper spelling

orthology is the study of the correct use of words

orthopedics is based on Greek *orthos*, "straight," and *paideia*, "child," and was originally the treatment and prevention of physical deformities in children

orthopraxy is another way of saying "right practice, right conduct" (orthodoxy is "right belief, rightness of beliefs")

orthoptics is treating visual defects by exercise and retraining in visual habits

orthorexia is an obsession with eating only "healthy" food

a librarian for the Academy of Motion Picture Arts and Sciences said the statues looked like her Uncle **Oscar** and a reporter heard this and the name stuck to the Academy Award

Latin *os*, "mouth" or "face" had a diminutive oscillum "little face" and this term was used for a mask of the god Bacchus that was hung as a charm in vineyards, swinging in the breeze—which evenually became *oscillare*, "swing," and then English **oscillate**

oscitancy is the act of yawning—and **pandiculation** is stretching and yawning

oscitation is drowsiness indicated by yawning or a state of not being attentive due to lack of interest

an **osmatic** animal relies mainly on its sense of smell

osmosis, the process of gradual or unconscious assimilation of ideas or knowledge, comes from Greek *osmos*, "push"

etymologically, the **osprey** is simply a "bird of prey"

the **ossature** is the arrangement of the bones of the skeleton

an **ossuary** (from Latin os, "bone") is any receptacle (urn, vault, etc.) for the bones of the dead

ostensible means literally "that can be shown," from Latin *ostendere*, "show"

otosis is the alteration of words because of a misunderstanding of sounds

{ **otter** is etymologically "water animal," from Indo-European base *udros*, which produced Greek *hudra/hydra*, then English *water* }

a group of peacocks is an **ostentation**

ostentiferous is "bringing omens or supernatural manifestations"

an **ostler** is a stableman at an inn

the adjective form of oyster is **ostracine**

in ancient Greece, when it was proposed that a person be sent into exile, a vote was taken and the method of registering the vote involved putting the name on a piece of broken pottery called *ostrakon*, so casting the vote was *ostrakizein*, giving us English **ostracism**

ostrich is from Latin *avis struthio*, "bird ostrich," from Greek *strouthos*, "**ostrich**, sparrow"

ostrichism is self-delusion, a refusal to cope with something, such as a threat—figuratively hiding one's head in the sand

a spy or listener is an **otacust**

other is part of a large Germanic word family expressing "alternative"

othergates means "in another manner; otherwise"

if one is unemployed or idle, they are **otiant**

if something is **otiose**, it serves no useful purpose

otiosity is another word for leisure or idleness

an ear, nose, and throat specialist is an **otorhinolaryngologist**

the ear-inspecting instrument is the **otoscope**

an **oubliette** is a secret dungeon with an opening only in the ceiling, often in a castle—from French *oublier*, "to forget"—for one is left in an **oubliette** to be forgotten

ouch once described the part of a ring in which the jewel was set

ought started out as the past tense of owe

Latin *uncia*, "twelfth" became **ounce** (a troy **ounce** is 1/12 of a pound)

our and **us** come from the same Proto-Germanic base "ons"

ourself was once used just like **ourselves** as the word self was plural as well as singular

oust came via French from Latin *obstare*, "to stand in the way"

ouster is a word once used for the act of bailing water out of a boat

out has a former comparative form in **utter** "complete"

farmlands at a distance from the farmhouse are the **outfield**

outlandish once meant "foreign"

an **outlier** is someone sleeping outdoors

the true etymology of **outrage** has nothing to do with out or rage, rather, it is a borrowing from French **outrage** "insult, **outrage**" based on Latin *ultra*, "beyond," and *agium*, a noun suffix; **outrage** first meant "lack of moderation"

outstanding as a noun once meant projection

oval is from Latin *ovum*, "egg"

Ovaltine was first Ovomaltine, from the eggs (Latin *ovo*) and malt it contained

Latin *ovum*, "egg" produced **ovary**, among a number of other words (oval, ovate, ovulate)

etymologically, **over** denotes "more up, upper"

an **overcome** is a crossing or passage

overconnectedness is an obsession with staying in constant touch with people and/or events via communications technology

an **overdog** is a person with a huge advantage or dominating position

overhand had an early meaning of "mastery, superiority"

overhead is the expense of maintaining property (e.g., paying property taxes and utilities and insurance), the cost of the upkeep or running of premises or a business

overkill first meant "excessive killing"

the upper lip is the **overlip**

to **overlook** and to **overshadow** both meant "to bewitch" at one time

overt first meant "open, not closed"

overture is from Latin *apertura*, "opening," and first meant "apperture, hole, orifice"

overweening is based on the old verb "to ween" meaning "to be of the opinion" or "to believe, think"

overwhelm originally meant "bury" or "drown" and the root of **overwhelm** is "over the helm"—stormy seas breaking over the side of a ship

overwrought is an archaic inflection of overwork

to **oviposit** is to lay an egg

ovoid means "resembling an egg"

ovulate (produce and discharge eggs) is a back-formation of ovulation

owe first meant "own, possess"

{ **owl** is from a Germanic base imitating the **owl's** call }

own implies acknowledging something in close relation to oneself

ox is traceable to Indo-European *uksin*, "male animal"

another word for armpit is **oxter** and to walk arm in arm is to **oxter**

Lavoisier believed **oxygen** was important in forming acids so he named it for Greek *oxys*, "acid," and French *gene*, "that which produces"

oxymoron (guest host, jumbo shrimp) is from Greek *óxmoron*, a compound formed from *oxs*, "sharp," and *mor?s*, "dull"

an unusually shrill voice is **oxyphonic**

oxytocia is quick childbirth

an **oxytone** is a word with the primary accent/stress on the last syllable

oy in Yiddish just means "oh" but **oy** veh means "woe"

an **oyer** is a criminal trial

oyez, a call for silence and attention, descends from Anglo-Norman **oyez**/*oiez* "to hear" or "hear ye"

the Greek word for **oyster** was *ostreon*, etymologically an allusion to its shell, from an Indo-European base *ost-*, "bone"

an **oysterage** is an oyster bed

ozone comes from Greek *ozein*, "smell, stink" and was called this when it was coined in 1840 due to its odd smell; however, colloquially, **ozone** is pure fresh air

ozostomia is another word for bad breath

{ **P** descended in a straightforward manner from the 17th letter of the ancient Near Eastern alphabet. }

pablum (a proprietary name for a mushy cereal) figuratively means any soft, easily digested food

one meaning of **pabulum** is "that which feeds a fire"

pace is from Latin *passus*, "stretch of the leg" or "step" and once meant "journey, route"

pachyderm is a collective term for animals with thick skin (elephant, rhinoceros, hippopotamus)

pacific and **pacify** trace back to Latin *pax*, "peace"

pacify can means "to subdue by armed action"

pack as in "influence the composition of" (a jury, meeting, etc.) is based on an obsolete verb meaning "making a secret agreement"

packet is a diminutive of pack

an alpaca and vicuña can produce a **paco-vicuña**

paction is the act of making a pact

pad is possibly borrowed from Low German or Dutch/Flemish **pad** "sole of the foot"

an aquatic animal's flipper can also be called a **paddle**—as can the foot of a duck or the wing of a penguin

a **paddling** of mallards is the collective noun

paddock is from Old English *pearroc*, "enclosure"

paddy as in "field" is from a Malay word meaning "rice in the straw or husk" (rice **paddy** is redundant)

a **paddywhack** is a childish temper tantrum

padlock's etymology is uncertain, but may come from *pad*, "wickerwork basket," perhaps from the similarity in shape between the hanging lock with closed hook and a basket with its handle

a **paean** is a song of praise or thanksgiving or an expression of praise or admiration

paella (rice dish) is Spanish for "frying pan" from Latin *patella*, "little pan"

pagan, from Latin *paganus*, first meant a country dweller or rustic and "belonging to a village"

page is from Latin *pagina*, "column of writing"

the first pageants were plays in a medieval mystery cycle or an act or scene in such a play; later, a **pageant** was a play with a religious theme

paggle is to hang loosely or bulge

to **paginate** is to count or order the pages in a document

pagoda comes from Persian *butkada*, "idol or god base"

pain (in English) originally meant punishment for a crime or offense—sometimes by losing one's head

rouge can also be called **paint**

pair is from Latin *par*, "equal"

paisley material is named after the town of **Paisley**, Scotland, where it was originally made

pajamas is from Persian *payjama* and Hindi *paejama*, "leg garment"; the original **pajamas** were loose-fitting pants and the matching top was only adopted when **pajamas** were brought back to the chillier European climate

Pakistan got its name from the initials of Punjab, Afghanistan, Kashmir plus the ending *-istan*, "place, country"

pal comes from the gypsy word *pral* or *phral*, "brother"

palace comes from Latin *palatium*, originally the name of one of the seven hills (Palatine) of Rome where the house of the emperor was located

palaver, self-seeking talk or blather, is from Portuguese *palavra*, "discussion, word, speech"—based on Latin *parabola*, "parable," from Greek *pard*, "across," and *bolein*, "to throw"

pale as in color comes from Latin *pallidus*, "turn **pale**"

geological time is divided into four great eras: **Paleozoic** "old life," Mesozoic "middle life," Cerozoic "recent life," and Precambrian "pre-Welsh"

palestral means pertaining to wrestling

a **palette** is the painter's mixing board or range of colors and a **pallet** is a makeshift bed of straw or portable platform used in warehouses for moving or storing goods; **palate** is the roof of the mouth and a sense of taste

etymologically, a **palfrey** is an "extra horse"

palimpsest can describe a manuscript or writing surface that has been reused, erased, or altered while retaining traces of its earlier form—and by extension, an object, place, or area that reflects its history

palindrome (word or phrase that reads the same backward as forward) is from Greek *palin*, "again, *back*," and *dromein*, "run"

a fence of pales is **paling**

palinoia is the compulsive repetition of an act until it is perfect

a **palisade** is a fence of pales (stakes), from Latin *palus*, "stake"

pall was first a cloth spread over a coffin, hearse, or tomb

the original **palladium** was a statue with magical powers, carved by the goddess Athena, who killed her childhood friend, the goddess Pallas

pallbearer is based on "pall," a cloth spread over a coffin, hearse, or tomb

if something is **palliate**, its true nature is concealed; to **palliate** is to attempt to abate the seriousness of an offense

something **pallid** is pale or wan (from Latin *pallere*, "to be pale"); **pallor** is paleness, especially of the face

palm, the plant, was named for its leaf being likened to a spread hand

the **palm** is the blade of an oar or paddle

palomino ultimately comes from Latin *palumba*, "wood pigeon"

the **palp** is the fleshy part of a fingertip

palpable first meant "able to be touched, felt, or handled"

the eyelid is also the **palpebra**; **palpebral** means "relating to the eyelids" and to **palpebrate** is to wink

palsy is another word for paralysis

the jack of clubs in cards is also called **pam**

pamper first meant "overindulge or cram with rich food"

pamphlet's root sense is "collection of love poems"; **pamphlet** should be pronounced PAM-fluht

the upper part of the skull has been called the **pan** or **brain pan**

panacea combines *pan-*, "all," and Greek *akos*, "remedy"

a **panache** can be a tuft or plume of feathers as a headdress or helmet

panary means pertaining to bread and **panivorous** is bread-eating

pancake is first attested in English around 1400 as a thin flat cake of batter, fried on both sides in a pan and usually served either flat or with several stacked

pancetta is an Italian diminutive for belly and it is the cured belly of pork

{ etymologically, **pancreas** (the gland) means "all flesh" }

panda may derive from Nepalese

a **pandect** is a complete digest of a particular branch of knowledge or a book of "everything"

pandemic is a stronger version of epidemic as in a **pandemic** outbreak, nearly everyone may be affected

pandemonium literally means abode of all demons (or hell), from the Greek *pan-*, "all," and *daimon*, "demon(s)"

pander started as a noun for a go-between in illicit love affairs—from the name of a Chaucer character (Pandare) who did this

pandiculation is an all-over stretching and yawning, as upon waking (from Latin *pandere*, "stretch")

Pandora is, literally, "all-gifted" in Greek

a **pane** originally was a "piece of cloth"—from Latin *pannus*—or a piece of cloth having several different colors or materials joined side by side (**panel** also originally meant the same, esp. one placed under a saddle)

a **panegyric** is a speech of praise, as a eulogy or encomium

paneity is the state of being bread

pang may be pain and sting combined, or is derived from prong

Pangaea was the single supercontinent before continental drift

sentences containing all twenty-six letters of the alphabet are known as **pangrams**

the **Panhandle** states are Florida, Texas, and Oklahoma

panic derives from Pan, Greek god of flocks and herds, who ruled the wilderness and its mysterious terrors and was believed to be the cause of any sudden groundless fear

a **panicle** is a loosely branching cluster of flowers

panification is conversion into bread

panjandrum is an invented word, coined in 1755 by English actor and playwright Samuel Foote to test the memory of actor Charles Macklin, who claimed to be able to memorize and repeat anything said to him

panmnesia is the belief that every mental impression remains in the memory

acorns and other pasturage for pigs is **pannage**

panniers are the baskets on a beast of burden or on the sides of the wheels of a bicycle, motorcycle, etc.

panoply first meant "complete protection for spiritual warfare"

panorama is made up of Greek *pan-*, "all," and *horama*, "view"

pansy derives from the French word *pensée*, "thought," because the flower seemed to have such a pensive face

it is the shock that makes you "gasp" that is behind the word **pant**, from Latin *phantasiare*, "gasp in horror"

pantaraxia are any actions aimed at keeping people on their toes

pantheon can describe a group of people particularly respected, famous, or otherwise significant in some capacity

a **pantomancer** sees omens or lessons in events and experiences

paper is derived from the Greek word *papyrus*

another way of saying "**kleenex**" is "**paper handkerchief**"

a box containing writing materials is a **papeterie**

papier-mâché is French for "chewed paper"

the bumps on a tongue are **papillae**

dandelions' tuft or fluff is **pappus**

paprika is derived from Hungarian/Serbo-Croatian *papar*, "pepper," as it is made from dried pimientos

par is Latin, literally "equal, equality"

para- as in paradox, paramedic, paramilitary—means "distinct from but analogous to"

para- in **parachute** and parasol means "defend, guard, shield"—and **parachute** is protection against "chute" fall

in ancient Rome, a *pantomimus* was a "mime artist" and the term was adoped as **pantomime**, literally "all imitator"

a **pantopragmatic** is one who meddles in everybody's business

Latin panis "bread" is the base of **pantry** (through Old French *paneterie*, "bread room or closet") and it originally was a room where bread was kept

pants comes from pantaloons—from a sixteenth century Italian comic called Pantalone, who wore strange trousers

panurgic means "able or ready to do anything"

papable means "eligible to be elected Pope"

paparazzi (plural) got their name from Paparazzo, a fictional freelance photographer in Fellini's 1959 film "La Dolce Vita"; paparazzo in Italian means "a buzzing insect"

a **parable** places a simple story in juxtaposition with a moral principle to draw a comparison

paracentral is "near the center"

the beginning of decline or decay is the **paracme**, the stage after one's peak

parade comes from a French word meaning "a showing" or "action of stopping a horse," originating from Latin *parare*, "to prepare"

the **paradiddle** drum rudiment (drum roll) is left right left left or right left right right

a **paradigm** is a very clear or typical example showing how something is to be done all the inflected forms of a word constitute its **paradigm**

Persian *pairidaeza*, "walled around" was borrowed into Greek (*paradeisos*, "park, pleasure ground") and became the word "**paradise**"

paradox is from Greek *para-*, "aside from, contrary," *doxa*, "opinion"—and it is something that seems to go against common sense but may still be true or is a person or thing with qualities that seem to be opposite

paraffin, coined from Latin *parum affinis*, "(having) little affinity"—resists chemical combination

a **paraffle** is an ostentatious display or flourish

to **paragate** is to wander through

the addition of a letter or syllable to the end of a word to give emphasis or modify the meaning is **paragoge**; also, the addition of an unneeded sound at the end of a word, like "r" on "idea"

paragon comes from Greek *parakone*, "sharpening stone, whetstone" and it came into English from a metaphor for "perfect example of virtue"

the ancient Greeks adopted the practice of placing a short horizontal mark under the first work in a line where a new thought occurred; this was called **paragraphos** from *para*, "beside," and *graphein*, "to write" and it became **paragraph**

parakeet is an anglicization of Old French *paroquet*

paralanguage includes intonation, hesitation noises, gesture, and facial expression

paralipomena are things added as a supplement

paralipophobia is a fear of having neglected some duty

parallel comes from Greek words meaning "beside" and "one another"

a **paralogism** is a piece of illogical or false reasoning, especially that appears or seems logical; to **paralogize** is to draw illogical conclusions from a series of facts

{ **paralysis** is from a Greek word meaning "disabled at the side" }

parameter is a quantity or mathematical variable that stays constant; **perimeter** is the outer boundary of an area

paramnesia can mean the inability to recall the meanings of common words

paramount means "primary, top" and **tantamount** means "equivalent to, same as"; **paramount** first meant "highest in jurisdiction"

paramour is from *par amour*, "by or through love" (French)

paranoia is from Greek *para*, "irregular," and *noos*, "mind"

paranumismatica are collectible items similar to coins and medals, like tokens

a **parapet** is a raised place or structure to conceal troops from the enemy's observation and fire

to **paraph** is to divide into paragraphs and the noun can mean a flourish made after a signature, especially to make it unique

an item of paraphernalia is a **paraphernal**

paraphernalia (Latin *pherne* "dowry") meant literally "beside the dowry" and was the property that a married woman was allowed (by law) to keep and deal with as her own

a **parapluie** is a great word for "umbrella"

a blunder that reveals a hidden motive is a **parapraxis**

{ **paraplegia** is from a Greek word meaning "strike at the side" }

parasite (from Greek meaning "one who eats at another table") first meant a person who lives at the expense of another person or of society in general

parasol is from Italian *para*, "guard or protect against," *sol*, "sun"

word formation involving both combination and derivation is **parasynthesis**, as in downhearted, formed from down plus heart plus -ed, not down plus hearted

parataxis is the placing of prepositions or clauses one after another, without indicating by connecting words the relation (coordination, subordination) between them, such as "Tell me, how are you?" or "Come sit here; I need you."

parboil actually comes from Latin "boil thoroughly" but the prefix became confused with one that means "part"

parcel first meant "small portion"

parcheesi descends from Sanskrit for "twenty-five," the highest throw in the game—and it was originally played with six cowries for dice

parchment is a blend of Latin *pergamina*, "writing material from Pergamum," and *Parthica pellis*, "Parthian skin"

a **parclose** is a railing or screen in a church that encloses an altar or separates off a side chapel—or a screen or railing that partitions off a space in a building

to **pare** the ground is to slice the turf off

pareidolia is the erroneous or fanciful perception of a pattern or meaning in something that is actually ambiguous or random—like the Man in the Moon or animals in cloud formations or religious images in tortillas

parel is physical or moral stature

parent as a Latin word meant "father or mother"

parenthesis derives from a Greek word translating to "put in beside"

Tahitian brings us **pareo** (wraparound skirt)

parergon is any subsidiary work or business apart from one's ordinary employment (moonlighting)—or a work that is a by-product of a larger work

parfait is literally French for "perfect"

pariah comes from Tamil *paraiyar*, "drummers of big drums"—who were despised for drunkenness and eating forbidden meat (in India)—so the word came to mean "social outcast"

parietal means of or relating to life within a college or university

the mutuel in **pari-mutuel** is French for "stake" or "wager" and the pari refers to an equal division

paring is done with a knife, **peeling** with the fingers

the etymological idea underlying **parish** is of "living nearby," from Greek *paroikos*, "living near"

park was originally a legal term for land held by royal grant for the keeping of game animals for royals to hunt

Paris was named for its indigenous clan, the Parisii

parka is from Russian meaning "pelt, skin jacket"

highways with median strips and plantings were first called **parkways** because they were left in a more natural state, like a park

parlay means to use one gain to make another; **parley** is to discuss (or as a noun, conference or discussion)

parliament is from French meaning "speaking" and its first meaning was "speech, conversation, discussion, debate" a **parlor** was first a room for conversation in a monastery or convent (from French *parler*, "to speak, talk")

parlous means "full of uncertainty; precarious"

Parmesan is French from Italian *parmigiano* (from Parma, Italy)

a collection of poems is a **parnassus**

a **parnel** is a priest's mistress

parody comes from a Greek word meaning "burlesque song or poem"

parol (note spelling) means "a spoken statement" or (as an adjective) "expressed orally"

parole is the actual linguistic behavior of a person, the practice of using a language

words derived from the same root, such as beautiful and beauteous, are **paronyms** or **conjugates**

a **paroxysm** is a sudden recurrence or attack, for example, of coughing

parp is the honking sound of a car horn

parquet is the orchestra pit or ground floor of an auditorium

parrot came into English as a diminutive form of the name Pierre "Peter"

a tame **parrot** is sometimes called a poll **parrot**, poll, or polly; a **parakeet** is a smaller slender **parrot**

parse, to break down a sentence, explaining the form and function of each part, is possibly from Middle English *pars*, "parts of speech"

parsimonious means extremely thrifty and frugal (from Latin *parcere*, "to spare, save")

parsimony is extreme unwillingness to spend money or use resources

the Greek root of **parsley** is selinon

parsnip comes from Latin *pastinare*, "to dig or trench the ground," and *napus*, "turnip"

parson and person started off as the same word, from Latin *persona*, but split eventually

a minister's or priest's residence is a **parsonage** or **rectory**

Latin *pars* meant "piece, side, share," etc., and it is a source of **part** (as well as many other words), though it was reborrowed from French in the thirteenth century

a pie may be divided into parts but each **part**, when offered to a person, becomes a **portion**, the **part** allotted to that person

a **part** is any of the components of a whole, a **portion** is a **part** allotted to or regarded as belonging to someone; a **piece** is a **part** separated from the whole; a **division** is a **part** formed by classifying, cutting, partitioning—and so is a **section**, though it is generally smaller; a **segment** is a **part** separated along natural lines of **division**, and a **fragment** is a small **part**

you **partake** of something and you **participate** in something

a **partan-face** is a sourpuss

a **parterre** is a decorative garden with paths between the beds of plants; the word also describes the back of the ground floor of a theater, often under the balcony (from French "on the ground")

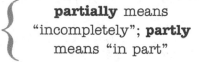

partially means "incompletely"; **partly** means "in part"

participation derives from Latin *participatus* meaning "made to share"

a verb acting as an adjective is a **participle** (a smoking gun) and the etymological idea underlying a **participle** is of a word that shares or "partakes" of the dual nature of an adjective and a noun (from Latin *particeps*, "partaker")

particle is a diminutive of part

particular, from a Latin word meaning "particle" first meant "belonging to or affecting a part"

a **partisan** is literally one who takes a "part" or "side" in a cause

partner came from *parcener*, "joint heir" from Anglo-Norman, from the earlier Latin *partitio*, "partition"

the root of the word **partridge** is "farter"— from the sound made by its wings when it flushes; in Middle English *partriche*, "fart bird" and its taxonomic name Perdixperdix is "fart fart (bird)"

a **passel** is a large number or group

a **passenger** was orignally a traveler or wayfarer in general—and often one on foot; the word meant simply "one who is passing or making passage"

passive first meant "suffering, exposed to suffering"

the word **Passover** literally means "pass over" as it commemorates the sparing of the Israelites from Egyptian bondage

passport originally was authorization to pass from a port, pass through a country

passion first meant the suffering of pain and is from Latin *passionem*, "suffering," as used to describe the sufferings of Jesus Christ

Latin *partitum*, "part, side" became **party** with the senses "political group" and, in the eighteenth century, "social gathering"

a matched set of necklace and earrings is a **parure**

parvanimity is "meanness"

pase is the cape movement a matador makes to attract the bull

pash is heavy rain or snowfall

pashmina is derived from a Persian word meaning "woolen"

pasimology is the study of gestures as a means of communication

the key unseen move in a magic trick is a **pass**

the **pass** is the counter in a restaurant between the waitstaff and the kitchen

passable means "barely satisfactory or able to be passed"; **passible** means "capable of feeling or suffering"

a **passage** is a one-way boat crossing; a **voyage** is a round trip journey by sea

to **passulate** is to dry grapes to make raisins (Latin passula "raisins")

past (adjective, noun) is the obsolete **past** participle of pass (verb)

pasta is literally "dough" or "**paste**" in Italian; **paste** first meant "dough" or "pastry"

pastel first pertained to the pigment or paste and evolved to mean light or pale colors

Louis Pasteur (1822–1895) discovered the process of fermentation called **pasteurization**; pasteurized milk has been heated to destroy pathogenic bacteria—and homogenized, also pasteurized, has been processed so that the fat globules have been broken up and distributed throughout

a **pastiche** is a work of art imitating another artist; as an adjective **pastiche** means "exhibiting or incorporating an amalgam of different styles" (from Italian *pasticcio*, "confused affair")

pastime is derived from "pass time"

the Latin word **pastor** means "shepherd," from an earlier root *pascere*, meaning "to feed, to graze" (**pasture** is derived from this root also)

pastose is an art term meaning "thickly painted"

pastrami, seasoned smoked beef, is Yiddish, from Rumanian *pastrama* and *pastra*, "preserve"

pastry is a derivative of paste and was coined in the sixteenth century as a collective term for food items made from flour-and-liquid mixtures

paté (French "paste") was originally baked in a crust and **terrine** (French "made in earthenware") was baked in a dish without a crust—and a **paté** is usually of finer consistency than a **terrine**

to **patefy** is to reveal or disclose

the metal plate used for serving bread in a church eucharist service or passed for collection of money in a church service is the **paten**

the word **patent** comes from Latin *patens*, "lying open," and they were first called "Letters **Patent**" meaning "open letters," which granted the holders with certain rights of monopoly

pathetic first meant "producing an effect on the emotions"

a **pathic** is a passive person or victim

pathology literally means "the study of suffering" but is actually used to describe the study of diseases

pathos (pronounced PAY-thos) is an English use of a Greek word for "suffering"

the horizontal bar of a cross is the **patible**

the stem of **patience** is Latin *pati*, "suffer"

a **patient** is, etymologically, one who is "suffering" from Latin *pati*, "suffer"

patio descends from Latin *patere*, "to lie open," and was adopted from Spanish for "inner courtyard"

a **patois** is a variety of language specific to a particular area, nationality, etc., which is considered to differ from the standard or orthodox version

patrial means having the right to live in the UK through the British birth of a parent or grandparent

{ **patriarch** is from Greek *patria*, "family," and *arkhes*, "ruling" }

patrimony first meant "the estate or property belonging by ancient right to an institution, corporation, class, etc."

Patriot is from Latin *patriota*, "fellow countryman" (from earlier Greek *pater*, "father") and this was its original meaning when it came into English in the late 1500s. Soon thereafter, it described a person who is willing to sacrifice his or her well-being for that of his or her country. It also means, "one who loves and defends a country's freedom or interests."

patrol comes from a French word meaning "paddle about in the mud"

patron derives from Latin *patronus*, which means "protector of clients" or "defender"

patter first meant "recite a prayer" as it derives from Latin *paternoster*, literally "Our Father," the Lord's Prayer

pattern comes from *patron*, "something serving as a model"

a **patzer** is a beginning chess player

if something is just completed or finished, you can say it is **paulopast**

to **paunch** is to swallow hastily or greedily

Greek *pauein*, "stop," passed into English via Latin *pausa*, and became **pause**

pave comes from Latin *pavire*, "to ram down to make a flat surface"

pavé a setting of jewels placed close together so that no metal is visible

pavement is from Latin *pavimentum*, "trodden-down or beaten floor";
pavement is a hard surface of which **asphalt** is one type

pavid means afraid or timid

a **pavilion** originally denoted a large decorated tent

pavonine means "pertaining to a peacock"

one's **paw** is one's handwriting or signature

to be **pawky** is to be lively, bold, uninhibited, and somewhat impertinent

pawn, the chess term, comes from Latin *pedo*, "foot soldier" (from *pes*, "foot")

a **pawpaw** is the same as a **papaya**

the first sense recorded for **pay** was "pacify" and it came to mean "pacifying a creditor"

Orthodox Jewish ringlets are called **payess**

cargo, baggage, and passengers are the **payload**

paynim is a name for a non-Christian or heathen

a **paysagist** is a painter of landscapes

pea comes from Greek *pison*, "pulse, pease"

the small wooden ball inside a referee's whistle is called a **pea**

peace is from Latin *pax*

peaceful means "characterized by peace, in a state of peace or tranquility"; **peaceable** means "disposed toward peace, inclined toward peacefulness"

peach derives from Latin *persicum malum*, "Persian fruit"

to **peach** is to betray secrets or give away one's accomplices

the original name of a **peacock** was pea, borrowed from Latin *pavo*; in the fourteenth century, the compounds **peacock** and **peahen** were created to distinguish the sexes

peafowl is the non-sex-specific version of peacock and peahen

the point of a beard is the **peak**

peak means "maximize," **peek** means "to peep or snoop," and **pique** means "to excite or irritate"

peal is from the word appeal

peanut takes its name from its resemblance to peas in a pod and has these synonyms: pinda, goober, groundnut, ground pea, earthnut, and monkey nut; **peanut** itself appeared in the early nineteenth century and is not a nut but a legume (pea)

pearl is a type size equal to five points, between ruby and diamond

peasant was first a person who lived in the country and worked the land

porridge of uncertain temperature is **pease**

the early English singular for pea was **pease**

the **peasecod** is another word for pod of the pea

a **pebble** is a high-spirited, hard-to-control person

the rough grainy feel of some paper is called **pebble**

pecan is borrowed from Illinois *pakani*, "nut that is cracked," and it was first spelled *paccan*

peccable means "capable of sinning" or "given to sinfulness"—the opposite of impeccable

peccadillo is a Spanish diminutive of *pecado*, "sin"

peccant means guilty of sinning while **peccable** means capable of sinning

peck can be slang for "food"

to **peckle** is to peck slightly or repeatedly

pecorino cheese is from ewe's milk, as pecora is Italian for "sheep"

pectination is the action of interlocking, like the teeth of two combs

pectoral was once a word for "breastplate"

peculate's root sense is "to embezzle"

the base of **peculiar** is Indo-European *peku*, "wealth expressed in heads of livestock," and Latin *pecu*, "cattle"—and the meaning was extended to "personal, private property"—so **peculiar** came to designate things that belonged to a person and no one else, then came to be applied to more abstract qualities and characteristics that were unique to a person (or group)

pedigerous means "having feet or legs"

French *pied de grue*, "foot of the crane"—gives us **pedigree**—because in a genealogy the vertical line divided into three branches resembles the foot of the bird called crane

pediment is another word for base or foundation

to operate something with your feet is to **pedipulate**

pedlar/peddler is probably a diminutive of ped "pannier, basket, hamper"

the raising of children is **pedotrophy**

peek first meant "look through a crevice"

a **peekapoo** is a cross between a Pekinese and poodle

{ cattle and sheep were an ancient medium of barter and exchange—and the word **pecuniary** is from Latin *pecu*, "cattle" }

pedagogue, from Greek *ped*, "child," and *agein*, "to lead" was a Roman slave who took children to school and on outings, but also taught them

pedal traces to Latin *pes*, "foot"

a **pedant** is a tiresome teacher who focuses only on details

peddle is a back-formation from peddler/pedlar, an itinerant trader in small goods

pedestal comes from Old Italian *piedestallo*, a conflation of *pie de stallo*, "foot of a stall"

pediatrician comes from Greek *pais/paidos*, "child," and *iatros*, "physician"

the stem of an apple is the **pedicel**

pedicure is from Latin *ped*, "foot," and *curare*, "attend to," and it once meant "one who treats feet; a chiropodist"

a baker's long-handled oven shovel for pizza, bread, etc., is a **peel**

an exceptional or noteworthy instance of a thing can be termed a "**peeler**"

peeler was first used to describe London police officers, for statesman Robert Peel, but soon the nickname switched to his first name—**bobby**

the **peen** is the end of a hammer head opposite the striking face; to **peen** is to bend or flatten with a hammer

to **peenge** is to complain in a whining voice

peepeye is another name for peekaboo

peer is based on Latin *par*, "equal," and it first meant "member of the nobility, person who is superior"

peeve is a back-formation from peevish "perverse, obstinate"

peevish, of animals, can mean "fond of being petted"

a **peg** is a segment of a citrus fruit

peignor is from French *peigner*, "to comb," because the negligee was originally worn while combing the hair

peirastic means tentative, experimental

to **pejorate** is to make worse; **pejorative**, a derogatory word, comes from a Latin base *peiorare*, "make worse"

Pekoe is tea picked so young that its leaves still have a coating of white down—Chinese *pek*, "white," and *ho*, "down"

pelage is the fur, hair, wool, etc., of a mammal

pelagic refers to the open sea, as opposed to shallow water near a coast; the **pelagic** environment is that in the water itself

pelf "money or goods taken" is from Old French *pelfre*, "booty," and is related to pilfer

pelican is probably based on a Greek word for "ax"—referring to the shape of its bill

parchment in a roll is a **pell**

etymologically, a **pellet** is a "little ball," from French *pelote*, from Latin *pilota*, "little ball"

a thin skin of film (or a thin scum on any liquid) that forms when oil paints dry is the **pellicle**

pellucid means "allowing the passage of light"

the main bunch of cyclists in a race is a **peloton** (originally a small body of soldiers)

pelsy means "trivial, trashy, of little value"

to attack with snowballs is to **pelt**

pelvis is literally "basin" in Latin

pen comes from Latin *penna*, "feather"

{ **penal** and **penalty** are based on Latin *poena*, "pain" }

penal means "relating to punishment" while **punitive** means "serving to punish"

penance as a form of apology for a mistake can be either voluntary or ordered by someone else

pence is a plural of penny

At first, **pencil** denoted a fine paintbrush and the word is derived from a diminutive of Latin *peniculus*, "brush; little tail"—which itself is actually a diminutive of *penis*, "tail." Chaucer also holds the distinction of having first used the word **pencil** (c 1386) as the instrument used in painting. By 1612, a **pencil** was a writing instrument—a thin cylinder with a tapering point made of various materials such as chalk, charcoal, graphite, plumbago, slate, etc. The amount of clay used determines the degree of hardness of the lead in a **pencil**, e.g., No.1 is soft, No. 2 is medium-soft, etc.

a light fixture suspended from a ceiling or the hanging part of an earring is a **pendant**

pendant is the noun; **pendent** is the adjective—meaning "hanging, suspended"

a pear-shaped glass (crystal) pendant on a lamp or chandelier is a **pendeloque**

pending can mean "hanging, overhanging"

a **pendule** is a pendulum clock

a **pendulum** is etymologically simply something that "hangs," from Latin *pendere*, "hang"

the **penetralia** or **penetral** are the innermost parts or deepest recesses of a place or thing, as of a building

penetrate is from Latin *penetrare*, "to get into, to affect or influence"

a non-flying member of an air force or a training aircraft used on the ground is called a **penguin**

the name *pen gwyn*, "white head" originally referred to the great auk in winter plumage and was misapplied to the animal we call **penguin**

penicils are the short tufts of hair or fur on caterpillars

penicillin is named for the mold's brushlike spore-bearing structures (Latin *peniculus*, "brush")

peninsula is literally (Latin) "almost an island"

penis means "tail" in Latin

penitentiary is an Americanism for a place where criminals work, pray, and read the Bible as "penitence" and it was once a place for giving penance

the **penknife** is so called since it was originally used for making or mending quill pens

{ **pennant** is a
blend of pendant
and pennon }

penne is pasta cut diagonally at the ends like an old-fashioned quill pen (Italian plural of *penna*, "quill, pen")

the sylvania in **Pennsylvania** is from Latin *silva*, "woods" (of William Penn)

penny comes from Germanic *panninggaz*, possibly from the root *pand-*, "pledge, security"

penny-wisdom is wisdom in small matters or carefulness in small expenditures (but not large ones)

Pensacola is Choctaw for "hair people"

payment for board and lodging or board and education, was once called **pension** and this word also referred to a relatively cheap boarding house; **pension** is, etymologically, something which is weighed out (Latin *pensio*, "payment," from *pendere*, "to weigh")

a chore as school punishment is a **pensum**

Pentecost means "fiftieth day," as it occurs on the seventh Sunday after Easter

a person with a strong dislike or aversion to their mother-in-law is a **pentheraphobe**

a shed or outhouse attached and sloping away from the main wall of a building was first called a **penthouse** (from French *pente*, "inclination, slope"); not until 1921 did it mean "apartment or small house built on the roof of a skyscraper"

a **pentimento** is a painting or drawing that has been painted over but still shows through

the **penultimate** is the one before the last; the one before that (second to last) is the antepenultimate

penumbra can describe any "gray area" where things are not all black and white, as well as the partial shadow surrounding a complete shadow, as in an eclipse

penurious is a synonym for "poor, in need"

people comes from Latin *populus*

people is a term equivalent to cows and horses—like a herd of humans; **persons** is used in regard to our external aspects and refers to a number of individuals

pepper comes from Sanskrit *pippali*, "long **pepper**"; **pep** is an abbreviation of **pepper**

pepperoni is from Italian *peperone*, "chile; red pepper"—as it is salami seasoned with this

in chemistry, the prefix **per-** relates to the maximum proportion of some element in combination, e.g., peroxide

peradventure is a great synonym for perhaps

perambulate first meant "to travel through and inspect and survey a territory"

the elements of **perceive** are Latin *per-*, "entirely," and *capere*, "take"

perceptible includes the prefix per- "through" so the word refers to whatever can be taken in through the senses

percolate is literally "to strain, to put through a sieve"—but can also mean walk or stroll

a **percontation** is a question or inquiry

something that is **perculsive** gives you a shock

percussion comes ultimately from Latin percutere "strike through; beat"

perdition is the state of complete ruin

to **perdure** is to continue, endure, keep going

peremptory comes from Latin *peremptorius*, "destructive," from *perimere*, "take away completely"; something **peremptory** takes away entirely a person's right to make further comments or requests

to **perennate** is to persist from season to season

perennial first meant "remaining leafy throughout the year"; plants living three or more years—dying aboveground and sending up fresh growth every year—are perennials

perestroika came from the mid-1980s Russia and literally means "rebuilding, reconstruction, reform"

something that is **perfect** is etymologically "completely made," from Latin *perficere*, "finish"

perfervid is "very fervid"—in other words, glowing

perfidy is breaching the faith or trust put in one

to **perform** is etymologically to provide or furnish completely

perfume derives from Latin *fumus*, "smoke," literally meaning "through smoke," as the first perfumes were obtained by the combustion of aromatic woods and gums—and their original use was in sacrifices to counteract the smell of burning flesh

perfume or parfum is 20–40 percent oil and the highest concentration; **eau de toilette** is 10–18 percent oil, and **cologne** or **eau de cologne** is 3–9percent oil

perfunctory is from Latin *per-*, "through," and *fungi*, "discharge, perform," meaning "getting through the doing"; to do something carelessly is to **perfunctorize** or **perfuncturate**

to **perfuse** is to cover with liquid or color

a **pergola** can be described as an arbor formed of growing plants trained over a trellis

perhaps is from Latin per "by means of" and Middle English *hap*, "chance, fortune"

on a citrus fruit, the **pericarp** is the white stuff just inside the zest—and it is also called the rind; the **mesocarp** is the juicy part you eat and it contains the juice sacs

periclitate is to put in danger or at risk

a tour or description of a region is **periegesis**

etymologically, **peril** means a "trying out of something" or an "experiment," from Latin *periculum*, "danger, experiment"

perimeter comes from *peri-*, "around," and *metron*, "measure"

period is from Greek meaning "orbit" or "course" or "recurrence"

peripatetic "itinerant" derives from the Greek *peripatos*, "a courtyard for walking about," and *peripateitikos*, "given to walking about"

reversed circumstances or a sudden change of events can be called **peripeteia**, **peripetia**, or **peripety**

the **periphery** at first was each of the three atmospheric layers formerly regarded as enveloping the earth

periplus is a word for a circuit, tour, or circumnavigation

persons who live within a polar circle are **periscii**

periscope can mean comprehensive summary, general view

perissology is redundancy or superfluity of words

{ a **periphrasis** is a figure of speech expressing the meaning of a word or phrase using a number of words instead of one or a few }

the digestive system's autonomic (automatic) contractions are **peristalsis**

periwinkle the plant gave its name to the bluish-purple color

if a person is **perjink** or **perjinkety**, they are (praised for being) precise or accurate or (criticized for being) prim and finicky

perjure is from Latin meaning "swear falsely"

perk (special privileges, rights) is an abbreviation of perquisite

perlection is the action of reading through something and to **perlegate** is to read through (a text)

the difference between **permeate** and **pervade** is that the former is affecting a surface, the latter an area; a characteristic of **penetrate** is that it is effected upon a solid substance

permit can be traced to Latin per-, "through," and mittere, "let go, send"

when the prefix per- "through, thorough" is added to mutation, the result is **permutation** "a thorough change"

to sail through is to **pernavigate**

to **pernoctate** is to stay up all night, pass the night somewhere; staying up all night to study, work, or party is **pernoctation**

the **peroration** is the concluding part of a speech, forcefully summing up what has been said

perpendicular was first an adverb meaning "at right angles"

perpension is consideration, careful thought

perpession is endurance of suffering

perplex is a back-formation of perplexed

to **perquest** is to search through; searching dictionaries for great words is called **perquesting** (also searching through books in general)

perscrutation is a thorough search or a diligent inquiry

persecute means "to harass or treat unjustly"; **prosecute** is "to bring legal action against" or "to pursue something until the end"

perseity is the quality or condition of existing independently

the recurrence of a tune or thought in the mind is **perseveration**

persevere should be pronounced puhr-suh-VEER

persiflage is taking a frivolous approach toward any subject (from French persifler, "to banter")

persimmon is from Algonquian pessem-mins/pasimenan, "small dried fruit"

the base of **persist** is Latin sistere, "stand"

the original meaning of **person** is "part played in a drama or in actual life"—a persona or guise—from Latin persona, "mask worn by actors"

personalia are personal matters

personality was first the quality of being a person and not a thing

personnel only dates from the 1960s, but it has already been replaced by "**human resources**"

the older word for the newer, more specialized microscope and telescope, was **perspective**—a glass that assisted sight in any way—and **perspective** first meant the "science of optics"

perspicacious is derived from the Latin word *perspicere*, "to look through" or "to see clearly," so **perspicacious** usually means having unusual power to see through or understand

perspicacity means shrewdness and applies to people; **perspicuity** means easily understood and applies to things

perspicuous means "plain to the understanding; clear"

perspiration and **perspire** come from Latin perspirare "breathe through"

if something is **perstreperous**, it is noisy

to **perstringe** is to criticize

persuade has the element -suade from Latin *suadere*, "advise, urge" plus the prefix per-, an intensive

to **persuade** is to get someone to do something; to **convince** is to get someone to think something

a name for an adjective that is usually defined with the phrase "of or pertaining to" is a **pertainym**

you are **pertinacious** if you are stubbornly persistent in pursuing your opinions or plans

⎰ the root -*turb* means basi- ⎱
⎱ cally "upset," so **perturb** ⎰
⎱ means "thoroughly upset" ⎰

peruke first meant a natural head of hair, then came to mean the opposite

peruse first meant "use up, wear out" as per- could mean "thoroughly"; **peruse** means to read or examine carefully—not to look over casually or quickly (the word for that is "skim")

pervious means "allowing passage through"—the opposite of **impervious**

the **pes** is the hind foot of an animal

pesade is the motion of a horse when, raising his forequarters, he keeps his hind feet on the ground without advancing (and it is also called **rearing**)

pessimal is the opposite of **optimal**

pessimism first meant "worst possible condition or state"

pest originally meant a fatal epidemic disease

pester first meant "clog" or "overcrowd"

pestle first was the leg of certain animals used for food

pesto (herb-based green sauce) comes from an Italian word meaning "crushed, pounded"

the first use of **pet** to refer to an animal was in 1539, and 1710 (dog, monkey, squirrel, parrot were mentioned) for one kept for pleasure or companionship

a leaf's stalk by which a leaf is attached to the stem is the **petiole** and the blade or expanded area of a leaf or petal is the **lamina**

petite can be used only in reference to a woman, not a man

a **petitor** is an applicant or candidate

the **petrel**, a gull-like seabird, is supposedly named after the apostle Peter because it flys close to the sea's surface, somewhat like Peter's reported "walking" on water

petrify comes from Latin *petra*, "rock"

petrol originally meant "mineral oil extracted from the ground" and it was not applied to the refined fuel until the nineteenth century; the word came from Latin **petroleum**, "rock oil" (*petr/petra*, "rock," and *oleum*, "oil")

a **petticoat** is literally French *pety cote*, "small coat," which was originally a tunic or chemise worn by men under a doublet

a **pettifogger** is an inferior lawyer, one who takes petty cases or uses unsavory practices

an early sense of **petulant** was "immodest"

the **petunia** is related to the tobacco plant, hence its name from Portuguese *petum*, "tobacco"

Indo-European *pu-*, "rotten; to rot" survives in the expressions **pew**!, **pee-u**!, and **phew**!

pew comes from a Latin term for "elevated place"; **pewage** is the annual rent once paid to a church for a **pew** space

pH means power/potency of hydrogen (ion)—the effective concentration of hydrogen in a solution

Ph.D. is Latin for Philosophiae Doctor

a **phaeton** is a rickety contrivance

habitual nail biting is **phaneromania**

a model of a baby used in obstetric demonstration is a **phantom**

pharaoh in Egyptian meant "great house"

pharmacy was formerly medicine or a medicinal preparation or treatment with drugs

pharology is the study of signal lights, especially lighthouses

a **phase** first described an aspect of the moon

a meteor can be described as a **phasm**

phat is a printing term meaning "profitable"—for advertising with a lot of white space and low composition costs

phatic speech is saying things like "Have a nice day," which are sociable instead of communicating ideas or information—and it also refers to speech consisting of noises rather than words

pheasant comes from Phasis, ancient name of River Rioni in Georgia from where the bird is said to have spread westward

phelloplastics is the art of carving or sculpting in cork

{ a **phememe** is a name given the smallest linguistic unit }

phenology is the study of the climate's role in recurring natural phenomena; **phrenology** is the study of skulls in relation to mental characteristics

phenomena (singular is phenomenon) are "things" though not generally "objects" and sometimes "strange or unusual things" as observed by the senses

Philadelphia contains the Greek *philos*, "loving," and *adelphos*, "brother"—and is the City of Brotherly Love

philamot is the color of a dead leaf, a brownish-orange

philander comes from a Greek adjective meaning "fond of men or one's husband"

the Greek term *ateles*, "free of charge" (from the days of post-marking "franking" letters) was combined with the prefix *phil-*, "loving, love of" to coin the word **philately** in 1865 for the hobby of collecting postage stamps

philharmonic is from Greek meaning "love" and "harmony" and the music use dates to the mid-1700s

philia is affection or love for friends or fellow human beings

the original **philippics** were a series of speeches by Demosthenes denouncing Philip of Macedon, then applied to Cicero's speeches against Mark Anthony, then became "fierce denunciation"

philistine comes from inhabitants of ancient seafaring Philistia of Palestine (first millennium BC), famed for their aggression; the notion of **philistine** as "boorish person" did not occur until the nineteenth century

the screwheads that look like an X on top are **Phillips™**

a **philobiblist** is a book lover

philocomal means "characterized by love of or attention to the hair"

if you are people-loving, you are **philodemic**

the **philodendron** is a tree-climbing plant and in Greek it meant "loving (*philos*) and "tree" (*dendron*)

someone who likes to hear themselves talk is a **philodox**

philology is a branch of linguistics dealing with changes in language over time and is literally "fondness of studying words"

a seeker of knowledge is a **philonoist**

instinctive and natural love for one's children is **philoprogeneity** or **storge**

one's **philosity** is the degree of body hair

a **philosopher** is literally a lover of wisdom—*philos*, "loving," and *sophos*, "wise"

philosophy is literally "love of wisdom"

natural love or affection is **philostorgy**

philter is another word for love potion

the groove/dent just under your nose is your **philtrum**

phiz means "face" and is a contraction of **physiognomy**

phlegm comes from Latin *phlegma*, "clammy moisture," and Greek *phlegma*, "inflammation"

phlegmatic first meant "abounding in phlegm" and now more commonly means "not easily excited; lacking enthusiasm; dull, sluggish"—supposedly the type of character one has from having an overabundance of phlegm

the surge of compounds (phobias) based on Greek *phobos*, "fear," started in the nineteenth century

the adjective form of seal is **phocine**

the **phoenix** may get its name from the red flames in which the fabulous bird perished, from Greek *phoinix*, "purple"

a **phoneme** is a word for a hallucination in which voices are heard

a **phoner** is an interview conducted by telephone, especially for a radio or TV program

Phonesthemic words are two or more words that share a speech sound and which have some similar certain meanings; **phonesthesia** (from Greek *phōnê*, "sound" + *aìsthesis*, "perception") or **sound symbolism** is the phenomenon and the speech sounds are known as phonesthemes. The **phonestheme** *gl-*, for example, is associated with the meaning "light" or "shining" in such words as glare, gleam, glimmer, glint, glisten, gloss, glow, glower.

the spots of light you see when you rub your eyes are called **phosphenes**

phosphorescent means "giving off a glow that continues after an energy source has stopped transmitting energy"

phosphorous comes from Greek *phosphoros*, "light-bearing"

Greek *phos*, "light" was the basis for **photo**

older terms for motion picture are **photodrama** and **photoplay**

photogenic was an earlier word for photographic—and it also originally meant "produced by light" or "producing light" and was used mostly in scientific or technical contexts

photography is literally "writing with light"

a **photon** is a powerful shot in racquetball

the Greek roots of **photosynthesis** combine to produce the basic meaning "to put together with the help of light"

phrase first meant "style or manner of expression"

word selection and arrangement is called **phraseology**

several clans may be combined into a larger group called a **phratry**

phreatic means pertaining to wells

to **phrenologize** is to discover a person's traits by studying the bumps on his or her skull

a **phrontistery** is a place for thought and study; a **phrontist** is a deep thinker to go **phut** is to break, become useless

phyllo derives from Greek *phullon*, "leaf" as the pastry is thin and leaf-like

phyllotaxy is the arrangement of leaves on a stem

phylogeny is the history of the development of a plant or animal

physical and **physician** come from Latin *physica*, "things related to nature"

physiology first meant "natural philosophy, natural science"

physics was first a term for natural science in general, especially the Aristotelian system

pi, a circle's circumference in relation to its diameter, was used in 1748 by Swiss mathematician Leonhart Euler (1707–83) to describe this, from Greek letter **pi** (from Hebrew "little mouth") as an abbreviation of Greek *periphereia*, "periphery"

piano is a shortened form of *pianoforte*, "soft and loud," which comes from the original Italian phrase *gravecembalo di piano e forte*, "harpsichord with soft and loud," which is how its inventor described it

Dutch *pekel*, "brine, **pickle**" gave us **pickle**—which was originally a spicy sauce with meat

a **pick-up** or **pick-up** dinner is one made up of leftovers

picnic was borrowed from French *piquenique*, originally denoting a sort of fashionable party to which everyone brought some food—though the notion of outdoor meal did not occur until the nineteenth century

movie patrons who bring their own snacks are called **picnickers** (slang)

edging with embroidered loops is **picot**

a flower that has one basic color edged with another is a **picotee**

pictorial first meant "pertaining to a painter or painting" as it derives from Latin *pictor* "painter"

picture is ultimately from Latin *pingere*, "paint"

picturesque is based on Italian *pittore*, "painter"—and the original meaning was "in the style of a painter"

pidgin is a crude auxiliary language with a tiny vocabulary; **creole** is developed out of a former **pidgin** and it is a real language with a large vocabulary

> **picayune** is from French *picaillon*, a copper coin that meant "cash"—and its first meaning was "a small coin of little value"

piazza is from Latin *platea*, "courtyard," **veranda** from Hindi "stockaded enclosure," and **porch** from Latin *porticus*, "entrance hall"

picaresque describes a situation that is impermanent or transitory

piccata means sliced, sautéed, and served in lemon, parsley, and butter

pick as in "pierce" comes from Latin *piccare*, "pierce, prick"

a **picket** is a pointed stake

pies were originally filled with a number of ingredients and this word may be connected to magpies, a bird that steals miscellaneous objects

piebald is being spotted with irregular patches of different colors, especially black and white; **skewbald** is spotted white and a color other than black

piece is probably from Latin *pecia/petai*, from an earlier Celtic *pett-*

piecemeal etymologically means "a piece taken one portion at a time"

pied means "having two or more different colors" and first had the sense "black and white like a magpie"

a **pier** is any structure that runs out and away from (usually right angle) to the shore and that vessels tie up to

the **pierogi** has variant spellings of perogi, pirogi, pierogie, or pierogy—from Polish **pierogi** "large piece of ravioli," from Russian pirog, "large pie"

respect due to a family or to one's homeland is **pietas**

a **piff** is something insignificant

pig originally meant just "young **pig**" until the sixteenth century (the word in Old and Middle English for this animal was swine)

pigeon comes from French pijon, from Latin pipine, "to peep, chirp"—and first meant "young dove"

in typography, an excessively wide space between words is a **pigeonhole**

people who classify things by instinct are **pigeonholers**

a **piggery** is a place where pigs are kept

piggesnye is an old term of endearment for one's sweetheart, literally, a darling pig's eye

a **piggin** is a milking pail with one long stave used as a handle

pigs have nothing to do with **piggyback** but is a folk etymology variation from pick-pack, pick-back, pick-a-back

a **pigment** (from Latin pingere, "paint") is a chemical that absorbs only certain colors from white light

in the seventeenth century, a **pigtail** was tobacco twisted into a thin rope which resembled the animal's tail

Pikachu is Japanese for "electric mouse"

a toll booth is called a **pike**

pilaf means "cooked rice" (Turkish)-so rice **pilaf** is redundant

pilaster first referred to a square or rectangular column or pillar

Pilates' own name for his system of exercise was contrology

the editing mark for "start a new paragraph" ¶ is called a **pilcrow**

pile as in carpet first referred to downy feather or hair

the fuzzy side of Velcro is the **pile** or **loop tape** and the nubby plastic side is the **hook tape**

pileated etymologically means "capped" like a mushroom but now refers to a bird with a crest on the top of the head from the bill to the nape

Latin pila, "ball" is the source of **piles** "hemorrhoids"

a **pileus** is a mushroom cap; the plural is **pilei**

originally **pilfering** was a serious matter, synonymous with plundering, but it came to mean "stealing small things"—and its source was Anglo-Norman pelfrer, "plunder, rob"

pilgarlic—a bald head or bald-headed man—derives from pilled, "with fluff removed"

the basic meaning of **pilgrim** was "traveler, homeless wanderer" and is from Latin peregrinum, "foreigner, stranger"

to form little balls of fiber, especially on a wool sweater, is to **pill**

pillage is from French piller, "plunder"

pillar is from Latin pila, "**pillar**," the source of compile, pilaster, and pile

the seat for the passenger behind the motorcyclist is the **pillion**

to **pillory** is to attack or ridicule publicly

pillow was based on an inflected form of Old English pyle, "**pillow**," from Latin pulvinus, "**pillow**"

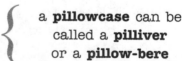
{ a **pillowcase** can be called a **pilliver** or a **pillow-bere** }

goose bumps cause **piloerection** or **hystriciasis** (hair standing on end)

pilose means "having soft hair"

pilosism or **hirsutism** is abnormal hairiness

pilot at first was a person steering a ship

pilsner is named from Pilsen, Czechoslovakia, where the water gave it its distinctive flavor

pimento is the standard spelling with **pimiento** as a variant

an olive stuffed with sweet red pepper is a **pimola**

pimp is derived from French *pimpant*, "speak seductively," and originally meant "little boy" or "servant"

a **pimpernel** is a plant of the primrose family

Latin *pinna*, "feather, wing, pointed peak" became Old English *pinn* before **pin** as "thin metal fastener"

a **pinafore** is etymologically a garment "pinned afore," pinned to the front of a dress for protection

piñata is Spanish for "jug, pot"

pince-nez is French, literally "(that) pinches (the) nose"

pindling means frail or puny; **piddling** means trivial or trifling

pine as in "languish" is from Old English **pine** "torture" from Latin *poena*, "penalty"

pine, **fir**, and **spruce** are quite different from each other—though they are all conifers; **pine** has clusters of long needle-shaped leaves, **spruce** is a type of **fir** and the only scientific difference between a **spruce** and a **fir** is that spruces have rectangular needles while firs have flat needle-shaped leaves

pineal, from Latin *pinea*, "pine cone" is a pea-sized gland in the brain and is pronounced PIE-nee-ul

originally, **pineapple** was the word for pinecone, since the cone is the fruit of the pine and apple had the former general meaning

"fruit"; **pineapple** is not "pine" or "apple" but is a very big berry and pineapples are also called "king pine" or "excellent fruit"

a **pinetum** is a pinetree plantation

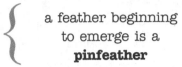

{ a feather beginning to emerge is a **pinfeather** }

to **pingle** is to nibble or pick at food, with little appetite

pinguefy means "to become fat" or "to fatten"; **pinguitude** is "fatness"

pink, the color, gets its name from **pink**, the flowering plant

if you **pink** your eyes, you half-shut them

several plants, including the carnation are called **pinks**—because the edges are pinked or notched as if by pinking shears

pinky or **pinkie** (finger) is from Dutch *pink*, "little finger"

the **pinna** is the "wing" of the ear, the broad upper part of the external ear

pinnate means "resembling a feather"

pinnipeds get their name from Latin *pinna*, "fin; wing," and *ped*, "foot"—i.e., having feet resembling fins

pinot is a variant of French *pineau*, a diminutive of pine, from the shape of the clusters of grapes

a small powerful spotlight is a **pinspot**

a towing vehicle's rear hook or bolt is the **pintle**

the vertical post or pin holding together the two halves or pieces of a door hinge is a **pintle**

a **pinwheel** was originally a mechanism in a clock

Pinyin, the standard system of romanized spelling for transliterating Chinese, literally means "spell sound" as this is the translation of Chinese into the Roman alphabet

pioneer was first used as a military term for an infantryman (French *pionnier*, "foot soldier")

pious was probably borrowed from Latin *pius*, "dutiful, kind"

an apple seed or lemon seed is a **pip**

pips are the spots on dominos and dice

the little bumps on a table tennis paddle are **pips**

the etymological notion underlying **pipe** is of a "piping" sound and the word is from Latin *pipare*, "chirp," from the base *pip-*, imitative of the sounds of young birds

piperaceous means "of the nature of pepper; pungent"

the stuff in black pepper that makes you sneeze is **piperine**

piperitious is another way of saying peppery

icing applied from a tube with a nozzle is **piping**

a **pippin** is a seed of a fruit

a **pippinface** is one with a round reddish face

piquant (pronounced PEE-kunt) first meant "sharp or stinging to the feelings"

piscation is fishing and a **piscator** is a fisherman

piscicapture is the catching of fish

piscifauna are the native fishes of an area or country

piscivorous is "fish-eating"

pish is said to reject, scoff, or deprecate; a **pisher** is a scoffer

pisiform is "shaped like a "pea""

a **pismire** is an ant and the word comes from the urinous smell of an anthill

squirreling away pennies, nickels, and dimes is **pismirism** and **pismire** can refer to the hoarding of small things

piss is probably an imitation of the sound of urinating

pissed first meant "intoxicated"

a track or trail beaten by a horse or other animal is a **piste** (French for "track" from Latin *pista*, "beaten track") and the word is also used for a course or run in skiing

piston comes from Latin *pistare*, "to beat or pound"—and became Italian *pistone*, variant of *pestone*, "great pestle"

pistol derives from Czechoslovakian meaning "whistle," and it evolved into the name of the firearm because of a resemblance in shape

a **pique** is a quarrel or feeling of enmity between two or more people

piranha is from Tupi words meaning "fish" and "tooth," as it has very sharp teeth

pirate derives from Greek *peirates/peiran*, "to attack" or "to attempt"

a canoe made from a tree trunk is a **pirogue**

pirouette is French, literally "spinning top"

pit "hole" comes from Latin *puteus*, "**pit**, well"; **pit** "fruit stone" may have been borrowed from Dutch **pit**

to put up a tent is to **pitch** it; to take down a tent is to **strike** it

pitch is movement up and down and **yaw** is movement side to side on a ship, airplane, or other conveyance

pitcher, the container, is from French pichier "pot"

pitchfork was originally pickfork

piteous is generally not used when speaking of people, **pitiable** means "able to be pitied," and **pitiful** most often means "insignificant; below contempt"

pitfall is from Old English elements meaning pit and trap, the original meaning being trapping animals in a pit that they fall into

pith first referred to the spongy cellular tissue in the stems and branches of many plants, and also the spongy white tissue lining the rind of citrus fruits

pithy once meant "strong, very alcoholic"

pitta/pita (the bread) traces back to Greek *pessein*, "bake, cook"

pittance (from Latin *pietas*) was originally a pious bequest or donation to a religious order

originally, **pituitary** was that "pertaining to phlegm or mucus"—now mainly refers to the gland

pity and **piety** shared the meanings "compassion" and "dutifulness, reverence" for a while

pixel is a blend of pix (pics) and el(ement)

pixilated can mean "led astray" or "confused, bewildered"

pizza is literally "pie" in Italian and *pizze* is a plural of **pizza**

pizzazz may have been invented by Diana Vreeland, 1930s editor of Harper's Bazaar magazine

plucking of a violin is **pizzicato**

placable is "of a tolerant nature"—the opposite of **implacable**

placard came from French *plaquier*, "to plate; lay flat"

place was, at first, more specific—meaning an open space in a town or a marketplace—derived from plaza

placebo is Latin for "I shall please" or "I shall be acceptable" and it first referred to a response in vespers and then the service itself, then came to mean purely palliative medicine

Latin **placenta** originally meant "flat cake" and it ultimately came from Greek *plax*, "flat surface"; its application to the organ in the uterus of a pregnant mammal came from its flat round shape

{ the material covering a zipper or fastener is called the **placket** }

plafond is an ornately decorated ceiling

the root word of **plagiarism** is Latin *plagiarius*, "kidnapper," and Greek *plagion*, "kidnapping"; **plagiarize** originally meant "kidnapping"

plagiarist once meant the kidnapper of a slave and **martial** a "kidnapper" of another's brain

plague is from Latin *plaga*, "stroke or blow," and it first meant this or "wound"

plaid from Scotch Gaelic meant "blanket" and was a fabric woven of different-colored yarns

the adjective **plain** once meant "flat"

an extensive area of flat open terrain can be called a **plain**, a **campagna**, or **champaign**

plainful means "distressing, grievous, pitiful"

plainsong etymologically means "clear singing" or "distinct chanting"

a **plaint** is an audible protest

plaintful means "mournful" and **plaintive** first meant "grieving, lamenting" (now "characterized by complaint" or "mournful, sad")

plaintiff once meant "person who complains of illness"

a **plait** is a twist of character, a quirk

plan is etymologically a design that has been "planted" on the ground; it was originally plant and not changed to **plan** until the sixteenth century

a plain metal disk from which a coin is made is a **planchet**

the movable pointer for a Ouija board is the **planchette** (French "small board")

plane is essentially the same word as **plain**, both ultimately coming from Latin *planus*, "flat" or "clear"

planet comes from Greek *planets*, "wanderer"

plangent describes the sound of the sea and its waves—reverberating and mournfully resonant

to **planish** is to make smooth and level

the idea underlying **plank** seems to be "flatness," from Latin *placa*, "slab," from *plancus*, "flat"

a **plank** is thicker than a **board**

water skiing was once called **plankgliding**

plankton comes from a Greek word meaning "drifting, wandering" as they are floating or drifting organisms

the urge to live a roaming and bohemian life is **planomania**

seeds and saplings were put into the soil and then stamped into the ground by early farmers, and the word **plant** is from Latin *planta*, "sole of the foot"

plantain of the banana family was originally named plantano "plane tree" by the Spaniards

the Latin word *plantatio*, "propagation of a plant, as from cuttings," is the source of **plantation**

plantigrade is literally walking (gradus) on the sole of the foot (planta)

to **plap** is to come down or fall with a flat, flapping impact

to **plapper** is to make the sound of boiling or bubbling

plaque comes from Dutch *plak*, "tablet"

plaque can cause **tartar** (also called dental calculus) and it is a soft deposit of saliva and bacteria which, when allowed to collect and harden, forms **tartar**

a synonym for puddle is **plash**

plasma first meant "form, mold, shape"

plaster originally referred to a bandage with medicine

plastic is from Greek *plastos*, "to form, mold"

a fencer's padded jacket is a **plastron**, also the name for a tortoise's or turtle's shell forming its underside

etymologically, a **plate** is something "flat," from Latin *plattus*, "flat," and Greek *platys*, "broad"

{ **plateau** can refer to an ornamented dish or tray for serving food }

a political candidate stands on a **platform** made up of planks to deliver his/her message—so figuratively the statement of what he/she believes is also the **platform** and its parts are planks

platina is the color of **platinum** (pale bluish gray); **platinum** (originally called **platina**) is ultimately derived from a Spanish diminutive of *plata*, "silver"

platitude first meant "flatness" or "dullness"

platonic is named for Plato, who expressed this idea in his "Symposium"

platoon means etymologically "little ball," from French *peloton*—and extended to "little cluster of people or group of soldiers"

platypus is "flat-footed" in Greek

plaudit is an act of applauding, a round of applause

plausible was once "that which obtained applause" (Latin *plausibilis*, "deserving applause or approval")

if people are **plausive**, they are applauding

play-on and **play-off** is music to get someone on or off a stage

plaza comes from Latin *platea*, "courtyard" or "street"

plead and **plea** (originally a lawsuit) go back to Latin *placitum*, "something pleasing both sides," and "decision, opinion," and it passed into French as "discussion, lawsuit"

to **pleach** is the braid hair

please descends from Latin *placere*, "please"

pleat is from Latin *plicitum/plictum*, "fold"

pleather is imitation leather made from polyurethane

the plebs were the "common people" of ancient Rome (possibly from Greek plethos "multitude") and English gets **plebeian** from this

originally, a **plectrum** was a device for tightening the strings of a harp and now is the piece used to pluck a guitar's strings; the plural is plectrums or plectra

pled can be the past participle of plead

the first meaning of **pledge** was as a legal term for a person acting as surely for another

a **pledget** is a small piece of paper or cotton used to absorb liquid—like when you cut yourself shaving—or it refers to a small mass of lint, such as that which collects in the navel

a **pleiad** is a group of seven illustrious persons

pleionosis is the exaggeration of one's own importance

the meaning behind epochs' names are **Pleistocene** "most recent," **Pliocene** "more recent," **Miocene** "moderately recent," and Oligocence "but a little recent"

plenary means "complete, entire, full"

pleniloquence is excessive talk and to **polylogize** is to talk too much

{ **plenilune** is a full moon or the time of the full moon }

plenitude is indicated when the amount in question is of something abstract, whereas concrete amounts motivate the use of "**plenty**" (both from Latin *plenus*, "full")

a **plenum** is an assembly of all the members of a committee or group—or a space completely filled with matter

the abdomen of a crustacean is the **pleon**

a **pleonasm** is the use of a word which merely repeats a bit of the meaning already present in an adjacent word—i.e., the use of redundant words together, e.g. exact same, close proximity, end result, minute detail

pleroma is fullness of being, plenitude

plethora originally described a medical condition in which there was believed to be too much blood in the body

plethora is too many of a good or bad thing and **surfeit** is too much of a good thing

Greek pleura "side" or "rib" came to be used for the "inner lining of the chest; lungs" and **pleuritis** or **pleurisy** is the inflammation of this area

the skin of a beaver is the **plew**

the little rubber-headed hammer doctors use to test reflexes is a **plexor**

plié (a ballet movement) is French, literally "bent"

plier(s), the tool, derives from the word ply

to **plight** is to make a pledge

a **plinth** is a squared base of a column, pedestal, piece of furniture, etc.

{ the shoe **plimsoll** is named after its resemblance to the **Plimsoll** line, the set of markings on the side of a ship showing loading levels }

ploce is the repetition of a word in an altered or more emphasized sense, e.g., "He who has, gets."

to **ploiter** or **potter** is to work ineffectively or dawdle

a **plongeur** is a dishwasher, busperson, or other menial worker in a restaurant or hotel

plonk is cheap or inferior wine (from French *vin blanc*)

a **plonker** is something large or substantial for its kind

a **plore** is an exhibit in a (science) museum which is hands-on

a **plosive** is a consonantal sound pro-duced from opening a previously closed oral passage, as when pronouncing the let-ter "p" as in pug

plot as in "secret scheme" comes from Old French *complot*

to **plounce** is to plunge into liquid

etymologically, the **plover** is the "rain bird," from Latin *pluvial*, "rain"

plow was borrowed from Old Norse *plogr*

pluck comes from Anglo-Saxon *pluccian*, "to pull out," and originally was used for the heart, liver, and lungs pulled out from animal carcasses

plum and **prune** are ultimately the same word, coming from Greek *proumnon*

plumb or **plummet** first meant a ball of lead

originally a **plumber** worked on lead pipes and the name comes from Latin *plumbum*, "lead"—also the origin of lead's symbol, Pb

plume comes from Latin *pluma*, "down, feathers," and it came to signify a single feather

a voice that is **plummy** is "thick-sounding, rich, fruity; with bass predominating"

plunder is from Dutch and etymologically denotes "rob of household goods" (plunde/plunne "household goods")

a **pluot** or **plumcot** is a plum/apricot hybrid

plural goes back to Latin *plus*, "more," from Indo-European *ple-*, "full"

plurennial means lasting for several years

plus is Latin for "more"

the term **plus** in mathematics is short for surplus

plush at first was a rich fabric with a long soft nap

a **pluteus** is a shelf for books or knick-knacks

plutonian means "grim, gloomy; harsh, unpleasing"

pluvial comes from Latin *pluvia* "rain"

a **ply** (from Latin *plicare*, "fold") is a thick-ness or any of the layers of a multilayer material, such as plywood

plywood is made of plies—thin layers of wood

pneumatic is etymologically "of the wind or breath" from Greek *pneuma*, "breath, wind"

pneumato- means "containing air" and **pneumo-** means "relating to the lungs" or "relating to air or gas"

pneumon, "lung" is part of **pneumonia**

pnigalion is a nightmare

if an animal **poaches**, it tramples or cuts up turf with its hoofs

one meaning of **poach** is to "ram or roughly push together" and another is to "sink into heavy wet ground while walking"

poach, the cooking term, is from French *pocher*, "to enclose in a bag"—as it is cooking while submerged in a special pan with the enclosure of the yolk in the white as in a bag

the machines used in paper-making are called **poachers**

a thin transparent envelope for keeping stamps is a **pochette**

pochismo is slang used by Mexican Spanish speakers along U.S. borders—consisting of English words given a Spanish pronunciation or form

pock has the plurals pocks and pox

pocket is a diminutive of French *poke*, "pouch"

originally, a **pocketbook** was a small book that would fit in a pocket

pococurante, from Italian "caring little," means indifferent or insouciant

a group of whales is a **pod** (also seals, dolphins); a small flock of birds can also be called a **pod**

a **podcast** is a digital recording of a radio broadcast (etc.), which one may download from the Internet to an iPod or other personal audio player

podex is another word for rump or fundament

podium comes from Greek *podion*, "small foot," as it is a footed structure

the original **Podunk**, Algonquian for "pocket of land," was the area between Hartford and Windsor, Connecticut

podware is the word for pulse plants having pods and pod is derived from that word

a fancy word for synonym ("one of various names for the same thing") is **poecilonym**

poecilonymy (also **polyonymy**) is the simultaneous use of several names or synonyms for one thing

a **poem** is etymologically "something created," from Greek *poein*, "create, make," and developed metaphorically via "literary work" to **poem**

to **poeteeze** is to write poety

po-faced may be a shortened form of poker-faced

pogonip is a dense winter fog containing frozen particles that is formed in deep mountain valleys of the western U.S.

pogonophobia is a fear of beards

pogonotomy is shaving

poinsettia is named for a U.S. botanist and diplomat, J.R. Poinsett (1779–1851)

sharp end is the etymological notion underlying **point**, from Latin *pungere*, "pierce, prick"

pointe is the extreme tip of the toe, especially referred to in ballet

the triangular partitions on a backgammon board are the **points** or **fleches**

point-blank's literal meaning is "white spot" and refers to the white spot in the center of a target

a **pointer** or **point man** was first a cowboy riding at the front of a herd of cattle

a **pointillist** is a painter who creates separate dots of pure color instead of mixed pigments; the pronunciation is PWAHN-tuhl-ist

poise actually means "equality of weight" or "balance, equilibrium"

the **poleyn** is the part of a suit of armor that protects the knee

poison and **potion** derive from Latin **potion**-, *potio*, "a drink, **potion**, poisonous drink," both coming into English through the Old French variant forms **poison**, "poisonous drink," and *pocion*, "drink, **potion**"

Pokemon is Japanese for "pocket monster"

poker derives from German *pochspiel*, a bluffing card game (*pochen*, "to brag or boast")

pole as a stake and measure derives from Latin *palus* "stake" while **pole** as in magnetic or extremity is from Greek *polos*, "axis, pivot"

polecat is synonymous with **skunk**

a **polemic** is a controversial argument or a person who partakes in them

polenta (baked cornmeal) comes from Latin meaning "pearl barley"

police had early senses "public order" and "prudent procedure"; **police** should be pronounced puh-LEES

at first, a **policy** was an organized, established form of government

policy "insurance document" is from a French word meaning "certificate, contract" and earlier Latin *apódissa/apódixa*, "a receipt or security for money paid"

polio is an abbreviation of poliomyelitis, from Greek *polios*, "gray," and *muelos*, "marrow," meaning "inflammation of the gray matter of the spinal cord"

poliosis is the graying of hair

{ **polish** comes from Latin *polire*, "make smooth and shiny" }

polite actually meant "polished" or "burnished" when it came into English

Greek *polis* originally meant "citadel"—as in Acropolis (high citadel) and "body of citizens" (from *polites*, "citizen," from *polis*, "city, state") and it has begotten **politic**, **politics**, **policy**, etc.

politician is borrowed from French *politicien*, "a political person, chiefly in the sinister sense; a shrewd schemer"

to **polk** is to dance the **polka**; **polka** is from Czech *pulka*, "half-step"

an early sense of **poll** was a count of heads or of votes, based on the original sense of **poll**, as "human head"; it evolved into its sense as a "census" and then as the "voting at an election"

to **poll** can mean "to cut the hair" or "to cut the top off a tree or plant" (a poller is a barber or tree-cutter)

pollen in Latin means "fine powder" and that was its original meaning in English

the **pollex** is the thumb or the big toe

pollincture is the washing, anointing, etc., of a dead body, in preparation for burning or burial (Latin *pollingere*, "to wash (a corpse)"

polliniferous is "bearing or producing pollen"

polliwog comes from poll "head" and wog "wiggle" and it is a synonym for **tadpole**

pollo is Spanish and Italian for chicken

pollute is based on Latin *lutum*, "mud," and it first meant "make morally impure"

polo is from Balti and means "ball"

poltergeist comes from German *poltern*, "make a noise or disturbance," and *Geist*, "ghost"

poltophagic means "chewing thoroughly"

poltroon is a word for a mean-spirited, worthless wretch

polygamous for animals means mating with more than one animal of the opposite sex

polyglot (written in or knowing many languages) is from Greek *polu-*, "many," and *glotto*, "tongue"

to **polylogize** is to talk excessively

polyloquent is talking about many things and **omniloquent** is talking about everything

a person of superior, wide-ranging knowledge is a **polymath** if something is described as compressed into a small space or is compact, it is **polymicrian**

polyonym is a synonym for synonym, meaning each of a number of words having the same or similar meaning

polyp is etymologically a "many-footed" creature (Greek *polu*, "much, many," and *pous*, "foot"), originally applied to the octopus but then broadened in meaning

polysemy refers to a word's "having more than one meaning" and it comes from Greek *poly-*, "many," and *sēmos*, "pertaining to meaning"; a **polysemant** is a word with more than one meaning

polytechnic is from Greek *polu-*, "many," and *tekhne*, "art"

the pulp of pressed apples is **pomace**

pomade was first apple cider, then a scented ointment (in which apples are said to have been originally an ingredient) for application to the skin; now **pomade** is for the head and hair

pomander is from Latin words pomme de ambre meaning "apple or ball of amber"

an apple is an example of a **pome** and it comes from Latin poma/pomum "apple"; actually, the fleshy part of an apple is the **pome** and the core is the "real" fruit

pomegranate is from Latin and literally means "apple having many seeds"

{ **pomiculture** is the cultivation of fruit trees and fruit }

the **pommel** is the rounded knob on the end of a sword or dagger, the handgrips on a vaulting horse, a ball at the top of a tower (etc.), or any rounded ornamental knob

pomp is from a Latin term meaning "solemn procession"

Louis XV's Madame de **Pompadour** (1721–64) lent her name to a cloak, fabric pattern, pink color, South American bird, and several hairstyles

pompeii is a moderate to deep reddish-brown

pompom is the preferred spelling, though pompon (from French "tuft") was the original

poncho is from Spanish as it was first a South American cloak

to **pond** is to accumulate water in a **pond**, which is really a small lake

ponder and **ponderous** come from the Latin base *pondus*, "weight"

pone as in corn **pone** (corn bread) comes from an Algonquian word for "bread"

the **pone** is the person who sits on the dealer's right in a card game

pont- words refer to bridges, the Greeks having regarded the sea as a bridge from land to land

in ancient Rome, the highest priests were called pontifex and it was adopted into Christian usage as "bishop" and then **pontiff** became the word for Pope

to **pontificate** first meant to perform the functions of a pontiff or bishop (Latin *pontificatus*, "office of a pontifex")

pontoon "floating structure" comes from Latin *ponto*, "bridge made of boats," from *pons*, "bridge"

pony probably comes from Latin *pullus*, "foal, young animal"

ponytails were once called cues

poodle originated in Germany as a water retriever, *pudel*, which is short for *pudel hund*, "puddle dog"

Pooh-Bah was originally a character in "The Mikado" (1885), a light opera

poop once had the meaning "to make an abrupt sound, as from a wind instrument"

poor comes from the Latin word "pauper"

pope is from Greek *pappas/papas*, "bishop, patriarch," a variant of *pappas*, "father"

barhopping is **popination**; **popinal** is pertaining to bars or restaurants

popinjay was an early name for a parrot

poplin may stand for the "Pope's linen"

the **popliteal** is the soft area behind the knee

a **popple** is a bubble that rises and breaks in boiling water; when water popples, it is rippling, rolling, or tumbling

when rain falls on water, the bubbling sound is called **poppling**

the **poppy** was first recorded in English around 700, from Latin *papaver*, which may be related to Latin *papula*, "papule," as the flower contains rounded capsules which contain many small round seeds

poppycock came from Dutch *pappekak*, "soft dung"

porch and portico go back to Latin *porticus*, "covered gallery or entry"

porcupine comes from Latin *porcus*, "pig," and *spina*, "thorn"

pore comes from a Greek word meaning "passage"

pork is from Latin *porcus*, "pig"

pork is traced to Indo-European *porkos*, "piglet"

porknell is a name for someone as fat as a pig

pornography is literally "writing about prostitutes" (Greek *porne* means "prostitute") and etymologically refers to the description of the life and manners of prostitutes and their patrons

porpoise is from Latin *porcus*, "pig," and *piscis*, "fish"

porreceous means "like a leek, of a leek" (Latin *porrum* "leek"); a **porret** is a young leek or onion

over the years, **popcorn** has also been called popped corn, parching corn, pot corn, cup corn, dry corn, and buckshot

popular goes back to Latin *populus*, "people"

popularity was once the wooing or courting of people's favor, not the actual attainment of people's favor

the earliest sense of **population** was "inhabited place, place that is populated"

only a place can be **populous**

porcelain is from Italian *porcellana*, "cowrie shell," and it led to its being the name for chinaware with comparable translucency and hardness

the little hole in the sink that lets water drain out instead of flowing over the side is the **porcelator**

porrect in botany and zoology means "extended forward and outward" as in **porrect** mandibles (there's also a verb **porrect** that means "to hold (a thing) out for acceptance")

porridge started out as pottage and was a beef and vegetable stew

port, the drink, is named for Oporto, a city in Portugal that is the chief **port** for the country's wines

port, as in lefthand side, was probably originally the side of a boat turned toward the **port** for cargo loading; **port** is the lefthand side (when facing forward) and **starboard** is the righthand side of a ship

a **portal** is an Internet site offering a directory of links to other sites

something's **portance** is its bearing or demeanor

a **portcullis** is the gate consisting of an iron or wooden grating that hangs in the entry to a castle or fortified town, that can be raised and lowered

the elements of **portend** are Latin pro- "forth" and tendere "to stretch"

a **portent** is that which portends or foretells something momentous

portentous can describe something amazing, marvelous, and extraordinary

a **porter**, from Latin porta "gate," is one who is in charge of a door or gate

a **porterhouse** was originally a place where **porter** (short for **porterhouse**) and other malt liquors were sold—and, coincidentally, steaks; Martin Harrison, the proprietor of a New York City **porterhouse**, popularized the **porterhouse** steak

portfolio comes from Italian for "carry" and "sheets or leaves of paper"

porthole is from Latin porta, "gate"

portico describes a covered walkway with a roof supported by columns and usually attached as a porch to a building

a **portiere** is a curtain in a doorway

portly was originally a complimentary term (based on "port") meaning "of dignified bearing; imposing"

a **portmanteau** movie is one with two distinct parts or aspects

portrait and **portray** come from por, "forward, from the front" and traire, "draw"

pose and **pause** come from Latin pausare, "**pause**, stop"

a **poser** is someone who sets test or exam questions or a difficult or perplexing question or problem; a **poseur** is a person who adopts an affected style or demeanor

posh had a great story of being an acronym for "port out, starboard home" and also one that it was from a slang term meaning "dandy, swell"—but the stories have not been substantiated

to **posit** is to assume as a fact or postulate

{ **position** comes from Latin positio, from ponere, "put, place" }

the word **positive** is based on Latin ponere, "put, place," and the original sense referred to laws being formally laid down

posse is an abbreviation of **posse** comitatus, Latin for "force of the country" a group of persons armed with legal authority

the word **possess** is based on Latin elements potis, "able, capable," and sedere, "sit"

to make possible is to **possibiliate**

possible ultimately derives from Latin posse, "be able"

possible means it could happen or be done; **probable** means it is likely to happen

a **possident** is someone who owns something

possum is from opossum, Algonquian for "little white creature"

Latin posita, "placed," gave us Italian posta, "station on a road," and became French poste, "a station for mail"—from the series of stations which fast horsemen traversed to deliver messages, giving us **post** as in "mail system"

a **post road** was one with a series of posthouses or stations for post-horses established; a road on which mail was carried

post-cenal means after-dinner

postcibal means "occurring after a meal" and **precibal** is "occurring before meal"

postdiluvian means "after a great flood"

poster got its name from being an advertisement affixed to a post

a back door or gate is a **postern**

post-haste is from the former direction on letters—haste, post, haste

posthumous (pronounced PAHS-chuh-mus) is based on Latin *postumus*, "last" or "late-born" (i.e., born after the death of the child's father)

a note or comment made in a margin is a **postil**

another way of saying subsequent is **postliminous**

postmeridian means related to or happening in the afternoon—same as post meridiem

post-partum is literally "after childbirth"

postpone is from Latin *post-*, "after," and *ponere*, "to place"

when a word like Alfredo follows a noun like fettuccine, it is a **postpositive**—i.e., a word that is pretty much always used after another

postulate (from Latin *postulare*, "ask") first meant "demand, require"

posture once meant "the relative position of one thing to another"

originally, a **posy** was a copy of verses or a poem presented to someone along with a bouquet of flowers or a motto inscribed inside a ring; now it is a small bunch of flowers given as a gift

pot was borrowed from Latin *pottus*, perhaps an alteration of *potus*, "drinking cup"

pot, as in marijuana, may be a shortened form of Mexican Spanish *potiguaya*

to strike a ball into a billiards pocket is to **pot** it; a stroke pocketing a ball is a **hazard**

potage (French "what is put in a pot") is thick soup; **pottage** "soup or stew" evolved into the word **porridge**

potamology is the science of rivers

potassium carbonate was originally obtained by burning wood or other vegetable matter, soaking the ashes in water, and evaporating that in iron pots—which was called in Dutch *potasschen*, "pot ashes," which was adopted into English as **potash**

a **potato** is also a hole in a sock through which flesh protrudes

batata in Taino was changed to *patata* and we made it **potato**; *batata* still means "sweet **potato**," though

the **potato** was once called an **earth apple**

pot-au-feu is "pot on the fire," a French stew of vegetables and beef

a **potent** is a support or crutch

potential is from Latin *potentia*, "power," from *posse*, "be able" (from which "power" comes from)

potluck comes from the practice of throwing leftovers in a pot and luck determining how good this stew would taste

a **potsherd** (also called **shard**, **sherd**) is any pottery fragment that has archaeological significance

potshot's meaning comes from shooting an animal purely for food (pot) rather than for simple conquest

POTUS is an abbreviation for President of the United States

one who is **potvaliant** is courageous from drinking liquor

a **pouf** or **pouffe** is a cushioned footstool

a **poult** is a young domestic fowl (like a turkey) being raised for food

poultry is derived from Latin *pullus*, "young animal" or "chicken"; a **pullet** is a young hen between the ages of chicken and mature fowl

to smooth down with pumice or sandpaper is to **pounce**

pound is (U.S.) slang for a five-dollar bill

potpourri comes from French *pot pourri*, which literally means "rotten pot" and was first a stew made of different kinds of meat

a **pousto** is "a place to stand"

pout is perhaps from Swedish *puta*, "be inflated"

powder comes from Latin *pulvis*, "dust"

power ultimately comes from Latin *posse*, "be able or powerful"

powwow is from Algonquian *powwaw* or Narragansett *powah*, "he dreams" and it originally referred to a shaman or Native American Indian priest and medicine man

pox is an alteration of *pocks*, "pustules"; **pox** used to be a common term for syphilis

practic is the action of doing some practical work (from Greek *prassein*, "experience, **practice**"), the base of the word "**practice**"

practical applies when what is in question is the conduct of affairs, whereas **pragmatic** applies when the question is the planning with respect to these affairs; **practical** is anything that can be done and is worth doing while **practicable** is anything that can be done—worthwhile or not

pragmatic first meant "busy" or "interfering"—from Greek *pragmatikos*, "active, businesslike, versed in affairs," and Latin *pragmaticus*, "skilled in business, especially law"

prairie descends from Latin *pratum*, "meadow"

a small prairie is a **prairillon**

praise first meant "set a price on, attach a value to"

prajna (Sanskrit "know directly") is direct insight into the truth not achieved by intellectual or rational means, taught by the Buddha

praline is named for a French field marshal/diplomat César du Plessis-Praslin (1598–1675), whose chef created this sweet

pram is an abbreviation of perambulator

prana is the breath of life, the breath as a life-giving force; **pranayama** is a yogic practice (Sanskrit from **prana** "breath" and *dyama*, "restraint") for breath control

prandial is relating to lunch or dinner, but mainly dinner; **postprandial** is relating to just after dinner

one's **prat** is one's buttocks, the base of the word **pratfall**; to **prat** is to push someone or something with the buttocks

to **prate** is to speak, also implying much and long

the practical application of a branch of learning is **praxis**; it also describes any "accepted practice"

pray comes from Latin *precari*, "ask for, entreat, **pray**"

preach comes from the Latin elements *prae*, "before," and *dicare*, "declare"

preantepenultimate is fourth from last

a **prebuttal** is a response formulated in anticipation of a criticism

precarious is from Latin *precarius*, "obtained by begging," and the root sense is "standing in the need of prayer"

precative refers to a word that expresses a wish or request

precede first meant "surpass in degree or quality"

preceding means "occurring immediately before the time of the utterance" while **previous** means "occurring at some time before the utterance"

a **precentor** is a person who leads or directs a choir or congregation in singing

a **precept** originally was an order or command—from Latin *capere*, "to take," thus a rule or principle that one takes in before doing something

precinct comes from Latin meaning "encircle, gird about"

precious was derived from Latin *pretium*, "price"

precipice once meant "a headlong fall" from Latin *praeceps*, "headlong, steep"

precipitate is from Latin *praecipitare*, "to throw or drive headlong"; **precipitation** first meant the action of falling or throwing down

precipitous "hasty, sudden and dramatic" is used in relation to physical or natural objects; **precipitate** "done with great haste" relates to human actions or processes

a **précis** is concise or abridged statement, a summary, an abstract

precise comes from Latin elements meaning *prae-*, "in advance," and *caedere*, "to cut"

a **precisian** is an overly precise person, a strict observer of rules and procedures

precocial means, of chicks, born covered with down and the eyes open and becoming almost immediately active

precocious was first a botany term for "flowering or fruiting early" and literally means "early ripened" (Latin *prae*, "before," and *coquere*, "to ripen")

precony is public commendation or praise

precursor is based on the Latin word *currere*, "run"

predecessor is from Latin *prae-*, "beforehand," and *decessor*, "retiring officer"

predicament is a term from Aristotelian logic and it first meant "thing which is predicated or asserted" as part of a proposition (from an earlier base meaning "category," referring to the ten categories or classes of predications formed by Aristotle)

predict (Latin *prae*, "pre-," and *dicere*, "say") first was "mention previously in speech or writing"

predispose differs from **dispose** by implying that the frame of mind is created some time before it becomes obvious

predormition is the period of semiconsciousness before sleep

pre-empt is from Latin elements meaning "in advance" and "buy"

{ **preen** is generally thought to be an alteration of prune "cut branches" }

preface and **foreword** were once considered the same (Latin *praefari*, "speak before," Germanic/Anglo-Saxon *vorwort*, "**preface**") but now **preface** is written by the author and **foreword** by someone else

to **prefer** one thing is etymologically to "carry it before" others, from Latin *praeferre*, "set before"

preferable should be pronounced PREF-uhr-uh-buhl

premature aging is **pregeria**

pregnant probably comes from *prae*, "before," and *gnasci*, "be born"

if something is graspable, it is **prehensible**

prehensile, from Latin *prehensus*, "to seize," describes an animal capable of grasping (and is pronounced pre-HEN-suhl)

prejudice originally meant harm or injury caused to a person resulting from a disregard of their rights; it is from Latin meaning "to judge beforehand"

preloved euphemistically means previously owned or secondhand

prelude comes from Latin *ludus*, "play" (play beforehand)

premier is from Latin *primarius*, "primary, first"

premiere is "first night" in French

premise comes from Latin *praemittere*, "send ahead"

premium first meant "prize, reward"

a **premonition** is literally a forewarning

having the end broken or bitten off is **premorse**

premundane is "before the creation of the world"

Latin *parare*, "make ready" is the source of **prepare** (with *prae-*, "before")

preponderate once meant "weigh more" and "have greater intellectual weight"

to **prepone** is to move something forward in time

preposition is from Latin meaning "put in front"

someone who makes a good first impression is **prepossessing**

preposterous derives from Latin *pre*, "before," *posterous*, "after," literally "with the hindside in front," which implied "putting the cart before the horse" and first meant "pertaining to reversing the true order or method of things"

being **prepunctual** is arriving earlier than the appointed time; the noun form is **prepunctuality**

prerogative comes from Latin *praerogare*, "ask before others," and came to mean "right to precedence, privilege"

presbycusis (or prebyacusis) is loss of hearing as part of the aging process

a **presbyope** is someone who is visually farsighted

the natural deterioration of vision due to aging is **presbyopia**, i.e., when you need, reading glasses

preschool is the noun (for the place) and **pre-school** is the adjective meaning "before school"

prescient is having foreknowledge, **parviscient** is having little knowledge, and **nescient** is lacking or disclaiming knowledge

prescribe is to set down as a rule or guide or recommendation while **proscribe** ("writing before") is to denounce or condemn, prohibit or forbid; tea and toast would be prescribed for an upset stomach while red-hot chili peppers would be proscribed (forbidden, labeled dangerous)

present, as in gift, comes from the verb "to **present** (give)"

presently means "soon, shortly, before long" while **at present** means "at the time of speaking"

preserve's -serve comes from Latin *servare*, "keep safe," and was combined with *prae-*, "before" to make "guard beforehand"

press as in "exert force, push" is from Latin *pressare*, from *premere*, "**press**"

prestidigitation is a borrowed French word meaning "sleight of hand"

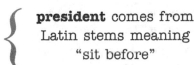

president comes from Latin stems meaning "sit before"

prestige first meant "illusion, conjuring trick" and **prestigious** (pronounced press-TIJ-us) once meant "of juggling, sleight of hand; illusory"

in music, **presto** (Latin *praesto*, "at hand") is faster than **allegro** ("cheerful, merry")

presumptive means "based on a presumption, based on grounds of probability" while **presumptuous** means "assuming an unwarranted, unauthorized responsibility" to **pretend** something is etymologically to "hold it out" as an excuse or as something it is not, from Latin *praetendere*

preterhuman is a synonym for superhuman and **preternatural** is a synonym for supernatural

a **preterist** lives in the past and is constantly nostalgic

past tense used to be called **preterit**

to **pretermit** is to pass over or ignore something

a **pretest** is a preliminary test or trial

pretext is from Latin *praetexere*, "to disguise," from *prae*, "in front," and *texere*, "weave"—as something serving to conceal plans

pretty originally meant "clever, crafty, cunning, sly"

pretzel descends from Latin *bracellus*, "bracelet," coming to English as *bretzel* from German, meaning "biscuit baked in the shape of folded arms"

etymologically, **prevaricate** means "walk crookedly" (from Latin *varus*, "knock-kneed")

an anticipation of others' needs is **prévenance**

prevent comes from Latin *praevenire* "come before"

use **preventive** "designed to prevent," not "**preventative**" (an unnecessary synonym)

prevernal refers to the period when winter is changing to spring

previous is from Latin *prae*, "pre-," and *via*, "way"—"leading the way"

originally, **prey** was that which is taken in war—booty, plunder

pribble is vain chatter

price comes from Latin *pretium*, "recompense"

prick can be a term of endearment or a term of abuse

a horse rider can be called a **pricker**

a candlestick with a spike for holding up the candle (or the spike itself) is called a **pricket**

rose plants have **prickles**, not thorns or spines, which are also called **emergences**

the Old English noun for "**pride**" was *pryto*, and it developed into "**pride**"

{ **pridian** is "of or relating to a previous day or yesterday; former" }

priest and **presbyter** both descend from Greek *presbuteros*, "elder"

prim etymologically means "first," from Latin *primus*

after **primary**, secondary, and tertiary come quaternary, quinary, senary, septenary, octonary, nonary, denary; words also exist for "twelfth order" (duodenary) and "twentieth order" (vigenary)

the Spanish word **primavera** literally means "Spring" and first referred to a tree native to Mexico and Central America, so called for its early flowering; the word ultimately derives from Latin *primus*, "first," and *ver*, "Spring," and the Italian culinary term **primavera** is short for alla **primavera** "in the style of springtime," which denotes anything served with a mix of fresh spring vegetables, such as asparagus, broccoli, carrots, peas, peppers, or zucchini

primaveral is "pertaining to early springtime"

in **prime** minister, **prime** means "most important"

prime is unusual since it can have virtually opposite meanings "preliminary, basic" or "lowest"—as well as "finest" and "highest"

a **primer** (pronounced PRIM-ur) is a small book on academic fundamentals

primeval is from Latin meaning "first age"—suggesting the earliest periods in the earth's history

the upper keyboard in a piano duet is **primo**; the lower is **secondo**

your earliest-known ancestor is your **primogenitor**; **primogeniture** is the condition of being the first-born of the children of the same parents

primrose is from Latin *prima rosa*, "first or earliest rose"

prince is derived from Latin *princeps*, "chief man" or "leading citizen"

the person who actually carries out a crime is the **principal**; an **accessory** (or secondary party) is someone who incites the crime or assists the **principal** before or after the crime

principle means fundamental as in beliefs or truths or understandings and it is always a noun; **principal** can be a noun or adjective meaning chief or of first importance

to **pringle** is to tingle persistently

Pringles (potato chips) got their moniker from a last name pulled out of the Cincinnati telephone book

to **prink** is to adorn oneself with ornaments

skin is said to **prinkle** when there is a tingling sensation, as in "pins and needles"

print comes from a Latin base meaning "to press" and it first was the impress of a seal or stamp

prior is from Latin **prior** "former, elder, superior"

prison is ultimately derived from Latin *prehendere*, "seize"

prissy may be a blend of prim and sissy

pristine formerly meant "of or belonging to the earliest period or state" or "original" (Latin *pristinus*, "ancient, former")

pritch is an offense taken

private comes from Latin *privatus*, "withdrawn from public life"

a **private language** is an exclusive one intelligible only to a restricted group of people; **idioglossia** is one invented by one child or by children in close contact, like twins

a **privateer** is a pirate with a mandate from a government

privilege derives from Latin *privus*, "private," and *leg/lex*, "law"

a **privilege** is a right that may be extended to a group or a number of people; a **prerogative** is a right that, customarily, is vested in a single person

privity is the state of being private or secret

privy can mean "withdrawn from public sight, knowledge, or use"—which may have brought the use of the word as a noun for "toilet, latrine"

prize is a variant of price

pro comes from Greek and Latin, where it means "before," "forward," or "for"—and as a prefix also means "earlier than," "front," and "in front of"

{ **primiparous** means "bearing a first offspring" or "having borne only one previous offspring" and it is used of animals as well as humans  }

priscan is "dealing with or existing in ancient times"

prism is from Greek *prisma*, "thing sawn"

proactive is the opposite or **reactive**

probably should be pronounced PRO-buh-blee

probate is from Latin *probatum*, "thing proved"—and **probate** is the official proving of a will

probation was first used to mean any examination, investigation, or testing

Latin probare "approve, **prove**, test" is the source of English **probe** and **prove**, from that came Latin probabilis "provable" which became English **probable**

probity is integrity, uprightness of character

a **problem** was originally a riddle or question for academic discussion, from Greek pro-, and ballein, "throw before"

the elephant's trunk was called **proboscis** from Greek proboskis, pro-, "in front," and boskein, "feed," because it is used for getting food, especially from branches

a marriage proposal can be called a **procation**

procedure, **process**, and **proceed** come from Latin procedere "to go forward"

{ a synonym for stormy and tempestuous is **procellous** }

procerity is a word for tallness

a **process** is a set or series of actions directed to some end or a natural series of changes; a **procedure** is a series of actions conducted in a certain manner, an established way of doing something

a choir entering a church is a **procession**; leaving is a **recession**

procinct is a state of readiness or preparation

proclivity (tendency, propensity) comes from Latin pro- and clivus "slope"

procrastinate comes from Latin meaning "defer until the morning" from the Latin base crastinus, "belonging to tomorrow" (cras, "tomorrow")

arbitrary imposition of conformity is **procrustean**

proctalgia or **rectalgia** is "pain in the backside"

proctor (exam supervisor) is actually a contraction of procurator

procure is from Latin pro-, "for," and curare, "look after"—making procurare "look after on the behalf of someone else; manage"

prodigal means recklessly wasteful or extravagant; farmers may make **prodigal** use of their soil and in a pointless war, lives can be lost on a **prodigal** scale

prodigious came to be applied to anything that is strange, amazing, or weird as well as anything extraordinary in amount, extent, or size

Latin prodige meant "an extraordinary sign or omen" and prodigium "portent, prophetic sign"—so **prodigy** was first an omen that was also considered extraordinary

prodigy refers to a person with exceptional talents, **protége** is a male who is guided or helped by someone, and **protégée** is the female version

an early sumptom of an attack or a disease is a **prodrome**

to **produce** something is etymologically to "lead it forward," from Latin producere

a **proem** is a preface or preamble to a document, while an **exordium** is the opening part of a speech or discourse

profane is Latin for pro, "before, outside," and fanum, "temple"—for those considered unholy and not allowed inside the temple

profer means "utter words"

profess comes from Latin profitieri, "declare publicly"

profession is from Latin professionem, at first a "declaration by a person entering a religious order"

professor is etymologically someone who "makes a public claim" to knowledge in a particular field

proficiency is achieved through hard work and maybe talent as well—but it is not genius or being gifted; a **proficient** is a person who is an adept or expert in a skill (etc.)

proficuous is the opposite of **frustraneous** (unprofitable, useless, vain)

profile is literally "draw in outline" or "shown by a thread" (pro "forth" and filum "thread")

profit goes back to Latin *proficere*, "advance, be advantageous"

to **profligate** is to overcome or overthrow

profound is based on Latin *fundus*, "bottom," as the word means "penetrating deeply into a subject" or "demanding much study or thought"

profugate is to drive or chase away

a **progenitor** is an ancestor or forefather (from Latin *pro-*, "before, forward, forth" + *gignere*, "to beget"

progeny is a word for children collectively

progeria is premature senility

the ultimate Latin root of **progress** is *gradus*, "step"

a **project** was at first a "preliminary design" as it is from Latin *projectum*, "something put forth"

prolegomenon are readings or exercises done for a further understanding or advance in knowledge in a subject

anticipation before something starts is **prolepsis**

proletarian is based on Latin *proles*, "offspring," as the Roman citizens of the lowest class were seen as serving the state only by producing offspring

prolix is literally "poured forth"

promenade came from French as a derivative of *se promener*, "go for a walk," from earlier Latin *prominare*, "drive forward"

anything daringly original or creative is **promethean**

{ **prominent** comes from Latin *prominere*, "jut out" }

promiscuous first meant "consisting of parts or elements of various kinds mixed together without order"

Latin *promittere* originally meant "send forth" but evolved to mean "say in advance, foretell" and then "cause to expect," hence, **promise**

promote suggests an encouraging or fostering and may denote an increase in status or rank—literally "move forward"

prompt comes from Latin *promere*, "bring out, show," which became *promptus*, "shown, manifest" and "ready; punctual"

promulgate is from an analogy drawn by the Romans between "milking" and "bringing into the light of day"—from Latin *pro-*, "forth, out," and *mulgere*, "milk"

the **pronaos** is the space in front of the naos—the body of a temple—enclosed by the portico; the **pronaos** can also be called the **vestibule**

pronate means turning the foot outward to take weight on the inner edge; the opposite is **supinate**, turning the foot so the weight is on the outer edge

prone is lying on your face (facing downwards)—which is also true for **prostate**, but only in expressing adoration or begging for protection; **supine** is lying on your back

to prance (like a goat) can be replaced by to **pronken**

pronograde is "moving on all fours"

pronoun is from *pro-*, "on behalf of," and *nomen*, "name"

pronounce is *pro-*, "forth, out," and *nuntiare*, "announce"

pronunciation should be pronounced proh-nuhn-see-AY-shun

the strength of alcohol is its **proof**

proot is a word of command to a donkey (etc.) to "go on, go faster"

there are three types of theatrical **prop**: set props, hand props, and personal props

propaganda comes from Latin *propagare*, "to increase or spread," and the word has its origin in the ecclesiastical "*congrezatio de* **propaganda** *fide*" or "congregation for propagating the faith"

a **propensity** is a tendency while a **predilection** is a partiality—thus, a **propensity** (from Latin meaning "hanging toward") is a behavioral predisposition whereas a **predilection** is a personal characteristic (from Latin meaning "choose or love before others")

proper first meant "inherent, intrinsic"

property and propriety are doublets, sharing the ancestor Latin *proprietas*, "ownership," a derivative of *proprius*

prophecy is what is foretold (noun) and to **prophesy** is "to foretell"

propinquity is closeness or nearness either physically (proximity) or spiritually (affinity)

propitiate means appease or make peace with

propitious means "being a sign of good things to come" and "likely to produce good results"

propone and **propound** are synonyms "put forward for consideration"

the **propositus** is the person from whom a line of descent originates

one would **propound** a plan (set forth for consideration something more extensive, substantial), but **propose** an idea (set forth for consideration)

a **proprietary** was originally a member of a religious order who held property

proprioception is the unconscious awareness of the movement and spatial position of one's body

a **proprium** is a characteristic distinctive to a person, an attribute that is essential to someone or something

props can mean "proper or due respect, credit" or "admiration"

to **prorump** is to break forth or burst out

propaedeutic is a subject or course of study that is an introduction to more advanced study or to an art or science

prophet comes from a Greek word meaning "interpreter" or "spokesperson for the will of a god"

prophylactic comes from Greek *prophulaktikos*, from *prophulassein*, "keep guard in front of a place"; washing the hands before meals is a **prophylactic** measure

prophylaxis's base is Greek *phulaxis*, "act of guarding"

the **proscenium** is the part of the theater space between the curtain or drop-scene and the orchestra, often including the curtain itself

prosciutto is Italian for ham (delicately flavored dry cured)

prose is from Latin *prosa*, "straight-forward discourse"

prosecute first meant "to follow up or pursue an inquiry or studies" or "to pursue to the end"

a **proselyte** is etymologically someone who "comes to" a new religion, from Greek *proseluthos*, "person who comes to a place"

prosody is the correct pronunciation of words

prosopography is the description of a person's appearance

the act of falling in love at first sight is **prosopolepsy**, which also means basing an opinion on the way someone looks

prospect is the action or fact of looking towards a distant object

prostate is the gland; **prostrate** means "lying face down"

prostitute is from Latin *prostituta*, "offer for sale"

protagonist is Greek for "first (important) actor" or "first struggler" and by extension is used for a person who drives the action in a situation or is the main character in a literary work; the **protagonist** is the hero or heroine and an **antagonist** is his/her principal opponent

anything quite variable or readily assuming many shapes, like an amoeba, is **protean**; **protean** "versatile, taking many forms," is from the Greek deity Proteus, who transformed himself into different creatures to avoid capture

protect comes from Latin *pro-*, "in front," and *tegere*, "cover"

protégé is from Latin meaning "protect" and it means "person under protection or patronage of another"

protein (pronounced PRO-teen, PRO-tee-un) comes from Greek *proteios*, "primary" as these compounds are essential to all living organisms

protervity is waywardness or stubbornness

protest was first used as a verb meaning "make a solemn declaration"

Protestant really is based on the word "**protest**" as the first Protestants repudiated obedience to the Roman Catholic Church; the word "**protest**" is Latin *pro-*, and *testari*, "be a witness" or "assert"

the **protext** is the preceding context in a piece of writing to that being referred to; also, a reason given in justification for a course of action that is actually not the real reason

a wedding song is a **prothalamion** or **epithalamium**

proto- has the basic meaning "first in time" or "first formed," so **protozoa** are among the most basic members of the biological kingdom and a **proton** is an elementary particle in all atomic nuclei

protocol was first a legal term for an agreement serving as the the legal authority for any subsequent deed or agreement based upon it; the word comes from Greek for the first sheet of a papyrus roll and now means "original record" or "original authority"

proto-language is any once-spoken language from which daughter languages descend

a **protonym** is "the first person or thing to have a certain name; that from which another is named"

a **protoplanet** is a whirling mass that is believed to give rise to a planet

protoplasm is a mixture of organic and inorganic substances, such as protein and water, and is regarded as the physical basis of life

a **prototype** is an original model on which something is patterned

protozoa/protozoans were originally animals having the simplest, most primitive form of their type

the common instrument for drawing and measuring angles is a **protractor**

a **protreptic** is a pep talk or exhortation; as an adjective, it is another word for "instructive" to thrust forward was an original sense of **protrude**

proud comes from Latin *prodesse*, "be good," "be of value"

Proustian refers to any sensory experience that provokes a flood of nostalgia

prove is from Latin meaning "honesty, integrity" is literally to "make (something) honest"

to **prove** dough is to aerate it during fermentation

provenance is a place of origin or a source

proverb, from *pro-*, "forth," and *verbum*, "word" is a saying put forth as a familiar truth; **proverbiology** is a set of proverbs or proverbs as a field of study

provide first meant "foresee"—literally, "look ahead" (Latin *pro-* and *videre*); **provident** first meant foreseeing, having foresight

providence can be an act of divine intervention

a **provitamin** is a substance which is converted into a vitamin within an organism

{ **provolone** comes from Italian *provola*, "buffalo's milk cheese" }

a **provost** is etymologically an official "placed before" or "put in charge" of others, from Latin *praepositus*, "superintendent"

the underlying notion of a **prow** is "being in front," from Greek *proira*, "front of a ship"

prowess first meant "bravery in battle"

proxemics studies the spatial relationships arranged by human beings

Latin *proximus* "nearest, next" evolved into the word *proximitas* "nearness" and then **proximity** in English

proxy is a contraction of procuracy ("authorized acting for another")

French **prude** femme "proud woman" gave us the word **prude**

prudent, "showing care and thought for the future," is a contraction of provident

the word **prudential** (from prudent) is patterned on evidential

prune, a dried plum, is from Greek *prou(m)non*, "plum"

prunk means "proud, vain"

prurient ("characterized by lust") first meant "itching, itchy"

a **pry** is an inquisitive person

after **PS** (Latin post scriptum) comes **PPS** and **PPPS**

psalm comes from Greek *psalmos*, "song sung to harp music"

pseade is a maneuver in which a horse raises its forequarters without moving forward

wrong or indistinct pronunciation or enunciation is **psellism**

the study of elections is **psephology**

a **pseudism** is a lie; a **pseudologist** is a liar

pseudo is a prefix meaning "counterfeit, deceptive, false" and it requires a hyphen when joined to a proper noun; **quasi** is a prefix meaning "resembling" or "in some manner" and it is usually hyphenated to a noun

pseudocyesis is a false or imaginary pregnancy

pseudonym is from Greek *pseudonumon*, "false name"

psilology is a love of trivial or vacuous talk

the sound of wind in the trees and rustling of leaves is **psithurism**

psoas is the name of the two large flexor muscles of the hip, from Greek literally "muscle of the loins," and is pronounced SO-AZ

a full-length adjustable mirror is called a **psyche**

psyche was so called for a Greek heroine, the name translating to "breath" or "life" or "soul"

the first appearance of pubic hair is **pubarche**

pubble is a synonym for "fat, plump"

puberty is from Latin *pubes*, "adult," and *implies*, "covered in hair"

pubescent refers to being in early adolescence

{ **public** means etymologically "of the people," from Latin *publicus* (influenced by *pubes*, "adult"), an alteration of *poplicus*, "of the people" }

---

psychedelic derives from Greek *psyche*, "soul," and *deloun*, "make manifest, reveal"; **psychedelic** now refers to any of a class of drugs that alter one's perception of reality and the word was coined in the late 1950s by Humphry Osmond, a British psychiatrist who researched the effects of mescaline and LSD

psychiatry is from Greek *psyche*, "mind," and *iatreia*, "healing"

psycho is an abbreviation of eight different words

psychoceramic is a slang term for "crackpot"

psychomachy is a conflict of the body with the soul

psychon is a hypothetical unit of nervous energy or mental activity

psychopathy first meant "mental illness"

psychurgy is mental energy

a substance that starts a sneezing bout is **ptarmic**

ptarmigan, an arctic grouse, was borrowed from Scottish Gaelic

ptero- is a prefix meaning "having wings"

pterodactyl is from Greek meaning "winged fingers"

ptomaine literally means "matter from a corpse," from Greek *ptoma*, "corpse," and *piptein*, "fall" ('fallen body")

to **publish** something is etymologically to "make it public" from Latin *publicare*, "make public"

puce is French, literally "flea (color)"

puck as a mischievous sprite comes from Old Norse *púki*, "a mischievous demon"

pucker has the underlying notion of being formed into "pockets"

originally **pudding** was a sausage—the stomach or intestine of a pig, sheep, etc.— stuffed with other food

puddingtime is another word for dinnertime

Old English had *pudd*, "ditch, furrow," and **puddle** was a diminutive formed from it

pudency means "bashfulness, modesty" (Latin *pudere* "make or be ashamed")

pudendum (external female genital organs) comes from a Latin word meaning "be ashamed"

pudic means "modest, chaste" and **pudicity** is "modesty, chastity"

pueblo is Spanish for "people," hence, a town or village

puerile is from Latin *puer*, "child" or "boy"

puffin probably comes from a Celtic language of the British Isles and the word no doubt comes from its plumpness

a **pugil** is what one can pick up with the thumb and first two (or sometimes three) fingers

pugil is boxer in Latin and it means "handful" in English; **pugilism** is another name for boxing

pugnacious (eager to fight) originated in Latin *pugnus*, "fist"

to **pugnozzle** is to move the nostrils and upper lip in the manner of a pug dog

puissant "omnipotent; immortal" is pronounced PWIH-suhnt or PYOO-uh-suhnt

puke appeared first in Shakespeare's **As You Like It** and is imitative of the sound

pulchritudinous means "very beautiful"

the adjective form of flea is **pulicine**

{ **pulicosity** is the condition of being full of fleas }

the main Old and Middle English word for "**pull**" was draw and **pull** itself did not come into its own until late in the sixteenth century

pull the plug first referred to an old-fashioned type of toilet

pulley is from Greek *polidion*, "little pivot or axis"

Pullman railway cars were named after George M. Pullman (1831–1897), their American designer

the etymological notion of **pullulate** is of "rapid new growth," from Latin *pullus*, "young animal"

pulmo, in **pulmonary**, is Latin for "lung"

pulp is the soft flesh of, say, the pads of the fingertips

classical Latin pulpitum "platform, stage" gave us **pulpit**

pulsar is a blend of puls(ating) (st)ar

pulsatilla can refer to the shaking of a flower in the wind

pulsus, "beating," in Latin is the base of **pulse**

pultaceous means "yielding"

puma is pronounced PYOO-muh

pumice, porous solidified lava, comes from Latin pumex "**pumice**," from Indo-European *poimo-*

pump's original use was nautical

pumpernickel comes from German words translating to "devil fart" because the dark bread is supposedly so coarse as to produce flatulence as powerful as the devil's

Pumpkin—the large fruit of the plant *Cucurbita pepo*—is a word evolved from the original English spelling of pompeon or pumpion or pompion to pumkin and finally to **pumpkin**. The word pompion came from Latin *pepo/peponem*, from Greek *pepon*, "large melon, edible gourd," from another word *pepon*, "cooked by the sun; ripe." Another spelling variant is punkin.

pumpkinification is pompous behavior or exaggerated praise

a **pumpkinseed** is a North American freshwater fish

pumps, the shoes, are so named for the sound they make

pun seems to be short for **pundigrion**, a short-lived term for "quibble, **pun**," perhaps from Italian *puntiglio*, "nice point, quibble"

punch has an obscure origin but stories include it being from Sanskrit *panca*, "five/five kinds of" as the drink had five ingredients

punctal means "pertaining to or having the nature of a point" (Latin *punctum*, "point")

a detail of etiquette is a **punctilio**; one who is **punctilious** is strictly observant of details and fine points

punctual (from Latin *punctum*, "point") can mean "pertaining to punctuation" or "of or relating to a point in space"

punctuate first meant "point out" and it and **punctuation** are from Latin *punctus*, "prick, point"; the present-day meaning comes from the insertion of "points" or dots into written texts to indicate pauses (once called "pointing")

pundit is from Sanskrit *pandita*, "learned, conversant with" or "scholar"

{ **pung** was once the name for a one-horse sled or wagon }

having a sharp taste is **pungent** and having a pleasingly sharp taste is **piquant**; **pungent** first meant "keenly painful or distressing"

Latin punire "**punish**" was derived from poena "penalty, punishment" and gave us **punish**

the loser in a court case is often directed to pay **punitive** damages, the money over and above the actual cost of the harm done to the other party

punt as in "kick" may be from **bunt** "push," now used in baseball meaning "hit the ball softly"

puny is from French *puis né*, "born after another"

pup can also refer to a young rat or baby dragon

in the fifteenth century, **pup** and **puppy** referred to a breed of dog that no longer exists; **puppy** originally referred to a lapdog, especially a lady's pet

the insect stage **pupa** is named for Latin *pupus*/**pupa**, "baby boy or girl doll"

pupil (from Latin *pupilla*) first meant "orphan, ward, minor"

the word **puppet** originally meant "doll" and a **puppet** usually goes on the hand and arm, while a **marionette** (or string **puppet**) is a jointed figure with strings or wires

purchase comes from the French *pourchasse*, meaning "to hunt, seek to obtain"

purdah can mean seclusion, isolation, even quarantine

a "**pure**" group of plants or trees means it consists of only one species

to decorate an edge or border is to **purfle**

purgatory is from Latin *purgatories*, "purifying," and it first meant a place or condition of spiritual cleansing

to **purge** a tree is to prune it; to **purge** a candle is to snuff it

purl is the murmuring or bubbling of water, as in a stream flowing over stones

the space between the thumb and the extended forefinger is the **purlicue**

purlieu comes from Anglo-Norman *puralee*, "act of walking around" or "area of land beyond a perimeter fixed by walking around," and was originally the borders or outskirts of a forest

purloin, to steal, is from Latin *pur/pro*, "forth," and *loign*, "far"

purple comes from Latin *purpura*, a **purple** shellfish used to make dye

purport is normally applied to things, not people

a word's "**purpose**" is its effect, import, or meaning

purposely means "intentionally, on purpose" while **purposefully** means "with a specific purpose or objective in mind"

purse traces back to Greek *bursa*, "leather"

purseproud is haughty on account of being wealthy

pursue's base is an alteration of Latin *prosequi*, "prosecute"

purvey first meant "foresee"

purblind can mean "totally blind" or "partially blind"

pus is a Latin term for the fluid product of inflammation; there is no etymological connection between **pus** and **pustule**; **pustule** is from Latin *pustula*, "blister"

push comes from Latin *pulsus*, the past participle of *pellere*, "beat, drive, **push**"

pusillanimous is from Latin meaning "weak, meager" and "soul"

puss, as mouth, is from Gaelic Irish *pus*, "mouth"

put is one of the most common English verbs, but its origins are uncertain; the golfing term *putt* (from Scottish) is essentially "**put**," just differentiated in spelling and pronunciation

putanism is another word for prostitution

putative is almost always used to express doubt or skepticism about a common belief

{ **putrefy** and **putrid** come from Latin *puter*, "rotten" }

putrilage is matter that is decomposing

puttanesca is Italian from *puttana*, "prostitute," as the sauce was said to have been created by them as something which could be cooked quickly between clients' visits

to **putter** was first to potter

cupids that make themselves useful, as in old paintings, are called **putti** (putto is singular)

miniature golf is also called **putt-putt** because you putt and putt again (and again)

etymologically, **putty** is something that comes from a pot—from French *potée*, "contents of a pot"

puzzle comes from Old French *opposaile*, "thing set before one," "bewildering thing"; **puzzle** (verb) first meant "be beset by difficulties"

a **puzzlepate** is someone overwhelmed or dumbfounded by simple ideas

pygmy derives from the Greek *pygmaios*, "dwarfish"—from *pygme*, "the distance from the elbow to the knuckles"

pylon is from Greek *pulon*, "gateway"

pyramid is from a Greek joke; the Arabic term was *pi-mar* and the Greeks punned it as *pyramis*, "stack of (Egyptian) wheat cakes"

Pyrex was first Py-right for its heatproof pie plate, but then was changed to match the names of other products of Corning

pyrology is the science of fire or heat

heartburn is actually **pyrosis**, caused by the presence of gastric secretions, called reflux, in the lower esophagus

pyrotechnic is from Greek *pyro*, "fire," which became part of pyrotechny "manufacture of bombs, gunpowder, firearms, etc."; the meaning of "fireworks" appeared in the seventeenth century

pysmatic is always asking questions

Python was first a terrible dragon or serpent which guarded an oracle at Delphi

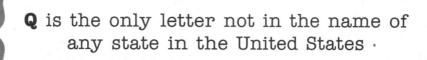

{ **Q** is the only letter not in the name of
any state in the United States · }

q.t. (or QT) is an abbreviation for "quiet"
(on the q.t.)

qi is from Chinese for "air, breath"

qu did not get firmly established in English
spelling until the thirteenth century

qua means "as; in the capacity of"

quack, as in doctor, is shortened from
quacksalver, one who quacks "boasts"
the virtues of salves and ointments

quadrangle is from Latin for "four
angles/corners" or "square (thing)"

a **quadrant** is a quarter of a circle or
sphere

a **quadrigamist** is someone who has married four times

quadrille paper, marked with small
squares, gets its name from Spanish
cuadrilla, "square block"

the best wine or liquor is **quadrimum**

the **quadrivium** was the liberal arts of the
Middle Ages: arithmetic, music, geometry,
and astronomy

quaesitum is the answer to a problem

something that is profit-oriented or money-
making is **quaestuary**

quaff comes from a German word for "eat
or drink immoderately"

quag is a marshy or boggy spot, especially covered with turf that gives way when
walked upon—and **quagmire** first meant
the same thing

quahog, pronounced coe-hog, is from
Narraganset *poquauhock*

the American **quail** is actually the **bobwhite**

quaint first described a person as being
"clever, ingenious" and once meant
"elegant, graceful, subtle"

a **quaker** is a light-colored underdevel-
oped coffee bean

the **Quaker** name perhaps alluded to
George Fox's direction to his followers to
"tremble at the name of the Lord" or from
the fits supposedly experienced by followers
moved by the Spirit

qualify first meant "to describe (something)
in a particular way"

qualitative refers to the characteristics or properties of quality and **quantitative** refers to the measure of something

quality comes from Latin *qualis*, "of what sort?"

qualmish is "affected with a qualm or qualms"

qualunquismo (from Italian) describes an attitude of indifference to political and social issues

quandary may come from Latin *quando*, "when"

quanked means overpowered by fatigue

quantity comes from Latin *quantus*, "how great, how much"

a small quantity is a **quantulum**

quarantine comes from Italian *quaranta*, "forty"—the number of days a ship was kept outside port if the ship's people had a contagious disease

the **quark** got its name from a James Joyce quote "Three quarks for Muster Mark," which was meaningless but catchy

quarrel once meant a square of glass (from Latin *quadrus*, "square," which came into Old French as **quarrel**)

quarry as an adjective can mean "square, squarely built"

a **quart** is a quarter of a gallon

a **quarter** is a limb and surrounding area of a quadruped

quarter goes back to Latin *quattuor*, "four" and its relatives

quarterback is so named because originally the player was positioned between the forwards (now the offensive line) and the halfbacks; the term was first recorded in print in 1895

quarternight is halfway between sundown and midnight

a **quarterpace** is a staircase landing at which the flights form a right angle

quartz derives from a Czech word meaning "hard"

quartz is the highest-scoring word in Scrabble (162 or 164) and **bezique** and **cazique** are the next-highest (161)

quash is from Latin *quatere*, "shake," and generally means "reject as invalid, especially by legal procedure" or "put an end to; suppress"

quassation is the act or process of being shaken or shaking

a crossroads can be called a **quatervois**

quaver came from the now obsolete Middle English *quave*, "tremble"

quay is of Celtic origin (*kagio-*)

queachy means "boggy, swampy"

queasy first meant "unsettled, uncertain"

a litter-bearing female cat is the **queen**

queer comes from a German root *quer*, "across, oblique, perverse"

the root sense of **quell** was "to kill" and "to die"

quench first meant extinguish a fire or light

one who seeks the advice of an astrologer is a **querent**; a **querent** or **querist** is one who inquires

querimonious is "full of complaints" or "given to complaining"; **querimony** is complaining or a complaint

to **querken** is to choke or suffocate

to be **querulous** is to be inclined to complain

a **query** is a single question; an **inquiry** (or enquiry) may be a single question or extensive investigation (series of questions)

a **query** differs from a **question** in that it suggests a reservation or disagreement

quesadilla is literally "little cheese pastry"

the thing or person inquired about is the **quesited**

question is from Latin *quaerere*, "seek, inquire"

a **questionist** is a habitual questioner

quetching is uttering moans

queue has the forms queued and queuing or queueing; queueing has five vowels in a row

queue is a braid or pigtail (from Latin *cauda*, "tail") or the tailpiece of a violin, and first meant "tail of a beast"

quibble once meant "to pun, to play on the sound of words"

quiche derives from German *kuchen*, "little cake"

quick's root sense is "alive" and "to live" and Old English added the sense "rapid"; the **quick** are "those who are living"

the **quick** is any tender or sensitive flesh as under the nails, around a sore or wound, or under a hoof

in **quicksand**, quick means "alive" as opposed to weight-bearing sand

the nature or essence of something can be described as its **quid** or **quiddity**

a **quiddity** is a quibble or trivial objection

to **quiddle** is to speak in a trifling way

a **quiddler** wastes as much time as possible at work

a **quidnunc** is a gossip or inquisitive person who always wants to know what is going on—and the only word that ends in "unc"; a synonym is **numquid**

quiescent means "motionless, inactive, at rest"

quiet is from Latin quies "**quiet**," from an Indo-European base *qwi-*, "rest"

quietism is calm acceptance of things

a **quiff** is a puff or whiff of wind or tobacco smoke

{ **quill** can be a curled piece of dried cinnamon or cinchona bark }

the whistle of a steam engine is a **quill**

originally, **quilts** were forms of bedding for lying on, not under (from Latin *culcita*, "cushion, mattress")

etymologically, **quince** is "fruit from Khania," a port on Crete from which quinces were exported

quincunx is a word to describe a basis of arrangement in planting trees, either in a single set of five or in combinations of fives

a **quinquagenarian** is 50–59 years old

quinsy is an almost obsolete term for "sore throat"

Aristotle thought there was a "fifth element or essence" that came before the other four (earth, air, fire, and water), which he called "quinta essentia," which gives us the words "**quintessence**" and "**quintessential**"; **quintessence** means "perfect manifestation"

quip originally was a sarcastic or sharp remark—or a curious or odd action

quirk was first a verb meaning "move jerkily"

any decoration on the side of socks or stockings is a **quirk** or **clock**

if something is **quisguous**, it is perplexing or puzzling

quisling is a word named for Norwegian fascist politician Vidkun **Quisling** (1887–1945), who aided German occupation of Norway in World War II

quisquilious and **quisquiliary** mean "having the nature of refuse or rubbish"

a **quit** is a point of departure

quite has the same origin as quit

quits in "call it **quits**" probably comes from a scribe's shortening of the medieval Latin quittus "discharged"

a **quiver** is a case for holding arrows

a set of surfboards is a **quiver**

quixotic means "visionary" or "naively idealistic"

quiz has a meaning "eccentric or odd person" and also "a practical joke; hoax"

quizzism is the practice of questioning or quizzing

quodammodotative is a "thing that exists in a certain way" (or an adjective meaning such)

a **quoddity** is a subtlety or quibble in an argument

a **quodlibet** is a question proposed as an exercise in philosophy (Latin, literally "what it pleases")

a **quodlibetarian** or **quodlibetary** is a person who talks or argues about any subject

a **quoin** is an external angle of a wall or building, one of the stones or bricks serving to form the angle, as a cornerstone

quomodo is means or manner

{ **quomodocunquize** is "to make money any way possible" }

quondam means "having been formerly"

a **quoob** is a queer, fool, and boob all in one

quop means "to throb with pain"

quorum was first the genitive plural of Latin *qui*, "who," and first referred to the "number of justices who need be present to try a case"

quota is from Latin *quot*, "how many"

quotation/quote was first a numbering or number; **quote** (verb) was to mark with numbers for chapters, references, etc.

one should use **quote** exclusively as a verb and use **quotation** as a noun

another way to say annual or yearly is **quotennial**

quotidian means "daily" or "everyday"

a **quoz** is a strange or absurd person or thing

QWERTY keyboards are named for the first six letters of the upper keyboard

the sound made in swallowing is a **qwick**

{ In England, an **R** was formerly used as a mark for rogues }

rabbi means "my master" in Hebrew

when **rabbit** came into English, it only applied to the young of the animal, with the adult **rabbit** being called a **cony**

rabid and **rabies** comes from Latin *rabere*, "be mad"

raccoon is from Algonquian *aroughcan* or *arocoune*, "he scratches with his hands"

a root of ginger is a **race**

race was originally used to denote a group with common features, a group connected by common descent or origin (from Italian *razza*)

raciones, Spanish "rations," are larger helpings of **tapas** (appetizers, Spanish "cover, lid")

rack (as in nerve-racking, **rack** one's brain) means to put under strain and does originate from the instrument of torture

rack is the linear gear and **pinion** is the circular gear in a mechanism

rack is destruction and **ruin** is destitution; in **rack** and **ruin**, **rack** is a variation of wrack and wreck

if you are **racked**, you are "tortured, strained, stretched, punished" (**racked** with guilt, nerve-**racked**); if something is

wracked (a variant of wrecked), it is "ruined, destroyed" (the Titanic was **wracked**)

racket (Arabic *rahet/rahah*, "palm of the hand") or **racquet** is fine for tennis and related games; the game resembling squash is spelled racquets in American English

racketeering/racketeer/racket come from the earlier grabracket, a confidence game in which a man grabbed money and ran while his accomplice distracted by making a **racket**

a **raconteur** or **raconteuse** is a teller of anecdotes, from French *raconter*, "relate"

racy in relation to wine or fruit means having a desirable quality or lively acidity

raddled is a word for "worn out, broken-down" or "showing signs of age"

if one has too much blush on the cheeks, they are **raddled** and **rubescent** means "blushing"

radiate (adjective) means having rays or parts coming out of a center (Latin *radius*, "ray, spoke")

radiators have a misleading name, as they actually work by convecting heat, not radiating it

radical first meant "forming the basis or root," "original, basic, fundamental"

radicchio is Italian for chicory

radices (singular **radix**) are the roots of words

radio is an abbreviation of radio telegraphy, the sending of messages by electromagnetic rays

the easy-to-grow **radish** takes its scientific name (*Raphanus sativus*) from Greek *raphanes*, "easily reared," though **radish** itself is derived from Latin *radix*, "root"

the **radius** is the outer arm bone and the **ulna** is the inner, longer arm bone

radon, a radioactive element, is based on the word radium but patterned on argon

raffish means "disreputable, low"

raffle was originally a dice game with three dice in which a triplet was the winning throw

raft meaning "large amount" is an alteration of raff "abundance"

rafter in construction is related to raft the floating platform

rag may be a back-formation of ragged (or raggy), which comes from Old Norse meaning "tufted"

rage traces back to Latin *rabia*, an alteration of *rabies*, "fury, madness"

raglan sleeves are named for a baron who lost his arm after the Battle of Waterloo

ragout is French and means "reinvigorate the appetite"

a **raid** was first a military expedition on horseback

the **rail** is the edge of a surfboard or sailboard

raillery is good-humored ridicule

railway was first recorded in 1776, but the first actual **railway** opened nearly 50 years later in 1825

raiment is aphetized (to shorten by removing an initial, usually unstressed vowel) from arrayment

rain hearkens to Gothic *rign*, probably ultimately from Proto-Germanic *rezna-*, and was first attested in English c 825, followed by rainbow c 1250, raindrop around 1400, rainstorm in 1816, rainy about 1834, and rainfall in 1854

rainbow comes from Old Norse *regnbogi* (becoming Old English *renboga*, *ren*, "rain" + *boga* "bend, bow") and is a bow or arch of the colors of the prism that is formed in the sky opposite to the sun by the reflection, double refraction, and dispersion of the sun's rays in falling drops of rain

if something is not washed away by rainfall, it is **rainfast**

to **raise** is "to bring something up"; to **rise** is "to get up"

from racemus, Latin for "cluster of grapes," came **raisin** "single grape"

raj is Hindi for "reign"

rake, as in stylish man, is an abbreviation of rakehell

a **rale** is an abnormal respiratory sound heard during a physical exam through a stethoscope

the source of **rally** is French re-, "again," and *alier*, "unite"

ram comes from Norse **ram**(m)*ir*, "strong"

the boughs or branches of a tree are the **ramage**

rambunctious, once rumbustious and robusteous, is probably based on Latin robus, "oak"—implying strength, and can describe a person or animal

a **ramekin** is a small lidless ceramic baking dish used for things like crème brûlée a fragment scraped off is a **ramentum**

if you are **ramfeezled**, you are worn out from work

ramiferous and **ramose** mean bearing branches

ramification is a subdivision of a complex; **ramify** means to form branches or subdivisions (both from Latin *ramus*, "branch")

if something is strangly scented, it is **rammish**

the adjective form of frog is **ranine**

a set of organ pipes is a **rank**

rankle comes from a French word meaning "festering sore"

a **rannygazoo** is a prank or trick

ransack is from Old Norse *rannsaka*, "to search for stolen goods"

ransom came through French from a Latin word meaning "redemption"

{ **randy**, from Scottish, means "lewd, lecherous" or "coarse, rude" }

ramp is an old synonym for tomboy

one of the elements of **rampage** is **ramp** "assume a threatening posture"

rampant is a word describing an animal, especially a lion rearing or standing on its hind legs

rampart is from Latin *re-*, "again," and *emparer*, "fortify," from the earlier *ante-*, "before," and *parare*, "prepare"

a tree whose top branches are dead is a **rampick**

ranch is from Spanish *rancho*, "group of persons eating together"

rancor "ill feeling, animosity" is from Latin *rancorem*, "rancidity, rankness"

a chasm formed by receding ice is **randkluft**

random first meant "headlong rush," from French *randir* "gallop"

a bookcase with a double face, as in a library, is a **range**

a **range** is a stove with spaces for cooking multiple items

range first referred to a line of people or animals

rant is from Dutch *ranten*, "rave, talk foolishly"

a **rantipole** is a wild or badly behaved person

hip-hop is **rap**, but not all **rap** is **hip-hop**; **hip-hop** has a particular beat and uses scratching and breaks/samples

rape originally referred to the violent seizure of property

the "seam" of the tongue is the **raphe**

the word **rapid** is from Latin *rapere*, "seize, take by force"

a turbulent, rock-obstructed river area is **rapid**(s) and steep rapids make a cataract

rapine means "the act or practice of seizing and taking away by force the property of others"

to descend a mountain is to **rappel**

rapport, from French *rapporter*, "bring back," is based on the notion of "return"

rapscallion is an alteration of rascallion, from the earlier **rascal**

raptor (from rapt "carried away by force") is an order of birds of prey, including the eagle, hawk, buzzard, owl, etc.

rapture (and **rapt**) derives from Latin *rapere*, "seize by force," which became the noun *raptura*, "seizure" or "ecstasy"

an egg that is cooked but still soft is described as "**rare**"

rare as in steak is an alteration of rear/rere "half-cooked"

rarefy also means "make or become thin"

a **rareripe** was originally simply a fruit or vegetable that ripened early

rariora is another word for rare books

rascal was first a collective noun for the soldiers of an army or for regular people of the lowest social class

the deep transverse creases across your wrist at the base of the palm are **rasceta** or **rascettes**

rash derives from Italian *raschia*, "itch"

rash (the adjective) suggests imprudence and lack of forethought; **reckless** implies disregard of possible consequences

a slice of bacon is a **rasher** (not several), a cube of bacon is a **lardon** or **lardoon**, and a side of bacon is a **flitch**

the **raspberry** probably takes its name from the English *rasp*, "to scrape roughly," from the thorned canes bearing the berries; it was first called the raspis-berry and has also been called a hindberry

a repetitive rapping or beating sound is **rataplan**

rate comes from Latin *rata*, "calculated, fixed"

a **rather** (noun) is a choice or preference

if you have approval, you have **ratihabition**

ratio is from Latin, literally "reckoning"

ratiocinate is a fancy word for "to reason"

ration is from Latin *ratio*, "calculation, computation," and in the Middle Ages took on the sense of "amount of provisions allotted to a soldier"

a **rationale** is given for a future course of action, whereas a **rationalization** is offered for a past action

a **rattle** is a succession of small noisy waterfalls forming rapids

raucous is based on Latin *raucus*, "hoarse"

the mass of eggs carried or deposited by a female fish is called the **raun**

raunchy can also mean "slovenly" or "inept"

ravage was first a flood or inundation

ravaged is "damaged, destroyed"; **ravished** is "carried off by force or emotion" or "raped"

ravel means the same as **unravel** - just like **flammable/inflammable**, **boned/deboned**

ratatouille, the eggplant dish, comes from French *touiller*, "to stir up"

rassasy is to satisfy a hungry person

rat is from Latin rattus, whose origin is unknown

to **raven** is to eat voraciously; **ravenous** came through French *ravines*, "seize by force," from Latin *rapere*

ravine first meant "violence" or "impetus," from French for "violent rush"

ravioli (plural of raviolo) derives from Italian *raviolo*, from *raviol/rafiol*, "meatball"

ravishing can mean "seizing on prey"

raw-gabbit is "speaking confidently on a subject of which one is ignorant"

one who noshes on crudites is a **rawist**

rawky means "foggy, damp, and cold"

to **rax** is to stretch oneself after sleep

raxed means "stretched as on awakening"

ray is distinguished from **beam** in that it describes a smaller quantity of light (**beam** being a collection of parallel rays)

raze, from French *raser*, "shave close," is from Latin *radere*, "scrape, scratch"—also giving us **razor**

to **razz** (harass, carp) comes from raspberry

RBIs is the proper plural of RBI

reach originally meant "stretch out the hand"

the **reach** is the stretch of a river that lies between two points or bends

react first meant "re-act" or "act in return; produce a response"

the first senses of **read** were "to believe, suppose, think" or "advise"

ready is from Latin *reri*, "to consider, take under advisement"

reaks are pranks or practical jokes

real was first a legal term pertaining to immovable property

realgar is another word for **arsenic**

realm traces to Latin *regimen*, "system of government," from *regere*, "rule"

realtor should be pronounced REEL-tuhr

ream is borrowed from Arabic *rizmah*, "bale, bundle"

a **ream** used to be 480 sheets of paper and now it is 500

rear, as in "back part," was first a military term

one **rears** children and **raises** crops

reason is from Latin ratio "thinking" and associated with the ideas of right order, proportion, or harmony

reave can mean to tear, split, cleave, or break into pieces

a **rebate** is a partial repayment, whereas a **refund** is a repayment of the total purchase price

rebel comes from re- and bellum "war"

rebellion is open resistance to a government or authority; **revolution** is a **rebellion** that succeeds in overthrowing the government and establishing a new one

rebuff comes from *re-* and Italian *buffo*, "gust, puff"; a **rebuffal** is an act of rebuffing

rebuke has the element bukier "beat, strike" from French

a **rebus** is a puzzle where you decode a message consisting of pictures representing syllables and words

to **rebut** a statement is to offer clear evidence or a reasoned argument against it; to **refute** a statement is to prove it wrong (neither means "contradict" or "deny")

recalcitrant comes from Latin *recalcitrare*, "kick out with the heels" (*calx*, "heel")

recant can mean "sing again"; the usual meaning of **recant** stresses the withdrawing or denying of something professed or taught

recap is short for **recapitulate** "repeat the headings" (literally)

receipt's first meaning was "a drug made according to a recipe" or a "recipe" for making food

to **receive** something is etymologically to "take it back," from Latin *recipere*, "regain"

to **recense** is to review or revise a text; scholarly editorial revision is **recension**

recent is from Latin *recens*, "fresh, new"

a recipe collection is a **receptary**

receptible is "able to be received; capable of receiving"

a **recidivist** "persistent offender" is etymologically someone who "falls back" and **recidivism** is literally "a falling back" especially into bad habits; **recidivation** is relapsing into crime, error, or sin

recipe, as a verb, was once used at the beginning of medical prescriptions and it first (in Latin) meant "take"—we are familiar with its use by physicians in the abbreviation R or Rx

reciprocal is based on the prefixes *re-*, "back," and *pro-*, "forward"

recision is the act of cutting back or pruning something

a **recital** is a musical performance by a soloist or two performers; a **concert** is a performance by a group

recite is from Latin *recitare*, "read out"

reckless is based on Old English *reck*, meaning "care, regard"

a **reckling** is the runt of a litter

reckon originally meant "give a list of, enumerate"

reclaim is from falconry "the act of calling a falcon back from flight"

réclame means "public acclaim or notoriety" or "self-publicity"

a part of a plant bent downwards is **reclinate**

a **recluse** is etymologically a person who is "shut up," from Latin *recludere*

Latin *recognosce*, "know again," became **recognize**

recoil is from French *reculer*, "move back" (from Latin *culus*, "buttocks")

recollect, from Latin *recolligere*, first meant "gather again"

an early sense of **recommend** (from Latin *commendare*) was "commit to the care of (God)"

reconcile comes from Latin elements meaning "bring together" and "back" (i.e., bring back together)

recondite "abstruse, obscure" means etymologically "hidden"

when you add water to dried or concentrated food, you **reconstitute** it

the Latin base of the word "**record**" is *cord*, "heart," and it first meant "get by heart, commit to memory"

both **recount** and **relate** mean "to tell, to give an account of" but **recount** adds the semantic component "in detail"

recoup first meant "cut short, interrupt"

recourse refers to turning to someone or something for help; **resort** is something you turn to after all other options have failed (and as a verb means to have **recourse**!)

recover and **recuperate** come from Latin *recuperare*, "**recover**, regain"—from *capere*, "take"

a **recreant** is a cowardly or disloyal person

recreation has older meanings of "refreshment by taking food" and "mental consolation or comfort"

recrement is any superfluous or useless part of a substance

recrimination is an accusation in retaliation for an accusation made against onself (or the making of such an accusation)

recruit has the Latin base crescere "grow, increase"

rectalgia or **proctalgia** is a pain in the behind

rectangle breaks down into Latin elements *rectus*, "right," and "angle"

rectify is based on Latin *rectus*, "right, straight"

{ to **recrudesce** is to break out again, literally and figuratively; **recrudescence** is the rediscovery or revival of something good or valuable }

to blend or dilute whiskey or other alcoholic spirits is to **rectify**

rectigrade describes walking in a straight line

rectilinear is used in physics to describe a motion in which speed remains constant and the path is a straight line

recto is the righthand page of a book or the front of a page; the opposite (or left-hand page) is the **verso**

someone easily hurt emotionally is **rectopathic**

a **rector** first was a ruler or governor, now generally a person conducting a religious service

the **rectrix** is a bird's strong tail feather used in directing flight

rectum is short for intestinum **rectum**

recubation is reclining in a near-horizontal position; to **recumb** is to "lean, recline, rest"

a **recumbent** is a person who is dependent on another

a **recusant** is a person who refuses to submit to authority or to comply with a command; **recuse** first meant "refuse" or "reject"

red is an ancient color term traceable to Indo-European reudh-

to **redact** is to put in writing, draw up a statement, etc.—including editing and revising this

redamation is loving in return

to **redd** is "to set in order; to clear"

rede can mean counsel or advice given by one person to another

redeem first meant "buy back" and one of its Latin elements is emere "buy"

redhibition is the return of defective merchandise

the derogatory term **redneck** came from the implied characteristic of this class of person being reactionary

redolent (an adjective) is customarily used of pleasant odors while **reek** (a verb) is used of odors that are sensorily unpleasing; **redolent**, "emitting a strong odor or smell," comes from Latin olere, "emit a smell"

redoubt has no connection to "doubt," but comes from French redoute and Latin reductus, "hidden place, refuge, stronghold"

redound is actually the base of redundant and it can means "to have a good or bad effect" and "to rebound or reflect"

reduce first meant "bring back or recall in memory" or "take back or refer (a thing) to its origin" (Latin reducere, "lead back"); **reduct** means "simplify"

etymologically, something that is **redundant** "overflows," from Latin redundare, "flow back, overflow"

a **reduplication** is the repetition of a word element with a small change, e.g., dilly-dally

redwoods are coastline trees while sequoias are inland trees and the wood of the **sequoia** is lighter and more brittle than that of the **redwood**

reebok is the Dutch name for a speedy South African antelope

reef is from Old Norse *rif*, "rib"

the word **reefer** may be related to Mexican Spanish *grifo*, "smoker of marijuana"

reek can mean "a haze of fine dust or snow"

smoking meat used to be called **reeking**

reeraw is a confused noise of loud laughter and singing, as at a drinking party

to **reeve** is to thread a rope through a hole or ring

refect first meant "refresh" especially with food or drink; **refection** is food and drink as refreshment

refer comes from Latin meaning "carry back" and a **referee** is a person to whom a matter or question is "carried back" for a decision

Referee originally referred to a person appointed by the British Parliament to examine patent applications (1621) and was formed from English *refer* and *-ee*. The sense of "an arbitrator or person to whom a dispute is referred" was first recorded in 1690; by 1840 the word acquired the further sense of "the judge of play in games and sports." Baseball, boxing, and cricket have umpires; basketball, hockey, rugby, and football have referees—and American football has both.

a **referendum** is a measure that is referred to the people

refine is based on the verb fine meaning "clarify"

to **reflect** something is etymologically to "bend it back," from Latin *reflectere*

refocillate means "refresh, revive"; **refocillation** is the restoration of strength by taking food or drink, total refreshment or revitalization

refossion is another word for "digging up"

refrain is based on Latin *frenum*, "bridle"

refrain means to choose not to do something or partake of something; **restrain**

means to immobilize by force or to forbid an action

refrigerator, **rigid**, **rigorous**, and **rigor mortis** all have the Indo-European base of *rig-*, "cold" (later Greek *rhigos*, "cold"); **refrigerator** is literally "thing that makes cold"

refuge is based on the Latin word *fugere*, "flee"

{ **refulgent** is shining with or reflecting a brilliant light }

refund first meant "pour back" and comes from Latin *re-*, and *fundere*, "to pour"

refurbish means to "clean up again," **refurnish** means "to provide with new furnishings," **redecorate** means "to add new decoration(s)," and **renovate** means "renew or restore to as-new condition"

refute means "to show conclusively to be false or illogical" and applies primarily to assertions or arguments; **confute** means "to prove wrong" and applies primarily to the person or agency making the assertion or argument

regal and **royal** both come from Latin *regalis*, "of or fit for a king, kingly" (from *reg-*, *rex*, "king"), **regal** through a French learned borrowing of the Latin word, and **royal** through Old French *roial*, derived from the same Latin word

regale (to entertain or lavish) is based on the Old French *gale*, "pleasure"

regard is from French *regarder*, "look back at, keep one's eyes on"

use "**regardless**," not "irregardless"

regatta is literally Italian for "contest, fight" and the word first referred to boat races in Venice

refreezing can be called **regelation**

regent is from Latin *regere*, "rule"

regime refers to a government, usually an authoritarian one

regimen was first a prescribed course of exercise, way of life, or diet—from Latin *regere*, "to rule"—and also first meant "government, rule" (as did **regiment**)

reiki is Japanese for "universal life energy"

reimburse is partly from Latin *imburse*, "put into a purse" (*bursa*, "purse")

a **rein** is etymologically something that "retains"

rejectamenta is a collection of things that have been rejected

{ **reindeer** is actually redundant, coming from Old Norse/Icelandic *hreinn*, "**reindeer**," and *dyr*, "deer," which translates to "**reindeer** deer" }

a **régisseur** is a director of a ballet or theater

register came from Latin *regesta*, "things recorded" (from *regerere*, "enter record")

regress is from Latin *re-*, "back," and *gradi*, "walk"

regret carries no explicit admission that one is responsible for an incident while **remorse** implies a sense of guilty responsibility and a greater feeling of personal pain and anguish

a person is **regretful**; a situation may be **regrettable**

regretfully means with feelings of regret; **regrettably** means unfortunately

regular first meant "subject to a religious rule" and was the opposite of secular

a base of **regurgitate** is gurges/gurgit "whirlpool" in Latin

rehabilitate first meant "to formally restore the former privileges, possessions, or rank of someone"

literally, **rehearse** is to re-harrow or "to go over again with a harrow"

reify is to convert mentally into a thing or to consider an abstract thing to be real

reign traces to Latin *reg/rex*, "king"

to cause joy was the early sense of **rejoice**

rejoin implies a sharp answer, but **retort** suggests the addition of criticism or an explicit charge

something that is **related** to something else is etymologically "carried back" to it, from Latin *referre*

a **relation** is any kind of connection or association between people or things; a **relationship** is a state or condition that results from a background of such connections or associations

relax is Latin *re-* and *laxus*, "lax"

relay first meant the provision of fresh hounds for tracking a deer

relegate can mean "send a person into exile"

relent and **resolve** originally meant "melt, dissolve" in literal (under the influence of heat) and figurative senses

relevant means "worthy of raising in the context of discussion"; **pertinent** means "applicable to the point at issue"

relic derives from Latin *reliquae*, "remains"

an animal or plant surviving in one area after becoming extinct elsewhere is a **relict**

relief (standing out) and **intaglio** (sunken) are opposites in art

relieve is from Latin *relevare*, "raise again," and metaphorically "alleviate, lighten"

religion comes from a Latin word meaning "reverence" and originally meant a life under monastic vows

a **reliquary** is a small receptacle for relics

relish first meant "odor, scent," then "taste, flavor"

reluctance is a feeling that is experienced; **recalcitrance** is an attitude that is shown

to be **reluctant** about doing something is literally to "struggle against" it, from Latin *reluctari*

rely first meant "gather together; assemble"

Latin *manere* meant "stay" and with *re-*, "back, in place," became **remain** in English

remainder is a general word for what is left over, while **residue** (and **residuum**) is the remains at the end of a process; **remnant** is a part left after the greater part has been removed

remark is from an intensified French word *marquer*, "observe, notice," i.e., "making a verbal observation"

rembrandt is a dark grayish brown

remeant is a synonym for returning

remedy comes from Latin *mederi*, "heal"

Latin *rememorari*, "recall to mind," became **remember**

to **remigate** is to row and **remex** is a rower (from Latin *remus*, "oar")

remission originally meant forgiveness or pardon for an offense or sin (and **remit** meant "forgive, pardon")

remnant is a contraction of the older word remenant

to **remonstrate** is to make plain or manifest, exhibit or show

remontant means "blooming more than once a year," such as some roses

a **remora** is a drag or hindrance (from Latin, literally "delay")

remorse is from the elements *re-* (intensive) and *mordere*, "to bite"

remote is from Latin *remotus*, the past participle of *removere*, "remove"

rémoulade seems to derive from French *rémola*, "horseradish," which came from Latin *armoracia*, "horseradish"

remove is from Latin *re-*, "again, back," and *movere*, "move," *removere*, "move back, move away"

remugient means "bellowing again"

remunerate has the element munus/muner "gift"

Renaissance is French *re-*, "again," and *naissance*, "birth" (from Latin *nasci*, "be born")

> **render** comes from Latin *reddere*, "give back," and then *rendere*

rendezvous is French for "present yourselves"

renegade first referred to a person who abandons one religion for another

renege (pronounced rih-NIG) first meant "desert" a faith or a person

renitent means "offering physical resistance"

renounce often equals **abjure** but may carry the meaning of disclaim or disown and may imply a sacrifice for a greater end

renovize is a blend of renovate and modernize

to be **renowned** is etymologically to be "named again" or be "famous," from Latin *re-*, "again," and *nomer*, "name"

rent comes from Latin *rendere*, "give back"

a person who makes income from rent is a **rentier**

repair is from Latin *reparare*, "put back in order"; **repair** as in "go" is ultimately the same word as repatriate, from Latin *repatriare*, "go home"

repandous is bent upward

repartee is from French for "reply readily"

repast (a delicious meal, a quantity of food) comes from Latin *pascere*, "feed" (and **repasture** means the same)

the -peat of **repeat** is from Latin *petere*, "go to, seek," and it combined with *re-*, "again, back" to make *repetere*, "go back to"
repeatedly is over and over again;

{ **repercussion** was first a medical term for "repressing an infection" }

reperible means "discoverable"

repertorium, which gives us **repertoire**, meant "catalog, inventory, collection" and later meant "a repository, store"—ultimately coming from *reperire*, "discover"

a **repertory** is etymologically a list of things "found," from reperire "find out" with the inner base of *per-*, "attempt"

repetitively is over and over but also tending to become boring or displeasing due to its sameness

replenish has the Latin base *plenus*, "full"

if something is **replete**, it is physically filled with something

replication can mean the action of folding something up or back—or the fold itself

reply is generally used when the answer is understood to be verbal—either written or oral; **response**, by contrast, has a more general application and may be used for a variety of reactions

to **report** something is etymologically to "carry it back," from Latin *reportare*—and the metaphorical sense of "bringing back news" also developed in Latin

repose is a state of restfulness and relaxation

reprehensible is usually applied to things, not people—the sin and not the sinner

represent is "present again," from Latin *re-*, "again, back," and *praesentare*, "present"

reprieve originally meant "send back to prison"

reprisal comes from the archaic meaning of **reprise** "to retake property by force"

to **repristinate** is to restore to an original state or condition

reproach comes from the Latin base *prope*, "near," which combined with *re-* to make *repropiare*, "bring back near," and evolved into its metaphorical sense of "bring somebody face to face with something for which they should be blamed"

Latin *re-*, "reversal of a previous condition" combined with *probare*, "approve, test" to create *reprobare* and then English **reprobate**

a **reprographer** is a person who makes copies of documents

to **reprove** is to reject or express disapproval of something

reptant means "crawling, creeping" (applicable to a lobster, crab) and **reptile** comes from Latin *repere*, "crawl, creep"

a **reptile** has dry scaly skin while amphibians have moist skin

a **republic** is a state or nation where the supreme power lies with its citizens; a **commonwealth** is an allied group of republics

republic comes from Latin *res*, "affair or thing," and *publica*, "public"

repudiate comes from a Latin word that means "divorce or abandon" and **repudiation** first meant "divorce of a wife"

repugn means "to strive against" or "be contradictory or inconsistent," giving us **repugnant**

repulsive describes a characteristic of a person or object; **repellent** describes an impression projected by a person or object— a person is **repulsive**, while a person's behavior is **repellent**

reputed is almost always used to describe suspected criminals

request comes from Latin *requirere* (as does require) "ask or search again" and it originally meant that

{ **require** includes the Latin element *quaerere*, "ask, seek" }

requital (pronounced rih-QUITE-uhl) is revenge or payback

to write in reply is to **rescribe**

rescue comes from Latin *excutere*, "shake out"—so it is the "shaking out" of a captive from the enemy

resemble goes back to Latin *similis*, "like," which became *similare*, "imitate"; the addition of the intensive prefix produced French *resembler*, "be very like" before English **resemble**

resent started out meaning "experience an emotion" and **resentment** first meant "strong return of good feeling"; it is a changeling word

the -side of **reside** has no connection to the general meaning of "side" but comes from Latin *sedere*, "settle," so **reside** is literally "settle back, remain in place"; **resident** comes from Latin elements meaning "sit back"

resign applies to the giving up of an unexpired office or trust and comes from Latin *re-*, "back, undo," and *signare*, "sign, seal"

to **resile** is to recoil, retreat, or draw back

resins, unlike sap, do not nourish a plant but are secreted in response to injury

resipiscence is recognition of one's own past errors or repentance for one's misconduct; **resipiscent** is "brought back to one's senses"

spiteful behavior manifested by inanimate objects is **resistentialism**

resolution is from the Latin *resolutio-*, from *resolvere* meaning "to loosen or dissolve again," (re- + solvere) which was the original meaning

resolve first meant "decompose, disintegrate, unloose" or "separate into constituent parts" (from Latin *solvere*, "dissolve, loosen"); the meaning "to determine or decide upon a course of action, etc.," was first used in English around 1523

resonance comes from a Latin word meaning "echo"

resonate means "to expand, to intensity, or amplify the sound of," whereas **resound** means "to throw back, repeat, the sound of"

respect goes back to *respectus*, from Latin *respicere*, "look back at" or "regard, consider" and this was the **respect**'s original meaning in English

respectably means "in a decent way," **respectfully** means "in a courteous way," and **respectively** means "in the order given or indicated"

a **respite** (pronounced RES-put) is a break or relief, especially from something difficult or disagreeable

resplendent is based on the verb resplend "to be radiant," from Latin *re-*, and *splendere*, "to shine"

respond suggests a quick reaction while **reply** implies a return commensurate with the original demand or question a person with a divorce action brought against them is the **respondent** and an involved adulterer is the **corespondent**

responsibility can lie only with people and not with things

to **respue** is to reject strongly

rest first meant a bed or couch

restaurant is a French word taken from the verb *restaurer*, "to restore," and was originally used to mean a food (like soup) that restores; it was first used to mean an eating establishment in Paris in 1763 and in the United States in 1827

restaurant owners are **restaurateurs** (no "n" is involved), a word taken directly from the French *restaurer*

resteteria was once a term for restroom

resting is a kind adjective for "between acting jobs"

restive, which now means "not wishing to rest" originally meant the opposite, "wishing to rest"

restive means impatient of fidgety under pressure or restraint; **restless** is being uneasy, unquiet, or unable to relax or rest

restoration is repairing a work that has been damaged through accident, decay, or neglect

résumé is from French, literally "resumed, taken on anew"

resurrect is a back-formation from resurrection

retail comes from a French word meaning "piece cut off"—because it is the sale of goods in small quantities

retaliate is to "repay in kind"—which could imply return of good as well as evil

retardataire means behind the times or characteristic of an earlier period

a **retch** is a long stretch of river

retch is to vomit or gag; **wretch** is a noun for a pitiable person

reticent is based on Latin *tacere*, "be silent" combined with *re-*, an intensive prefix

reticulate or **carcellate** means "having crossed lines"

reticule, an older term for a small hand-bag, alludes to the fact that they were originally made of netted fabric—Latin *rete*, "net" became *reticulum*, "netted bag"

retina is from Latin *rete*, "net," as there is a net of nerves making up this layer of the eyeball

a **retinue** is etymologically "that which is retained"

retiracy is another word for retirement

retire is from the French *retirer re-*, "back," and *tirer*, "throw," and its first sense was "withdraw to a place of safety or seclusion"

retract applies to the withdrawing of a promise, an offer, or an accusation

retral means "situated at or towards the back"

retreat goes back to *retrahere*, "draw back"

a **retreatant** is a person taking part in a retreat

retrench originally meant "dig a new trench as a second line of defense"

to **retrieve** something is etymologically to "refind" it, from Latin *retrover*, "find again"

a nation **retrocedes** a territory by giving it back to the country it origanlly belonged to

{ **retrogress** is the opposite of progress and it often implies an unexpected or undesirable decline from a higher or more advanced level }

retrograde can mean "in a direction contrary to the previous motion" or "tending or inclined to go back or to revert"

retroition is the action of returning or a re-entrance

a **retronym** is a word formed from an older word by attaching a previously unnecessary modifier—a noun that has been forced to take on an adjective in order to stay up-to-date, e.g., guitar now has versions like acoustic guitar

retroussé refers to a nose turned up at the tip

return is from Latin re-, "back," and tornare, "turn on a lathe," making retornare "turn back"

to **reune** is to hold or attend a reunion

rev is an abbreviation of revolution

revamp originally referred to shoes—vamp being the covering of the instep

reveal is based on Latin that means "lifting of a veil"

veins are **revehent** because they "carry back" blood to the heart

a **revenant** is one who returns after a long exile

revenge is personal and **justice** is societal

revenue first meant "return to a place"

an early sense of **reverberate** was "beat or drive back"

revere is from Latin vereri, "hold in awe or fear," plus the intensive re-

reverie first meant "delight, joy" and "revelry"

a **reverist** is one inclined to dream, especially daydream

a lapel or cuff's reverse side that is showing is the **revers**

a **reversal** is a word that becomes another word when read backwards (live becomes evil)

a reverse dictionary, one starting with definitions and leading to the headwords, can be called a **reversicon**

a retaining wall can also be called a **revetment**

review traces back to revoir, "see again"

revise first meant "look again, look back, reflect on"

{ **revoke** first meant "bring back to a belief or a way of life" }

to **revolt** is to refuse to obey the constraints imposed by another; to **rebel** is to attempt to replace those constraints by a set of one's own

revolution derives from Latin revolutio, meaning the movement of a thing from one place to another

revolve and **rotate** are synonyms in everyday writing, but not in scientific/technical writing: the Earth revolves around the Sun and rotates upon its axis

reward was originally used interchangeably with **regard**, coming from Anglo-Norman rewarder through French regarder

rhapsody is, literally, dispersed pieces or songs loosely sewn or strung together (Greek rhapsoidia, from rhaptein, "to stitch," and oide, "song, ode")

rhathymia is the state of being cheerful and optimistic

rhematic is pertaining to the construction of sentences or the formation of words

a **rhetor** is a teacher of rhetoric or a master of it

in Greece, a rhetor was a "public speaker" or "orator," going back to Indo-European wer-, "say, speak," and giving us **rhetoric**

Greek rheuma, "flow, stream" (rheum being a watery discharge) was transferred to denote "watery discharge from the body" and borrowed into English for **rheumatic** and **rheumatism**

a **rhinarium** is the hairless habitually moist nose of some mammals, as the antelope

the rhine in **rhinestone** is the Rhine River and **rhinestone** is a translation of French *caillou du Rhin*; it was originally the word for a type of rock crystal found in or near the Rhine and now denotes artificial colorless gems of high luster that are cut to imitate diamonds

rhinoceros comes from Greek *rhin-*, "nose," and *keras*, "horn"; the correct plural is **rhinoceroses**

the red nose of a drunk is called **rhinophyma** or **grog blossom**

> **rhododendron** is from Greek *rhodo*, "rose," and *dendron*, "tree"

something that is **rhonchisonant** is imitative of the noise of snorting

rhubarb appears to come from Latin *rha*, "**rhubarb** root" and *barbarum*, "foreign"

a **rhumb** is any of the thirty-two points on a marine navigational compass

rhyme is from Latin *rhythmus*, "rhythm," from Greek *rhein*, "to flow"

rhythm traces to Greek *rhuthmos*, "recurring motion," and it was later applied to recurring accents in verse and music

rib is Germanic, from prehistoric *rebjo*

ribald was first a noun for "retainer or dependent of low status"

a **ribble** is a wrinkle or furrow

rice derives from Greek *oryza*, but is ultimately from Sanskrit *vrihi-s*, "**rice**"

rich first meant "powerful"

a **rick** is a stack of hay, corn, peas, etc., covered with thatching for protection

rickety is based on the name of the disease rickets

ricochet is French meaning "the skipping of a stone on water"

rickshaw is from Japanese, literally "man power carriage"

ricotta (cheese) literally means "recooked" in Italian

the expanse of one's mouth is the **rictus** (Latin "open mouth")

rid was borrowed from Old Norse *rythja*, from the earlier Germanic *rudjan*

riddle is a hole made by a bullet

ride is Germanic with connections to Celtic languages, but that is all that is known

if someone is **rident** or **riant**, they are radiantly cheerful

in Old English, **ridge** was the word for "back" as part of the body, human or animal

a short musical phrase (a group of notes forming a distinct unit within a longer passage) is often called a **riff** or a **lick**

a shallow part of a stream or river is the **riffle**

to shuffle two piles of cards into one is to **riffle**

rif/riff, "spoil, strip," and *raf*, "carry off" combined to *rif et raf* in French, then went to English *riff and raff* "everything, every scrap," then **riffraff**

rifle was first **rifle** gun, a gun with rifles "spiral grooves" inside the barrel

another word for "to break wind" is **rift**

rift figuratively means "to come back unpleasantly to the memory"

a ship's **rig** is the arrangement of masts, sails, etc.; the **rigging** is the system of ropes or chains supporting these

rigatoni comes from Italian *rigare*, "to mark with lines, to make fluting"

right goes back to the Indo-European base *reg-*, "move in a straight line" or "direct"; the use of the word as the opposite of left derives from the notion that the **right** hand is the "correct" hand to use

if something is somewhat rigid or a little stiff, it is **rigidulous**

rigmarole may be a colloquial alteration of ragman roll "a catalog, list"

rigor first meant a sudden feeling of chill at the onset or height of a fever

rigorism is extreme strictness

riley has two meanings: thick and turbid, angry and irritable

rill is a small brook, rivulet, or stream—and also the long, narrow trenchlike valleys on the surface of the moon

the **rims** are the edges of the tongue

a **riparian** is someone who lives on a river bank

ripe is the bank of a river or a seashore

a **ripienist** is a musician who plays only with others, never alone

a **riposte** is a counterstroke, such as a snappy retort (from Italian riposta "reply, response")

broken foundation stones are called **riprap**

riptides are actually currents, not tides

rise is from Germanic meaning "go up"

the vertical piece connecting two threads of a stair is the **riser**

something **risible** is laughable, ludicrous, comical

English acquired **risk** from French *risquè*, from Italian *riscare*, "run into danger" or *risco*, "steep rock or reef," but that is all that is known

 rind is the hard or tough covering on oranges, grapefruit, and watermelon; once removed, skin or **rind** is usually known as **peel**

rime is another word for frost or frozen mist

a **rimple** is a ripple or wrinkle

rinbombo is a rare word for a booming roar

a piece of or the whole outer bark of a tree is the **rind**

boxing started off in circles—and when Marcus of Queensbury introduced a set of rules in 1867, he also introduced the roped-off square which continued to be called the "**ring**"

ringer in "dead **ringer**" means "a double or counterpart"—so the phrase means "exact double"

ringworm is an infection that makes ring-like marks on the skin, but there are no worms involved; it is caused by a fungus

risorgimento is a time of renewal or revival

risotto means "little rice" in Italian

a **ristra** is a string of dried chiles or other foodstuffs

a **rite** is an established form of religious or otherwise solemn practice; a **ritual** is a prescribed form for carrying out the ceremonies associated with such a practice (both from Latin *ritus*, "ceremony")

ritzy is derived from the luxurious Ritz hotels

originally, **rivals** were people who lived on opposite sides of a river (Latin *rivus*) or stream

wood that has been split (as opposed to sawed) is **rived**

river is the finest grade of diamond

rivulet is from Latin *rivulus*, a diminutive of *rivus*, "stream"

a **rixatrix** or **termagent** is a quarreling woman

to **rizzle** is to relax after a heavy meal

road first meant "riding" or "hostile incursion on horseback"—a sense preserved in "inroads"

if a vehicle is **roadable**, it is suitable for being driven on public roads

roadster first referred to a horse, cycle, or horse-drawn carriage for use on the roads

roar first pertained to humans; later, to lions and other animals

roary is hazy or not clear

roast originally meant "cook before a fire" before it meant "cook in an oven"

an adult chicken is a **roaster**

rob goes back to Germanic *roub-*, "to break"

robe's history is related to "rob" as it first came from regarding clothes as booty

robin is a shortening of **robin** redbreast and comes from a diminutive or nickname for Robert

robot derives from Czech *robota*, "forced labor"

a **robot** is a fully mechanical conscience-less device; an **android** is an autonomous humanlike **robot**

robust comes from Latin meaning "oak" and "oaken"

rock as in "stone" was borrowed from Old French *rocque*, but that is all that is known

rock as in "sway" is from Germanic *rukk-*, "move"

rocket once meant "small rock"

rococo is an alteration of French *rocaille*, a type of pebble- or shell-work

rod is probably related to Old Norse *rudda*, "club"

rodent comes from Latin *rodere*, "gnaw"

rodeo is Spanish for "a going around, especially a cattle ring" from *rodear*, "to go around"

rodomontade, loud bragging, got its name from Rodomonto, a loud bragging Moorish king of epics

roe is a term for the patterned alternation of light and dark streaks in the grain of wood

rogue probably comes from Latin *rogare*, "ask, beg"

to **roil** is to perturb, disturb, or disorder

roin is an old word for scab

{ do you know a **roinous** person? (mean, nasty, contemptible) }

to **roister** is to enjoy oneself noisily; a **roisterer** is a swaggering reveler

rold means "stout, strong," or "rough, violent" or "large, unwieldy"

role comes from a French word (*roule*) that first referred to the roll of paper on which the actor's part was written

a **roleo** is a logrolling contest (roll and rodeo)

Rolfing is named for the U.S. physiotherapist who developed the massage technique

roll ultimately is derived from Latin *rotulus*, "small wheel," diminutive of *rota*, "wheel"; **roll** in English first meant "rolled-up parchment"

rollick may be a blend of romp and frolic

romance is from Old French meaning "the vernacular tongue" or "a work composed in the vernacular tongue"

rom-com means "romantic comedy"

romp is perhaps an alliteration (repetition of the same consonant sound in the stressed or initial syllables) of ramp

another word for sexually desirable is **rompworthy**

the cross of the crucifixion (of Christ) was a **rood** or **crucifix**

roof has the plurals roofs and rooves

in chess, the **rook** is also called the **castle**

{ **rookie** comes from Civil War slang "reckie," which was short for "recruit" }

the Old English word for "**room**" was *cofa* but it simply meant "space," and the modern sense did not emerge until the fifteenth century; **room** comes from Germanic *rumaz*, "spacious," but that is all that is known of its history

rooped is a synonym for hoarse

a false report made to damage the reputation of a political candidate is a **roorback**

roost is traced back to Middle Dutch and Flemish roest

root (of a plant) is a word borrowed from Old Norse *rot*, from the Indo-European base *wrot-/vrot-*, which also produced Latin *radix*, "**root**"

rootage is a system of roots

root-bound describes a plant whose roots have outgrown their container, thwarting new growth

the **roozles** is wretchedness of mind or miserableness

a bunch of onions is a **rope**

rope is from Germanic but the ultimate origin is unknown; a **stirrup** is etymologically a "climbing **rope**"

a **ropewalk** is a place where ropes are made

Roquefort is the name of the village in southwest France where it was created

in croquet, to strike another ball with your own is to **roquet**

roral means dewy, **roric** is pertaining to dew, **roriferous** is generating dew, and **rorulent** means covered with dew

originally, **rosary** was a "garden of roses" (from Latin *rosarium*) and evolved to mean a set of devotions or prayers consisting of recitation or chanting

a long string of beads for prayer is a **rosary**; a short string is a **chaplet**

the Old English form **rose** came from Latin *rosa*, "red," which may have been an adoption of the Greek word *rhodon*, "**rose**."

rosé is French for "pink" and elliptical from *vin rosé* "pink wine"

roseate can mean rose-colored, rose-scented, or just plain rosy

rosemary comes from Roman *ros marinus*, "sea dew"

a **rosery** is a rose garden or rosebed

a **rosette** (a diminutive of rose) is a decoration consisting of a bunch of ribbons or other material, concentrically arranged to look like a rose

the rosy light of dawn is **rosicler**

roster was originally a list of duties for military personnel

rostrum is Latin for "beak" and first referred to part of the Rome Forum decorated with bird beaks and used as a platform for speakers

rot is from Germanic *rutjan*, and may be ultimately from Latin *rudis*, "rough"

the adjective **rotate** means "wheel-shaped"

rote is the roar of surf crashing into the shore

rotisserie first meant a restaurant or shop specializing in roasted or barbecued meat

a round building or hall is a **rotunda**

the gentle cooing of doves is **roucoulement**

a **roué** is one who leads a life of pleasure and sensuality

rough is from Germanic *rukhwaz*, "shaggy, hairy, **rough**," but that is all that is known

> **roughage** was first the unused or refuse part of a crop

rough-and-tumble was originally boxing slang

roughing-in is the installation of plumbing and electrical wiring

a **rough-rider** breaks in horses

a roll of coins wrapped in paper is a **rouleau**

roulette formerly described a hair-curling device or a massage roller

round goes back to Latin rotundus **"round"**

a tubular-style hairbrush is a **roundbrush** (or round brush)

rouse is a shake, especially of a bird's feathers

rout comes from Proto-Romance word meaning "broken or partial company" as it first meant a band of people or pack of animals

routine is related to **route**, as it means "a regular course"

a **roux** (French "browned butter") is a mixture of flour and fat used to thicken sauces, gravies, and soups

rove originally meant "to shoot arrows at randomly selected marks or targets"—a method of improving the archer's sense of range

rover is from Middle Dutch **rover**, literally "sea robber" and that transferred to "wanderer"

row as in oars is from Germanic *ro-*, "steer," and **row**, "orderly line" is from Germanic *raigwa*

rowdy is related to row "loud noise or commotion"

the pig's snout is a **rowel**

the **rowel** is the spiked revolving disk on a spur

royal is from Latin *regalis*, a derivative of *rex*, "king"

a card game to break a tie is a **rubber**

rubber in the sense of the latex of the **rubber** plant is so called because you can rub out pencil marks with it, not the other way around

rubble came from Anglo-Norman *robel*, "bits of broken stone," from earlier French *robe*, "loot, odds and ends stolen"

rube is a pet form of the name Reuben

a person can be described as **rubicund** if their complexion tends to be ruddy or flushed

rubigenous is rusted or rust-colored

rubric first meant a heading or section of text written in red to stand out; the title of a category is the **rubric**

ruby is from Latin *ruber*, "red"

a frill of gathered ribon as a trimming is a **ruche**

a **ruck** or **ruckle** is a heap or a pile

rucksack comes from German *Rucken*, "back," and "sack"

ruckus is probably a blend of rumpus and ruction

a **ruction** is a disturbance or riot

rudder first meant "paddle" or "oar"

to **ruddle** is to cause to flush or blush

rude derives from Latin *rudis*, "uncultivated" and it first meant "uneducated, ignorant"

rudera are the ruins of a building

something growing in dumps or garbage sites is **ruderal**

rudiment is from Latin *rudis*, "unlearned, untrained," and is patterned on elementum "element"

rue (noun) is regret, repentance, sorrow

the space between the bed and the wall is the **ruelle**

the tendency to turn red or reddish is **rufescence** or **rubescence**

the fur or fake fur along the edge of the hood of a coat is the **ruff**

rum was once known as rumbo, rumbowling, rumbustion, rumbullion—from a Devonshire word meaning "uproar"

rumaki may be an alteration of Japanese *harumaki*, "spring roll"

rumbustical and **rumbustious** mean "boisterous, unruly, overbearing"

ruminant, an animal that chews the cud, derives from Latin *rumen*, "throat, gullet" (as does **ruminate**)

rummage comes from French *arrumage*, "act of arranging a ship's cargo," and the word first referred to the arranging of casks in the hold of a vessel

a large wine glass is a **rummer**

rumor in Latin means "noise"

a continuous low drumbeat is a **ruffle**, a continuous even drumbeat is a **tattoo**, a continuous loud drumbeat is a **drumroll**

ruffian comes from Italian *roffia*, "beastly thing"

rufous means "reddish-brown"

rug was first a name for a type of coarse wool

rugby is named for the public school in Warwickshire where it was first played

a hairy or shaggy animal was once called "**rugged**"

rugose means marked by *rugae* (Latin *ruga*, "wrinkle") or wrinkles

ruin traces back to Latin *ruere*, "fall"

rule is one of many words from Latin *regula*, "straight stick, ruler"

ruly means obedient, the opposite of **unruly**

to **rump** is to snub, give the cold shoulder

the ancestry of **run** is unknown, though it does come from Germanic and may be linked to Sanskrit *rnoti*, "he moves"

a combination of fork, spoon, and sometimes knife is the **runcible**, also known as a **spork**

a ladder rung can also be called a **rundle**

rune (ancient alphabet letter) is from Old English *run*, "secret, mystery"

runnel is a synonym for brooklet, rivulet, rill, or trickle

a blade of a skate or sled is a **runner**; the supports on which a drawer slides are the runners

rainwater not absorbed by the earth is **run-off**

rupestrian means written in stone

rural comes from Latin *rur/rus,* "the country," from an Indo-European ancestor meaning "open space" (and **rustic** comes from this, too)

rurban is a blend of rural and urban

rurigenous means born in the country or being from the country

a **ruse** was first a detour or doubling back of a hunted animal to avoid capture

the original sense of **rush** was "force out of place; drive back" with no implied speed or eagerness

russet goes back to Latin *russus,* "red," and Indo-European *reudh-,* "red"

etymologically, **rust** means "reddened"

rustication is a trip to the country

rusticity is lack of refinement or sophistication

rut is a word describing the roaring of the sea, especially in breaking on the shore

rutabaga is from Swedish *rotabagge,* "root bag"—and it is also called Swedish turnip

ruth, "compassion, pity," is part of **ruthless** and **ruthful**

rutilant or **rutilous** means "glowing with reddish light"

Rx comes from Latin, with the R standing for "take this" and the x for Jupiter, the Roman god of medicine

Sabbath is from Hebrew *shabbath*, "rest"

sabbatical literally means "pertaining to the Sabbath" and "pertaining to every seventh year"; an old Hebrew custom Shabath said that every seven years farmers were supposed to give the fields a year's rest, which became the term **sabbatical**

to **sabbatize** is to enjoy a period of rest

sabeline is another name for the fur of the sable

saber is from Polish *szabla* or Hungarian *szablya*

the **sable**, of Slavic origin, is related to the Russian word *sobol*, and came through Latin *sabellum*, to become **sable**

the wooden shoes pictured on little Dutch boys and girls are **sabots**

the box from which cards are dealt at a casino is a **sabot** or **shoe**

sabotage is based on the **sabot**, a military weapon that consisted of a wooden disk attached to a spherical projectile

sabulous is another word for "sandy"

the rapid intermittment movement of the eyes, as in a tennis match or when they shift from one object to another or when the eyes move to fix on one point after another in the visual field, is called **saccade** (from French "flick of a sail"); periods in between are known as fixations and reading is a series of **saccades** and fixations

the artificial sweetener is **saccharin**; the adjective "excessively sweet" is **saccharine**

sacerdotal means "pertaining to the priesthood, pertaining to a priest"

sachem is derived from Algonquian *sachim* or *Narragansett sachima*, "he prevails over"

a **sachet** is etymologically a "little sack" (a small packet of perfumed matter)

sack, "large bag" was borrowed from Latin *saccus*, from Greek *sakkhos*, "rough cloth used for packing," which was of Semitic origin

sacrament was originally a military oath taken by Roman soldiers not to desert their standard, turn their back on the enemy, or abandon their general

sacred is from Latin *sacer*, "holy, **sacred**"

sacrifice is from Latin *sacrificium*, related to *sacrificus*, "sacrificial," from *sacer*, "holy, sacred"

sacrilegious (often misspelled!) and **sacrilege** are from Latin *sacrilegus*, "take sacred things" (which is a crime)

sacrosanct means literally "made holy by a sacred rite," and was originally reserved for things of the utmost holiness

the **sacrum** gets its name from Greek meaning "sacred bone," from the belief that the soul resides in it

sad first meant "satisfied" or "settled"

the rounded part on the top of a book of matches is the **saddle**

saddle shoes were named for the brown or black "saddle" across the middle

sadism is derived from the Marquis de Sade (1740–1814), who described sexual depravity in his novels and plays

safari is from Swahili, from Arabic *safar*, "journey, trip"

{ **safe** once referred to a box or cupboard where provisions were kept }

safe and **secure**, now nearly synonymous, used to be more different; **secure** was subjective, man's own sense of the absence of danger, while **safe** was objective, the fact of such absence of danger

an ingredient in an insecticide or fungicide that reduces its harmfulness to plants, etc., is a **safener**

a **safety** in football is the player(s) who occupies the deepest position in order to receive a kick, defend against a forward pass, or stop a ball carrier

saffron comes from the **crocus** and the Greek word for **saffron** is *krokos*, which became English **crocus**; the word is ultimately from Arabic *azzafaran*, "be yellow"

sag is from German *sacken*, "settle, subside"

saga is Old Norse for "narrative"

sagacious first meant "acute in perception, especially with the sense of smell"

sage takes its name from Latin *salvia*, "healing plant"; **sage**, the person, is from Latin *sapere*, "be wise"

the **sages** of Greece used to be called *sophoi*, "wise men," but that was thought to be too arrogant and was changed to *philosophos*, "lover of wisdom"— **philosopher**

to **saginate** is to fatten

Sahara comes from Arabic *sahra*, "desert" (so **Sahara** Desert is redundant)

sahib is Arabic for "friend" or "lord, master"

sail once specifically meant "to travel on a ship with sails," later "to travel on any ship," and figuratively "to go through effortlessly," as in "to **sail** through the exam"

saint comes from Latin *sanctus*, "holy"

saké, the Japanese alcoholic drink, may derive from *saka mizu*, "prosperous waters"

salacious goes back to Latin *salire*, "to jump," from the antics of animals and birds in their mating ritual

salad is a shortened version of Latin *herba salata*, "salted vegetables" (from Latin *sal*, "salt")

a poker for the fireplace is the **salamander**

salami is the plural of *salame*, "salt pork," a derivative of the Italian verb *salare*, "salt"

salary is from Latin *salarium*, originally prize money given to Roman soldiers to buy salt; a person receiving regular payment for work is receiving a **salary**, while one who is paid by the hour or for an amount of work done is being paid a **wage**

sale is from Old Norse *sala*, from Germanic *sal-*

salient (noticeable, prominent) is from Latin *salire*, "to leap"

saliva is a Latin word

sallow describes a complexion that is sickly yellow or brownish yellow

to **sally** is etymologically to "jump"

salmagundi was first a dish of chopped meat and eggs, highly seasoned and served with lemon juice and olive oil

the Indo-European ancestor of **salmon** is *lax* (source of English lox "smoked **salmon**")

salmonella takes its name from its identifier, veterinary pathologist Daniel Salmon (1850–1914)

saloon is from a family of words for "large room," Germanic *salaz*

salsa is Spanish and Italian for "sauce"

salt is that which gives liveliness or individuality to a person's character, life, etc.

to be **saltant** is to be dancing, jumping, or leaping

a **saltation** is an abrupt transition (from Latin *saltatio*, "to leap")

{ **salut** is French for "(good) health" and *salud* is Spanish for this }

a **salute** is a kiss given in greeting

if something is healthful, it is **salutiferous**

salvage was originally compensation to people who saved ships or goods from danger

the main semantic element of **salve** is "healing," but the etymological meaning is "oily substance"

a greeting upon meeting is the **salvediction**

a **salver** is a tray or dish on which a drink, letter, calling card, etc., is offered

a barrage of applause or cheers is a **salvo**

sam is a verb meaning "bring or collect things or people together"

the winged seeds of maple trees are called **samaras**, or **keys**

sambuca gets its name from Italian *sambuco*, "elder," the liqueur's original flavoring

same comes from Indo-European *somos*, "**same**," which produced Greek *homos* and Latin *similis*

a **samovar**, a decorated tea urn, is from Russian, literally "self-boiler"

sample is actually an apheretic form of "example"

samurai first referred to members of the military in feudal times

sanctimonious can mean holy and sacred in character, or pretending or assuming holiness and sanctity

sanction originally meant "make holy," that is, "give official church approval to"

Latin *sanctus*, "holy," preceded sancire, "consecrate," and gave us **sanctity**

a **sanctum** is a private room

sand is from Indo-European *samdam*, "crush, grind"

sandal is from Greek *sandalon*, "wooden shoe"

sandhi is the process where the form of a word changes due to its position, e.g. the change from "a" to "an" before a vowel

the person who holds the child during the circumcision ceremony is the **sandik** or **sandek**

there is no sand in **sandpaper**

sandwich is named for the fourth Earl of **Sandwich**, a gambling man who wanted a handheld lunch brought to him so he did not have to leave the gaming table

sane is from Latin *sanus*, "healthy"

sang-froid (pronounced SAHN-FRWAH) is French for "cold blood" and means "coolness in danger or disturbing circumstances"

{ **sangria** is Spanish for "bleeding," as the drink is dark red }

sanguinary can mean "imposing the death penalty freely"

sanguine, from Latin *sanguis*, "blood," comes from the old notion of the four humors or bodily fluids, coming to mean "cheerful, confident, or optimistic," and is pronounced SANG-wuhn

sanitude is a healthy condition

Sanka, the decaffeinated coffee, is an abbreviation of French *sans caffeine*, "without caffeine"

sap, as in "plant juice," is from Germanic *sappam*, which became Latin *sapa*, "new wine," before **sap**

sapid and **saporous** mean full of flavor, lively, interesting

sapient came from Latin *sapere*, "be wise"; **savor** is from Latin *sapere*, "to have a flavor"

saponaceous means "evasive, slippery" or "soapy"

sapphire is from Greek *sappheiros*, "lapis lazuli" or "blue stone"

if you have bad breath, you are **saprostomous**; **ozostomia** is foul-smelling breath

sarcasm is from Greek *sarkasmos*, from *sarkazein*, "tear flesh" or "speak bitterly"

a **sarcast** is a sarcastic writer or speaker

sarcastic means "derisive, tauntingly contemptuous" while **sardonic** means "bitterly scornful, cynically disdainful"

to dig up weeds, especially with a hoe, is to **sarcle**

sarcophagus is from Greek *sarko*, "flesh," and *phagos*, "eating," because it was once believed that the stone swallowed the corpse and wooden coffin

the process of canning small herrings was invented on the island of Sardinia; hence, **sardines**

sardonic is from Greek *sardanios*, "mocking, scornful"

sarong is literally "sheath," from Malay

sartage is the clearing of woodland by setting fire to trees

a **sartor** is a tailor, hence **sartorial**

a **sash** was first (from Arabic *shash*) a roll of silk, linen, or gauze worn about the head, a turban

sashay is an American corruption of French *chassé*, "chase, pursue," as the steps follow/chase each other

sashimi, thinly sliced raw fish with a sauce, is a compound formed from *sashi*, "pierce," and mi, "flesh"

satan derives from Hebrew, meaning "plot against"

satchel first referred to a small bag

sateen is an alteration of "satin" on the pattern of "velveteen"

satellite first meant "an attendant on a person of importance"

satiate comes from Latin *satis*, "enough"

satin is from an Arabic word meaning "pertaining to the town of Zaitun" in China, where it was first made

satire is from Latin *satura*, "poetic medley," in which things were held to ridicule

the state of enough having been said is **satisdiction**

satisfy comes from a Latin base of *satis*, meaning "enough"

satori (spiritual enlightenment) is Japanese for "awakening"

saturate first meant "to satisfy or satiate"

Saturday was literally "Saturn's day"— Saturn being worshipped as the harvest god

a **saturnalian** appetite is unrestrained

a **saturnine** person is sluggish, cold, and gloomy in temperament

satyr, (pronounced SAY-tur) in Greek mythology, was any of a class of lustful, drunken, woodland gods

sauce is from Latin *salsus*, "salted food"

saucer was originally a small dish on which sauce was served

sauerbraten is literally (German) "sour roast meat," and sauerkraut is "sour cabbage or vegetable"

sauerkraut is literally "sour cabbage," though *kraut* generally means "leafy plant," but is a dialect word for "cabbage"

saunter originally meant "muse, daydream"

a **savant** is a person of learning or science

save is from Latin *salvus*, "unharmed"

savoir-faire is French, literally "know how to do," and it is the ability to act appropriately in social situations; the phrase is a pair of verbs in French and it can only be used as a noun in English

savvy is a corruption of Spanish *sabe/saber*, "to know"

saw, as in saying, derives from the same Germanic ancestor as **saga**

sawbuck for a ten-dollar bill comes from the frame of a **sawbuck**/sawhorse, which rested on X-shaped supports, resembling Roman numeral X for "ten"

a **sawyer** is a person who saws timber

Antoine (Adolphe) Sax (1814–1894) devised the **saxophone**

say is from Indo-European base *seq-*, "point out" or "**say**"

say, **speak**, and **tell** are nearly synonyms, but **say** is usually followed by a statement or words actually uttered

sayonara is Japanese, literally "if it be so"

scab first pertained to any skin disease in which pustules or scales were formed and is from Old Norse *skabbr*, "crust over a wound"

English got **scabbard** from Anglo-Norman *escaubers*, "sword protection"

a synonym for an idle person is **scabber-lotcher**

sausage's name goes back to Latin *salsus* "salted" while wurst is from Latin *veriere* "roll, turn," a reference to its cylinder shape

sauté, a form of French *sauter*, means "to leap or cause to toss"

savage comes from Latin *silvaticus*, "wild woodland"

scabrous is "rough with minute points or knobs"

if something is **scacchic**, it is pertaining to chess

scaevity is another word for unluckiness

historically, **scaffold** and **catafalque**, "coffin stand," are identical

a **scalawag** or **scallywag** was a white Southerner who supported reconstruction after the U.S. Civil War—or a man who would not work

the Latin elements of **scald** are *ex-*, "thoroughly," and *calidus*, "hot"

a preacher who delivers a fiery sermon is a **scaldabanco**

scale, from Old Norse *skal*, "bowl," first meant "drinking cup" before it meant "weighing instrument"; **scale**, as in graduated values, is from Latin *scala*, "ladder"

scallions get their name from the Palestinian seaport of Ascalon and were first *caepa Ascolonia*, "Ascalonian onions"

scallopini in veal **scallopini** is a diminutive of *scallapo*, "thin slice"

> { **scalp** originally meant "top of the head; cranium" }

scalpel comes from Latin *scalprum*, "chisel"

to **scamander** is to wander about or meander

a **scamp** was once a highwayman and as a verb meant "rob on the highway"

scampi are not shrimp but rather a species of lobster; **scampi** is actually the plural of "scampo"

for centuries, **scan** meant "to analyze, examine with great care," and first meant "analyze the meter" of a line of verse

scandal is based on Greek *skandalon*, "stumbling block, trap"

scansorial is "pertaining to climbing"

scant comes from an Old Norse word meaning "brief, short"

a **scantle** is a small portion

scantling means "measured or prescribed size" or "a set of standard dimensions"

during Yom Kippur, a high priest symbolically lays the sins of the people on the head of one goat and then allows it to escape—so it was the escape goat, now called **scapegoat**

the etymological idea of **scapegrace** is "one who escapes the grace of God"

scapular means "pertaining to the scapula, the shoulder blade"

scar traces back to Greek *eskhara*, "hearth" or "scab"

scarab is from Greek *karabos*, "horned beetle"

a **scaramouch** is a boastful but cowardly person, from the name of a character in Italian farce

scarce is from Latin *excarpsus*, "picked out" or "rare"

the shank of a golf club can be called the **scare**

scarify is from Greek *skariphasthai*, "to scratch an outline," and now means "to break up the surface of"

scarlet was first a name for any rich or brightly colored cloth

to **scarp** is to slope, cut a steep face

to **scarper** means "to leave in haste, escape, run away" (from Italian)

scart is a gust of wind or a strip of cloud and can also mean "to scratch or scrape"

the first **scarves** were worn around the waist or over the shoulder by soldiers for carrying things; **scarves** and **scarfs** are correct plurals for **scarf**

scat is slang for whiskey

stilts for walking in a filthy place are called **scatches**

scathe comes from Germanic, meaning "harm, injury"

scatology is based on Greek *skat-*, "dung"

to **scatter** first meant "to squander goods"

scaturient describes something that flows or gushes out

insincere talk can be called **scaum**

if you have large ankles, you are **scaurous**

a fireplace spade is a **scavel**

scavenge first meant "clean out dirt"

scavenger started as a term for an official in the East India Company or a person employed to clean streets and was first spelled "scavager"

other terms for wicked are **scelestious** or **scelestic**

the surge of a wave or the sea is the **scend**; to **scend** is to pitch or surge up in a heavy sea

scene is based on Greek *skene*, "booth, stage, tent"; a **scenite** is a person who lives in a tent

scenery was originally theatrical—"a stage depiction of nature"—and it came to be applied to nature itself; **scenic** first pertained to the theatre and meant "dramatic, theatrical"

a **scenographer** is a person who designs or paints theatrical scenery

scent comes from Latin *sentire*, "feel, perceive"

scepsis is a skeptical attitude about philosophy and **skeptic** is based on Greek for "consider, observe"

{ **scepter** is based on Greek for "lean on, prop oneself" }

scevity is a way to say unluckiness

schadenfreude is German for "harm" and "joy" or "shameful joy," enjoyment of another's misfortune, as experienced when you see two Mercedes Benz collide

something done impromptu or offhand is **schediasm**

schedule goes back to Greek *skhede*, for "leaf of papyrus," and started out meaning a ticket or brief note

scheme is from Greek *skhema*, "figure, form," and first referred to a figure of speech, especially a figure of rhetoric, denoting a way of deviating from the ordinary use and order of words to create special effect

schemozzle or **shemozzle** is a muddle or complication

schism should be pronounced SI-zuhm

winged seeds that fall from maple trees are called **schizocarps**

schizophrenia is from Greek, meaning "split mind"

schlemiel is from a Bible character Shelumiel, a military leader who lost all the time

schlep is also spelled **schlepp**, **shlep**, or **shlepp**

schmaltz was first a name for melted chicken fat (German, "dripping, lard")

schnapps' etymology is German for "dram of liquor, especially gin," from Dutch, meaning "gulp" or "mouthful"

schnitzel is a diminutive of *sniz*, "slice," in German and also means "escalope"

an esoteric collection of learned words is **scholasms**

scholastic is based on a Greek word for "devote one's leisure to learning"

a **scholiast** is an annotator or commentator

School traces back to Greek *skhole*, "lectureplace," but earlier it meant "leisure," "learned discussion," and "study." This very old word appeared in English by 1000 AD and it has cognates in nearly all Celtic, Romance, and Teutonic languages. It became Latin *schola*, "**school**," and then Old English *scól*.

school, as in fish, is simply a variation of "shoal"

to **schoon** is to "sail, skim" or "glide"; from this came **schooner**

a **schooner** is a tall glass for beer

domesticated dog poop is called **schumber**; wild dog poop is **lesses**

schuss, a straight downhill ski run, is literally German for "a shot"

a **schwa** is German and it is synonymous with *sheva*, which is Hebrew for "emptiness"

sciamachy is fighting with shadows

having huge feet is **sciapodous**

{ **sciatic** in **sciatic** nerve is from Greek, meaning "relating to the hips, hip joints" }

scibility is the power of knowing

science is from Latin *scientia*, "knowledge," (from *scire* "know"); **sciental** is "concerning or having knowledge"

scientist was not used until 1840; up until then it had been "natural philosopher"

a curved sword is a **scimitar**

a **scintilla** is a "piddling amount"

scintillation is the process of giving off flashes or sparks

sciolists "amateurs" or "pretenders to knowledge"get the most out of superficial knowledge—radio shows, newspapers, magazines, shallow books

a **scion** is either a descendant or heir—or a shoot or twig of a plant

the scrap metal after coins have been cut is called **scissel** (from French for "clip with shears")

scission is an act of cutting or dividing

scissors comes from *cisorium*, "cutting instrument"; **shears** describes a large implement (over 6 inches of blade) and **scissors** describes a smaller one

knowledge has the synonym **sciture**

the adjective form for squirrel is **sciurine**

scraping a golf club along the ground before hitting the ball is called **sclaffing**

the whites of your eyes are the **sclera**

scoff may be of Scandinavian origin or from Dutch *skof/skuf*, "mockery, jest"

scold first meant a woman who used coarse language

sconce first meant "portable lantern"

scone is a Scottish contraction of the Middle Dutch *schoonbrot*, "beautiful or fine bread"

to **scoon** was "to skim or skip across water like a flat stone," giving us "scooner," which was later spelled **schooner**

the act of skipping a rock across the water is **scoon** or **scooning**

scoop was first a utensil for pouring liquid—from a German word for "waterwell bucket"

the newspaper term **scoop** may have come from poker because if there is a big pot and you are the winner, you "**scoop**" up the chips

a person who rides a scooter is a **scooterist**

scope first meant "target for shooting" from Greek *skopos*, "target"

visual has the synonym **scopic**

scorch may come from Old Norse, meaning "shriveled"

score was first a notch used to keep count, as on a stick

scorn is from Latin *escarnire*, from Germanic *skarnjan*, "deride, mock"

Scotch, meaning Scottish, only dates to the 1600s, while **scotch** from hopscotch is from the 1400s, a verb meaning "cut a line or gash in"

the art of writing in the dark is **scoteography**

scotfree ("payment-free") is from Scandinavian for "a payment or reckoning" plus "free"

scour evolved from "take care of" into "cleaning," as it was ultimately from Latin *curare*, "take care of"

scourge is based on Latin *ex-*, "thoroughly" and *corriga*, "whip"

scout comes from the Latin *ausculture*, "to listen," then became Old French *escoute*, "a spy"

a barge that transports refuse is a **scow**

> **Scrabble** was originally called "Lexiko" and then "Criss-crosswords"

a **Scrabbler** is someone who plays Scrabble

scrag can describe a tree stump or a projecting branch or outcrop

scram is probably an abbreviation of scramble

to **scranch** is to crunch or crush noisily

scrap used to mean a plot or sinister scheme

scrape is either from Old Norse *skrapa* or Middle Dutch *schrapen*, from a shared Germanic base *skrap-*, "scratch"

scrapiana is a word to describe literary scraps or cuttings

scrappage is the discarding of something that is worn out or has been superseded

another word for **scrapple** (the food) is **ponhaus**

a **scrat** is a person who scrapes and saves

scratch is a line or mark for a starting position in some games, which is the origin of the phrase "from **scratch**"

scratch may be a blend of "scrat" and "cratch"

to **scrattle** is to scrape away or remove snow by scratching

scrawl may be a combination of "scribble" and "sprawl"

the shrill cry of the eagle is a **scream**

screaming-meemies were originally German artillery shells that let off a high-pitched whine before exploding

scree is a mass of small loose stones that form or cover a slope on a mountain

the longest one-syllable word is **screeched**

a **screed** is, figuratively, a harangue

screed is a cut or broken fragment

screen comes from a German word meaning "bar, barrier, fence"

a **screenager** is a young person comfortable with computers and new technology (screen + teenager)

screw comes ultimately from Latin *scrofa*, "female pig"—probably in allusion to the pig's curly tail

screwball started out as a cricket and baseball term, then took on its slang meanings

scribable means "suitable for being written on"

scribacious means "fond of writing"

scribble is a diminutive of Latin *scribere*, "write"

scribblement is illegible handwriting

{ **scribe** is part of a large set of words from Latin *scribere*, "write" }

a librarian was originally a **scribe** or **copyist**

a tiny portion, like a second helping, is a **scrid**

to wriggle and struggle is to **scriggle**

scrim is a word used figuratively to mean a veil or screen, something that conceals what is happening

to **scrimshank** is to shirk duty

carved ivory, shells, or whalebone are **scrimshaw**

to **scrinch** is to sit closely or to bunch together

an archivist can also be called a **scriniary**

scrip can be a scrap of paper with writing on it

scrippage is one's baggage and personal belongings

handwriting, as distinct from print, is **script**

scription is another word for handwriting

a **scriptorium** is a room set apart for writing

scripturient means having a strong desire or compulsion to write or to be an author

to **scriven** is to write busily or hastily

scrod is a young cod or haddock weighing less than three pounds

scroddled describes pottery made of different colored clays for a marbled or mottled effect

a **scrofulous** person is morally corrupt

scroll goes back to Germanic *skrautha*, "something cut," which evolved into Latin *scroda* and French *escroe*, "strip of parchment," before finding its way into English

scrooge comes from the character in Charles Dickens's "A Christmas Carol"

scroop is the rustle of silk

to **scrouge** is to cause discomfort to a person by coming too close

scrounge first meant to live off of or sponge off of someone else; **scrounge** is a variant of scrunge, "steal"

the sky can be called **scrow**

scrub first meant "to dry one's body by rubbing vigorously" before it meant "to clean by rubbing vigorously"

scrub, as in brush or undergrowth or stunted trees and shrubs, is a variant of shrub

scruffy is derived from the word "scurf"

to **scrumble** is to scrape or scratch (something) out of or from

scrummage is a synonym for "scrimmage"

scrump is something withered or shriveled or dried up and a **scrumple** is a wrinkle or crease

scrunch is a combo of squeeze and crunch

scruple comes from a French word meaning "anxiety," from Latin *scrupulous*, "pebble," figuratively a cause of uneasiness; a **scrupulist** is a person with moral scruples

something **scrutable** is that which can be understood through scrutiny

scrutate means "search out, investigate"

a **scrutator** or **scrutineer** examines or investigates thoroughly (**scrutiny**), especially officially, and comes from Latin *scrutari*, "search through rags"; the etymological notion of **scrutinize** is of ragpickers searching through garbage for things of use or value (from Latin *scruta*, "rubbish")

to **scruttle** is to save money with difficulty

scry is to foretell the future with a crystal ball

scuba is an acronym for Self-Contained Underwater Breathing Apparatus

tiny clouds that seem to have broken away from bigger clouds are called **scuds**

the **scullery**, now a small kitchen, was at first the department of a household responsible for dishes and utensils (from Latin for "wooden dish or platter") or the room where dishes were washed

sculpture is from Latin *sculpere*, "carve, scratch"

scum is etymologically a "layer on top" of something

to **scumble** is to give a softer or duller effect to a picture by applying a very thin coat of opaque paint; **scumbling** is softening the lines or colors of a drawing by rubbing lightly with the finger

the beveled inner edge of a window frame or door jamb is the **scuncheon**

an illogical hostile feeling or feeling of antagonism toward someone is a **scunner**; if a teacher takes a **scunner** to you, it means he/she has a dislike of you for no reason

the **scupper** is an opening of a ship's deck level to allow water to run off

to **scurf** is to ridicule

{
scurrilous is derived from a Latin word meaning "buffoon"
}

scurry is an abbreviation of hurry-**scurry**, which was a reduplication of hurry

a rabbit or deer tail is a **scut**

a fish's scales provide it with a **scute**, "armor plate"

scuttle, "to run in quick, hurried steps," may be a combination of scud and shuttle

scuttlebutt was a water container (butt) with a small hatch (scuttle) on a ship for drinking from—and the word originally denoted gossip centered around this item

scuzz is probably an abbreviation of "digusting"

Scylla is a sea monster and **Charybdis** is a whirlpool

scythe is ultimately from Indo-European *sek-*, "cut"

sea first referred to the continuous body of salt water covering a large part of the earth's surface; now **sea** generally denotes either a large body of salt water wholly or partly enclosed by land, or a large body of fresh water

a **lobster** was once called a **sea crayfish**

the Caspian **Sea** and the Dead **Sea** are actually lakes

seal, the animal, is from Germanic *selkhaz*; **seal**, "impressed mark," is from Latin *sigillum*, a diminutive form of *signum*, "little mark or picture"

a young seal is a **seal-calf**

a **sealer** is a seal hunter and seal hunting is called **sealing**

the **sealine** is the horizon of the sea

a **seam** is etymologically a joint made by sewing

the place where planks join is the **seam**

séance is "a sitting" in French, from Latin *sedere*, "to sit"

search derives from Latin *cicare*, "go around," from *circus*, "circle"

seared means quickly browned over high heat, often with butter, to seal in juices and flavor

a **season** is not capitalized unless personified in poetry, and this is part of the trend in English toward fewer initial capital letters

season derives from Latin *sation*, "time of sowing; seed time," and was long used just for the time of year when seed was sown; the divisions of the year into four separate seasons dates only to the twelfth century

seasonal means "pertaining to the seasons" or "periodical"; **seasonable** means "suitable to the season"—so **seasonal** refers to a characteristic of an event or phenomenon, whereas **seasonable** offers a judgment about that characteristic

a shore can also be called the **seastrand**

seat first referred to the action of sitting

a **seat-stick** is a walking stick with an attached folding seat

sebum is the secretion of acne

seclude first meant "obstruct access to" from Latin se-, "apart," and claudere, "to shut"

 second (as in order) comes from Latin *secundus,* "following"

etymologically, something that is **secret** is "separated" from others, i.e. hidden, and it comes from Latin secretus, an adjectival form of secernere, "separate"

a desk with a small bookcase on top is a **secretary**

secretary comes from Latin meaning "confidential officer" and first denoted a person entrusted with private or secret matters, such as a confidant; **secretary** should be pronounced SEK-ruh-tair-ee

sect is from Latin secta, literally "following"

if something is capable of being cut easily with a knife, it is **sectile**

section is a U.S. measurement for one square mile of land

section is based on Latin secare, "cut," and **sector** is Latin for "cutter"

the root of **secular** is "temporal"—opposed to the eternity of the church—and it means "not connected to a religion"

secure originally meant "carefree" and "over-confident"

sedate was first a medical term meaning "not sore or painful"; **sedative** is also from Latin sedare, "settle"/sedere, "sit," as is **sediment** and **sedentary**

seder is the Hebrew word for "order, procedure" and it is the ceremonial Jewish dinner held on the first night of Passover

sederunt is prolonged sitting—as for discussion, reading, or relaxation

the **sedge** is etymologically the plant with "cutting leaves"

seats by the altar for church clergy are called the **sedile**(s)

sedition's origin is se-, "apart" and itio, "a going"

seduce first meant "to persuade someone to abandon their duty" (from Latin se-, "apart, away," and ducere, "to lead")

sedulous is "diligent and persistent"

see, as in "perceive visually," is from prehistoric Germanic sekhwan, from Indo-European seq-, and etymologically is "follow with the eyes"

seed is from Proto-Indo-European se-, "to sow"

when a plant or crop runs to seed, it looks shabby, hence, **seedy**

originally, **seem** meant "be suitable" and was borrowed from Old Norse soema, "conform to, honor"

seersucker is from Persian shir u shakar, "milk and sugar"

seethe first meant "cook a food by boiling or stewing," or to be subjected to this

segment was first a term in geometry

segregate comes from Latin segregare, "to separate from the flock"

segue, from Latin sequi, "to follow," is pronounced SEG-way and is the seamless transition from one thing to another

seism is another word for earthquake

seismic is from Greek *seismos*, "shock or earthquake," from *seiein*, "to shake"

seize is from feudal times, "take possession of property," from Latin *sacire*, "claim"

are you afraid of sun light flashing through trees or dazzling reflections off of water? that is **selaphobia**

selcouth means rare, strange, unusual, wonderful

seldom's underlying meaning is "strange and rare"

select is from Latin *legere*, "choose" with the prefix *se-*, "apart"

self is a Germanic word from *selba-*, but that is all that is known; in medieval English, **self** referred not to an inner personal identity but to the generic idea of sameness

{ **self-deprecating** does not correspond to any accepted sense of deprecate }

sell-through is the ratio of the quantity of goods sold by a retail outlet to the quantity distributed by it

seltzer is from Niederselters, Germany, where the sparkling mineral water was found and originally called *selterser wasser* (selters water)

selvage is apparently from self + edge, for an edging sewn to a material to keep it from unraveling

a basic irreducible meaning unit (like "cat" or "sit") in a language is a **semanteme** or **sememe**

semantic is based on Latin *sema*, "sign, mark" and it means "concerning word meaning," and **semasiology** is a synonym for semantics

semaphore is from Greek *sema*, "signal" and *phoros*, "bearing"

semen is from a Latin base of *serere*, "sow"

if something is **semese**, it is half-eaten

semester first meant six months, as it comes from Latin *semestris*, "of six months"

a **semicolon** tells you that there is still some question about the preceding full sentence—something needs to be added and more information is to come; the first printed **semicolon** was the creation of Aldus Manutius in 1494, though medieval scribes used a symbol similar to this to indicate abbreviations

seminal means "of or pertaining to a seed(s)"

a **seminary** was first a piece of ground for a garden, from Latin *seminarium*, "seed plot" or "nursery"

semiology is a synonym for sign language

semiopathy is a tendency to read humorously inappropriate meanings into signs

semiotics is the study of signs and symbols and their use or interpretation

a single quotation mark may also be called a **semiquote**

semisomnous means "half asleep"

semolina is the diminutive of Italian *semola*, "bran," from Latin *simila*, "finest flour"

sempiternal means "eternal, everlasting"

senary is the number six or a set of six things

senate is actually based on Latin *senex*, "old man," so the body is literally "gathering of old men," while senex is also the base of **senectitude**, "old age," and **senile**

send is from the prehistoric Germanic *santhjan*, and etymologically means "cause to go"

someone growing old can be described as **senescent**

senior is Latin, a comparative form of *senex*, "old"

a week is a **sennight**

sense comes from Latin *sentire*, "feel"; **sensible** first meant "perceptible by the senses"

sensiferous means "conveying sensation"

the **sensorium** is the seat of common sense, the center of the brain to which sense impressions are transmitted by the nerves from the organs

sensuous usually implies gratification of the senses for the sake of aesthetic pleasure; **sensual** usually describes gratification of the senses or physical appetites as an end in itself

sentence once meant "way of thinking; opinion" or "sense, meaning"

sententious means "full of meaning" and has the same root as "sentence" (Latin *sentential*, "opinion, maxim")

the ability to feel is **sentience**

sentiment is from Latin *sentimentum*, "feeling," from *sentire*, "feel," and it originally meant "feeling" or "opinion"

The names of the months **September**, **October**, and **November** are rooted in Latin. **September** is from *septem*, "seventh month" of the early Roman calendar, though it is now the ninth month in the Gregorian calendar. **October** (*octo*) is Latin for "eighth month" (now tenth) and **November** (*novem*) is Latin for "tenth month" (now eleventh in the Gregorian calendar). In Old English, **September** was called "harvest month."

septic comes from Greek *sepein*, "make rotten"

a **septuagint** is a group of seventy

the wall between the nostrils is the **septum** and the bulbous parts of the nostrils are **alae**

sepulcher comes from Latin *sepelire*, "to bury with religious observance"

sequacious is "following in regular order" and is synonymous with subservient

a **sequela** is a pathological condition resulting from a previous disease or injury

sequence is from Latin *sequi*, "follow"

 sequin, from Arabic *sikkah*, "die for coining," originally was applied to certain gold coins such as the Italian *zecchino*, "little mint"

sentry is probably short for the obsolete centrinell "**sentry**," from Italian *sentinella*

the tiny green leaves on a strawberry are the **sepals**

etymologically, **separate** means "arrange apart," from Latin *se-*, "apart," and *parare*, "arrange (in advance), make ready"

punctuation marks are traditionally either "**separators**" or "**terminators**"

sepia, a cuttlefish, is the origin of the brown pigment prepared from a secretion of the fish

sequoia are named for **Sequoia**, a nineteenth-century Cherokee Indian scholar

a **seraglio** is a place of confinement, as for a harem or other polygamous household

a Mexican blanket-like shawl is a **serape**

the highest-ranking angel is a **seraph**

serein is rain falling from a cloudless sky

serenade is, literally, music performed on a clear night (Italian *sereno*, "open air")

serendipity comes from a Persian fairy tale ("Three Princes of Serendip") about itinerant heroes constantly discovering valuable or pleasant things that they were not seeking

serene first pertained to weather, "calm, clear, fair"

serge is a durable twilled woolen or worsted fabric

the Latin base of **sergeant** is *servire*, "serve"

sericulture is the raising of silkworms for the purpose of making raw silk

Latin *series*, "succession of things connected together" gave us **series** in English

the cross of a T is the **serif**

the tiny lines at the ends of characters in typography are called **serifs**; when there are none, as on O, they are **sans serif**

serious is from Latin *serius*, "grave, **serious**"

sermon first simply meant "talk, discourse"

a short sermon is a **sermuncle**

serotinal is "of or relating to the latter and usually drier part of summer"

a **serpent** is etymologically a "crawling" animal, from Latin *serpere*, "crawl, creep"

serrated is from Latin *serra*, "saw"

to crowd together closely is to **serry**

servant once meant "admirer, wooer"

serve is from Latin *servire*, "**serve**," from *servus*, "slave"

the formal delivery of a legal document is **service**

someone who speaks **serviceable** Spanish is not fluent in it but gets by pretty well

the word **sesame** is of Semitic origin

sesamoid is having the shape of a sesame seed

sesqui- is the combining form meaning "one and a half" and is used mainly to describe anniversaries like sesquicentennial, "150th"

sesquipedalian etymologically means "a foot and a half long"

session originally was a place for sitting, the act of sitting, the state of being seated

in the "Oxford English Dictionary," the word "**set**" has 58 noun uses, 126 verb uses, and 10 adjective uses (and counting)

to **set** is to place something; to **sit** is to be seated

a badger's burrow is a **sett**

settee comes from settle but was influenced by "set(y)e down"

settle "bench" is the source of the verb

seven is from the Indo-European base *septm*, "**seven**"

Seven-Up (7-Up) supposedly has seven "natural" flavors that the company describes as having "wallop" (thereby, "up")

several traces back to Latin *separ*, "different, separate"

severe is a descendant of Latin *severus*, "rigorous"

sew comes from Germanic *siwjan* and became Latin *suere*

sewer first referred to a watercourse for draining marshy land (from French *seuwiere*)

sex ultimately comes from Latin *sexus*, "either of two divisions of organic beings distinguished as male and female respectively," derived from *secare*, "to cut, divide" (English sect, section, dissect, and insect are based on the same Latin root)

the use of the word **sex** for sexual intercourse was first recorded in the works of DH Lawrence

sexile is to force your college roommate to leave when you wish to "entertain" a guest

a **sextant** is etymologically an instrument based on a "sixth" of a circle

sexton is from Latin, literally, "person in charge of holy vessels"

shabbify is to make shabby

shabby once described weather that was bad or inclement but not violently stormy

shack is from the Aztec word *xacatli*, "wooden hut"

the **shaddock** commemorates a Captain **Shaddock**, commander of an East India Company ship who left seeds of this in Jamaica

shade and **shadow** originated in Old English *sceadu*, which traces back to Indo-European *skotwa*

shade/shadow and **mead/meadow** are historically the same words in two forms

a **shaft** is a ray of light

shag originally meant "rough, untidy hair"

to **shail** is to stumble or walk in a shambling way

cracks in wood caused by wind and frost are called **shakes**

shake is also a measure of time, with one **shake** equal to one-hundred-millionth of one second

the **Shakers** got their name from the shaking and convulsive movements they made during worship

about one/tenth of the words **Shakespeare** used were original, created by him—approximately 29,066 unique words and usages

{ the tall, cylindrical marching band hat, as for a drum major, is a **shako** }

the etymological meaning of **shall** is "owe"

shallot is etymologically the onion from Ascalon, an ancient port in Palestine

to **shamble** is to walk awkwardly

shambles first meant "meat market" and shamble was the table or stall on which meat was placed for sale

shamefaced, "held firm by shame," was an alteration by folk etymology of the earlier shamefast, from Old English *scamfæst*, "bound by shame," a compound of *scamu*, "shame" and *fæst*, "fastened, bound"

shammocking is an adjective describing walking with an unsteady or clumsy gait; **shammock** describes one who is idle or worthless

shampoo is from the Hindu *champo*, "to massage"

the word seamróg, which gave us **shamrock**, is a diminutive of Irish *seamar*, "**clover**"

to **shandy** is to digress

shandygaff is beer mixed with ginger ale; beer mixed with a soft drink is a **shandy**

shanghai gets its name from the nineteenth-century practice of drugging someone and taking that person aboard sailing ships on the trade route from **Shanghai** to San Francisco

Shangri-La was in Tibet

each half of a pair of scissors is a **shank**

shank once meant "the remainder, the rest" as in "**shank** of the evening"

the **shank** is the stem of a wine glass

chantier ("workshop") was the name the early French settlers gave to the hut in the Canadian forest which served as their headquarters; **shanty** is a corruption of *chantier*

shape's first meaning was creation or the created universe

share, as in portion, etymologically denotes something "cut up" or divided among people

sharp and **shear** goes back to Germanic *skarpaz* and Indo-European *sker-*, "cut"

the **Shar-Pei**'s name is from Chinese, *sha pi*, literally "sand fur"

shawl is from Urdu and Persian for a material first made in Kashmir from the hair of the **shawl**-goat

SHAZAM stood for Solomon's wisdom, Hercules's strength, Atlas's stamina, Zeus's power, Achilles's courage, and Mercury's speed

she is the traditional pronoun referring to a ship and other vehicles, because the seafaring man depends upon the ship and it is dear to him

a pig less than a year old is a **sheat**

sheath seems to have first been a split stick that a sword could be inserted into

shebang may come from an Irish name for a speakeasy—"shebeen," so the "whole shebeen" was the whole drinking establishment; **shebang** also first meant "hut, shed, dwelling"

sheen first described "a beautiful person"

Sheetrock is a brand name and should be capitalized; **plasterboard** is the generic equivalent

shenanigans may come from Irish *sion-nachuighim*, "I play the fox"

to pour a drink for someone is to **shench**

shepherd is a compound of sheep and herd

sherbet was originally a drink of sweetened fruit juice, coming from Arabic *sharbah*; **sherbet** should be pronounced SHUHR-buht

sheriff comes from Old English *scirgerefa*, the royal office of a shire, becoming *shire reeve*, then **sheriff**

sherpa literally means "inhabitant of an eastern country"

sherry gets its name from Jerez, Spain, originally spelled *Xeres* and pronounced SHERIS

shiatsu is Japanese, literally "finger pressure"

a **shibboleth** is a word used as a test to detect an interloper or foreigner by its mispronunciation; also, a **shibboleth** is something once thought important that is now regarded as old-fashioned or useless

{ **sheer** first meant "bright, shining" (applied to light or water), or "exempt, blameless," or "pure, unmixed" (applied to concrete things) }

sheikh is from Arabic *shaikh*, "old man"—a title of respect for leaders of Arab tribes—and has other spellings: sheik, shaik, shaykh

the underlying meaning of **shelf** is "piece of split wood for standing things on"

shell's underlying meaning is "covering that splits off or is peeled off"

shellac is a lacquer melted into thin plates of varnish

shellpad is another name for tortoise

shelter may come from "sheltron," a body of troops which protected itself in battle with a covering of joined shields

a turtle's shell is the **shield**

shiitake is Japanese for "evergreen beech, chinquapin" (*shii*) and "mushroom" (*take*)

the accomplice in a con game is the **shill**

shillelagh is named for a town in Ireland

shilly-shally comes from "Shill I? Shall I?" as "shill" is a weak form of "shall"

a **shim** is a wedge-shaped piece of wood or other material used to level something, as under a table leg to stop it from wobbling

you **shimmy** when you shake or vibrate; you **shinny** up a pole or rope

shin's underlying meaning seems to be "thin piece"

at a rough party, men often began to fight and dig their boots into each others' shins, hence, **shindig**

shingle is from Latin *scandula*, "roof tile"

shingles, from the chicken pox virus, causes a rash around the middle of the body and the name is from Latin *cingulus*, "belt, girdle"

shingles, as in roofing tiles, comes from Latin *scindula*, "wooden roofing tile"

ship is from Germanic *skipam*, but that is all that is known

shiraz, a red wine, is named for **Shiraz**, Iran, and is an alteration of French *syrah*, from the belief that the vine was brought from Iran by the Crusaders

shirk once meant "sponger"

an act of **shirking** can be called a "**mike**"

to bake eggs is to **shirr** them

shirt probably comes from a base meaning "short garment" (and short and **shirt** are related to "skirt")

a **shirtwaist** is a shirt cut to look like a feminized version of a man's shirt

shish kebab takes its name from Turkish *sis*, "skewer," and *kebap*, "roast meat"—also spelled shish kebob, shish cabob—and the pieces of meat themselves are called kebabs

the word **shit** is from an Indo-European root meaning "to cut, divide," with the root sense "stuff divided from the body"

shittle means unstable, inconstant

shivaree, a mock serenade, originally meant "headache" in its Latin form

shives are splinters or fragments broken from a larger mass, as a slice of bread

shiver is etymologically the "chattering of the teeth"

shoal is a synonym for "school," in referring to a large number of fish swimming together

{ an encounter between two charging hostile forces is a **shock** }

shod means "wearing shoes"

the part in a person's hair is the **shoding** or **shed**

shoe comes from Anglo-Saxon *sceo*, meaning "to cover"

a Japanese rice-paper screen is a **shoji**

at first, **shop** designated a small retail establishment and **store** was applied only to a large establishment; now the differences are blurred

shopgrifting is buying an item, using it, and then returning it for a full refund

shore is the general word for an edge of land directly bordering a body of water; **coast** is limited to land along a sea or ocean

etymologically, something **short** has been "cut off"

shortbread, **shortcake**, and **short pastry** are made with shortening—"short" in this case meaning that the added fat makes the dough easily crumbled

shortcoming earlier meant "failure to reach the required or expected amount"

shortening, the culinary term, refers to fats used in making breads, cakes, pastry, etc.— because they make mixtures "short" or tender

failure to satisfy demand is **shortfall**

a **short-short** is a short story with a surprise ending

a **shot** of liquor is a fluid dram of the substance—and this term is fairly new, dating to 1928 (PG Wodehouse)

should started out as the past tense of shall

a **shovel** is literally an instrument for shoving

the curled end of a ski is the **shovel**

show originally meant "look at"

show-how is a step-by-step demonstration of how some action should be performed

to **shram** is to be numb or shrink with cold

Royal Artillery lieutenant Henry **Shrapnel** (1761–1842) created a hollow bomb capable of distributing lead pellets and grapeshot across a wide area while in flight

a **shred** is etymologically a "cut"

shrew once described any malicious or mischievous person

shrewd first meant "vicious"

shrift means "absolution, penance" and **short shrift** first meant a brief penance given to someone condemned to die

English seems to have acquired **shrimp** by adapting German or Old Norse *schrimpfen*, "to shrink, shrivel up"

shrine is from an Old English word for "cabinet, chest," from Latin *scrinium*, "book chest"

wrinkles of skin were once called **shrinks**

to **shrip** means to clip, prune, or trim

to **shrive** is to hear a confession; the verb's other tenses are shrove and shriven

a **shrivel** is a shrunken thing

shroud is the word for the branches of a tree providing shade

shrubbage is another word for shrubbery

shruff is refuse wood or other material

shrug first meant "to move the body from side to side," "fidget," or "cower"

shucks refers to corn **shucks**, once considered a worthless part of corn

shudder is a frequentative of a Germanic word meaning "shake"

shuffle first meant "deal dishonestly or surreptitiously"

shumai are small steamed dumplings, usually stuffed with seafood or vegetables

shun began with the stronger meanings of "abhor, loathe"

shut is from the Germanic base that produced "shoot," and the underlying notion is the "shooting" of a bolt across a door to fasten it

{ the bars of a gate are often called **shuttles** }

the object hit in badminton is the **shuttlecock**

shy was first used to describe horses as "easily frightened"

shylock comes from a Shakespeare character in "The Merchant of Venice"

shyster may derive from German *Scheuster*, a lawyer who uses unprofessional practices, from *Scheisse*, "excrement," or may refer to a Mr. Scheuster, an unscrupulous lawyer of the 1840s

a **sialagogue** is anything that makes the mouth water; **sialogogic** is causing one to salivate

sialoquent pertains to someone who is spitting while speaking

Siberia means "sleeping land"

words of drinking and swallowing are **sibilant** or **popping** and sh, b, and p are common starts to these words

sibling originally meant "relative," not specifically a brother or sister

sibship is a relationship between siblings

sibylline is prophetic in a mysterious fashion; **orphic** is mystic, esoteric, or entrancing

sic, "thus, so," bracketed and usually set in italics, is used to indicate that a preceding word or phrase in a quoted passage is reproduced as it appeared in the original passage and meaning "the foregoing mistake was made by the writer/speaker"; it should be positioned right after the error to which it refers

a **siccative** is a substance causing drying, especially when mixed with oil paint, etc.

the six on a dice or on a dice roll is called **sice**

sickle is based on Latin *secare*, "to cut"

sick'm or **sicém**, used to incite an attack, is merely a colloquial form of "seek him" or "seek 'em"

the etymological meaning of **side** seems to be the "long" surface of something, as opposed to the ends, top, or bottom

a box within an article or book is a **sidebar**

sideburns were first called burnsides, named for Civil War general Ambrose Burnside

one's **profile** is also **sideface**

sidekicker came before **sidekick**; incidental criticism, a passing or indirect attack, is often termed **sidekick**

in **sidelong** and **headlong**, -long is just a variant of -ling (expressing direction)

sienna is a pigment that is either naturally yellowish-brown or reddish-brown when burnt (burnt **sienna**)

sierra is a mountain range with a sawtoothed appearance and **sierra** means "saw" or "mountain range" in Spanish

the word **siesta**, an afternoon sleep or rest, comes from Latin *sexta hora*, literally "the sixth hour"

a selective or purifying process can be called a **sieve**—and **sift** means "to pass through a **sieve**"

a synonym for whisper (as a verb) is **siffilate**; speaking in whispers is **siffilating**

a **sight** is a measurement or observation taken with an optical device

the **sight** is the area enclosed by a picture frame

a **sigil** is a sign or image considered to have magical powers

sigla are the words for signs and abbreviations representing words

 the earliest attested uses of **sign** in English go back to the thirteenth century, with some specialized uses, such as math, dating from the eighteenth century

sidereal means "pertaining to the stars" (Latin *sidus*, "star")

sidetrack was first used for a railway siding or a minor track or path

sidewalk's original meaning was "a stroll" and then "a path running parallel to a main one"

a passing place in a canal is a **siding**

to **sidle** is to move along with one side forward (derived from sidelong)

siege derives from Latin *sedere*, "to sit"—as this tactic involved surrounding a place and sitting there until the enemy broke down from lack of aid and supplies

signal is from Latin *signalis*, "of a **sign**" from *signum*, "mark, token" (the latter from which **sign** is derived)

a person signing an agreement is a **signatory**

signature is from Latin *signatura*, "sign manual"

lack of flavor in a distilled spirit or lack of scent in a flower, perfume, or spice is a **silence**

silent is from Latin *silere*, "be silent"

something performed in silence is **silential**

the person whose job it is to maintain quiet order in a courtroom is the **silentiary** a **silentium** is a place where silence is imposed (library, religious retreat)

silhouette is named for Etienne de **Silhouette**, an eighteenth-century French author and politician

silicon is the chemical element; **silicone** is any of the chemical compounds of **silicon**

silk comes from Greek *Seres*, the name given to people of Far Eastern countries from which **silk** first came

silkworms are not worms; they are caterpillars

sill originally denoted "the foundation of a wall"

silly first meant "deserving of pity or sympathy" and comes from Old English *soelig*, "happy"

a **silo** was first an underground chamber or pit for storing grains or roots

silt probably originally referred to mud in salt flats of a river—and may be related to "salt" etymologically

silva is the arboreal population of a geographical region (what "fauna" is to animals)

the word **silver** may be of oriental origin

simian "apelike, monkeylike" is from Latin *simia*, "ape," which is from *simus*, "snubnosed"; not only apes and monkeys can be **simian**—a person may have a **simian** style of eating a banana

similar traces back to Latin *similis*, "like, **similar**"

a **simile** likens one thing to another dissimilar thing and once meant "resemblance, similarity"; a **metaphor** acts as if the two compared things are identical and substitutes one for the other

simmer means "be at a heat just below the boiling point"

to **simper** is to smile in a silly or self-conscious way

etymologically, **simple** means "same-fold" or "single"

simple means "plain, uncomplicated"; **simplistic** means "characterized by a forced, unwarranted simplicity"

in the original sense of the word, a **simulacrum** was simply a representation of something, such as an oil painting or marble statue

since is a contracted form of Middle English *sithenes*, "**since**"

sincere is from Latin *sincerus*, "clean, pure"

sinciput is the front of the head

sine is from Latin *sinus*, "curve, fold, hollow"

a **sinecure** is a job that pays well but demands little work

if ears **sing**, they are affected by a buzzing sound

single is from Latin *singulus*, "**single**," with the elements *sim-*, *go-*, *lo-*, and **singular** is from Latin *singularis*, "solitary, **single**"

a **singult** is a sob or a hiccup

sinister comes from Latin "to the left"—as left was associated with bad omens

> **sink** originally meant only "go below water," not "cause to go below water"

sinus is from Latin meaning "bend, curve" or "bay"

sip is probably a modification of "sup"

the **sipapu** is the hole in the floor of a Native American *kiva*, from which ancient ancestors "emerge" into the present

sipes are the fine lines or grooves cut into the tread of tires that allow the tire to flex and give better traction on wet surfaces

sipid—of pleasing taste, flavor, or character—is the opposite of **insipid**

a **sippet** is a small piece of toast or bread served in soup or used for dipping in gravy or sauce; the bread in French onion soup is called a **sippet**

a **siquis** is a public notice

sir is a short form of **sire**, which originally came from Latin *senior*

a dog has a **sire** (father) and a **dam** (mother) (from "dame")

siren first meant an imaginary snake or a part-woman/part-bird creature that mythically lured sailors to death on rocks along the shore

sirloin comes from French *surlonge sur*, "above," and *longe*, "loin" ("the cut of meat above the loin")

{ **sirocco**, from Arabic, is literally "east wind" }

sisal is the fiber of the Mexican *agave* plant used for cordage or rope

sissy first meant "sister"

sister is part of a large word family from Indo-European *swesor*

the female equivalent of the word brethren is **sistren**

sit is from the Proto-Indo-European base *sed-* "to **sit**"

sitar is from Persian and Urdu *sih*, "three" and *tar*, "string"

site is from Latin *situs*, "local position"

the time allotted for service and consumption of a complete meal, especially at a restaurant, is a **sitting**

situate goes back to Latin *situatus*, "placed," from *situs*, "position"

the Indo-European ancestor of **six** was *seks*

a **sixsome** is a group of six persons

size is a shortening of "assize"

sizzard is heat with high humidity

a **sizzle** is the half hiss, half sigh of an animal—or the effervescence of beer

skank and **skanky** may have originated in Black English as meaning "nasty; sluttish" or "low life"

skate is an old word for a mean or contemptible person

The word **skate** was originally plural and comes from Dutch *schaats*, which derived from an Old French word for "stilt," but the connection is unclear. **Skate** appeared in English in the mid-seventeenth century. **Ski**, in English by 1755, was borrowed from Norwegian, and ultimately from Old Norse for "snowshoe." And **sled** came from Flemish and Germanic *sledde* between 1325–1388 for a "vehicle for transporting heavy goods" and is related to sledge and sleigh.

skedaddle may come from the Irish word *squedadol*, "scattered"

a **skein** is a length of yarn wound into a loose coil, specifically 360 feet long

to **skelder** is to beg or to live by begging

skeleton is from Greek *skeletos*, "dried up"

the Greek *skeptikoi* were "the inquirers" or "the hesitants," the followers of the Greek philosopher Pyrrho of Elis (c 300 BC), giving us **skepticism** and **skeptic**

a **skerry** is a small rugged or rocky island—or a stretch of rocks usually covered at high tide

sketch traces back to Greek *skhedios*, "done extempore"

though both a **sketch** and **skit** are short entertaining presentations, a **sketch** is usually serious and unrehearsed while a **skit** is typically rehearsed and comical

skew comes from askew

ski is derived from Old Norse *skith*, "stick of wood, snowshoe"; the plural is **skis** or **ski**

to **skice** is to frisk about like squirrels in spring

a **skid** is a wooden roller used as part of a set to move logs or other heavy objects

skiddoo was the invention of T.A. "Tad" Dorgan, the cartoonist (who also came up with hot dog)

skill, from Old Norse, first meant "knowledge"

skillet may come from Latin *scutella*, diminutive of *scutra*, "dish, platter"

the **skin** is the outermost layer of an aircraft's structure

skin is the term for the thin, tight covering on carrots, potatoes, grapes, and peaches—but also the thicker covering of bananas and avocados

skin is the general term for an animal's outer covering; the layer of fur, hair, or wool is the **coat**; **hide** is the tough **skin** of certain large animals that is tanned and made into leather; and **pelt** is untanned **skin** of fur-bearing animals

{ **skinny** first meant "pertaining to or affecting the skin" }

skip was once the term for footman or manservant

Middle Dutch *schip* had a derivative *schipper*, "captain of a small ship," that became English **skipper**

skirl is the distinctive sound of a bagpipe

skirmish is derived from Italian *scaramuccia*

the whirr of birds in flight is **skirr**

skirt derives from Old English *scyrte*, "shirt"

the ice cream at the base of a scoop of ice cream in a cone is the **skirt**

a **skite** is a contemptible person

skosh, as in small amount, comes from Japanese *sukoshi*

skulduggery is from Scottish *skulduddery*, "unchaste behavior"

to **skulk** is to move stealthily, hide, or lurk in a sneaky way

the **skull** is the bony framework while the **cranium** is all the bones of the **skull** except for one, the mandible/lower jaw

skullduggery is from Scottish *sculduddery*, "obscenity"

skunk is from Algonquian *seganku* or *segonku*, "animal that sprays or squirts" or "urinating fox"

sky comes from Old Norse *sky* meaning "cloud" and at first referred only to clouds

sky-hook means "wishful thinking"

skyscraper as a word existed for about 100 years, originally as the name of a small triangular sail on square-riggers before it was used in the context of a building

an artist's block or palette for grinding or mixing colors is a **slab**

slacks (as in pants) probably comes from Latin *laxus*, "loose"

slalom is from Norwegian *sla*, "sloping" and *lam*, "track"

a **slam** is the winning of every trick in a card game

slander is spoken defamation; **libel** is written, visual, or broadcast defamation

slang started out as the special vocabulary of the underworld and other disreputable persons; the origin of the word **slang** is unknown!

a lean, long person or thing is a **slangrel**

to **slangwhang** is to use abusive or violent language

slant is a variant of "slent," an older word

slanting can be said fancier: **slantindicular**

slapstick is named for the use of two sticks slapped together off-stage to accentuate a comic's onstage pratfall

the **slash** is also called a virgule, diagonal, separatrix, slant, and solidus

a salmon after spawning is a **slat**

an area of quiet water between areas of disturbed water or an interval of fair weather is a **slatch**

{ **slaughter** is from Old Norse meaning "butcher's meat" }

slave comes from Latin *sclava* or *sclavus*, "Slav, Slavonic (captive)," as these people were reduced to this via conquest in the ninth century

slaver means "to have a craving" or "to go in eager pursuit"

etymologically, **slay** means "hit"

sleaze was first used in 1967

sleazy first meant "rough, having projecting fibers" and then indicated that a fabric was thin or flimsy

sleck is soft mud or ooze

sledge of sledgehammer once meant "heavy hammer" on its own

sleek is a variant form of slick

to **sleepaway** is to die without disease, to die peaceably

an underdog with a chance is a **sleeper**

sleet is snow that has partially thawed as it falls

a protective cover for a record is a **sleeve**

sleeveless once meant "paltry, petty, frivolous"

sleigh is from Dutch

sleuth comes from Old Norse meaning "track, trail"

slew is from Irish for "crowd, multitude"

slice comes from Old French *esclice*, "splinter," from *esclicier*, "reduce to splinters, shatter"

slickrock is a smooth, slippery rock

slight first meant "even, level" or "smooth"

AIDS is called **Slim** in central Africa

slime is related to Latin *limus*, "mud, **slime**"

slip, as in pottery, derives from a Norwegian word for "slime on fish"

loose slippers were once called slipshoes and the careless forgot to change them before going outdoors; hence the word **slipshod**, which first meant "wearing slippers"

slip-slopping is the "misnaming and misapplication of a hard word"

slister is to idle away time, be lazy

slither is loose stones on a hillside or any smooth slippery mass

generally, **slobs** can be called: jeeter, slammock, muck-scutcheon, slubberdegullion, or tatterdemalion

a messy eater is a **slobberchops**

etymologically, **sloe** is probably blue-black fruit

slogan is from Scottish-Gaelic *slaugh*, "army" and *gairm*, "shout"—since the first slogans were actually battle cries

to **slonk** is to swallow greedily

to **sloom** is to sleep heavily and soundly; to **slumber** is to sleep lightly

another word for sluggish is **sloomy**

the noun **slope** did not appear until the seventeenth century

slosh may be slop and slush combined

slot's original meaning in English was "bar" or "rod" rather than "an opening" as it came from German *schloss*, "lock, clasp"

sloth derives from the word "slow"

a **slough** (pronounced SLAU, like plow) is a state of despair or dejection; deep depression can be called the **slough of despond**

slovenly first meant "low, base" from **sloven** "a person of low character"

the etymological base of **slow** is "dullness, sluggishness"

a lump on a thread or yarn is a **slub**

slushy ice on the surface of the sea is **sludge**

the garden **slug** takes its name from Scandinavian *sluggje*, "heavy, slow person"; **slug** was originally slothfulness personified

to **slug** can mean "to hunt for slugs"

a **slugabed** is a late riser

a **sluice** is etymologically a device for "excluding" water, from Latin *excludere*, "shut out"

slum can mean "nonsensical talk or writing"

a **slum** and a **ghetto** are different—if everyone is ethnically similar, it is a **ghetto**, and if everyone is basically poor, it is a **slum**

slumgullion is an insignificant person

a **slummocker** is an awkward or careless person

slur first meant "thin, fluid mud" and later became a verb meaning "smear" or "disparage"

slurry is semi-liquid mud, cement, or manure

slush may be imitative of sludge

slut comes from Middle English for "mud" or Norwegian *slutr*, "impure water"

sly comes from Old Norse meaning "able to strike"

smack, "hit," first meant "open the lips noisily"—borrowed from German or Dutch *smacken*, which is imitative of the sound

smarmy is from smarm, "to behave in a flattering or toadying manner"

smart started out as a verb and the adjective first meant "painful, stinging" before "clever"

a **smartism** is a witty saying or aphorism

smack and mash may have combined to make **smash**

a **smatchet** is a nasty child or person

smaze is a mixture of smoke and haze

smear's original notion seems to be "butter"

smectic means "cleansing, detergent"

smegma once meant soap or anything that cleanses or scours

a **smell-feaste** is one who appears uninvited to share in a feast

a **smellfungus** or **swelp** is a complainer who finds fault with everything

to melt ore and extract metal is to **smelt**

to **smile** can mean to laugh gently

a **smilet** is a little smile

smith is literally "craftsman, worker"

smithereens is from Irish *smidirin*, "fragment"

another word for contagious is **smittlish**

an artist's garment is a **smock**

honeycombed stitching on clothes is called **smocking**

a **smockster** is a go-between

smog is a blend of smoke and fog

a **smoothie** is a thick drink made of fruit puréed in a blender with yogurt, juice, etc.

{ a **smooch** is a deliberate smudge made with the fingers on a drawing to produce shading }

smorgasbord is Swedish for *smorgas*, "bread and butter" or "open sandwich," and *bord*, "table"

smug was more complimentary at first, meaning "trim and neat" or "smooth and sleek"

smur is drizzly fog

smut comes from German *smutzen*, "to smear, stain"

snack first meant "bite, snap (of a dog)," from Dutch meaning "to bite"

snafu is an acronym for "Situation Normal—All F–ed Up"

snag literally first meant a stump on a tree trunk or a piece of timber underwater that obstructed navigation

snail is from a Germanic base Jmeaning "crawl"

snake's name comes from Old High German and Norse words meaning "crawler" or "creeper," from Latin meaning "crawl"; **serpent** and **snake** mean the same thing and **reptile** is the general word for the class that includes snakes

the **snapdragon**'s flowers supposedly look like the mouth of a dragon

snapshot first referred to a quick or hurried shot taken without deliberate aim, especially at a rising bird or quickly moving animal

{ a **snarge** is a total jerk }

snark is a blend of snake and shark by Lewis Carroll—and is a synonym for "snore" or "snort"

to be **snarky** is to be irritable and short-tempered

snaste or **snot** is the burnt part of a candle wick

a **snattock** is a fragment or scrap

to **snawk** is to smell

snazzy is a combination of snappy and jazzy

a **sneaker** is a glass of brandy

sneakers got their name because they don't squeak like leather shoes do

a **sneb** is a reprimand or a snub

the Old English word for "**sneeze**" was *fnesan* and there was (now obsolete) verb neeze "**sneeze**"—which bridged a gap and created **sneeze**, which is imitative of the sound

a window catch or latch is a **snib**

a small cut or mark is a **snick**

snide first meant "counterfeit, imitation"

a **snipe** is the discarded stub of a cigar or cigarette

to **snirtle** is to attempt to suppress one's laughter, to snicker, laugh quietly and mockingly

breath going through the nose is **snoach**

Oxford freshmen who were not of noble birth once had to register as *sine nobilitate*, abbreviated to s.n.o.b., which may have given us the word "**snob**"

snockered is one of the many words meaning "drunk"

a **snofari** is an expedition into a cold, snowy region

snogging is kissing and cuddling

snollygosters are sleazy politicians or lawyers

snoop is from Dutch *snoepen*, "eat on the sly" and it first meant "steal and eat in a clandestine manner"

to **snoove** is to glide and move steadily forward

like **snort**, which originally meant "snore," **snore** is from a Germanic base imitative of the sound

snorkel is from German *schnorchel*, "air intake, spiral"

to **snouch** someone is to snub or treat with scorn

snout first referred to the trunk of an elephant

snout and **muzzle** are used for dogs and horses, and include the mouth, nose, jaws

snow (technically, a mineral) is of Teutonic origin, from an Indo-European root shared by the Latin words *niv-/nix* and Greek *nipha*; the spelling **snow** first appeared in English around 1200

snow-blossom is another word for snowflake

a **snowcat** is a tracked vehicle for snow travel

snowman is the name of a clay-modeling technique in archaeology

snozzle is one of the slang terms for "nose"

to **snudge** is to nestle, be snug and quiet

snuff first described the charred part of a candle wick

snug can also mean bar of a public house

snug originally was a nautical term meaning "compact" or "shipshape, prepared for bad weather"

a **snuggery** is a cozy or comfortable room

snuggle is a frequentative (denoting repeated or recurrent action or state) of the verb snug

a **snurge** is an obnoxious person

dodging an unpleasant duty is **snurging**

to **snurl** is to turn up one's nose in scorn

to **snurt** is to expel mucus when sneezing

when animals poke around with their noses, that is **snuzzling**

if something is **snying**, it has an upward curve

to **soak** bread is to bake it thoroughly

soap is a slang synonym for flattery

soap is an organic compound; **detergent** is a synthetic cleaning agent

soar is from Latin *ex-*, "from," and *aura*, "air"

soba are thin buckwheat noodles in Japanese cuisine

sober originally meant "moderate, avoiding excess" (in both eating and drinking)

the ever-serious-minded solemn person is a **sobersides**

sobriquet in French is literally "a tap under the chin" and means "nickname, epithet" in English

soccer is a shortened form of Assoc./Association and it is aphetic, i.e. shortened by the dropping of a letter/ syllable from the beginning of a word

soceraphobia is aversion to your in-laws

sociable, **social**, **society**, etc., originate in Latin *socius*, "companion, fellow," or "colleague"

socialism is the more loosely defined term and encompasses **communism**

the original meaning of **society** was companionship or fellowship and the word derived from Latin *societas*, "companionship," and *socius*, "companion, friend, associate"

> **sock** first referred to a light shoe, like a slipper (from Latin *soccus*)

a **sockdolager** is a decisive blow or sizzling retort, a climax or crescendo

socket is from Middle English, first as "head of a spear, resembling a plowshare," from an Anglo-Norman French diminutive of French *soc*, "plowshare"

the **socket** is the part of the head of a golf club into which the shaft is fitted

in the sixteenth–seventeenth century, **soda** was a synonym for headache

soda may get its name from Persian for "saltwort" or "salt marsh"

food that is **sodden** is heavy or doughy from improper cooking

the term **sodomy** commemorates the Palestinian city of Sodom, a hotbed of vice according to the Bible

sofa comes from Arabic *soffah*, originally a raised part of the floor made comfortable for sitting with carpets and cushions

the underside of any architectural structure is the **soffit** (from suffix, formed as *sub-*, "under" and *figere*, "fix")

sofrito is a sautéed mixture of seasonings and finely chopped vegetables, such as onions, garlic, and peppers, used as a base for many Spanish, Caribbean, and Latin American dishes

radiation is termed "**soft**" if it has little penetrating power

soft first meant "agreeable, pleasant"

softball was originally known as kitten ball, mush ball, and diamond ball

the convention of using "**softwood**" or "**hardwood**" to identify a tree is not necessarily an indication of its hardness but simply whether it is a conifer or a flowering tree

a **sog** is a drowsy state or a doze

soigné means "well cared for, very well groomed" and can be applied to things like gardens as well as people; **soignée** is the feminine form

soil may trace back to Latin *solium*, "seat" or *solum*, "ground"

soirée derives from French *soir*, "evening"

sojourn is from Latin *sub-* and *diurnum*, "day," and it first meant "temporary stay" or a "delay"

solace is a form of comfort given to one who is in sorrow or distress; **consolation** is an act of offering such comfort or the result of such comfort having been provided

solanaceous is pertaining to peppers, tomatoes, eggplants, etc., of the nightshade family

a box made in the form of a book is a **solander**

solar is from Latin *solaris*, from *sol*, "sun"

solarium first meant "sundial"

solatium is monetary compensation for emotional suffering, grief, inconvenience, etc.

to **solder** something is etymologically to make it **solid**; **solid** comes from Latin *solidus*, "**solid**, whole"

soldier gets its name from Latin *solidus*, a gold coin of the Roman empire that was the pay of the empire's army

sole (of a foot) is from Latin *solea*, "sandal," as is the fish of this name (from its tongue shape)

in Soloi, Greece, a corrupt form of Athenian Greek was spoken, leading to the Greek word *soloikos*, "speaking incorrectly," which became **solecism**

solein means "done alone, in solitude"

solemn first meant "associated with religious rites," from Latin meaning "celebrated on a fixed date"

the **soleplate** is a metal plate forming the base of an iron, machine saw, or other machine

the **sol-fa** syllables are doh, ray, mi, fah, sol, lah, te—for the notes of the major musical scale

solfeggio and **gamut** are words formed on the sequence of musical notes

solferino is a purplish-pink color

solicit first meant "disturb, make anxious" and also "manage, attend to (business)"

{ **solicitous** can mean "full of anxiety; troubled" }

solipsism is the philosophy that the self is the only reality that can be proven to exist

solitaire (the card game) in North America is known as "patience" elsewhere

Latin *solus*, "alone," gave us **solitude**

a **solitudinarian** wants to be alone, thank you

{ a **solivagant** is a person who wanders alone }

solo has the plurals solos and soli

solstice is derived from the Latin *sol*, "Sun," and *stitium*, "stoppage," as the Sun appears to stand still on the first day of winter

the original meaning of **soluble** was medical, "not suffering from constipation"; it can now also mean "able to be solved or explained"

a **solute** is a substance dissolved in another substance, which is the **solvent**

solve first meant "loosen," from Latin *solvere*, "free, unfasten"

soma is the body of an organism

somber and **sombrero** are from Latin *sub-* and *umbra*, "shade" ("under the shade")

somersault comes from Provençal *sobre*, "above" and *saut*, "leap"

sommelier, a wine steward, is pronounced suh-mull-YAY

sonar is an acronym from SOund NAvigation and Ranging

song and **sing** come from prehistoric Germanic *sanggwaz*

the making of sound is **sonification**

sonnet is from Italian *sonetto*, a diminutive of *suono*, "sound"

in Old English, **soon** meant "straightaway"

people who crossed the border into Oklahoma Territory sooner than was allowed for its settlement became known as **Sooners**

soot is etymologically something which "sits" on something, like film settling on a surface

sooth, "true, truth," or "that which is" is part of **soothsayer**; it is related to **soothe**, which once meant "assent to be true; say yes to" or "to prove or show a fact to be true"

sop originally denoted a piece of bread, cake, etc., dipped into water, milk, wine, etc.

sophiology is the science of educational activities

sophism derives from Greek *sophos*, "wise" and **philosophy** is from "philosophia" (love of wisdom)

sophisticate originally meant "mix with a foreign or inferior substance"; **sophistication** once meant adulteration or counterfeiting of something

sophisticated originally meant "worldly wise"

sophistry is based on Greek *sophos*, "clever, wise"

sophomore is probably from Greek *sophizesthai*, "become wise," pertaining to sophism, specious but fallacious argumentation serving as a university exercise

sophomoric includes the roots *soph-*, "wise," and *moros*, "fool,"—so the contrast between wisdom and ignorance is built right into the word

sophrosyne is self-control, prudence, temperance

to **sopite** is to lull or put to sleep

deep sleep is **sopor**

soporific, "tending to cause sleep," is from Latin *sopor*, "sleep"

soprano is based on Latin *supra*, "above"

if something is **sorbile**, it is liquid and drinkable

a **sorcerer** is etymologically a drawer of "lots" from Latin *sors*, "lot"; **sort** comes from this "piece of wood used for drawing lots" and developed metaphorically into "condition" or "class"

sordid can mean "filthy, dirty," physically

a mute for an instrument is a **sordino**

sore as a noun first meant generally "physical pain and suffering"

the adjective form of shrew is **soricine**

sororal is the female equivalent of **fraternal**

{ getting together with other women is **sororizing** (Latin *soror*, "sister") }

SOS stands for nothing; the letters were chosen to be a distress signal because the nine keystrokes were simple to transmit and recognize in Morse Code

a **sot** is a drunkard

soufflé, French for "puffed up," comes from Latin *subflare*, "to puff or blow up from below," and also describes types of puffing, like breathing and inflating things with air—and a murmuring breathing sound

a soft rustling or murmuring sound—like the deep sigh of a sleeping baby—is **soughing**

the Latin word for **soul** is *anima*, which is found in English "*animated*"; **soul** in this ancient usage is always associated with motion

a sea inlet that is long and separates an island from a mainland is a **sound**

sounding-board was a board used to determine the depth of water

soup is from French *soupe* and maybe Latin *suppa* (from *suppare*, "soak"); **soup** originally denoted a piece of bread soaked in liquid, then broth poured onto bread

soupçon means "just a suspicion of a trace"

a **sour** is a mixed drink consisting of whisky, brandy, or gin (etc.), lemon or lime juice—hence the name, and sugar

a **source** is etymologically something that has surged up, from Latin *surgere*, "rise"

sourdough is named from the practice of prospectors who carried a lump of sour dough from each biscuit-baking to start fermentation of the next batch

to **souse** something is etymologically to steep it in salt; **soused** first meant "pickled, steeped in brine"

the band trimming on robes and pajamas is **soutache**

the **South** states of the U.S. include Virginia, West Virginia, Kentucky, North Carolina, South Carolina, Tennessee, Georgia, Alabama, and Mississippi—and sometimes Arkansas

south seems to come from the Germanic root *sunth/sunthaz*, "sunny"

the **Southeast** U.S. states are South Carolina, Georgia, Alabama, and Florida

the first baseball fields were positioned a certain way to maximize daylight (there were no night games)—so left-handers" arms were on the south side—hence, earning them the **southpaw** nickname

Texas, Arizona, and New Mexico constitute the **Southwest** U.S.

souvenir is literally "remember" in French, from Latin *subvenire*, "occur to the mind"

the Greek dish **souvlaki** derives from *souvla*, "skewer"

sovereign is literally "above" (Latin *super*) and reign through Old French *soverain*

to **sowl** is to pull roughly by the ear or ears

soy, from Japanese *shoyu*, is *shi*, "salted beans," and *yu*, "oil"

sozzled is a word meaning "intoxicated"

spa was originally a watering-place in Liége, Belgium, celebrated for its mineral springs

space is from Latin *spatium*, "distance," or "period"

space-time is time and three-dimensional space regarded as fused in a four-dimensional continuum which includes all events

a nail with a hook or eye as the head—sometimes used in surveying—is a **spad**

spade is from Latin *spatha*, "broad flat instrument"

Spandex is actually named for "expand"

spandy means "very good, fine"

spang means "directly, completely," as in "I hit it **spang** on the head"

spangle comes from an archaic noun, spang, meaning "a glittering ornament"

spaniel comes from French *espaigneul*, "Spanish"—though the Irish were first to use them as hunting dogs and probably got them from Spain

a fast horse or a person is a **spanker**

a timed-released capsule is also a **spansule**

{ **spam**, as in email, gets its name from the Monty Python sketch where the word is repeated many times }

to **call a spade a spade** is based on an ancient Greek expression, literally "to call a fig a fig, a trough a trough," which became another Greek word for digging tool, which was then translated to "**spade**"

spades in a deck of cards has nothing to do with **spades** as tools but comes from Spanish *espada*, "sword"

spaghetti, "small cords/little strings," is diminutive of *spago*, "cord, string"; the singular is *spaghetto* and slang terms are **spaggers** and **spag**

a **spall** is a splinter or chip of rock; **spalling** is breaking up stone or rock with a hammer

SPAM, as in the food, combines SP from spice and AM from ham

span was originally the distance between the tip of the thumb and tip of the little finger

spanakopita is Greek for "spinach pie"

spanandry is scarcity of males in a population

a **sparable** is a headless nail used for soles and heels of shoes

spareribs has nothing to do with "spare" ("extra") as we know it; it is from German *ribbesper*, "ribspear," for pickled pork ribs roasted on a spit—but the name changed through folk etymology

sparge is the action of sprinkling or splashing (as is **spargefication**)

a **sparkler** is a miniature firework

sparkling wine is the generic term for any wine that is naturally or artificially effervescent; **asti spumante** is artificially effervescent wine from Asti (*spumante*, "sparkling"), while **Champagne** is naturally effervescent wine from Champagne

sparks is a colloquial term for an electrician

sparrow-fart is daybreak

sparse derives from Latin *sparsus/spargere*, "scatter"; **sparse** first described widely spaced writing

spasm and **spastic** derive from Greek *span*, "draw, pull"

a baby oyster and bees' eggs are each called a **spat**

a **spate** is a sudden flood or rush, an out-pouring

spats (the shoe covering) is a shortening of spatterdashes

to **spattle** is to flip or turn something over (from Dutch for "spatula")

spatula comes from Latin *spathula*, a diminitive of *spatha*, "a broad blade to stir mixtures"

spawn comes from Anglo-Norman *espaun-dre*, "spread out," ultimately from Latin *expandere*, "expand"

spay is a shortening of a French word meaning "cut with a sword"

speakable is "capable of being spoken or spoken about"—as opposed to unspeakable

in **speakeasy**, the easy means "softly"—because people either spoke quietly about them or in them

specimen comes from Latin *specere*, "look (at)"

specious means "seeming to be correct or logical"

spectacle is from Latin *specere*, "look at"

the word **spectacular**, from spectacle, is patterned on other pairs like oracle/oracular

spectrophobia is fear of looking in a mirror

spectrum is literally Latin for "apparition, image of something"

speculate, from Latin meaning "look, see," once meant "look or gaze at (a thing)"

speed is from a Germanic base that begat Old English *spowan*, "prosper, succeed," its early meaning

speed is the distance an object travels during a unit of time; **velocity** is the distance an object travels in a specified direction during a unit of time

spelaean or **spelean** means "living or occurring in a cave"

specialization refers to the process of becoming specialized; **specialty** refers to a special pursuit, occupation, or product

a swelling of the uvula is a **spean**; a **spean** is another name for a prong of a fork

an asparagus stick is a **spear**

the sting of a reptile or insect is a **spear**

spearmint is so named for its shape

special comes from French *specialist*, "of a particular type"

species is a subgroup of **genus** and you capitalize a **genus**, but not a **species** (which is properly pronounced SPEE-sheez)

specificity refers to a character of definiteness or explicitness in a description or account; **specification** refers to an item of definiteness in such a description

speleology, the study of caves, derives from Greek *spelynx*, "cave"; a **speleothem** is any structure formed in a cave, like a stalactite or stalagmite

spell (the verb) is from Old French *espeler*, "read out"

spellbind is "bind with a spell"

Not until primers like "McGuffey's Readers" and dictionaries like Noah Webster's came along did uniform **spelling** become established. Before that, there was much orthographic variation, even among the more educated.

spelt is used for the past tense of spell in Britain

a **spelunker** is a cave explorer, more correctly called a **speleologist**, from Latin *spelunca*, "cave" and Greek *spelynx*, "cave"

spend is a blend of Latin *pendere*, "pay, weigh," and *expendere*, "pay out"

a **spendthrift** is one who spends the "thrift" or earnings/wealth of another

sperate means "hopeful, promising"

sperm is etymologically something that is "sown" like seed, from Greek *sperma*, "seed"

an act of spitting is a **spet**

spew first meant "vomit"

SPF stands for sun protection factor and **SPF** numbers on a package can range from as low as 2 to as high as 60; the **SPF** rating is calculated by comparing the amount of time needed to produce a sunburn on protected skin to the amount of time needed to cause a sunburn on unprotected skin, e.g. with **SPF** 15, it multiplies the initial burning time by 15, so it takes about 2.5 hours for that person's skin to turn red

if you are **sphairistic**, you are playing tennis

an erroneous or mistaken belief is a **sphalm**

spharistike (Greek for "let's play") was the original name for lawn tennis

sphere comes from Greek *sphaira*, "ball"

a synonym for "to appropriate" is **spheterize**

sphincter, the anus-controlling muscle, comes from Latin *sphiggein*, "bind tight"

a **sphinx** is body of lion, wings of eagle, head of woman; **sphinx** has two plurals—sphinxes and sphinges

the device that measures your blood pressure is the **sphygmomanometer**

a figure-eight bandage or wrap is a **spica**

spica is a spikelet, as on a wheat stalk

the word **spice** traces back to Latin *species*, "goods, wares," which went to French and

first meant "usually sweet items used in cooking"

to **spiculate** a pencil is to sharpen it

a frying pan with a long handle is a **spider**

spider comes from a German word that literally means "female spinner"

the framework of a lampshade is the **spider**

a **spiderweb** is called a **cobweb** because cob is a form of cop, an old word for "spider"

spiel is derived from German for "game" or "play" and is speech intended to trick someone into doing something

spike is probably borrowed from Dutch *spiker*, "long sharp piece"

the device for tapping sap from maple trees to sap pails is a **spile**

the modern sense of **spill** is a metaphor for the early sense "shedding blood"

spinach may come from Persian *aspanakh/ispanak*, perhaps related to the Latin *spina*, "spine," because of its prickly seeds

spine, from Latin *spina*, "prickle, thorn" (or "backbone"), first referred to sharp outgrowth on a plant

Giovanni Spinetti (fl. c.1503) created the small harpsichord-like instrument we call the **spinet**

{ **spinney** is another word for "small wood, thicket" }

a **spinosity** is a rude remark

spinster first pertained to a woman who spun cotton, wool, etc., for a living or one who had spun herself a set of body, table, and bed linen—and later was used as a legal designation for an unmarried woman

the activity or product of making fiber into yarn is **spinstry**

spiracle was first "breath, spirit" and came to mean a small opening, like a pore

spiral is from Latin *spiralis*, "coiled"

in Old English, **spire** meant "stalk" or "stem"

a **spire** is the tall pointed roof of a tower or the tall pointed structure on top of a **steeple**; a **steeple** is the tower plus the **spire**

spirit is from Latin *spirare*, "breathe"

spissated is a synonym for thickened

something's **spissitude** is its density or thickness

to **spit** (imitative of its sound) means to expel saliva; **expectorate** means to dredge up and expel phlegm

spondulicks is slang for "cash, money"

sponge is from Latin *spongia* and Greek *sphoggos*, "water growth"

spongeous means "having holes"

sponsor comes from a Latin stem meaning "promise solemnly"

the word **spoof** was invented by a British comedian (Arthur Roberts 1852–1933) for a hoaxing game

spoon first came into English meaning "chip, splinter" or "thin piece of wood"

spoor is the trail of a wild animal—footprints, fur, odors, sounds, or dung

sporadic means etymologically "scattered like seed"

spoonerisms, unintentional interchanges of sounds in two or more words, is named for Rev. William Archibald Spooner (1844–1930)

spite is from French *despit*, "ill will, scorn," from Latin *despicere*, "look down on"

spizzerinctum is personal drive or motivation

splash and spatter are combined into **splatter**

splenative is a synonym for irritable

splendid is from Latin *splendere*, "shine"

a six-ounce bottle of a beverage, like Champagne, is a **split**

split originally referred exclusively to a ship breaking up on rocks

a **splodge** or **splotch** is an irregular stain; **splotch** may be a combination of spot and blotch

a **spod** is a studious person who is quite socially inept or dull or a person who pursues an unfashionable, technical, or esoteric interest with obsessive dedication

spoil (noun) is from Latin *spolium*, "skin stripped from a killed animal"

spore comes from Greek *speirein*, "to sow"—for the small bodies by which ferns, mosses, and mushrooms reproduce

a **spore** is a lone reproductive cell capable of producing a plant without combining with another cell; a **seed** develops from sexual recombination of genes from within one plant or two separate plants

the fur-covered pouch on a kilt is a **sporran**

sport is actually a shortening of the noun disport, "diversion from serious duties"

a small playful animal is a **sportling**

sportulary means dependent on donations

spouse is from Latin *sponsus*, "bridegroom," and *sponsa*, "bride," based on Latin *spondere*, "to make a ritual pledge"

a synonym for adultery is **spousebreach**

a block placed behind a car wheel to keep it from rolling down a hill is a **sprag** young salmon can be **sprag** but also, in chronological order, parr, smolt, grisle, and alevin

a **sprain** involves one or more ligaments; a **strain** involves a tendon or muscle

spraint is the word for otter droppings

spread may be from Latin *spargere*, "scatter, sprinkle"

spread-eagle first described a navy man who was lashed to the rigging for flogging

it is thought that **spree** comes from the Scots' *spreath*, "cattle raid"

sprezzatura is the art of doing a difficult thing with grace, thereby making it look easy

the season of **spring** was first called Lent, but by the sixteenth century took its new name, based on the notion of something beginning or rising, like water "springs" from the ground

a cow about to give birth is a **springer**

the colored **sprinkles** on food like doughnuts, ice cream, and cupcakes are also called "jimmies"

> { **sprite** started out simply as a variation of spirit }

spritzer is from German, meaning "splash"

spruce is the Old English (aliteration) name for Prussia; **spruce**, the tree, was originally **spruce** fir, literally the "Prussian fir"

Spruce or **Spruceland** are actually other names for the country of Prussia

the word **spud** comes from the kind of spade (spuddle) with which potatoes were dug out

to **spuddle** is to go about a trifling business as if it were of great importance

another word for thickset is **spuddy**

spumante (Italian "sparkling") takes its name from Italian *spuma*, "foam"

spume is any type of foam, especially that produced by ocean waves against rocks

spunk may be a blend of spark and the obsolete sense of funk, "spark"

each of the main roots of a tree is a **spur**

spurious first meant "born out of wedlock," based on Latin *spurius*, "false"

sputnik is literally "traveling companion" in Russian

sputum is expectorated matter

spy is from French *espie*, "person who watches," from Latin *specere*, "behold, look"

a cushion of a sofa or car seat is a **squab**

to **squabash** is to defeat with cutting criticism

a **squadron** is etymologically a "square" and the sense of "military group" comes from an earlier "square formation of troops"; the word was borrowed from Italian *squadrone*, from Latin *quadrare*, "square"

to dirty something through handling is to **squage**

a **squall** is a violent wind that comes in suddenly, but does not last long, and is often accompanied by rain or snow

squalor is the state of being squalid

a fish or snake can be **squamous** or **squamulose** (covered with minute scales)

square is from Latin *exquadra*, "out of four"

squash, the veggie, is a shortened form of Narragansett *asquutasquash*, "eaten raw," (from *asq*, "raw, uncooked")

squash, the verb, is an alteration of quash and means, generally, to "crush, squeeze, or suppress"

someone who **squats** is etymologically "forced together," from Latin *coactire*, "press together"

squaw was borrowed into English in Massachusetts by settlers and meant "younger woman"

squdge means "hug tightly"

to **squiggle** can mean to shake a liquid or to squeeze paint from a tube

squeam is what a squeamish person feels

squelch originally was a heavy crushing fall onto something soft

squelch or **squidge** is the sucking sound made on wet muddy ground

a **squib** is a type of small firework that burns with a hissing sound before it explodes with a loud bang

to **squiddle** is to waste time with idle talk

a **squillion** is a very large number of something

to **squinch** is to contort one's face and is probably a blend of squint and pinch

squinny is to look at with partly closed eyes, look askance at

squint is short for the obsolete "asquint," which may have come from Dutch *schuin*, "sideways, sloping"

squire is etymologically a "shield carrier" from Latin *scutarius*, "shield carrier," from *scutum*, "shield"

a half-suppressed laugh is a **squirk**

a **squirl** is a flourish in handwriting

squirrel comes from Greek *skiouros*, from *skia*, "shadow," and *oura*, "tail"

{ squirt and squash may have combined to make **squish** }

to squeeze and crush is to **squiss**

squit is idiotic talk

sqush is to squeeze messily

stable at first housed cattle, too, and was not specifically for horses

stadium was first a unit of length equal to 600 Greek or Roman feet, c 185 meters, and then was used to describe a course for racing that was this length

staff is from Germanic *stabaz*, "stick"; the sense of **staff** as employees probably is an allusion to the carrying of a **staff** of office by a person in charge

minor figures or details added to a painting are the **staffage**

to go in **stag** meant to "go naked," which influenced the later "**stag** party"

stage derives from Latin *stare*, "stand"

stagnate comes from Latin *stagnum*, "pool"; a stagnant pool is a **stagnum**

in Old English, **stair** meant a whole flight of steps, not a single one

a **stairway** does not necessarily have a handrail or balustrade, but a **staircase** does

stake "post" comes from a Germanic base meaning "pierce, prick"

stalactite is derived from a Greek word meaning "dripping, dropping"—but the base of **stalagmite** means the same thing; **stalagmites** are formed on the ground (point up) while **stalactites** hang from the ceiling (point down)

a **stale** is someone or something used as a decoy

stale first referred to alcoholic drinks that had stood for a long time or were aged or strong

stalemate is a term from chess

stalemate does not end—it is the outcome (stale in **stalemate** is from Anglo-Norman meaning "be placed"); a **standoff** or **deadlock** can end

the **stalk** in a car is the flexible arm holding the mounting by which a seatbelt is secured

a finger of a glove is a **stall**

stallion first referred to a promiscuous person

stalwart came from Old English *stoel-wierthe*, with *stoel* meaning "place" and *wierthe* meaning "worth, worthy," so it could literally be interpreted as "able to stand someone in good stead"

stamen, Latin for "thread of warp," first referred to the warp of a fabric until Pliny applied it to a lily—**stamina** is the plural of this and it first meant "the essential or original elements of something"

to **stammer** is to etymologically be "impeded" in speech

stamp originally meant "crush into small pieces; pound" and "imprint with design by pressure" came into play in the sixteenth century—it being the semantic basis of postage **stamp**

{ **stampede** is from Mexican Spanish *estampida*, "crash, uproar" }

stanch is a verb that means "to stop a flow" while **staunch** is an adjective meaning "steady, loyal"

a **stanchion** is a vertical support beam or post

a growth or array of one type of tree or plant in an area is a **stand**

standard is etymologically complicated—developed by *aphesis* (loss of an initial letter) from Latin *extendere*, "stretch out"—applied first to a flag stretched out from its pole; the sense of "criterion, norm" is probably a metaphor of the notion of "royal **standard**" or banner as being the point from which an authority's commands are issued

a **standee** is a person who is standing

a husband with marital problems is a **stangster**

Italian *stanza* means "a stopping place" and it is a division of a poem or song

technically, a **stanza** is a succession of lines that form a poem or song and a **verse** is either a single line of writing or a series of lines in a song

staphylococcus is from Greek words *staphule*, "bunch of grapes," and *kokkos*, "berry," as the bacterium occur in grapelike clusters

staple first referred to an emporium or mart or a center of trade

star came from the Indo-European *ster-*, "**star**" which was the source of Latin *stella* and Greek *aster*, both meaning "**star**"

starboard is the righthand side and **port** is the lefthand side when facing forward on a ship or boat

Starbucks gets its name from Starbuck, the coffee-loving first mate in Herman Melville's *Moby-Dick*

the etymological notion of **stare** is "fixity" or "rigidity," from a Germanic base meaning "be rigid"

if an animal's hair stands on end, it is **staring**

starling is a diminutive of *stoer*, the Old English name of the bird

if something is **star-litten**, it is lighted by stars

start originally meant "caper, jump, leap" and evolved into its other meanings, not meaning "begin" until the end of the eighteenth century

starve is from Old English *steorfan*, "to die"

stash may be a blend of store and cache

stasiology is the branch of knowledge dealing with political parties

stasis is a period of inactivity or equilibrium (Greek "stoppage")

stat, the medical direction meaning "immediately," is an abbreviation of Latin *statim*

statal means "referring to a state"

state is from Latin *status*, "way of standing; condition, position"; the political sense comes from Latin expressions, including "status"

stateside refers to the continental United States

static once meant "the science of weighing," from Greek *statike* (*tekhne*); the adjective is from Greek *statikos*, "causing to stand"

a **station** is etymologically a "standing," hence, a "place for standing," from Lation statio "standing"

the original "stationers" or "**stationery**" were booksellers who had a regular "station" or shop at a university, unlike most booksellers who were itinerant vendors

stationery is paper and office supplies; **stationary** indicates "in a fixed position"

statistic comes from a German noun describing knowledge dealing with the constitutions and resources of the states of the world

{ the stationary part of a motor is the **stator**; the turning part is the **rotor** }

statue, **stature**, **status** are all based on Latin *stare*, "to stand"

something's **stature** is its normal standing height

staunch first meant "impervious to water"

a **stave** is a rung of a ladder or a curved slat of wood forming part of a barrel

stay, "stop," comes from Latin *stare*, "stand"

stays were originally strips of whalebone glued together and inserted into bodices to stiffen them

stead "place" comes from prehistoric Germanic *stadiz*, from Indo-European, meaning "stand"

steady was derived from stead "place" and it etymologically means "fixed in one place"

steak seems to be related to Old Norse *steikja*, "roast on a spit," and *stikna*, "be roasted"

steal comes from a Germanic base which also gave us **stalk**

stealth is the action or practice of stealing

steam originally denoted "vapor given off by something hot"

a **steam room** is moist air; a **sauna** is dry air

steel is carbon and iron

steep "precipitous" originally meant "very high"

steeple is etymologically a "high" tower

the horse race known as **steeplechase** is so called because originally the riders used a distant steeple as a landmark and goal

steer "young ox" comes from Germanic meaning "strength, sturdiness"

castrated male cows raised for beef are **steers**; castrated males raised as draft animals are **oxen**

the recovery period after childbirth can be called **stegmonth**

a **stein** is defined as a large earthenware beer mug and the German root is literally "stone"

stele or **stela**, from archaeology, is Greek for "standing block or stone"

stellar, relating to stars, is from Latin *stella*, "star"; **stellate** means "in a radiating pattern like a star"

stelliscript is a word for "what is written in the stars"

the **stem** of a tree is etymologically the upright part, the part that "stands" up, from its Germanic base *sta-*, "stand"

stencil was originally a verb meaning "decorate with bright colors," from Latin *stincilla/scintilla*, "spark"

Homer introduced **Stentor**, a very loud herald, in the *Iliad*—which gives us **stentor** "person with a loud voice" and **stentorian**, which originally meant "loud, booming"

step in stepchild (etc.) does not mean "one **step** removed" but goes back to a meaning of **step**, "bereaved"

a **steppe** is a large, semiarid, treeless, but grass-covered plain found in southeastern Europe and in Siberia

stereo comes from Greek *stereos*, "solid," and it was first part of the compound noun *stereometry*

a brick foundation for a building is a **stereobate**

sterile goes back to Indo-European *ster-*, which became Latin *sterilis* before English **sterile**

the British **sterling** is based on a word for "star" because the early Norman pennies had a small star on them

stern, the nautical term, probably comes from Old Norse *styra*, "to steer"

sternum comes from Greek *sternon*, meaning "chest"

the act or sound of sneezing is **sternutation**

sternway is the backward movement of a ship

stertorous is an adjective for "snoring"

stet is Latin for "let it stand," a notation to ignore a correction made to a text

stethoscope is from Greek *stethos*, "breast" and *skopein*, "look at"

John B. **Stetson** (1830–1906) created the **Stetson** hat worn in the American West

stew is from Old French *estuver*, "to steam," and first meant a stove, heated room, hot bath, or cauldron

steward is based on Old English *stig*, "hall, house," and *weard*, "ward"

the longest word typed entirely with one hand is **stewardesses**

sthenic is "marked by excessive energy, especially nervous energy"

a **stich** is a line of poetry

sticker is the full retail price of a car

stickler first described a referee or umpire

stiction means "static friction"

stiff goes back to Germanic *stifaz*, "inflexible"

stifle was probably from Old French *estouffer*, "choke, smother," from Latin *stuppare*, "plug, stop up"

stigma is literal Greek meaning "a mark made by a pointed instrument or brand" the art of punctuation is **stigmeology**

a **stile** is a set of steps that allows people to climb over a fence or wall—or a vertical section of a door or window frame

stiletto (diminutive of Italian *stilo*, "dagger") was first a short dagger before it was a type of shoe

still was used as an adverb in Old English meaning "not changing physical position," and this evolved metaphorically to "never changing" or "always" and then "until now"

stillatitious means "falling in drops"

stilly means "quietly" or "with little movement"

a **stimulant** is a drug; a **stimulus** is anything encouraging an action (but rarely is it a drug)

stimulate is from Latin *stimulus*, "pointed stick for goading animals"

stinko means "extremely drunk"

a **stipe** is a stalk or stem of a seaweed, fungus, or fern frond

{ **stick** comes from Germanic meaning "be sharp, pierce, prick"; the piercing notion led to "becoming fixed in something" and then "adhering" }

stipend comes from Latin elements which translate to "wages" and "to pay"

the etymological basis of **stipulate** has to do with an ancient custom of breaking a straw to seal a bargain, from Latin *stipulari*, "bargain, demand"

the etymological connotations of **stir** are "agitation, disturbance" and a secondary development is the mixing of ingredients

stirrup is literally a rope to step up by, from Old English *stig*, "path, step" and *rap*, "rope"

stitch was first a noun meaning "prick, sting"

stochastic means "random"

liquid used as a base for soups is **stock**

{ **stock** was originally a tree trunk or stem }

the block from which a large bell hangs is a **stock**

playing cards that remain undealt are called the **stock** or **talon**

a **stocking** is a white marking on the lower part of a horse's leg

stocky is a derivative of stock, which first meant "trunk, block of wood" in Old English

a **stogie** (or **stogy**) is named for the Conestoga wagon—as drivers of the wagons rolled tobacco into thin ropes for smoking on long trips, and they are now long, thin cigars

stoic derives from the Stoa Poikile in Athens, which was a portico (*stoa*) painted (*poikile*) with scenes of the destruction of Troy

stoke is a back-formation from stoker

a **stole** is a long or wide fur or scarf worn around a woman's shoulders

stolid means being unemotional and insensitive

stomach comes from Greek *stomakhos*, "gullet"

to be **stomachous** is to be angry, bitter, and disdainful

stomata (singular **stoma**) are microscopic breathing pores on plant surfaces or mouth-like parts of animals

stone is from a Germanic base meaning "solidity" or "stiffness"

to **stonewall** comes from Confederate General Thomas J "**Stonewall**" Jackson from the First Battle of Bull Run (1861)

stooge was first a stagehand or assistant, then such a person serving as a foil or straight man for a lead character

stool's etymological meaning is "stand," from Germanic

an entrance stairway to a building is a **stoop**

the original meaning of **stop** was "close an opening, plug"

a drain plug is a **stop** or **stopper**

store is a shortened version of the obsolete *astor*, "stock of provisions, supplies"

storge is natural love, especially of parents for their children

a **storiette** is a very short story

storiology is the branch of knowledge dealing with the origin and development of legends and tales

stork is etymologically the "stiff-legged bird" and it may be related to "stark," referring to the bird's rigid stance

etymologically, a **storm** is probably a "violent disturbance or agitation" and its meteorological meaning seems to be secondary

a "**story**" was first a "history or an historical account" (from Latin *historia*, "history")

the basin of holy water is called a **stoup** or an **aspersorium**

stout is from a seventeenth-century expression "a **stout** beer" or "a **stout** ale," meaning a strong one; it did not mean a specific type of beer until the nineteenth century

stove, from Middle English "hot-air sweating room," is descended from Latin *extufa/extufare*, possibly from Greek *typhein*, "to give off smoke"

stow is a shortening of bestow

straight is the archaic past participle of stretch

strain comes from Latin *stringere*, "draw tight"

a **strait** is a narrow sea channel and is usually singular

strait in **strait-laced** means "of limited spacial capacity"

strange is a shortening of Old French *estrange*, from Latin *extraneus*, "external, **strange**"

stranger was originally a foreigner, from Old French *estrangier*, from Latin *extraneus*, "person outside"

strangle implies a focus on the result of this process, whereas **strangulate** focuses on the process itself

stratagem comes from a Greek word meaning "be a general" and it is a deception or trick used to gain advantage over an enemy

strategy comes from Greek elements meaning "to lead an army" and it is planning for a war, battle, contest, or competition

straticulate means "arranged in thin layers"

stratum and **strata** in Latin are literally "something spread or laid down"

straw is etymologically something "strewn" on the floor

strawberries got their name because the plant "strews" its runners along the ground; the **strawberry**'s seeds are actually individual fruits and it is termed an aggregate fruit

streak is from Germanic meaning "touch lightly," and it first meant "mark"

streaky describes bacon with alternating strips of fat and lean

a **stream** is smaller than a **river**, a **creek** is smaller than a **stream** but larger than a **brook**; **stream**, **brook**, **creek**, and **rivulet** are applied interchangeably to any small **river**

streck means "in a straight coarse; directly"

street comes from Latin *strata*, "something laid"; **road** is a general term, whereas **street** is narrower in sense and chiefly urban in application: A **street** typically has buildings on either side and is paved

one nine-letter word having one vowel is **strengths**

strepent and **strepitent** mean "noisy"

stress is a shortening of distress or may partially be from Old French *estresse*, "narrowness, oppression," from Latin *strictus*, "drawn tight"

stretch originally meant "lengthening the limbs" or making them more stiff by stretching

a rod between chair legs is a **stretcher**

streusel comes from a German word meaning "to sprinkle"

{ a **stria** is a narrow groove or thin channel, band, or line }

strict comes from Latin *stringere*, "draw tight"

stride has an underlying meaning of "great effort, severity"

strident is from Latin *stridere*, "make a harsh noise; creak"

stridulation is the noise of crickets

strift is an act of striving

the adjective form of owl is **strigine**

strike is from Germanic, meaning "touch lightly"—that evolved into the more violent modern sense

string is etymologically something that has been pulled "taut, stiff"

stringent often means simply "**strict**, strictly regulated" and also "tight or constricted" and emphasizes the narrowness of what is permitted (while **strict** emphasizes the sternness with which something is enforced)

strive seems to be from Old French *estriver*, "quarrel, **strive**"

strong is from Germanic, meaning "severe" or "stiffness, tautness"

a **strop** is a strip of leather used to sharpen a razor

a stanza of a poem or verse is a **strophe** (Greek, literally "turning")

stropping is the cat's habit of sharpening its claws

structure comes from Latin *struere*, "build"

strudel literally means "whirlpool, eddy"— because of its spiral cross-section

the adjective form of ostrich is **struthionine**

stuff first referred to material for making clothes

a **stull** is a hunk or piece of something edible

to **stultify** can mean "to cause to appear stupid or foolish"

stum is the same as **must** in wine fermentation—unfermented or partly fermented grape juice

stumble is from the Germanic base *stum-/stam-* "check, impede"

a pipe's bowl and shank is the **stummel**

cutting down trees is easier than removing the remaining stumps; if someone could not remove a stump, they were "**stumped**" (or "puzzled")

stumping comes from the time of barnstorming politicians who stood on tree stumps to make speeches

stun etymologically means "leave thunderstruck" and comes from Latin *extonare*, "stupefy"

---

 to be **stultiloquent** is to be given to foolish talk or babbling; an instance of speaking foolishly or foolish babbling is **stultiloquy**

---

stubble first referred to stalks left in the ground after reaping

stubborn originally meant "implacable, untameable"

the nubs—square, round, or otherwise—that make up the tread of a sneaker sole are called **studs**

studio is from Latin *studium*, "zeal, devotion, eagerness"

study is based on Latin *studium*, "painstaking application, zeal" (from *studere*, "to be zealous"); **study**'s earliest uses are surprising: "affection, friendliness," an "occupation or pursuit," and "a state of reverie or abstraction; state of perplexity"

stupendous is from Latin *stupere*, "to be stunned"

another name for a stupid person is **stupex**

at one time, **stupid** meant "stunned with surprise," as it comes from Latin *stupere*, "to be amazed"

stupid refers to lack of ability while **ignorant** refers to lack of knowledge

someone who is **sturdy** is etymologically "drunk as a thrush," from Latin *exturdire*, (with that same meaning)

stuthious is the adjective for ostrich

sty, as for pigs, is probably the same word as Old English *stig*, "hall"

style first referred to stylus, a sharp-pointed writing instrument and also to "a written work"

another word for **acupuncture** is **stylostixis**

the **stylus**, or **point**, of a record player is held by the **cartridge**; the base of the turntable is called the **deck**

a **stymie** in golf is obstructing another's ball

suaviation is another word for kissing

Subaru is Japanese for "unite" and is also the common name for the Pleiades, in the constellation Taurus

subaudition is the act of understanding something that is implied but not overly expressed; the act of reading between the lines or otherwise understanding a message that is implicit is **subaudition**

words with a, e, i, o, u once each in reverse order are **subcontinental**, **uncomplimentary**, and **unnoticeably**

subdue is from Latin *subducere*, "draw from below"

subfusc is dark or dusky in color

a **subingression** is a subtle or unseen entrance

subitary is "suddenly or hastily done or made"

subjacent means lying directly under

to **subject** something is etymologically to "throw it under"; the modern sense "topic" is from the notion "that which is operated on by something else"

subjugate is from Latin *subjugare*, "bring under a yoke"

in chemistry, to **sublimate** is to change from a solid to a gas or from a gas to a solid without becoming a liquid

sublime is from Latin *sublimis*, "exalted, lofty"

the Latin word *limen* means "threshold," so something **subliminal** exists just below the threshold or border of conscious awareness

to **suborn** is to induce another to commit an unlawful act

subpoena is literally "under penalty"

subsequent means occurring after: "**subsequent** to the cable installation, the TV worked better"

subside implies the ceasing of turbulence or agitation

substance first referred to the essential nature of something

substantial means considerable or sizeable; **substantive** means actual or firm

substantive should be pronounced SUHB-stuhn-tiv

substitute should only be followed by "for"

subscribe first meant "sign at the bottom of a document"

a **substrate** is the surface on which an organism lives or moves

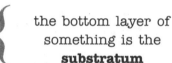

{ the bottom layer of something is the **substratum** }

the ultimate source of **subtle** is Latin *subtilis*, "finely woven," a weaving term, from *sub tela*, "beneath the lengthwise threads of a loom"

to **subtract** something is etymologically to "pull it away," from Latin *subtrahere*, "pull away"

subtrahend is the amount subtracted in a math problem

to **subumber** means "to shelter"

suburb is from Latin elements meaning "near to" and "city"

subversion is literally the "turning over" of something—what was on top is turned under

fruit preserved in sugar is **succade**

sullage is waste from household sinks, showers, and baths, but not toilets; also figuratively meaning filth or refuse

the permanent teeth that erupt to replace baby teeth are called **succedaneous** teeth—substitute teeth

to **succeed** someone is to etymologically "go next to them" or "follow them"; this evolved into "doing well, prospering"

success first meant "result or outcome," whether good or bad

> **succor** is assistance or relief in time of distress

succotash—cooked corn, lima beans, and butter—comes from Narragansett *msiquatash*

succulent is from Latin *succus*, "juice"

someone who **succumbs** to something is etymologically "lying down under"

etymologically, **such** means "so formed"

suck is part of a large Indo-European family *seug-/seuk-*, which imitates the sound

a **sucker** originally was "baby still at the breast" and took a metaphorical meaning "gullible person" later

sudden is from Latin *sub-*, "up to," and *ire*, "come, go," making *subitus*, "come or go up stealthily"

sudoku is a number/logic puzzle consisting of a nine-by-nine grid of squares, each divided into nine three-by-three squares; it originated in New York but the name is Japanese *Su*, "number," and *doku*, "single, unmarried," and was first called "number place puzzle"

suds was probably borrowed from Middle Dutch *sudse*, probably from a Germanic base meaning "boil"

sue, from Latin *sequi*, "follow," first meant "follow, go in pursuit of"

gants de **suede** is French for "gloves of Sweden" but now refers to the undressed kidskin that we know as **suede**

suet is from Latin *sebum*, "tallow"

to **suffer** something is etymologically to "hold or sustain it from underneath," from Latin *sufferre*, "sustain"

sufficient first meant "legally satisfactory"

suffocate is from Latin elements meaning "below" and "throat"

suffrage is from Latin *suffragium*, "voting tablet"

suffuse means "to spread over or through as fluid or light does; to flush or fill"

sugar traces back to Arabic *sukkar* or Sanskrit *sarkara*, through Old French *cucre*

to **suggest** something is etymologically to "carry it under," from Latin *sub-*, "under" and *gerere*, "bring, carry"

suggestion started out as "prompting to evil, temptation by the devil"

to **sugillate** is to beat black and blue; a **suggilation** is a black-and-blue mark

suit originally meant "body of followers, retinue" and then "set of things in general"; a **suitor** is etymologically a "follower" and first meant "frequenter of a place" (from Latin *secutor*)

sukiyaki derives from *suki*, "slice, spade" and *yaki*, "broil, grill"

sulk was a back-formation of sulky (from obsolete *sulke*, "sluggish")

the root sense of **sullen** is "alone, self-enclosed"

Arabic **sultan** meant "ruler," from Aramic *shultana*, "power"

sultry comes from the obsolete *sulter*, "swelter"

sum is from Latin *summus*, "highest"

sumi-e is Japanese for "ink painting"

The word **summer** derives from Old Norse *sumar*, but ultimately is from Proto-Germanic. By the late 1500s to early 1600s, it locked into its current spelling. The term **midsummer** actually refers to the day of the **summer** solstice as well as the "middle of **summer**." Its formation was patterned on words like midday, midnight, and midwinter.

a **sump** is any low-lying land or pit that receives and collects drainage water, as a cesspool

etymologically, **sumptuous** denotes "costly, expensive" from Latin *sumptus*, "expense"

the language used to describe the **Sun**'s course, its rising and setting, etc., is based upon the old view of the **Sun** as a body moving through the zodiac, rising above, passing across the heavens, and sinking below the horizon, etc.

columna lucis was translated to Old English *sunnebeam*, "sun post," to **sunbeam**

the **Sunbelt** states of the U.S. are Florida, Louisiana, Texas, New Mexico, Arizona, California, and sometimes Georgia

a **suncatcher** is a window ornament, especially of colored glass

Sunday is from Latin *Dies Solis*, "Sun's Day"

sundry can mean "having an existence apart; separate"

sup is a small bite or mouthful

super is from Latin *super* "above"

superannuated is disqualified due to advanced age or infirmity

if a building or monument is **superb**, it is of magnificent proportions and grand in aspect or decoration

supercilious, "haughty," comes from Latin *super*, "above," and *cilium*, "eyebrow," i.e. "with raised eyebrows"

a **superette** is a small supermarket

superficial literally means "of the surface," from Latin *superficies*, "surface" (*super-*, "above," and *facies*, "face")

Superglue is a trade name; the generic term is "**contact adhesive**"

superincumbent means "on the surface of" or "lying or resting upon"

the word **superman** was used by George Bernard Shaw as an attempt to translate the German Übermensch, a term coined by Nietzsche

supermundane refers to that which is above the earth, transcendent, and unearthly

supernal means "celestial, heavenly"

supernatant means "swimming on the surface"

{ **sundae** is an alteration of Sunday—either because leftover ice cream was sold on Sunday or the dish was only served on that day }

sunflowers are so named because they resemble the full sun and they turn in every direction daily, whether the sun is out or not

sunscreen works chemically to filter UV rays; **sunblock** works physically to deflect UV rays

supernova refers to a star's explosive death

an actor with a nonspeaking role is a **supernumerary**

supersede first meant "postpone"

to **supinate** is to turn the hand and forearm so the palm faces upward

supine is lying face upward, **prone** and **prostrate** are lying face downward—and **prostrate** suggests throwing oneself down, while **recumbent** is lying flat in any position

supper started out as a meal of soup and bread and was originally spelled souper

supplant literally means "trip up," from Latin *supplantare*, "trip up, overthrow"

go has an unusual past tense, formed from a different root than its present tense, which is a process called **suppletion**; **suppletion** is the replacement within a series of inflected forms of one form by an unrelated form—an extreme example of this being be/am/are/was

someone who **supplicates** is etymologically "bending or folding up underneath" or "kneeling to pray"

{ **supplosion** is stamping the feet in disapproval }

supply is from Latin *supplere*, "complete, fill up"

support is from Latin *supportare*, "bring, carry, convey"

suppose seems to come from Latin *supponere*, "put under"

suppositious means "supposed, assumed, hypothetical"; **supposititious** means "spurious, phony, bogus"

suppository is literally "something placed underneath"

suppurate is a verb for "create or secrete pus"

supputation is the act of computing or calculating

supreme is ultimately from Latin *supra*, "above" which begat *supremus*, "highest," before **supreme**

sural pertains to the calf of the leg

to **surbate** is to tire the feet with excessive walking

sure and **secure** are doublets from Latin *securus*, "without care," but one came directly into English while the other became *sur* in Old French, before "**sure**"

surf the Net originated from the term channel-**surf** for TV

surface was coined in French and modeled on Latin *superficies*, "**surface**"

surfeit can mean overindulgence, especially in food or drink

to **surge** first meant "come to anchor"

surgeon is from Greek *kheir*, "hand," and *ergon*, "work"

Surinam was formerly Dutch *Guiana*

surly originally meant "lordly; majestic"

surnames were not widespread until the thirteenth century and grew from the custom of adding the place of domicile or provenance, trade, or some descriptive characteristic to the Christian name to aid in identification

surprise was first an unexpected seizure or attack

surquidry is another word for arrogance

surrender is etymologically to "give up," from French *surrendre*, "deliver over, give up"

surreptitious is based on Latin elements meaning "secretly" and "seize"

a **surrogate** is etymologically someone who has been "asked" to take the place of another, from Latin *subrogare*, "nominate an alternative candidate"

surround first meant "overflow"

to **survey** something is etymologically to "oversee" it, from Latin *supervidere*

survive comes from Latin *super*, "in addition" and *vivere*, "live"

with its prefix *sus-*, "up," **susceptible** refers to what "takes up" or absorbs like a sponge

sushi in Japanese means "it is sour"; the *su* in **sushi** means "vinegar" and the one ingredient common to all **sushi** is vinegared rice

suspect is from Latin *suspicere*, "look up at," which evolved metaphorically to "look up to" and "look at secretly," then "look at distrustfully"

to **suspend** something is etymologically to "hang it up"

suspenders in the UK is **garters** in the U.S.; **braces** in the UK are **suspenders** in the U.S.

to **suspire** is to sigh

to **suss**, an abbreviation of suspect, is to figure or work out, discover the truth about

soft whispering or muttering is **susurrus**

sutile means "made by sewing"

a seamlike joint of a bone, fruit, or shell is a **suture** (from Latin *suere*, "sew")

swab, as in "mop the decks," is a back-formation from swabber, "sailor who mops the decks," from a Germanic base meaning "splash"

swaddle is derived from swathe

a **swadge** is a chunk or mass

to **swaff** is to come one over another, like waves upon a shore

swag is one's goods carried in a pack or bundle

swain, now jocular for "lover," was once a word for swineherd

swale is another word for wetlands or a depression in a wet area

swallow, the bird, is based on a root word meaning "swirl" or "flash"

swami is Sanskrit for master or prince

a **swamp** (from Germanic meaning "fungus" or "sponge") is wetland that's more wet than land and supports surface-breaking plants and trees like cypresses

the **swan** got its name for the unmusical sound it makes; their singing during their final minutes begat the word "**swansong**"

a **swapword** is a compound word where the first and last parts can be swapped to make a new word

sward is the rind of bacon or pork

a faint or sudden loss of consciousness can also be called a **swarf**

{ **swarf** is metal particles removed by a cutting, filing, or grinding tool }

swarm may go back to an Indo-European base which is behind Latin *susurrus*, "hum," and Sanskrit *svarati*, "it sounds"

swarthy goes back to the Indo-European base that begat Latin *sordidus*, "dirty"

to **swarve** is to choke with sediment

swashbuckle is a back-formation from **swashbuckler**, originally a warrior who struck his shield with his sword as a sign of aggression (swash, "hit," and buckler, "shield")

swasivious means "agreeably persuasive"

swastika means "benediction or well-being" and was originally a good-luck sign

swat "slap" was first a variant of squat

a path cut by a mower is a **swath**

sway implies influences that are not resisted or irresistible, with resulting change in character or course of action

to **sweal** is to set fire to, burn, or cause to dry or wither; also, of a candle, to melt away

swear originally meant "take an oath"

swot originally was a dialectal variant of **sweat**

a **sweater** was first clothes worn by a person or horse during exercise to induce sweating

an original meaning of **sweating** was doing tedious work for low wages—so **sweatshop** was where that took place

swedge means "to leave without paying"

sweep comes from a Germanic base meaning "bend, swing" and **swipe** originally was a dialectal variant of **sweep**

the allusion of **sweepstakes** is that one sweeps or takes all the stakes in a game

sweet is from Indo-European *swad-*; the noun **sweet** for "confectionery" is presumably short for sweetmeat

The sweet potatoes and yams in the stores are the same vegetable, and a **sweet potato** is a root but a russet potato is a tuber; true yams are not sold anywhere except a handful of specialty grocers—sweet potatoes are inside every mislabeled **yam** can. Black slaves brought to North America saw the resemblance of the **sweet potato** to their native plant, the true yam or nyami; hence, our misnamed **sweet potato**.

sweetmeat is made from fruit and **sweetbread** is made from meat (and is not sweet)

a slow wave that does not break is a **swell**

swelt means "be overpowered or oppressed by heat," hence **swelter**

swerked is troubled or gloomy

> **swerve** is related to Middle Dutch *swerven*, "to stray"

a **swesby** is one who can be relied upon

swidden is an area cleared for cultivation by the slash-and-burn method

the etymological meaning of **swift** seems to be "moving along a course," with speed as a secondary development

swims is the longest word with 180-degree symmetry

swindler and **swindle** are from German *Schwindler*, "promoter of wild schemes; cheat"

swine is the collective (and ancestral) term for domesticated pigs and hogs; a **hog** is 120 pounds and ready for market, while a **pig** is immature and weighs less

swing comes from Germanic, meaning "violent circulatory movement"; the sense of "oscillate" did not emerge until the sixteenth century

swink is hard labor and to **swink** is to labor or work hard at something; **forswunk** is utterly exhausted from hard labor

swipe is probably wipe and sweep combined

the bushy tip of a cow's tail is the **switch**

Switzerland is actually Confédération Helvétique in French, which gives the initials of CH for the country's symbol

a **swivet** is a state of agitation

swizz can be a disappointment or swindle

swop and **swap** originally meant "strike; hit"

sword's etymological meaning may be "stinger; causer of pain"

a nickname for the **swordfish** is **broadbill**

to **swot** is to work or study at school or college

the wealthy inhabitants of Sybaris, an ancient Greek colony in Italy, gave their name to **sybarite,** "pleasure-seeker"

the **sycamore** is etymologically "fig mulberry" or "mulberry mulberry," from Greek *sukomoros*, (from *moron*, "mulberry," and Greek *sukon*, "fig," or Hebrew *shiqmah*, "mulberry")

sycophant was originally an informer or a slanderous accuser

a **syllabary** is a collector of words

syllable's Greek base meant "bring together," as it is a unit of pronunciation without interruption

the word **syllabus** is the result of a misprint, originally from Greek *sittuba*, "label; table of contents," but in Cicero's "Letters to Atticus," it was spelled syllabos and it was later changed to **syllabus**

a **sylloge** is a collection or summary

a **syllogism** is etymologically something "reasoned together" or "inferred"

sylvans are native or inhabitants of forests or woods

symbiosis is communal living

symbol first meant "summary of doctrine; a creed"

symmetry is formed from *sym-* and *metron*, "measure"—and symmetrical is patterned after geometrical

sympathy means the stimulation in a person of feelings that are similar in kind to those that affect another person; **empathy** means a mental or affective projection into the feelings or state of mind of another person

symphony originally meant "harmony" or "a sounding together," and was not used for a piece of music or a band until the late eighteenth century

the moderator or chair of a symposium is a **symposiarch**; a master of ceremonies on a TV awards show is technically a **symposiarch**

symposium originally meant "drinking party"

symptom comes from a Greek base meaning "fall upon, happen to"

synagogue is from Greek elements meaning "coming together"

synapse is Greek for "clasp together"

synchroneity is the state of happening, existing, or arising at the same time

in 1953, **synchronicity** is the name given by the Swiss psychologist Carl Jung to the phenomenon of events which coincide in time and appear meaningfully related but have no discoverable causal connection

a word shortened by omitting a sound or letter is a **syncope**

a combining of different things is **syncrasy**

a **syndicate** was originally a "body of syndics" or delegates, from Greek *sundikos*, "public advocate"

a **synecdoche** is a figure of speech in which a part is made to represent the whole or vice versa, as in "Chicago won by six runs" (meaning "Chicago's baseball team"); it is pronounced suh-NEK-duh-kee

synergy can mean "the whole is greater than the sum of the parts"

synesthesia is the commingling of the five senses

syngenesophobia is dislike or fear of relatives

 syndrome is from Greek elements meaning "run together" and is a group of **symptoms**; **Synopsis** literally means "seeing together"

the root of **synod** is "(assembly come to) by road" (Greek *hodos*, "road")

a **synodite** is a traveling companion

a **synonymicon** is a lexicon of synonyms

synopsis is from *syn-* and Greek *opsis*, "view," ("seeing together")

one's personal set of understood syntactical constructions is one's **syntacticon**

 the pattern of word arrangement in sentences is **syntax**

a go-with-the-flow person is a **syntone**

syphilis takes its name from a poem by Girolamo Fracastoro (1483–1553) about a shepherd's death from a pox, the first sufferer of this disease

Syrah and **Shiraz** are the same wine grape

syringes get their name for the cylindrical shape, from Greek *surigx*, "pipe"

the throat part producing a bird's voice is the **syrinx**

syrup gets its name from Arabic *sarab*, "beverage," at first having the medicinal sense

syssarcosis is the joining of two or more bones by muscle

a meal shared with others is **syssition**

a **system** is etymologically something that is "brought together," from Greek *sustema*, "combined or organized whole, formed from many parts"

something affecting the body generally is **systemic**

systemic means "deep-seated, integral, built into the system"; **systematic** means "periodic, occurring with regularity"

a **syzygy** occurs when all the planets of the solar system align

{ **T cushion** is the technical name for the removable cushion in a stuffed chair, which looks like a broad, squat T }

the flap of a shoe is the **tab**

tabac, the color, is French for tobacco

tabanid refers to any bloodsucking insect, like a horsefly

Tabasco is made from chiles picked near the **Tabasco** River

the common **tabby** cat derives its name from silk with a wavy pattern, from Arabic *utabi*, the name of the quarter in Baghdad where the silk was made

a **tabernacle** was first a portable tent sanctuary for the Ark of the Covenant during a time of exodus by the Israelites

tabernacle and **tavern** are both derived from Latin *taberna*, "hut or booth"

the socks with the separate big toe worn by the Japanese are called **tabi**

tablature comes from an Italian word for "set to music"

Latin *tabula*, "plank, **table**" or "list," is the source of **table**—and in the past, **table** was applied to the board used for games such as chess and backgammon, which is the origin of "turn the tables"

table tennis is often called by its trademarked name, **Ping-Pong**

a **tableau** is a graphic or vivid description

tablet is from Old French *tablete*, from a diminutive of Latin *tabula*, "list, plank, **tablet**"

tabloid, first a proprietary name of a medicinal tablet, became popular as a term for "compressed or summarized news"

taboo is from Tongan *tabu*, "set apart," and was brought into English by the explorer Captain Cook in 1777

a **taboret** is an artist's multi-drawer cabinet table for tools and materials

tacenda are things not to be mentioned or made public, things better left unsaid; **tacit** means "unspoken, silent" or "implied, inferred"

tachometer is literally a "speed measurer," from the Greek root *tach*, "speed"

tachycardia, from the Greek root *tach*, "speed," is a medical condition in which the heart races uncontrollably

tachygraphy is the art or practice of quick writing, as shorthand

an early meaning of **tacit** was "wordless, noiseless" (from Latin *tacere*, "be silent")

taciturn means habitually untalkative

tack, the fastening, comes from French *tache*, "nail, fastening"
tackle derives from German *takel*, from *taken*, "lay hold of"

taco in Spanish means "roll, wad" or "stopper"

tact first referred to the sense of touch (from Latin *tactus*, "touch, sense of touch"); **taction** in the action of touching

an illustration used to fill the page at the end of a chapter (etc.) is a **tailpiece**

Taiwan was formerly Formosa

take was borrowed from Old Norse *taka*, probably from the Germanic root *tækanan

use **take place** for scheduled events; use **occur** when something is accidental

the winged sandals seen in pictures of some gods and goddesses are **talaria** (singular is talar)

a **tale** is etymologically something that is "told"

 tactic is etymologically "arrangement, setting in order," from Greek *tassein*, "put in order" or "arrange in battle formation"

tactical comes from Greek *taktikos/taktos*, "arranged, ordered"

tactual means "arising from or due to touch" and **tactile** means "capable of, allows for being touched"

tad first referred to a mean person

tadpole literally means "toad head" and **polliwog** is "wiggling head"—each meaning the tailed legless larva of an amphibian

tae-bo is Korean for "leg boxing"

taffeta goes back to Persian *taftah*, "silken cloth, linen clothing"

taffy is actually the same as **toffee**—just a variant spelling

tahini, a paste of sesame seed, is from Arabic *tahana*, "crush, grind"

tail is from an Indo-European root meaning "something long and thin"

the original **tailgates** were gates that dropped down at the tails of wagons

tailor comes from French *tailleur*, "cutter" (of cloth)

a **talent**, from Greek *talanton*, "balance, weight," is from *tal*, "to lift or bear," and was an ancient unit of weight—eventually acquiring a figurative meaning of inclination of the will or disposition

talion is punishment corresponding to the nature of a crime

talisman is derived from Greek *telesmon*, "consecrated object"

talk is derived from the Germanic base of tale or tell

talkingstock (patterned after laughingstock) is one who is the object of much conversation

the early meaning of **tall** was "quick" as it comes from Old English *getoel*, "quick, ready"; the meaning "of great height" did not develop until the sixteenth century

tally comes from a Latin word for "cutting; rod or stick" and it was first such a thing that was scored to represent a debt or payment

Talmud means "instruction" in Hebrew

talon is the part of the bolt that goes in the lock

the **talons** are the claws of a bird of prey

talon is from the Latin word for "ankle" and **talus** is the human ankle bone

talus is rock fragments piled up at the base of a cliff or steep slope

an embroidery or needlepoint frame is a **tambour**

the rolling top of a rolltop desk is the **tambour**

tambourine is from Persian *tabir*, "drum"

tame came from Indo-European *dom*, "**tame**, subdue"

the **tam-o'-shanter** hat is named after the hero of a poem by the same name, written by Scotsman Robert Burns

{ **tamper** first meant "to work in clay" or "temper in clay" }

tampon is a variant of a French word meaning "plug, stopper"

tan comes from a Latin word for "oak" and the word first referred to the crushed bark of the oak or other trees, especially in its use to convert hides into leather

tandem, from Latin, was literally "eventually, at length" and then metaphorically "acting conjointly"; in the 1880s it was transferred from a two-horse carriage to a bicycle with two seats, one behind the other

the tongue of a snake is the **tang**—as is the pin or a buckle or prong or tine of an implement

a **tangelo** is a hybrid of a tangerine and pomelo

contact at a single point is a **tangent**

tangent is a sudden divergence, something which "touches" the original subject

but then veers off in another direction; **tangential** means "touching lightly; incidental"

a **tanger** is a person who has a noticeable effect on others

tangerines got their name from Tangiers, Morocco, where they were first imported

tangible means literally "touchable," from Latin *tangere*, "touch"—it is literally something that can be touched but also can be a feeling so strong that it seems "touchable"

tanglefoot is slang for an intoxicating beverage, especially whiskey

tango is an American Spanish alteration of *tangu*, "to dance," from Africa

a **tangram** is a square cut into seven pieces to be reassembled into different figures (a Chinese toy puzzle)

tank may have come from Gujarati *tanku* or Marathi *tanke*, "underground cistern," from Sanskrit *tadaga*, "pond"

a **tankard** was first a large tub for carrying liquid

a **tanling** is a person tanned by the sun

a **tansu** is a Japanese chest of drawers or cupboard

tantalize is based on Tantalus, Lydian king of Greek mythology; he killed his son and the punishment was the provision of fruit and water to him, which he could never reach

tantamount is from an earlier verb of the same spelling, meaning "amount to as much"—from Italian *tanto montare*

fanfare on a trumpet or horn is **tantara**

the smallest pig in a litter is the **tantony**

tao or **dao** (pronounced DOW, DAU) is Chinese for "path, way" or "right way of life"

tapas, from *tapa*, Spanish for "cover, lid," are snacks to accompany wine, etc.

tapénade, a spread of capers, comes from Provençal *tapéno* "capers"

taper is a dissimilated form of Latin *papyrus*, the pith of which was used for candle wicks; now it is a long slender candle

tapestry is based on French *tapis*, "carpet"

the **tapetum** is the reflective layer of choroid in the eyes of some animals which aids night vision and makes the eyes glow in the dark

taphonomy is the study of the processes (burial, decay, preservation) that affect animal and plant remains as they become fossils

tapioca comes from Tupi-Guarani *tipi*, "residue," and *ok/og*, "squeeze out"

a **tapis** is any cloth with colorful designs

taps, the bugle call for lights out, was originally a drum roll and got its name from the tapping of the drums; **taps** are also called **last post**

tapster is another name for bartender

a **taqueria** is a taco restaurant

tar is etymologically a substance produced from trees, from Indo-European *drew*, "tree"

a **taradiddle** is a little lie

the **tarantula** is named for Taranto, a town in southern Italy

the male equivalent of hysteria is **tarassis**

taratantara is pretentious talk

{ the sound of a bugle or trumpet can be called **taratantara** }

tardigrade means "walking or moving slowly or sluggishly"

tardy are from Latin *tardus*, "slow"

tare is the container's weight deducted to find the contents' weight

target is a diminutive of an archaic synonym, targe, and originally was a round shield

tariff is from Arabic *ta'rifah*, "notification, explanation," and was first a multiplication or arithmetic table (literally "list of charges")

tarmac (another word for "runway") and **macadamization** are named for John L. McAdam (1756–1836), Scottish engineer

a **tarn** is a small mountain lake, often created by glaciers

tarnish descends from French *terne*, "dark, dull"

tarpaulin—originally cloth treated with tar—comes from tar and pall

a **tarriance** is a delay or procrastination—or a temporary stay at a place or a sojourn

tarry can mean "a short story" or "a sojourn"

plaid and **tartan** are synonymous in informal use

tartle (from Scottish) is to hesitate in recognizing a person or thing, as happens when you are introduced to someone whose name you cannot recall; so you say, "Pardon my **tartle**!"

tartufo is the Italian word for "truffle"

task comes from Latin *taxare*, "censure, charge"

Tasmania is named for Dutch navigator Abel Tasman (1603–1659)

tassel was first a clasp and it was an Old French word

tasseography is the art of divination by means of reading tea leaves

taste also had the sense "touch" in the beginning and may be a blend of Latin *tangere*, "to touch," and *gustare*, "to **taste**"

tasteful can mean "having many different tastes or hobbies"

tat are worthless articles

the edge of a handkerchief is the **tat**

tatter or tatters is a scrap of cloth, from Old Norse *totrar*, "rags"

tattersall is named for Richard **Tattersall** (1724–1795), an English horseman and founder of a company whose horse blankets used the pattern

tattoo in the military sense was originally written tap-too, from a Dutch word meaning "close the tap" (of a cask) which was told to soldiers when they were expected to return to their quarters

taunt is from French for "tit for tat" as it is a provoking remark

taupe is from French, literally "moleskin" or "mole"

another way of saying redundant is **tautological**

a **tautonym** is a "name that repeats itself"—as in some two-word classification terms (taxonomic binomials), such as gorilla gorilla—and it also denotes words with two identical parts, like tutu or muumuu

tavern is derived from Latin *taberna*, "inn, tavern"

a **taw** is a large marble

taw is a square-dance partner or the starting line in any sport or race

to **taw** is to prepare a natural product for use

tawdry is short for **tawdry** lace—a lace or ribbon worn as a necklace of the sixteenth and seventeenth centuries—which is itself a contraction of "St. Audrey's lace" for a patron saint who wore showy necklaces

tax is from Latin *taxare*, "censure, charge, or compute"

taxi is an abbreviation of taximeter and taxicab

taxicab is a combination of Greek *taxa*, "charge, cost," and French *cabriolet*, "cab"

the stuffing of dead animals is called **taxidermy**

the fare device in taxis is the **taximeter**

taxonomy, a scheme of classification, is from Greek *taxis*, "arrangement," and *nomia*, "distribution"; for plants, the **taxonomy** in descending order is division, class, order, family, genus, species, and for animals, phylum, class, order, family, genus, species

{ a **tazza** is a saucer-shaped cup, especially one mounted on a foot }

tazzled is another word for entangled

Amoy Chinese *t'e* became "**tea**," coming through Malay *te/the* into Dutch and then to English

teach in Old English (c 888) first meant "to present or point out; instruct" and the word is of Germanic origin; the word **teacher** was first used to mean "that which points out or shows," and then quickly became used in the sense of "instructor"

teak comes from Malayalam *tekka* as the tree grows in India's monsoon forests

teal the color comes from **teal** the duck

team as a noun once meant "the bearing of children"

to comb hair toward the roots to bulk it up is to **tease** or **backcomb**; to **tease** wool or another fiber is to pull it apart into separate fibers

a tool for raising the nap of something is a **teasel**

a **teaspoon** is five milliliters

technical is based on **technic**, an adjective meaning "pertaining to art," from Greek *tekhne*, "art"

a **technicism** is a technical term or expression

technicity is the extent to which a person, group, or culture is technically adept

to **technicize** is to make technical

technification is the adoption or imposition of technical methods

a **technolator** is a person unduly worshipful of technology and electronic gadgets

technology, from Greek *tekhnologia* and its root *tekhne*, "art or craft," meant "systematic treatment"—as a study of the arts

tectonic also means "related to building or construction"; **tectonics** can mean the production of practical and beautiful buildings

to **ted** is to turn over and spread out for drying

teddy, as in bear, was named for U.S. President Theodore Roosevelt (1858–1919), who enjoyed bear-hunting

tee is a Scottish golf term, a shortening of the earlier teaz, which has no known origin

teem first meant "give birth to" or "be or become pregnant"

teemful is fruitful, productive, prolific

teen as the suffix **-teen** originated as an inflected form of ten; **teen** as a noun was

tegestology is collecting of beer mats or coasters

a **telarian** is a webmaking spider

the word **telecommuting** came into the language in 1973

the study of design in nature is **teleology**, but the word's basic meaning is "the study of ends or purposes"—attempts to understand the purpose of a natural occurrence by looking at its results

a **telepheme** is a telephone message or telephone communication

telephone is from Greek *tele*, "afar," and *phone*, "sound, voice," and it was first called the speaker telegraph

telescope is created from elements meaning "at a distance" and "looking"

telesis is progress through wise and conscious planning or the intelligent direction of effort toward a goal

television literally means "see at a distance"

 as far back as Old English, **tell** has had another sense "to count one by one" and it is often used to describe counting off rosary beads

derived from this in the seventeenth century with teenage in 1921 and teenager in 1941

teenful means troublesome or irritating

teeter comes from Old Norse *titra*, "shake, shiver"

teetotal is total plus "tee" as an emphatic extension (reproducing the first letter)—thereby meaning "total total" (reduplication) in reference to total abstinence, first used to refer to this by Richard Turner in a speech in 1833

Teflon, a combo of tetra and fluoro and on, is patterned on nylon and rayon

a **teller** was originally someone who kept the tallies (Anglo-French *talier*) and counted the money

tellurian means of or inhabiting the earth

telmatology is the branch of geography concerned with wetlands

telos is an ultimate end or object

temerarious is acting rashly or recklessly

someone who behaves with **temerity** is etymologically "acting in the dark," from Latin *temeritas*, "rashness," from *temere*, "blindly" or "rashly"

temper, originally a proportionate mixture, is from Latin *temperare*, "to mix correctly; regulate" or "to keep within limits"

tempera is short for Italian *pingere a tempera*, "painting in temper," from the verb *temperare*, "to mix properly"—referring to the egg yolk emulsion used as a binder

temperance is from Latin *temperantia*, "moderation," from *temperare*, "restrain, keep within limits"; however, historically, **temperance** has usually meant the prohibition of all alcoholic drink

temperature first described a "state of being mixed or tempered" and was once a mean between two opposites or a temperate condition

a **tempersome** or **tempery** person has a quick temper

tempest is from Latin *tempestas*, simply "period of time" and it gradually came to mean "bad weather, storm"

template first meant a horizontal piece of timber in a wall, or spanning a window or doorway, to take and distribute the pressure of a girder, or of joists or rafters, i.e., a frame or framework

temple is from Latin *templum*, "open, consecrated space"

tempo derives from Latin *tempus*, "time"; the plural of **tempo** is tempi

a **tempo** is a turn at chess

the word **temporal** derives from Latin and **chronological** is from Greek; **temporal** is "having to do with time as opposed to eternity, having to do with earthly life as opposed to heavenly existence, having to do with time as opposed to space" while **chronological** is "arranged according to **temporal** order"

temporary is from Latin *temporarius*, from *tempus*, "time"

to **temporize** is to draw out a discussion to gain time

tempt first meant "put to the test" and "attempt"

tempura is not a Japanese name—but a name that evolved from Portuguese *tempero*, "seasoning"

temulent means drunken or intoxicated; **temulency** is intoxication

ten and the family of "ten" words go back to Indo-European *dekm*

tenable means "holdable," "capable of being held or defended; reasonable"

tenant comes from Latin *tenere*, "to hold"

tend, as in tending a flock, is short for "attend"; **tendance** is looking after or caring for something

tendent is "having a tendency to or towards"

tendentious or **tendential** means "having an underlying purpose"

tender goes back to the Indo-European root *ten*, "stretch"

tenderloin is the most tender cut of meat—in beef, from below the short ribs and made up of the psoas muscle

tendon is based on Greek *teinein*, "stretch"

tendresse is a feeling of fondness or love

tendril is etymologically a "tender shoot"

a **tenebrio** is a person who lurks in the dark (tenebrity is "darkness")

tenebrous means gloomy or dark

tenement first meant "holding as a possession"

 Tennessee's name is from Spanish *Tenaqui*, a Cherokee settlement

tennis is from French *tenez*, "take, receive," which was originally called out by the server to the opponent

a **tennist** is one who plays tennis

tenor, as in general sense or meaning, is from Latin, literally "continuous course"

tenor, the voice, is between baritone and alto or countertenor; **tenorino** is a high **tenor**

tense is from Latin *tendere*, "stretch"

tension was first a medical term for the condition of being physically strained

tent comes from a Latin word for "stretch" as early tents were made from cloth or skins stretched on poles

tentacle goes back to a Latin word *tentare*, "to feel"

an experiment or attempt can be called a **tentamen**

a **tenter** is a type of framework for stretching cloth—and on which **tenterhooks** are used; figuratively, a **tenterhook** is something on which something is stretched

someone's **tenue** is their general appearance, bearing, or manner

tenuous comes from Latin *tenuis*, "thin"

tenure always emphasizes the notion of holding on to something

a **teocalli** is a Mexican temple standing on a truncated pyramid

tepee is from Sioux or Dakota *tipi*, "tent, dwelling," from *ti*, "to dwell," and *pi*, "to use for"

tephra are rock fragments ejected by a volcano (Greek literally "ashes")

tepid is from Latin *tepere*, "be warm"

tequila's name comes from **Tequila**, Mexico, a center for its production—and it is a variety of mescal, from the agave plant

terdiurnal is three times a day

to **terebrate** is to bore or penetrate

tergiversate comes from Latin elements meaning "turn one's back"

terikayi is Japanese, from *teri*, "gloss," and *yaki*, "grill, roast"

term, **terminal**, **terminate**, and **terminology** come from Latin *terminus*, "boundary, end"; terms, specialized words or expressions, tend to have precise boundaries of meaning and each field has its own **terminology**

termagant was introduced in medieval morality plays as a violent, turbulent, overbearing person in long flowing robes

a **terminus** is simply the end or conclusion of something, but a **terminal** is a structure or installation erected at a **terminus**

a **termitarium** is a termites' nest

terpsichorean means pertaining to dance and **euterpean** means pertaining to music

terrace is from Latin *terra*, "earth," as is **terrestrial**, **terrier**, and **territory**

terrain was once the exercise training ground for horses at a riding school

a **terran** is an earth inhabitant

the word **terrapin** comes from the Algonquin *toarebe* or *turupem*, meaning "little turtle"

{ the ring on an animal collar for attaching a leash is the **terret** }

terribilità is the emotional intensity of an artist

terrible and **terrific** once meant "causing terror"

a **terrier** is a dog that "takes the earth" or unearths its prey (Latin *terra*, "earth")

terrine is French, literally "made of earthenware"—ultimately from Latin *terra*, "earth"

terror is stronger than **horror**, though it usually lasts for a shorter time

terry is the cloth with raised uncut loops of thread on both sides, used especially for towels—but the word's origin is unknown

use **terse** to characterize brevity or succinctness of expression in a person; **concise** is used to characterize this in a message

terve is an old word for "turn upside-down"

to **tesselate** is to form into a mosaic pattern

tessera, the pieces used in making a mosaic, comes from Greek *tesseres*, "four," for the four corners of these pieces; the plural is tesserae

test was first a pot (cupel) used to treat alloys or ore and it comes from Latin *testu/testum*, "earthen pot"

a **testament** is a document in which something is testified to (will, covenant, book of the Bible); a **testimonial** is a written or spoken expression of regard for a person's service or accomplishments

the canopy over a bed is the **tester**

testicle comes from Latin *testis* with the same meaning, possibly from *testa*, "pot, shell"

to express one's personal religious belief is to **testify**

testify comes from Latin *testis*, "witness," from Indo-European roots meaning "three" and "stand"—i.e., a witness was a third person standing by; when a witness gives **testimony**, he is literally "standing as a third party" to the defendant and the plaintiff—and **testimony** originally referred to the tablets containing the Ten Commandments

testudinate means "slow-moving; like a turtle" (from Latin *testudo*, "tortoise") and it also describes something curved or vaulted like a turtle shell

testy means etymologically "heady," from French *teste*, "head," and Latin *testa*, "tile, earthenware pot" which was a humorous word for "head"

a **tête-à-tête** is an S-shaped sofa on which two people can sit face to face

the furthest extent of one's knowledge is their **tether**

a **tetrahedron** is also known as a **pyramid**

a **tetralogy** is a set of four connected artistic, literary, or musical works—such as Vivaldi's "Four Seasons"

the earliest **tetrapods**, "four-footed animals," were mammal-like reptiles that evolved before the dinosaurs; **tetrapods** today include humans

the dish **Tetrazzini** was named for an Italian opera singer, Luisa **Tetrazzini** (1871–1940)

Texas is from Native American texia, "ally, friend" (of the Apaches)

a **text** is literally "something woven" from Latin *textus*, "tissue," from *texere*, "to weave"—and its first definitions refer to "the words and sentences of the Holy Scripture"

nudists call people who wear clothes "**textiles**"

texture once referred to a woven fabric, from Latin *texere*, "to weave"

the distinctive quality of a piece of music is its **texture**

the suffix **-th** as in growth, health, ruth, aftermath etc.,—means "process of" or "result of"

Thailand was formerly Siam

than is ultimately the same word as **then** and the two were used interchangeably until the end of the seventeenth century

thanatism is the belief that at death the soul also dies

thanatopsis is thinking about death

the noun **thank** originally meant "thought," then "thoughtfulness," before "gratitude"

a hollow or rut across a road is colloquially called "**thank-you-ma'am**"

In current usage, **that** refers to persons or things and **which** is used chiefly for things.

The standard rule says that one uses **that** only to introduce a restrictive or defining relative clause—one that identifies the person or thing being talked about. An example is "The fort **that** Keir built has to be taken down" and the clause "**that** Keir built" describes which fort has to be taken down, i.e., it is restrictive. In contrast, **which** is used only with nonrestrictive or nondefining clauses. This type of clause gives additional information about something that has already been identified in the context. An example is "The students have been complaining about the assigned novel, **which** is hard to understand." The clause "**which** is hard to understand" is nonrestrictive as it does not indicate the specific novel being complained about. In a sentence including a nonrestrictive clause, the sentence would still be clear even if the clause were omitted. One will find that **which** sounds more natural than **that** in such a sentence, which is a great double-check of the grammar. Some people very strictly use **that** only in restrictive clauses and **which** in nonrestrictive clauses. However, even in good prose one will find the use of **which** in restrictive clauses in very common and considered grammatically acceptable. An example is "I would like to find a website **which** will tell me all about writing a research paper.

to **thatch** a building is literally to "cover" it, from Indo-European *tog/teg*, "cover"

thaw was first used as a verb in English as "the melting of a frozen liquid or sub-stance," having come from the Scandinavian languages, Old Norse, Norwegian, Swedish, and Danish; a form of this word was first attested c. 1000

in the late Old English period se was replaced by **the**, perhaps a version of "that," and it followed other definite articles by changing to beginning with th-

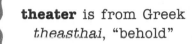

{ **theater** is from Greek *theasthai*, "behold" }

theft is the action of a thief

a **theic** is one who drinks too much tea

caffeine in tea is technically called **theine**

the Old English forms of hie, hiera, and him were replaced at the end of the period by **they**, **their**, and **them**—which came from Old Norse

theme is from Greek meaning "proposition"

then was formed from the ancient demonstrative base tha, which is also the base of that and there"

the opposite of **nowadays** is **thenadays**

the palm of the hand and the sole of the foot are called the **thenar**, which is also the name for the ball of muscle (**thenar** eminence) at the base of thumb

theology is, literally "discourse on god"

the etymological underpinnings of **theory** is "looking," from Greek *theoria*, "contemplation, speculation, theory" or "sight, spectacle"

therapy comes from Greek *therapeuein*, "attend, administer treatment"

therein contains ten other words: the, there, he, in, rein, her, here, ere, **therein**, and herein

thermal's first sense was "relating to hot springs"—from Greek *therme*, "heat"; a **thermal** is also a rising current of warm air used by birds to carry them aloft

thermesthesia is sensitivity to heat

thermometer comes from Greek *therme*, "heat," and *metron*, "measure"

thermos is Greek for "warm, hot"

thermostat is Greek *therme/thermo*, "heat, hot," and *states/stat*, "constant, set"

to be **thersitical** is to be loudmouthed or foulmouthed; **clamant** is loud and insistent

thesaurus comes from a Greek word, *thesaurus*, meaning "storehouse, treasury," and its original sense was "dictionary or encyclopedia" but this was narrowed to the current meaning with the appearance of Roget's in 1852, now a treasury or storehouse of synonymous or related words

these/those are the plural forms of this/that, and behave in the same way

thesis first referred to beating musical time with one's hand or foot

thesis is for a master's degree and a **dissertation** is for a doctorate

the word **thespian** is a tribute to Thespis, a tragedian of the sixth century BC

the English language unfortunately lacks a simple singular pronoun which does not specify gender, so many use "**they**" instead of "he" or "she" or "he/she"

thick-eyed means absorbed in deep thought

{ **thief** has the underlying meaning of "crouching, furtive person" }

to **thig** is to beg or cadge

thigh is etymologically the "plump" part of the leg, from an Indo-European base meaning "swell" or "fat"

being **thigmotropic** pertains to a plant that coils around something, like a string or stake

thimble is an alteration of "thumb bell"

thimblerig is the sleight-of-hand game with three inverted cups

thin denotes etymologically "stretched"

in Old English, **thing** meant "court, assembly, council"

think is from Old English *thencan* and etymologically has the meaning "causing images, reflections to appear in one's brain"

a **thirl** is a hole, opening, or perforation

the etymological notion under **thirst** is of being "dry"

thirty, written 30, indicates the end of a story in journalism, first used in Morse Code for its distinctive . . .

this is descended from an Old English demonstrative adjective *thes*, from the earlier Germanic *tha*

thither means "there," "to that place," and **whither** is "where," "to what place"

thole means be subjected or exposed to something evil

thong first meant "shoelace"

thorns, also called stem-spines, are modified branches or stems that are usually squatter than spines and may produce leaves, unlike spines

thoroughbred and **purebred** are virtually synonymous, both referring to animals that have been bred from the best blood through a long line and whose pedigrees have been recorded for a number of generations; **pureblooded**, **registered**, and **pedigreed** are used in a similar sense

originally, **those** was the plural of this

from Middle English, **thou** was the second-person pronoun used to address another and ye was used to address more than one person (the objective singular was **thee**)—and this evolved into using **thou/thee** for familiar persons and ye/you for others as a sign of respect

English borrowed **though** from Old Norse *thoh*, coming from Germanic *tha* plus a suffix meaning "and"

thousand is an ancient noun originally meaning "several hundreds"

to **thrack** is to cram or pack full

the **thread** is the degree of stickiness reached in boiling clarified syrup for confectionery

threat was a word for a throng or crowd of people

three goes back to a prehistoric Indo-European base of *trejes*

threshold is from thresh "stamping" or "treading"—as something you do as you go through a door

thribble means "three times as much or many"

thrift first meant "acquired wealth, prosperity, success"

thrill originally was a verb meaning "pierce, penetrate"

to **thring** is to move in a crowd, especially pressing or crushing

thrive was borrowed from Old Norse *thrifask*, "grasp for oneself" and then "prosper"

throat is the "devouring capacity of any destructive thing, such as war, a plague, etc."

throne is from Greek *thronos*, "elevated seat"

the etymological notion of **throng** is of "pressing together" from a Germanic base *thringg* "press"

through and **thorough** were originally variants of the same word meaning "to pass between, among, across, by means of"

through is used in reference to a movement or passage that proceeds linearly; **throughout** to a movement or passage that proceeds spatially

rainfall reaching the ground through trees (etc.) is **throughfall**

the original sense of **throw** was "twist, turn" as in throwing a pot on a potter's wheel and it is not known how it evolved into "hurl, project"

if you are **thrunched**, you are displeased or very angry

thrush, the bird, is from Germanic *thruskjon*, which produced Latin *turdus*, "**thrush**"

{ **thrust** was borrowed from Old Norse *thrysta*, "compress, thrust" }

thud first meant "blast or gust of wind; violent wind"

thag, Sanskrit for "cheat," eventually became **thug**

thumb was *thuma*, "thick, swollen," in Old English

etymologically, **thunder** is "noise," from the Indo-European *ton/tn*, "resound"

a **thurible** is a container in which incense is burnt, a censer

thurification is the act of burning incense

Thursday is Thor's Day, the Germanic god of thunder (Thunor)

to **thutter** is to make a dull, repetitive sound

a seat in a rowboat is a **thwart**

thyme is from Greek *thumon*, from the verb *thuein*, "burn sacrificially," as the leaves are quite aromatic; we pronounce the "th" in **thyme** as T because it passed into English from French with that pronunciation

thyroid comes from the Greek *thyreoid*, meaning shield-shaped; when early anatomists discovered the two broad quadrilateral plates joined in the human throat to form the "Adam's apple," the part was so-named for its resemblance to a shield

a **tiara** was originally the turban-like head-dress worn by Persian kings as well as lords and priests

a spontaneous reaction or a whim can be called a **tic**

tick, the insect, may be related to Armenian *tiz*, "bug"

tick as in "sound of a clock," "mark of cor-rectness," originally meant "light touch, tap" and its modern senses are recent develop-ments; **tickle** is probably a derivative of this version of **tick**

ticket comes from Old French *estiquet*, "label, note"

the strong cloth used to cover mattresses, pillows, etc. is **ticking**

tic-tac-toe (or **tick-tack-toe**) is the North American term for noughts and crosses

a **tidal wave** is caused by the gravitation-al effect of the moon and is on the surface (no deeper than thirty feet), while a **tsunami** is triggered by an earthquake, landslide, volcano, or meteorite and extends from the surface to the ocean floor

tidbit comes from British titbit, "small small"

to **tiddle** is to indulge to excess

a **tiddlywink** originally was an unlicensed public house or pawn shop, then a game played with dominoes

the seven canonical hours of the church were called tides—and **tide** is used with other words to denote a definite interval of time: noontide, Eastertide, even-tide, summertide, etc. (and comes from an Indo-European root meaning "to divide")

the mark left in the bathtub when the water is let out is the **tidemark**

tidings probably comes from Old Norse *tithindi*, "news of events"

tidy comes from tide, which in Old English meant "time period"—and **tidy**'s original meaning was "timely, opportune"

the word **tie** ("band, cord, rope") came into Old English by 800 CE in the form *teah*, *teag*, or *teagum*, developed from Proto-Germanic; the word **necktie** dates from around 1838 when it first hit the fashion scene as a narrow band of material worn around the collar (neck) of a shirt and tied in front

tie-dyed means tied in knots, then dyed with several colors

tier is from French *tire*, "order, sequence"

{ **tiercels**, hens, and eyas are father, mother, and baby hawks }

tiff is weak or diluted liquor; to **tiff** is to drink liquor slowly or sip it

a petty fight is a **tiff** or **spat**

something insubstantial or flimsy can be called **tiffany**

a light midday meal or midmorning snack can be called a **tiffin**; eating or drinking outside of mealtimes is **tiffing**

tiger came through Old French and Latin from Greek *tigris*, presumably from an ear-lier oriental word

tight as in sleep **tight** may be from the sense "soundly, roundly" of the 1700s

tight first meant "healthy, vigorous"

the choice of **tight** or **tightly** depends on whether it is the result or the application that is emphasized; if it is an enduring state, you would use **tight**

when a lion and tiger get together, a baby is a **tigon**, **tiglon**, or **tigron**

the adjective form of tiger is **tigrine**

a **tiki** is a human shape carved on art and objects

tikka, a Hindi word, is an Indian kebab

a domino or a playing piece in Scrabble or mah-jong is called a **tile**

the etymological notion of **till** "cultivate the soil" is "striving to obtain a goal," from Germanic *tilam*, "aim, purpose"

tilt originally meant "fall over," from Germanic *taltaz*, "unsteady," long before it was "slant"

tilth is another name for agricultural work or soil cultivation

etymologically, **tinge** is "moisten, soak" from its Latin source

tingle is from Middle English, possibly a variant of tinkle, and the original meaning was "response to a loud noise" and "response to hearing something shocking"

a **tinker** is an itinerant peddler or repairer of kettles, pots, etc.

{ the food dish called **timbale** (French "kettledrum"), which is drum-shaped, is probably named for the timbal drum (kettledrum) }

timber originally referred to a building as well as to building material

time originally denoted "delimited section of existence; period," from Old Teutonic *timon*, from *ti*, "to stretch, extend," from an Indo-European base meaning "cut up, divide"

timeful is another word for seasonable or timely

to record a television program for later viewing is to **time-shift**

timid is used of a person's character or disposition; **timorous** is used of a person's action or behavior

timpani (plural of timpano) is from Latin *tympanum*, "drum"

if cans were really made of **tin**, you could crush them with your hand

tinct is a poetic term for "color" or "coloring matter"; **tint** is an alteration of **tinct**, "to color"

tincture can mean an imperfect knowledge of an art or science

tinder is from a Germanic base meaning "ignite, kindle"

tinfoil was replaced by **aluminum foil** in the 1920s

ringing in your ears is called **tinnitus** or **acouasm**

tinsel comes from Latin *stincilla*, "spark"

tintinnabulate and **tintinnabulation** are from a Latin word *tintinnabulatus*, "having a bell or bells"

tine (adjective, noun) meaning "very small" gave us **tiny**

tip, as in gratuity for service, first meant "give, hand, or pass" and probably comes from the earlier meaning for **tip** of "culmination"

the **tipe** is the highest point of something

the **tippee** receives tips from the **tipper**

to **tippet** is to move on tiptoe

tipple first meant the retail sale of alcoholic drink (a back-formation of **tippler**) and to **tipple** means to drink alcohol regularly

tirade is from Italian *tirata*, "volley"

tiramisu is from an Italian phrase *tira mi su* meaning "pick me up"—probably from its' containing coffee and liqueur

in Old English, **tire** meant "fail, cease, come to an end"

the repetitive melodic sound of songbirds is called **tirra-lirra**

an outburst of temper is a **tirret**

tissue was first used to describe a rich cloth or material, often woven with gold or silver

tissue is a collection of cells that form a thin but tough structure and each type of **tissue** has a special function; a **membrane** is a thin layer of **tissue**

a **titch** means something tiny

originally, **tithe** meant "tenth"

titillate is from Latin *titillare*, "to tickle"

titivate means "to make decorative additions to"

title is from Latin *titulus*, "inscription, placard"

the **titmouse** is actually a bird

dot your i with a **tittle**

titubant means "staggering, unsteady"

{ a **tittynope** is a small quantity of anything left over }

tizzy is possibly a blend of tipsy and dizzy

tmesis is the separation of a compound word by an intervening (medial) word or part of a word (like abso-bloody-lutely or abso-posi-lutely)

to comes from prehistoric West Germanic **to**, from Indo-European *do*; **too** is historically the same word as **to** and they were not differentiated until the sixteenth century

all **toads** are **frogs**, but not all **frogs** are **toads**

to **toad-eat** is to behave servilely, to fawn over someone; **toady** is said to be a contraction of toad-eater

toadstools were named for their stool-like shape and the association between poisonous fungi and the supposedly poisonous toad

toady first meant "little or young toad"

a **toast** referred to the seventeenth century banquet custom of choosing a lady to drink to—with her name flavoring the drink like pieces of spiced **toast** formerly placed in drinks or wine

if someone is **toast**, their skills have eroded and career possibly finished

the verb **toast** originally meant "parch, scorch"—from Latin *torrere*, "parch"

a **toaster** is a person who accompanies reggae music by speaking or shouting

tobacco comes from the Carib word *tabaco*, which meant the reed pipes in which the natives smoked the dried leaves—but it came to represent the leaves and then the **tobacco** plant

toboggan comes from Canadian French from Micmac *tobakun* or Abnaki *udabagan*, "sled, sleigh"

the sport of **tobogganing** is also called hurley-hacket

a **tock** is more resonant than a **tick**

a **tod** is a unit of weight in wool

today is a combination of the preposition "to" and the noun "day"

todder is the spawn of a frog or toad

toddy is the juice obtained by tapping certain palms (from Hindi *tari*, "juice of palmyra palm")

the outer edge of a spoon is the **toe**

the tip of the head of a golf club or hockey stick is the **toe**

to slant a nail is to **toe** it

the indented space under kitchen counters is the **toe-hole** or **kick space**

stuff found between your toes is **toe-jam** or **gronk**

toffee is an alteration of **taffy**

tofu, Japanese for bean curd, is Chinese *doufu*, from *dou*, "beans," and *fu*, "rot, sour" (rotten beans)

toga is from Latin *tegere*, "to cover"; if some-one is wearing a **toga**, they are **togate**

the etymological idea of **together** is of "gathering" things into one group, to and gad, "association, company"

togethering is taking a vacation with your extended family and friends

toggle was first a boat pin passed through a rope loop to secure it

toggery is clothes collectively

togs (clothes) comes from Latin *toga*, from *tegere*, "to cover"

toil comes from Latin *tudiculare*, "stir about," from *tudicula*, "machine for crush-ing olives"

toilet was first a fabric wrapper for clothes—especially for hairdressing or makeup appli-cation

a **token** is etymologically something that "shows" you something, from a base mean-ing "show, sign"

Tokyo's elements mean "east(ern) capital; **Kyoto** means "capital city"

to **tolerate** something is to etymologically "bear" it

toll traces back to Greek *telos*, "tax"

Toltec is from the Nahuatl language, literally "person from Tula" (an ancient **Toltec** city)

the adjective form for armadillo is **tolypeutine**

say TOE-mah-toe for **tomato** are historically correct as it was Mayan *xtomatl*, with three syllables, though the ultimate source is prob-ably Nahuatl *tomatl*

a **tomb** is any place of burial, but to most it means a chamber or vault in the earth; the word is derived from Latin *tumba* and Greek *tymbos*, "sepulchral mound"

a **tombolo** is a sandbar extending from an island to the mainland or another island

tomboy was first an uncouth or boisterous boy

adult male cats are **tomcats** and adult female cats are **cattas**

tome comes from Greek *tomos*, "roll of papyrus," and was originally a word for one volume of a larger work

tomfoolery is from Thome Fole, formerly a common name for a half-wit

tommy in tommyrot is British for "bread, foot"

tomorrow was formed on the model of today from the preposition to "at, on" and *morgenne*, a form of Old English *morgan*, "morning" (which evolved into morn and morrow)

ton comes from tun/tunna "a large wine vessel or cask"

tonant means "loud, thundering"

a **tondo** is a circular easel painting

 a **tone** is a color variation with more variations than a shade—having to do with the value of hue or its chroma (saturation or purity)

tomatoes were first called tomates, from French/Spanish and when tomatoes first came to England, they were called love apples because they looked like apples and were considered aphrodisiacs; those who

tongs comes from a base meaning "bite"

tongue first had the general meaning "part of the body"; the pin of a buckle is the **tongue**

tongueshot is one's vocal range

tonic first meant "pertaining to tone; relating to tension"

the word **Tonka** means "great" in Dakota Sioux, a Native American tribe of Minnesota—and the trucks were created in Minnesota

the interior of a car behind the front seat is the **tonneau**

tonsure is the shaved part of the head of a member of a religious order

the **Tony** Award is named after U.S. actress Antoinette Perry (1888–1946)

tony is an abbreviation of high-toned, "of cultivated elegance"

toodles and **toodle-oo** as "goodbye" come from French "*a tout a l'heure*"

tool comes from a Germanic base meaning "prepare"

etymologically, a **tooth** is an "eater," from Indo-European *ed*, "eat"

the **tooth-fee** is the gift given a child upon the appearance of the first tooth, an ancient Nordic custom, and also is the word for the gift or money given when a child loses baby teeth

tooth-music is the sound of chewing

to **tootle** is to toot continuously, as notes on a wind instrument

tootlish is muttering in a childish way

top is from Germanic *toppaz*, "tuft of hair on **top** of the head"

to **tope** is to drink liquor copiously and habitually

Topeka is Dakotan for "good place to dig potatoes"

a **toper** or **tosspot** is a chronic drinker of alcohol

topesthesia is using touch to determine where one is

topiary is derived from Latin *topiarius*, "ornamental gardener" and shrubs and trees that are trimmed are **topiary**

topic originally meant "a set or book of general rules or ideas," from Greek *ta topika*, "matters concerning commonplaces"—the name of a treatise by Aristotle (from Greek *topos*, "place")

toploftical means "haughty"

a **topo** is a photograph of a mountain that has possible routes for climbing marked on it

topography combines top with graph, "write, describe"—and **topography** describes or shows the features of a place on a map or chart and is also the term used to describe the features of a surface

topology is the branch of botany dealing with plant habitats

toponym, a place name, was coined in the 1890s from the combining forms *top(o)* (from Greek *topos*, "place") + onym

a chef's hat is a **toque** or toque blanche

a **tor** is a rocky hill or a rock heap on a hilltop

torch is from Latin *torquere* and first referred to tarred twists of frayed rope

toreador, a bullfighter, is from Spanish *torear*, "fight bulls"

toric means "doughnut-shaped" and a doughnut-shaped figure is a **torus**; a **toric** contact lens has two different curves instead of one

torment comes from a Latin word for an instrument of torture

torment suggests persecution or the repeated inflicting of suffering or annoyance; **torture** adds the implication of causing unbearable pain or suffering

tornado's original sense was "a tropical thunderstorm" and was possibly an alteration of Spanish *tronada*, "thunderstorm";

tornado was first a violent thunderstorm in the tropical Atlantic and the term **twister** is slang for **tornado**

the original **torpedo** was a flat electric ray fish, the electric ray (in Latin *torpedo* meant "numbness, stiffness")

torpid means mentally or physically inactive; **torpor** is mental or physical inactivity or sluggishness

a hanging mass of foliage is a **torrent**

torrid means "very hot and dry"

Torschlusspanik is a sense of alarm or anxiety at the passing of life's opportunities

the tendency to untwist after being twisted is **torsibility**; **torsibility** is also the degree to which something can be twisted

{ **torsion** was first a synonym for colic or any twisting in the body }

torso also means something that is mutilated or left unfinished, as a piece of writing

torso is the stump of a cabbage or core of an apple or pear

torte comes from Italian *torta*, "cake"

tortellini ("little cakes," as it is diminutive of *tortello*, "cake") are rolled **tortelli**—and **tortelli** are small pasta packets of cheese or vegetables

tortilla is the Spanish diminutive of *torta*, "cake"

the original and true **tortoiseshell** of eyeglass frames, combs, etc., is from the shell of the hawksbill turtle; **tortoiseshell** is now made synthetically

tortoni ice cream was named for an Italian café owner in Paris

tortuous is "winding, crooked, full of twists and turns" and **torturous** (based on "torture") is "painful, characterized by suffering"

torus is the cuplike part of a flower from which the floral leaves grow

Tory, now the name of the British Conservative party, once meant Irish outlaw, from *toraidhe*, "outlaw, fugitive"

an igloo tunnel is the **tossut**

tot in tater tot means "a very small object, a small quantity of something"

total is from Latin *totus*, "whole"

totem is from a North American Indian word for "animal image"

the **toucan**'s name is imitative of its call

the etymological idea of **touch** is "striking of a bell," from Latin *toccare*, "hit, knock" or "make sound by striking something, as a bell"

touché in fencing is the acknowledgment of a hit by the opponent

toupee was first a curl or lock of artificial hair, from French *toup*, "tuft"

a **tour** is one's turn to do something

the phenomenon of **tourism** or traveling for recreation accompanied the development of transportation and exploration in the Near East as early as 3000 BCE and earlier in the Far East and the term in English dates from 1811

diarrhea of a tourist is called **tourista** or **turista**

tournament (and **tourney**) are based on Latin *torus*, "turn"

tournedo means "to turn the back" in French because the dish originally was not placed upon the table but passed behind the backs of guests

tournure is a word for grace and poise

to **touse** is to pull or handle roughly

to **tousle** is to dishevel or make something untidy; to **tussle** is to scuffle

the etymological idea of **tout** is "projecting, sticking out" from a Germanic base meaning this

tow is the fiber of flax, hemp, or jute prepared for spinning

the suffix of -ward/-wards in "**towards**" is from Indo-European *wert*, "turn," so **towards** literally is "turning to" something

towel once referred to a table napkin

a group of giraffes is a **tower**

towhead, for a blonde-haired person, is from tow, meaning "unworked flax fiber," which is light yellow in color

a **town** was originally a group of dwellings surrounded by a hedge or hill (from German *zaun*, "hedge, enclosure") and first meant "enclosed piece of ground, field"

toxic comes from Greek *toxikon pharmakon*, "poison for arrows" (from *toxon*, "bow")

toy originally described a funny story or remark—then a trick or frivolous entertainment

to **toze** is to pull apart, unravel, or separate the fibers of

trabeated means "constructed with beams"; **trabeation** is the use of beams in construction

tracasserie is a state of annoyance or a petty quarrel

trace first was "the way or path an animal, person, or thing takes; a course"

trace and **trade** both originally meant "path, course"

track was borrowed from Old French *trac*, from Middle Dutch *trek*, "pulling," or *trekken*, "pull"

a **trackway** is a path formed by the repeated treading of animals or people

tract first meant "duration or course (of time)" before it was applied to area or land

tract, as in written work, is an abbreviation of Latin *tractatus*, "discussion, treatise"

a **tractate** is a literary work treating a particular subject, i.e., a treatise

traction and **tractor** trace back to Latin *tractus*, "drawing, pulling," and *trahere*, "draw, pull"

{ **tractive** refers to power exerted in pulling, especially by a machine }

trade originally meant "track, way" and only in the sixteenth century did it become "buying and selling"

a **trade-last** is an exchange in which somebody repeats an overheard compliment to the complimented person if that person will first offer an overheard compliment about the other

TM is a **trademark**, but R is a **registered trademark** (with the U.S. Patent Office)

a **trademark** is a name, symbol, or other depiction identifying a product and the first trademarks were stamps and symbols used by ancient cultures to indicate who had made goods; a **trade name** is the name of the maker, not the product, but has the status of a **trademark**

tradition and **treason** derive from Latin *tradere*, "to deliver, hand over, betray"; **tradition** first was "orally given information or instruction"

to **traduce** is to slander or betray

traffic can only be traced to Italian *traffico* and *trafficare*, "trade," but that is all that is known

the word **tragedy** comes from Greek *tragos*, "goat," and *ode*, "song" (goat song)

the peacock's fan is called the **train**—which is not its tail

trait is a stroke of a pen or pencil

traitor comes from Latin *tradere*, "hand over"

the fleshy cartilage between your ear and temple is the **tragus** and the downward notch is the **intertragic notch**

tralatitious is "traditional, handed down from generation to generation" and can also mean "characterized by transference, either figurative or metaphorical"

tram is from German or Dutch *trame*, "balk of timber, beam" and first referred to the shafts of a cart

trampoline comes from Italian *trampoli*, "stilts"; small trampolines are called trampolets

to **tranont** is to sneakily change position

transcend is from Latin *trans*, "across," and *scandere*, "climb," and **transfer** is from *trans*, "across," and *ferre*, "to bear"

a **transept** is either of two lateral arms of a cruciform church

transgressive pertains to going beyond or stepping over a line of general acceptability

transhumance is seasonal movement of livestock to different pasture

transient, **transit**, and **transition** are related—based on Latin *trans* and *ire*, "to go"

transilient is "passing from one thing or condition to another"

transistor is a blend of transfer and resistor

early on, **translate** meant "transfer"

translucent is from *trans*, "through," and *lucere*, "to shine"

translucent means light passes through but without clarity; **transparent** means light passes through with clarity

a **transom** is a small hinged window hung over a door or another window

etymologically, something that is **transparent** allows the light to "appear

through" it, from Latin *transparere*, "be seen through"

if something is **transpicuous**, it is easily seen through or understood

transpire had an early sense of "emit as vapor through the surface"—from *trans*, "through," and *spirare*, "breathe"

transplant first meant "to reposition a plant"

transvestite is from Latin *trans*, "across," and *vestire*, "clothe," and because it is so acceptable for women to wear men's clothing, the word **transvestite** is generally applied only to men

miscellaneous items of little value (think "tag sale") are **trantlums** or **trantles**

trapeze and quadruped both etymologically mean "four feet," with **trapeze** coming from Greek *trapezion*, "small table"—and its use for gymnastic equipment alludes to the quadrilateral shape formed by the ropes and crossbar with the roof or support

trappings are etymologically "drapery" and it was originally an ornamental covering for a horse

the original sense of **trash** was "things broken, snapped, or lopped off; broken or torn pieces, as twigs, etc."

trattles are the rounded droppings of animals like rabbits and sheep

trauma comes from Greek meaning "a wound"

travel, from Latin *trepaliare*, "torture," evolved into "journey" from the allusion to the inevitable trouble of medieval **travel**

travelogue is a combination of travel and monologue

traveltainted is fatigued with travel

travesty was first an adjective meaning "dressed ridiculously" and now means "an inferior or distorted imitation" as well as a "broadly comic imitation in art, drama, or literature"

trawl was likely borrowed from Dutch *traghelen*, "drag," from Latin *trahere*, "pull"

a **tray** is the drawer for storing a body at a mortuary

treachery has no etymological connection with traitor or treason; it was borrowed from French *trecherie*, a derivative of *trichier*, "cheat"

treacle was first an antidote against venom

the steps of an escalator are the **tread-boards**

the **treadle** is the foot-operated pedal for a potter's wheel

treason first had the simpler meaning of "betrayal"

treasure is based on Greek *thesauros*

treat is from Latin *tractus/tractare*, forms of *trahere*, "drag, pull," which metaphorically changed to "deal with, discuss, handle"

treble and triple come from Latin *triplus*, "threefold"

tree is part of a large Indo-European group based on *deru/doru*—"oak"

driving something to or up a tree is "**treeing**"

treen means "made of wood; wooden"

a design of three leaves, petals, or lobes is **trefoil** (as a clover), four is **quatrefoil**, and five is **cinquefoil**

trek is from South African Dutch *trek/trekken*, "pull" or "travel," (and **trigger** also descends from this)

trellis is literally "three-ply" or "three warp threads"

tremble is from the base trem, "shake"

tremendous is based on Latin *tremere*, "to tremble"

the **trench** coat was created in the first World War—a soldier's long padded or lined waterproof overcoat

{
trenchant is "effective, forceful" (from French *trenchier*, "to cut")
}

a **trencher** is a platter or tray for serving food

a **trenchermate** is a dining companion

if someone is **trenching**, they are feasting or pigging out

to **trend** is "to turn around, revolve, rotate"

trepid means "fearful, trembling"

the root of **trespass** is "to pass through (go beyond) God's commandments"

tress was originally a braid of hair

trestles are removable table legs

triage is a French word, from *trier*, "separate out"—and came to mean the assessment of the wounded from battle or the act of sorting according to quality

trial is from an Old French verb meaning "to sift or cull"

trial-size is a small size of a product

tribe may refer to the three divisions of early Romans (Latin *tribus*), the Latins, Sabines, and Etruscans

tribulation's base is Latin *tribulum*, "threshing board"

tribunal originally referred to a seat or raised platform for judges, from *tribunus*, "head of a tribe"

tribute is from Latin *tributum*, "divide between or assign to tribes"

trice can mean "an instant"

triceps means "three-headed"

an obsolete word for hairball is **trichobezoar**

something that is **trichogenous** produces hair

trichology is the science of hair

trick is from French *trique/triche/trichier*, "cheat," probably form Latin *tricari*, "play tricks, make difficulties"

a **tricolor** is a flag of three different colors—in equal horizontal or vertical bands

the three-cornered hat of early Americans was a **tricorn**

trifle in the pudding sense gets its name from being a "light" confection

trifle is from French *truffle/truffe*, "deceit, trickery"

a **trilapse** is a third downfall, **relapse** being the second

a **trilemma** is a problem situation with three possible solutions

a **trilling** is one of a set of three

trilobite, a Palaeozoic fossil, is pronounced TRY-luh-bite

to **trim** is to maintain an aircraft at a steady altitude

trimenon is a three-month period

a **trimmer** is one who sits on the fence or remains neutral about political issues

trindle means "cause to revolve"

a group of goats is a **trip**

tripe is synonymous with garbage and bad writing

triphibious means capable of operating on land, sea, or in the air

triplasian means "threefold, triple"

examples of **triplets** are capital, cattle, chattel, all ultimately from Medieval Latin *capitale*, "property," and salary, sauce, sausage, all ultimately from Latin *sal*, "salt"

tripod and **trivet** are from Greek, both literally "three" and "foot"

triquetous means having three acute angles

triskaidekaphobia is the fear of Friday the 13th

tristful means "full of melancholy or sadness"

trite is from Latin *tritus*, "worn," a form of *terere*, "to rub, wear down"

tritical means "of a trite nature," possibly a blend of trite and critical

triumph probably derives from Greek *thriambos*, "hymn to Bacchus"

the word **trivia** derives from Latin *tri*, "three," and *via*, "ways," and in Roman times, at the intersection of any three streets were kiosks where information was posted for travelers—but which were totally ignored by the citizens—hence the meaning; **trivia** is actually plural and should take "these" instead of "this" (etc.)

trivial comes from the Trivium (grammar, rhetoric, logic), which was less prestigious (more "**trivial**") than the Quadrivium (astronomy, music, geometry, arithmetic)

troche is another word for tablet or pill

{ a **trod** is a footprint or footstep }

a **troll** was originally a witch or sorceress

fishing from a moving boat is **trolling**

trollop "untidy, slovenly woman" may be connected with the word "troll"

troop is from Latin *troppus*, "flock," and is a group of people or animals; **troupe** is a company of actors or performers

a **trope** is a figurative or metaphorical use of a word or phrase

trophy once referred to the display of weapons taken from a defeated army (from Greek *trope*, "a rout")

tropic originally meant "turning" (point)—as in an eclipse or solstice (from Greek *trope*, "turning")

tropism is the leaning of plants toward light and heat

trot and **tread** seem to have been derived from the same Germanic base

troth, as in pledging one's **troth** in marriage, is a variant of "truth"

a **troubadour** is etymologically someone who "finds" or "composes" songs, from Provençal *trobador/trobar*, "compose"

trouble derives from Latin *turbidus*, "turbid"

trouble-mirth is one who spoils another's enjoyment

etymologically, a **trough** is something made of "wood," from Indo-European *dru*, "tree, wood"

the singular of **trousers** is **trouse**

trousseau is the French diminutive of truss or bundle—the thing that tramps or runaways carry tied to a stick over their shoulders

a **trousseau** was first a bunch of keys

a troutlet or troutling is a young or small **trout**

trowel is from Latin *trulla*, "scoop"

a **truant** was originally a "beggar" or "vagrant," from French *truant*, "vagabond"

truce is historically the plural of the noun version of the adjective "true"

the ball on top of a flagpole is the **truck**

truck was formed by combining *trochos*, "wheel," and *trechein*, "to run," and originally the word referred to a wooden wheel

to be **truculent** is to be cruel and destructive

the **trudgeon** is a swimming stroke like the crawl, with a scissors movement of the legs added

true is from Old English *treowe/trywe*, "loyal, steadfast," and **truth** from *triewth/treowth*, "constancy, faithfulness"

the underlying meaning of **true** is "faithful, firm, steadfast," from the Germanic base *treww*, "like a tree"

truffle (Latin *tufer/trufe*, "tuber") is both an edible fungus growing underground and a type of chocolate; the chocolate **truffle** is so named because the finished candy somewhat resembles the black and white truffles used for cooking

a shallow oblong basket for vegetables is a **trug**

trullization is laying on plaster with a trowel

{ **trump**, as in cards, is an alteration of "triumph" }

trumpery are small household articles of little worth

truncate is from Latin *truncare*, "maim"

a **trunk** as a box or chest was originally made from a tree trunk

a bunch of fruit is a **truss**

trust was probably borrowed from Old Norse *traust*, "confidence; help," and shares the same base as true and truth

if you consider, balance, or weigh something, you **trutinate**

try originally meant "separate, sift out" from French *trier*, "separate, sift"

a **tryma** is a nut with a hard fibrous outer layer separating its rind from the inner layer—like a hickory or walnut

tryst comes from Scottish as a variant of an old word, *trist*, "an appointed place or station in hunting," and now means a "secret meeting of lovers"

tsar or **czar** is from Latin *Caesar*; **kaiser** in German is also derived from this

Japanese **tsunami** literally means "harbor wave" and can also be called a seismic sea wave

tuba is the Latin word for "trumpet"

tubers are different from bulbs and corms in that they have no basal plate or enveloping leaves

tuberose means "bearing tubers"

tuck first meant "punish, torment" or "chastise"

a **tucket** is a trumpet flourish or signal

an unripened ear of corn is a **tucket**

Tuesday is Tiw's or Tyr's Day—the Germanic god of war in Old Norse

{ a **tuffet** is a footstool or low seat—or a small grassy mound or hillock }

the **tuft** is the tassel on a mortarboard

tuition first meant taking care of something, then teaching or instruction, especially for a fee

tulip takes its name from a Latinized version of Arabic for "turban" in allusion to the shape of the flower

tulle is the starched netting used for veils, gowns, and ballet costumes

tumble is from German *tummelen*

tumblers at first were glasses made with a rounded or pointed base so they would not stand upright and had to be emptied in one swig

tumblification is the pitching and rolling of a ship in a storm

tumid means "swollen, swelling"

the life of the party is a **tummler**

tumor is from Latin *tumere*, "swell"

the sling for carrying a load on one's back that has a strap going over the forehead is called a **tumpline**

tumult applies only to people, while **turmoil** is confusion and agitation for people and things; **tumultuous** can describe things and people

tumultuary describes "being without order or system"

a **tumulus** is the mound of earth placed over a tomb, synonymous with **barrow**

tune is an alteration of tone

a **tunic** is a bulb with leaves tightly wrapped around an embryonic plant located at their center, e.g., onions, tulips, daffodils, Easter lilies

tunicate means "clothed in concentric layers," like the bulb of an onion

tunnel began as a tubular net for catching birds, deriving from French *tonne*, "tun, cask"

turban comes from Persian *dulband/tuliband*, "tulip," because a **turban**'s shape resembles the tulip

turbid means "unclear or murky" as in liquids; **turgid** means "swollen or distended," especially in relation to physical bodies

Latin *turbo*, "whirl, whirling thing," brought us **turbine**

turd is an ancient word, etymologically denoting something "separated" from the body, as an excretion

to **turdefy** is to turn into a turd

tureen (serving dish) is an alteration of terrine, from French *terrin*, "earthen"

turf is the institution or practice of horse racing

a **turfite** is a devotee of horse racing or one who makes a living from it

turkey was originally the name for African guinea fowl and eventually for the Western hemisphere fowl with which the earlier fowl was confused; **turkey** is short for turkeycock or turkeyhen

the powdered root of the **turmeric** plant is the chief ingredient in curry and its French name, *terre merite*, "worthy of the earth," became English **turmeric**

the ultimate source of **turn** is Greek *tornos*, "lathe"

tutoyant means "intimate, affectionate"

tutti-frutti is Italian for "all fruits"

tutu is a childish alteration of French *cucu*, diminutive of *cul*, "buttocks"

{ etymologically, a **turnip** may be a "turned neep," neep being a word used for turnips or swedes (vegetables) }

the hook of a clothes hanger is the **turnback**

turngiddy means dizzy from spinning around

turnpike comes from the poles or bars, "pikes," which were swung on a pivot across roads and had to be "turned" before vehicles or horsemen could pass; they were set up to insure collection of tolls

turpentine originally denoted the "resin of the terebinth," the resin being Latin *terbenthina resina*

turpitude is baseness or depravity—not integrity

turquoise comes through French and means "Turkish stone," so named as it was first found in Turkestan

a **turret** is a small or subordinate tower, usually one forming part of a larger structure

if something is **tursable**, it is portable

turtle is applied to those living in water and **tortoise** to those that live on land while terrapins live in fresh water; **turtle** and **tortoise** may come from the Latin root *tort*, with reference to the animals' twisted feet

a **turtlet** is a baby turtle

tussiculation is a hacking cough

tussock is a clump of grass

tutelary is "acting as a guardian"

tutor was first a caregiver, custodian, or protector (Latin *tuere*, "look after")

Tuvalu was formerly Ellice Islands

the **tuxedo** is so named from where it was first worn—**Tuxedo** Park, New York

a bunch of flowers is a **tuzzymuzzy**

twaddle is empty or trivial talk

twee is "excessively sweet, mawkish"

tweed is from twilled, meaning "woven"

the **tweeter** is the small speaker for high-frequency sounds and the **woofer** is the large low-frequency speaker

etymologically, **twelve** probably means "two over"

twenty is etymologically "two tens"

twenty-twenty is being able to read all the eye chart letters and numbers from twenty feet away

twice was formed from Old English *twige*, "**twice**," and the ending -s (as in always, once, etc.)

twiddle first meant "occupy oneself with trivial matters"

a **twiffler** is a plate intermediate in size between a dessert plate and a dinner plate

twig is etymologically a "forked branch," from a base twi, "two"

twilight is the time of two lights, the fading sunset and the emerging light of the moon and stars, and there are three sequential stages of **twilight**: civil

twilight, nautical **twilight**, and astronomical **twilight**

twin originally meant "double"

Twinkies were named for a billboard seen by their creator which said "Twinkle Toe Shoes"

twirl may be a blend of twist and whirl

twisel is a point or part at which something divides into branches—a fork

twist is from a base meaning "two," and rope, originally made from two strands, is something to which this word would have been applied

the game **Twister** was originally called Pretzel

a bicycle grip that may be twisted to change the gears is a **twist-grip**

a **twit** is a tangled thread—or a pregnant goldfish

a **twitten** is a narrow path between two walls or hedges

twitter-light is an old word for twilight

to **twizzle** is to spin around

two is an ancient word from Indo-European *duwo*

a **two-tone** fog signal (breeoooo) is a **diaphone** fog signal

tycoon comes from Japanese *tai*, "great," and *kun*, "prince, lord," from Chinese *da*, "great," and *jun*, "prince, ruler"

tyke is a term of contempt for a dog, especially a low-bred dog

{ when the abdomen swells with air or gas, that's **tympanites** }

type is from Greek *tupos*, "figure, image"

typhoon comes from Chinese dialect *tai fung*, "big wind"

a **tyrology** or **tirology** is a set of instructions for beginners (tyros)

tyronic is "exhibiting inexperience, acting as a tyro/beginner"

{ for many centuries, **U** and **V** were interchangeable, not separated in English dictionaries until c. 1800 }

ubication or **ubiety** is the condition or fact of being in a certain place or position or art of occupying a new place

ubiquitous is from Latin **ubique**, "everywhere," and **ubique** means "in any place whatsoever, anywhere and everywhere"; **ubiquity** was first in English, then **ubiquitous**

U-boat is the Anglicized spelling of German *U-Boot*, an abbreviation of *Untersee-Boot*, "undersea boat" (the difference in capitalization is that all German nouns are capitalized)

ug means fear or dread

ughten is the part of the night immediately before daybreak—early morning

ugly is from Old Norse *uggligr*, "be feared," from *ugga*, "feel or fill with dread"

ugsomeness can be used to mean "loathing" or "ugliness, loathsomeness"; it is derived from Old Norse *ugga*, "to fear or dread"

a **ukase** (from Russian) is an authoritative decree by the government, an edict

ukulele means "jumping flea" in Hawaiian

ullage is the term to describe the amount of space in a wine bottle that is not filled

ulterior is from a Latin word literally meaning "further, more distant"

the **ultima** is the last syllable of a word

ultimatum in Latin means "the last part" and we use it to mean "final offer or demand"

ultion is another word for revenge

an **ultracrepidarian** is one who gives opinions on matters beyond their knowledge

ultramarine was first a blue pigment made from lapis lazuli, imported from Asia by sea, so in Latin it was *ultramarinus*, "beyond the seas"

ultramontane means "beyond the mountains"

ultrasound or **ultrasonography** work on the principle that sound is reflected at different speeds by tissues or substances of different densities

ultraviolet has a wavelength shorter than that of violet light but longer than the longest X-rays

ultroneousness is free will

the howl or wail of an animal is **ululation**

besides salt, bitter, sour, and sweet—some say there is a fifth taste category known as **umami**, found in soy products and Asian foods

umber is a darkish brown mineral containing manganese and iron oxides used for coloring paint; when crushed and mixed with paint it produces an olive color known as raw umber and when crushed and burnt it produces a darker tone known as burnt umber

pattern of twenty, thirty, etc.

unanimous is based on Latin *unus*, "one," and *animus*, "mind"

to describe two things as equally stupid, use **unasinous**

unaware is an adjective that means "not being aware of something" and **unawares** is an adverb meaning "by surprise; unexpectedly"

unbeer means "impatient"

to **unbosom** is to reveal in confidence

uncle is from Latin *avunculus*, "mother's brother, maternal **uncle**"

the only fifteen-letter word that can be spelled without repeating a letter in **uncopyrightable**

unconscious first meant "unheeding" (the mind not fully present to itself) and the mind as threatened by an unknown part of itself

an **umberment** is a multitude

umbilical is from Latin *umbilicus*, "navel"

umbra is the darkest part of a shadow

umbrage is from Latin *umbra*, "shadow," and originally it meant "shade, shadow" in English—then shadowy suspicion, then came to mean displeasure or resentment at a slight or insult

if something is **umbratile**, it stays or lives in the shade or indoors, is reclusive and retiring

etymologically, an **umbrella** is a "little shadow"

umpire was once noumpere/numpire, coming from French *nonper*, "not equal"

in early Morse Code,—or umpty, meant "large, many," which helped create the words **umpteenth** and umpteen

umpty was an indefinite number—on the

uncouth once meant "unknown, uncertain," "remote, desolate," and "foreign, strange"

unction was borrowed from Latin *unctio/unguere*, "anoint"

unctuous originally meant "oily, greasy" and now has metaphorical meanings

an **undecennial** is an eleventh anniversary

under originated as a comparative form meaning "lower"

underdog first meant "the beaten dog in a fight"

underground begins and ends with "und"

undermine originally was from the practice of tunneling under the foundation of a castle to weaken the walls—and eventually was used for any underhanded method to defeat an enemy

underprivileged first meant lacking some legal right(s)

an **understander** is a person who plays a supporting role in an acrobatic troupe

undertaker once meant "one who takes up a challenge"

undulate is from Latin *unda*, "wave"

unemployment was first used of something not being put to use

unexceptional is ordinary and not outstanding; **unexceptionable** means not open to objections

a fancy name for a fingernail is **unguicule**

unicorn is from a Greek wild ox known as *monokeros*, "one horn," which in Latin became *unicornis*

something that is **uniform** has literally only "one form," from Latin *unus*, "one," and *forma*, "form"

unigeniture is the condition of being an only child

uninterested means "having no interest in, being indifferent to"; **disinterested** means "having no personal interest or stake in; being unbiased toward"

union is from Latin *unus*, "one," from Indo-European *oinos*

the word **unique**'s absolute sense of "being only one of its kind" of "having nothing like it anywhere"—means it cannot be modified with adverbs like "really," "quite," or "very'"

unison is from Latin *uni*, "one," and *sonus*, "sound"

unit was formed from Latin *unus*, probably on the analogy of digit and used as a math term to replace unity as a translation of Euclid's *monas*, "indivisible number"

universe denotes etymologically "turned into one" or "indivisible, whole," from Latin *universus* (*unus*, "one," and *versus/vertere*, "turn")

university is from Latin *universitas*, "whole"

an **unjustified** act is one for whose justification no past event or development can be adduced; an **unjustifiable** act is one for whose justification no future event or development can be adduced

unkempt is a variant of unkembed, from kemb, "comb"

  the root of **unkind** is "not of our (gracious and honorable) sort"

to **unlay** is to untwist a rope

unmeeching is not cringing or whining

unproductive is achieving poor results while **nonproductive** is achieving no results

unsane is not quite the same as insane as it implies "not quite normal; unwise or unreasoning"

unsatisfied implies that a wish, need, or expectation that previously existed has not been satisfied; **dissatisfied** implies no such prior existence, but simply registers a failure to be satisfied

unwieldy originally meant "feeble, weak" from Old English *wielde*, "active, vigorous"

up is from Indo-European up, which also produced over and the prefixes hyper- and super-

upbraid originally meant "throw something up against someone as a fault," from English braid, which used to mean "throw"

upholster comes from uphold, as upholder originally meant "a repairer of furniture"

uproar is from Middle Dutch *op*, "up," and *roer*, "confusion"

the rapid flow of water up onto the beach face following the breaking of surf is the **uprush** or **swash**

upset first meant "set up; raise, erect"

upshot's first meaning was "a final shot in a match at archery"

upstage in theater is "towards the rear of the stage" and **downstage** is "towards the audience"; **stage left** and right are left and right as the audience views the stage

an **upstart** is etymologically someone who has "started up" in the sense of "jump, rise, spring"

uranium is named for Ouranos, ancient sky god of Greek mythology

uranomania is the delusion that one is descended from heaven

urban is from Latin *urbs*, "city"

urban refers to a city; **urbane** means polished and smooth, as in a person's demeanor

the original meaning of **urchin** was "hedgehog" (from Latin *ericius*, "hedgehog") and "goblin" or "elf"

urge and **urgent** are from Latin *urgere*, "compel, drive, press"

{ **urheimat** is the location where a people or language originated }

urine is from Latin *urina* or Greek *ouron*

URL is uniform resource locator

to be **urled** is to be stunted in growth or dwarfish

the male equivalent of a lesbian is an **urning**

an **urtext** is the original or earliest version of a text

the difference between **use** and **usage** consists primarily in the fact that the former has a specific, the latter a general sense

usher was originally a term for a doorkeeper

a synonym for sunburned is **ustulate**

usual means, etymologically, that which is commonly "used" or employed or commonly obtained—from Latin *usualis*

usucaption is the acquisition of property by right of long possession and enjoyment

usufruct is a concept from Latin *usus et fructus*, "use and enjoyment," and now means "the right to use or enjoy something"

etymologically, **usurp** is to "seize it for one's own use"

etymologically, **usury** is the "use" of money lent

Utah might be Navaho for "higher land"

utensil was once a collective term for domestic implements or containers

uterus is from Latin *uterus*, "belly, womb"

a dog bred for **utility** is one intended for a particular use such as hunting or herding

utilize means to make the best use of something that was not intended for the job

utopia comes from two Greek words meaning "good place" and "no place, nowhere"—coined by Thomas More in 1516

utter first meant "outer, outward"

uvate is another way of saying grape jam

the "stalactite" in the back of your throat is your **uvula** (diminutive of Latin *uva*, "grape," which it resembles)

uxorial is "pertaining to a wife" and **uxorious** is "overly fond of one's wife"

{ **V8** is named for its juice content: tomato, celery, carrot, spinach, lettuce, watercress, beet, and parsley }

vacant is from Latin *vacare*, "be empty"

vacation is a word coming from Latin *vacation/vacatio*, from *vacare*, "to be free, empty; to be at leisure," and around 1395, this term entered Old English, meaning "rest and freedom from any activity"

a **vaccary** is a place where cows are kept—a dairy farm

vaccimulgence is a fancy word for "milking of cows"

vaccinate and vaccine are from Latin *vacca*, "cow"—as the first vaccination was based on the observance that people who had gotten cowpox were unlikely to catch smallpox

vaccination and **inoculation** are synonymous

Latin *vacuus*, "empty, void," gives us **vacuum**, **vacuous**, **vacate**

vagabond was a criminal and then a rogue before a wanderer

vagarious means erratic and unpredictable in behavior or direction

a **vagary** is an odd or eccentric idea

vagation is the action of wandering, straying, or departing from the proper or regular course

vagile means free to move about, the opposite of **sessile**

vagina is Latin for sheath or scabbard

vagitus is the first cry of a newborn

vagrant comes from Latin *vagari*, "wander"

to **vague** means "to roam, wander"

vain's early sense of "devoid of real worth" comes from its Latin base of *vanus*, "empty, without substance"

vair is the type of fur found on gray and white squirrels

a curtain hung along the top edge of a window or door is a **valance**

valediction is from Latin *vale*, "goodbye," and *dicere*, "to say"

a closing address is **valedictory** and **valedictorian** means "farewell"; a welcoming address is **salutatory** a **valentine** formerly was a person chosen as a sweetheart or special friend, named for either of two Italian saints

valet (pronounced VAH-lut) came from French *vaslet/varlet*, "a warrior in service to his feudal lord"

a **valetudinarian** is someone who is unnecessarily anxious about their health

early senses of **valiant** were "robust" and "well-built"

van is a shortening of caravan

the word **vandal** comes from the destructive Germanic tribe of the fourth-fifth centuries CE

a blade of a propeller, turbine, or windmill is a **vane**

vane's literal sense is "flat thing"

vanguard is a shortening of French *avan(t) garde*, "before guard"

 vanilla was thought to be an aphrodisiac because its pod resembled the vagina—and the word **vanilla** comes from the Spanish for "little vagina"

valid and **value** come from Latin *valere*, "be strong"

a **valise** is an overnight bag or piece of hand luggage

valley is from Latin *vallis*, "**valley**"

valuation means "an estimated value" whereas **evaluation** means "the estimating of value"; thus, a **valuation** measures something's worth and an **evaluation** is the process of examination that results in a measurement

a color's **value** is its brightness, its **chroma** is its strength, and its **hue** is its position in the spectrum

a **valve** is either of two leaves (sides, parts) of a folding or double door

vamoose comes from Spanish *vamos*, "let us go"

the part of a sock or stocking covering the foot and ankle is the **vamp**

Theda Bara's performance in the movie *The Vampire* brought us the word **vamp** "seductive woman"

vampire is from *ubyr*, "witch," in a Russian language

vanilla can mean "having no special features"

if something is like or containing vanilla, it is **vanillic**

vaniloquence is much talk or babbling

vanish is from Latin *evanescere*, "die away"

vanquish comes from Latin *vincere*, "conquer"

Vanuata was formerly New Hebrides

vapid first described drinks as "lacking in flavor or taste"

vapor is from Latin *vapor*, "heat, steam"

vapulatory means related to flogging

miscellaneous things can be called **varia**

another word for **varicose vein** is **varix** (with the plural varices)

variegated can mean "having variety in character, form, etc."

a **varietist** is someone whose attitudes or activities are not what most people would consider normal

varnish may have gotten its name from a city in Libya—Berenike—which became *vernix*, "odorous resin," in Latin

varsity is actually a shortened form of "university" (first, it was versity), which was its original meaning

{ **vary** is from Latin *varius*, "speckled, variegated; changeable" }

vase is from Latin *vas*, "vessel"

Vaseline gets its name from the German word for water, the Greek word for oil, plus the suffix -ine

vast comes from Latin *vastus*, "immense" or "void"

vastation is the opposite of **devastation**—a renewal

vat is from Germanic *fatam*, "barrel, vessel"

the **Vatican** is named for the hill it is built on in Rome: Vaticanus

vaudeville comes from a French composer's calling his songs "*chanson du Vau de vire*" (song of the valley of Vire—in Normandy)—later shortened to "*vau de ville*"

vault is from Latin *volvere*, "roll, turn"

veal is from Latin *vitellus*, a diminutive of *vitulus*, "calf"

a run before a leap is a **vease**, **feeze**, or **pheese**

vector is Latin for "carrier, traveler"; a carrier of disease or germs is a **vector**

veer can mean "to let out gradually a line or rope"

a **vegan** eats no animal products in any form

a **vegetable** (from Latin *vegetabilis*, "animating, life-giving") may be described as any plant or plant part, other than a sweet fruit, suitable for eating; the word

vegetable has very little meaning in describing plants botanically, other than to suggest their horticultural nature or culinary use—and it was first an adjective meaning "having the life of a plant"

vegetable sponge is another name for **loofah**

vegetarian was popularized by the formation of the Vegetarian Society in England in 1847

if something is **vegete**, it is healthy and active, flourishing in respect to health and vigor

vehement once described pain or temperature as being "high, intense"

a **vehicle** is etymologically something that "carries" (from Latin *vehere*)

the source of **veil** is Latin *velum*, "curtain, sail, **veil**"

vein is from Latin *vena*, "blood vessel"

Velcro gets its name from French *vel(ours) cro(ché)* "hooked velvet"

veld is Dutch for "field" and it means "open grassland" in English

velleity describes a mild desire, wish, or urge that is too slight to lead to action

vellicating or **vellication** is a twitching, jerking, or convulsive movement

the short downy hair on the face and other parts of the body prior to puberty is **vellus**

velvet's root is Latin *villus*, "hairy, shaggy"

venal is "corruptible, unscrupulous"; **venial** is "forgivable; not criminal"

vend is from Latin *vendere*, "sell"

veneer and **furnish** are both from Old French *fournir*

to **venenate** is to poison

venereal is from Latin *venus*, "love," and *venereus*, "of sexual love or intercourse"; **venereal** disease is now called a **sexually transmitted disease** (STD)

terms of **venery** (or venereal nouns) are expressions referring to groups of animals; **venery** is also the practice or sport of hunting

venison's origin is Latin *venatio*, "game hunting," and it first referred to the meat of any animal killed in the chase—now just deer eaten as food is **venison**

venom comes from Latin *venenum*, the love potion Venus used to attract people to each other—but later, *venenum* came to describe "poison"

vent is from Latin *exventare*, "let out air"

a fingerhole on a flute or other wind instrument is a **ventage** or **ventil**

the belly or abdomen of a mammal is the **venter**

a stone shaped or altered by windblown sand is a **ventifact**

ventilate is based on Latin *ventus*, "wind"

ventriloquism comes from *venter*, "belly," and *loqui*, "to speak," as early on people believed ventriloquists spoke by using air in their stomachs

ventripotent is a way of saying fat-bellied

venture is a shortening of adventure

venturesome implies an eagerness for dangerous undertakings

venue in French is literally "a coming" and **venue** was first an attack or call to attack

veranda is from Portuguese *varanda*, "balustrade, railing"

a **verb** expresses action or being

to repeat words or phrases, usually unconsciously, is to **verbigerate**

verdant can mean "inexperienced"

verdict is from Latin *ver*, "true," and *dictum*, "to say"

verdigris is etymologically "green of Greece"

green plant life or trees is **verdure**

verge is the technical term for the male reproductive organ of invertebrate animals

verisimilitude means basically "like the truth"

verjuice is the acid juice of green or unripe grapes, crabapples, or other sour fruit

{ **vermiculture** is the farming of earthworms for compost or fishing }

vermin was first a collective term for reptiles/snakes or other yukky animals

Vermont is French for "green mountain"

vermouth is named for the herb wormwood (German *Wermuth*), which was then borrowed into French as *vermout*

spring fever is also called **vernalagnia**

vernile means "servile, slavish"

vernissage originally indicated the adding of finishing touches by artists; now it is used to mean "private viewing" of an artwork

verse's root is "turning"—as a plow at the end of a furrow—because of the way poetry is written and formatted

versed "practiced" is based on Latin *versare*, "be engaged in"

a short sentence said or sung by a minister is a **versicle**

versicolor means "having various hues"

versimilitude is the appearance of being real or true

version, from Latin *vertere*, "turn," means "act or instance of turning something"

verso (Latin "on the turned (leaf)") is the lefthand page and **recto** the righthand page of an open book

greenery as cover or food for deer is **vert**

vertebrate comes from Latin *vertebratus*, "jointed"

vertical first meant "directly overhead"

vertiginous is "revolving or turning as if on an axis"

vertigo is the sense of whirling and loss of balance (dizziness) from looking down from a great height

verve first meant special talent for writing

very is from Latin *verus*, "true"

big blisters are called **vesicles** and small ones are **bullae**

Latin *vesper* meant "evening" and **vespers** are etymologically "time when the sun goes down," as the Romans believed the evening star was Vesper (or Hesper)

vespertine describes flowers, insects, etc. that are opening or active in the evening

a **vespiary** is a wasps' nest

vessel was once a collective term for table utensils

vest was originally a robe or gown and it comes from Latin *vestire*, "to clothe, dress," and *vestis*, "clothing, garment"

vestal is "chaste, virginal"

vestibule in from Latin *vestibulum*, "entrance court"

vestige comes from Latin *vestigium*, "footprint"

vestment are the ritual robes of the clergy

{ a **vestry** is a church room used for classes or meetings }

to **vesuviate**, from Mount Vesuvius, is to erupt, and a match for lighing cigars was once called a **vesuvian**

to **vet** is to evaluate expertly

vetanda are forbidden things

veteran derives from Latin *vetus*, "old"

veterinary derives from Latin *veterinae*, "cattle, beast of burden"

veto is Latin for "I forbid"

vexillology is the study of flags (from Latin *vexillum*, "flag")

via (pronounced VIE-uh or VEE-uh) means "by way of" not "by means of"

viaduct is based on Latin *via*, "way" on the pattern of aqueduct

viaggiatory is an adjective meaning "traveling about"

an article of food is a **viand**

vibrate comes from Latin *vibrare*, "move quickly to and fro; shake"

hair in the nostrils or whiskers on a cat are **vibrissae**

vicar is etymologically a substitute or representative for someone else

vicarious is from Latin *vicarious*, "substitute"

the earliest sense of **vice** in English was "winding staircase" (deriving from French *vis*, "screw")

vicennial is "occurring once every twenty years"

viceroy is from French *vice*, "standing in the place of," and *roi*, "king"

vichyssoise is shortened from créme vichyssoise, "iced cream soup of Vichy" (a town in France)

vicinage is another word for neighborhood

vicinal, from Latin *vicus*, "group of houses," means "of or pertaining to a neighborhood"—hence, **vicinity**

{ **vicious** first meant pertaining to or characterized by vice }

sudden or unexpected changes in life are **vicissitudes**

victim originally denoted a person or animal killed as a sacrifice

victory is from Latin *vincere*, meaning "defeat"

a female victor is a **victress**

victual is from Latin *victualia*, "provisions"—and is properly pronounced VIH-tuhl

vicuña, a South American mammal with silky fleece and resembling the llama, is pronounced vie-KOON-yuh

videnda are things worth seeing or which ought to be seen

video, from Latin *videre*, "to see," is patterned on audio

a **vidiot** is an undiscriminating viewer of television or video recordings

viduage is another word for widowhood

vie is a shortened version of envie, "make a challenge"

view is etymologically something "seen"

the part you look through on a camera is the **viewfinder**

vigil is literally Latin for "awake"; **vigilant** and **vigilante** (through Spanish **vigilante** "watchman") are from Latin *vigilans*, "keep awake"

vignette is French "a little vine," from the vinelike decorations in early books; sketches or pictures on product labels are called vignettes

Viking came from vik / vic, "camp, village," since the Vikings made temporary camps during their raids of foreign countries

vile first meant "of low status, quality, or price"

to **vilify** is to say defamatory things about someone

vilipend means "consider as having little value; treat contemptuously"

villa first denoted a "country house" (from Latin)

villain was a farm laborer and, hence, an uneducated person, before the meaning evolved

vim is the same as **vigor**

VIN is your Vehicle Identification Number (so **VIN** number is redundant)

vinaceous is "of the color wine red" and **violaceous** is "of the color violet"

vinaigrette is a diminutive form of French *vinaigre*, "vinegar"; in British English it is known by the name "French dressing" (vinegar is, literally, "sour wine")

vincible means conquerable

vincula are links, ties, and bonds

vindicate is from Latin *vindicare*, "claim, defend, revenge"

vine came through Old French from Latin *vinea*, "**vine**, vineyard" (from *vinum*, "**wine**"); **wine** was an early Old English borrowing from Latin *vinum*, "**wine**"

vinegar is from French *vyn egre*, based on Latin *vinum*, "wine," and *acer*, "sour"

vintage is etymologically the "taking away of wine" and the word's ultimate source is *vindemia*, "grape gathering"

violate is from Latin *violare*, "to treat with violence"

violet, from Latin *viola*, "**violet**," probably originated in a pre Indo-European Mediterranean language

violin is from Latin *vitula*, "stringed instrument"—from Vitula, a Roman goddess of joy and victory; her name also gave us **fiddle**

viper is from Latin *vivus*, "alive," and *parere*, "bring forth" (because a snake gives birth to live young)

a loudmouthed overbearing woman is a **virago**

virescent is "beginning to be green" or "tending toward green"

virgin is from Latin *virgo*, "maiden, young woman"

Virginia was named for England's Queen Elizabeth I (1533–1603), the "Virgin Queen"

a **virgule**, the forward slash as between and/or, is from Latin *virgula*, "little rod"

viridescent is green or slightly green

viridity is the quality or state of being green (as foliage, grass)

to go in circles or a circuit is to **viron**

knowledge of or a taste for antiques is **virtu**

virtue, which meant at first a desirable male attribute (derived from Latin *vir*, "man"), was extended over time to apply to both sexes

virulent can mean "full of malice" or "antagonistic"

virus was a Latin word meaning "poison" or "slimy liquid" and it first meant "venom of a snake"

a **visa** is etymologically something "seen," from Latin *visa*, "things seen"

visage is a literary term that may refer to either the shape of the face or the impression it gives or the mood it reveals—and is not restricted to humans but may describe things like a town

visagiste is a fancy word for makeup artist

vis-à-vis means "face-to-face" in French and is used to mean "compared, contrasted with"

visceral is "pertaining to the response of the body as opposed to the intellect," but it can also mean "extremely emotional" (in a negative way)

viscerotonic is having a sociable, easy-going, comfort-seeking personality

viseme is the movement of the lips when pronouncing phonemes

a **visit** is an instance of visiting; a **visitation** is an act of visiting—with **visitation** carrying the connotation of an unexpected or undesired occurrence

visnomy is a person's face or expression, especially as an indication of character and mind

a **visor** is etymologically something that covers the face, from Anglo-Norman *viser*, from *visus*, "appearance, sight"

vista is literally Italian for "view"

vital is from Latin *vitalis* and *vita*, "life"

vitamin is Latin *vita*, "life," and *amine*, because vitamins were originally thought to contain an amino acid

vitative means "loving life"; **vitativeness** is a "love of life" and is also the seat of the instincts of self-preservation

another word for egg yolk is **vitellus** and **vitelline** is egg-yolk yellow

vitiate is "to make imperfect; spoil"

viticulture comes from Latin *vitis*, "vine"; **vintner** from Latin *vinum*, "wine"

to **vitilitigate** is to contend noisily or argue

a **vitrailist** is a designer or maker of stained glass

vitreous is from Latin *vitrum*, "glass," and *vitreus*, "clear, transparent"

vitriol first meant "sulfuric acid"

vittate means "longitudinal/lengthwise stripes"

vittles is a very old English word and it is not a corrupt pronunciation of victuals (but rather vice versa)

to **vituperate** is to verbally abuse; **vituperation** implies fluent and sustained abuse

the adjective form for calf is **vituline**

vivacious can mean "long-lived"

a **viver** is a fish pond

vivid is from Latin *vividus*, "full of life"

a **vixen** is a female fox

a **vizard** is a mask or masked person

vocabular means "of or pertaining to words"

vocabulation is one's selection and use of words

vocation is "a calling" from Latin *vocare*, "to call"

voculation is correct pronunciation

voda is Russian "water" and **vodka** is the diminutive "little water"—as alcoholic beverages have sometimes been called the "water of life"

a vodka martini can be called a **vodkatini**

fog mixed with volcanic fumes (as in Hawaii) is **vog**

the etymological meaning of **vogue** is being borne along by the "waves" of fashion; **vogue** first was applied to rowing as "going along smoothly"

voice is from Latin *vox*, "voice"

the **voice box** is the **larynx**

void means empty; **devoid** means empty, but empty only after something has been taken away

the **void** is the space into which the rounded projection or **nub** is placed to form a lock in a jigsaw puzzle

a **voidee** is a last-minute snack

another word for neighborhood is **voisinage**

a **volar** pain is in the sole of the foot or palm of the hand

volatile was a collective term for birds or creatures that fly, from Latin *volare*, "to fly"

volcano gets its name from Vulcan, the Roman god of fire

the meadow or field mouse is also called a **vole**

to **volitate** is to fly aimlessly here or there

volition is from Latin *vola*, "I wish"

a bad shot that turns out well in golf is known as a **Volkswagen** in golfing slang

to hit a ball before it bounces (in many sports) is to **volley**

Alessandro Volta (1745–1827) built the first battery and **volt** is named for him

a **volte-face** is reversal, as in policy, or an about-face

voluble is "flowing with speech, talkative"— and a **voluble** person has words "rolling" off his or her tongue

ancient books were written on sheets of paper that were rolled and **volume** was originally the name of a scroll or roll of papyrus (Latin *volvere*, "to roll up")

volunteer is from Latin *voluntas*, "free will, will"

a **voluptuary** is one totally into luxury and sensual pleasure

voluptuous is from Latin *voluptas*, "pleasure," and *voluptuosus*, "giving pleasure"

volutation is the action of turning something over in one's mind

Volvo derived from Latin for "I roll"

vomit is from Latin *vomere*

a large passageway in an athletic stadium (or an amphitheatre) for entry/exit is called a **vomitorium** or **vomitory**; the plural is vomitories or vomitoria

the word **vowel** comes from Latin *vocalis*, "using the voice," *littera*, "letter"—and vowels are spoken without much interference or shaping in the mouth

voyage first described a "journey by sea or land," from Latin *viaticum*, "provisions for a journey"; the phrase boon voyage ("prosperous journey") was altered to bon voyage late in the seventeenth century

voyeur is French for "one who sees"

{ **votal** means "associated with or having the nature of a vow" }

voodoo derives from West African *vodu*, "demon"

the lean of a downhill skier is called **vorlage**

vortical means "moving in a vortex"

Vote is from Latin *votum*, "vow, wish," which was the word's original meaning in English. The word had a number of (now) obsolete meanings before it took on the sense (in the fifteenth century) of "a formal expression of one's opinion or approval or disapproval of a matter, especially a candidate, motion, or proposal."

vouch originally meant "call as a witness"

vouchsafe etymologically means vouch in the sense of "warrant" and first meant "to confer or bestow (a thing, favor, etc.) on a person"

a **VPN** (virtual private network) is a private computer network that is configured within a public network (a carrier's network or the Internet)

a small cavity in a rock is a **vug** or **vugg** or **vugh**

the "Vulgar" in **Vulgar** Latin stands for "of the people"

vulgar is an example of pejoration, of a word developing negative meaning over time; it first meant "common, ordinary"

vulgate is accepted everyday speech

vulnerable is from Latin *vulnus*, "wound"

to **vum** is to swear or vow

{ the letter **W** is the only letter that does not have just one syllable; it has three }

wabbit means "tired out, exhausted"

wabi-sabi is "solitude, loneliness" in Japanese and pertains to art with a mood of spiritual solitude as in Zen philosphy

wacky is based on the noun whack

waddle is probably wade and toddle combined

wade once meant "move onward" and "penetrate" as it came from a Germanic word meaning "go (through)"

wadi can mean a "dry riverbed" or a "stream or oasis"

wafer and **waffle** come from German *wafel*, from an early Germanic word *wabo*, "honeycomb"

waft comes from wafter as a back-formation, for "convey by water; convoy"

wafture is "a wave of the hand, the act of waving"

wage once meant "pledge, security" and **wager** was defined as "solemn pledge" or "undertaking," from French *wagier*, "to pledge"

wagon comes from Dutch *wagen*

waif originally described something found by happenstance and belonging to nobody; it can also describe a flag marking the position of a harpooned whale

wail comes from an Old English word meaning "woe"

the root of **wainscotting** is "wagon siding"

a wagon builder is a **wainwright**

waist is etymologically "girth to which one has grown"

wait first meant "to watch with hostile intent"

a **waitron** is a person, male or female, who waits on tables at a restaurant

to **waive** something is etymologically to make a "waif" of it (abandon it)

a **wake** is a watch or vigil over the body of a dead person

a corduroy rib or ridge is a **wale**

walk first meant "roll," "toss," or "move about; go" (from Old English *wealcan*, "to roll")

wall comes from Latin *vallum*, "rampart"

wallet was first a bag for holding goods for a journey, a bag for provisions

to **wallop** can mean "to bubble up in boiling" or "boil with a noisy bubbling sound"

to **wallow** is etymologically to "roll" about

the runt of a litter is a **wallydrag**

if something **walms**, it is bubbling up

wanderlust is German for "to wander" and "desire" (the desire to wander)

wane suggests the fading or weakening of something good or impressive

the root of **want** is Latin *vanus*, "empty, lacking"

wanton's root is "not well-reared"

to **wantonize** is to flirt or dally with

a **wap** is a piece of string wrapped around something

to **wapper** is to blink one's eyes

{ Old English *walhhnutu* (from *wealh*, "foreign"), meaning "foreign nut, nut of the Roman or Persian lands" became **walnut** }

walrus comes from Dutch and means "sea horse"

waltz comes from German *walzen*, "to revolve, dance"

wamble or **womble** is the churning or grumbling of the stomach; to **wamble** is to move unsteadily with a weaving or rolling motion

Algonquian *wampumeage*, "white string of beads," brings us **wampum**

a fringed western shirt is a **wamus**

wan can mean "bland" or "uninterested"

wand is etymologically a "bendable" stick, from Old Norse *vondr*, "thin straight stick" (from earlier Germanic)

to **wander** is etymologically to "turn" off the right path

wanderjahr is literally "wander year" (German) and refers to a year of wandering or travel

war, first coming into Old English (c. 1154) as *werre* or *warre*, from Anglo-Norman French *guerre*, is ultimately of Germanic origin

warble has the underlying notion of "whirling around" and for sounds that took on the meaning "whirl of notes; trill"

the ridge in a lock or keyhole or the corresponding notched part of a key is the **ward**

warden is from Middle English, originally a guardian or protector, from French *guarden*, "guardian"

wardrobe comes from French *garderobe*, "keep robe"

ware originally meant "commodities"

a **wark** is an ache or pain

warm shares an Indo-European base with Latin *formus*, Greek *thermos*, and Sanskrit *gharma*

warn is from prehistoric West Germanic *war*, "watch, be on one's guard" or "take care"

warp is lengthways and **weft** is crossways

the **warp** are parallel strands; strands threaded over and under are **weft** or **woof**

a **warple** or **warple** way is a country lane

warrant was first a defender or protector

a **warren** is etymologically a "fenced-off" area, from Gaulish *varrenna*, "area bounded by a fence"

a **warth** is a shore or stretch of coast

the adjective ware "aware, conscious" gives us the word "**wary**"

wasabi and **daikon** are Japanese horseradish and radish

the suffix -**wash** denotes a deliberate attempt to change the appearance of something, patterned on "whitewash"

a **wasm** is an "ism" that has gone out of fashion, an obsolete theory

WASP stands for White Anglo-Saxon Protestant

{ **wasp**, the insect, traces back to an Indo-European root meaning "weave" }

wassail comes from the Middle English *waes haeil*, "be in good health" or "be fortunate," and wassailing was the Old English custom of toasting the holiday and each other's health and a **wassail** is a festivity involving the drinking of much alcohol and the name of the spiced apple beverage used in such this activity

a word like **Wassup**? can be labeled as a **pronunciation spelling**—and it is also a **phatic** term, one that creates an atmosphere of goodwill

a **wastrel**, either a wasteful or worthless person, is derived from the verb "waste" (from Latin *vastus*, "desert, waste") and pronounced WAYS-trul

a group of nightingales is a **watch**

the Indo-European root of **water** means "wet"

the transparency and luster of a diamond is its **water**

a hose attachment that disperses rather than concentrates water (as a **nozzle** does) is a **water breaker**

a **watermelon** is really a berry and it was first written as two words

watersmeet is a junction of two rivers

800 numbers were called **WATS** lines, for Wide-Area Telephone Service, from 1929 to 1979

Scottish engineer James Watt (1736–1819) refined the steam-powered piston engine and the electrical unit **watt** is named for him

the **wattle** is the fleshy part hanging from the neck of a turkey or other bird

to **waught** is to drink down in great gulps

wave "movement of the sea" seems to be an alteration of an earlier *wawe*, "wave," from Old English *woeg*, "motion, wave"

a stray animal is a **wavenger**

wax (verb) is from Old English *weaxan*, "to become" or "to grow"

wax (noun) originally referred specifically to "beeswax" and the word's underlying etymological reference is to the combs being "woven" from **wax** by the bees

the **waxwing** has small red tips on the end of the secondary feathers of the wings that look like blobs of sealing wax

waxy can mean "angry, irritated, vexed"

the most frequently used noun in English seems to be **way**

a **waypoint** is a stopping place on a journey

the **wayside** is the edge of a road

the original meaning of **wayward** was "turning away" or "turned away"

if one is good at not getting lost, then one is **waywise**

> **WD-40** stands for "Water Displacement-40th attempt"

weak is from a Germanic base meaning "give way, yield"

wealth is from well or weal plus -th, patterned after health

the etymological notion of **wean** is "becoming accustomed" and we use it as a verb meaning "to cause to give up something"; the verb **ween** means "to think, suppose, or imagine something"

baby seals are called **weaners**

weapon is from prehistoric Germanic *woepnam*, but no more is known for certain

weapons-grade is an extreme version of something

weasel is based on a root meaning "seep, exude" for the powerful musk it secretes

weather goes back to the Indo-European base *we*, "blow"; **wither** may have originated as a variant of **weather**

weaved is rare as a form of **weave**, which has **wove** and **woven**

Web should be capitalized in **World Wide Web**, **Web**, and **Web** site, though **website** is a common spelling now; **Internet** should also be capitalized

the Old English word for "one who weaves" was **webster**

the root sense of **wed** is "to pledge, to espouse" and **wedlock**'s "lock" is from Old English *lac*, "condition of being committed to"

a **wedding** is etymologically a ceremony at which people "promise" to marry each other

a **weddinger** is a wedding guest but can also be used to describe anyone in the wedding party

Wednesday is Woden's day—for Odin of Norse mythology

wee, "small," was originally a noun, Old English *weg/wege*, which meant "weight," and it shifted to mean "small amount"

the word **weed** comes from the Old English *wiod*, a variant of a Saxon term for "wild"

week comes from prehistoric Germanic *wikon*, probably from *wik*, "bend, change, turn," and it may originally have meant "time change"

weekend is literally "the end of a week"

weep is probably imitative of the sound of wailing or lamentation

weevil comes from Old English *wifel*, "beetle," and *boll* (first spelled *bowl*) refers to the pod of the cottonplant, which the beetle attacks

weigh first meant "carry, lift, bear, raise up"

a **weir** is etymologically a structure for "hindering" the flow of water, from Old English *werian*, "defend, protect" or "hinder"

weird (as a noun) originally meant "fate, destiny" and (adjective) "having the power to control destiny"—and it is spelled with "ei"

welcome first referred to a person whose arrival was desirable or pleasing

weld and **well** (verb) originally meant "boil, melt" but **weld** evolved to mean "fuse metal by healing"

welfare was originally the phrase wel fare—first meaning "happiness" or "prosperity"

well is an adverb to describe an activity; **good** is an adjective to describe a condition or state

the **Wellington** boot is named after a British prime minister Arthur Wellesley, first—Duke of **Wellington** (1808–1814)—as well as other articles of clothing

well-taken means "accurate, shrewd" of a comment or argument

a **welt** is a narrow piece of leather stitched into a shoe between the sole and the upper

Weltanschauung is German for "world perception, worldview"

a **wen** is another word for a boil or sebaceous cyst on the skin

wench first referred to a child with unformed character

wend started off meaning "turn" but broadened to "go"

Wendy's was named for Dave Thomas's (the founder) daughter

in **werewolf**, the first element is probably Old English wer, "a man"

weskit is a vest, shortened from wainscoat

west shares an Indo-European root with Greek hesperos and Latin vesper, "evening"

the states of the U.S. **West** (or **Far West**) are California, Nevada, Arizona, Utah; sometimes Oregon, Idaho, New Mexico, and Wyoming

wet is closely related to water and comes from the same prehistoric base

wetback, a derogatory term for illegal immigrant from Mexico, alludes to getting wet swimming the Rio Grande to cross the frontier

wetware is human brain cells—as opposed to computer software

wey is a former unit of volume for weighing cheese

whack can mean a large quantity or amount

whale is from prehistoric Germanic khwal

whammy is from "wham" and became associated in the 1950s with the cartoon "Li'l Abner" in which Evil-Eye Fleegle could "shoot a **whammy**" meaning "put a curse on somebody" by pointing a finger with one eye open and a "**double whammy**" with both eyes open

a **whangdoodle** is a person who eagerly attacks things he/she dislikes

a **wharf** is any structure that is built along and parallel to a shore and that vessels tie up to

what traces back to Indo-European qwod, which also produced Latin quod, "**what**"

wheaten is the color of wheat, a pale yellow or fawn

wheel is etymologically something that "goes around"

the barrow of **wheelbarrow** is related to bear, "carry"

the cement/asphalt barriers or bars in parking lots are called **wheelguards**

the sound of a sword drawn from its sheath is a **wheep**

wheeze is probably from Old Norse hvaesa, "to hiss"

whelk comes from Old English wioluc, "turns"

{ **whelk** is a euphemism for pimple }

to **whelm** can mean to throw something over violently or in a heap upon something else so as to cover, smother, or crush it

the Anglo-Saxon **whelp** lost out to puppy

whem is a blemish or spot

when and **where** were formed from the ancient base qwo, also the source of what, who, etc.

whence means "from where," so no need to say "from **whence**"

use **whether** for a choice between alternatives

a knife-sharpening stone is a **whetstone**

which is from Latin *qui*, "who"

to **whicker** is to utter a half-suppressed laugh

a **whiffle** is an unimportant thing

while is from Germanic *khwilo*, from Indo-European *qwi*, meaning "rest"

{ another word for trinket is **whim-wham** }

if an arrow **whines**, it whistles through the air

whip was first a verb meaning "move quickly"

whipsnapper, a cheeky person with nothing better to do than snap whips, became **whippersnapper**

a cross between a greyhound and a terrier is a **whippet**

whisk is from a Germanic base *wisk*, meaning "move quickly"

a **whiskerando** is a heavily whiskered man

a beard-growing contest is a **whiskerino**

whiskers was originally a bundle of feathers, twigs, etc. used for whisking (from "whisk") and then came to denote the projecting hairs or bristles of mammals

Gaelic *uisgebeatha*, "water of life," was respelled *whiskybal*, then shortened to **whiskey**; the Scots and Canadians spell **whisky** without the "e," the Irish and Americans spell **whiskey** with the "e"

a **whisp** is a slight gust of wind or a light rain shower

whisper is from a base which imitated a hissing sound

the game of **whist** was originally called whisk, from "whisking away" the cards after the tricks had been taken

whistle first meant "play on a pipe"

whistness means silence

white noise is noise made from a blend of all audible frequencies

white traces to Indo-European *kwitnose/kwidnos* and it is technically not a color but a combination of all colors; **wheat** is etymologically "**white**" grain

a **whitlow** is an inflammation near a fingernail or toenail

Use **who** when a nominative pronoun is appropriate, and **whom** when an objective pronoun is appropriate. **Who** is a nominative pronoun (meaning it acts as a subject) and is used: 1) as the subject of a verb, as in "It was Paul **who** rescued the dog."; 2) as the complement of a linking verb, as in "They know **who** you are." **Whom** is an objective pronoun (meaning it serves as an object) and is used: 1) as the object of a verb, as in "**Whom** did you see?" and 2) as the object of a preposition, as in "That is the group to **whom** the credit belongs." **Who** and **whom** seem to cause more difficulty than other pronouns. Thus, when in doubt, substitute him and see if that sounds right. If him is OK, then **whom** is OK. For example: "You talked to **whom**? You talked to him." It would be incorrect to say "You talked to he," and few native English speakers would make that mistake.

a **whole** comprises its **parts**, a **whole** consists of its **parts**, a **whole** is composed of its **parts**, **parts** constitute a **whole**

to **whoofle** is to snort, gurgle, or snuffle

whoops is probably an alteration of upsy-daisy

a **whore** is etymologically a "lover," from an Indo-European base that also produced words meaning "dear" and "lover" and "randy"

whorl is a variant of whirl and first meant "small flywheel"

why is from Indo-European base of *qwei*, a form of *qwo*

wich, found in many place-names (Greenwich, Keswick), may comes from Old English *wic*, "a settlement," but also seems to originally have been locations of salt pits

wicked is probably based on Old English *wicca*, "witch"

wicker is typically made of willow and is from Swedish *viker*, "willow"

a **wicket** was originally a small gate and etymologically the word apepars to denote something that "turns" as on a hinge

widdershins means "in a direction opposite of the usual one," but can also mean "unlucky'"

wide traces to Indo-European *wi*, "apart, away"; **width** was coined probably on the analogy of breadth

a **widger** is a spatula used in gardening to transplant seedlings

widget may be an alteration of gadget

widow is from an Indo-European root meaning "be empty"

to **wield** something is etymologically to "command" or "rule" and that is what it first meant in English

wieldy means "easily controlled or handled" and once meant "agile, nimble"

wiener is German, an adjective from *Wien*, "Vienna"; **Wiener** schnitzel is literally "Vienna cutlet"

wife originally meant simply "woman" but by Old English it was "married woman"

wig is a shortening of periwig

a **wight** is a spirit or ghost

{ **wigwam** is from Ojibwa *wigwaum* and Algonquian *wikiwam*, "their house" }

wiki comes from Hawaiian *wikiwiki*, "fast, speedy"

the radio code **wilco** means "will comply"

wild marjoram is another term for **oregano**

wilderness etymologically denotes the "condition of being a wild animal," from Old English *wild deor*, "wild animal," but it came to mean "wild land"

the **wildtrack** or **room tone** consists of the barely audible noises that make up a background sense of quiet

a **williwaw** is a sudden violent squall

willy-nilly is a contraction of "will I, nill I"

wimp did not come into the language until 1920, and was not used widely until the 1960s

a nun's headgear is a **wimple**

win's Germanic base gave it its first meaning of "to labor, strive, work"

in horse racing results, there is **win**, **place**, **show**, and **also-ran**

wince first meant "kick restlessly" due to impatience or pain

wind goes back to an Indo-European base meaning "blow"

wind moves horizontally, while a **draft** moves vertically

a row of trees acting as a fence is a **windbreak**

a step in a spiral staircase is a **winder**

a branch or tree blown down by the wind is a **windfall**

window is from Old Norse *vindr*, "wind," and *auga*, "eye"; Norsemen kept their doors closed in winter and relied on a hole ("eye") in the roof for ventilation

leaves or snow heaped up by the wind is a **windrow**

wine comes from Latin *vinum*, probably from a lost Mediterranean language word *win/woin*, "**wine**"

wing was borrowed from Old Norse *voengir*, from Indo-European *we*, "blow"

a **wingding** can be a fit or spasm, an outburst

a bow tie's ends are called the **wings** and the middle is the **crosspiece** or **crossknot**

wink is the closing of the eyes for sleep

a **winker** is a tiddlywinks player

Winnebago translates to "filthy water people" and **Mohawk** to "Man-Eaters"

etymologically, to **winnow** grain is to separate it from the chaff by means of the "wind"

winsome's derivation is Old English *wynn*, "joy, pleasure"

The word **winter** comes from an old Germanic word that means "time of water" and refers to the rain and snow—as well as low temperatures—of the season in middle and high latitudes. In the Northern Hemisphere, it is commonly regarded as extending from the **winter** solstice (the year's shortest day), December 21 or 22, to the vernal equinox, the start of spring. The word **winter** came into English c. 888.

wire may derive from Latin *viere*, "plait, weave"

Wisconsin is Algonquian for "grassy place, beaver place"

wise comes from an Indo-European base meaning "see" and "know," which also produced the English words idea, vision, and wit

wiseacre comes from Dutch *wijsseggher*, "soothsayer"

wish comes from prehistoric Germanic *wunskjan*, from Indo-European meaning "think, suppose"

the **wishbone** of a turkey used to be called the **merrythought**; the forked bone between the neck and breast of a bird is technically the **furcula**

{ **wisteria** is named for professor of anatomy Caspar Wistar (1761–1818) }

wit originally meant "mind, judgment, sense, understanding"

in Old English, **witch** was actually *wicca* and originally (c. 890) was a man who practiced magic or sorcery, which we now call wizard; by the year 1000, **witch** came to be defined as "a female magician or sorceress"

a **with** is a tough but supple twig or slender branch, as of a willow

with once meant "against" and denoted opposition

wither is a differentiated and special use of Middle English *wederen*, "to expose to weather"

a person who tries to be funny but is not is a **witling**

witness first meant "knowledge, understanding"

a **wittol** is a man who tolerates his wife's adultery

a **witwanton** is a would-be comedian who is not funny

witzelsucht is a feeble attempt at humor; **witzelsuchting** is making a weak attempt at being funny or humorous

wizard was a philosopher or sage and was based on "wise" and "-ard"

begone in **woebegone** meant "beset" or "surrounded," so the word meant "beset by woe"

wok derives from a Cantonese word meaning "pan"

a **wold** is open rolling hills or open country

wolf is an ancient word from Indo-European that came into Greek as *lukos* and Latin as *lupus*

wolfing is hunting for wolves

a **woman** is etymologically a "wife-man" or "female person"

womb once referred to the abdomen or stomach

wonton is an alteration of Cantonese *wan t'an*, "pastry"

woo is a word that may have arisen as the imitation of the sounds associated with the soft murmuring of lovers

the early meaning of **wood** is probably "collection of trees, forest"

woodness is madness or insanity—from Old English *wood*, "out of one's mind"

to **woodshed** is to practice in an isolated place

woofits is an unwell feeling or moody depression

wool is from Indo-European *wina*, which also produced Latin *lana*

wopsy means tangled, disordered, uneven

Worcester grocers Lea and Perrins coined the term for their **Worcestershire** (also Worcester) sauce

the Germanic base of **word** is related to Latin *verbum*, "**word**"

to **wordify** is to put into words

work shares its Indo-European base with Greek *ergon*

workaholic was coined in the late 1960s by Wayne Oates, an American pastoral counselor, from work + a(lco)holic

world first meant "(a period of) human existence" or "age or life of man" and "ancient place of man's sustenance"

the ligament under a dog's tongue is the **worm**

the spiral thread of a screw or corkscrew is the **worm**

there are no worms or wood involved in **wormwood**, which is an alteration of the word wermod, a plant used for making vermouth and absinthe and medicine

the original meaning of **worry** was attack by a dog on sheep, literally "to choke, strangle" and figuratively "harass"

worse is from Germanic *wersizon*, a comparative formation of *wers*, "confuse"

worship, from Old English meaning worth and ship, first was defined as "dignity, worth" and its root meaning is "turning reverence toward someone/something"

worsted (pronounced WOOS-tid) is a yarn or fabric first made in Worstead, England

a **wough** is a wall or partition of a house

would goes back to wold, the Old English past tense of will; **would** have is the correct phrase (not **would** of)

a **wowser** is a self-righteous snob

a **wrack** is a mass of high, thick fast-moving cloud

seaweed and vegetation cast ashore is called **wrack**

to **wrangle** can mean "to scream with passion"

{ to **wreathe** is to make a wreath or move in a repeatedly curving course—when smoke wreathes, it is moving in a curling motion }

the past tense and past participle of wreak is always **wreaked**

a **wreath** is a single turn or coil of a coiled thing

wreck goes back to Indo-European *wreg* and it produced *wrek/wrekan*, "drive," and then Old English wreak before **wreck**

wrench comes from an old word meaning "to deceive"

wrinkle may be a back-formation from wrinkled, from Old English *gewrinclod*, "sinuous, winding; serrated"

the **wrist** of the foot is the instep or ankle

all Western Indo-European languages except English derive the verb for "to **write**" from Latin *scribere*; English **write** comes from *a roo wreid*, "to cut, sketch an outline"

writhen is "twisted or contorted out of shape"

wrizzled is marked with creases, corrugations, or wrinkles

a **wro** is a nook, corner, or secluded spot

{ **wrong** originally meant "crooked, twisted, bent" }

to **wrong-foot** is to disconcert by doing something unexpected

wroth and **wrath** are adjective synonyms for "wrathful, angry"; **wrothful** is angry or stirred up

wrought is the archaic past and past participle forms of "work"

wry once meant "contorted"

wurp is a stone's throw

wurst as in liverwurst and bratwurst means "to mix up" as these meats are mixed with various seasonings

the rustling of wind among branches is **wuther**

Wyoming is Algonquian *mache-weaming*, "at the big flats"

{ in medieval times, most people were illiterate and signed documents with an **X**, which they then kissed to prove sincerity— so **X** became associated with a kiss }

x is the horizontal axis and **y** is the vertical

in mathematics, there are three unknown quantities: **X**, **Y**, and **Z**

xanthodontous is having yellow teeth

a guidebook for visitors is a **xenagogy**

xenial or **xenian** pertains the the relationship between host and guest, also between two persons of different countries or between a person and a foreign country

xenodochial means hospitable to strangers

xenon is etymologically the "strange" gas, named by its discoverer in 1898

xeres is another word for sherry

Greek *xeros* meant "dry" and **xerography**, invented in the 1940s, is a photographic reproduction process not using liquid developers

x-height is the height of lower-case letters

the initial letter X in **Xmas** (Christmas) is the Greek letter chi of Khristos "Christ"

puzzled by his discovery, Roentgen named it **X-ray** because X was used as a symbol for the unknown in math—**X-ray** is a translation of German X-Strahlen, from x, "unknown," and *Strahl*, "ray"

XXX and **OOO** added at the end of a letter for kisses and hugs probably originated in the Middle Ages when illiterate people would sign an X for their name and then kiss the paper as a sign of good faith

from the Greek *xylon*, "wood," **xylem** in a plant is what we think of as "wood"

xylophone is from Greek *xylo*, "wood," and *phonos*, "sound," as originally it was made of wooden bars

{ **Y** is the only letter commonly used as both vowel and consonant in English. The vowel is the elder by more than 2,000 years. }

yacht comes from Dutch *jaghtschip*, "hunting ship" or "ship for chasing"

yaffle can mean "bark sharply like a dog," "mumble or talk indistinctly," or "eat or drink noisily or greedily"

yahoo was a brutish race of people in Jonathan Swift's "Gulliver's Travels"

yakitori is Japanese *yaki*, "cook, grill," and *tori*, "bird," as it is a chicken kebab

the word **yam** can be traced back to the Senegal *nyami*, "to eat"

to **yamph** is to bark, especially by a small dog

yang is the male or active/positive force in Chinese philosophy; **yin** is the female or dark/negative force

Yankee probably comes from Dutch *Janke*, a diminutive of the name Jan, "John," that was used as a derisive nickname

a **yantra** is a geometrical diagram used like an icon, especially in meditation

yap means hungry, **yaply** is hungrily, **yapness** is hunger

yard first had the general meaning of "home, house" or "land, region"

yare means "prepared, ready"

yarn comes from an Indo-European base with descendants like Greek *khorde*, "string"

yatter is another word for idle chatter or small talk

to deviate from a course momentarily is to **yaw**

yawn is from an Indo-European base that also gave us gape

yawning can also be called **oscitation**, **hiation**, and **pandiculation**

a **yazzihamper** is a disliked person

ye is an archaic way of writing "the"; in actuality, **ye** from Anglo-Saxon or Old English is pronounced THUH, like "the"

year's root sense is "what passes"

yeast is etymologically a substance that causes "fermentation"

yeepsen is anything that can be held in two hands, a double handful

a **yegg** is a safecracker or burglar yellow jackets and hornets are actually types of wasps

yellow and **green** come from the same Proto-Indo-European base, *ghel/ghol*

yemeles means "careless, negligent"

in-yan was the Chinese expression for "craving for opium" and **yen** first meant "craving of an addict for a drug"; this became *yan* and, eventually, **yen**, for a "powerful craving"

yen as in the currency of Japan comes from the Chinese word *yuan*, meaning "round thing" or "dollar"

a **yenta** or **badaud** is a gossiper and blabbermouth

yeoman, a ship's clerk, is a contraction of yengman, "young man"

cupping of the hands is called **yepsen**

the yester of **yesterday** and yesteryear was a word on its own meaning

yodel is from Bavarian *jodln*, "to utter the syllable jo (yo)"

yoga is Sanskrit and Hindi for "union"—of body and mind

yoghurd—now **yogurt**, yoghurt—was the original Turkish name of this fermented milk

yoicks is an exclamation of excitement or exultation

the etymological idea of **yoke** is of "joining" two animals together

yokel is a figurative use of English dialect **yokel**, "green woodpecker"

yolk comes from an Old English word meaning "yellow"

yes is descended form Old English *gese*; it was first used as a response to negative questions while yea was used for positive questions

"**yesterday**," but by Old English it had become a collocation with "day"

a **yesterfang** is something that was caught or taken yesterday

yestreen is yesterday evening

yield first meant "payment"

Yippies were a radical outgrowth of the Hippies

yips is the pressure that affects golf players, a state of nervousness

another word for whining is **yirning**

to **yisse** is to desire or covet

ylem is the primordial matter from which neutrons, protons, etc. were formed

a **yock** is a hearty laugh

yoctosecond is the smallest designated unit of time (a decimal and twenty-three zeroes)

yonk is an indefinitely long time

yonside is the furthest side, the other side

a **yoop** is a convulsive or sudden sob

to **yote** is to pour liquid on

you was originally the accusative and dative form of ye, "**you**," and it eventually ousted thou

young goes back to Indo-European *juwen*, which produced Latin *juvenis*

yo-yo was once called bandalore

the name **Yucatan** comes from Maya for "listen to how they speak"

yule first referred to December and January

yuppie is an acronym from "young urban professional," coined in 1984

{ For every one-thousand uses of E (the most-used letter), we use **Z** twenty-two times. **Z** is the least-used letter in printed English. }

zaftig is "full-figured," from Yiddish *zaftik*, "juicy"

a round meditation cushion is a **zafu**; a hard rectangular one is a **gomden**

the **Zamboni** ice resurfacer machine is named for Frank J. Zamboni, who invented it

zany comes from Italian *zanni*—a buffoon who mimicked a character or clown in the *commedia dell'arte*

zap is probably a combination of zip and slap—and was first used in comic strips

the dance performed by rhythmic heel stamping is the **zapateado**

zarf is Arabic for "vessel" and it is a cup-shaped holder for a coffee cup

zazen is sitting meditation in Zen Buddhism; *za* is Japanese for "sitting" and *zen* is "meditation (from Chinese *chan*, "quietude," from Sanskrit *dyana*, "meditation")

zeal and jealousy come from the base of Latin *zelus* and Greek *zelos*, "**zeal**, ardor, jealousy"

zebra is literally "wild ass" in Spanish and Italian, and may derive from Latin *equiferus*, "wild horse"

the adjective form of zebra is **zebrine**

zee (U.S.) and **zed** (UK, Canada) are names for the letter Z, which is also called **izzard** and **uzzard**

zeitgeist (pronounced TSIGHT-guyst) is the defining spirit or mood of a particular period of history (from German *Zeit*, "time" and *Geist*, "spirit")

zelator is another word for zealot

Zen is from Sanskrit *dhyana*, "meditation" from a Proto-Indo-European root meaning "to observe, see"

zendo, the meditation room of a Zen monastery, is zen and do, "hall"

zenith derived from Arabic *samt ar-ras*, "the way or road above one's head"; **zenith** technically is the point directly above the observer and **nadir** is the point directly below

zephyr is a breeze from the west or gentle breeze, based on the ancient Greek name for the west wind

Count von **Zeppelin** (1838–1917) built the airship named for him

zero and **cipher** come from Arabic *sifr*, "empty"

zest can be traced back only to French *zeste*, "orange or lemon peel"

zetetic means "asking, questioning"

zetetic (adjective) means "inquiring, investigating" and "proceeding by inquiry or investigation" or (noun) "inquirer"

a **zig** or a **zag** is one leg of a zigzag

a **ziggurat** is a tower in the form of a terraced pyramid

zigzag probably comes from German *ziche*, "to dodge about," and *zacke*, "a jagged edge"

zillion is based on Z as a symbol for "unknown quantity" plus "million"

finger cymbals that belly dancers use are **zills**

Zimbabwe, "walled grave," was formerly Rhodesia

the **zinnia** got its name from Linnæus, who named it for J. G. Zinn, a German botanist (1727–1759)

a news display on a screen affixed to a building is a **zipper**

ziraleet is a sudden expression of joy, an exultation

zita is the singular form of **ziti**; this tubular pasta's name is Italian, plural of zito, alteration of zita, probably short for *maccheroni di zita*, literally, "bride's macaroni"

a **zizz** is a nap

zob is a worthless person

zodiac is from Greek *zodiakos*, "circle of little animals"

the toy Viewmaster™ is technically a **zoetrope**

zoilism is destructive or carping criticism

zombie was originally the name of a snake god in the voodoo cult of West Africa and the Caribbean and later applied to a reanimated corpse

a **zonkey** is the offspring of a zebra and donkey

zoo is a back-formation from zoological garden

zoology is Greek *zoion*, "animal" and *logic*, "discourse, treatise," and first referred to the medical science of remedies derived from animals; **zoology** should be pronounced zoh-OL-uh-jee

{ an animal disease that can be transmitted to humans is **zoonosis** }

zoonters! is an expression of surprise

zori, a type of flip-flop, is Japanese, literally, *so*, "grass, straw," and *ri*, "footwear"

Zorro means "fox" in Spanish

zucchini is the plural of Italian *zucchino*, "courgette," diminutive of *zucca*, "gourd"

a **zuche** is a tree stump

zugzwang is a situation in chess where all the moves open to one player will cause damage to his position

a **zumbooruk** is a swiveling gun mounted on a camel; the gunner who uses it is the **zumboorukchee**

zwieback means "twice baked," as it is a baked biscuit that is sliced and toasted

zydeco first appeared in the 1940s and is the Creole pronunciation of French *"les haricots"* from the song title *"Les Haricots Son pas Salès"*

a **zythepsary** is a brewhouse

zyzzyva, a type of weevil, is the last word in many dictionaries

{ **Miscellaneous** came into English around 1615, from Latin *miscellus*, "mixed" }

The Cat in the Hat has 220 "words"

a lazy person's set of epithets: drotchel, drumble, affler, loblolly, lollard, lollpoop, scobberlotcher, ragabash, faineant, and flutch

a special word is used for the cry, call, or sound of many animals: apes gibber; asses bray; bears growl; beetles drone; bulls bellow; calves, sheep, and lambs bleat; cocks crow and crows caw; cows and oxen low; deer bell; eagles, vultures, hawks, and peacocks scream; falcons chant; guinea pigs and hares squeak; ravens croak; sparrows chirp; swallows twitter

almost all of the hundred most common words in our modern vocabulary come from Old English and three are from Old Norse (their, them, they)

Arabic-derived words related to plants are: couscous, lilac, henna, apricot, coffee, spinach, cork, artichoke, tarragon, cotton, carob, jasmine, lime, caraway, lemon, tamarind, orange, loofah, aubergine, alfalfa, hashish, camphor, saffron

at least half of the words in any sample of modern **English** writing will be of Anglo-Saxon origin

Benjamin Franklin drew up the first list of American slang terms for drunkenness (228)

between 1500–1650, about ten thousand to twelve thousand words were coined, of which about half still exist

black, white, red, yellow, and green are Anglo-Saxon in origin, but blue, brown, orange, and violet entered English via Norman French

by a child's second birthday, he/she is hoovering up new words at a rate of one every two hours

by the time children enter school, they command thirteen thousand words; a typical high school graduate knows sixty thousand—a literate adult, twice that

capitals that look the same in lowercase are: C, O, P, S, U, V, W, X, Z

Charles A. Dana of the "New York Sun" was credited with inventing zowie, bam, socko, yurp, plop, wow, wam, glug, oof, whap, bing, flooie, and grrr

cloud, draft, hail, rain, sleet, snow, storm, wind, and flood are all traceable to Germanic

coined by Shakespeare (to name a few): alligator, dawn, lonely, drug, eyeball, undress, puke, domineering, inaudible, pander, amazement, leapfrog, bedroom, hint, submerge

colors seem to have gotten their names in this order: black, white, red, yellow, green, blue, brown, purple, pink, orange, gray

drink/drench, sit/set, lie/lay, fall/fell are pairs where one verb comes from a prehistoric Germanic causative

English is a much harder language for computers to understand than Japanese or Italian or Spanish due to inconsistency in the way words sound and are spelled—and the fact that some verbs may be nouns and vice versa, identifiable only by their position in a sentence. There is also the complexity of English idioms

English is the only language that has books of synonyms like Roget's Thesaurus

English often incorporated the same word from two languages with slightly different spellings

English speakers can recognize a word in two hundred, milliseconds or less from its onset, i.e., approximately one-fifth of a second from its beginning (usually well before the whole word has been heard)

English words of Latin or Greek origin have rather unpredictable plurals, and each one usually depends on how well-established that particular word is; it may also depend on whether the Latin or Greek form of the plural is either easily recognizable or pleasant to the speaker of English

eponyms from inventors are: biro, braille, bunsen, celsius, derrick, diesel, Fahrenheit, galvanize, guillotine, joule, Morse, ohm, pasteurize, pavlovian, Richter, salmonella, saxophone, silhouette, volt, watt, zeppelin

every time you open a newspaper, you will be faced with at least one word with un- that you have never seen before, one with -ness, and one with -ly

fifty words account for 50 percent of all the words in our speech—and they all have only one syllable

Humpty Dumpty said that we are the masters and words are our servants

if you notice in etymologies that some German words are capitalized, it is because they are nouns

if you speak English, you know parts of at least a hundred different languages

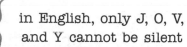

in English, only J, O, V, and Y cannot be silent

in the sixteenth century, there was a fashion to make spellings reflect word history— so if a word originated in Latin or Greek, letters might be added to show the relationship: g was added to reign since it was from Latin *regno*, b was added to debt to show it came from Latin *debitum*

it has been said that just forty-three words account for fully half of all the words in common use and that just nine account for fully one-quarter of all the words in almost any sample of written English: and, be, have, it, of, the, to, will, you

it takes the brain about one-quarter of a second to find a word to name an object

it took Noah Webster twenty years to write his dictionary

Japan has four written languages and one spoken language

language is the cheapest way of expressing identity

less than 3 percent of Old English are loan words from other languages

letters that can be written in one stroke: B, C, D, G, I, J, L, M, N, O, P, R, S, U, V, W, Z

letters with no enclosed areas: C, E, F, G, H, I, J, K, L, M, N, S, T, U, V, W, X, Y, Z

many scientific and technical adjectives are Latinate (canine, cardiac) while the nouns are Old English or Middle English (dog, heart)

many words for animals come from Old English and some of these had no special plural or lost it during the Old English period

Mary Anning was a young paleontologist who is commonly held to be the source of the famous tongue twister "she sells sea shells on the seashore"

more redundancies: added bonus, closed fist, spoiled rotten, revert back, prior history, sum total, end result, true fact, bare naked, unique individual, total abstinence, join together, advance warning, lag behind, close proximity, exact same, exact replica

more than half of all the words adopted into English from Latin now have meanings quite different from their original ones

most of our specifically American spelling rules came from Noah Webster

most of the English archaisms surviving in America seem to be derived from the dialects of eastern and southern England, from which most of the original English settlers came

names starting out with Fitz come from a word meaning "son"

no Chinese last names are more than one syllable long

number-plus-word nouns generally take a hyphen: six-pack, nine-iron, eight-ball

only one thousand words make up 90 percent of all writing

only about 4,500 Old English words survived—which is only about 1 percent of the total in the "Oxford English Dictionary"

only four English words end in -dous: tremendous, horrendous, stupendous, and hazardous

only the letters "a" and "g" have two modern print lowercase forms; every other letter has just one essentially the same for all typefaces

other Anglo-Saxon nouns have an Anglo-Saxon adjective as well as a Latinate adjective: earth/earthly/terrestrial, mother/motherly/maternal, time/timely/temporal

our extraordinarily complex language is built on forty-four distinctive sounds that combine into hundreds and thousands of meaningful word elements

{ over one thousand languages have contributed to modern English }

paired words from Latin and Greek include compassion—sympathy, transparent—diaphanous, revelation—apocalypse

quantifying the meanings of common words, the American scholar GK Zipf said, "Different meanings of a word will tend to be equal to the square root of its relative frequency."

redundancies include: add on to, bare naked, betwixt and between, bits and pieces, brand name, close proximity, fine and dandy, free gift, future plans, head honcho, great big, ISBN number, leave of absence, look and see

even more redundancies: manual dexterity, name brand, old geezer, past experience, personal friend, pick and choose, PIN number, plan ahead, prior notice, quagmire (marsh marsh), reindeer (reindeer deer), reiterate, rice paddy, rules and regulations, scheduled appointment, skin rash, so on and so forth, temper tantrum, time clock, time period, unexpected surprise, up above, vast majority, VIN number, whys and wherefores, wrack and ruin, young child

rule of thumb: if you think a punctuation mark is needed, then it probably is!

Seize each new word as if it was a shining toy! The more words you read, the more words you will know.

70 percent of all English words are made with ten letters: A, D, E, H, I, N, O, R, S, T

some collective terms are: a drift of bees, a cloud of flies, a dissimulation of small birds

some common words derived from Arabic: alcohol, rook, algebra, sequin, mattress, giraffe, amber, crimson, gazelle, hazard, arsenal, lute, sofa, zero, alcove, safari, sherbert, alkali, candy, syrup, check, admiral, magazine

some paired words from Old English and Latin are shepherd—pastor, feeling—sentiment, handbook—manual, anger—ire, freedom—liberty

some words with the most senses in dictionaries are: set, take, through, strike, serve, run, draw, cut, cast, point

some words with vowels in alphabetical order: affectiously, half-seriously, pareciously

sometimes an old meaning is preserved in a phrase or expression: neck, meaning "a parcel of land," is retained in neck of the woods

{ strictly speaking, only adverbs modify; nouns and adjectives qualify }

synonyms for an easy college course are: pud, crip course, crip, easy A, sleep course, cruise course, fluff, bluff, punt, or skate

technical matters have the highest concentration of borrowed classical (Greek and Latin) vocabulary

ten English nouns have double u's: continuum, duumvir, duumvirate, individuum, lituus, menstruum, mutuum, muumuu, residuum, vacuum

the fifty U.S. states derive their names from six basic sources: twenty-eight from Native American languages, eleven from English, six from Spanish, three from French, one from Dutch, and one for the Father of this Country

the ancients divided a play into protasis, epitasis, catastasis, and catastrophe—introduction, continuance, heightening, and conclusion

the birds that can imitate human speech are the budgerigar, mynah, and parrot

the don't in the DONT WALK sign is usually misspelled, since the apostrophe is missing

the dot over the lowercase i is derived from a diacritical mark, like an accent mark, used in Latin to indicate "i" in places where it might be mistaken for part of another letter; this is also why English has the rule that i is not the final letter of a word but must be changed to y

the earliest Americanisms were probably words borrowed from Native American languages for natural objects that had no counterparts in England

the earliest known use of any punctuation is credited to Aristophanes of Byzantium (the librarian of Alexandria) c. 200 BCE

the first Spanish loanwords in American English were mainly Spanish adaptations of Native American terms: tobacco, hammock, tomato, tapioca, chocolate, barbecue, canoe

the five most frequently used letters in English are e, t, o, a, n and the five least frequently used are k, j, x, z, q

the five most persuasive words in English are said to be: discover, easy, guarantee, health, and results

the Hawaiian alphabet has only twelve letters—the shortest alphabet in the world: A, E, I, O, U and H, K, L, M, N, P, W. Until the 1820s, it was only a spoken language and now it is nearly extinct

the "L" is not pronounced in almond, alms, balm, calm, palm, psalm, qualm, and salmon in much of standard English, except in New England

the meaning of a spoken word is accessed by a listener's brain in about a fifth of a second, the meaning of a printed word in about an eighth of a second

the more words you know, the more choices you can make; the more accurate, vivid, and varied your speaking and writing will be

the richness of the English vocabulary and the wealth of available synonyms means that English speakers can often draw shades of distinction unavailable to non-English speakers

the speed of "normal" speech is about six syllables a second (about three or more words)

the surviving words from Anglo-Saxon are among the most fundamental words in English: man, wife, child, brother, sister, live, fight, love, drink, sleep, eat, house, etc.—as well as: and, at, but, for, in, on, to

the top ten most common verbs in English are be, have, do, say, make, go, take, come, see, get—and they are all irregular

the words spelled with most short lowercase letters include curvaceousness, necromancers, reassurances

the words spelled with most tall lowercase letters include highlight and hillbilly

there are forty-odd common prefixes and suffixes in English

there are ninety-six "official" two-letter word playable in Scrabble, from aa to yo

there are five vowel letters but twenty shades of vowel sounds

there are many sets of triplet synonyms from Anglo-Saxon/Latin/Greek and also Anglo-Saxon/Norman French/Latin-Greek like cool-calm-collected and foretell-predict-prophesy

there are many words for one's behind, including: peach, fundament, spankit, prat, dowp, bubble, quoit, croupon, bahakas, hinderlings, nates, rusty-dusty, and sit-upon

there are no irregular verbs in Esperanto

there are ten body parts with three letters: leg, ear, rib, arm, hip, gum, eye, jaw, toe, lip

there are words that rhyme with purple (hirple, curple), orange (Blorenge, sporange), and silver (wilver, chilver); these words all have half rhymes (also known as "imperfect rhyme" or "near rhyme")

there is a statistic that only 1 percent of all "new" words are, in fact, entirely new; the vast majority of neologisms are new takes on the old

there is a tendency in English to adopt a foreign adjective form for an Anglo-Saxon noun, so fingers are not fingerish but digital, eyes are ocular not eyeish—and other such pairs are mouth/oral, book/literary, water/aquatic, house/domestic, moon/lunar, son/filial, sun/solar, church/ecclesiastical, town/urban

these letters have no curved lines: A, E, F, H, I, K, L, M, N, T, V, W, X, Y, Z

these letters have no straight lines: C, O, S

{ these letters look the same upside-down: H, I, N, O, S, X, Z }

these words are rarely used in the singular: trivia, paparazzi, auspices, timpani, minutiae, graffiti, scampi, scruples, measles

three common words start with dw: dwarf, dwell, dwindle

vet was clipped from veterinarian and also from veteran; van, clipped from caravan; cab from cabriolet, exam from examination, fan from fanatic, pants from pantaloons, brig from brigantine, canter from Canterbury gallop

when a verb does not agree in number with the subject, that is because it has been "attracted" to the noun closest to it in the phrase and agrees with that noun instead of the subject

words back-formed from their apparent opposites include couth from uncouth, kempt from unkempt, ept from inept

words can be alphabetized two ways— word-by-word or letter-by-letter; in the former, a shorter word will precede all others beginning with the same letters even if the word is followed by another word—and in the latter all letters are taken as a sequence with hyphens and spaces ignored

words ending in -cracy, -crat, and -cratic come from Greek *kratos*, "power, dominion"

words with a, e, i, o, u once in alphabetical order are abstemious, abstentious, annelidous, arsenious, casesious, fracedinous, and facetious

you can lowercase the shared common noun element in phrases like Third and Main street and the Justice and Labor departments

{ **Of Interest to Word Nerds** }

Etymology Terminology

The underlying meaning of **etymology** is finding the underlying or true meaning of words (from Greek *etumo*, "real, true," and *etumon*, "true thing"). **Notation** is the old term for the explanation of a word on the basis of its etymology; **derivation** and **word history** are also synonyms for **etymology**.

The earliest known form of a root word is an **etymon**, the original or primary meaning of a word.

Folk etymology is a term for words and phrases that have resulted from changes based on "folk" or "popular" notions. A folk etymology arises when a word is assumed to derive from another because of some association of form or meaning, but in fact the word has a different derivation.

A **back-formation** is a word that is formed from what appears to be its derivative (e.g., *edit* from *editor*). Back-formation occurs when speakers of a language assign a regular derivational structure to a word, although a part of this structure, namely the base, did not previously exist. If this new base becomes a word of the language, it is called a back-formation.

A **cognate** (from Latin *cognatus*, "born together") is a word having the same etymological derivation as another (e.g., English *father*, German *Vater*, and Latin *pater*). The term also refers to genetically related languages descended from the same ancestral root.

Derivation is the process of forming a word from another word or base, as by the addition of an affix (specifically a noninflexional one). A **derivative** is a word formed in this way, e.g., the adding of -ial, -able, -ability, -ible to a root or primitive form.

A **diminutive** is a word denoting something small or endearing of its kind. There are many words denoting a smaller or affectionate version of an original (e.g., auntie, sonny, starlet). Diminutiveness is sometimes contained in etymologies and is not evident to those using the words (e.g., catkin, originally "little cat"). Examples of diminutives are cigarette from cigar, rivulet from river, and princeling from prince. Diminutives are also formed by the addition of a combining form like mini-.

A **word element** is any ultimate minimal element of speech having a meaning as such. A **root** or **root word** is one of those ultimate elements of a language that cannot be further analyzed—a primary word or form from which others are derived.

Indo-European is the parent language that developed around 4000 BCE and evolved into the separate languages now spoken in most of Europe and as far east as northern India. This is the group of languages from which most modern European languages are derived, as well as Sanskrit and Farsi. It is assumed that the dispersal of these languages must have occurred through large-scale migrations of people. Attempts have been made to identify the carriers of Indo-European languages with groups recognizable in the archaeological record.

A **proto-language** is a hypothetical parent language from which actual languages or dialects have been derived, e.g., proto-Indo-European, from which the major family developed.

Getting to the Root of a Word

A good question is how to find roots in a dictionary. Dictionaries usually divide words into syllables. The division into syllables is done mainly to help the reader decide where to hyphenate at the end of a line. Dictionaries also indicate pronunciation, including marking where the accent falls in words with more than one syllable. But roots are not labeled as such. Rather, dictionaries give etymological ("word history") information from which the user is supposed to figure out what the root forms are. From this information, how do we find the roots? Looking at a word's etymology, we can start to investigate the root. We must find the ultimate source of the word—the very last italicized word or words in the etymology. Let's look at an example:

> **municipal** *adjective* Latin *municipalis* of a municipality, from *municip-*, *municeps* inhabitant of a municipality, from *munus* duty, service + *capere* to take [*Merriam-Webster's Online Dictionary*]

> The roots of this word are *munus* and *capere*.

How Etymologies Are Researched

The general principles involved in present-day etymology are:

1. The earliest form of a word, or word element, must be ascertained, as well as all parallel and related forms.
2. Every sound of a given word, or word element, must be compared with the corresponding sound in the form (often called its etymon) from which it is derived.
3. Any deviation in the previously established phonetic correspondences for the language of which the word is a part must be plausibly and rationally explained.
4. Any shift in meaning that has occurred in the historical transmission of the word must also be explained.

5. Words that present non-native sounds, or combinations of sounds, that appear isolated in the language, or that demonstrate marked deviation from the usual phonetic correspondences, are probably borrowed rather than inherited, and the language of origin must be determined.

How Many English Words Are There?

The mind is crammed to the rafters with words: by age two, about two hundred; by seven, over 1,300 words; in college, 75,000 words; post-college somewhere between fifty thousand and 250,000 words. The estimates vary widely, as does the definition of what it means to "know" a word, but you get the idea. Everyone agrees that the mental lexicon is vast. The current edition of the *Oxford English Dictionary* has around 229,000 entries. Estimates of the number of words in English place the total around one million.

How New Words Come into Being

The process of changing an existing word or word sequence to form a new word is called *modification*. The formation of abbreviations and acronyms, back-formations, clipped forms, and so on, are common modifications. All words, whether they are nouns, verbs, adjectives, or other parts of speech, seem able to undergo modification. Certain modifications, such as doublets (*guarantee/warranty*), are historical oddities due to different routes of transmission of a word from a single source. Others, such as those modified by folk etymology (for example, *muskrat*, from an Algonquian word unrelated to either *musk* or *rat*) are the product of simple misunderstanding. Rather than English having specific rules for these modifications, there are a number of totally free processes, and any word can undergo one or more of these as the need arises. A good book about this topic is *The Life of Language* by Sol Steinmetz and yours truly (Random House).

How to Choose a Dictionary/Dictionaries

It is impossible for any single dictionary to satisfy the needs of everyone. People need to know that dictionaries use two basic but very different ordering schemes: historical and frequency of use. They need to know how to decipher the abbreviation systems describing etymologies and pronunciations in a standard dictionary. Dictionaries also differ in the way they illustrate or clarify the meaning and use of entries. Some dictionaries offer staff-written examples of how words are used in context, either in sentence fragments or as complete sentences. Others include quotations from noted speakers and writers. The presence and frequency of illustrative examples may be a significant aid in improving young native speakers' understanding and use of words.

Further, all good dictionaries provide usage labels and status labels to show how various words, definitions, spellings, and pronunciations are categorized or restricted. Many dictionaries go beyond this, offering simple descriptions to advise readers about particularly troublesome or confusing areas of grammar and usage. There may be paragraph-length "usage notes" or "synonym studies." This added descriptive information lets the readers make informed choices based on knowledge of the situation and the available alternatives. A dictionary provides the *what* in a person's quest for language improvement—the tens of thousands of words that can be used in hundreds of thousands of ways to help people convey clearly and artfully any idea they might ever want to express to anyone else in speech or writing. Everyone needs to first understand that there is not something called "*the* dictionary" and that every dictionary is different.

How to Find a Word When You Have Tip-of-the-Tongue Syndrome

Reverse dictionary searches (http://www.onelook.com) may be even more useful. A search on "apple beverage" can return such possibilities as: cider, applejack, calvados, brandy, toddy, wassail, and redstreak. These two methods are about finding the missing word, the one that is on the tip of your tongue but won't come out.

How to Find a Word You Cannot Spell

You know alphabetical order, so that is a big tool for finding words. Say you want to learn how to spell "separate." You know it begins with an "s" and it is followed by a vowel. You open the dictionary to the letter "S" and choose the vowel you think is most likely, "e," so you are looking under "se." You sound out the word and figure out that the next likely letter is "p," so you are now looking under "sep." You will find "separate" pretty quickly as you read down the list of words in the dictionary.

The problem is harder when you do not know the first letter of the word. For instance, for a word like "catamaran" you would start either in "c" or "k" and follow the same procedure by sounding out and trying to figure out the next letter or letters. You will learn a great deal about spelling by doing this, and though it may seem tedious, it is good to go through this exercise and learn the correct spelling. It is equally important to read the entry's definitions when you find the correct spelling. Doing so reinforces your learning and sets that word in your memory.

Remember that correct spelling is key to conveying what you mean in writing. Sometimes a word appears in a dictionary as an inflected form of an entry word or as a derivative or run-on. By learning all the features of your dictionary, you'll know to check all parts of an entry and will often find spellings in other parts of a dictionary entry than the headword itself.

How to Learn New Words

If you want to learn new words, you have to take a couple of things into consideration. What is your reason for wanting to improve your vocabulary? For a purpose, like the SAT? Or for fun and general self-improvement? Whatever your objective, it pays to read about different approaches toward achieving it. For example, there are books that offer methods for increasing one's vocabulary for SAT test-taking. Also, you can examine how you learn best, especially when it comes to word-based information. Some people need to use what they learn in order for it to stick, as in conversation and writing. Others succeed by taking quizzes. Still others are good at memorizing.

Word-of-the-day offerings of websites like Dictionary.com and page-a-day calendars are most beneficial for those who are learning for fun and self-improvement. This low-key approach is a great habit to get into. However, just reading about a word does not make it stick. The best method for learning a word-of-the-day is to use it; for example, by writing about it to someone, jotting it down in a new-word notebook, making a flash card, or telling others at the dinner table about the word. If you use the new-word notebook approach, each day you choose a new word from the notebook and use it when talking or find a way to write about it. We tend to remember words more easily when we read about them in a meaningful context, when we see that they are useful and worth remembering, and also when they have been fully explained. Knowing how to use a word is just as important as knowing its meaning. Most word-of-the-day offerings supply the definition and an example sentence or two. Studies have shown that a new word will stay in your vocabulary if it is regularly reinforced through use and reading. Word quizzes are a fast, fun way to build vocabulary. It's a great idea to take along a quiz book when you have to wait in places like a dentist's office. Keeping a quiz book in the car and on the bedside table is good practice, too.

Language List Used in Etymologies

Anglo-French: the form of French used in medieval England

Anglo-Norman: the form of Anglo-French used by Normans living in England after the Conquest (1066)

Central Middle English: the form of English spoken from about 1250–1400

Early Middle English: the form of English spoken from about 1100–1250

Early Modern English: the form of English spoken from about 1500–1660

Germanic: the original Indo-European language from which developed modern German, English, Dutch, the Scandinavian languages, and a few others such as Flemish

Greek: the language spoken by the ancient Greeks until about 200 AD

Indo-European: the parent language that developed around 4000 BC and evolved into the separate languages now spoken in most of Europe and as far east as northern India

Late Greek: the form of Greek spoken from about 200–600 AD

Late Latin: the form of Latin spoken from about 200–600 AD

Late Middle English: the form of English spoken from about 1400–1500

Latin: the language spoken by the ancient Romans until about 200 AD

Medieval Latin: the form of Latin used for liturgical and literary purposes from about 600–1500

Middle Dutch: the form of Dutch spoken from about 1100–1500

Middle English: the form of English spoken from about 1100/1150–1500

Middle French: the form of French spoken from about 1300–1600

Middle Greek: the form of Greek spoken from about 600–1500

Middle High German: the form of German spoken in southern Germany from about 1100–1500 (so named because the land is higher than in the north; became modern standard German)

Middle Low German: the form of German spoken elsewhere than in southern German from about 1100–1500

Modern English: the form of English spoken and written by 1700

New Greek/Modern Greek: the form of Greek spoken since about 1500

New Latin: the form of Latin used from about 1500 for scientific and learned texts

Old English (or Anglo-Saxon): the form of English spoken in medieval times until about 1100/1150

Old French: the form of French spoken in medieval times until about 1300

Old High German: the form of German spoken in southern Germany until about 1100

Old Norse: the common language of Scandinavia and Iceland spoken until about 1350

Old North French: the dialects of Old French spoken mainly in Normandy and Picardy

Romance: the original Indo-European language that developed around 300 AD from Latin, then into French, Italian, Spanish, Portuguese, and Romanian

Sanskrit: the ancient sacred language of India, dating from about 1200 BC

Vulgar Latin: the informal spoken language of ancient Rome that was the main source of the Romance languages

The Importance of Latin and Greek Roots

English is a living language that is growing all the time. One way that English expands is when words are incorporated from other languages. New words are also created when words or word elements, such as roots, prefixes, and suffixes, are combined in new ways. Many English words and word elements can be traced back to Latin and Greek. In ordinary life, knowing Greek and Latin components of English enhances understanding and facilitates communication. In the sciences, particularly in areas of medicine, it is extremely important.

Latin was the language spoken by the ancient Romans. As they conquered most of Europe, the Latin language spread throughout the region. Over time, the Latin spoken in different areas developed into separate languages, including Italian, French, Spanish, and Portuguese. These languages are considered "sisters" to English as they all descended from Latin, their "mother" language. Many Latin words came into English indirectly through French and into English directly, though, too. Monks from Rome brought religious vocabulary as well as Christianity to England beginning in the sixth century. From the Middle Ages onward, many scientific, scholarly, and legal terms were borrowed from Latin.

Most people do not know that Ancient Greek (along with Latin) is the major building block of SAT vocabulary. The Greek language has contributed to the English vocabulary in four ways: directly, as an immediate donor; indirectly, through other intermediate language(s); as an original donor (mainly through Latin and French); and with modern coinages or new Greek.

Learning the root of one word often gives a clue to dozens or even hundreds more. For example, if you learn that syn/sym/syl mean "together, with," you have a clue to more than 450 words and their derivatives. As you become more aware of how these roots make up words, you'll find you can understand unfamiliar words, even without a dictionary.

The Joys of Looking Things Up

Not all dictionaries contain the same words, are written for the same purposes, or contain the same features or types of information. They are also written for different levels—elementary, intermediate, high school, college; and then there are the huge, hulking, unabridged dictionaries. Even those big guys in the library, though, do not contain every word in the English language. And if you think Internet dictionaries are bigger and better, think again.

The very first thing you should do with any dictionary (or any type of reference book) is to read the short "Guide to the Dictionary" or "How to Use the Dictionary" section in the front of the book. These are short instructions. You will find that, like anything else, if you do not read the instructions it is going to be harder for you to proceed. Dictionaries have to use abbreviations and other conventions to save space because there are so many words in English and so much information about them that lexicographers provide. There are also many symbols, and dictionaries use different typefaces to signal different things.

The word in boldface is called the entry word or headword. After the headword, you will see the pronunciation. In most dictionaries, you will need to refer to the pronunciation guide to understand the symbols and you will also need to practice to learn how to read a pronunciation. You will also see syllabification in the beginning of an entry—this tells you how the word can be broken up by syllable, especially when you are writing or typing. Next you will see an abbreviation indicating the part of speech, so that you know you are using the right word or definition for your sentence. For instance, if you are using the word *sketch* in a sentence as a verb, you need to read the dictionary entry for the *verb* form of that word.

Then there are the definitions, the meat of the dictionary. Most definitions are written so that you can substitute them in your sentence for the word itself. Yes, they are long—but you will see that it works if you try it. Consider this sentence: "They dug up a skeleton at the archaeological site." In a dictionary, you would find a definition for skeleton like "the bones supporting the muscles and internal organs of any animal with a backbone." You can substitute that in your sentence to make sure you are using an appropriate word, and an appropriate meaning of that word: "They dug up the bones supporting the muscles and internal organs of any animal with a backbone at the archaeological site."

Many dictionaries offer sample phrases and sentences along with the definitions. This gives you added information. Not only do you get to see how a word is used in a sentence, but the example itself may tell you about the type of noun or subject that works best with a verb, or it may tell you the kind of object a verb may take—great information that is somewhat hidden but is really useful to you once you know it's there. Some dictionaries include usage notes that describe in detail how a word is used and how it compares and contrasts to other words that mean nearly the same thing, or to other words with which the original word can be confused. For example, in the entry for *like*, a usage note would tell you when are the times to use *like* and when it is better to use *as*.

At the end of most dictionary entries you will find run-ons or derivatives. These words, though not defined, are different forms of the entry word. For "skeleton" there is *skeletonlike*. Learning what a run-on means may require an extra step; in this case, looking up the suffix *–like*, which means to "be like a <something>" or "be like that of a <something>," so *skeletonlike* means to "be like a skeleton."

One of the coolest features in dictionaries is the etymology—a word's origin and/or history. We are all fascinated by words like "Halloween" or "octopus" or "democracy"—how did they originate? Some dictionaries offer an origin for every word and, though you may be surprised at all the abbreviations, this is something you will learn to use easily with practice.

{ About the Author }

Dr. Barbara Ann Kipfer is the author of many list and reference books. She has an MPhil and PhD in Linguistics from University of Exeter, a PhD in Archaeology, an MA in Buddhist Studies from Greenwich University, and a BS in Physical Education from Valparaiso University. A lexicographer and part-time archaeologist, Barbara is the Managing Editor of Dictionary.com, Thesaurus.com, and Reference.com for Lexico LLC. Her websites are word-nerd.com and thingstobehappyabout.com.

THE CONSTITUTIONAL

THOUGHT OF

THOMAS JEFFERSON

DAVID N. MAYER

UNIVERSITY PRESS OF VIRGINIA

Charlottesville and London

THE UNIVERSITY PRESS OF VIRGINIA

Copyright © 1994 by David N. Mayer

FIRST PUBLISHED 1994
First paperpack edition 1995

Library of Congress Cataloging-in-Publication Data
Mayer, David N.
    The constitutional thought of Thomas Jefferson / David N. Mayer.
      p. cm.
    Adaptation of thesis (Ph.D.)—University of Virginia, 1988.
    Includes bibliographical references and index.
    ISBN 0-8139-1484-1 (cloth). ISBN 0-8139-1485-x (paper)
    1. Jefferson, Thomas, 1743–1826—Political and social views.
    2. United States—Politics and government—1775–1783.   3. United
    States—Politics and government—1783–1809.   4. United States—
    Constitutional history.   I. Title.   II. Series.
    E332.M38   1994
    973.4'6'092—dc20   93-29649
    [347.30735]   CIP

PRINTED IN THE UNITED STATES OF AMERICA

To My Mother and Father

CONTENTS

PREFACE

So much has been written about Thomas Jefferson that the author of yet another book about him feels compelled to offer some explanation. Jefferson himself probably would have been surprised at the scope and persistence of Jefferson scholarship in light of his oft-repeated observations that "the only full and genuine journal" of his life would be found in his letters and that out of this "voluminous mass" of some 18,000 letters which he wrote and which have been preserved, "a selection may perhaps be made of a few which may have interest enough to bear a single reading." Yet it is the sheer volume of the legacy of Jefferson writings, coupled with the importance of his place in American history as well as what Merrill Peterson has called "the obstacle of the man himself," that has posed so great a challenge to generations of students of Jefferson's thought.[1]

The lack of a thorough study of his constitutional thought is a surprising omission in Jefferson scholarship. Jefferson was a central figure in virtually every significant constitutional issue of his age, from the time of the outbreak of the American Revolution to the crisis over states' rights at the time of the Missouri Compromise. In addition, Jefferson was a first-rate scholar of the law: during this crucial period in Western history, "the Age of the Democratic Revolution," as R. R. Palmer has called it,[2] he had, arguably, one of the finest legal minds on either side of the Atlantic. Yet there has been no comprehensive study of Jefferson's ideas about government—a study which would take into account his views of law, individual rights, and governmental administration, within the context of Anglo-American constitutionalism.[3] The omission is especially striking in light of the appearance of several books focusing on the constitutional thought of Jefferson's contemporaries.[4]

A full study of Jefferson's constitutionalism has special significance at this time because of the recent celebration of the bicentennials of both the Constitution and the Bill of Rights. Although he was not present at the Constitutional Convention, Jefferson nevertheless properly may be regarded as one of the founders because of the central role he played in the key issues that surfaced during the first four decades of government under the Constitution—issues many of which persist to this day.

A brief identification of some of the more important questions that concerned Jefferson helps reveal the comprehensive nature of the perennial interest in his ideas about the Constitution. Jefferson's espousal of a federal Bill of Rights was instrumental in the adoption of that important early addition to the document framed in Philadelphia. His articulation of the establishment clause of the First Amendment as erecting a "wall of separation" between church and state has become the classic statement of that principle in constitutional law. His concern about the president's perpetual eligibility for reelection was reflected in the two-term limitation followed in practice for nearly 150 years and finally made mandatory by the Twenty-second Amendment. His insistence on maintaining, while president, the executive's full powers as an independent, coordinate branch of the federal government helped establish the "strong" model of that office and set precedents that have not been overlooked in contemporary struggles between the president, Congress, and the courts. His espousal of a strict interpretation of the powers granted Congress under the Constitution, and the corresponding powers retained by the states, has been influential among advocates of states' rights both before and after the Civil War. And his thoroughgoing republicanism, which stressed the right of each generation to free itself from the limitations imposed by preceding generations, continues to pose challenging questions about the continued vitality of the Constitution itself and the need for constitutional change.

The existence of studies of the constitutional thought of Jefferson's contemporaries makes the case for a study of Jefferson's constitutionalism especially compelling. Americans often speak of the Founding Fathers as if they were a homogeneous group and of the establishment of the Constitution as if it were an act clear in its purpose and its result. Yet as Forrest McDonald has shown in *Novus Ordo Seclorum*, the story of the intellectual origins of the Constitution is remarkably multifaceted. And in many important respects Jefferson's constitutionalism is distinguishable from that of the other founders, including not only his adversaries Alexander Hamilton and John Marshall (and, to some extent, John Adams) but also his friend and frequent collaborator James Madison.

This book takes a fresh persective on Jefferson's thought, free from

the "liberalism" versus "civic republicanism" debate that has so dominated early American scholarship in recent years.[5] Rather than trying
to force it into either of these paradigms, this book instead seeks to
explain comprehensively Jefferson's constitutional thought on its own
terms. Jefferson described himself, first and foremost, as a "whig,"
and also as a true "federalist" and a "republican." This study of Jefferson's thought argues that Jefferson's constitutional thought is best
understood as Whig, federal, and republican, in the sense that Jefferson meant each of those terms—a fairly precise sense, whose full
meaning has become obscured in our day.

These three essential aspects of his thought may be summarized
simply. Jefferson viewed constitutions primarily as devices by which
governmental power would be limited and checked, to prevent its
abuse through encroachment on individual rights (the Whig aspect of
his thought). His preferred system for doing this was one in which
governmental power was divided into distinct spheres (the federal aspect), each of which was in turn subdivided into distinct branches
(legislative, executive, and judicial) equally accountable to the "rightful" majority will of the people (the republican aspect). The inter-
relationships—and, at times, tensions—between these three essential
aspects of Jefferson's constitutional thought explain his response to
the particular constitutional issues and problems of his time.

This book also shows that Jefferson's mature constitutional theory
did not develop suddenly or in isolation from historic events; rather, it
evolved gradually, shaped by the circumstances of his time. The first
five chapters show this evolution, starting with the English radical
Whig tradition that determined Jefferson's understanding of English
constitutionalism during the Revolutionary era. In the 1780s and 1790s
Jefferson's experiences, first as a commentator upon early American state and federal constitutions and then as a participant in the
first political party struggles, further determined the contours of his
constitutional thought by adding to its Whig foundations the other
two essential elements of federalism and republicanism. Chapters 4
and 5 argue, in particular, that Jefferson's role as leader of the Republican opposition forced him to articulate a constitutional theory
distinguished by its strict adherence to principles of federalism and
separation of powers. Finally, as chapter 5 further shows, in the years
following his retirement from the presidency, Jefferson took federalism and separation of powers even more seriously, tying them to a

radical republicanism which required the people to be active participants not only in politics but also in constitutional law.

The last five chapters of the book show how the evolving relationships between the Whig, federal, and republican aspects of his
thought explain Jefferson's approach to particular constitutional topics. Simultaneously, these chapters also explain many of the apparent
contradictions in Jefferson's thought: the "dark side" of his record with
regard to civil liberties; his strict interpretation of some provisions of
the Constitution, in contrast with his loose (and often inventive) construction of other provisions; both the strong and the weak sides of
his exercise of presidential powers; and, perhaps most importantly,
the connection between his seemingly conservative nostalgia for "first
principles" and the radical populism of his advocacy of frequent constitutional change. This study of Jefferson argues that rather than to
try to force his ideas into our modern notions of what it means to
be "conservative" or "liberal"—or, indeed, into modern historians'
notions of a "civic republican" or "liberal" paradigm—the best way to
understand Jefferson's thought is on its own terms, which permitted
him to be at once both conservative and progressive.

In explaining Jefferson on his own terms, I have made liberal use
of Jefferson's own words. His writings—especially his private correspondence, where he wrote with a frankness often lacking in his
public writings—more often than not speak for themselves, in that
unique "felicity of expression" for which John Adams credited him.
Generally, where multiple published versions of Jefferson's writings
exist, I have used the text of the most reliable version. For most Jefferson writings before 1793, citations are made to the Princeton edition
of *Papers* which, when complete, will be the definitive collection of
Jefferson writings and correspondence. For published writings after
May 1793, generally the Ford edition is cited in preference to the Lipscomb and Bergh edition because of its greater reliability, although it is
less complete. The texts generally are quoted literally; that is, spelling,
punctuation, and capitalization generally have not been modernized.
For example, Jefferson's usual use of "it's" as the possessive is retained throughout. Exceptions include capitalization at the beginning
of sentences and punctuation at the end of sentences. Occasionally,
abbreviated words and phrases are spelled out, where literal transcrip-
tions of a text may be unclear; brackets are used where the missing
letters or words that are supplied are conjectural.

The book is adapted from my doctoral dissertation, "The Constitutional Thought of Thomas Jefferson" (University of Virginia, 1988). Portions of chapters 1–3 of the dissertation have been published in my article "The English Radical Whig Origins of American Constitutionalism," *Washington University Law Quarterly* 70 (1992): 131–208.

This study of Jefferson's constitutional thought could not have been completed without help from many sources. The dissertation upon which it is based was the culmination of a decade-long study of Jefferson's life and writings that began with the research for an undergraduate honors thesis at the University of Michigan and continued through my studies at both Michigan Law School and graduate school at the University of Virginia. It accordingly has profited from the insights of many of my former teachers who introduced me, in sometimes subtle but almost always profound ways, to various aspects of Jefferson's intellectual life and the broader canvas of scholarship against which it must be understood. These include William W. Abbot, Thomas A. Green, the late William R. Leslie, Shaw Livermore, Jr., Dorothy Ross, J. Mills Thornton, and Calvin Woodard.

My dissertation adviser at the University of Virginia, Merrill D. Peterson, read the rough draft of the text in its entirety and offered advice patiently and generously. His insights on Jefferson and the Jeffersonian world have been invaluable to me. The drafts of various dissertation chapters were also read by Charles W. McCurdy, my graduate adviser at the University of Virginia; Leonard Liggio, Walter Grinder, and Jeremy Shearmur, of the Institute for Humane Studies at George Mason University; and Mark Greenwold, a former colleague at the Washington, D.C., law firm of Pierson Semmes and Bemis. Their comments, questions, and suggestions were all helpful to me. Revision of the dissertation into this book benefited from the advice of David O'Brien and Peter Onuf, of the University of Virginia.

Although during my years in Charlottesville I did not have the privilege of studying with the late Dumas Malone, I must acknowledge the importance of his work in helping shape my studies. His monumental six-volume biography *Jefferson and His Time* is not only a model of scholarship for all historians but is—and will continue to be—an indispensable guide for all serious students of Jefferson and his time.

I also must acknowledge that the completion of this book, and the dissertation upon which it is based, would not have been possible without the support, financial and otherwise, provided by several institutions. The Thomas Jefferson Memorial Foundation and the University of Virginia provided me with fellowships during the first three years of my graduate study at the university. After I moved to the Washington, D.C., area to practice law, for three years, with the Georgetown firm of Pierson Semmes and Finley (now Pierson Semmes and Bemis), the partners accommodated my wishes to work on a part-time basis during my third year with the firm, so that I could make some further progress on my dissertation. The Institute for Humane Studies at George Mason University—administering a grant generously provided by Freedom Newspapers, Inc.—selected me as the R. C. Hoiles Postdoctoral Fellow for 1987–88, an appointment which gave me the opportunity to devote substantially all my time and energies to completion of the dissertation. The institute and its staff deserve special thanks in addition for their helpfulness in countless ways and for providing an atmosphere especially conducive to scholarship and free inquiry.

More recently, Capital University Law and Graduate Center has provided research assistance for the task of revising the dissertation into a book manuscript. Rod Smith, the former dean of the Law School, has been especially supportive of this book project; I thank him and my other colleagues at Capital University for their helpfulness and encouragement. I also thank Elizabeth Gaba and Dennis McGuire for editorial and research assistance.

Finally, I thank my parents, Anna and Nicholas Mayer, whose love and support throughout the years cannot be adequately acknowledged with words alone. Without them, none of my studies would have been possible.

THE CONSTITUTIONAL

THOUGHT OF

THOMAS JEFFERSON

1

Bold in the Pursuit

of Knowledge

The Education of an

American Real Whig

In an especially candid letter to James Madison in 1826, Thomas Jefferson outlined his criteria for the appointment of a law professor at the University of Virginia:

In the selection of our Law Professor, we must be rigorously attentive to his political principles. You will recollect that before the revolution, Coke Littleton was the universal elementary book of law students, and a sounder whig never wrote, nor of profounder learning in the orthodox doctrines of the British constitution, or in what were called English liberties. You remember also that our lawyers were all whigs. But when his black-letter text, and uncouth but cunning learning got out of fashion, and the honeyed Mansfieldism of Blackstone became the students' hornbook, from that moment, that profession (the nursery of our Congress) began to slide into toryism, and nearly all the young brood of lawyers now are of that hue. They suppose themselves, indeed, to be whigs, because they no longer know what whigism or republicanism means. It is in our seminary that the vestal flame is to be kept alive; it is thence it is to spread anew over our own and the sister States.[1]

This letter demonstrates quite unambiguously Jefferson's disdain for Blackstone. It also reveals in clear terms that Jefferson's own constitutional principles, as he described them, were those of a "whig," and that he considered the choice of a "whig" as law professor to be vital in ensuring that the "vestal flame" of republicanism be kept alive at the university to which he devoted the last years of his life.

Jefferson used the phrase *vestal flame* quite deliberately. Just as the Vestals of ancient Rome, in their little round temple in the Forum, carefully tended the sacred fire, ensuring that it never went out, so too the law professors at the university would carefully tend the flame of "whigism," keeping it lighted by instructing the young men who would be their students and who would carry the fire, in turn, into the halls of state legislatures, Congress, and the courts—whence, he hoped, the flame would "spread anew" over the United States.

It is significant that in his letter to Madison, Jefferson expressed the key distinction in terms of "whigism" and "toryism": the professor to be chosen was one who had learned the law from the sound "whig" principles of Coke, and not one of the new breed of lawyers who imbibed the "honeyed Mansfieldism" of Blackstone's *Commentaries,* with its Tory "hue." The distinction was not merely academic; to an American of the Revolutionary generation, the words *Whig* and *Tory* had, of course, precise meanings. But use of these terms was not limited to the context of the struggle for independence and the division of the people into Patriots and Loyalists during the Revolution. Jefferson used the terms also to distinguish his own party of Republicans from the Federalists during the party struggle of the 1790s.

The form of constitutionalism that Jefferson identified as "whig" was based on a profound distrust of concentrated political power and, with it, an especially intense devotion to the ideal of limited government. Its fundamental principle, for which Jefferson used the word *jealousy,* received its most cogent expression in a paragraph appearing in his draft of the Kentucky Resolutions in 1798. There he wrote, "Confidence is everywhere the parent of despotism—free government is founded in jealousy, and not in confidence; it is jealousy and not confidence which prescribes limited constitutions, to bind down those whom we are obliged to trust with power. . . . In questions of power, then, let no more be heard of confidence in man, but bind him down from mischief by the chains of the Constitution." The contrast between "jealousy" and "confidence" reveals the essential difference between a Whig and a Tory, as Jefferson saw it: the Whig, zealously guarding liberty, was suspicious of the use of governmental power and so cautioned "jealousy," while the Tory, who in Jefferson's mind was less zealous in his devotion to liberty, desired "confidence" in government. The Whig stance assumed not only that governmental power was inherently dangerous to individual liberty but also, as Jefferson put it, that "the natural progress of things is for liberty to yeild, and government to gain ground." The governments in Europe, he believed, "have divided their nations into two classes, wolves and sheep." If the people of America become "inattentive to the public affairs," he warned, "you and I, and Congress, and Assemblies, judges and governors shall become wolves. It seems to be the law of our general nature, in spite of individual exceptions." [2]

This "Whig tradition of political pessimism," as one historian has called it,[3] had its direct antecedents in English opposition thought of the seventeenth and eighteenth centuries. It was in this tradition that Jefferson's early intellectual life was steeped. To a remarkable degree, the essentials of his constitutional thought were fixed in his mind at a relatively young age, in the crucial years preceding the American Revolution, before his thirty-third birthday. To understand fully Jefferson's thought, one must therefore take into account the education he received as a boy, a college student, and a young lawyer in colonial Virginia in the middle of the eighteenth century.

Thomas Jefferson, Student

Late in life Jefferson said that from the age of fourteen, when his father died, his whole care and direction were thrown on himself "entirely, without a relation or friend qualified to advise or guide me." The statement is exaggerated, for Jefferson had inherited not only an estate and an established position in Virginia society but also a far more important legacy: the formal education for which his largely self-taught father had scrupulously provided. From the age of nine until the year of his father's death, young Thomas attended the Reverend William Douglas's Latin school, where he learned "the rudiments" of Latin and Greek, as well as some French. Tradition has it that Peter Jefferson's dying instruction was that his son should continue his classical education, and this he did at the school of the Reverend James Maury, whom the younger Jefferson later described as a "correct classical scholar." After two years of study with Maury, Jefferson was able to read ancient authors in the original Greek and Latin, a "sublime luxury" for which he was effusively grateful and in which he continued to indulge throughout his long life.[4] At Maury's school Jefferson no doubt also became familiar with some English literature, history, geography, and mathematics, for Maury had a library of some four hundred volumes, which was considered large at that place and time.

In the spring of 1760 Jefferson went to Williamsburg, where he studied for two years at the College of William and Mary and then began preparation for the practice of law. The void in Jefferson's life that had been created when his father had died was filled during his Williamsburg years by two mature counselors who, it is no exaggeration to say, "fixed the destinies" of his life, William Small and George Wythe.[5]

Dr. William Small, from Scotland, was professor of natural philosophy at the college; as Jefferson described him in his autobiography, he was "a man profound in most of the useful branches of science, with a happy talent of communication, correct and gentlemanly manners, and an enlarged and liberal mind." It was truly Jefferson's "great good fortune" to have studied under Small, for he was at Williamsburg for only a few years. The only professor who was not an Anglican clergyman, Small was appointed also to fill the chair in moral philosophy that—by another stroke of luck—had become vacant when the incumbent was dismissed for rowdiness. Thus, Jefferson studied not only physics, mathematics, and natural history but also logic, ethics, rhetoric, and belles lettres with this gentleman who exposed the young man to the scientific rationalism of the Enlightenment. "From his conversation," Jefferson noted, "I got my first views of the expansion of science, and of the system of things in which we are placed."[6]

It was under the tutelage of George Wythe that Jefferson began the study of law. Like Small, Wythe was a true man of the Enlightenment. One of the more distinguished members of the bar of the General Court, Wythe was a self-educated native Virginian with a keen legal mind and a passion for classical studies. One English traveler, who met Wythe a few years before Jefferson began studying with him, described Wythe as a man who had a "perfect knowledge" of Greek and of ancient philosophy and such a character "as would have dignified a Roman senator, even in the most virtuous times of the republic." As Jefferson completed his years of study and prepared to enter upon "the business of life," Wythe remained Jefferson's "faithful and beloved mentor" as well as his "most affectionate friend."[7]

Jefferson's later recollection that during his Williamsburg days he was a "hard student" is in accord with the independent recollections of his contemporaries as well as the program of studies he later prescribed for young men interested in preparing for the law. His boyhood friend John Page recalled that Jefferson "could tear himself away from his dearest friends to fly to his studies." It is easy to imagine that the man who later would admonish his own daughter, "It is wonderful how much may be done, if we are always doing," himself had followed the rigorous dawn-to-bedtime reading schedule he suggested to "a young friend" in preparing for the law: a study of the physical sciences, ethics, and religion before 8 A.M.; four hours of law study after breakfast; history in the afternoon; and literature in the evening. The study plan reflects Jefferson's belief that "carrying on several studies at a time is attended with advantage. Variety relieves the mind, as well as the eye, palled with too long attention to a single object." Noting further that "a great inequality is observable in the vigor of the mind at different periods of the day," he believed that advantage should be taken of this fact "in marshalling the business of the day."[8]

Although it is questionable whether Jefferson adhered to such a regimen while in Williamsburg—where practical activities, such as attendance at court and the drafting of pleadings, and social diversions are known to have consumed much of his time—it is nevertheless likely that Jefferson did follow such a rigorous schedule of reading during most of 1763 and 1766, when he was at home in Albemarle County.[9]

As the generous amount of time scheduled for other readings indicates, Jefferson—presumably influenced by Wythe's guidance—believed that law was not to be studied in an intellectual vacuum but rather must be read in conjunction with the "other branches of science, and especially history," which he considered "as necessary as law to form an accomplished lawyer." Thus, interspersed with his purchases of lawbooks in 1764 and 1765 were purchases of such books as Milton's *Works*, Hume's six-volume *History of England*, Robertson's *History of Scotland*, Stith's *History of Virginia*, Sterne's *Sermons*, Bacon's *Philoso-*

phy, and *The Thoughts of Cicero*. [10] And in addition to the books Jefferson considered important enough to own, he undoubtedly found many other books in Wythe's library, to which he had access, which further supplemented his readings purely in the law. The reading lists he later compiled for prospective law students contain ample selections in history, politics, ethics, religion, natural law, physics, literature, criticism, rhetoric, and oratory.

The essence of law study for Jefferson was, literally, "reading law." Jefferson criticized the concept of apprenticeship, the prevailing mode of legal education in his day. As he cautioned the father of a prospective law student in 1769, "I always was of opinion that the placing a youth to study with an attorney was rather a prejudice than a help" because the attorney would be tempted to encroach on the student's studies with legal business. "The only help a youth wants," he added, "is to be directed what books to read, and in what order to read them." Apparently this was Wythe's method of instruction, and Jefferson's preference for it helps explain his efforts to promote more formal methods of legal education. While governor of Virginia, Jefferson reorganized the curriculum at William and Mary to establish the first law professorship in America, a chair which was filled by his old law preceptor Wythe, whom he heartily recommended as "one of the greatest men of the age" and "the pride of the Institution." [11]

A vital complement to the readings themselves was the practice of digesting, or "commonplacing," a method of analyzing cases which modern law students will no doubt recognize. Jefferson recommended this method of study with his characteristic concern for practicality, noting that it was "doubly useful" because it also helped the student acquire "the most valuable of all talents, that of never using two words where one will do." He applied this practice in his own studies, not only to law cases but to other readings that "merited" commonplacing. [12]

Jefferson kept three commonplace books; they are untitled manuscripts but by convention are referred to as the literary commonplace book, the legal commonplace book, and the equity commonplace book. [13] Although no clear criteria for determining what books "merited" commonplacing are apparent, and therefore the entries cannot be relied upon to reflect his student work in its entirety, the commonplace books confirm that Jefferson did read certain books during this critical period in his life. [14] For example, the frequent entries of passages from Henry Home, Lord Kames (whose name Jefferson usually spelled "Kaims"), in both the equity and legal commonplace books, demonstrate clearly Jefferson's familiarity with the works of this Scottish jurist and philosopher.[15] Various entries in the legal commonplace book indicate sources for Jefferson's hostility to feudalism and the law of entails, as well as for the Whigs' "Saxon myth" version of English history to which Jefferson wholeheartedly subscribed.[16] Thus, Jefferson's commonplace books, and particularly the legal commonplace book, may be used to help determine certain contours in his readings in history, law, and government.

Evidence found in Jefferson's commonplace books, supplemented by his lists of recommended readings for prospective law students[17] and his library catalogues, thus identify certain works as important in helping to shape Jefferson's thought, in various fields of inquiry and at various stages in his life. Those readings which were most important in shaping Jefferson's Whig constitutionalism in the crucial years prior to the Revolution may be divided into three groups: texts that espoused the "orthodox doctrines" of English law, primarily the works of Sir Edward Coke; Real Whig histories; and Real Whig political tracts. Each of these groups of works merits close examination.

"Orthodox" Texts: The Training of a Whig Lawyer

The first law text that Wythe directed Jefferson to read was Sir Edward Coke's *Commentary upon Littleton*, commonly referred to as simply "Coke on Littleton," which constitutes the first of four parts of the *Institutes of the Laws of England*. This difficult work was written in the form of a commentary, with a formidable mass of the author's criticism and learned notes heaped around the text. In the preface Coke forewarned the reader about "this pain-full and large volume," whose complexity of subject matter was rendered even more formidable by the "uncouth" style to which Jefferson later referred in his 1826 letter to Madison.

Struggling in the winter of 1762 with this crabbed treatise, Jefferson exclaimed to his old college chum John Page, "I do wish the Devil had old Cooke, for I am sure I never was so tired of an old dull scoundrel in my life." Contemporaries such as John Adams, whose legal mentor, Jeremiah Gridley, had directed him to read Coke, shared Jefferson's exasperation with this book. As Dumas Malone has observed, "The technical study of the law was then a 'dreary ramble,' as John Adams said, for books that smoothed the student's path did not exist. Textbooks of the modern sort were unknown, and Blackstone's famous *Commentaries* had not yet appeared." [18]

The text that Coke had chosen for his commentary in the first part of his *Institutes* was written sometime in the 1470s by Sir Thomas Littleton for the instruction of his son Richard. It was a brief black-letter treatise on the land law, describing the customs that since time out of mind had surrounded the ownership and inheritance of English real property—a matter of the first importance in Virginia as well as in England.[19] Coke's English translation of the text began with Littleton's definition of the most important of the estates in land at common law, the fee simple: "Tenant in Fee-simple is he which hath Lands or Tenements to hold for him and his heirs for ever." Coke's commentary on the text took the form of an almost word-for-word exegesis, for he deemed Littleton's every phrase worthy of comment and exposition. "Certain it is," wrote Coke, "that there is never a period, nor (for the most part) a word, nor an &c but affordeth excellent matter of learning." Thus, in the notes in an adjoining column, Coke noted that the word *tenant* was derived from the Latin verb *teneo* "and hath in the law five significations." [20]

The example was not lost upon this particular student. The influence of Coke's style is plainly evident in many of Jefferson's writings; as Dumas Malone has observed, the influence is most obvious in the manuscript for his bill for proportioning crime and punishments, "in the notes which first accompany and then invade the columned text." The example set by Coke is also discernible in Jefferson's lifelong penchant to delve into what Coke had called the "rough mines of hidden treasure," as is aptly illustrated by his disquisition attacking the generally held view that Christianity was a part of the English common law. Jefferson was never a mere passive reader. Rather, he was actively engaged intellectually with what he read, frequently digesting it in his commonplace books, writing marginal notes in the books themselves, or incorporating into his writing ideas he had so gained. For most of his life he remained a student, "bold in the pursuit of knowledge, never fearing to follow truth and reason to whatever results they lead, and bearding every authority which stood in the way." [21]

In the course of time Jefferson studied the other three volumes of

Coke's *Institutes*. The second volume, or "part," as Coke entitled it, was a commentary on Magna Carta and some thirty-eight other important charters and statutes of the realm. Typical of the tone of the second *Institute* was Coke's exposition of the thirty-ninth clause of Magna Carta: "No free man shall be taken or imprisoned, or disseised or outlawed or exiled or in any way ruined, . . . except by the lawful judgment of his peers or by the law of the land." "Upon this chapter," wrote Coke, "as out of a roote, many fruitful branches of the law of England have sprung." "The law of the land," to Coke, meant the due process of the common law: hence, for example, all monopolies were against Magna Carta, "because they are against the liberty and freedome of the subject, and against the law of the land." Further, Coke declared, a man "cannot be sent against his will into Ireland, to serve the King; which being an exile is prohibited by this Act." It is little wonder that Coke's near contemporary Thomas Hobbes attacked the *Institutes* on the grounds that Sir Edward seemed "on purpose to diminish . . . the King's authority." The same Whig constitutionalism that so appalled that advocate of monarchical sovereignty no doubt was immensely satisfying to Jefferson.[22]

The third *Institute* contained an account of the criminal law. It was the most readable of the four *Institutes*, and it was also probably the least politically controversial at the time of its original publication, 1644. Coke, drawing frequently upon his own experience as attorney general under Elizabeth and James I for anecdotal embellishment, defined each crime and gave its history and the penalty that the law prescribed. He strongly criticized the cruelty of current penalties, arguing that "great and extreame punishments" had little deterrent effect. Jefferson took extensive notes on the third *Institute* in his legal commonplace book, and it is probable that the substance of Coke's commentary as well as the style worked an important influence on the bill for proportioning crime and punishments on which Jefferson worked in 1776–79.[23]

In the fourth and last *Institute*, a description of the jurisdiction of the various courts in England, Coke championed the common law courts of King's Bench, Common Pleas, Exchequer, and Chancery, emphasizing that their "proper roots" lay in the common law, not in royal prerogative. It was "Coke the parliament man all over again," Catherine Drinker Bowen has noted. The parliament held in the third year of Charles I—the parliament of 1628, of the Petition of Right—

was the *"benedictum parliamentum,* the blessed parliament," to Coke because it had asserted the supremacy of law in its protests against the king's actions. Again, though not evidenced in the commonplace books, the influence on Jefferson is clear.[24]

After making his way through Coke's *Institutes,* Jefferson undoubt edly concluded that the constitution—the "law of the land," rooted in custom since time immemorial—limited the powers of all officers of government, including the monarch. His belief that such limitations were part of an unwritten "ancient constitution" was further strengthened by his reading of Whig history.

Some brief observations on Jefferson's other law reading should be made. After the *Institutes,* Jefferson turned to the reports—Coke's and others'—and to the abridgments, primarily Matthew Bacon's *New Abridgment* and *General Abridgment of Cases in Equity.*[25] Jefferson emphasized the importance of obtaining a knowledge of the state of the law at four important stages of its development by using Bracton, Coke, Bacon, and Blackstone, supplemented by the reports intervening between these writers. The laws of England, "in their progress from the earliest to the present times," he noted, "may be likened to the road of a traveller, divided into distinct stages or resting places, at each of which a review is taken of the road passed over so far." He regarded Bracton's "most able work, complete in its matter and luminous in its method," and Bacon's "sound digest" as highly as Coke's learned and authoritative "jumble." Blackstone's *Commentaries,* though "the most lucid in arrangement" and "classical in style," Jefferson considered to be lacking, in that it was "only an elementary book" which, unlike the other three great treatises, did not present "all the subjects of the law in all their details" and therefore required supplementation.[26]

Blackstone's treatise, which was not completed until two years after Jefferson was admitted to practice, did not form a part of Jefferson's own law study; nevertheless, he was familiar with the *Commentaries* at the time of the Revolution.[27] As he wrote Judge John Tyler in 1812, part of his disdain for the *Commentaries* was based on his concern that it had been "perverted . . . to the degeneracy of legal science. A student finds there a smattering of everything, and his indolence easily persuades him that if he understands that book, he is master of the whole body of law." He added that the difference between modern students of Blackstone and "those who have drawn their stores from the deep and rich mines of Coke, Littleton, seems well understood even by the unlettered common people, who apply the appellation of Blackstone lawyers to these ephemeral insects of the law." [28]

Jefferson's views on the undesirability of the *Commentaries* as a law text stemmed from more than simply an "old school" bias, however; his dislike of Blackstone's "elegance" was more than merely a dissatisfaction with Blackstone's style. The full context of his letter to Tyler shows that Jefferson regarded "Blackstone lawyers," those "ephemeral insects of the law," as politically dangerous, as well as bad lawyers. As his 1826 letter to Madison indicates, what Jefferson particularly found objectionable about Blackstone's treatise was its Tory "hue."

Finally, it should be noted that Jefferson's careful study of the common law and equity persuaded him of the value of keeping the two types of law distinct. Undoubtedly influenced by Coke's supreme regard for the common law, Jefferson firmly believed that law should be objective and that rights should be placed on "sure ground": "Relieve the judges from the rigour of text law, and permit them, with pretorian discretion, to wander into it's equity, and the whole legal system becomes incertain." Jefferson therefore opposed efforts to allow the Virginia courts of common law to perform the discretionary functions of chancery, considering such a reform as "worse than running on Scylla to avoid Charybdis," since "nine tenths of our legal contestations are perfectly remedied by the Common law, and can be carried before that judicature only." He was quite critical of Lord Mansfield's "revolution" in English law, reviving in the courts of common law the practice of "construing their text equitably," which had rendered the law "more uncertain under pretence of rendering it more reasonable" and had made the Chancery useless by administering justice in the same way in the courts of common law. Needless to say, Jefferson was extremely well versed in common law pleading, which was the heart of a lawyer's practice at the time. [29]

Rights of Englishmen:
The Whig Approach to History

"It has ever appeared to me," Jefferson wrote to the English radical Whig John Cartwright in 1824, "that the difference between the Whig and Tory of England is that the Whig deduces his rights from the Anglo-Saxon source, and the Tory from the Norman." He congratulated Cartwright for deducing the English constitution from its "rightful root, the Anglo-Saxon," and added that "although this constitution was violated and set at naught by Norman force, yet force cannot change right. A perpetual claim was kept up by the nation, by their perpetual demand of a restoration of their Saxon laws; which shows they were never relinquished by the will of the nation. In the pullings and haulings for these ancient rights, between the nation, and its kings of the races of Plantagenets, Tudors, and Stuarts, there was sometimes gain, and sometimes loss, until the final reconquest of their rights from the Stuarts."[30]

This passage nicely illustrates the extent to which Jefferson's historical vision was shaped by the romantic view that historians have called the "Whig interpretation" of English history.[31] The Whig historians had an idealized model of government, which they believed was introduced into northern Europe by the barbarian tribes that settled there, and saw in that model the original constitution. To the Whig historians the whole of English constitutional history since the Conquest was the story of a perpetual claim kept up by the English nation for a restoration of Saxon laws and the ancient rights guaranteed by those laws.

Jefferson's devotion to the Whig version of history is evident in his contempt for David Hume's *History of England*, which he regarded as "an apology" for the arbitrary acts of the Stuart monarchs. Jefferson was convinced that Hume's work "undermined the free principles of the English government, has persuaded readers of all classes that these were usurpations on the legitimate and salutary rights of the crown, and has spread universal toryism over the land." In later years when a "republicanized" Hume—John Baxter's *New and Impartial History of England*—became available, he recommended it instead of the Tory "poison" of Hume.[32]

To form a composite version of the Whig understanding of English history and the original constitution, five works are particularly useful. Jefferson read and recommended these works, and they probably were vital in shaping his view of English law and the constitution on the eve of the Revolution. Jefferson read the multivolume *History of England* written by Paul de Rapin, sieur de Thoyras, as a youth and recommended it as the "most faithful" general history of England.[33] He read both Sir John Dalrymple's *History of Feudal Property in Great Britain* and the anonymous *Historical Essay on the English Constitution*, which has been attributed to Obadiah Hulme, and abstracted them in his legal commonplace book.[34] Although he did not abstract Henry Care's *English Liberties* and George St. Amand's "Historical Essay on the Legislative Powers of England," they were included in his second library, and he had likely read them by the time he drafted the Declaration of Independence.[35]

According to the Whig historians, "whilst all the rest of Europe groaned under the galling yoke of tyranny and oppression," the tribes of Germany preserved their native political liberty in a model of government "as far superior to the Greek and Roman commonwealths, as these surpassed the governments of the Medes and Persians." Citing Tacitus's *Germania*, the Whig historians described as the key element of this "Gothick model of government" the general assemblies, where all important matters were decided and where outstanding men were chosen as leaders to determine the affairs of lesser consequence.[36]

As the German tribes increased in number, they conquered neighboring territories for the settling of their people, some of whom, "distinguished by the name of Saxons," settled in England "about the year four hundred and fifty."[37] After destroying the native Britons or driving them westward into Wales, the Saxons distributed the lands among the various tribes, who had settled as "little republics," paralleling the political organization that had prevailed in their native lands.

The land conquered by the Saxons "was vested in the collective body of the people, and not in any one person." This fact was significant, for it demonstrated to the Whig historians that feudalism as understood in the ninth and tenth centuries was "unknown to our Saxon ancestors before the Norman invasion." Not only were the Saxon feudal tenures rather undeveloped, but also a great deal of the land continued to be allodial, not held by feudal tenures at all.[38]

With so many lands held allodially in Saxon England, "it was necessary to subject in a political capacity those who were not subjected in a feudal." Within each Saxon kingdom the allodial lands were divided into counties, or shires, which were in turn divided into wapentakes, or hundreds, and these were subdivided into boroughs and rural tythings. Each of these "little republics" was self-governing, and within each all those to whom lands were apportioned had a say in the government. Over time, as the population grew and the seven Saxon kingdoms merged into one, the people's "native right of being governed by laws made by themselves" came to be exercised indirectly, through their representatives. Those representatives were the presiding judges or magistrates, who were elected annually within each borough or tything. These *wites*, or wise men, as they were called, along with the king's thanes and the bishops and abbots as representatives of the clergy, comprised the witenagemot, or Saxon parliament.[39]

This parliament was literally an assembly of "wise men," an assembly of "all the presiding judges of the nation, earls, bishops, and *wites*, or the annual magistrates of the tythings or boroughs, who represented all the proprietors of land in their respective tythings." A key characteristic of the Whig historians' "Gothick model of government," then, was the fact that each piece of land—or, equivalently, every proprietor of land—was represented, directly or indirectly, in the assembly. Just as the lands conquered by the Saxons were taken by the whole collective body and distributed to all who had a right to share in the conquest, so too was the making of laws entrusted to the whole nation, as represented in the assembly.[40]

The Saxons "had only one mode of government," whether for a town, a wapentake, a shire, or a kingdom: government by representatives, elected annually by each inhabitant of the respective district who "paid his shot and bore his lot." Each level of government had its equivalent of a court of council to make laws, a court of law to enforce laws, and a chief magistrate to administer the laws. The chief magistrate's power was circumscribed by the laws, and this limitation applied equally as well to kings, the chief magistrates of the nation, the only difference being the duration and the compass of authority: the magistrate's was annual and confined to the walls of the town, while the king's was for life and extended over the whole kingdom. Thus, the English constitution in its original form—as it was under the Saxons—was "an intimate union between the prince and the people," connected by the witenagemot, the assembly of wise men "who represented the whole nation." [41]

The Whig historians argued that the conquest of England by William, duke of Normandy, "contaminated the purity of the English constitution" by mixing with the old Saxon laws, "founded on the principles of liberty," the new establishment of the Normans, founded on "the principles of slavery." [42] Although the English constitution continued to be fundamentally a union between the crown and the people, connected by a parliament nominally representative of the whole nation, the character of that union was greatly altered in two respects under the weight of the "Norman yoke." First, the imposition of Norman feudalism so changed the composition of Parliament that it no longer served as an adequate check upon the power of the king. Thus, although the executive authority in theory continued to be confined to a certain sphere of action prescribed by the law, it in fact was quite arbitrary. Second, the dilution of the elective power of the people made Parliament less and less representative of the will of the nation. In time, the Whig historians declared, it came to reflect the will of the sovereign and of certain factions that had come to power.

The Whig historians argued that under the Saxons feudalism had not fully developed: their rear vassals had no clearly defined feudal holdings (Dalrymple noted that their grants of land were not hereditary, for example), and even the vassals "of the crown," properly speaking, held not of the crown but of the realm. William of Normandy, however, "came from a country where the greater power of the prince had soon rivetted the feudal duties of the crown vassals, and had given time and room for the rights of the rear vassals to ripen." William redistributed the lands of his former Saxon opponents among his own confederates, who held of the crown by a service and who in turn enfeoffed their own immediate followers with some portions of land under reservation of a service. A Norman chief, or baron, was placed over most tythings, alongside the existing Saxon earls, to undermine their power. The estates of the Norman chiefs were called baronies, and the barons recognized no superior but the king. The distinction between allodial and feudal lands was eliminated, since both were held by military tenures. All the fiefs of the nation, lower as well as higher, became hereditary and acquired firmness, and subsequently there developed the feudal incidents such as escheats, wards, and marriages, to which "the independency of the Saxons would never have submitted." Only the boroughs were left in the same condition as in Saxon times; at least at the beginning of William's reign, they continued to be governed by magistrates whom they chose annually.[43]

Although "every spot of land" was still represented in Parliament, it was represented in Norman times through either a barony or a borough rather than through some tything, as in Saxon times. The rural tythings were no longer represented by *wites* chosen annually; rather, they were represented by the barons. "Greater" barons were personally summoned to Parliament, while "lesser" barons, after Magna Carta, were summoned generally and were represented indirectly by the knights of the shires, chosen at the county courts by the lesser barons of each shire. Thus did the government fall into the hands of "a new order of men, with new authority derived from the king." William, in creating the new seats in Parliament, amassed a great deal of power; he "put his finger upon the great artery of the constitution, and stopped the circulation of all power arising from the Saxon principles of government."[44]

Church property was seized, taxes were imposed heavily, and a great portion of Hampshire was depopulated to make room for the Conqueror's New Forest. Rule of law was replaced by the arbitrary rule of one man. Even the boroughs, which continued to be represented in Parliament by men of their own choosing (called burgesses instead of *wites*, probably because they were not always the magistrates), periodically succumbed to the power of the crown: the towns were frequently forced to surrender their rights of self-government and then to repurchase them in order to pay for the wars that medieval English kings were fond of waging. In addition, because parliamentary seats did not change with demographic patterns, over a period of centuries the boroughs became quite unevenly represented: deserted boroughs retained their seats, while new commercial towns, such as Birmingham, had hardly any representatives at all. By the time of the Tudors, every spot of land was still represented, but the representation had lost the logical simplicity it once had under the Saxons.[45]

To the Whig historians Duke William's "conquest" of England was no less a conquest because he "accepted" the crown under color of a legitimate claim and began his reign by taking the usual oath of the Saxon kings. Although he and many of his successors "seduced" the English people by this "seeming indulgence," the king's oath taking— like the fiction of an elective monarchy—showed the Whig historians that by insisting on the restoration of the ancient mode at the beginning of every reign, the English people "kept up a title to their Saxon privileges" which even the Norman kings "acknowledged . . . to be just." Some of William's successors—Henry I, most notably— confirmed the ancient Saxon privileges and renounced the unjust prerogatives of their predecessors. In addition, Magna Carta signified an end to the distinction between Norman and Saxon by demonstrating that the Norman lords, as anxious as the Saxons to be secured in their acquisitions free of the arbitrary power of the crown, had by degrees "put on the English genius, wholly addicted to liberty." Yet in spite of these partial restorations of Saxon laws, much arbitrary power continued to be vested in the crown. The heavy weight of the "Norman yoke" continued to be felt long after the two races had merged.[46]

The Whig historians' concern for the constitutionally legitimate maintenance of the union between the crown and the people extended not only to the composition of Parliament but also to its duration. Just as the representation of every man who "paid his shot and bore his lot" helped ensure that the consent of Parliament was every man's consent (or, at least, the consent of every proprietor of land), annual elections kept that consent legitimate. The annual exercise of the elective power, to at least one Whig historian, was "the quintessence, the life and soul of [the Saxons'] constitution, and the basis of the whole fabrick of their government, from the internal police of the minutest part of the country, to the administration of the government of the whole kingdom." The House of Commons was representative of the people only insofar as it was "constitutionally so, that is, for one year; agreeable to the ancient law of the land, and confirmed by a statute, of Edward III, which declares, 'that parliaments should be holden every year, or oftener, if need be, for the redress of divers mischiefs and grievances that daily happen.' "[47]

Even after the Norman establishment had changed the composition of Parliament so that there were knights and burgesses instead of *wites*, it appeared to the Whig historians that annual parliaments were the rule from the time of Edward III until Henry VIII lengthened his parliaments as "the most effectual means for rendering the members obedient to his will." Annual parliaments were restored by Mary Tudor and continued until the Triennial Act in the reign of Charles I. From then on, new parliaments were not held more often than every three years. No Parliament at all met for eleven years under Charles I; the "long," or "rebel," Parliament continued itself for some twenty years; Charles II's "pensioned" Parliament continued for eighteen years; the Triennial Act was reinstituted under William III, only to be repealed under George I and replaced by the Septennial Act. Moreover, by the law in the reign of Anne making a landed qualification for members of the Commons, Parliament was converted into "a down-right rank aristocracy of the rich in land," composed of the "RICH MEN" rather than the "WISE MEN."[48]

Dilution of the elective power of the people, coupled with the inadequacy of representation, resulted in a Parliament which no longer represented the nation. A Parliament which sat for three or seven years instead of one lacked "that confidence between the commons and the people, which had been the support of the constitution for many ages." The Whig historians pointed to such examples as the rapid and complete transition back to popery under Mary Tudor and the shifts in control of the 1647–48 Parliament between Independents and Presbyterians to show that "the determination of a Parliament is not always a convincing proof of the approbation of the whole English nation."[49] In the ebb and flow of the political tides under the houses of Tudor, Stuart, and Hanover, Parliament fell under the influence of monarchs, armies, and corrupt ministers.

Although the extent of the royal prerogative—the constant occasion of quarrels between Parliament and the Stuarts, with each side "pulling and hauling" for what it considered its ancient right—was resolved by the constitutional settlement following the "glorious" Revolution of 1688, the restoration of the ancient Saxon constitution was not completed to the satisfaction of the Whig historians. The influence of the Hanoverian court in the election of members of Parliament, in part occasioned by the division into Whig and Tory parties; the unequal representation of boroughs in Parliament; the lack of instructions binding members of Parliament to the wills of their constituencies; the purchasing of boroughs; bribery and corruption at elections; and, of course, the lack of annual elections: these were the sad facts that troubled the Whig historians concerned with preserving the English constitution according to its original "mixed" character. They raised their banner—"where annual election ends, there slavery begins"—and called for Englishmen to defend their constitutional rights and liberties by organizing legal associations, "the only effectual remedy the people of England have now left, for the redress of their grievances."[50]

Rights of Men: The Whig
Approach to Government

Jefferson was interested in the Saxons not only because they were "our ancestors" but also because their system of government was "the wisest and most perfect ever yet devised by the wit of man." Like other

Whigs he admired Tacitus as "the first writer in the world without exception" because his works, including the description of the Saxons in *Germania*, were a "compound of history and morality of which we have no other example."[51]

Thomas Gordon, whose translation of Tacitus was read by Jefferson and his contemporaries, appended to Tacitus's works political disquisitions on such subjects as human nature and the corruptions of public office. Man, he observed, is disposed to both goodness and evil; the people are "often patient under oppression, while men in power have a miserable infatuation . . . to push that power and the people's patience as far as either will go." The Saxons, a people "pure and independent" and distinguished by a sort of noble rudeness, had the sagacity to decide all great matters themselves. What few matters were left to their leaders to decide were entrusted to splendid men who procured obedience "not so much by the force of their authority as by that of their example."[52]

Whig historians recognized that the Saxons "founded their government upon the common rights of mankind." They "made the elective power of the people the first principle of [their] constitution, and delegated that power to such men, as they had most reason to confide in." But they were cautious because they knew well "the degenerating principles of mankind; that power makes a difference in the temper and behaviour of men, and often converts a good man in private life, to a tyrant in office." For this reason, "they never gave up their natural liberty, or delegated their power, of making laws, to any man, for a longer time than one year." The executive authority, which was more fixed than the legislative, they confined within a certain sphere of action prescribed by the laws, so that it could not operate to the injury of any individual and could be controlled by the parliament.[53]

As J. G. A. Pocock has shown, Whiggism followed in part from the "common-law version" of history, but some of the more radical Whigs "went on to reject history altogether and aver that the criterion by which any government must be judged was not its antiquity, but its rationality." These radical Whigs were the three generations of "Commonwealthmen" whom Caroline Robbins has described. They called themselves "Real Whigs" or "Independent Whigs," to distinguish themselves from the mainstream of the eighteenth-century Whig political party and to avow a kinship with mid-seventeenth-century republicans such as James Harrington and Algernon Sidney.

They had a strong influence on Jefferson and his contemporaries, the Americans of the Revolutionary generation.[54]

From the Real Whigs' standpoint, the Saxon constitution was in itself noble because it was based on "the natural rights of mankind." The fact that it was also the original English constitution was simply a happy coincidence. As one of these Whigs, Algernon Sidney, wrote, "The English nation has always bin governed by itself or its representatives"; it mattered not whether the assemblies "were frequent or rare; composed of many or few persons, sitting together in one place, or in more; what name they had; or whether every free man did meet and vote in his person, or a few were delegated by many." All that mattered was that the Saxons "ordered all things according to their own pleasure," for "that which a people does rightly establish for their own good, is of as much force the first day, as continuance can ever give to it; and therefore in matters of the greatest importance, wise and good men do not so much inquire what has bin, as what is good and ought to be." [55]

Pocock has suggested that because they were not bound by historical precedent, the Whig philosophers of government were not troubled by a dilemma which confronted the Whig historians: they were not forced to choose between parliamentary sovereignty and monarchical sovereignty because the appeal to rationality led them to the concept of popular sovereignty. From that concept, the Whig philosophers derived the notions about natural rights and the remodeling of governments that eventually underlay the case for American independence as asserted in Jefferson's Declaration.

Six works demonstrate the Whig approach to government. These too are works with which Jefferson was familiar and whose ideas helped shape his understanding of the English constitution on the eve of the Revolution. Jefferson and most other members of the Continental Congress owned James Burgh's *Political Disquisitions;* Jefferson later included the work on his library list for the University of Virginia and recommended it in a letter to his son-in-law Thomas Mann Randolph, Jr.[56] Robert Molesworth's *Account of Denmark,* Granville Sharp's *Declaration of the People's Natural Right to a Share in the Legislature,* and Trenchard and Gordon's *Cato's Letters* were all included both in Jefferson's second library and on his University of Virginia list.[57]

Finally, though certainly not least in order of importance, were Locke's and Sidney's treatises on government. The influence of John

Locke has been greatly exaggerated by some scholars and unjustifiably trivialized by others.[58] The evidence from Jefferson's own writings, however, is that Locke was among the more influential authors whom Jefferson read.[59] He usually mentioned Locke's treatise together with Algernon Sidney's *Discourses on Government:* he recommended both in 1771 as necessary parts of a gentleman's library, and later in life he specifically mentioned both as "elementary books of public right" that helped shape the "harmonizing sentiments" of American Whigs in 1776 and that continued to reflect American libertarian principles.[60]

The Whig philosophers of government began, logically, with an understanding of human nature. Man, "whom we dignify with the honorable title of *Rational*," is much more frequently influenced by his passions; and chief among these passions is self-love, for "it is impossible for any Man to act upon any other motive than his own interest." In their natural state all men have an equal right to their natural freedom; reason teaches mankind that all being equal and independent, no one ought to harm another in his life, liberty, or possessions.[61] As Jefferson recalled in his last letter, written on the eve of the fiftieth anniversary of American independence, God did not intend that the greatest part of mankind should be born with saddles on their backs while a favored few were born with crowns on their heads, booted and spurred to ride the others to death.[62]

Men being naturally equal, "none ever rose above the rest but by Force or Consent." Reason leads men to see that "they cannot well live asunder"—"since we cannot endure the Solitude, Barbarity, Weakness, Want, Misery, and Dangers that accompany it whilst we live alone"—"nor [can we live] many together, without some Rule to which all must submit." Accordingly, men mutually agree to restrain their natural liberty by submission to laws; "this general consent of all to resign such a part of their Liberty as seems to be for the good of all, is the voice of Nature, and the act of Men (according to Natural Reason) seeking their own Good." The consent must be mutual since "the equality in which men are born is so perfect, that no man will suffer his natural liberty to be abridged, except others do the like."[63]

Men consent to give up their free natural state by "agreeing with other Men to joyn and unite into a Community for their comfortable, safe, and peaceable living one amongst another, in a secure Enjoyment of their Properties," that is, their lives, liberties, and estates. The end of civil society is to avoid and remedy the inconveniences necessarily arising in the state of nature, in which every man is the judge in his own case. Civil society, therefore, is based on consent, and it is consent which is the ground of all lawful, just, and peaceable govern-ment.[64] The people may choose whatever form of government they wish—democracy, aristocracy, monarchy, or mixed—but regardless of the form, all the lawful authority, legislative and executive, origi-nates from the people. According to the Whig model of government, "power in the *people* is like light in the sun: native, original, inherent, and unlimited by anything human. In governors, it [power] may be compared to the reflected light of the moon; for it is only borrowed, delegated, and limited by the intention of the people, whose it is, and to whom governors are to consider themselves as responsible, while the people are answerable only to God." The coercive power of law proceeds from the authority of the legislative power, which is in turn delegated by the people.[65]

Civil liberty, as understood by the Whig philosophers of govern-ment, thus meant being under no other legislative power but that established by consent in the commonwealth and being under the dominion of no law but that which the legislature shall enact accord-ing to the trust placed in it. Freedom under government is to have a standing rule to live by, common to everyone in society and made by the legislative power erected in society. Freedom under government is also not to be subject to the inconsistent, arbitrary rule of another. Again, "the *consent* of the whole *people*, as far as it can be obtained, is indispensably *necessary* to every law, by which the whole *people* are to be bound." Otherwise, the Whig writers warned, "the whole people are enslaved to the *one*, or the *few*, who frame the laws for them." The consent of the people similarly binds the magistrate who enforces the law: he "can have no other just power than what the Laws give"; "he ought not to take what no Man ought to give, nor exact what no Man ought to perform."[66]

Consent alone, however, is not the sole basis of legitimate govern-ment; it is a necessary, but not a sufficient condition. To be legitimate, the exercise of legislative power must accord with the ends of political society: the further security of one's life, liberty, and possessions. It is not merely the will of the majority; for if it were, a society where all peaceful men are protected would become instead "a conspiracy of the Many against the Minority." "The sole end of man's entering into political Societies" being "mutual protection and defense," "whatever Power does not contribute to these Purposes, is not Government but Usurpation." [67]

The Whig philosophers were aware not only of the good that may come from the rational use of government but also of the evil that may come from its abuse. "Such is the perverse disposition of man," that government, "this most useful institution, has been generally debauched into an engine of oppression and tyranny over those, whom it was expressly and solely established to defend"—so much so that "in almost every age and country, the *government* has been the principal grievance of the people." Everyone in civil society "ought to be upon his Guard against another, that he not become the Prey of another." Where the "publick passions"—"every Man's particular Warmth and Concern about publick Transactions and Events"—are well regulated and honestly employed, there is good government; but where they are "knavishly raised and ill employed," there is that bane of all good Whigs, "Faction." Positive laws "can never entirely prevent the Arts of crafty Men to evade them"; they can only lessen or qualify evil, not abolish it. New laws are daily made, and new occasions for more laws are daily arising. Law being "a sign of the Corruption in Man," many laws are "signs of the Corruption of a State." [68]

To the Real Whigs it was the right and duty of every citizen to be watchful of those in power, since "considering what Sort of Creature Man is, it is scarce possible to put him under too many Restraints, when he is possessed of great Power." "Those who are in the Possession of Power, as all Magistrates are, ought above all other Men, to be narrowly watched and checked with Restraints stronger than their Temptations to break them." All in society should behave, argued the Whig writers, in the spirit of what Burgh called "a true and independent Whig": one who, among other things, "scorns all implicit faith in the state, as well as in the church," and "claims a right of examining all publick measures, and if they deserve it, of censuring them." One rash law may overturn the country at once since "the Liberty, the Property, nay the Virtue, Credit, and Religion of his Country" are in the legislator's or the magistrate's hands. "Such is the Misfortune of Mankind, and so uncertain is the Condition of human affairs, that the very Power given for Protection, carries in it a sufficient Power to destroy, and so readily does Government slide, and often start, into Oppression!" The example of Denmark, which had changed into an absolute monarchy in the mid-seventeenth century, convinced the Whig writers that this was no idle fear.[69]

As the people are the fountain of power, and their good the object of government, so are the people "the last resource when governors betray their trust." "He that institutes, may also abrogate": the people choose the form of government, and therefore they only can be "fit Judges of the performance of the Ends of the Institution." The people are "often patient under oppression"; only "a long train of abuses" would cause them to rebel.[70] The general revolt of the people, when it occurs, accordingly cannot be called a rebellion; it is merely their "resisting oppression, and vindicating their own Liberty." As the Whigs saw it, it would be "a most wicked and absurd position" to say that the whole people can never be in a situation "to defend and preserve themselves, when there is no other Power in Being to protect and defend them; and much more so, that they must not oppose a tyrant."[71]

The Whig writers thus anticipated a natural right of revolution which Jefferson and his colleagues at the Second Continental Congress would exercise in 1776.

2

Causes Which Have Impelled

Us to the Separation

The Logic of the

American Revolution

When forced, therefore, to resort to arms for redress, an appeal to the tribunal of the world was deemed proper for our justification," Jefferson wrote to Henry Lee in 1825, explaining the purpose of his most famous work. "This was the object of the Declaration of Independence. Not to find out new principles, or new arguments, never before thought of, not merely to say things which had never been said before; but to place before mankind the common sense of the subject, in terms so plain and firm as to command their assent, and to justify ourselves in the independent stand we are compelled to take. Neither aiming at originality of principle or sentiment, nor yet copied from any particular and previous writing, it was intended to be an expression of the American mind, and to give to that expression the proper tone and spirit called for by the occasion." "All its authority," he added, "rests then on the harmonizing sentiments of the day, whether expressed in conversation, in letters, printed essays, or in the elementary books of public right, as Aristotle, Cicero, Locke, Sidney, &c." With respect to "our rights, and the acts of the British government contravening those rights, there was but one opinion on this side of the water," Jefferson further asserted. "All American whigs thought alike on these subjects."[1]

Jefferson was not alone in his reading of English Whig writers on history and government and the classical authors to whom they frequently alluded. Colonial Americans were thoroughly familiar with the chronicles of the collapse of the Roman republic and the rise of the empire by Plutarch, Livy, Cicero, Sallust, and Tacitus; the writings of Coke and other seventeenth-century common lawyers; the works of Locke, Sidney, Rapin, Trenchard and Gordon, Molesworth, and other Real Whigs of the late seventeenth and early eighteenth centuries; and the writings of their contemporaries, Burgh and other British Radicals of the 1760s and 1770s.[2]

Devouring Real Whig opposition thought, Americans held a "comprehensive theory of politics"—a "pattern of ideas and attitudes"— that they shared with their ideological brethren across the water. Like the Real Whigs in the mother country, American Whigs dissented from the general complacency of eighteenth-century politics and, insisting instead that government was inherently threatening to liberty, called for vigilance against the abuse of governmental power. Associated with this inherent suspicion of government was another concept, also derived from Real Whig thought: the veneration of the English constitution as the great protector of the subjects' liberties. It is in the joining of these two concepts in American thought—in the interpretation that Americans gave to the new regulations imposed by the British government on the colonies after 1763—that the roots of the colonies' rebellion may be found. The Americans saw nothing less than a conspiracy which threatened the destruction of the English constitution and the rights and privileges embedded in it. As Edmund Burke described the American Whig temperament in a memorable speech, "They augur misgovernment at a distance, and snuff the approach of tyranny in every tainted breeze."[3]

What was true of colonial Americans generally was also true of Virginians. Charles Sydnor has noted the remarkable extent to which Virginia lawyers were familiar with English constitutional history, observing that some of the great names—and one might add, the great deities in the Real Whig pantheon—were "perhaps better known in America than in England in the 1770s." Indeed, a Virginia college founded in that decade was named for John Hampden and Algernon Sidney. More importantly, the Virginia gentry venerated their traditions of representative government and consent. The "most valuable Part of our Birthright as Englishmen," Richard Bland asserted, was the "vital Principle in the Constitution" that "all men" were "only subject to Laws made with their own Consent." The House of Burgesses, as the agency through which the governed gave their consent to laws, was the "natural" guardian of their rights, Virginians believed.[4] Indeed, Virginia's heritage of self-government ran deep: representative government had already existed in the Old Dominion for well over a hundred years when Jefferson was born. No doubt Jefferson held the values that Virginians generally shared, and these values helped shape his reaction to the crisis with Britain as it emerged in the 1760s and 1770s.

Jefferson's first acquaintance with the developing crisis with Britain was as an observer—while a law student in Williamsburg in 1765, he listened at the Capitol to Patrick Henry's oration against the Stamp Act—but he soon became an active player in Virginia's protests against the actions of the British government. In 1769 he was a member of the House of Burgesses when, in "common cause" with the Massachusetts house, it protested Parliament's right to impose the Townshend duties on the colonies. He was also one of the members who, after the governor had dissolved the Burgesses, defiantly reassembled at the Raleigh Tavern and drew up articles of "Association" against the use of merchandise imported from Britain. A few years later, while Jefferson was again a burgess and the Boston port bill of 1774 again "excited our sympathies for Massachusetts," he "rummaged over" Rushworth's *Historical Collections* and the parliamentary records of Stuart times for "the revolutionary precedents and forms of the Puritans of that day" in order to help "cook up" a resolution for a day of fasting and prayer, to arouse the people "from the lethargy into which they had fallen, as to passing events." The governor again dissolved the assembly, and the burgesses again retired to Raleigh Tavern where, as before, they signed an association and passed resolves. Jefferson also attended a meeting of the Committee of Correspondence that ordered letters sent to similar committees in the other colonies calling for a general congress. As Dumas Malone has noted, Jefferson thus "helped translate the local grievance of Boston into a common cause, and unquestionably he himself was among the first to be electrified."[5]

The freeholders of Albemarle County, meeting in Charlottesville toward the end of July 1774, reelected Jefferson and John Walker as their delegates and adopted resolutions that Jefferson had drawn up. These declared in unmistakable terms the right of Americans to be governed by laws to which they had given consent in their own colonial legislatures, insisting that "no other legislature whatever may rightfully exercise authority over them." The resolutions further declared that "these their natural and legal rights" frequently had been "invaded" by Parliament, most recently by the act closing the port of Boston. "All such assumptions of unlawful power" were "dangerous to the rights of the British empire in general," the resolutions concluded, noting Virginians' readiness to join the "common cause" of Americans on behalf of "their constitutional rights."[6]

Jefferson elaborated these ideas, expecting to present them to the convention in Williamsburg, but was stricken ill on the road and had to turn back. He sent on his ideas, in the form of resolutions which were to be moved as instructions to the Virginia delegates to Congress and then, Jefferson hoped, embodied by Congress in an address to the king. In August 1774 his resolutions were published anonymously as an essay entitled *A Summary View of the Rights of British America.*[7] These were the circumstances in the summer of 1774 under which Jefferson, at age thirty-one, wrote his chief literary contribution to the patriot cause prior to the Declaration of Independence.

The Case for the Redress American Grievances: The *Summary View* and Jefferson's "True Ground"

Despite Jefferson's statement in his letter to Henry Lee that "all American whigs thought alike" on the subject of their rights, by Jefferson's own admission he carried the Real Whig doctrines of representation and consent much further than most of his contemporaries in 1774. He took what years afterward he would call the "true ground," "the only one orthodox or tenable," the complete denial of any parliamentary authority over the colonies. He believed that "the relation between Great Britain and these colonies was exactly the same as that of England and Scotland, after the accession of James, and until the union, and the same as her present relations with Hanover, having the same executive chief, but no other necessary political connection." "In this doctrine, however," Jefferson added in his autobiography, "I had never been able to get any one to agree with me but Mr. Wythe." The other Virginia patriots—Edmund Randolph, Richard Henry Lee and Francis Lightfoot Lee, Robert Carter Nicholas, Edmund Pendleton— "stopped at the half-way house of John Dickinson, who admitted that England has a right to regulate our commerce, and to lay duties on it for the purposes of regulation, but not of raising revenue." For this ground, Jefferson maintained, "there was no foundation in compact, in any acknowledged principles of colonization, nor in reason."[8]

The fullest statement of what Jefferson considered the Americans' "true" constitutional ground for claiming an infringement of their rights is found in his *Summary View of the Rights of British America*. In this essay, as in the Albemarle Resolutions, he stated the American position (as he understood it) in legal terms. The *Summary View* was written as "an humble and dutiful" address to George III for the redress of injured rights that, as the title suggests, belonged to British America.[9] It was written, therefore, as a legal brief—or, more precisely, as a bill in equity.[10] But it was also, as Anthony Lewis has shown, a "chart of political union," a plan for harmonizing imperial relations "which accepted fearlessly the logic in the facts" of the relationship between Britain and the colonies in America.[11] The starting point of Jefferson's argument was historical, but it concluded in a much broader context—one which provided not only the justification of American independence but also the rationale for the federal union that the new American nation ultimately would adopt as the form of its constitution.

At first glance the *Summary View* reads like a Whig history. Indeed, as Trevor Colbourn has observed, the document was "the first graphic illustration of the political use Jefferson made of his careful reading of the past, and specifically the past of his English forefathers." Jefferson, "behaving more like an archaelogist than a revolutionary," placed American rights in a historical context which far antedated the seventeenth-century settlements in America. He went back to "our Saxon ancestors," referring to them in two contexts, both of which were crucial to the argument presented in the *Summary View*. The first concerned that general right "which nature has given to all men, of departing from the country in which chance, not choice has placed them, of going in quest of new habitations, and of there establishing new societies," under new laws. The second concerned specifically the crown's grant of lands in America.[12]

The right of expatriation being "a right which nature has given to all men," Jefferson saw the English settlement of America as exactly parallel to the Saxon emigration. "America was conquered, and her settlements made and firmly established, at the expense of individuals, and not of the British public. Their own blood was spilt in acquiring lands for their settlement, their own fortunes expended in making that settlement effectual. For themselves they fought, for themselves they conquered, and for themselves alone they have right to hold." He further pointed out that "no shilling was ever issued from the public treasures" of the British crown for the assistance of the Americans "till of very late times, after the colonies had become established on a firm and permanent footing." Jefferson thus asserted that British Americans, like their Saxon forebears, "conquered" lands for themselves and therefore were entitled to govern those lands and themselves "under such laws and regulations as to them shall seem most likely to promote their public happiness." [13]

He then argued that the British emigrants to America "thought proper to adapt that system of laws under which they had hitherto lived in the mother country, and to continue their union with her by submitting themselves to the same common sovereign, who was thereby made the central link connecting the several parts of the empire thus newly multiplied." As Jefferson would later write in his draft of the Declaration of Independence, in a passage detailing "the circumstances of our emigration and settlement here" which Congress would delete from the final draft, the Americans had "adopted one common king, thereby laying a foundation for perpetual league & amity" with the British people; but "submission to their parliament was no part of our constitution, nor ever in idea, if history may be credited." From this line of argument came the fundamental constitutional point made by the *Summary View*, that "the true ground" on which the Americans could consider the objectionable acts of Parliament over the colonies to be void "is that the British parliament has no right to exercise authority over us." [14]

The second reference in the *Summary View* to the Saxons, in conjunction with Jefferson's discussion of crown land grants in America, raised the Whig historians' familiar view that Saxon lands were allodial until William the Conqueror first introduced generally the system of feudalism, after which "the Norman lawyers soon found means to saddle" the populace "with all the other feudal burdens." In the Norman Conquest, Jefferson saw the origin of the principle that "all lands in England were held either mediately or immediately of the crown," to which he took exception in regard to the Saxon laws of possession. Particularly in America, which "was not conquered by William the Norman, nor its lands surrendered to him or any of his successors," possessions of land were "undoubtedly of the Allodial nature." But since the first American colonists "were laborers, not lawyers," they were early persuaded to believe "the fictitious principle that all lands belong originally to the king" and accordingly "took grants of their own lands from the crown." This error did not waive the right, however, and the *Summary View* in part called for George III to declare that he had no right to grant lands of himself.[15]

Taken together, these references to "our Saxon ancestors" made clear that the rights of British America that Jefferson was asserting were rights which had a solid historical foundation, which he sought to prove. Indeed, Jefferson's continuing effort to provide legal precedent for Americans' "natural, conventional, and chartered" rights is revealed in his *Notes on the State of Virginia,* where he reproduced in its entirety the text, "from the records," of the Articles of 12 March 1651 under which the Virginia Cavaliers surrendered to the authority of the "government of the common wealth of England." Before laying down their arms in submission to Cromwell and Parliament, he observed, the Virginians in this "solemn convention" sought to secure "their most essential rights"—among them free trade and exemption from taxation but by their own assembly—rights that nevertheless were violated by subsequent kings and Parliaments.[16]

There are other respects in which the *Summary View* reflected the Whig approach to history. The long list of examples of British iniquities that Jefferson included was plainly reminiscent of the Whig historians' principal bugbear, the notion of a continuous effort on the part of the crown to deprive the people of their liberties. It was not just the crown, however, but the crown together with Parliament that threatened the Americans' constitutional rights as transplanted Englishmen, "expatriated men," entitled to their liberties. Jefferson's list of grievances started with the Stuart monarchs' "dividing and dismembering" of the American colonies among their "favorites and followers" and continued through the various acts of Parliament concerning the American colonies, beginning with the Navigation Acts of the seventeenth century and continuing up through recent acts in the reign of George III. Among the statutes for which Jefferson expressed contempt was an act passed in the fifth year of the reign of George II forbidding an American "to make a hat for himself of the fur which he has taken perhaps on his own soil," "an instance of despotism to which no parallel can be produced in the most arbitrary ages of British history." These acts, Jefferson contended, provided evidence of a conspiracy. "Single acts of tyranny may be ascribed to the accidental opinion of a day; but a series of oppressions, begun at a distinguished period, and pursued unalterably thro' every change of ministers, too plainly prove a deliberate, systematical plan of reducing us to slavery."[17]

The *Summary View* also reflected the approach of the Whig historians in its implicit recognition of English government as fundamentally a union between crown and people, connected by their legislature. American grievances as stated in the *Summary View* and later in the Declaration accordingly focused upon actions by the king outside the legitimate sphere of executive authority. He was, after all, "no more than the chief officer of the people, appointed by the laws, and circumscribed with definite powers to assist in working the great machine of government erected for their use." Chief among the grievances was the king's cooperation in the extension of "many unwarrantable incroachments and usurpations, attempted to be made by the legislature of one part of the empire" upon another part. Parliament's statutes concerning America were "the acts of power assumed by a body of men foreign to our constitutions, and unacknowledged by our laws." The *Summary View* called for the king, "as yet the only mediatory power between the several states of the British empire, to recommend to his parliament of Great Britain the total revocation of these acts." Indeed, Jefferson implored George III to "open [his] breast . . . to liberal and expanded thought" and not let his name be "a blot in the page of history." Reminding the king that his counselors were parties too, he urged George III to ignore them and "do your duty": "The whole art of government consists in the art of being honest."[18]

Jefferson's use of the past in the *Summary View*, however, as Trevor Colbourn has noted, was not conservative; Jefferson used the past "as Bolingbroke prescribed—'philosophy teaching by examples'—as an illustration of dangers to be avoided, and democratic delights to be recaptured."[19] It is with his reference to the king's role as "mediatory power" between the "several states" of the British empire that Jefferson's analysis in the *Summary View* clearly surpassed a merely historical approach. Nothing in English Whig history suggested that Parliament could be considered but one of several legislatures that connected the king with the "British" people: Parliament, after all, was the only representative assembly known to English history before the colonization of America.

Obadiah Hulme's treatment of the constitutional right of the British parliament to tax "our distant provinces" in America, in his *Historical Essay on the English Constitution* (1771), aptly illustrated the limitations of a purely historical approach, even that of a Whig. Hulme differed from Jefferson in his basic factual premise; the lands in America, he argued, were "acquired at the expence of the people of England" and hence are "at all times, subject to the order and direction" of Parliament. America was colonized "for the general good of the whole community, and not for the particular good of the settlers," who had "placed themselves, for the enjoyment of these lands, . . . at such a distance, they have put it out of their own power to be electors." Having no representatives in Parliament, the people of the colonies are "precisely, and literally, in the same situation as the people in these great towns" of Birmingham and Manchester, which also have no (or, actually, little) elective power. But "in every other respect, they may receive the full benefit of the constitution, as much as any man at home." All that is important is that there is "a competent number of electors, in every place of election, so as to secure a constitutionally free, and independent house of commons." Even one who cannot exercise the right of election "may always receive the full benefit of a government founded upon the principles of election, as much as if he were an elector, so long as he is bound by no other law than those are, who do exercise the power of election." The electors "must of necessity take care of [the nonvoter's] interest, at the same time they take care of their own," Hulme assumed, adhering to the classic balanced government theory that the House of Commons existed to check the king and Lords, and that its doing so constituted the only important political interest of the king's subjects. He thus saw the American colonies as the constitutional equivalents of the Saxon shires: independent as to internal matters (including, interestingly enough, the expense of the administration of government within the colony) but along with the other parts of the empire obliged, "by all the laws of justice, equity, and reason, as well as the constitution," to contribute their share to "the national expence of the state, necessarily incurred for the defence, protection, and government of the whole community in general." [20]

Hulme's approach, although in a strict constitutional sense the classic Whig approach, may be considered naive in several respects. What was especially absurd was his assertion that the people's interest in sharing in the legislative power was essentially the same throughout the British empire. Certainly the existence of many of the disagreeable statutes mentioned in the *Summary View*—laws giving certain British merchants monopolies over colonial trade, laws prohibiting American manufactures, and laws making American lands subject to the demands of British creditors, for example—suggested that conflicts of interest did exist. Hulme could not admit that America and England might be separate political communities because he was bound by the past, by historical precedent and by the traditional constitutional model of balanced government: England had always been one nation, even during the Norman Conquest, and the House of Commons—in spite of its deficiencies—had always represented the commons of the nation.

The case made by *A Summary View* for the redress of American grievances, therefore, was not compelled by English history, even that of the Whig historians. It is true that in calling for the monarch to confine his powers within certain bounds and in calling for a legislative assembly more representative of the will of the nation, Jefferson put forth the traditional Whig demands for a restoration of liberties derived in fact from the English constitution. Specifically, the American as an Englishman had "a fixed fundamental right born within him, as to the freedom of his person and property in his estate, which he cannot be deprived of" but by the laws of the land; and this freedom from arbitrary power also carried with it the "fundamental privilege" of a parliament where "no new laws bind the people of England, but such as are by common consent agreed on." [21] But in arguing that the privilege required that the American colonies have their own legislatures, independent of and equal to the English Parliament, Jefferson moved beyond a merely historical analysis of the rights of Englishmen.

Jefferson's idea of a British empire of several peoples, each with its own independent legislature, connected through a common sovereign (as were England and Scotland after the accession of James I and until the Act of Union) was a novel one. It was totally unacceptable to English Whigs, even those who were considered friends of America;

with the exception only of the more farsighted of the radicals, such as Burgh or Cartwright, they viewed the British imperial bond as one in which Parliament held "full power and authority . . . to bind the colonies and people of America . . . in all cases whatsoever," as the Declaratory Act had stated in 1766.[22] Jefferson's vision of the British empire was ahead of its time, prefiguring the British Commonwealth of the late-nineteenth and twentieth centuries.[23] The reluctance of many American Whigs to accept Jefferson's position in 1776 accounts for the deletion of the relevant passage of his Declaration of Independence from the final version approved by Congress. Jefferson's unique position on "the circumstances of our emigration and settlement here"— particularly the argument that America was settled without the help of the English crown—was by no means orthodox history.

The case made by Jefferson's *Summary View* did not need to rest on such dubious historical grounds, however. Even if one saw the American colonists as Englishmen rather than "expatriated men," the Real Whig approach to government provided an analysis which made Jefferson's argument for the "true" constitutional ground of the Americans' grievances especially compelling. To those Whigs who had a view broadened by the appeal to rationality rather than mere historical precedent, the rights of Englishmen included the rights of man in general. That was so because their Saxon ancestors founded their model of government upon the "natural rights of mankind." The legitimacy of the constitution was measured by the extent to which it approximated the idea of the Saxon mode, making the elective power of the people the fundamental principle. As the consent of the people was "indispensably *necessary* to every law, to which the whole *people* are to be bound," the most compelling Whig argument for the American case in 1774—and, ultimately, for American independence—was the inadequacy of consent in the then-existing structure of government in the British Empire.[24]

This argument also was presented in 1774 by British radical Whigs. In discussing the shortcomings of the post-Conquest English constitution, James Burgh—unlike Hulme—did not stop with the inadequate state of representation in Parliaments and the excessive length of their periods; he went on to assail Parliament's taxation of the American colonies in spite of the complete absence of representation for them in that body. "We have seen Parliament stamp the *Americans*, then unstamp them, and then tax them in a new manner. Parliament has not, in these sudden doings and undoings, followed the sense of the people"; rather, as it was in former times "overawed by the authority of *kings*," it has lately been "too much swayed by *ministerial* influence." The Americans, whose friendship England ought to cherish, have been enslaved by a Parliament having in view the object of "enlarging the power of the court by increasing the number of places and pensions for their dependents." As Granville Sharp also pointed out, "the *Inequality of Representation*" in the English Parliament "affords no just argument for setting aside the *Representation* of the people in other parts of the British Empire; because experience teaches us that even a *defective Representation* is better than none at all." [25]

Both Burgh and Sharp were aware of the absurdity in contending that the electors on the island of Britain adequately represented the interests of the American colonists. After all, the people of Manchester, though inadequately represented in Parliament, had never been exclusively subjected to a tax as had the American colonists, who had no representation at all. For the inhabitants of "one part of the empire" to determine a question or enact a law "for the particular advantages of that *one part*, though to the manifest detriment and injury of another part," without the representation of the latter would make the former "*judges in their own cause*; a circumstance that would be literally *partial*, the very reverse of justice and *natural equity*." The taxing of the colonies without their consent violated Magna Carta and the Bill of Rights because it violated that natural right which they were partially designed to protect, of "having a share in the legislature" and thereby being able to give consent. The making of laws for the subjects of any part of the British Empire without their participation and assent was, in short, "INIQUITOUS and therefore unlawful, . . . unjust in its principles, rigorous in its execution, and pernicious in its operations alike to the mother-country and the colonies." [26]

Behind Burgh's and Sharp's analysis of the "striking absurdities" in the "*British* house of commons proposing to tax the unrepresented colonies in *America*" was an awareness of the fact that England and America were two separate political societies. The hypothetical tax exclusively levied on the people of Manchester "would be more plausible than a *British* parliament's taxing *America:* because the members cannot be supposed competent judges of the abilities of the colonists to bear taxes; whereas they are undoubtedly judges of the ability of their own countrymen," Burgh argued. Noting the sad example of the union of Great Britain and Ireland, Sharp concluded that "the *Representation of the People,* in every part of the British Empire, is absolutely necessary to constitute an *effectual Legislature,* according to the fundamental principles of the English Constitution; for none of them, *separately,* can be esteemed as *competent Legislature* to judge of the other's *Rights,* without the highest injustice and *iniquity."* [27]

The idea that Americans were not simply transplanted subjects of the British king but a separate, sovereign people was implicit throughout Jefferson's *Summary View* and its reference to the Americans as "expatriated men." The rights that Jefferson claimed on their behalf, therefore, were not only rights derived from the English constitution, as is suggested by the repeated references to natural rights in the document: "those rights which god and the laws have given equally and independently to all"; "a right, which nature has given to all men," of expatriation; "the exercise of free trade" possessed by the American colonists "as of natural right"; "a free people, claiming their rights as derived from the laws of nature, and not as the gift of their chief magistrate." Thus, although the approach of the *Summary View* might have been based on Jefferson's understanding of Whig history, its analysis is much more than merely historical. The case for the redress of American grievances in 1774, like the case for American independence in 1776, was based not only on the rights of Englishmen but also on the rights of man.

The Case for American Independence: Jefferson's Declaration and Its "Harmonizing" Logic

Although as late as August 1775 Jefferson wrote of "looking with fondness toward a reconciliation with Great Britain," he also identified his "first wish" as "a restoration of our just rights." And though he described himself as "sincerely one of those" who still wish for a reunion with Britain and who "would rather be in dependence on Great Britain, properly limited, than on any nation upon earth," he also remained adamant in his view of the "true ground" of American grievances. Rather than submit to "the right of legislating for us assumed by the British parliament," he defiantly noted that he would "lend [his] hand to sink the whole island in the ocean." He wrote this letter to John Randolph, a Loyalist who was returning to Britain, in order to help Randolph open the eyes of Englishmen to the true state of affairs in America.[28]

Jefferson's hopes for reconciliation were based on his belief that the king and ministry could be persuaded of the true state of American affairs: that the patriot opposition was not a small faction but rather encompassed "the body of the people," and that they meant to "insist rigorously" on their rights. Yet Jefferson recognized that "even those in parliament who are called friends to America"—men such as Burke or Fox—"seem to know nothing of our real determinations." As time passed, Jefferson became convinced that the equal adamancy of the British government made a political solution impossible. In a letter to his former teacher Dr. Small written in May 1775 shortly after Jefferson had received news of the battles at Lexington and Concord, he wrote, almost despairingly, of the "haughty deportment" of the British government. He particularly lamented the fact that the king, "the only mediatory power . . . instead of leading to a reconciliation his divided people, should pursue the incendiary purpose of still blowing up the flames, as we find him constantly doing, in every speech and public declaration."[29]

By late November, Jefferson was convinced that the king was "the bitterest enemy we have," and he again warned John Randolph, in unmistakable terms, of the probable consequences. Still maintaining that "there is not in the British empire a man who more cordially loves a union with Great Britain than I do," he swore, "by the god that made me, I will cease to exist before I yield to a connection on such terms as the British parliament propose; and in this, I think I speak the sentiments of America." Speaking further for all Americans, he assured Randolph that "we want neither inducement nor power, to declare and assert a separation. It is will, alone, which is wanting, and that is growing apace under the fostering hand of our king."[30]

British intransigence alone, however, does not explain the failure of the attempt to resolve the crisis within the bounds of the law. An equally important factor was the inability of Americans to present a united front in making the case for the redress of their grievances. In stating both the constitutional grounds for their grievances and their proposed solutions for redressing them, American Whigs differed among themselves—as, no doubt, Jefferson was keenly aware.[31] At the Second Continental Congress meeting in Philadelphia in 1775–76, his authorship of the *Summary View* enhanced his reputation as not only a writer with a demonstrable "felicity of expression" but also an exponent of the radical position. But Jefferson acknowledged that he was unable to get any of his fellow Virginians except Wythe to agree with him on the "true ground" for opposing the lawfulness of parliamentary legislation, the absolute denial of any parliamentary authority over the colonies. Jefferson's view of the basis for the Americans' status as subjects of the crown—that the settlers had quit their allegiance upon emigrating to America and had then voluntarily agreed to again become subjects of the king—was similarly unique; it distinguished Jefferson's position in the *Summary View* from that of two other important pamphlets which appeared in 1774, John Adams's *Novanglus* and James Wilson's *Considerations on the Nature and Extent of the Legislative Authority of the British Parliament*, both of which held that the Englishmen who settled in America had never renounced allegiance to the British monarch and therefore remained subjects of the king. Despite the broad canvas of Jefferson's work—purporting to speak for all British America—the *Summary View* expressed no consensus but rather Jefferson's almost singular view of the case for the redress of American grievances.

Jefferson was far more successful in speaking for "all American whigs" in stating in the Declaration of Independence the "harmonizing sentiments" explaining the actions of 2 July 1776, the day Congress voted to approve the resolution of independence. Part of his success in making the Declaration "an expression of the American mind" must be attributed not to Jefferson but to Congress, in its deletion of certain passages of Jefferson's draft—particularly three long passages that stated his unique views detailing "the circumstances of our emigration and settlement here," denouncing the British people as "unfeeling brethren," and condemning George III for having "waged cruel war against human nature itself" by permitting slavery to exist in the colonies.[32]

The more important reason, however, explaining the success of the Declaration in speaking for all American Whigs in 1776 was in the very nature of Jefferson's assignment as primary draftsman for the committee of five appointed by Congress on 11 June. By that time, the die had been cast: members of Congress had come around to the standard of Thomas Paine's *Common Sense*, had given up hope of getting the king to intercede on their behalf and effect a reconciliation, and had voted on 10 and 15 May to recommend to the states that they establish new governments founded on "the authority of the people." Most importantly, the king himself had made it possible for Americans to dissolve their allegiance by declaring the colonies in rebellion and out of his protection and then, in fact, waging war against the colonies. Questions that earlier had divided American Whigs, questions about the nature of their rights as transplanted subjects of the king—Were they "expatriated men" or had they always been subjects of the British monarch? Were they subject to the authority of Parliament; if so, what was the source of that obligation, and to what extent did it bind them?—were no longer relevant after they had de facto renounced allegiance to the king and assumed the status of a free and independent people.

What remained was to withdraw allegiance formally, and the actions of the king had made the justice of such a formal renunciation evident to the members of Congress. As Jefferson put it, in summarizing the arguments advanced in Congress by the advocates of independence, "the question was not whether, by a declaration of independence, we should make ourselves what we are not; but whether we should declare a fact which already exists":

> That as to the people or parliament of England, we had alwais been independant of them, their restraints on our trade deriving efficacy from our acquiescence only & not from any rights they possessed of imposing them, & that so far our connection had been federal only, & was now dissolved by the commencement of hostilities;
>
> That as to the king, we had been bound to him by allegiance, but that this bond was now dissolved by his assent to the late act of parliament, by which he declares us out of his protection, and by his levying war on us, a fact which had long ago proved us out of his protection; it being a certain position in law that allegiance & protection are reciprocal, the one ceasing when the other is withdrawn.

Moreover, Jefferson noted, an exact parallel could be drawn between the present circumstances and the Glorious Revolution of 1688, except that "James the IId. never declared the people of England out of his protection yet his actions proved it & the parliament declared it."[33] Thus, the situation that warranted a formal withdrawal of allegiance from George III was compelling. With the exception of passages cut by Congress, for the obvious reason that they did not "harmonize" with that body's general views, Jefferson's draft of the Declaration brilliantly downplayed those issues that had divided the Patriots and stated the case for American independence in terms on which they could all agree—and thus expressed, in a quite literal sense, the "harmonizing sentiments" of American Whigs of the day.

Analytically, Jefferson's Declaration began where his *Summary View* ends: the case for the redress of American grievances having failed, it was time to put forth the case for American independence. Yet, as Thomas Grey has noted, the case for independence "could not be made in legal terms" but rather had to be based upon extralegal considerations of utility and political philosophy.[34] The theory is familiar: all men, created "equal & independant" with respect to their natural rights, institute governments to secure those rights; the "just powers" of government deriving from "the consent of the governed," it is the right of the people "to alter or to abolish" government whenever it has become "destructive of these ends" and when "a long train of abuses & usurpations" makes it clear that there is no other way for the people to restore their liberties.[35] The ideas expressed were, as Jefferson said in his 1825 letter to Henry Lee, the "harmonizing sentiments" of the day. The language used was strikingly similar to that used not only by Locke and Sidney, both of whose works Jefferson specifically mentioned as the "elementary books of public right" on which the authority of the Declaration rested, but also by other Whig writers on government.[36]

The Declaration did not merely state general principles, however; it was drafted to explain why it had become "necessary" for the American people to exercise the ultimate right to which "the laws of nature & of nature's god entitle them." In presenting this argument in the Declaration, Jefferson did more than merely express Whig ideas about government; he also sought "to place before mankind the common sense of the subject, in terms so plain and firm as to command their assent, and to justify ourselves in the independent stand we are compelled to take." As Wilbur Samuel Howell has shown, Jefferson employed the language of eighteenth-century logic and rhetoric to present the case for American independence. The ideas expressed in the Declaration were given "added persuasive power by their adherence to the best contemporary standards of mathematical and scientific demonstration," probably reflecting the influence of William

Duncan, whose *Elements of Logick* Jefferson almost certainly read while under the tutelage of William Small, who had been a student of Duncan at Marishal College, Aberdeen.[37]

Howell has shown how Jefferson's Declaration, following the principles of Duncan's *Logick*, constitutes a demonstration, or proof, proceeding from self-evident truths in the order of a syllogism. The argument begins with a major premise, the "self-evident" propositions of the second paragraph. The adjective *self-evident* has a precise meaning: as Duncan had expressed it, it refers to a proposition that "admits not of any Proof, because a bare Attention to the Ideas themselves, produces full Conviction and Certainty."[38] Such were the "truths" that "all men are created equal & independant, that from that equal creation they derive rights inherent & inalienable, among which are the preservation of life, & liberty, & the pursuit of happiness; that to secure these ends, governments are instituted among men, deriving their just powers from the consent of the governed; that whenever any form of government shall become destructive of these ends, it is the right of the people to alter or to abolish it, & to institute new government, laying it's foundation on such principles & organising it's powers in such form, as to them shall seem most likely to effect their safety & happiness." By founding the syllogistic argument of the Declaration on the self-evident propositions of this major premise, Jefferson gave his argument the highest standard of proof, the logical certainty required to "command the assent of mankind."

Jefferson gave the argument added persuasiveness by utilizing corollaries, which flow "naturally and of themselves," as Duncan said they should, from the propositions, reinforcing the argument of the syllogism as a whole. Thus, for example, the proposition stating the right of the people to alter or abolish government has as its corollary the proposition that "governments long established should not be changed for light & transient causes." "But," Jefferson further noted, "when a long train of abuses & usurpations, begun at a distinguished period, & pursuing invariably the same object, evinces a design to subject them to arbitary power," it is both the right and the duty of the people to "throw off such government & to provide new guards for their future security."

Next in the order of argument is the minor premise: that "the history of his present majesty, is a history of unremitting injuries and usurpations, . . . all of which have in direct object the establishment of an absolute tyranny over these states." The minor premise connects with the major premise through the corollaries: having borne with "patient sufferance" the abuses of George III, the colonies now must bow to "the necessity which constrains them to expunge their former systems of government." That necessity proceeds from the duty "to throw off" tyrannical or arbitrary government, when "a long train of abuses and usurpations" evinces such a design.

⟨ The main body of the Declaration, the list of eighteen specific injuries and usurpations—or counts, if one wishes to draw an analogy to a bill of indictment—alleged against George III, specified the "facts" to be "submitted to a candid world" in proof of the minor premise. The listing of these facts also accorded with Duncan's principles of syllogistic proof; they constituted the scholia, or particulars needed to illustrate the subject and complete the reader's information, in the manner of annotations upon a text. The difference is that in the Declaration these were not marginal glosses or footnotes but the main body of the text.[39]

The list of counts against the king has a logic of its own, as Garry Wills has shown. The list has four distinct parts, three of which were modeled after earlier lists of grievances, including the *Summary View* and the preamble from Jefferson's draft of the Virginia Constitution.[40] The first twelve counts related to the misuse of executive powers, including such offenses as the disallowance or suspension of colonial legislation, dissolving assemblies, making judges dependent on the king's will, keeping standing armies, and making the military superior to the civil power. The thirteenth count charged that the king had "combined with others to subject us to a jurisdiction foreign to our constitutions and unacknoleged by our laws"—in other words, Parliament—"giving his assent to their pretended acts of legislation." Acts of Parliament were not cited by statute but by the type of grievance they represented. Among the eight types of parliamentary offenses charged were restrictions on the colonies' trade, the imposition of taxes "without our consent," and the deprivation of the benefits of trial by jury. Counts fourteen through eighteen related to what Garry Wills has characterized as "war atrocities"; they included charges that the king had "abdicated government" by withdrawing his governors and declaring the colonies out of his allegiance and protection and had made war on the colonies, using not only British troops but "foreign mercenaries," "merciless Indian savages," and the Americans' own slaves. The nineteenth and final count against the king related the fact that "in every stage of these oppressions" the Americans had petitioned for redress, but their "repeated petitions have been answered by repeated injury." The king, therefore, was shown to be "a tyrant" and "unfit to be the ruler of a people who mean to be free."

As John Phillip Reid has shown, many of the counts against George III in the Declaration state constitutional grievances "previously litigated and established as [offenses] in British constitutional law" in such milestones of Whig constitutionalism as the Petition of Right of 1628 and the Bill of Rights of 1689. These include standing armies, quartering troops, taxation without the consent of elected representatives, and the use of martial law against civilians. Moreover, the general charge represented by counts fourteen through eighteen— making war on his own people—was "one of the most serious constitutional grievances that could be made in English constitutional law." [41] However, many of the other charges against George III were peculiar to the American quarrel with the mother country. Even the familiar offense of taxation without consent had a peculiar twist: the king was charged for giving his assent to taxes imposed by Parliament, an offense which was unknown to the seventeenth-century English constitutional struggles.

It is not surprising that the list of counts against the king reflected Jefferson's thorough understanding of English history and constitutional law. This part of the Declaration indeed may be, as Reid has suggested, "more legal than we thought," but its context must not be overlooked. [42] These were "facts submitted to a candid world" for proof that George III governed arbitrarily, as a tyrant. The fact that the king acted contrary to English law and the constitution was, of course, relevant, but the nature of the charges against the king need not be so narrowly characterized. The Americans' rights under the English constitution were relevant, but so too were their basic, natural rights as men. George III violated not only his original compact but also the Lockean social compact by making his government of the colonies "destructive of the ends" for which it was established. And, in declaring themselves independent, the Americans were exercising not merely their right to rebel, under Whig constitutional theory, but also their right to institute new government, under Real Whig political theory that based all government on the consent of the governed.

Finally, the argument of the Declaration reached the conclusion that followed from its major and minor premises: the American states through their representatives in Congress "reject and renounce all allegiance & subjection to the kings of Great Britain & all others who may thereafter claim by, through, or under them." Further, as Jefferson originally wrote, they "utterly dissolve & break off all political connection which may have heretofore subsisted between us & the people or parliament of Great Britain"—thus nicely accommodating the various positions taken by American Whigs with respect to the source and nature of parliamentary authority over the colonies by leaving the question open.[43] Congress then declared the colonies to be "free and independent states," with full power to "levy war, conclude peace, contract alliances," and perform all other acts appropriate to such a status.

With this conclusion the argument of the Declaration was complete. It declared the "causes which impel" American independence, as the opening sentence of the Declaration summarized: "One people," the American colonists, being denied their natural and constitutional rights under the British Empire, must of necessity "dissolve the political bands which have connected them with another" people, the British, "and . . . assume among the powers of the earth the separate and equal station to which the laws of nature & of nature's god entitle them." Congress's omission of the later sections detailing "the circumstances of our emigration and settlement here" and denouncing "the unfeeling brethren" of Britain may have deprived the Declaration of some of its original Jeffersonian character, but the omissions were not fatal. The passages expressing Jefferson's unique understanding of the history of the settling of America and of the loss of the bonds of affection between the two peoples were not essential to the meaning of the Declaration as a political document, reflective of Whig ideology; nor were they essential to the logical development of the Declaration's argument. The opening sentence of the Declaration, which was not altered by Congress, said it all.

Postscript to the Revolution: The American Whig Perspective and the Irrelevance of Blackstone

The "harmonizing sentiments" of American Whigs in 1776 as revealed in Jefferson's Declaration of Independence were a combination of the Whig approaches to history and government. As an American Whig,

Jefferson in his understanding of English history was impressed with "that excellent Equilibrium of power, or mixt government, *limited by law*," which his Saxon ancestors "most zealously asserted, and transmitted to [him] as [his] best *Birthright* and *Inheritance*." [44] But he was not limited by historical precedent; he admired the Saxon mode of government for its rationality, its consonance with what he understood to be the rights of man, under the laws of nature. Most of all, he esteemed the notion of consent, "the free Representation of the people in the legislature," as essential to any legitimate government. Thus when he found himself in a situation in which English history furnished no adequate precedent through which to obtain a redress of his grievances, he abandoned history and turned to philosophy, asserting his general rights as a man in addition to his particular rights as a member of the British Empire.

The theory of government articulated in the Declaration, by focusing upon popular consent, modified significantly the concept of sovereignty, changing its locus from the government to the people. The notion of an ultimate supremacy of the people, as it was suggested by Locke in his *Second Treatise* or by Burgh in his *Political Disquisitions*, was a sharply limited one; as Bernard Bailyn has observed, it was a supremacy which was "normally dormant and exercised only at moments of rebellion against tyrannical government," such as the Glorious Revolution. [45] Even then, the ultimate right of the people to dissolve and reconstruct their government was never seriously suggested, at least by Locke. If Parliament did derive sovereignty from the people, that grant was irrevocable. It was not so in American Revolutionary ideology. The notion of the ultimate supremacy of the people carried over into the uniquely American notion of sovereignty seated in the people. [46]

When, for example, the Massachusetts General Court announced in 1776 that the sovereign power "resides always in the body of the People" and that it "never was, or can be delegated, to one Man or a few," it was expressing a wholly new concept of republican government. Gordon Wood has aptly described it as the "disembodiment of government" because it separated sovereignty, the locus of ultimate political power in the society, from government. The legislature represented the people for certain purposes only, and not to all intents and purposes whatever. Its powers were limited to those that the people, who always remained sovereign, had conferred; and the written constitution served as a documentation of this ad hoc conferral of powers from people to government. This notion of popular sovereignty and the view of government that it entailed was indeed the crucial issue of the Revolution.[47] Englishmen could never conceive that the statutes of Parliament and the statutes of colonial legislatures could be given equal application in the colonies, because they saw sovereignty, by definition undivisible, as vesting in Parliament. Jefferson had no problem with the idea of two legislatures for one geographical area. As he saw it, the powers of government might be divided in any manner without destroying Hobbes's notion of the indivisibility of sovereignty because sovereignty vested in the people rather than in the government. That crucial perception, when it became generally understood in America, would come to underlay the federal system of government embodied in the Constitution and to help pave the way for the development of judicial review in the early nineteenth century.

As the notion of sovereignty developed from a rudimentary notion of parliamentary sovereignty, sovereignty derived from the people, to the notion of popular sovereignty, sovereignty seated in the people, so too developed the related concepts of law and constitutionalism. The source of law eventually became not merely the description of what is and has been but rather the measure of what ought and ought not to be. The Revolutionary achievement of the Americans in 1776 was to establish firmly that this was the direction in which the development of legal and political theory was headed.

The full measure of that achievement may be assessed by returning to Jefferson's admonition to Madison in 1826 that the law professor selected for the University of Virginia ought to be a good Whig, not one of Tory "hue," weaned on the "honeyed Mansfieldism" of Blackstone. One can grasp most readily the full significance of the change in constitutionalism made possible by the American Revolution—the shift from parliamentary sovereignty to popular sovereigny—by considering the basis for Jefferson's charge that the study of Blackstone's *Commentaries* could cause young lawyers to "slide into toryism."

Most obviously, the Tory sentiments of Blackstone may be found in his position with respect to the "plantations" in America, which he found to be subject to the authority of Parliament. Blackstone, like Jefferson, supposed that the common law of England, as such, had no authority in America; and Blackstone was careful to note that only acts of Parliament in which the colonies were particularly named would bind them. But in analyzing the American colonies as conquered territories subject to the king's authority and in arguing that some acts of Parliament could bind them, Blackstone took a position particularly objectionable to the author of the *Summary View* and the Declaration of Independence. An extract from Jefferson's legal commonplace book shows his awareness of Blackstone's concept of sovereignty as an essential part of the argument of those who alleged that Parliament had power to make laws binding the American colonies.[48] The way in which that concept was used to assert parliamentary jurisdiction was not the only feature of Blackstone's view of sovereignty that was objectionable to Jefferson; the view itself, and its relation to Blackstone's arguments about the nature of law generally and of English law in particular, was what Jefferson and others found to be the Tory "hue" of Blackstone's treatise.

The *Commentaries* was Tory in Jefferson's eyes for two additional reasons. The first, and more obvious, was that despite some superficial similarities to Whig histories, the *Commentaries* in general sought to glorify what the Real Whigs considered to be a corrupt English constitution. Blackstone equated with the Glorious Revolution of 1688–89 the permanent reestablishment of the ancient constitution. Yet the tone of the final chapter of the *Commentaries*, if not that of the entire work, was more than a glorification of the past; it was, in fact, a glorification of the present state of English law, the "noble monument of ancient simplicity" with all the "excrescences," however "troublesome," that later generations had added. It was not the constitution of the mid-eleventh century but the constitution of the mid-eighteenth century that he referred to as "this noble pile." As Daniel Boorstin has noted, Blackstone was endeavoring to make English law not only a "science" but also a mystery. Although he shared with Whig historians the primitivistic conviction that the original form of the legal system had been one of pure and rational simplicity, Blackstone also argued that "through all of legal history there ran a mysterious purpose which was of its own force improving institutions," a Providence "at once so mysterious and so powerful that in comparison men were bound to be either bungling or insignificant." Blackstone left the would-be reformer in the position of only "a powerless spectator of a happy story." He illustrated the tangible result of that story, the "noble pile" of mid-eighteenth-century England, with all its perfection and complexity, with the "sublime" symbol of "an old Gothic castle."[49]

A second, and far more important, reason why Jefferson considered the *Commentaries* Tory is evident in Blackstone's concept of sovereignty. Blackstone argued that different societies may constitute their governments variously, but all forms of government have in common the essential attribute of sovereignty: however constituted, "there is and must be in all of them a supreme, irresistible, absolute, uncontrolled authority, in which the *jura summi imperii*, or the rights of sovereignty, reside." He followed classical political thought in seeing advantages and disadvantages in the three "pure" forms of democracy, aristocracy, and monarchy and hence concluding that the best form is a mixed government, combining the benefits of the other three yet avoiding their basic flaws. Not surprisingly, he identified the English government as such a mixed form and argued that the legislative power, and "(of course) the supreme and absolute authority of the state," is therefore vested in Parliament, the jurisdiction of which is "so transcendent and absolute, that it cannot be confined, either for causes or persons, within any bounds." As described by Blackstone, Parliament "hath sovereign and uncontrolable authority in making, confirming, enlarging, restraining, abrogating, repealing, reviving, and expounding of laws, concerning matters of all possible denominations, ecclesiastical or temporal, civil, military, maritime, or criminal." Parliament, Blackstone concluded, "can, in short, do every thing that is not naturally impossible; and therefore some have scrupled to call it's power, by a figure rather too bold, the omnipotence of parliament. True it is, that what they do, no authority upon earth can undo." [50]

Nor was Blackstone willing to recognize an inherent supreme power in the people to remove or alter the legislature when they find it acting contrary to the trust reposed in it, as Locke had argued in the *Second Treatise of Government*. "However just this conclusion may be in theory, we cannot adopt it, nor argue from it, under any dispensation of government at present actually existing." Such a "devolution of power, to the people at large," argued Blackstone, would dissolve "the whole form of government" established by that people, reducing all individuals to a state of nature—"their original state of equality"—and repealing "all positive law whatsoever before enacted." Blackstone solemnly declared that "no human laws will . . . suppose a case, which at once must destroy all law, and compel men to build afresh upon a new foundation; nor will they make provision for so desperate an event, as must render all legal provisions ineffectual."

Yet, as Forrest McDonald has noted, that is the "case" and "event" that the Continental Congress brought into being by declaring the independence of the thirteen American states.[51]

Blackstone's concept of an omnipotent Parliament and his refusal to recognize any constitutional right of revolution led him to the inevitable conclusion that "the power of parliament is absolute and without control." He regarded the only practical check upon the power of Parliament, the separation of the executive from the legislative power, as a means of restraining executive power only; he identified the independence of the legislative power with the liberty of the subject. And, again, by Blackstone's definition of civil or political liberty, there was no contradiction in this, for it was the sovereign, omnipotent Parliament which was to decide how far to restrain individual liberty as "necessary and expedient for the general advantage of the public." Hence it followed from Blackstone's argument that "neither judicial disallowance of acts of Parliament nor yet the right of revolution has either legal or constitutional basis."[52]

After 1776 Jefferson and some of his contemporaries viewed Blackstone's concept of sovereignty as not only logically deficient but also wholly irrelevant to the American experience. Indeed, in 1803 St. George Tucker, a judge on the Supreme Court of Errors of Virginia and George Wythe's successor as professor of law at the College of William and Mary, published an "Americanized" version of the *Commentaries,* so extensively annotated that it expanded Blackstone's original four volumes into five. It was this version of Blackstone that Jefferson would later recommend to prospective law students. As Robert M. Cover has noted in his review of Tucker's 1803 edition, "If any ideological issue can be specified as having been at the heart of the American Revolution it was whether sovereignty is indeed indivisible, unconditional, and legislative." From the American perspective, Cover pointed out, Blackstone, "like Dante's Virgil, worked under the insurmountable handicap of living before the Great Event."[53]

To Jefferson, sovereignty in the sense meant by Blackstone properly resided only in "the People." Popular sovereignty was a matter Jefferson took seriously, for it was at the heart of the American Revolution: the foundation of the American republic lay in the principle enunciated in the Declaration of Independence, that governments derive their just powers from "the consent of the governed." This principle, in turn, lay at the heart of the philosophy of government espoused by the Whig writers whose ideas helped shape Jefferson's thought by the eve of the Revolution. "All lawful authority, legislative and executive," argued James Burgh, "originates from the people": "Power in the *people* is like light in the sun, native, original, inherent, and unlimited by anything human. In governors, it may be compared to the reflected light of the moon; for it is only borrowed, delegated, and limited by the intention of the people, whose it is and to whom governors are to consider themselves responsible, while the people are answerable only to God. . . . And happy is that people, who having originally so principled their constitution, that they themselves can without violence to it, lay hold of its power, wield it as they please, and turn it, when necessary, against those to whom it was entrusted, and who have exerted it to the prejudice of its original proprietors." The latter idea had been expressed ninety years earlier by the republican martyr Algernon Sidney, who in his *Discourses concerning Government* had said that "all human Constitutions are subject to corruption, and must perish, unless they are timely renewed and reduced to their first principles," and that "Good Governments admit of Changes in the Superstructures, whilst the Foundations remain unchangeable." Burgh followed Sidney's suggestion, and anticipated American constitutionalism, when he proposed that "in planning a government by representation, the people ought to provide against their own *annihilation*. They ought to establish a regular and constitutional method of acting by and from *themselves,* without, or even in opposition to, their *representatives,* if necessary."[54]

To the Whig philosophers of government, the absence of such a method was the greatest weakness in the English constitution. Extraordinary tyrannies in English history required extraordinary acts, often involving bloodshed. The "glorious" Revolution of 1688–89— all the more glorious because bloodless—was made possible only because James II abdicated the government; it was not clear what, if anything, could be done against legislative tyranny in England. As Burgh observed, "Our ancestors were provident; but not provident enough. They set up parliaments, as a curb on *kings* and *ministers;* but they neglected to reserve to themselves a regular and constitutional method of exerting their power in curbing *parliaments,* when necessary."[55] It was for want of such a constitutional remedy that the

Americans declared their independence in 1776, and it was the perceived need of providing such a constitutional remedy that made the
work of constitution making during the Revolution so important.

C. H. McIlwain has noted that "the Whigs brought on the English
Revolution, but the American doctrine of 1774 [and 1776] was really
a new revolt against one of the main principles of 1688," the doctrine
of the supremacy of Parliament, the doctrine of sovereignty found
in Blackstone.[56] The Americans, in breaking from the British Empire,
could carry Whig doctrines several steps further by establishing forms
of government through which the people could exercise "a regular and
constitutional method of acting by and from themselves," as Burgh
and other English Real Whig writers had urged.

3

Our Revolution Commenced on

More Favorable Ground

The Foundations of

Republican Government

Our Revolution commenced on more favorable ground," Jefferson explained to the English radical Whig John Cartwright in 1824. "We had no occasion to search into musty records, to hunt up royal parchments, or to investigate the laws and institutions of a semibarbarous ancestry. We appealed to those of nature, and found them ongravod on our hoarto."[1]

He thus expressed, nearly a half century later, the sense of exhilaration that he and his contemporaries felt in 1776, at the prospect of creating new forms of government after declaring the independence of the American states. Independence gave American Whigs a glorious opportunity, one which "the greatest lawgivers of antiquity" would have envied, John Adams wrote: "How few of the human race would have ever enjoyed an opportunity of making an election of government, . . . for themselves or their children! When, before the present epocha, had three millions of people full power and a fair opportunity to form and establish the wisest and happiest government that human wisdom can contrive?" Thomas Paine put it most succinctly in *Common Sense* when he informed Americans, "We have it in our power to begin the world over again."[2]

This chapter examines Jefferson's efforts to establish the foundation—the "favorable ground"—for republican government during the decade and a half after the Declaration of Independence. During these years he served in the governments of both of the new political societies that he had helped bring into being in 1776, the Commonwealth of Virginia and the United States of America; and he served in a variety of capacities, as a member of both the Virginia legislature and Congress, as governor, and as a diplomat in Europe.

If one common link can be discerned in the various types of public service in which Jefferson was involved during these years, it was the effort to establish in America a republican form of government which would last. Not only his work in the making of constitutions and in reforming law but also his service as a diplomat—and particularly his efforts to negotiate treaties of commerce—had in view his desire to ensure the success of what he would later call the "experiment of self-government" that he and his colleagues had launched in Philadelphia in 1776.

This chapter focuses primarily on Jefferson's activities as constitution maker and law reformer, showing his understanding of republicanism. The term is incapable of precise definition; Jefferson not only used it in ways that differed from his contemporaries but in different ways himself. Later in life he said that the foundation of republican government was "the equal right of every citizen, in his person and property, and in their management"; and he declared that the degree of "the control of the people over the organs of their government" was "the measure of its republicanism." At about the same time he defined a republic as a representative democracy, in which "the mass of individuals composing the society . . . reserve to themselves personally, the exercise of all rightful powers to which they are competent, and to delegate those to which they are not competent to deputies named, and removable for unfaithful conduct, by themselves immediately."[3] Jefferson thus thought of republicanism as not only a constitutional and political system but also a social system, what he sometimes referred to as "self-government." While his fuller elaboration of the constitutional and political aspects of republicanism came in later decades—following Jefferson's involvement in the party struggles of the 1790s, the focus of the next two chapters—his concept of republicanism as a social theory, or of self-government, was formulated at a much earlier stage and helped to give meaning to his reform efforts of the 1780s.

"Novices in the Science of Government": Considering the Virginia Constitution

Jefferson in 1776 was keenly aware of the importance of the making of state constitutions, describing it as "a work of the most interesting nature and such as every individual would wish to have his voice in." Indeed, he added, "in truth it is the whole object of the present controversy" because instituting "a bad government" would not have justified the risk and expense of the Revolution. By the accidents of history, however, Jefferson was absent both when the constitution of his native Commonwealth of Virginia was written in 1776 and when the Constitution of the United States was written in 1787. On the first occasion, when he was in Philadelphia as a delegate to the Continental Congress, Jefferson transmitted the resolution adopted by Congress on 15 May 1776 urging the several states to adopt a form of government independent of the authority of the British crown. Stressing the importance of the work as "the whole object of the present controversy," Jefferson hoped that "should our Convention propose to establish now a form of government perhaps it might be agreeable to recall for a short time their delegates."[4] This hope of being recalled was in vain; and while Jefferson was busy drafting the Declaration of Independence, the convention in Williamsburg adopted a constitution which was largely the work of George Mason.

Although he was not present, Jefferson's influence was felt to a degree in the framing of the Virginia Constitution of 1776. By mid-June, before he began work on the Declaration of Independence, Jefferson had drafted a constitution which he entrusted to George Wythe for the convention in Virginia. By the time Wythe arrived in Williamsburg, however, it was too late for the convention seriously to consider Jefferson's draft: the weather was hot, the delegates were tired, and they already had adopted Mason's Declaration of Rights as well as Mason's basic plan of government. Jefferson's draft was drawn upon for amendments; and a part of it, the preamble, containing charges against the king and foreshadowing the similar bill of indictments found in the main text of the Declaration, was adopted almost as

Jefferson had written it.[5] In its essence—the structure of government and the basis of representation—however, the constitution adopted in Williamsburg differed fundamentally from Jefferson's draft.

What Jefferson's countrymen established was a system of government which, with one important exception, closely resembled the constitutional and political system of colonial Virginia. In the place of the royal governor was one who was elected annually by the General Assembly and whose executive powers were largely stripped away, as was typical of the American Whig reaction against executive authority in the framing of state constitutions during the Revolution. The old Governor's Council, which had exercised both executive and legislative functions, was replaced by an executive Council of State, chosen by the assembly, and an upper legislative house elected by the people, which, following Jefferson's suggestion, the convention called the Senate. The two houses of the assembly, the Senate and the House of Delegates, selected the judges as well as the governor and therefore dominated the government. Property qualifications for the electorate were retained; so too was the outmoded county-based system of representation, which heavily favored the older tidewater counties at the expense of the newer, rapidly growing western counties. The net result was, in Dumas Malone's words, an "aristocratic republic" in which the old colonial elite—the wealthy planters in the eastern, tidewater region—continued to hold a predominate share of the political power.[6]

Jefferson's draft, in contrast, would have extended the suffrage to freeholders possessing only a quarter of an acre in town or twenty-five acres in the country and to all residents who had paid taxes to the government for two years or more. This suffrage provision, coupled with a provision granting fifty acres of land to every man of full age who did not already have that many, would have resulted in near-universal adult white male suffrage. (Women and slaves were not included in the political community known to Jefferson and his contemporaries.) Representation in the lower house would have been based on the distribution of voters (thus, practically, on population), a system far more equitable and favorable to Jefferson's own piedmont region. As J. R. Pole has observed, these provisions indicated that "the author of the affirmation that governments derived their just powers 'from the consent of the governed' had done some purposeful thinking about the meaning of consent" by penetrating to the principle of equal representation of individuals.[7]

In Jefferson's plan the assembly as a whole would have wielded less power: it would have shared some appointive powers with the governor, whom Jefferson called "the administrator," and whose powers were defined as "those formerly held by the king," but with a long list of exceptions. The election of both the administrator and the Senate would have been confined to the more representative lower house.

The constitution of the Senate was a troubling point for Jefferson, who struggled in his various drafts to find a basis for distinguishing the upper house from the annually elected popular assembly. As Merrill Peterson has noted, Jefferson apparently was still influenced by the Old World norms of the one, the few, and the many: "The English theory of balanced government hung in his mind, a ruin from the past, for which he could find no satisfactory place in the political creed of the Revolution." After originally providing for life appointment of senators, he finally decided on election of the senators by the popular body for staggered terms of nine years, with one-third removed every three years and incapable of reelection. Jefferson rejected the solution, adopted by many of the first state constitutions, of composing the upper house of men of "distinguished property." His Senate would have been aristocratic by virtue of its wisdom, not its wealth; as he explained to Edmund Pendleton in the summer of 1776, he sought to have the "wisest men" chosen and did not think "integrity the characteristic of wealth." To ensure that truly wise men would be chosen, he would have the senators chosen by the lower house, which he called the House of Representatives; he believed "a choice by the people themselves is not generally distinguished for it's wisdom."[8]

Jefferson's draft also included a section on "Rights Private and Public" which not only was a bill of rights but also embodied a number of far-reaching reforms. "Full and free liberty of religious opinion" would be guaranteed and the Anglican church disestablished; freedom of the press, except for private libel actions, would be absolute; and "no person hereafter coming into this country" would be held in slavery "under any pretext whatever."[9] The significance of reforms relating to religious freedom and freedom of press became evident when a federal bill of rights came under consideration; the provision concerning slavery here deserves some explanation.

As someone who remained a slaveowner all his life but who nevertheless repeatedly declared his abhorrence of slavery, Jefferson was at best ambivalent about the "peculiar institution." His failed effort to include in the Declaration of Independence a condemnation of slavery and the slave trade probably convinced him—if indeed he needed to be convinced—that an institution which had been established in Virginia for a century and a half could not be abolished easily. Apparently, however, he was aware that the "self-evident" truths he had enunciated precluded the continued existence of slavery. His proposal to forbid further importation of slaves, though falling short of total emancipation, may be viewed as a feasible first step toward the ultimate extinction of slavery in Virginia.[10]

Two more reforms proposed in Jefferson's draft constitution of 1776 anticipated provisions similar to those that later either would be included in some other state constitutions or would be proposed for the federal Bill of Rights. These are the provisions requiring that juries try all factual questions, "whether of Chancery, Common, Ecclesiastical, or Marine law," and guaranteeing a freeman's right to use arms while forbidding standing armies.[11]

The Virginia Constitution of 1776 neither embodied nor envisioned such reforms. Moreover, it contained no article for future amendment or revision. Jefferson's draft, in contrast, contained an unprecedented clause that "these fundamental laws and provisions of government" could be altered by the vote of the people of two-thirds of the counties, all voting on the same day.[12] Thus, despite his apparent difficulty in transcending the British theory of balanced government, Jefferson nevertheless was far ahead of his countrymen in anticipating a constitutionalism based fully upon popular sovereignty. The form of popular ratification that Jefferson proposed had no parallel in any of the first state constitutions; indeed, it anticipated by some four years the system of popular ratification first utilized to approve the Massachusetts Constitution of 1780.

In his 1824 letter to Cartwright, Jefferson noted that despite the "more favorable ground" on which the Revolution commenced, he and his fellow American Whigs "did not avail themselves of all the advantages of our position." Inexperienced in the exercise of self-government and unschooled in its principles and forms, "when forced to assume it, we were novices in its science." Thus the early state constitutions established "some, although not all its important principles": among them, that "all power is inherent in the people; that they may exercise it by themselves, in all cases to which they think themselves competent, . . . or they may act by representatives, freely and equally chosen; that it is their right and duty to be at all times armed; that they are entitled to freedom of person, freedom of religion, freedom of property, and freedom of the press."

In many other respects, Jefferson added, the early state constitutions were flawed. In particular, the constitution in Virginia—which he stressed was "not only the first of the States, but, I believe I may say, the first of the nations of the earth, which assembled its wise men peaceably together to form a fundamental constitution," committed to writing—was nevertheless "very imperfect." [13] Jefferson's understanding of the various ways in which the Virginia Constitution of 1776 was "imperfect" is revealed most clearly in the analysis he included in his *Notes on the State of Virginia*.

Jefferson prepared the *Notes on Virginia* in 1781–82 in response to a questionnaire by a French diplomat, François, marquis de Barbé-Marbois, who was seeking to gather information for his government about the various American states. The twenty-three queries propounded by Barbé-Marbois, rearranged somewhat by Jefferson for purposes of organization, furnished the topics and mode of treatment in the book. Geographical materials predominate; indeed, the natural history section comprises about one-fourth of the whole book as finally published.[14] To the student of Jefferson's thoughts on government, however, it is Query XIII, regarding the Virginia Constitution, together with Query XIV, concerning the laws of Virginia, which are the most interesting parts of the work.

In the *Notes on Virginia* and elsewhere, Jefferson made clear his understanding of what a constitution is: that it is a fundamental law which defines and limits the powers of the ordinary legislature and which cannot be altered or affected by ordinary legislation. Hence, a true constitution must be established by the people themselves, acting through special agents appointed for that particular purpose, in a constitutional convention or the equivalent. This concept of the term *constitution* fundamentally differed from the concept that prevailed in eighteenth-century England, which was descriptive rather than prescriptive, and it evolved out of the concept that American Whigs had worked out in the 1760s and 1770s.[15] It is not clear exactly when Jefferson came to hold this peculiarly American concept of *constitution*; his reference in the Declaration of Independence to Parliament as a body foreign to "our constitution" may be viewed as either an early expression of the more modern sense of the term or merely a reflection of the broader Whig principle that government must derive its legitimacy from the consent of the governed.

By the time Jefferson wrote the *Notes on Virginia*, however, his concept of a constitution had crystallized. He viewed as one of the "very capital defects" of the Virginia Constitution of 1776 the fact that it was enacted by, and therefore could be altered by, the ordinary legislature.[16] The constitution was adopted by a convention of delegates chosen at the annual election in April 1776. That election, in turn, was conducted pursuant to an ordinance passed in July 1775 by the convention of delegates who had been elected in April of that year. Neither in July 1775 nor in April 1776, Jefferson argued, were the ideas of independence from Britain and the establishment of a new form of government "opened to the mass of the people." How then, he asked, could the delegates elected in 1776, chosen "for the year, to exercise the ordinary powers of legislation," have created a permanent or perpetual constitution, irrevocable by subsequent assemblies? "Had an unalterable form of government been meditated, perhaps we should have chosen a different set of people" than the delegates elected in April 1776, Jefferson noted. Indeed, he cited the practice of "the other states in the Union," in which the people chose special conventions to form permanent plans of government, unalterable by ordinary legislation.[17]

As understood by Jefferson, Virginia's so-called constitution of 1776 was not, properly speaking, a constitution at all.[18] The delegates to the convention, in order to organize the de facto government of Revolutionary Virginia more effectively—and to manage the "great contest" in which they were engaged with Britain—thought it proper to pass an ordinance of government. But, he argued, evidence showed that the delegates themselves considered it alterable. The instrument itself "pretends to no other higher authority than the ordinances of the same session" and does not say that it shall be perpetual or unalterable. Nor, he added, does the fact that they chose to call it "a Constitution or Form of government" change its true character. Moreover, the convention itself and subsequent assemblies had passed legislation contrary to the ordinance of government.[19]

The omnipotence of the legislature was another major concern Jefferson had with the 1776 Virginia Constitution. Its other five "capital defects" that he enumerated in *Notes on the State of Virginia* all involved, in one way or another, the legislative branch: two involved the system of representation; two, the powers of the legislature; and the other, the composition of the two houses of the legislature.

Representation was defective, Jefferson argued, in two ways. First, "the majority of the men in the state, who pay and fight for its support, are unrepresented in the legislature." And, second, "among those who share the representation, the shares are very unequal," with the tidewater counties having a disproportionately greater representation. He noted that 19,000 "fighting men," living in the area between the seacoast and the falls of the river, "possess" exactly half the Senate and just slightly less than a majority of the House of Delegates, and that these 19,000 men living in one part of the state, therefore, "give law" to upwards of 30,000 living in the more western parts of the state.[20]

The composition of the two houses of the legislature was defective, Jefferson argued, because the Senate was "too homogeneous" with the House of Delegates, since its members were chosen "by the same electors, at the same time, and out of the same subjects" and therefore were "men of the same description" as the members of the lower house. This ran counter to the purpose for a bicameral legislature, as Jefferson understood it, which was "to introduce the influence of different interests or different principles." The result was that Virginians "do not therefore derive from the separation of [their] legislature into two houses, those benefits which a proper complication of principles is capable of producing, and those which alone can compensate the evils which may be produced by their dissensions."[21]

The concern for proper structural safeguards—what we today call checks and balances—suggested by Jefferson's rationale for a bicameral legislature is made manifest in his discussion of the next "capital defect" in the Virginia Constitution: that "all the powers of government, legislative, executive, and judiciary, result to the legislative body." This concentration of powers in the same hands was to Jefferson "precisely the definition of despotic government." It does not matter that the powers are exercised by many men rather than just one: "173 despots would surely be as oppressive as one." Nor does it matter that they are chosen by the electors: "An *elective despotism* was not the government we fought for; but one which should not only be founded on free principles, but in which the powers of government should be so divided and balanced among several bodies of magistracy, as that no one could transcend their legal limits, without being effectively checked and restrained by the others."[22]

Jefferson's discussion of this defect thus far suggested his adherence to the classic eighteenth-century ideal of the balanced constitution. But, as the sentence that follows makes clear, he also had in mind a quite different doctrine, the comparatively new doctrine of the separation of powers. The convention that passed the "ordinance of government," Jefferson observed, "laid its foundation on this basis, that the legislative, executive and judiciary departments should be separate and distinct, so that no person should exercise the powers of more than one of them at the same time." Jefferson was paraphrasing the declaration that began the 1776 constitution, which has been described as "the clearest, most precise statement of the doctrine" of separation of powers that had appeared anywhere at that time.[23]

Jefferson clearly recognized that it was the separation of powers that formed the basis of the institutional structure of government. He viewed the actual structure of the Virginia government, however, as not in keeping with this theory. The reason why "all the powers of government, legislative, executive, and judiciary," though in theory assigned by the Virginia Constitution to separate and distinct departments, in fact "result to the legislative body" was that "no barrier was provided between these several powers." Because the assembly appointed the governor and the judges, "no opposition is likely to be made" if the legislature assumes executive and judiciary powers. Even if there were opposition, he added, it might not be effectual: the legislature "may put their proceedings into the form of an act of assembly, which would render them obligatory on the other branches."

Jefferson observed that the legislature in fact had assumed executive and judiciary powers through "the direction of the executive, during the whole time of their session," a practice which was becoming "habitual and familiar," and through the passage of private laws, by which the legislature "in many instances, decided rights which should have been left to judiciary controversy." Although these acts had been done "with no ill intention," he warned that the integrity of the men who presently held such powers was no safeguard against future dangers to liberty. "Mankind soon learn to make interested uses of every right and power which they possess, or may assume," he observed, adding that Americans should look forward to the not-too-distant time when their political systems would be as corrupt as the British. "Human nature is the same on every side of the Atlantic, and will be alike influenced by the same causes. The time to guard against corruption and tyranny, is before they shall have gotten hold on us." He concluded with one of his favorite metaphors: "It is better to keep the wolf out of the fold, than to trust drawing his teeth and talons after he shall have entered." [24]

The final "capital defect" of the Virginia Constitution of 1776 that Jefferson identified in his *Notes on the State of Virginia* was the legislature's power to determine its own quorum. By a vote on 4 June 1781 the House of Delegates determined to follow the precedent of the British Parliament ("one precedent in favor of power is stronger than a hundred against it") in fixing its own quorum, at forty members. The precedent thus established was a dangerous one, he argued; "if they may fix it at one number, they may at another, till it loses its fundamental character of being a representative body." This final defect identified by Jefferson was in a sense the capstone of all the other defects. For when it is considered that there was "no legal obstacle to the assumption by the assembly of all the powers legislative, executive, and judiciary," and that "these may come to the hands of the smallest rag of delegation," he pointed out, the legitimacy of any acts of the legislature may be questioned [25]

Printed as an appendix to the *Notes on the State of Virginia* was another proposed constitution, drafted by Jefferson in 1783, which he offered as a new frame of government without the defects of the 1776 constitution. The 1783 draft constitution also reflected Jefferson's experience with the actual operation of Virginia government, for three years as a legislator and two years as governor.

As in his 1776 draft constitution, Jefferson provided for liberal suffrage and equitable representation, proportionate to the number of electors in each district. He retained the district system for the election of senators, but they were to be elected not by the House of Delegates but by the electorate operating through senatorial electors. Elections were to be held every three years instead of annually, and the senatorial term lengthened to six years, with half the Senate subject to change at each general election. As in his 1776 draft, Jefferson rejected the notion that the Senate should be representative of propertied men, choosing rather to differentiate it from the House of Delegates by its smaller size, its longer term, and its indirect mode of election—which, presumably, would assure that its members would be wiser than those of the more numerous and popularly chosen lower house.[26]

The provisions concerning the office of governor especially reflected Jefferson's own frustrating experience as governor of Virginia during the critical years of the Revolutionary War. Although still chosen by joint ballot of both houses of the General Assembly, the governor in Jefferson's 1783 draft constitution was made more independent of that body by being given a single five-year term. He was invested with "the Executive powers," which were broadly defined as "those powers . . . necessary to carry into execution the laws" and not by nature legislative or judicial, with some limitations. The Council of State was retained, but its function was reduced to virtually the status of an advisory board, and the governor was given ultimate command of "the whole military of the state, whether regular or militia." The governor, in short, was a vastly more effective executive officer than Jefferson, acting under the inherent constraints imposed by the 1776 constitution, had been. Not annually elected by the General Assembly or rigidly separated from it, Jefferson's governor could exercise real executive powers rather than being enjoined merely to implement the laws of the Commonwealth. Moreover, the governor could exercise his powers individually, not as merely head of a plural executive composed of the governor together with the Council of State. Nor would his direction of the military forces within the state be compromised by the obstinacy of local militia captains or regular army commanders (such as General von Steuben), as Jefferson's had been.[27]

Despite language that stated emphatically the principle of the separation of powers, Jefferson's draft contained important exceptions to this principle: exceptions which constituted those "barriers" to the effective exercise of powers that the principle of checks and balances required. The governor, with the advice of the council, could call the legislature at a different time or place in case of danger "from an enemy or from infection." Although still not invested with the veto power, the governor, together with two councillors and three high judicial officers, constituted a Council of Revision—patterned after that of the New York Constitution of 1777—which could reject bills passed by the legislature. And a Court of Impeachments was created, before which "any member of the three branches of government may impeach any member of the other two for any cause sufficient to remove him from his office." [28]

Jefferson's 1783 draft constitution contained no bill of rights specifically designated as such, but it did contain important express limitations on the power of the legislature. Jefferson sought to guarantee freedom of religion, exemption from ex post facto laws and bills of attainder, and other important rights, as well as reforms such as the gradual abolition of slavery. Most importantly, in light of his criticisms of the 1776 constitution in the *Notes*, his proposed constitution expressly denied the General Assembly the power to infringe the constitution. It would be adopted by a specially authorized constitutional convention, and it could be amended by another specially elected convention when called for by two-thirds of each of two of the three branches of government.[29]

Jefferson's explanation for the defects in the 1776 Virginia Constitution—and, one may add, for the gradualness of his realization of some of them as defects—was not only that American Whigs were "novices" in the "science of government," but also that they were, in a literal sense, Whigs. In breaking away from political union with the British Empire, Americans also rejected the monarchical form of government. In so doing, they shared with seventeenth-century English Whigs the emphasis on legislative powers at the expense of the executive powers claimed and exercised by the Stuart monarchs as part of their royal prerogatives. As Jefferson explained to a correspondent in 1816, referring to the era of the American Revolution: "In truth, the abuses of monarchy [under George III] had so much filled all the space of political contemplation, that we imagined everything republican that was not monarchy. We had not yet penetrated to the mother principle, that 'governments are republican only in proportion as they embody the will of the people and execute it.' Hence, our first constitutions had no leading principles in them." [30]

For the rest of his life, Jefferson remained, in Merrill Peterson's words, "a declared enemy of the Virginia Constitution" of 1776. In 1784 he wrote Edmund Pendleton that he had "long wished to see a convention called" in order to correct the fundamental defects; but at about the same time, he indicated in a letter to James Madison his doubts that the needed reforms could be made so long as Patrick

Henry (whom he regarded as "the great obstacle" to a new constitution) was alive. Over thirty years later the 1776 constitution remained in effect, and Jefferson continued to deride the "gross departures" from "genuine republican canons" that were found in that "first essay of our Revolutionary patriots at forming a Constitution."[31]

"A Foundation Laid for a Government Truly Republican": Republican Reformation in Virginia

During the decade or so after 1776, Jefferson's efforts to commence the Revolution on "more favorable ground" were not confined to his drafts of a constitution for Virginia. In the realms of law reform and policy-making, as in constitution making, he saw an opportunity to help ensure the preservation of the Revolutionary achievement of republican government. As he observed in *Notes on Virginia*, although the "spirit of the times" was good, it "may alter, will alter. Our rulers will become corrupt, our people careless." He concluded that "the time for fixing every essential right on a legal basis is while our rulers are honest, and ourselves united."[32]

In 1776 Jefferson began his efforts to revise Virginia law comprehensively. Some of his proposals help to more fully reveal his understanding of the purpose of law and government generally. Many of the changes he proposed were fundamental, just as fundamental as those he sought to institutionalize through his draft constitutions. Individually they warrant some close attention; collectively they show the comprehensive plan of a man whose vision of republicanism had been shaped not only by Real Whig ideas but also by the complementary ideas of the eighteenth-century Enlightenment.

Within a few days after taking his place in the Virginia legislature in October 1776, Jefferson drafted two bills: one for the abolition of the law of entail and the other for a general revision of the laws of the Commonwealth. The bill for the abolition of entails was passed promptly; the bill for the revision of the laws was also passed, and Jefferson was appointed to the Committee of Revisors—composed finally of him, Edmund Pendleton, and George Wythe—that would labor for two and a half years before reporting a total of 126 bills for legislative consideration and possible enactment.[33]

Jefferson later recollected that in 1776 he was persuaded that "our whole code [of law] must be reviewed, adapted to our republican form of government; and, now that we had no negatives of Councils, Governors, and Kings to restrain us from doing right, it should be corrected, in all its parts, with a single eye to reason, and the good of those for whose government it was framed." When the committee met in Fredricksburg early in 1777 to settle the plan of operation, disagreement immediately arose on the first question, "whether we should propose to abolish the whole existing system of laws, and prepare a new and complete Institute, or preserve the general system, and only modify it to the present state of things." Ironically it was Pendleton, "contrary to his usual disposition in favor of ancient things," who favored the more radical approach. Jefferson, along with Wythe and Mason, urged caution, warning that the formulation of a completely new code would be "an arduous undertaking" as well as dangerous: "When reduced to a text, every word of that text, from the imperfection of human language, and its incompetence to express distinctly every shade of idea, would become a subject of question and chicanery, until settled by repeated adjudications; and this would involve us for ages in litigation, and render property uncertain, until, like the statutes of old, every word had been tried and settled by numerous decisions, and by new volumes of reports and commentaries." Here Jefferson spoke as a student of the common law, a careful reader of Coke's *Institutes*; to him, as Merrill Peterson has observed, law was a science based on experience as well as reason, and he was suspicious of system making heedless of the historic fabric of the law. Thus he moderated his impulse to correct the law "with a single eye to reason"; and the committee, in fact, followed a middle course, recasting the existing body of law while simultaneously introducing new principles.[34]

The moderate approach followed by Jefferson and the committee in many ways resembled the approach to law that had been followed by the Real Whig writers: on the one hand, it was a historical approach which admired an idealized ancient system and sought to restore its pure principles from the corruptions of later generations; and, on the other hand, it was a rational, or philosophical, approach which entailed a willingness to depart from precedents altogether and to institute change based upon the wisdom gained from historical experience. It was, in short, an approach to reform which was at once conservative and progressive, looking backward as well as forward.

Two of the changes that Jefferson and his colleagues proposed nicely illustrate the nature of this impulse. The reform of land law was a pragmatic change, one that would free the ownership of land from archaic legal entanglements and thus facilitate transfers. It also would give freer range to individual talent and virtue in all ranks of society. At the same time, however, it would restore the ancient Saxon law of allodial, rather than feudal, landholding and thus return Virginians to "that happy system of our ancestors, the wisest & most perfect ever yet devised by the wit of man, as it stood before the 8th century." [35]

The bill for proportioning crime and punishments benefited from Jefferson's reading of Cesare Beccaria and other Enlightenment writers who deplored the general severity of punishments—particularly the vast array of crimes that were subject to punishment by death—and urged more humane and rational punishments, proportionate to the particular crime. Convinced that Virginia criminal law was "too sanguinary," Jefferson proposed that capital punishment be abolished, except for treason and murder, and that other felonies be punished either by hard labor on roads, canals, and other public works or by the *lex talionis*. Abolition of the death penalty for the crimes of rape, polygamy, and sodomy, for example, was an advance; but the punishment that Jefferson substituted—"if a man, by castration; if a woman, by cutting thro' the cartilage of her nose a hole of one half inch diameter of the least"—seemed almost as inhumane in Jefferson's time as it does today. He explained to George Wythe that in resorting to the *lex talionis* he had "strictly observed the scale of punishments settled by the Committee" as well as followed his own policy of going back to the simple ancient precedents. His bill indeed was scattered with citations to the old English law, reminiscent of the clutter in Coke's *Institutes*. Jefferson clearly was embarrassed, and he observed to Wythe that "an eye for an eye, and a hand for a hand," although "a restitution of the Common law" to the simplicity that generally seemed advantageous, "will be revolting to the humanised feelings of modern times." He noted particularly that punishment by maiming, "atho' long authorised by our law," had been "long since repealed in conformity with public sentiment"; and he urged reconsideration of the whole matter. Several years later in his autobiography he stated, rather disingenuously, that he did not remember how the "revolting principle" of *lex talionis* came to obtain the committee's approbation. [36]

Only a fraction of the bills proposed by Jefferson and the Committee of Revisors actually became law; and some of the more important, such as the Statute for Religious Freedom, were not passed until some years later, while Jefferson was abroad. Nevertheless, Jefferson in later years took pride in the effort itself. Pointing to four of these bills— the ones abolishing entail, abolishing primogeniture and providing for equal partition of inheritances, supporting religious freedom, and promoting general education—he said that he considered them "as forming a system by which every fibre would be eradicated of ancient or future aristocracy; and a foundation laid for a government truly republican." He added that "all this would be effected, without the violation of a single natural right of any one individual citizen."[37] These bills, along with some of Jefferson's additional proposals that closely related to them, warrant closer attention. Viewed in the fuller context of Jefferson's republicanism as it had been formulated by the time of the Revolution and was elaborated in later decades, the proposals help reveal what Jefferson had in mind when he referred to "a government truly republican."

"A Just Degree of Union among Individuals": Republicanism and the Ideal of Self-Government

Jefferson's bill for establishing religious freedom provided that no one should be compelled "to frequent or support any religious worship, place, or ministry whatsover," nor should anyone in any way suffer "in his body or goods" on account of his religious opinions or belief; rather, "all men shall be free to profess, and by argument to maintain, their opinions in matters of religion, and that the same shall in no wise diminish, enlarge, or affect their civil capacities." It thus sought not only to abolish the establishment of the Anglican church in Virginia but to affirm, in the broadest possible terms, the separation of church and state. It did this by taking the high ground—as Jefferson later stated, the bill was drawn in "all the latitude of reason and right"— declaring that "the opinions of men are not the object of civil government, nor under its jurisdiction."[38] By thus drawing a line between the public realm, subject to regulation by civil government, and the private realm, free of all civil restraints, Jefferson's bill exemplifies a key aspect of his republican theory.

This aspect of Jefferson's republicanism derives from the word *republican*, as used in the literal sense, *res publica*. It posited government and society as two separate autonomous spheres: a realm of politics which encompassed what was truly of common interest, on the one hand, and on the other, a sphere in which individuals could fashion their lives as they saw fit, through voluntary social relationships. By thus positing a distinction between the public and private realms, republicanism set a limit to political power. Outside that limit, individuals literally governed themselves. Republicanism, or self-government, thus envisioned a society of individuals who acted, as Jefferson would later express it in a 1801 letter to Joseph Priestley, "under the unrestrained and unperverted operation of their own understandings," and it viewed expansively "the degree of freedom and self-government in which a society may venture to leave it's individual members." [39] As the frequent descriptions of America's mission in his writings indicate, republican government, or self-government, as Jefferson understood it, was a new idea—a concept of government and its relation to society which was unknown to the world of classical politics. It was, in fact, an idea which came to fruition during the Enlightenment; indeed, it is in his understanding of the concept of self-government that the contribution of Enlightenment ideas to Jefferson's political thought can be most clearly seen.

Essential to Jefferson's understanding was the concept that Yehoshua Arieli has described as the idea of the "natural society." This was the idea that there was a natural order of social life, separate and distinct from civil government. It assumed, on the one hand, such related ideas as the natural sociability of man, a natural identity of interests, and the spontaneous growth of social order and, on the other hand, the concepts of individual rights, majority rule, and the distrust of political power. Thomas Paine expressed the basic idea most plainly in his *Common Sense* when he described the distinction between society and government: "Society is produced by our wants and government by our wickedness; the former promotes our happiness *positively* by uniting our affections, the latter *negatively* by restraining our vices. . . . Society in every state is a blessing, but Government, even in its best state, is but a necessary evil; in its worst . . . an intolerable one." When these words were published early in 1776, Paine was seeking to rid Americans of the fear that dissolving their allegiance to the British crown would throw their society into anarchy. He did this by postulating the autonomy of social life and by reconciling freedom with social order, "not through the coercive powers of the state but by the very nature of man's wants and affections," Arieli has noted in describing Paine's argument. "Not freedom, but uncontrolled power and authority, endangered society. The functions of government were limited and represented only a small part of the activities of society, which were unlimited and capable of infinite development."[40]

The idea of natural society was more fully developed in Paine's *Rights of Man*, the book that generated a storm of controversy in Europe when it appeared in London in 1791 as a counterpoint to Edmund Burke's *Reflections on the Revolution in France*. The contest between Paine and Burke was revived in America a few months later when an American edition of Paine's work was printed. Jefferson found himself at the center of controversy when his laudatory statement recommending Paine's work as antidote to "the political heresies which have sprung up among us" and expressing confidence that "our citizens will rally a second time round the standard of Common Sense" appeared in the publisher's preface.[41] The controversy is less important here than its cause: Jefferson's statement shows that he fully identified with Paine's views and that he associated those views with American orthodoxy. An important part of Paine's argument concerned the idea of natural society. Elaborating upon the ideas he had expressed in *Common Sense*, Paine quite explicitly distinguished society and government, arguing that a "great part of that order which reigns among mankind is not the effect of Government" but has its origin in "the principles of society" and "the natural constitution of man." Indeed, he further argued, the operations of government often disturb or destroy the "natural propensity to society"; thus does government itself become "the cause of the mischiefs it ought to prevent."[42]

It was not from Paine, however, that Jefferson derived his concept of self-government; rather, Paine merely expressed in an especially cogent way a concept which many enlightened thinkers, on both sides of the Atlantic, had grasped by the time of the American and French revolutions. The idea of natural society was a synthesis of Enlightenment ideas: Lockean natural rights doctrine, Scottish moral sense philosophy, deistic natural religion, and the economic theories developed by British and French antimercantilists.[43] All these sources helped shape Jefferson's understanding of the concept of self-government.

The distinction between political and natural society was not based on Locke, although certain elements were implicit in his description of the state of nature. For Locke, the natural state preceded political society and was superseded by it; in Paine's and Jefferson's thought, both states existed simultaneously.[44] The chief impetus for the enlargement of the idea of a natural society came from a pupil of Locke, and the grandson of the founder of the Whigs, Anthony Ashley Cooper, the third earl of Shaftesbury. Through Shaftesbury's influence the idea that sociability was an essential attribute of human nature found its way into the thought of the leading exponents of the Scottish school of moral philosophy: Francis Hutcheson, David Hume, Adam Smith, Adam Ferguson, Dugald Stewart, Thomas Reid, and Henry Home, Lord Kames. Of these thinkers, it was Kames who most influenced Jefferson's thought; it was Kames's moral philosophy and jurisprudence, together with the deistic natural religion of Henry St. John, Viscount Bolingbroke, which most visibly shaped the moral philosophy on which Jefferson's understanding of natural society and, more broadly, his concept of self-government rested.

In his legal commonplace book Jefferson abstracted much of Kames's *Historical Law Tracts,* including an excerpt from Kames's tract on the history of property which stated in especially cogent terms the moral philosophy associated with the concept of natural society. "Man by his nature is fitted for society, and society, by it's conveniences, is fitted for man. The perfection of human society consists in the just degree of union among individuals, which to each reserves freedom and independency, as far as is consistent with peace and good order." [45] Jefferson's idea of the natural fitness of man for society (and society for the needs of man) was based on a simple moral philosophy premised on an innate "moral sense," existing in man's heart more than in his head and thus independent of education, religion, state, and even reasoning.[46] As Jefferson explained to his nephew Peter Carr, "Man was destined for society. His morality therefore was to be formed to this object. He was endowed with a sense of right & wrong merely relative to this. This sense is as much a part of his nature as the sense of hearing, seeing, feeling," though it is given to human beings in varying degrees and may be strengthened "by exercise." Attending lectures in moral philosophy is "lost time," he noted, since mere "Common sense" is all that is required to ascertain moral truths: "State a moral case to a ploughman and a professor," and the former will decide it at least as well as the latter because "he has not been led astray by artificial rules." The only "exercises" in moral philosophy that Jefferson prescribed for Carr, accordingly, were to "read good books," such as the works of Laurence Sterne, and to "lose no occasion of exercising your dispositions to be grateful, to be generous, to be charitable, to be humane, to be true, just, firm, orderly, courageous &c." [47]

In believing morality to be "instinct[ual] and innate," Jefferson expressly rejected what he called "the principles of Hobbes," which based morality on convention. He similarly rejected egoism, or interest, as a basis of morality; indeed, he argued that self-love is "no part of morality" but rather is "the sole antagonist of virtue, leading us constantly by our propensities to self-gratification in violation of our moral duties to others." Good acts give men pleasure because "nature hath implanted in our breasts a love of others, a sense of duty to them, a moral instinct," Jefferson maintained. Nevertheless, he also noted that where the moral sense is lacking or imperfect in some men, the defect may be supplied by "education," "sound calculation," "the rewards and penalties established by the laws," and "the prospects of a future state of retribution." Thus he acknowledged that the moralist, legislator, and preacher may play useful roles in inculcating morality in some individuals. [48]

The other important influence on Jefferson's understanding of the concept of a natural society, and of the idea of innate human sociability that it entailed, was Bolingbroke. As a young man, Jefferson filled his literary commonplace book with lengthy passages from the *Philosophical Essays*, and at nearly eighty he still regarded Bolingbroke as a great advocate of human liberty and a writer of the highest order. It was not Bolingbroke's "politics of nostalgia" which most impressed Jefferson; it was, rather, Bolingbroke's epistemology and "natural religion." [49] In Bolingbroke's writings Jefferson found the admonition basic to his method of inquiry, in all fields of knowledge: "No hypothesis ought to be maintained if a single phenomenon stands in direct opposition to it," he wrote, copying Bolingbroke. This was the method that Jefferson followed in his religious studies and recommended to Peter Carr, whom he advised to read the Bible as one would read Tacitus or Livy, using reason as his "only oracle." It was also the method that he followed in his study of human nature. Jefferson was primarily an empiricist: experience, not theory, was his guiding light. [50]

Although Bolingbroke's version of moral sense philosophy had no discernible effect on Jefferson's—Bolingbroke founded the moral sense on self-interest—it arrived at the same conclusion, the inherent sociability of man, upon which the concept of a natural society rested. As against both Hobbes and Locke, Bolingbroke argued that man is by nature social, not solitary, and that the origins of civil society lay in man's natural sociability. "Self-love begat sociability; and reason, a principle of human nature, as well as instinct, improved it," Bolingbroke argued. In addition, Bolingbroke expressed a notion which could only be described as that of enlightened self-interest—what Tocqueville later called "self-interest rightly understood"—when he argued that "a due use of our reason makes social and self-love coincide." Although Jefferson disagreed with these ideas, he undoubtedly approved of another observation made by Bolingbroke, "Sociability is the great instinct, and benevolence the great law of human nature."[51] From his ideas of the natural sociability and innate morality of man, Jefferson derived similar conclusions concerning the compatibility of interests in society.

The "just degree of union among individuals" that Jefferson envisioned for civil society was one that kept distinct the public and private spheres. Self-government, as he understood the concept, accordingly had two interrelated meanings, as Yehoshua Arieli has observed. The term "referred to the structure in which individuals managed their own affairs and met their common needs either directly in the economic, social, and religious spheres, or indirectly through their representatives in the political sphere." At the same time the term also "connoted the power and the right of the individual to guide his own destiny according to his own reason and his own innate morality, to pursue happiness without impinging on the same right of others." Within the latter meaning, Jefferson's concept of self-government also "comprised all the inalienable rights of man."[52]

"A Natural Aristocracy among Men": Republicanism and the Equality of Rights

Jefferson's bills for the abolition of entail and primogeniture were two of the other bills that he later identified as eradicating aristocracy and laying a foundation for "a government truly republican." English common law had permitted a landholder to limit the line of descent of his estate to his eldest son and the heirs of that son's body, or to the heirs begotten by a particular marriage, or in any other special way to restrict its transmission. The abolition of such entails, Jefferson noted, "would prevent the accumulation and perpetuation of wealth, in select families." Similarly, the abolition of primogeniture meant that estates of persons who died intestate would pass jointly to descendants or other relatives, rather than following the common law rule under which the eldest son would succeed to the entire estate. The rule had been established in feudal times as a device to help ensure the perpetuation of great estates; Jefferson undoubtedly regarded it as a relic of the past, inherently unfair and inappropriate to Virginia, where land was comparatively plentiful. Repeal of the rule "removed the feudal and unnatural distinctions which made one member of every family rich, and all the rest poor, substituting equal partition, the best of all Agrarian laws." These measures, he added, were accomplished "without the violation of a single natural right of any one individual citizen." In a letter to John Adams he also observed that the laws "laid the axe to the root of Pseudo-aristocracy"—an exaggeration of their real effect but a description that is nevertheless revealing.[53]

Jefferson's interpretation of these particular reforms is an apt illustration of another key aspect of his republican theory, the relationship between the ideal of natural society and the theory of natural rights. The two were closely interrelated; indeed, as Arieli has argued, the uniqueness of the Jeffersonian concept of self-government lay in the fact that the egalitarian and libertarian doctrine of natural rights was "grafted" onto the ideal of a natural society, to yield a new concept of a natural order of freedom. The primary aim of civil society, under this view, was to ensure the freedom and independence of the individual and his rights. Locke's concept of the state of nature was enlarged; the law of nature—that mankind, "being all equal and independent, no one ought to harm another in his life, health, liberty, or possessions"—was fully applied to civil society as well as natural society. "The individual, then, lost neither his freedom nor his independence as a member of society; they were, rather, established for each and all on a surer basis." Those rights in the exercise of which the individual was self-sufficient remained his natural rights; those which required collective protection became civil rights and were made the objects of government.[54]

Throughout Jefferson's writings there is evidence of his awareness of this link between natural and civil rights. In 1816, discussing the "rightful limits" of legislators' power, Jefferson maintained that "their true office is to declare and enforce only our natural rights and duties, and to take none of them from us": "No man has a natural right to commit aggression on the equal rights of another; and this is all from which the laws ought to restrain him; every man is under the natural duty of contributing to the necessities of society; and this is all the laws should enforce on him; and, no man having a natural right to be the judge between himself and another, it is his natural duty to submit to the umpirage of an impartial third." He added, "When the laws have declared and enforced all this, they have fulfilled their functions, and the idea is quite unfounded, that on entering into society we give up any natural right." He reiterated these ideas in a letter he wrote during his presidency to the French economist Jean Baptiste Say. "So invariably do the laws of nature create our duties and interests, that when they seem to be at variance, we ought to suspect some fallacy in our reasoning." Indeed, Jefferson believed that nature had so resolved the age-old tension between individual self-interest and the welfare of the community that, as he told Say, "the rights of the whole can be no more than the sum of the rights of individuals." [55] Many years later, in a report which he prepared as chairman of the Commissioners for the University of Virginia, Jefferson expressed a similar idea in describing, as one of the basic principles of government, "a sound spirit of legislation, which, banishing all arbitrary and unnecessary restraint on individual action, shall leave us free to do whatever does not violate the equal rights of others." [56]

Fundamental to Jefferson's political philosophy was the idea that no government could legitimately transgress natural rights. In order for law to be binding, it not only must proceed from the will of properly authorized legislators but also must be "reasonable, that is, not violative of first principles, natural rights, and the dictates of the sense of justice." In the final paragraph of his bill for establishing religious freedom, for example, Jefferson added a declaration that the rights therein asserted were "the natural rights of mankind," and that although the legislature which enacted the bill had no constitutional power to restrain subsequent legislatures, any future act repealing it or narrowing its operation would be "an infringement of natural right." [57]

Jefferson had given particularly eloquent expression to the doctrine of natural rights in his original draft of the Declaration of Independence, where he had maintained the "sacred & undeniable" truths that all men were created "equal & independant," that from that equal creation they derived "rights inherent & inalienable, among which are the preservation of life, & liberty & the pursuit of happiness," and that "to secure these ends, governments are instituted among men." These were ideas that were commonplace among the Whig Patriots of Revolutionary-era America. The influence of Locke is evident, but Locke was not the only—nor, arguably, was he the most important— source for the doctrine of natural rights. As Jefferson had indicated in his 1825 letter to Henry Lee, in writing the Declaration he had sought to "harmonize" the views of all American Whigs; and to the extent that he drew upon any particular sources, they were those "elementary books of public right" by "Aristotle, Cicero, Locke, Sidney, &c." Speculation as to who may be fairly included among those *cetera* has been a fertile field for scholars; in addition to the Real Whig writers on government and the moral sense philosophers, they have attributed Jefferson's ideas to the leading figures of natural law jurisprudence— Hugo Grotius, Samuel von Pufendorf, Emmerich de Vattel, and Jean Jacques Burlamaqui.[58]

Jefferson believed that the identification of natural rights, like the identification of right and wrong, was too important a matter to be left to reason alone. Accordingly, he based his natural rights doctrine, like his moral philosophy, on intuitive, innate sense. Referring to the right of expatriation, he held that "the evidence of this natural right, like that of our right to life, liberty, the use of our faculties, the pursuit of happiness, is not left to the feeble and sophistical investigations of reason, but is impressed on the sense of every man." Natural rights are not claimed "under the charters of kings or legislatures, but under the King of kings," he added.[59] Like moral truths, they were "self evident," and their origin lay in the constancy of human nature. As he would later say, nothing is unchangeable but the inherent rights of man.

What rights did Jefferson regard as natural rights? The Declaration of Independence stated three of them: the preservation of life, liberty, and the pursuit of happiness. Elsewhere in his writings Jefferson referred to others. His *Summary View of the Rights of British America*, for example, described expatriation as a natural right, and his bill for religious freedom described the freedoms it protected as natural rights.

Whether or not Jefferson regarded property as a natural right is a matter of much debate among scholars. Much of the discussion centers upon the meaning of "pursuit of happiness" and upon the possible implications of Jefferson's substitution of it for property—

the third element of Locke's trinity, "life, liberty, and estate"—in the Declaration of Independence. One problem, as Forrest McDonald has observed, is that it is by no means clear whence Jefferson derived the concept, or whether he thought of it independently. McDonald noted that Jefferson may have drawn the idea from its likely source, the Swiss jurist Jean Jacques Burlamaqui, directly or indirectly, through James Wilson's pamphlet *Considerations on the Authority of the British Parliament*, Blackstone's *Commentaries*, John Adams's *Thoughts on Government*, George Mason's Virginia Declaration of Rights, or even from Burlamaqui's source—Aristotle.[60] The similarity of the language used in Jefferson's original draft of the Declaration to Mason's Declaration of Rights has been noted by many scholars. The first paragraph of Mason's Declaration stated, "That all men are born equally free and independent and have certain inherent natural rights of which they can not by any compact, deprive or divest their posterity: among which are the enjoyment of life and liberty, with the means of acquiring and possessing property, and preserving and obtaining happiness and safety." Mason's formulation, indeed, suggests that "pursuit of happiness," as used by Jefferson, was a kind of generic term for a bundle of rights that included property rights.

Another problem lies in the apparently contradictory record left in Jefferson's writings. On the one hand, Jefferson did omit property from the natural rights named in the Declaration; and a decade later, when Lafayette submitted to him a draft declaration of rights for France, he even more deliberately urged the omission of property (although he retained "the power to dispose of . . . the fruits of [one's] industry").[61] In addition, in a letter written in 1813, Jefferson emphatically denied that inventors had "a natural and exclusive right" to their inventions. "If nature has made any one thing less susceptible than all others of exclusive property," he argued, "it is the action of the thinking power called an idea, which an individual may exclusively possess as long as he keeps it to himself; but the moment it is divulged, it forces itself into the possession of every one, and the receiver cannot dispossess himself of it." Society "may give an exclusive right to the profits arising from them, as an encouragement to men to pursue ideas," but such a right would be entirely utilitarian, "according to the will and convenience of the society, without claim or complaint from anybody." He similarly viewed rules of inheritance as purely conventional and utilitarian. "The laws of civil society indeed for the encouragement of industry, give the property of the parent to his family on his death, and in most civilized countries permit him even to give it, by testament, to whom he pleases. . . . But this does not lessen the right of that majority to repeal whenever a change of circumstances or of will calls for it. Habit alone confounds what is civil practice with natural right." [62]

On the other hand, Jefferson understood the origin of property rights, generally, as natural. In his abstract of Kames's tract on the history of property, after describing the "perfection of human society" as a "just degree of union among individuals," Jefferson further noted that in order to approach this ideal, society must avoid becoming too lax or too rigid; especially, society must adapt its expectations to man's "remarkable propensity for appropriation." A society where "every man shall be bound to dedicate the whole of his industry to the common interest . . . would be unnatural and uncomfortable, because destruction [*sic*] of liberty and independency; so would be the enjoyment of goods of fortune in common." Besides going against man's natural propensities, a communion of goods, Jefferson added, would leave no room for generosity, benevolence, and charity: "These noble principles, destitute of objects and exercise, would forever lie dormant." [63]

At various times in his life Jefferson described the right to property in ways consistent with the view suggested in these notes. In 1816 he expressed his belief that "a right to property is founded in our natural wants, in the means by which we are endowed to satisfy those wants, and the right to what we acquire by those means without violating the equal rights of other sensible beings." At about the same time, Jefferson argued that extra taxation of the wealthy, in order to produce a greater equality of possessions, would violate natural law. "To take from one, because it is thought that his own industry and that of his fathers has acquired too much, in order to spare to others, who, or whose fathers have not exercised equal industry and skill, is to violate arbitrarily the first principle of association, 'the *guarantee* to every one of a free exercise of his industry, and the fruits acquired by it.'" He expressed a similar principle in his Second Inaugural Address, where he said that it was the policy of his presidency that "equality of rights [be] maintained, and that state of property, equal or unequal, which results to every man from his own industry, or that of his fathers." [64] These statements strongly suggest that Jefferson viewed property—at least with respect to possessions acquired by labor—as a natural right.

A further complication in understanding Jefferson's view of property, and the possible distinction between it and the pursuit of happiness, is that Jefferson viewed the latter, by its very nature, as incapable of precise definition: "If [God] has made it a law in the nature of man to pursue his own happiness, he has left him free in the choice of place as well as mode; and we may safely call on the whole body of English jurists to produce the map on which Nature has traced, for each individual, the geographical line which she forbids him to cross in pursuit of happiness." Thus he suggested that each man was the best judge of his own way to pursue happiness; that this extended to place, as well as mode, explained why he regarded expatriation as a natural right—indeed, as a variation of the basic right of the pursuit of happiness.[65]

One may similarly regard property rights—since the acquisition, possession, and transfer of property is one of the modes by which men pursue their happiness—and, by doing so, help resolve the apparent inconsistency in Jefferson's statements regarding property. It is useful to view Jefferson's theory of rights not as one which sharply differentiated natural and conventional rights but rather as one in which there existed various categories of rights, some of which were intermediate, partaking of the qualities of both natural and conventional rights. Property rights may be viewed as such intermediate rights, particularly if one assumes, as some scholars have, that Jefferson was influenced by the natural law doctrines of Burlamaqui.[66] Jefferson was familiar with Burlamaqui's treatise *Principles of Natural and Politic Law*, first published in 1747.[67] Burlamaqui viewed property as an "adventitious" (as opposed to original, or God-given) right which nevertheless was also a natural right because it derived from what he called a secondary natural law. He maintained that property existed in a state of society which antedated civil government and that it was a right which civil government was instituted to protect. These Burlamaquian ideas help explain why Jefferson could consistently regard property as both a natural and a civil right, and why he omitted it from his enumeration of the inherent and inalienable rights of man in the Declaration of Independence.[68]

The significance of Jefferson's understanding of the rights to property and the pursuit of happiness lies not so much in his view of the content of these rights—or how they ought to be categorized—but rather in his recognition of the basic principles that they were rights possessed equally by all men and that government existed to protect these rights. Real Whig thought had an egalitarian emphasis—for example, in its idealization of the Anglo-Saxon model of allodial land titles and of equal representation of all who bore arms and paid taxes. Enlightenment thought clearly added a broader philosophical context to these Whig ideas. Here it was not only natural rights doctrine but also the new science of political economy—the ideas of the British and French antimercantilists, Adam Smith, J. B. Say, and A. L. C. Destutt de Tracy—that helped shape the vision of a "natural society" which lay at the heart of Jefferson's philosophy of limited government.[69]

Against this background Jefferson's bills for the repeal of entail and primogeniture can be better understood. In his 1813 letter to John Adams, Jefferson maintained that "there is a natural aristocracy among men," grounded in virtue or talents, from which he distinguished the "artificial aristocracy founded on wealth and birth, without either virtue or talents." Like Adams, Jefferson affirmed that he considered the natural aristocracy "the most precious gift of nature for the instruction, the trusts, and government of society," adding, "May we not even say that that form of government is the best which provides the most effectually for a pure selection of these natural aristoi into the offices of government?" But Jefferson questioned Adams's scheme of balanced government, arguing that "to put the Pseudo-aristoi into a separate chamber" would be to arm them for mischief, "increasing instead of remedying the evil." Jefferson then argued that "the best remedy is exactly that provided by all our constitutions, to leave to the citizens the free election and separation of the aristoi from the pseudo-aristoi, and of the wheat from the chaff." He went on to summarize his proposals for the revision of the laws of Virginia—abolition of entail and primogeniture, a system of public education, and the administration of government through local units, or wards—suggesting that "Science is progressive" and that new means, other than balanced orders in government, may be devised to "lay the axe to the root of Pseudo-aristocracy."[70]

As Ralph Lerner has observed, Jefferson's Virginia was "a republic with a sharp eye for making distinctions and discriminations. There are citizens and aliens, rich and poor, masters and servants, slave-owners and slaves, and what can be called anomalies." Yet, as Lerner further noted, notwithstanding these distinctions, "the entire body of laws may be seen as forming a mantle of procedural safeguards for all." It was, in short, a society of "unequals in a republic of equals."[71]

It was equality under the law—equality in the possession of basic rights, whether natural rights such as the pursuit of happiness or civil rights such as those concerning the ownership and transmission of property—that concerned Jefferson, not the equality or inequality of conditions. An aristocrat himself, he took for granted that men were unequal in talents and virtue—hence his genuine belief in the existence of the "natural aristocracy" discussed in his 1813 letter to Adams. Only great disparities in wealth concerned him: the kind of disparities that he believed, after his mission to France, differentiated Europe from America. "There is no such thing in this country as what would be called wealth in Europe," he observed after his return to the United States. "The richest [Americans] are but a little at ease, & obliged to pay the most rigorous attention to their affairs to keep them together," he added, drawing upon his own experience with debts and the fluctuations of income. "I am myself a nailmaker," he added, alluding to his manufacturing efforts at Monticello.[72]

Jefferson's abhorrence of the "enormous inequality" of landholding that he viewed in France was based upon his belief that in encouraging the establishment of a "pseudo-aristoi" of landed property interests, the laws of France violated the "first principle of association," the equitable distribution of property according to industry. "Wherever there is in any country, uncultivated lands and unemployed poor, it is clear that the laws of property have been so far extended as to violate natural right," he observed in a letter to Madison written in 1785. Considering that the enormous inequality in landholding in France had produced "so much misery to the bulk of mankind," Jefferson added that "legislators cannot invent too many devices for subdividing property, only taking care to let their subdivisions go hand in hand with the natural affections of the human mind." He suggested two such possible devices: the first, changing the law of descents, as he had done in Virginia; the second, a kind of progressive taxation.[73]

Jefferson's bills to abolish entail and primogeniture were modest proposals, designed to remedy what was, comparatively speaking, a modest problem of unequal landholding in Virginia. Together with the provision for the fifty-acre grants in his 1776 draft constitution, these bills were designed to ensure that all Virginians (or, at least, all adult white male Virginians) could find employment as independent yeoman farmers, in a republic of freeholders that resembled the Anglo-Saxon society Jefferson had idealized. Reiterating an extraordinary statement he had made in the *Summary View*, in the letter to Madison he declared that "the earth is given as a common stock for man to labor and live on. If, for the encouragement of industry we allow it to be appropriated, we must take care that other employment be furnished to those excluded from the appropriation." Otherwise, he added, "the fundamental right to labour the earth returns to the unemployed." It was "too soon" yet for such an expedient to be resorted to in Virginia—as he later confidently predicted, America had "room enough for all descendents to the 1000th and 1000th generation"—but it was "not too soon to provide by every available means that as few as possible shall be without a little portion of land. The small landholders are the most precious part of a state."[74]

An important exception to the egalitarian vision of Jefferson's agrarian republic, of course, was the institution of slavery. From his concept of property rights followed the conclusion that the possession of human beings was an illegitimate form of property. Property, he wrote, "is founded in our natural wants" and included "the right to what we acquire . . . without violating the equal rights of other sensible beings." As John C. Miller has observed, "No dialectical ingenuity can reconcile chattel slavery with such a definition of property." Perhaps that is an added reason why Jefferson substituted "pursuit of happiness" for "property" in the Declaration: he "deliberately, although only by implication, excluded property in slaves from the rights of man." Nevertheless, he could not transcend the circumstances in which he was born; as Miller noted, Jefferson was "never able to wholly cast aside the prejudices and the fears which he had absorbed from his surroundings toward people of color." Thus, he did not free himself from dependence upon slave labor and eventually gave up even his modest efforts to rid Virginia of "this great political and moral evil."[75]

Foundations of Republican Government: The Revolution and Beyond

In sum, Jefferson's efforts to reform law and government in the 1770s and 1780s were shaped by his evolving understanding of republicanism. Viewing the Revolution as an unprecedented opportunity to establish the foundations for a government "truly republican," Jefferson saw the first priority to be the framing of new plans for government, based firmly on the consent of the people, within each of the states. In his own state, or "country" as he usually referred to Virginia, he found the constitution that had been framed in 1776 to be deficient in several respects. First and foremost, it failed as a constitution—as fundamental law that would bind, and therefore limit, legislative power—because it had not been adopted by a special convention. Second, the constitution imperfectly implemented the very principle that it declared to be its chief device for controlling power, the doctrine of the separation of powers. Too much power was concentrated in the legislature—a state of things which Jefferson fully realized after his unhappy experience as governor—and the legislature itself was imperfectly constituted, chiefly in its unequal representation of the people, a third basic defect. Jefferson sought to correct these defects, and to that end he himself drafted constitutions that he proposed to offer as alternatives.

Republicanism, however, meant more than simply abolishing monarchy and framing a constitution which would effectively check the abuse of power through the institutions that it established. Basic to Jefferson's Whig thought was his fear of political power, his conviction that—as he would later express it—"the natural progress of things is for liberty to yeild and government to gain ground." A written constitution was an important safeguard, one that Whigs on the other side of the Atlantic lacked, but it alone was insufficient, he believed. The American Revolution "commenced on more favorable ground" because it permitted not only the establishment but also the continuing functioning of a government truly based upon popular sovereignty: a government accountable to the people in its day-to-day operations and a people watchful of the government and jealous of their rights. To further this latter end, Jefferson sought to supplement the 1776 constitution with a series of legislative reforms (some of them duplicating provisions in his draft constitutions) that would foster the conditions and inculcate the principles which were consistent with republicanism.

Of the various reforms proposed by Jefferson and his fellow revisors, the more important of them, he later said, formed "a system" by which the foundations for republican government would be laid through eradicating "every fibre" of "ancient or future aristocracy." His reference to aristocracy—by which he meant the "Pseudo-aristocracy" that he later condemned, in contrast to the "natural aristocracy" of talents and virtue that he valued throughout his life—suggests a broader context of republicanism, as Jefferson understood it, against which his reform efforts must be understood.

Jefferson's social theory taught him that the people were not to be feared. Although pessimistic about human nature where the exercise of political power was involved, he considered man "made for society" and "endowed with a sense of right and wrong relative to this." The concept of natural society envisioned a republic of self-governing men, in which a whole realm of human concerns was beyond the pale of government control. His Statute for Religious Freedom was designed to protect what Jefferson at this time regarded as the most obvious of these concerns; it did so by establishing religious freedom, as he wrote in *Notes on Virginia*, "on the broadest bottom."

Jefferson's republicanism also encompassed his convictions, shared alike with Real Whig writers and Enlightenment theorists, that man was born with certain inalienable natural rights; that government, deriving its just powers from the consent of the governed, existed to protect those rights; and that all men equally possessed the same rights and merited similar protections. Although women and blacks (freedmen as well as slaves) were disfranchised in Jefferson's republic, he embraced the doctrine of equality before the law more fully than many of Virginia's elite. Men of talent and virtue, who comprised the "natural aristocracy" that Jefferson so valued as leaders of his republic, could be found in every social class, the poor and obscure as well as the wealthy and well-known. To ensure preservation of the republic of independent farmers—to recapture the mythical Anglo-Saxon republic that he so idealized, at least during the Revolutionary period—Jefferson proposed the abolition of those features of positive law, such as entail and primogeniture, that perpetuated artificial distinctions and the "Pseudo-aristocracy" of wealth and birth.

What remain to be considered are two other significant proposals that Jefferson as legislative draftsman put forth in the Revolutionary period. These are his Virginia bill on education and his efforts, in both the Virginia legislature and in Congress, to establish governments in the western territories.

His bill for the more general diffusion of knowledge was the last of the four bills that Jefferson in his autobiography considered the foundation for "a government truly republican." It was in a sense the capstone of his efforts, for in the long run it would serve as the most effective of the means by which, first, all citizens would remain vigilant of their liberties while, second, those few whose talents and virtue made them peculiarly well suited for political leadership would find their way into public service. The accomplishment of both these objectives, he believed, was too important to be left to chance; it therefore was an appropriate responsibility for government.

As Jefferson later described it, the bill sought to "diffuse knowledge more generally through the mass of the people" by the establishment of primary schools, in districts called "hundreds," where all children would receive at least three years of instruction in reading, writing, and arithmetic at public expense. The reading in this first stage would be chiefly historical: the "most useful facts from Grecian, Roman, European, and American history" would be instilled into young minds, enabling them "to know ambition under every disguise it may assume; and knowing it, to defeat its views." Thus would the people be made "safe depositories" of political power, "qualified to understand their rights, to maintain them, and to exercise with intelligence their parts in self-government."[76]

The bill also provided that from each school "the boy of best genius" whose parents were too poor to give him further education would be chosen to attend, at public expense, intermediate grammar schools where Greek, Latin, geography, and higher mathematics would be taught. There would be twenty such schools, erected in different parts of the state, and in each one, every year or two, the "best genius" of the boys would be selected and continued for a total of six years. By this means, Jefferson noted in his description of the plan in *Notes on Virginia*, "twenty of the best geniuses will be raked from the rubbish annually, and be instructed, at the public expense, as far as the grammar schools go." At the end of six years' instruction, half the students would be dismissed, and the others, "chosen for the superiority of their parts and disposition," would be continued for three additional years of study in "all the useful sciences" at the College of William and Mary.

Jefferson's stress on public education was tied directly to his republicanism and the assumptions that underlay his concept of self-government. As he later observed, a civilized nation could not be both ignorant and free.

The other legislative proposal that warrants mention here, as part of his overall efforts to establish the foundations of republicanism in Revolutionary-era America, is his plan for establishing government in the West. As a legislative draftsman in Virginia, Jefferson had sought to provide for the orderly settlement of western territory and the establishment of representative government in it; his efforts included the largely unsuccessful attempt, through his bill to establish a land office, to keep Virginia's unappropriated lands from becoming monopolized by speculators. Of greater significance here, however, are his efforts at the national level.

In 1784 Jefferson prepared for Congress his "Report of a Plan of Government for the Western Territory" in which he outlined a scheme for organizing the region north of the Ohio, which Virginia had ceded to the United States, into new republics and admitting them into the Union "on an equal footing with the . . . original states." Two features of the plan are especially significant. First, the plan divided the whole territory into distinct states and within each state allowed for successive stages of government—a temporary government during the earliest period of settlement, followed by a permanent government after the population reached 20,000 free inhabitants—with self-government, by "free males of full age," at each stage. When the number of free inhabitants was as great as that of the least populated of the thirteen original states, the state could be admitted on equal footing into Congress. Second, both the temporary and permanent governments within the new states were to be "in republican forms"; they were specifically prohibited from admitting into citizenship any person holding a hereditary title. Other noteworthy features of the plan were that the states were to remain "for ever" a part of the United States and that after 1800 slavery and involuntary servitude in any of the states were prohibited.[77] Thus the republic of equals that Jefferson had envisioned for Virginia also formed the basis of his vision for an expanding union of self-governing commonwealths.

Jefferson's proposals for public education in Virginia and for establishing governments in the West relate to one other important aspect of his republicanism: republicanism as a democratic—that is, as a majoritarian, as well as an egalitarian—theory. Jefferson's commitment to majority rule was clear, and it formed an essential premise in his constitutional thought, particularly as it developed into a more mature theory of constitutionalism in the decades after his return from France. That aspect of his republican thought and its relationship to his evolving constitutionalism must be understood in the context of the events of the 1790s.

4

The Interesting Experiment

of Self-Government

The Evolution of Republican

Constitutionalism

Writing to Benjamin Franklin in the summer of 1777, Jefferson observed that the people of Virginia "seem to have deposited the monarchical and taken up the republican government with as much ease as would have attended their throwing off an old and putting on a new suit of clothes. Not a single throe," he asserted, "has attended this important transformation."[1] But Jefferson exaggerated the ease with which his countrymen would exchange monarchy for republicanism. The decade of the 1780s was, as he and others later described it, "the age of experiments in government"[2] and an age of constitution making in America; yet Jefferson's experience with the actual operation of government both in Virginia and at the Continental Congress, followed by his experience as a diplomat in Europe, made clear to him that experimentation must continue. He and his contemporaries were, as he recognized, "novices" in the "science of government." They struggled with the forms of government appropriate for a society in which sovereignty rested with the people, on whose consent the government was founded. Forms, moreover, were not the sole concern of the founders' "science of government"; principles also were important.

If Jefferson had not been fully aware of the importance of principles, as well as forms, in the constitution of government when he returned to the United States late in 1789, he would soon become so aware. During the next decade of his public career, his continued experience with the operation of government—first as secretary of state and then as vice president—colored as it was by his involvement in the emerging political party system, further shaped his constitutionalism. The party struggles of the 1790s forced Jefferson, as the acknowledged head of the Republican opposition to Federalist programs, to articulate the grounds of opposition in constitutional terms. That was so because, as he saw it, the difference between the parties was not simply a disagreement over policy, over men and measures, but rather a genuine struggle between adherents to fundamentally different principles of government. The political party struggle of the 1790s, as he understood it, thus was an important catalyst which hastened the process that had begun in Jefferson's mind in the 1760s: the synthesis of Real Whig and Enlightenment ideas into a constitutionalism which was self-consciously "republican."

This chapter traces this evolution of Jefferson's constitutional theory. The first section discusses his initial reaction to the new federal Constitution: "neither Federalist nor Antifederalist," he viewed the Constitution ambivalently, fearing certain features of the document though in general supporting the stronger national government that it created. His experience as minister to France from 1785 to 1789 imbued him with an abhorrence of monarchy and an appreciation of republicanism as a democratic—that is, as an egalitarian and a majoritarian—political system. His understanding of the benefits of republicanism while in France, reinforced by his experience as secretary of state in the early 1790s, is discussed in the second section of the chapter. The third section explores Jefferson's reaction to key political events in the crucial decade of the 1790s. His central role in the Republican opposition provided the impetus for his articulation of a republican constitutionalism which wedded his republican political theories to his view of the federal Constitution. At the same time, he also developed a theory of political parties which made his experience of the 1790s meaningful and shaped his expectations for his own presidency and the decades following.

"Neither Federalist nor Antifederalist": Considering the Federal Constitution

Having been absent from America since 1784, serving as American minister to France, Jefferson played no part in the events that led to the Constitutional Convention in Philadelphia in 1787.[3] Indeed, he was largely out of touch with the sense of urgency felt by many of his countrymen with respect to the need to reform, if not replace, the Articles of Confederation. While friends such as Madison viewed with alarm Shays's Rebellion, seeing the turbulent scenes in Massachusetts as portending a crisis in civil government, Jefferson—from his vantage point in France, on the eve of its far more turbulent revolution—was untroubled. He discounted fears of anarchy, seeing as a sign of strength, rather than weakness, the occurrence of just one rebellion during eleven years of government under the Confederation.[4]

Notwithstanding his relative calm, Jefferson clearly perceived defects in the Articles of Confederation that called for amendment—and amendment in the direction of strengthening national powers. As early as 1784 he expressed the conviction that "nothing can preserve our Confederacy unless the band of Union, their common council be strengthened." Jefferson repeatedly stated his awareness of defects in the Articles. He saw three principal features that were lacking: the requisite degree of unity needed for conducting foreign affairs and regulating interstate and foreign commerce; separation of powers; and a mode of coercing states that failed to observe their obligations. As he put it, "My idea is that we should be made one nation in every case concerning foreign affairs, and separate ones in whatever is merely domestic. That the Federal government should be organized into Legislative, executive and judiciary as are the state governments, and some peaceable means of enforcement devised for the federal head over the states."[5]

The most serious defect, in Jefferson's opinion, was that relating to commerce. The Articles of Confederation failed to grant Congress the power to regulate the commerce of the several states. This "want of power in the federal head" he identified as "the flaw in our constitution which might endanger its destruction." Having "no original and inherent" power over commerce, Congress could exercise such power only indirectly, by virtue of the ninth article, which authorized it to enter into treaties of commerce with foreign nations. "The moment these treaties are concluded," he argued, "the jurisdiction of Congress over the commerce of the states springs into existence, and that of the particular states is superseded so far as the articles of the treaty may have taken up the subject." As an American minister his own object in the formation of treaties with European countries was "to take the commerce of the states out of the hands of the states, and to place it under the superintendence of Congress, so far as the imperfect provisions of our constitution will admit," until such time as "the states shall by new compact make them more perfect." Jefferson's hope was that the United States could say "to every nation on earth, *by treaty,* your people shall trade freely with us, and ours with you, paying no more than the most favoured nation." By this policy Congress could "put an end to the right of individual states acting by fits and starts to interrupt our commerce or embroil us with any nation."[6]

Although Congress could try to regulate uniformly the foreign commerce of the several states through its treaty power, Jefferson recognized that such a system was "too imperfect." Until a treaty was made with any particular nation, the commerce of any one of the states with that nation could be regulated by the state itself. Moreover, even when a treaty had been made, the regulation of commerce was taken out of the hands of the several states only so far as it was covered or provided for by that convention or treaty. But treaties "are very imperfect machines for regulating commerce in the detail"; by their nature they "are made in such general terms, that the greater part of the regulations would still result to the legislatures." There were two principal objects in the regulation of commerce, he argued: first, to lay such duties, restrictions, or prohibitions on the goods of a particular nation as to oblige that nation to concur in just and equal arrangements of commerce; and second, to lay such uniform duties on articles of commerce throughout all the states as may raise the funds necessary for public expenses. These objects could not be accomplished by the states acting separately; therefore, it followed that the commerce of the states "cannot be regulated to the best advantage but by a single body, and no body so proper as Congress."[7]

With regard to the supposed lack of coercive power against delinquent states—in enforcing, for example, contributions of money—Jefferson took the position that it was "not necessary" that the Articles give Congress that power expressly; Congress could exercise the enforcement power "by the law of nature." This was so because the Confederation was a compact among the several states; and as in any other contract, "the right of compulsion naturally results to the party injured by the breach." Thus, "when any one state in the American Union refuses obedience to the Confederation by which they have bound themselves, the rest"—acting through Congress—"have a natural right to compel them to obedience."[8] Consequently, under Jefferson's view at the time, amendment of the Articles of Confederation in order to authorize such coercion against the states was not really necessary.

Jefferson, however, did acknowledge the need for "a federal government which could walk upon it's own legs, without leaning for support on the state legislatures." Years later, when writing his autobiography, he regarded the "fundamental defect" of the Confederation to be the fact that "Congress was not authorized to act immediately on the people, & by its own officers. Their power was only requisitory, and these requisitions were addressed to the several legislatures, to be by them carried into execution, without other coercion than the moral principle of duty." This in effect gave each state legislature a negative on every measure of Congress, he argued, "a negative so frequently exercised in practice as to benumb the action of the federal government, and to render it inefficient," particularly in "pecuniary and foreign concerns." Moreover, notwithstanding his characterization of the Articles as a compact among the states, Jefferson regarded the Confederation as a true constitution. He referred to it as "the American Constitution" and considered it to be "a part of the law of the land, and superior in authority to the ordinary laws, because it cannot be altered by the legislature of any one state."[9]

Finally, with regard to the lack of separation of powers, he argued that in order "to enable the Federal head to exercise the powers given it, to best advantage," it should be organized as the state governments were, more or less, "into Legislative, Executive and Judiciary" departments, each exercising the appropriate powers. The legislative and judiciary were "already separated"; the executive, he argued, "should also be." The want of such a separation had "done more harm than all the [other] federal defects put together." Perhaps because he had not yet formulated a coherent constitutional theory of separation of powers, however, the reason for his concern was more practical than theoretical. "Nothing is so embarrassing nor so mischievous in a great assembly as the details of execution," he observed, drawing upon his own experience as a delegate to the Continental Congress, where "the smallest trifle" often occupied as much attention as the most important legislation. The result of Congress's exercise of executive powers—the reason why he referred to it as "the greatest cause of evil to us"— was that it "in fact place[s] us as if we had no federal head, by diverting the attention of that head from great to small objects." To remedy this problem he proposed a "Committee of the states" to function as an executive committee, but in late 1786 he expressed doubt whether Congress could ever have "self-denial enough" to go through with this distribution of executive powers to a separate body.[10]

Jefferson therefore sympathized with the effort to strengthen federal power through amendments to the Articles of Confederation; but despite his explicit recognition of one critical "flaw" and at least two other more easily remediable "defects" in the Articles, he regarded the Confederation as "a wonderfully perfect instrument." And although the Articles failed to establish fully the general plan that Jefferson thought desirable for the government of the United States— "to make the states one as to everything connected with foreign nations, and several as to everything purely domestic"—he observed in the summer of 1787 that "with all the imperfections of our present government, it is without comparison the best existing or that ever did exist."[11]

He nevertheless held a favorable attitude toward the Constitutional Convention. He was sincere in expressing his high opinion of the statesmen who met in Philadelphia when he referred to the convention as "really an assembly of demigods." While the convention was sitting, he wrote to George Washington, its presiding officer, and urged that the great objects should be "to make our states one as to all foreign concerns, preserve them several as to all merely domestic, to give to the federal head some peaceable mode of enforcing their just authority, [and] to organize that head into Legislative, Executive, and Judiciary departments."[12] These recommendations were in full accord with the defects Jefferson had perceived in the Confederation and the reforms necessary to correct them. He had no idea, however, of the extent to which the convention would go in reforming the national government. Because the convention held its deliberations behind closed doors and swore its members to secrecy, months passed before Jefferson learned of the outcome.

Jefferson's initial reaction when a copy of the Constitution came to him in France was one of surprise and uncertainty. In November 1787 he wrote to John Adams, "How do you like our new constitution? I confess there are things in it which stagger all my dispositions to subscribe to what such an assembly has proposed." He particularly objected to the office of president, which he characterized as "a bad edition of a Polish King" because the incumbent could be elected "from 4 years to 4 years, for life," making the office "worthy of intrigue, of bribery, of force, and even of foreign interference." With respect to the last problem, he feared that "it will be of great consequence to France and England, to have America governed by a Galloman or Angloman," and that once in office such a president, "possessing the military force of the Union, without the aid or check of a council," would not be "easily dethroned." He indicated his opinion that "all the good of this new constitution might have been couched in three or four new articles, to be added to the good, old and venerable fabric" of the Articles of Confederation, "which should have been preserved even as a religious relique." On the same date he wrote to Adams's son-in-law: "There are very good articles in it: and very bad. I do not know which predominate." Jefferson's basic doubt, as he expressed it to another correspondent several months later, was whether the convention had "run from one extreme to another." "Our government wanted bracing," he observed, while warning that "we must take care . . . not to brace too high."[13]

Jefferson's ambivalence toward the Constitution was clear. The simplest characterization of his stance was one he himself made in a letter written in December 1787: "As to the new Constitution I find myself nearly a Neutral. There is a great mass of good in it, in a very desirable form: but there is also to me a bitter pill, or two."[14] Later, after the struggle over ratification had crystallized into a political party struggle, Jefferson explicitly denied adherence to either side. "I am not a Federalist," he protested, emphasizing his desire never to submit "the whole system of my opinions to the creed of any party of men"; but he added, "I am much further from [the party] of the Antifederalists," explaining that he "approved, from the first moment, of the great mass of what is in the new constitution" despite some points of disapprobation. He concluded, "I am neither federalist nor antifederalist; . . . I am of neither party, nor yet a trimmer between parties."[15]

Perhaps the most thorough exposition of Jefferson's views on the new Constitution is found in a letter to James Madison. Jefferson first stated what he liked about the document:

> I like much the general idea of framing a government which should go on of itself peaceably, without needing continual recurrence to the state legislatures. I like the organization of the government into Legislative, Judiciary and Executive. I like the power given the Legislature to levy taxes; and for that reason solely approve of the greater house being chosen by the people directly. For tho' I think a house chosen by them will be very illy qualified to legislate for the Union, for foreign nations &c. yet this evil does not weigh against the good of preserving inviolate the fundamental principle that the people are not to be taxed but by representatives chosen immediately by themselves. I am captivated by the compromise of the opposite claims of the great and little states, of the latter to equal, and the former to proportional influence. I am much pleased too with the substitution of the method of voting by persons, instead of that of voting by states: and I like the negative given to the Executive with a third of either house, though I should have liked it better had the Judiciary been associated for that purpose, or invested with a similar and separate power.

He thus expressed his basic satisfaction with the strengthened national government established by the Constitution, the separation of powers, the bicameral organization of the Congress, and—at least with respect to the president's veto power—the system of checks and balances; these elements comported with his own general idea of what a good constitution should provide (as evidenced by his 1783 draft constitution for Virginia) as well as his understanding of what was needed to remedy the defects in the Articles of Confederation.[16]

He then specified what he did not like about the Constitution. There were two chief defects that Jefferson noted. The first was the absence of a bill of rights, something which "the people are entitled to against every government on earth, general or particular, & what no just government should refuse, or rest on inference." The second was the absence of rotation in office, particularly in the case of the president. As in his letter to Adams, he predicted to Madison that the president, if perpetually eligible for reelection, would be "an officer for life," and that the European nations therefore would attempt to influence elections in America.[17]

He acknowledged to Madison that he was at a loss as to how to correct these two defects, whether to hope for amendment or to consider another convention, and he expressed his willingness to acquiesce in whatever public opinion demanded. "After all, it is my principle that the will of the Majority should always prevail. If they approved the proposed Convention in all it's parts, I shall concur in it chearfully, in hopes that they will amend it whenever they shall find it work wrong."[18]

In other correspondence at this time, Jefferson identified the same two basic defects in the proposed constitution.[19] After further reflection, by early February 1788 he decided not to press the objection to the perpetual reeligibility of the president, perceiving no objections in America (given the high regard for General Washington, whom everyone expected would be elected the first president) and "therefore no prospect of a change of that article." He was still astonished by the omission of a bill of rights, however; he despaired to find "such a change wrought in the opinions of our countrymen since I left them" that they would "be contented to live under a system which leaves to their governors the power of taking from them" fundamental rights. "This is a degeneracy in the principles of liberty to which I had given four centuries instead of four years." Determined to press this point, he hoped that nine states would ratify the Constitution so that it would go into force, but that four states would reject it until a bill of rights was added. "Were I in America," he advised one correspondent, "I would advocate it warmly till nine should have adopted & then as warmly take the other side to convince the remaining four that they ought not to come into it till the declaration of rights is annexed to it." Such a course of action "would be the happiest turn the thing could take," since it would at once "secure all the good" of the new Constitution and yet "procure so respectable an opposition as would induce the accepting states to offer a bill of rights."[20]

To his own mind, Jefferson leaned more to the Federalist than to the Antifederalist side in the struggle over ratification, since he did approve of "the great mass" of what was in the Constitution. Nevertheless, the fact that he found in the lack of a bill of rights and in the perpetual reeligibility of the president two "bitter pills" which made it difficult for him to swallow the whole in practice brought the weight of his influence down on the Antifederalist side of the scale. By the time the Virginia ratifying convention met in June 1788, eight states had ratified and a ninth ratification was expected from New Hampshire. Patrick Henry, leading the opposition to ratification, appealed to the convention to follow Jefferson's advice and reject the Constitution until it was amended by the addition of a bill of rights. Jefferson's advice caused some embarrassment to Madison, who led the proponents of ratification in the Virginia convention and was thus forced to explain Jefferson's views.[21]

By summer Jefferson in fact had changed his advice. Near the end of May he wrote: "I learn with great pleasure the progress of the new Constitution. Indeed I have presumed it would gain on the public mind, as I confess it has on my own." He rejected his earlier proposal that four states should withhold ratification until a bill of rights was added and now favored the course followed by Massachusetts, the sixth state to ratify, of ratifying the Constitution but at the same time proposing amendments to be added afterwards. To a young American touring Europe, he wrote that rejection of the Constitution "would drive the states to despair and bring on events which cannot be foreseen" and that its adoption "is become absolutely necessary." "It will be easier to get the assent of 9 states to correct what is wrong in the way pointed out by the constitution itself, than to get 13 to concur in a new convention and another plan of confederation." In July he wrote Madison: "I sincerely rejoice at the acceptance of our new constitution by nine states. It is a good canvas, on which some strokes only want retouching."[22]

Jefferson thus overcame his reservations and accepted the Constitution. Despite his qualms about crucial omissions in the document, he was unreservedly enthusiastic about the process by which the new national government was created. He gloried in the fact that his country had changed its constitution peaceably, by assembling conventions instead of armies: "We can surely boast of having set the world a beautiful example of a government reformed by reason alone, without bloodshed," he wrote in 1788. A few months later he informed Richard Price, "Our new constitution . . . has succeeded beyond what

I apprehended it would have done," furnishing "new and consolatory proof that wherever the people are well informed they can be trusted with their own government; that whenever things get so far wrong as to attract their notice, they may be relied on to set them to rights." [23]

The adoption of the Constitution thus confirmed the prediction he had made to Price some four years earlier, that the American people were becoming "universally sensible" of the essential defect in the Articles of Confederation—"the want of power in the federal head"— and that the defect would be "immediately redressed, and redressed radically." Although the process had taken somewhat longer than he had so optimistically predicted in the winter of 1785, the denouement further confirmed Jefferson's overall confidence in the people. "Our motto is truly 'nil desperandum,'" he then had observed: "The happiness of governments like ours, wherein the people are truly the mainspring, is that they are never to be despaired of. When an evil becomes so glaring as to strike them generally, they arouse themselves, and it is redressed." This character of the American governments, he had added, "has kept my mind in perfect quiet as to the ultimate fate of our union." [24]

Jefferson's enthusiasm over the country's acceptance of the Constitution helped him be more sanguine about the document itself. "The constitution too which was the result of our deliberations, is unquestionably the wisest ever yet presented to men," he wrote in the spring of 1789. He wrote approvingly of "our new government" to the leading Antifederalist of his own state, George Mason, and sought to reassure him both as to the Constitution itself and as to the prospect for "some amendments, further than those which have been proposed," which would fix it "more surely on a republican basis." "To secure the ground we gain, and gain what more we can, is I think the wisest course," he added. "I think much has been gained by the late constitution; for the former one was terminating in anarchy, as necessarily consequent to inefficiency. . . . In general I think it necessary to give as well as take in a government like ours." [25] When he wrote these hopeful lines, Jefferson had returned to America and was in New York, embarking upon his new duties as the first secretary of state of the new government of the United States.

"The Will of the Nation":
Republicanism and Majority Rule

Jefferson frequently—and particularly during his years in France—alluded to the comparative superiority of republican America to the monarchical states of Europe. The "vaunted scene of Europe," the refinement of European manners and the fine arts that so enchanted Jefferson, did not blind him to the fact that "the general fate of humanity" there was "most deplorable." While in France as diplomatic minister, he had an opportunity to observe that despite the "finest soil upon earth, the finest climate under heaven," and a highly benevolent people, France still labored under misery, because the "kings, nobles, and priests" loaded the people's minds with "ignorance and prejudice." "The truth of Voltaire's observation offers itself perpetually, that every man here must be either the hammer or the anvil," he noted. "Much, very much inferior this to the tranquil permanent felicity with which domestic society in America blesses most of it's inhabitants." The "high ground" upon which the American people stood was made possible by the unique circumstances of the nation's founding and by geography. Our people, Jefferson believed, "could not have been so fairly put into the hands of their own common sense had they not been separated from their parent stock and kept from contamination . . . by the intervention of so wide an ocean." [26]

He wrote to James Monroe that a trip to France would "make you adore your own country, it's soil, it's climate, it's equality, liberty, laws, people and manners." "My god! How little do my countrymen know what precious blessings they are in possession of, and which no other people on earth enjoy. I confess I had no idea of it myself," he exclaimed. "Come then and see the proofs of this," he invited Monroe, "and on your return add your testimony to that of every thinking American, in order to satisfy our countrymen how much it is their interest to preserve uninfected by contagion those peculiarities in their government and manners to which they are indebted for these blessings." [27]

Chief among the "peculiarities" in American government that Jefferson credited for America's "blessings" was republicanism. In this sense republicanism meant a system antithetical to the monarchical system that Jefferson viewed firsthand in Europe. The author of the Declaration of Independence, who in that document condemned George III as a tyrant, claimed that although he was "much an enemy" to monarchy before he came to Europe, he was "ten thousand times more so" since he had seen it for himself. "There is scarcely an evil known in these countries which may not be traced to their king as it's source, nor a good is not derived from the small fibres of republicanism existing among them," he wrote to George Washington, explaining his "dislike" of what he regarded as the monarchical feature of the new federal Constitution, the perpetual reeligibility of the president. Several years later, he wrote to a fellow Whig Patriot of the Revolution generation, Samuel Adams: "Your principles have been tested in the crucible of time, and have come out pure. You have proved that it was monarchy, and not merely British monarchy, you opposed. A government by representatives, elected by the people at *short* periods, was our object; and our maxim at that day was, 'where annual election ends, tyranny begins.' " [28]

When he distinguished republican government from monarchy, he emphasized not simply the element of representation of the people but rather the concept of popular sovereignty in its fullest implications: a government founded on consent both in theory and in practice. To Jefferson, the Real Whig maxim, "Where annual election ends, there tyranny begins," thus had come to symbolize his adherence not merely to a Whig version of history which idealized the supposed "Gothick model of government" but more fundamentally to a constitutional theory which stressed the will of the majority as the only legitimate basis of political power.

The type of government that the Americans substituted for monarchy—government not only founded in theory upon the consent of the governed but continually responsible to the will of the people in all its branches—was unprecedented in both its form and its principles. Classical politics based government only on force; modern governments, on either force or corruption, Jefferson came to believe. Republican government as it existed in the United States, in contrast, was founded on the enlightened doctrines of the modern age. "The equal rights of man, and the happiness of every individual, are now acknowledged to be the only legitimate objects of government"; and "the only device by which these rights can be secured," he later would write, was "government by the people, acting not in person, but by representatives chosen by themselves." Republicanism, Jefferson maintained, was "the only form of government which is not eternally at open or secret war with the rights of mankind."[29]

News of such "tumults in America" as Shays's Rebellion did not shake Jefferson's confidence or pride in American republicanism. Although he considered the citizens' resort to arms to be "acts absolutely unjustifiable," he benignly concluded that such turbulence was the price that America paid for its republicanism. Weighed against the oppression of monarchy, it "becomes nothing," he noted, adding that he was not at all discouraged: the rebellion in Massachusetts was the first in the thirteen American states after eleven years of independence, which he calculated to amount to "one rebellion in a century and a half for each state." "What country ever existed a century and a half without rebellion?" he asked. Thus the rebellion became evidence that the American "experiment" would be successful in proving to the world that "men may be trusted to govern themselves without a master."[30]

Two of Jefferson's letters commenting on Shays's Rebellion early in 1787 are especially deserving of mention. To James Madison he expressed the hope that the governmental authorities in America would not act too harshly in putting down such turbulence because it "prevents the degeneracy of government, and nourishes a general attention to the public affairs." Thus, he concluded, "a little rebellion now and then is a good thing, . . . a medicine necessary for the sound health of government." Two weeks earlier, in a letter written to Edward Carrington, Jefferson similarly urged tolerance. "The people are the only censors of their governors; and even their errors will tend to keep these to the true principles of their institution. To punish these errors too severely would be to suppress the only safeguard of public liberty." Jefferson also contrasted America with Europe, arguing that societies without governments (such as that he believed the American Indians had) enjoyed greater happiness than those, like most in Europe, where under the pretext of governing, one class of people preyed upon another like "wolves and sheep." He urged his correspondent, "Cherish therefore the spirit of our people, and keep alive their attention. Do not be too severe upon their errors, but reclaim them by enlightening them. If once they become inattentive to the public affairs, you and I, and Congress, and Assemblies, judges and governors shall all become wolves."[31]

Jefferson's observations about the abuse of political power—which led him to be particularly wary of those in power and comparatively confident in the body of the people—explain his early enthusiasm for the French Revolution. Even after the Reign of Terror, Jefferson was extraordinarily tolerant of what he perceived to be the people's efforts to restore their liberties. Although he later "lamented" that these efforts had been "attended with the diffusion of so much blood," in early 1793 he indulged in hyperbole in writing about the Revolution to a protégé: "The liberty of the whole earth was depending on the issue of the contest, and was ever such a prize won with so little innocent blood? My own affections have been deeply wounded by some of the martyrs to this cause, but rather than it should have failed, I would have seen half the earth desolated. Were there but an Adam and an Eve left in every country, and left free, it would be better than as it now is."[32]

As Adrienne Koch has observed, "One looks in vain for any fear of the majority in Jefferson's writings." He regarded the *lex majoris partis,* the law of the majority, as the natural law of every society of men. Founded in "common law as well as common right," the law of the majority was also, according to Jefferson, the fundamental law in any society that recognized "equal rights"; it was therefore the "vital principle of republics," where, as he stated in a 1787 letter to Madison, "the will of every one has a just influence."[33] Recognition of this principle explains his acceptance of the Constitution after popular ratification despite his qualms about certain features, particularly the absence of limitations on presidential terms. This principle also was what he emphasized as the distinguishing feature of American self-government as well as "the only sure guardian of the rights of man" in his eloquent reply to a welcoming address from his Albemarle neighbors upon his return from France. "Let us then, my dear friends, for ever bow down to the general reason of the society," he said, observing that it was safe, "even in it's deviations, for it soon returns again to the right way."[34]

Majoritarianism thus was an essential component of Jefferson's republicanism. As one scholar has observed, Jefferson believed that the will of the majority was the only principle of government and of order in society that did not involve the appeal to force, and he clearly saw "a dichotomy of this sort: either the will of the majority or force." As understood by Jefferson, republicanism was "the political expression of reason, tolerance, arbitration, and the acceptance of majority will, even if the majority's decision is not as each individual would have it, because it is the opposite of resorting to force." Later in his life, years after the French Revolution had been followed by the rise and fall of Napoleon Bonaparte, Jefferson drew upon this history as proof that "the will of the society enounced by the majority of a single vote, as sacred as if unanimous, is the first of all lessons in importance, yet the last which is thoroughly learnt. This law once disregarded, no other remains but that of force, which ends necessarily in military despotism." [35]

Because Jefferson's principle of acquiescence in the will of the majority was, to use Adrienne Koch's term, basically "anti-force," he qualified it by also holding that the majority will must not be "oppressive," and that the rights of minorities must be maintained, through the principle of a "fair majority" or the "rightful will" of the majority. As he stated this "sacred principle" in his First Inaugural Address, "Tho' the will of the majority is in all cases to prevail, that will, to be rightful, must be reasonable." [36]

Except for these qualifications, however, Jefferson's devotion to the principle of majority will was absolute. Unlike many of his contemporaries, particularly John Adams and James Madison, he harbored few fears of majority tyranny.[37] Undoubtedly it was Jefferson's comparatively optimistic view of human nature—his idea of natural society and the other premises associated with his concept of self-government, such as the existence of a "moral sense"—that underlay his confidence in the will of the majority. He accordingly was unshakable in his beliefs that majority rule was ordained by nature and common sense as the appropriate foundation for order in civil society, and that its only alternative was force and the despotism to which the use of force inevitably leads.

Jefferson's stress on majority will as the operative principle of republicanism was not mere theory; it had many interesting practical applications as a guide to political policy. During his tenure as secretary of state, Jefferson found two occasions to apply this principle to questions of public policy. The first arose in one of the first constitutional opinions he wrote for President Washington. At issue was the question whether the president should veto the bill that transferred the seat of government to the Potomac in 1800. Arguing in favor of the bill, Jefferson bottomed his constitutional argument on the exercise by each house of Congress of its "natural right of governing itself":

"When a certain description of men are to transact together a particular business, the times and place of their meeting and separating, depend on their own will; they make a part of the natural right of self-government." Since the right of adjournment was not given by the Constitution but was "a natural right," like all other natural rights, it could be "abridged or modified in it's exercise" by law, he concluded.[38]

The second, and far more important, implementation of Jefferson's principle of majority will while he was secretary of state was the position he took on the United States' recognition of the government of France after the Revolution there had deposed Louis XVI. Writing to Gouverneur Morris, the American minister in Paris, Jefferson observed, "It accords with our principles to acknowledge any government to be rightful which is formed by the will of the nation substantially declared." Somewhat later, after he had concluded from newspaper reports that the French Convention was sufficiently authorized to form a new government—and thus was the organ through which the will of the French nation was "substantially declared"—Jefferson, with Washington's concurrence, was more explicit in his instructions, both to Morris and to Thomas Pinckney, the American minister in London. To the latter, he emphasized that recognition of the new French government by the United States was compelled by what he called "the Catholic principle of republicanism": "We certainly cannot deny to other nations that principle whereon our government is founded, that every nation has a right to govern itself internally under whatever forms it pleases, and to change those forms at it's own will; and externally to transact business with other nations thro' whatever organ it chuses, whether that be a king, convention, assembly, committee, president, or whatever it may be. The only thing essential is the will of the nation."[39]

An even fuller explication of this "Catholic principle of republicanism" and its consequences for American foreign policy as seen by Jefferson may be found in his opinion, written in 1793, concerning the validity of the Franco-American treaties of 1778. These treaties contained articles that could have jeopardized the effort of the United States to remain neutral in the war between Britain and France. Primarily because he was anxious to avoid war with Britain at all costs, Secretary of the Treasury Alexander Hamilton took the position that the treaties were contracts with Louis XVI only and accordingly should be considered void, or at least suspended. Following a heated cabinet discussion, in which Jefferson and Attorney General Edmund Randolph opposed Hamilton and stood by the treaties, written opinions were submitted to President Washington.

In his opinion Jefferson sought to respond to Hamilton's argument from the law of nations, based largely upon a quotation from Vattel which suggested grounds for renouncing the alliance. Jefferson marshaled contrary authorities (including other quotations from Vattel himself) upholding the sanctity of treaties regardless of changes in the form of government. He prefaced his discussion of the law of nations, however, with a recitation of the "principles" that governed the case:

> I consider the people who constitute a society or nation as the source of all authority in that nation, as free to transact their common concerns by any agents they think proper, to change these agents individually, or the organisation of them in form or function whenever they please; that all the acts done by those agents under the authority of the nation, are the acts of the nation, are obligatory on them, and enure to their use, and can in no wise be annulled or affected by any change in the form of government, or of the persons administering it. Consequently the Treaties between the US. and France, were not treaties between the US. and Louis Capet, but between the two nations of America and France, and the nations remaining in existence, tho' both of them have since changed their forms of government, the treaties are not annulled by these changes.

For the validity of these principles, Jefferson appealed not merely to the authority of the treatise writers but more fundamentally to the standard of reason. He argued that "the same moral duties" that exist between individuals exist also between societies, and that the "true fountains of evidence" for these duties lie in "the head and heart of every rational and honest man." There are circumstances, such as when performance becomes impossible or self-destructive, that excuse the nonperformance of contracts. Such circumstances were not applicable to this case, he maintained. Absent these circumstances, compacts between nations, like those between individuals, remained obligatory despite the changes affecting one or both of the parties.[40]

Years later, Jefferson used a similar argument in responding to the Federalists' contention that the English common law (particularly concerning the crime of seditious libel) was in force in federal courts. "It is the will of the nation which makes the law obligatory; it is their will which creates or annihilates the organ which is to declare & announce it. . . . The law being law because it is the will of the nation, is not changed by their changing the organ through which they chuse to announce their future will; no more than the acts I have done by one attorney lose their obligation by my changing or discontinuing that attorney." He noted that this doctrine had been "in a certain degree sanctioned" by the federal government, "for it is precisely that on which the continuation of obligation from our treaty with France was established." He urged that a consistent application of the doctrine would lead to the conclusion that the common law was in force only in the states, where it had been adopted by the will of the people, "manifested by the organs we constituted."[41]

"A Mild and Safe Corrective of Abuses": Republicanism and the Political Party Struggles of the 1790s

One of the advantages of popular government, of which Jefferson was distinctly aware, was that it afforded a means of redressing grievances against the government without the resort to force; it provided, as he would later put it in his First Inaugural Address, "a mild and safe corrective of abuses which are lopped by the sword of revolution where peaceable remedies are unprovided."[42] It was his enthusiasm for popular, as opposed to monarchical, government, that caused him to be relatively untroubled about Shays's Rebellion in 1787. And in 1788 Jefferson applauded the peaceable adoption of the Constitution, boasting that America had "set the world a beautiful example of a government reformed by reason alone, without bloodshed." Jefferson's involvement in the political party struggles of the 1790s, however, was the experience that, more than any other in his life, confirmed his confidence in republican government—and in the people.

Jefferson at first probably shared with his contemporaries a contempt for political parties; eighteenth-century Americans viewed parties, or "factions," as evil and, like Washington in his Farewell Address, condemned the "baneful effect" of party spirit.[43] Indeed, one of Jefferson's earliest references to political parties is highly critical. Declaring himself a neutral bystander in the struggle over ratification of the Constitution, he protested: "I am not a Federalist, because

I never submitted the whole system of my opinions to the creed of any party of men whatever in religion, in philosophy, in politics, or in any thing else where I was capable of thinking for myself. Such an addiction is the last degradation of a free and moral agent. If I could not go to heaven but with a party, I would not go there at all."[44] Part of Jefferson's reason for applauding the ratification of the Constitution, one may safely conclude, was that it removed the source of discord that had divided Americans into Federalists and Antifederalists. Thereafter, he may be assumed to have thought, Americans would be united in adherence to republican principles and devotion to the federal system created by the new Constitution.

If, however, Jefferson returned to America to his new post as President Washington's secretary of state with expectations of political tranquillity or unanimity, such expectations were quickly dispelled. Years later, he recalled experiencing a sense of shock soon after his arrival in the new national capital:

> When I arrived at New York in 1790, to take a part in the administration, being fresh from the French revolution, while in its first and pure stage, and consequently somewhat whetted up in my own republican principles, I found a state of things, in the general society of the place, which I could not have supposed possible. . . . The revolution I had left, and that we had just gone through in the recent change of our own government, being the common topics of conversation, I was astonished to find the general prevalence of monarchical sentiments, insomuch that in maintaining those of republicanism, I had always the whole company on my hands, never scarcely finding among them a single co-advocate in that argument, unless some old member of Congress happened to be present. The furthest that any one would go, in support of the republican features of our new government, would be to say, "the present constitution is well as a beginning, and may be allowed a fair trial, but it is, in fact, only a stepping stone to something better."[45]

One must allow for Jefferson's proneness to exaggeration, especially in the retrospection of old age; yet this description accords well with his observations at the time in his correspondence.[46] For Jefferson, Madison, and the other leaders of what would become the Republican party opposition, it is clear that opposition arose because of their perception that the administration was moving dangerously toward monarchy; it is also clear that the economic program of the secretary of the treasury, Alexander Hamilton, sparked this perception.

The story of the rise of the Republican party during Washington's presidency and of Jefferson's emergence as its leader is a complicated one. It is useful here to trace the evolution of Jefferson's perception of the Federalist administration, of the Republican opposition to it, and of the principles that divided the two parties. His writings reveal in quite explicit terms his perception of the party struggle as a battle, not only between competing ideologies but also between competing theories of constitutionalism.

Beginning early in 1791 Jefferson in his correspondence wrote of the emergence of "a sect" which was "preaching up and pouting after an English constitution of king, lords, and commons." The members of this sect "declare they espoused our new constitution, not as a good and sufficient thing itself, but only as a step to the English constitution, the only thing good and sufficient in itself, in their eye," he maintained. Although he ominously noted that the members of this sect comprised many "high and important characters" in government, including a phalanx of "stock-jobbers and king-jobbers" in Congress, he declared them to be "preachers without followers." The "great mass" of the American people were "untainted with these heresies" and "firm and unanimous in their principles of republicanism," he further maintained; and he confidently predicted that at the next election "the voice of the people" would make itself heard and "cleanse" the government. On this assumption, he said, he built his hopes "that we have not laboured in vain, and that our experiment will still prove that men can be governed by reason."[47]

Clearly, Jefferson regarded Alexander Hamilton as the leader of this "sect."[48] Although it is difficult to date precisely the origins of his suspicions of Hamilton—and indeed they probably evolved over time, as he and the secretary of the treasury came increasingly into conflict— by August 1791 he was sufficiently suspicious of Hamilton's motives to note, in a memorandum later incorporated into his memoirs, a conversation which had taken place. According to Jefferson's account, Hamilton expressed his opinion that "the present government is not that which will answer the ends of society, by giving stability and protection to it's rights, and that it will probably be found expedient to go into the British form." Jefferson believed that Hamilton "was not only a monarchist, but for a monarchy bottomed on corruption." [49] He regarded the "British form" that Hamilton so admired to be tantamount to the style of government that mid-eighteenth century English Real Whigs so condemned: one that relied, as an administrative system, upon the maintenance of a kind of symbiosis—a link of influence, patronage, and personal relationships—between the king's ministers and the two houses of Parliament. This was what Jefferson condemned as "corruption," and he interpreted Hamilton's "schemes"—the assumption bill, the bank bill, and the other parts of his financial program that the secretary of the treasury was skillfully guiding through Congress—to be the means by which the "corrupt" British system of government could be introduced into the United States. [50]

In an extraordinary letter he wrote to President Washington in the fall of 1792, Jefferson elaborated his grievances against Hamilton. He avowed that he had "utterly, in my private conversations, disapproved of the system of the Secretary of the treasury" and that "this was not merely a speculative difference." Hamilton's economic system "flowed from principles adverse to liberty, & was calculated to undermine and demolish the republic, by creating an influence of his department over the members of the legislature," Jefferson charged. "The object of these plans taken together is to draw all the powers of government into the hands of the general legislature, to establish means for corrupting a sufficient corps in that legislature to divide the honest votes & preponderate, . . . & to have that corps under the command of the Secretary of the Treasury for the purpose of subverting step by step the principles of the constitution, which he has so often declared to be a thing of nothing which must be changed." He then responded to Hamilton's accusations, among them, that Jefferson had written letters from Europe to friends in America opposing the Constitution. This charge, Jefferson maintained, was "most false," arguing that he was the true supporter of the Constitution and especially of its "parts most vitally republican." Hamilton, he reminded Washington, had argued for a monarchy at the Constitutional Convention, as Jefferson had learned from Madison's notes on the debates. Reiterating this latter point in a subsequent conversation with Washington, Jefferson accused Hamilton of trying to destroy the separation of powers—or, as he put it, "the equilibrium of the three great bodies Legislative, Executive, & Judiciary"—by undermining the independence of Congress. Through its most powerful arm, the Treasury Department, the executive "had swallowed up the legislative branch," he argued.[51]

These statements to Washington in the fall of 1792 indicate the substance of Jefferson's charges against Hamilton as well as his own characterization of the opposition to Hamilton and his programs. The "republican interest," as he called it late in 1792, thus was actuated by a desire, first, to keep the exercise of powers by Congress within the boundaries drawn by the Constitution and, second, to preserve the independence of Congress from the "influence and patronage of the Executive." He furthermore identified the "republican interest" with public opinion, confidently predicting that the elections would produce "a decided majority" in its favor and that "the tide of this government" was at its fullest and, from the beginning of the next session of Congress, would "retire and subside into the true principles of the Constitution." Early in 1793 he wrote to his friend and protégé, William Short, in France, that except for the Hamiltonian party, "this country is entirely republican, friends to the constitution, anxious to preserve it and to have it administered according to it's own republican principles."[52]

The year 1793 was another turbulent one for the secretary of state. Direct conflict again arose within the cabinet, primarily in the area of foreign policy and particularly with respect to the problem of American neutrality. Jefferson opposed Hamilton on the question of the continuing validity of the treaties of 1778 with France. Although he acquiesced in Washington's Proclamation of Neutrality, he regarded it as an illegitimate exercise of executive powers and an impingement on the prerogatives of Congress. The new French minister, Edmond Charles Genet, proved an embarrassment to Jefferson and others friendly to France; when Genet's activities and statements threatened to involve the United States in the Anglo-French war, Jefferson prepared papers demanding the diplomat's recall. These controversies aggravated the division between Federalists and Republicans and reinforced their mutual accusations, that the former were promoting the cause of Britain, the latter the cause of France, and neither for the good of the United States. This perception was not dispelled by Jefferson's last major act as secretary of state, his Report on Commerce, which urged retaliation in kind against discriminatory British trade practices. He submitted it to Congress in mid-December, just before his resignation at year's end.[53]

Jefferson did not return to Philadelphia until 1797 when, having placed second to John Adams in electoral votes, he assumed his duties as vice president of the United States. During his absence, despite his stated determination to retire fully to "family, farm and books," Jefferson nevertheless continued to be involved in politics. As the decade progressed, he found himself increasingly assuming the position of leader of the Republican party; and he certainly was an active and interested observor of key political events, particularly the controversy generated by the treaty that John Jay had negotiated with Great Britain. The Jay Treaty was quite favorable to Britain; among other things, the United States gave up for ten years the right to impose any tonnage or tariff discrimination against British ships or goods— thereby completely undermining the linchpin of Madison's and Jefferson's commercial policy.[54] Jefferson saw the Jay Treaty as a partisan maneuver, another attempt of the pro-British, antirepublican faction to entrench themselves, against the public interest and in defiance of popular opinion.

By the time Jefferson received a copy of the treaty, it had been approved by the Federalist-controlled Senate but had yet to be considered by the House of Representatives, which had to pass on the appropriations measures implementing the treaty. In the newspapers and in Congress, the Federalists took the position that the House had no choice but to enact whatever enabling legislation was necessary, regarding the treaty as a fait accompli, the supreme law of the land, since it had received the approbation of the Senate and the president. Republicans, however, insisted that all matters in the treaty normally requiring the concurrence of both houses of Congress and the president should be referred to the House, which should be free to reject these, either by explicit action or by refusing to pass legislation carrying them into effect. A concerted campaign in opposition to the treaty arose in Virginia by late summer 1795; and although he took no active part in this campaign, Jefferson shared the sentiments of his fellow Virginia Republicans. He wrote Madison: "A bolder party-stroke was never struck. For it certainly is an attempt of a party, which finds they have lost their majority in one branch of the legislature, to make a law by the aid of the other branch and of the executive, under color of a treaty, which shall bind up the hands of the adverse branch from ever restraining the commerce of their patron-nation," Britain. To another correspondent he described it even more succinctly as an "infamous act, which was nothing more than a treaty of alliance between England and the Anglomen of this country against the legislature and people of the United States."[55]

At about the time of the controversy over the Jay Treaty, in a series of notes written for the benefit of a foreigner seeking information about the United States, Jefferson summarized the machinations of Hamilton and the other "anti-republicans," over the course of the past several years, as an elaborate scheme "of strengthening all the features of the government which gave it a resemblance to an English constitution, of adopting the English forms & principles of administration, and of forming like them a monied interest, by means of a funding system, not calculated to pay the public debt, but to render it perpetual, and to make it an engine in the hands of the executive branch of the government which, added to the great patronage it possessed in the disposal of public offices, might enable it to assume by degrees a kingly authority." He hopefully added that it was "inevitable" that both houses of Congress, "once brought to act on the true principles of the Constitution, backed by the people, will be able to defeat the plan of sliding us into monarchy, & to keep the Executive within Republican bounds."[56]

The most famous, or infamous, statement of Jefferson with respect to the parties of the 1790s appeared in his letter to Philip Mazzei in the spring of 1796. Jefferson wrote that "an Anglican monarchical aristocratical party has sprung up, whose avowed object is to draw over us the substance, as they have already done the forms, of the British government." The "main body of our citizens, however, remain true to their republican principles," he added, but he emphasized how formidable the antirepublican party was—and thus painted a dismal picture of the United States government:

> Against us are the Executive, the Judiciary, two out of three branches of the legislature, all the officers of the government, all who want to be officers, all timid men who prefer the calm of despotism to the boisterous sea of liberty, British merchants & Americans trading on British capital, speculators & holders in the banks & public funds, a contrivance invented for the pur-

poses of corruption, & for assimilating us in all things to the rotten as well as the sound parts of the British model. It would give you a fever were I to name to you the apostates who have gone over to these heresies, men who were Samsons in the field & Solomons in the council, but who have had their heads shorn by the harlot England.

"In short," he concluded, "we are likely to preserve the liberty we have obtained only by unremitting labors and perils." But he confidently predicted that "we shall preserve it," and once awakened from the "first sleep which succeeded our labors," the American people would "snap the Lilliputian cords" with which the antirepublican party had been entangling them. Jefferson later explained that in his reference to "forms" he meant the ceremonies—"the birthdays, levees, processions to parliament, inauguration pomposities, etc."—that he so disliked about the Washington administration and, later, the Adams administration; but the frank tone of the letter, when it became public, caused him much embarrassment.[57]

Through the end of the decade Jefferson continued to adhere to his perception of the party struggle—the Federalist leadership as a "sect," preaching antirepublican "heresies" that the vast majority of the American people did not share—despite the fact that it took much longer to "cleanse" the government than he had predicted. Certainly by the time of the presidential election of 1796 he had come to the realization that the "sect" he had identified earlier in the decade was in fact a political party. Still, he did not regard the opposing groups as parties in the modern sense; he justified his partisan activities as being in the public interest but was unwilling to acknowledge the same motives in his political foes, although he did later maintain that some of those who called themselves Federalists had been duped by the party leaders, the antirepublican sect. Convinced that the principles at stake would determine the very survival of republicanism, he expressed little tolerance for trimmers between parties. As he wrote late in 1795, "Where the principle of difference is so substantial and as strongly pronounced as between the republicans and Monocrats of our country, I hold it as honorable to take a firm and decided part, and as immoral to pursue a middle line, as between the parties of honest men and rogues, into which every country is divided."[58]

In the highly partisan and warmly contested election campaign of

1796, Jefferson was pitted against John Adams: one was the leading candidate of the Republican party and the other, of the Federalists. Adams became president with only three more electoral votes than Jefferson. As vice president, Jefferson presided over the Senate, but he had no role in Adams's Federalist-controlled administration; accordingly, he was free to provide direction to the opposition party. With Federalist majorities in both houses of Congress, the nation had both its first party government and, for the first time, an uninhibited opposition party. And with Madison in retirement in Virginia, the burden of Republican party leadership fell on Jefferson, who took an active role as a center for unity in the party.[59]

The events of Adams's presidency intensified party animus; it was a time when, Jefferson said, party animosities "raised a wall of separation between those who differ in political sentiments" and when men of opposite parties crossed the street to avoid having to touch their hats as they passed. The "unremitting labors and perils" to which Jefferson had referred in his letter to Mazzei came to pass, as war between Britain and France raged on and anti-French hysteria, egged on by the Federalists, pushed the United States to the brink of war with France. At the beginning of April 1798, with war measures pending in Congress, Jefferson wrote: "The present period . . . is the most eventful ever known since that of 1775, and will decide whether the principles established by that contest are to prevail, or give way to those they subverted."[60]

The day after Jefferson wrote this letter, President Adams submitted to Congress the papers relating to the failed mission to France, exposing the so-called XYZ affair, wherein three anonymous agents of Talleyrand, the French foreign minister, demanded bribes as the price of negotiation. Jefferson wrote scathingly of the "X.Y.Z. dish cooked up by [John] Marshall," one of the American commissioners. He urged the printing and distribution of handbills to "expose the dupery" practiced on the people and thus to bring about "the resurrection of their republican spirit" and "a reduction of the administration to constitutional principles."[61]

Following the XYZ imbroglio, the war hysteria came to a crisis point in 1798, with the passage in Congress of a series of statutes known collectively as the Alien and Sedition Acts: the Naturalization Act, raising from five to fourteen years the residency requirement for citizenship; the Alien Enemies Act, empowering the president to confine or banish aliens of an enemy country during time of war; the so-called Alien Friends Act, authorizing the president summarily to deport aliens deemed dangerous to the peace and safety of the United States; and the Sedition Act, making it criminal, among other things, to publish "any false, scandalous and malicious writing" against the government, Congress, or the president. Jefferson took an active, though hidden, role in opposing these measures and secretly drafted the Kentucky Resolutions of 1798, protesting the acts as unconstitutional. As in his opposition to Hamiltonian financial programs, his arguments centered around a strict interpretation of federal powers under the Constitution and adherence to the principle of separation of powers.[62]

By the time of the Alien and Sedition Acts crisis of 1798, Jefferson had arrived at an important conclusion with respect not only to the party struggle of the 1790s but also to the nature of political parties generally. This is revealed in a letter he wrote to John Taylor of Caroline County, Virginia, in the summer of 1798, at the height of the anti-French war hysteria and at the time when the omnibus alien and sedition bill was being considered in Congress. Taylor had suggested to Jefferson that Virginia and North Carolina escape from the "saddle" of Massachusetts and Connecticut by leaving the Union. Jefferson responded by urging caution and patience. The present situation was not a natural one, he argued; the Federalists, or "anti-republicans," had won an artificial preponderance because of the "irresistable influence and popularity" of George Washington, which Hamilton had exploited. This in time would correct itself, he assured Taylor: "The body of our countrymen is substantially republican through every part of the Union. . . . A little patience, and we shall see the reign of witches pass over, their spells dissolve, and the people, recovering their true sight, restore their government to it's true principles. . . . If the game runs sometimes against us . . . we must have patience till luck turns, & then we shall have an opportunity of winning back the *principles* we have lost, for this is a game where principles are at stake." He added that party division was not a sufficient reason for secession:

> In every free & deliberating society there must, from the nature of man, be opposite parties & violent dissensions and discords; and one of these, for the most part, must prevail over the other for a longer or shorter time. Perhaps this party division is neces-

sary to induce each to watch & delate to the people the proceedings of the other. But if on a temporary superiority of one party, the other is to resort to a scission of the Union, no federal government can ever exist. If to rid ourselves of the present rule of Massachusetts & Connecticut we break the Union, will the evil stop there? . . . Seeing, therefore, that an association of men who will not quarrel with one another is a thing which never existed, from the greatest confederacy of nations down to a town meeting or a vestry, seeing that we must have somebody to quarrel with, I had rather keep our New England associates for that purpose than to see our bickerings transferred to others.

As Richard Hofstadter has noted, Jefferson thus gave as concise a statement of the function of parties as any of his contemporaries, and it seems that he came close to accepting the dynamics underlying a two-party system.[63]

In other letters written during this period, Jefferson similarly suggested that the two-party division was not to be feared. Early in 1797 he further suggested that a division between republicans and monarchists was inevitable: "Where a constitution, like ours, wears a mixed aspect of monarchy and republicanism, its citizens will naturally be divided into two classes of sentiment, according to their true tone of body or mind, their habits, connections & callings, induce them to wish to strengthen either the republican or monarchical features of the constitution." And, a year later, he described the party division this way:

It is now well understood that two political Sects have arisen within the U.S. the one believing that the executive is the branch of our government which most needs support; the other that like the analogous branch in the English Government, it is already too strong for the republican parts of the constitution; and therefore in equivocal cases they incline to the legislative powers: the former of these are called federalists, sometimes aristocrats or monocrats, and sometimes tories, after the corresponding sect in the English Government of exactly the same definition: the latter are stiled republicans, whigs, jacobins, disorganizers &c. . . . Both parties claim to be federalists and republicans, and I believe with truth as to the great mass of them: these appellations therefore designate neither exclusively, and all the others are slanders, except those of whig and tory which alone characterize the distinguishing principles of the two Sects as I have before explained them.[64]

The ideas that the real party division was between "tories" and "whigs" and that party division was inevitable were developed more fully in Jefferson's mind later, after his retirement from the presidency, when he would suggest that such a division was rooted in man's nature. It should be noted, however, that in postulating the party division in terms of differences in "sentiment," Jefferson was slowly reconciling himself to the idea of a party system while still continuing to believe that the true nonrepublicans—and not those who had been "duped" by them—were a distinct minority among the people of the United States.

Later in life, when he looked back to the party struggle of the 1790s, Jefferson declared that the Republicans were not "a mere set of grumblers, and disorganisers, satisfied with no government, without fixed principles of any, and, like a British parliamentary opposition, gaping after loaves and fishes, and ready to change principles, as well as position, at any time, with their adversaries." The Republicans rather were "in truth endeavoring to keep the government within the line of the Constitution, and prevent it's being monarchised in practice." This was "the real ground of the opposition which was made to the course of administration" during the Federalist era. "It's object was to preserve the legislature pure and independant of the Executive, to restrain the administration to republican forms and principles, and not permit the constitution to be construed into a monarchy, and to be warped in practice into all the principles and pollutions of [the Federalists'] favorite English model." He concluded, "The contests of that day were contests of principle, between the advocates of republican, and those of kingly government, and . . . had not the former made the efforts they did, our government would have been, even at this early day, a very different thing from what the successful issue of those efforts have made it."[65]

5

We Are All Federalists,

We Are All Republicans

The Republican "Revolution"

of 1800 and Beyond

The Republican party's electoral victory in 1800 was, to Jefferson, a "second American Revolution"; it represented the American people's decisive repudiation of the principles of monarchy (principles that Jefferson associated with the Federalist party leadership), just as their action in 1776 had shown that they had repudiated the forms of monarchy. To put it another way, the happy denouement of the great political drama of the 1790s, as viewed by Jefferson, was that the principles as well as the forms of the American constitutions, federal and state, were firmly established as those appropriate to a society in which sovereignty rested with the people.

By the time he became president, Jefferson's understanding of the constitutional dimensions of republicanism—the principles and forms appropriate to a government founded upon the consent of the people—had become fully articulated and integrated into his overall philosophy of government. The constitutional devices that he emphasized—chiefly federalism and the separation of powers—were linked to his concept of republicanism. The result was Jefferson's vision of the "experiment in self-government" that the American constitutions sought to establish, however imperfectly: a theory that would combine into one coherent whole the Whig, federal, and republican components of Jefferson's thought. This was the constitutional theory to which Jefferson adhered with remarkable scrupulousness during his two terms as president—despite certain extraordinary circumstances that severely challenged his principles—and which he continued strenuously to advance after his retirement from public office.

This chapter traces these final stages of the evolution of Jefferson's constitutional thought. Beginning with his accession to the presidency in 1801, the first section discusses Jefferson's efforts to conciliate political party differences by pursuing a policy which was both federal and republican—a policy, he believed, which would not only carry the support of the vast majority of the American people but also would help restore the Constitution to its true principles. Jefferson's view of the significance of the Republican electoral triumph, the "revolution," of 1800 thus is explained in constitutional, as well as political, terms. The second section of the chapter presents Jefferson's mature constitutional theory, developed by the time of his presidency and further articulated in its clearest terms after his retirement.

The "Revolution" of 1800: Republicanism from Opposition to Ascendancy

As he had applauded the peaceable adoption of the Constitution in 1788–89, Jefferson hailed the Republican electoral triumph in 1800. He later described it as "the revolution of 1800," explaining that it was "as real a revolution in the principles of our government as that of 1776 was in its form; not effected indeed by the sword, as that, but by the rational and peaceable instrument of reform, the suffrage of the people. The nation declared its will by dismissing functionaries of one principle, and electing those of another, in the two branches, executive and legislative, submitted for their election."[1] Jefferson's election to the presidency and the election of Republican majorities in both houses of Congress, replacing the Federalist majorities that had controlled Congress during the Adams administration, brought a complete transfer of power, thus fulfilling Jefferson's optimistic prophecies in his 1798 letter to John Taylor that "the reign of witches" would pass and the people would restore the government to its "true principles."[2]

In his presidential inaugural address on 4 March 1801, Jefferson announced, "We are all republicans: we are all federalists." As Dumas

Malone has noted, Jefferson did not capitalize the key words and thus turn them into party names, as later editors would take the liberty of doing. His meaning was clear in the context of his previous statements: that "every difference of opinion is not a difference of principle," and that "we have called by different names brethren of the same principle." He meant that nearly all Americans favored a republican rather than a monarchical form of government and accepted the federal system, as contrasted with a consolidated national government on the one hand and a confederacy of fully sovereign states on the other. He differentiated the Federalist leaders, whom he considered monarchists, from their followers, drawn from the great mass of the people, who like their Republican brethren were attached to the Constitution and the maintenance of a federal, republican government. It was to this latter group—the true federalists, in the sense described—that he took a conciliatory tone in his First Inaugural Address, where he defined and declared to them "the ground on which we could rally."[3]

Among the principles that he stated in the First Inaugural, as part of this common ground, was the "vital principle of republics": "absolute acquiescence in the decisions of the majority." Related to this principle were two others: "a jealous care of the right of election by the people," which he described as "a mild and safe corrective of abuses"; and the "sacred principle" that "though the will of the majority is in all cases to prevail, that will to be rightful, must be reasonable," with the equal rights of the minority protected. Consistent with these principles, Jefferson expressed toleration even for monarchists, asserting that the republic was strong enough to withstand dissent:

> If there be any among us who would wish to dissolve this Union or to change it's republican form, let them stand undisturbed as monuments of the safety with which error of opinion may be tolerated where reason is left free to combat it. I know, indeed, that some honest men fear that a republican government cannot be strong; that this government is not strong enough. But would the honest patriot, in the full tide of successful experiment, abandon a government which has so far kept us free and firm, on the theoretic and visionary fear that this government, the world's best hope, may by possibility want energy to preserve itself? I trust not. I believe this, on the contrary, the strongest govern-

ment on earth. I believe it is the only one where every man, at the call of the laws, would fly to the standard of the law, and would meet invasions of the public order as his own personal concern. Sometimes it is said that man cannot be trusted with the government of himself. Can he, then, be trusted with the government of others? Or have we found angels in the forms of kings to govern him? Let history answer this question.

Perhaps no more eloquent testament of Jefferson's confidence in the efficacy of republican government can be found in all his writings. It should be added, however, that at this stage he could afford to be magnanimous because the "revolution of 1800" had borne out his belief that the political and constitutional principles held by him and his party were also held by the majority of the people.[4]

Jefferson's assumptions that the true monarchists were a small minority and that the body of the people were "all federalists, all republicans" also underlay his policy on appointments and removals from office. Having experienced firsthand in the 1790s "the formidable phalanx opposed to the republican features of our constitution," as president he now sought to form a republican phalanx, composed of "the talents & virtues of our country." This, of course, entailed the removal of some Federalists from office, particularly in light of the virtual Federalist monopoly on certain types of offices—a situation that had been aggravated by President Adams's last-minute, or "midnight," appointments. If all his predecessor's appointees were kept in office, Jefferson argued, "the constitutional remedy by the elective principle becomes nothing" and the will of the majority would be thwarted. He nevertheless resisted pressure from fellow Republicans calling for the wholesale removal of Federalists from office and instead adopted a moderate policy. "Midnight" appointments were considered nullities, and officers guilty of official misconduct were proper subjects of removal; but "good men, to whom there is no objection but a difference of political principle, practiced on only as far as the right of a private citizen will justify," were not to be removed. This was a policy of conciliation, and behind it lay Jefferson's hopeful expectation that by following a moderate course, his administration could win the support of the main body—the "honest part"—of "those who were called federalists" and thus be able to "obliterate, or rather to unite, the names of federalists and republicans."[5]

Jefferson quite deliberately sought to accomplish two potentially conflicting goals: on the one hand, "to preserve principle" and, on the other, "to treat tenderly those who have been estranged from us." This conciliatory policy was not self-contradictory to Jefferson's mind because he continued to distinguish the Federalist leaders—"the leaders of the late faction, whom I abandon as incurables"—from their followers, whom he considered to be real republicans as well as federalists but who had been driven over to the Federalist party by the XYZ affair and other "manoeuvres." His hope was that by gaining their support his administration would "unite a great mass of confidence, and bid defiance to the plans of opposition meditated by leaders who are now almost destitute of followers."[6] In other words, Jefferson sought to destroy opposition by tolerating differences of opinion.

Richard Hofstadter has discerned an ambivalence in Jefferson's view of political parties. On the one hand was a persistence in classical eighteenth-century antiparty views, as evidenced by Jefferson's almost defensive description of the Republican opposition and by the anger with which he once wrote that Hamilton was "daring to call the republican party a *faction*." On the other hand, Jefferson on occasion made shrewd observations on the realities of human nature and the American political system.[7] He long espoused a psychological conception of the origin of parties, the idea that there is a "natural" human tendency to divide into two parties—called "whigs and tories, republicans and federalists, aristocrats and democrats, or by whatever name you please"—and that the basic difference between the two sides was always the degree to which one's fear of the people or one's "cherishment" of them was uppermost.[8] When he seemed most receptive to the toleration of these party differences—as, for example, in his 1798 letter to Taylor—Jefferson even suggested that party division could serve a useful purpose, inducing each party to hold the other accountable to the people. He nevertheless hoped to see the demise of the Federalist party; and indeed, after the successful conclusion of the War of 1812, he reported with apparent delight the virtual annihilation of Federalism.[9] Thus, Hofstadter has concluded, "abstractly, Jefferson accepted the idea of political division and the reality that opposition would be embodied in the form of parties; but concretely he could never see the legitimacy of any particular opposition in his own country."[10]

The apparent ambivalence in Jefferson's view of political parties can be explained by emphasizing that in Jefferson's view the parties of the 1790s were actuated by fundamentally different, and indeed irreconcilable, principles. Years after his retirement from the presidency, Jefferson continued to regard the difference between the Republicans and Federalists as fundamental, in terms of both political ideology and constitutionalism. Indeed, the features that Jefferson associated with republicanism in America—both as a social system of self-government and as a democratic political theory—were the features that in his mind differentiated the parties.

In what was perhaps his fullest description of the basis of the party division, in a letter he wrote to Judge William Johnson in 1823, Jefferson first traced the origins of Federalism to "the doctrines of Europe": "that men in numerous associations cannot be restrained within the limits of order and justice, but by forces physical and moral, wielded of kings, hereditary nobles, and priests" who kept the people down by "hard labor, poverty and ignorance," taking from them their earnings "to maintain their privileged orders in splendor and idleness, to fascinate the eyes of the people, and excite in them an humble adoration and submission, as to an order of superior beings." Those who held these beliefs in the years after 1787 formed the antirepublican sect that constituted the core of the Federalist party, a sect which Jefferson considered anathema to the Constitution: he believed their "steady object" was to undermine the "equilibrium" that the framers at the 1787 Convention had endeavored to draw between the federal government and the states. He then contrasted the Federalist agenda with the object of the Republican party:

> Ours, on the contrary, was to maintain the will of the majority of the convention, and of the people themselves. We believed, with them, that man was a rational animal, endowed by nature with rights, and with an innate sense of justice; and that he could be restrained from wrong and protected in right, by moderate powers, confided to persons of his own choice, and held to their duties by dependence on their own will. . . . We believed that men, enjoying in ease and security the full fruits of their own industry, enlisted by all their interests on the side of law and order, habituated to think for themselves, and to follow their reason as their guide, would be more easily and safely governed than with minds nourished in error, and vitiated and

debased, as in Europe, by ignorance, indigence, and oppression.

"The cherishment of the people then was our principle, the fear and distrust of them, that of the other party," he concluded.[11] Thus the party struggle of the 1790s was to Jefferson nothing less than the struggle of the American "experiment" with self-government to succeed and prove to the rest of the world its efficacy.

The full significance of the "revolution of 1800" to Jefferson is dramatically illustrated by the frequent references in his post-1801 correspondence to this experiment, whose success he identified as the primary object of his administration. One of the best examples is a letter he wrote to Dr. Joseph Priestley during his first term as president, in which Jefferson described the advantageous situation of America:

> Our people in a body are wise, because they are under the unrestrained and unperverted operation of their own understandings. Those whom they have assigned to the direction of their affairs, have stood with a pretty even front. If any one of them was withdrawn, many others entirely equal, have been ready to fill his place with as good abilities. A nation, composed of such materials, and free in all it's members from distressing wants, furnishes hopeful implements for the interesting experiment of self-government; and we feel that we are acting under obligations not confined to the limits of our own society. It is impossible not to be sensible that we are acting for all mankind; that circumstances denied to others, but indulged to us, have imposed on us the duty of proving what is the degree of freedom and self-government in which a society may venture to leave it's individual members.[12]

About a year later he wrote another correspondent of his awareness that Americans were not "acting for ourselves alone, but for the whole human race." "The event of our experiment is to shew whether man can be trusted with self-government. The eyes of suffering humanity are fixed on us with anxiety as their only hope, and on such a theatre for such a cause we must suppress all smaller passions and local considerations. The leaders of federalism say that man can not be trusted with his own government. We must do no act which shall replace them in the direction of the experiment. We must not by any departure from principle disgust the mass of our fellow citizens who have confided to us this interesting cause."[13] The "interesting cause," of proving to the world the efficacy of self-government, Jefferson described in particularly eloquent terms in 1809, upon his retirement from the presidency, when he noted that "the station which we occupy among the nations of the earth is honorable, but awful. Trusted with the destinies of the solitary republic of the world, the only monument of human rights, and the sole depository of the sacred fire of freedom and self-government from hence it is to be lighted up in other regions of the earth, if other regions of the earth shall ever become susceptible to its benign influence, all mankind ought then, with us, to rejoice in its prosperous, and sympathize in its adverse fortunes, as involving everything dear to man." He then urged Americans to strive "to maintain harmony and union among ourselves," despite their differences of opinion in politics, religion, and other matters, in order to "preserve from all danger this hallowed ark of human hope and happiness."[14]

When divisions appeared in the ranks of Republicans during the second term of Jefferson's presidency, he indicated that he was not surprised, suggesting that differences in "shades" of republicanism by themselves were not evil.[15] But, as his advocacy of harmony indicates, he also feared that intraparty schisms could provide a handle for the restoration of Federalists to power. Partly for this reason, he viewed with alarm the split among Virginia Republicans in 1808, when some of the more "ardent" Republicans, believing that Madison's principles were insufficiently pure, supported James Monroe instead to succeed Jefferson.[16] Even after his retirement from the presidency, he continued to urge that Republicans remain united. In 1811 he wrote William Duane, "We ought not to schismatize on either men or measures"; rather, he advised, Republicans should support President Madison's measures even if they disagreed with them, so long as the administration did not violate fundamental republican principles. At stake was the great mission that had been entrusted to America, to show by its example the efficacy of self-government. "The last hope of human liberty in this world rests on us," Jefferson reminded Duane. "We ought, for so dear a state, to sacrifice every attachment and every enmity."[17]

"The True Spirit of the Constitution":
Republicanism and the Division of Powers

Jefferson regarded the great political contest of his lifetime to be, as he put it, "contests of principle between the advocates of republican, and those of kingly government." His understanding of republicanism—as it had developed in his mind through the decades of the 1780s and 1790s and beyond—was multi-faceted, encompassing elements of a social philosophy (the concepts of natural society and self-government) as well as of a political philosophy (the concepts of natural rights, equality, and representative democracy). The difference between republicanism and monarchy or aristocracy, as Jefferson understood those terms, involved more than simply the forms of government; it involved also the principles of government, the underlying views of human nature and social theory that shaped public policy. It is significant, then, that at least by the time of his presidency, Jefferson distinguished the Republicans from the Federalists by describing them as "whigs" and "tories" by nature: the former had confidence in the people's capacity for self-government and accordingly were willing to hazard the "interesting experiment"; the latter, lacking this confidence, desired the heavy hand of government in all things.

What remains to be considered is how constitutionalism in general, and the federal Constitution in particular, related to Jefferson's theory of the political parties: how constitutional theories fit into his definitions, and more importantly, how his understanding of the party struggle—evolving as it did over time—shaped his constitutional theories.

The party struggle of the 1790s helped reinforce, on the one hand, Jefferson's low opinion of the English constitution—"that kind of Halfway house" between monarchy and republicanism, as he described it[18]—and, on the other, his high regard generally for the federal Constitution. By associating the Federalist "sect" with a conspiracy to transform into a monarchy the form of government established by the Constitution, Jefferson came to regard the Republican party as the true "republican interest," defending the Constitution, while simultaneously viewing its "true principles" or "true spirit" as republican. So close were these identities that given Jefferson's niggardly use of capital letters, it is often unclear in his writings (even from the context) whether by "republican" he meant the concept or the party.

Jefferson maintained that "tho' written constitutions may be violated in moments of passion or delusion, yet they furnish a text to which those who are watchful may again rally & recall the people; they fix too for the people the principles of their political creed."[19] The terrain on which the party struggles of the 1790s were fought was largely constitutional. This was especially true with respect to those battles in which Jefferson was personally involved: among them, Hamilton's Report on Public Credit and the bank bill, the related problems of American neutrality and recognition of republican France, Hamilton's Report on Manufactures, the Alien and Sedition Acts—all concerned the scope and exercise of federal powers. In articulating his opposition to Federalist measures, Jefferson himself had relied on the text of the Constitution—and particularly its provisions for the division of powers between the federal and state governments and among the three branches of the federal government—for both his lance and his shield.

Summarizing in retrospect the difference between the parties, Jefferson maintained that the Republicans were "steadily for the support of the present constitution," adding that "they obtained at its commencement, all the amendments to it they desired."[20] He was exaggerating with respect both to himself and to the more "ardent" Republicans, the Old Republicans of his own state, many of whom were former Antifederalists and who continually pressed for more constitutional amendments, before and after 1801. Jefferson himself was not an opponent of the Constitution; in 1788–89 he called himself "neither federalist nor antifederalist" but made clear his general support for the Constitution, with two exceptions. One of these, the lack of a bill of rights, was quickly remedied; the other, the perpetual reeligibility of the president, remained a "monarchical" feature which continued to disturb him but which also was remedied, in practice, through Washington's refusal to seek a third term—a tradition that Jefferson and his successors (at least until Franklin D. Roosevelt) followed. If other clauses of the Constitution disturbed Jefferson (those relating to the Senate and to the judiciary, particularly, provoked his later criticism), he did not articulate such concerns during the struggles of the 1790s. As the English Real Whigs had symbolically identified their ideal constitution with the "ancient constitution," the "Gothick" model of their Anglo-Saxon forebears, so Jefferson symbolically identified his ideal "republican" constitution with the federal Constitution.

Behind Jefferson's articulation of Republican opposition in constitutional terms were two fundamental ideas that he had derived from his readings in history and government and that had been confirmed by his own experience with government, in Virginia and in France, in the 1780s. The first was the idea he expressed in 1787, when he noted that European governments had divided the people into two classes, wolves and sheep, and warned that if the people of the United States should become inattentive to public affairs, all officers of government, including himself, would become wolves.[21] The second was the idea, directly derived from mid-eighteenth century Real Whig writers such as James Burgh, that the American Revolution had provided a "more favorable ground" for the preservation of liberty by making it possible for the constituent power of the people—popular sovereignty—to act as a continuing check on the exercise of power by those in government through the device of a written constitution. That was so because, as Jefferson put it, the constitution furnished "a text" which specified both the legitimate scope of powers and the principles upon which the government was constituted; it furnished, in short, a standard against which the people could hold those in power accountable.

Perhaps the finest expression of these ideas—the distrust of political power and the use of a constitution as a standard to hold it in check—may be found in the eighth of the Kentucky Resolutions that Jefferson drafted in 1798. There he wrote, "Free government is founded in jealousy, and not in confidence; it is jealousy, and not confidence which prescribes limited constitutions, to bind those whom we are obliged to trust with power: . . . our Constitution has accordingly fixed the limits to which, and no further, our confidence may go." "Let no more be heard of confidence in man," Jefferson concluded, "but bind him down from mischief by the chains of the constitution."[22]

What did Jefferson regard as the essential principles—the most vital of the "chains"—of the Constitution? One of his clearest statements of these appeared in a letter he wrote to Elbridge Gerry early in 1799, in which he outlined many of the political principles and policies that he would later reiterate in his 1801 presidential inaugural address. He declared that "with sincere zeal" he wished "an inviolable preservation of our present federal constitution, according to the true sense in which it was adopted by the States, that in which it was advocated by it's friends, & not that which it's enemies apprehended." The statements that followed made clear what Jefferson regarded as the "true sense" of the Constitution: "I am opposed to the monarchising it's features by the forms of it's administration, with a view to conciliate a first transition to a President & Senate for life, & from that to a hereditary tenure of these offices, & thus to worm out the elective principle. I am for preserving to the States the powers not yielded by them to the Union, & to the legislature of the Union it's constitutional share in the division of powers; and I am not for transferring all the powers of the States to the general government, & all those of that government to the Executive branch." Thus he identified three distinct constitutional principles essential for the preservation of the Constitution: first, republicanism, in the sense of representative democracy ("the elective principle"); second, federalism, or "the division of powers" between the states and "general government"; and third, the separation of powers among the three branches, executive, legislative, and judicial, of the general government. These principles of constitutionalism were "unquestionably the principles" not only of himself but "of the great body of our fellow citizens," Jefferson maintained.[23]

Focusing on one of these principles, the separation of powers, M. J. C. Vile has argued that it received "its most complete and its most impressive intellectual expression" in Jeffersonian Republicanism, and that in turn it was "the highest and most consistent expression of the philosophy of Jeffersonian Republicanism." The principle articulated in Jeffersonian constitutionalism, Vile has noted, was "the pure doctrine" of the separation of powers, distinguishable from the doctrine of checks and balances; in this form, it became the foundation of Jefferson's constitutional thought, though rather late in his life.[24] It was his pure separation of powers doctrine, together with the principles of federalism and republicanism, that provided Jefferson ultimately with a coherent republican theory of the Constitution.

James Madison in *Federalist* No. 48 sought to defend the system of checks and balances embodied in the federal Constitution against the anticipated criticism that it ran afoul of the principle of separation of powers. He did so by citing Jefferson's *Notes on Virginia*, where it had been demonstrated, Madison argued, that the constitutionally mandated separation of powers provided no effective check upon legislative usurpation. "Unless these [the legislative, executive and judiciary] departments be so far connected and blended, as to give to each a constitutional controul over the others, the degree of separation which the maxim requires as essential to a free government, can never in practice, be duly maintained."[25] Madison thus expressed a truism about the impracticality of a pure doctrine of separation of powers that subsequent American history has verified: neither this doctrine nor the doctrine of checks and balances in its pure form (with the departments of government, free of popular control, exerting checks upon each other) caught on in the United States; rather, both doctrines—separation of powers together with checks and balances, in a kind of hybrid—became in the nineteenth century the basis of American constitutionalism. At the time Jefferson presumably agreed with Madison: Jefferson's early reaction to the Constitution was that he "liked" certain features, such as the executive veto, that were elements of checks and balances theory incompatible with a pure separation of powers theory (for the simple reason that the veto is an exercise of legislative power). To be at all workable, a pure separation of powers model of government would seem to require making each branch of government subject to popular control. This is precisely the system that Jefferson apparently envisioned later in life, perhaps as early as the beginning of his presidency but not fully articulated until years later, in his retirement.

During his presidency Jefferson espoused the so-called tripartite doctrine, which held that each branch of the federal government was entitled independently to interpret the Constitution as to the functions assigned to it.[26] This doctrine provided the rationale under which Jefferson as president challenged the authority of the Supreme Court to decide the meaning of the Constitution when it applied to the other branches of government. It also provided the justification for Jefferson's early presidential order to discontinue prosecutions begun under the Sedition Act of 1798, which he deemed unconstitutional. The constitutional basis for Jefferson's tripartite doctrine was a pure theory of separation of powers, in which each branch of government was kept within the bounds of its assigned powers not by an elaborate system of checks and balances but by the independence of the branches from each other and by the dependence of each upon the will of the people.

Jefferson's fullest articulation of a pure theory of separation of powers, tied to his understanding of republicanism, can be found in a series of letters he wrote in the year 1816. In his correspondence Jefferson explored the topic of republicanism, which he considered to be an unprecedented idea. "The introduction of this new principle of representative democracy has rendered useless almost everything written before on the structure of government," he observed. "The full experiment of a government democratical, but representative, was and is still reserved for us. The idea (taken, indeed, from the little specimen formerly existing in the English constitution, but now lost) has been carried by us, more or less, into all our legislative and executive departments; but it has not yet, by any of us, been pushed into all the ramifications of the system, so far as to leave no authority existing not responsible to the people; whose rights, however, to the exercise and fruits of their own industry, can never been protected against the selfishness of rulers not subject to their control at short periods." He added: "My most earnest wish is to see the republican element of popular control pushed to the maximum of its practicable exercise. I shall then believe that our government may be pure and perpetual."[27] Thus did Jefferson indicate his desire to fully implement the Real Whig notion of government founded, in all its branches, on popular will, with frequent (preferably annual) elections.

In a letter to Pierre Samuel Du Pont de Nemours, Jefferson explained that Americans were "constitutionally and conscientiously democrats," observing that under the system of self-government individuals "reserve to themselves personally the exercise of all rightful powers to which they are competent, and . . . delegate those to which they are not competent to deputies named, and removable for unfaithful conduct, by themselves immediately." This "proximate choice and power of removal," he added, "is the best security which experience has sanctioned for ensuring an honest conduct in the functionaries of society"—for preventing those in power from becoming wolves. He similarly wrote a few years earlier to another correspondent that "unless the mass [of the people] retains sufficient control over those intrusted with the powers of their government, these will be perverted to their own oppression, and to the perpetuation of wealth and power in the individuals and their families selected for the trust." He added, "Whether our Constitution has hit on the exact degree of control necessary, is yet under experiment."[28]

The "essence of a republic," Jefferson wrote Du Pont, consisted of "action by the citizens in person, in affairs within their reach and competence, and in all others by representatives, chosen immediately, and removable by themselves." Governments were "more or less republican in proportion as this principle enters more or less into their composition." In a letter to John Taylor, he used slightly different language that also stressed the elements of democracy and majoritarianism. Acknowledging that the term *republic* was "of very vague application, in every language"—"Witness the self-styled republics of Holland, Switzerland, Genoa, Venice, Poland"—he advanced his definition: "Were I to assign to this term a precise and definite idea, I would say, purely and simply, it means a government by its citizens in mass, acting directly and personally, according to rules established by the majority; and that every other government is more or less republican, in proportion as it has in its composition more or less of this ingredient of the direct action of the citizens." Noting that such a government was "restrained to very narrow limits of space and population," he doubted whether such a "pure republic" would be practicable beyond the extent of a New England township. "The first shade" from this pure republic "would be where the powers of the government, being divided, should be exercised each by representatives chosen either *pro hac vice,* or for such short terms as should render secure the duty of expressing the will of their constituents." This he considered "the nearest approach to a pure republic, which is practicable on a large scale of country or population." [29]

Jefferson then proceeded to examine the Virginia and the federal constitutions, noting that they exhibited various "shades of republicanism," again using direct popular control as the standard: "The further the departure from direct and constant control by the citizens, the less has the government of the ingredient of republicanism." First considering the Virginia Constitution, he observed that the "purest republican feature" was the House of Delegates, which was annually elected. The Senate was "equally so the first year, less the second, and so on"; and the governor, "still less, because not chosen by the people directly" but by the legislature. "The Judiciary," he said, was "seriously anti-republican, because for life"; and he condemned the "vicious constitution of our county courts," those "self-appointed, self-continued" institutions, comprised of justices of the peace "holding their authorities for life," "to whom the justice, the executive administration, the taxation, the police, the military appointments of the county, and nearly all our daily concerns are confided." [30]

Turning then to the federal Constitution, Jefferson observed to Taylor that the House of Representatives was "mainly republican" (no doubt because it was elected biennially) but the Senate "scarcely so at all, as not elected by the people directly, and so long secured even against those who do elect them." The executive was "more republican than the Senate, from its shorter term, its election by the people in *practice*, (for they vote for A only on an assurance that he will vote for B), and because, *in practice also*, a principle of rotation seems to be in a course of establishment." As for the federal judiciary, it was sufficient for him to observe that it was "independent of the nation, their coercion by impeachment being found nugatory"; hence, by his definition it was not republican at all. Summing up his analysis of both the Virginia and federal constitutions, he concluded, "If, then, the control of the people over the organs of their government be the measure of its republicanism, . . . it must be agreed that our governments have much less of republicanism than ought to have been expected; in other words, that the people have less regular control over their agents, than their rights and interests require."[31]

Jefferson voiced similar criticisms of the Virginia Constitution in more detail in his letter to Samuel Kercheval in July 1816. This letter is especially important because it contains an exposition of Jefferson's ideas regarding constitutional change, including a series of amendments to the Virginia Constitution that he desired "to secure self-government by the republicanism of our constitution, as well as by the spirit of the people." "The true foundation of republican government," as he defined it in this letter, "is the equal right of every citizen, in his person and property, and in their management." From this premise he derived what he referred to as the "mother principle, that 'governments are republican only in proportion as they embody the will of their people, and execute it.'" On this basis he criticized the inequality of representation in the Virginia legislature, as constituted by the 1776 ordinance of government; and he indicated that additional years of "experience and reflection" had "more and more confirmed" in his mind the importance of equal representation. Again he restated his definition: "A government is republican in proportion as every member composing it has his equal voice in the direction of its concerns (not indeed in person, which would be impracticable beyond the limits of a city, or small township, but) by representatives chosen by himself, and responsible to him at short periods." He suggested further, "Let us bring to the test of this canon every branch of" the constitution. It was by this standard that he condemned each "republican heresy" in the 1776 Virginia Constitution. Interestingly, he also specifically criticized the provision empowering the legislature alone to appoint certain officers of government. "Nomination to office is an executive function," he noted. "To give it to the legislature, as we do, is a violation of the principle of separation of powers."[32]

In these letters Jefferson expressed his criticisms of the Virginia and federal constitutions as insufficiently "republican" and suggested a more comprehensive and direct implementation of the principle of popular election and control in all branches of government (including the judiciary). He thus was articulating the principles of constitutionalism he identified before 1800 but now carried to their logical conclusion. What resulted was a constitutional theory which turned on the pure doctrine of the separation of powers, one in which checks and balances provided by one branch on the other offered protections that were negligible compared to the check provided by popular control. Of course, additional checks on the federal government were provided through the states: thus federalism also was a vital device of constitutionalism in Jefferson's theory of the federal Constitution.

Apart from these 1816 letters and other writings elaborating the tripartite doctrine, the best evidence of Jefferson's embrace of a virtually pure separation of powers theory is indirect. He enthusiastically read and recommended two works that quite clearly espoused the most radical version of separation of powers: the *Commentary and Review of Montesquieu's Spirit of Laws* by the French philosopher and *économiste* Antoine Louis Claude Destutt de Tracy and *An Inquiry into the Principles and Policy of the Government of the United States* by a fellow Republican, John Taylor of Caroline County, Virginia. Close examination of the ideas advanced in both of these works suggests the extent to which Jefferson's republican constitutionalism, by the second decade of the nineteenth century, had departed from the traditional balanced government model.

Jefferson's reaction to Montesquieu's *Spirit of the Laws* as a text on government changed over time, and his change in attitude may be traced through his own readings as well as through the various lists of recommended readings that he compiled for aspiring law students over the years. Jefferson's abstracts from the *Spirit of the Laws* in his legal commonplace book were culled from practically every book and chapter—although curiously omitting the discussion in book 11 of the English constitution and Montesquieu's theory of the separation of powers—and he devoted more pages to the Frenchman than to any other single writer. Yet as early as 1790, in a letter to his son-in-law Thomas Mann Randolph, he denounced the work as containing as many political "heresies" as truths. To William Duane in 1811 he confessed: "I had with the world, deemed Montesquieu's work of much merit; but saw in it, with every thinking man, so much of false principle and misapplied fact, as to render its value equivocal on the whole." To the same man, in the previous year, he had described the *Spirit of the Laws* as "a book of paradoxes," abounding in "inconsistencies, apocryphal facts and false inferences." He also had suggested the reason for his dislike: Montesquieu's "predilection for monarchy and English monarchy in particular, has done mischief everywhere, and here also, to a certain degree."[33]

Jefferson's disenchantment with Montesquieu likely began during his years in Paris, where reform-minded Frenchmen of the late 1780s divided into two hostile camps, one comprising those who from Montesquieu had come to admire the balanced constitution of England—the Anglomanes—and the other, comprising Turgot's followers, who spurned the English example and rallied to the slogan "one king, one nation, one house." It was this last group, the Americanistes, with whom Jefferson identified; and this debate over constitutional reform in France, and the use of British and American models, may have initiated the process of Jefferson's political estrangement from John Adams.[34] The Americanistes were drawn from the ranks of the Economistes, who disliked England's mercantilism as much as its constitution.

Shortly after his retirement from the presidency, Jefferson undertook the translation of a manuscript by the French philosopher and *économiste* Destutt de Tracy. He prevailed on his friend William Duane to publish it anonymously, and in due course Destutt de Tracy's *Commentary and Review of Montesquieu's Spirit of Laws* appeared in Philadelphia. Jefferson had an exalted opinion of the work, describing it as "the most profound and logical work" addressed to the present generation and predicting that it would reduce Montesquieu to his true value. Although he did not agree with Destutt de Tracy in everything, he wished to see the *Review* "in the hands of every American student, as the elementary and fundamental institute" of the science of government; and he included it as a basic text on government in the lists of recommended readings that he drew up in his later years.[35]

Destutt de Tracy refuted Montesquieu chapter by chapter. In the

Spirit of the Laws, Montesquieu had divided governments into three types, each with its own governing principle: republican, with either virtue (if a democratic republic) or moderation (if an aristocratic republic); monarchical, with honor; and despotic, with fear. Destutt de Tracy regarded Montesquieu's threefold classification of governments as "essentially erroneous" and instead divided all governments into two classes, "national" and "special," according to whether civil rights were common to all or were particular and unequal. Destutt de Tracy favored a particular form of general government, the "representative democracy," a form unknown in Montesquieu's time and one which rendered obsolete Montesquieu's injunction that republics must be small in physical territory, for representative government renders democracy "practicable for a long time and over a great extent of territory."[36]

Destutt de Tracy was especially critical of Montesquieu's concept of virtue, which he described as consisting in "voluntary privations, in self-denials," and characterized as "false and fluctuating," for "no human being is so constituted by nature." A representative government, he argued, "should . . . allow a free course to all inclinations which are not depraved, and to every kind of industry which is not incompatible with good order and morals." Such a government "tends to equality"; it "encourages talent, by all the members of society possessing an equal and unrestrained right to exercise their faculties; and it opens to all alike the roads to fortune and to honor." It is not necessary to "incommode" the people with sumptuary laws, which are "always an abuse of authority"; it is sufficient, he wrote, that "no efforts be made to impede men in their reasonable pursuits or natural inclinations," since a society is happily regulated where it is "happy from the absence of unnecessary regulation." Destutt de Tracy recognized certain kinds of luxury as pernicious but emphasized that "industry properly so called"—including manufactures "of utility and necessity"—is "without danger, and very advantageous."[37]

Critical of the other "economical scientists," Smith and Say, for their agrarianism—the "false idea of a sort of magical virtue attributed to the earth"—Destutt de Tracy defined production as simply the giving of greater utility, a definition which was "equally applicable to the farmer, manufacturer, and merchant." The source of national wealth lies in "the exercise of the human faculties," and in this he considered both "intellectual" as well as manual labor. Commerce he defined as exchange, and he regarded it "not only the foundation and basis of society" but also "the fabric itself" of society, "for society is nothing more than the continual exchange of mutual succours, which occasion the concurrence of the powers of all for the more effectual gratification of the wants of each." Commerce, far from being an evil, is "the author of all social good"; there is nothing immoral about industrious persons seeking "only rewards for their talents, by means of free agreements entered into with good faith and guaranteed by the laws." The industrious man "does more good to humanity, often even without knowing it, than the most humane idler, with all his zeal."[38] "All labor is productive which produces property greater in value than the amount of the expenses employed in procuring it." There is "a complete similitude" to the labor of the trader, farmer, and manufacturer: "The one is not more or less *essentially productive* than the other."[39]

As Joyce Appleby has noted, Destutt de Tracy's book and Jefferson's high regard for it indicate that Jefferson's mature opinion on matters of political economy was closer to the liberal than to the civic humanist style of thinking and therefore casts doubt on scholarly efforts to construe Jeffersonian Republicanism as an American version of the English Country party. At the very least, it indicates that by the 1810s Jefferson had departed from the simple agrarian views he held in the 1780s and had come to embrace market capitalism.[40]

It was in book 11 of Destutt de Tracy's treatise, "Of the Laws Which Establish Public Liberty in Relation to the Constitution," that he took to task Montesquieu's constitutionalism, first arguing that Montesquieu failed to solve the basic problem, that of identifying "the best means of distributing the power of society [or, rather, of government], so as to be most favorable to liberty," and then positing his own solution to this problem.[41]

Destutt de Tracy began by defining liberty as "nothing else than the power of executing the will, and accomplishing our desires," which he equated with happiness, the gratification of one's desires. From this basic premise he concluded that "the government under which the greatest liberty is enjoyed, whatever may be its form, is that which governs the best, for in it the greatest number of people are the happiest." It was not the form of government in itself that is important, he argued; rather, it was the result: "The only circumstance . . . which renders any one social organization preferable to another, is its being better adapted to render the members of society happy."[42]

Borrowing from Montesquieu the idea that each kind of government had its own unique "moving, or rather conservative principle," Destutt de Tracy concluded that "the *principle of government founded on the rights of man, is reason.*" He then outlined three "fundamental laws," or "fundamental principles," of "all governments truly rational." The first was that laws were "formed for the governed, not the governed for them," and that therefore "they only exist in virtue of the will of the majority of those governed, and should change when the will changes." From this first principle two corollaries followed: that no one should be forced to stay in a given society's territory who does not wish to live under its laws; and that no hereditary power be established, nor "any class constituted with exclusive privileges or honors, nor any class depressed or degraded to profit another." The second principle was that "there should never be a power in society which cannot be changed without violence, nor any such that when it is changed all must change with it." From this principle, he argued, follows the separation of executive, legislative, and judicial (or "conservative") powers. The third, and final, fundamental principle was that government must always "have in view the conservation of the independence of the nation, the liberty of its members, and such security for every individual as to supercede the idea of fear internal or external." This principle implied, among other things, the obligation of government not to interfere with citizens' religious opinions or "their right of declaring their sentiments upon any subject whatever."[43]

Destutt de Tracy was especially critical of Montesquieu's "prepossession in favor of English institutions and ideas," and particularly the "erroneous and indefensible" system of balanced powers. Montesquieu, he argued, overlooked his own basic observation that there are three kinds of public functions—"willing," or making, laws; executing laws; and judging laws—and that these three great functions, or even two of them, could not be united in the same person or persons "without the greatest danger to the rest of the citizens." Montesquieu's English bias, Destutt de Tracy maintained, led him in the first place to forget that the legislative, executive, and judicial functions are "properly only delegated trusts," for there is "by *right,* only one power in society, and that is the will of the nation or society, from which all authority flows." It also led Montesquieu to overlook the fact that in England "there exists really no more than *two* powers instead of three," that is, the legislative and executive, and that "these two powers, by uniting" (as king in Parliament), "are legally competent to the change of the public established laws, and even those which determine their relations and existence." Destutt de Tracy, in short, argued that Montesquieu ignored the fundamental attribute of English constitutionalism, parliamentary sovereignty.[44]

This oversight in turn led Montesquieu into the fundamental error of assuming that the English "really enjoy liberty" because of their form of government. Rather, Destutt de Tracy maintained, to the extent that the English people enjoy liberty, it originates in "certain received usages in their civil and criminal proceedings," not in positive laws; "liberty is not truly established by their political laws" at all. That is to say, England has not resolved "the great problem . . . of the distribution of the powers of society, so that neither of them may trespass on the authority of the other, or the limits assigned them by the general interests; and that it may always be easy to keep them within bounds, or to bring them back by peaceable and legal means." The honor of solving that problem, he further argued, ought to be claimed by the United States of America, "the constitution of which determines what should be done when the executive, or when the legislative, or when both together, go beyond their legitimate powers, or are in opposition to each other; and when it becomes necessary to change the constitutional act of a state, or of the confederation itself." [45]

Perhaps Jefferson had Destutt de Tracy's criticism of Montesquieu in mind when, in his 1816 letter to John Taylor, he ascribed the want in the American constitutions of republicanism, in the full sense he was advocating, "not to any want of republican dispositions in those who formed their constitutions, but to a submission of true principle to European authorities, to speculators on government, whose fears of the people have been inspired by the populace of their own great cities, and were unjustly entertained against the independent, the happy, and therefore orderly citizens of the United States." [46]

Although Destutt de Tracy's review of Montesquieu certainly affirmed Jefferson's republicanism, as well as his abhorrence of the English form of balanced government, it offered little in the way of a theory of constitutionalism which Jefferson could apply directly to the American constitutions. Despite the high praise that he bestowed on the American constitution, Destutt de Tracy outlined as his solution to the basic problem of government an idealized constitution which resembled the federal Constitution (or the typical American state constitution) only in its broadest outlines.[47] Indeed, the features of Destutt de Tracy's proposed constitution—and particularly his espousal of a plural executive—were the parts of the book with which Jefferson explicitly disagreed.

Much more relevant to Jefferson's theory of the federal Constitution was John Taylor's *Inquiry into the Principles and Policy of the Government of the United States*, first published in 1814, a book which particularly impressed Jefferson when he read it in 1816. Writing to Taylor, Jefferson said that he saw in it "much matter for profound reflection; much which should confirm our adhesion, in practice, to the good principles of our constitution, and fix our attention on what is yet to be made good." Putting his finger on the most significant aspect of Taylor's book, Jefferson added, "You have successfully and completely pulverized Mr. Adams' system of orders, and his opening the mantle of republicanism to every government of laws, whether consistent or not with natural right." He later wrote another correspondent that he was "indebted" to Taylor's *Inquiry* for "many valuable ideas, and for the correction of some errors of early opinion." [48] It is likely that Taylor's critique of Adams helped shape Jefferson's republican constitutionalism, particularly his adherence to the doctrine of separation of powers.

John Adams had written his three-volume *Defence of the Constitutions of Government of the United States of America* in 1787–88 in an effort to refute those Americanistes, and Turgot in particular, who were advocates of simple forms of government with unicameral legislatures, by demonstrating that the virtue of the American constitutions consisted in their resemblance to the complex form of the British balanced constitution. Although Adams's basic concern in the first volume of the *Defence* was the problem of aristocracy, by the time he reached the third volume, he was equally concerned with the problem of majority tyranny (no doubt in response to news of Shays's Rebellion). His solution to both problems—putting aristocrats in a separate legislative house, where, along with a strong executive, they could mutually check the power of the democratic house—struck many observers, among them Jefferson, as smacking too much of an admiration for monarchy. Indeed, Adams had argued that the American governments were, like that "most stupendous fabric of human invention," the English constitution, "monarchical republics." [49]

Taylor thought Adams's critique of Turgot, and therefore also his defense of the American constitutions, misdirected because in Taylor's view it was not the organization of the legislature but the moral tendencies that its legislation generated which determined whether the government was good or bad. Taylor's basic premise was that the "true value and real superiority" of American governmental policy consist in its "good moral principles." Taylor recognized that self-love is the dominant motive in man, and that from self-love come man's propensities toward both good and evil—the propensity to do good to oneself and the propensity to do evil to others for the sake of doing good to oneself. Government, said Taylor, was a "moral agent," actuated by good or evil moral qualities, corresponding to the principles upon which it is founded. Monarchy, aristocracy, and democracy are all forms of government founded in evil moral qualities; they tend to excite the propensity in man to injure others for one's own benefit.[50]

The English policy of mixed government, Taylor argued, did not correct this problem; indeed, by balancing the three orders against one another, it aroused jealousies between social classes and excited the evil qualities of avarice and ambition. Like that of so many other nations, the English policy was founded on "authority," defined by Taylor as the substitution of the understanding and honesty of others for one's own. In vesting government with virtually unlimited powers, in order to control the passions that stimulate individuals to injure each other, this policy tended to stimulate further wrongdoing, by the governors themselves—or the parties aspiring to become governors.[51]

Like Jefferson, Taylor attributed the prosperity and good order of America to the absence of jealous and rival orders, and thus the lack of any need to balance them. The "true legal policy of the United States," according to Taylor, does not legislate virtue and vice, knowledge and ignorance, or wealth and poverty; rather, it allows each man, guided by his own self-interest, to acquire the fruits of his own labor. "The basis of our policy," said Taylor, "is the constancy of nature in her moral as well as her physical operations." Knowing that self-love is the dominant motive in man, the American policy relied not on force or fraud but on reason; it sought not so much to balance but to reduce political power, through the elective principle and representation and by the separation of powers at various levels into various branches. Thus, "by balancing man with man, and by avoiding the artificial combinations of exclusive privileges, no individual of these equipoised millions, would be incited by a probability of success, to assail the rest."[52]

Adams's basic error, according to Taylor, was to consider the American division of powers the same as his, or the English, balance of orders, when the two principles are really "opposite and inimical." He thus summed up the basic difference between Adams and the Jeffersonians: "Our policy divides power, and unites the nation in one interest; Mr. Adams's divides a nation into several interests, and unites power." Having thus distinguished the American policy as the division, rather than the balancing, of power, Taylor then proceeded to analyze the Constitution of the United States, which he criticized for having mixed in, with the "good moral principles" of division of powers, certain "evil moral principles" or "elements of force or fraud" associated with the theory of balance. Taylor followed the separation of powers to its logical conclusion and accordingly rejected the controlling links and balances between the branches of government that were an essential part of the balanced government model, which had been incorporated into the Constitution. The Constitution, rather, he argued, should bestow upon each officer and department only that portion of power needed to fulfill his or its proper function and to ensure the dependence of all of them upon the nation. The Constitution failed to observe this principle in several respects, Taylor argued, among them, the power of the executive. He attacked the granting of "kingly powers" to the president, in particular the patronage power, military and diplomatic powers, and the power to appoint judges.[53]

Taylor's attack upon judicial review was particularly bitter. "The people were supposed to be the only source for altering the constitution, according to our policy; but it is exposed to a power of construction, not responsible to the people. Legislative, executive and judicial powers shall be separate and distinct, yet the judges can abolish or make law by precedent," Taylor observed. As a substitute for giving to federal judges the exclusive right of declaring law void, he offered two alternative solutions to the problem of controlling the exercise of legislative power. One was to retain judicial review—that is, to continue to permit the judges to declare laws unconstitutional—but to correspondingly "exalt" the judicial power into the status of a branch of government "which would be conformable to our principle of division": to make the judiciary elective and so responsible to the people.

The other solution, the one Taylor regarded as the best way to check Congress, was the federal system of government: "the mutual right of the general and state governments to examine and controvert before the publick each others' proceedings." Thus, as M. J. C. Vile has observed, summing up Taylor's system, the separation of powers and federalism became interlocking elements in a thoroughgoing philosophy of the division of power. Power is divided between government and people, between state and federal governments, and, within each government, between the legislative, executive, and judicial branches. Each element of this divided system of government was to be sole judge of the rightness of its own actions, subject to the overriding power of the people.[54]

Except perhaps to the extent that Taylor pushed to its logical extreme the doctrine of separation of powers—and particularly in applying it against the presidency and judicial review—the *Inquiry* probably did not introduce Jefferson to significant new ideas. Taylor's book, however, undoubtedly helped reinforce, clarify, and synthesize ideas that Jefferson had been formulating in his own mind in the four decades since 1776. Vile is probably right in arguing that "the coherence of Jefferson's views in and after 1816 must surely be due, in part at least, to the major work of John Taylor."[55] The system of division of powers that Taylor expounded is useful to understanding Jefferson's mature theory of the Constitution, however, primarily because it so well explains the constitutional theory that Jefferson had developed and articulated as his own.

6

Certain Fences against Wrong

The Federal Constitution
and the Bill of Rights

I sincerely rejoice at the acceptance of the new constitution by nine States," Jefferson wrote Madison on the last day of July, 1788. "It is a good canvas, on which some strokes only want retouching." Jefferson focused on two defects that needed "retouching." To one, the perpetual reeligibility of the president for election, he grudgingly acquiesced despite his firm belief that it would lead to monarchy. Amendment of the Constitution to limit presidential terms was necessary, Jefferson urged, because "if it does not take place erelong, it assuredly never will. The natural progress of things is for liberty to yeild and government to gain ground."[1]

Recognition of this tendency as the "natural progress of things" probably convinced Jefferson, as it did most Antifederalists, that the more urgent matter was the absence of a bill of rights, his other major objection to the proposed Constitution. "A bill of rights," he urged Madison, "is what the people are entitled to against every government on earth, general or particular, and what no just government should refuse, or rest on inference." Madison had to be convinced, since he shared with Alexander Hamilton, James Wilson, and others the view—which had dominated at the Philadelphia convention—that

a bill of rights was unnecessary because the federal government established by the Constitution was to be a government of strictly limited
powers. Whether or not Jefferson actually convinced Madison on the
merits, the addition of a bill of rights became a political necessity since
its absence was the most important single objection to the Constitution. To the extent that his arguments on behalf of a bill of rights were
effective in persuading Madison of the need to amend the Constitution, Jefferson should share credit for the addition of the first ten
amendments to the Constitution.[2]

This chapter examines Jefferson's views regarding the Bill of Rights.
The first section focuses on Jefferson's correspondence with Madison
between October 1787 and March 1789, a critical seventeen-month
period during which Jefferson's arguments on behalf of a federal bill
of rights helped to overcome Madison's skepticism of bills of rights
as mere "parchment barriers." This section of the chapter also discusses the types of rights that Jefferson, in his correspondence with
Madison and others, suggested for inclusion in the Bill of Rights. He
classified constitutional rights generally into two categories: natural
rights and civil rights, or "fences against wrong." The last two sections of the chapter are devoted, respectively, to the most important
examples of these two types of rights: religious freedom and freedom
of the press. Jefferson's early views are compared to his later views—
including the actions he took (or refrained from taking) during his
presidency—in an effort to better explain his understanding of these
First Amendment rights.

"What the People Are Entitled To against Every
Government": Jefferson's Case for the Bill of Rights

The omission of a bill of rights from the new federal Constitution
was not accidental; as Leonard Levy has noted, it was "a deliberate
act of the Constitutional Convention." Roger Sherman expressed the
framers' theory most succinctly when he stated on the floor of the
Convention that a bill of rights "is unnecessary."[3] James Wilson, Alexander Hamilton, and other Federalists elaborated the theory during
the struggle for ratification and argued further that the addition of a
bill of rights to the Constitution would be "dangerous."

The basic argument was set forth by Wilson in a speech delivered in
Philadelphia on 6 October 1787 and soon printed and widely distrib-

uted—so widely that a copy eventually reached Jefferson in Paris. The people of the states, Wilson noted, had vested in their governments all the powers and rights "which they did not in explicit terms reserve," but the case was different as to the federal government, whose authority rested on positive grants of power expressed in the Constitution. For the federal government, "the reverse of the proposition prevails, and everything which is not given, is reserved" to the people or to the states. Rejecting Antifederalist charges that specific provisions were necessary to protect freedom of the press and religious freedom, Wilson argued that since the federal government was not granted power over such liberties, a formal declaration would have been "merely nugatory." A formal declaration of rights would be not only "absurd" but also harmful, he further argued; the attempt to delineate limits on the extent of powers could "imply" that some degree of power had been granted: "A bill of rights annexed to a constitution is an enumeration of the powers reserved. If we attempt an enumeration, everything that is not enumerated is presumed to be given. The consequence is, that an imperfect enumeration would throw all implied powers into the scale of the government; and the rights of the people would be rendered incomplete."[4]

Hamilton further developed these arguments in *Federalist* No. 84, first published in May 1788. Observing that bills of rights were, in their English origin, "stipulations between kings and their subjects" that reserved "rights not surrendered to the prince"—such as the Magna Carta and the Bill of Rights of 1689—he argued that they had "no application" to constitutions founded upon the power of the people. Further, he noted, "a minute detail of particular rights is certainly far less applicable" to the proposed federal Constitution, "which is merely intended to regulate the general political interests of the nation," than it would be to the state constitutions, which concern "the regulation of every species of personal and private concerns." A bill of rights, therefore, was "unnecessary" in the federal Constitution; furthermore, adding a bill of rights "would even be dangerous": "It would contain various exceptions to powers not granted; and, on this very account, would afford a colorable pretext to claim more than were granted. For why declare that things shall not be done which there is no power to do? Why, for instance, should it be said that the liberty of the press shall not be restrained, when no power is given by which restrictions may be imposed?" Even if the enumeration of specific rights did not confer a regulating power, it could "furnish, to men disposed to usurp, a plausible pretence for claiming that power." Hamilton finally noted that many provisions protecting individual rights were in the body of the Constitution—among them the Article I, section 9, provisions protecting the writ of habeas corpus and prohibiting bills of attainder, ex post facto laws, and titles of nobility and the Article III, section 2, provisions assuring trial by jury in criminal cases and defining narrowly the crime of treason. He concluded therefore "that the Constitution is itself, in every rational sense, and to every useful purpose, A BILL OF RIGHTS."[5]

Wilson's and Hamilton's arguments failed to persuade the Antifederalists, who viewed with alarm the national government that would be established under the Constitution: a government which not only would possess more powers than did the Confederation government but, by operating directly on individuals, would also exercise those powers more effectively. The "necessary and proper" clause particularly provoked concern. Advocates of a bill of rights saw that clause as the source of undefined and unlimited powers that would accrue to the national government in the absence of a bill of rights. The Federalist arguments that a bill of rights was unnecessary in the federal Constitution, or even that it would be "dangerous," did not allay this fear.

The difficult question that so dominated the debate over the Constitution in America was taken up, as Ralph Ketcham has put it, "less polemically and more subtly," in Jefferson's correspondence with Madison.[6] In his exchange of ideas with Madison on this vitally important question, Jefferson presented the case for the addition of a bill of rights in broad terms that revealed his understanding of the nature of the new federal Constitution.

In a long letter of 24 October 1787 transmitting the proposed Constitution to Jefferson in Paris, Madison sought to summarize the deliberations of the convention. Among other topics, Madison discoursed on one which particularly concerned him: the difficult problem of protecting the rights of a minority in the face of the power of a potentially tyrannical majority. "The great desideratum in Government," he observed, "is, so to modify the sovereignty as that it may be sufficiently neutral between different parts of the Society to controul one part from invading the rights of another, and at the same time sufficiently controuled itself, from setting up an interest adverse to that of the entire Society." Madison anticipated the argument he would make in *Federalist* No. 10: "If then there must be different interests and parties in Society; and a majority when united by common interest or passion can not be restrained from oppressing the minority, what remedy can be found in a republican Government, where the majority must ultimately decide, but that of giving such an extent to its sphere, that no common interest or passion will be likely to unite a majority of the whole number in an unjust pursuit." Thus, he observed, the solution to the problem of majority tyranny in a republic was to broaden the "sphere" of government. In the "extended Republic of the United States," he optimistically predicted, "the General Government would hold a pretty even balance between the parties of particular States, and be at the same time sufficiently restrained by its dependence on the community, from betraying its general interests."[7]

Madison did not mention a bill of rights. In part, this was because his basic concern was "to secure individuals against encroachments on their rights" by the states. It was the injustice and mutability of state laws, he maintained, that brought about the Constitutional Convention. But Madison recognized the concern over the powers to be exercised by the new national government. "It may be asked how private rights will be more secure under the guardianship of the General Government than under the State Governments, since they are both founded on the republican principle which refers the ultimate decision to the will of the majority," he conceded. Madison's response to this concern, however, focused wholly upon what he conceived to be the crucial distinction between the states and the national government, "the extent within which they will operate." A "full discussion" of this point, such as he would endeavor to provide in *Federalist* No. 10, would at once "unfold the true principles of Republican Government" and address the problem of majority tyranny.[8]

Jefferson replied at once, in his letter of 20 December, with his impressions of the new Constitution, both positive and negative. Only in a postscript did he reply to Madison's point about the mutability of state laws; there he agreed that "the instability of our laws is really an immense evil," and he suggested as a solution adding to the state constitution certain procedural safeguards—a one-year delay between the engrossing and the passing of a bill or a two-thirds vote rather than a simple majority for passage. Jefferson did not expressly respond to Madison's long discourse on the tyranny of majorities at the state level. He did note, as he similarly observed in other correspondence at this time, that he thought that "the late rebellion in Massachusetts has given more alarm than I think it should have done," and that in his view such insurrections could not be prevented by "any degree of power in the hands of government." He stressed his hope that "the education of the common people will be attended to," noting that he was "convinced that on their good sense we may rely with the most security for the preservation of a due degree of liberty." It was to the people, then, and not to a more effective national government, that Jefferson pointed in suggesting the solution to the problem identified by Madison. "I own I am not a friend to a very energetic government. It is always oppressive," he observed.[9]

Jefferson emphasized the two features of the proposed Constitution that he most disliked. As to the omission of a bill of rights, he clearly indicated that he had read James Wilson's speech of 6 October and was not persuaded by the argument. "To say, as Mr. Wilson does that a bill of rights was not necessary because all is reserved in the case of the general government which is not given, while in the particular ones all is given which is not reserved, might do for the Audience to whom it was addressed, but is surely gratis dictum, opposed by strong inferences from the body of the instrument, as well as from the omission of the clause of our present confederation which had declared that in express terms." Nor was Jefferson sympathetic to the argument that bills of rights were somehow inappropriate for republican governments: "A bill of rights is what the people are entitled to against every government on earth, general or particular, and what no just government should refuse, or rest on inference." Mentioning particular rights, he urged that they be provided for "clearly and without the aid of sophisms," in a bill of rights.[10]

Madison did not respond to this letter for nearly ten months. During that period, when he was heavily engaged in the ratification struggle, he moved slowly and quite reluctantly toward a willingness to add a bill of rights to the Constitution after its ratification. Although as late as March 1788 he wrote to one correspondent of his still "powerful reasons . . . against the adoption of a Bill of Rights," by the time the Virginia ratifying convention met in June 1788 Madison had agreed to support a bill of rights. The influence of the Baptist preacher John Leland has been cited to explain Madison's acceptance of a bill of rights; but, as one scholar has noted, his statements at the convention indicated that "Madison thought the diversity spawned by free government a surer protection for natural rights than mere statement of them on a piece of paper." [11]

In the fall Madison received another letter, dated 31 July, in which Jefferson continued to insist on the addition of a bill of rights, referring to the "general voice from North to South" that called for it. Sensing Madison's qualms about a bill of rights, Jefferson stressed that "the few cases wherein these things may do evil, cannot be weighed against the multitude wherein the want of them will do evil." He concluded with his hope that "a bill of rights will be formed to guard the people against the federal government, as they are already guarded against their state governments in most instances." [12]

When Madison finally responded in October 1788 to Jefferson's letters calling for a bill of rights, he was candid about his position. Summarizing the debate in America, he observed that some sought "further guards to public liberty and individual rights . . . from the most honorable and patriotic motives," but many others continued to think the addition of a bill of rights "unnecessary . . . and misplaced in such a Constitution." Although Madison now disassociated himself from the latter view—writing, "My own opinion has always been in favor of a bill of rights; provided it be so framed as not to imply powers not meant to be included in the enumeration"—he admitted that he still did not regard "the omission a material defect." He said he supported a bill of rights, supposing it might be "of some use, and if properly executed could not be of disservice," but he had not "viewed it in a very important light" for four reasons. First, he agreed somewhat, "though not in the extent argued by Mr. Wilson," that rights were reserved by the manner in which federal powers are granted. Second, he feared that some essential rights, especially religious freedom, might somehow be limited by the language used to state them. Third, he suggested that the limited powers of the federal government and the "jealousy" of the state governments would uniquely "afford a security" against infringements by federal authority. Fourth, and finally, he argued that "experience proves the inefficacy of a bill of rights on those occasions when its controul is most needed." [13]

On this last point, the most important of the four, Madison expounded at length. Pointing particularly to Virginia's experience with the establishment of religion, Madison noted that "repeated violations of these parchment barriers have been committed by overbearing majorities in every State." "Wherever the real power in a Government lies, there is the danger of oppression," he observed. "In our Governments the real power lies in the majority of the Community, and the invasion of private rights is *chiefly* to be apprehended, not from acts of Government contrary to the sense of the constituents, but from acts in which the Government is the mere instrument of the major number of the constituents." Madison emphasized, "This is a truth of great importance, but not yet sufficiently attended to," and suggested to Jefferson that it "is probably more strongly impressed on my mind . . . than on yours which has contemplated abuses of power issuing from a very different quarter." A bill of rights would be a useful, even a necessary, check against abuses of power in a monarchy; but such a "solemn charter of popular rights" would not be effectual against a tyrannical majority in a popular government.[14]

Madison did not yet foresee that judicial review, the authority of the courts to declare statutes (however popular) unconstitutional, could become the most important use for a bill of rights in a popular government and indeed the means whereby individual rights could be secured against the tyranny of the majority. At this time he saw only two uses for a bill of rights that would recommend "the precaution," although in a popular government it was, as he maintained, "less essential than in other Governments." One was that the "political truths" declared in such a bill of rights would "acquire by degrees the character of fundamental maxims of free Government" and thus "incorporated with the national sentiment" could exert a subtle force to "counteract the impulses of interest and passion." The other was that on the few occasions where oppression may arise not from the interested majorities of the people but from the government, a bill of rights would be "a good ground for an appeal to the sense of the community" and thus would function as it would against tyranny in a monarchy. Although Madison saw "no tendency in our governments to danger on that side," he admitted that it would be prudent to guard against it, "especially when the precaution can do no injury."[15]

Presumably Madison already had in mind the inclusion of an article similar to the Ninth Amendment in the Bill of Rights, as finally ratified, which would—at least in theory—guard against the dangers of enumerating rights.[16] Although he recognized difficulties in phraseology—he warned against "absolute" statements of certain rights, such as habeas corpus, which might need to be overruled in emergencies—Madison evidently did not see a bill of rights as "dangerous," in the sense that Wilson and Hamilton argued it could be, but only as unnecessary.[17] Again, to Madison it was the "extended sphere" of the federal government alone that would provide the most effectual guard against oppression and the invasion of rights.

Replying five months later, Jefferson wrote that he was happy that Madison on the whole now favored a bill of rights, and he sought more fully to bring him around by answering each of the four "objections" Madison had raised.[18]

To the first argument, that rights were reserved by the manner in which the federal powers were granted, Jefferson agreed that a constitution could "be so formed as to need no declaration of rights," and he noted that he had endeavored to draft his 1783 proposed constitution for Virginia "to reach all the great objects of public liberty, and did not mean to add a declaration of rights." But, he emphasized, in a constitution like the new federal Constitution, "which leaves some precious articles unnoticed, and raises some implications against others," a declaration of rights "becomes necessary, by way of supplement." Unlike Wilson and Hamilton, Jefferson saw no essential difference between the federal Constitution and the various state constitutions. He maintained that the federal Constitution "forms us into one state as to certain objects, and gives us a legislative and executive body for these objects" and "should therefore guard us against their abuses of power within the field submitted to them."

Second, to Madison's fear that a positive declaration of some essential rights might not have "the requisite latitude," Jefferson replied succinctly: "Half a loaf is better than no bread. If we cannot secure all our rights, let us secure what we can."

Third, to the argument that the "jealousy" of the state governments would afford sufficient protection for rights, Jefferson answered that such jealousy was a "precious reliance," but that the state governments were "only agents" and "must have principles furnished whereon to found their objections." A bill of rights, he argued, would be "the text whereby they will try all the acts of the federal government." He added that it was "necessary to the federal government also," for "by the same text they may try the opposition of the subordinate governments."

Finally, to Madison's fourth argument, that "experience proves the inefficacy of a bill of rights," Jefferson did not agree. He observed that "tho it is not absolutely efficacious under all circumstances, it is of great potency always, and rarely inefficacious." A bill of rights might occasion "inconveniences" because it may "cramp government in it's useful exertions," but these would be "short-lived, moderate, and reparable" evils. The inconveniences of the want of a bill of rights, however, would be "permanent, afflicting, and irreparable" and "in constant progression from bad to worse."

Jefferson agreed with Madison's emphasis upon the legislature as the branch of government from which tyranny would most likely ensue, and he corrected Madison's misimpression. "The executive in our governments is not the sole, it is scarcely the principal object of my jealousy. The tyranny of the legislatures is the most formidable dread at present, and will be for long years." Believing that Americans were steeped in republicanism and that "apostacy from that to royalism is unprecedented and impossible," Jefferson downplayed his fears of monarchy, at least for the time being. The tyranny of the executive "will come in it's turn," he predicted, "but it will be at a remote period."

Jefferson made a further argument to Madison on behalf of a bill of rights which deserves particular mention. An argument "which has great weight with me," he wrote, was "the legal check which it puts into the hands of the judiciary." Noting that the judiciary "is a body, which if rendered independent, and kept strictly to their own department merits great confidence for their learning and integrity," he pointed to "Wythe, Blair, and Pendleton," some of Virginia's distinguished jurists, and asked, "What degree of confidence would be too much for a body composed of such men?" This argument apparently quite impressed Madison, who alluded to it in the debates in Congress over the proposed bill of rights, predicting that "independent tribunals of justice will consider themselves in a peculiar manner the guardians of those rights" stipulated by the declaration.[19]

Jefferson concluded his case for a bill of rights by acknowledging what he knew had been an important consideration in Madison's skepticism, that some Antifederalists were using the cry for a bill of rights as a lever either to prevent ratification or to include among the proposed amendments restraints on federal powers. Jefferson wrote that he hoped that the addition of a bill of rights "will be done in that way which will not endanger the whole frame of government, or any essential part of it." Still, he emphasized, it should be added. "The

Declaration of rights is like all other human blessings alloyed with some inconveniences, and not accomplishing fully it's object. But the good in this case vastly outweighs the evil." [20]

In his correspondence with Madison and others, Jefferson clearly had in mind certain rights that needed protection. His letter to Madison of 20 December 1787 urged that a bill of rights should expressly guarantee "freedom of religion, freedom of the press, protection against standing armies, restriction against monopolies, the eternal and unremitting force of the habeas corpus laws, and trials by jury in all matters of fact triable by the laws of the land and not by the law of Nations." [21] He listed the same six rights—jury trial in civil cases, habeas corpus, prohibition against standing armies, freedom of the press, religious freedom, and "freedom of commerce"—in his correspondence during the winter of 1787–88 and in his letter to Madison of 31 July 1788. [22] In a later letter, commenting on a draft of proposed amendments which Madison had sent him, Jefferson suggested changes in the articles dealing with freedom of the press, juries, habeas corpus, monopolies, and standing armies—again indicating that these five rights, as well as religious freedom, were the matters that most concerned him. [23]

Jefferson did not need to explain fully to his close friend Madison his reasons for wanting to protect these particular rights. A fuller explanation for the bill of rights he was proposing, and of the theoretical basis for this mode of protecting individual rights, appeared in letters which he wrote to two other, perhaps more skeptical, correspondents in March 1789 and December 1790.

In the earlier letter, written to David Humphreys, Jefferson explained why he considered it a "defect" in the Constitution that "important rights" were not "explicitly secured by a supplementary declaration." His basic reason was grounded in his Whig distrust of governmental power and related particularly to his observation in 1788 that the "natural progress of things" was for "liberty to yeild and government to gain ground." A declaration of rights, "as a supplement to the constitution where that is silent," was needed to secure certain kinds of rights. [24]

Jefferson described three classes of rights. First, there are "rights which it is useless to surrender to the government, and which governments have yet always been fond to invade"; these were "the rights of thinking, and publishing our thoughts by speaking or writing;

the right of free commerce; the right of personal freedom." Second, there are "instruments for administering the government, so peculiarly trust-worthy, that we should never leave the legislature at liberty to change them." These included "trials by the people themselves, that is to say, by jury," which the new Constitution failed to secure fully in the judicial department. Finally, there are "instruments so dangerous to the rights of the nation, and which place them so totally at the mercy of their governors, that those governors, whether legislative or executive, should be restrained from keeping such instruments on foot, but in well-defined cases"; such an instrument was a standing army. Thus Jefferson revealed the reasoning underlying his choice of the six articles he had earlier proposed for inclusion in the federal declaration of rights.

To Noah Webster in December 1790 Jefferson gave a slightly different explanation which even more explicitly revealed his understanding of the nature of these rights. He began with what he characterized as the "universal and almost uncontroverted position" that "the purposes of society do not require a surrender of all our rights to our ordinary governors: that there are certain portions of right not necessary to enable them to carry on an effective government, and which experience has nevertheless proved they will be constantly incroaching on, if submitted to them." As an example of one of these "unceded portions of right," he cited freedom of religion. Jefferson then observed that there were also "certain fences which experience has proved peculiarly efficacious against wrong, and rarely obstructive of right, which yet the governing powers have ever shown a disposition to weaken and remove." As examples of such "fences against wrong" he cited trial by jury, habeas corpus laws, and a free press. Both categories of rights, he instructed Webster, were "delineated . . . in instruments called declarations of rights and constitutions" and were adopted by conventions that the people "appointed for the express purpose of reserving these rights, and of delegating others to their ordinary legislative, executive and judiciary bodies." Thus the declaration of rights, like the constitution establishing the frame of government, is "fixed and unalterable" by the ordinary legislature; and "none of the reserved rights can be touched without resorting to the people to appoint another convention for the express purpose of permitting it."[25]

Jefferson's letters to Madison, to Humphreys, and especially to

Webster show that his arguments for a bill of rights emerged from his general social theory and particularly from his understanding of natural rights theory. In his advocacy of a federal bill of rights, he in effect transformed the traditional Anglo-American view of bills of rights—documents that enumerated, for greater protection, rights created by tradition or some other "higher law" basis—to a view compatible with Real Whig and Enlightenment theories. The federal Bill of Rights, like the comparable declarations of rights found in state constitutions, was meant by Jefferson to more effectually secure against the encroachments of governmental power both reserved "natural rights," in the sense of rights that inhere in individuals despite the institution of government, and "fences," or means of protecting natural rights.

Furthermore, as Adrienne Koch has observed, Jefferson's 1790 letter to Webster shows a further development of his natural rights theory, by recognizing the distinction between reserved natural rights and acquired ones, or "fences." Jefferson placed both "unceded portions of right" and "fences against wrong" in written instruments and made no distinction between declarations of rights and constitutions; he regarded both as instruments for safeguarding the rights not surrendered by the sovereign people to their governors. In this way, every individual's claim to rights is made, as Koch noted, "a real privilege and a sturdy fence." "Only the owners of fences," she further observes, "can arrange for their removal." The compelling thought here, as elsewhere in Jefferson's constitutionalism, is distrust of power.[26]

The Bill of Rights, as finally adopted and ratified, differed significantly from the federal bill of rights that Jefferson had proposed. The Seventh Amendment preserves the right of trial by jury in civil suits, but far less comprehensively than Jefferson had proposed. There are no provisions expressly concerning standing armies or the writ of habeas corpus, but it may be argued that the provisions concerning the people's right to keep and bear arms in the Second Amendment, the quartering of troops in the Third Amendment, and "due process" in the Fifth Amendment were inspired by ideas similar to Jefferson's. Monopolies are not mentioned at all in the first eight amendments. Of Jefferson's six articles, then, only two—one of them an "unceded portion of right" and the other a "fence against wrong," according to the distinction he raised in the letter to Webster—were included in the Bill of Rights. These were, respectively, the religious freedom clause and the free press clause of the First Amendment. Because of Jefferson's special regard for the freedoms protected by them and because of his image as a champion of freedom of opinion and expression generally, both rights deserve closer examination.

"A Wall of Separation Between Church and State": Jefferson and Religious Freedom

Jefferson was a remarkably consistent and zealous defender of religious freedom. Even Leonard Levy, the scholar who has been most critical of Jefferson's record in civil liberties matters—and who has labored hard to portray Jefferson's "dark side"—concedes that his "record on religious liberty was really quite exceptional" for its consistency in adherence to "profoundly libertarian" values.[27] The extent to which Jefferson valued freedom of religion and took pride in his endeavors in furtherance of that cause is illustrated by the fact that his authorship of the Virginia Statute for Religious Freedom was one of only three achievements for which he wanted to be remembered in his epitaph.[28]

The constitution that Jefferson proposed for Virginia in 1776 included the provision, "All persons shall have full and free liberty of religious opinion; nor shall any be compelled to frequent or maintain any religious institution."[29] Thus Jefferson sought to protect, in the terminology of modern constitutional law, both the "free exercise" of religion and freedom from an "establishment" of religion. Because Jefferson's draft arrived too late for serious consideration, the convention instead adopted James Madison's language providing that "all men are equally entitled to the free exercise of religion, according to the dictates of conscience" but rejected Madison's additional proposal that would have ended the state's Anglican establishment. Continued pressure by evangelical groups, primarily the Presbyterians and Baptists, resulted in further legislative action to relieve dissenters, but the General Assembly refrained from comprehensive action that would decisively and explicitly separate church and state.[30]

As a member of the Committee on Religion in the Virginia legislature, Jefferson found himself in the thick of political battle, which he later described as one of "the severest contests in which I have ever been engaged." Late in 1776 he drafted a series of notes relating to the disestablishment of the Church of England, including a set of proposed resolutions.[31] Included were extensive notes on

Locke and Shaftesbury. Those on Locke are particularly interesting, for they show Jefferson's awareness of the principles upon which Locke's theory of toleration rested and thus suggest an important source of Jefferson's own principles. Some of these relate to the nature of religion itself, stressing the importance of individual volition: "No man has *power* to let another prescribe his faith. . . . The life and essence of religion consists in the internal persuasion or belief of the mind." Other notes concern the nature of government and stress that religious conformity does not lie within the sphere of objects of legal compulsion, properly considered: "The care of every man's soul belongs to himself. . . . Laws provide against injury from others; but not from ourselves. . . . I cannot be saved by a *worship* I disbelieve and abhor."

The notes, moreover, indicate that Jefferson went further than Locke, who in advocating religious toleration had drawn the line at Catholics, atheists, and others whose opinions he viewed as subversive of civil authority. "Locke denies toleration to those who entertain opinions contrary to those moral rules necessary for the preservation of society," he observed, adding parenthetically, "It was a great thing to go so far . . . but where he stopped short, we may go on." These notes indicate that Jefferson had in mind the widest possible latitude for religious freedom, extending it not only to all Christians, whether Catholic or Protestant, but also to Jews, "Mahamedans," "Pagans," and atheists.[32]

Jefferson's ideas crystallized into his bill for establishing religious freedom, which he drafted in 1777 early in his work as a revisor of the Virginia laws. He later reflected that he had drawn the document "in all the latitude of reason and right," and that despite "some mutilations in the preamble" as enacted, it proved "its protection of opinion was meant to be universal."[33] The first paragraph consisted of a long preamble—over three times longer than the other two paragraphs of the bill combined—stating in passionate terms the principles upon which Jefferson based his understanding of the broad scope of religious freedom.

Freedom of opinion, he maintained, was a natural right. Like Locke's, Jefferson's argument turned on observations about the nature of religion as well as the proper role of government. The bill began by recognizing that God "created the mind free" and that therefore "all attempts to influence it by temporal punishments, or burthens, or by civil incapacitations, tend only to beget habits of hypocrisy and meanness, and are a departure from the plan of the holy author of our religion," who chose "[to extend it by its influence on reason alone]." It deplored the "impious presumption" of legislators and rulers, both civil and ecclesiastical, who "have assumed dominion over the faith of others, setting up their own opinions and modes of thinking as the only true and infallible, and as such endeavoring to impose them on others." This, it stated, "hath established and maintained false religions over the greatest part of the world and through all time." Religious tests for public office were not only violations of natural right but also a corruption of religion itself, "by bribing, with a monopoly of worldly honours and emoluments, those who will externally profess and conform to it." Other forms of religious establishment were equally condemned. The bill declared that to compel a man to furnish contributions of money for the propagation of opinions that he disbelieves and abhors was "sinful and tyrannical," and moreover that to force him to support teachers of even his own "religious persuasion" was to deprive him of that "comfortable liberty" of giving his contributions to whomever he considers most fit.[34]

Jefferson went beyond Locke, however, in separating more completely religious opinion from the proper concerns of government. "The opinions of men are not the object of civil government, nor under its jurisdiction," Jefferson's text declared. Although the legislature struck out this broad general statement, it retained his argument that "to suffer the civil magistrate to intrude his powers into the field of opinion and to restrain the profession or propagation of principles on the supposition of their ill tendency is a dangerous fallacy, which at once destroys all religious liberty, because he being of course judge of that tendency will make his opinions the rule of judgment, and approve or condemn the sentiments of others only as they shall square with or differ from his own." Accordingly, the preamble rejected the notion that the supposed bad "tendency" of certain opinions justified governmental action and instead made the difference between opinions and actions the crucial distinction. "It is time enough for the rightful purposes of civil government for its officers to interfere when principles break out into overt acts against peace and good order," the preamble noted, thus establishing a standard which would later become important in constitutional law.[35]

The ideas justifying religious freedom in the preamble of Jefferson's bill to a great extent reflected his own religious views. Although his political enemies labeled Jefferson an atheist, his religion may be best described as deism: the God in which he professed belief was Nature's God, the Creator to which he referred in the Declaration of Independence, the God of the Enlightenment.[36] He considered himself a true "Christian," but this was in no accepted theological sense. It was to moral philosophy, rather than theology, that Jefferson referred when he described himself as "a disciple of the doctrines of Jesus," "sincerely attached to his doctrines" of benevolence and ascribing to him "every *human* excellence . . . believing that he never claimed any other." Jefferson took religion seriously and later in life entered upon serious, systematic religious studies.[37] But, as he frequently maintained, he regarded religion as a wholly personal, or private, matter; and since he maintained that government should be concerned with conduct alone, the religious opinions of others did not concern him as a statesman.[38]

Following the long preamble, the heart of the bill was contained in the second paragraph, the enacting clause, which provided that "no man shall be compelled to frequent or support any religious worship, place, or ministry whatsoever, nor shall be enforced, restrained, molested, or burthened in his body or goods, nor shall otherwise suffer, on account of his religious opinions or belief; but that all men shall be free to profess, and by argument to maintain, their opinions in matters of religion, and that the same shall in no wise diminish, enlarge, or affect their civil capabilities." Thus Jefferson sought to erect, as he would later put it, "a wall of separation between Church and State."

This remarkably comprehensive definition of religious freedom was followed by the third, and final, paragraph of the bill, which made a statement equally remarkable in light of Jefferson's overall constitutional theory: "And though we well know that this Assembly, elected by the people for the ordinary purposes of legislation only, have no power to restrain the acts of succeeding Assemblies, constituted with powers equal to our own, and that therefore to declare this irrevocable would be of no effect in law; yet we are free to declare, and do declare, that the rights hereby asserted are of the natural rights of mankind, and that if any act shall be hereafter passed to repeal the present, or to narrow its operation, such act will be an infringement of natural right." Thus Jefferson emphasized that this was no ordinary bill. It did not establish freedom of religion in the sense of creating it as an adventitious right, under positive law; rather, it acknowledged that freedom as an inalienable, natural right that no future legislature or court had legitimate authority to deny.[39]

Jefferson's bill was first introduced in the General Assembly in 1779, after he had become governor. At the same time a second bill, entitled "A Bill concerning Religion," was introduced by Patrick Henry. In contrast to Jefferson's bill, which sought to remove religion altogether from the jurisdiction of civil government, this bill proposed a general assessment, declared the Christian religion to be the "established Religion" of Virginia, and provided articles of faith to which church members must subscribe in order to be incorporated as an established church. It endeavored, in short, to replace the former establishment of the Church of England with an establishment of the multiple forms of the Christian religion. Neither Henry's bill nor Jefferson's could muster a majority in the legislature. Thus the question whether Virginia would truly separate church and state or rather merely create a multiple, nonpreferential establishment of Christianity remained unresolved for several years.[40]

Not until 1786, while Jefferson was in France, did the Virginia legislature—acting under James Madison's leadership and in response to an overwhelming popular movement—finally enact Jefferson's bill, in a slightly modified form. Near the end of 1786 Jefferson, with obvious pride, reported to Madison that the Virginia statute "has been received with infinite approbation in Europe, and propagated with enthusiasm." He added that "it is comfortable to see the standard of reason at length erected, after so many ages, during which the human mind has been held in vassalage by kings, priests, and nobles," and also that "it is honorable for us, to have produced the first legislature who had the courage to declare, that the reason of man may be trusted with the formation of his own opinions."[41]

The text of Jefferson's bill for establishing religious freedom was printed as an appendix to his *Notes on the State of Virginia*. In discussing the bill in the *Notes*, he again drew a sharp line between the private realm of religious opinion and the realm of civic concerns. "Our rulers can have authority over such natural rights only as we have submitted to them," Jefferson argued, noting that "the rights of conscience we never submitted, we could not submit," because men are answerable for them to God only. "The legitimate powers of government extend to such acts only as are injurious to others. But it does me no injury for my neighbour to say there are twenty gods, or no god. It neither picks my pocket nor breaks my leg." He added that government-imposed uniformity is neither possible nor desirable since "difference of opinion is advantageous to religion," that reason and free inquiry are "the only effectual agents against error," and that it was "error alone which needs the support of government," since "truth can stand by itself." [42]

As in the preamble to his bill, Jefferson's argument for religious freedom here dovetailed with his own convictions, his confidence in the efficacy of reason as a sure guide to truth. For this reason primarily he encouraged diversity. As he stated in the *Notes on Virginia,* diverse opinions, when loosened, "will support the true religion by bringing every false one to their tribunal, to the test of their investigation." But he also encouraged diversity because he saw the futile effort to impose uniformity as the cause of political oppression: "Millions of innocent men, women, and children, since the introduction of Christianity, have been burnt, tortured, fined, imprisoned; yet we have not advanced one inch toward uniformity. What has been the effect of coercion? To make one half the world fools, and the other half hypocrites. To support roguery and error all over the earth." [43]

When Jefferson, in his letter to Madison of 20 December 1787, expressed his great disappointment that the Constitution included no explicit guarantee of rights, the first such right that he listed was freedom of religion. Jefferson surely had in mind the kind of broad statement of "natural right" expressed in his bill. Although the language finally adopted by Congress in proposing what would become part of the First Amendment—stating that "Congress shall make no law respecting the establishment of religion, or prohibiting the free exercise thereof"—was far less explicit than the language of the Virginia statute, Jefferson interpreted it to be just as comprehensive a guarantee. In other words, he understood the First Amendment freedom of religion clause, like the Virginia statute, to erect "a wall of separation between Church and State." This guarantee encompassed both an absolute free exercise of religion and an absolute prohibition of an establishment of religion. It meant, as Jefferson put it in his letter to Madison in 1786, to leave the formation of religious opinions solely to "the reason of man."

Jefferson on several occasions deliberately expressed this broad interpretation of the First Amendment, an interpretation consistent with the broad principles of his bill for religious freedom. In what was the pretext for perhaps his most famous utterance, he wrote Benjamin Rush at the height of the electoral campaign in 1800, when Jefferson was being violently castigated by the Federalist clergy of New England, that their "hope of obtaining an establishment of a particular form of Christianity through the United States" would be doomed by his election. "They believe that any portion of power confided to me, will be exerted in opposition to their schemes. And they believe rightly: for I have sworn upon the altar of God, eternal hostility against every form of tyranny over the mind of man." [44]

As president, Jefferson faithfully adhered to these principles and to his broad view of the rights guaranteed by the First Amendment. He departed from the precedent set by his predecessors, Washington and Adams, by refusing to recommend or designate any day for national prayer, fasting, or thanksgiving. Early in his presidency, after he had received an admiring address from a group of Baptists in Danbury, Connecticut, Jefferson took advantage of the opportunity which their address presented to publicize his views in his reply. He stated his position in memorable terms:

> Believing with you that religion is a matter which lies solely between man and his God, that he owes account to none other for his faith or his worship, that the legislative powers of government reach actions only, and not opinions, I contemplate with sovereign reverence that act of the whole American people which declared that their legislature should "make no law respecting an establishment of religion, or prohibiting the free exercise thereof," thus building a wall of separation between Church and State. Adhering to this expression of the supreme will of the nation in behalf of the rights of conscience, I shall see with sincere satisfaction the progress of those sentiments which tend to restore to man all his natural rights, convinced he has no natural right in opposition to his social duties.

In his draft of the letter Jefferson added that since Congress was prohibited by the First Amendment from enacting laws respecting religion, and the executive was authorized only to execute legislative acts, he had refrained from ordering "even occasional performances of devotion." Although he followed the advice of his attorney general, Levi Lincoln, and deleted this passage for political reasons, Jefferson's declaration that the First Amendment mandated a "wall of separation" between church and state remained to be cited by subsequent generations as a general constitutional principle.[45]

Jefferson again found an opportunity to express his position in a letter he wrote in his second term. "I consider the government of the U.S. as interdicted by the Constitution from intermeddling with religious institutions, their doctrines, discipline, or exercises. This results not only from the provision that no law shall be made respecting the establishment, or free exercise of religion" but also from the Tenth Amendment, "which reserves to the states the powers not delegated to the U.S.," he observed. To recommend a day of fasting and prayer, even if such a recommendation was sanctioned by nothing other than public opinion, would violate this prohibition, Jefferson argued. "Fasting & prayer are religious exercises. The enjoining them an act of discipline," no less "*a law* of conduct for those to whom it is directed" merely because it may be a recommendation only, and not an actual executive order. The president could not "*indirectly* assume to the U.S. an authority over religious exercises which the Constitution has directly precluded [the federal government] from." As Leonard Levy has noted, "Only a totally principled commitment to the privacy and voluntary nature of religious belief explained so exquisite a constitutional conscience."[46]

After his retirement Jefferson continued to apply the principle of the separation of church and state consistently. When the question of whether there existed a federal common law arose—an issue which threatened to involve the federal judiciary in matters he regarded as properly beyond their cognizance—Jefferson dug into his lawbooks, supplementing research he had done in the late 1770s and entered into his legal commonplace book, to disprove the thesis that Christianity was a part of the English common law.[47]

A more practical and significant application of the principle of separation of church and state arose in Jefferson's efforts on behalf of educational reform. His proposals for a comprehensive plan for public education in Virginia excluded sectarian influence at all levels. His 1817 draft of a bill for the establishment of public elementary schools enumerated only secular subjects in the curriculum, specified that ministers should not serve as "visitors" or supervisors, and provided that "no religious reading, instruction or exercise, shall be prescribed or practised" in violation of the tenets of any sect or denomination.[48] In the report that Jefferson prepared in 1818 as chairman of the Commissioners for the University of Virginia, he explained why a wholly secular curriculum had been adopted: "In conformity with the principles of our [Virginia] Constitution, which places all sects of religion on an equal footing . . . we have proposed no professor of divinity . . . [having] thought it proper . . . to leave every sect to provide, as they think fittest, the means of furnishing instruction in their own particular tenets."

Under the pressure of criticism, in 1822 Jefferson, as rector of the university, and the Board of Visitors, among them Madison, reluctantly agreed to a plan to permit "some pious individuals . . . to establish their religious schools on the confines of the University, so as to give their students ready and convenient access and attendance on the scientific lectures of the University." The report noted that the plan would thus provide places where university students could worship, "but always understanding that these schools shall be independent of the University and of each other." Such an arrangement would meet the objections raised to the "chasm" that existed as a result of the exclusion of religion from the university curriculum and yet "leave inviolate the constitutional freedom of religion, the most inalienable and sacred of all human rights, over which the people and authorities of this state . . . have ever manifested the most watchful jealousy."[49]

"Inestimable Liberty" and "Demoralising Licentiousness": Jefferson and Freedom of the Press

Among those rights which Jefferson considered "useless to surrender to the government and which governments have yet always been fond to invade" was that "of thinking, and publishing our thoughts by speaking and writing." As Dumas Malone has noted, the broad principles expressed in Jefferson's bill for religious freedom were not limited to the subject of religion but asserted complete intellectual liberty. Malone has concluded that to Jefferson "freedom of thought was an absolute," and it extended not only to religious opinion but to all opinion, including political opinion. Leonard Levy has questioned this conclusion, arguing instead that Jefferson's "threshold of tolerance for hateful political ideas" was "less than generous." That Jefferson fell far short of libertarian standards, even those of his own day, with respect to freedom of the press constitutes an important part of Levy's indictment of Jefferson's overall record on civil liberties.[50]

It is not surprising that historians could take two such apparently contradictory views of Jefferson's record with respect to freedom of the press. Unlike his record on religious freedom, which is basically clear and consistent in its adherence to thoroughgoing libertarian principles throughout his public career, Jefferson's record on freedom of the press is more complex and less susceptible to easy generalization. This is especially so because his understanding of the nature of this freedom and the aspects of it that he chose to emphasize changed over time. Nevertheless, there emerges from Jefferson's writings a general theory of freedom of the press, quite libertarian in emphasis, which accorded with Jefferson's republicanism in a significant way.

Before considering Jefferson's views, it is important to note that freedom of the press, as it is generally understood today, is a relatively modern notion in Anglo-American law. Leonard Levy has argued that there was no genuinely libertarian theory of freedom of the press in America until a number of Jeffersonian Republicans articulated such a theory in response to the Sedition Act of 1798. Neither the Revolution nor the First Amendment superseded the law of seditious libel, claimed Levy: "Libertarian theory from the time of Milton to the ratification of the First Amendment substantially accepted the right of the state to suppress seditious libel."[51]

According to Levy, the First Amendment left intact the common law of seditious libel in the states, restricting only the power of the federal government. It also left intact the Blackstonian concept that freedom of the press meant merely freedom from prior restraint, a freedom "so narrowly understood that its constitutional protection did not, per se, preclude the enactment of a sedition law." The Sedition Act of 1798, in part, made it a crime for any person to "write, print, utter or publish . . . any false, scandalous and malicious writing or writings against the government of the United States, or either house of the Congress of the United States, or the President of the United States, with intent to defame [any of them] . . . or to excite against them . . . the hatred of the good people of the United States, or to stir up sedition within the United States, or to excite any unlawful combinations therein, for opposing or resisting any law of the United States, or any act of the President of the United States, . . . or to resist, oppose, or defeat any such law or act." The statute thus clearly created a federal statutory crime of seditious libel. The extreme partisan nature of the act is evidenced by its timing—enacted at the height of the public hysteria against France in the summer of 1798—as well its own provisions, which protected offices of the United States that were controlled by the Federalist party and stipulated that the act would expire on 3 March 1801, the last full day of the Adams administration. Yet the act was also, Levy has noted, "the very epitome of libertarian thought since the time of Zenger's case," for it incorporated everything that American libertarians had ever demanded: a requirement that criminal intent be shown, the power of the jury to decide whether the accused's statement was libelous as a matter of law as well as of fact, and truth as a defense. "By every standard the Sedition Act was a great victory for libertarian principles of freedom of the press—except that libertarian standards abruptly changed because the Republicans immediately recognized a Pyrrhic victory." [52]

The Sedition Act provoked Republicans to develop a new libertarian theory about the scope of liberty of expression, applicable to political as well as religious expression. The "new libertarianism" began to emerge in the speeches by Republican congressmen in the House debates on the sedition bill, and it was further developed by defense counsel in Sedition Act prosecutions. The "new libertarianism" reached its most reflective and systematic expression in a group of tracts and books that challenged the very concept of seditious libel as a crime, advocating instead a near-absolute freedom of political expression, limited only by the law of defamation. These writings identified by Levy include George Hay's *Essay on the Liberty of the Press* (1799), James Madison's *Report* on the Virginia Resolutions for the Virginia House of Delegates (1800), and Tunis Wortman's *Treatise concerning Political Enquiry, and the Liberty of the Press* (1800). [53]

It is against this background—the delayed emergence of what Levy has called "a new promontory of libertarian thought jutting out of a stagnant Blackstonian sea" [54]—that one must assess Jefferson's views. His earliest known statements on freedom of expression reflected his contemporaries' double standard as to the distinction between religious and political opinions. Jefferson's thoroughgoing libertarianism with respect to religious freedom was based partly on the notion that religious belief is a private matter and partly on the principle that government intervention is unwarranted since a diversity of religious opinions harms no one. Neither of these reasons led Jefferson to a libertarian position with respect to freedom of expression of political opinions. What is remarkable about Jefferson's early views, however, is the extent to which he struggled with the difference between religious and political opinions and, in trying to arrive at a workable distinction, toyed with the complete rejection of seditious libel altogether—well in advance of the "new libertarianism" of the 1790s.

Jefferson's reservations about the scope of political expression are evident in the caveats he inserted in his religious liberty clause in the first two drafts of his 1776 proposed Virginia constitution. In the first draft, after declaring that no person should be compelled to frequent or maintain any religious service or institution, he added, "but seditious behavior to be pun[isha]ble by civil magistrate accdg to the laws already made or hereafter to be made." On reconsideration he bracketed these words. In his second draft he added the following clause about liberty of religious opinion and then crossed it out: "but this shall not be held to justify any seditious preaching or conversation against the authority of the civil government." [55]

Jefferson omitted this restrictive clause from the third and final draft, however. In addition, the same clause on freedom of the press, with minor changes in wording, appeared in all three of his drafts in 1776. "Printing presses shall be free, except (so far as they or their managers shall be subject themselves to the private action of any individual) where by commission of private injury they shall give cause of private action," he wrote in the first draft. In the second and third drafts he wrote, "Printing presses shall be free, except so far as by commission of private injury" cause may be given of "private action." [56] The clause is important as the earliest known expression of Jefferson's position with respect to freedom of the press.

Together with the omission of the restrictive caveat to the religious liberty clause, the "except" clause in the free press provision in the final draft suggests that Jefferson in fact viewed this freedom quite broadly. It is true that Jefferson placed limitations on the freedom of expression of political and other nonreligious opinions while not putting any limitations on the expression of religious opinions. But Jefferson's final draft suggests that in 1776 he already had begun to anticipate the ideas of the "new libertarians" of the years following 1798, in conceiving of a free press as one limited only by the law of libel to protect private reputations against malicious falsehoods.

Jefferson's draft constitution for Virginia in 1783 proposed that the press "shall be subject to no other restraint than liableness to legal prosecution for false facts printed and published." The phrase "legal prosecution" is ambiguous. It might refer to any legal cause of action, civil as well as criminal, and thus Jefferson might have meant only to allow private causes of action for personal defamation, as he did in the final draft in 1776. However, even if Levy is right in arguing that the language "explicitly opened the door to criminal prosecutions,"[57] Jefferson's failure to challenge the substantive law of criminal libel in 1783 is understandable, given the fact that no one in America did so until after 1798.

Jefferson's years in Europe as minister to France helped strengthen his appreciation for freedom of the press. He deplored an attack on John Jay which appeared in the New York newspapers, yet he explained to one correspondent why "it is however an evil for which there is no remedy": "Our liberty depends on the freedom of the press, and that cannot be limited without being lost. To the sacrifice of time, labor, fortune, a public servant must count upon adding that of peace of mind and even reputation." To Jay himself Jefferson repeated these sentiments, pointing out that "it is a part of the price we pay for our liberty" and that such a sacrifice of "quiet" is "better than European bondage." He argued that freedom of the press must be absolute because such freedom was necessary to political liberty, which "cannot be guarded but by freedom of the press nor that be limited without danger of losing it."[58]

Jefferson's position at this time is perhaps best known from a certain hyperbolic statement he made in the context of his reaffirmation of his confidence in the people. Writing to a correspondent about the "tumults in America," primarily Shays's Rebellion, Jefferson confidently noted that the way to prevent "these irregular interpositions of the people" is to give them full information of public affairs through the newspapers. "Were it left to me to decide whether we should have a government without newspapers, or newspapers without a government, I should not hesitate a moment to prefer the latter," he wrote from Paris.[59]

To the extent that Jefferson's statements in 1786 and 1787 indicate a rejection of the law of even private libels when a public official is attacked, his libertarianism exceeded that of the "new libertarians" fourteen years later and indeed anticipated a development which did not come in constitutional law until the twentieth century.[60] These statements, however, may be regarded as exaggerated and therefore as less than accurate indicators of Jefferson's true position with respect to freedom of the press. His exchange of ideas about the Bill of Rights with Madison and others better indicates Jefferson's view of freedom of the press and suggests that notwithstanding the above comments, Jefferson in the 1780s continued to view this freedom in less absolute terms than he viewed religious freedom.

Jefferson wrote Madison in July 1788, when he was still arguing for the need for a federal bill of rights: "A declaration that the federal government will never restrain the presses from printing anything they please, will not take away the liability of the printers for false facts printed. The declaration that religious faith shall be unpunished does not give impunity to criminal acts dictated by religious error."[61] The full context of these statements should not be ignored. One must also note, again, that the words "liability" and "impunity" are ambiguous and might refer only to private causes of action for personal defamation, and that it is also unclear whether by "criminal acts" Jefferson meant overt acts or the mere expression of opinion. The statements do show, however, that he regarded the scope of the freedoms that would later be explicitly protected by the First Amendment as something less than absolute.

A stronger implication that Jefferson had not yet discarded the concept of seditious libel follows from the language of an amendment which he suggested to Madison in a letter in August 1789. Madison had proposed an amendment providing: "The people shall not be deprived or abridged of their right to speak, or write, or to publish their sentiments; and the freedom of the press, as one of the great bulwarks of liberty, shall be inviolable." Jefferson said he liked that proposal, but he suggested the following alteration: "The people shall not be deprived or abridged of their right to speak or write or otherwise to publish anything but false facts affecting injuriously the life, liberty, property or reputation of others or affecting the peace of the confederacy with foreign nations."[62] The first part of the "false facts" clause refers to private causes of action for personal defamation; the second, however, is unquestionably a recognition of the concept of seditious libel. Jefferson was suggesting only a limited recognition of that concept—not liability for any "false facts" that would bring the government into disrepute but only for those which would "affect" the national peace. Levy is nevertheless quite right in inferring serious consequences from Jefferson's recommendation during controversies such as those that later emerged over Jay's Treaty, the Louisiana

Purchase, or the embargo.[63] But Jefferson's proposal for what would become the First Amendment was made in 1789, several years before these problems in American foreign policy materialized and ten years before the emergence of a truly libertarian conception of freedom of the press. In confining that freedom to "anything but false facts," Jefferson was in fact adhering to the epitome of post-*Zenger* libertarianism, recognizing that truth should be an absolute defense to prosecutions for libel.

The most revealing bit of evidence of Jefferson's view of freedom of the press at this time is the distinction he drew between it and religious freedom in his 1790 letter to Noah Webster. He described two classes of rights that ought to be protected in a federal bill of rights: on the one hand were those "portions" of natural rights that the people had not ceded to the government; on the other were "certain fences which experience has proved peculiarly efficacious against wrong." He classed freedom of religion in the first category and freedom of the press, along with trial by jury and habeas corpus, in the second. Both categories of rights needed protection, Jefferson argued, because both were susceptible to usurpation by government; hence, in a sense, the distinction is merely academic. The fact that Jefferson so distinguished the two freedoms, however, suggests that unlike religious freedom, freedom of the press was not in the highest category of "inalienable and sacred," or God-given, rights but rather, like trial by jury and habeas corpus, was a means for vindicating natural rights.

The troublesome distinction between opinions and actions posed problems for Jefferson. He maintained that the legitimate powers of government were limited to "such acts only as are injurious to others" and did not extend to religious opinion because "it does me no injury for my neighbour to say there are twenty gods, or no god." Was not the expression of nonreligious opinion—particularly if it involved libels upon the character of individuals—a different matter, to which the legitimate powers of government may extend? Jefferson's correspondence of the 1780s suggests some equivocation between a liberal theory of a free press, which would permit individual causes of action for defamation as well as make criminal certain well-defined abuses, and an absolutely libertarian theory.

In the context of Republican opposition to Federalist administrations in the 1790s, Jefferson returned to the kind of absolute libertarian stance he had assumed in reaction to European despotism in 1786.

In a letter to President Washington responding to Hamilton's charges that Jefferson had used Philip Freneau's *National Gazette* as an organ for criticizing Hamilton's financial programs, Jefferson went beyond a simple denial to frame an eloquent appeal on behalf of an unrestricted freedom to criticize the government: "No government ought to be without censors; and where the press is free, no one ever will. If virtuous, it need not fear the fair operation of attack and defence. Nature has given to man no other means of sifting out the truth either in religion, law, or politics. I think it as honorable to the government neither to know, nor notice, it's sycophants or censors, as it would be undignified and criminal to pamper the former and persecute the latter." Several years later, during the Adams administration when the Republicans were in danger of being silenced as the opposition party, Jefferson again emphasized the importance of a free press, this time tying it to "the improvement of science," in the very broad sense which that term meant to him. "To preserve the freedom of the human mind then and the freedom of the press, every spirit should be ready to devote itself to martyrdom; for as long as we may think as we will, and speak as we think the condition of man will proceed in improvement."[64]

Jefferson was particularly alarmed at the introduction into Congress of the bill for a federal sedition law in 1798, recognizing its aim as "the suppression of the Whig presses." He wrote Madison on 6 June that the Federalists' alien and sedition bills were "so palpably in the teeth of the Constitution as to show they mean to pay no respect to it." Republican fears that the Sedition Act would be used to silence Republican newspapers in the months preceding the election of 1800 were justified by the enforcement pattern: of the seventeen verifiable indictments—fourteen under the act, three under the common law (two before, one after passage of the act)—most cases came to trial in the spring of 1800, with the strictest enforcement in areas either thoroughly Federalist (such as New England) or in states where Federalist supremacy was threatened (such as New York and Pennsylvania).[65]

Jefferson's constitutional argument against the Sedition Act, as embodied in his draft of the Kentucky Resolutions of 1798, emphasized federalism. The Constitution expressed the states' determination "to retain to themselves the right of judging how far the licentiousness of speech and of the press may be abridged without lessening their useful freedom, and how far those abuses which cannot be separated from their use should be tolerated, rather than the use be destroyed." This intention was manifest in the text of the Constitution, Jefferson argued. The power over freedom of speech or press was not delegated to the United States, nor was it prohibited to the states; therefore, by the "general principle" of limited federal powers and by the express provision of the Tenth Amendment, such power was reserved to the states or to the people. In addition, Jefferson noted, the First Amendment specifically withheld "libels, falsehoods, and defamation, equally with heresy and false religion," from the cognizance of "federal tribunals." [66]

Federalism was a tactically useful argument as a means of denying federal jurisdiction over libels; even Tunis Wortman, author of the "preeminent" treatise expressing the "new libertarian" view described by Levy, used the federalism argument. Yet, though the Kentucky Resolutions were primarily expressions of states' rights, Jefferson did not avoid the question of the legitimacy of seditious libel—that is, whether government ought to punish libels. Indeed, he implied a repudiation of the concept when he wrote in the eighth resolution that "free government is founded in jealousy, and not in confidence" and that "it is jealousy and not confidence" that calls for constitutions "to bind down those whom we are obliged to trust with power." [67]

By thus repudiating the concept of confidence in government, Jefferson put himself squarely at odds with the dominant Federalist view which provided the philosophical justification for seditious libel generally and specifically the rationale for the Sedition Act. As James Morton Smith has observed in his study of the act, the Federalists contended that election of officials by the people served as a continuing vote of confidence in those leaders, the "constituted authorities" who directed public affairs until the next election. To find fault with these authorities was to undermine public confidence in the government itself, as the Federalists saw it. By identifying the administration with the government, and the government with the Constitution, the Federalists concluded that criticism of their administration was an attempt to subvert the Constitution and to overthrow the government. To bring the president or other high governmental figure into disrepute was criminal because the stability of the government depended on public confidence. [68]

The Republicans, on the other hand, followed Jefferson in rejecting such confidence altogether. The public could examine the conduct of the "constituted authorities" and could denounce it as well as praise it; public opinion was in a continuous process of formulation and could be constitutionally registered in speeches or in the press. Thus, the Republican challenge to the Sedition Act turned on two points: the states' rights argument—which Smith has viewed as "a realistic defense of free speech and a free press" because the immediate threat to civil liberties came from the federal statute—and the repudiation of the very concept of seditious libel. That more basic challenge to the act, which culminated in the "new libertarian writings" identified by Levy, vigorously defended the freedom of the press as necessary to a free republican form of government.

Levy has argued that Jefferson in power "behaved in ways that belied" the Jeffersonian libertarian sentiments of 1798.[69] His statements and actions with respect to the Sedition Act (which by its own terms expired on the day he took office as president, 4 March 1801), however, suggest that Jefferson as president consistently adhered to a qualified form of the "new libertarian" view.

In his First Inaugural Address, President Jefferson generously stated, "If there be any among us who would wish to dissolve this Union or to change its republican form, let them stand undisturbed as monuments of the safety with which error of opinion may be tolerated where reason is left free to combat it." With a due regard for legal proprieties, the president ordered the discontinuance of the prosecution of William Duane, editor of the Republican newspaper the Philadelphia *Aurora*. More importantly, in March 1802 he wrote his attorney general, Levi Lincoln, upholding the sentiments he had expressed in his inaugural address the preceding year. "While a full range is proper for actions by individuals, either public or private, for slanders affecting them," Jefferson noted, "I would wish much to see the experiment tried of getting along without public prosecutions for *libels*. I believe we can do it. Patience and well doing, instead of punishment, if it can be found sufficiently efficacious, would be a happy change in the instruments of government."[70] That the pursuit of such an "experiment" remained a policy of his administration is suggested by a letter Jefferson wrote to Judge John Tyler more than two years later: "No experiment can be more interesting than that we are now trying, and which we trust will end in establishing the fact, that man may be governed by reason and truth. Our first object should therefore be, to leave open to him all the avenues of truth. The most effectual hitherto found, is the freedom of the press. It is, therefore, the first shut up by those who fear the investigation of their actions. The firmness with which the people have withstood the late abuses of the press, the discernment they have manifested between truth and falsehood, show that they may safely be trusted to hear everything true and false, and to form a correct judgment between them." [71] In leaving to the people the discernment between truth and falsehood, Jefferson's stated policy was fully consistent with the precepts that underlay the "new libertarian" view of freedom of the press.

Jefferson was painfully aware of the attacks on him that had appeared in Federalist papers during the election of 1800 and continued during his administration. [72] As he wrote to a French correspondent in 1803: "Our newspapers, for the most part, present only the caricatures of disaffected minds. Indeed, the abuses of the freedom of the press have been carried to a length never before known or borne by any civilized nation." Yet, reporting the "happy change" in the policy of the administration, he added that "as yet, we have found it better to trust the public judgment, rather than the magistrate, with the discrimination between truth and falsehood." Fortunately, he noted, "hitherto the public judgment has performed that office with wonderful correctness." [73]

Only two weeks after this letter, however, Jefferson expressed misgivings about the public capacity to distinguish truth and falsity. He addressed an "entirely confidential" letter to Governor Thomas McKean of Pennsylvania, a letter which—as Levy has noted—removes any doubts whether he believed libels could be punished by the states. The Federalists, he wrote, "having failed in destroying the freedom of the press by their gag-law, seem to have attacked it in an opposite form, that is by pushing it's licentiousness & it's lying to such a degree of prostitution as to deprive it of all credit. And the fact is that so abandoned are the tory presses in this particular that even the least informed of the people have learnt that nothing in a newspaper is to be believed. This is a dangerous state of things, and the press ought to be restrained to it's credibility if possible." To do this, Jefferson suggested "the restraints provided by the laws of the states," adding that he had "long thought that a few prosecutions of the most prominent offenders would have a wholesome effect in restoring the integrity of the presses. Not a general prosecution, for that would look like persecution, but a selected one." He transmitted with the letter a sample of an offending newspaper which, he added, "appears to me to offer as good an instance in every respect to make an example of, as can be selected." The identity of the paper that Jefferson sent McKean is not known, but some five months later an indictment for libel was brought against Joseph Dennie, editor of the *Port-Folio*. Dennie was a merciless satirist whose barbs were frequently directed at the president—in particular, Jefferson's alleged relationship with Sally Hemings—but the passage cited in the libel action was a tirade against democracy. The case, many times postponed, was not tried until Jefferson's second term, and Dennie was acquitted.[74]

In thus explicitly warranting a state libel prosecution, Jefferson did not repudiate the declared policy of his administration with respect to federal prosecutions. In an undated memorandum of 1801 intended as a message to the Senate explaining abandonment of the Duane prosecution, Jefferson expressed his wish "to secure to the press that degree of freedom in which it remained under the authority of the states, with whom alone the power is left of abridging that freedom, the general government being excluded from it." In a letter to Abigail Adams in September 1804, explaining his opinion of the "unconstitutionality and subsequent nullity" of the Sedition Act, Jefferson emphasized that "while we deny that Congress [has] a right to control the freedom of the press, we have ever asserted the right of the states, and their exclusive right to do so." This, he explained to Mrs. Adams—who was still very sensitive about the libels that had been directed against her husband during his presidency—was the solution to the problem of "the overwhelming torrent of slander which is confounding all vice and virtue, all truth and falsehood." All states have provisions "for punishing slander, which those who have time and inclination resort to for the vindication of their character," and those state laws generally "appear to have made the presses responsible for slander as far as is consistent with their useful freedom."[75]

The few libel prosecutions of Federalist journalists that occurred during Jefferson's first term were tried in state courts. Two of these are worthy of note: the previously discussed Pennsylvania prosecution of Joseph Dennie for seditious libel against the state and the United States and the New York prosecution of Harry Croswell, editor of the New York Federalist newspaper *The Wasp*, for the crime of seditiously libeling the president. That Jefferson supported such prosecutions is evident in his suggestion to Governor McKean that there be a "selected" prosecution of "the most prominent offenders" and in his added remark that "if the same thing be done in some other of the states it will place the whole band more on their guard." As Dumas Malone has observed, however, there is no ground for holding Jefferson responsible for these particular state cases, other than in his failure to protest; and to protest would not have been in line with his general policy of noninterference in state matters.[76]

In his Second Inaugural Address on 4 March 1805, Jefferson made public the fullest explanation of his policy respecting freedom of the press. He began his three-paragraph discussion of the subject by taking note that "during this course of administration, and in order to disturb it, the artillery of the Press has been levelled against us, charged with whatsoever it's licentiousness could devise or dare." These "abuses of an institution so important to freedom and science" were to be regretted "inasmuch as they tend to lessen it's usefulness and to sap it's safety." The abuses of the press might "perhaps"— in his draft Jefferson first wrote "indeed" but then substituted this softer word—have been "corrected by the wholesome punishments reserved to, and provided by, the laws of the several states against falsehood & defamation." But, he added, "public duties more urgent press on the time and attention of public servants," thus leaving the offenders to their punishment "in the public indignation." An "experiment" had been "fairly and fully made" to determine "whether freedom of discussion, unaided by power, is not sufficient for the propagation and protection of truth" and "whether a government, conducting itself in the true spirit of it's constitution with zeal and purity, and doing no act which it could be unwilling the whole world should witness, can be written down by falsehood & defamation."[77]

Thus far the Second Inaugural read like a "new libertarian" treatise; the contrast with the Federalist view is evident. Jefferson, nevertheless, went on to emphasize the role that state libel laws could play within the context of this libertarian "experiment":

> No inference is here intended that the laws provided by the states against false & defamatory publications should not be enforced. He who has time renders a service to public morals & public tranquility, in reforming these abuses by the salutary coercions of the law. But the experiment is noted to prove that since truth & reason have maintained their own ground against false opinions,

in league with false facts, the Press, confined to truth, needs no other legal restraint. The public judgment will correct false reasonings & opinions, on a full hearing of all parties; and no other definite line can be drawn between the inestimable liberty of the press, and it's demoralising licentiousness. If there be still improprieties which this rule would not restrain, it's Supplement must be sought in the censorship of Public opinion.

The Second Inaugural, then, did more than reiterate Jefferson's steadfast denial of federal authority over freedom of the press: it revealed that when pressed to draw a line between "the inestimable liberty" and the "demoralising licentiousness" of the press, Jefferson came down on the libertarian side. He would leave to the marketplace of ideas, and ultimately to "the censorship of public opinion," the restraint of falsehoods. At the same time he left to anyone "who has time" the option of "reforming" the "abuses" of the press through the "salutary coercions of the law." He referred specifically to state laws "against false & defamatory publications" and the "wholesome punishments" which those laws provided.[78]

Notwithstanding this clear repudiation of seditious libel prosecutions, Levy has charged Jefferson with hypocrisy for condoning the so-called Connecticut libel cases. These prosecutions were undertaken in a federal court by a judge appointed by Jefferson and under a federal common law of seditious libel which Jefferson had declared in the Kentucky Resolutions should be "withheld from the cognizance of federal tribunals." In instituting the prosecutions, local Republicans, District Judge Pierpont Edwards included, probably sought to retaliate for Federalist prosecution of Republican newspaper editors in the state courts, which the Federalists controlled. The federal grand jury, handpicked by a Republican marshal and charged by Judge Edwards, returned indictments against Judge Tapping Reeve of the Connecticut Supreme Court for articles he had published in the Litchfield *Monitor*, a Federalist paper; against Thaddeus Collier, publisher of the *Monitor*; against Hudson and Goodwin, editors of the Federalist *Connecticut Courant* of Hartford; and against Thaddeus Osgood, a candidate for the ministry, and the Reverend Azel Backus, for sermons they had preached. The case against Judge Reeve was not prosecuted, and the trials of the other five defendants were postponed until the September 1807 session. At the session of the circuit court in April 1808, the district attorney dropped all the libel indictments except those against Hudson and Goodwin, which were referred to the Supreme Court as a test case. After a delay of four years, the Court issued a decision. In a brief opinion for the majority, Jefferson's appointee, Justice William Johnson, held that the courts of the United States had no jurisdiction over common-law criminal libels, thus settling the question whether there was a federal common law of crimes.[79]

The Federalist claim that Jefferson instigated the federal prosecutions, a claim made in the "Hampden" pamphlet on which Levy extensively relied for his account of the cases, was, as Malone has argued, "wholly without factual foundation." Jefferson's own later testimony, in a letter to Wilson Cary Nicholas written in June 1809, was that the prosecutions "had been instituted without my knowledge" and that they were "disapproved by me as soon as known and directed to be discontinued." Still later, in an 1814 letter to his former postmaster general, Gideon Granger, Jefferson wrote that the prosecutions instituted in Connecticut were "too inconsistent" with the stated principles of his administration "to be permitted to go on," but that he had wished the prosecutions to be dismissed "with all possible respect to the worthy citizens who had advised them, and in such way as to spare their feelings which had been justly irritated by the intemperance of their adversaries." Contemporary evidence, though not entirely clear, seems consistent with these statements, showing that he had expressed his desire to dispense with seditious libel prosecutions although he was sympathetic with and considerate of the local feelings that prompted the Connecticut cases.[80] While he can be justly charged with waiting too long to intervene, he eventually did direct the discontinuance of all but the test cases against Hudson and Goodwin.

The Connecticut libel cases aside, Jefferson's record was untarnished in terms of federal restraints on freedom of the press; his administration did indeed repudiate the policy of the preceding administration. Jefferson, however, consistently maintained the power of the states to "confine the press to truth." It is unclear whether he had in mind state criminal prosecutions for seditious libel, as in the Dennie and Croswell cases, or private suits for damages for personal defamations. His reference to "wholesome punishments" in the Second Inaugural, when seen in the context of his other statements on the power of the states to control libels, suggests that he was thinking of the latter.[81] The "wholesome punishments" and "salutary coercions of the law" that he mentioned in the address were actions—whether civil or criminal—begun at the instance of individuals in their capacities as private citizens, and not actions for seditious libel begun at the instance of the government.

The Second Inaugural Address was consistent with Jefferson's mature views on the question of freedom of the press. Late in his life, in an 1823 letter to a French correspondent in which Jefferson listed the principles of the American constitutions, he included "freedom of the press, subject only to liability for personal injuries." He added that "this formidable censor of the public functionaries, by arraigning them at the tribunal of public opinion, produces reform peaceably, which must otherwise be done by revolution" and is also "the best instrument for enlarging the mind of man, and improving him as a rational, moral, and social being." Levy has recognized this as "the wisest remark he ever made on the subject," Jefferson's "final testament on freedom of the press—a reflex of the best Enlightenment theory" as well as a statement which "catapulted Jefferson into the ranks of the most advanced libertarians, for no one had ever advocated a wider freedom than that which was restrained only by liability for 'personal injuries.' "[82] What Levy has failed to recognize is the degree to which this remark was consistent with Jefferson's earlier statements—if not as far back as his 1776 draft constitution for Virginia, at least as far back as his presidency. The 1823 remark was a particularly eloquent elaboration of what Jefferson referred to in the Second Inaugural as the "inestimable liberty" of the press.

It remains to be considered what Jefferson had in mind when he referred to the "demoralising licentiousness" of the press. His views of the press overall help explain his actions while in office, particularly the letter to Governor McKean and the delay in ordering the discontinuance of the Connecticut libel prosecutions.

It is more than mere coincidence that in both 1803 and 1807, at about the same times Jefferson wrote McKean and was allowing the Connecticut prosecutions to drag on in federal court, he expressed negative opinions about the state of the press. In his letter to McKean he indicated his concern that the "licentiousness" of the Federalist press raised the danger that "even the least informed of the people have learnt that nothing in a newspaper is to be believed." In June 1807 in reply to John Norvell, a young man from Kentucky who had asked his opinion about the proper conduct of a newspaper, Jefferson sent a "hasty communication" which revealed a mood of extreme disillusionment. "It is a melancholy truth," he observed, "that a suppression of the press could not more completely deprive the nation of its benefits, than is done by its abandoned prostitution to falsehood. Nothing can now be believed which is seen in a newspaper. Truth itself becomes suspicious by being put into that polluted vehicle." Jefferson added that "the man who never looks into a newspaper is better informed than he who reads them, inasmuch as he who knows nothing is nearer to truth than he whose mind is filled with falsehoods and errors." Noting that only "general facts, such as that Europe is now at war, that Bonaparte has been a successful warrior," might be culled from newspapers, and that "no details can be relied on," Jefferson suggested that editors divide their papers into "four chapters"— "Truths," "Probabilities," "Possibilities," and "Lies"—and explained that the first chapter would be "very short, as it would contain little more than authentic papers, and information from such sources as the editor would be willing to risk his own reputation for their truth." The reform-minded editor, in addition, should "set his face against the demoralizing practice of feeding the public mind habitually on slander, & the depravity of taste which this nauseous aliment induces." Jefferson deplored the fact that "defamation is becoming a necessary of life; insomuch, that a dish of tea in the morning or evening cannot be digested without this stimulant." Statements similar in intensity, though not quite as detailed, appear in Jefferson's correspondence in the years after his retirement.[83]

Jefferson understandably was upset at libels directed against him personally or at his administration. It was not vanity or mere sensitivity.[84] As Levy has recognized, Jefferson was not a relativist: confident in the rightness of his convictions, he could not consider Federalist libels as anything but falsehoods. Indeed, he frequently described antirepublican ideas as "heresy"—perhaps a deliberate word, for in his 1776 notes on religion he had defined a heretic as "an impugner of fundamentals." Levy emphasized Jefferson's conviction that the great American experiment in self-government was in nearly constant danger, even in times of Republican administration of the government, and found in Jefferson's complete identification with that experiment the source of his intolerance.[85] The explanation for Jefferson's negative views of the press, however, is not so simple. As Dumas Malone has noted, Jefferson "drew a blanket indictment" against all newspapers, Republican as well as Federalist, and "pronounced a plague on both houses." [86]

The important fact about Jefferson's statements concerning the deplorable state of the press in his day lies in his conception of what was "demoralising" about its "licentiousness." Jefferson was not concerned about the loss of popular confidence in the government in the sense in which the Federalists were. Although his political convictions—his complete unwillingness to consider Federalism compatible with republicanism—undoubtedly colored his understanding of what constituted "falsehood" and "errors," Jefferson's concern about libels was not for loss of popular confidence in the government but rather for loss of popular confidence in the newspapers themselves. His concern was not for the stability of government but for its responsibility to the people whom it represented. "Free government is founded in jealousy, and not in confidence," he wrote in the Kentucky Resolutions, and that sentiment permeates all his political writings.

Jefferson valued a free press—indeed considered its liberty "inestimable" in value—because, as he wrote in 1823, it functioned as a "formidable censor of public functionaries, by arraigning them at the tribunal of public opinion." This was the "useful" freedom of the press. When, because of the extent of its libels, the press became a "polluted vehicle," it could no longer serve this function; as Jefferson noted in his letter to Norvell in 1807, nothing could be believed and truth itself became suspect. This was what was "demoralising" about the licentiousness of the press in Jefferson's day.

His remarks were equally applicable to Republican newspapers, just as his concern about responsibility in government was equally directed at Republican administrations. As he wrote to Edward Carrington in 1787, "The people are the only censors of their government." Should they become inattentive to public affairs, "you and I, and Congress, and Assemblies, judges, and governors shall all become wolves." People must be kept informed; newspapers should "penetrate the whole mass of the people," and "every man should receive those papers and be capable of reading them." This was the context in which Jefferson made his remark that "were it left to me to decide whether we should have a government without newspapers, or newspapers without a government, I should not hesitate a moment to prefer the latter." [87] Subsequent experience, if it would not cause

Jefferson to reconsider his choice, would at least prompt him to add the qualification that the newspapers must be trustworthy.

Jefferson's libertarianism was not unqualified; for him, freedom of the press was not an end in itself. He was concerned about the success of the American republican "experiment," and it was only within the context of that larger mission that during his presidency he was willing to hazard another "experiment," that the press "confined to truth" through the operation of state libel laws "needs no other legal restraint." Madison and the other "new libertarians" may have been more absolute in the language by which they articulated the freedom of the press, but their rationalization of that freedom was hardly more consistent or sophisticated than was Jefferson's. "Our people in a body are wise, because they are under the unrestrained and unperverted operation of their own understandings," he wrote to Joseph Priestley in 1802, adding that this was indispensable to "the interesting experiment of self-government." [88] As the Second Inaugural Address reveals, his confidence in the people led him to adopt a libertarian stance which was equal to the standards set by the "new libertarians" of his time. Because the people were "wise," he was willing to leave to "the censorship of public opinion"—and not to government—the important task of maintaining the "useful" freedom of the press.

7

The True Theory of
Our Constitution

Federalism and the Limits

of Federal Power

Among the principles Jefferson espoused in his First Inaugural Address were these interrelated ones: "the support of the state governments in all their rights, as the most competent administrations for our domestic concerns, & the surest bulwarks against anti-republican tendencies," on the one hand, and "the preservation of the General government, in it's whole constitutional vigour, as the sheet anchor of our peace at home, & safety abroad."[1] Taken together, the two principles of federalism reveal the tension at the heart of Jefferson's theory of the Constitution: the attempt to balance the centrifugal and centripetal forces that underlay the government of the United States, as he understood it.

Jefferson described the Constitution as "a compact" of the several states in which they "agreed to unite in a single government as to their relations with each other and with foreign nations, and as to other articles particularly specified" (for example, the coining of money and establishment of post offices), but "retained at the same time, each to itself, the other rights of independent government comprehending mainly their domestic interests." This was, Jefferson said shortly before he was elected president, "the true theory of our Constitution . . . surely the wisest and best, that the States are independent as to everything within themselves, and united as to everything respecting foreign nations. Let the general government be reduced to foreign concerns only, and let our affairs be disentangled from those of all other nations, except as to commerce, which the merchants will manage the better the more they are left free to manage for themselves, and our general government may be reduced to a very simple organization and a very unexpensive one—a few plain duties to be performed by a few servants." Under Jefferson's view, the whole field of government in the United States was divided into two departments, "domestic" and "foreign," each department having "distinct directories, coordinate and equally independent and supreme, in its own sphere of action." To the state governments were reserved "all legislation and administration, in affairs which concern their citizens only"; to the federal government was given "whatever concerns foreigns, or the citizens of the other states." The "foreign," or federal, sphere, moreover, was strictly limited to the few functions enumerated in the Constitution.[2]

It should not be surprising that Jefferson viewed the federal government as dealing with "foreign" matters; as late as 1792, he still referred to Virginia as "my country."[3] Nor should it be surprising that he viewed the government of the United States as a true federal system, with such a clear division between the state, or "domestic," sphere and the national, or "foreign," sphere. This view of the Constitution, though most clearly expressed in his writings after 1800, was one he long held. Certainly he viewed the United States government under the Articles of Confederation this way. Indeed, as early as 1774, in his *Summary View of the Rights of British America,* Jefferson had envisioned federalism as the desired form of union for America. More clearly than any of his contemporaries, he saw the constitution of the British Empire as one in which sovereign powers were divided between the local and imperial spheres.

What did change over time was not the essential theory of federalism but the side of the balance that Jefferson chose to emphasize. During his service as American minister in the Confederation period, the difficulties he had in negotiating commercial treaties with the nations of Europe made him painfully aware of the need for a stronger national government with full powers to regulate the foreign commerce of the several states. His stress at that time was on the problems arising from the centrifugal forces at work in the infant nation. His own efforts as a diplomat were directed at the enhancement of federal powers, and he supported the effort to amend the Articles of Confederation to accomplish this end. Furthermore, his earliest critical comments on the Constitution of 1787 related not to the reduction in powers of the states but to the lack of safeguards for individuals. When this problem was remedied by the Bill of Rights, he became a loyal supporter of the Constitution, believing it provided a practicable equilibrium.

After his return to the United States, however—and indeed, from the time he began his tenure as secretary of state in 1790 until the end of his life—his emphasis was almost always on the danger of encroachments by the federal government on the states. His fears of the Hamiltonian system and a monarchist conspiracy heightened his awareness of centripetal dangers to American republicanism. Writing to a fellow Virginian in 1791, he urged that the state government be strengthened as a means of preserving the equilibrium of the Constitution against such dangers:

> I wish to preserve the line drawn by the federal constitution between the general & particular governments as it stands at present, and to take every prudent means of preventing either from stepping over it. Tho' the experiment has yet not had a long enough course to shew us from which quarter incroachments are most to be feared, yet it is easy to foresee from the nature of things that the incroachments of the state governments will tend to an excess of liberty which will correct itself (as in the late instance) while those of the general government will tend to monarchy, which will fortify itself from day to day, instead of working it's own cure, as all experience shews. I would rather be exposed to the inconveniencies attending too much liberty than those attending too small a degree of it.[4]

If by 1791 he still was unsure "from which quarter incroachments are most to be feared," the events of the decade of the 1790s surely convinced him that the greatest need was to keep within check the powers of the federal government, and thus to resist the designs of the Hamiltonians.

Jefferson therefore came to regard the states, as he put it many years later, as "the true barriers of our liberty in this country" and "the wisest conservative power ever contrived by man." From the context of this statement, it is clear that what he sought to conserve was individual liberty, against what he elsewhere described as "the natural progress of things," for liberty to yield and government to gain ground. Jefferson was constantly on guard against the danger of tyranny, and he found in the federal system an effective device against this danger:

> Seventeen distinct States, amalgamated into one as to their foreign concerns, but single and independent as to their internal administration, regularly organized with legislature and governor resting on the choice of the people, and enlightened by a free press, can never be so fascinated by the arts of one man, as to submit voluntarily to his usurpation. Nor can they be constrained to be by any force he can possess. While that may paralyze the single State in which it happens to be encamped, sixteen others, spread over a country of two thousand miles diameter, rise up on every side, ready organized for deliberation by a constitutional legislature, and for action by their governor, constitutionally the commander of the militia of the State.

"The republican government of France was lost without a struggle," he added, because it lacked such provincial organizations; the governments of the United States, in contrast, he confidently maintained, "present such obstacles to an usurper as forever to stifle ambition in the first conception of that object." Thus, to Jefferson, federalism was the most effectual means for preserving republicanism, particularly in a republic as extensive as the United States.[5]

Jefferson regarded the principle of federalism, as he understood it, as "the radical idea of the constitution of our government," the distinctive and defining feature of the federal Constitution. What makes his view of federalism particularly important to his constitutional thought is that Jefferson also adopted it as a canon of constitutional interpretation. "The best general key for the solution of questions of power between our governments," he maintained, "is the fact that 'every foreign and federal power is given to the federal government, and to the States every power purely domestic.'" "Whenever a doubt arises to which of these branches [state or federal] a power belongs, I try it by this test," he said in his later years.[6] His theory of constitutional interpretation thus may properly be regarded as contextual, and the theory of federalism provided the context—the principle that Jefferson understood as the overall design, or purpose, of the Constitution; the premise upon which it was based—within which he resolved questions of allocations of power.[7]

This chapter focuses on the principle of federalism and its application in Jefferson's overall theory of the Constitution. The two best expositions of Jefferson's federal theory of the Constitution and the rule of constitutional interpretation that it entailed—his opinion on the constitutionality of the bank bill and his draft of the Kentucky Resolutions of 1798—are examined in detail. Jefferson's presidency also is examined, in an effort to help explain the apparent inconsistency between the principles of strict construction he espoused in the 1790s and certain exercises of federal power that he supported (or, at least, in which he acquiesced) during his presidency and after his retirement.

The Limits of Congressional Powers:
The Case against the Bank

In a report submitted to Congress early in 1791, Secretary of the Treasury Alexander Hamilton proposed the creation of the Bank of the United States. This quasi-public institution, modeled on the Bank of England, was to be a corporation chartered by Congress but privately administered. It would be capitalized largely on public credit, however: out of the $10 million total, $2 million was to be furnished directly by the government and three-fourths of the remainder, furnished by the investing public, was subscribable in government securities. The bank, moreover, would perform important public services: it would be the depository of government funds; and its notes, payable upon demand in specie and receivable for all payments owed to the United States government, would become the principal circulating medium in the Republic.

Congress enacted the bank bill virtually as it had been proposed by Hamilton despite a heated debate in the House of Representatives, where James Madison led the opposition. If Jefferson, who was preoccupied by his State Department duties, expressed reservations about Hamilton's proposal, they were not evidenced in his writings until early February 1791.[8] By the middle of the month, however, Jefferson was presented with the opportunity to scrutinize the bank bill when President Washington asked his secretary of state for a formal opinion on its constitutionality. Deeply troubled by the objections that had been raised by Madison in his speeches in Congress, Washington was unwilling to sign the bill without first resolving the constitutional question. He first had asked his attorney general, Edmund Randolph, who issued an adverse opinion. Jefferson's brief opinion agreed with the conclusion that had been reached by Madison and Randolph: the creation of the Bank of the United States was beyond the legitimate powers of Congress.

Jefferson began his opinion by listing the things undertaken by the bill: first, to form the subscribers into a corporation which would be empowered, in various ways, to change the common law; second, to give to the corporation what amounted to a monopoly, "the sole and exclusive right of banking under the national authority"; and third, to give to the corporation a power "to make laws paramount to the laws of the states," for such a construction of its powers would be necessary to protect the institution from the control of the state legislatures.[9] These observations provided a legal context which was important as a background to Jefferson's constitutional argument as well as to his ultimate recommendation, that President Washington exercise his veto power against the bill.

He then stated the gravamen of his constitutional argument. Citing the language of the Tenth Amendment, that "all powers not delegated to the U.S. by the Constitution, not prohibited by it to the states, are reserved to the states or to the people," Jefferson considered this provision to be "the foundation of the Constitution." It reiterated the general principle of federal powers expressed by the language of Article I: that the legislative powers of the federal government, vested in the Congress of the United States, were limited to those "herein granted" in the Constitution. "To take a single step beyond the boundaries thus specifically drawn around the powers of Congress, is to take possession of a boundless field of power, no longer susceptible of any definition."[10]

The rest of Jefferson's opinion shows what he regarded those "boundaries drawn about the powers of Congress" to be: they were the words of Article I, the enumerations of congressional power, construed (as Jefferson would later put it) "according to the plain and ordinary meaning of its language, to the common intendment of the time and those who framed it." "The incorporation of a bank, and other powers assumed by this bill, have not . . . been delegated to the

U.S. by the Constitution," Jefferson concluded, arguing that they were neither "among the powers specially enumerated" nor "within either of the general phrases" of Article I. These were the only possibilities he mentioned.[11]

Taking the first three clauses of Article I, section 8, one by one, he argued that the bill laid no taxes, borrowed no money, and regulated no commerce. On the latter point, particularly, Jefferson elaborated. The creation of a bank, he maintained, was exactly like the creation of a bushel of wheat or the mining of precious metals; and the creation of a subject of commerce was not the same as the regulation of commerce. "To erect a thing which may be bought and sold, is not to prescribe regulations for buying and selling." And, he further argued, even if it were a regulation of commerce, it would be void because it extended as much to the internal commerce of every state as to the external, while "the power given to Congress by the Constitution, does not extend to the internal regulation of the commerce of a state (that is to say of the commerce between citizen and citizen) which remains exclusively with it's own legislature; but to it's external commerce only, that is to say, it's commerce with another state, or with foreign nations or with the Indian tribes." He concluded the first part of the argument by noting that "still less are these powers covered by any other of the special enumerations."[12]

He then considered the two "general phrases" of Article I, the general welfare clause and the necessary and proper clause, which he also interpreted quite literally. The relevant language of the first clause of Article I, section 8, empowers Congress "to lay . . . taxes . . . to . . . provide for the . . . general welfare of the United States." This Jefferson interpreted to mean "to lay taxes *for the purpose* of providing for the general welfare." In other words, the general welfare clause was a statement of the purpose for which the specific power of laying taxes was to be exercised, not a grant to Congress of "a distinct and independent power to do any act they please, which might be for the good of the Union." To interpret it as the latter, Jefferson observed, "would render all the preceding and subsequent enumerations of power completely useless" as it would, in effect, "reduce the whole instrument to a single phrase," of empowering Congress to do whatever it pleased.[13]

Jefferson's argument against a broad construction of the general welfare clause rested on two basic grounds. First, such a sweeping interpretation of the clause would run against the "established rule

of construction," that where a phrase will bear either of two meanings, it should be given "that which will allow some meaning to the
other parts of the instrument, and not that which would render all
the others useless." Second, such a broad interpretation would be
contrary to the intent of the Constitution, as evident both in the text
itself and in the circumstances of its framing and ratification. "Certainly," Jefferson maintained, no such "universal power" was meant to
be given Congress: the Constitution "was intended to lace them [Con-
gress] up straitly within the enumerated powers, and those without
which, as means, these powers could not be carried into effect." The
powers assumed in the bank bill could not fairly be considered legitimate means to the effectuation of the enumerated powers, Jefferson
further argued, relying on a piece of historic information undoubtedly
furnished him by Madison: the power of Congress to incorporate a
bank—"the very power now proposed *as a means*"—was considered
and "rejected *as an end*" by the Constitutional Convention.[14]

The second "general phrase" was the last clause of Article I, section 8, which empowers Congress "to make all laws which shall
be necessary and proper for carrying into execution the foregoing
powers," that is, the enumerated powers. They can all be carried into
execution without a bank, Jefferson argued; "a bank therefore is not
necessary, and consequently not authorised by this phrase." The argument, of course, turns on the meaning of the adjective *necessary*, which
Jefferson contrasted with *convenient*. Acknowledging that a bank could
"give great facility, or convenience, in the collection of taxes" and that
bank bills "may be a more *convenient* vehicle than treasury orders" for
the transfer of funds between the states and the treasury, he nevertheless denied that the bank was necessary. Pointing, for example, to the
practice then followed in Philadelphia, where the existing bank had
entered into arrangements with the treasury for the receipt and transfer of debts to the United States, Jefferson maintained that this single
example disproves "that *necessity* which may justify the assumption of
a non-enumerated power as a means for carrying into effect an enumerated one. The thing may be done, and has been done, and well
done without this assumption; therefore it does not stand on that degree of *necessity* which can honestly justify it." Moreover, "if such a
latitude of construction be allowed to this phrase as to give any non-
enumerated power, it will go to every one, for there is no one which
ingenuity may not torture into a *convenience, in some way or other*, to

some one of so long a list of enumerated powers." The Constitution restrained Congress "to the *necessary* means, that is to say, to those means without which the grant of the power would be nugatory"; otherwise, the necessary and proper clause "would swallow up all the delegated powers, and reduce the whole to one phrase as before observed" in Jefferson's discussion of the general welfare clause.[15]

Returning to the points made in the beginning of his opinion, Jefferson then clinched his constitutional argument by contrasting the alleged benefits of the bank with the great legal changes that he argued would result from passage of the bank bill into law. "Can it be thought that the Constitution intended that for a shade or two of *convenience*, more or less, Congress should be authorised to break down the most antient and fundamental laws of the several states, such as those against Mortmain, the laws of alienage, the rules of descent, the acts of distribution, the laws of escheat and forfeiture, the laws of monopoly?" The purpose of his summary of the bank bill as, in effect, a reform of the common law of the several states thus became clear: it underscored the importance of his distinction between necessary and convenient means. "Nothing but a necessity invincible by any other means"—certainly not mere convenience, he argued—"can justify such a prostration of laws which constitute the pillars of our whole system of jurisprudence." [16]

Jefferson's opinion on the constitutionality of the bank bill thus presented a theory of interpretation of the Constitution which assumed that the legislative powers of the United States, vested in Congress under Article I, were strictly limited to those powers enumerated in section 8 of that article: the specially enumerated powers (including the general welfare clause, which he construed as a qualification on the power to lay and collect taxes, and not as an independent power) as well as those corollary powers that were "necessary and proper" to carry into execution the enumerated powers. He interpreted "necessary and proper" fairly strictly, although the opinion on the bank bill suggests that he realized that the line between those means that were absolutely necessary and those that constituted mere conveniences was not a clear one and that, in most questions, the power proposed would likely fall somewhere between these two poles. Jefferson's definition of "necessary means"—"those means without which the grant of the power would be nugatory"—clearly, however, put the burden on the proponents of a new federal measure. Where the measure proposed clearly interfered with state law, as Jefferson argued was the case with the bank bill, "nothing but a necessity invincible by any other means" could justify it.

As Dumas Malone has observed, the theory of constitutional interpretation revealed in Jefferson's opinion on the bank bill must be understood within the context of his general attitude toward public law. "To him laws in general, and constitutions in particular, were shields against tyranny; and he coupled a positive faith in human beings with a predominantly negative attitude toward political agencies and institutions."[17] Jefferson certainly was no foe to change; after all, he was the man who believed that each generation has the right to govern itself and who accordingly favored the revision of constitutions every twenty years. He nevertheless feared new interpretations of existing law—by any public functionary, legislative, executive, or judicial—as the instrumentality of change. Whig principles of government had taught him that it was the inevitable tendency of those in power, however well intentioned, to seek to expand their powers at the expense of individual liberties. For this reason he tended to be a literalist, even with respect to statute law, but particularly with respect to fundamental law as embodied in constitutions.

To say that Jefferson was a literalist or a strict constructionist, however, is insufficient to describe his theory of interpretation. Again it should be emphasized that it was the context of a particular constitutional provision within the overall purpose of the federal Constitution, and not the text of the provision alone, that mattered to Jefferson. He indeed was a strict constructionist with regard to most of the powers granted Congress in Article I, section 8, especially where federal powers could preempt state law. Nevertheless, he could interpret federal powers under the Constitution quite liberally in matters involving foreign affairs, which he regarded as an exclusive responsibility of the national government since the time of the Articles of Confederation. He also could be quite liberal in interpreting power-restraining or rights-guaranteeing provisions of the Constitution, at times following the literal meaning of the text in apparent disregard of the framers' actual intent.[18] In analyzing the bank bill, however, Jefferson clearly adhered to the Article I, section 8, enumeration of powers, interpreted quite strictly according to the framers' intentions as he understood them.

After he received Jefferson's opinion on the bank bill, President

Washington then turned to his secretary of the treasury, presenting Hamilton with Jefferson's and Randolph's objections for rebuttal. Hamilton's lengthy, discursive opinion is remarkable both for its thoroughness—he responded to each of Randolph's and Jefferson's arguments—and for its comprehensiveness, in expounding a theory of broad construction which contrasted sharply with Jefferson's theory of interpretation.[19]

Hamilton's opinion was based on the fundamental idea that "every power vested in a government is in its nature *sovereign*, and includes, by *force* of the *term*, a right to employ all the *means* requisite and fairly *applicable* to the attainment of the *ends* of such power; and which are not precluded by restrictions & exceptions specified in the constitution; or not immoral, or not contrary to the essential ends of political society." The power to erect corporations such as the Bank of the United States was "unquestionably incident" to sovereign power, he argued; therefore, the criterion of constitutionality was "the *end*, to which the measure relates as a *mean[s]*": "If the end be clearly comprehended within any of the specified powers, & if the measure have an obvious relation to that end, and is not forbidden by any particular provision of the Constitution—it may safely be deemed to come within the compass of the national authority." In other words, the question as Hamilton framed it was whether the corporation being established sufficiently related "to any of the acknowledged objects or lawful ends of the [federal] government." He found that this particular corporation, the bank, had a "natural relation" to the powers to collect taxes and to regulate national trade. He therefore concluded that the incorporation of the bank was a constitutional measure and that the objections to the bank bill were "ill-founded."[20]

Hamilton dismissed Jefferson's argument as to the meaning of *necessary* as an "erroneous" conception of the meaning of the word. *Necessary*, as it is commonly used, "often means no more than *needful, requisite, incidental, useful,* or *conducive to*," he argued. To understand the word as Jefferson did "would be to give it the same force as if the word *absolutely* or *indispensibly* had been prefixed to it." Such a construction "would beget endless uncertainty & embarrassment," he maintained, noting that "few measures of any government would stand so severe a test." To insist upon such a requirement, moreover, would "make the criterion of the exercise of any implied power a *case of extreme necessity*." That kind of necessity, to Hamilton, was "rather a rule to justify the overleaping of the bounds of constitutional authority, than to govern the ordinary exercise of it." Jefferson's restrictive interpretation of the word *necessary*, Hamilton added, would be contrary to a "sound maxim of construction," that governmental powers "ought to be construed liberally, in advancement of the public good."[21]

In response to Jefferson's Tenth Amendment argument, Hamilton conceded that the federal government had only those powers delegated to it, but he identified three classes of powers that were delegated to the federal government under the Constitution. In addition to the "express powers," specified in Article I, there were "implied powers"; that is, powers which were the instruments or means to the carrying out of any of the specified powers. The power to erect a corporation was such a power. There were also, he added, "resulting powers," powers that resulted from "the whole mass of the powers of the government, and from the nature of political society," such as the power to possess sovereign jurisdiction over conquered territory. He further maintained that "how much is delegated in each case, is a question of fact to be made out by fair reasoning & construction upon the particular provisions of the constitution—taking as guides the general principles & general ends of government."[22]

Hamilton, like Jefferson, thus posited a theory of interpretation of the Constitution which was contextual. To both, interpretation was not a rigidly mechanical process, focused on the text of particular provisions of the document; rather, it was a process in which the plain meaning of the terms employed in the text was to be understood in light of the overall purposes of the document. But it was here, in their basic view of the federal Constitution, that Hamilton and Jefferson differed fundamentally—a difference which lay at the heart of the divergence in their theories of interpretation. Jefferson posited a fairly strict theory which presumed against the exercise of federal powers in doubtful cases and, indeed, excluded from "the ordinary exercise of constitutional authority" the exercise of implied powers. Hamilton posited a theory of liberal construction with the opposite effect. As Merrill Peterson has observed, while both men wished for a strong Union, "one sought its strength in the trust of the states and the people, the other in the amplitude of the general government's powers." Jefferson believed in federalism as the only secure foundation of the Union, while Hamilton, who regarded the Constitution as a "frail and worthless fabric," had little faith in the principle and worked to shrink the powers of the states.[23]

The debate between Jefferson and Hamilton was a strictly private one, conducted in writing and for the president's eyes only. Faced with the conflicting opinions of his advisers, Washington delayed as long as the law would allow him before he signed the bill, thus resolving the question in favor of the measure's constitutionality. Ironically, it may have been a part of Jefferson's opinion—his view of the limited scope of the veto power—that helped Washington overcome his qualms about the bank bill. Jefferson maintained that the presidential veto power was "the shield provided by the constitution" to protect, among other things, the rights of the states, and that the bill involved "the case of a right remaining exclusively with the states"—presumably, the power to erect corporations. (That the bank would also affect in other ways the common law of the states, as Jefferson asserted in his prefatory observations, subtly underscored this point.) He nevertheless advised that "unless the President's mind on a view of every thing which is urged for and against this bill, is tolerably clear that it is unauthorised by the constitution," he should give the benefit of doubt to Congress and sign the bill. Jefferson added, probably more to reinforce his negative assessment of the bill than as a mere aside, that "it is chiefly for cases where they [Congress] are clearly misled by error, ambition, or interest, that the constitution has placed a check in the negative of the President." [24]

Jefferson's and Hamilton's now-famous conflicting opinions did not become public until 1807, when they were printed in an appendix to John Marshall's *Life of George Washington*. Not coincidentally, Marshall incorporated Hamilton's arguments in his opinion in the case *McCulloch v. Maryland,* in which the constitutionality of the bank was upheld and Hamilton's doctrine of implied powers was enshrined in constitutional law.

Washington did follow Jefferson's advice in vetoing the apportionment bill in the spring of 1792. This first exercise of the presidential veto power involved a fairly straightforward problem of constitutionality, and Jefferson's opinion and the brief veto message that he drafted for Washington manifest quite clearly Jefferson's constitutional scruples. The Constitution declared (Article I, section 2) that representatives and direct taxes were to be apportioned among the several states "according to their respective numbers," with each state having at least one representative and the number of representatives not exceeding one for every 30,000 people. The bill, Jefferson observed, "without explaining any principle at all, which may shew it's conformity with the constitution," arbitrarily apportioned representatives among the states. His calculations showed the same ratio had not been applied to each state; therefore, the bill did not apportion representatives among the states proportionate to their populations, as the Constitution required. Moreover, the bill allotted to eight states one representative for every 27,770 people—thus exceeding the limit of one for every 30,000, if that provision was interpreted to apply to the states individually, which Jefferson considered to be a natural interpretation. He followed the canon "where a phrase is susceptible of two meanings, we ought certainly to adopt that which will bring upon us the fewest inconveniencies" and concluded that a contrary interpretation of Article I, section 2, would be "an inconvenient exposition of it's words." His brief draft of the president's veto message merely identified the two provisions of the bill that were inconsistent with the Constitution.[25]

In 1792 Hamilton's Report on Manufactures again raised constitutional issues, this time involving the general welfare clause more fully. The report, which Hamilton had submitted at the end of 1791, proposed that manufactures be given federal aid through such devices as protective tariffs, bounties, and the exemption from duties of certain imports of raw materials. Hamilton's sweeping assertions regarding the general welfare clause in connection with the provision for bounties particularly appalled both Madison and Jefferson.[26] Jefferson told President Washington that Hamilton's report and its assertions posed "a very different question from that of the bank, which was thought an incident to an enumerated power." The general welfare clause, as Jefferson understood it, was not a separate grant of power to Congress; rather, it merely specified the purpose for which the taxation power was to be exercised. To interpret it, as he saw Hamilton doing, to give Congress the right to exercise all powers that may be for the general welfare—"that is to say, all the legitimate powers of government, since no government has a legitimate right to do what is not for the welfare of the governed"—would be a "sham limitation," he argued.[27]

Congress did not act on Hamilton's report, but Jefferson's abhorrence of a loose construction of the general welfare clause survived and was reasserted years later. In 1815 he wrote: "I hope our courts will never countenance the sweeping pretensions which have been set up under the words 'general defence and public welfare.' These words only express the motives which induced the Convention to give to the ordinary legislature certain specified powers which they enumerate, . . . and not to give them the unspecified also; or why the specification? They could not be so awkward in language as to mean, as we say, 'all and some.' And should this construction prevail, all limits to the federal government are done away." He added that "this opinion, formed on the first rise of the question, I have never seen reason to change, whether in or out of power; but on the contrary, find it strengthened and confirmed by five and twenty years of additional reflection and experience." [28]

"The True Barriers of Our Liberty": The Kentucky Resolutions

One of the foundations for Jefferson's theory of federalism was his notion that "the true barriers of our liberty in this country are our State governments." [29] This idea was no mere abstraction; Jefferson gave it concrete application in the crisis year of 1798 when, faced with the Alien and Sedition Acts and a Federalist-dominated national government, he and some fellow Republicans turned to the states, to the legislatures of Virginia and Kentucky, to challenge the legislation as unconstitutional.

An episode in his home state shows Jefferson's willingness to use the state legislature to criticize actions of the federal government. Late in May 1797 a federal grand jury had returned a presentment, or formal accusation of crime, against Samuel J. Cabell, the congressman from Jefferson's own district, for seditious libel, or as the presentment put it, for disseminating "at a time of real public danger . . . unfounded calumnies against the happy government of the United States" in a circular letter to his constituents. The grand jury presentment was extraordinary since it was the first case of seditious libel against the United States founded wholly upon the common law, as more than a year would pass before the introduction of the Sedition Act in Congress. Jefferson drafted an anonymous petition to the Virginia House of Delegates condemning the presentment and calling for the impeachment and punishment of the grand jurors by the legislature.[30]

Jefferson's draft petition argued that the grand jury presentment violated, first, the privileges of Congress (because it concerned a communication made by Cabell to his constituents in the exercise of his function as a representative), second, the constitutional principle of separation of powers (because it in effect made the legislative branch subject to the cognizance and coercion of the judiciary, of which the grand jury was a part), and third, the "natural right" of free correspondence between citizens. It was in order to protect this third right, particularly, that Jefferson turned to the Virginia legislature. The Virginia Constitution empowered the House of Delegates to impeach officers "offending against the State," and the grand jurors' "crime" was of "that high and extraordinary character" for which the constitution had provided this extraordinary procedure.[31]

Jefferson explained in a letter to James Monroe his reasons for directing the petition to the Virginia assembly rather than to Congress, as Monroe had suggested. "The system of the General government, is to seize all doubtful ground. We must join in the scramble, or get nothing. Where first occupancy is to give a right, he who lies still loses all. Besides, it is not right for those who are only to act in a preliminary form, to let their own doubts preclude the judgment of the court of ultimate decision. We ought to let it go to the Ho[use] of delegates for their consideration, & they, unless the contrary be palpable, ought to let it go to the General court, who are ultimately to decide on it." He concluded, "It is of immense consequence that the States retain as complete authority as possible over their own citizens." Although Jefferson apparently was uncertain about the specific means of redress and the exact procedures to follow to obtain it, it is significant that he regarded the General Court, the highest judicial authority of the state, as the body "who are ultimately to decide on it." As Dumas Malone has noted, at this stage, with both the executive and judicial branches of the federal government manned by Federalists and with Congress itself rather uncertain, "he saw no recourse except to the states." Regarding the matter at issue—Congressman Cabell's freedom to communicate with his constituents in Albemarle County—as a matter pertaining to Virginia rather than to the federal government, he was convinced that the state needed to assert its authority, to preclude the Federalist-dominated national government from seizing "all doubtful ground."[32]

Against this background, one can more fully understand Jefferson's response the following year to the even more ominous threats to freedom that were posed by the Alien and Sedition Acts. Jefferson saw these laws not only as attempts to stifle Republican criticism of the administration—to suppress the "whig presses" and their contributors, supporters and friends—but also as "an experiment on the American mind, to see how far it will bear an avowed violation of the constitution." In addition to his observation that the laws were "palpably in the teeth of the Constitution," he described the acts as "worthy of the 8th and 9th century," which despite his affection for Anglo-Saxon England, he did not mean as a compliment.[33]

The Kentucky and the Virginia Resolutions were drafted by Jefferson and Madison in response to the rather extraordinary political circumstances in 1798; both sets of resolutions were drafted in secrecy and introduced in the Kentucky and Virginia legislatures through intermediaries, respectively, John Breckinridge and John Taylor. Explaining the secrecy under which the Resolutions were drafted, Adrienne Koch has suggested that the war fever that brought on the Alien and Sedition Acts would have mounted to a new high if the principal author of the Kentucky Resolutions had been publicly identified as Vice President Jefferson. Indeed, she argued, Jefferson and Madison probably were aware that Jefferson himself might be charged with sedition.[34] Although Jefferson and Madison acted in close collaboration with one another, Jefferson's draft of the Kentucky Resolutions was the more radical of the two, in expressing the principle that the states might nullify—that is, treat as void—acts of Congress that they deemed unconstitutional.

Like his draft of the Declaration of Independence, Jefferson's Kentucky Resolutions put forth an argument in the form of a syllogism. The resolutions accordingly began by stating the major premise, setting forth Jefferson's theory of the Union as a compact among the states. The several states composing the United States of America "are not united on the principle of unlimited submission to their General Government"; rather, "by a compact under the style and title of a Constitution for the United States . . . they constituted a General Government for special purposes,—delegated to that government certain definite powers, reserving, each State to itself, the residuary mass of right to their own self-government." Each state "acceded as a State" to the compact, and each state was "an integral party, its co-States forming, as to itself, the other party." [35]

From this general theory of the Union, Jefferson derived two basic corollary principles. First, since it was created by the compact for special, limited purposes only, "whensoever the General Government assumes undelegated powers, its acts are unauthoritative, void, and of no force." Second, the government created by the compact could not be "the exclusive or final judge of the extent of the powers delegated to itself" because "that would have made its discretion, and not the Constitution, the measure of its powers." Accordingly, "as in all cases of compact among powers having no common judge," each party—that is, each state—has an equal right to judge for itself, "as well of infractions as of the mode and measure of redress." [36]

If Jefferson had not reached this conclusion on his own, the idea might have come from John Taylor, who wrote to him early in the summer of 1798: "The right of the state governments to expound the Constitution might possibly be made the basis of a movement toward its amendment. If this is insufficient, the people in state conventions are incontrovertibly the contracting parties, and, possessing the infringing rights, may proceed by orderly steps to attain the object." [37] Jefferson did not distinguish between conventions and legislatures at this juncture, perhaps as a matter of expediency. Again, the experience of the Cabell case, as well as the Virginia General Assembly's continuing experience with such resolutions of protest since the Revolution, showed him that the legislature could be relied upon as an instrument for expressing the voice of the people.

Five resolutions in Jefferson's draft—the second through the sixth—stated the minor premises of his overall argument. They were devoted to proving the unconstitutionality of the Alien and Sedition Acts. In the second, third, and fourth resolutions is evident the same theory of strict construction that Jefferson posited in his case against the constitutionality of the bank. The Tenth Amendment confirmed the basic principle, that powers not delegated to the United States by the Constitution, nor prohibited by it to the states, are reserved to the states, or to the people. The Constitution specified the crimes, such as treason and counterfeiting, over which the United States had jurisdiction; the creation, definition, and punishment of all other crimes were reserved, "and, of right, appertain[ed] solely and exclusively" to the states, "each within its own territory." Similarly, because no power over the freedom of speech or press was delegated to the United States by the Constitution—which indeed declared, in the First Amendment, that "Congress shall make no law . . . abridging the freedom of speech or of the press"—all lawful powers respecting these freedoms remained with the states. Jefferson's position was that the Constitution reserved to the states alone the power of judging "how far the licentiousness of speech and of the press may be abridged without lessening their useful freedom, and how far those abuses which cannot be separated from their use should be tolerated, rather than the use destroyed." Finally, no power over alien friends having been delegated to the United States or prohibited to the individual states by the Constitution, "alien friends are under the jurisdiction and protection of the laws of the State wherein they are." He concluded in the fourth resolution, with respect to the Alien Friends Act, as he had concluded in the second and third resolutions with respect to the Sedition Act, that it was "altogether void, and of no force."[38]

The fifth and sixth resolutions presented rather novel constitutional arguments. In the fifth resolution Jefferson departed from his canon of original intention and engaged in what he must have been aware was a literal but nonoriginalist interpretation of the language in Article I, section 9. This section provided that "the migration or importation of such persons as any of the states now existing shall think proper to admit, shall not be prohibited by the Congress prior to the year 1808." Although Madison's notes on the debates in the Constitutional Convention would have revealed to Jefferson what was generally understood to be the intent of this clause—to protect the slave trade—Jefferson took the "such persons" phrase quite literally and argued that "this commonwealth [Kentucky] does admit the migration of alien friends," the subject of the Aliens Act. The act, therefore, was void because it violated Article I, section 9: "A provision against prohibiting their migration, is a provision against all acts equivalent thereto, . . . [and] to remove them when migrated, is equivalent to a prohibition of their migration."[39] Thus, Jefferson was not above resorting to ingenious constitutional arguments when making his case for the limitation of governmental powers.

In the sixth resolution he argued that the procedures of the Alien Act—particularly its provision empowering the president to order deportations—violated the Fifth Amendment's due process clause and the Sixth Amendment rights to a jury trial, held in public, with benefit of counsel and the opportunity to cross-examine witnesses. The act also violated the principle of separation of powers, Jefferson argued, in that it transferred the judiciary power, "the power of judging," from the courts, where Article III vested it, to the president, "that magistrate of the general government who already possesses all the Executive, and a negative on all Legislative powers." For these reasons, he again concluded, the act was "not law, but utterly void, and of no force." [40]

The seventh resolution was a blanket condemnation of all "proceeedings of the General Government" that had been undertaken under color of the general welfare and necessary and proper clauses. The broad construction applied to those clauses "goes to the destruction of all limits prescribed" to the power of the federal government by the Constitution, he argued, reiterating in concise language the arguments he had raised against Hamiltonian measures during Washington's administration. "Words meant by the instrument to be subsidiary only to the execution of limited powers, ought not to be so construed as themselves to give unlimited powers, nor a part to be so taken as to destroy the whole residue of that instrument." The resolution declared the entire class of all such unconstitutional measures to be "a fit and necessary subject of revisal and correction" later, "at a time of greater tranquillity," while those specified in the preceding resolutions "call for immediate redress." [41]

Finally, in the eighth and ninth of his draft resolutions, Jefferson stated the conclusion of his overall argument. This conclusion was inevitable by the logic of a syllogism premised on the idea that each state, as a party to the Constitution, had an equal right to judge for itself "as well as infractions as of the mode and measure of redress." Two modes of redress, one rather mild and the other fairly radical, were specified in his resolutions.

The milder mode of redress was called for in the first clause of the eighth resolution and in the ninth resolution: the appointment of "a committee of conference and correspondence" to communicate to the legislatures of the other states the preceding resolutions. The committee also would assure sister states of Kentucky's devotion to the Union, properly limited: "that this commonwealth . . . considers union, for specified national purposes . . . to be friendly to the peace, happiness, and prosperity of all the States . . . [but] that it does also believe, that to take from the States all the powers of self-government and transfer them to a general and consolidated government, without regard to the special delegations and reservations solemnly agreed to in that compact, is not for the peace, happiness or prosperity of these States."

The more radical mode of redress was then suggested in the further clauses of the eighth resolution. "In cases of an abuse of the delegated powers, the members of the general government, being chosen by the people, a change by the people would be the constitutional remedy," the resolution continued; "but," as here, "where powers are assumed which have not been delegated, a nullification of the act is the rightful remedy." This followed, Jefferson argued, from the "natural right" of each state "in cases not within the compact . . . to nullify of their own authority all assumptions of power by others within their limits." Although this right could be exercised individually by each state, the resolution made clear that "this commonwealth, from motives of regard and respect for its co-States, has wished to communicate with them on the subject," since "they alone," as parties to the federal compact, were "solely authorized to judge in the last resort of the powers exercised under it," Congress being not a party but "merely the creature of the compact." [42]

The eighth resolution did not end there. To underscore the importance of the issues at stake, Jefferson added a parade of horribles that would result from permitting the Alien and Sedition Acts to stand. Congress could make criminal any act it pleased, empowering the president to summarily judge and outlaw any inhabitants of the states—not just "friendless" aliens but even citizens, and perhaps even members of the legislatures, governors, and judges of the several states—for whatever reason, good or bad, public or personal. "These and successive acts of the same character, unless arrested at the threshold, necessarily drive these States into revolution and blood, and will furnish new calumnies against republican government, and new pretexts of those who wish it to be believed that man cannot be governed but by a rod of iron," the resolution warned. Next came the passage that, as previously noted, may be regarded as the most succinct expression of the touchstone of Jefferson's constitutionalism. Declaring that "it is jealousy and not confidence which prescribes limited constitutions, to bind down those whom we are obliged to trust with power," he further urged, "Let the honest advocate of confidence read the Alien and Sedition acts, and say if the Constitution has not been wise in fixing limits to the government it created, and whether we should be wise in destroying those limits." This was the context in which Jefferson summed up, "In questions of power, then, let no more be heard of confidence in man, but bind him down from mischief by the chains of the Constitution."

The eighth resolution then concluded with a reiteration of the invitation to other states to concur "in considering the said acts as so palpably against the Constitution as to amount to an undisguised declaration that the compact is not meant to be the measure of the powers of the General Government, but that it will proceed in the exercise over these States, of all powers whatsoever," seizing the rights of the states and "consolidating them in the General Government, with a power assumed to bind the States . . . in all cases whatsoever," by laws made "not with their consent, but by others against their consent," thus surrendering "the form of government we have chosen."[43]

If one accepts the Republican arguments that the Alien and Sedition Acts were dangerously partisan and blatantly unconstitutional, it is easy to see why Jefferson and others were so alarmed in 1798. Jefferson wrote over twenty years later that "at the time when the representatives of our country were so much alarmed at . . . the federal ascendancy in Congress, in the executive and judicial departments, it became a matter of serious consideration how head could be made against their enterprises on the constitution." The leading Republicans decided that they would "take a stand in the State legislatures"— which were not a part of the Federalist monopoly of offices—"and endeavor there to arrest their progress."[44] Thus, to a great extent the resolutions must be understood in light of the extraordinary political circumstances that necessitated recourse to the state legislatures.

Although the political circumstances of 1798 were unique, it does not follow that the general course of action represented by the Kentucky Resolutions was also unusual. Dumas Malone has pointed out that, ironically, Alexander Hamilton had predicted in *Federalist* Nos. 26 and 28 that the state legislatures would be "not only vigilant but suspicious and jealous guardians of the rights of the citizens against encroachments from the federal government," and that they would "readily communicate with each other in the different States, and unite their common forces for the protection of their common liberty." Indeed, insofar as one can limit Jefferson's resolutions, and certainly Madison's, to merely a declaration of the unconstitutionality of acts of Congress, one may even suggest that Hamilton went even further, in arguing that the state legislatures would be "not only the voice, but if necessary, the ARM of discontent"—whatever he may have meant by that.[45] Since at least the time of the Stamp Act crisis in 1765, legislative resolutions protesting unconstitutionality (whether of acts of Parliament or of Congress) were considered a normal mode of redress of grievances. Jefferson's call for a "committee of conference and correspondence" in his eighth resolution and his argument that Congress (like Parliament) had assumed an illegitimate power to bind the states "in all cases whatsoever" suggest the Revolutionary parallel.[46]

What was radical in Jefferson's draft of the Kentucky Resolutions was the passage in the eighth resolution declaring "nullification" the rightful remedy. The resolutions as introduced in and passed by the Kentucky legislature omitted this troublesome word; although they still declared the Alien and Sedition Acts contrary to the Constitution and therefore "void," the specific actions they called for were relatively mild. The official Kentucky Resolutions of 1798 contained a new eighth resolution, instructing the state's senators and representatives to seek a prompt repeal of these unconstitutional statutes in Congress; and the new ninth resolution, an edited version of Jefferson's original eighth, called upon the other states to concur in declaring the acts void and of no force and demanding that Congress repeal them.[47]

Although the evidence suggests that the scenario Jefferson posited in his eighth draft resolution was not mere rhetoric but an expression of his genuine fears, he indicated in November 1798 his desire not to "push the matter to extremities" but rather to await the adoption of Madison's Virginia Resolutions and the result of the appeal made by both sets of resolutions to the other states.[48] In less than a year, however, he was prepared to set in motion the machinery to intensify the campaign against the Alien and Sedition Acts. The disappointing response of the northern states to the Kentucky and Virginia Resolves, coupled with the truly frightening prospect that the Federalist judiciary might allow prosecutions for seditious libel under the "formidable" doctrine of a federal common law, prompted Jefferson to propose a new, dangerous strategy. He urged that further resolutions be drawn up, again inviting the other states to join Kentucky and Virginia in making "a firm protestation against the principle &

the precedent" and "a reservation of the rights" resulting from these "palpable violations" of the Constitution. The resolutions would then declare the ultimate determination of the two states, "were we to be disappointed in this, to sever ourselves from that union we so much value, rather than give up the rights of self-government which we have reserved, & in which alone we see liberty, safety & happiness." As in 1774–75, when he said that he would rather see the American colonies declare their independence than continue being subjected to violations of their rights by the British government, so was Jefferson, in August 1799, raising the threat of disunion.[49]

Madison, to whom Jefferson broached this dangerous strategy, undoubtedly exerted a moderating influence on him, and the extreme proposal was dropped. By the spring of 1800, when political developments in the middle states were more encouraging, Jefferson returned to the optimistic spirit in which he had written to John Taylor some two years earlier, when he maintained that "resort to a scission of the Union" was not an answer, that the body of the citizens were substantially republican, and with "a little patience" they would "see the reign of witches pass over, . . . and the people . . . restore their government to its true principles."[50]

"A Few Plain Duties Performed by a Few Servants": Federal Powers under Republican Administrations

The dual principles of federalism—the "support of the state governments in all their rights," for the administration of domestic matters, and the "preservation of the general government, in it's whole constitutional vigour," for the administration of foreign matters—were among the fundamental principles that Jefferson identified in his First Inaugural Address as the true creed and the policy that would guide his administration. The notable achievement of Jefferson's presidency was to remain faithful to this creed, by and large, and thus reverse the policies of the preceding Federalist administrations that he viewed as destructive of federalism, the "true theory" of the Constitution.

The easiest reversal concerned the Sedition Act. Although the statute by its own terms had expired on 4 March 1801, the day Jefferson was inaugurated, prosecutions of William Duane, editor of the Philadelphia *Aurora*, and others were still pending. Jefferson, exercising his doctrine that each of the three branches of government was competent to judge the constitutionality of its own acts, authorized the dismissal of these prosecutions on the ground that the statute on which they were based was unconstitutional.

Reversal of other parts of the Federalist domestic program, and particularly the Hamiltonian financial system, proved far more difficult. Since its establishment in the early 1790s Hamilton's financial system, including the hated Bank of the United States, had become a fixture in the American economy. Jefferson ruefully explained his dilemma: "When this government was first established, it was possible to have kept it going on true principles, but the contracted, English, half-lettered ideas of Hamilton destroyed that hope in the bud. We can pay off his debt in 15 years; but we can never get rid of his financial system. It mortifies me to be strengthening principles which I deem radically vicious, but this vice is entailed on us by the first error. In other parts of our government I hope we shall by degrees to introduce sound principles and make them habitual." He concluded, "What is practicable must often controul what is pure theory; and the habits of the governed determine in a great degree what is practicable." Although he acquiesced in the continued existence of the Bank of the United States, Jefferson never overcame his hostility to it. He urged his secretary of the treasury, Albert Gallatin, to bring the bank to "perfect subordination" by reducing it to equal footing with other banks. He also encouraged the patronage of Republican state banks. These efforts on Jefferson's part, however, were basically rhetorical, and Gallatin's pragmatic acceptance and use of the bank thus "controlled theory."[51]

There were some aspects of the Hamiltonian system that could be, and were, corrected in Jefferson's administration. In the 1790s Jefferson had complained of the "chaos" in the accounts of Hamilton's Treasury Department, which rendered it difficult to determine whether sums appropriated were applied to their specific objects. Republicans had argued that this violated that section of the Constitution requiring that no money be drawn from the treasury but in consequence of appropriations made by law. "The accounts of the United States ought to be, and may be made as simple as those of a common farmer, and capable of being understood by them," Jefferson argued. Accordingly, as president, Jefferson encouraged Gallatin to follow his idea of "kneading all [Hamilton's] little scraps & fragments into one batch." By thus simplifying the treasury accounts, Jefferson pointed out to Gallatin, "we might hope to see the finances of the Union as clear and intelligible as a merchant's book, so that every member of Congress, and every man of any mind in the Union, should be able to comprehend them, to investigate abuses and consequently control them."[52]

Jefferson otherwise sought to ameliorate the pernicious effects of the Hamiltonian system by embarking upon a thoroughgoing program of economy in government and retirement of the national debt. In his first annual message, in December 1801, he declared that it was his administration's policy "to reduce expenses to what is necessary for the useful purposes of government," and he described those concerns which he regarded as appropriate for the federal government. "When we consider that this government is charged with the external and mutual relations only of these states; that the states themselves have principal care of our persons, our property, and our reputation, constituting the great field of human concerns, we may well doubt whether our organization is not too complicated, too expensive; whether offices and officers have not been multiplied unnecessarily, and sometimes injuriously to the service they were meant to promote."[53]

The restoration of peace in Europe during Jefferson's first term made possible—at least for a few years—this reduction of the federal government, for it not only lessened pressures to build up the nation's defenses but also augmented revenues through the increase in foreign trade. Thus Jefferson's policy benefited from fortunate circumstances; as Dumas Malone has observed, "he could have congratulated himself that his administration began in 1801 instead of 1797, when the launching of such an experiment in democratic and economical government as his would hardly have been possible." It should be emphasized, however, that Jefferson's policy of reduction in government was not based merely on the expectation of continued peace in Europe but rather was integral to his concept of a limited federal government.[54]

Jefferson's policy may be divided into four closely related parts, one of which already has been discussed, the reform of treasury accounts through the use of specific, rather than general, appropriations. The other three parts of the program were: tax reduction, definite provision for retirement of the national debt, and strict economy in government. Each warrants a brief examination.

Despite Gallatin's advice recommending delay, Jefferson advocated the immediate repeal of all internal taxes, dating back to Hamilton's excise on whiskey. In suggesting this to Congress in his first annual message, Jefferson recognized that "the changes of foreign relations now taking place so desirably in the world" had favorably affected the prospects for revenue—both "to provide for the support of government" and "to pay the interest on the public debts and to discharge the principals"—through tariffs and imposts alone. Although war and other "untoward events" might change these prospects, he argued that "sound principles will not justify our taxing the industry of our fellow citizens to accumulate treasure for wars to happen we know not when, and which might not perhaps happen but from the temptations offered by that treasure."[55]

In addition to the repeal of internal taxes, Jefferson also enthusiastically endorsed the plan prepared by Gallatin to pay off the entire national debt—some $83 million—within sixteen years by annual appropriations of $7.3 million. During the eight years of Jefferson's administration the debt actually was reduced by almost a third; extraordinary expenses not foreseen at the beginning of his presidency —chiefly, the increased naval costs associated with the Barbary Wars and the $15 million Louisiana Purchase—forced the modification of Gallatin's plan. Nevertheless, the plan to extinguish the debt was largely successful because of the large increase in revenue from import duties that accompanied the growth in American commerce during this period.[56] The increased revenues actually created a surplus later in the administration, prompting Jefferson to recommend a constitutional amendment permitting expenditures for roads and other internal improvements.

The idea of a long-term national debt was part of the Hamiltonian financial system that Jefferson especially abhorred. He condemned it as a violation of natural rights, incompatible with his conviction that "the earth belongs to the living generation." It also was linked in his mind to the corrupt English system of government and thus was contrary to sound principles of public policy, as well. In 1798 he expressed support of a constitutional amendment, removing from the federal government the power of borrowing, in order to obtain "the reduction of the administration of our government to the genuine principles of its constitution."[57] One of the clearest statements of his aversion to public debt appeared a few months after his retirement from the presidency, in a letter to Gallatin. "I consider the fortunes of our republic as depending, in an eminent degree, on the extinguishment of the public debt before we engage in any war: because, that done, we shall have revenue enough to improve our country in peace and defend it in war, without recurring either to new taxes or loans. But if the debt should once more be swelled to a formidable size, its entire discharge will be despaired of, and we shall be committed to the English career of debt, corruption, and rottenness, closing with revolution." Concluding that "the discharge of the debt is vital to the destinies of our government," he urged Gallatin to remain in President Madison's cabinet. "We shall never see another President and Secretary of the Treasury making all other objects subordinate to this."[58]

Even during and after the War of 1812, he continued to urge that the debt be paid off and that the government adhere to the pay-as-you-go principle. He urged "a wise rule . . . 'never to borrow a dollar without laying a tax in the same instant for paying the interest annually, and the principal within a given term; and to consider that tax as pledged to the creditors on the public faith.' " The tax "will awaken the attention of the people and make reformation and economy the principles of the next election. The frequent recurrence of this chastening operation can alone restrain the propensity of governments to enlarge expense beyond income."[59] Since Jefferson found high taxes equally as abhorrent as debts, the implications of this principle in practice mandated economy in government: without economy, there would be public debt; with public debt, there must be taxation, "and in its train wretchedness and oppression."[60]

Thus associated with the goals of tax reduction and the discharge of the national debt was the fourth policy of Jefferson's administration, economy in government. Abolition of internal taxes made possible the elimination of the internal revenue service employed to collect them; this resulted in a significant decrease in the Department of Treasury, by far the largest of the executive departments. Jefferson also recommended reductions in the army, navy, and diplomatic corps. The most dramatic reductions took place in the navy, for which expenditures fell in 1802 to $915,000, half the level of the first year of Jefferson's presidency, although they rose again because of the war against the Barbary states.[61]

By these four policies—treasury reform, tax reduction, retirement of the debt, and economy in government—then, Jefferson sought to accomplish the objective he had stated in his First Inaugural Address and reiterated elsewhere in his writings at the start of his presidency: to restore the constitutional equilibrium between the states and federal government by keeping the latter "a wise and frugal government" limited to its sphere. But did Jefferson as president act in a manner wholly consistent with the principles of federalism and constitutional interpretation that he had elaborated in the 1790s, in his opinion on the bank and in the Kentucky Resolutions?

Critics of Jefferson, both past and present, have argued that he did not adhere to these principles; and they have pointed to other programs of his administration—chiefly, the Louisiana Purchase, the embargo, and internal improvements—that seem to have more than made up for the reductions in government with dramatic exercises of federal powers in ways that appear wholly inconsistent with Jeffersonian doctrines. For example, Joseph Story, writing in 1833, argued that the purchase of Louisiana and the embargo were "the most remarkable powers, which have been exercised by the government, as auxiliary and implied powers, and which, if any, go to the utmost verge of liberal construction." At the end of the nineteenth century, Henry Adams similarly argued that the purchase of Louisiana was a precedent "too striking to be overlooked," an act "which he [Jefferson himself] said made blank paper of the Constitution." With respect to the embargo, Adams argued that "no one could doubt that under the doctrine of States-rights and the rules of strict construction the embargo was unconstitutional."[62] These particular charges, and the broader issue of consistency that they involve, warrant closer examination.

It is true that Jefferson as president apparently departed from some of the principles of strict construction of federal powers that he had espoused in his opinion on the bank in 1791. There he had maintained that federal powers were strictly limited to those enumerated in Article I and the corollary powers that were "necessary and proper"— in the fairly restrictive sense in which he defined *necessary*—to the exercise of enumerated powers. He thus had posited a fairly strict theory of constitutional interpretation that presumed against the exercise of federal powers in doubtful cases and that indeed excluded the exercise of implied powers from the ordinary exercise of constitutional authority. As president, however, Jefferson sanctioned some exercises of federal powers which can only be explained in terms of either a looser definition of "necessary and proper" or Hamiltonian "implied powers."

Two cases in point involved the establishment of the United States Military Academy at West Point, New York, and Jefferson's controversial plan to establish a dry dock for the navy. Before his presidency Jefferson had questioned the constitutional authority of Congress to set up a military academy; yet in 1802, under authority of a congressional act of that year, he set up a small school for military engineers at West Point.[63] Establishment of such an institution was not among the enumerated powers of Congress. It could be justified only as an exercise of a power implied from the Article I, section 8, powers to raise and support armies and to erect "forts, magazines, arsenals, dock-yards, and other needful buildings." Jefferson did point to Congress's power to provide and maintain a navy as the constitutional basis for his proposal in 1802 to construct in the Washington Navy Yard a dock in which vessels could be "laid up dry and under cover from the sun"—an economy measure that Federalist congressmen quickly derided as a "visionary scheme." He similarly considered an act for the building of piers in the Delaware River as an adjunct to the power to provide and maintain a navy since, he maintained, that power was tantamount to the power "to provide receptacles for it, and places to cover and preserve it."[64]

In both these cases Jefferson tied the projects directly to enumerated powers. In contrast, shortly before his presidency, when he criticized a House bill incorporating a company for the Roosevelt copper mines in New Jersey, he pointed out that the incorporation fell "under the *sweeping clause* of the Constitution, and supported by the following pedigree of necessities. Congress are authorized to defend the country: ships are necessary for that defence: copper is necessary for ships: mines are necessary to produce copper: companies are necessary to work mines: and 'this is the house that Jack built.'"[65] This was the same kind of reasoning with respect to the necessary and proper clause that he had condemned in his opinion on the bank. Creation of a corporation, whether a bank to assist the government in its financial operations or a mining company to assist in national defense, was too remote a means to the enumerated ends. The corps of engineers and the dry dock, in Jefferson's mind at least, were so closely tied to enumerated powers that though strictly speaking they were warranted under the necessary and proper clause, he thought of them as tantamount to the enumerated powers.

What is even more important to remember, however, is the contextual nature of Jefferson's theory of constitutional interpretation. It was the context of a particular constitutional provision, within the overall purposes of the federal Constitution, and not the text of the provision alone, that mattered. What concerned him about the bank bill, apart from its association with Hamilton's overall system—a consideration that mattered, to be sure—was his perception that the Bank of the United States would interfere with state law in a variety of ways. He was concerned, in short, because the bank bill, as he saw it, threatened federalism by establishing a corporation with powers that would impinge upon the sphere of state authority reserved by the Tenth Amendment. Where Jefferson perceived no federalism problem, he could espouse a fairly liberal theory of interpretation, embracing even implied powers. This was especially so in the realm of foreign affairs, which he had regarded as an exclusive responsibility of the national government since the time of the Articles of Confederation.

With these general observations in mind, one can best understand the far more important issues involving the Louisiana Purchase, the embargo, and internal improvements. Here too, the inconsistency between his constitutional theory and his sanctioning of expansive federal powers was more apparent than real.

The purchase of Louisiana and its attendant constitutional difficulties are discussed more fully in the next chapter, in the context of executive powers, because Jefferson regarded the matter as one in which he acted within his discretionary powers as president. Consistent with his strict interpretation of Article I powers, he held genuine doubts regarding the constitutionality of the acquisition (or, more strictly speaking, the incorporation of the acquisition into the United States). Although he eventually acquiesced in the Louisiana Purchase without the constitutional amendment that he believed was necessary to sanction it, what is noteworthy is the degree to which he agonized over what may be fairly regarded as a technical question. Indeed, he was willing to jeopardize the acquisition of Louisiana, despite its immense strategic importance, in order to save the principle of strict construction. That he ultimately regarded the purchase of Louisiana as an act of executive discretion is a quite telling fact. It suggests that Jefferson understood it to be an instance of the exercise of implied powers, which (as Hamilton correctly had pointed out in his opinion on the bank bill) was, under Jefferson's theory, essentially an extraconstitutional act: "a case of extreme necessity," as Hamilton put it in his opinion, or "a necessity invincible by any other means," as Jefferson put it in his.

Rather than showing hypocrisy, Jefferson's reluctant acquiescence in the Louisiana Purchase and his rationalization of it as an extraconstitutional act of executive discretion demonstrate the seriousness of his constitutional scruples. He was loath to imply federal powers to acquire new territory and incorporate it into the United States even though these clearly were not powers which could be exercised by the states. Thus, unlike the bank bill, the Louisiana Purchase did not jeopardize the principle of federalism; it did not threaten any powers reserved to the states by the Tenth Amendment. By dramatically increasing the size of the United States, however, it did have profound political implications for the other states, among them one that Jefferson lived to witness—the controversy surrounding the admission of Missouri into the Union as a slave state in 1820. And, as Joseph Story's and Henry Adams's criticisms so vividly illustrate, the acquisition of the Louisiana territory did set a precedent for broad exercise of federal powers.

The embargo on foreign trade that was implemented in Jefferson's second term posed even greater constitutional questions about which, ironically, Jefferson apparently was not troubled at all. The embargo was his answer to the resumption of war between Britain and France in 1803 and the resulting difficulty in maintaining American neutral rights. The combined effect of Britain's Orders in Council and Napoleon's Berlin Decree was that by late 1807 American ships, seamen, and merchandise were subject to seizure by both belligerent powers.[66] The measure that Jefferson recommended and Congress enacted with astonishingly little debate—the complete interdiction of foreign trade—thus was essentially a defensive measure designed to remove the danger of war. As Jefferson explained the policy in a private letter to John Taylor of Caroline, "The embargo keeping at home our vessels, cargoes & seamen, saves us the necessity of making their capture the cause of immediate war; for if going to England, France had determined to take them; if to any other place, England was to take them. Till they return to some sense of moral duty therefore, we keep within ourselves. This gives time, time may produce peace in Europe: peace in Europe removes all causes of difference, till another European war: and by that time our debt may be paid, our revenues clear, & our strength increased."[67] As this letter suggests, Jefferson's abhorrence of public debt was an important calculation in his decision:

because war would necessarily entail debt, embargo—at least for a certain length of time—was the lesser evil.

The embargo that Jefferson called for, however, was indeterminate; and as time passed, the policy behind the embargo shifted. What had begun as a defensive measure to avoid war became an offensive measure, a weapon of economic pressure against the belligerents, particularly the British. Evolution of the embargo policy into that of a great "experiment" in economic coercion was not surprising, since commercial discrimination was a policy which Jefferson long had supported and in conjunction with Madison in 1793–94 had recommended as the way to deal with British restrictions on American commerce.[68]

Was the embargo a constitutional exercise of Congress's power to regulate foreign trade? Arguing that it could be so justified only by "the most liberal construction of the constitution," Joseph Story (who as a member of Congress in 1808 advocated repeal of the embargo) in his 1833 *Commentaries on the Constitution* emphasized that the embargo suspended commerce wholly for an unlimited period of time. The argument against the constitutionality of the embargo, as Story summarized it, was that "the power to regulate did not include the power to annihilate commerce, by interdicting it permanently and entirely with foreign nations." However, a federal district court judge in Massachusetts—ironically, a Federalist—upheld the embargo as a constitutional exercise of the power to "regulate" commerce, reasoning that all regulation involved partial prohibitions and that the degree or extent of the prohibition rested with the discretion of Congress. The court further observed that the embargo also could be regarded as a constitutional adjunct to the legitimate exercise of Congress's power to declare war: "If Congress have the power, for purposes of safety, of preparation, or counteraction, to suspend commercial intercourse with foreign nations, where do we find them limited as to the duration more than as to the manner and extent of the measure?"[69]

Although these are the words of a Federalist judge, they could have been said by Jefferson, who expressed no doubts that the power of Congress to regulate commerce could embrace commercial discrimination, nonintercourse, or embargo—all policies that, at one time or another in his public career, he advocated as legitimate exercises of federal power. Where trade with foreign nations was involved, Jefferson perceived no conflict between Congress's powers under Article I, section 8, and the rights reserved to the states under the Tenth Amendment: the former were plenary.

The final, and least troubling, area of apparent inconsistency between Jefferson's professed constitutional theory and his record as president concerns the issue of internal improvements. In his Second Inaugural Address, after reporting favorably on the abolition of internal taxes and the sufficiency of the revenue from import duties, Jefferson suggested a use for surplus revenues after the redemption of the public debt. The surplus, "by a just repartition among the states, and a corresponding amendment of the constitution," might be applied *"in time of peace"* to "rivers, canals, roads, arts, manufactures, education, and other great objects in each state." Over a year later, in his sixth annual message, Jefferson made a more definite proposal. Given (at least for the time being) a treasury surplus and debt retirement proceeding on schedule, despite the outlay for Louisiana, he suggested that Congress apply the surplus revenue "to the great purposes of the public education, roads, rivers, canals, and such other objects of public improvement as it may be thought proper to add to the constitutional enumeration of federal powers." He was proposing this for the consideration of Congress, even before the debt was fully discharged, because he said he wanted to give sufficient time for Congress to propose, and the states to ratify, a constitutional amendment. He added, "I suppose an amendment of the Constitution, by consent of the States, necessary, because the objects now recommended are not among those enumerated in the Constitution, and to which it permits the public monies to be applied."[70]

Clearly Jefferson recognized that he was recommending an enlargement of the functions of the federal government. His statements in his 1806 message to Congress, however, suggest that he saw internal improvements as matters that legitimately fell under the purview of the national government, not the states. "By these operations new channels of communication will be opened between the States; the lines of separation will disappear, their interests will be identified, and their union cemented by new and indissoluble ties," he declared. Although his "true theory" of the Constitution called for all "domestic" matters to be left under the purview of the states, it also gave the federal government jurisdiction over "foreign" matters; commerce between the states was, to Jefferson, a "foreign" matter. In matters of political economy as well as foreign policy, Jefferson was a nationalist; indeed, it has been argued that the distinguishing feature of Jeffersonian Republicanism, in terms of political economy, was the extent to which it envisioned the national market system as the means to achieving economic prosperity, political unity, and social stability.[71]

Jefferson nevertheless felt that amendment of the Constitution was necessary to give Congress these powers: that, in other words, the appropriation of moneys for such projects as he proposed in 1806 was neither an enumerated power nor a power which could be fairly implied from an enumerated power. Article I, section 8, did authorize Congress to establish post roads; and Article IV, section 3, authorized Congress to "dispose of and make all needful rules and regulations respecting the territory" of the United States. Perhaps because he saw it warranted under these provisions, Jefferson approved of an ad hoc internal improvements project conceived by Gallatin and instituted during his administration: construction of the National Road, from Cumberland, Maryland, to Ohio, financed from a fund established when Ohio became a state in 1802.[72] This project differed, certainly in degree and perhaps in kind, from the comprehensive plan Jefferson suggested to Congress in 1806, and it therefore did not set a precedent for general internal improvements legislation. Except for a Senate resolution calling on Gallatin to submit a report on a comprehensive plan of national roads and canals, Congress did not act on Jefferson's proposal: the continuing risk of war forced both the administration and Congress to shelve the plan.[73]

After his retirement from the presidency, Jefferson continued to advocate internal improvements projects, but he was still adamant concerning the necessity of a constitutional amendment. When President Madison vetoed an internal improvements bill in 1817, Jefferson approved, writing that the bill was "negatived by the President, on constitutional, and I believe, sound grounds; that instrument not having placed this among the enumerated objects to which they are authorized to apply the public contributions." He added that a constitutional amendment extending national powers to this object would be "a better way of obtaining the end, than by strained constructions, which would loose all the bands of the constitution." He wrote Albert Gallatin—who on this point did not share Jefferson's and Madison's constitutional scruples—that while the Federalists believed that such an appropriation was legitimate under the general welfare clause of the Constitution, "our tenet ever was, and, indeed, it is almost the only landmark which now divides the federalists from the republicans, that Congress had not unlimited powers to provide for the general welfare, but were restrained to those specifically enumerated." The general welfare clause, he again argued, was not an independent grant of power; it was rather a limitation on the purposes for which Congress may exercise the power of raising money. Madison's veto of the bill was "a fortunate incident" since it should spur the states to call for a constitutional amendment in which they would "concede the power" to appropriate for internal improvements and expressly grant it to Congress with appropriate modifications, such as requiring that the expenditures in each state be proportionate to the "federal ratio" of representation. Such an amendment, Jefferson believed, would not only prevent future logrolling in congressional appropriations but would "settle forever" the meaning of the general welfare clause, "this phrase, which, by a mere grammatical quibble, has countenanced the General Government in a claim of universal power." It would also be "a national confirmation of the grounds of appeal" to the people of the various states for the resolution of questions of constitutional interpretation, he added.[74]

Still later in life, when he was especially concerned about what he perceived as a movement to consolidate powers in the federal government,[75] he continued to insist that amending the Constitution would be a "wiser and safer" means of authorizing federal appropriations for internal improvements than interpreting it by "elaborate construction," using "a little sophistry on the words 'general welfare'" to strip the states of their reserved powers. By this time John Quincy Adams was president and, in his first annual message to Congress in December 1825, advocated a plan for massive internal improvements. Jefferson drafted a declaration for the General Assembly of Virginia affirming the principles of federalism and protesting federal attempts to authorize internal improvements projects within the states as "usurpations" of state powers.[76] Thus, near the end of his life Jefferson reaffirmed the principles of federalism that he had formulated at the very beginning of government under the Constitution.

Considered in its entirety, then, Jefferson's record during and after his presidency was remarkably consistent with his earlier stated views of the "true theory" of the Constitution. In advocating federal internal improvements projects, he usually maintained that federal appropriations for such projects required an amendment to the Constitution specifically authorizing them. The purchase of Louisiana and the embargo certainly were dramatic exercises of federal power; but notwithstanding Jefferson's qualms about the constitutionality of the former, both concerned matters that were properly federal under his view of the Constitution. His understanding of the "true theory" of the Constitution, after all, turned not only on the preservation of the rights of the states but also, as he put it in his First Inaugural Address, on "the preservation of the General government, in it's whole constitutional vigour"—the other half of the equilibrium that critics such as Joseph Story and Henry Adams have overlooked, causing them erroneously to characterize Jefferson's theory of federalism as simply the "Virginia school" dogma of states' rights.

8

Bound by the Chains of

the Constitution

The Presidency and

Executive Power

Jefferson generally has been regarded as one of the half dozen or so most able presidents in American history, despite his apparent "lingering Whig biases" for the limitation of executive powers. Nevertheless, his own experience with the presidency was a far from happy one: like his predecessor Washington and so many of his successors, Jefferson suffered a decline in political fortunes during his second term in office, culminating in the disastrous policy of the embargo. When he retired from office, observing ruefully that nature had intended him for the "tranquil pursuits of science," not the "boisterous ocean of political passions" on which circumstance had obliged him to steer his bark, he no doubt recalled his own characterization of the presidency as "a splendid misery."[1]

Critics in his own day and in more recent times have charged Jefferson with hypocrisy for failing to follow the republican principles he had espoused in the 1790s after he himself came into power. Some of these charges, concerning Jefferson's apostasy from a supposed states' rights theory of federalism, have been discussed in the previous chapter. Here the focus is on Jefferson's view of executive power, both as he saw it while an opposition leader in the 1790s and as he exercised it while president. The classic criticism was made by Henry Adams at the end of the nineteenth century. Jefferson, whom Adams derisively characterized as "the philosopher president," wielded executive authority "more complete than had ever before been known in American history," particularly in foreign affairs, where his authority was "little short of royal." "If Jefferson's favorite phrase was true,—that the Federalist differed from the Republican only in the shade more or less of power to be given the Executive,—it was hard to see how any President could be more Federalist than Jefferson himself," Adams argued.[2]

Beginning with an examination of Jefferson's early views of executive power and the presidency during the 1780s and 1790s, this chapter then evaluates Jefferson's actions during his presidency to determine whether in fact Jefferson did behave in ways that were inconsistent with positions he took earlier. It shows that the critics' charge of hypocrisy, like that of apostasy from states' rights, is untenable, for a similar reason: it was based on a faulty premise. Adherence to a weak Whig model of executive powers was no more an essential aspect of Jefferson's constitutionalism than was adherence to a weak states' rights model of federal powers. Instead, separation of powers and federalism, respectively, were the key principles. Just as Jefferson's view of the proper division of powers between the states and federal government was consistent with his support of broad powers within a clearly identified federal sphere, so too was his view of separation of powers consistent with a strong presidency within a clearly defined executive sphere. Where the Constitution assigned powers exclusively to the president, Jefferson vigorously exercised them; where powers were assigned to or shared with other branches, however, Jefferson both preached and exercised restraint, quite strictly. In sum, he regarded the president, like the federal government generally and all its other parts, as "bound by the chains of the Constitution."

Early Views of Executive Power and the Presidency

Perhaps the earliest expression of Jefferson's understanding of executive power was his interpretation of the British monarchy in his *Summary View of the Rights of British America*. There he described the king as an officer, "circumscribed with definite powers," who assisted "in working the great machine of government," subject to the people's "superintendence." He primarily held "the executive powers" within each state, which he wielded simultaneously along with the same kind of power for the whole empire. As "the only mediatory power between . . . states," Jefferson wrote, the king had the duty to receive protests and to redress grievances through "exercise of his negative power," to veto acts of Parliament that extended beyond its legitimate sphere. This theory of the British monarchy—a theory that was more or less peculiar to Jefferson—thus provided a rationale for the appeal to George III to redress American grievances, the object of the *Summary View*.

His view of the British monarchy in 1774 no doubt had been influenced to some degree by the Whig historians and writers on government that Jefferson and his contemporaries so avidly read in the decade or two before the Revolution. Two of the staples of Whig thought were the ideas that the essence of the British constitution—in its pure Anglo-Saxon mode—was the union between king and people, cemented by a parliament properly representative of the people; and that the whole of English constitutional history since the time of the Norman Conquest consisted of the struggle to preserve this ideal from the corruptions wrought by William the Conqueror and his successors. The great English constitutional struggles of the seventeenth century, culminating in the "Glorious Revolution" settlement of 1688–89, helped to restore the monarchy to its proper place in the constitutional system, but—at least as the Real Whigs saw it—much reform was still necessary, particularly on the parliamentary side, to restore the old union between crown, Parliament, and the people in its proper balance.

With American independence it was possible, as Jefferson put it, to found government on "more favorable ground." Americans, however, had no experience with a republican executive; consequently, their first constitutions were the imperfect products of "novices in the science of government." Jefferson's experience as governor of Virginia during the Revolution convinced him of the need for a stronger executive power, more independent of the legislature, than that provided for in the Virginia Constitution of 1776. In his *Notes on Virginia* he criticized those features of the constitution responsible for the relative weakness of the executive, which he sought to remedy in his own draft constitution of 1783 and later explained as a product of Whiggism. "In truth, the abuses of monarchy had so filled all the space of political contemplation, that we imagined everything republican that was not monarchy. We had not yet penetrated to the mother principle, that 'governments are republican only in proportion as they embody the will of the people and execute it.' "[3] This broad principle of republicanism, at least as it had evolved in Jefferson's mind by the time of his return to the United States in 1789, coupled with the principle of separation of powers, furnished the basis for his earliest perceptions of the new executive office for the federal government that had been created at the Philadelphia convention in 1787.

Jefferson had recognized that the absence of a separate executive department was a fundamental weakness of the national government under the Articles of Confederation. His own efforts as a diplomat in Europe had been hampered by the uncertainties resulting from the vesting of both executive and legislative powers in the Congress. Years later he would point to this experience in explaining his preference for a single over a plural executive.[4]

He therefore approved of Article II of the proposed federal constitution in 1787, writing to Madison that he liked, among other features of the plan, "the organization of the government into Legislative, Judiciary and Executive" and "the negative given to the Executive with a third of either house"—in other words, the president's veto power.[5] He expressed concern, however, that the convention, in strengthening the executive through creation of the office of president, had gone too far. Significantly, what concerned Jefferson was not the power vested in the presidency but the degree to which the president would be accountable to the people.

Of particular concern to Jefferson in 1787–88 was what he characterized as "the abandonment of the necessity of rotation in office," namely, the perpetual eligibility of the president for reelection. "Experience concurs with reason in concluding that the first magistrate will always be re-elected if the constitution permits it," he maintained. He therefore feared that this would make the president an officer for life, essentially an elective monarch—an evil in itself and but one step away from a return to hereditary monarchy. He also feared the possibility of foreign intervention in American elections, observing: "The importance to France and England to have our government in the hands of a Friend or foe, will occasion their interference by money, and even by arms. Our President will be of much more consequence to them than a king of Poland."[6]

Jefferson grudgingly acquiesced in the perpetual eligibility of the president, despite his firm belief that it could lead to monarchy, when he realized that it had excited virtually no objection in America. "After all, it is my principle that the will of the Majority should always prevail," he wrote Madison. Noting that Americans' "jealousy" was "only put to sleep by the unlimited confidence" they had in Washington, whom everyone expected to be elected president, he concluded that amendment of the Constitution to correct this flaw would have to wait until "inferior characters" succeeded Washington in that high office and "awaken us to the danger which his merit has led us into."[7]

At the time Jefferson said that he desired either an amendment providing a two-term limitation or, even better, a single seven-year term, which he heard had been proposed at the convention. Once Washington had set the precedent of voluntary retirement after two terms, Jefferson expressed his desire that the practice would become an unwritten constitutional tradition. During his own presidency, soon after his reelection, he declared his intention to retire at the end of his second term, observing that "the danger is that the indulgence and attachments of the people will keep a man in the chair after he becomes a dotard, that reelection through life shall become habitual, and election for life follow that."[8] Despite this tradition—which Jefferson's successors Madison and Monroe also followed—as late as 1824 he continued to support constitutional amendments to limit the presidential term and to place the choice of the president effectively in the hands of the people.[9]

Jefferson's concern about the duration of the president in office was tied directly to his republicanism. By the time of his return to the United States in 1789, he had come to regard republicanism in terms of the accountability of the government, in all its branches, to the will of the people. Simultaneously, he had come to regard separation of powers as an essential principle of constitutionalism. This was certainly so by the time he received a copy of the first volume of John Adams's *Defence of the Constitutions of the United States*, when he wrote the author that "the first principle of a good government" was the separation of powers—"a distribution of its powers into executive, judiciary, and legislative, and a subdivision of the latter into two or

three branches." Significantly, his first, favorable reaction to Adams's
Defence was prefaced by that remark. "It is a good step gained," he
noted, "when it is proved that the English constitution, acknowleged
to be better than all which have proceeded it, is only better in proportion as it has approached nearer to this distribution of powers. From
this last step is easy, to shew by a comparison of our constitutions
with that of England, how much more perfect they are." [10]

Jefferson's tenure as Washington's secretary of state helped force
him to formulate a theory of separation of powers applicable to the
new federal government that had been created by the Constitution.
The office he assumed entailed many responsibilities: in addition to
his most important function of conducting foreign affairs, the secretary of state was responsible for the safekeeping of the records of government, the handling of federal commissions, and the promulgation
of laws. He also served as the president's medium of communication
with the states and those federal officials who did not fall within the
jurisdiction of the Departments of War and Treasury. Thus he wrote to
governors and, in the absence of a department of justice, to judges and
marshals. In the conduct of foreign affairs he worked closely with the
chief executive in formulating and implementing policy; he similarly
served as the medium of communication between foreign countries
and the president. [11]

What was significant about Jefferson's experience as secretary of
state was that the office was so directly associated with the presidency;
the secretary of state was the president's spokesman, subordinate and
responsible to the chief executive by law. As such, it became part of
the province of his office, working with Washington, to arrive at a
practical definition of the scope of presidential powers and thus to
demarcate the lines along which powers were separated. The status of
Alexander Hamilton as secretary of the treasury was rather different,
for he was expected to be closer to Congress than either of the heads
of the other departments, State and War. The act creating his office
provided that he give information to the legislative branch on request,
that he digest and prepare plans respecting the revenue and the support of the public credit, and that he report to Congress periodically. It
is little wonder that, from Jefferson's perspective as secretary of state,
Hamilton was working too closely with Congress, violating the principle of separation of powers and thereby working the "corruption" of
the legislature in the manner of a British minister. [12]

An important clue to Jefferson's early view of the importance of keeping powers separated may be found in his 1790 report on the government of the Northwest Territory. The governor, Arthur St. Clair, and the secretary as acting governor had issued certain orders and proclamations regulating the conduct of citizens in the territory—for example, prohibiting them from entertaining any strangers without notice to military officers. Jefferson condemned these regulations as being "beyond the competence of the Executive of the said government" in that "they amount in fact to laws, and as such could only flow from it's regular legislature." Further noting that "it is the duty of the General government to guard it's subordinate members from the encroachment of each other, even where they are made through error or inadvertence, and to cover it's citizens from the exercise of powers not authorized by the laws," he urged that the attorney general issue an opinion to be communicated to the territorial governor to guide his future conduct.[13]

Execution of the laws enacted by the legislature was, of course, but one of the many responsibilities assigned to the president under Article II of the Constitution. The Constitution in fact did not implement a pure theory of separation of powers but rather coupled the principle of separation with the nearly antithetical principle of shared powers; and even with respect to the distinction between lawmaking and the execution of the laws, the line was somewhat blurred. The president, though the executive, was given under the Constitution what may be regarded as certain legislative powers: chiefly, the negative, or veto, on acts of Congress. Similarly, powers that might be considered strictly executive—the appointment power and the treaty-making power—were not given to the president alone but were to be shared with the Senate. His perception of the scope of the president's authority in these areas of shared power reveals Jefferson's early views of presidential power most tellingly.

Jefferson viewed the veto power narrowly. He advised President Washington to veto the bank bill only if his mind were "tolerably clear that it is unauthorised by the constitution." In his opinion on the bank bill he described the president's veto power as "the shield provided by the constitution to protect against the invasions of the legislature 1. the rights of the Executive. 2. of the Judiciary. 3. of the states and state legislatures." Although Jefferson himself was quite certain that the bank bill was a case involving a right remaining exclusively with the states and therefore "one of those intended by the constitution to be placed under [the president's] protection," he also suggested that the president to some extent should defer to the legislature. "If the pro and con hang so even as to balance" the president's judgment— as, for instance, when Washington had before him Hamilton's favorable opinion on the bank bill balanced against the negative opinions of Randolph, Jefferson, and Madison—"a just respect for the wisdom of the legislature would naturally decide the balance in favour of their opinion."[14]

When Washington followed the advice of his secretary of state and exercised the first of only two vetoes while in office, it was with respect to the congressional apportionment bill. Arguing that the bill was clearly unconstitutional because it violated the apportionment provisions, Jefferson urged that the bill be vetoed even if it could be saved from the constitutionality problem by an "inconvenient exposition" of the language of the Constitution. He thus took a somewhat broader view of the scope of the veto power, believing, Dumas Malone has argued, that it was "high time that the presidential veto should be used, in order to give assurance that the President was guarding the Constitution."[15]

Still, Jefferson tended to see constitutional objections as the only legitimate ground for the use of the veto power. As he perceived it, the veto power was not legislative. He viewed the Constitution as vesting the legislative power completely in the Congress and thus considered the veto to be roughly analogous to the powers of the Council of Revision that was a part of the New York Constitution and that he himself had proposed for Virginia. As observed above, his earliest comments to Madison regarding the Constitution were generally favorable, and among those features that he liked was "the negative given to the Executive with a third of either house." He added that he "should have liked it better had the Judiciary been associated for that purpose, or invested with a similar power." This underscores Jefferson's view that the veto power should be used only in safeguarding the Constitution, not for reasons of policy. As president, Jefferson cast no vetoes at all; and the early chief executives generally were quite conservative in use of the veto power and reluctant to substitute their judgment on policy matters for that of the Congress.[16]

Jefferson's views, while he was secretary of state, of the scope of executive power in the realm of foreign affairs were more mixed. A pattern can be discerned, however. While Jefferson took a fairly broad view of the president's discretion in the conduct of foreign affairs generally, he also recognized that Congress could not be excluded from policy-making altogether and suggested that in certain areas, where powers were in fact shared between the legislative and executive branches, presidential discretion was quite limited. Apparent throughout Jefferson's writings in this period is his effort to comply strictly with the allocations of power made by the Constitution: to keep separate those powers that were clearly assigned to one branch rather than another and to caution deference to the judgment of the other branch where powers were to be shared.

An especially revealing indication of Jefferson's effort to comply strictly with the constitutional allocation of powers was an opinion he gave President Washington on diplomatic appointments early in his tenure as secretary of state. Jefferson prefaced his opinion with the general observation that "the Constitution has divided the powers of government into three branches, Legislative, Executive and Judiciary, lodging each with a distinct magistracy," with certain exceptions. He advised Washington that "the transaction of business with foreign nations is Executive altogether" and accordingly belongs to the president, "*except* as to such portions of it as are specially submitted to the Senate" by the Constitution. Such exceptions, moreover, "are to be construed strictly." Thus, when confronted with the question whether the Senate had the right to negative the grade of a diplomatic appointment, as well as the person to be appointed, Jefferson concluded that it did not. Article II, section 2, of the Constitution gives the appointment of diplomats to the president and Senate jointly, but it leaves to the president alone the power of nomination. Determining the destination of a foreign mission and the character, or grade, of the persons to be employed in it were matters decided before the act of nomination and therefore were beyond the scope of the Senate's powers, he reasoned. "The Senate is not supposed by the Constitution to be acquainted with the concerns of the Executive department. It was not intended that these should be communicated to them; nor can they therefore be qualified to judge of the necessity which calls for a mission to any particular place, or of the particular grade, more or less marked, which special and secret circumstances may call for. All this is left to the President. They are only to see that no unfit person be employed." Jefferson added that it would be "a breach of trust, an abuse of the power confided to the Senate," for it to negative the grade of a diplomatic appointment, in effect, through continual rejection of the person nominated by the president. He concluded, "If the Constitution had meant to give the Senate a negative on the grade or destination, as well as the person, it would have said so in direct terms, and not left it to be effected by a sidewind. It could never mean to give them the *use* of one power through the *abuse* of another." [17]

Similarly broad statements regarding the executive nature of matters involving foreign affairs may be found in Jefferson's communications with foreign nations, as President Washington's representative. When, upon the death of Benjamin Franklin, the French National Assembly sent a message of condolence to the Congress addressed to "The President of Congress," Jefferson through the agency of William Short gave instructions about the proper constitutional distinction to be observed in future communications. "Let it be understood that Congress can only correspond through the Executive, whose organ in the case of foreign nations is the Secretary of state. The President of the U.S. being co-ordinate with Congress, cannot personally be their scribe." Some two years later, when the volatile French minister to the United States, Genet, threatened to deal directly with Congress, Jefferson in effect reprimanded him. The president "being the only channel of communication between this country and foreign nations, it is from him alone that foreign nations or their agents are to learn what is or has been the will of the nation," he wrote Genet.[18]

It must be emphasized, however, that these statements in defense of executive prerogatives concerned only "the transaction of business" with foreign nations, strictly speaking—not the making of foreign policy. In that broader context Jefferson clearly recognized that certain powers were allocated to Congress, as well as to the president, under the Constitution: the power to declare war, given to both houses of Congress alone, and the treaty-making power, given to the Senate in conjunction with the president. His statements, while secretary of state and after his retirement, concerning Washington's Neutrality Proclamation and the Jay Treaty clarify Jefferson's understanding of the limits of executive prerogative in the realm of foreign policy.

As Dumas Malone has noted, Jefferson favored the policy of American neutrality in the war between Britain and France; in the cabinet meetings at which the administration's policy was hammered out, his doubts related wholly to the desirability of a presidential proclamation and to its form and timing. The proclamation that Washington issued in April 1793 scrupulously avoided use of the word *neutrality* and thus met with Jefferson's approval. Congress was not in session, and all had agreed that the president's summoning of Congress to special session would unwisely cause alarm; given this situation, Jefferson was concerned that the proclamation not bind the United States in such a way as to undercut the power to declare war, vested alone in Congress by Article I, section 8, of the Constitution. A presidential declaration of neutrality was, as he saw it, tantamount to a declaration of no war, which was as much beyond the competence of the executive as a declaration of war. The executive had no authority to do more than "declare the actual state of things to be that of peace," which is what Washington's proclamation essentially did.[19]

As in so many other aspects of his political and constitutional thought, Jefferson's views were shaped by the dialectic with Hamilton. Jefferson suspected that his colleague wanted to bind the future conduct of the country—to ensure that the United States would not go to war against Britain—by executive act, pressing executive powers to their limit. His fears were borne out when Hamilton, under the pseudonym "Pacificus," wrote for newspaper publication a series of papers defending the concept of a neutrality proclamation. Arguing that the president could make such a proclamation by virtue of his role as commander in chief when Congress was not in session, Hamilton sought to assign the initative in matters of foreign policy to the executive. At Jefferson's urging Madison, under the signature "Helvidius," wrote a series of essays in response. The argument of Helvidius was an elaboration of Jefferson's constitutional position: that because the power to decide between war and peace was assigned by the Constitution to Congress, the president could not initiate a policy which would confront Congress with a fait accompli.[20]

Jefferson's concern that the prerogatives of Congress not be undercut was rooted not only in his adherence to the Constitution but in his conviction that the Article I, section 8, provision empowering Congress to declare war was wise policy. In the 1789 letter to Madison in which he expounded the idea that "the earth belongs to the living," Jefferson also had written approvingly of the Article I provision giving Congress the power to control the purse strings for the military by limiting appropriations to two-year periods: "We have already given . . . one effectual check to the Dog of war by transferring the power of letting him loose, from the Executive to the Legislative body, from those who are to spend to those who are to pay."[21] Congressional control of the purse strings also was a relevant fact in the next major constitutional issue, the political dispute that arose following Senate ratification of the treaty between the United States and Great Britain that John Jay had negotiated in London.

By the time of the Jay Treaty controversy, Jefferson had resigned from the office of secretary of state. His role in the controversy was that of an observer, from the distance of Monticello, rather than as an active participant; nevertheless, in his correspondence with Republican leaders he expressed his disgust not only of the provisions of the treaty itself but also of the partisan maneuver that he perceived behind it. He described the treaty as "unconstitutional" and took the position that even after the president signed it, the House might oppose it as "constitutionally void."[22] He also expressed his full sympathy with the opposition campaign that arose in Virginia and its constitutional argument that a treaty did not become "the supreme law of the land" unless and until the House of Representatives approved those provisions normally requiring the concurrence of both houses of Congress.[23] These included certain limitations on the power of Congress to regulate commerce (the treaty prohibited for ten years any discrimination against British ships or goods), as well as the appropriations that would be required to put the treaty into full effect.

Later in life Jefferson claimed that he had been in "entire concurrence of opinion with Mr. Madison and others who maintained the rights of the House of Representatives" on the question of ratifying Jay's Treaty. Denying that his position was broader than that of Madison and the other Republicans in Congress, he argued that he agreed with them that "the subjects which were confided to the House of Representatives in conjunction with the President and Senate, were exceptions to the general treaty power given to the President and Senate alone." The right of the House of Representatives arose only whenever a treaty stipulation would interfere with a law; in such a situation, the consent of the House of Representatives was necessary to give it effect. This rule, Jefferson maintained, derived from the basic canon of construction that "an instrument is to be so construed as to reconcile and give meaning and effect to all its parts"; here, the treaty-making provision of the Constitution was being reconciled with the provisions requiring the concurrence of both houses of Congress for the making of laws. To this general rule requiring the concurrence of the House of Representatives in certain circumstances there was "but the single exception of war and peace," he further maintained. The Constitution "expressly requires the concurrence of the three branches to commit us to the state of war, but permits two of them, the President and Senate, to change it to that of peace, for reasons as obvious as they are wise."[24]

Jefferson's early views of executive power are far from absolutely clear, and indeed they evolved over time, shaped by political circumstances. Nevertheless, some general conclusions can be drawn. Jefferson recognized that Article II, section 1, of the Constitution vested "the executive power" in the president and that diplomacy was generally an executive matter. However, he distinguished the transaction of business with foreign nations from the making of foreign policy. The former was wholly executive and therefore a matter of presidential discretion; but the latter, although executive in theory, was in certain important aspects—most notably, the making of treaties—assigned jointly to the president and the Senate by an exception to the general rule specified in the Constitution. Moreover, he also recognized that Article I vested in the two houses of Congress "all legislative powers herein granted," including the powers to declare war and to make appropriations. Reading the Constitution as a whole, he sought to give equal effect to all its provisions. This effort led him to see further limitations on the exercise of executive discretion, to ensure that the prerogatives of Congress not be undercut in practice by actions taken by the president alone.

It would be misleading, therefore, to characterize Jefferson's view of executive power as favoring either a strong or a weak presidency. Neither label adequately comprehends his overall view; and the position he took with respect to any particular issue can be fully assessed only by taking into account all the circumstances, including the relative stance of his contemporaries. Although in contrast to Alexander Hamilton he may be regarded as a proponent of legislative supremacy—or, more precisely, of severely limited executive power— his record as secretary of state lends little support for the thesis that his perception of the scope of executive power was a narrow, Whig view. Hamilton himself later testified that while they "were in the administration together, [Jefferson] was generally for a large construction of the Executive authority."[25] Taking quite seriously the constitutional separation of powers, Jefferson favored an executive which was both vigorous and limited: an executive which exercised its powers fully but within its proper sphere. It is against this standard that the record of his own presidency must be assessed.

President Jefferson and Congress: Separation of Powers and Coordination of Government

Jefferson's presidency, as both its admirers and its critics have observed, was remarkable both for the effectiveness of Jefferson's personal leadership in dealing with Congress and for his scrupulous adherence to the principle of separation of powers.[26] These two apparently contradictory accomplishments were made possible to a great extent by the force of Jefferson's own intellect, character, and personality.[27] However, the key to understanding Jefferson's relationship with Congress lies not only in Jefferson's leadership qualities but also in the constitutional theory that guided the relationship: his republican constitutionalism. That theory, when Jefferson put it into practice as president, made possible a fine-tuned relationship which permitted coordination to the degree required for the effective functioning of government, but without sacrificing the independence of the branches.

It has been observed that the constitutional separation of powers was "reflected and accentuated" in the residential and social pattern of the governmental community in Washington during Jefferson's administration. Legislators lived and worked on Capitol Hill, spatially separated from executives, who lived and worked in the neighborhood of the President's House; members of the federal judiciary, when in town, also lived and worked on Capitol Hill but associated almost exclusively with one another. Thus the separation of powers became "the separation of persons."[28]

The geographical metaphor is apt, for Jefferson as president sought to keep his constitutional distance from the Congress. He could hardly have done otherwise without opening himself to charges of hypocrisy by his enemies or backsliding from his friends and followers, for the Republicans in the 1790s had been sharply critical of what they perceived as Federalist attempts to institute an English monarchical and ministerial system. Consequently, early in his administration Jefferson declared that he would abandon "all those public forms and ceremonies which tended to familiarize the public idea to the harbingers of another form of government." These included the annual speech to Congress, which Jefferson found too reminiscent of the king's opening of Parliament. In sending a written message rather than delivering it in person, he broke with the precedent that George Washington had set and started a tradition which lasted more than a century, until Woodrow Wilson's presidency.[29] He also dispensed with his predecessors' practices of holding birthday balls and weekly levees, as well as appointing public days for fasting and thanksgiving. These reforms were important symbolic acts, suggesting that as president Jefferson— the "Man of the People," as he was called—did not seek to overawe Congress in the way his precedessors did. The result was to give to the presidency a democratic flavor: the Federalist ideal of a remote dignitary shielded by protocol was transformed into an unceremonious chief executive who was open, accessible, even familiar.[30]

Similarly, in all of his formal dealings with Congress—particularly his annual messages and confidential messages dealing with foreign policy—Jefferson took an extremely deferential tone. He customarily spoke only in generalities, both in describing problems that ought to command the attention of the "Supreme Council of the nation" and in suggesting the solutions that it should adopt. For example, in his 1804 annual message Jefferson observed to Congress: "Whether the great interests of agriculture, manufacturing, commerce, or navigation, can, within the pale of your constitutional powers, be aided in any of their relations; whether laws are provided in all cases where they are wanting . . . in fine, whether anything can be done to advance the general good, are questions within the limits of your functions which will necessarily occupy your attentions." Even when his administration had specific programs in mind, the tone of his messages suggested otherwise. One of the best examples was Jefferson's confidential message to Congress in December 1805 concerning the negotiations with Spain for purchase of Florida, where the formal message only hinted vaguely at the administration's request for a $2 million appropriation. The so-called Two Million Act eventually was approved by Congress but at the cost of alienating John Randolph of Roanoke, the volatile Republican leader in the House, who opposed the merits of the policy and was offended because the president had not stated in his message precisely how much he wanted and what he wanted it for.[31] Jefferson's excessive deference to Congress was a factor in the failure of his embargo policy: proceeding under the fiction that the policy was Congress's, not the administration's, Jefferson never adequately explained it so as to gain public support.

Jefferson held a quite narrow view of the executive power, strictly speaking. On one occasion he wrote, "I am but a machine erected by the constitution for the performance of certain acts according to the laws of action laid down for me." Although he was trying to explain to his good friend Dr. Benjamin Rush why he had appointed someone else as director of the mint, the statement may justly be regarded as an expression of Jefferson's attitude regarding the exercise of power generally.[32] For example, when Jefferson as president refused to designate a day of national prayer, fasting, or thanksgiving, he explained his position by noting that Congress was prohibited by the First Amendment from acts respecting religion and that the president was authorized only to execute its acts. He also argued that the First Amendment prohibited him from even the mere recommendation of a day of fasting or prayer because he could not "*indirectly* assume to the U.S. an authority over religious exercises which the Constitution has directly precluded them from."[33] These arguments assumed a view of executive power which saw it limited in its exercise both by constitutional restraints and by law. In matters of domestic policy, Jefferson generally seemed inhibited from action by the notion that he was "but a machine"; and even in foreign policy, where he undoubtedly felt freer in his conduct, his options frequently—and particularly during his second term—were limited by external circumstances he could not control.[34]

These observations notwithstanding, Jefferson went far beyond his predecessors in developing the policy-making role of the president. Although his formal constitutional powers were limited to the initial recommendation of measures to Congress and the veto, Jefferson—without employing force or corruption—used to full advantage informal, extraconstitutional tools to mobilize support for his own ideas; and indeed, the fact that he never used the veto power illustrates how well he could work with Congress through informal means.

In his careful study of the operation of the executive and legislative branches of government during the years 1801–9, Noble Cunningham has concluded that "Jefferson brought to the presidency the most system in administration and the strongest leadership that the office had yet experienced." Despite the emphasis that Jefferson placed on the theory of separation of powers between the executive and legislative branches, in the actual process of government the lines of separation were quite blurred.[35] Among the informal tools that Jefferson utilized in dealing with Congress, three deserve special notice: his own sizable personal skills of persuasion; his willingness and ability to use legislative lieutenants on the floor of Congress; and his role as leader of the Republican party, coupled with his popular support.

In his administration of government, as in his personal relationships, Jefferson strove to maintain harmony. This was true not only within the executive branch, where Jefferson's cabinet—in stark contrast to Washington's—had few frictions, but also with respect to his relations with Congress, including its Federalist members. Jefferson used a social activity, the dinner hour, as a tool for governing: individual members of Congress were invited to the White House in small groups—usually of either one party or the other—and with the invitations issued not by the president but by "Th: Jefferson." At these informal gatherings matters of public policy could be discussed amicably, and Jefferson's wishes could be made known. By such means the channels of communication between the executive and legislative branches were kept open, and the barriers of distance—both geographical and constitutional—were somewhat overcome.[36]

Jefferson also employed lieutenants—congressional leaders who functioned, in effect, as the president's agents—to help ensure passage of administration measures. In this he had a mixed record of success: things went a bit more smoothly with the leaders he employed in the Senate, Stevens Thomson Mason, Wilson Cary Nicholas, and John Breckinridge, than with those in the House, where the key man, John Randolph of Roanoke, the eccentric chairman of the Ways and Means Committee, was not cut out for the role. What is important here, however, is not the political circumstances that affected the success or failure of this method but Jefferson's own understanding of the method itself. As he explained it in an especially frank letter written to a loyal supporter, Jefferson observed that he sought to employ a man of "talents, integrity, firmness, & sound judgment . . . to take the lead in the H. of R. to consider the business of the nation his own business, to take it up as if he were singly charged with it and carry it through." He added that he did not expect the House leader to relinquish his own judgment and instead support the administration in all its measures; but "where he does not disapprove of them, he should not suffer them to go off in sleep, but bring them to the attention of the house and give them a fair chance." Because of John Randolph's break with the administration, he was aware of criticisms of this practice of employing a "backstairs man," but some liaison between the president and Congress was necessary for government to function effectively. Otherwise, he noted, "if the Executive is to keep all other information to himself, & the house to plunge on in the dark, it becomes a government of chance & not of design."[37]

Perhaps the most important means by which Jefferson bridged the gap between the legislative and executive branches was his role as undisputed head of the Republican party, reinforced by the nation's popular support. As Cunningham has found, the Jeffersonian Congresses were quite open, receptive, and responsive to their constituencies. Jefferson's popularity in the nation no doubt helped in his dealings with the Republican majorities in Congress; and his success in doing so, both publicly and behind the scenes, can be gauged by the bitterness of Federalist complaints of his unseen control of Republican "puppets" in Congress.[38]

In his studies of Jefferson's presidency, Robert Johnstone has concluded that Jefferson's "greatest contribution" to the development of the presidency was "his perception of the office as a potentially popular one." Jefferson "combined the constitutional powers of the presidency with a 'political' power grounded on popular support," and by this means he used the presidency as a vehicle for the furtherance of majority rule. This was a significant change from the conception of the presidency held by the framers and by Jefferson's Federalist predecessors: the conception, drawn from the English model of balanced government, of the executive as the branch of government designed to check the more popular branches. Jefferson's conception of the presidency, in contrast, emphasized the popular base of the president's authority, its direct relationship to the consent of the governed. It was a conception of executive power that, if not drawn directly from, was probably at least shaped by Jefferson's reading of those Whig historians and writers on government who viewed the Anglo-Saxon ideal of kingship as that of the link between the people and the government. The president, Jefferson once wrote, should "lead things into the channel of harmony between the governors and governed." Somewhat less obliquely, he later stated: "In a government like ours, it is the duty of the Chief Magistrate, in order to enable himself to do all the good which his station requires, to endeavor, by all honorable means, to unite in himself the confidence of the whole people. This alone, in any case where the energy of the nation is required, can produce a union of the powers of the whole, and point them in a single direction, as if all constituted but one body and one mind."[39] This understanding was basic to Jefferson's exercise of presidential powers.

As Johnstone and other scholars have observed, Jefferson's conduct of the presidency in many respects followed the example set by Washington. This was particularly true in the realm of foreign affairs, where Jefferson himself while secretary of state had defended executive powers and prerogatives, arguing, for example, against substantive involvement by the Senate in the appointing power. As president Jefferson asserted the exclusive power of the executive to conduct diplomacy, defended his right to control outside access to privileged information, and protected members of the administration—including himself—from investigative and judicial subpoenas.

An apt example of Jefferson's exercise of executive prerogative in an area he regarded as wholly assigned to the president under the Constitution was his rejection in 1807 of a treaty which James Monroe and William Pinkney had negotiated with Great Britain. Whether or not the treaty was a good one has been a matter of some dispute, in Jefferson's day and today.[40] Jefferson considered the treaty inadequate, chiefly in the absence of a provision dealing with the British practice of impressment, one of the chief grievances of the United States, whose satisfactory resolution both Jefferson and Secretary of State James Madison regarded as the sine qua non of an acceptable treaty. He and Madison received a copy of the treaty on 3 March, the day before the expiration of the Ninth Congress, and Jefferson promptly decided that the treaty was unacceptable and that consequently he would not submit it to the Senate for its approval. He accepted full responsibility for the rejection of the treaty and later cited it as an instance where the president was to act "ultimately and without appeal," independent of the other branches of government. He felt that under the circumstances to submit the treaty to the Senate "would be a mockery of them." "The Constitution had made their advice necessary to confirm a treaty, but not to reject it." Not everyone agreed with this decision, he noted, but "I have never doubted its soundness."[41]

Behind Jefferson's exercise of executive prerogative in the realm of foreign affairs, however, was his distinctively republican idea that it was the duty of the chief executive to "unite in himself the confidence of the whole people." To the extent that Jefferson "favored a large construction of the Executive authority," as his adversary Hamilton had recognized, he did so because he understood presidential leadership to be firmly tied to electoral responsibility to the people. This concept of the presidency was reflected in his continuing concern over the length of the presidential term in office and the president's perpetual eligibility for reelection. Jefferson was especially concerned that the president remain closely tied to the will of the nation because only in that way—by the president serving in fact as well as symbolically as a "man of the people"—could the vigorous executive leadership that Jefferson advocated, and while in office practiced, be kept safe.

In distinguishing his constitutional theory from that of the Federalists, Jefferson emphasized not only separation of powers—the independence of each branch of government from the others—but also republicanism, the dependence of government on the consent of the people. The Republicans sought "to preserve an entire independence of the executive and legislative branches of each other, and the dependence of both on the same source—the free election of the people." [42] If in practice Jefferson as president in his relations with Congress did not preserve the "entire independence" of the executive and legislative branches, it was in part because he recognized the necessity of presidential leadership, to avoid "a government of chance & not of design." But it was also because both he and Congress were equally accountable to the people, a fact which permitted departures in practice from the strict theory of separated powers.

One can fully appreciate the importance of republicanism as a device for softening the sharp lines of the separation of powers theory, and therefore making feasible a workable coordination between the legislative and executive branches, when one considers, in contrast, the strained relationship between Jefferson and the Federalist-dominated federal judiciary, the branch of government that was not subject to the elective control of the people. Indeed, as chapter 9 shows, it was in the executive-judicial relationship that Jefferson's strict theory of separation of powers, his so-called tripartite doctrine, was most evident. As Jefferson later put it, "The three departments having distinct functions to perform, must have distinct rules adapted to them. Each must act under its own rules, those of no one having any obligation on either of the others." [43]

The remaining two sections of this chapter discuss, in two contexts, Jefferson's continued adherence, while himself in power, to the view of the presidency that he had arrived at in the 1790s: an executive of limited powers, vigorously exercised. The first context concerns Jefferson's recognition of limitations on executive powers imposed by the Constitution itself. The second concerns his recognition of the principle of executive prerogative; that is, the idea that in certain extraordinary circumstances, the president has the right—indeed, the obligation—to depart from a strict adherence to the written law. This doctrine of emergency power, like the principle of separation of powers, must be understood within the fuller context of Jefferson's republicanism. Not only the "chains of the Constitution," strictly speaking, but also the elective power of the people, to whom the president was ultimately responsible, provided a check on the exercise of presidential powers, whether ordinary or extraordinary.

Constitutional Scruples and the Limits of Executive Power: War with Tripoli and the Louisiana Purchase

The "chains of the Constitution," mentioned in Jefferson's Kentucky Resolutions, that bound down the president comprised both the limits on the powers of the federal government, generally, imposed by the constitutional enumeration of federal powers and the limits on presidential powers imposed by the principle of separation of powers. Two events of Jefferson's first term as president—the war with the Barbary states and the purchase of Louisiana—provide good illustrations of his recognition of both kinds of limitations on the exercise of presidential powers.

The only outright military conflicts that occurred during Jefferson's administration were with the Barbary states on the north coast of Africa. For many years Tripoli, Algiers, Tunis, and Morocco had preyed on American shipping in the Mediterranean, reaping profits from the seizure of ships and vessels and from holding hostages for ransom. The United States had paid tribute to these powers while it had no navy and during the Adams administration while the navy was preoccupied by the quasi-war with France. After that ended in September 1800, however, President Adams sent the frigate *George Washington* to the Mediterranean with instructions to convoy and defend American vessels. Seizure of the *George Washington* by Algiers and news that one or more of the powers might declare war on the United States prompted Jefferson to send a naval squadron to the Mediterranean.[44]

Orders issued by the secretary of the navy to the commander of the squadron, Commodore Richard Dale, stated that the president had ordered the Mediterranean cruise under authority of an act of Congress which stipulated that six frigates be kept in constant service in time of peace. Dale was instructed to determine whether any or all of the Barbary powers had declared war on the United States. If he should find that all of them had, he was to distribute his force according to his judgment "so as best to protect our commerce & chastise their insolence—by sinking, burning or destroying their ships & Vessels wherever you shall find them." If only the bey of Tripoli had declared war—which was in fact the case—Dale was only to blockade that port.

On the first day of August one of the ships under Dale's command, the schooner *Enterprise,* while on a supply mission, encountered a Tripolitan cruiser which it engaged in battle and defeated. Following the orders he had received from Dale, the captain of the *Enterprise* then disabled the Tripolitan vessel and released it and its crew. Although Dale's orders permitted the taking of prisoners, tactical considerations—the fact that the *Enterprise* was en route to Malta to obtain water for the squadron—explained why the vessel had not been captured.

Jefferson's response to these circumstances has been cited frequently to support a restrictive view of executive war powers.[45] In his first annual message to Congress he attributed the release of the captured Tripolitan vessel to constitutional rather than tactical considerations. "Unauthorized by the Constitution, without the sanction of Congress, to go beyond the line of defence, the vessel, being disabled from committing further hostilities, was liberated with its crew." He then urged Congress to "consider whether, by authorizing measures of offence, also, they will place our force on an equal footing with that of its adversaries." This latter statement expressed what one modern commentator has described as "one of the most restrictive interpretations of executive war powers ever uttered by an American president."[46]

In response to this invitation to act, Congress duly passed legislation that gave explicit authorization to the president to capture and make prizes of Tripolitan vessels. He had sent Congress, as he stated in the message, "all material relevant on this subject, that, in the exercise of this important function confided by the Constitution to the Legislature exclusively, their judgment may form itself on a knowledge and consideration of every circumstance of weight." As in 1793 when he questioned the propriety of Washington's issuance of a proclamation of neutrality, Jefferson sought to have the executive branch avoid acting in such a way that might compromise the power to declare war assigned exclusively to Congress by the Constitution.[47] Thus he took the position, as controversial in his own time as it is in ours, that the president lacked the power to act offensively against a nation which had both declared and made war on the United States. Privately, Jefferson may have agreed with the contrary position taken by some of his cabinet members.[48] Nevertheless, the position that he took publicly in his message to Congress implied that he wished the decision committing American navy forces to hostilities in the Mediterranean not be a unilateral one but one in which Congress shared.

The extremely limited nature of Jefferson's position is underscored by the criticisms of Alexander Hamilton, writing in the *New York Evening Post* as "Lucius Crassus." Hamilton agreed that it was the province of Congress, when the nation was at peace, to change that state into a state of war; but when a foreign nation declared or made war upon the United States, he argued, a declaration by Congress, if not nugatory, was at least unnecessary.[49]

Equally controversial have been Jefferson's constitutional scruples with respect to the Louisiana Purchase. Here, unlike in the Barbary War, Jefferson ultimately decided not to air his qualms publicly. He thus left himself open to the charge of hypocrisy, which Henry Adams later leveled against Jefferson in his *History*, where he argued that the purchase of Louisiana was a precedent "too striking to be overlooked," one that gave a "fatal wound to 'strict construction,'" by "an act which he said made blank paper of the Constitution."[50] These charges were possible only because Jefferson was so troubled by the issue of constitutionality.

What is truly significant about Jefferson's actions regarding Louisiana is not that he ultimately relented—although his rationale for accepting the addition of Louisiana to the United States without a constitutional amendment is in itself quite revealing—but rather that he was so deeply troubled by what may fairly be regarded as a mere technical question. It is especially significant that the question so troubled Jefferson—and his writings give ample evidence of the real agony with which he dealt with the issue—that he was willing to lose, and indeed came dangerously close to losing, the magnificent opportunity that the Louisiana treaty presented.[51]

Jefferson had long understood that possession of New Orleans was key to controlling navigation of the Mississippi River, and that free navigation of the Mississippi was in turn vital to the commercial life of the developing West. The retrocession of Louisiana, along with the Floridas, from Spain back to France in 1802 was a matter of deep concern to the Jefferson administration; Jefferson was so troubled by the idea of Napoleon controlling the Mississippi that he even threatened a possible alliance with Britain to protect American interests.[52] In his diplomatic efforts Jefferson sought to acquire only New Orleans; but in the spring of 1803 Talleyrand, the French foreign minister, offered Robert Livingston and James Monroe, the American representatives, all of Louisiana—a vast territory whose addition would more than double the size of the United States. It was an unexpected bonus, and at the price agreed upon—$15 million—could be considered a bargain; but the immediate importance of the treaty to Jefferson, when he first received news of its signing in Paris, was that it secured New Orleans and thereby the control of the Mississippi. That this was absolutely vital to the interests of the United States was the premise upon which Jefferson and his administration based all their thinking; understanding that this was their premise is in turn a necessary backdrop to the constitutional issues involved.

The Louisiana treaty actually raised two basic questions of constitutionality: the power to acquire new territory by treaty and the power to incorporate into the Union new states formed from territory acquired since ratification of the Constitution. In an opinion received by Jefferson on 13 January 1803, Secretary of the Treasury Albert Gallatin offered some "hasty and incomplete" constitutional arguments: first, "that the United States as a nation have an inherent right to acquire territory"; second, "that whenever the acquisition is by treaty, the same constituted authorities in whom the treaty-making power is vested have a constitutional right to sanction the acquisition"; and third, "that whenever the territory has been acquired, Congress have the power either of admitting into the Union as a new state, or of annexing to a State with the consent of that State, or of making regulations for the government of such territory." He further pointed out that if it were not the case that the power of acquiring territory by treaty was delegated to the United States, under the Tenth Amendment such power would be reserved to the people alone, since the Constitution expressly prohibited the states from making treaties. Such a construction of the Constitution would preclude the United States from ever enlarging its territory. Would it not be "a more natural construction to say that the power of acquiring territory is delegated to the United States by the several provisions which authorize the several branches of government to make war, to make treaties, and to govern the territory of the Union," he asked.[53]

Gallatin's arguments somewhat satisfied Jefferson, who replied that he saw "no constitutional difficulty as to the acquisition of territory" and viewed as "a question of expediency" whether territory, having been acquired, "may be taken into the Union by the Constitution as it now stands." He cautioned, however, that he thought "it will be safer not to permit the enlargement of the Union but by amendment of the Constitution."[54]

The constitutional question was necessarily held in abeyance while the administration awaited word from its negotiators in Paris. As Malone has noted, for Jefferson to have suggested difficulties and voiced scruples to Congress at this stage "would have been to borrow trouble." When news of the cession reached him in July, however, he faced an agonizing dilemma. "Recognizing as he did the supreme importance of the undisputed control of the inland waterways, he had no hesitancy in accepting the whole of Louisiana, but the sheer size of the cession inevitably magnified and accentuated the constitutional question."[55]

Gallatin's argument did not overcome Jefferson's constitutional scruples as to the incorporation of new states formed from territory acquired since the ratification of the Constitution. In communications with the chief executive officers and in several private letters in July and August, Jefferson continued to maintain that an amendment to the Constitution was necessary. Obliged to convene Congress earlier than usual in order to ratify the treaty of cession within the short period it allowed, he thought that Congress should be supplied with all the available information respecting the treaty, including the constitutional difficulty. As he observed to one correspondent, Congress would be "obliged to ask the people for an amendment of the Constitution, authorizing their receiving the province into the Union, and providing for its government; and the limitations of power which shall be given by that amendment, will be unalterable but by the same authority."[56]

Jefferson again stated the need for a constitutional amendment in a letter he wrote to one of the men of '76, John Dickinson, in early August. "Our confederation is certainly confined to the limits established by the revolution. The general government has no powers but such as the constitution has given it; and it has not given it a power of holding foreign territory, and still less of incorporating it into the Union. An amendment of the Constitution seems necessary for this." He added, "In the meantime, we must ratify & pay our money, as we have treated, for a thing beyond the constitution, and rely on the nation to sanction an act done for its great good, without its previous authority."[57]

As this letter indicates, there had emerged in Jefferson's mind a conflict between constitutional scruples and expediency. He laid bare his thoughts in a letter to Senator John Breckinridge of Kentucky. On the one hand he stressed that the exclusive right to the navigation of the Mississippi was "very important to our peace," and that both houses of Congress accordingly must "see their duty in ratifying and paying for" the cession "so as to secure a good which would otherwise probably be never again in their power." But he also observed that Congress "must then appeal to *the nation* for an additional article to the Constitution," retroactively approving its act; and he repeated what he had written to Dickinson, that "the Constitution has made no provision for our holding foreign territory, still less for incorporating foreign nations into our Union." He then described in striking language—and by way of a legal analogy—the dilemma that he as president faced:

> The Executive in seizing the fugitive occurrence which so much advances the good of their country, have done an act beyond the Constitution. The Legislature in casting behind them metaphysical subtleties, and risking themselves like faithful servants, must ratify & pay for it, and throw themselves on their country for doing for them unauthorised what we know they would have

done for themselves had they been in a situation to do it. It is the case of a guardian, investing the money of his ward in purchasing an important adjacent territory; & saying to him when of age, I did this for your good; I pretend to no right to bind you: you may disavow me, and I must get out of the scrape as I can: I thought it my duty to risk myself for you. But we shall not be disavowed by the nation, and their act of indemnity will confirm & not weaken the Constitution, by more strongly marking out its lines.

The "act of indemnity" to which he referred was, of course, an amendment to the Constitution.[58]

In the summer of 1803 Jefferson made at least two known attempts to draft an amendment, the first preceding and the second following receipt of the treaty. His latter draft, which he sent to Attorney General Lincoln at the end of August, provided: "Louisiana, as ceded by France to the U.S. is made a part of the U.S. Its white inhabitants shall be citizens, and stand, as to their rights & obligations, on the same footing with other citizens of the U.S. in analogous situations. Save only that as to the portion thereof lying North of an East & West line drawn through the mouth of the Arkansas river, no new State shall be established, nor any grants of land made, other than to Indians in exchange for equivalent portions of land occupied by them, until authorised by further subsequent amendment to the Constitution shall be made for these purposes." An additional paragraph stipulated that Florida, "whenever it may be rightfully obtained," should also become part of the United States and its white inhabitants, citizens.[59]

Two points are worth noting about Jefferson's draft amendment. First, by failing to mention a grant of authority to acquire new territory by treaty, Jefferson in effect conceded that the general government possessed that power under the Constitution. Apparently he continued to be convinced, as he had observed to Gallatin earlier in the year, that there was "no constitutional difficulty" as to the acquisition of territory. Second, the draft underscores what Jefferson's correspondence over the summer of 1803 indicated: that his chief concern was the lack of constitutional authority for holding newly acquired territory and incorporating it into the Union. His draft amendment made Louisiana part of the United States but it was narrowly drawn,

denying Congress the authority to grant lands in the unsettled northern section of the newly acquired province until given such authority
by another amendment. Thus the power that would be granted by
his own proposed amendment would be sharply limited, confined to
correction of the constitutional difficulty.

Malone has observed that no important adviser or supporter of
Jefferson apparently urged either the necessity or the practicality of
such a constitutional procedure, however. Indeed, Jefferson's close
friend Senator Wilson Cary Nicholas argued strongly against it, saying
that a declaration from Jefferson that the treaty exceeded constitutional authority would lead to its rejection by the Senate or at least to
the charge of his willful breach of the Constitution.[60]

Jefferson's reply to Nicholas's letter, stating in particularly striking
terms his lingering constitutional scruples, has been one of the most
often quoted of Jefferson's writings on constitutional matters. He first
addressed Nicholas's argument that Article IV, section 3, providing
for the admission of new states into the Union, with some exceptions,
ought to be interpreted broadly: "When I consider that the limits of
the U.S. are precisely fixed by the treaty of 1783, that the Constitution expressly declares itself to be made for the U.S., I cannot help
believing that the intention was not to permit Congress to admit into
the Union new States, which should be formed out of the territory
for which, and under whose authority alone, they were then acting. I
do not believe it was meant that they might receive England, Ireland,
Holland, &c. into it, which would be the case on your construction."
He then stated his basic theory of constitutional interpretation, the
theory that underlay all his concerns:

> When an instrument admits two constructions, the one safe, the
> other dangerous, the one precise, the other indefinite, I prefer
> that which is safe & precise. I had rather ask an enlargement of
> power from the nation where it is found necessary, than to as-
> sume it by a construction which would make our powers bound-
> less. Our peculiar security is in possession of a written Constitu-
> tion. Let us not make it a blank paper by construction. I say the
> same as to the opinion of those who consider the grant of the
> treaty making power as boundless. If it is, then we have no con-
> stitution. If it has bounds, they can be no others than the defini-

tions of the powers which that instrument gives. It specifies and delineates the operations permitted to the federal government, and gives all the powers necessary to carry these into execution.

Conceding the likelihood that the framers' enumeration of powers was "defective"—for "this is the ordinary case of all human works"— he urged, "Let us go on then perfecting it, by adding by way of amendment to the constitution, those powers which time & trial show are still wanting." In the present case, he concluded, it was "impor- tant . . . to set an example against broad construction by appealing for new power to the people." With particular reference to this letter, one scholar has observed that "probably no other president in Ameri- can history has expressed greater doubt about the constitutionality of his own actions. His caution testifies to the seriousness with which Jefferson treated constitutional issues." [61]

Jefferson's letter to Nicholas also contained, however, a recognition of the practical difficulties against which Nicholas had warned as well as another disturbing development. Jefferson had learned from Robert Livingston that the Spanish, who had not yet delivered Louisiana to the French, might be having second thoughts; he noted that an "un- usual letter" had been written to Madison from the marques de Casa Yrujo, the Spanish envoy, warning that "if we give the least open- ing, they will declare the treaty void." He therefore thought "what- ever Congress shall think it necessary to do, should be done with as little debate as possible, & particularly so far as respects the consti- tutional difficulty." In letters written to other correspondents in late August, Jefferson similarly cautioned that "the less that is said about the constitutional difficulties, the better," and he urged that Congress do what was necessary "in silence." Thus, as he concluded in his letter to Nicholas, although he considered it important "to set an example against broad construction," he was willing to acquiesce in political necessity: "If, however, our friends shall think differently, certainly I shall acquiesce with satisfaction; confiding, that the good sense of our country will correct the evil of construction when it shall produce ill effects." [62]

Jefferson thus dropped the matter, not because he had given up strict construction but because he was following his friends' advice not to press the constitutional problem, realizing that it could jeopardize a treaty so vital to the nation's security. "What is practicable must often control what is pure theory; and the habits of the governed determine in a great degree what is practicable." Jefferson took solace in what he regarded as the "good sense" of the people, not to permit this one precedent to destroy the whole edifice of enumerated powers upon which constitutional limitations on the federal government rested.

There was another possible source of solace for Jefferson on this point. In September, he received a letter from Thomas Paine, who reassured his friend that his concern over the constitutional question was exaggerated. First, he noted, "the cession makes no alteration in the Constitution; it only extends the principles over a larger territory, and this certainly is within the morality of the Constitution, and not contrary to, nor beyond, the expression of intention of any of its articles." Paine further asserted that "the idea of extending the territory of the United States was always contemplated, whenever the opportunity offered itself," for during the Revolution many people thought "that Canada would, at some time or other, become a part of the United States."[63] These remarks concerning the foreseeability of the addition of Louisiana to the United States probably did not move Jefferson. He viewed questions of original intent rather strictly; and as he wrote in his letter to Nicholas, when new circumstances arose Jefferson's solution was not to reinterpret existing constitutional language but to make amendments explicitly to take into account the changes.

In arguing that the Louisiana cession was "within the morality of the Constitution," however, Paine had hit the nail on the head. One can only speculate to what extent this argument helped Jefferson overcome his constitutional scruples, but Paine had injected into the constitutional debate a refreshing bit of common sense. If a new power had been added by construction to those powers assigned by the Constitution to the federal sphere, it was only the power to add to the domain of what Jefferson, who had long since concluded that the American system of republican government was particularly well suited for an extensive territory, as early as 1780 aptly referred to as "the Empire of liberty."[64] The denouement of the Louisiana matter, as Jefferson observed in a letter written a few months later to another friend, Joseph Priestley, was "happy"; and Jefferson with pride spoke of "this duplication of area for extending a government so free and economical as ours" as "a great achievement."[65]

Laws "of Higher Obligation": Executive Prerogative and the Presidency

At the time of the Louisiana crisis Jefferson recognized, as he put it in his August 1803 letter to John Breckinridge, that in "seizing the fugitive occurrence" that the treaty offered "which so much advances the good of [the] country," he as president had acted "beyond the Constitution." The metaphor of the guardian who had "risk[ed] [him]self" by the unauthorized investment of his ward's money hinted at another way of rationalizing the purchase of Louisiana which, surprisingly, Jefferson did not articulate until after his retirement: the theory of executive prerogative. When, in relation to other constitutional questions largely pertaining to the events of his second term, Jefferson did discuss this theory, it added another new aspect to his conception of executive powers within a republican system of government.

In a letter written in 1810 former president Jefferson discussed the question, "whether circumstances do not sometimes occur, which make it a duty in officers of high trust, to assume authorities beyond the law." It was a question, he wrote, which was "easy of solution in principle, but sometimes embarrassing in practice." He then stated the principle, in a passage which subsequent generations of historians, political scientists, and other commentators have frequently cited out of context: "A strict observance of the written laws is doubtless *one* of the high duties of a good citizen, but it is not *the highest*. The laws of necessity, of self-preservation, of saving our country when in danger, are of higher obligation. To lose our country by a scrupulous adherence to written law, would be to lose the law itself, with life, liberty, property and all those who are enjoying them with us; thus absurdly sacrificing the end to the means." He gave several examples: during the battles of Germantown and Yorktown, General Washington's army fired on citizens' homes, for "the laws of property must be postponed to the safety of a nation"; when the British invaded Virginia, Jefferson himself as governor "took horses, carriages, provisions and even men by force"; and, as a hypothetical case, "a ship at sea in distress for provisions" might follow "the law of self-preservation" in taking supplies from another ship by force. "In all these cases," Jefferson observed, "the unwritten laws of necessity, of self-preservation, and of the public safety, control the written laws of *meum* and *tuum*." [66]

Exercise of extraordinary powers pursuant to these "unwritten laws" was not for governmental officers "charged with petty duties," he emphasized. "Where consequences are trifling, and time allowed for a legal course," the written law must be adhered to; otherwise, "the example of overleaping the law" would be "of greater evil than a strict adherence to its imperfect provisions." Only high government officials justifiably might act beyond the written Constitution, and even they only when extraordinary circumstances impose upon them this "higher obligation": "It is incumbent on those only who accept of great charges, to risk themselves on great occasions, when the safety of the nation, or some of its very high interests are at stake. An officer is bound to obey orders; yet he would be a bad one who should do it in cases for which they were not intended, and which involved the most important consequences." He noted, "The line of discrimination may be difficult, but the good officer is bound to draw it at his own peril, and to throw himself on the justice of his country and the rectitude of his motives." [67]

Jefferson's doctrine of higher obligation probably derived from John Locke, with whom the notion of the executive power, as conceived in modern constitutionalism, had originated. Jefferson may well have taken the opportunity afforded by his retirement to reread Locke's works. In his *Second Treatise* Locke observed that where the legislative and executive powers were in separate hands—as they were in "moderated Monarchies, and well-framed Governments"—"the good of the Society requires, that several things should be left to the discretion of him, that has the Executive Power." This discretionary power he called "Prerogative" and defined as the power to act "for the publick good, without the prescription of the Law, and sometimes even against it." It arose of necessity, first, from the fact that the legislators could not foresee, and provide by laws for, all contingencies. The executive, "having the power in his hands, has by the common Law of Nature, a right to make use of it, for the good of the Society, in many Cases, where the municipal Law has given no direction, till the Legislative can conveniently be Assembled to provide for it." The prerogative also arose from the fact that in some cases, even though there existed an applicable rule of law, the rule must be disregarded. "'Tis fit," noted Locke, "that the Laws themselves should in some Cases give way to the Executive Power, or rather to this Fundamental Law of Nature and Government, *viz.* That as much as may be, *all* the Members of the Society are to be *preserved*." [68]

The further examples Jefferson provided in his 1810 letter more clearly indicate both the nature of the extraordinary circumstances that would justify "overleaping the law" and the officer who might so act. Two of the examples involved presidential acts; the other involved the response to the Burr conspiracy by General James Wilkinson. The first, "an hypothetical case" involving the purchase of the Floridas in the autumn of 1805, presented constitutional difficulties analogous to those involved in the purchase of Louisiana. "Suppose it had been made known to the Executive of the Union in the autumn of 1805, that we might have the Floridas for a reasonable sum, that that sum had not indeed been so appropriated by law, but that Congress were to meet within three weeks, and might appropriate it on the first or second day of their session." Ought the president, "for so great an advantage to his country, to have risked himself by transcending the law and making the purchase?" If there was the danger that "a John Randolph" might protract the debates in Congress until the following spring, by which time new circumstances would change the mind of the other party, then the president ought to have acted and his action "would have been approved," Jefferson concluded.[69]

His next example was an actual case. Following attack by a British man-of-war on the American frigate *Chesapeake* off Norfolk on 22 June 1807, Jefferson in consultation with his cabinet ordered purchases of timber for gunboats and other military supplies even though Congress had not authorized the appropriations. Although Jefferson sought not to push matters too far, war between Britain and the United States was an imminent possibility and some preparations had to be made; furthermore, Congress was not in session. After Congress convened in the fall, Jefferson sent his annual message describing the situation and explaining, among other things, the emergency purchases of supplies that had not been legally authorized. Congress subsequently appropriated funds to cover the expenditures but not without heated debate between John Randolph, who argued that the president ought to have immediately convened Congress, and defenders of Jefferson's actions, who argued that the "doctrine of 1801" (no expenditures without specific appropriations) was properly subordinated to the president's duty to act in an emergency because "the safety of the nation is the supreme law."[70]

The final example Jefferson cited in his 1810 letter was the Burr conspiracy and his defense of General Wilkinson's actions. Based on the information Jefferson received about the western conspiracy that involved the former vice president, Aaron Burr—which he afterward said indicated that Burr's plans involved severing the Union west of the Alleghenies as well as an attack on Mexico—the president issued a proclamation calling for the supression of the enterprise and the arrest of the conspirators. General Wilkinson, who himself was probably implicated in the conspiracy, at some point deserted it and on his own authority ordered the arrest and detention of some of the conspirators, circumventing local judicial authorities who had ordered their release on writs of habeas corpus.[71] Jefferson maintained that Wilkinson's actions ought to be judged "according to the circumstances under which he acted" and the officer's own understanding of them—a kind of subjective good faith standard.[72] Perhaps a similar idea was relevant to Jefferson's rather tortured attempt later in life to defend his drafting of a bill of attainder against the traitor Josiah Phillips in 1778.[73]

The doctrine of executive prerogative, as expounded by Jefferson in 1810, thus concerned extraordinary acts required, literally, to save the nation—where, as he put it, "the safety of the nation, or some of its very high interests are at stake." One indication of how exceptional the circumstances were that would legitimately permit "overleaping the law" is Jefferson's omission from his list of examples of exercises of prerogative powers one that his critics might cite: the enforcement of the embargo. Although Jefferson's enforcement of the embargo occupies an important part of Leonard Levy's indictment of Jefferson's record in matters of civil liberties,[74] and although indeed the draconian nature of executive actions during this period can hardly be denied, it is important to note that Jefferson's actions were entirely authorized by Congress. A series of enforcement measures, each more extreme than the preceding, passed Congress almost without debate—a sign of the administration's effectiveness in getting what it wanted from Congress—and granted Jefferson increasingly greater powers.[75] Prior to passage of the fifth enforcement act, Jefferson wrote Gallatin, the cabinet member under whose jurisdiction the enforcement of the embargo fell, that "this embargo law is certainly the most embarrassing one we have ever had to execute." As Dumas Malone has noted, "Because of the logic of developing circumstances and the sheer momentum of a policy of control once initiated and consistently adhered to, the whole trend of the embargo laws was toward the increase of executive authority." Nevertheless it is worth repeating, for the sake of emphasis, that in enforcing the embargo, Jefferson stayed within the confines—admittedly, quite broad confines—of the law.[76]

Jefferson's presidency, in sum, exhibited instances of the exercise of executive powers that were unparalleled; yet it also simultaneously exhibited a sense of caution in exercising questionable powers—a concern by the president over the constitutionality of his own actions—which also probably has not been matched in American history. Above all, Jefferson's presidency shows the evolution of his republican ideology into a republican constitutionalism that, to be sure, valued the written constitution and its provisions for dividing power as important safeguards, but that also envisioned the ultimate, and the most fundamental, check on governors to be the elective power of the people. "We shall all become wolves," he had warned in 1787. "Let no more be heard of confidence in man, but bind him down by the chains of the constitution," he declared in 1798. About a decade later, at the close of his presidency, after such momentous decisions as the acquisition of Louisiana and the dangerous (and eventually disastrous) policy of embargo, he was sensitive to the fact that he had acted as an agent of the people, answerable to them for the exercise of whatever discretionary authority that the Constitution and laws of the United States had vested in him.

9

A Solecism in a Republican Government

The Judiciary and Judicial Review

Perhaps no single aspect of Jefferson's constitutional thought better illustrates the interplay of republicanism with federalism than does his view of the judicial branch of the national government. It certainly is the aspect of his constitutional thought that seems to have changed most dramatically over time. Jefferson's writings of the 1780s suggest that he reposed "great confidence" in the judiciary as a protector of rights and that he believed in judicial review—or something very much like judicial review—as an effective "legal obstacle," or "legal check," against legislative tyranny. At about the time he became president, however, Jefferson apparently switched his position; he criticized the federal judiciary as a "stronghold" of the Federalist party and proposed a theory of concurrent review emphasizing the independent roles of the president and Congress as interpreters of the Constitution. After he retired from the presidency, moreover, Jefferson's negative opinions of the federal judiciary intensified. By the 1820s he came to regard the judiciary as a "corps of sappers and miners" working to undermine federalism, and he described the independence of the Marshall Court as "a solecism, at least in a republican government."[1]

Having noted the scholarly debate over the question whether Jefferson's position on judicial review had changed by the time of his presidency, Dumas Malone concluded that there was undoubtedly a change in emphasis, arguing that Jefferson's fears of judicial power "varied with circumstances." That Jefferson was at first more hospitable toward judicial review may indeed be explained by Malone's observations that "he generally opposed such tyrannies as seemed most menacing at a particular time" and that in the late 1780s, when he seemed to favor vigorous judicial review, Jefferson was not so concerned about the danger of judicial tyranny as he was later, when John Marshall headed the federal judiciary.[2] More fundamentally, however, Jefferson's views of judicial review and of the appropriate role of the judiciary evolved as his overall constitutional theory—particularly with respect to federalism and the separation of powers—evolved.

As it has been argued in previous chapters, Jefferson's constitutionalism gradually moved from an earlier balanced government model with some emphasis on separation of powers, his constitutional view at the time of *Notes on Virginia*, to the quite self-consciously republican constitutionalism, with decided emphases on the division of powers and popular control, that he espoused most explicitly after his retirement. During the crucial period of transition—the decades of the 1790s and early 1800s—as Jefferson formulated his mature constitutional theory, the same dialectic with Federalism that helped to shape other aspects of his thought also helped shape his views of the judiciary. His conflict with Marshall, like his conflict with Hamilton, provided the impetus for Jefferson to refine his earlier, rather nebulous views, which approved of judicial review in some form, into a thoroughgoing critique of the robust form of judicial review that Jefferson perceived the federal judiciary to be expounding. He did so in response to the circumstances of the time, to be sure; but he also did so because the premises that underlay his idea of republicanism were fundamentally challenged by the jurisprudence of John Marshall.

A "Legal Check into the Hands of the Judiciary": Early Views of Judicial Review

There is substantial ambiguity in Jefferson's earliest statements regarding the judiciary. Like most Americans of the time, Jefferson in 1776 had not worked out the difficult problem of determining the role a judiciary should play in a republican government. He did not advocate an elective judiciary; his draft constitution for Virginia provided that judges would be appointed and hold their offices during good behavior. He did argue, however, that a judge should be "a mere machine," dispensing "equally and impartially" the law formulated by the elected representatives of the people.[3]

Jefferson valued an independent judiciary, but not necessarily—at least not at this very early stage—as a check upon the legislature. Among his criticisms of the Virginia Constitution of 1776 in *Notes on Virginia* was that it provided "no legal obstacle to the assumption by the assembly of all the powers legislative, executive, and judiciary." To remedy this fault, in 1783 he proposed a new constitution which would be paramount to ordinary legislative acts; indeed, it would contain the explicit provision that the General Assembly "shall not have power to infringe this constitution" or to abridge certain specified civil rights. To enforce this provision, he provided for a special Council of Revision, consisting of representatives of the executive and judicial branches, which would have the power to veto legislation.[4] By implication, then, Jefferson did not envision judicial review—that is, the power of the courts to invalidate, or to declare null and void, unconstitutional legislation. He sought to provide that sort of check upon the legislature before the fact, by the veto of the Council of Revision, rather than after the fact, by the ordinary courts, which presumably would be obligated to enforce laws that had withstood this prior scrutiny.

Jefferson nevertheless did endorse the more limited concept of concurrent review—that is, the power of the courts not to invalidate but merely to refuse to enforce (in the cases presented to them) legislative acts that they deemed unconstitutional. In 1784 he listed, among the "rational and necessary" objects for which he had long wished to see a state constitutional convention called, these reforms: "To make the Executive and Judiciary branches independent of the Legislative; to give them some controul over the laws by forming them into a Council of revision as in New-York; . . . [and] the making our constitution paramount the powers of the ordinary legislature so that all acts contradictory to it may be adjudged null." His use of the verb *adjudged*, as well as his separate mention of the Council of Revision, suggests that he envisioned at least concurrent review.[5]

At the same time, however, Jefferson was quite concerned about the abuse of judicial discretion, as his statement that a judge should be "a mere machine" indicates. He was particularly apprehensive of the exercise of equity powers, which he believed should be confined to courts of equity, like the Chancery in England, separate from the courts of common law. The common law, as written law, had the merits of certainty as well as fairness, for it contained rules equally applicable to all; equity—that is, adjudication according to "the spirit and reason," rather than the letter, of the law—lacked certainty and was therefore dangerous. To permit the courts, even when prompted by the desire to do justice in individual cases, to extend the text of the law according to its equity would be "worse than running on Scylla to avoid Charybdis," Jefferson argued. "Relieve the judges from the rigour of text law, and permit them, with pretorian discretion, to wander into it's equity, and the whole legal system becomes incertain." Nothing could be worse, he maintained, than to allow, as England seemed to be doing under the "revolution" wrought by Judge Mansfield, "the courts of Common law to revive the practice of construing their text equitably."[6]

Some of Jefferson's earliest statements expressing apparent support of judicial review, in some sense, appeared in his correspondence with James Madison at about the time of the drafting and adoption of the Constitution. Madison had favored strongly a proposal to give Congress a negative, or veto, over state legislation "in all cases whatsoever," as a means to ensure that treaties entered into by the federal government with foreign powers would not be undercut by the states. Jefferson in response observed that this proposal was too broad: it failed, he said, "in an essential character, that the hole and the patch should be commensurate." Madison's proposal would "mend a small hole by covering the whole garment"; not more than one out of a hundred state acts concern the confederacy, Jefferson maintained. He then suggested an alternative which he considered "as effectual a remedy, and exactly commensurate to the defect": to permit "an appeal from the state judicatures to a federal court, in all cases where the act of Confederation controlled the question." He gave as an illustration the case of a British creditor who sues for his debt in Virginia. "The defendant pleads an act of the state excluding him from their courts; the plaintiff urges the Confederation and the treaty made under that, as controuling the state law; the [state] judges are weak enough to decide according to the views of their legislature." In such a case, Jefferson maintained, "an appeal to a federal court sets all to rights." To the argument that the federal courts thus would "encroach on the jurisdiction of the state courts," he answered that "there will be a power, to wit Congress, to watch and restrain them." To place the authority in Congress, as Madison advocated, however, would leave "no power above them to perform the same office."[7]

When he received a copy of the proposed federal Constitution late in 1787 and wrote Madison to comment on its features, Jefferson mentioned that he would have "liked it better had the Judiciary been associated" with the executive in holding the power to veto legislation "or invested with a similar and separate power." As Wallace Mendelson has observed, this indicates obviously that Jefferson wanted the judiciary to have some part in a veto, or "legal obstacle," against unconstitutional legislation; and "whether it was the council-of-revision type, *or* a separate judicial veto, did not seem to matter."[8]

Significantly, in 1789, while corresponding with Madison about the need for a bill of rights to be incorporated into the Constitution, Jefferson noted an argument in favor of such a declaration of rights "which has great weight with me": "the legal check which it puts into the hands of the judiciary." The "legal check" that he had in mind apparently was some sort of judicial veto, but it is unclear whether he meant to endorse judicial review by the federal courts. He wrote: "This [the judiciary] is a body, which, if rendered independent and kept strictly to their own department, merits great confidence for their learning and integrity. In fact, what degree of confidence would be too much, for a body composed of such men as Wythe, Blair and Pendleton?" The reference to three prominent Virginia jurists suggests that it was the state, not the federal, courts that Jefferson had in mind; the clause referring to the judiciary being "kept strictly to their own department" might imply the more limited concept of concurrent review rather than judicial review. His further statements that the declaration of rights would be "the text by which they [the states] would try all the acts of the federal government" and that "the jealousy of the subordinate governments is a precious reliance," suggest indeed that Jefferson gave equal emphasis to federalism as a means to check Congress in its exercise of national powers.[9] The letter to Madison nevertheless shows that Jefferson did recognize, and apparently value, the role that the courts could play in safeguarding the rights of individuals.

At about the same time, however, Jefferson also expressed fear of the "partiality" of judges; and, accordingly, he emphasized the importance of juries. As he explained to one correspondent, "Permanent judges acquire an Esprit de corps, that being known they are liable to be tempted by bribery, that they are misled by favor, by relationship, by a spirit of party, by a devotion to the Executive or Legislative." Hence he believed it "better to leave a cause to the decision of cross and pile, than to that of a judge biased to one side; and that the opinion of 12 honest jurymen gives still a better hope of right." Acknowledging the common law rule limiting juries to questions of fact, Jefferson nevertheless maintained that if the jurors thought the judges to be "under any bias whatever," they might "take upon themselves to judge the law as well as the fact." He added that by the exercise of this power, juries have been "the firmest bulwarks of English liberty." [10]

The right to trial by jury was one of the six rights that Jefferson urged for inclusion in a federal bill of rights. He already had begun formulating his concept of republicanism as the inclusion of the people into every department of government "as far as they are capable of exercising it"; and he clearly regarded juries as the means by which this principle could be realized in the judicial branch. For that reason, he was especially concerned that the French revolutionaries include in their proposed declaration of rights a guarantee of jury trial, which he called "the only anchor, ever yet imagined by man, by which a government can be held to the principles of it's constitution." [11] Direct citizen participation in government through such devices as the jury, therefore, was as important to Jefferson as the independence of judges in safeguarding constitutional rights.

After his return to the United States and during his tenure as Washington's secretary of state, Jefferson apparently took pains to maintain the independence of the federal judiciary. In one of his earliest acts as secretary of state, he returned some papers that he had received relating to the action of Georgia on British debts, explaining to the British recipient, "The validity of the laws in question being purely a judiciary question, will, by our Constitution, [have] to be decided on by the Federal Court, before whom the parties interested will of course take care to bring it." Several months later, when the Swedish consul complained that an American admiralty court had taken cognizance of a complaint of some Swedish sailors against their captain for cruelty, Jefferson similarly invoked the doctrine of separation of powers in explaining why the executive branch could do nothing. "This question lies altogether with the Courts of Justice; . . . the Constitution of the United States having divided the powers of Government into three branches, legislative, executive and judiciary, and deposited each with a separate body of Magistracy, forbidding either to interfere in the department of the other, the Executive are not at liberty to intermeddle in the present question," he wrote to the consul. "It must be ultimately decided by the Supreme court if you think proper to carry it into that." Pursuant to Washington's instructions, Jefferson even formally requested the Supreme Court to issue advisory opinions, a request that Chief Justice Jay declined.[12]

The political party struggle of the 1790s provided further occasions for Jefferson to formulate a theory of constitutionalism which laid great stress on separation of powers doctrine. By 1797, at the time he drafted the petition to the Virginia legislature protesting the federal grand jury's presentment of Samuel Cabell for seditious libel, concern over Federalist machinations involving the courts prompted Jefferson to rely on this doctrine for his basic argument. Each of the three branches of government, legislative, executive, and judiciary, "in the discharge of their functions, should be free from the cognizance or coercion of the co-ordinate branches," he wrote. Thus the grand jury presentment violated not only the "natural right" of constituents to communicate with their representative but also "that wise and cautious distribution of powers made by the constitution between the three branches," for the presentment would give, in effect, a "complete preponderance" to the judiciary over the legislature.[13]

It was the crisis of 1798, generated in the wake of the Alien and Sedition Acts, that prompted Jefferson to push the principle of separation of powers to its logical conclusion respecting the judicial branch: the doctrine of concurrent review, or what scholars have designated as Jefferson's tripartite theory of constitutionalism. In his draft of the Kentucky Resolutions, he took issue with the Federalist claim that the United States Supreme Court was the exclusive and final arbiter of constitutional questions. To give this authority to a branch of the government created by the Constitution, he maintained, would be to make "it's discretion, and not the Constitution, the measure of it's powers." It should be added that in another of the resolutions, he argued that the Alien Act unconstitutionally had deprived the courts of "the judicial power" by empowering the president to deport aliens without benefit of trial. Thus, Jefferson's concern for separation of powers cut both ways.[14]

Another of the arguments Jefferson advanced in the Kentucky Resolutions deserves special attention. In the second resolution he argued that the Constitution "delegated to Congress the power to punish treason, counterfeiting the securities and current coin of the United States, piracies, and felonies committed on the high seas, and offences against the law of nations, and no other crimes whatsoever." "The power to create, define, and punish such other crimes is reserved, and, of right, appertains solely and exclusively to the respective States, each within its own territory," he maintained.[15] This principle closely followed from the fundamental constitutional argument of the resolutions: that the federal government was one of limited powers, enumerated in the Constitution itself. All other powers, by the principle of the federal compact as well as the additional safeguard of the Tenth Amendment, remained with the states.

If it was unconstitutional for Congress to make sedition a crime, then Jefferson believed it was similarly unconstitutional for the federal courts to try persons for the offense of sedition under the common law. After this in fact had been attempted, and Federalists advanced the general doctrine that there existed a federal common law of crimes, Jefferson interpreted the suggestion as, essentially, the final blow in a campaign by the Federalists to destroy the federal, republican system of government established by the Constitution. He described this "dangerous doctrine" as "the most formidable" one advanced by the Federalists. "All their other assumptions of un-given powers have been in the detail. The bank law, the treaty doctrine, the sedition act, alien act, the undertaking to change the state laws of evidence in the state courts by certain parts of the stamp act, &c., &c., have been solitary, unconsequential, timid things, in comparison with the audacious, boldfaced and sweeping pretension to a system of law for the U.S., without the adoption of their legislature, and so infinitely beyond their power to adopt." Hence, it was not only the doctrine of a federal common law of crimes that concerned Jefferson. His fear of the incorporation into federal jurisprudence of the common law in civil causes was equally great, for the same reason: it would destroy federalism, as Jefferson understood it, for giving federal judges jurisdiction coextensive with the common law would give them general jurisdiction over all cases and persons, leaving nothing to the states.[16] Adoption of a federal common law, whether criminal or civil, also represented the destruction of republicanism, as Jefferson understood it, for it would substitute the will of the judges for the will of the nation as the basis of law.

In the suppressive atmosphere of 1798 and 1799, on the eve of the 1800 electoral campaign, the federal judiciary thus was revealed in Jefferson's mind as an institution which posed threats to liberty at least as formidable as those that had been posed by the Hamiltonian system. The stage was set for Jefferson's near-complete parting of the ways with the federal judiciary and for his complete rejection of the doctrine of judicial review.

President Jefferson and the Judiciary

"The revolution of 1800," Jefferson wrote to Spencer Roane in 1819, "was as real a revolution in the principles of our government as that of 1776 was in its form; not effected indeed by the sword, as that, but by the rational and peaceable instrument of reform, the suffrage of the people."[17] By the "revolution" of 1800, Jefferson of course meant the Republican victory in the elections of that year: it was revolutionary because, in late-eighteenth century American politics, differences ran deep. To Jefferson and his fellow Republicans much more was at stake in 1800 than political offices; to them, as the name of their party suggested, the question was whether American government would remain republican, in principles as well as form. The result of those elections was a vindication of republicanism; for, as Jefferson wrote to Roane, "the nation declared its will by dismissing functionaries of one principle [the Federalists] and electing those of another, in the two branches, executive and legislative, submitted to their election." But the vindication of principles was necessarily incomplete; for, as Jefferson added, "over the judiciary department, the constitution had deprived them [the people] of their control."

To Jefferson's dismay the federal judiciary was monopolized by Federalists. Moreover, the Supreme Court was headed by John Marshall, who had been appointed chief justice late in the Adams administration and whose decisions would later represent to Jefferson nothing less than an effort to preserve, and to entrench into the law, the hated principles of that "Anglican monarchical aristocratical party." Referring to his political foes early in the first congressional session of his presidency, Jefferson wrote: "On their part, they have retired into the judiciary as a stronghold. There the remains of federalism are to be preserved and fed from the treasury, and from that battery all the works of republicanism are to be beaten down and erased." If indeed, as Jefferson's language suggests, this prepared the ground for a battle, it was the Republican side that first attacked, early in 1802, by repealing the Judiciary Act of 1801. The Republicans "leveled the outworks that had been erected during the final days of the Adams administration, thus restoring the *status quo ante bellum*," as Dumas Malone has put it, continuing the metaphor.[18]

Repeal of the Judiciary Act of 1801 was one of the first and most striking acts of what at least one scholar has called "Jefferson's attack on the federal judiciary." The Judiciary Act of 1801 had abolished the old system of the Supreme Court justices riding circuit in the far reaches of the Union and in its place created a new system of circuit courts with sixteen judgeships vested with trial jurisdiction in all cases in law and equity arising under the Constitution and laws of the United States. Though not apparently partisan in substance, the act was an avowedly partisan Federalist measure in its intent and effects: it would expand the jurisdiction of the federal courts, facilitating the transfer of litigation from the states to the federal bench; it also would create several new offices, filled by Federalists appointed in the waning days of the Adams administration, from which they were irremovable. As Jefferson saw it by December 1801, "By a fraudulent use of the Constitution, which has made judges irremovable, they have multiplied useless judges merely to strengthen their phalanx."[19]

Jefferson did not immediately press for the repeal of the act, for he began his administration urging a policy of moderation and conciliation. He withstood demands by Edmund Pendleton and other Old Republicans for amendments to the Constitution, which among other things would change the tenure of judges from life to a limited term of years. Instead, Jefferson merely exercised his power to remove Adams's "midnight" appointments of Federalist attorneys and marshals. He thus did not seek to undermine judicial review or independence directly but rather followed a cautious, moderate course to weaken the Federalist monopoly over the federal judiciary through actions that were clearly within his prerogatives as president. His desire not to alienate moderate Federalists even prompted him to withhold a statement of his tripartite doctrine that he had planned to make public in his first annual message; he confined to private correspondence his denial of the judiciary's right ultimately to determine constitutional questions. He also acted to end the prosecutions that the Adams administration had begun under the Sedition Act against James T. Callender and William Duane, taking pains, however, not to exceed his authority before he remitted Callender's unexpired sentence and discontinued the prosecution against Duane.[20] Despite this cautious approach Jefferson's actions were subjected to scathing criticisms in the Federalist press, which argued that he had violated the Constitution by interfering with the prosecutions.

Two additional developments that were particularly disturbing may have prompted Jefferson to take the further step of initiating the effort to repeal the Judiciary Act of 1801. Only months after his inauguration two of the Federalist judges of the new Circuit Court for the District of Columbia instructed the Republican district attorney to institute a common law prosecution against the *National Intelligencer*, the administration newspaper, for publishing an attack on the judiciary. The grand jury returned a presentment, but the district attorney refused to act, and subsequently the grand jury refused to indict.[21] No doubt Jefferson viewed with alarm this resurrection of the doctrine of federal common law crimes. Even more ominous, however, was an episode that took place in the December term of the Supreme Court. William Marbury and three other justices of the peace of the District of Columbia whose commissions Jefferson had refused to deliver decided to test the legality of the administration's decision by instituting an original action before the Supreme Court, petitioning for writs of mandamus requiring Secretary of State James Madison to deliver the commissions. Chief Justice Marshall granted the plaintiffs' preliminary motion to require Madison to show cause why the writs should not be issued against him, and then he assigned the fourth day of the next term for hearing arguments. The *Marbury* case convinced Jefferson that there existed a real and immediate danger of judicial control over the acts of the executive. On the very day that Marshall delivered his ruling on the preliminary motion, Jefferson wrote angrily of the judiciary as a Federalist "stronghold."[22]

Jefferson then moved from his prior cautious approach and took the step of recommending to Congress—in that oblique way which characterized his formal dealings with that body—that it consider repeal of the 1801 act. In his annual message he stated simply, "The judiciary system of the United States, and especially that portion of it recently erected, will of course present itself to the contemplation of Congress." At the same time he laid before Congress a hastily prepared report, full of inaccuracies, of the number of cases decided by the federal courts since their establishment and the number of cases pending at the time of the adoption of the 1801 act. By thus breaking his silence and taking leadership on the issue, Jefferson managed to unite the various Republican factions that had been bickering in Congress and thus made the movement for repeal "the President's measure."[23]

As Richard Ellis has persuasively argued, the evidence does not support the charge that Jefferson either considered or intended the repeal of the Judiciary Act of 1801 to be the first step in an assault on the federal judiciary. What Congress did in repealing the 1801 act, as Jefferson saw it, was only to "restore our judiciary to what it was while justice & not federalism was its object." Political considerations no doubt entered into his reluctance to take the offensive, as they clearly did with respect to his decisions not to press for constitutional amendments and to delete from his annual message an explicit repudiation of judicial review.[24] More fundamentally, however, Jefferson's cautious approach reflected his constitutional principles. His quarrel was not with judicial independence from the other branches of government, as has been suggested,[25] but rather with judicial independence of the will of the nation. As Jefferson later put it, "A judiciary independent of a king or executive alone, is a good thing; but independence of the will of the nation is a solecism, at least in a republican government."[26] Jefferson's constitutional theory, in fact, relied upon the independence of the judiciary as a guardian of individual rights against executive and legislative tyranny; his quarrel with the judiciary was that under the control of Federalists, it failed to fulfill this vital function and had become the destroyer rather than the protector of the Constitution and citizens' liberties.[27]

The constitutional theory that scholars have designated as Jefferson's tripartite doctrine was fully developed in Jefferson's mind by the time of his presidency. He explained his doctrine in a letter written to Abigail Adams in 1804, defending his actions in discontinuing prosecutions and pardoning offenders under the Sedition Act:

> You seem to think it devolved on the judges to decide on the validity of the sedition law. But nothing in the constitution has given them a right to decide for the executive, more than to the Executive to decide for them. Both magistracies are equally independant in the sphere of action assigned to them. The judges, believing the law constitutional, had a right to pass a sentence of fine and imprisonment, because that power was placed in their hands by the constitution. But the Executive, believing the law to be unconstitutional, was bound to remit the execution of it; because that power has been confided to him by the constitution.

The Constitution, he concluded, "meant that it's co-ordinate branches should be checks on each other" and that to give the judiciary the right to decide questions of constitutionality "not only for themselves in their own sphere of action, but for the legislative and executive also in their spheres, would make the judiciary a despotic branch." [28] Jefferson's theory of the nature of executive power emphasized that the president was "bound by the chains" of the Constitution and compelled to act accordingly, except in those extraordinary circumstances where a higher, unwritten law might govern. The president's general duty to obey the Constitution in practice required him to interpret the Constitution, for, as Jefferson later put it, his obligation was "to execute what was law," and this obligation therefore "involved that of not suffering rights secured by valid laws, to be prostrated by what was no law." [29]

Perhaps the most eloquent statement of Jefferson's doctrine was found in a passage he included in the draft of his first annual message to Congress but omitted after certain members of his cabinet advised him that it was too controversial. In the passage Jefferson, citing his oath of office and his corresponding duty to exercise his "free & independent judgment," declared the Sedition Act to be "in palpable & unqualified contradiction to the constitution" and therefore "a nullity." According to Jefferson's marginal note, he left out the passage because he thought it "capable of being chicaned, and furnishing the opposition something to make a handle of." [30] Notwithstanding the political reasons for its removal, the passage stated Jefferson's constitutional theory in clear terms:

> Our country has thought proper to distribute the powers of it's government among three equal & independent authorities, constituting each a check on one or both of the others, in all attempts to impair it's constitution. To make each an effectual check, it must have a right in cases which arise within the line of it's proper functions, where, equally with the others, it acts in the last resort & without appeal, to decide on the validity of an act according to it's own judgment, & uncontrouled by the opinion of any other department. We have accordingly, in more than one instance, seen the opinions of different departments in opposition to each other, & no ill ensue. The constitution, moreover, as a further security for itself, against violation even by a concurrence of all the departments, has provided for it's own reintegration by a change of the persons exercising the functions of those departments.

Jefferson did not seem at all troubled by the fear of conflicts arising from the departments' divergent interpretations of the Constitution. In part, this may have been due to the fact that in his day, for all practical purposes, the legislature and the executive continued to determine for themselves whether or not they were acting within the bounds of the Constitution. The last sentence in this passage suggests a further, more important reason why Jefferson was so untroubled about each department deciding for itself the meaning of the Constitution: if a truly difficult conflict arose between two or more branches, it could be resolved by the only ultimate arbiter of constitutional questions, the people, acting in their elective capacity. Through their periodic choosing of officers for two of the three departments of national government, the people have an opportunity to reintegrate the Constitution, by demonstrating their approval or disapproval of those branches' interpretation of it.

Indeed, in his marginal insert Jefferson broadened his rationale for declaring the Sedition Act a nullity into a general principle, declaring that "succeeding functionaries have the same right to judge of the conformity or non-conformity of an act with the constitution, as their predecessors who past it, for if it be against that instrument, it is a perpetual nullity." Yet, a check against the right of each succeeding president to interpret for himself the constitutionality of an act was the fact that "uniform decisions . . . sanctioned by successive functionaries, by the public voice, and by repeated elections would so strengthen a construction as to render highly responsible a departure from it."[31] These ideas may help explain why Jefferson did not seek to repeal the Alien and Sedition Acts formally: he was convinced of their unconstitutionality, and he thought the public concurred with his judgment. He decided at the last minute that it was unnecessary to press the point by making his stance public through his first annual message because he understood the Republican electoral victory—the "revolution"—of 1800 to be evidence of public disapproval of the Federalists' entire program.

Because he found the exception of the judges from this elective check "quite dangerous enough," Jefferson was particularly disturbed by the notion that judges were the ultimate arbiters of all constitutional questions. That notion, he emphasized repeatedly, was a "very dangerous one" which would "place us under the despotism of an oligarchy."[32]

Jefferson's tripartite doctrine was not without its problems, the chief one being how to decide when a department of government should act "for itself" and thus act "ultimately and without appeal." Jefferson recognized that "the judges certainly have more frequent occasion to act on constitutional questions, because the laws of *meum* and *tuum* and of criminal action, forming the great mass of the system of law, constitute their particular department."[33] It is not clear to what extent he was suggesting something truly revolutionary in arguing that the president and Congress might decide "for themselves" the constitutional validity of laws "prescribing" their actions when at the same time he conceded that "questions of property, of character and of crime" were "ascribed to the judges, through a definite course of legal proceeding." Laws involving such questions "belong" to the judges, who "decide on them ultimately and without appeal" and therefore "of course decide *for themselves*."[34] Jefferson used the verb *belong*, which suggests that particular laws may be classified as legislative, executive, or judicial in nature. If in so doing one finds that the vast majority of acts of Congress belong to the judicial category, Jefferson's theory would require that the Supreme Court ultimately determine the constitutionality of most laws enacted by Congress. Jefferson's formula therefore might carve an exception which would ultimately swallow much of the rule that he meant to offer in opposition to the proposition that the judiciary is invested with exclusive authority to decide the constitutionality of laws.

The Supreme Court's 1803 decision in *Marbury v. Madison* affords an interesting opportunity to assess Jefferson's doctrine. Marshall had presented the issues before the Court in terms of three questions: First, has Marbury a right to the commission? Second, if he has a right and that right has been violated, does the law afford him a remedy? and Third, if he does have a remedy, is it a mandamus issuing from this Court? Taking these questions in order, Marshall then gave his opinion in two parts: first, holding that Marbury indeed did have a right to the commission, a right which had been violated by the Jefferson administration's decision to withhold it; but second, holding that the Court could not remedy the situation by issuing a mandamus because that section of the Judiciary Act of 1789 which authorized the Court to do so had unconstitutionally added to the Court's original jurisdiction under Article III.[35] Historically the second part of opinion, the true holding of the Court, has been considered the more important as an explicit assertion of judicial review; at the time, however, it was the first part of the opinion, the obiter dictum on the rights of federal appointees with its implied criticism of Jefferson, that caused controversy when the opinion was announced.

Jefferson's summary of the case, in his 1823 letter to Justice William Johnson, emphasized that most of the opinion was "merely an *obiter* dissertation of the Chief Justice," an instance of Marshall's "very irregular and very censurable" practice of "travelling out of his case to prescribe what the law would be in a moot case not before the court."[36] Jefferson's main point of disagreement with Marshall was in his understanding of the common law. Because as he saw it Marbury's commission was not a deed until it was delivered, Jefferson considered his nondelivery of the commission as an instance where he was acting within his discretion as president, ultimately and without appeal.

Implicit in Jefferson's criticism of the decision is his agreement with the true holding of the Court, that it lacked original jurisdiction to issue the mandamus. For Jefferson, of course, it was the principle of separation of powers and not Article III of the Constitution that deprived the Court of jurisdiction. Indeed, referring explicitly to the Marbury case in a 1819 letter to Spencer Roane, he noted that the federal judges "cannot issue a mandamus to the President or legislature, or to any of their officers," explaining, "the constitution controlling the common law in this particular."[37]

The interesting question is whether Jefferson would have conceded the Court's authority to declare a part of the Judiciary Act of 1789 unconstitutional and therefore void. Assuming that Jefferson agreed with Marshall that "it is emphatically the province and duty of the judicial department to say what the law is," would it have been consistent with his tripartite theory to conclude that merely by the Court's declaring it so, section 13 of the Judiciary Act was void? The holding in *Marbury*, in a strict sense, accords with Jefferson's view of the proper balance of powers between the departments. Because the Court was construing a portion of the Judiciary Act, which concerned its jurisdiction, the Court was acting ultimately and without appeal, under Jefferson's theory. Marshall was stating a really quite narrow principle: that if a law and the constitution are in conflict and if both apply to a particular case so that the court must decide in accordance with one or the other, the court must determine which of the two conflicting rules govern. "This is of the very essence of judicial duty," Marshall wrote. "Courts, as well as other departments" are bound by the Constitution; therefore, the Court must hold the law to be void. Jefferson could hardly have disagreed with the principle of judicial review in this narrow sense.[38]

The Court's decision in *Marbury*, then, was a kind of Pyrrhic victory for Jefferson: its result accorded logically with his own constitutional theory; and even though historically it has been interpreted as an affirmation of the Court's right ultimately to interpret the Constitution, the second part of Marshall's opinion did not assert the claim either that the power of review was solely within the Supreme Court's province or that the Court's judgment was superior to that of other branches. It was the first part of the opinion—the obiter dictum with its implicit accusation that Jefferson was guilty of dereliction of duty in withholding the commissions—that stirred his ire.

Marbury was not the last conflict that Jefferson would have with the federal judiciary during his presidency, but what followed fell far short of an administration-sponsored assault on the judiciary. The evidence suggests that Jefferson gave only lukewarm support to the two Republican efforts to impeach Federalist judges that occurred during his presidency: the successful impeachment and conviction of the insane Judge John Pickering of the federal district court of New Hampshire and the impeachment and acquittal of Supreme Court Justice Samuel Chase.

Early in February 1803 Jefferson sent to the House of Representatives a communication containing evidence against Pickering, noting that the complaints he had received against the judge were "not within Executive cognizance" and that he was accordingly transmitting the documents to the House, "to whom the Constitution has confided a power of instituting proceedings of redress if they shall be of opinion that the case calls for it." Although he was determined to see Pickering removed, Jefferson in private expressed doubts about the expediency of impeachment and suggested that he would prefer to see the Constitution amended to permit removal of judges from office by the president upon application by Congress. Impeachment also posed constitutional difficulties, particularly in Judge Pickering's case: insanity and intoxication, not his guilt for "high crimes and misdemeanors," called for his removal from the bench.[39]

Jefferson's role in initiating proceedings against Justice Chase, though less formal, was more direct. Chase had become notorious to Republicans for his partisan harangues from the bench—particularly during the sedition trial of Callender in Richmond—and his charge to a grand jury in Baltimore in May 1803 apparently was the final straw. Chase attacked, among other things, the doctrines of natural rights and equality of rights. The central part of his charge condemned the repeal of the Judiciary Act of 1801, the recent change in the Maryland Constitution establishing universal manhood suffrage, and proposals for further changes in the state judiciary—all of which, he said, "take away all security for property and personal liberty" and would cause the constitution to "sink into a mobocracy, the worst of all possible governments." Hearing of Chase's wholesale repudiation of virtually all the principles that he believed the American Revolution had stood for, Jefferson sent a clear hint in a letter he wrote to a Maryland congressman that the House initiate impeachment proceedings, which it did. Consistent with his adherence to the principle of separation of powers, Jefferson took no part in the proceedings in Congress, whose disappointing outcome added a sour final note to his otherwise quite successful first term. He later said, without specific reference to Chase's acquittal, that impeachment was "an impracticable thing, a mere scare-crow," and that the "only remaining hold" on federal judges was "public opinion."[40]

In the treason trial of Aaron Burr, however, Jefferson was intimately involved in all stages of the proceeding, one which again put him in direct conflict with John Marshall.[41] Because the overt treasonable acts that Burr was accused of committing took place on Blennerhassett's Island, which was under the jurisdiction of Virginia, venue for the case lay with the federal circuit court in Richmond, where Marshall presided. A direct challenge to Jefferson's doctrine of separation of powers was raised when Marshall granted the defense motion to issue a subpoena *duces tecum* to the president, requiring him to produce certain papers he had received from General Wilkinson as well as copies of orders respecting Burr that had been issued to military officers. Although Jefferson's personal attendance in Richmond was not requested, he saw that issuance of such a subpoena set a precedent which could undermine the separation of powers, as he explained in a letter to George Hay, the United States attorney and chief prosecutor in the case:

> If the Constitution enjoins on a particular officer to be always engaged in a particular set of duties imposed on him, does not this supersede the general law, subjecting him to minor duties inconsistent with these? The Constitution enjoins his constant agency in the concerns of six millions of people. Is the law paramount to this, which calls on him on behalf of a single one? . . . The leading principle of our Constitution is the independence of the legislature, executive and judiciary of each other, and none are more jealous of this than the judiciary. But would the executive be independent of the judiciary, if he were subject to the *commands* of the latter, and to imprisonment for disobedience; if the several courts could bandy him from pillar to post, keep him constantly trudging from north to south and east to west, and withdraw him entirely from his constitutional duties?[42]

By thus raising a doctrine that in modern times has been called executive privilege, Jefferson was adamant in refusing to submit to the subpoena. Not wanting to create a constitutional deadlock, however, he sought to resolve the impasse by proposing a solution which would avoid a confrontation with the judiciary without yielding his executive prerogatives. Through Hay he made clear that his personal attendance at Richmond was out of the question and, further, that as to the disclosure and publication of government papers, the president "of course, from the nature of the case, must be the sole judge." At the same time he took steps to make the desired papers available. The production of documents sufficiently satisfied the subpoena so that further resolution of the executive privilege issue was not required at this stage of the trial.[43]

Jefferson made no secret of his convictions that Burr was guilty of treason and that the Federalists—Chief Justice Marshall included—had made "Burr's cause their own."[44] He reacted with outrage at the outcome of the Burr trial: Marshall, contradicting the position he had taken in the habeas corpus case of two of Burr's co-conspirators, Dr. Justus E. Bollmann and Samuel Swartwout, only a few weeks before, defined treason so narrowly that the jury was compelled to return a verdict that Burr was "not proved to be guilty by any evidence submitted to us."[45] Viewing the decision almost entirely in political rather than legal terms, Jefferson declared that it was "equivalent to a proclamation of impunity to every traitorous combination which may be formed to destroy the Union" and showed that rather than having "fixed laws to guard us equally against treason & oppression, . . . we have no law but the will of the judge." He then predicted that the "scenes which have been acted at Richmond" could have the happy result of producing an amendment to the Constitution "which, keeping the judges independent of the Executive, will not leave them so, of the nation."[46]

An amendment to the Constitution which Jefferson might have been expected to welcome—calling for the appointment of federal judges for terms of years and their removal on joint address of two-thirds of both houses of Congress—was introduced early in the next session of Congress but went nowhere. Jefferson apparently did nothing to advance it, although he had suggested to Congress in his annual message that it consider the Burr case and decide "whether the defect was in the testimony, in the law, or in the administration of the law" and whether Congress might "apply or originate the remedy."[47]

The outcome of the Burr trial thus was to confirm Jefferson's abhorrence of Federalist control of the judiciary, and particularly his disdain for Marshall, and to set the stage for the extremely critical opinions that he would express after his retirement.

Virginia against the Court: Jefferson and the Old Republican Campaign of the 1820s

"The judiciary of the United States is the subtle corps of sappers and miners constantly working underground to undermine the foundations of our confederated fabric," Jefferson wrote on Christmas Day, 1820, to Thomas Ritchie, editor of the Richmond *Enquirer*. "They are construing our constitution from a co-ordination of a general and special government to a general and supreme one alone. . . . A judiciary independent of a king or executive alone, is a good thing; but independence of the will of the nation is a solecism, at least in a republican government." A few months later Jefferson described the federal judiciary to another correspondent as "an irresponsible body . . . working like gravity by night and by day, gaining a little to-day and a little to-morrow, and advancing its noiseless step like a thief, over the field of jurisdiction, until all shall be usurped from the States, and the government of all be consolidated into one." [48]

At the time he wrote these letters, Jefferson was becoming involved in a campaign of rhetoric conducted by a group of Virginia Republicans in reponse to a series of decisions handed down by the Supreme Court, including *McCulloch v. Maryland* (1819) and, most importantly, *Cohens v. Virginia* (1821). The Virginians involved in this campaign—Ritchie, Judge Spencer Roane of the Virginia Supreme Court of Appeals, John Taylor of Caroline, and others—were "Old Republicans," especially ardent proponents of Jeffersonian Republicanism. By 1820 this group had gained control of the Republican party in Virginia and had launched an attack upon the Court so violent as to prompt Chief Justice Marshall to warn "the friends of the Union" about "a deep design to convert our government into a mere league of States." [49]

Marshall incorrectly identified Jefferson as the head of the attack: Jefferson was in fact more like a convert to the cause—awakened, he said, by the Missouri question—although it was true that the principles espoused by the Old Republicans in the early 1820s were akin to the constitutional doctrines espoused by Jefferson in his Kentucky Resolutions of 1798. [50] Marshall was also wrong in assuming that the attacks upon the Court were prompted by ambition and personal resentment. Certainly Jefferson had little regard for the chief justice, and many of his criticisms of the Court arose from his suspicions of the "crafty" judge. For example, he bemoaned Marshall's abandonment of the English practice of the justices issuing opinions seriatim because the new practice instituted by Marshall, the opinion of the Court, masked differences between the justices under the cloak of a collegiate decision.[51] In spite of such suspicions of Marshall, however, Jefferson and the Old Republicans were genuinely motivated by principles. For them the struggle against the Court in the early 1820s was, like the struggle against the Federalist party in the late 1790s, "a game where principles are at stake."[52]

The Virginia campaign against the Marshall Court began in the newspapers and was immediately occasioned by the Court's decision in *McCulloch v. Maryland* in 1819. The case concerned a tax that the state of Maryland had levied upon the Baltimore branch of the second Bank of the United States, which Congress had chartered in 1816. James McCulloch, the branch's head cashier, sued to block collection of the tax. The Court sustained the second bank and nullified the Maryland tax. Writing the opinion for the unanimous court, Marshall—who had been writing his *Life of Washington* and thus had access to Washington's papers—drew on Hamilton's earlier arguments about the constitutionality of a national bank. Like Hamilton, Marshall found that the national government possessed implied as well as enumerated powers and that the standard for judging the constitutionality of the former was whether or not they served the latter. "Let the end be legitimate, let it be within the scope of the constitution, and all means which are appropriate, which are plainly adapted to that end, which are not prohibited, but consistent with the letter and spirit of the constitution, are constitutional." Like Hamilton also, Marshall interpreted the language of the Constitution broadly: "It is a constitution we are expounding . . . intended to endure for ages to come, and consequently, to be adapted to the various crises of human affairs."[53]

After the Court's decision a series of critical essays appeared in the Richmond *Enquirer* under the pseudonym "Amphictyon" in late March and early April 1819. The last week of April, Marshall responded anonymously with essays signed by "A Friend to the Union" in the Philadelphia *Union.* In response to these essays Judge Roane of the Virginia Court of Appeals wrote his critique of the *McCulloch* opinion in his essays signed "Hampden," which appeared in the Richmond *Enquirer* in June 1819.

Much of what Roane discussed in the "Hampden" essays concerned the merits of the case, the Court's finding that Congress had the power to charter the Bank of the United States.[54] For present purposes the essential part of the "Hampden" articles was the argument contained in the fourth and last essay, concerning the jurisdiction of the Supreme Court. Judge Roane bottomed his objections to the Court's exercise of appellate jurisdiction upon his view of federalism, "that our government is a *federal*, and not a consolidated government." Arguing that the powers of the general government resulted from a compact, the parties to which were the peoples of the several states, acting in their highest sovereign capacity, Roane emphasized that it was not the people of the United States, as one people, who were sovereign but rather the peoples of the several states—"such people being competent, and *they* only competent, to alter the pre-existing governments operating in the said states." The Constitution being a compact among the peoples of the several states, then, only the parties to the compact—the peoples of the several states—might impartially and competently judge whether the compact had been violated. As a subordinate department of the general government, the Supreme Court certainly was not competent to decide whether or not the general government had usurped powers reserved by the Constitution to the states, Roane argued. Considering the *McCulloch* case to be a contest between "the head and one of the members of our confederacy," he emphatically rejected the Supreme Court's claim of exclusive right to determine the controversy. While the head might be entirely disinterested in relation to disputes between its members—and recognizing this, the Constitution had in fact given the Supreme Court the express right to decide controversies between states—it is not disinterested in relation to disputes between it and a member. The Supreme Court could not be given the power to decide such a dispute without violating "the principle which forbids a party to decide his own cause," argued Roane; and therefore, no such power should be implied merely from the general words extending the jurisdiction of the Court to "all cases arising under the constitution."[55]

The publication of Roane's essays occasioned Jefferson's letter of 6 September 1819 informing Roane that he had read them "with great approbation" and that, with one exception, he subscribed "to every tittle of them." The one exception concerned the power of the judiciary with respect to the other departments of the federal government. In that area Jefferson went even further than Roane in denying the Court's power exclusively to interpret the Constitution. Roane, citing the *Federalist Papers*, had stated that "the judiciary is the last resort in relation to the other departments of the government, but not in relation to the rights of the parties to the compact under which the judiciary is derived," that is, the states. If this were true, the Constitution would be "a mere thing of wax," Jefferson observed. "My construction of the Constitution is very different from that you quote," he wrote. "It is that each department is truly independent of the others, and has an equal right to decide for itself what is the meaning of the Constitution in the cases submitted to its action; and especially, where it is to act ultimately and without appeal." Jefferson then referred to three events from his administration as examples of cases in which the president was acting ultimately and without appeal: his pardoning of those who had been convicted under the Sedition Act, his withholding of the commission from Marbury, and his failure to submit to the Senate for ratification the Monroe-Pinkney treaty with Britain of 1806.[56]

It is clear that by 1820 Jefferson was taking the position that the Constitution erected no single tribunal to determine ultimately all constitutional questions, because the framers knew that "to whatever hands confided, with the corruptions of time and party, its members would become despots." The Constitution rather "more wisely made all the departments co-equal and co-sovereign within themselves." "When the legislative or executive functionaries act unconstitutionally, they are responsible to the people in their elective capacity. The exemption of the judges from that is quite dangerous enough," he noted, concluding that to make judges the ultimate arbiter of all constitutional questions would be "very dangerous" and "would place us under the despotism of an oligarchy." The only "safe depository of the ultimate powers of the society" was "the people themselves."[57]

A couple of months after writing this in the fall of 1820, Jefferson received a copy of John Taylor's *Construction Construed and Constitutions Vindicated*. Taylor wrote his book largely in response to the *McCulloch* decision, but its publication in late 1820 gave it a certain relevance to the developing constitutional crisis that another case, *Cohens v. Virginia*, represented to many Virginians. Its importance in Jefferson's eyes is stressed by the fact that Jefferson, who was ordinarily quite adverse to having his political opinions exposed to the public eye, yielded to Spencer Roane's request that he write a public recommendation of the book. He described the book as containing "the true political faith to which every catholic republican should steadfastly hold. It should be put in the hands of our functionaries, authoritatively, as a standing instruction, and the true exposition of our constitution, as understood at the time we agreed to it." He also acknowledged reading Taylor's book with "edification" as well as "great satisfaction."[58] It is likely that *Construction Construed and Constitutions Vindicated* helped shift the focus of Jefferson's constitutional thought from his persistent, almost anachronistic, concern for presidential or congressional autonomy to the more immediate concern for state autonomy, or what later came to be known as states' rights.

More explicitly than either Roane or Jefferson, Taylor dealt with the question of the scope of the federal judicial power in relation to the judicial power of the states. Taking up the supremacy clause of Article VI of the Constitution, Taylor argued that it was intended "equally and coextensively to protect and secure the powers delegated to the federal government, and those reserved to the states"; and that it was not intended to extend the power of the federal judiciary in any degree whatsoever. By declaring every law of Congress constitutional, the Supreme Court could extend its own jurisdiction—"a limitation of which, attended with a power to extend it without controul, by a supreme power over the state courts, would be no limitation at all; since the power of supremacy would destroy the co-ordinate right of construing the constitution, in which resides the power of enforcing the limitation." In plainer English, "a jurisdiction, limited by its own will, is an unlimited jurisdiction." Since the supremacy clause was intended to work as a limitation upon the federal government as well as upon the states, and since the power to construe the Constitution was the equivalent of the power to enforce the limitation, the federal Supreme Court could not have the exclusive right to interpret the Constitution without violating the supremacy clause.[59]

It followed that both the federal and the state judiciaries had the right to interpret the Constitution, but that neither had the right to do so with finality. Taylor argued that the federal judicial power "stands in the same relation to the state judicial power, as the federal legislative power does to the state legislative power; and if either be independent of the other whilst acting in its own sphere, both must be independent of the other." Thus, he noted, "if Congress cannot repeal or enjoin state laws, the supreme federal court cannot enjoin or abrogate state judgments or decrees. If the federal legislative power be limited, the federal judicial power must also be limited." Conceding the right of judicial review in the strict sense—that is, the right of a court to refuse to enforce an act of the legislature that the court deemed to be unconstitutional—Taylor limited the exercise of this function to the appropriate "sphere." "Certainly" judges can declare unconstitutional laws void, he noted, but the constitutionality of state laws "cannot legitimately be decided by federal courts, since they are not a constituent part of the state governments, nor have the people of the state confided to them any such authority." In fact, he added, "the spheres of action of the federal and state courts are as separate and distinct, as those of the courts of two neighboring states." Because neither the state nor federal governments are sovereign, "the right of construing the constitution within their respective spheres, is mutual between the state and general governments."[60]

The immediate practical effect of Taylor's constitutional arguments was to deny the Supreme Court appellate jurisdiction over cases arising in state courts. In the case of *McCulloch v. Maryland*, that would seem to mean that McCulloch had no further recourse after the high court of Maryland upheld that state's tax upon the Baltimore branch of the Bank of the United States. Conflicting constructions of similar state laws throughout the nation seems the inevitable result. But that result did not trouble Taylor. That his interpretation may lead to clashing constructions "is not a good reason for overturning our system for dividing, limiting, and checking power, if that system be a good one." Uncertainty over the validity of particular laws might cause occasional inconvenience; but that inconvenience was nothing when weighed against the immense benefits to be gained from a federal system in which the state and federal governments function as the Constitution's "coordinate guardians, designed to check and balance each other."[61]

Writing a few months after he first read Taylor's book, Jefferson echoed Taylor in calling "a fatal heresy" the notion that "either our State governments are superior to the federal, or the federal to the States." He described the federal system this way:

> The people, to whom all authority belongs, have divided the powers of government into two distinct departments, the leading characters of which are foreign and domestic; and they have appointed for each a distinct set of functionaries. These they have made co-ordinate, checking and balancing each other, like

the three cardinal departments in the individual States: each equally supreme as to the powers delegated to itself, and neither authorized ultimately to decide what belongs to itself, or to its coparcenor in government. As independent, in fact, as different nations, a spirit of forbearance and compromise, therefore, and not of encroachment and usurpation, is the healing balm of such a Constitution; and each party should prudently shrink from all approach to the line of demarcation, instead of rashly overleaping it, or throwing grapples ahead to haul to hereafter.

Thus, just as Jefferson saw the three branches of government as independent, with each "supreme" in its own sphere, he also saw the two great "departments" as equally so. And just as he had concluded with respect to disagreements among the three branches, he maintained that if contradictory views of the Constitution arise between the states and federal government, neither is to decide, but rather the final appeal is to the people—"to their employers peaceably assembled by their representatives in convention."[62]

Cohens v. Virginia provided Virginians with an even better vehicle for mounting an intense and focused anti-Court campaign. In addition, the case involved a new element which promised to rouse Virginia resentment against the Court: the claim of federal review jurisdiction over state courts where the state itself was a party. Philip and Mendes Cohen had been convicted of selling tickets for a District of Columbia lottery in violation of a Virginia statute prohibiting the sale of lottery tickets not authorized by the laws of Virginia. The Cohens had raised as a defense the act of Congress authorizing the D.C. lottery. Although the controversy on the merits of the case persisted, spurred on by an opinion letter issued in June 1820 by William Pinkney and four other lawyers, emphasis shifted to the jurisdictional question after a writ of error pursuant to section 25 of the Judiciary Act of 1789 was obtained from Chief Justice Marshall.[63]

Virginia's two lawyers in the case, Philip Pendleton Barbour and Alexander Smyth, limited their arguments before the Supreme Court to the jurisdictional challenge, moving to dismiss the writ of error for want of jurisdiction. Chief Justice Marshall, in his opinion for the Court denying the motion to dismiss, articulated a stridently nationalistic view of the Constitution. "The general government, though limited as to its objects, is supreme with respect to those objects." The federal judiciary department is authorized by the Constitution to decide "all cases of every description, arising under the constitution or laws of the United States," not excepting cases in which a state may be a party. "The United States form, for many and for most important purposes, a single nation," Marshall argued; "in many respects the American people are one; and the government which is alone capable of controlling and managing their interests in all these respects, is the government of the Union." That government "for all these purposes" is "complete" and "to all these objects" is "competent." The states are "constituent parts of the United States," "members of one great empire—for some purposes sovereign, for some purposes subordinate." Hence, he concluded, the exercise of appellate power over those judgments of the state tribunals which may contravene the Constitution or laws of the United States is "essential to the attainment of these [national] objects." [64]

Having thus decided against Virginia's contention that it had no jurisdiction on the writ of error, the Court proceeded to determine the merits of the case. Two questions were involved: whether the act of Congress, properly construed, authorized the sale of lottery tickets even where such sale was prohibited by state law; and if so, whether Congress had constitutional power to authorize such sale. The Court decided the case on the merits in favor of the Commonwealth, holding that Congress did not intend to authorize sale of the tickets in Virginia, even if it had the power to do so. [65]

It was a Pyrrhic victory for Virginia, and the Old Republicans were all the more convinced by the language of Marshall's opinion that the Court was determined to encroach on the sovereignty of the states and to destroy the federal principle upon which the Union was based. Ritchie's *Enquirer* warned that "the Judiciary power, with a foot as noiseless as time and a spirit as greedy as the grave, is sweeping to their destruction the rights of the States" and advocated a repeal of section 25 of the Judiciary Act as "the most advisable and constitutional remedy for the evil." Jefferson warned that the federal judiciary was "advancing its noiseless step like a thief, over the field of jurisdiction, until all shall be usurped from the States, and the government of all be consolidated into one." [66]

Jefferson's theory of federalism helps explain his fear that the *Cohens* decision was a harbinger of consolidation. In writing Justice Johnson about the decision, Jefferson prefaced his remarks about that danger with a discussion of his two canons of construction of the Constitution. First, "the capital and leading object" of the Constitution "was to leave with the States all authorities which respected their own citizens only, and to transfer to the United States those which respected citizens of foreign or other States; to make us several as to ourselves, but one as to all others." Second, "on every question of construction, carry ourselves back to the time when the Constitution was adopted, recollect the spirit manifested in the debates, and instead of trying what meaning may be squeezed out of the text, or invented against it, conform to the probable one in which it was passed." Trying the Cohens case by these two canons, Jefferson concluded, first, that as it was between a citizen and his own state and under a law of his state, "it was a domestic case, therefore, and not a foreign one." Second, he asked rhetorically, "Can it be believed, that under the jealousies prevailing against the General Government, at the adoption of the Constitution, the States meant to surrender the authority of preserving order, of enforcing moral duties and restraining vice, within their own territory?" This being the present case—the Cohens being prosecuted under "the ancient law of gaming"—it followed then, quite clearly as Jefferson saw it, that Virginia's exercise of police power was valid. "Laws are made for men of ordinary understanding, and should therefore be construed by the ordinary rules of common sense," he maintained, asserting that any contrary reading of the Constitution—one that would deny the states "the moral rule of their citizens"—would be "a licentiousness of construction . . . hanging inference on inference, from heaven to earth, like Jacob's ladder." [67]

Jefferson's view of federalism, then, led him to the conclusion that the judicial power of the United States could not extend to cases between a state and its own citizens, even where, as in *Cohens*, a federal question was involved. In response to Marshall's point that "there must be an ultimate arbiter somewhere," Jefferson argued that "the ultimate arbiter is the people of the Union, assembled by their deputies in convention at the call of Congress, or of two-thirds of the States. Let them decide to which they mean to give an authority claimed by two of their organs." [68]

Jefferson's two "canons" provided, as he suggested, a general rule of thumb for determining the limit of federal jurisdiction. They were not meant to constitute a full theory of interpretation and, indeed, do not withstand hard analysis as such. [69] Of the two, only the second is a true canon of interpretation, and Jefferson was not wholly consistent in urging that the text of the Constitution be construed in accordance with the "probable [meaning] in which it was passed." He frequently suggested that the *Federalist Papers* should be regarded as an authoritative guide to intent; and as his opinion on the bank bill shows, he also relied on Madison's notes of debates in the Constitutional Convention. However, he adhered more closely to original intent when construing the power-granting clauses of the Constitution. As the Kentucky Resolutions illustrate, he could ignore the framers' intent altogether in construing power-limiting, or rights-guaranteeing, provisions, following instead the literal text of the Constitution. Thus both his commitment to originalism and the form of originalism to which he adhered would vary with the circumstances.[70]

Jefferson was far more consistent in adhering to his first canon, which amounted to a contextual theory of constitutional interpretation, the context being his understanding of the Constitution as a compact among the states to form a national government for specified purposes. The division of government into two departments, "domestic and foreign," was the "radical idea of the character of the constitution of our government" and the standard by which he resolved federalism questions.[71] Indeed, he even maintained that the Constitution, being "a compact of many independent powers," was not really a constitution "formed by a single authority, and subject to a single superintendence and control" and that therefore judicial interpretation of its text "by inferences, analogies, and sophisms, as they would on an ordinary law," was inappropriate.[72]

Jefferson was led by the logic of his republican principles to link federal judicial review with disunion because of the anticipated reaction of the people in the several states against attempted consolidation. He predicted that "a few such doctrinal decisions, as barefaced as that of the Cohens, happening to bear immediately on two or three of the large States" might cause the states to join "in arresting the march of government" and "to bring back the compact to its original principles, or to modify it legitimately by the express consent of the parties themselves, and not by the usurpation of their created agents." The nationalists "imagine they can lead us into a consolidated government, while their road leads directly to its dissolution," he ominously warned.[73] It was no mere coincidence that the Court's "assaults on the Constitution" in the early 1820s reminded Jefferson of the crisis of the late 1790s, and particularly of the Alien and Sedition Acts crisis of 1798. He believed that the same dangers—either consolidation or civil war—threatened at both times.[74] Nevertheless, once more Virginia was largely unsuccessful in getting other states to join in the campaign on behalf of states' rights.

More than merely an abstract devotion to states' rights lay behind Jefferson's and the Virginia Old Republicans' dread of consolidation. Jefferson found particularly troublesome the "irresponsibility" of the judiciary: judicial offices being nonelective and (as the painful effort to remove Justice Chase had shown) impeachment being an ineffective check, the judiciary was effectively insulated from popular will. And, since Jefferson defined republicanism by the degree to which government was responsive to the public will, to him the federal judiciary and especially the Supreme Court represented a fatal blemish on a constitution which was otherwise quite republican in form.

In his autobiography Jefferson noted with approbation the independence of the judiciary that had been secured after the English Glorious Revolution, when judicial tenures were changed from the king's pleasure to good behavior; but he suggested that the American constitutions had taken judicial independence too far by making a vote of impeachment "so impossible . . . that our judges are effectually independent of the nation." He did not want to go back to the old English system of making the judges dependent on the executive, he said; but he deemed it "indispensable to the continuance of this government that they should be submitted to some practical & impartial controul: and that this, to be imparted, must be state and federal authorities." Appointing honest men to judgeships was not enough; "all know the influence of interest on the mind of man, and how consciously his judgment is warped by that influence." Add to this bias the judicial "esprit de corps," the notion that "it is the office of a good judge to enlarge its jurisdiction," and the absence of responsibility, "and how can we expect impartial decision between the General government, of which they are themselves so eminent a part, and an individual state from which they have nothing to hope or fear." He also noted the tendency of judges—here he clearly had Marshall in mind—"of going out of the question before them, to throw an anchor ahead and grapple further hold for future advances of power."[75]

It was not only the "irresponsibility" of the judicial office that troubled Jefferson, however; it was the substance of the Court's decisions—its upholding of exercises of Congress's power—that raised the specter of consolidation. Jefferson's choice of the adjective *foreign* to describe the federal "department" of government was not odd, since he considered all "domestic" concerns to belong to the states. This was no merely arbitrary line of demarcation: the "wholesome distribution of powers established by the Constitution" represented to Jefferson yet another attempt to preserve republicanism by keeping government decentralized and closer to the people. He wrote Justice Johnson in 1823 that he wished "never to see all offices transferred to Washington, where, further withdrawn from the eyes of the people, they may more secretly be bought and sold as at market." As he had written in the summer after the *Cohens* decision, he feared consolidation because it threatened to destroy all that the American Revolution had achieved:

> To this [consolidation] I am opposed: because when all government, domestic and foreign, in little as in great things, shall be drawn to Washington as the centre of all power, it will render powerless the checks provided of one government on another, and will become as venal and oppressive as the government from which we separated. It will be as in Europe, where every man must be either pike or grudgeon, hammer or anvil. Our functionaries and theirs are wares from the same work-shop; made of the same materials and by the same hand. If the States look with apathy on this silent descent of their government into the gulf which is to swallow all, we have only to weep over the human character formed uncontrollable but by a rod of iron, and the blasphemers of man, as incapable of self-government, become his true historians.[76]

During this period, Jefferson's fear of national consolidation began to overcome his habitual optimism. The controversy over the admission of Missouri into the Union aroused him; "like a fire-bell in the night," he said, it filled him with terror, at the "knell of the Union." "I regret that I am now to die in the belief that the useless sacrifice of themselves by the generation of 1776, to acquire self-government and happiness to their country, is to be thrown away by the unwise and unworthy passions of their sons, and that my only consolation is to be, that I live not to weep over it."[77]

Jefferson did not see the Missouri question as primarily a dispute about slavery, although he certainly recognized the implications of Congress's effort to impose restrictions on Missouri prior to statehood. As he wrote to Albert Gallatin, "If Congress once goes out of the Constitution to arrogate a right of regulating the condition of the inhabitants of the States, its majority may, and probably will next declare that the condition of all men within the US. shall be that of freedom, in which case all the whites South of the Patomak and Ohio must evacuate their States; and most fortunate those who can do it first." Thus, to the dangers of consolidation generally were added in Jefferson's mind the fear of abolitionism that he shared with other southern slaveowners. Like many southerners too during this period (including his friend James Madison), he subscribed to the notion of "diffusion," the proposition that the expansion of slavery into the western territories offered the best means of improving the condition of slaves and hastening their eventual emancipation. Indeed, he said that if there was any morality in the question, it was on the southern side "because by spreading them over a large surface, their [the slaves'] happiness would be increased, & the burthen of their future liberation lightened by bringing a greater number of shoulders under it."[78]

He preferred to interpret the Missouri dispute as a Federalist "party trick," an effort to divide the Republican party geographically and thus regain the presidency. If sectionalism was a mere "party trick," however, it was one to which Jefferson himself apparently succumbed, for he was more avowedly southern in this period than any other in his life. Indeed, his efforts to establish the University of Virginia were in large part motivated by a desire to provide southern and western students with a "proper," or republican, seminary of learning as an alternative to northern institutions.[79]

In this highly charged political atmosphere, consolidation replaced monarchy as Jefferson's greatest object of dread; and in this, he viewed the old party struggle of the 1790s as continuing, in a new form. "An opinion persists that there is no longer any distinction, that the republicans & Federalists are completely amalgamated, but it is not so. The amalgamation is of name only," he warned. The Federalists, with their party extinguished after the Battle of New Orleans, "finding that monarchy is a desperate wish in this country, they rally to the point which they think next best, a consolidated government. Their aim is now therefore to break down the rights reserved by the constitution to the states as a bulwark against that consolidation, the fear of which produced the whole of the opposition to the Constitution at it's birth." He noted that he was unsure which was worse, "a consolidation or dissolution of the states," because "the horrors of both are beyond the reach of human foresight."[80]

In the 1820s, therefore, as during his presidency, Jefferson was animated by an opposition not to judicial review per se but to what he perceived as its misuse by an unaccountable Supreme Court dominated by John Marshall. It was not the general act of the Supreme Court's ruling on the constitutionality of particular laws passed by Congress or state legislatures but the specific act of the Supreme Court's approval (or disapproval) of certain laws with which Jefferson disagreed. His was a result-oriented approach, to which he had been pushed by the force of political circumstances—by his abhorrence of Marshall—at the price, perhaps, of logical inconsistency.

James Madison, in contrast, remained a consistent proponent of judicial review, in a much broader sense than that recognized by his old friend and collaborator. Though concurring with the Old Republicans in their fear of the consolidating tendency of the Court, Madison disagreed with some of the more radical proposals, such as Spencer Roane's advocacy of repeal of the Court's appellant jurisdiction in cases arising from state courts. Madison wrote Roane in June 1821 that "the problem of collision between the federal & State powers, especially as eventually exercised by their respective tribunals" was "the Gordian Knot of the Constitution." "If the knot cannot be untied by the text of the Constitution, it ought not certainly to be cut by any political Alexander," he wrote; and while the Constitution should be construed as far as possible so as to "obviate the dilemma of a Judicial rencounter or a mutual paralysis," nevertheless "on the abstract question whether the federal or State decisions ought to prevail, the sounder policy would yield to the claim of the former." He later explained his position to Jefferson:

> Believing as I do, that the General Convention regarded a provision within the Constitution for deciding in a peaceable and regular mode all cases arising in the course of operation, as essential to an adequate system of government; that it intended the authority vested in the Judicial Department as a final resort in relation to the States for cases resulting to it in the exercise of its functions . . . and that this intention is expressed by the

Articles declaring that the Federal Constitution and laws shall be the supreme law of the land and that the Judicial Power of the United States shall extend to all cases arising under them . . . thus believing, I have never yielded my original opinion indicated in the *Federalist* No. 39, to the ingenious reasonings of Col. Taylor against this construction of the Constitution.

In *Federalist* No. 39 Madison had stated that the federal Supreme Court was "the tribunal which is ultimately to decide" controversies between the federal and state governments, and that "some such tribunal is clearly essential to prevent an appeal to the sword and a dissolution of the compact." Thus Madison refused to join in the Virginia Old Republicans' campaign against the Marshall Court in the early 1820s, just as he would criticize some of them and their fellow nullifiers when they exploited the Jeffersonian legacy in their challenge to the federal tariff law at the end of the decade, after Jefferson's death.[81]

Conclusion: Jefferson versus Marshall

John Marshall was intensely suspicious of the Old Republicans' challenge to the Court's authority and particularly of the role that he assumed Jefferson played in that challenge. He too feared disunion, and like Madison he associated the danger not with the presence of an ultimate arbiter but with its absence. Just as the Old Republicans perceived a conspiracy led by Marshall to consolidate the powers of government in Washington, so Marshall perceived a "deep design" led by Jefferson to "convert our government into a mere league of states." Like other Federalists, Marshall interpreted the challenge to the Court as a challenge to law itself. The intensity of feelings on both sides of the judiciary debate paralleled that of the Federalist-Republican party struggles of the 1790s and derived from the same source: a shared concern for the survival of the republican form of government, along with a fundamental difference in outlook which made real debate or genuine dialogue impossible.[82]

In a perceptive essay Julian Boyd has observed that "Marshall and Jefferson—kinsmen, products of the Virginia Piedmont, students of the law under George Wythe—became inexorable protagonists of two opposed views of man and society." Marshall and Jefferson were equally committed to the ideal of a government which would secure individual natural rights, or "interests," but they disagreed profoundly as to the means by which this would be accomplished. As Robert Faulkner has noted, Marshall found in law and government—in the regulation of commerce "according to the needs of commerce itself and of a commercial society"—the "primary condition for a proper nation." He was a nationalist to the extent that he saw the United States, as he said in *Cohens*, as "one nation" whose government must be adequate to the nation's "exigencies." Although G. Edward White has shown that Marshall's theory was less expansive in practice when cases testing the scope of national power came before the Court, the theory was indeed consolidationist in its assumptions; Marshall's chief concern was the preservation of the Union against centrifugal forces.[83] Jefferson, on the other hand, believing as he did in the ideal of the natural society and in the virtue of localized government, could perceive only a few legitimate exigencies requiring federal legislation. To Jefferson, the American republican experiment was literally one in self-government: as he put it, it would prove to the world "what is the degree of freedom and self-government in which a society may venture to leave it's individual members." Governmental coercion need hardly play a role in the ideal society that Jefferson envisioned, "for the mutual workings of an independent and industrious citizenry would be almost self-sufficient." His view of society itself challenged "all the 'order' for which Marshall stood."[84] In this sense, Federalist charges that the Republicans were "lawless" were true.

A second important difference between Marshall and Jefferson was their attitude toward a concept which is best called responsibility. Marshall shared with Alexander Hamilton a theory of political conduct which, as Gerald Stourzh put it, "opposed to the corrupting tendencies of power the sobering influence of responsibility." Marshall perceived the Supreme Court as a kind of "guardian of the republic," or as he said in *Cohens*, "that tribunal which is destined to unite and assimilate the principles of natural justice and the rule of national decision." Jefferson, on the other hand, suspected that such an assumption—that the Supreme Court knew what was right for the nation—came too perilously close to "playing God."[85] He was steeped in what Stourzh called "the Whig tradition of political pessimism," which saw all men—regardless of their character or circumstances—as inherently susceptible to the corruptions of power and therefore denied the notion of responsibility, or trust and confidence in any public officeholders. "We shall all become wolves," Jefferson once warned; no man can be trusted with the government of others.[86]

Because Jefferson was unwilling to trust any single man or group of men in the governance of society, he reposed a great deal of confidence in the people themselves. Another part of his Whig inheritance was a favorable attitude toward a frequent "resort to first principles." His devotion to such reforms as rotation in office, frequent elections, and short legislative sessions and to such devices as the amending process and constitutional conventions reflected not only his view of republican government as government by the people but also his conviction that a frequent recurrence to fundamental principles was vital to the preservation of republicanism in all its vigor. This conviction underlay both his sanguine attitude toward extralegal resort to first principles—as expressed in his statement that "a little rebellion now and then is a good thing," for example—and his opposition to the Supreme Court as an ultimate arbiter of constitutional questions.

Like John Taylor, Jefferson was willing to accept the clashing of opinions on constitutional questions, which would be inevitable under their constitutionalism, because he thought that such disagreements were preferable to other dangers that threatened the Union. Regardless of what one might think of the feasibility of a legal system without a final arbiter of constitutional questions, it must be remembered that Jefferson did recognize a final arbiter: the states in their highest sovereign capacity; that is, the people of the several states. The question is not how to effectuate a system with no highest tribunal but rather how to effectuate a legal system which has as its highest tribunal the people themselves. One answer is found in the passage that Jefferson omitted from his first annual message to Congress, where he suggested that differences of opinion between departments of government might ultimately be settled through the elective power of the people, which would function as a mode by which the Constitution would "reintegrate" itself "by a change in the persons exercising the functions of those departments." Another answer is found in Jefferson's letter to Judge Roane recommending Taylor's *Construction Construed*. There Jefferson noted that when differences of opinion arise between different sets of servants, the appeal is to "their employers peaceably assembled by their representatives in convention." Jefferson, though not an advocate of "frequent and untried changes in laws and constitutions," nevertheless denied that he was a man who looked at constitutions with "sanctimonious reverence . . . like the ark of the covenant, too sacred to be touched."[87] Accordingly, he favored revisions of laws and constitutions, as the need arose. A full treatment of his criticisms of the federal judiciary cannot ignore either this fact or his sentiments favoring a literal reading of constitutional language, which implied that it is better to revise the Constitution explicitly by amendment than implicitly by construction.

Jefferson's view was clearly distinct from that of Marshall, who in *McCulloch* argued that the Constitution was "intended to endure for ages to come." Jefferson, with his Whig heritage of distrust of law and government, looked to the people rather than to the courts when he thought of adapting the Constitution, or of determining the application of its provisions, to new circumstances. Always suspicious of men in power, he sought, in the words of the Kentucky Resolutions, to "bind [them] down from mischief by the chains of the Constitution." Considering the republican form and principles of the American governments and the "salutary distribution of powers" that the Constitution had established as the "two sheet anchors of our Union," Jefferson was particularly reluctant to entrust so important a role as the interpretation of the federal Constitution to any one body of men—especially to a Supreme Court dominated, as it then was, by John Marshall. Hence he preferred that constitutional difficulties remain unresolved or that the mode of resolving them remain awkward and uncertain, rather than having mutual jealousies give way to confidence in the government at Washington.

10

Hand in Hand with the

Progress of the Human Mind

Constitutional Change

and the Preservation

of Republicanism

In one of the most significant letters he ever wrote, Jefferson in 1816 declared to Samuel Kercheval his position with regard to the issue of constitutional change. "Some men look at constitutions with sanctimonious reverence, and deem them like the arc of the covenant, too sacred to be touched. They ascribe to the men of the preceding age a wisdom more than human, and suppose what they did to be beyond amendment." As a member of the Revolutionary generation, he "knew that age well," but he also knew that "forty years of experience in government is worth a century of book-reading." He therefore declared "preposterous" the idea that constitutions ought to remain unchanged despite changes in circumstances and the greater political wisdom that a society gains through experience. "I am certainly not an advocate for frequent and untried changes in laws and constitutions," he wrote, observing that it was possible to accommodate oneself to "moderate imperfections" and to find "practical means of correcting their ill effects." "But," he added, "I know also, that laws and institutions must go hand in hand with the progress of the human mind," and that "as that becomes more developed, more enlightened, as new discoveries are made, new truths disclosed, and manners and opinions change with the change of circumstances, institutions must advance also, and keep pace with the times." To Kercheval, author of a pamphlet advocating the calling of a convention to write a new constitution for Virginia, Jefferson expressed his support. Let Virginians follow the example of people in their sister states and "avail ourselves of our reason and experience, to correct the crude essays of our first and unexperienced, although wise, virtuous, and well-meaning councils," he concluded. And, he added, "let us provide in our constitution for its revision at stated periods," suggesting nineteen or twenty years as the appropriate period, revealed by mortality tables as the average lifetime of a generation.[1]

From the early 1780s until the end of his life, Jefferson was generally a consistent and frequent advocate of constitutional change. Indeed, the hallmark of Jefferson's constitutional thought—the one aspect that most distinguished his ideas from those of nearly all his contemporaries, Republicans as well as Federalists—was his high degree of receptiveness to constitutional change, at both the state and national levels. He was an active critic of the Virginia Constitution of 1776 from almost its inception—in other words, for most of his active political life. The generally strict theory of interpretation that Jefferson applied to the federal Constitution had as its corollary an emphasis upon explicit change through amendment, rather than accommodation through interpretation, as the vehicle for adding to federal powers, as his proposals with respect to the Louisiana Purchase and internal improvements, for example, indicate. In addition, Jefferson was sympathetic to more far-reaching reforms at the national level. Although he did not press for amendments at the beginning of his presidency, as some Old Republicans wished he would, he did indicate support for the calling of a new federal convention, not only during the electoral crisis of 1800 but in later years to meet other exigencies. Constitutional conventions, in short, held no terrors for Jefferson. As Julian Boyd has observed, Jefferson "anticipated that forms of government would come and go, being changed as often and as drastically as changing circumstances required"; to him "the danger to be feared was not so much imperfection in the fabric as a failure in the people to discern the nature of the imperfection and to demand its remedy."[2]

This chapter traces the evolution of Jefferson's favorable attitude toward constitutional change, showing its relation to his understanding of republicanism. It is in his theory of constitutional change and the associated assumptions that Jefferson made his most distinctive contributions to American constitutionalism.

"Resort to First Principles": Popular Sovereignty and Whig Constitutionalism

The impulse toward constitutional reform and innovation was not original with Jefferson, nor was it—as one might assume—solely a product of Enlightenment thought. Rather, the basis for this impulse may be traced to the ideas of the Real Whig writers on government, including not only the mid-eighteenth-century constitutional reformers such as James Burgh and John Cartwright but also the seventeenth-century republican philosophers of government, particularly Algernon Sidney. Indeed, it was Sidney whom Jefferson echoed in his letter to Samuel Kercheval when he observed, "We might as well require a man to wear still the coat which fitted him when a boy as civilized society to remain forever under the regimen of their barbarous ancestors." Sidney, whose *Discourses concerning Government* Jefferson consistently recommended as an elementary text on government, had asked similarly, "If men are not oblig'd to live in Caves and hollow trees, to eat Acorns, and go naked, why should they be forever oblig'd to continue under the same form of Government that their ancestors happen'd to set up in the time of their ignorance?"[3]

Behind both Jefferson's and Sidney's observations was the basic idea expressed by the Real Whig writers on government: that government was an artificial contrivance, erected by the people of a society and deriving its powers from their consent. Some Whig writers went further to suggest that it was a defect in the English constitution that it could not be changed by the constituent power of the people. Indeed, they anticipated American constitutionalism by proposing, in James Burgh's words, "a regular and constitutional method of acting by and from *themselves*, without, or even in opposition to their *representatives*, if necessary."[4]

Also behind the idea of the necessity of constitutional change was the Whig premise that power corrupts, even in the best-constituted governments. To writers such as Sidney and Burgh, the notion that there existed a perfect constitution was absurd; "all human Constitutions are subject to corruption, and must perish, unless they are timely renewed, and reduced to their first principles," wrote Sidney. Although the abhorrence of "corruption," both as the notion apparently was held by Sidney and as it has been interpreted by modern scholars, was essentially a conservative impulse, motivated by a reverence for the existing constitution and a desire for its preservation, it also provided a rationale for change. As Sidney observed, "Corruptions slide in insensibly; and the best Orders are sometimes subverted by malice and violence; so that he who only regards what was done in such an age, often takes the corruptions of the State for the institution." He concluded, "We are not therefore so much to inquire after that which is most antient, as that which is best, and most conducing to the good ends to which it was directed." Because government was instituted to obtain justice and to preserve liberty, "we are not to seek what Government was the first, but what best provides for the obtaining of Justice, and preservation of Liberty. For whatever the Institution be, and how long soever it may have lasted, 'tis void, if it thwarts, or does not provide for the ends of its establishment."[5]

The "resort to first principles" to which Burgh, Sidney, and other writers referred was an idea derived originally from Machiavelli, but it was taken far beyond the ideological confines of classical republicanism by some of the Real Whigs of the late-eighteenth century and their American counterparts. Despite their frequent references to an ideal Anglo-Saxon constitution that they sought to preserve against the corruptions of the modern English system of government, many of these Whigs, like Sidney, took reason rather than antiquity as their standard. The "first principles" to which they sought to return were not merely those which identified an idealized Anglo-Saxon or "Gothick" constitution but included the fundamental principles of popular sovereignty and government by consent of the governed: principles that underlay all forms of free government. Referring by example to constitutional change in ancient Rome, Sidney observed that "there is no disorder or prejudice in changing the name or number of Magistrates, whilst the root and principle of their Power"—the sovereignty of the people—"continues." This is the context of his statement that all human constitutions are subject to corruption and must perish unless timely renewed and reduced to first principles.[6]

The process of reverting to first principles, moreover, could involve both frequent elections and popular tumults; as Sidney pointed out, either could remedy the insolence of office and the corruptions of power. Jefferson's complacent reaction to Shays's Rebellion, for example, can be best understood in this context. As he wrote to Edward Carrington and to James Madison in 1787, such "tumults" or "irregular interpositions of the people" would keep the governors of society "to the true principles of their institution." Hence "a little rebellion" now and then was a good thing, "as necessary in the political world as storms in the physical" and "a medicine necessary for the sound health of government."[7]

However, Jefferson saw as a strength of American republican government the fact that such extralegal resort to first principles was not really necessary. That was so because the American constitutions had institutionalized the process of reverting to first principles, in two ways. The first, for which nearly all the early state constitutions provided, involved devices such as frequent election and rotation in office that the Real Whig parliamentary reformers had advocated so earnestly in the 1770s and 1780s. The second, and far more innovative, way involved further devices such as the amending process and the constitutional convention, by which "the people might recurr to first principles in a Regular Way, without hazarding a Revolution in the Government."[8]

The idea of orderly constitutional change through the devices of the constitutional convention and the amendment process was invented in America during the decade or so after 1776. It did not develop easily, however; as Merrill Peterson has observed, "there was a good deal of fumbling and stumbling before the idea of institutionalized constitutional change was clearly grasped." Of the eleven original early state constitutions, nine contained no provision for amendment; seven contained no provision for change by way of a convention; and five contained neither provision. A typical provision, that of the Pennsylvania Constitution of 1776, created a Council of Censors to be elected and to meet every seven years to determine whether the constitution has been preserved, where and how it had failed or been violated, and whether a convention should be called for the purpose of making corrective amendments. As Peterson has observed, the purpose of such a provision was not to innovate, to adapt the constitution to changes in circumstance, but to preserve inviolate the original constitution; it was a provision still within the classical republican paradigm of decline.[9]

Jefferson's early ideas about constitutions, however, were not limited by the confines of classical republicanism; and in his reading of

Sidney, Burgh, and other radical Whig writers on government he was quick to grasp the implications of popular sovereignty with respect to constitutional change. Jefferson regarded the "more favorable ground" on which the American Revolution rested to be the opportunity that it gave Americans to devise new forms of government, based not on the "musty records" of the past but on the light of reason. Yet he was aware that the American experiments with constitution making were indeed experiments and that the constitutions created in 1776 and the years following were far from perfect. He was well ahead of his contemporaries in making provision for progressive constitutional change in his draft constitutions for Virginia, although he too did not immediately hit upon the device of a provision for regular amendments to the constitution. His final 1776 draft contained an unprecedented provision permitting "repeal or alteration" of the provisions of the constitution "by the personal consent of the people." Under Jefferson's plan, the legislature would propose changes that would be submitted to the people, meeting in their respective counties and all voting on the same day; approval by two-thirds of the counties would be necessary for the changes to be effective. His 1783 draft contained a provision permitting a convention, authorized by the government and elected by the people, to be called "for altering this Constitution or correcting breaches of it," although—despite the recent example of the Massachusetts Constitution of 1780—he did not provide for popular ratification of the convention's changes.[10]

Jefferson's *Notes on the State of Virginia* elaborated his criticisms of the Virginia Constitution of 1776, among them, that the constitution could be altered by the ordinary legislature. It was in the context of this criticism that he first called for a constitutional convention "to fix our form of government."[11] His 1783 plan was printed as an appendix to *Notes on Virginia* and thus may be regarded as representative of Jefferson's position with respect to constitutional change in the mid-1780s.

James Madison, in a rare instance of public disagreement with his friend, attacked Jefferson's position in 1788, in *Federalist* No. 49. Madison first recognized that Jefferson's provision for periodic change through conventions elected by the people followed from the logic of popular sovereignty. "As the people are the only legitimate fountain of power, and it is from them that the constitutional charter, under which the several branches of government hold their power, is derived; it seems strictly consonant to the republican theory, to recur to the same original authority, not only whenever it may be necessary to enlarge, diminish, or new-model the powers of government; but also whenever any one of the departments may commit encroachments on the chartered authorities of the others." But, Madison continued, there were "insuperable objections" against such a recurrence to the people "as a provision in all cases for keeping the several departments of power within their constitutional limits." [12]

Among the objections cited by Madison was that too frequent appeals to the people to "new-model" government would "in great measure deprive the government of that veneration, which time bestows on every thing, and without which perhaps the wisest and freest governments would not possess the requisite stability." The reason of man might be a sufficient reliance in "a nation of philosophers," but in an ordinary nation something more is required to maintain the necessary reverence for the laws. Another objection put forward by Madison was that a frequent reference of constitutional questions to the decision of the whole society raised "the danger of disturbing the public tranquility by interesting too strongly the public passions." [13]

If, as Merrill Peterson has suggested, Jefferson and Madison had aired their disagreement on this issue during earlier discussion of a new Virginia constitution, [14] it marked the beginning of a line of development in Jefferson's constitutional thought which would take it rather far afield from that of Madison and most of his other contemporaries. Jefferson's ready embrace of the idea of periodic change in the constitution, not only for the purposes of correcting abuses but also for making substantive changes in the fundamental plan of government, shows that by the eve of the federal Convention of 1787, he had taken to its logical conclusion the Real Whig notion of recurrence to first principles. The device of a constitutional convention became, to Jefferson, the American solution to the problem perceived by Burgh and Sidney—the need for some "regular and constitutional method" by which the sovereign voice of the people could be heard—transforming from the realm of pure theory to the real world of practical politics the notion that government was founded on the consent of the people.

Jefferson's praise for the new federal Constitution—praise that focused more on the process by which the form of government was changed than on the substance of the changes themselves—provides added evidence of his acceptance of the idea of constitutional change. He was applauding not only the fact that change had been accomplished peaceably, without bloodshed, but also that it had come through the will of the people having been heard.

During the following two decades, Jefferson would take the idea of constitutional change even further, embracing frequent change and rejecting Madison's concerns for stability and public tranquillity. Far from acknowledging these as legitimate concerns that cautioned against frequent constitutional change, Jefferson would come to advocate a quite radical position: one favoring frequent and regular change, with active citizen involvement in debates over fundamental political questions—one that no doubt made his prudent friend's head spin.

"The Earth Belongs to the Living": Natural Rights, Progress, and Reform

In a letter that Jefferson wrote to Madison from Paris in September 1789 (and redrafted early in 1790), he developed the theory that furnished the basis for his advocacy of frequent constitutional change, the theory of "the sovereignty of the living generation." This theory—otherwise identified by the expression Jefferson used in his letter, that "the earth belongs to the living"—was, Julian Boyd has argued, "the one great addition to Jefferson's thought that emerged from his years of residence at the center of European intellectual ferment" and "an idea that exerted a compelling influence over him for the remainder of his life." [15]

The basic question that Jefferson raised in the letter to Madison— "whether one generation of men has a right to bind another"—probably arose during the course of conversations that Jefferson had with Thomas Paine in Paris during the winter and spring of 1788. [16] Implicit in his discussion of this question is a basic element of Jefferson's political thought, a notion that Jefferson and Paine shared: the distinction between natural and civil rights.

Jefferson began his argument on the "self evident" principle, " '*that the earth belongs in usufruct to the living*,' that the dead have neither powers nor rights over it." Whatever powers or rights a person has while alive cease after his death, he observed, using property rights as an example:

The portion occupied by any individual ceases to be his when [he] himself ceases to be, and reverts to the society. If the society has formed no rules for the appropriation of it's lands in severality, it will be taken by the first occupants. These will generally be the wife and children of the decedent. If they have formed rules of appropriation, those rules may give it to the wife and children, or to some one of them, or to the legatee of the deceased. So they may give it to his creditor. But the child, the legatee, or creditor takes it, not by any natural right, but by a law of the society of which they are members and to which they are subject. Then no man can, by *natural right*, oblige the lands he occupied, or the persons who succeed him in that occupation, to the paiment of debts contracted by him. For if he could, he might, during his own life, eat up the usufruct of the lands for several generations to come, and then the lands would belong to the dead, and not to the living, which would be the reverse of our principle.

Then, observing that "what is true of every member of the society individually, is true of them all collectively, since the rights of the whole can be no more than the sums of the rights of individuals," Jefferson turned to the question of the rights and powers of a generation. "Let us suppose a whole generation of men to be born on the same day, to attain mature age on the same day, and to die on the same day, leaving a succeeding generation in the moment of attaining their mature age all together. . . . Each successive generation would, in this way, come on, and go off the stage at a fixed moment, as individuals do now. Then I say the earth belongs to each of these generations, during it's course, fully, and in their own right." From this he concluded that "no generation can contract debts greater than may be paid during the course of its own existence," not only because this would violate the basic principle, by making the earth belong to the dead and not the living generation, but also because generations, unlike individuals, have no superiors, no laws of the society, governing them. Rather, "by the law of nature, one generation is to another as one independent nation is to another."[17]

He then took his hypothetically clean distinction between the generations and reduced it to actual practice. "What is true of a generation all arriving to self-government on the same day, and dying all on the same day, is true of those in a constant course of decay and renewal," with the exception that with generations changing daily by births and deaths, the only constant term—the standard for measuring the life of a given generation—was the life expectancy of a majority of those at full age at the time a contract was entered into. Turning to tables of mortality, he calculated that nineteen years was the average lifetime of a generation and therefore "is the term beyond which neither the representatives of a nation, nor even the whole nation itself assembled, can validly extend a debt." [18]

Similarly, he argued—and here he reached the most important implication of the principle—"no society can make a perpetual constitution, or even a perpetual law." "The earth belongs always to the living generation. They may manage it then, and what proceeds from it, as they please, during their usufruct. They are masters too of their own persons, and consequently may govern them as they please. But persons and property make the sum of the objects of government. The constitution and the laws of their predecessors extinguished then in their natural course with those who gave them being. This could preserve that being till it ceased to be itself, and no longer." He concluded, "Every constitution, then, and every law, naturally expires at the end of 19 years. If it be enforced longer, it is an act of force, and not of right." [19]

Jefferson regarded the principle that the earth belongs to the living as one "of very extensive application and consequences" in France and in the United States; but in submitting it to Madison's consideration in early 1790, he ostensibly directed it to the matter of public debts, which was occupying Madison's attention as a member of Congress. He urged Madison to establish the principle in the first law for appropriating the public revenue, denying the validity of long-term debts. He also suggested that the duration for rights in the law to be passed for protecting copyrights and inventions be nineteen, rather than fourteen, years. [20]

Madison replied politely to Jefferson, noting that the idea was "a great one" that suggested many "interesting reflections to legislators," particularly with respect to public debts; but he was firm in raising some practical objections to the application of the doctrine to a constitution. Here he reiterated objections he had raised to Jefferson's provision for change in his 1783 draft constitution for Virginia: that a "Government so often revised" might become "too mutable" to be venerated or might "engender pernicious factions." With respect to laws that might bind succeeding generations, Madison asked whether "the *improvements* made by the dead form a debt against the living who take the benefit of them." Debts may be incurred for purposes that benefit the unborn as well as the living; indeed, they may be incurred principally for the benefit of posterity, and such may be the case of the debt of the United States, Madison observed. If benefits can be passed from one generation to the next, equity demands the descent of obligations from one to another; and "all that is indispensible in adjusting the account between the dead and the living is to see that the debits against the latter do not exceed the advances made by the former." Finally—in perhaps the most devastating part of his reply to Jefferson's proposal—Madison argued that there was no way the theory could be applied practically. Noting that "all the rights depending on positive laws, that is, most of the rights of property" would be subject to redefinition at the end of the term, he foresaw "the most violent struggles . . . between those interested in reviving and those interested in new-modelling the former state of property." Anarchy, the depreciation of property values, and discouragement of industry would be among the other ill effects.[21]

The only escape from the difficulties of Jefferson's theory, both theoretical and practical, that Madison could see was "the received doctrine that a tacit assent may be given to established Constitutions and laws, and that this assent may be inferred, where no positive dissent appears." Jefferson had anticipated the implied consent, or tacit assent, argument in his letter to Madison, arguing that the power of repeal was not an equivalent because under no form of government could the will of the majority always be obtained fairly and without impediment and that, therefore, "a law of limited duration is much more manageable than one which needs a repeal." Madison did not directly respond to this argument but instead raised the question, "whether it be possible to exclude wholly the idea of tacit assent, without subverting the foundation of civil Society?" He noted that the voice of the majority binds the minority, not under a law of nature—which would rather require unanimity—but rather under this principle of tacit assent. Although he said he did not mean to impeach "either the utility of the principle in some particular cases, or the general importance of it in the eye of the philosophical Legislator," he concluded that

Jefferson's theory was not likely to sway many members of Congress: the "spirit of philosophical legislation" was not in fashion, and "our hemisphere must be still more enlightened before many of the sublime truths which are seen thro' the medium of Philosophy, become visible to the naked eye of the ordinary Politician." [22]

Jefferson did not persist in pushing his radical doctrine, largely because he soon found that more urgent problems—namely, the challenges posed first by Hamilton's financial program and later by other Federalist measures throughout the 1790s—dictated his stance, in contending for the preservation of the federal Constitution against these perceived threats. He nevertheless continued to voice his support for the idea of constitutional change by applauding the fact that the American constitutions were capable of adapting to changed circumstances when such adaptation was necessary. [23] More importantly, as the decade passed, he affirmed his belief in the idea of progress with increasing intensity.

In his 1799 letter to Elbridge Gerry where Jefferson enumerated his political and constitutional principles, differentiating them from those of the Federalists, he declared his belief in progress. As he put it, "I am for encouraging the progress of science in all it's branches; and not for raising a hue and cry against the sacred name of philosophy; for awing the human mind by stories of raw-head & bloody bones to a distrust of its own vision, & to repose implicitly on that of others; to go backwards instead of forwards to look for improvement; to believe that government, religion, morality, & every other science were in the highest perfection in ages of the darkest ignorance, and that nothing can ever be devised more perfect than what was established by our forefathers." Similarly, later in the same year, Jefferson stated that like Condorcet he believed that the mind of man was "perfectible to a degree of which we cannot as yet form any conception." He therefore branded as "cowardly" the idea that the human mind was incapable of further advances, calling it "precisely the doctrine which the present despots of the earth are inculcating, & their friends here re-echoing; & applying especially to religion & politics; 'that it is not probable that any thing better will be discovered than what was known to our fathers.'" [24]

Adherence to the idea of progress did not come suddenly to Jefferson in the 1790s: he had long believed in progress, as is evidenced, for example, by his efforts during the Revolution to reform Virginia

law, and particularly his efforts to reform the criminal code by bringing punishments more in line with the recommendations of Beccaria
and other Enlightenment writers. Jefferson particularly emphasized
his belief in progress, however, in the 1790s when he distinguished his
principles from those of the Federalists. In later years he continued to
espouse his convictions that immense advances had yet to be made in
science and the arts and that the happiness of the human race would
advance "to an indefinite, although not to an infinite, degree."[25]

It was not until long after his retirement from the presidency, in a
letter written in 1823, that Jefferson returned to the idea that the earth
belongs to the living, reiterating the argument that he had presented
to Madison—but with two important differences. He no longer referred to nineteen years, or any other time period, as the lifetime of
a generation; and he apparently accepted Madison's tacit assent argument. Noting that although society had found it "more convenient to
suffer the laws of our predecessors to stand on our implied assent,"
he noted that nevertheless "this does not lessen the right" of new
generations to repeal old laws if they wish. Without abandoning the
basic principle that the earth belongs to the living, Jefferson softened
the doctrine somewhat, transforming it from a rationale for periodic,
radical change into a rationale for change whenever circumstances or
the will of the majority calls for it. Similarly, in a letter written to John
Cartwright in 1824, he again affirmed the basic idea that the earth belongs to the living, arguing that "a generation may bind itself as long
as its majority continues in life; when that has disappeared, another
majority is in place, holds all the rights and powers their predecessors
once held, and may change their laws and institutions to suit themselves." This is the context in which he concluded, "Nothing then is
unchangeable but the inherent and unalienable rights of man."[26]

During the three and a half decades between the time of his original letter to Madison and these slightly modified reaffirmations of the
idea, much had happened to shape Jefferson's constitutional thought.
The most significant development was the evolution of Jefferson's
republicanism, spurred on and shaped by the Federalist-Republican
party struggles of the 1790s. One result was his particular emphasis
on progress and with it the opportunity of each generation to improve
upon the institutions established by past generations. These notions
supplemented the natural rights theory that had formed the original basis for the idea of the "sovereignty of the living generation."

Another, and possibly more important, notion that also entered into Jefferson's rationale for change was the idea that republican government must be responsive to the will of the majority.

"The Full Experiment": Republicanism, Federalism, and Constitutional Change

During the 1790s Jefferson did not push for change in the federal Constitution largely because the nature of the Republican opposition to the Federalist administrations of government during the presidencies of Washington and Adams caused him to stand for the Constitution's preservation. As he explained in 1791 to a fellow Virginian, who had asked what should be done about a new frame of government, "I wish to preserve the line drawn by the federal constitution between the general & particular governments as it stands at present, and to take every prudent means of preventing either from stepping over it. . . . It is important to strengthen the state governments; and as this cannot be done by any change in the federal constitution, (for the preservation of that is all we need contend for,) it must be done by the states themselves, erecting such barriers at the constitutional line as cannot be surmounted either by themselves or by the general government." He then recommended specific changes in the government of Virginia that would, among other things, strengthen the executive and dignify the judiciary.[27]

With respect to the United States Constitution, Jefferson's position throughout the 1790s was consistent with the advice he gave in this letter: he sought not to change the Constitution, either through the amendment process or through implicit change by way of construction or interpretation. Indeed, he strongly opposed the latter means of change, advancing rather the theory of strict construction of federal powers. Not until the electoral crisis of February 1801, when the tie in electoral votes between Jefferson and Aaron Burr placed the contest for the presidency in the House of Representatives, did Jefferson suggest in his writings that a second constitutional convention might be necessary to reform the Constitution.

The threat that the Federalists might succeed in preventing the constitutional election of the president raised in Jefferson's mind the specters of the dissolution of the government and rebellion—evils that could be obviated by the immediate calling of a convention, which Jefferson and his friends proposed to do if it proved necessary. The crisis ended with Jefferson's election on the thirty-sixth ballot; nevertheless, looking back on these events just shortly after his inaugural, he observed that "a convention, invited by the Republican members of Congress . . . would have been on the ground in eight weeks, would have reformed the Constitution where it was defective, and wound it up again." He also said that "this peaceable and legitimate resource, to which we are in the habit of implicit obedience, superseding all appeal to force, and being always within our reach, shows a precious principle of self-preservation in our composition." [28] As in his reaction to the adoption of the federal Constitution, he was again applauding constitutional change by way of a convention and popular ratification as a peaceable alternative to the resort to force.

Eventually the addition of the Twelfth Amendment to the Constitution resolved the "defect" in the mode of choosing a president that had given rise to the crisis of 1801. This was the last amendment to the United States Constitution in Jefferson's lifetime; indeed, over sixty years would pass before the addition of the Thirteenth Amendment. This was not as Jefferson would have liked it; several times during and after his presidency he urged amendments to the Constitution.

Only in one respect was Jefferson, while president, apparently loath to propose amendments to the Constitution: he resisted demands put forward by Old Republicans that he do so at the beginning of his administration. John Randolph expressed the feelings of these ardent Virginia Republicans when he observed, "In this quarter we think that the great work is only begun: and that without *substantial reform*, we shall have little reason to congratulate ourselves on the mere change of *men*." Edmund Pendleton, in a pamphlet entitled *The Danger Not Over*, published in October 1801, proposed a series of constitutional amendments designed to institutionalize the "revolution of 1800." Among other things, these amendments would provide that the president's duration in office be restricted to a single four-year term, that senators serve a shorter term and be removable by their constituents, that judges be appointed by Congress and removable by vote of both houses, that members of Congress and judges be prohibited from receiving appointments while in office, and that limitations be placed on the power to borrow money. Although Jefferson was probably sympathetic to these pleas, his policy of moderation and conciliation as well as practical political considerations prevented him from supporting the Old Republicans.[29]

While he was president, Jefferson did propose amendments to the Constitution to sanction the Louisiana Purchase and to permit Congress to appropriate money for internal improvements projects. His qualms about the constitutionality of the Louisiana treaty prompted him to draft an ad hoc amendment to permit such a purchase retroactively; but as with the Old Republican demands for comprehensive constitutional change, practical political considerations mitigated against the effort. In his letter to Wilson Cary Nicholas in September 1803 in which Jefferson warned that loose construction would make the Constitution "a blank paper," Jefferson nevertheless presented his rationale for change. "Nothing is more likely," he noted, than that the original enumeration of federal powers was "defective," for this was "the ordinary case of all human works." He then suggested, "Let us go on then perfecting it, by adding, by way of amendment to the Constitution, those powers which time and trial show are still wanting."[30]

It was after his retirement from the presidency that Jefferson was most explicit in calling for constitutional change, both federal and state. Although he wrote to one correspondent in 1813 that the Republican party was "steady for the support of the present constitution"— and that having "obtained at its commencement all the amendments to it they desired," they were "perfectly reconciled to it"—he nevertheless noted that some Republicans, perhaps himself included, sought "to popularize it further, by shortening the Senatorial term, and devising a process for the responsibility of judges, more practicable than that of impeachment."[31] What was most significant in prompting Jefferson to desire amendments to both the Virginia and United States constitutions during his later years was his full realization of the implications of republicanism.

Jefferson's fullest articulation of his theory of republican government appeared in a series of letters written in 1816. He defined republicanism, variously, as "the equal right of every citizen in his person and property, and in their management"; as "action by the citizens in person, in affairs within their reach and competence, and in all others by representatives, chosen immediately, and removable by themselves"; or as "a government by its citizens in mass, acting directly and personally, according to rules established by the majority." Under these definitions, and particularly the last, the American constitutions proved wanting. "The full experiment of a government democratical, but representative, was and is still reserved for us," he observed; it had not been "pushed into all the ramifications of the system, so far as to leave no authority existing not responsible to the people." His "earnest wish," he said, was "to see the republican element of popular control pushed to the maximum of its practicable exercise."[32]

In his 1816 letter to Samuel Kercheval, where he identified the "mother principle" of republicanism—that "governments are republican only in proportion as they embody the will of their people, and execute it"—Jefferson also confessed his belief that the first American constitutions "had no leading principles in them." He was extremely critical of the Virginia Constitution of 1776, and he explained its "defects" by observing that Americans in 1776 were novices in the science of government. Similarly, in his 1816 letter to John Taylor, he analyzed both the federal and Virginia constitutions, finding that they exhibited only various "shades" of republicanism, depending on how far each of their departments was from the direct and constant control by the citizens. "If, then, the control of the people over the organs of their government be the measure of its republicanism . . . it must be agreed that our governments have much less of republicanism than ought to have been expected," he concluded.[33]

To Kercheval, Jefferson proposed a series of amendments to the Virginia Constitution. These included near-universal male suffrage; equal representation in the legislature; popular election of the governor, judges, and sheriffs; and division of the counties into wards. He also urged periodical amendments of the constitution: "Let us provide in our constitution for its revision at stated periods," suggesting nineteen years as the period shown by mortality tables as the average life of a generation. These "loose heads of amendment," he said, he was throwing out for consideration; their object was "to secure self-government by the republicanism of our constitution, as well as by the spirit of the people; and to nourish and perpetuate that spirit." With much understatement Jefferson added, "I am not among those who fear the people." Here he went on to observe that he believed that "laws and institutions must go hand in hand with the progress of the human mind." He also noted that the present generation had the right "to choose for itself the form of government it believes most promotive of its own happiness; consequently, to accommodate to the circumstances in which it finds itself, that received from its predecessors."[34]

In this 1816 letter to Kercheval, Jefferson thus presented a rationale for constitutional change which combined all the principles upon which his advocacy of change had rested: the idea that the earth belongs to the living, the idea of progress, and republicanism. In a subsequent letter to Kercheval he added an additional justification. Although expressing his determination not to "intermeddle" in the question of a constitutional convention, which he said had become "a party one"—and although he said he was willing to live under the present constitution if a majority of his fellow Virginians preferred it—he declared his conviction that "for the sake of future generations (when principles shall have become too relaxed to permit amendment, as experience proves to be the constant course of things) I wish to have availed them of the virtues of the present time to put into a chaste & secure form, the government to be handed down to them."[35] This was reminiscent of his observation in *Notes on Virginia* that the time to secure the liberties of the people was while the Revolutionary spirit was still high, an awareness of practical considerations which was rather inconsistent with his notions of frequent, continuing amendment. On balance, however, Jefferson in 1816 was continuing to take a position which was quite distinct from that taken by Madison, who had warned that frequent change would lessen the people's veneration of constitutions and lead to social turbulence. Jefferson, as he said, did not fear the people; nor did he fear the prospects of public controversy over constitutional questions, although he personally preferred to stay out of the fray.[36]

With respect to the federal Constitution, Jefferson voiced support for several amendments whose general thrust was to preserve the Constitution in the federal, republican form that Jefferson believed constituted its "true theory." One of his most explicit statements favoring amendments to the Constitution appeared in a letter he wrote late in life, when he declared that "the real friends of the constitution in its federal form, if they wish it to be immortal, should be attentive, by amendments, to make it keep pace with the advance of the age in science and experience." He proposed three "great amendments":

"the limitation of the term of presidential service"; "the placing the choice of president effectually in the hands of the people"; and "the giving to Congress the power of internal improvement, on condition that each State's federal proportion of the monies so expended, shall be employed within the State."[37]

One other amendment that he supported, omitted from this list but nevertheless one that he particularly emphasized during his retirement years, was some provision to make the federal judiciary more accountable to popular will. Exactly what provision Jefferson desired is unclear. In his autobiography he suggested submitting the judges to "some practical & impartial controul," compounded of "a mixture of state and federal authorities." At about the same time he indicated his support of proposals to appoint judges for fixed terms, with reappointability at the approbation of Congress.[38] Earlier he had indicated his support of proposals to make the judges removable by the president in conjunction with both houses of Congress. Clearly he considered impeachment an ineffective device.

Perhaps more important than Jefferson's advocacy or support for particular constitutional amendments was his advocacy of the general principle that constitutional problems ought to be resolved not through ingenious construction—whether as an exercise of executive prerogative, as in the Louisiana Purchase, or as an exercise of judicial interpretation, as in Chief Justice Marshall's opinion in *McCulloch v. Maryland*—but rather through appeals to the people. He envisioned either an informal process—the will of the people "reintegrated" into the Constitution through the electoral process—or the formal process of constitutional conventions and amendments.

During the Virginia campaign against the claim that the United States Supreme Court was the ultimate arbiter of constitutional questions, Jefferson emphasized the position that he had earlier claimed in the Kentucky Resolutions, that the ultimate arbiter was the people themselves. As he stated to Justice Johnson in 1823, "The ultimate arbiter is the people of the Union, assembled by their deputies in convention, at the call of Congress, or of ⅔ of the states." Or, as he wrote to another correspondent a few years earlier, when the *Cohens* case was before the Supreme Court, "I know no safe depository of the ultimate powers of the society but the people themselves; and if we think them not enlightened enough to exercise their control with a wholesome discretion, the remedy is not to take it from them, but to inform their discretion by education. This is the true corrective of abuses of constitutional power."[39]

"The True Corrective of Abuses of Constitutional Power": Citizen Participation and Education

The notion that the control by the people over their government, according to their own "wholesome discretion," informed by education, constituted the "true corrective" of abuses of power is distinctively Jeffersonian. Indeed, the emphasis that Jefferson placed on popular participation and control—making the people themselves a vital element in constitutionalism—was the preeminent hallmark of Jefferson's constitutional thought.[40] None of his contemporaries, with perhaps the exception of John Taylor of Caroline, quite so emphasized this element. It in fact underlay many of the other aspects of his constitutional thought. Both the pure theory of separation of powers as well as the theory of federalism that Jefferson espoused were ultimately derived from his thoroughgoing republicanism. With each branch of the federal government and each state in the Union determining constitutional questions, potentially in conflict with one another, some common ground was necessary; and that common ground—in effect, the glue that held Jefferson's constitutional system in place—was the active participation of the people in constitutional questions.

It has been shown that Jefferson regarded America's great mission to be proving to the world the efficacy of republican government, the "interesting experiment of self-government" that he referred to in his 1802 letter to Priestley. In that letter he indicated what he perceived as a prerequisite, or precondition, of his system of republican constitutionalism: that the people be wise, by being "under the unrestrained and unperverted operation of their own understandings." The emphasis on education is a recurrent theme in Jefferson's political writings. While in France he wrote to George Wythe back in Virginia, admonishing him to "preach, my dear Sir, a crusade against ignorance; establish and improve the law for educating the common people."[41] Many years later he observed, "If a nation expects to be ignorant and free, in a state of civilization, it expects what never was and never will be." And in one of his more poetical expressions of his confidence in the education of the people as a means of preserving liberty, he wrote, "Enlighten the people generally, and tyranny and oppressions of body and mind will vanish like evil spirits at the dawn of day."[42]

An important element of Jefferson's proposals for republican reform of Virginia's laws during the Revolution was the establishment of a system of public education. The purpose for his "Bill for the More General Diffusion of Knowledge," as he explained it in *Notes on Virginia*, was that of "rendering the people the safe, as they are the ultimate guardians of their own liberty." "Every government degenerates when trusted to the rulers of the people alone. The people themselves therefore are its only safe depositories. And to render even them safe their minds must be improved to a certain degree." Jefferson's bill sought to do this through a two-tier system of publicly supported education. All citizens would receive a basic schooling in reading and writing at the "hundred schools"; there they would also learn "the most useful facts" from ancient and modern history. The emphasis on historical education was quite deliberate, Jefferson explained: "History by apprising them of the past will enable them to judge of the future; it will avail them of the experience of other times and other nations; it will qualify them as judges of the actions and designs of men; it will enable them to know ambition under every disguise it may assume; and knowing it, to defeat its views." Beyond this basic schooling, the best students would receive advanced training suitable to prepare the "natural aristocracy" for public service: by this means, "those persons, whom nature hath endowed with genius and virtue, should be rendered by liberal education worthy to receive, and able to guard the sacred deposit of the rights and liberties of their fellow-citizens, and that they should be called to that charge without regard to wealth, birth, or other accidental condition or circumstance."[43]

Ensuring that "genius and virtue," not accidental circumstances such as wealth and birth, should be the foundations of the republic's leaders—in other words, ensuring that the natural, not the "pseudo," aristocracy should lead the republic—was one important reason for public support of education. Another, as Jefferson explained later in connection with his proposal for a national university, was to ensure that all sciences necessary to the improvement and preservation of the nation be nourished.[44] Most fundamentally, however, Jefferson regarded education as too important to be left to chance; the very survival of republican government depended on it.

In later years Jefferson coupled education with one other proposal, which he considered equally necessary to the preservation of republicanism: his proposed system of local government by wards. These "little republics," he said, would be the main strength of the greater ones.[45] Jefferson's proposal was to divide the counties into wards of such size that every citizen can attend meetings, when called on, and act in person. The government of each ward would take care of "all things relating to themselves exclusively": a justice, a constable, a military company, a school, the care of the poor, the maintenance of local public roads, the choice of jurors, and so on. Such a system, he declared, not only would relieve the county administration of most of its business but would do it better. Moreover, the ward system, "by making every citizen an acting member of the government, and in the offices nearest and most interesting to him, will attach him by his strongest feelings to the independence of his country, and its republican constitution." These wards, like the townships of New England— or the hundreds of Anglo-Saxon England, according to the Whig view—have proved themselves "the wisest invention ever devised by the wit of man for the perfect exercise of self-government, and for its preservation." He envisioned the marshaling of government into four levels: first, "the general federal republic, for all concerns foreign and federal"; second, the state, for what relates to its own citizens exclusively; third, "the county republics," for the duties and concerns of the county; and finally, "the ward republics, for the small, and yet numerous and interesting concerns of the neighborhood." By this system of division and subdivision, Jefferson maintained, "all matters, great and small, can be managed to perfection."[46]

He similarly explained the rationale for the ward system in a letter to Joseph Cabell in 1816:

> The way to have good and safe government, is not to trust it all to one, but to divide it among the many, distributing to every one exactly the functions he is competent to. Let the national government be entrusted with the defence of the nation, and its foreign and federal relations; the State governments with the civil rights, laws, police and administration of what concerns the State generally; the counties with the local concerns of the counties; and each ward direct the interests within itself. It is by dividing and subdividing these republics from the great national one down

through all its subordinations, until it ends in the administration of every man's farm and affairs by himself; by placing under every one what his own eye may superintend, that all will be done for the best.

"What has destroyed liberty and the rights of man in every government which has ever existed under the sun?" Jefferson asked. "The generalizing and concentrating all cares and powers into one body." The "secret" of maintaining freedom, he suggested, was to make the individual alone "the depository of the powers respecting himself, so far as he is competent to them, and delegating only what is beyond his competence by a synthetical process, to higher and higher orders of functionaries, so as to trust fewer and fewer powers in proportion as the trustees become more and more oligarchical."[47]

The system of republics thus described would accomplish this and thereby itself become a vital element of constitutionalism. "The elementary republics of the wards, the county republics, the States republics, and the republic of the Union, would form a gradation of authorities, standing each on the basis of law, holding every one its delegated share of powers, and constituting truly a system of fundamental balances and checks for the government," he explained. "Where every man is a sharer in the direction of his ward-republic, or of some of the higher ones, and feels that he is a participator in the government of affairs, not merely at an election one day in the year, but every day; when there shall not be a man in the State who will not be a member of some one of its councils, great or small, he will let the heart be torn out of his body sooner than his power be wrestled from him by a Caesar or a Bonaparte," he also observed. Emphasizing the importance with which he viewed the subject, he noted that "as Cato then concluded every speech with the words 'Carthago delenda est,' so do I every opinion, with the injunction, 'divide the counties into wards.' "[48]

One further advantage would be gained by the ward system, of immediate importance to the problem of resolving constitutional questions. "A general call of ward meetings by their wardens on the same day through the State, would at any time produce the genuine sense of the people on any required point, and would enable the State to act in mass," as New Englanders do in their town meetings, he noted.[49]

Jefferson thus envisioned, as a vital element of constitutionalism—

indeed, as the most effective check on the abuse of governmental power—the active involvement of citizens in the government itself. In the wards citizens would gain practical education in government that, together with the education they received through formal schooling, would constitute the "two hooks" upon which "the continuance of republican government hung."[50] An educated, actively involved citizenry would be both self-reliant and vigilant: they would manage directly those affairs to which individuals were alone competent; at the same time, they would keep a close watch over their elected officials, to whom they had entrusted all other affairs, and make certain that they did not turn into wolves.

A full understanding of Jefferson's ideas regarding constitutional change—and indeed, of his constitutional thought generally—must take into account his dual emphasis on education and participation. The essentially negative view of politics that Jefferson held thus ultimately influenced his constitutional thought in a profound way.[51] He regarded as truly modest the achievements of his generation, believing that subsequent generations, learning from additional experience, would improve on the founders' handiwork, with the problem of maintaining a free government becoming far simpler as subsequent generations hit upon better and better solutions. Hence he recommended that each generation create anew its constitutions—a recommendation that reveals both his assumptions that constitution making was a relatively simple matter and that the people, as a whole, were fully competent to the task. Although a preeminent member of what Dumas Malone has called the "great generation," Jefferson disclaimed its greatness.[52]

Jefferson's view of constitutionalism, in the final analysis, was one which placed less emphasis on mechanics—the written enumeration of powers, division of powers, checks and balances, and so on—than it did on the character of the people themselves. "Where is our republicanism to be found? Not in the constitution, but merely in the spirit of the people."[53] Or, as Jefferson put it more rhapsodically by quoting a poem,

> "What constitutes a State?
> Not high-raised battlements, or labor'd mound,
>   Thick wall, or moated gate;
> Not cities proud, with spires and turrets crown'd;

No: men, high minded men;
Men, who their duties know;
But know their rights; and knowing, dare maintain.
These constitute a State." [54]

Conclusion

Government "Founded in Jealousy, and Not in Confidence"

This study of Jefferson's constitutional thought has examined on its own terms his stance as a Real or True Whig, which was the label that he applied to his constitutionalism. When Jefferson described himself as a Whig, he used the term in a fairly precise sense, whose full meaning was known to eighteenth-century Americans but has become obscured in our day. That meaning, in the context of constitutionalism, is epitomized by the passage in the eighth of Jefferson's Kentucky Resolutions of 1798, where he wrote that "free government is founded in jealousy, and not in confidence," and that accordingly, the purpose of constitutions is to limit government, "to bind down those whom we are obliged to trust with power."

The principle of jealousy was rooted in a basic premise of the Whig canon: the idea that political power is of necessity antithetical to individual liberty. This premise gave rise to the distrust of government, and particularly the distrust of concentration in the powers of government, which was the hallmark of eighteenth-century radical Whig ideology. Whig constitutionalism, generally, sought to render political power safe through various checks and limitations institutionalized in the constitution itself. Jefferson's constitutionalism, particularly, sought to do this through use of a written constitution and through the division, or separation, of governmental powers. He perceived the basic principle of the federal Constitution to be the division of all governmental powers into two distinct spheres—the national government for "foreign" matters and the states for all "domestic" concerns—each of which was in turn subdivided into three separate and autonomous functional branches.

These were the specific constitutional means through which Jefferson sought to render safe governmental power—to "bind" down from "mischief" those in power by "the chains of the constitution." This basic principle helps to explain the various aspects of Jefferson's constitutionalism, ranging from his views of the British constitution, which led him to support the American Revolution; to his views of the federal Constitution of 1787, which led him to demand a federal bill of rights, to espouse a federalism which saw the states as "the true barriers of our liberty," and to criticize the claim that the United States Supreme Court should be the ultimate arbiter of constitutional questions.

Jefferson's constitutionalism, however, was based on more than theories of limited federal government and the separation of powers. His peculiar Whig stance also involved more fundamental premises about the nature of law and of government generally. From his Whig constitutionalism Jefferson also derived the premise that "the natural progress of things is for liberty to yeild, and government to gain ground" and the related idea that the institutional safeguards provided by a constitution were necessary but not sufficient guarantees of individual freedom. "The ground of liberty is to be gained by inches," he wrote; "we must be contented to secure what we can get from time to time, and eternally press forward for what is yet to get." [1] Only through a literal application of the concept of popular sovereignty in the actual practices of government—only through the active, continual involvement of the people in their government—could liberty effectively be secured from the encroachments of those in power. Hence followed other distinctive aspects of Jefferson's constitutional thought: for example, his emphasis upon the electoral process as "a mild and safe corrective of abuses"; his tripartite doctrine of separation of powers, which envisioned each of the three autonomous branches of government as equally competent to judge its own powers because it was equally accountable to the people; his peculiar understanding of the purpose of a free press, which had little tolerance for "licentiousness"; and—perhaps the most distinctive aspect of his thought—his advocacy of frequent legal and constitutional change, through the explicitly democratic processes of formal amendment and popular ratification.

All of these ideas presupposed a society in which all of the people were as concerned about public affairs as they were about their private lives—not because they subsumed the latter to the former, but because, as Jefferson put it in his First Inaugural Address, "every man . . . would meet invasions of the public order as his own personal concern." Unlike other Anglo-American Whigs of his day, who could be advocates of either a republican form of government or a limited, or constitutional, monarchy, Jefferson was a thoroughgoing republican. Indeed, he went much further than his contemporaries (even such like-minded contemporaries as his friend Madison) in espousing a republicanism which emphasized as its touchstone popular participation in all aspects of government—including the most fundamental ones, the interpretation and amendment of constitutions. Jefferson's Whig constitutionalism, in short, was also peculiarly republican. It rested on radically new views of human nature and society and of the relationship between society and government—views that encompassed the full meaning of what Jefferson referred to as "self-government."

The truly revolutionary character of Jefferson's notion of self-government may be seen most clearly by contrasting it with the views of the great English conservative Edmund Burke. In his criticism of the French Revolution, Burke derided the undertaking of forming a new government by identifying the problem as a kind of paradox. "To make a government requires no great prudence. Settle the seat of power; teach obedience; and the work is done. To give freedom is still more easy. It is not necessary to guide; it only requires to let go the rein. But to form a *free government*; that is, to temper together these opposite elements of liberty and restraint in one consistent work, requires much thought, deep reflection; a sagacious, powerful, and combining mind." Burke's answer to the problem lay in the notion of the "ancient constitution": because no one man, or even one generation of men, could be relied upon to be sufficiently "sagacious" to achieve the proper balance of liberty and restraint required by good government, the solution was to preserve "as an inheritance from our forefathers" the British constitution—inherited crown and peerage, plus a House of Commons and people possessing inherited liberties, franchises, and privileges—which was, argued Burke, the "only security for law and liberty."[2]

As Burke saw it, government existed as "a contrivance of human wisdom to provide for human *wants*," and among these is the want, reckoned "out of civil society," of a "sufficient restraint upon the passions" of individuals. "Society requires not only that the passions of individuals should be subjected, but that . . . the inclinations of men should frequently be thwarted, their will controlled, and their passions brought into subjection." Since this can be done only by "a power out of themselves," government is required to provide the necessary restraints.[3] Underlying this conception of government was a Hobbesian view of man, driven by self-interested passions that necessarily pit individuals one against another and that require the powerful coercive force of a Leviathan to set things right. Hence, to Burke, liberty and restraint were opposites, and the formulation of a "free government" was a difficult task indeed.

Jefferson's philosophy of government rested upon an entirely different premise which saw individual freedom not as a threat to the social order but rather as the very cement that binds society together. His view in a sense resolved Burke's paradox by reconciling liberty and restraint through a redefinition of government itself. As he so cogently expressed it in the second paragraph of the Declaration of Independence, everyone is created with "certain inalienable rights, among which are life, liberty, and the pursuit of happiness." In order "to secure these rights," government is instituted among men, deriving its "just powers from the consent of the governed." Government thus defined is not merely consonant with liberty: its very legitimacy is measured by the extent to which it fosters man's rights to life, liberty, and the pursuit of happiness. The Revolution was justified accordingly, for "whenever any form of government becomes destructive" of the ends for which it is instituted, "it is the right of the people to alter or abolish it" and to institute new government better suited to the role of protecting individual rights.

The problem in government, as Jefferson saw it, was not to make men moral; that would be absurd, Jefferson believed, since the "moral faculty," the capacity for doing good to others, was inherent in man's nature. The problem in government, rather, was to maintain a social environment in which it was possible for individuals to be moral, to live harmoniously and benevolently together in society. Government did this not by directing persons' lives through ordering society from above but instead by providing the underlying structure that made it possible for society to order itself. Thus Jefferson espoused a limited government: a "wise and frugal government, which shall restrain men from injuring one another, which shall leave them otherwise free to regulate their own pursuits of industry and improvement, and shall not take from the mouth of labor the bread it has earned." Such a government, by minimizing the temptations to use coercive power for self-aggrandizement, would appeal to the good side of human nature. A well-governed society was one that maintained "the just degree of union among individuals, which to each reserves freedom and independency, as far as is consistent with peace and good order." Such a society, Jefferson believed, furnishes proof of "the degree of freedom and self-government in which a society may venture to leave it's individual members."

To say that Jefferson's philosophy of government transcended traditional concepts, however, is of course not to say that it lacked ambiguities of its own. Indeed, some may question whether Jefferson even had a political philosophy, that is, a comprehensive and consistent set of ideas about government. Jefferson's public life was filled with many apparent conflicts and contradictions that seem to make questionable the existence of a Jeffersonian philosophy, at least as a constant over time. In many areas of his thought other than politics, Jefferson was quite unsystematic. This is especially true with respect to ethics, for Jefferson's musings about a "moral sense" inherent in man hardly rise to the level of a true ethical philosophy.[4] Yet with respect to his thinking about government—despite the indication of change, or evolution, in Jefferson's thought, as well as the accommodation of his ideas to changed circumstances—the evidence does show that Jefferson held certain basic tenets to which he consistently adhered for the greater part of half a century, from the time of the American Revolution until his death in 1826. The aggregate of those tenets can be described as a philosophy—as something more than the general humanitarian impulse that permeated Jefferson's life.

One reason why it is so difficult to identify a Jeffersonian philosophy of government is that Jefferson himself deliberately sought to avoid formulating one. As Merrill Peterson has noted, "He never attempted to throw his own thought into a system, in part because he distrusted all theoretical systems." His distrust was especially deep with respect to politics, which he regarded as far less personally satisfying than such pursuits as farming, agriculture, and music. Throughout his life Jefferson deliberately downplayed his public service. For example, in 1800 he drafted a list of his services that emphasized his role in introducing olive trees and upland rice into South Carolina. "The greatest service which can be rendered any country is," he wrote, "to add a useful plant to its culture."[5] At various stages of his life, Jefferson expressed his desire to retire permanently from the turbulent world of politics to the far more tranquil and pleasurable world of his "farm, family, and books"; and he thus "retired" at least four times in his life.[6] Avowals of his aversion to political controversy permeate his private correspondence, highlighting the irony that this man, who was so very private, was also so intimately and extensively involved with the public life of the American republic during its first half century.

Another, related reason why the existence of a systematic Jeffersonian philosophy of government may be questioned is that Jefferson wrote no treatise or any other single work containing an exposition of his philosophy. In order to find Jefferson's philosophy of government, one must survey all his writings—the vast body of Jefferson's correspondence and other private papers as well as his public writings—in order to cull from them those passages which best reveal his systematic thought. This is true even though Jefferson and his contemporaries were aware that the American Revolution opened "a whole new chapter in the history of man," an experiment "to shew whether men can be trusted with self-government," and that as political leaders and spokesmen for the American republic, they were not acting for themselves alone "but for the whole human race."[7]

Why then did not Jefferson make his philosophy explicit, in a single, comprehensive treatise? There are at least three equally plausible explanations. The first is that Jefferson, realizing the radical nature of this new philosophy, as well as the potentially violent opposition from "monarchist" sects, refrained from writing such a treatise because of his personal rule to "never enter into dispute or argument with another." Jefferson once remarked that his great wish was "to go on a strict but silent performance of my duty; to avoid attracting notice, and to keep my name out of the newspapers, because I find the pain of a little censure, even when it is unfounded, is more acute than the plea-sure of praise."[8] Jefferson's aversion to controversy, arising thus out of his Epicurean aversion to pain, kept him continually on guard against the publication of his private correspondence. Particularly after his retirement from public office, he constantly urged discreet use of his communications, due to his "wish to avoid all collisions of opinion with all mankind."[9]

This aversion to controversy explains, in part, Jefferson's failure to take a stand against slavery beyond the criticisms of the institution that he voiced in the *Notes on the State of Virginia*. Late in life, when a young Virginia neighbor, Edward Coles, called upon Jefferson to support a plan for gradual emancipation, he refused, finding an ap-propriate analogy in Homer's *Iliad:* "This, my dear sir," he wrote Coles, "is like bidding Old Priam to buckle [on] the armour of Hector. . . . The enterprise is for the young." He therefore left to future genera-tions the difficult problem that he once likened to holding "the wolf by the ears": "We can neither hold him, nor safely let him go. Justice is in one scale, and self-preservation in the other." Thus did Jefferson rationalize his decision to countenance the injustice of slavery, the greatest failure of both his private and public life. As John Miller has observed, "in spite of his real and abiding abhorrence of the 'pecu-liar institution,' he was too much the political pragmatist, too intent upon achieving lofty but realizable goals, and too much the product of his background as a Virginia slaveowner to grapple with this par-ticular example of man's tyranny over man with the same fervor he had displayed in contending against British tyranny."[10]

It seems clear, then, that a man so wary of expressing a controver-sial opinion even in personal letters would certainly not want to write and publish an entire treatise honestly and completely espousing his views on the most controversial of subjects, politics. He was reluctant to publish his book *Notes on Virginia* for this very reason. The unpleas-ant controversy generated by the unauthorized publication in 1791 of Jefferson's note commending Thomas Paine's *Rights of Man* no doubt reinforced his wariness.[11]

A second explanation for Jefferson's failure to make his philosophy explicit in the form of a treatise is that his authorship of such a work did not seem, to his mind, necessary. Before the publication of Destutt de Tracy's *Review of Montesquieu*, Jefferson recognized that "there does not exist a good elementary work on the organization of society into civil government: I mean a work which presents in one full and comprehensive view the system of principles on which such an organization should be founded, according to the rights of nature."[12] Lack of a single work, however, did not mean that there were no sources. The philosophy of the American Revolution, he believed, was obvious: it was rooted in Anglo-Saxon precedents, recognized by good Whigs on both sides of the Atlantic, and consistent with Enlightenment ideas accepted by men of letters everywhere. The Declaration of Independence, which Jefferson said "contained no new ideas" but merely expressed "the harmonizing sentiments of the day," the consensus among American Whigs, contained in Jefferson's rough draft a "reminder of the Circumstances of our Emigration and Settlement here," which like the similar argument found in Jefferson's *Summary View of the Rights of British America* compared the American colonists to their Saxon ancestors and their political rights to the natural rights that the Saxons (according to the Whig historical view) enjoyed. As Jefferson saw it, the American Revolution was fought for these lost Saxon liberties; hence, the principles of American government generally might be found in a study of history and in the Real Whig tracts that glorified the natural superiority of the ancient "Gothick" constitution.

Even after the political party struggles of the 1790s forced the Jeffersonian Republicans to articulate what they perceived to be the true nature of the Revolution of 1776, Jefferson thought it unnecessary to do so personally. Other "fellow-labourers" in "the holy cause of freedom,"[13] less averse to controversy, were willing to enter the lists during crucial periods of ideological combat with the Federalists. When a Federalist-controlled Congress enacted the Sedition Act of 1798, for example, a number of Jeffersonian Republicans responded with a group of publications which gave systematic expression to a libertarian view of First Amendment freedom of the press. And the political heresies that Jefferson found in John Adams's three-volume magnum opus, *A Defence of the Constitutions of Government of the United States,* were eventually refuted by John Taylor of Caroline in his major work, *An Inquiry into the Principles and Policy of the Government of the United States* (1814). Similarly, two of Taylor's later books—*Construction Construed and Constitutions Vindicated* (1820) and *New Views of the Constitution* (1823)—voiced the disapprobation of the Marshall Court which Virginia Jeffersonians generally shared in the 1820s.

Jefferson's belief in some sort of Whig consensus on the principles of government also provides evidence for a third explanation for the lack of a comprehensive text of Jeffersonianism: that such a text was unnecessary because whether or not these principles were spelled out in written form, Jefferson was convinced that they nevertheless were known and believed in by the American people. On a number of occasions when he had cause to despair—when Federalist "monarchists" controlled the government, when constitutional defects such as the perpetual reeligibility of the president and the life tenure of federal judges were not corrected, and when an amendment was not added to the Constitution authorizing the Louisiana Purchase—Jefferson found assurance in "the good sense of the people." "Where, then, is our republicanism to be found? Not in our constitution certainly, but merely in the spirit of the people. That would oblige even a despot to govern us republicanly." [14]

This confidence in the people, which was the hallmark of Jefferson's constitutional thought and in many ways one of its strengths, was also its greatest weakness. It blinded him to the possibility—a very real possibility, as American history has shown—that individual liberty is as threatened by government when it acts according to the will of the people as when it does not. Political power corrupts those who hold it—the people as well as their governors. Contemporaries of Jefferson, like his good friend and frequent collaborator James Madison, who were more aware of the dangers of majority tyranny, were also therefore more realistic defenders of individual rights than he.

Jefferson was born into Virginia's gentry class; and that circumstance, coupled with other aspects of his life as well as the traits of his mind, helped imbue him with a high degree of self-confidence that had few parallels, even in the "great generation" of Revolutionary Americans. His optimism and idealism led him to assume that people in general were equally self-assured and competent, as well as benevolent.

He had confidence in the people because he believed that they were committed to republicanism, if not in abstract political philosophy, at least in sentiment and habit; and that with a certain amount of education, the people's commitment could be relied upon to set things right. This conviction was bolstered by an equally passionate conviction held by Jefferson as an Enlightenment man of letters: a belief in the naturalness and simplicity of republicanism. Jefferson thought that true political principles, like basic truths in religion, ethics, and the other branches of "science," were discoverable merely by clear thinking. He held this naive faith in the obviousness of republicanism despite evidence, even in his own time, to the contrary. "All eyes are opened, or opening, to the rights of man," he wrote in his last letter, commemorating the fiftieth anniversary of American independence. "May it be to the world, what I believe it will be, (to some parts sooner, to others later, but finally to all,) the signal of arousing men to burst the chains under which monkish ignorance and superstition had persuaded them to bind themselves, and to assume the blessings and security of self-government." [15]

Ironically, then, one may argue that it is Jefferson's own faith in the obvious truth of his philosophy of government which makes it necessary for scholars today to continue to seek to understand it. This study of Jefferson's constitutional thought is but another chapter in that continuing quest.

NOTES

SELECT BIBLIOGRAPHY

INDEX

NOTES

Abbreviations

Cappon	Lester J. Cappon, ed., *The Adams-Jefferson Letters* (1959; reprint, 2 vols. in 1, New York: Clarion, 1971)
Commonplace Book	Gilbert Chinard, ed., *The Commonplace Book of Thomas Jefferson* (Baltimore: Johns Hopkins Press, 1926)
Ford	Paul Leicester Ford, ed., *The Writings of Thomas Jefferson*, 10 vols. (New York: Putnam's, 1892–99)
L&B	Andrew A. Lipscomb and Albert Ellery Bergh, eds., *The Writings of Thomas Jefferson*, 20 vols. (Washington, D.C.: Thomas Jefferson Memorial Association, 1904)
LC	Jefferson Papers, Manuscripts Division, Library of Congress
Lib. Am.	Merrill D. Peterson, ed., *Thomas Jefferson: Writings* (New York: Library of America, 1984)
Literary Book	Douglas L. Wilson, ed., *Jefferson's Literary Commonplace Book* (Princeton, N.J.: Princeton Univ. Press, 1989)
Malone	Dumas Malone, *Jefferson and His Time*, 6 vols. (Boston: Little, Brown, 1948–81)
MHS	Jefferson Papers, Coolidge Collection, Massachusetts Historical Society
Papers	Julian P. Boyd et al., eds., *The Papers of Thomas Jefferson*, 25 vols. to date (Princeton, N.J.: Princeton Univ. Press, 1950—)
TJ	Thomas Jefferson
UVa	Jefferson Papers, Special Collections Department, University of Virginia Library

Preface

1. TJ to Robert Walsh, 5 Apr. 1823, UVa; TJ to Francis A. Van der Kemp, 11 Jan. 1825, Ford, 10:337; Peterson, *Jefferson and the New Nation*, viii.

2. Palmer, *Age of the Democratic Revolution*, 4.

3. The only book-length study of Jefferson's constitutionalism, Caleb Perry Patterson's *Constitutional Principles of Thomas Jefferson*, was first published in 1953. Although Patterson's book has some valuable insights into certain aspects of Jefferson's ideas about government—particularly his views on judicial review in the federal courts—it is far from being a comprehensive study of Jefferson's constitutional thought.

4. For example, Faulkner, *Jurisprudence of Marshall*; Morgan, *Madison on the Constitution and the Bill of Rights*; and Stourzh, *Hamilton and the Idea of Republican Government*.

5. Elsewhere I have argued that "liberalism" versus "civic republicanism" is a false and misleading debate with respect to early American constitutional thought. See Mayer, "English Radical Whig Origins of American Constitutionalism." For a recent example of this debate's influence on Jefferson scholarship, see Sheldon, *Political Philosophy of Jefferson*.

1. "Bold in the Pursuit of Knowledge": The Education of an American Real Whig

1. TJ to James Madison, 17 Feb. 1826, Ford, 10:375–76.

2. TJ, Draft of the Kentucky Resolutions, [Oct.] 1798, ibid., 7:304; TJ to Edward Carrington, 27 May 1788, 16 Jan. 1787, *Papers* 13:208–9, 11:48–49.

3. Stourzh, *Hamilton and the Idea of Republican Government*, 96–97.

4. TJ to Thomas Jefferson Randolph, 24 Nov. 1808, Autobiography, [6 Jan. 1821], and TJ to Joseph Priestley, 27 Jan. 1800, Ford, 9:231, 1:3, 7:413; TJ to John Brazier, 24 Aug. 1819, L&B, 15:209.

5. TJ, Autobiography, [6 Jan. 1821], Ford, 1:4. Although the quoted phrase as used by Jefferson referred to Small alone, it is equally applicable to Wythe.

6. Ibid.

7. Malone, 1:69; TJ, Autobiography, [6 Jan. 1821], Ford, 1:4.

8. Malone, 1:56–58; TJ to Martha Jefferson, 5 May 1787, *Papers* 11:348–49; TJ to Bernard Moore, revised as an enclosure in Jefferson to John Minor, 30 Aug. 1814, Ford, 9:480–85. See also TJ to Dabney Terrell, 26 Feb. 1821, L&B, 15:318–22.

9. Dewey, *Thomas Jefferson, Lawyer*, 15–17.

10. TJ to John Garland Jefferson, 11 June 1790, *Papers* 16:480–81; TJ to Dabney Terrell, 26 Feb. 1821, L&B, 15:318–22; Dewey, *Thomas Jefferson, Lawyer*, 14, citing the records of the *Virginia Gazette*.

11. TJ to Thomas Turpin, 5 Feb. 1769, to Ralph Izard, 17 July 1788, *Papers* 1:23–24, 13:372.

12. TJ to John Minor, enclosure (to Bernard Moore, revised), 30 Aug. 1814, Ford, 9:483; TJ to Thomas Cooper, 10 Feb. 1814, L&B, 14:85.

13. The manuscripts of the literary and legal commonplace books are now in the possession of the Library of Congress. The equity commonplace book has never

been published; the manuscript is in the Jefferson Collection, Henry E. Huntington Library, San Marino, Calif., and recently has been described in Dumbauld, "Thomas Jefferson's Equity Commonplace Book."

14. Douglas Wilson has identified the time periods during which the notebooks were kept as well as the dates of the entries themselves (Wilson, "Thomas Jefferson's Early Notebooks").

15. The fact that Jefferson copied so prodigiously from Lord Kames's *Principles of Equity* in the equity commonplace book—over 30,000 words, or nearly half the entire manuscript—supports the conclusion reached by Wilson, that Kames was Jefferson's "principal guide and mentor in the world of equity" (ibid., 449–50).

16. These entries are the long extracts from Lord Kames's *Historical Law Tracts* (entry nos. 557–68), followed immediately by a series of long entries (nos. 569–84) from Sir John Dalrymple's *History of Feudal Property* and somewhat later by a series of extracts from Sir Henry Spelman's *Glossarium Archaiologicum,* William Sumner's *Treatise of Gavelkind,* and Blackstone's *Commentaries* (nos. 733–40) (*Commonplace Book,* 95–162, 186–93).

17. TJ to Robert Skipwith, 3 Aug. 1771, to Peter Carr, 28 Mar. 1790, to Thomas Mann Randolph, Jr., 30 May 1790, to John Garland Jefferson, 11 June 1790, *Papers* 1:76, 16:276, 448, 480; to John Norvell, 14 June 1807, to John Minor, 30 Aug. 1814, Ford, 9:71, 480; to Joseph C. Cabell, 2 Feb. 1816, UVa.

18. TJ to John Page, 25 Dec. 1762, *Papers* 1:5; Malone, 1:69–70.

19. A substantial portion of Jefferson's law practice concerned land law. See Dewey, *Thomas Jefferson, Lawyer,* 30.

20. Coke, *First Part of the Institutes, or, A Commentary upon Littleton,* 1:1a.

21. Malone, 1:72; *Commonplace Book* (entry nos. 873 and 879), 351–56, 359–63; TJ to Thomas Cooper, 10 Feb. 1814, Lib. Am., 1321.

22. Coke, *Second Part of the Institutes,* 45, 47; Bowen, *Lion and the Throne,* 514–15.

23. Bowen, *Lion and the Throne,* 517–18. Entries 30–68 of Jefferson's commonplace book were taken from the third *Institute* (*Commonplace Book,* 68–75).

24. Bowen, *Lion and the Throne,* 520–21. Only three entries in the legal commonplace book—items 76–78—are drawn from the *Fourth Institute* (*Commonplace Book,* 75).

25. The reports and abridgments read and recommended by Jefferson are ably described in Dumbauld, *Jefferson and the Law,* 14–17.

26. TJ to Thomas Cooper, 16 Jan. 1814, L&B, 16:54–59.

27. Citations from the *Commentaries* appear in the legal commonplace book; and both the numerous annotations in his set of the 1770 edition, now in the Library of Congress, and the references to Blackstone in the marginal notes that Jefferson wrote in many of his books, some of which are preserved today, attest to the fact that Jefferson carefully studied Blackstone.

28. TJ to Judge John Tyler, 17 June 1812, L&B, 13:166–67.

29. TJ to Philip Mazzei, [28] Nov. 1785, *Papers* 9:67–71. Frank Dewey has noted

that the lawbooks Jefferson purchased in 1764 and 1765 were of a decidedly practical nature, indicating his thorough study of common law pleading (Dewey, *Thomas Jefferson, Lawyer*, 13–14, citing *Virginia Gazette* Day Books).

30. TJ to John Cartwright, 5 June 1824, L&B, 16:42, 44.

31. Colbourn, "Jefferson's Use of the Past," 59, citing, inter alia, the pioneering essay by Herbert Butterfield, *The Englishman and His History* (Cambridge: Cambridge Univ. Press, 1944).

32. TJ to John Norvell, 14 June 1807, Ford, 9:71; to William Duane, 12 Aug. 1810, Lib. Am., 1227–29; to [George Washington Lewis], 25 Oct. 1825, L&B, 16:124–28. See also Wilson, "Jefferson vs. Hume."

33. TJ to [George Washington Lewis], 25 Oct. 1825, L&B, 16:125. See also Colbourn, "Jefferson's Use of the Past," 60 n. 14.

34. *Commonplace Book* (entry nos. 569–84, 803–5), 135–62, 296–98. Wilson's dating of the entries places Jefferson's reading of Dalrymple before 1773 but his reading of Hulme in the late 1770s (Wilson, "Thomas Jefferson's Early Notebooks," 446–47). Although attributed to Allan Ramsay in library catalogs, *An Historical Essay on the English Constitution* (1771) was almost certainly not written by Ramsay; Caroline Robbins has traced its authorship to Obadiah Hulme (Robbins, *Eighteenth-Century Commonwealthman*, 363).

35. See, for example, the libraries' book lists found in the appendix to Colbourn, *Lamp of Experience*, 217–21. Care and St. Amand, along with Dalrymple and Hulme, were also included in Jefferson's "fourth" library, the catalogue for the University of Virginia (ibid., 219–21 [excerpted from the *1828 Catalogue of the Library of the University of Virginia*, ed. William H. Peden (Charlottesville, Va., 1945)]).

36. St. Amand, "Historical Essay," ii–iv; Hulme, *Historical Essay*, 3; Tacitus, *Germania*, in *Works*, trans. Gordon, 323–25, 328. See also Molesworth, *Account of Denmark*, 42–43.

37. Hulme, *Historical Essay*, 3; St. Amand, "Historical Essay," xiii.

38. St. Amand, "Historical Essay," viii; Dalrymple, *History of Feudal Property*, 7–10, 12–13, 15–16. Jefferson's entries in the legal commonplace book closely follow Dalrymple's text.

39. Dalrymple, *History of Feudal Property*, 11; Hulme, *Historical Essay*, 12–16; St. Amand, "Historical Essay," xlv–xlvii, l, lix.

40. Rapin, *History of England* 1:xiv–xvi, 2:32–33 (note by Tindal), 34. From this, Whig historians concluded that the House of Commons was always a part of Parliament.

41. Hulme, *Historical Essay*, 27–30; Rapin, *History of England* 1:xiii.

42. Hulme, *Historical Essay*, 8, 38.

43. Dalrymple, *History of Feudal Property*, 16–19, 269.

44. Rapin, *History of England* 2:33–34 (note by Tindal); Hulme, *Historical Essay*, 40, 47–48.

45. Rapin, *History of England* 2:33; Hulme, *Historical Essay*, 58–59, 75–76.

46. Rapin, *History of England* 2:76–77, 162–63, 464; Hulme, *Historical Essay*, 60, 71.

47. Hulme, *Historical Essay*, 7, 115.

48. Ibid., 107–28.

49. Ibid., 139; Rapin, *History of England* 7:24–25, 10:483–523.

50. Rapin, *History of England* 7:24, 12:264–66; Hulme, *Historical Essay*, 153–57, 161.

51. TJ to Edmund Pendleton, 13 Aug. 1776, *Papers* 1:492; TJ to [George Washington Lewis], 25 Oct. 1825, L&B, 16:124.

52. Tacitus, *Works*, trans. Gordon, 2:92–94, 101–2, 323–25.

53. Hulme, *Historical Essay*, 5–6.

54. Pocock, *Ancient Constitution and the Feudal Law*, 232. See Robbins, *Eighteenth-Century Commonwealthman*; Mayer, "English Radical Whig Origins of American Constitutionalism"; Bailyn, *Ideological Origins of the American Revolution*, 34–35; Toohey, *Liberty and Empire*.

55. Hulme, *Historical Essay*, 4; Sidney, *Discourses concerning Government*, 379–83.

56. TJ to Thomas Mann Randolph, Jr., 30 May 1790, *Papers* 16:448–49.

57. Jefferson also abstracted Molesworth in *Commonplace Book* (entry no. 754), 212–13.

58. Compare Becker, *Declaration of Independence* with Wills, *Inventing America*. Wills's study has been decisively refuted by Hamowy, "Jefferson and the Scottish Enlightenment."

59. See Colbourn, *Lamp of Experience*, 217–18; Perkins, Buchanan & Brown to TJ, 2 Oct. 1769, TJ to Thomas Mann Randolph, Jr., 30 May 1790, *Papers* 1:34, 16:449; TJ to John Norvell, 14 June 1807, Ford, 9:71.

60. TJ to Robert Skipwith, 3 Aug. 1771, *Papers* 1:79; TJ to Henry Lee, 8 May 1825, Ford, 10:343; Minutes of the Board of Visitors of the University of Virginia, [4 Mar. 1825], L&B, 19:460–61.

61. Burgh, *Political Disquisitions* 1:1; Trenchard and Gordon, *Cato's Letters* 1:245, 4:4; Locke, *Two Treatises of Government*, ed. Laslett, 309–11 (*Second Treatise*, chap. 2).

62. Burgh, *Political Disquisitions* 1:3; Sidney, *Discourses concerning Government*, 406; TJ to Roger C. Weightman, 24 June 1826, Ford, 10:391–92.

63. Trenchard and Gordon, *Cato's Letters* 2:275; Sidney, *Discourses concerning Government*, 23–24, 151, 437.

64. Locke, *Two Treatises of Government*, 369, 374–75 (*Second Treatise*, chaps. 7, 8); Trenchard and Gordon, *Cato's Letters* 2:53–54; Sidney, *Discourses concerning Government*, 23.

65. Burgh, *Political Disquisitions* 1:3–4; Sidney, *Discourses concerning Government*, 457.

66. Locke, *Two Treatises of Government*, 324 (*Second Treatise*, chap. 4); Burgh, *Political Disquisitions* 1:2–3; Sidney, *Discourses concerning Government*, 250; Trenchard and Gordon, *Cato's Letters* 2:56. See also Sharp, *Declaration*, 2–3, 9–10.

67. Burgh, *Political Disquisitions* 1:2–3; Trenchard and Gordon, *Cato's Letters* 1:67, 2:73.

68. Burgh, *Political Disquisitions* 1:1–2; Trenchard and Gordon, *Cato's Letters* 2:235, 241, 253.

69. Trenchard and Gordon, *Cato's Letters* 1:88, 262, 3:76, 234; Burgh, *Political Disquisitions* 1:xvi–xvii; Molesworth, *Account of Denmark,* 44, 46–47, 52–54, 69–73.

70. Burgh, *Political Disquisitions* 1:3–4; Sidney, *Discourses concerning Government,* 15; Gordon, "Discourses on Tacitus" (Discourse 9), in Tacitus, *Works* 2:94; Locke, *Two Treatises of Government,* 463–64 (*Second Treatise,* chap. 19).

71. Sidney, *Discourses concerning Government,* 413–14; Trenchard and Gordon, *Cato's Letters* 2:17.

2. "Causes Which Have Impelled Us to the Separation": The Logic of the American Revolution

1. TJ to Henry Lee, 8 May 1825, Ford, 10:343. See also TJ to James Madison, 30 Aug. 1823, ibid., 268.

2. Colbourn, *Lamp of Experience,* 21–56; Bailyn, *Ideological Origins,* 22–54.

3. Bailyn, *Ideological Origins,* 47, 54, 94–95, 117; Edmund Burke, Speech on Conciliation with America, 22 Mar. 1775, in *Writings and Speeches of Burke,* 12 vols. (Boston: Little, Brown, 1901), 2:125.

4. Sydnor, *American Revolutionaries in the Making,* 17–18; Greene, "Society, Ideology, and Politics," 44–47.

5. TJ, Autobiography, [6 Jan. 1821], Ford, 1:9–10; Malone, 1:172–73.

6. Resolutions of the Freeholders of Albemarle County, 26 July 1774, *Papers* 1:117–18.

7. Malone, 1:181; *Papers* 1:135 (editorial note).

8. TJ, Autobiography, [6 Jan. 1821], and TJ to John W. Campbell, 3 Sept. 1809, Ford, 1:12, 9:258; Answers to François Soule's Queries, 13–18 Sept. 1786, *Papers* 10:378–79.

9. TJ, Draft of Instructions to the Virginia Delegates in the Continental Congress, manuscript text of *A Summary View of the Rights of British America,* [July 1774], *Papers* 1:121–35.

10. Peter C. Hoffer has argued that Jefferson drafted the Declaration of Independence in the form of a bill in equity (Hoffer, *Law's Conscience,* 72–77). This argument is more convincingly applied to the *Summary View* since it, unlike the Declaration, is in fact written as a petition to the king for the redress of grievances.

11. Lewis, "Jefferson's *Summary View.*"

12. Colbourn, "Thomas Jefferson's Use of the Past," 66; *Summary View,* in *Papers* 1:121–22, 132–33.

13. *Summary View,* in *Papers* 1:122. Jefferson also drafted a "Refutation of the Argument (that the Colonies were Established at the Expense of the British

Nation)," written in response to the king's speech of October 1775 (*Papers* 1:277–84). A probable source influencing Jefferson's view that the American settlers had the natural rights of "expatriated men" was Richard Bland's *Inquiry into the Rights of the British Colonies* (1766) (Lewis, "Jefferson's *Summary View*," 41–42).

14. *Summary View*, in *Papers* 1:122–23, 125; "Original Rough Draught" of the Declaration of Independence, ibid., 426.

15. *Summary View*, ibid., 132–33.

16. TJ, *Notes on the State of Virginia* (1787 ed.), Query XIII, Lib. Am., 238–42.

17. *Summary View*, in *Papers* 1:124–25.

18. Ibid., 121–22, 129–34.

19. Colbourn, "Jefferson's Use of the Past," 68.

20. Hulme, *Historical Essay*, 5, 18, 179–81, 185–86, 193–96.

21. Care, *English Liberties*, 4.

22. Declaratory Act, 6 George III, c. 12 (1766), in *Sources of English Constitutional History*, ed. Carl Stephenson and Frederick G. Marcham (New York: Harper and Row, 1972), 2:659–60. John Cartwright flatly dismissed the prevalent doctrine, that one "central supreme authority" must exist for legislation, and urged instead, paralleling Jefferson's idea, that a treaty of alliance should be concluded among all the dominions, united under a common king (*American Independence: The Interest and Glory of Great Britain* [Philadelphia, 1776]).

23. It has been argued that the Commonwealth model of empire was not politically feasible in the eighteenth century. See J. G. A. Pocock, "1776: The Revolution against Parliament," in *Three British Revolutions*, ed. Pocock, 281–82.

24. Burgh, *Political Disquisitions* 1:2–3.

25. Ibid., 1:29, 2:274, 288; Sharp, *Declaration*, 7–8.

26. Burgh, *Political Disquisitions* 2:310, 328; Sharp, *Declaration*, 2–3, 11–12.

27. Burgh, *Political Disquisitions* 2:310; Sharp, *Declaration*, 25–27. The Irish example was frequently invoked in the pre Revolutionary debate over the rights of Americans. See generally McIlwain, *American Revolution*, chap. 2.

28. TJ to John Randolph, 25 Aug. 1775, *Papers* 1:240–42. The fact that Jefferson's letter came into the possession of the second earl of Dartmouth, secretary of state for the colonies during the years 1772–75, indicates that Randolph brought it to the attention of British government authorities (*Papers* 1:243 [editorial note]).

29. Ibid., 241; TJ to William Small, 7 May 1775, ibid., 165–66.

30. TJ to John Randolph, 29 Nov. 1775, ibid., 269. Jefferson's conviction that George III was hostile to America was strengthened over time. See, for example, TJ to Richard Henry Lee, 22 Apr. 1786, to John Jay, 23 Apr. 1786, to James Madison, 25 Apr. 1786, to John Page, 4 May 1786, ibid., 9:398, 402, 433, 445–46.

31. For the lack of harmony between Jefferson and John Dickinson, see ibid., 1:187–92 (editorial note).

32. On the "unfeeling brethren" and slavery passages, see Wills, *Inventing America*, 71–75; Miller, *Wolf by the Ears*, 7–9.

33. TJ, Notes of Proceedings in the Continental Congress, [7 June–1 Aug. 1776], *Papers* 1:311.

34. Grey, "Origins of the Unwritten Constitution," 890.

35. The text used here is Jefferson's "original Rough draught" of the Declaration, *Papers* 1:423–27. For the evolution of the text, see Boyd, *Declaration of Independence,* and Munves, *Jefferson and the Declaration of Independence.*

36. The phrase "equal & independant" is especially revealing in showing the extent to which Jefferson's theory followed the Whig tradition; it is also strikingly similar to Locke's statement in the *Second Treatise.* During the second stage of the evolution of the text, "& independant" was deleted by Jefferson himself or by the committee of five (Boyd, *Declaration of Independence,* 29). Possible explanations for the change, both theorizing that the change was more literary than substantive, are found in Becker, *Declaration of Independence,* 198, and White, *Philosophy of the American Revolution,* 77 n.23.

37. TJ to Henry Lee, 8 May 1825, Ford, 10:343; Howell, "Declaration of Independence and Eighteenth-Century Logic."

38. Howell, "Declaration of Independence and Eighteenth-Century Logic," 474, quoting from Duncan's *Logick,* as it appears in [Robert Dodsley], *The Preceptor* (London, 1748), 2:96–97.

39. Howell, "Declaration of Independence and Eighteenth-Century Logic," 479–81.

40. Wills, *Inventing America,* 68–71; TJ, First Draft of the Virginia Constitution, [before 13 June 1776], *Papers* 1:337–40.

41. Reid, "Irrelevance of the Declaration," 84–87.

42. Ibid., 84.

43. The final version approved by Congress was even less specific, or more accommodating of different views. The wording was changed to conform with Richard Henry Lee's resolution: Congress declared that the colonies "are & of right ought to be free & independent states; that they are absolved of all allegiance to the British crown, and that all political connection between them & the state of Great Britain is, & ought to be, totally dissolved" (Munves, *Jefferson and the Declaration of Independence,* 107, 117). The nature of the "political connection" was not identified.

44. Sharp, *Declaration,* 14–15.

45. Bailyn, *Ideological Origins,* 201.

46. Wood, *Creation of the American Republic,* 372–89.

47. Proclamation of the General Court, 23 Jan. 1776, in *Massachusetts, Colony to Commonwealth: Documents on the Formation of Its Constitution, 1775–1780,* ed. Robert J. Taylor (Chapel Hill: Univ. of North Carolina Press, 1961; reprint, New York: Norton, 1972), 20; Wood, *Creation of the American Republic,* 383–89; Bailyn, *Ideological Origins,* 198.

48. Blackstone, *Commentaries* 1:104–5; *Commonplace Book* (entry no. 832), 316–17

(abstracting James Wilson's *Considerations on the Nature and Extent of the Legislative Authority of the British Parliament* [1774] and citing Blackstone, *Commentaries* 1:48–49).

49. Blackstone, *Commentaries* 4:436, 3:268; Boorstin, *Mysterious Science of the Law*, 25, 74–75, 82, 104.

50. Blackstone, *Commentaries* 1:48–49, 143, 156–57.

51. Ibid., 1:157; McDonald, *Novus Ordo Seclorum*, 59.

52. Blackstone, *Commentaries* 1:121, 140–41, 157; Corwin, *"Higher Law" Background of American Constitutional Law*, 85–86.

53. Robert M. Cover, review of St. George Tucker ed. of Blackstone's *Commentaries*, 5 vols. (1803; reprint, S. Hackensack, N.J., 1969), *Columbia Law Review* 70 (1970): 1475, 1479.

54. Burgh, *Political Disquisitions* 1:3–4, 6; Sidney, *Discourses concerning Government*, 117, 134.

55. Burgh, *Political Disquisitions* 1:6.

56. McIlwain, *American Revolution*, 150, 160.

3. "Our Revolution Commenced on More Favorable Ground": The Foundations of Republican Government

1. TJ to John Cartwright, 5 June 1824, L&B, 16:44.

2. John Adams, "Thoughts on Government," in *Works*, ed. Adams, 4:200; Thomas Paine, *Common Sense*, in *Complete Writings of Paine*, ed. Foner, 1:45.

3. TJ to Samuel Kercheval, 12 July 1816, to John Taylor, 28 May 1816, to P. S. Du Pont de Nemours, 24 Apr. 1816, Ford, 10:39, 30, 22.

4. TJ to Thomas Nelson, 16 May 1776, *Papers* 1:292.

5. George Wythe to TJ, 27 July 1776, ibid., 476–77; Malone, 1:236–37. As Jefferson explained it later in life, "my Preamble became tacked to the work of George Mason" (TJ to Augustus B. Woodward, 3 Apr. 1825, Ford, 10:342).

6. Malone, 1:238–39; Virginia Constitution as Adopted by the Convention, 29 June 1776, *Papers* 1:377–83.

7. TJ, Third Draft Constitution, [before 13 June 1776], *Papers* 1:356–64; Malone, 1:238–39; Pole, *Political Representation in England and the Origins of the American Republic*, 288–89.

8. Peterson, *Adams and Jefferson*, 22, 42; TJ, First, Second, and Third Drafts of the Virginia Constitution, [before 13 June 1776], TJ to Edmund Pendleton, 26 Aug. 1776, *Papers* 1:341–42, 348–50, 358–60, 503–5.

9. TJ, Third Draft of the Virginia Constitution, [before 13 June 1776], *Papers* 1:363–64.

10. See Miller, *Wolf by the Ears*, 7–11, 17.

11. TJ, Third Draft of the Virginia Constitution, [before 13 June 1776], *Papers* 1:362–63.

12. Ibid., 364.

13. TJ to John Cartwright, 5 June 1824, L&B, 16:44.

14. The text of *Notes on the State of Virginia* generally cited here is that as given by Ford, 3:85–295, which follows the original edition of 1782 (printed in Paris in 1784) and gives in footnotes the important variations in other editions. What may be regarded as the definitive edition of the *Notes on the State of Virginia*, Jefferson's revised text printed in London by John Stockdale in 1787, may be found in Lib. Am., 123–325. On Jefferson's authorship of the *Notes* and the *Notes* themselves as literary text, see Malone, 1:373–89, 2:94–106; Ferguson, *Law and Letters in American Culture*, 34–58.

15. See Bailyn, *Ideological Origins*, 175–89; Wood, *Creation of the American Republic*, 260–68; Adams, *First American Constitutions*, 18–22.

16. TJ, *Notes on the State of Virginia*, Ford, 3:222, 225. Jefferson's view was not accepted by the Virginia courts (Dumbauld, "Jefferson and American Constitutional Law," 373 n. 9).

17. TJ, *Notes on the State of Virginia*, Ford, 3:229. The best example of other states' practices is Massachusetts (Adams, *First State Constitutions*, 86–93).

18. See TJ to Diodati, 3 Aug. 1789, *Papers* 15:326–27.

19. TJ, *Notes on the State of Virginia*, Ford, 3:225–29; TJ, Answers to Démeunier's Additional Queries, [ca. Jan.–Feb. 1786], *Papers* 10:28–29.

20. TJ, *Notes on the State of Virginia*, Ford, 3:222–23.

21. Ibid., 223.

22. Ibid., 223–24.

23. Ibid., 224; Vile, *Constitutionalism and the Separation of Powers*, 119.

24. TJ, *Notes on the State of Virginia*, Ford, 3:224–25.

25. Ibid., 229–31.

26. TJ, Draft of a Constitution for Virginia, [May–June 1783], *Papers* 6:294–305.

27. Ibid.; Peterson, *Jefferson and the New Nation*, 173–74; Malone, 1:305–51.

28. TJ, Draft of a Constitution for Virginia, [May–June 1783], *Papers* 6:297, 301, 302–3.

29. Ibid., 298, 304–5.

30. TJ to Samuel Kercheval, 12 July 1816, Ford, 10:37.

31. Peterson, *Adams and Jefferson*, 23; TJ to Edmund Pendleton, 25 May 1784, to James Madison, 8 Dec. 1784, to William Short, 16 Oct. 1792, *Papers* 7:293, 557–58, 24:491; TJ to Samuel Kercheval, 12 July 1816, Ford, 10:37. The Virginia constitution of 1776 was not replaced until 1830, four years after Jefferson's death.

32. TJ, *Notes on the State of Virginia*, Query XVII, Lib. Am., 287. Although the passage quoted concerned particularly the need for guaranteeing religious freedom, it had wider application to all of Jefferson's reform efforts.

33. For the text of the 126 bills reported by the Committee of Revisors, see *Papers* 2:305–657.

34. TJ, Autobiography, [6 Jan. 1821], Ford, 1:57–59; Peterson, *Jefferson and the New Nation*, 111. See also Jefferson's criticism of the thesis advanced by the independent settlers of Vermont that the Revolution had dissolved the "social contract" and with it all the laws of the colonies (TJ to Edmund Randolph, 15 Feb. 1783, *Papers* 6:247–48, 249–50 [editorial note]).

35. TJ to Edmund Pendleton, 13 Aug. 1776, *Papers* 1:491–92.

36. Peterson, "Jefferson and the Enlightenment," 120–21; TJ to George Wythe, 1 Nov. 1778, and A Bill for Proportioning Crimes and Punishments in Cases Heretofore Capital, *Papers* 2:229–30, 492–504; TJ, Autobiography, [6 Jan. 1821], Ford, 1:60; Malone, 1:271.

37. TJ, Autobiography, [6 Jan. 1821], Ford, 1:68–69.

38. Ibid., 62; TJ, A Bill for Establishing Religious Freedom, *Papers* 2:545–46. The Virginia legislature omitted the phrase that declared "the opinions of men are not the objects of civil government," but Jefferson considered this to be the basic principle of the bill.

39. TJ to Joseph Priestley, 19 June 1802, Ford, 8:158–59.

40. Arieli, *Individualism and Nationalism in American Ideology*, 90–93, 97.

41. On the controversy over the *Rights of Man*, see *Papers* 20:268–90 (editorial notes), and Malone, 2:351–70. Two important consequences of the controversy were Jefferson's estrangement from John Adams and, because of the latter's identification with the antirepublican "heresies" to which Jefferson referred, Adams's undeserved but enduring reputation as a monarchist.

42. Paine, *Rights of Man*, pt. 2, in *The Essential Thomas Paine*, ed. Foner, 228–30.

43. Arieli, *Individualism and Nationalism in American Ideology*, 97, 123–24.

44. Ibid., 99.

45. *Commonplace Book* (entry no. 559), 107–8.

46. See the "dialogue between my Head and my Heart," in TJ to Maria Cosway, 12 Oct. 1786, *Papers* 10:450.

47. TJ to Peter Carr, 10 Aug. 1787, ibid., 12:14–15.

48. TJ to Thomas Law, 13 June 1814, to Francis W. Gilmer, 6 June 1816, to John Adams, 14 Oct. 1816, L&B, 14:140–41, 15:24–25, 76–77.

49. *Literary Book*, 24–50, 156–57. See also Peterson, "Jefferson and the Enlightenment," 102–111.

50. TJ to Peter Carr, 10 Aug. 1787, *Papers* 12:14; Lehmann, *Thomas Jefferson: American Humanist*, 73–83; Chinard, "Introduction," in *Commonplace Book*, 53–54, 63–64.

51. Bolingbroke, *Works of Lord Bolingbroke* 4:146–47, 181–99, 297, 369, 371.

52. Arieli, *Individualism and Nationalism in American Ideology*, 133.

53. TJ, Autobiography, [6 Jan. 1821], Ford, 1:68–69; TJ to John Adams, 28 Oct. 1813, Cappon, 389.

54. Arieli, *Individualism and Nationalism in American Ideology*, 85–86. This distinc-

tion between natural rights, as "rights of personal competency," and civil rights, as "rights of compact," was made by Paine, but it was almost certainly recognized by Jefferson (Chinard, *Jefferson*, 80–83).

55. TJ to Francis W. Gilmer, 7 June 1816, Ford, 10:32; TJ to Jean Baptiste Say, 1 Feb. 1804, L&B, 11:2–3, cited in Appleby, *Capitalism and a New Social Order*, 97.

56. TJ, Report of the Commissioners for the University of Virginia, 4 Aug. 1818, Lib. Am., 459–60.

57. Beitzinger, "Philosophy of Law of Four Founding Fathers," 11. As Beitzinger noted, this implies, for example, that retroactive penal laws would be contrary to "natural right" and not binding, even if there were no constitutional prohibition of them. Jefferson similarly held that civil rights could not be transgressed by government. For example, he later wrote that a legislature "can neither pass a law that my head shall be stricken from my body without trial, nor my freehold taken from me without indemnification, and when not necessary for a public use" (TJ to James Monroe, 8 Jan. 1811, L&B, 19:181–82).

58. See, for example, Koch, *Philosophy of Jefferson*, 147–48; Ferguson, *Law and Letters in American Culture*, 42.

59. TJ to John Manners, 12 June 1817, L&B, 15:124–25.

60. McDonald, *Novus Ordo Seclorum*, ix–x. See also Chinard, "Introduction," in *Commonplace Book*, 42; Harvey, *Jean Jacques Burlamaqui*, 121–24; White, *Philosophy of the American Revolution*, 213–20.

61. Lafayette's Draft of a Declaration of Rights, *Papers* 15:230–31, 232–33 (editorial note).

62. TJ to Isaac McPherson, 13 Aug. 1813, to Thomas Earle, 24 Sept. 1823, L&B, 13:333–36, 15:470–71.

63. *Commonplace Book* (entry no. 559), 107–8.

64. TJ to P. S. Du Pont de Nemours, 24 Apr. 1816, to Joseph Milligan, 6 Apr. 1816 (enclosure), L&B, 14:490, 466; TJ, Second Inaugural Address, 4 Mar. 1805, Ford, 8:347.

65. TJ to John Manners, 12 June 1817, L&B, 15:124–25.

66. Harvey, *Jean Jacques Burlamaqui*, 121–24; White, *Philosophy of the American Revolution*, 213–20.

67. Invoice enclosed in Perkins, Buchanan & Brown to TJ, 2 Oct. 1769, *Papers* 1:34; Cunningham, *In Pursuit of Reason*, 16–17; Koch, *Philosophy of Jefferson*, 17–18.

68. See White, *Philosophy of the American Revolution*, 217–20.

69. While it is true that the republican order Jefferson envisioned in the 1780s was based on a primarily agricultural society, composed of small independent farmers, Jefferson's agrarianism was neither a constant nor an indispensable attribute of his republicanism. Jefferson's changing political economy is discussed more fully in chap. 5, in the context of his later reading of Destutt de Tracy's treatises.

70. TJ to John Adams, 28 Oct. 1813, Cappon, 388–91.

71. Lerner, *Thinking Revolutionary*, 63–64. Among the "anomalies" Lerner cited were free nonwhites, whom "A Bill Declaring Who Shall Be Deemed Citizens of This Commonwealth" (no. 55) overlooked, and who therefore, being neither citizens nor aliens, were outlaws (see *Papers* 2:476–78).

72. TJ to Démeunier, 29 Apr. 1795, Ford, 7:12.

73. TJ to James Madison, 28 Oct. 1785, *Papers* 8:682.

74. *Summary View*, and TJ to Madison, 28 Oct. 1785, *Papers* 1:133, 8:682. In a later letter to Madison, he predicted that "our governments will remain virtuous for many centuries; as long as they are chiefly agricultural; and this shall be as long as there are vacant lands in any part of America" (TJ to Madison, 20 Dec. 1787, ibid., 12:442). As noted in chap. 5, Jefferson's position changed, becoming less agrarian as circumstances changed during and after his presidency. Nevertheless, the idea that expansion across space would ensure the preservation of republican government was an important aspect of Jefferson's thought, particularly during the 1780s. See McCoy, *Elusive Republic*.

75. Miller, *Wolf by the Ears*, 3, 7, 16; TJ, *Notes on the State of Virginia*, Lib. Am., 214.

76. TJ, Autobiography, [6 Jan. 1821], Ford, 1:69; TJ, *Notes on the State of Virginia*, Query XIV, Lib. Am., 271–74.

77. Revised Report of the Committee, 22 Mar. 1784, *Papers* 6:607–9. The plan, approved by Congress on 23 April 1784 in a revised form (with the antislavery clause deleted) as the Ordinance of 1784, was eventually superseded by the Northwest Ordinance of 1787.

4. "The Interesting Experiment of Self-Government": The Evolution of Republican Constitutionalism

1. TJ to Benjamin Franklin, 13 Aug. 1777, *Papers* 2:26.

2. TJ to John Adams, 28 Feb. 1796, Cappon, 259–60.

3. As Dumas Malone has noted, Jefferson made a significant, though indirect, contribution to the Constitution through the books which he bought in Paris and shipped to Madison in America, to assist Madison's study of ancient and modern confederacies (Malone, 2:87). In addition, Jefferson played a key role in the addition of the Bill of Rights to the Constitution, as shown in chap. 6.

4. See, for example, TJ to William S. Smith, 13 Nov. 1787, *Papers* 12:356–57.

5. TJ to James Madison, 1 July 1784, to John Blair, 13 Aug. 1787, ibid., 7:356, 12:28. See also TJ to Joseph Jones, 14 Aug. 1787, to George Washington, 14 Aug. 1787, ibid., 12:34, 36.

6. TJ to Richard Price, 1 Feb. 1785, to James Monroe, 17 June 1785, ibid., 7:630–31, 8:230–31. Edward Dumbauld has argued that Jefferson thus "was apparently the first advocate of employing treaties as a means of increasing federal power

over matters otherwise within the exclusive control of the state governments" (Dumbauld, "Jefferson and American Constitutional Law," 379).

7. TJ, Answers to Questions Propounded by Démeunier, 24 Jan. 1786, *Papers* 10:14–17.

8. Ibid., 19; TJ to Edward Carrington, 4 Aug. 1787, ibid., 11:678–79. James Madison held the same view (Madison to TJ, 16 Apr. 1781, ibid., 5:473).

9. TJ to Richard Price, 8 Jan. 1789, ibid., 14:420; Autobiography, [6 Jan. 1821], Ford, 1:108; TJ to George Weedon, 10 Apr. 1781, to John Adams, 23 Feb. 1787, *Papers* 5:402, 11:177. Late in 1777, while a member of the Virginia House of Delegates, Jefferson had drafted a bill to explicitly give the Articles of Confederation the force of law within the Commonwealth (ibid., 2:111).

10. TJ to James Madison, 16 Dec. 1786, to Edward Carrington, 4 Aug. 1787, to Joseph Jones, 14 Aug. 1787, ibid., 10:603, 11:679, 12:34. The "separated" judiciary consisted of the Court of Appeals in Cases of Capture, the first federal court, which had been created by Congress in 1780 to review decisions of state admiralty courts in prize cases (William F. Swindler, "Of Revolution, Law and Order," *Supreme Court Historical Society Yearbook, 1976* [Washington, D.C., 1976], 16–24).

11. TJ, Answers to Questions Propounded by Démeunier, 24 Jan. 1786, to Edward Carrington, 4 Aug. 1787, *Papers* 10:19, 11:679.

12. TJ to John Adams, 30 Aug. 1787, to George Washington, 14 Aug. 1787, ibid., 12:69, 36. As early as 16 Dec. 1786, in a letter to James Madison, Jefferson described "the outline of the proper division of powers between the general and particular [state] governments" as one intended "to make us one nation as to foreign concerns, and keep us distinct in Domestic ones" (ibid., 10:603).

13. TJ to John Adams, 13 Nov. 1787, to William Stephens Smith, 13 Nov. 1787, to Edward Rutledge, 18 July 1788, ibid., 12:350–51, 356, 13:378.

14. TJ to Edward Carrington, 21 Dec. 1787, ibid., 12:445. See also TJ to James Madison, 20 Dec. 1787, to Carrington, 27 May 1788, ibid., 12:439–41, 13:208.

15. TJ to Francis Hopkinson, 13 Mar. 1789, ibid., 14:650–51.

16. TJ to James Madison, 20 Dec. 1787, ibid., 12:439–41. See also TJ to Francis Hopkinson, 13 Mar. 1789, ibid., 14:650.

17. TJ to James Madison, 20 Dec. 1787, ibid., 12:440.

18. Ibid., 442.

19. See, for example, TJ to George Washington, 2 May 1788, to Edward Carrington, 27 May 1788, to Francis Hopkinson, 13 Mar. 1789, ibid., 13:128, 208–9, 14:650–51.

20. TJ to William Stephens Smith, 2 Feb. 1788, ibid., 12:558. See also TJ to James Madison, 6 Feb. 1788, to Alexander Donald, 7 Feb. 1788, ibid., 569–71.

21. Rutland, *Birth of the Bill of Rights*, 130; Malone, 2:172–74.

22. TJ to Edward Carrington, 27 May 1788, to William Carmichael, 3 June 1788, to Thomas Lee Shippen, 19 June 1788, to James Madison, 31 July 1788, *Papers* 13:208, 232, 277, 442. By the time of his letter to Madison, Virginia had become the

tenth state to ratify the Constitution, on June 25. Madison had convinced Jefferson that calling a second constitutional convention (as New York had urged) would be dangerous and undesirable. See TJ to Madison, 18 Nov. 1788, ibid., 14:188.

23. TJ to Edward Rutledge, 18 July 1788, to Richard Price, 8 Jan. 1789, ibid., 13:378, 14:420.

24. TJ to Richard Price, 1 Feb. 1785, ibid., 7:630–31.

25. TJ to David Humphreys, 18 Mar. 1789, to George Mason, 13 June 1790, ibid., 14:678, 16:493.

26. TJ to Charles Bellini, 30 Sept. 1785, to George Wythe, 13 Aug. 1786, ibid., 8:568–69, 10:244–45. See also TJ to John Adams, 28 Feb. 1796, Cappon, 259–60 (wishing for "an ocean of fire" to more completely separate America from Europe).

27. TJ to James Monroe, 17 June 1785, *Papers* 8:233.

28. TJ to George Washington, 2 May 1788, ibid., 13:128; TJ to Samuel Adams, 26 Feb. 1800, Ford, 7:425.

29. TJ to A. Coray, 31 Oct. 1823, L&B, 15:480; TJ to John Adams, 28 Feb. 1796, Cappon, 259–60; TJ to William Hunter, the Mayor of Alexandria [Response to an Address of Welcome], 11 March 1790, *Papers* 16:225. By "the people," Jefferson meant no particular class but rather "the mass of individuals composing the society" (TJ to P. S. Du Pont de Nemours, 24 Apr. 1816, Ford, 10:22–23).

30. TJ to James Madison, 30 Jan. 1787, to David Hartley, 2 July 1787, to William S. Smith, 13 Nov. 1787, to Madison, 20 Dec. 1787, *Papers* 11:92–93, 526, 12:356–57, 442. The letter to Smith was written at a time when Jefferson, who had just received a copy of the proposed federal constitution, feared that the convention "has been too much impressed by the insurrection in Massachusetts" and in the effort to create a stronger national government had gone too far, "setting up a kite to keep the hen yard in order." It is in the context of this fear that he observed: "[W]hat country can preserve it's liberties if their rulers are not warned from time to time that their people preserve the spirit of resistance? Let them take arms. The remedy is to set them right as to facts, pardon and pacify them. What signify a few lives lost in a century or two? The tree of liberty must be refreshed from time to time with the blood of patriots and tyrants. It is it's natural manure."

31. TJ to James Madison, 30 Jan. 1787, to Edward Carrington, 16 Jan. 1787, ibid., 11:92–93, 48–49.

32. TJ to Démeunier, 29 Apr. 1795, Ford, 7:13; TJ to William Short, 3 Jan. 1793, *Papers* 25:14. See also Malone, 3:39–53.

33. Koch, *Philosophy of Jefferson*, 150; TJ to James Madison, 30 Jan. 1787, *Papers* 11:92–93.

34. TJ to James Madison, 20 Dec. 1787, to David Humphreys, 18 Mar. 1789, Reply to the Citizens of Albemarle, 12 Feb. 1790, *Papers* 12:442, 14:678–79, 16:178–79. See also TJ to William Findley, 24 Mar. 1801, Ford, 8:27.

35. Koch, *Philosophy of Jefferson*, 150–51; TJ to F. H. A. von Humboldt, 13 June 1817, Ford, 10:88.

36. Koch, *Philosophy of Jefferson*, 151, citing TJ to President Washington, 9 Sept. 1792, and to Thomas Seymour, 7 Feb. 1807; First Inaugural Address, 4 Mar. 1801, LC. The need for "a respect for the rights of the minority" was another lesson that Jefferson derived from the unhappy history of the French Revolution (TJ to William Bache, 2 Feb. 1800, UVa).

37. Compare, for example, James Madison to TJ, 24 Oct. 1787, *Papers* 12:276–79; John Adams, *A Defence of the Constitutions of Government of the United States of America*, in *Works*, ed. Adams, 4:301, 399–400, 504, 6:7–62, 68, 88–90, 110.

38. TJ, Opinion on the Constitutionality of the Residence Bill, 15 July 1790, *Papers* 17:195.

39. TJ to Gouverneur Morris, 7 Nov. 1792, Notes on the Legitimacy of Government, 30 Dec. 1792, and to Thomas Pinckney, 30 Dec. 1792, ibid., 24:593, 802, 802–3.

40. TJ, Opinion on the French Treaties, 28 Apr. 1793, ibid., 25:608–18.

41. TJ to Edmund Randolph, 18 Aug. 1799, Ford, 7:383–87.

42. TJ, First Inaugural Address, 4 Mar. 1801, LC.

43. See Hofstadter, *Idea of a Party System*, 2–4, 27.

44. TJ to Francis Hopkinson, 13 Mar. 1789, *Papers* 14:650.

45. TJ to William Short, 8 Jan. 1825, Ford, 10:332–33.

46. For example, Jefferson wrote to Madame d'Houdetot on 2 April 1790 that he found in New York "a philosophic revolution, philosophically effected" (*Papers* 16:292).

47. TJ to George Mason, 4 Feb. 1791, to Thomas Paine, 19 June 1791, to Lafayette, 16 June 1792, ibid., 19:241, 20:312, 24:85.

48. See TJ to James Madison, 21 Sept. 1795, Ford, 7:32.

49. TJ, Notes of a Conversation with Alexander Hamilton," 13 Aug. 1791, *Papers* 22:38–39; TJ, Anas, [4 Feb. 1818], Ford, 1:165–66. See also TJ to Benjamin Rush, 16 Jan. 1811, Ford, 9:295–96.

50. Although many historians have drawn a parallel between the Jeffersonian Republicans and the "Country" party of early eighteenth-century England, it is important to note that the "Country" concerns of the first and second generations of Real Whigs were distinguishable from the concerns of the third generation, of the 1760s and 1770s, the generation closest (both in time and in ideology) to American Real Whigs (see Kramnick, "Republican Revisionism Revisited," 629, 635, 661). The "corruption" that Jefferson condemned was not quite the same as that condemned by Bolingbroke; it was much closer to that condemned by James Burgh and the Real Whig reformers of the mid-century. Hamilton's "schemes" subverted the Constitution not so much because they destroyed its "balance," but because they circumvented public opinion and therefore made the Congress a less representative—a less accountable—body. In this light, Jefferson's characterizations of the Federalists as an "anti-republican" party can be best understood, as can his condemnation of the "paper men"—the "bank directors and stock-jobbers"

in Congress who were attached to Hamilton and his policies by ties of financial interest (see TJ, Note of a Conversation with George Washington, 10 July 1792, *Papers* 24:210, 211 [describing corruption in Congress as "a legislature legislating for their own interests in opposition to those of the people"]).

51. TJ to the President of the United States (George Washington), 9 Sept. 1792, and Notes of a Conversation with George Washington, 1 Oct. 1792, *Papers* 24:351–59, 435; Malone, 2:459–69. On Jefferson's access to Madison's notes, and Hamilton's speech in the Constitutional Convention, see *Papers* 19:548–49 (editorial note); Madison, *Notes*, 129–39.

52. TJ to Thomas Pinckney, 3 Dec. 1792, to William Short, 3 Jan. 1793, *Papers* 24:696, 25:15.

53. See Malone, 3:55–161; Peterson, *Jefferson and the New Nation*, 479–516. See also Peterson, "Jefferson and Commercial Policy"; Nelson, *Liberty and Property*.

54. See Charles, *Origins of the American Party System*, 91–122; Malone, 3:246.

55. Malone, 3:250–53; Peterson, *Jefferson and the New Nation*, 550–51; TJ to James Madison, 21 Sept. 1795, to Edward Rutledge, 30 Nov. 1795, Ford, 7:32–33, 40.

56. Notes on Professor Ebeling's Letter of 20 July 1795, Ford, 7:46–47.

57. TJ to Philip Mazzei, 24 Apr. 1796, to James Madison, 3 Aug. 1797, ibid., 7:75–76, 164–67. The text of Jefferson's letter to Mazzei was leaked to the popular press and made the subject of heated Federalist attacks and demands for explanations. In the version published in the Philadelphia newspapers, the text referred to the "form," rather than the "forms," of the British government, thereby implying his opposition to the government itself—to the Constitution. Reference to "the Samsons in the field and Solomons in the council" also was interpreted as an attack on the venerable Washington himself, and until rather late in life Jefferson was compelled to clarify his opinion of Washington. No explanation was sufficient for Jefferson's Federalist enemies, however, who continued for many years to attach notoriety to the letter. At a crucial moment in 1801, when the electoral vote tie put Jefferson in contest with Aaron Burr for the presidency, John Marshall observed to Hamilton, "The morals of the author of the letter to Mazzei cannot be pure" (Malone, 3:302–5).

58. TJ to W. B. Giles, 31 Dec. 1795, Ford, 7:43.

59. See Cunningham, "Political Parties," in *Jefferson: A Reference Biography*, ed. Peterson, 303; Malone, 3:478; Charles, *Origins of the American Party System*, 90.

60. TJ to Edward Rutledge, 24 June 1797, Ford, 7:155; TJ to Mrs. Angelica Church, 11 Jan. 1798, LC (wrongly dated as October 1792 in Ford, 6:115); TJ to Edmund Pendleton, 2 Apr. 1798, Ford, 7:229.

61. TJ to Edmund Pendleton, 29 Jan. 1799, Ford, 7:336. See also Malone, 3:368–94.

62. The partisan nature of the Alien and Sedition Acts of 1798 and their threat to civil liberties are ably detailed in Smith, *Freedom's Fetters*.

63. TJ to John Taylor, 4 June 1798, MHS (misdated as June 1 in Ford, 7:264);

Hofstadter, *Idea of a Party System*, 114–15. See also TJ to Thomas Lomax, 12 Mar. 1799, to Edward Livingston, 30 Apr. 1800, Ford, 7:373–74, 443.

64. TJ to James Sullivan, 9 Feb. 1797, Ford, 7:117; TJ to John Wise, 12 Feb. 1798, quoted in Malone, 3:364–65.

65. TJ, Anas, [4 Feb. 1818], Ford, 1:156–57, 165.

5. "We Are All Federalists, We Are All Republicans": The Republican "Revolution" of 1800 and Beyond

1. TJ to Spencer Roane, 6 Sept. 1819, Ford, 10:140.

2. Of course the election of 1800 was not this simple; even victory brought another ordeal—the tie in electoral votes between Jefferson and Aaron Burr, the Republican vice-presidential candidate. The tie was eventually broken, on the thirty-sixth ballot, in the House of Representatives, according to the procedures specified in the Constitution. The harrowing experience spurred the Republicans to sponsor the Twelfth Amendment, which was adopted by Congress in 1803 and ratified by a sufficient number of states to take effect in time for the presidential election of 1804. Thus, as Richard Hofstadter has observed, the election of 1800 led to "a decisive step . . . toward constitutional recognition of the role played by parties in the federal government" (*Idea of a Party System*, 139 n.17).

3. TJ, First Inaugural Address, 4 Mar. 1801, LC; TJ to Henry Knox, 27 Mar. 1801, to Levi Lincoln, 11 July 1801, to P. S. Du Pont de Nemours, 18 Jan. 1802, Ford, 8:36, 67, 126; Malone, 4:20.

4. TJ, First Inaugural Address, 4 Mar. 1801, LC.

5. TJ to Gideon Granger, 31 Oct. 1801, LC; TJ to Thomas McKean, 2 Feb. 1801, to William Giles, 23 Mar. 1801, to James Monroe, 7 Mar. 1801, to Horatio Gates, 8 Mar. 1801, Ford, 7:487, 8:25, 9–10, 11–12. See also Malone, 4:69–89. Given the Federalist monopoly of the judicial branch, the offices of U.S. attorneys and marshals were an exception to Jefferson's general policy on removals. He regarded the replacement of Federalists with Republicans in these offices—"the doors of entrance into the courts"—as "indispensably necessary as a shield" for Republican citizens (TJ to William Giles, 23 Mar. 1801, Ford, 8:25).

6. TJ to Horatio Gates, 8 Mar. 1801, Ford, 8:11–12.

7. Hofstadter, *Idea of a Party System*, 204; TJ to Madison, 29 June 1792, *Papers* 24:133.

8. TJ to Henry Lee, 10 Aug. 1824, Ford, 10:317. In 1797–98 Jefferson had begun to accept the idea of these two parties being inevitable in any free society, but it was after his presidency that Jefferson most fully articulated this idea. He believed that the division between Whigs and Tories was based in human nature: the "weakly, timid man" who feared the people was a Tory by nature; the "healthy, strong and bold" man who cherished them, was a Whig (See TJ to Joel Barlow,

3 May 1802, to Lafayette, 4 Nov. 1823, Ford, 8:150, 10:281; TJ to John Adams, 27 June 1813, Cappon, 335).

9. See, for example, TJ to Albert Gallatin, 8 Sept. 1816, to Lafayette, 14 May 1817, Ford, 10:65, 83.

10. Hofstadter, *Idea of a Party System*, 205.

11. TJ to William Johnson, 12 June 1823, Ford, 10:226–28.

12. TJ to Joseph Priestley, 19 June 1802, ibid., 8:158–59.

13. TJ to Governor Hall, 6 July 1802, ibid., 8:156–57. See also TJ to John Dickinson, 6 Mar. 1801, to Joseph Priestley, 21 Mar. 1801, to Roger C. Weightman, 24 June 1826, Ford, 8:8, 22, 10:391–92; TJ to Rev. Samuel Knox, 12 Feb. 1810, L&B, 12:359; TJ to John Adams, 12 Sept. 1821, Cappon, 575.

14. TJ, Reply to the Citizens of Washington, 4 Mar. 1809, L&B, 16:347–48.

15. TJ to Thomas Cooper, 9 July 1807, Ford, 9:102. See also Ellis, *Jeffersonian Crisis*; Risjord, *Old Republicans*.

16. See Malone, 5:149, 549; Ammon, "Monroe and the Election of 1808 in Virginia"; Mayer, "Of Principles and Men."

17. TJ to William Duane, 28 Mar. 1811, Ford, 9:310.

18. TJ to George Mason, 4 Feb. 1791, *Papers* 19:241.

19. TJ to Joseph Priestley, 19 June 1802, Ford, 8:159–60.

20. TJ to John Melish, 13 Jan. 1813, ibid., 9:374–75.

21. TJ to Edward Carrington, 16 Jan. 1787, *Papers* 11:48–49.

22. TJ, "Fair Copy" of the Kentucky Resolutions, [Nov. 1798], Ford, 7:304–5.

23. TJ to Elbridge Gerry, 26 Jan. 1799, ibid., 327.

24. Vile, *Constitutionalism and the Separation of Powers*, 161, 164.

25. Madison, *Federalist* No. 48, [1 Feb. 1788], in *The Federalist*, ed. Cooke, 332–36.

26. Dumas Malone followed other scholars in calling Jefferson's doctrine the "tripartite theory" (Malone, 4:152).

27. TJ to Isaac H. Tiffany, 26 Aug. 1816, L&B, 15:66.

28. TJ to P. S. Du Pont de Nemours, 24 Apr. 1816, Ford, 10:22–23; TJ to F. A. Van der Kemp, 22 Mar. 1812, L&B, 13:135.

29. TJ to P. S. Du Pont de Nemours, 24 Apr. 1816, to John Taylor, 28 May 1816, Ford, 10:24, 28–29.

30. TJ to John Taylor, 28 May 1816, Ford, 10:29–30. On Jefferson's opposition to the county courts, the customary institution of local government in Virginia, see Roeber, *Faithful Magistrates and Republican Lawyers*, 163–71, 239–40.

31. TJ to John Taylor, 28 May 1816, Ford, 10:30. Jefferson's reference to "A" and "B," of course, concerns the method devised under the Constitution for the election of the president, the Electoral College.

32. TJ to Samuel Kercheval, 12 July 1816, ibid., 37–45.

33. *Commonplace Book*, 9, 31–36, 257–96; TJ to Thomas Mann Randolph, Jr., 30 May 1790, *Papers* 16:449; to William Duane, 12 Aug. 1810, L&B, 12:408.

34. Appleby, "What Is Still American in the Political Philosophy of Jefferson?" 290–91, and "Jefferson-Adams Rupture and the First Translation of Adams's *Defence.*"

35. Malone, 6:208–10; TJ to Thomas Cooper, 16 Jan. 1814, L&B, 14:54.

36. Montesquieu, *Spirit of the Laws*, trans. Nugent, 2–28 (books 2 and 3); Destutt de Tracy, *Commentary and Review*, trans. Jefferson, 9, 12, 19. For Jefferson's refutation of Montesquieu's principle that a republic could be preserved only over a small territory, see, for example, TJ to François d'Ivernois, 6 Feb. 1795, Lib. Am., 1024; TJ to Nathaniel Niles, 22 Mar. 1801, Ford, 8:24; TJ to François Marbois, 14 June 1817, Lib. Am., 1410.

37. Destutt de Tracy, *Commentary and Review*, trans. Jefferson, 20, 41–42, 68–71.

38. Ibid., 232–33. Tracy's comments on the "moral effects" of commerce are particularly interesting. Commerce, besides being "the author of all social good," according to Tracy, is "the only bond among men; the source of all their moral sentiments; and the first and most important cause of the improvement of their mutual sensibility and reciprocal benevolence."

39. Ibid., 185–88, 192, 205–6, 213–14, 232–33. The French text is more explicit in revealing Tracy's equation of the work of all three—the farmer, manufacturer, and merchant—as forms of "industry": "Ce lumineux principe est également applicable aux industries agricole, manufacturière et commerçante." In describing commerce as "the fabric itself" of society, again the French text is more explicit: it is "l'essence, qu'il est la société elle-même" (Destutt de Tracy, *Commentaire sur L'Esprit des Lois de Montesquieu* [Paris, 1819; reprint, Geneva: Slatkine, 1970], 286, 313–14). Destutt de Tracy elaborated many of these arguments in his *Treatise of Political Economy*, which Jefferson also translated and helped get published, late in 1818. See Malone, 6:210, 305–7.

40. Appleby, "What Is Still American in the Political Philosophy of Jefferson?" 294–97, 301–309. See also Koch, *Philosophy of Jefferson*, 184–85. The clearest evidence that Jefferson's position changed over time is Jefferson's own statement of explanation, in a letter to Benjamin Austin dated 9 Jan. 1816, in which he stated that "changed circumstances" in the thirty years since he had written *Notes on Virginia* had taught him that "manufactures are now as necessary to our independence as to our comfort," and that "we must now place the manufacturer by the side of the agriculturist" (Ford, 10:10). See also TJ to J. Lithgow, 4 Jan. 1805, LC, discussed in Malone, 5:24.

41. See generally Destutt de Tracy, *Commentary and Review*, 94–157.

42. Ibid., 100–101.

43. Ibid., 147–48, 154–55.

44. Ibid., 101–3, 117.

45. Ibid., 107.

46. TJ to John Taylor, 28 May 1816, Ford, 10:30–31.

47. Destutt de Tracy's ideal constitution had a unicameral legislature and a

plural executive. The third branch, the "conservative body," resembled the U.S. judiciary in having lifetime tenures, but its multifaceted "preserving power" extended beyond judicial review of constitutionality. In his translation of the treatise, Jefferson likened it to the "council of censors" in the Pennsylvania constitution of 1776 (Destutt de Tracy, *Commentary and Review*, 138 n.14).

48. TJ to John Taylor, 28 May 1816, to Thomas Ritchie, 25 Dec. 1820, Ford, 10:28, 169–70. The importance of Taylor's *Inquiry* as a critique of John Adams's *Defence of the Constitutions of Government of the United States* is discussed in Wood, *Creation of the American Republic*, 587–92, and Vile, *Constitutionalism and the Separation of Powers*, 167–72.

49. Adams, *Defence*, in *Works*, ed. Adams, 4:406, 427–29, 556. For Jefferson's criticisms of Adams's *Defence*, see TJ to Paine, 29 June 1791, *Papers* 20:308; TJ to William Short, 8 Jan. 1825, L&B, 16:92.

50. Taylor, *Inquiry*, vi, 76, 78–79, 165.

51. Ibid., 512, 644.

52. Ibid., 402, 422, 633.

53. Ibid., 171 73, 428.

54. Ibid., 203, 209, 217, 649; Vile, *Constitutionalism and the Separation of Powers*, 170–71.

55. Vile, *Constitutionalism and the Separation of Powers*, 166.

6. "Certain Fences against Wrong": The Federal Constitution and the Bill of Rights

1. TJ to James Madison, 31 July 1788, to Edward Carrington, 27 May 1788, *Papers* 13:442, 208–9.

2. TJ to James Madison, 20 Dec. 1787, ibid., 12:440; Rutland, *Ordeal of the Constitution*, 199–217, and *Birth of the Bill of Rights*, 119–25; Levy, "Bill of Rights," 258–89. See also TJ to Joseph Priestley, 19 June 1802, Ford, 8:159.

3. Levy, "Bill of Rights," 258; Madison, *Notes*, 630, 640.

4. Wilson, Address to a Meeting of the Citizens of Philadelphia, 6 Oct. 1787, in *The Bill of Rights: A Documentary History*, ed. Bernard Schwartz, 2 vols. (New York: Chelsea House, 1971), 1:528–29.

5. *The Federalist*, ed. Cooke, 576–81. Leonard Levy has shown that Hamilton's arguments were inconsistent. The notion that the Constitution already included sufficient guarantees of rights "opened the Federalists to devastating rebuttal"; their argument that a partial enumeration would be dangerous thus "boomeranged" against them (Levy, "Bill of Rights," 270–71, 274–76).

6. Ketcham, "Dilemma of Bills of Rights in Democratic Government," 38–39.

7. James Madison to TJ, 24 Oct. 1787, *Papers* 12:278–79.

8. Ibid., 276.

9. TJ to James Madison, 20 Dec. 1787, ibid., 442.

10. Ibid., 440. The "clause of our present confederation" was Article II of the Articles of Confederation, which provided: "Each state retains . . . every Power, Jurisdiction and right, which is not by this confederation expressly delegated to the United States, in Congress assembled" (*Documents of American History*, ed. Commager, 1:111).

11. James Madison to George Lee Turberville, 1 Mar. 1788, *Papers of Madison*, ed. Hutchinson, 10:550; Ketcham, "Dilemma of Bills of Rights in Democratic Government," 40–41.

12. TJ to James Madison, 31 July 1788, *Papers* 13:442–43.

13. James Madison to TJ, 17 Oct. 1788, ibid., 14:18–19.

14. Ibid., 19–20.

15. Ibid.

16. For Madison's suggested version of what became the Ninth Amendment, as it read when he proposed amendments in the First Congress, see Madison, Speech in the U.S. House of Representatives, 8 June 1789, *Papers of Madison*, ed. Hutchinson, 12:201–2. As finally adopted, the Ninth Amendment provides: "The enumeration in the Constitution, of certain rights, shall not be construed to deny or disparage others retained by the people."

17. James Madison to TJ, 17 Oct. 1788, *Papers* 14:21.

18. TJ to James Madison, 15 Mar. 1789, ibid., 659–61.

19. Ibid., 659; Madison, Speech in the U.S. House of Representatives, 8 June 1789, *Papers of Madison*, ed. Hutchinson, 12:207.

20. TJ to James Madison, 15 Mar. 1789, *Papers* 14:659, 661. For Jefferson's opposition to the meeting of a new constitutional convention, see TJ to James Madison, 18 Nov. 1788, to John Paul Jones, 23 Mar. 1789, ibid., 188, 688.

21. TJ to James Madison, 20 Dec. 1787, ibid., 12:440. By "monopolies," Jefferson meant the term as it was fairly well understood under English law; that is, laws or regulations which granted exclusive privileges to certain persons. Jefferson may have been particularly concerned about monopolies during his stay in France because of his effort to bring about the abolition of the French tobacco monopoly (see Malone, 2:38–44).

22. TJ to William Stephens Smith, 2 Feb. 1788, to James Madison, 31 July 1788, *Papers* 12:558, 13:442–43.

23. TJ to James Madison, 28 Aug. 1789, ibid., 15:367–68. Jefferson's suggested language with respect to freedom of the press, the proposed Article 4, is discussed in the last section of this chapter. The proposed Article 7 would have provided for jury trial of "all facts put in issue before any judicature," excepting admiralty, courts martial, and impeachments. Proposed Article 8 would have defined, with great particularity, the procedures under which the writ of habeas corpus may issue as well as the limitations upon its suspension. Proposed Article 8 would have permitted monopolies "to persons for their own productions in literature & their own inventions in the arts"—i.e., for copyrights and patents—for a given term of

years, "but for no longer term and no other purpose." Proposed Article 10 would have required that all United States troops be disbanded "at the expiration of the term for which their pay and subsistence shall have been last voted by Congress."

24. TJ to David Humphreys, 18 Mar. 1789, to Edward Carrington, 27 May 1788, ibid., 14:678–79, 13:208–9.

25. TJ to Noah Webster, Jr., 4 Dec. 1790, ibid., 18:132–33. For the context of this letter, see ibid., 134 (editorial note); Wood, *Creation of the American Republic*, 376–77.

26. Koch, *Philosophy of Jefferson*, 141–42.

27. Levy, *Jefferson and Civil Liberties*, 15, 21.

28. The other two were his authorship of the Declaration of Independence and his founding of the University of Virginia (TJ, Epitaph, [1826], LC).

29. TJ, Third Draft of the Virginia Constitution, [before 13 June 1776], *Papers* 1:363.

30. Levy, *Establishment Clause*, 51–53; Curry, *First Freedoms*, 134–39.

31. TJ, Autobiography, [6 Jan. 1821], Ford, 1:53. Jefferson's notes are printed in *Papers* 1:525–58, with a useful editorial note discussing the confused state of the documentary record.

32. TJ, Notes on Locke, ibid., 545–48.

33. TJ, Autobiography, [6 Jan. 1821], Ford, 1:62. He noted that an amendment inserting the words "Jesus Christ" into the preamble's declaration that coercion is a departure from the plan of "the holy author of our religion" was rejected by a "great majority" of the legislature, "in proof that they meant to comprehend, within the mantle of its protection, the Jew and the Gentile, the Christian and the Mahometan, the Hindoo, and Infidel of every denomination."

34. TJ, A Bill for Establishing Religious Freedom, *Papers* 2:545–46. In this text passages of Jefferson's document that did not appear in the bill as enacted are enclosed in brackets.

35. Ibid. See also *Reynolds v. United States*, 98 U.S. 145, 164 (1879), a Supreme Court decision upholding the imposition of criminal sanctions upon Mormons who practiced polygamy; Little, "Jefferson's Religious Views."

36. See, for example, TJ to John Adams, 11 Apr. 1823, Cappon, 591–94. See also Malone, 2:110–11; Peterson, *Adams and Jefferson*, 120–23.

37. TJ to Benjamin Rush, 21 Apr. 1803, to Charles Thomson, 9 Jan. 1816, Ford, 8:223–28, 10:5–6; TJ to John Adams, 12 Oct. 1813, Cappon, 383–86; *Jefferson's Extracts from the Gospels*, ed. Dickinson W. Adams (Princeton, N.J.: Princeton Univ. Press, 1983).

38. See, for example, TJ to Mrs. Samuel H. Smith, 6 Aug. 1816, L&B, 15:60; TJ to John Adams, 11 Jan. 1817, Cappon, 506.

39. TJ, A Bill for Establishing Religious Freedom, *Papers* 2:546–47.

40. Levy, *Establishment Clause*, 53–60; Curry, *First Freedoms*, 139–48.

41. TJ to James Madison, 16 Dec. 1786, *Papers* 10:603–4.

42. TJ, *Notes on the State of Virginia,* Query XVII, Lib. Am., 285.

43. Ibid., 286. Elsewhere in his writings, there is support for the proposition that Jefferson valued diversity for its own sake. See, for example, TJ to Charles Thomson, 29 Jan. 1817, Ford, 10:75–76 (deploring the "singular anxiety which some people have that we should all think alike" and declaring that in a world without variety, where "all move strictly uniform, catholic & orthodox, what a world of physical and moral monotony it would be!").

44. TJ to Benjamin Rush, 23 Sept. 1800, Ford, 7:460.

45. TJ to Nehemiah Dodge and others, a Committee of the Danbury Baptist Association, in the State of Connecticut, 1 Jan. 1802, L&B, 16:281–82; Malone, 4:108–9; TJ to Nehemiah Dodge, &c. (draft), 31 Dec. 1802, LC; Levi Lincoln to TJ, 1 Jan. 1802, LC; *Everson v. Board of Education,* 330 U.S. 1, 16 (1947).

46. TJ to Rev. Samuel Miller, 23 Jan. 1808, Ford, 9:175; Levy, *Jefferson and Civil Liberties,* 7.

47. TJ to Thomas Cooper, 10 Feb. 1814, Lib. Am., 1321–29; *Commonplace Book* (entry nos. 873, 879), 351–56, 359–63; Wilson, "Jefferson's Early Notebooks," 447–48; TJ to John Cartwright, 5 June 1824, L&B, 16:42–52.

48. Dumas Malone has noted that Jefferson deleted these provisions from the bill on the advice of friends, among them Judge Spencer Roane and Thomas Ritchie, who thought them politically unwise (Malone, 6:270).

49. TJ, Plan for Elementary Schools, 9 Sept. 1817, L&B, 17:425; TJ, Report of the Commissioners for the University of Virginia, 4 Aug. 1818, Lib. Am., 467; Minutes of the Board of Visitors of the Commonwealth of Virginia, 7 Oct. 1822, L&B, 19:413–16.

50. TJ to David Humphreys, 18 Mar. 1789, *Papers* 14:678; Malone, 1:278, 3:393; Levy, *Jefferson and Civil Liberties,* 44–45.

51. Levy, *Emergence of a Free Press,* x–xii.

52. An Act in addition to the act, entitled "An act for the punishment of certain crimes against the United States" (Sedition Act), approved 14 July 1798, sec. 2, in *Documents of American History,* ed. Commager, 1:177–78; Levy, *Emergence of a Free Press,* 128–30, 201, 266–72; Levy, "Liberty and the First Amendment," 32.

53. Levy, *Emergence of Free Press,* 309–17, 327–32, 335–37; Levy, "Liberty and the First Amendment," 32–35.

54. Levy, "Liberty and the First Amendment," 22.

55. TJ, Drafts of the Virginia Constitution, [before 13 June 1776], *Papers* 1:344, 353.

56. Ibid., 344–45, 353, 363. Levy has ignored this clause in his discussion of the 1776 drafts of the Virginia constitution (Levy, "Civil Liberties," in *Jefferson: A Reference Biography,* ed. Peterson, 336).

57. Levy, *Jefferson and Civil Liberties,* 46.

58. TJ to James Currie, 28 Jan. 1786, to John Jay, 25 Jan. 1786, *Papers* 9:239, 215.

59. TJ to Edward Carrington, 16 Jan. 1787, ibid., 11:49.

60. George Hay in the second edition of his *Essay on the Liberty of the Press* in 1803 recognized the validity of criminal proceedings against notorious libelers of private persons, an important exception to his belief in "absolute" freedom and his repudiation of seditious libel (Levy, *Emergence of a Free Press*, 315). The privileged nature of defamatory statements made without malice about public officers was first recognized as a constitutional mandate by the Supreme Court in *New York Times v. Sullivan*, 376 U.S. 255 (1964).

61. TJ to James Madison, 31 July 1788, *Papers* 13:442–43.

62. James Madison to TJ, 30 June 1789, TJ to Madison, 28 Aug. 1789, ibid., 15:229, 367.

63. Levy, *Jefferson and Civil Liberties*, 49.

64. TJ to the President of the United States (George Washington), 9 Sept. 1792, *Papers* 24:357; TJ to William Green Munford, 18 June 1799, Lib. Am., 1064–65.

65. TJ to James Madison, 26 Apr. 1798, L&B, 10:31–32; TJ to Madison, 6 June 1798, Ford, 7:266–67; Smith, *Freedom's Fetters*, 185–87.

66. TJ, "Fair Copy" of the Kentucky Resolutions, [Nov. 1798], Ford, 7:294–95 (Third Resolution). It should be noted that the very act of drafting these Resolutions was in violation of the Sedition Act; for this reason, and other, even more compelling political considerations, Jefferson's authorship of the Kentucky Resolutions was kept quite confidential. See Malone, 3:395–424; Koch and Ammon, "Virginia and Kentucky Resolutions."

67. Ford, 7:304 (Eighth Resolution); Levy, *Legacy of Suppression*, 265 n.46.

68. Smith, *Freedom's Fetters*, 67 n.11, 143, 148–49, 177, 332–33.

69. Levy, *Emergence of a Free Press*, 280–81.

70. TJ, First Inaugural Address, 4 Mar. 1801, to Robert R. Livingston, 31 May 1801, to Edward Livingston, 1 Nov. 1801, to Albert Gallatin, 12 Nov. 1801 (with enclosed rough draft of a message prepared for the Senate), to Levi Lincoln, 24 Mar. 1802, Ford, 8:4, 56–58, 139.

71. TJ to Judge John Tyler, 28 June 1804, L&B, 11:33.

72. See, for example, TJ to Peregrine Fitzhugh, 23 Feb. 1798, Ford, 7:208–9 ("I have been for some time used as the property of the newspapers, a fair mark for every man's dirt."). The attacks continued, and intensified with the adoption of the embargo, during Jefferson's second term as president. See Malone, 5:13–14, 605–6.

73. TJ to M. Pictet, 5 Feb. 1803, L&B, 10:357.

74. TJ to Gov. Thomas McKean, 19 Feb. 1803, Ford, 8:218–19; Malone, 4:230.

75. TJ, memorandum (no date), Ford, 8:56–57; TJ to Abigail Adams, 11 Sept. 1804, Cappon, 279.

76. Malone, 4:228–33.

77. TJ, fair copy of Second Inaugural Address, 4 Mar. 1805, and draft of Second Inaugural Address, [before 4 Mar. 1805], LC.

78. Ibid. (fair copy).

79. Levy, *Jefferson and Civil Liberties*, 60–67; Malone, 5:388; *United States v. Hudson and Goodwin*, 7 Cranch 32, 34 (1812).

80. Malone, 5:372, 376, 379; TJ to Wilson Cary Nicholas, 13 June 1809, to Gideon Granger, 9 Mar. 1814, to Thomas Seymour, 11 Feb. 1807, Ford, 9:253–54, 456–57, 29–30.

81. See TJ to Levi Lincoln, 24 Mar. 1802, Ford, 8:139; TJ to Abigail Adams, 11 Sept. 1804, Cappon, 279.

82. TJ to A. Coray, 31 Oct. 1823, L&B, 15:489; Levy, *Jefferson and Civil Liberties*, 69.

83. TJ to John Norvell, 11 June 1807, to Walter Jones, 2 Jan. 1814, to James Monroe, 1 Jan. 1815, L&B, 11:224–26, 14:46, 226; TJ to John Adams, 21 Jan. 1812, Cappon, 577–78.

84. On Jefferson's sensitiveness, see Malone, 1:133, 2:248.

85. Levy, *Jefferson and Civil Liberties*, 163–64, 167; TJ, Notes on Heresy, [1776], *Papers* 1:553. On Jefferson's tendency to describe political differences in religious terms, see Malone, 2:356–57.

86. Malone, 5:384.

87. TJ to Edward Carrington, 16 Jan. 1787, *Papers* 11:49.

88. TJ to Joseph Priestley, 19 June 1802, Ford, 8:158–59.

7. "The True Theory of Our Constitution": Federalism and the Limits of Federal Power

1. TJ, First Inaugural Address, 4 Mar. 1801, LC.

2. TJ to James Madison, 24 Dec. 1825, to Gideon Granger, 13 Aug. 1800, to Edward Livingston, 4 Apr. 1824, Ford, 10:350, 7:451–52, 10:300; TJ to John Cartwright, 5 June 1824, L&B, 16:42.

3. TJ to Archibald Stuart, 9 Sept. 1792, to Charles Clay, 11 Sept. 1792, *Papers* 24:351, 367.

4. TJ to Archibald Stuart, 23 Dec. 1791, ibid., 22:436.

5. TJ to A. L. C. Destutt de Tracy, 26 Jan. 1811, to Gideon Granger, 13 Aug. 1800, Ford, 9:309, 7:451–52.

6. TJ to Robert J. Garnett, 14 Feb. 1824, to Edward Livingston, 4 Apr. 1824, ibid., 10:295, 300.

7. Although most of his efforts were aimed at preventing the intrusion by the federal government into the sphere of the states, Jefferson realized the rule could cut both ways. See TJ to Joseph C. Cabell, 31 Jan. 1814, ibid., 9:451–52 (cautioning against a proposal that the state add qualifications to those prescribed by the Constitution for members of Congress).

8. TJ to Thomas Mann Randolph, Jr., 11 Jan. 1790, to George Mason, 4 Feb. 1791, *Papers* 18:489, 19:241–42.

9. TJ, Opinion on the Constitutionality of the Bill for Establishing a National Bank, 15 Feb. 1791, *Papers* 19:275–76.

10. Ibid., 276.

11. TJ to James Madison, 24 Dec. 1825, Ford, 10:352; TJ, Opinion on the Constitutionality of the Bill for Establishing a National Bank, 15 Feb. 1791, *Papers* 19:276–77.

12. TJ, Opinion on the Constitutionality of the Bill for Establishing a National Bank, 15 Feb. 1791, *Papers* 19:276–77.

13. Ibid., 277.

14. Ibid. Jefferson's description of the debates in the Convention suggests that he was relying on Madison's oral account rather than consulting Madison's notes on the proceedings. The notes show that Madison himself proposed that Congress be granted the power to grant charters of incorporation and that after it was suggested that the creation of banks would excite the interests of the cities of Philadelphia and New York and thus divide the states, the proposal was amended (on George Mason's motion) to limit it to the establishment of canals only. In the more limited form of a power to authorize canal companies, the proposal was rejected (Madison, *Notes*, 638–39 [Fri. 14 Sept. 1787]). Later in 1791, probably during the summer, when Madison had finished his "little task" of correcting and revising his notes, Jefferson arranged to have his own copy of the notes transcribed by his nephew and future son-in-law, John Wayles Eppes (*Papers* 19:548–49 [editorial note]).

15. TJ, Opinion on the Constitutionality of the Bill for Establishing a National Bank, 15 Feb. 1791, *Papers* 19:278–79.

16. Ibid., 279.

17. Malone, 2:342.

18. See Jefferson's interpretation of the Article I, section 9, migration or importation clause in connection with the Alien Acts of 1798 and his interpretation of the First Amendment establishment clause, expanding the meaning of "establishment" effectively to require a "wall of separation" between church and state. Jefferson's constitutional rights theory closely approximated what one scholar has identified as a "power-constraint" conception, as opposed to the "rights-powers" conception that many Federalists (among them, Alexander Hamilton and James Wilson) held. See Randy Barnett, "Introduction: James Madison's Ninth Amendment," in *The Rights Retained by the People: The History and Meaning of the Ninth Amendment*, ed. Barnett (Fairfax, Va.: George Mason Univ. Press, 1989), 4–19.

19. Alexander Hamilton, An Opinion on the Constitutionality of an Act to Establish a Bank (Final Version), 23 Feb. 1791, *Papers of Hamilton*, ed. Syrett, 8:97–134.

20. Ibid., 98, 100–101, 107.

21. Ibid., 102–3, 105.

22. Ibid., 100.

23. Peterson, *Jefferson and the New Nation*, 434–35; Alexander Hamilton to Gouverneur Morris, 29 Feb. 1802, *Papers of Hamilton*, ed. Syrett, 25:544.

24. Malone, 2:348; TJ, Opinion on Constitutionality of the Bill for Establishing a National Bank, 15 Feb. 1791, *Papers* 19:280.

25. TJ, Opinion on the Bill Apportioning Representation, 4 Apr. 1792, *Papers* 23:370–76; TJ, Draft of President's Message Vetoing Apportionment Bill, 5 Apr. 1792, Ford, 5:501.

26. For Madison's objections, see Koch, *Jefferson and Madison*, 128–29.

27. TJ, Memorandum of a Conversation with George Washington, 1 Mar. 1792, to George Washington, 9 Sept. 1792, *Papers* 23:187, 24:353.

28. TJ to Spencer Roane, 12 Oct. 1815, Ford, 9:531.

29. TJ to A. L. C. Destutt de Tracy, 26 Jan. 1811, ibid., 309.

30. TJ, Petition to the Virginia House of Delegates, Aug. 1797, ibid., 7:158–64.

31. As an alternative to impeachment, Jefferson also suggested the revival of *praemunire*, an English common law writ subjecting to punishment people who introduced foreign (papal) authority against the authority of the crown. See Levy, *Freedom of the Press from Zenger to Jefferson* (Indianapolis: Bobbs-Merrill, 1966), 343.

32. TJ to James Monroe, 7 Sept. 1797, Ford, 7:173; Malone, 3:336–37. With his name kept out of the business, Jefferson's petition was presented to the House of Delegates, which passed a resolution condemning the presentment of the grand jury but adopted no punitive measures (Malone, 3:336).

33. TJ to James Madison, 26 Apr. 1798, Ford, 7:245; TJ to T[homas] M[ann] R[andolph], 9 May 1798, LC; TJ to Madison, 6 June 1798, Ford, 7:266–67.

34. Koch and Ammon, "Virginia and Kentucky Resolutions"; Koch, *Jefferson and Madison*, 186. Jefferson's and Madison's authorship of the Kentucky and Virginia Resolutions was not generally known until it was revealed in 1814 in Taylor's *Inquiry*, p. 174n.

35. TJ, "Fair Copy" of the Kentucky Resolutions, [Nov. 1798], Ford, 7:289–91.

36. Ibid., 291–92.

37. John Taylor to TJ, 25 June 1798, *Branch Historical Papers* 2:271–76, cited in Malone, 3:404.

38. TJ, "Fair Copy" of the Kentucky Resolutions, [Nov. 1798], Ford, 7:293–96.

39. Ibid., 296–97.

40. Ibid., 297–99.

41. Ibid., 299.

42. Ibid., 300–302.

43. Ibid., 304–6.

44. TJ to —— Nicholas, 11 Dec. 1821, L&B, 15:350.

45. Malone, 3:397.

46. An even more direct comparison can be made with the stance Jefferson took much later against the federal judiciary's "assaults on the Constitution," when he

pointed to the danger of dissolution should the Supreme Court continue to usurp from the states the right to construe the Constitution. See chap. 9.

47. Resolutions of the Kentucky Legislature, approved 16 Nov. 1798, in Ford, 7:288 (opposite). The changes were probably made by Breckinridge; however, when a revised version of Jefferson's draft was reintroduced the following year, the word "nullification" did appear in the Kentucky Resolutions of 1799 (Koch and Ammon, "The Virginia and Kentucky Resolutions," 158).

48. TJ to James Madison, 17 Nov. 1798, to John Taylor, 26 Nov. 1798, Ford, 7:288–90 and note. Madison's Virginia Resolutions were even more moderate than the resolutions adopted by Kentucky, for they omitted the critical word "null," which Madison distrusted (Koch, *Jefferson and Madison*, 190–91).

49. TJ to James Madison, 23 Aug. 1799, W. C. Rives Papers, LC, quoted in Koch, *Jefferson and Madison*, 196–98. In their replies the northern states generally disavowed the constitutional principles of the Virginia and Kentucky Resolutions and argued that constitutionality of acts of Congress ought to be determined by the judiciary rather than by state legislatures. See, for example, New Hampshire Resolution of 15 June 1799, in *Documents of American History*, ed. Commager, 1:185.

50. TJ to John Taylor, 4 June 1798, MHS.

51. TJ to P. S. Du Pont de Nemours, 18 Jan. 1802, to Albert Gallatin, 13 Dec. 1803, Ford, 8:127, 285. See also TJ to Gallatin, 7 Oct. 1802 and 12 July 1803, ibid., 172, 252. There was no attempt to repeal or impair the Bank's charter, and at Gallatin's urging additional branches were established.

52. William Branch Giles's Resolutions on the Secretary of the Treasury, 27 Feb. 1793, *Papers* 25:294–95; TJ to James Madison, 6 Mar. 1796, to Albert Gallatin, 1 Apr. 1802, Ford, 7:61–62, 8:140–41.

53. TJ, First Annual Message, 8 Dec. 1801, Ford, 8:125.

54. Malone, 4:95, 102.

55. TJ, First Annual Message, 8 Dec. 1801, Ford, 8:125.

56. Malone, 4:105–6.

57. TJ to John Wayles Eppes, 24 June 1813, to John Taylor, 26 Nov. 1798, Ford, 9:389, 7:310. See also TJ to James Madison, 21 June 1792, to A. Donald, 5 Mar. 1793, *Papers* 24:105–6, 25:318.

58. TJ to Albert Gallatin, 11 Oct. 1809, Ford, 9:264.

59. TJ to John Wayles Eppes, 24 June 1813, to Albert Gallatin, 26 Dec. 1820, ibid., 9:389, 10:176–77.

60. TJ to Samuel Kercheval, 12 July 1816, ibid., 10:41–42. Jefferson's explanation is worth quoting in full: "We must make our election between *economy and liberty, or profusion and servitude*. If we run into such debts, as that we must be taxed in our meat and in our drink, in our necessaries and our comforts, in our labors and our amusements, for our callings and our creeds, as the people of England are, our people, like them, must come to labor sixteen hours in the twenty-four, give the earning of fifteen of these to the government for their debts and daily

expenses; and the sixteenth being insufficient to afford us bread, we must live, as they now do, on oatmeal and potatoes; have no time to think, no means of calling the mismanagers to account; but be glad to obtain subsistence. . . . This example leads us to the salutary lesson, that private fortunes are destroyed by public as well as by private extravagance. And this is the tendency of all human governments. A departure from principle in one instance becomes a precedent for a second; that second for a third; and so on, till the bulk of the society is reduced to be mere automatons of misery, to have no sensibilities left but sinning and suffering."

61. Cunningham, *Process of Government under Jefferson*, 97–98; Malone, 4:102–3.

62. Story, *Commentaries*, 459 (book 3, chap. 27); Adams, *Administrations of Jefferson*, 389, 1110.

63. Malone, 5:510; TJ, memorandum of 23 Nov. 1793, Ford, 1:269–70.

64. TJ, Second Annual Message, 15 Dec. 1802, to Albert Gallatin, 13 Oct. 1802, Ford, 8:186, 174; Malone, 4:263. Another potential precedent for broad construction was the beginning of the United States Coastal Survey under the auspices of Jefferson's administration and pursuant to an 1806 appropriation for the survey of the coast between Cape Hatteras and Cape Fear. (Peterson, *Jefferson and the New Nation*, 857). Like the establishment of West Point, such a project could only be rationalized as the exercise of implied powers.

65. TJ to Robert R. Livingston, 30 Apr. 1800, Ford, 7:446.

66. Malone, 5:481; Perkins, *Prologue to War*, 69, 148.

67. TJ to John Taylor, 6 Jan. 1808, LC.

68. See Peterson, "Jefferson and Commercial Policy"; Spivak, *Jefferson's English Crisis*; Nelson, *Liberty and Property*, 173–75.

69. Story, *Commentaries*, 463 (book 3, chap. 27); *United States v. The William*, 28 F. Cas. 614 (D. Mass. 1808) (No. 16,700), quoted in Henry Adams, *Administrations of Jefferson*, 1112–13.

70. TJ, Second Inaugural Address, 4 Mar. 1805, Sixth Annual Message, 2 Dec. 1806, Ford, 8:344, 494.

71. TJ, Sixth Annual Message, 2 Dec. 1806, ibid., 494; Nelson, *Liberty and Property*, xiv; Appleby, *Capitalism and a New Social Order*.

72. Peterson, *Jefferson and the New Nation*, 857; Malone, 5:555–57.

73. Malone, 4:557–58. See also Carter Goodrich, *Government Promotion of American Canals and Railroads* (New York: Columbia Univ. Press, 1960), 27–31.

74. TJ to George Ticknor, [May?] 1817, to Albert Gallatin, 16 June 1817, Ford, 10:80–81, 91–92; James Madison, Veto Message, 3 Mar. 1817, in *Mind of the Founder*, ed. Meyers, 307–9. Gallatin had always been less troubled than Jefferson about the constitutional problem; he once observed that he was "not quite so orthodox . . . as my Virginia friends [on] the U.S[.] Bank & internal improvements" (Gallatin, Autobiographical Sketch [1849], quoted in Nelson, *Liberty and Property*, 132).

75. See, for example, TJ to William F. Gordon, 1 Jan. 1826, Ford, 10:358.

76. TJ to Edward Livingston, 4 Apr. 1824, to William B. Giles, 26 Dec. 1825, ibid., 256, 301; TJ, Draft Declaration and Protest of the Commonwealth of Virginia, on the Principles of the Constitution of the United States, and on the Violations of Them, Dec. 1825, Lib. Am., 482–86.

8. "Bound by the Chains of the Constitution": The Presidency and Executive Power

1. Ralph Ketcham, "Executive Leadership, Citizenship and Good Government," *Presidential Studies Quarterly* 17 (1987): 276; TJ to P. S. Du Pont de Nemours, 2 Mar. 1809, Lib. Am., 1203; TJ to Elbridge Gerry, 13 May 1797, Ford, 7:119.

2. Adams, *Administrations of Jefferson*, 48, 354, 439, 467.

3. TJ to Samuel Kercheval, 12 July 1816, Ford, 10:37.

4. TJ to John Adams, 28 Sept. 1787, *Papers* 12:189; TJ to A. L. C. Destutt de Tracy, 26 Jan. 1811, Ford, 9:305.

5. TJ to James Madison, 20 Dec. 1787, *Papers* 12:439–41.

6. Ibid.; TJ to Edward Carrington, 27 May 1788, to Alexander Donald, 7 Feb. 1788, ibid., 13:208–9, 12:571.

7. TJ to James Madison, 20 Dec. 1787, to Edward Carrington, 27 May 1788, ibid., 12:439–41, 13:208–9. See also TJ to William Carmichael, 12 Aug. 1788, ibid., 13:502.

8. TJ to William Short, 20 Sept. 1788, ibid., 13:619; TJ to John Taylor, 6 Jan. 1805, Ford, 8:339. In the latter, he wrote that he had changed his mind about the single seven-year term, viewing seven years as "too long to be irremovable" and believing that "there should be a peaceable way of withdrawing a man in midway who is doing wrong." Service for eight years with a power to remove at the end of the first four, he said, "comes nearly to my principle as corrected by experience."

9. See TJ to Robert J. Garnett, 14 Feb. 1824, Ford, 10:295.

10. TJ to John Adams, 28 Sept. 1787, *Papers* 12:189.

11. See Malone, 2:269–85.

12. Ibid., 270.

13. TJ, Report of Secretary of State on Executive Proceedings in the Northwest Territory, 14 Dec. 1790, and enclosure, *Papers* 18:188–90; see also editorial note at pp. 168–69.

14. TJ, Opinion on the Constitutionality of the Bill for Establishing a National Bank, 15 Feb. 1791, ibid., 19:279–80.

15. TJ, Opinion on the Bill Apportioning Representation, 4 Apr. 1792, ibid., 23:370–76; Malone, 2:441.

16. Adams, like Jefferson, cast no vetoes at all; Monroe vetoed only one piece of legislation. The only early president to exercise the veto power with any frequency

was Madison, who vetoed seven bills in all. Thus in the forty-year period (1789–1829) covered by the first six presidential administrations, there were a total of only ten vetoes. It was Andrew Jackson's presidency that marked a radical change in use of the veto power (Richard A. Watson, "Origins and Early Development of the Veto Power," *Presidential Studies Quarterly* 17 [1987]: 407–8).

17. TJ, Opinion on Powers of the Senate respecting Diplomatic Appointments, *Papers* 16:378–80.

18. TJ to William Short, 8 Mar. 1791, ibid., 19:424–25; ibid., 102 (editorial note); TJ to Edmund Charles Genet, 22 Nov. 1793, Ford, 6:451. See also TJ to Genet, 31 Dec. 1793, Ford, 6:495–96.

19. Malone, 3:69; TJ to James Madison, 23 June, 29 June 1793, Ford, 6:315, 327; Washington's Proclamation of Neutrality, 22 Apr. 1793, in *Documents of American History*, ed. Commager, 1:163.

20. Malone, 3:110–11; Peterson, *Jefferson and the New Nation*, 494; TJ to James Madison, 7 July 1793, Ford, 6:338; five "Helvidius" essays, 24 Aug.–18 Sept. 1793, *Papers of Madison*, ed. Hutchinson, 15:64–73, 80–87, 95–103, 106–10, 113–20.

21. TJ to James Madison, 6 Sept. 1789, *Papers* 15:397.

22. TJ to James Monroe, 6 Sept. 1795, to James Madison, 26 Nov. 1795, Ford, 7:28, 38.

23. Jefferson avidly followed the debate in the House of Representatives in March and April 1796. He was particularly impressed with the arguments of Albert Gallatin, who observed that Federalist arguments, taken to their logical conclusion, would give the president and Senate the power to legislate under the guise of treaty making without regard to the House. Jefferson described Gallatin's speech as "worthy of being printed at the end of the Federalist, as the only rational commentary on the part of the constitution to which it relates," i.e., the treaty-making provision of Article II, section 2 (TJ to James Madison, 26 Mar. 1796, ibid., 68; Malone, 3:251, 256).

24. Jefferson to ——, 13 Mar. 1816, L&B, 14:444–45.

25. Alexander Hamilton to James A. Bayard, 16 Jan. 1801, *Papers of Hamilton*, ed. Syrett, 25:319–24.

26. See, for example, Malone, 4:xviii; McDonald, *Presidency of Thomas Jefferson*, 166.

27. See McDonald, *Presidency of Thomas Jefferson*, 167.

28. Malone, 5:xii; Young, *Washington Community*, 78.

29. TJ to Nathaniel Macon, 14 May 1801, Ford, 8:51.

30. See Malone, 4:xviii, 93.

31. TJ, Fourth Annual Message, 8 Nov. 1804, Ford, 8:332; Peterson, *Jefferson and the New Nation*, 813–19; Malone, 5:71–72.

32. TJ to Benjamin Rush, 13 June 1805, LC; Malone, 5:20.

33. TJ to Nehemiah Dodge and Others, a Committee of the Danbury Baptist

Association in the State of Connecticut, 1 Jan. 1802 (draft), LC; TJ to Rev. Samuel Miller, 23 Jan. 1808, Ford, 9:175.

34. See Malone, 5:xiii, xvi.

35. Cunningham, *Process of Government under Jefferson*, 322.

36. Malone, 4:60–62, 91, 112; Cunningham, *In Pursuit of Reason*, 255.

37. TJ to Barnabus Bidwell, 5 July 1806, LC. See also Malone, 5:164–66; Peterson, *Jefferson and the New Nation*, 690–91.

38. Cunningham, *Process of Government under Jefferson*, 321; Peterson, *Jefferson and the New Nation*, 691–92.

39. Robert M. Johnstone, Jr., "The Presidency," in *Jefferson: A Reference Biography*, ed. Peterson, 352; TJ to James Monroe, 10 July 1796, to John Garland Jefferson, 25 Jan. 1810, Ford, 7:89, 9:270. See also Robert M. Johnstone, Jr., *Jefferson and the Presidency: Leadership in the Young Republic* (Ithaca, N.Y.: Cornell Univ. Press, 1978).

40. See Malone, 5:395–414; Peterson, *Jefferson and the New Nation*, 860–65; Perkins, *Prologue to War*, 114–39; Spivak, *Jefferson's English Crisis*, 53–67; Donald R. Hickey, "The Monroe-Pinkney Treaty of 1806: A Reappraisal," *William and Mary Quarterly*, 3d ser., 44 (1987): 65–88.

41. TJ to Spencer Roane, 6 Sept. 1819, Ford, 10:140.

42. TJ to John F. Mercer, 9 Oct. 1804, L&B, 11:54.

43. TJ to Governor James Barbour [of Virginia], 22 Jan. 1812, Ford, 9:337.

44. See Malone, 2:27–32, 4:97–99; Sofaer, *War, Foreign Affairs, and Constitutional Power*, 208–24; Turner, *War Powers Resolution*, 19–24.

45. See, for example, Robert Scigliano, "The War Powers Resolution and the War Powers," in Joseph M. Bessette and Jeffrey Tulis, *The Presidency in the Constitutional Order* (Baton Rouge: Louisiana State Univ. Press, 1981), 138, cited in Turner, *War Powers Resolution*, 40 n.61.

46. TJ, First Annual Message, 8 Dec. 1801, Ford, 8:118–19; Turner, *War Powers Resolution*, 20.

47. TJ, First Annual Message, 8 Dec. 1801, Ford, 8:119. See also George Washington to the Senate and House of Representatives, 28 Nov. 1792, *Papers* 24:674 (draft written by Jefferson requesting Congress to "definitively" declare that hostilities existed between the United States and the Chickamauga Cherokees, who had been attacking American settlers in the Southwest Territory).

48. At a cabinet meeting on 15 May 1801, the treasury secretary, Albert Gallatin, maintained that "the ex[ecuti]ve can not put us in a state of war, but if we be put into that state either by the decree of Congress or of the other nation, the command & direction of the public force then belongs to the [executive]." All but Attorney General Levi Lincoln agreed that if war existed, naval captains could search for and destroy enemmy vessels (TJ, Anas, [15 May 1801], Ford, 1:293–94).

49. Malone, 4:98.

50. Adams, *Administrations of Jefferson*, 363, 389.

51. See Malone, 4: chaps. 14–17; Brown, *Constitutional History of the Louisiana Purchase,* esp. 22–29.

52. TJ, Report on Negotiations with Spain, 18 Mar. 1792, *Papers* 23:302; Malone, 2:310; TJ to Robert R. Livingston, 18 Apr. 1802, Ford, 8:143–47.

53. Gallatin, *Writings,* ed. Adams, 1:111–14, quoted in Brown, *Constitutional History of the Louisiana Purchase,* 21–22.

54. TJ to Albert Gallatin, [Jan. 1803], Ford, 8:241n.

55. Malone, 4:313.

56. TJ to William Dunbar, 17 July 1803, Ford, 8:254–55n. See also TJ to Benjamin Austin, 18 July 1803, LC; TJ to T[homas Mann] R[andolph], 15 July [18]03, MHS.

57. TJ to John Dickinson, 9 Aug. 1803, Ford, 8:262–63.

58. TJ to John C. Breckinridge, 13 Aug. 1803, ibid., 244n.

59. TJ, Drafts of an Amendment to the Constitution, [July 1803], ibid., 241–45 (right col.); Malone, 4:314–15.

60. Malone, 4:318, summarizing Wilson Cary Nicholas to TJ, 3 Sept. 1803, reproduced in Brown, *Constitutional History of the Louisiana Purchase,* 26–27.

61. TJ to Wilson Cary Nicholas, 7 Sept. 1803, Ford, 8:247–48; Richard E. Ellis, "Constitutionalism," in *Jefferson: A Reference Biography,* ed. Peterson, 131.

62. TJ to Wilson Cary Nicholas, 7 Sept. 1803, to James Madison, 18 Aug. 1803, to Thomas Paine, 18 Aug. 1803, to Levi Lincoln, 30 Aug. 1803, Ford, 8:247–48, 245–46n. See also Malone, 4:321–22; Robert W. Tucker and David C. Hendrickson, *Empire of Liberty: The Statecraft of Thomas Jefferson* (New York: Oxford Univ. Press, 1990), 167–71.

63. Thomas Paine to TJ, 23 Sept. 1803, quoted in Malone, 4:321.

64. TJ to George Rogers Clark, 25 Dec. 1780, *Papers* 4:237–38.

65. TJ to Joseph Priestley, 29 Jan. 1804, Ford, 8:294–95.

66. TJ to J. B. Colvin, 20 Sept. 1810, L&B, 12:418. See also Malone, 5:277–78.

67. TJ to J. B. Colvin, 20 Sep. 1810, L&B, 12:421–22.

68. Locke, *Two Treatises of Government,* ed. Laslett, 421–22 (*Second Treatise,* chap. 14, sec. 159–60). See also Harvey C. Mansfield, Jr., "The Modern Doctrine of Executive Power," Thomas L. Pangle, "Executive Energy and Popular Spirit in Lockean Constitutionalism," and Morton J. Frisch, "Executive Power and Republican Government—1787," *Presidential Studies Quarterly* 17 (1987): 244–51, 259–64, 284–86.

69. TJ to J. B. Colvin, 20 Sept. 1810, L&B, 12:419–20.

70. See Malone, 5:415–38, 462; Sofaer, *War, Foreign Affairs, and Constitutional Power,* 172–73. See also TJ to Thomas Mann Randolph, 18 June 1801, LC, cited in Malone, 4:103; Peterson, *Jefferson and the New Nation,* 876; Cunningham, *In Pursuit of Reason,* 297.

71. See Malone, 5:215–66, which cites the clasic 1954 study by Thomas Perkins Abernathy, *The Burr Conspiracy.*

72. TJ to J. B. Colvin, 20 Sept. 1810, L&B, 12:420–21.

73. TJ to L. H. Girardin, 12 Mar. 1815, L&B, 14:271–78, discussed in Malone, 6:220–24.

74. Levy, *Jefferson and Civil Liberties*, chaps. 5, 6.

75. See Malone, 5:561–657; Peterson, *Jefferson and the New Nation*, 883–916.

76. TJ to Albert Gallatin, 11 Aug. 1808, Ford, 9:202; Malone, 5:581–82.

9. "A Solecism in a Republican Government": The Judiciary and Judicial Review

1. TJ to Thomas Ritchie, 25 Dec. 1820, Ford, 10:169–70.

2. Malone, 4:151, 152 n.46, 2:163.

3. TJ, Third Draft of a Constitution for Virginia, [before 13 June 1776], TJ to Edmund Pendleton, 26 Aug. 1776, *Papers* 1:361, 505. See also TJ, Draft of a Constitution for Virginia, [May–June] 1783, ibid., 6:300.

4. TJ, Draft of a Constitution for Virginia, [May–June] 1783, ibid., 6:302–3. The veto of the Council of Revision could be overridden by a two-thirds vote of both houses of the General Assembly.

5. TJ to Edmund Pendleton, 25 May 1784, ibid., 7:292–93. On the difference between concurrent review and judicial review, see Mendelson, "Jefferson on Judicial Review," 328.

6. TJ to Philip Mazzei, Nov. 1785, *Papers* 9:70–71. On Mansfield, see McDonald, *Novus Ordo Seclorum*, 114–15; Waterman, "Mansfield and Blackstone's Commentaries."

7. James Madison to TJ, 19 Mar. 1787, TJ to Madison, 20 June 1787, *Papers* 11:219–20, 480–81. See also Dumbauld, "Jefferson and American Constitutional Law," 377–78.

8. TJ to James Madison, 20 Dec. 1787, *Papers* 12:439–41; Mendelson, "Jefferson on Judicial Review," 329.

9. TJ to James Madison, 15 Mar. 1789, *Papers* 14:659–60.

10. TJ to the Abbé Arnoux, 19 July 1789, ibid., 15:282–83.

11. Ibid.; TJ to Thomas Paine, 11 July 1789, ibid., 269.

12. TJ to Sir John Temple, 11 Aug. 1790, to Charles Hellstedt, 14 Feb. 1791, ibid., 17:333, 19:272–73; TJ to John Jay, 18 July 1793, John Jay to George Washington, 8 Aug. 1793, *The Founders' Constitution*, ed. Kurland and Lerner, 4:257–58.

13. TJ, Petition to the Virginia House of Delegates, Aug. 1797, Ford, 7:158–64.

14. TJ, "Fair Copy" of the Kentucky Resolutions, [Nov. 1798], ibid., 292, 298 (First and Sixth Resolutions).

15. Ibid., 293–94.

16. TJ to Edmund Randolph, 18 Aug. 1799, ibid., 383–87. See also "Symposium: Federal Common Law of Crime," *Law and History Review* 4 (1986): 223–336 (articles by Kathryn Preyer, Robert C. Palmer, and Stephen Presser).

17. TJ to Spencer Roane, 6 Sept. 1819, Ford, 10:140.

18. TJ to John Dickinson, 19 Dec. 1801, L&B, 10:302; Malone, 4:458–59.

19. George Lee Haskins, pt. 1 of Haskins and Johnson, *Foundations of Power*, 136; TJ to John Dickinson, 19 Dec. 1801, L&B, 10:302.

20. Ellis, *Jeffersonian Crisis*, 39–40; Kathryn Preyer, "Jurisdiction to Punish," *Law and History Review* 4 (1986): 223, 238.

21. Haskins, *Foundations of Power*, 161–62.

22. TJ to John Dickinson, 19 Dec. 1801, L&B, 10:302. Marshall, as former acting secretary of state, himself contributed to the chain of events that culminated in *Marbury*. See Haskins, *Foundations of Power*, 183–84.

23. TJ, First Annual Message, 8 Dec. 1801, Ford, 8:123; Ellis, *Jeffersonian Crisis*, 45–52.

24. Ellis, *Jeffersonian Crisis*, 42–43, 51–52; TJ to M. Volney, 20 Apr. 1802, LC.

25. Haskins has asserted that "the concept of an independent judiciary was a thorn in the flesh of eighteenth-century-minded persons, like Jefferson" (*Foundations of Power*, 286).

26. TJ to Thomas Ritchie, 20 Dec. 1820, Ford, 10:169–70.

27. See Peterson, *Jefferson and the New Nation*, 693.

28. TJ to Abigail Adams, 11 Sept. 1804, Cappon, 279–80. He was responding to a letter from Mrs. Adams, complaining that one of the first acts of Jefferson's administration was "to liberate a wretch," namely James Thomson Callender, who was punished for a libel against Mr. Adams. In an earlier letter Jefferson noted that he released Callender and others who were suffering punishment or prosecution under the Sedition Act "because I considered and now consider that law to be a nullity as absolute and as palpable as if Congress had ordered us to fall down and worship a golden image" (TJ to Abigail Adams, 22 July 1804, ibid., 275).

29. TJ to Wilson Cary Nicholas, 13 June 1809, Ford, 9:254.

30. TJ, Draft of First Annual Message to Congress, 8 Dec. 1801, LC. See also Cunningham, *In Pursuit of Reason*, 246, citing Secretary of the Navy Robert Smith to TJ, received 21 Nov. 1801, LC.

31. TJ, Draft of First Annual Message to Congress, 8 Dec. 1801, LC.

32. TJ to William Charles Jarvis, 28 Sept. 1820, L&B, 15:277–78.

33. Ibid., 278.

34. TJ to W. H. Torrance, 11 June 1815, Ford, 9:517–18.

35. *Marbury v. Madison*, 5 U.S. (1 Cranch) 153 (1803).

36. TJ to Justice William Johnson, 12 June 1823, Ford, 10:226–32.

37. TJ to Spencer Roane, 6 Sept. 1819, Ford, 10:141–42.

38. *Marbury v. Madison*, 5 U.S. (1 Cranch) 153, 177–78, 180 (1803).

39. See Peterson, *Jefferson and the New Nation*, 795; Ellis, *Jeffersonian Crisis*, 70–75; Malone, 4:459–64.

40. Lerner, *Thinking Revolutionary*, 109–15; Malone, 4:405; TJ to Joseph H. Nicholson, 13 May 1803, LC; Ellis, *Jeffersonian Crisis*, 83–107; TJ to Thomas Ritchie, 25 Dec. 1820, Ford, 10:170–71.

41. See Malone, 5:291–346.

42. TJ to George Hay, 20 June 1807, Ford, 9:59–60.

43. TJ to George Hay, 17 June 1807, ibid., 57.

44. TJ to William Branch Giles, 20 Apr. 1807, ibid., 42.

45. In the earlier case Marshall appeared to adhere to the common law rule of "constructive treason": if a body of men actually assembled "for the purpose of executing a treasonable design," he declared, "all those who perform any part, however minute, or however remote from the scene of action, and who are actually leagued in the general conspiracy, are to be considered traitors" (*Ex Parte Bollmann*, 8 U.S. [4 Cranch] 125, 126–27 [1807]). In his instructions to the Burr jury, however, Marshall emphasized the constitutional requirements of "levying war" and proof by the testimony of two witnesses to the same overt act, thus rejecting the doctrine of constructive treason and, in effect, directing the jury to acquit Burr because of the insufficiency of the evidence (Peterson, *Jefferson and the New Nation*, 871–73; Haskins, *Foundations of Power*, 258–60).

46. TJ to James Wilkinson, 20 Sept. 1807, to William Thomson, 26 Sept. 1807, Ford, 9:142–43. See also TJ to John W. Eppes, 28 May 1807, ibid., 68.

47. Malone, 5:367; TJ, Seventh Annual Message, 27 Oct. 1807, Ford, 9:163–64.

48. TJ to Thomas Ritchie, 25 Dec. 1820, Ford, 10:169–70; TJ to Charles Hammond, 18 Aug. 1821, L&B, 15:331–32. See also TJ, Autobiography, [6 Jan. 1821], Ford, 1:113.

49. Risjord, *Old Republicans*, 1–3, 179; Ellis, *Jeffersonian Crisis*, 19–21; John Marshall to Joseph Story, 18 Sept. 1821, in Charles Warren, *The Supreme Court in U.S. History*, rev. ed., 2 vols. (Boston: Little, Brown, 1935), 1:562–63.

50. Dumas Malone identified "a definite body of constitutional doctrine that could be designated as Virginian" (Malone, 6:355–57). Henry Adams similarly identified "the Virginia school," and he argued that "the essence of Virginia republicanism lay in a single maxim: THE GOVERNMENT SHALL NOT BE THE FINAL JUDGE OF ITS OWN POWERS" (Adams, *Administrations of Jefferson*, 174).

51. See TJ to Thomas Ritchie, 25 Dec. 1820, to Justice William Johnson, 27 Oct. 1822, Ford, 10:169–70, 222–26; Herbert A. Johnson, pt. 2 of Haskins and Johnson, *Foundations of Power*, 382–83.

52. TJ to John Taylor, 1 June 1798, Ford, 7:265.

53. *McCulloch v. Maryland*, 4 Wheat. (17 U.S.) 400, 415 (1819).

54. In the first three essays Judge Roane gave a detailed critique which compared quite closely with the arguments advanced by Jefferson in his 1790 opinion on the constitutionality of the bank (Spencer Roane, "Hampden," in *John Marshall's Defense of McCulloch v. Maryland*, ed. Gunther, 107–38).

55. Ibid., 138, 140–42, 148–49, 152–53.

56. TJ to Spencer Roane, 6 Sept. 1819, Ford, 10:141–42.

57. TJ to William Charles Jarvis, 28 Sept. 1820, ibid., 160–61.

58. Cunningham, *In Pursuit of Reason*, 334, citing Jefferson's letter to Roane of

6 Sept. 1819; TJ to Spencer Roane, 27 June 1821, L&B, 15:327–28. See also TJ to Archibald Thweat, 19 Jan. 1821, Ford, 10:184.

59. Taylor, *Construction Construed and Constitutions Vindicated*, 124–31.

60. Ibid., 132, 135–36, 144.

61. Ibid., 144, 159.

62. TJ to Spencer Roane, 27 June 1821, L&B, 15:328–29.

63. Section 25 permitted the Supreme Court by writ of error to review a final judgment or decree of the highest court of a state in certain cases, among them (as in the Cohens case) "where is drawn in question the validity of a statute of, or an authority exercised under, any State, on the ground of their being repugnant to the constitution, treaties, or laws of the United States, and the decision is in favor of their validity" (Judiciary Act of 1789, [24 Sept. 1789], in *Documents of American History*, ed. Commager, 1:154).

64. *Cohens v. Virginia*, 6 Wheaton 264, 381–82, 414–15, 422–23 (1821).

65. Id. at 447.

66. Richmond *Enquirer*, 23 Mar., 6 Apr. 1821, quoted in Warren, *History of Supreme Court*, 552; TJ to Charles Hammond, 18 Aug. 1821, L&B, 15:331–32.

67. TJ to William Johnson, 12 June 1823, Ford, 10:226–32.

68. Ibid., 232.

69. For Joseph Story's stunning refutation of Jefferson's two canons, see Story, *Commentaries on the Constitution of the United States*, 3 vols. (Boston, 1833), 1:390–92 n.1 (book 3, chap. 5).

70. Elsewhere Jefferson stated his canon of interpretation as follows: "Construe the Constitution according to the plain and ordinary meaning of its language, to the common intendment of the time and those who framed it" (TJ to James Madison, 24 Dec. 1825, Ford, 10:352). Modern scholars have identified different forms of originalism: strict textualism, or literalism; strict intentionalism; and moderate originalism. The last regards the text of the Constitution as authoritative but treats many of its provisions as inherently open-textured—in other words, while guided by original understanding, it is more concerned with the adopters' general purposes than with their specific intentions. See Paul Brest, "The Misconceived Quest for Original Understanding," *Boston University Law Review* 60 (1980): 204, 205. Plausible arguments can be made that, at various times and in various contexts, Jefferson adhered to all three forms of originalism.

71. See TJ to Edward Livingston, 4 Apr. 1824, Ford, 10:300.

72. TJ to Edward Livingston, 25 Mar. 1825, L&B, 16:113.

73. Ibid.

74. See TJ to —— Nicholas, 11 Dec. 1821, L&B, 15:350–52.

75. TJ, Autobiography, [6 Jan. 1821], Ford, 1:111–13. At about this time Jefferson was proposing, as a remedy for making "republican" the judiciary, appointments for six-year terms, with a reappointablity by the president with approbation of both houses of Congress (TJ to James Pleasants, 16 Dec. 1821, Ford, 10:197).

76. TJ to Judge William Johnson, 12 June 1823, to Charles Hammond, 18 Aug. 1821, L&B, 15:450–51, 331–32.

77. TJ to John Holmes, 22 Apr. 1820, Ford, 10:157.

78. TJ to Albert Gallatin, 26 Dec. 1820, ibid., 177; McCoy, *Last of the Fathers*, 265–66. See also Miller, *Wolf by the Ears*, 221–52.

79. See TJ to Charles Pinckney, 30 Sept. 1820, L&B, 15:280; TJ to Lafayette, 4 Nov. 1823, Ford, 10:81; Malone, 6:384.

80. TJ to William Johnson, 27 Oct. 1822, Ford, 10:225–26.

81. James Madison to Spencer Roane, 29 June 1821, *Mind of the Founder*, ed. Meyers, 362–68; Madison to TJ, 27 June 1823, *The Writings of James Madison*, ed. Gaillard Hunt, 9 vols. (New York: Putnam's, 1900–1910), 9:143; Madison, *Federalist* No. 39, [16 Jan. 1788], in *The Federalist*, ed. Cooke, 256; McCoy, *Last of the Fathers*, 139–51.

82. See John Howe, "Republican Thought and the Political Violence of the 1790s," *American Quarterly* 19 (1967): 147–65.

83. Boyd, "Chasm That Separated Thomas Jefferson and John Marshall," 18; Faulkner, *Jurisprudence of John Marshall*, 27–28, 45, 81–82, 97, 104–112; G. Edward White, *The Marshall Court and Cultural Change, 1815–1835*, abridged ed. (New York: Oxford Univ. Press, 1991), 519.

84. Faulkner, *Jurisprudence of Marshall*, 178, 187. Faulkner exaggerated Jefferson's commitment to egalitarianism. His statement that Jefferson "could not have written [as Marshall did] that government's first object was the protection of the 'unequal faculties of accumulating property' " (p. 176) overlooks many passages in Jefferson's writings, including a memorable one in his Second Inaugural Address, saying exactly that.

85. Stourzh, *Hamilton and the Idea of Republican Government*, 180; Faulkner, *Jurisprudence of Marshall*, 68–70, 215; Kerber, *Federalists in Dissent*, 153.

86. Stourzh, *Hamilton and the Idea of Republican Government*, 97–104, 182–86; TJ to Edward Carrington, 16 Jan. 1787, *Papers* 11:49.

87. TJ to Samuel Kercheval, 12 July 1816, Ford, 10:39.

10. "Hand in Hand with the Progress of the Human Mind": Constitutional Change and the Preservation of Republicanism

1. TJ to Samuel Kercheval, 12 July 1816, Ford, 10:42–43.

2. Boyd, "Chasm That Separated Jefferson and Marshall," 10.

3. TJ to Samuel Kercheval, 12 July 1816, Ford, 10:43; Sidney, *Discourses concerning Government*, 16.

4. Burgh, *Political Disquisitions* 1:6.

5. Sidney, *Discourses concerning Government*, 365.

6. Niccolò Machiavelli, *The Prince and the Discourses*, ed. Max Lerner (New York:

Modern Library, 1950), 397–402 (book 3, chap. 1); Sidney, *Discourses concerning Government*, 117.

7. Sidney, *Discourses concerning Government*, 365; TJ to Edward Carrington, 16 Jan. 1787, to James Madison, 30 Jan. 1787, *Papers* 11:48–49, 92–93.

8. Stourzh, *Hamilton and the Idea of Republican Government*, 36–37 (quoting "Sentiments of the Town of Roxbury on the Constitution of Civil Government proposed by Conventions," May 1780).

9. Peterson, *Jefferson, the Founders, and Constitutional Change*, 5–6.

10. TJ, Third Draft of a Constitution for Virginia, [before 13 June 1776], and Draft of a Constitution for Virginia, [May–June 1783], *Papers* 1:364, 6:304. See also Willi Paul Adams, *First American Constitutions*, 86–93.

11. TJ, *Notes on the State of Virginia*, Query XIII, Lib. Am., 251.

12. Madison, *Federalist* No. 49, [2 Feb. 1788], in *The Federalist*, ed. Cooke, 339–40.

13. Ibid.

14. Peterson, *Jefferson and Madison and the Making of Constitutions*, 12.

15. TJ to James Madison, 6 Sept. 1789, enclosure in TJ to Madison, 9 Jan. 1790, *Papers* 15:392–97; ibid., 384 (editorial note).

16. See Koch, *Jefferson and Madison*, 81–88; *Papers* 15:384–90 (editorial note).

17. TJ to James Madison, 6 Sept. 1789, ibid., 392–95.

18. Ibid., 394.

19. Ibid., 395–96.

20. Ibid., 397.

21. James Madison to TJ, 4 Feb. 1790, ibid., 16:147–49.

22. Ibid., 149–50; TJ to James Madison, 6 Sept. 1789, ibid., 15:396.

23. See, for example, TJ to Benjamin Vaughan, 11 May 1791, to Noah Webster, Jr., 4 Dec. 1790, ibid., 20:392, 18:133, 134 (editorial note).

24. TJ to Elbridge Gerry, 26 Jan. 1799, Ford, 7:329; TJ to William Green Munford, 18 June 1799, Lib. Am., 1064–65. See also Robert Nisbet, *History of the Idea of Progress* (New York: Basic Books, 1980), 198, 210–11. Jefferson even seemed to flirt with the radical libertarianism, or anarchism, of William Godwin. Although he himself did not affirm what he regarded as "Godwin's doctrine"—that man "may in time be rendered so perfect that he will be able to govern himself in every circumstance so as to injure none, to do all the good he can, to leave government no occasion to exercise their powers over him, & of course to render political government useless"—he nevertheless did not denounce it as absurd. He did state, however, that he did not, "with some enthusiasts, believe that the human condition will ever advance to such a state of perfection as that there shall no longer be pain or vice in the world" (TJ to Bishop James Madison, 31 Jan. 1800, to P. S. Du Pont de Nemours, 24 Apr. 1816, Ford, 7:419–20, 10:25).

25. See, for example, TJ to Benjamin Waterhouse, 3 Mar. 1818, Ford, 10:103–4;

TJ to Cornelius Camden Blatchly, 21 Oct. 1822, L&B, 15:399–400; TJ to John Adams, 15 June 1813, Cappon, 332.

26. TJ to Thomas Earle, 24 Sept. 1823, to John Cartwright, 5 June 1824, L&B, 15:470–71, 16:42.

27. TJ to Archibald Stuart, 23 Dec. 1791, *Papers* 22:435–36.

28. TJ to James Monroe, 15 Feb. 1801, to Joseph Priestley, 21 Mar. 1801, Ford, 7:491, 8:22. See also Peterson, *Jefferson, the Founders, and Constitutional Change*, 12–13.

29. John Randolph to Joseph H. Nicholson, 26 July 1801, cited in Richard E. Ellis, "The Persistence of Antifederalism after 1789," in *Beyond Confederation*, ed. Beeman, 303; Malone, 4:118–19; Ammon, "Monroe and the Election of 1808 in Virginia," 35–36. See also John Taylor to Wilson Cary Nicholas, 10 June 1806, in Mayer, "Of Principles and Men," 360–63.

30. TJ to Wilson Cary Nicholas, 7 Sept. 1803, Ford, 8:247–48.

31. TJ to John Melish, 13 Jan. 1813, ibid., 9:374–75.

32. TJ to Samuel Kercheval, 12 July 1816, to P. S. Du Pont de Nemours, 24 Apr. 1816, and to John Taylor, 28 May 1816, ibid., 10:37–39, 24, 28–29; TJ to Isaac H. Tiffany, 26 Aug. 1816, L&B, 15:66.

33. TJ to John Taylor, 28 May 1816, Ford, 10:29–30.

34. TJ to Samuel Kercheval, 12 July 1816, ibid., 39–41, 43.

35. TJ to Samuel Kercheval, 8 Oct. 1816, ibid., 47.

36. See Malone, 6:349–50, 441–43.

37. TJ to Robert J. Garnett, 14 Feb. 1824, Ford, 10:295.

38. TJ, Autobiography, [6 Jan. 1821], ibid., 1:111–12; TJ to William T. Barry, 2 July 1822, L&B, 15:389; TJ to James Pleasants, 26 Dec. 1821, Ford, 10:198.

39. TJ to Judge William Johnson, 12 June 1823, Ford, 10:231–32; TJ to William Charles Jarvis, 28 Sept. 1820, L&B, 15:277–78.

40. See Yarbrough, "Republicanism Reconsidered," 88.

41. TJ to Joseph Priestley, 19 June 1802, Ford, 8:158–59; TJ to George Wythe, 13 Aug. 1786, *Papers* 10:245.

42. TJ to Col. Charles Yancey, 6 Jan. 1816, to P. S. Du Pont de Nemours, 24 Apr. 1816, Ford, 10:4, 24–25. In the letter to Du Pont, he expressed his approbation of a provision, supposedly in the Spanish constitution, that no person could aquire the rights of citizenship until he could read and write. "It is impossible sufficiently to estimate the wisdom of this provision," he observed, calling it the "most effectual" means of preserving constitutional government.

43. TJ, *Notes on the State of Virginia*, Query XIV, Lib. Am., 274; TJ, A Bill for the More General Diffusion of Knowledge, *Papers* 2:526–27.

44. TJ, Sixth Annual Message, 2 Dec. 1806, Ford, 8:494.

45. TJ to Governor John Tyler, 26 May 1810, L&B, 12:391.

46. TJ to Samuel Kercheval, 12 July 1816, Ford, 10:41.

47. TJ to Joseph C. Cabell, 2 Feb. 1816, Lib. Am., 1380.

48. Ibid., 1380–81.

49. TJ to John Adams, 28 Oct. 1813, Cappon, 390.

50. TJ to Joseph C. Cabell, 31 Jan. 1814, Ford, 9:451.

51. Jean Yarbrough has observed that what set Jefferson apart from his colleagues was his rather low opinion of all political activity. His heroes were not the classical lawgivers but rather the philosopher-scientists Bacon, Newton, and Locke. "Not even the glorious activities of founding a republic could alter his essentially negative view of politics" (Yarbrough, "Republicanism Reconsidered," 91).

52. Dumas Malone, "The Great Generation," *Virginia Quarterly Review* 23 (1947): 108–22.

53. TJ to Samuel Kercheval, 12 July 1816, Ford, 10:39.

54. TJ to John Taylor, 28 May 1816, ibid., 30.

Conclusion: Government "Founded in Jealousy, and Not in Confidence"

1. TJ to Charles Clay, 27 Jan. 1790, *Papers* 16:129.

2. Edmund Burke, *Reflections on the Revolution in France* (1790; reprint, Baltimore: Penguin Books, 1973), 373–74, 117–20.

3. Ibid., 151.

4. For example, see TJ to Peter Carr, 10 Aug. 1787, *Papers* 12:15; TJ to Thomas Law, 13 June 1814, L&B, 14:138–43. See also Hamowy, "Jefferson and the Scottish Enlightenment," 522 n.67.

5. Peterson, *Adams and Jefferson,* 41; TJ, Memorandum ("Services to My Country"), [ca. 1800], Lib. Am., 703.

6. See, for example, TJ to P. S. Du Pont de Nemours, 2 Mar. 1809, Lib. Am., 1203; TJ to Edmund Randolph, 16 Sept. 1781, *Papers* 6:118.

7. TJ to Governor Hall, 6 July 1802, Ford, 8:156–57.

8. TJ to Thomas Jefferson Randolph, 24 Nov. 1808, ibid., 9:231–32; TJ to Francis Hopkinson, 13 Mar. 1789, *Papers* 14:651.

9. TJ to Charles Yancey, 6 Jan. 1816, Ford, 10:4. See also, for example, TJ to George Logan, 20 June 1816, to Joseph Delaplaine, 26 July 1816, to John Adams, 27 June 1822, ibid., 27, 56, 218.

10. TJ to Edward Coles, 25 Aug. 1814, to John Holmes, 22 Apr. 1820, ibid., 9:477–79, 10:157; Miller, *Wolf by the Ears,* 279.

11. TJ to James Madison, 11 May 1785, to Charles Thomson, 21 June 1785, *Papers* 8:147–48, 245; editorial note, ibid., 20:268–90.

12. TJ to John Norvell, 14 June 1807, Ford, 9:71; TJ to Joseph C. Cabell, 2 Feb. 1816, Lib. Am., 1378.

13. TJ, Response to Address of Welcome by the Citizens of Albemarle, 12 Feb. 1790, *Papers* 16:179.

14. TJ to Samuel Kercheval, 12 July 1816, Ford, 10:39.

15. TJ to Roger C. Weightman, 24 June 1826, ibid., 390–92. See also TJ to John Adams, 4 Sept. 1823, ibid., 270 (continuing to hope that France and other nations eventually would succeed in following the American example, "to recover the right of self-government").

SELECT BIBLIOGRAPHY

Primary Sources

Manuscript Collections

Jefferson, Thomas. Papers. Manuscripts Division, Library of Congress.
——. Papers. Coolidge Collection, Massachusetts Historical Society.
——. Papers. Special Collections Department, University of Virginia Library.

Published Collections of Papers and Documents

Adams, Charles Francis, ed. *The Works of John Adams.* 10 vols. Boston, 1850–56.
Boyd, Julian P., et al., eds. *The Papers of Thomas Jefferson.* 25 vols. to date. Princeton, N.J.: Princeton Univ. Press, 1950–.
Cappon, Lester J., ed. *The Adams-Jefferson Letters.* Chapel Hill: Univ. of North Carolina Press, 1959. Reprint. New York: Clarion, 1971.
Chinard, Gilbert, ed. *The Commonplace Book of Thomas Jefferson.* Baltimore: Johns Hopkins Press, 1926.
——. *The Literary Bible of Thomas Jefferson.* Baltimore: Johns Hopkins Press, 1928.
Commager, Henry Steele, ed. *Documents of American History.* 9th ed. 2 vols. New York: Appleton-Century-Crofts, 1973, vol. 1.
Foner, Philip S., ed. *The Complete Writings of Thomas Paine.* 2 vols. New York: Citadel Press, 1945.
Ford, Paul Leicester, ed. *The Writings of Thomas Jefferson.* 10 vols. New York: Putnam's, 1892–99.
Hutchinson, William T., et al., eds. *The Papers of James Madison.* 17 vols. Chicago: Univ. of Chicago Press, and Charlottesville: Univ. Press of Virginia, 1962–91.
Kurland, Philip B., and Ralph Lerner, eds. *The Founders' Constitution.* 5 vols. Chicago: Univ. of Chicago Press, 1987.
Lipscomb, Andrew A., and Albert Ellery Bergh, eds. *The Writings of Thomas Jefferson.* 20 vols. Washington, D.C.: Thomas Jefferson Memorial Association, 1904.
Meyers, Marvin, ed. *The Mind of the Founder: Sources of the Political Thought of James Madison.* Rev. ed. Hanover, N.H.: Univ. Press of New England, 1981.
Peterson, Merrill D., ed. *Thomas Jefferson: Writings.* New York: Library of America, 1984.
Syrett, Harold C., et al., eds. *The Papers of Alexander Hamilton.* 26 vols. New York: Columbia Univ. Press, 1961–79.

Wilson, Douglas L., ed. *Jefferson's Literary Commonplace Book*. Princeton, N.J.: Princeton Univ. Press, 1989.

Other Printed Sources

Blackstone, William. *Commentaries on the Laws of England*. 1765–69. Reprint. 4 vols. Chicago: Univ. of Chicago Press, 1979.

Bolingbroke, Henry St. John, Viscount. *The Works of Lord Bolingbroke*. 1844. Reprint. 4 vols. London: Frank Cass, 1967.

Burgh, James. *Political Disquisitions*. 3 vols. London, 1774–75.

Care, Henry. *English Liberties, or The Free-Born Subject's Inheritance*. 6th ed. Providence, R.I., 1774.

Coke, Edward. *The First Part of the Institutes of the Laws of England, or, A Commentary upon Littleton*. 1st American ed. (from 19th London ed.) 2 vols. Philadelphia: Robert H. Small, 1853.

——. *The Second Part of the Institutes of the Laws of England*. London: E. & R. Brooke, 1797.

Cooke, Jacob E., ed. *The Federalist*. Middletown, Conn.: Wesleyan Univ. Press, 1961.

Dalrymple, John. *An Essay towards a General History of Feudal Property in Great Britain*. London, 1759.

Destutt de Tracy, Antoine Louis Claude. *A Commentary and Review of Montesquieu's Spirit of Laws*, trans. Thomas Jefferson. Philadelphia: William Duane, 1811.

Gordon, Thomas, trans. *The Works of Tacitus*, vol. 2. London, 1731.

Gunther, Gerald, ed. *John Marshall's Defense of McCulloch v. Maryland*. Stanford, Calif.: Stanford Univ. Press, 1979.

Hulme, Obadiah. *An Historical Essay on the English Constitution*. London, 1771.

Laslett, Peter, ed. John Locke, *Two Treatises of Government*. 1960. Reprint. New York: Cambridge Univ. Press, 1963.

Madison, James. *Notes of Debates in the Federal Convention of 1787*. 1966. Reprint. New York: Norton, 1969.

Molesworth, Robert. *An Account of Denmark*. London, 1694.

Rapin, Paul, sieur de Thoyras. *The History of England*, trans. N. Tindall. 4th ed. 12 vols. London, 1757–62.

St. Amand, George. "An Historical Essay on the Legislative Power of England." In *A Complete Collection of the Lords' Protests*, vol. 2. London, 1767.

Sharp, Granville. *A Declaration of the People's Natural Right to a Share in the Legislature, Which Is the Fundamental Principle of the British Constitution of State*. London, 1774.

Sidney, Algernon. *Discourses concerning Government*. London, 1698.

Story, Joseph. *Commentaries on the Constitution of the United States*. Abridged ed. Boston, 1833. Reprint. Durham, N.C.: Carolina Academic Press, 1987.

Taylor, John. *Construction Construed and Constitutions Vindicated*. Richmond: Shepherd & Pollard, 1820.

———. *An Inquiry into the Principles and Policy of the Government of the United States.* Fredericksburg, Va.: Green and Cady, 1814.

Trenchard, John, and Thomas Gordon. *Cato's Letters.* 4 vols. London, 1724.

Secondary Sources

Books

Adams, Henry. *History of the United States of America during the Administrations of Thomas Jefferson.* 1903. Reprint. New York: Library of America, 1986.

Adams, Willi Paul. *The First American Constitutions: Republican Ideology and the Making of State Constitutions in the Revolutionary Era.* Chapel Hill: Univ. of North Carolina Press, 1980.

Appleby, Joyce. *Capitalism and a New Social Order: The Republican Vision of the 1790s.* New York: New York Univ. Press, 1984.

Arieli, Yehoshua. *Individualism and Nationalism in American Ideology.* Baltimore: Penguin Books, 1964.

Bailyn, Bernard. *The Ideological Origins of the American Revolution.* Cambridge, Mass.: Harvard Univ. Press, 1967.

Banning, Lance. *The Jeffersonian Persuasion: Evolution of a Party Ideology.* Ithaca, N.Y.: Cornell Univ. Press, 1978.

Becker, Carl L. *The Declaration of Independence.* 1922, 1942. Reprint. New York: Vintage Books, 1958.

Beeman, Richard, et al., eds., *Beyond Confederation: Origins of the Constitution and American National Identity.* Chapel Hill: Univ. of North Carolina Press, 1987.

Boorstin, Daniel. *The Mysterious Science of the Law.* Reprint. Gloucester, Mass.: Peter Smith, 1973.

Bowen, Catherine Drinker. *The Lion and the Throne: The Life and Times of Sir Edward Coke.* Boston: Little, Brown, 1957.

Boyd, Julian P. *The Declaration of Independence.* Princeton, N.J.: Princeton Univ. Press, 1945.

Brown, Everett S. *The Constitutional History of the Louisiana Purchase.* Berkeley: Univ. of California Press, 1920.

Buel, Richard, Jr. *Securing the Revolution: Ideology in American Politics, 1789–1815.* Ithaca, N.Y.: Cornell Univ. Press, 1972.

Charles, Joseph. *The Origins of the American Party System.* 1956. Reprint. New York: Harper and Row, 1961.

Chinard, Gilbert. *Thomas Jefferson: The Apostle of Americanism.* 2d ed. rev. Boston: Little, Brown, 1939.

Colbourn, H. Trevor. *The Lamp of Experience: Whig History and the Intellectual Origins of the American Revolution.* 1965. Reprint. New York: Norton, 1974.

Corwin, Edward S. *The "Higher Law" Background of American Constitutional Law.* 1928, 1929. Reprint. Ithaca, N.Y.: Cornell Univ. Press, 1955.

Cunningham, Noble E., Jr. *In Pursuit of Reason: The Life of Thomas Jefferson*. Baton Rouge: Louisiana State Univ. Press, 1987.

——. *The Process of Government under Jefferson*. Princeton, N.J.: Princeton Univ. Press, 1978.

Curry, Thomas J. *The First Freedoms: Church and State in America to the Passage of the First Amendment*. New York: Oxford Univ. Press, 1986.

Dargo, George. *Roots of the Republic: A New Perspective on Early American Constitutionalism*. New York: Praeger, 1974.

Dewey, Frank L. *Thomas Jefferson, Lawyer*. Charlottesville: Univ. Press of Virginia, 1986.

Dumbauld, Edward. *Thomas Jefferson and the Law*. Norman: Univ. of Oklahoma Press, 1978.

Ellis, Richard E. *The Jeffersonian Crisis: Courts and Politics in the Young Republic*. 1971. Reprint. New York: Norton, 1974.

Faulkner, Robert. *The Jurisprudence of John Marshall*. Princeton, N.J.: Princeton Univ. Press, 1968.

Ferguson, Robert. *Law and Letters in American Culture*. Cambridge, Mass.: Harvard Univ. Press, 1984.

Harvey, Ray Forrest. *Jean Jacques Burlamaqui: A Liberal Tradition in American Constitutionalism*. Chapel Hill: Univ. of North Carolina Press, 1937.

Haskins, George Lee, and Herbert A. Johnson. *Foundations of Power: John Marshall, 1801–1815*. Vol. 2 of the Oliver Wendell Holmes Devise *History of the Supreme Court of the United States*. New York: Macmillan, 1981.

Hayek, Friedrich A. *The Constitution of Liberty*. Chicago: Univ. of Chicago Press, 1960.

Hill, C. William, Jr. *The Political Theory of John Taylor of Caroline*. Rutherford, N.J.: Fairleigh Dickinson Univ. Press, 1977.

Hofstadter, Richard. *The Idea of a Party System: The Rise of Legitimate Opposition in the United States, 1780–1840*. Berkeley: Univ. of California Press, 1972.

Hoffer, Peter C. *The Law's Conscience: Equitable Constitutionalism in America*. Chapel Hill: Univ. of North Carolina Press, 1990.

Kerber, Linda K. *Federalists in Dissent: Imagery and Ideology in Jeffersonian America*. Ithaca, N.Y.: Cornell Univ. Press, 1970.

Kettner, James. *The Development of American Citizenship, 1608–1870*. Chapel Hill: Univ. of North Carolina Press, 1978.

Koch, Adrienne. *Jefferson and Madison: The Great Collaboration*. 1950. Reprint. New York: Oxford Univ. Press, 1970.

——. *The Philosophy of Thomas Jefferson*. 1943. Reprint. Gloucester, Mass.: Peter Smith, 1957.

Leder, Lawrence. *Liberty and Authority: Early American Political Ideology, 1689–1763*. 1968. Reprint. New York: Norton, 1976.

Lehmann, Karl. *Thomas Jefferson, American Humanist*. New York: Macmillan, 1947.

Lerner, Ralph. *The Thinking Revolutionary: Principle and Practice in the New Republic.* Ithaca, N.Y.: Cornell Univ. Press, 1987.

Levy, Leonard W. *Emergence of a Free Press.* New York: Oxford Univ. Press, 1985.

——. *The Establishment Clause: Religion and the First Amendment.* New York: Macmillan, 1986.

——. *Jefferson and Civil Liberties: The Darker Side.* Cambridge, Mass.: Harvard Univ. Press, 1963.

——. *Legacy of Suppression: Freedom of Speech and Press in Early American History.* 1960. Reprint. New York: Harper and Row, 1963.

McCoy, Drew R. *The Elusive Republic: Political Economy in Jeffersonian America.* Chapel Hill: Univ. of North Carolina Press, 1980.

——. *The Last of the Fathers: James Madison and the Republican Legacy.* New York: Cambridge Univ. Press, 1989.

McDonald, Forrest. *Novus Ordo Seclorum: The Intellectual Origins of the Constitution.* Lawrence: Univ. Press of Kansas, 1985.

——. *The Presidency of Thomas Jefferson.* Lawrence: Univ. Press of Kansas, 1976.

McIlwain, Charles H. *The American Revolution: A Constitutional Interpretation.* 1923. Reprint. Ithaca, N.Y.: Cornell Univ. Press, 1958.

Malone, Dumas. *Jefferson and His Time.* 6 vols. Boston: Little, Brown, 1948–81.

Miller, John C. *Alexander Hamilton and the Growth of the New Nation.* New York: Harper and Row, 1959.

——. *The Federalist Era.* New York: Harper and Row, 1960.

——. *The Wolf by the Ears: Thomas Jefferson and Slavery.* New York: Free Press, 1977.

Morgan, Robert J. *James Madison on the Constitution and the Bill of Rights.* New York: Greenwood Press, 1988.

Munves, James. *Thomas Jefferson and the Declaration of Independence.* New York: Scribner's, 1978.

Nelson, John R. *Liberty and Property: Political Economy and Policymaking in the New Nation, 1789–1812.* Baltimore: Johns Hopkins Univ. Press, 1987.

Palmer, R. R. *The Age of the Democratic Revolution: A Political History of Europe and America, 1760–1800.* Princeton, N.J.: Princeton Univ. Press, 1959.

Perkins, Bradford. *Prologue to War: England and the United States, 1805–1812.* Berkeley: Univ. of California Press, 1961.

Peterson, Merrill D. *Adams and Jefferson: A Revolutionary Dialogue.* New York: Oxford Univ. Press, 1976.

——. *The Jefferson Image in the American Mind.* New York: Oxford Univ. Press, 1962.

——. *Jefferson and Madison and the Making of Constitutions.* Charlottesville: Univ. Press of Virginia, 1987.

——. *Thomas Jefferson, the Founders, and Constitutional Change.* Claremont, Calif.: Claremont Institute, 1984.

——. *Thomas Jefferson and the New Nation.* New York: Oxford Univ. Press, 1970.

——, ed. *Thomas Jefferson: A Reference Biography.* New York: Scribner's, 1986.

Pocock, J. G. A. *The Ancient Constitution and the Feudal Law.* 1957. Reprint. New York: Norton, 1967.

——. *Three British Revolutions: 1641, 1688, 1776.* Princeton, N.J.: Princeton Univ. Press, 1980.

Pole, J. R. *Political Representation in England and the Origins of the American Republic.* Berkeley: Univ. of California Press, 1971.

Randall, Henry S. *The Life of Thomas Jefferson.* 3 vols. New York: Derby & Jackson, 1858.

Reid, John Philip. *In Defiance of the Law: The Standing-Army Controversy, the Two Constitutions, and the Coming of the American Revolution.* Chapel Hill: Univ. of North Carolina Press, 1981.

Risjord, Norman K. *The Old Republicans: Southern Conservativism in the Age of Jefferson.* New York: Columbia Univ. Press, 1965.

Robbins, Caroline. *The Eighteenth-Century Commonwealthman: Studies in the Transmission, Development, and Circumstance of English Liberal Thought.* Cambridge, Mass.: Harvard Univ. Press, 1959.

Roeber, A. G. *Faithful Magistrates and Republican Lawyers: Creators of Virginia Legal Culture, 1680–1810.* Chapel Hill: Univ. of North Carolina Press, 1981.

Rutland, Robert. *The Birth of the Bill of Rights, 1776–1791.* Rev. ed. Boston: Northeastern Univ. Press, 1983.

——. *The Ordeal of the Constitution: The Antifederalists and the Ratification Struggle of 1787–1788.* 1966. Reprint. Boston: Northeastern Univ. Press, 1983.

Sheldon, Garrett Ward. *The Political Philosophy of Thomas Jefferson.* Baltimore: Johns Hopkins Univ. Press, 1991.

Sisson, Daniel. *The American Revolution of 1800.* New York: Knopf, 1974.

Smith, James Morton. *Freedom's Fetters: The Alien and Sedition Laws and American Civil Liberties.* Ithaca, N.Y.: Cornell Univ. Press, 1956.

Sofaer, Abraham. *War, Foreign Affairs, and Constitutional Power.* Cambridge, Mass.: Ballinger, 1976.

Sowerby, E. Millicent. *Catalogue of the Library of Thomas Jefferson.* 5 vols. 1952–59. Reprint. Charlottesville: Univ. Press of Virginia, 1983.

Spivak, Burton. *Jefferson's English Crisis: Commerce, Embargo, and the Republican Revolution.* Charlottesville: Univ. Press of Virginia, 1979.

Stourzh, Gerald. *Alexander Hamilton and the Idea of Republican Government.* Stanford, Calif.: Stanford Univ. Press, 1970.

Sydnor, Charles E. *American Revolutionaries in the Making* [originally published as *Gentlemen Freeholders*]. 1952. Reprint. New York: Free Press, 1965.

Toohey, Robert E. *Liberty and Empire: British Radical Solutions to the American Problem, 1774–1776.* Lexington: Univ. Press of Kentucky, 1978.

Turner, Robert F. *The War Powers Resolution: Its Implementation in Theory and Prac-tice*. Philadelphia: Foreign Policy Research Institute, 1983.

Vile, M. J. C. *Constitutionalism and the Separation of Powers*. Oxford: Claren-don, 1967.

Weymouth, Lally, ed. *Thomas Jefferson: The Man, His World, His Influence*. New York: Putnam's, 1973.

White, Morton. *The Philosophy of the American Revolution*. New York: Oxford Univ. Press, 1978.

Wills, Garry. *Inventing America: Jefferson's Declaration of Independence*. Garden City, N.Y.: Doubleday, 1978.

Wood, Gordon. *The Creation of the American Republic, 1776–1787*. Chapel Hill: Univ. of North Carolina Press, 1969.

Young, James Sterling. *The Washington Community, 1800–1828*. New York: Colum-bia Univ. Press, 1966.

Articles and Essays

Ammon, Harry. "James Monroe and the Election of 1808 in Virginia." *William and Mary Quarterly*, 3d ser., 20 (1963): 33–56.

Appleby, Joyce. "The Jefferson-Adams Rupture and the First Translation of John Adams's *Defence*." *American Historical Review* 73 (1978): 1084–91.

———. "The New Republican Synthesis and the Changing Political Ideas of John Adams." *American Quarterly* 25 (1973): 578–95.

———. "What Is Still American in the Political Philosophy of Thomas Jefferson?" *William and Mary Quarterly*, 3d ser., 39 (1982): 287–309.

Banning, Lance. "Republican Ideology and the Triumph of the Constitution." *William and Mary Quarterly*, 3d ser., 31 (1974): 167–88.

Beitzinger, Alfons. "The Philosophy of Law of Four American Founding Fathers." *American Journal of Jurisprudence* 21 (1976): 1–19.

Boyd, Julian P. "The Chasm That Separated Thomas Jefferson and John Mar-shall." In *Essays on the American Constitution*, ed. Gottfried Dietze, 3–20. Englewood Cliffs, N.J.: Prentice-Hall, 1964.

Colbourn, H. Trevor. "Thomas Jefferson's Use of the Past." *William and Mary Quarterly*, 3d ser., 15 (1958): 56–70.

Cronin, Thomas E., ed. "The Origins and Invention of the American Presidency." *Presidential Studies Quarterly* 17 (1987): 225–432.

Dumbauld, Edward. "Thomas Jefferson and American Constitutional Law." *Journal of Public Law* 2 (1953): 370–89.

———. "Thomas Jefferson's Equity Commonplace Book." *Washington and Lee Law Review* 48 (1991): 1257–83.

Greene, Jack P. "Society, Ideology, and Politics: An Analysis of the Political Culture of Mid-Eighteenth-Century Virginia." In *Society, Freedom, and Con-*

science: The Coming of the Revolution in Virginia, Massachusetts, and New York,
ed. Richard M. Jellison, 14–76. New York: Norton, 1976.

——. "An Uneasy Connection: An Analysis of the Preconditions of the American Revolution." In *Essays on the American Revolution,* ed. Stephen G. Kurtz and James H. Hutson, 32–80. New York: Norton, 1973.

Grey, Thomas C. "Origins of the Unwritten Constitution: Fundamental Law in American Revolutionary Thought." *Stanford Law Review* 30 (1978): 843–93.

Hamowy, Ronald. "Jefferson and the Scottish Enlightenment." *William and Mary Quarterly,* 3d ser., 36 (1979): 503–23.

Howell, Wilbur Samuel. "The Declaration of Independence and Eighteenth Century Logic." *William and Mary Quarterly,* 3d ser., 18 (1961): 463–84.

Ketcham, Ralph. "The Dilemma of Bills of Rights in Democratic Government." In *The Legacy of George Mason,* ed. Josephine F. Pacheco, 29–59. Fairfax, Va.: George Mason Univ. Press, 1983.

Koch, Adrienne, and Harry Ammon. "The Virginia and Kentucky Resolutions." *William and Mary Quarterly,* 3d ser., 5 (1948): 145–76.

Kramnick, Isaac. "Republican Revisionism Revisited." *American Historical Review* 87 (1982): 629–64.

Levy, Leonard W. "Bill of Rights." In *Essays on the Making of the Constitution,* 2d ed., ed. Leonard Levy, 258–306. New York: Oxford Univ. Press, 1987.

——. "Liberty and the First Amendment, 1790–1800." *American Historical Review* 68 (1962): 22–37.

Lewis, Anthony M. "Jefferson's *Summary View* as a Chart of Political Union." *William and Mary Quarterly,* 3d ser., 5 (1948): 34–51.

Little, David. "Thomas Jefferson's Religious Views and Their Influence on the Supreme Court's Interpretation of the First Amendment." *Catholic University Law Review* 26 (1976): 57–72.

Mayer, David N. "The English Radical Whig Origins of American Constitutionalism," *Washington University Law Quarterly* 70 (1992): 131–208.

——. "Of Principles and Men: The Correspondence of John Taylor of Caroline with Wilson Cary Nicholas, 1806–1808," *Virginia Magazine of History and Biography* 96 (1988): 345–88.

Mendelson, Wallace. "Jefferson on Judicial Review: Consistency through Change." *University of Chicago Law Review* 29 (1962): 327–37.

Peterson, Merrill D. "Thomas Jefferson and Commercial Policy, 1783–1793." *William and Mary Quarterly,* 3d ser., 22 (1965): 584–610.

——. "Thomas Jefferson and the Enlightenment: Reflections on Literary Influence." *Lex et Scientia* 11 (1975): 89–127.

Preyer, Kathryn, et al. "Symposium on the Federal Common Law of Crime." *Law and History Review* 4 (1986): 223–336.

Reid, John Phillip. "The Irrelevance of the Declaration." In *Law in the American*

Revolution and the Revolution in the Law, ed. Hendrik Hartog, 46–89. New York: New York Univ. Press, 1981.

Thayer, James B. "The Origin and Scope of the American Doctrine of Constitutional Law." *Harvard Law Review* 7 (1893): 129–56.

Waterman, Julian S. "Jefferson and Blackstone's Commentaries." *Illinois Law Review.* 27 (1933): 629–59.

——. "Mansfield and Blackstone's Commentaries." *University of Chicago Law Review* 1 (1934): 549–71.

Wilson, Douglas L. "Jefferson vs. Hume." *William and Mary Quarterly,* 3d ser., 46 (1989): 49–70.

——. "Sowerby Revisited: The Unfinished Catalogue of Thomas Jefferson's Library." *William and Mary Quarterly,* 3d ser., 41 (1984): 615–28.

——. "Thomas Jefferson's Early Notebooks." *William and Mary Quarterly,* 3d ser., 42 (1985): 433–52.

Yarbrough, Jean. "Republicanism Reconsidered: Some Thoughts on the Foundation and Preservation of the American Republic." *Review of Politics* 61 (1979): 61–95.